PROBLEMS, CASES, AND READINGS

ENVIRONMENTAL POLICY LAW

FOURTH EDITION

by

THOMAS J. SCHOENBAUM
Dean and Virginia Rusk Professor of Law
University of Georgia School of Law

RONALD H. ROSENBERG
Professor of Law
Marshall-Wythe School of Law
College of William and Mary

HOLLY D. DOREMUS
Professor of Law
University of California at Davis
School of Law

NEW YORK, NEW YORK
FOUNDATION PRESS
2002
Mat #17361600

Foundation Press, a division of West Group, has created this publication to provide you with accurate and authoritative information concerning the subject matter covered. However, this publication was not necessarily prepared by persons licensed to practice law in a particular jurisdiction. Foundation Press is not engaged in rendering legal or other professional advice, and this publication is not a substitute for the advice of an attorney. If you require legal or other expert advice, you should seek the services of a competent attorney or other professional.

TEXT IS PRINTED ON 10% POST
CONSUMER RECYCLED PAPER

PREFACE

Environmental law is no longer a new field. Few people today would be surprised to learn that the law addresses a variety of environmental problems. Many attorneys consider at least a portion of their practice to be "environmental" in some sense; personal injury litigation, real estate transactions, corporate counseling and other practices all raise environmental issues. Environmental law proved its staying power in the mid-1990s, when advocates of deregulation gained a majority in Congress but were unable to significantly relax federal environmental laws.

Although it has in some respects matured over the last two decades, environmental law remains an exciting and controversial field. Environmental problems typically share a number of characteristics that complicate attempts to find legal solutions to them. Human activities can affect the environment at great distances, crossing state and international boundaries. Environmental harms often result from the combination of a number of different actions, and even different types of action, none of which would be problematic in isolation. It is frequently difficult to predict the environmental consequences of action, or even to measure them. It is equally difficult to agree on the value of environmental harm, or how it should be compared with the economic costs of preventing it. Because of the threat of irreversible or catastrophic harm, environmentalists often argue for early, precautionary, responses. On the other hand, proposals for economically costly regulation face substantial resistance where their benefits cannot be clearly demonstrated.

We take a very broad view of environmental law, encompassing the regulation of private and public land use and protection of wildlife as well as pollution control and remediation. We believe that artificially separating pollution law from the regulation of natural resources can obscure important conceptual similarities. Each instructor, of course, must determine the appropriate scope of coverage for his or her class. This casebook is designed to facilitate that kind of selection. It provides sufficient breadth for any introductory environmental or natural resources law course.

Environmental law remains highly complex. Students who aspire to practice environmental law must gain a sense of that complexity, and the confidence to address it. They must learn something of the science, economics, and philosophy used to evaluate environmental controversies. They must become familiar with regulations and the basics of administrative law, as well as statutes and judicial opinions. They must understand that state and local law, although still not as important as federal law, plays an increasingly important role as the federal courts take an increasingly restrictive view of federal powers.

At the same time, environmental law remains subject to continual modification. Although there have been few amendments to the major federal environmental statutes in the last few years, judicial opinions and regulatory changes have continued apace. Since the details will surely change, we believe it is most productive for teachers and students to focus on the larger picture. We have struck a balance by focusing in detail on those portions of the statutes covered that raise particularly interesting or important conceptual issues. Throughout, we highlight perpetual controversies such as the nature of human relationships to nature, the appropriate extent of individual control over natural resource use, and the degree of certainty needed to support regulatory intervention.

We have included in each chapter a number of problems designed to provide a concrete focus for classroom discussion. These problems help students develop and test their facility with the materials in the text and the concepts underlying those materials.

The development of such a comprehensive set of materials necessarily reflects the combined efforts of many people. We are grateful for the excellent research assistance of Olga Brand, Malcolm Milne, Aram Durphy, Paulla Hyatt, Christine Ichimura, and Kenneth Weatherwax. Jack Ayer, Robert Miller and Clifford Rechtschaffen generously read and provided helpful comments on portions of the manuscript. The University of Georgia School of Law, Marshall-Wythe School of Law at the College of William and Mary, and the University of California, Davis, School of Law provided invaluable institutional and financial support. Special appreciation for word processing, proofreading and editorial support should be given to Ms. Debbie Fitzpatrick, Ms. Della Harris and Ms. Felicia Burton of the College of William and Mary. Finally, we owe a tremendous debt of gratitude to Yanfang Tang and Gordon Anthon for patience, encouragement and support during the course of this project.

THOMAS J. SCHOENBAUM
ATHENS, GEORGIA

RONALD H. ROSENBERG
WILLIAMSBURG, VIRGINIA

HOLLY DOREMUS
DAVIS, CALIFORNIA

ACKNOWLEDGEMENTS

The following copyrighted material has been reproduced with permission of the copyright holder:

Andreen, William L., Beyond Words of Exhortation: The Congressional Prescription for Vigorous Federal Enforcement of The Clean Water Act, 55 Geo. Wash. L. Rev. 202 (1987), reprinted with permission.

Andreen, William L., In Pursuit of NEPA's Promise: The Role of Executive Oversight in the Implementation of Environmental Policy, 64 Ind. L.J. 205, 245-247 (1989), reprinted with permission.

Andrews, Richard N.L., The Unfinished Business of National Environmental Policy, in Environmental Policy and NEPA: Past, Present, and Future, 85 (Ray Clark and Larry Canter eds, 1997), reprinted with permission.

Baxter, William F., People or Penguins: The Case for Optimal Pollution, 4-12 (Columbia University Press 1974), reprinted with permission.

Bear, Dinah, NEPA at 19: A Primer on an "Old" Law with Solutions to New Problems, 19 Envtl. L. Rep. 10060, 10061-10065 (1989). © 1989, Environmental Law Institute, reprinted with permission.

Beldon, Roy, Clean Air Act 63-72 (2001) © 2001, American Bar Association Publishing, reprinted with permission.

Blumm, Michael C., Public Choice Theory and the Public Lands: Why "Multiple Use" Failed, 18 Harv. Envtl. L. Rev. 405, 406-408 (1994) © 1994 by the President and Fellows of Harvard College and the Harvard Environmental Law Review, reprinted with permission.

Brunet, Edward, Debunking Wholesale Pivate Envorcement of Environmental Rights, 15 Harv. J.L. & Pub. Pol'y 311, 313-323 (1992), reprinted with permission.

Commission for Racial Justice, United Church of Christ, Toxic Wastes and Race in the United States, 13 (1987), reprinted with permission.

Coquillette, Daniel R., Mosses from an Old Manse: Another Look at Some Historic Property Cases About the Environment, 64 Cornell L. Rev. 761, 792 (1979), reprinted with permission.

Cross, Frank B., Common Law Conceits: A Comment on Meiners & Yandle, 7 Geo. Mason L. Rev. 965, 966-981 (1999), reprinted with permission.

Doremus, Holly, Patching the Ark: Improving Legal Protection of Biological Diversity, 18 Ecology L.Q. 265, 269-281 (1991), reprinted with permission.

Ecosystem Management in the United States: An Assessment of Current Experience, Steven Yaffee, Ali Phillips, et al, eds. © 1996 The Wilderness Society. Published by Island Press, Washington, D.C. and Covelo, California.

Funk, William, Bargaining Toward the New Millennium: Regulatory Negotiation and the Subversion of the Public Interest, 46 Duke L. J. 1351 (1997), reprinted with permission.

Gatto, Marino & DeLeo, Giulio A., Pricing Biodiversity and Ecosystem Services: The Never-Ending Story, 50 BioScience 347, 354 (2000), reprinted with permission.

Germany's Polluter Pays Concept Could Be Applied to U.S. Industry, 17 Int'l Env't Rptr. (BNA) 368 (1994), reproduced with permission from International Environment Reporter, Vol. 17, No. 8, p. 368 (April 20, 1994). © 1994 by The Bureau of national Affairs, Inc. (800-372-1033) <http//www.bna.com>.

Goplerud, III, Peter, Water Pollution Law: Milestones from the Past and Anticipation of the Future, 10 Nat. Res. & Envt. 7-12 (1995) © 1995 American Bar Association, reprinted with permission.

Hamilton, James T. and Viscusi, W. Kip, Calculating Risks: The Spatial and Political Dimensions of Hazardous Waste Policy 240-42 (1999) © 1999 The MIT Press, reprinted with permission.

Hardin, Garrett, The Tragedy of the Commons, reprinted with permission from 162 Science 1243, 1244-1245, 1247 (1968). © 1968 American Association for the Advancement of Science.

Harter, Philip J., Fear of Commitment: An Affliction of Adolescents, 46 Duke L. J. 1398 (1997), reprinted with permission.

Heinzerling, Lisa, Discounting Our Future, 34 Land & Water L. Rev. 39, 44 (1999), reprinted with permission.

Hill, Randolph L., An Overview of RCRA: The "Mind-Numbing" Provisions of the Most Complicated Environmental Statute, 21 Envtl. L. Rep. 10254, 10268-10269 (1991), © 1991 Environmental Law Institute®, Washington, DC. Reprinted with permission from ELR® - The Environmental Law Reporter®. All rights reserved.

Houck, Oliver, The Clean Water Act TMDL Program: Law, Policy and Implementation 87-94 (2000) © 2000 Environmental Law Institute, reprinted with permission.

Karkkainen, Bradley C., Information as Environmental Regulation: TRI and Performance Benchmarking, Precursor to a New Paradigm? 89 Geo. L.J. 257, 287-333 (2000) © 2000, reprinted with permission. Reprinted with permission of the publisher, Georgetown Law Journal.

Krieger, Martin H., What's Wrong With Plastic Trees, reprinted with permission from 179 Science 446, 446-453 (1973) © 1973, American Association for the Advancement of Science.

Lazarus, Richard J., Restoring What's Environmental About Environmental Law in the Supreme Court, 47 UCLA L. Rev. 703, 744-748 (2000). Originally published in 47 UCLA L. Rev. 703. © 2000, The Regents of the University of California. All Rights Reserved. Reprinted with permission.

Leopold, Aldo, A Sand County Almanac: with other Essays on Conservation from Round River, 218-240, © 1949, 1953, 1966, renewed 1977, 1981 by

Oxford University Press. Used by permission of Oxford University Press, Inc.

Lipeles, Maxine I., 4 Environmental Law 501 (3d ed. 1997) © 1997 Anderson Publishing Company, reprinted with permission.

Meiners, Roger & Yandle, Bruce, Common Law and the Conceit of Modern Environmental Policy, 7 Geo. Mason L. Rev. 923, 946-959 (1999), reprinted with permission.

Meyer, Judy L., The Dance of Nature: New Concepts in Ecology, 69 Chi.-Kent L. Rev. 875, 875-886 (1994), reprinted with permission.

Noss, Reed F., Some Principles of Conservation Biology, As They Apply to Environmental Law, 69 Chi.-Kent L. Rev. 893, 895 (1994), reprinted with permission.

Paustenback, Dennis J., Health Risk Assessment: Opportunities and Pitfalls, 14 Col. J. Envtl. L. 397, 405 (1989), reprinted with permission.

Rechtschaffen, Clifford, The Warning Game: Evaluating Warnings Under California's Proposition 65, 23 Ecology L.Q. 303, 313-348 (1996), reprinted with permission.

Reed, Phillip D., Law of Environmental Protection 11-54 to 11-59 (1995) © 1995 West Publishing Co., reprinted with permission.

Reitze, Jr., Arnold W., Air Pollution Law 60-61 (1995) © 1995 The Michie Company, reprinted with permission.

Rodgers, Jr., William H., Environmental Law 338-9, 343 © West Publishing, reprinted with permission.

Sagoff, Mark, We Have Met the Enemy and He Is Us or Conflict and Contradiction in Environmental Law, 12 Envtl. L. 283, 283-308 (1982), reprinted with permission.

Salzman, James, Sustainable Consumption and the Law, 27 Envtl. L. 1243, 1273 (1997), reprinted with permission.

Salzman, James, Thompson, Barton H. & Daily, Gretchen, Protecting Ecosystem Services: Science, Economics, and Law, 20 Stan. Envtl. L.J. 309, 312 (2001), reprinted with permission.

Sax, Joseph, Introduction to Symposium: Environmental Law: More Than Just a Passing Fad, 19 U. Mich. J.L. Ref. 797, 804 (1986), reprinted with permission.

Shavell, Steven, Liability for Harm Versus Regulation of Safety, 13 J. Legal Stud. 357, 357-365 (1984) © 1984 by The University of Chicago. All rights reserved.

Stewart, Richard B., Pyramids of Sacrifice? Problems of Federalism in Mandating State Implementation of National Environmental Policy. Reprinted by permission of The Yale Law Journal Company and William S. Hein Company from The Yale Law Journal, Vol. 86, pages 1196-1272.

Tarlock, A. Dan, Environmental Law: Ethics or Science? 7 Duke Envtl. L. & Pol'y F. 193, 194-195, 221-223 (1996).

Thornton, Robert D., Searching for Consensus and Predictability: Habitat Conservation Planning Under the Endangered Species Act of 1973, 21 Envtl. L. 605, 621-624 (1991), reprinted with permission.

Torres, Gerald, Introduction: Understanding Environmental Racism, 63 U. Colo. L. Rev. 839, 839-840 (1992), reprinted with permission.

SUMMARY OF CONTENTS

*

TABLE OF CONTENTS

xiii

CHAPTER FOUR. Who's in Charge of Environmental Decisions? --- 160

Sec.

*

TABLE OF CASES

Principal cases are in bold type. Non-principal cases are in roman type. References are to Pages.

GLOSSARY OF ACRONYMS

2,4-D	2,4-dichlorophenoxyacetic acid
2,4,5-T	2,4,5-trichlorophenoxyacetic acid
AAIA	Airport and Airway Improvement Act
AHLA	American Heart and Lung Association
ALJ	Administrative Law Judge
ANPR	advanced notice of proposed rulemaking
APA	Administrative Procedure Act
AQI	Air Quality Index
ARAR	applicable or relevant and appropriate standards, limitations, criteria and requirements
BACT	best available control technology
BART	best available retrofit technology
BAT	best available technology economically achievable
BCT	best conventional pollutant control technology
BDAT	best demonstrated available technology
BDT	best demonstrated technology
BLM	Bureau of Land Management
BMP	backcountry management plan
BPA	Bonneville Power Administration
BPT	best practicable control technology currently available
BRT	Biological Review Team
CAA	Clean Air Act
CANT	Citizens Against Nuclear Trash
CEC	Claiborne Enrichment Center
CEO	chief executive officer
CEQ	Council on Environmental Quality
CERCLA	Comprehensive Environmental Response, Compensation and Liability Act of 1980
CERCIS	Comprehensive Environmental Response, Compensation and Liability Information System

CFCs	chloroflurocarbons
CFR	Code of Federal Regulations
CMA	Chemical Manufacturers Association
CO	carbon monoxide
CRS	Congressional Research Service
CTGs	control technique guidelines
CWA	Clean Water Act
DDT	dichlorodiphenyltrichloroethane
DHR	Rhode Island Division of Harbors and Rivers
DMF	Massachusetts Division of Marine Fisheries
DMR	discharge monitoring reports
DNA	deoxyribonucleic acid
DOE	Department of Energy
DOJ	Department of Justice
DOT	Department of Transportation
DTF	Dithiocarbamate Task Force
DWP	Los Angeles Department of Water and Power
EA	environmental assessment
EAB	Environmental Appeals Board
EIS	environmental impact statement
EPA	Environmental Protection Agency
EPCRA	Emergency Planning and Community Right-to-Know Act of 1986
ESA	Endangered Species Act of 1973
ESU	evolutionarily significant unit
FAA	Federal Aviation Administration
FDA	Food and Drug Administration
FEIS	final environmental impact statement
FEMAT	Forest Ecosystem Management Assessment Team
FERC	Federal Energy Regulatory Commission
FFD	factors for decline
FFDCA	Federal Food, Drug and Cosmetic Act
FHA	Federal Highway Administration
FIFRA	Federal Insecticide, Fungicide, and Rodenticide Act
FIP	Federal Implementation Plan
FLPMA	Federal Land Policy and Management Act
FONSI	finding of no significant impact
FPC	Federal Power Commission

FRCP	Federal Rules of Civil Procedure
FWS	Fish and Wildlife Service
GGS	giant garter snake
HCP	habitat conservation plan
HRS	Hazard Ranking System
HSWA	Hazardous and Solid Waste Amendments of 1984
HUD	Department of Housing and Urban Development
ITP	incidental take permit
IWC	International Whaling Commission
LAER	lowest achievable emission rate
LES	Louisiana Energy Services
LCRs	land coverage rights
LDRs	land disposal restrictions
LRMP	land and resource management plan
LULUs	locally undesirable land uses
LFAS	low frequency active sonar
MCC	Minnesota Conservation Club
MCLs	maximum contaminant levels
MOA	memorandum of agreement
MUSYA	Multiple Use Sustained Yield Act
NAACP	National Association for the Advancement of Colored People
NAAQS	National Ambient Air Quality Standard
NBAR	non-binding allocation of responsibility
NBC	Natomas Basin Conservancy
NCP	National Contingency Plan
NEPA	National Environmental Policy Act
NFMA	National Forest Management Act
NFP	Northwest Forest Plan
NIMBY	not in my back yard
NMFS	National Marine Fisheries Service
NPL	National Priorities List
NPS	National Park Service
NRC	Nuclear Regulatory Commission
NRDC	Natural Resources Defense Council
NO2	nitrogen dioxide
NOAA	National Oceanic and Atmospheric Administration
NOI	notice of intent
NOX	nitrogen oxides

NPDES	National Pollutant Discharge Elimination System
NPS	nonpoint source
NSO	no surface occupancy
NSPS	new source performance standard
NWP	nationwide permit
NWPA	Nuclear Waste Policy Act
NWRTB	Nuclear Waste Technical Review Board
O3	ozone
OCSRI	Oregon Coastal Salmon Restoration Initiative
OIRA	Office of Information and, Regulatory Affairs
OMB	Office of Management and Budget
OPR	Office of Protected Resources
PCBs	polychlorinated biphenyls
PILT	Payment in Lieu of Taxes Act
PM	particulate matter
PMN	premanufacture notification
POTW	publicly owned treatment works
PSD	prevention of significant deterioration
PSI	Pollutant Standards Index
RACT	reasonably available control technology
RCRA	Resource Conservation and Recovery Act
RD	remedial design
RFG	Reformulated Gasoline Program
RFP	reasonable further progress
RIA	Regulatory Impact Analysis
RI/FS	remedial investigation/feasibility study
ROD	record of decision
RPAR	rebut table presumption against registration
RQ	reportable quantities
SEP	Supplemental Environmental Project
SEZ	stream environment zone
SIP	State Implementation Plan
SO2	sulfur dioxide
SWANCC	Solid Waste Agency of Northern Cook County
SWDA	Solid Waste Disposal Act
SWMA	Solid Waste Management Act
TCLP	Toxicity Characteristic Leaching Procedure
TDRs	transferable development rights

TCNOR	Texas Committee On Natural Resources
TMDL	total maximum daily load
TRI	Toxic Release Inventory
TSCA	Toxic Substances Control Act
TSDF	treatment, storage and disposal facility
TVA	Tennessee Valley Authority
UST	underground storage tank
UWC	Universal Widget Company
VOCs	volatile organic compounds
WQLS	Water Quality Limited Segment
WQS	Water Quality Standards

*

ENVIRONMENTAL POLICY LAW

*

PART I

INTRODUCTION

In this part we present the background themes and legal underpinnings of environmental law. Chapter 1 begins with an explanation of what sets environmental law apart from other policy topics, and highlights perspectives from ecology, economics, and philosophy.

In Chapter 2, we address the doctrines developed by the common law to address resource allocation and pollution problems. Despite the great expansion of statutory environmental law in the late 20th century, the common law remains important, especially in the area of toxic torts.

Nonetheless, modern environmental law is primarily a public law subject, administered by federal and state governmental agencies. Understanding environmental law, therefore, requires some exposure to the basics of administrative law. Chapter 3 provides that background.

Decisions affecting the environment are made by individuals and by government at all levels. Chapter 4 addresses the allocation of environmental decisionmaking power between federal and state governments, and between government and the marketplace.

CHAPTER ONE

ENVIRONMENTAL POLICY PERSPECTIVES

SECTION 1. WHAT IS ENVIRONMENTAL LAW?

The environment is where we live; it encompasses all our surroundings—physical, biological, and social. The physical environment includes such things as the air we breathe; the water we drink, grow crops with, and use in industrial processes; the soils that nourish our agriculture and support our buildings; and the storms, floods, and earthquakes that disrupt our lives. The biological environment includes the plants, animals, and micro-organisms that provide food, clothing, beauty, and companionship as well as disease and, occasionally, danger. Our surroundings also include the social and cultural environment—the form of our cities, the economic and ethnic diversity of their human populations, and the relationships among individuals and groups.

Environmental law is the regulation of human activities affecting the physical and biological environment, "a set of rules for managing the interface between humans and * * * the larger ecological systems within which human social and economic systems are nested." Jonathan Baert Wiener, Law and the New Ecology: Evolution, Categories, and Consequences, 22 Ecology L.Q. 325, 337 (1995). It includes governmentally-imposed limitations on pollution of the air, water and land; requirements that past pollution be remediated; protection of various aspects of nature, including wetlands and endangered species; and allocation of natural resources among competing uses. Although not directly aimed at the social and cultural environment, environmental law inevitably affects those aspects of our surroundings as well. Choices we make about air pollution, for example, affect the cost of electricity, the types of automobiles available, and the compactness of our cities. Concerns about the socio-cultural environment may also determine how we choose to attack environmental problems. We may, for example, want to find ways of dealing with hazardous waste that not only protect the air and water but also treat communities equitably.

This casebook concentrates on federal environmental law, both to avoid becoming mired in the variable details of state programs and because federal initiatives have been the major driving force behind the great expansion of environmental regulation that began in the 1970s. It is important to keep in mind, however, that environmental law occurs at both larger and smaller geographic scales. A number of treaties and international agreements address environmental concerns that cross international boundaries, such as emissions of ozone-destroying chemicals and distribution of the waters of international rivers. State law operates in combination with federal law in many environmental contexts, imposing additional limitations as well as implementing federally-determined goals. Local governments also play an important role, primarily as an outgrowth of their traditional regulation of land use and waste disposal.

Environmental law encompasses a wide range of problems, each of which could be addressed by multiple regulatory strategies. It is easy to get lost in the bewildering details of environmental regulation. The details are vitally important to the outcome of particular disputes, and anyone who wishes to become an environmental lawyer must learn how to master them. But to understand environmental policy, you must also see the larger picture. A good place to begin is to look for common characteristics of environmental problems that affect policy choices.

Richard J. Lazarus, Restoring What's Environmental About Environmental Law in the Supreme Court

47 UCLA L. Rev. 703, 744–48 (2000).

What makes environmental law distinctive is largely traceable to the nature of the injury that environmental protection law seeks to reduce, minimize, or sometimes prevent altogether. Environmental law is concerned, in the first instance, with impacts on the natural environment. Hence, although some environmental laws are concerned about human health effects, as are many other types of laws (e.g., food and drug, worker safety, Medicare, and food stamp programs), environmental law is concerned only about human health effects resulting from impacts on the natural environment. And, of course, many environmental laws are concerned only with those impacts and not with possible human health effects at all.

A common denominator, therefore, for environmental law is the *ecological injury* that serves as the law's threshold and often exclusive focus. That common denominator is also the primary source of the special challenges environmental law presents for lawmaking. Ecological injury has several recurring features that render its redress through law especially difficult. * * *

1. *Irreversible, Catastrophic, and Continuing Injury*: Environmental law is often concerned about the avoidance of irreversible, catastrophic results. The destruction of an aquifer upon which a community depends for drinking water, the erosion of soil necessary for farming that required centuries to develop, and the destruction of the ozone layer are not possibilities to be lightly taken. Such potential downsides render enormously costly any errors in decision making. Yet, while errors are costly, so too can be delays in decision making. Even the best resolution is worth little if

it is developed too late to prevent a chain of events inexorably leading to ecological disaster.

Finally, a closely related trait of some environmental injury is its continuing nature. Environmental law must address harm that increases over time. The harm is dynamic and not static in character. An oil spill addressed quickly may be confined to manageable dimensions. But conversely, if not quickly addressed, it may rapidly and exponentially increase in scope to overwhelming dimensions. Legal regimes that are inherently cautious and slow to react do not readily lend themselves to the quick action often necessary in the ecological context.

2. *Physically Distant Injury*: Ecological injury is often not physically confineable. Actions in one location may have substantial adverse effects in very distant locations. This may be because the pollutants actually travel from one place to another. Or it may be as the result of the adverse impacts of activities in one locale on a global commons, upon the viability of which many regions are dependent.

Long-range transportation of airborne pollutants is an example of the former. The ozone layer in the upper atmosphere exemplifies the transboundary implications of degradation of a commons resource, as the destruction of the ozone layer by activities in one part of the world can have serious environmental and human health effects in other parts of the world. Global warming presents a similar physical dimension.

For each, the associated challenges for the establishment of any legal regime are great, especially because the costs of control are imposed in one area and the benefits are enjoyed in a very different area. Such a distributional mismatch renders the adoption, implementation, and enforcement of the necessary transboundary legal rules very difficult. This is certainly true in the international arenas, but even far more localized spreadings of causes and effects between states and counties resist ready political resolutions.

3. *Temporally Distant Injury*: Much of the injury environmental law seeks to address is not imminent. Sometimes actions now may trigger the injury, but the injury itself will be realized only in the distant future. Sometimes the injury will be realized now and will increase, inexorably, over time. To the extent that the latter is occurring, this temporal character to some environmental injury may become, as a practical matter, irreversible and thus collapse into the first feature of ecological injury described above.

This temporal feature of ecological injuries poses challenges to legal doctrine and lawmaking analogous to those presented by the "physically distant" characteristic discussed above. The same distributional mismatch is presented but even more problematically, because the benefits to be enjoyed will generally inure only to future generations lacking any representation in current lawmaking fora. Such intergenerational effects raise issues regarding the propriety of "discounting" the value of future benefits (including human lives) in selecting environmental controls today. Even more fundamentally, however, the intergenerational dimension to ecological injury raises basic questions regarding the moral responsibilities that current generations have to safeguard the interests of future generations.

4. *Uncertainty and Risk*: There is much uncertainty associated with environmental injury, which poses even further challenges for lawmaking. The primary source of this uncertainty is the sheer complexity of the natural environment and, accordingly, how much is still unknown about it. This uncertainty expresses itself in our inability to know beforehand the environmental impact of certain actions. It equally undermines our ability to apprehend, after the fact, what precisely caused certain environmental impacts.

The inevitable upshot is that environmental laws that seek to prevent harm are directed to risk rather than to actual impact. It similarly means that environmental laws that seek to assign responsibility for harm that has already occurred are limited in their ability to do so.

Because, moreover, environmental law is concerned with risk, there is an inherently psychological dimension to the injury being redressed. The injury is not confined to that which occurs if the risk is itself realized. There is often psychological harm resulting from the risk itself, whether or not ever realized. For this same reason, by failing to address that mental dimension, one can increase the associated injury even if the numerical probability of the risk's physical realization remains the same.

5. *Multiple Causes*: Ecological injuries are rarely the product of a single action at an isolated moment of time. Putting aside the pervasive uncertainty issues, environmental harms are more typically the cumulative and synergistic result of multiple actions, often spread over significant time and space. This is primarily traceable to the sharing inherent in any common natural resource base, which is the object of so many simultaneous and sporadic actions over time and space.

6. *Noneconomic, Nonhuman Character*: Many of the ecological injuries resulting from environmental degradation are not readily susceptible to monetary valuation and have a distinctively nonhuman character. There is simply no readily available market analogue. The nonexclusive nature of the natural resources at stake is often one factor prompting resistance of valuation. Even more generally, the decision to protect the ecological interest in question may have been deliberately made notwithstanding any notion of economic value. It could, of course, be ultimately rooted in notions of uncertainty and concerns about adverse human health affects— e.g., the after-the-fact discovery that the DNA of a subspecies of fly would have cured the common cold. But it may instead be, and often is, based on the deeper notion that there are certain results—such as species extinction or resource destruction—that humankind should strive to avoid because they fall beyond its legitimate authority.

Other kinds of injury that resist ready monetary valuation are the adverse human health effects that can result from environmental degradation, although these valuation issues are shared by all laws designed to

safeguard human health. For some economists, *all* human health effects of
this kind must be susceptible to such valuation for the simple reason that
tradeoffs are inevitably made in any allocation of limited societal resources.
Nothing has infinite value, and each decision has opportunity costs related
to opportunities thereby foregone. But some environmental laws reflect a
very different philosophy, which posits that there are some adverse human
health effects that are presumptively out of bounds for policymakers. For
those who share that policy view, economic valuation and tradeoffs are
therefore not legitimate topics for policy discussion.

NOTES AND QUESTIONS

1. *Characteristics of Environmental Problems.* What characteristics does
Professor Lazarus identify as typical of environmental problems? Do all
environmental problems share all these characteristics? Is any one characteristic common to all environmental problems? Do you agree with Lazarus
that these characteristics make "redress through law especially difficult"?
How do they complicate the search for legal solutions to environmental
problems?

Can you think of any other characteristics that should be added to the
list? Are there often many victims as well as many causes of environmental
harm? How might that make legal redress more difficult to obtain? Another
common feature, implicit in Lazarus' discussion of the non-economic, nonhuman character of environmental harms, is that environmental problems
frequently implicate difficult tradeoffs between conflicting, deeply-held
values. These values are explored in more detail in Section 4 below. It is
worth thinking for a moment at this point, however, about the difficulty of
arriving at public policy positions in the face of deep moral divisions in
society. Consider, for example, the struggles over abortion, rights to die,
and other issues that are the subject of strong moral beliefs. How should
individual values be translated into public policy? Should a strong societal
consensus be required? To what extent does such a consensus exist with
respect to environmental problems?

2. *The Precautionary Principle.* As Professor Lazarus points out, two
common features of environmental problems are the possibility of irreversible or catastrophic harm, and the existence of substantial uncertainty
about the likelihood of such harm. One possible response to those conditions is application of the "precautionary principle," a general exhortation
to proceed cautiously which can be framed in various ways. One common
statement of the principle is that activities should not proceed until their
potential adverse effects are understood. Another is that the burden of
proof should rest with the proponent of an environmentally risky activity to
show that it will not be harmful, rather than with the government to show
that it will cause harm.

The precautionary principle has many proponents, particularly in
international law. It has been incorporated, in various forms, into many
treaties and international agreements, such as the 1992 Rio Declaration on
Environment and Development. But it also has its critics. Interpreted too

broadly, the principle could lead to paralysis, since adverse impacts are rarely fully understood, and proving the absence of harm is almost impossible. See Christopher D. Stone, Is There a Precautionary Principle?, 31 Envtl. L. Rep. 10790 (2001).

Who should bear the burden of proof in environmental decisions? Your answer is likely to depend on the relative values you assign to economic activity and the environment. The precautionary principle can be seen as a healthy recognition of our ignorance, designed to encourage additional inquiry and learning where the value of information is very high. It can also be seen as an unwarranted block on development, placing an unjustified premium on environmental values compared to others. Do we need a special rule for dealing with low or uncertain probabilities of catastrophic or irreversible harm? Are the tools used to evaluate ordinary risks (discussed further in Chapter 7, Section 1) sufficient for extra-ordinary risks?

3. *Psychological Harm.* Professor Lazarus argues that because "environmental law is concerned with risk, there is an inherently psychological dimension to the injury being redressed." Should environmental law concern itself with psychological harms? Consider first bystanders who inhale a chemical suspected to be toxic in the wake of a train derailment. Even if they never develop physical symptoms as a result, should they be compensated for their fear of cancer? Does it matter how rational that fear is, that is, whether and to what extent it is supported by evidence that the inhaled chemical may indeed cause cancer? Next, consider the desire of people who will never visit Alaska to have the Alaska National Wildlife Refuge remain pristine. Should that desire be factored into the decision to allow or forbid oil drilling in the refuge? How should it be weighed against the economic needs, or even the esthetic preferences, of local residents?

Section 2. Insights from Ecology

Because the defining characteristic of environmental problems is injury, or threatened injury, to the non-human natural world, environmental law has long looked to ecology for insight and justification. In the 1960s and 1970s, a major inspiration for environmental law was the image of humankind upsetting the "balance of nature," with potentially disastrous results.

Ecology began to move away from that image many years ago. Law has only recently followed.

Judy L. Meyer, The Dance of Nature: New Concepts in Ecology

69 Chi.-Kent L. Rev. 875, 875–886 (1994).

I. Natural Systems are Open and Continuously Changing; They are not at Equilibrium.

The classical paradigm in ecology conceives of an ideal ecosystem that is either at equilibrium, stable, or moving toward stability. * * * [E]arly ecological thinkers conceived of an ideal system that was stable, and they viewed nature as striving to achieve that ideal. In the field of plant ecology, individuals sought to identify the stable, self-perpetuating, climax community in an area and the well-defined stages leading to that climax. In the field of theoretical ecology, mathematical modelers solved their equations for the equilibrium condition.

Empirical data in several disciplines of ecology did not necessarily fit this classical paradigm. Natural communities were found to have multiple persistent states rather than a local climax, and there were multiple successional pathways—that is, several ways of getting there. Ecologists recognized that terrestrial and aquatic ecosystems in nature were frequently subjected to a wide range of disturbances including fires, windstorms, insect outbreaks, floods, and droughts. These disturbances alter succession and influence the distribution and abundance of species in the ecosystem.

* * * Discoveries like these have led to a paradigm shift in ecology.

The contemporary paradigm recognizes that ecosystems are open and not necessarily in equilibrium. It recognizes disturbance to be a natural and necessary part of ecosystems. It recognizes that systems are influenced by and can, in fact, be controlled by events occurring in neighboring or even distant ecosystems. The focus of the contemporary paradigm is on process rather than endpoint—on the trajectory of change rather than on the final endpoint. It recognizes historical contingency: the state of the system today depends on what happened yesterday as well as decades ago.

* * *

The classical view of nature is of a system striving for equilibrium, which implies that systems will maintain themselves in balance if they are protected from human disturbance. This view results in a very different conservation and management strategy than the strategy that would result from the non-equilibrium paradigm. * * * Rather than simply protecting the endpoint, we need to preserve the processes that generate the desired result. Disturbance * * * is an essential part of the process.

* * *

The lack of stable endpoints in nature has implications for how we write regulations and assess the impacts of human activity. Consider the issue of preserving water quality. Over the past decade, we have achieved considerable water quality improvement by strict end-of-pipe regulations. As we begin to tackle the problems of nonpoint pollution, it will be necessary to shift our regulatory emphasis to maintaining the ecological integrity of the rivers receiving the runoff. We cannot do this by establishing some threshold value of a metric or series of metrics that rivers have to achieve to be considered of high quality. Regardless of what we choose for this metric, it will vary with region, season, and year. * * *

Danger lurks in misinterpretation of the new paradigm: if change is a part of nature, then can we view anthropogenic change as just part of the natural way? Absolutely not; the new paradigm is not a license for environmental abuse. Anthropogenic change differs from natural change in both quality and rate. It is more rapid and often of a type never before experienced by natural ecosystems. Anthropogenic change is acceptable only if that change is within limits. * * * We can use natural rates of change to help set acceptable limits for anthropogenic change. One important role for ecological science is to determine natural rates of change—to understand intrinsic variation in ecological phenomena over long periods of time.

II.   Linkages are Extensive in the Landscape * * *

* * * Our history of dealing with problems of eutrophication or acidification of lakes has taught us that activities in one part of the landscape greatly influence other parts. * * * Our laws need to recognize these natural connections in the landscape. As an example, we know that in many landscapes, streams and groundwater are linked physically, chemically and biologically. Yet * * * [i]n some cases, a pipe that pumps water from a stream is subject to a different set of laws than a pipe that pumps water from the ground a few feet from the channel. This makes little ecological sense. * * *

III.   Indirect Effects can be as Significant as Direct Effects in Natural Systems.

This concept is another expression of the connectedness of ecological systems. Ecologists have long observed the importance of direct effects in ecosystems: for example, the response of lakes to nutrient additions from municipal wastewater. Yet it is not just these direct, "bottom-up" effects that influence aquatic ecosystems. "Top-down" and indirect effects are often equally important; altering higher trophic levels affects lower trophic levels in a "trophic cascade." A simple description of a lake food web illustrates how this trophic cascade can be manipulated by lake managers. In a lake, algae are fed on by herbivorous zooplankton, which are fed on by planktivorous (plankton eating) fish like bluegill, which become food for piscivorous fish like bass. As bass numbers increase (for example, from stocking), bluegill numbers decrease, large herbivorous zooplankton like Daphnia increase and graze heavily on algae, which then decrease.

* * * It is important that regulators and managers recognize the multiplicity of control points in natural systems. Controlling nutrient inputs is important, but the structure of the food web will influence the effectiveness of that control measure.

* * *

V.   Organisms not only Adapt to the Environment, They Modify it.

* * * [W]e often forget how interdependent the physical and biological systems are on our planet. We readily accept a determining role for physical factors (for example, climatic influences on vegetation), but we forget the extent to which physical factors are influenced by biological activity. * * *

* * * A global circulation model does a decent job of predicting global patterns of temperature and rainfall when rates of evapotranspiration are what one would expect from a vegetated planet. But if the effects of plant evapotranspiration are removed from the model, it no longer provides reasonable predictions of global patterns of rainfall and temperature: it predicts no rain in Scotland and summer temperatures of forty-five degrees Celsius (one hundred and thirteen degrees Fahrenheit) in Chicago. Clearly the biosphere has a marked influence on our climate.

This example of global temperature and precipitation patterns brings me to my final point, which is that ecology is global. Humans are altering a highly interconnected biosphere, and the actions of another state or nation can have major implications for our environment in the United States. Even if United States resource management were fully enlightened and environmental laws rigorously enforced, we would not be guaranteed a sustainable biosphere. It is critical that environmental law maintain a global perspective.

NOTES AND QUESTIONS

1. *Insights From the "Old Ecology."* Despite its revolutionary nature, the non-equilibrium paradigm leaves undisturbed, and may even reinforce, several key concepts from the "old ecology." One is the idea of *interconnectedness*. Ecology, old and new, teaches that there are many important interconnections in the ecological landscape, not all of which are obvious at first glance. The flow of energy, water, and nutrients through ecosystems forms a complex web of linkages connecting communities and individuals across time, space, and species lines.

While it is not precisely true that everything is connected to everything else, there are enough connections that impacts can propagate across the landscape. A well-known example is the effect of removing the starfish *Pisaster ochraceus* from the rocky intertidal zone on the Pacific coast. The starfish is the top predator in these systems, preying on sessile, filter-feeding barnacles and mussels. In the presence of the starfish, these communities include some fifteen species. When all the starfish are removed from an area, the barnacles move in, and are eventually crowded out by the mussels. More surprisingly, the overall number of species in the intertidal community falls to eight, as algae are physically crowded out, and invertebrates cannot find either space or food. See R.T. Paine, Food Web Complexity and Species Diversity, 100 American Naturalist 65 (1966).

A second, related concept is that of *complexity*. Ecosystems are complicated and, almost without exception, poorly understood. It is often difficult to predict with any confidence the effects, quantitative and qualitative, of perturbations. Prior to the starfish experiment described above, for example, scientists would not have expected starfish removal to dramatically alter the community's algal composition.

A third concept is *the importance of scale*, in relation to time, geography, and extent of impacts. While disturbance on one scale may be an integral part of ecosystem functioning, the same disturbance on a larger scale may drastically alter the system. For example, small fires distributed across a landscape mosaic may increase the diversity of habitats and, therefore, of species. A large fire in the same area, however, may have a very different effect, eliminating species that depend on forested habitat. As the scale of reserves shrinks, managing them to allow disturbance at an appropriate scale but avoid disturbance at a catastrophic scale becomes more complicated. The temporal scale of disturbances is also important. Global temperatures have always fluctuated; the earth has gone through both warmer and cooler periods in the past. The ability of animals and plants to respond to temperature changes depends critically upon the speed with which those changes occur.

2. *People and Nature.* An enduring puzzle for environmental policy is how to deal with the dual status of people as 1) product of, and part of, nature; and 2) conqueror of nature, with far greater ability to control and alter nature than any other species. What implications did the old "balance-of-nature" paradigm have for the role of human beings in and with respect to nature? Precisely how do the implications of the non-equilibrium paradigm differ? Are human effects on other species or the natural world generally different from other "natural" effects in ways relevant to environmental policy and, in particular, the role of law? What limits should the law put on anthropogenic impacts on the natural world?

SECTION 3. INSIGHTS FROM ECONOMICS

A. ALLOCATING SCARCE RESOURCES: EFFICIENCY AND MARKETS

Environmental problems are problems of competition among conflicting demands for scarce resources. Air pollution would not be a problem if the atmosphere were large enough to provide a sink for all the waste people want to vent to it, and at the same time provide clean air for all who wish to breathe it. The same is true of endangered species—if there were enough habitat to satisfy both development and conservation desires, there would be no endangered species controversies.

Given that natural resources are scarce compared to human demands, we must make choices about their allocation. Welfare economists tell us that under certain circumstances a well-functioning decentralized market, driven by the self-interested decisions of individual participants, will allocate scarce resources efficiently. Efficiency in this sense has a particular meaning. An efficient allocation maximizes individual preference satisfaction, aggregated across society. The most stringent definition of efficiency is "Pareto efficiency." An allocation is Pareto-efficient if any change in that allocation would reduce at least one person's preference satisfaction. A change that makes at least one person better off and no one worse off (because the winners compensate the losers) is "Pareto-superior." Perfect markets should achieve Pareto-efficient allocation of resources because transactions are voluntary. The fact that Seller is willing to sell, and Buyer to buy, a resource at a given price in a voluntary market exchange proves that Seller prefers the money to the resource, and Buyer prefers the resource to the money. Assuming an ideal market, their transaction makes both better off and no one else worse off. The market achieves levels of efficiency that would be very difficult to duplicate by central government regulation because individuals, who know their own preferences best, make the key decisions.

In order for a market to allocate resources efficiently, it must meet several criteria. Buyers and sellers must have *full information* about all relevant characteristics of the goods or services exchanged. There must be large numbers of buyers and sellers in the market, so that there is *no collusion or monopoly power*. There must be *no externalities*, that is costs or benefits of the transaction that are not paid or realized by the participants. There must be *well-defined and enforceable property rights* to the resources traded. Finally, *transaction costs* must be sufficiently low to allow mutually beneficial transactions to occur. See Steven C. Hackett, Environmental and Natural Resources Economics: Theory, Policy, and the Sustainable Society 33–34 (1998).

Reliance on the market to allocate environmental resources is subject to two major criticisms. The first, explored in Section 3(B), below, is that markets for environmental resources rarely satisfy the criteria for efficient allocation. The second, considered in Section 4, is that efficiency is not the only, or necessarily the highest, societal goal.

B. MARKET FAILURE AND MARKET CORRECTION

Garrett Hardin, The Tragedy of the Commons

162 Science 1243, 1244–45, 1247 (1968).

The Tragedy of Freedom in a Commons

The tragedy of the commons develops in this way. Picture a pasture open to all. It is to be expected that each herdsman will try to keep as many cattle as possible on the commons. * * *

As a rational being, each herdsman seeks to maximize his gain. Explicitly or implicitly, more or less consciously, he asks, "What is the utility *to me* of adding one more animal to my herd?" This utility has one negative and one positive component.

1. The positive component is a function of the increment of one animal. Since the herdsman receives all the proceeds from the sale of the additional animal, the positive utility is nearly + 1.

2. The negative component is a function of the additional overgrazing created by one more animal. Since, however, the effects of overgrazing are shared by all the herdsmen, the negative utility for any particular decision-making herdsman is only a fraction of –1.

Adding together the component partial utilities, the rational herdsman concludes that the only sensible course for him to pursue is to add another animal to his herd. And another; and another.... But this is the conclusion reached by each and every rational herdsman sharing a commons. Therein is the tragedy. Each man is locked into a system that compels him to increase his herd without limit—in a world that is limited. Ruin is the destination toward which all men rush, each pursuing his own best interest in a society that believes in the freedom of the commons. Freedom in a commons brings ruin to all.

* * *

In an approximate way, the logic of the commons has been understood for a long time, perhaps since the discovery of agriculture or the invention of private property in real estate. But it is understood mostly only in special cases which are not sufficiently generalized. Even at this late date, cattlemen leasing national land on the western ranges demonstrate no more than an ambivalent understanding, in constantly pressuring federal authorities to increase the head count to the point where overgrazing produces erosion and weed-dominance. Likewise, the oceans of the world continue to suffer from the survival of the philosophy of the commons. Maritime nations still respond automatically to the shibboleth of the "freedom of the seas." Professing to believe in the "inexhaustible resources of the oceans," they bring species after species of fish and whales closer to extinction.

The national parks present another instance of the working out of the tragedy of the commons. At present, they are open to all, without limit. The parks themselves are limited in extent—there is only one Yosemite Valley—whereas population seems to grow without limit. The values that visitors seek in the parks are steadily eroded. Plainly, we must soon cease to treat the parks as commons or they will be of no value to anyone.

What shall we do? We have several options. We might sell them off as private property. We might keep them as public property, but allocate the right to enter them. The allocation might be on the basis of wealth, by the use of an auction system. It might be on the basis of merit, as defined by some agreed-upon standards. It might be by lottery. Or it might be on a first-come, first-served basis, administered to long queues. These, I think, are all the reasonable possibilities. They are all objectionable. But we must choose—or acquiesce in the destruction of the commons that we call our national parks.

Pollution

In a reverse way, the tragedy of the commons reappears in problems of pollution. Here it is not a question of taking something out of the commons, but of putting something in—sewage, or chemical, radioactive, and heat wastes into water; noxious and dangerous fumes into the air; and distracting and unpleasant advertising signs into the line of sight. The calculations of utility are much the same as before. The rational man finds that his share of the cost of the wastes he discharges into the commons is less than the cost of purifying his wastes before releasing them. Since this is true for everyone, we are locked into a system of "fouling our own nest," so long as we behave only as independent, rational, free-enterprisers.

The tragedy of the commons as a food basket is averted by private property, or something formally like it. But the air and waters surrounding us cannot readily be fenced, and so the tragedy of the commons as a cesspool must be prevented by different means, by coercive laws or taxing devices that make it cheaper for the polluter to treat his pollutants than to discharge them untreated. We have not progressed as far with the solution of this problem as we have with the first. Indeed, our particular concept of private property, which deters us from exhausting the positive resources of the earth, favors pollution. The owner of a factory on the bank of a stream—whose property extends to the middle of the stream—often has difficulty seeing why it is not his natural right to muddy the waters flowing past his door. The law, always behind the times, requires elaborate stitching and fitting to adapt it to this newly perceived aspect of the commons.

* * *

Mutual Coercion Mutually Agreed Upon

The social arrangements that produce responsibility are arrangements that create coercion, of some sort. Consider bank-robbing. The man who takes money from a bank acts as if the bank were a commons. How do we prevent such action? Certainly not by trying to control his behavior solely by a verbal appeal to his sense of responsibility. * * *

The morality of bank robbing is particularly easy to understand because we accept complete prohibition of this activity. We are willing to say "Thou shalt not rob banks," without providing for exceptions. But temperance also can be created by coercion. Taxing is a good coercive device. To keep downtown shoppers temperate in their use of parking space we introduce parking meters for short periods, and traffic fines for longer ones. We need not actually forbid a citizen to park as long as he wants to; we need merely make it increasingly expensive for him to do so. * * *

* * * To many, the word coercion implies arbitrary decisions of distant and irresponsible bureaucrats; but this is not a necessary part of its meaning. The only kind of coercion I recommend is mutual coercion, mutually agreed upon by the majority of the people affected.

To say that we mutually agree to coercion is not to say that we are required to enjoy it, or even to pretend we enjoy it. Who enjoys taxes? We all grumble about them. But we accept compulsory taxes because we recognize that voluntary taxes would favor the conscienceless. We institute and (grumblingly) support taxes and other coercive devices to escape the horror of the commons. * * *

———

The Tragedy of the Commons illustrates the consequences of market failure. The grazing commons in Hardin's essay violates two of the requirements for efficient markets: it lacks well-defined property rights, and it permits externalization of costs. These two flaws are connected. In the absence of defined, enforceable limits on each herder's rights to the commons, herders can externalize a portion of the costs of their use, while internalizing the full benefits. As a result, every herder has an incentive to overutilize the resource.

The commons example can be generalized to all "collective" or "public" goods, defined as goods which cannot be supplied to one person without also making them available to others. The classic example of a collective good is national defense, since one person cannot be protected against a missile strike without also protecting her neighbors. Clean air is another obvious example—if the air is healthy for one person, it is necessarily healthy for others nearby. Can you think of other environmental collective goods?

Because the supply of collective goods cannot be limited to those who pay, the market system breaks down. No one consumer will pay the full price of the good, because no one consumer can realize the full benefit. Moreover, individual consumers expecting that others will pay may rationally decide to "free ride," paying nothing but expecting to enjoy the benefits because others will pay. If everyone thinks that way no one will pay, and the good simply will not be supplied. Collective goods are therefore overconsumed and undersupplied in the market.

How can collective good problems like the tragedy of the commons be solved? What solutions does Hardin suggest in the national park context? In the pollution context? Why are those suggestions different?

Because the problem is one of market failure, the solution is societal intervention in some form to correct that failure. Intervention can take many different forms.

1. *Command-and-control regulation.* The government (or any other authority with the power to impose sanctions) can step in to create enforceable standards for use of or access to the commons. In the pollution context, the government sets standards for allowable emissions. To be effective, those standards must be backed by mechanisms for detecting and punishing violations, which may impose significant administrative costs.

Command-and-control is the predominant strategy employed by our current environmental law system. Environmentalists have traditionally favored the command-and-control system, while economists have long questioned the efficiency of centrally-determined, uniform standards.

2. *Privatizing the commons.* Property owners who realize both the costs and the benefits associated with caring for and exploiting resources have incentives to use those resources efficiently. If the grazing commons is divided into individual property allotments, from which the owner can exclude other herders' livestock, the perverse incentives to over-exploit the resource should disappear. This solution is promoted by advocates of "free-

market environmentalism." See generally Terry L. Anderson & Donald R. Leal, Free Market Environmentalism (2001).

Of course, some resources are more easily privatized than others. Fencing portions of a pasture is straightforward, although it entails some costs. Dividing the air into individual allotments seems much more difficult. With some ingenuity, this too can be done, at least for some purposes. An example is Title IV of the Clean Air Act, which sets up a system of tradable permits for SO_2 emissions, a major cause of acid rain, from power plants and other major sources. The program essentially sets a cap on the extent to which those sources can use the atmosphere to dispose of their SO_2, allocates the allowable SO_2 increment among existing sources, and allows those sources to trade with one another, setting up a market for SO_2 emissions.

Clear, secure, tradable property rights allow a private market, with the benefits of decentralized decisionmaking, to flourish. Under a command-and-control system, all polluters must install the same equipment or control pollution to the same level. Tradable permits allow those able to control pollution at less cost to profit from that ability by selling their excess credits to those less able to reduce emissions. If the market works well, the same level of pollution control will be reached at less cost than under a command-and-control regime.

This type of market also allows environmentalists to satisfy their preferences for clean air, provided they are willing to pay the going price. They can purchase and retire, rather than use, the credits, thereby reducing allowable emissions. Various nonprofit organizations, including environmental law societies at several law schools, have bought and retired SO_2 credits.

3. *Economic incentives.* Instead of establishing standards and issuing permits, government can force users of collective goods to bear the costs of their actions through taxes or fines. Taxes have the drawback of not assuring a specific level of control. It can also be difficult to determine the appropriate amount of a tax or charge if the goal is to induce specific levels of behavior modification. But taxes offer the advantage of facilitating individually adaptive responses much the same way that private rights do. Firms able to reduce emissions pay lower taxes, and therefore enjoy a competitive advantage. Investment and innovation in pollution control is directly rewarded.

Fines, taxes, and fees are negative economic incentives, designed to force the producers of environmental costs to internalize those costs in their decisions. Government can also use positive economic incentives, subsidies, to help the producers of environmental benefits internalize the value of those benefits. Environmental subsidies include federal payments to local governments for wastewater treatment plants and tax credits for pollution control equipment.

C.   COST-BENEFIT ANALYSIS

To many economists, the proper goal of regulation is correction of market failure or, put another way, achievement of the efficient distribution of resources in the absence of an ideal market. Cost-benefit analysis provides, in theory at least, an objective mechanism for determining whether a proposed regulation is efficient.

The concept of efficiency employed in cost-benefit analysis differs from the Pareto efficiency described earlier. Without a market, it can be exceedingly difficult to ensure that no one is made worse off by a regulation (economists would say the transaction costs of arranging for winners to compensate losers can be very high). Recognizing that, economists have developed an alternative, less stringent, efficiency criterion known as Kaldor–Hicks efficiency. An allocation decision satisfies this criterion if the aggregate gains in preference satisfaction exceed the aggregate losses. A change that imposes heavy losses on a small number of people will nonetheless be efficient in the Kaldor–Hicks sense if it provides a very small benefit to a large number of people.

While this might seem unfair at first glance, it has substantial intuitive appeal when we think resources are inappropriately distributed but transaction costs or other factors will prevent the market from redistributing them efficiently. Consider, for example, land reform in nations where ownership is concentrated in a small elite class. Government redistribution of land to the larger peasant class would be Kaldor–Hicks efficient if the new owners would value the land more highly than the old ones. Yet lack of resources, and perhaps social taboos, would prevent the peasants from ever obtaining the land in the market. Under the circumstances, it may seem appropriate for government to step in and transfer the land to the peasants, particularly if the wealthy owners are allowing the land to sit idle. We may not even be sympathetic if the government does not compensate those owners for the loss of their land.

Cost-benefit analysis tests for Kaldor–Hicks efficiency by comparing the total societal costs of a policy with the total societal benefits, using dollars as the common metric. Future costs and benefits are *discounted* to present value. When both costs and benefits are strictly monetary, discounting is non-controversial (although there may be fierce arguments about the discount rate). It simply reflects the uncontroverted fact that money received later is worth less than money received earlier. If you doubt that, consider being asked to choose between getting $500 today and getting $500 five years from now. Most people would opt for the former without hesitation. Discounting becomes highly controversial, however, when applied to non-monetary benefits such as years of life saved by restricting use of a toxic chemical, or a river left free-running by not building a dam. Will those be worth more or less in the future than today? The answer is not obvious: we could not "invest" a river today to generate more rivers in the future. On the other hand, keeping the river free may cost us money we could otherwise invest.

The discounting decision, and the choice of discount rate, often have enormous impacts on the outcome of cost-benefit analyses because environmental costs and benefits are typically realized over long time frames.

> [T]he present value of a benefit of $1 million to be received in ten years from now is $900,000 if one uses a 1% discount rate, but only $390,000 if one applies a 10% discount rate. Discounted at 10%, one dollar received fifty years from now is worth slightly less than a penny today—a difference of two orders of magnitude. Even more dramatic, if one discounts present world GNP over two hundred years at 5% per annum, it is worth only a few hundred thousand dollars, the price of a good apartment. Discounted at 10%, it is equivalent to a used car.

Lisa Heinzerling, Discounting Our Future, 34 Land & Water L. Rev. 39, 44 (1999) (internal quotation marks omitted).

Like discounting, cost-benefit analysis itself is straightforward and non-controversial when both costs and benefits are readily measured in dollars. But in the environmental context, many costs and benefits are not readily monetizable. Many, perhaps most, environmental amenities are not traded in any existing market, and many people are uncomfortable with assigning a monetary price to those amenities. What is the value, for example, of a clean river, an unspoiled view, or healthy air? Many people would intuitively describe those things as priceless.

Economists, however, have developed techniques for assigning prices to a wide range of environmental amenities. The normative objections to using such prices to make policy decisions are considered below, in Section 4. Setting those aside for the moment, a major technical challenge remains. How can we estimate the monetary value of environmental goods and services for which no market exists? Economists generally use *contingent valuation* or *hedonic pricing* to estimate consumer willingness to pay for those goods and services in a hypothetical market.

Contingent valuation relies on surveys asking respondents whether they would be willing to pay specified amounts to ensure a specific policy outcome. For example, to determine the value of protecting salmon runs from extinction, residents of the Pacific northwest might be asked if they would pay $5, $50, or $500 annually to protect salmon. Contingent valuation has been criticized on several grounds, including: that people who have never thought about the question may simply pick an answer at random, revealing little about their true preferences; that people may not be prepared to express their environmental values in terms of money; and that people may overstate their willingness to pay because they do not actually have to come up with the money.

Hedonic pricing uses information from actual markets to infer the value of environmental amenities. For example, analysts can compare the value of parcels of land differing in only one characteristic, such as scenic beauty, air quality, or access to environmental amenities. The price differential reflects the value of the environmental characteristic. This method has the advantage of reflecting real market behavior, but it cannot determine values for many environmental goods. In particular, it cannot reflect existence values, the extent to which people care about aspects of the environment they do not expect ever to use. No real market can be used to estimate the value of the Alaska National Wildlife Refuge to people in the lower forty-eight who do not wish to go to Alaska, but enjoy knowing that the refuge exists in a relatively pristine condition. The difficulty of estimating environmental benefits is often compounded by uncertainties about the extent or probability of environmental harm and long time horizons for the appearance of injury. For a more detailed explanation of these techniques, see Steven C. Hackett, Environmental and Natural Resources Economics: Theory, Policy, and the Sustainable Society 110–117 (1998).

Assuming the technical challenges can be surmounted, many environmentalists remain uncomfortable about using cost-benefit analysis to evaluate environmentally protective regulations. Critics of cost-benefit analysis are skeptical that environmental values can, or should, be monetized. They fear that benefits for which no monetary value can be generated will be effectively ignored in the decision. They also point out that cost-benefit analysis is as much art as science, leaving a great deal of room for subjective guesses. As Professor Daniel A. Farber points out: "Except in extreme cases, the result of a cost-benefit analysis often turns on a series of discretionary judgments; competent, reasonable analysts can come up with quite different but equally defensible answers." Daniel A. Farber, Revitalizing Regulation, 91 Mich. L. Rev. 1278, 1282 (1993). Particularly when it is carried out by the Office of Management and Budget, an agency widely regarded during the Reagan–Bush years as hostile to regulation, environmentalists suspect that cost-benefit analysis may be slanted against environmental protection.

Environmentalists have also vigorously criticized the goal of cost-benefit analysis, achieving Kaldor–Hicks efficiency, that is maximizing aggregate societal welfare. Why might environmentalists disagree with efficiency as a decision criterion? What other goals might environmental regulation have? Much has been written about the appropriate use and shortcomings of cost-benefit analysis as a tool for determining public policy, in the environmental context and others. Some recent examples include: Symposium, Cost–Benefit Analysis: Legal, Economic, and Philosophical Perspectives, 29 J. Legal Stud. 913–1152 (2000); Matthew D. Adler and Eric A. Posner, Rethinking Cost–Benefit Analysis, 109 Yale L.J. 165 (1999); Lisa Heinzerling, Regulatory Costs of Mythic Proportions, 107 Yale L.J. 1981 (1998); David M. Driesen, The Societal Cost of Environmental Regulations: Beyond Administrative Cost–Benefit Analysis, 24 Ecology L.Q. 545 (1997).

D. THE INTERFACE OF ECONOMICS AND ECOLOGY: ECOSYSTEM SERVICES

In addition to a range of material goods, nature supplies humanity with an array of useful services, such as waste decomposition and detoxification, air and water purification, crop pollination, pest control, and flood control. The importance of these ecosystem services was recognized long ago; the national forest system was established in the late 19th century not only to ensure the nation a lasting timber supply, but also to protect water supplies and reduce flood danger.

Recently, ecologists and economists have worked to bring ecosystem services systematically into environmental policy decisions. This effort may help increase public awareness of ecosystem functions which are easily taken for granted. Because ecosystems services are collective goods for which markets do not currently exist and cannot easily be created, however, properly valuing them in environmental decisions is extraordinarily difficult. In addition to facing the usual difficulties of non-market valuation, it requires a level of ecological understanding that may be difficult to obtain. For discussions of the valuation problem, see, e.g., Gretchen C. Daily et al., The Value of Nature and the Nature of Value, 289 Science 395 (2000); N.E. Bockstael et al., On Measuring Economic Values for Nature, 34 Envt'l Sci. & Tech. 1384 (2000); R.K. Turner et al., Ecosystem Services Value, Research Needs, and Policy Relevance: A Commentary, 25 Ecological Economics 61 (1998); Robert Costanza et al., The Value of the World's Ecosystem Services and Natural Capital, 387 Nature 253 (1997); James Salzman, Valuing Ecosystem Services, 24 Ecology L.Q. 887 (1997).

Despite the challenges, many economists, ecologists, and policy analysts are enthusiastic about the ecosystem services approach. As one group explains:

> An explicit ecosystem services perspective provides two obvious benefits. The first is political. Understanding the role of ecosystem services powerfully justifies why habitat preservation and biodiversity conservation are vital, though often overlooked, policy objectives. While a wetland surely provides existence and option values to some people, the benefits provided by the wetland's nutrient retention and flood protection services are both universal and undeniable. Tastes may differ over beauty, but they are in firm accord over the high costs of polluted water and flooded homes.

> The second benefit is instrumental. Efforts to capture the value of ecosystem services may spur institutional designs and market mechanisms that effectively promote environmental protection at the local, regional, national, and international levels. To realize this potential, however, we must first create market mechanisms and institutions that can capture and maximize service values. If given the opportunity, natural systems can, in many cases, quite literally "pay their way." The key challenge is how to make this happen.

James Salzman, Barton H. Thompson & Gretchen Daily, Protecting Ecosystem Services: Science, Economics, and Law, 20 Stan. Envtl. L.J. 309, 312 (2001).

Not everyone shares this enthusiasm, however. Knowledge of ecosystem services can provide greater accuracy to cost-benefit determinations, but does not necessarily overcome skepticism about whether cost-benefit analysis is an appropriate basis for environmental policy decisions. Consider the view of two ecologists:

> [E]conomists should recognize that cost-benefit analysis is only part of the decisionmaking process and that it lies at the same level as other considerations. Ecologists should accept that monetary valuation of biodiversity and ecosystem services is possible (and even helpful) for part of its value, typically its use value. We contend that the realistic substitute for markets, when they fail, is a transparent decision-making process, not old-style cost-benefit analysis. The idea that, if one could get the price right, the best and most effective decisions at both the individual and public levels would automatically follow is, for many scientists, a sort of Panglossian obsession. In reality, there is no simple solution to complex problems. We fear that putting an a priori monetary value on biodiversity and ecosystem services will prevent humans from valuing the environment other than as a commodity to be exploited, thus reinvigorating the old economic paradigm that assumes a perfect substitution between natural and human-made capital.

Marino Gatto & Giulio A. DeLeo, Pricing Biodiversity and Ecosystem Services: The Never–Ending Story, 50 BioScience 347, 354 (2000).

NOTES AND QUESTIONS

1. *Cost-Benefit Analysis in Agency Decisions.* As we shall see in subsequent chapters, some environmental laws forbid consideration of costs in setting environmental standards. In a world of scarce resources, can a policy forbidding consideration of costs ever be justified? Does Congress truly expect agencies to impose regulations that will wreak economic havoc? For one view of the origin and consequences of such statutory mandates, see John P. Dwyer, The Pathology of Symbolic Legislation, 17 Ecology L.Q. 233 (1990).

Since 1981, federal agencies have been required by executive order to prepare cost-benefit analyses of major regulations. Executive Order 12866, issued by Bill Clinton and currently in effect, mandates that each agency "assess both the costs and benefits of the intended regulation and, recognizing that some costs and benefits are difficult to quantify, propose or adopt a regulation only upon a reasoned determination that the benefits of the intended regulation justify its costs." Exec. Ord. 12866, § 1(b)(6) (Sept. 30, 1993). The executive order does not purport to alter agencies' statutory responsibilities or authority, so agencies are not to base their regulatory decisions on the cost-benefit analysis if a statute forbids consideration of costs. Is there any point to requiring a cost-benefit analysis of such regulations?

Where the applicable statute does not forbid consideration of costs, what role should cost-benefit analysis play in regulatory decisions? Should cost-benefit analysis be required? Should it be determinative? Can you think of circumstances under which it would be appropriate to adopt a regulation that failed a cost-benefit analysis?

2. *Discounting and Obligations to Future Generations.* Should discounting be applied to non-monetary costs and benefits in evaluating environmental policy? Do obligations to future generations argue for or against discounting? For discussion of these issues, see Heinzerling, supra; Richard L. Revesz, Environmental Regulation, Cost-benefit Analysis, and the Discounting of Human Lives, 99 Colum. L. Rev. 941 (1999); Daniel A. Farber & Paul A. Hemmersbaugh, the Shadow of the Future: Discount Rates, Later Generations, and the Environment, 46 Vand. L. Rev. 267 (1993); Tyler Cowen & Derek Parfit, Against the Social Discount Rate, in Justice Between Age Groups and Generations 144 (Peter Laslett & James S. Fishkin eds., 1992).

SECTION 4.   THE ROLE OF VALUES

Ecology and economics are useful tools for understanding the natural world and human behavior, both integral aspects of environmental problems. They are widely accepted, by persons on both sides of the political spectrum, as means to improve the odds of achieving societally-determined ends. When their practitioners tout them, implicitly or explicitly, as methods for determining societal goals, however, they become controversial. A key reason for the continuing controversy over environmentally protective regulation is that it implicates a fundamental clash of deeply held values. As the following excerpts illustrate, ecologists and economists often find themselves on opposite sides of this value divide.

Aldo Leopold, A Sand County Almanac: With Other Essays on Conservation from Round River

218–240 (Oxford University Press 1949, 1977, 1981).

The first ethics dealt with the relation between individuals; the Mosaic Decalogue is an example. Later accretions dealt with the relation between the individual and society. The Golden Rule tries to integrate the individual to society; democracy to integrate social organization to the individual.

There is as yet no ethic dealing with man's relation to land and to the animals and plants which grow upon it. * * * The land-relation is still strictly economic, entailing privileges but not obligations.

The extension of ethics to this third element in human environment is, if I read the evidence correctly, an evolutionary possibility and an ecological necessity. * * *

All ethics so far evolved rest upon a single premise: that the individual is a member of a community of interdependent parts. His instincts prompt him to compete for his place in the community, but his ethics prompt him also to co-operate (perhaps in order that there may be a place to compete for).

The land ethic simply enlarges the boundaries of the community to include soils, waters, plants, and animals, or collectively, the land.

This sounds simple: do we not already sing our love for and obligation to the land of the free and the home of the brave? Yes, but just what and whom do we love? Certainly not the soil, which we are sending helter-skelter downriver. Certainly not the waters, which we assume have no function except to turn turbines, float barges, and carry off sewage. Certainly not the plants, of which we exterminate whole communities without batting an eye. Certainly not the animals, of which we have already extirpated many of the largest and most beautiful species. A land ethic of course cannot prevent the alteration, management, and use of these "resources," but it does affirm their right to continued existence, and, at least in spots, their continued existence in a natural state.

In short, a land ethic changes the role of *Homo sapiens* from conqueror of the land-community to plain member and citizen of it. It implies respect for his fellow-members, and also respect for the community as such.

* * *

One basic weakness in a conservation system based wholly on economic motives is that most members of the land community have no economic value. Wildflowers and songbirds are examples. Of the 22,000 higher plants and animals native to Wisconsin, it is doubtful whether more than 5 per cent can be sold, fed, eaten, or otherwise put to economic use. Yet these creatures are members of the biotic community, and if (as I believe) its stability depends on its integrity, they are entitled to continuance.

When one of these non-economic categories is threatened, and if we happen to love it, we invent subterfuges to give it economic importance. At the beginning of the century songbirds were supposed to be disappearing. Ornithologists jumped to the rescue with some distinctly shaky evidence to the effect that insects would eat us up if birds failed to control them. The evidence had to be economic in order to be valid.

It is painful to read these circumlocutions today. We have no land ethic yet, but we have at least drawn nearer the point of admitting that birds should continue as a matter of biotic right, regardless of the presence or absence of economic advantage to us.

* * *

To sum up: a system of conservation based solely on economic self-interest is hopelessly lopsided. It tends to ignore, and thus eventually to eliminate, many elements in the land community that lack commercial value, but that are (as far as we know) essential to its healthy functioning. It assumes, falsely, I think, that the economic parts of the biotic clock will function without the uneconomic parts. * * *

A land ethic, then, reflects the existence of an ecological conscience, and this in turn reflects a conviction of individual responsibility for the health of the land. Health is the capacity of the land for self-renewal. Conservation is our effort to understand and preserve this capacity.

* * *

The "key-log" which must be moved to release the evolutionary process for an ethic is simply this: quit thinking about decent land-use as solely an economic problem. Examine each question in terms of what is ethically and esthetically right, as well as what is economically expedient. A thing is right when it tends to preserve the integrity, stability, and beauty of the biotic community. It is wrong when it tends otherwise.

William F. Baxter, People or Penguins: The Case for Optimal Pollution

4–12 (Columbia University Press 1974).

* * * Recently scientists have informed us that use of DDT in food production is causing damage to the penguin population. For the present purposes let us accept that assertion as an indisputable scientific fact. The scientific fact is often asserted as if the correct implication—that we must stop agricultural use of DDT—followed from the mere statement of the fact of penguin damage. But plainly it does not follow if my criteria are employed.

My criteria are oriented to people, not penguins. Damage to penguins, or sugar pines, or geological marvels is, without more, simply irrelevant. One must go further, by my criteria, and say: Penguins are important because people enjoy seeing them walk about rocks; and furthermore, the well-being of people would be less impaired by halting use of DDT than by giving up penguins. * * *

[T]his attitude does not portend any massive destruction of nonhuman flora and fauna, for people depend on them in many obvious ways, and they will be preserved because and to the degree that humans do depend on them.

* * *

I reject the proposition that we *ought* to respect the "balance of nature" or to "preserve the environment" unless the reason for doing so, express or implied, is the benefit of man.

I reject the idea that there is a "right" or "morally correct" state of nature to which we should return. The word "nature" has no normative connotation. Was it "right" or "wrong" for the earth's crust to heave in contortion and create mountains and seas? Was it "right" for the first amphibian to crawl up out of the primordial ooze? Was it "wrong" for plants to reproduce themselves and alter the atmospheric composition in favor of oxygen? For animals to alter the atmosphere in favor of carbon dioxide both by breathing oxygen and eating plants? No answers can be given to these questions because they are meaningless questions.

* * *

From the fact that there is no normative definition of the natural state, it follows that there is no normative definition of clean air or pure water—hence no definition of polluted air—or of pollution—except by reference to the needs of man. The "right" composition of the atmosphere is one which has some dust in it and some lead in it and some hydrogen sulfide in it—just those amounts that attend a sensibly organized society thoughtfully and knowledgeably pursuing the greatest possible satisfaction for its human members.

* * *

People enjoy watching penguins. They enjoy relatively clean air and smog-free vistas. Their health is improved by relatively clean water and air. Each of these benefits is a type of good or service. As a society we would be well advised to give up one washing machine if the resources that would have gone into that washing machine can yield greater human satisfaction when diverted into pollution control. We should give up one hospital if the resources thereby freed would yield more human satisfaction when devoted to elimination of noise in our cities. And so on, trade-off by trade-off, we should divert our productive capacities from the production of existing goods and services to the production of a cleaner, quieter, more pastoral nation up to—and no further than—the point at which we value more highly the next washing machine or hospital that we would have to do without than we value the next unit of environmental improvement that the diverted resources would create.

Mark Sagoff, We Have Met the Enemy and He Is Us *or* Conflict and Contradiction in Environmental Law

12 Envtl. L. 283, 283–308 (1982).

In a course I teach on environmental ethics, I ask students to read the Supreme Court opinion in *Sierra Club v. Morton*[, 405 U.S. 727 (1972)]. In that case environmentalists challenged a decision by the Forest Service to lease the Mineral King Valley, a wilderness area in the middle of Sequoia National Park, to Walt Disney Enterprises, to develop a ski resort. But let the Court describe the facts:

> The final Disney plan, approved by the Forest Service in January 1969, outlines a $35 million complex of motels, restaurants, swimming pools, parking lots, and other structures designed to accommodate 14,000 visitors daily.... Other facilities, including ski lifts, ski trails, a cog-assisted railway, and utility installations, are to be constructed on the mountain slopes and in other parts of the valley.... To provide access to the resort, the State of California proposes to construct a highway 20 miles in length. A section of this road would traverse

Sequoia National Park, as would a proposed high-voltage power line. . . .

I asked how many of the students had visited the wilderness at Mineral King or thought they would visit it as long as it remained a wilderness. No one raised a hand. Why not? Too many mosquitoes, someone said. Not enough movies, said another. Another offered to explain in technical detail the difference between chillblain and trench foot. * * *

Then I asked how many students would like to visit the Mineral King Valley if it were developed in the way Disney planned. Every hand went up. * * *

I brought the students to order by asking if they thought the government did the right thing in giving Disney Enterprises a lease to develop Mineral King. I asked them, in other words, whether they thought that environmental policy, at least in this instance, should be based on the principle of maximizing the satisfaction of consumer demand. Was there a connection between what the students as individuals wanted for themselves and what they thought we should do, collectively, as a nation?

The response was unanimous, visceral, and grim. All of the students believed that the Disney plan was loathsome and despicable; that the Forest Service had violated a public trust by approving it; and that the values for which we stand as a nation compel us to preserve the little wilderness we have for its own sake and as an historical heritage for future generations.

The consumer interests or preferences of my students are typical of those of Americans in general. Most Americans like a warm bed better than a pile of wet leaves. They would rather have their meals prepared in a kitchen than to cook them over a campstove. Disney's market analysts knew all this. They found that the resort would attract over 14,000 tourists a day, in summer and winter alike, which is a lot more people than now hike into Mineral King. Moreover, tourists would pay to use the valley; backpackers just walk in.

You might suppose that most Americans approved of the Disney proposal; after all, it would service their consumer demands. * * *

Yet the public's response to the Disney project was like that of my students—visceral and grim. Public opinion was so unfavorable that Congress acted in 1978 to prohibit the project, by making the Mineral King Valley a part of Sequoia National Park. * * *

Economists have given us a sophisticated array of tools for measuring the costs and benefits associated with various public works projects. These techniques generally help us to determine "consumer surplus"—that is, the amount that consumers are willing to pay for a project less the amount that the project will cost. The idea behind these techniques seems to be this: the use of resources that generates the greatest consumer surplus over the long run is the use that ought to be made of them. One such use, I believe, would be the development of a Disney resort at Mineral King.

One problem with economic techniques of "cost-benefit analysis," however, is that they may fail to register ideological or ethical convictions citizens entertain about the very things that interest them as consumers. * * *

The things we cherish, admire, or respect are not always the things we are willing to pay for. Indeed they may be cheapened by being associated with money. It is fair to say that the worth of the things we love is better measured by our *unwillingness* to pay for them. Consider love itself. A civilized person may climb the highest mountain, swim the deepest sea, or cross the hottest desert for love, sweet love. He might do anything, indeed, except be willing to pay for it.

* * *

The things we are unwilling to pay for are not worthless to us. We simply think we ought not to pay for them. Love is not worthless. We would make all kinds of sacrifices for it. Yet a market in love—or in anything we consider "sacred"—is totally inappropriate. These things have a *dignity* rather than a *price*. The things that have a dignity, I believe, are in general the things that help us to define our relationship with one another. The environment we share has such a dignity. The way we use and the way we preserve our common natural heritage helps to define our relation or association with each other. It also helps to define our association with generations in the future and in the past.

A. Dan Tarlock, Environmental Law: Ethics or Science?

7 Duke Envtl. L. & Pol'y F. 193, 194–95, 221–23 (1996).

The principal argument of this article is that environmental law and management should derive their primary political power and legitimacy from science, not ethics. This is a deliberately provocative statement because it runs counter to the pluralistic justification for environmental law, which posits that environmentalism can be sustained from multiple sources of legitimacy all of which are equal. * * * Pluralism has served the environmental movement well. If science does not support a position, the problem may be reclassified as ethical. As environmentalism matures, however, questions of legitimacy become more important and the pluralistic basis of environmentalism becomes more problematic by making legitimacy too contingent. The easy regulatory actions have been taken, and future actions intrude more deeply into personal choice and conflict more directly with the pursuit of other firmly rooted cultural interests.

* * *

Ethics are not a substitute for scientific analysis, and thus environmental law and environmentalism are more contingent than many would prefer them to be. Any principles derived from science remain subject to revision in light of new evidence. Ethics can legitimately, however, bridge the gap between scientific uncertainty and the risks of inaction pending further research through the adoption of the cautionary principle. Environmentalism does represent a profound shift in our world-view of our physical surroundings. Through science we have increasingly come to see natural processes as phenomena to be respected rather than manipulated. This new-found respect can support laws, enacted in advance of conclusive scientific evidence, which recognize the value of new resource functions. * * * However, as long as we value rationality (an open question with respect to some strains of modern environmentalism), science will continue to serve an important checking function. The need for some scientific justification, however probabilistic, for environmental regulation is necessary to constrain the potential arbitrariness and unfairness that can result from the substitution of intuition for verification.

* * *

The central project of environmental law has been to marry wonder to power. Environmentalism's central insight has been to demonstrate the need to supplant the Enlightenment view that humans are sovereign over nature with one which appreciates the many instrumental as well as intrinsic values of nature. In short, nature is both a commodity and a source of delight and wonder to be valued by different standards from the past. Environmental law's mission has been to counter the traditional bias in favor of the early and rapid exploitation of nature by using principles and procedures which try to sustain biodiversity over time. To many environmentalists this seems a modest if not incorrect objective, but it is Herculean in light of the continued dominance of the view that nature is a commodity for present consumption. The principal argument of this paper is that if environmental law is to succeed in this effort, there is no escape from the development of a science-based management. Biodiversity management can be informed by values which reflect the heightened appreciation of the functions that natural systems perform, but the management choices that are made must be grounded in science and recognized as contingent. Modification of management strategies and adjustment to new information, not the recognition of the rights of nature, will characterize the future of environmental law.

NOTES AND QUESTIONS

1. *Ecology and Values.* Does the new ecology undermine Leopold's call for a land ethic? His description of that ethic?

2. *Economics and Values.* To what extent do Leopold and Baxter agree? Exactly how do their views differ? Is Baxter's view of "economic" value broader than Leopold's? Is it broad enough to support Leopold's call for a land ethic?

3. *Obligations to Future Generations and the Possibility of Substitution.* Many people agree that the present generation has some obligation to take the needs of future generations into account. There is disagreement, however, about the definition of intergenerational equity. Economists tend to think of it as obliging us to consider future human welfare, in the sense of the opportunity to satisfy aggregate individual preferences. They also tend to view resources, including environmental resources, as inherently subject to substitution, so that if we run out of oil, or scenic vistas, we will find something else to satisfy our desires for energy and esthetic pleasure. In this light, intergenerational equity requires that we provide the future with a robust stock of aggregate capital, but it does not matter how much of that capital is natural. Ecologists are far less likely to see natural capital as replaceable by means of human ingenuity. They therefore equate intergenerational equity specifically with the maintenance of natural capital for future generations. This same disagreement haunts debates over "sustainable development." See, e.g., Robert M. Solow, Sustainability: An Economist's Perspective, in Economics of the Environment: Selected Readings (Robert Dorfman and Nancy Dorfman, eds., 3d ed. 1993); Emery N. Castle et al., The Economics of Sustainability, 36 Natural Res. J. 715, 716–17 (1996); Bryan G. Norton & Michael A. Toman, Sustainability: Ecological and Economic Perspectives, 73 Land Econ. 553, 555 (1997).

4. *Are Citizens Different From Consumers?* Do you agree with Professor Sagoff that people approach decisions differently, and may arrive at different conclusions, in the contexts of consumer and societal choices? Would you patronize a ski resort at Mineral King? Would you vote in favor of permitting such a ski resort there? What accounts for the willingness of Sagoff's students to visit the ski resort, but their unwillingness to allow its construction? Would their response be different if the land had been privately owned? Should it be? Can economics account for "citizen preferences"? Will willingness-to-pay surveys include those preferences? How else might they be measured? Should societal decisions depend only upon the *intensity* of preferences, or is their *basis* and *justification* more important?

5. *Preference Shaping.* The quest for economic efficiency depends upon the assumptions that individuals know their own preferences best, and that individual preferences deserve societal respect. It turns out, however, that preferences can be shaped, deliberately by techniques such as advertising, and unconsciously by experiences and information.

The malleability of preferences particularly complicates the search for long-term environmental policies. Consider the following excerpt:

> * * * The ecology movement seeks to have man's environment valued in and of itself and thereby prevent its being traded off for the other benefits it offers to man. * * *

> [But] [w]hat is considered a natural environment depends on the particular culture and society defining it. * * *

> * * * What a society takes to be a natural environment is one. * * *

> It is likely that we shall want to apply our technology to the creation of artificial environments. It may be possible to create environments that are evocative of other environments in other times and places. It is possible that, by manipulating memory through the rewriting of history, environments will come to have new meaning. Finally,

we may want to create proxy environments by means of substitution and simulation. In order to create substitutes, we must endow new objects with significance by means of advertising and by social practice. Sophistication about differentiation will become very important for appreciating the substitute environments. We may simulate the environment by means of photographs, recordings, models, and perhaps even manipulations in the brain. What we experience in natural environments may actually be more controllable than we imagine. Artificial prairies and wildernesses have been created, and there is no reason to believe that these artificial environments need be unsatisfactory for those who experience them.

Rare environments are relative, can be created, are dependent on our knowledge, and are a function of policy, not only tradition. It seems likely that economic arguments will not be sufficient to preserve environments or to suggest how we can create new ones. Rather, conscious choice about what matters, and then a financial and social investment in an effort to create significant experiences and environments, will become a policy alternative available to us.

What's wrong with plastic trees? My guess is that there is very little wrong with them. Much more can be done with plastic trees and the like to give most people the feeling that they are experiencing nature. We will have to realize that the way in which we experience nature is conditioned by our society—which more and more is seen to be receptive to responsible interventions.

Martin H. Krieger, What's Wrong With Plastic Trees? 179 Science 446, 446–53 (1973). Is there something wrong with plastic trees, even if people could be persuaded to enjoy them as much as the real thing? Does the malleability of preferences make it more or less important to protect the environment?

6. *The Search for Rationality.* Economists and ecological scientists tend to share the view that environmental policy decisions should be "rational" in a particular sense—that they should be arrived at and defended on objective grounds. Professor Tarlock argues that science can provide that rationality. Do you agree that environmental (or other) policy decisions must be grounded in some objective measure? What are the benefits of objective decisionmaking? What might be its shortcomings?

To what extent can science make environmental decisions more rational? Precisely what role does Tarlock suggest should be assigned to science? What role(s) would Leopold and Baxter have science play?

One well-known practitioner of conservation biology, a discipline devoted to determining how biological resources might best be protected, writes:

A distinguishing feature of conservation biology is that it is mission oriented. Underlying any mission is a set of values. Philosophers of science now recognize that no science is value free, despite all we were taught in school about the strict objectivity of the scientific method. Conservation biology is more value-laden than most sciences because it is not concerned with knowledge for its own sake but rather is directed toward particular goals. Maintaining biodiversity is an unquestioned goal of conservation biologists. * * *

Underlying the goals of conservation biology, whether general or specific, is the fundamental value assumption that biodiversity is good and ought to be preserved. * * *

Reed F. Noss, Some Principles of Conservation Biology, As They Apply to Environmental Law, 69 Chi.-Kent L. Rev. 893, 895 (1994). Does this confession undermine the usefulness of science as a basis for environmental decisionmaking?

CLASS DISCUSSION PROBLEM: SHOULD A HIGH–LEVEL RADIOACTIVE WASTE FACILITY BE SITED AT YUCCA MOUNTAIN?

The United States does not currently have a permanent repository for high-level nuclear waste. About ninety percent of high level waste is spent fuel from nuclear power plants; the rest comes from defense sources such as nuclear submarines. Each of the roughly one hundred nuclear reactors currently operating in the United States produces twenty to thirty metric tons (a metric ton is 1,000 kilograms, about 2,200 pounds) of spent nuclear fuel annually. As of September 2000, 42,000 metric tons of spent fuel were stored at more than seventy locations across the country. Spent nuclear fuel is very hot and highly radioactive. It contains both short-lived and long-lived radioactive components.

The federal government proposes to create a permanent high-level radioactive waste repository at Yucca Mountain, Nevada. Waste would be packaged in thick metal containers, which would be sealed and placed in tunnels averaging 1000 feet below the surface. Although the Department of Energy (DOE) describes the location as "remote," it lies less than 100 miles from Las Vegas, one of the fastest growing metropolitan areas in the nation. Yucca Mountain is also far away from most of the nation's commercial nuclear reactors, which are concentrated in the eastern portion of the country. See Figures 1 and 2.

Nonetheless, Yucca Mountain is an attractive site for climatic and other reasons. Water infiltration in a repository could corrode the containers in which the waste will be placed. Water can also carry radioactive materials to groundwater, and thence out into the environment. This risk is lower at Yucca Mountain than in many other locations, because annual rainfall is less than six inches and ground water lies 1000 feet below the proposed tunnels. In addition, Yucca Mountain, which like more than 80% of Nevada is federally-owned, sits at the southwest corner of the Nevada Test Site. Originally established for nuclear weapons testing, the Test Site is one of the largest restricted-access areas in the United States.

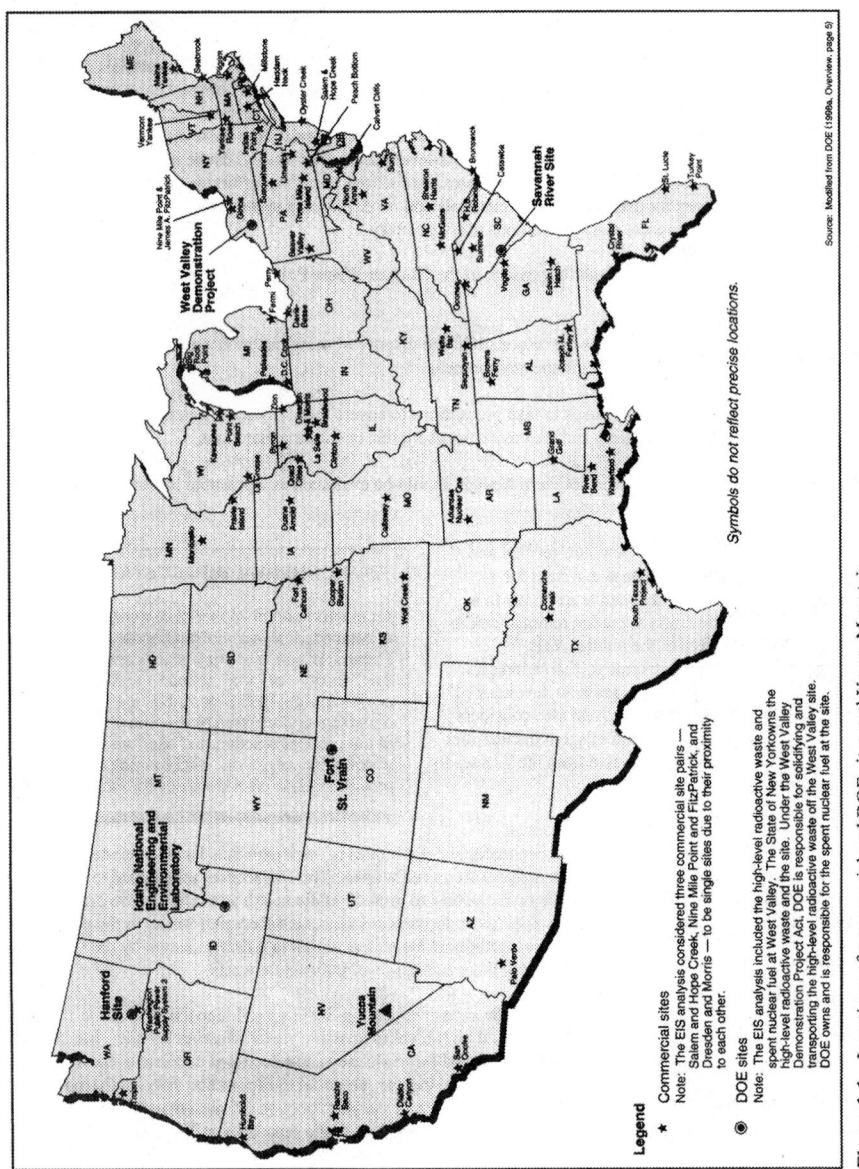

Figure 1-1. Locations of commercial and DOE sites and Yucca Mountain.

The route to a permanent high-level nuclear waste repository has been long and winding. The nuclear power industry began with the expectation that spent fuel would be reprocessed for reuse. In the 1970s, however, Presidents Ford and Carter prohibited reprocessing because of fears that the purified plutonium produced in reprocessing could be stolen for weapons use. President Reagan lifted the ban in 1981, but reprocessing remains uneconomical for commercial reactors.

Faced with a growing stockpile of spent fuel and no permanent disposal method, Congress passed the Nuclear Waste Policy Act (NWPA) in 1982. The NWPA adopted deep underground storage as the nation's strategy for high-level radioactive waste disposal, and directed the DOE to identify three potential repository sites. See 42 U.S.C. § 10132(b). The NWPA also imposed a fee on commercial generation of nuclear power to pay for construction and operation of a disposal site. 42 U.S.C. § 10222. In return for payment of this fee, generators were assured that the DOE would dispose of their waste no later than 1998. 42 U.S.C. § 10222(a)(5)(B).

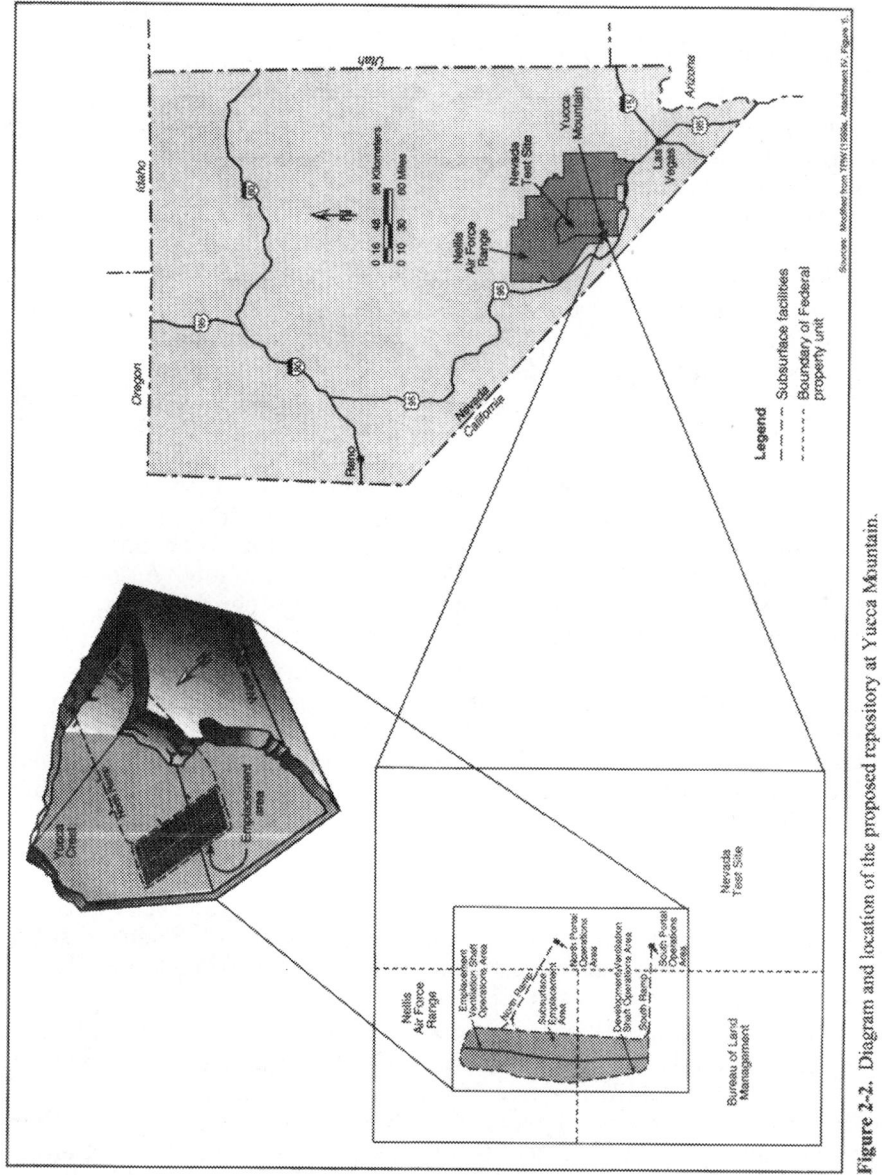

Figure 2-2. Diagram and location of the proposed repository at Yucca Mountain.

In 1986 the Secretary of Energy recommended, and the President approved, characterization of sites in Nevada (Yucca Mountain), Texas, and the state of Washington. In 1987, however, faced with strong political objections to the Texas and Washington sites, Congress amended the NWPA to designate Yucca Mountain as the only site for further characterization. 42 U.S.C. § 10172(a). If Yucca Mountain proves unsuitable, the DOE must seek further direction from Congress. Legislation limits the Yucca Mountain site to no more than 70,000 metric tons of waste, considerably less than the expected national inventory of spent fuel by 2030.

The siting process involves a series of decisions. If the DOE determines, after studying the site, preparing an environmental impact report, and holding public hearings in the vicinity, that the Yucca Mountain site is suitable for development of a high-level radioactive waste depository, it will recommend the site to the President. The President then must decide whether to forward that recommendation to Congress. If Nevada objects to developing the site, Congressional approval would be required for development. Following Congressional approval, the DOE must submit a license application to the Nuclear Regulatory Commission (NRC), which will evaluate the proposal for compliance with standards issued by the Environmental Protection Agency.

EPA issued standards for a Yucca Mountain repository in June 2001. See 66 Fed. Reg. 32074 (June 13, 2001), to be codified at 40 C.F.R. part 197. The standards require that, for 10,000 years after the repository opens, at a point 11 miles from the repository: 1) human exposure through groundwater not exceed 4 millirems per year (the same as the national standard for drinking water); and 2) human exposure through all routes not exceed 15 millirem per year. For comparison, a roundtrip journey by air from New York to Los Angeles exposes each passenger to 2 to 5 millirems. Background exposures in the United States, including both natural and man-made sources, average about 360 millirems annually. According to EPA, lifetime exposures of an additional 15 millirems per year will produce no more than 3 fatal cancers per 10,000 exposed persons.

Since 1987, the DOE has performed extensive site characterization studies. In 1999, DOE issued a draft Environmental Impact Statement which concluded that development of a high-level waste repository at Yucca Mountain should proceed. The DOE estimates that emplacement of waste at Yucca Mountain would begin about 2010 and capacity would be reached about 2033. The entire site would be permanently sealed fifty to three hundred years later. Radioactivity levels are expected to decrease by about five orders of magnitude during the first 100,000 years, as the short-lived radionuclides disappear. Thereafter, EPA believes that radioactivity levels will remain virtually constant. A National Academy of Sciences study concluded that human exposures would peak between 200,000 and 800,000 years after the repository is established.

Despite the extensive recent studies, considerable controversy remains about the suitability of Yucca Mountain as a repository site. One area of concern is seismic stability. Yucca Mountain lies within a region of earthquake faults, some of which have been active as recently as 1993. The DOE contends that there is little likelihood that earthquakes would affect either the operation of the repository while it is accepting waste or groundwater levels after closure. The Nevada Agency for Nuclear Projects disagrees, however, citing studies that suggest the rate of ground movement along local fault lines is more than ten times greater than estimated by the DOE. A second concern is the potential for volcanic activity in the region. Several volcanic eruptions have occurred within a few miles of the site in the past one million years; one may have been as recent as 20,000 years ago. The DOE and Nevada disagree about the likelihood of a future eruption. The third area of dispute is the region's hydrology, which determines the likelihood and speed at which radionuclides could reach groundwater. Scientists have recently discovered that isotopes created by nuclear tests in the Nevada desert in the 1950s have traveled much faster than previously predicted. Computer models have suggested that, if a waste package were penetrated, radionuclides could reach the water table within 100 years or less. In addition, a scientist formerly with the DOE, now working for the state of Nevada, has produced a study suggesting that earthquakes could trigger rapid rises in groundwater at the site, bringing the water table much closer to the repository. The DOE commissioned a review of that study by the National Academy of Sciences, which concluded that there was no evidence to support the claims. See James E. Mielke, Proposed High-level Nuclear Waste Repository: Yucca Mountain Site Characterization Process (CRS Report for Congress 1999).

EPA's performance standards for Yucca Mountain are also controversial. The state of Nevada's Nuclear Projects Agency and a coalition of environmental groups have brought a lawsuit, claiming that the standards should cover the period of peak exposure rather than being limited to 10,000 years in the future. They also argue that exposure limits should be set at the boundary of the site, rather than 11 miles away. The DOE, NRC, and the nuclear industry, on the other hand, view EPA's standards as unnecessarily stringent. They argue that the all-pathways standard should be set at 25 millirems per year, and that no separate standard is needed for groundwater.

Towards the end of the Clinton administration, Congress passed a bill that would have accelerated opening of the Yucca Mountain site and removed EPA from the process. President Clinton vetoed the bill, and an override effort fell just short. The nuclear industry had hoped the Bush administration would move the Yucca Mountain facility forward, but when Democrats gained the Senate majority in early 2001 their leadership declared the issue dead for the time being.

Nonetheless, there is considerable pressure to open a permanent repository. Many states with nuclear power plants are unhappy with the current system of on-site storage. A lawsuit brought by several nuclear power generators has lent even greater urgency to the search for a permanent repository. The Federal Circuit has held that the DOE breached contracts under the Nuclear Waste Power Act to begin disposal services by 1998. Maine Yankee Atomic Power Co. v. United States, 225 F.3d 1336 (Fed.Cir. 2000). Damages, estimated already to be in the tens of billions of dollars, continue to mount as long as the United States is unable to accept waste for disposal.

Should a high-level nuclear waste repository be developed at Yucca Mountain? Suppose you were the President, and the Secretary of Energy recommended development of the Yucca Mountain site. How would you decide whether to endorse that recommendation or not? If the site goes forward, should EPA's recently-promulgated standards govern the licensing decision? If not, how should those standards be revised?

NOTES AND QUESTIONS

1. Which of the features Professor Lazarus identifies as characteristic of environmental disputes does the Yucca Mountain problem display? How do those features complicate the decision?

2. *Cost-Benefit Analysis.* Would cost-benefit analysis be helpful? What would you identify as the major costs and benefits of the Yucca Mountain proposal? How readily could either costs or benefits be quantified? Would cost-benefit analysis overlook any factors important to the decision?

3. *Who Should Decide?* What role should Nevada and local residents play in the siting decision? What role should residents of areas with reactors at which waste is currently stored play? Is it equitable to site a nuclear waste repository in Nevada, a state without any civilian nuclear power plants?

4. *Comparison to Alternatives.* The Yucca Mountain decision cannot be made in isolation. If Yucca Mountain is not available, some alternative strategy for nuclear waste disposal will be needed. Currently, spent fuel is stored on-site at reactors, many of which are nearing their capacity. Several states have objected to the current practice, and threatened to restrict expansion of on-site storage beyond present levels. How should the limited availability of additional on-site storage affect the Yucca Mountain decision? Should the decision take into account the possibility that reactors might have to shut down if a permanent disposal solution is not found soon? In evaluating that possibility, how should the likelihood that those reactors would be replaced by fossil-fuel power plants, which contribute far more to global warming, be factored in?

Should the United States consider disposal methods other than geologic isolation, such as sub-seabed, space, or Antarctic ice disposal? What advantages and disadvantages do you see in those possibilities? Note that sub-seabed and Antarctic disposal are currently prohibited by international agreements to which the United States is a party.

Should the U.S. encourage reprocessing of spent nuclear fuel? Does any form of permanent disposal inappropriately export the heaviest risks to future generations? See Kristin Shrader–Frechette, Equity and Nuclear Waste Disposal, 7 J. Ag. & Envtl. Ethics 133 (1994).

5. *Socioeconomic Impacts.* Nevada contends that fears of nuclear disaster could severely disrupt its economy, which depends heavily on tourism in the Las Vegas region. What weight should decisionmakers give that possibility? Does it matter whether actual risks would justify tourist fears?

6. *Scientific Uncertainty.* Like many environmental problems, the Yucca Mountain decision includes some areas of substantial scientific uncertainty and disagreement. Many of these uncertainties cannot be resolved by experiments or additional observations, because they require forecasts into the distant future. How should these uncertainties be factored into the decision? Should the "precautionary principle" be applied? What exactly would that mean in this case?

7. *What is the Relevant Time Frame?* Should EPA have specified acceptable radiation exposures from the repository for more than 10,000 years? Should the agency have applied its standards to the period of maximum exposure, thought to be more than 200,000 years in the future? Would such standards have any meaning or effect? Can we possibly predict human activities that might lead to exposure that far into the future? As points of reference, consider that 10,000 years ago was near the dawn of human civilization, and that modern human beings evolved only about 100,000 years ago. If a cost-benefit analysis were prepared for Yucca Mountain, should health effects in the distant future be subject to discounting?

CHAPTER TWO

ENVIRONMENTAL COMMON LAW

Before enactment of the numerous federal and state statutes that currently form the major part of the *corpus* of environmental law, environmental problems were addressed, if at all, by the common law. Today, despite the existence of many detailed environmental statutes, the common law remains relevant. It provides the flexibility to address new technologies or newly-recognized harms not yet covered by statutory law, and it allows recovery of compensatory damages, a remedy generally not available through environmental statutes.

CLASS DISCUSSION PROBLEM: OAK RIVER POLLUTION

James Cunning owns a 200–acre farm located on the Oak River in Tennessee. James diverts water directly from the river for his livestock and, in dry periods, to irrigate his crops. A shallow well located close to the river provides the family's water. Tennessee law gives riparian owners the right to divert water for domestic and agricultural purposes.

Recently, Oak River has become polluted with foul-smelling chemicals that discolor the water. Several of James' farm animals have died, and his crop yields are down. Neighbors along the river have voiced similar complaints. In addition, the number of fish in the stream has decreased, and several area residents have been diagnosed with leukemia or other cancers. James fears for his health and that of his family. He also worries that the value of the farm, the family's only substantial economic asset, is sharply declining.

James and his neighbors believe the Fox Pulp and Paper Mill, located upstream in Canton, North Carolina, is responsible for the pollution. Fox, the largest employer in the region, discharges wastes containing lead, arsenic, chlorine, and chlorinated organic compounds into the Oak River. North Carolina has issued Fox a discharge permit, which requires the mill to control the color and smell of its discharge but does not address metals, chlorine, or chlorinated compounds. State and federal statutes, as well as a Canton town ordinance, forbid discharge of dangerous chemicals to waters. State and local officials, however, have told James nothing can be done about the chemical discharges.

Does James have a remedy under the common law? What barriers will a common law action face? If James came to you for legal advice, what counsel would you offer? In answering those questions, consider the following cases and materials.

SECTION 1.   COMMON LAW ENVIRONMENTAL DOCTRINES

A.   NUISANCE

Nuisance, which potentially covers pollution of air, water, or land by almost any route, has been called the "common law backbone" of modern environmental law. William H. Rodgers, Environmental Law 113 (2d ed. 1994). The common law recognizes two loosely distinct causes of action, for private nuisance and public nuisance.

1.   PRIVATE NUISANCE

A private nuisance is an unreasonable and substantial interference with the use and enjoyment of land. The influential Restatement (2d) of Torts, § 822, calls for liability for acts that are either: (a) intentional and unreasonable, or (b) unintentional and otherwise actionable under the rules controlling liability for negligent or reckless conduct, or for abnormally dangerous conditions or activities. Acts are considered "intentional" if they are substantially certain to produce harm, whether or not the actor desires that harm. Intention is therefore established if an invasion continues after the defendant has been made aware of the harm. Id. § 825.

An invasion is "unreasonable" if the gravity of the harm outweighs the utility of the conduct or the harm is serious and the economic burden of compensation would not make the conduct infeasible. Id. § 826. Factors to be considered in determining the gravity of the harm and the utility of the conduct include: the extent and character of the harm; the social value of the plaintiff's use of land and defendant's conduct; the suitability of each to the character of the locality; and the burden on plaintiff and defendant, respectively, of avoiding the harm. Id. §§ 827–28.

The balancing of utilities rule, followed in most American jurisdictions, is a 19th-century modification of the old common law rule of *sic utere tuo ut alienum non laedas* (use your own property so as not to injure that of another). Prior to the industrial revolution, substantial injury to the enjoyment of property was actionable without regard to fault or the social utility of the defendant's conduct. As expanding populations led to increasingly frequent land use conflicts, and industrial uses took on greater economic importance, courts adjusted the doctrine of nuisance. The location and social utility of defendant's conduct became important elements in determining whether there was a nuisance and, if so, what relief would be granted. See Louise A. Halper, Untangling the Nuisance Knot, 26 B.C. Envtl. Aff. L. Rev. 89, 101–115 (1998); Joel Franklin Brenner, Nuisance Law and the Industrial Revolution, 3 J. Legal Stud. 403, 408–420 (1974). Activities that might be a nuisance in a rural agricultural area could now continue in the industrial towns. In the famous words of Justice Sutherland, a nuisance came to be seen as "merely a right thing in the wrong place, like a pig in the parlor instead of the barnyard." Euclid v. Ambler

Realty Co., 272 U.S. 365, 388 (1926). Even in a relatively unsullied area, an activity with great economic or social value might be found not to be a nuisance, or not to justify injunctive relief.

Were these changes a necessary adjustment to a changed economy, or an unjustified subsidy for wealthy entrepreneurs? Consider the following statement from Daniel R. Coquillette, Mosses from an Old Manse: Another Look at Some Historic Property Cases About the Environment, 64 Cornell L. Rev. 761, 792 (1979):

> This old common law doctrine was decent and humane compared to the hardened attitudes of the nineteenth century. The balancing of utilities doctrine * * * permitted the industrial user to externalize the costs of his pollution. Such a legal doctrine offered no economic incentive for the active user of property to develop technology that would prevent such side effects. * * * It was an unjust way of forcing public investment in industrial growth, regardless of how desirable that investment might have seemed.

2.   PUBLIC NUISANCE

A public nuisance is an unreasonable interference with the interest of the community or the rights of the general public. The doctrine has been used to protect public morals from prostitution, drug use, and gambling, as well as public health, safety and convenience. Traditionally, public nuisance actions could be brought only by public authorities, or by a private citizen who had suffered injury different in kind from that suffered by the general public. The Restatement (2d) of Torts, § 821C, allows a private citizen who has standing to sue "as a representative of the general public, as a citizen in a citizen's action or as a member of a class in a class action" to maintain an action to abate a public nuisance (but not to recover damages) without having to satisfy the special injury requirement.

B.   TRESPASS

Whereas nuisance protects the right to use and enjoyment of land, trespass protects the right to exclusive possession. Any non-privileged, knowing physical invasion of land without the possessor's permission is a trespass. The trespasser is liable for actual damages done, and for nominal damages if there is no actual harm. William B. Stoebuck & Dale A. Whitman, The Law of Property 411 (3d ed. 2000).

Trespass and nuisance shade into one another in environmental pollution cases. There appears to be a trend to merge the two. In Bradley v. American Smelting & Refining Co., 104 Wash.2d 677, 709 P.2d 782 (1985), for example, the court held that a group of landowners could sue in both trespass and nuisance for damages to their property caused by microscopic airborne particles from a nearby copper smelter. Jurisdictions which allow trespass claims for pollution, however, typically add a requirement that the plaintiff demonstrate substantial damage. See id. at 790–91. Other jurisdictions continue to insist that trespass actions are not available without a tangible physical invasion. See Adams v. Cleveland–Cliffs Iron Co., 237 Mich.App. 51, 602 N.W.2d 215 (1999) (holding that Michigan law does not permit trespass action for "intangible" intrusions by airborne particles, noise, or vibrations).

C.   NEGLIGENCE

An important limitation of trespass doctrine is the requirement that the defendant act with knowledge that harm is substantially certain to result. Trespass does not cover unexpected, accidental harm. See United Proteins, Inc. v. Farmland Industries, Inc., 259 Kan. 725, 915 P.2d 80 (1996). Negligence, the broadest category of tort liability, and strict liability fill the gap. Both concepts have been imported into nuisance law by Restatement (2d) of Torts, § 822, which imposes liability for acts that are either: 1) intentional; or 2) unintentional but actionable under the doctrines of negligence or strict liability. But negligence and strict liability remain far broader than nuisance, covering personal injuries as well as harm to interests in land.

Conduct is negligent if it creates an unreasonable risk of harm to others. A cause of action based on negligence has four elements:

(1) a legal duty owed by the defendant to the plaintiff;

(2) a breach of that duty;

(3) harm; and

(4) a causal relationship between the breach and the harm.

D.   STRICT LIABILITY

Most jurisdictions recognize liability for damages caused to persons or property by abnormally dangerous activities without requiring any showing of fault. Whether an activity is abnormally dangerous is determined by balancing several factors, including:

(a) existence of a high degree of risk of some harm to the person, land or chattels of others;

(b) likelihood that the harm will be great;

(c) inability to eliminate the risk by the exercise of reasonable care;

(d) extent to which the activity is not a matter of common usage;

(e) inappropriateness of the activity to the place where it is carried on; and

(f) extent to which its value to the community is outweighed by its dangerous attributes.

Restatement (2d) of Torts, § 520.

Justifications for imposing liability without fault include: forcing those who engage in dangerous activities to internalize the costs of those activities; spreading the costs of otherwise devastating individual losses across a wide group; avoiding unfairness by imposing the costs of injury on the person who benefits from the injurious activity; deterring highly dangerous activities; and reducing the administrative costs associated with proving negligence. See Joseph H. King, Jr., A Goals-Oriented Approach to Strict Tort Liability for Abnormally Dangerous Activities, 48 Baylor L. Rev. 341, 350–61 (1996). By contrast to negligence, which is a determination for the jury, whether or not an activity is abnormally dangerous is a matter of law decided by the court. Restatement (2d) of Torts, § 520, comment l.

Indiana Harbor Belt Railroad Co. v. American Cyanamid Co.

United States Court of Appeals, Seventh Circuit, 1990.
916 F.2d 1174.

■ POSNER, CIRCUIT JUDGE.

American Cyanamid Company, the defendant in this diversity tort suit governed by Illinois law, is a major manufacturer of chemicals, including acrylonitrile, a chemical used in large quantities in making acrylic fibers, plastics, dyes, pharmaceutical chemicals, and other intermediate and final goods. On January 2, 1979, at its manufacturing plant in Louisiana, Cyanamid loaded 20,000 gallons of liquid acrylonitrile into a railroad tank car that it had leased from the North American Car Corporation. The next day, a train of the Missouri Pacific Railroad picked up the car at Cyanamid's siding. The car's ultimate destination was a Cyanamid plant in New Jersey served by Conrail rather than by Missouri Pacific. The Missouri Pacific train carried the car north to the Blue Island railroad yard of Indiana Harbor Belt Railroad, the plaintiff in this case, a small switching line that has a contract with Conrail to switch cars from other lines to Conrail, in this case for travel east. The Blue Island yard is in the Village of Riverdale, which is just south of Chicago and part of the Chicago metropolitan area.

The car arrived in the Blue Island yard on the morning of January 9, 1979. Several hours after it arrived, employees of the switching line noticed fluid gushing from the bottom outlet of the car. The lid on the outlet was broken. After two hours, the line's supervisor of equipment was able to stop the leak by closing a shut-off valve controlled from the top of the car. No one was sure at the time just how much of the contents of the car had leaked, but it was feared that all 20,000 gallons had, and since acrylonitrile is flammable at a temperature of 30° Fahrenheit or above, highly toxic, and possibly carcinogenic, the local authorities ordered the homes near the yard evacuated. The evacuation lasted only a few hours, until the car was moved to a remote part of the yard and it was discovered that only about a quarter of the acrylonitrile had leaked. Concerned nevertheless that there had been some contamination of soil and water, the Illinois Department of Environmental Protection ordered the switching line to take decontamination measures that cost the line $981,022.75, which it sought to recover by this suit.

[The complaint] asserts that the transportation of acrylonitrile in bulk through the Chicago metropolitan area is an abnormally dangerous activity, for the consequences of which the shipper (Cyanamid) is strictly liable to the switching line, which bore the financial brunt of those consequences because of the decontamination measures that it was forced to take. [The District Court granted summary judgment on that issue to the plaintiff switching line.]

The question whether the shipper of a hazardous chemical by rail should be strictly liable for the consequences of a spill or other accident to the shipment en route is a novel one in Illinois * * *.

The parties agree that the question whether placing acrylonitrile in a rail shipment that will pass through a metropolitan area subjects the shipper to strict liability is, as recommended in Restatement (2d) of Torts § 520, comment l (1977), a question of law, so that we owe no particular deference to the conclusion of the district court. They also agree * * * that the Supreme Court of Illinois would treat as authoritative the provisions of the Restatement governing abnormally dangerous activities. The key provision is section 520, which sets forth six factors to be considered in deciding whether an activity is abnormally dangerous and the actor therefore strictly liable.

The roots of section 520 are in nineteenth-century cases. The most famous one is Rylands v. Fletcher, 1 Ex. 265, *aff'd*, L.R. 3 H.L. 300 (1868), but a more illuminating one in the present context is Guille v. Swan, 19 Johns. (N.Y.) 381 (1822). A man took off in a hot-air balloon and landed, without intending to, in a vegetable garden in New York City. A crowd that had been anxiously watching his involuntary descent trampled the vegetables in their endeavor to rescue him when he landed. The owner of the garden sued the balloonist for the resulting damage, and won. Yet the balloonist had not been careless. In the then state of ballooning it was impossible to make a pinpoint landing.

Guille is a paradigmatic case for strict liability. (a) The risk (probability) of harm was great, and (b) the harm that would ensue if the risk materialized could be, although luckily was not, great (the balloonist could have crashed into the crowd rather than into the vegetables). The confluence of these two factors established the urgency of seeking to prevent such accidents. (c) Yet such accidents could not be prevented by the exercise of due care; the technology of care in ballooning was insufficiently developed. (d) The activity was not a matter of common usage, so there was no presumption that it was a highly valuable activity despite its unavoidable riskiness. (e) The activity was inappropriate to the place in which it took place—densely populated New York City. The risk of serious harm to others (other than the balloonist himself, that is) could have been reduced by shifting the activity to the sparsely inhabited areas that surrounded the city in those days. (f) Reinforcing (d), the value to the community of the activity of recreational ballooning did not appear to be great enough to offset its unavoidable risks.

These are, of course, the six factors in section 520. They are related to each other in that each is a different facet of a common quest for a proper legal regime to govern accidents that negligence liability cannot adequately control. The interrelations might be more perspicuous if the six factors were reordered. One might for example start with (c), inability to eliminate the risk of accident by the exercise of due care. The baseline common law regime of tort liability is negligence. When it is a workable regime, because the hazards of an activity can be avoided by being careful (which is to say, nonnegligent), there is no need to switch to strict liability. Sometimes, however, a particular type of accident cannot be prevented by taking care but can be avoided, or its consequences minimized, by shifting the activity in which the accident occurs to another locale, where the risk or harm of an accident will be less (e), or by reducing the scale of the activity in order to minimize the number of accidents caused by it (f). By making the actor strictly liable—by denying him in other words an excuse based on his inability to avoid accidents by being more careful—we give him an incentive, missing in a negligence regime, to experiment with methods of preventing accidents that involve not greater exertions of care, assumed to be futile, but instead relocating, changing, or reducing (perhaps to the vanishing point) the activity giving rise to the accident. The greater the risk of an accident (a) and the costs of an accident if one occurs (b), the more we want the actor to consider the possibility of making accident-reducing activity changes; the stronger, therefore, is the case for strict liability. Finally, if an activity is extremely common (d), like driving an automobile, it is unlikely either that its hazards are perceived as great or that there is no technology of care available to minimize them; so the case for strict liability is weakened. * * *

Against this background we turn to the particulars of acrylonitrile. Acrylonitrile is one of a large number of chemicals that are hazardous in the sense of being flammable, toxic, or both; acrylonitrile is both, as are many others. A table in the record * * * contains a list of the 125 hazardous materials that are shipped in highest volume on the nation's railroads. Acrylonitrile is the fifty-third most hazardous on the list. Number 1 is phosphorus (white or yellow), and among the other materials that rank higher than acrylonitrile on the hazard scale are anhydrous ammonia, liquified petroleum gas, vinyl chloride, gasoline, crude petroleum, motor fuel antiknock compound, methyl and ethyl chloride, sulphuric acid, sodium metal, and chloroform. The plaintiff's lawyer acknowledged at argument that the logic of the district court's opinion dictated strict liability for all 52 materials that rank higher than acrylonitrile on the list, and quite possibly for the 72 that rank lower as well, since all are hazardous if spilled in quantity while being shipped by rail. Every shipper of any of these materials would therefore be strictly liable for the consequences of a spill or other accident that occurred while the material was being shipped through a metropolitan area. * * *

[W]e can get little help from precedent, and might as well apply section 520 to the acrylonitrile problem from the ground up. To begin with, we have been given no reason * * * for believing that a negligence regime is not perfectly adequate to remedy and deter, at reasonable cost, the accidental spillage of acrylonitrile from rail cars. [A]lthough acrylonitrile is flammable even at relatively low temperatures, and toxic, it is not so corrosive or otherwise destructive that it will eat through or otherwise damage or weaken a tank car's valves although they are maintained with due (which essentially means, with average) care. No one suggests, therefore, that the leak in this case was caused by the inherent properties of acrylonitrile. It was caused by carelessness—whether that of the North American Car Corporation in failing to maintain or inspect the car properly, or that of Cyanamid in failing to maintain or inspect it, or that of the Missouri Pacific when it had custody of the car, or that of the switching line itself in failing to notice the ruptured lid, or some combination of these possible failures of care. Accidents that are due to a lack of care can be prevented by taking care; and when a lack of care can * * * be shown in court, such accidents are adequately deterred by the threat of liability for negligence. * * *

The district judge and the plaintiff's lawyer make much of the fact that the spill occurred in a densely inhabited metropolitan area. Only 4,000 gallons spilled; what if all 20,000 had done so? Isn't the risk that this might happen even if everybody were careful sufficient to warrant giving the shipper an incentive to explore alternative routes? Strict liability would supply that incentive. But this argument overlooks the fact that, like other transportation networks, the railroad network is a hub-and-spoke system. And the hubs are in metropolitan areas. Chicago is one of the nation's largest railroad hubs. In 1983, the latest year for which we have figures, Chicago's railroad yards handled the third highest volume of hazardous-material shipments in the nation. * * * With most hazardous chemicals (by volume of shipments) being at least as hazardous as acrylonitrile, it is unlikely—and certainly not demonstrated by the plaintiff—that they can be rerouted around all the metropolitan areas in the country, except at prohibitive cost. Even if it were feasible to reroute them one would hardly expect shippers, as distinct from carriers, to be the firms best situated to do the rerouting. * * * It is no more realistic to propose to reroute the shipment of all hazardous materials around Chicago than it is to propose the relocation of homes adjacent to the Blue Island switching yard to more distant suburbs. It may be less realistic. Brutal though it may seem to say it, the inappropriate use to which land is being put in the Blue Island yard and neighborhood may be, not the transportation of hazardous chemicals, but residential living. The analogy is to building your home between the runways at O'Hare.

The case for strict liability has not been made. * * *

The judgment is reversed (with no award of costs in this court) and the case remanded for further proceedings, consistent with this opinion, on the plaintiff's claim for negligence.

Leaf River Forest Products, Inc. v. Ferguson

Supreme Court of Mississippi, 1995.
662 So.2d 648.

■ PITTMAN, JUSTICE.

* * *

In 1984 the Leaf River Paper Mill began operation in New Augusta, Perry County, Mississippi. The mill is located on the Leaf River, which eventually combines with the Chickasawhay River to form the Pascagoula River. The mill processes timber into a paper pulp product for domestic and foreign sale. In 1985 2,3,7,8–tetrachlorodibenzo-p-dioxin ("dioxin"), a toxic substance, was detected in the sludge, or solid waste material, produced by certain paper mills in Maine. It was subsequently determined that this type of dioxin was a by-product of the pulp-making process, particularly resulting where chlorine was used to bleach pulp to make it whiter. Dioxin was eventually found in the effluent, or waste water, and sludge produced by the Leaf River mill. Testing for dioxin was subsequently performed on fish caught in the Leaf River. As a result of these tests the Mississippi Department of Wildlife and Fisheries closed the Leaf, Pascagoula and Escatawpa Rivers to commercial fishing from October 1990 to January 1991, and issued consumption advisories for fish caught from the Leaf and Pascagoula Rivers. The consumption advisory for the Pascagoula was lifted in December 1990, but remained in effect for the Leaf River.

On March 1, 1991, [Thomas Ferguson, Jr., and his wife, Bonnie Jane Ferguson] filed suit in Jackson County Circuit Court against Leaf River Forest Products, Inc.; Warren Richardson; Acker Smith; Great Northern Nekoosa Corporation; and Georgia–Pacific Corporation. The plaintiffs alleged that the defendants, through the operation of the Leaf River mill, had discharged toxic chemicals into the Leaf River, causing injury to the plaintiffs, who lived along the Pascagoula River. The complaint was based on negligence, strict liability, nuisance and trespass. The plaintiffs alleged that they had suffered emotional distress and were entitled to actual and punitive damages totaling approximately $560,000,000.00. [T]he Fergusons' property was approximately one hundred twenty-five miles downriver from the mill. * * *

PLAINTIFFS/APPELLEES

Thomas Ferguson, Jr., was born in Georgia but had lived in south Mississippi since 1945. In 1960, Ferguson purchased fifteen acres of land on the Pascagoula River. He cleared the land and built bayous, two boat sheds, a house, a bait shop and a trailer park. He had hoped to leave the property to his son. He stated that he could no longer swim or fish in the river and he had developed a fear of cancer, as he had eaten large amounts of fish caught in the Pascagoula before knowing about the dioxin problem. Ferguson also stated that his property had flooded several times recently and this had worsened his fear that his property was contaminated with dioxin.

Ferguson testified that if he had known that the mill was discharging dioxin into the river, he would have made "different arrangements with [his] lifestyle." He had first noticed the river water getting darker in 1986–87. Ferguson had seen Dr. Charlton Stanley, a psychologist, and Dr. Donald Guild, a psychiatrist, but had not taken the medicine prescribed for him. He had not been informed of any kind of evaluation or diagnosis until his pretrial deposition was taken. Ferguson had not had his property or his well water tested for dioxin, and had not tried to sell his property. He had not had his blood tested for determination of dioxin levels. Ferguson had a separate fear of cancer claim in asbestos-related litigation, and he had been tested in connection with that particular claim.

Bonnie Jane Ferguson, wife of Thomas Ferguson, Jr., was born and raised in south Mississippi. She was a housewife and she also ran their marina, which included collecting the rent and keeping the records of the rent money. She stated that over the past few years the river had gotten darker, a light coffee color, and the fish did not bite like they once had. She had first noticed the change in the color of the river in 1985. Her greatest sense of loss came from the belief that the property she and her husband had planned to leave to their son was now worthless. She had declined Leaf River's offer to pay for her blood to be tested, stating that if dioxin was in her system and could not be removed she did not want to know about it. She claimed to have developed a fear of cancer because of the large amount of catfish she had eaten which had been caught in the Pascagoula. The fear was not something that paralyzed her or kept her from functioning.

We must note a lack of evidence as to substance on the Ferguson's property or dioxin in their body. The Fergusons testify only to a mental fear, a fear without foundation in fact. * * *

APPELLEES' EXPERTS

Dr. Arnold Schecter, physician and professor of preventative medicine at the State University of New York, Binghamton, referred to 2,3,7,8–tetrachlorodibenzodioxin, or dioxin, as a "super toxin," because a very tiny amount would produce increased ill effects in an animal. Schecter testified that dioxin was fat-soluble, that it could enter the body through breathing, ingestion or through contact with the skin; that the dioxin in food that was eaten and not eliminated through waste would be absorbed into the bloodstream and throughout the body's organs; and that dioxin was a persistent compound, with an estimated half-life of seven years. Schecter testified that studies showed that human health effects resulting from exposure to dioxin included several different cancers; malformation and death of unborn children; weakening of the immune system; liver damage; lipid alteration; damage to the central nervous system; skin rashes; and learning disabilities. Schecter felt that there was no doubt that dioxin caused cancer in humans. He had visited with the appellees for less than an hour before trial and had reviewed a number of fish studies performed by the State of Mississippi as well as medical and psychological tests concerning the appellees. He stated that he felt that, based on a reasonable degree of medical probability, the appellees' fear of developing cancer from eating fish from the Pascagoula River was reasonable. Schecter agreed that a comprehensive medical evaluation, including blood tests, was the best method of determining exposure to dioxin, and stated that he had his own blood and fat tested for dioxin after he became involved with a chemical cleanup in Binghamton, New York. He could not say that the appellees' health was actually at risk because of their exposure to dioxin. He also did not know the level of dioxin in the appellees' bodies, either before or after their alleged exposure due to eating fish from the river.

Dr. Arthur Hume, a member of the Department of Pharmacology and Toxicology at the University of Mississippi, was accepted as an expert in toxicology and chemistry. Hume testified that tests had shown that dioxin had a harmful effect on all the different systems in a mammal's body, with the most notorious effect being its ability to damage the immune system. Recent toxicological evidence had convinced Hume that dioxin was a human carcinogen, and Hume also believed that appellees, who had eaten fish from the Pascagoula River, had a reasonable basis for fear of an increased chance of contracting cancer. Dr. Hume agreed that no one could know the level of dioxin in the fish eaten by the appellees, however he maintained that it was probable that the fish had dioxin in them. Hume also agreed that the best way to measure increases in dioxin levels after exposure was to take fat or blood samples and test them. * * *

Dr. Charlton Stanley, a psychologist, was admitted as an expert in the field of human psychology and particularly in the area of human psychological effect of environmental disasters. Dr. Stanley had seen the Fergusons on May 13, 1991. He interviewed them jointly, and took a history. He found that the Fergusons' primary fear besides contracting cancer was not being able to leave something of value, their property, to their son. Stanley believed that the Fergusons suffered from an adjustment disorder. He believed that the Fergusons' fears and distress were genuine and reasonable under the circumstances. Dr. Stanley had not informed the Fergusons of his findings concerning them and it was his understanding that they had not sought any follow-up psychotherapy or counseling.

Guy Blankinship was accepted as an expert in the field of real estate appraisal. Blankinship based his appraisal of the Ferguson property, totaling approximately 14 acres, on 6.1 acres facing the Pascagoula. He estimated a market value of $12,000.00 per acre, for a total of $73,200.00, and stated that the diminution in value of the property due to the presence of dioxin in the Leaf River and the stigma involved with the river was $65,000.00. Blankinship did not know whether dioxin was actually on the Fergusons' property. He had recommended to them that they have the property tested, but they had not tested the property.

TESTING FOR DIOXIN

As the Fergusons did not have themselves or their property tested for the presence of dioxin, they relied on tests of wildlife in the area of the Leaf River to support their claims of emotional distress and nuisance. Appellants used the same test results in an effort to repudiate these claims. The testing took place from 1988 to 1990. The majority of the test results dealt with fish caught in the vicinity of the Leaf River mill. The earlier results showed detectable levels, in parts per trillion or quadrillion, of dioxin in fish caught on the Leaf River. Some of the later results showed a reduction of dioxin levels in the fish tested. None of the testing of fish took place in the vicinity of the Fergusons' property. The testing sites closest to the

Fergusons' property were at Merrill, approximately eighty miles upriver from the Fergusons. * * *

APPELLANTS' EXPERTS

Lee M. Thomas had served as the Environmental Protection Agency's assistant administrator in charge of waste programs, such as the Super-fund, from 1983–1985, and had served as administrator of the EPA from 1985 until 1989. Thomas was offered as an expert "on the topic of government regulation generally and specifically in EPA's regulation of dioxin." * * * Thomas denied that the Leaf River was the most polluted, in terms of dioxin, in the country, and denied that the paper industry had ever approached him about weakening dioxin regulations. He further denied that there was data showing dioxin to be a human carcinogen.

Dr. Kenneth Dickson served as a professor of aquatic ecology at the University of North Texas in Denton, Texas. He was accepted as an expert in the fields of aquatic ecology and aquatic biology. Dickson testified that he had examined several studies done concerning the Leaf and Pascagoula Rivers and offered the following conclusions: (1) the Leaf and Pascagoula Rivers were in good condition; (2) the rivers had made a remarkable recovery from pollution problems of the 1950s–60s; (3) there was "no impact on the ecological health of the aquatic communities downstream of the mill, compared to upstream of the mill." He stated that it was extremely unlikely that the mill's effluent could have any effect on aquatic life 100 to 125 miles below the mill. He also labeled as unlikely the effluent from the mill causing a color change in the river 100 miles down river.

James Davis, Jr. was called as an expert real estate appraiser. Davis denied that the Ferguson property had decreased in value due to alleged dioxin contamination or to the 1990 fishing advisory, saying that this had not been born [sic] out by comparable sales in the area.

Dr. Wood Hiatt, professor of psychiatry at the University of Mississippi, had reviewed Dr. Stanley's file and the tests that Dr. Stanley had administered to the Fergusons. Dr. Hiatt found it unacceptable that the Fergusons had been seen together by Dr. Stanley instead of being evaluated as individuals. Dr. Hiatt found that the Fergusons' fear of cancer was not reasonable, as they had refused to have themselves tested to determine if they had potentially dangerous levels of dioxin in their bodies.

Dr. John Doull, professor of toxicology and pharmacy at the University of Kansas, specialized in pesticides, which included work with dioxin. Dr. Doull agreed that dioxin had caused cancer in some animals at high doses but had decreased breast cancer in other animals at low doses. Doull stated that the United States had been much more conservative in setting dioxin standards than the other industrialized nations. He testified that the Fergusons, considering the distance they lived downriver from the mill, should have no basis for concern for their health. Doull labeled the State of Mississippi's standard on dioxin as very conservative and denied that the Fergusons had any increased risk of developing cancer.

Dr. Renate Kimbrough, a physician who had worked for several governmental agencies, including the Center for Disease Control, the Food and Drug Administration, and the Environmental Protection Agency, was accepted as an expert in public health and epidemiology. She was familiar with the ten to fifteen major studies done on dioxin exposure. Kimbrough testified that there had been no convincing study showing an excess of cancer in those exposed to many times the levels of dioxin alleged to be present in the Leaf and Pascagoula Rivers. She further stated that it would be important to test the blood of the plaintiffs to see whether they had been exposed at all, and to see whether their levels were any different than a normal person's. * * * Kimbrough testified that, assuming dioxin levels of four parts per trillion in fish around the Leaf River mill, and assuming that the plaintiffs lived one hundred miles downriver, she would not expect the plaintiffs to have anything other than normal background exposure. She denied that eating fish from the Leaf or Pascagoula River would pose any health risk. Kimbrough agreed that people who ate large amounts of fish regularly would get higher exposure rates, but not necessarily increased risk. * * *

The jury found in favor of the defendants on the trespass count. As to nuisance, the jury found for the Fergusons, awarding $10,000.00 each. On the emotional distress count the jury found for the Fergusons, awarding $90,000.00 each. In addition, the jury awarded $3,000,000.00 in punitive damages to the Fergusons. * * *

I. WHETHER THE EMOTIONAL DISTRESS VERDICT BELOW MUST BE REVERSED * * *

Appellants argue both that the Fergusons failed to show that they were exposed to dioxin and that the cause of action for fear of future disease does not exist or is not compensable. Assuming there is such a cause of action, appellants argue that there is insufficient evidence to show that appellees' fear is reasonable.

This state recognizes recovery for both negligently and intentionally inflicted emotional distress * * *.

[I]n a case of simple, or ordinary "garden variety negligence," even in the absence of physical injury accompanying the negligent conduct, if there is a resulting physical illness or assault upon the mind, personality or nervous system of the plaintiff which is medically cognizable and which requires or necessitates treatment by the medical profession, this Court has followed the modern tendency and held a legal cause of action exists. This assumes, of course, the test of reasonable foreseeability is also satisfactorily met.

It would be impossible to enumerate all the ways in which emotional distress could be inflicted. However, this Court has never allowed or affirmed a claim of emotional distress based on a fear of contracting a disease or illness in the future, however reasonable.

In this case, there is a lack of evidence proving exposure of the appellees to a dangerous or harmful agent and the record is devoid of any medical evidence pointing to possible or probable future illness. Certainly, if one is to recover for emotional distress predicated on potential future illness there must be substantial proof of exposure and medical evidence that would indicate possible future illness.

The appellees fail in their proof on both counts; therefore, this is not a case to allow recovery for emotional distress based on a fear of occurrences in the future. The Fergusons will be able to pursue a cause of action against the appellants if any disease caused by alleged exposure to dioxin manifests itself in the future. Their claim based on fear of future disease is at best, premature. * * *

II.   WHETHER THE NUISANCE VERDICT BELOW MUST BE REVERSED * * *

The appellees alleged, in their second amended complaint, that the appellants had discharged "into the waters of the Leaf River, and the East and West Pascagoula Rivers dark and foul smelling effluent in sufficient quantities that the color of the river is often altered as far downstream as waters adjacent to plaintiffs' property in Jackson County, Mississippi." * * *

Appellants argue that the nuisance verdict cannot stand because (a) appellants failed to prove dioxin from the mill was actually on or near their property and (b) damage from stigma, or public perception alone, is not recoverable. Appellants rely first on *Shutes v. Platte Chemical Co.*, 564 So.2d 1382 (Miss.1990). The Shutes alleged that Platte Chemical, immediately adjacent to the Shutes' property, had committed trespass and had caused a nuisance. The Shutes reported dying vegetation, and also stated that they could smell the plant, and that it made their eyes water and their noses run. The Shutes proved that linuron, a herbicide, was actually present in their soil. The only plant in the area producing linuron was that belonging to Platte. The trial court granted a directed verdict in favor of Platte. This Court reversed, finding that the Shutes had presented sufficient evidence to establish a jury question. The differences between the proof offered in *Shutes* and in this case are manifest. The Shutes proved that the only entity in the vicinity of their property producing linuron was Platte Chemical, and that linuron was actually on their property. The Shutes testified as to the actual physical effect Platte Chemical had on their health and on their property. The Fergusons produced no proof of this type. * * *

The Fergusons argue that their nuisance claim was based not only on "the dioxin problem, but is also based on the unsightly discoloration of the water, river banks, and sand bars caused by Defendants' injection of the darkening effluent into the Leaf River." * * *

There was testimony that the Pascagoula had darkened, and river banks and sand bars had also been discolored. * * * There was no testimony that the Fergusons' property had been darkened, or that the river had left a dark residue on their land or their buildings. There was no testimony showing the appellants to be the cause of this color change except that the change had been noticed after the appellants began operation of the mill. Some of the appellees' witnesses noticed the color change around 1985; others did not until 1990. Guy Blankinship never mentioned any damage to the property except for the condition of the river and the resulting stigma. We find that the evidence presented is insufficient to constitute a significant interference with the Fergusons' use and enjoyment of their property. We further find that mere stigma, supported by tests showing dioxin contamination no closer than eighty river miles north of the alleged damage, is not sufficient evidence of compensable injury.

[The Fergusons also alleged public nuisance.] "To recover damages [for public nuisance] the plaintiff usually must have sustained harm different in kind, rather than in degree, than that suffered by the public at large." Comet Delta[, Inc. v. Pate Stevedore Co.], 521 So.2d [857,] 861[(Miss.1988)]; but see Ronald J. Rychlak, *The Role of Common–Law Remedies for Environmental Wrongs: Private Nuisance*, 59 Miss. L.J. 657, 659 n. 12 (1989) (public nuisance requirement of different kind of harm under attack as "relic"). If one were to assume that the darker water of the Pascagoula and stains on riverbanks and sandbars were enough to qualify as an unreasonable interference with [public rights], there is still the matter of a harm different from that suffered by the public at large which the Fergusons must have endured. A reduction of recreational or aesthetic use or enjoyment of the river is the same injury that the general public would suffer. Appellees argue that part of their emotional distress damages results from the diminution of value of their property and their inability to leave something of value to their son. This is a different kind of damage than that suffered by the general public which could be compensable as the result of a public nuisance. However, the verdict form showed that the jury awarded the Fergusons $10,000.00 each for nuisance damages. The jury awarded the Fergusons $90,000.00 each for emotional distress. Emotional distress may not serve as a component of the nuisance award where it was separately awarded. * * * As with their emotional distress claim, the Fergusons' nuisance claim cannot stand due to a failure of proof.

■ McRae, Justice, dissenting:

The majority's ruling is contradictory to the long established principal [sic] of law in this state that physical impact or injury is not necessary to prove intentional, or even negligent infliction of emotional distress. This case should at least be remanded for a new trial under the majority's holding since a plaintiff was not required under existing law to prove physical impact in a claim for emotional distress. * * *

In concluding that the plaintiffs' fears are too remote, the majority incorrectly distinguished the plaintiffs' fears from their emotional distress. The plaintiffs' emotional distress in this case is the fear that they will become sick in the future. The fear and the emotional distress are merely two different ways of describing the same injury. The fear of future illness is only a more specific way of characterizing the emotional distress suffered by the plaintiffs. The emotional distress in the present case is not "based on the fear of a future illness" as indicated by the majority. The emotional distress, or fear, is instead based on the fish kills, discoloration of the water, and foul odors among other things caused by the Leaf River pollution.

To determine the validity of an emotional distress claim, we look to the conduct of the defendant or the nature of the act to determine whether it intentionally, or with reasonable foreseeability, evokes outrage. The fear, or emotional distress, in the case at hand was not based on abstract fear, but was instead based upon concrete physical scientific evidence that the river was knowingly contaminated by and through the conduct of Leaf River. Since it is virtually impossible to produce physical scientific evidence that will prove the existence of abstract fear, a plaintiff's evidence of emotional distress will never be persuasive if the concepts of fear and emotional distress are considered separate injuries as in the case before us. The misinterpretation of the emotional distress claims before this Court has led the majority to reinstate the impact rule in an attempt to find some physical evidence proving abstract fear. The conclusion that the fear, or the emotional distress, was too remote is merely another way of stating that the plaintiff's fear of serious illness cannot be believed. However, the jury has already decided otherwise. * * *

The majority reverses the nuisance claim for lack of sufficient evidence demonstrating that the contamination existed as far downstream as the Ferguson property. Again, the majority fails to afford the Fergusons the benefit of all favorable inferences that may be reasonably drawn from the evidence. * * * Both Bonnie and Thomas Ferguson testified that the water changed color at the location of their property. * * * The wildlife consumption advisories and commercial fishing ban directly impacted the Ferguson property, and signs were posted to that effect both north and south of the property.

It was reasonable for the jury to conclude from this evidence that dioxin was present in the area of the Ferguson property despite the absence of scientific data specifically from the site of their property. Giving the plaintiffs the benefit of all favorable inferences to be drawn, as is required where the jury has returned a verdict for the plaintiffs, we must conclude that the evidence sufficiently established all of the elements of private nuisance.

Walsh v. Town of Stonington Water Pollution Control Authority

Supreme Court of Connecticut, 1999.
250 Conn. 443, 736 A.2d 811.

■ NORCOTT, JUSTICE.

The defendants, the town of Stonington water pollution control authority and the town of Stonington, appeal from a jury verdict in favor of the plaintiffs, Joseph Walsh, Jr., Claire Walsh, James Stewart and Ruth Stewart, awarding them damages in the framework of a common-law private nuisance cause of action for harm caused by odors emanating from the defendants' operation of a sewage treatment plant (plant) on land located near the plaintiffs' residences. * * *

The record discloses the following relevant facts. The plaintiffs, who are two married couples living on parcels of land abutting the defendants' plant brought an action against the defendants alleging, inter alia, that they had created, maintained and permitted a continuing nuisance to exist that harmed the plaintiffs' respective properties. The manifestation of the alleged nuisance consisted of insects and unreasonable odors that arose from the operation of the plant.

Shortly after the plant began processing septage, "the [water pollution control authority] applied to the [state Department of Environmental Protection] for a renewal of its discharge permit. The [commissioner of environmental protection] appointed a hearing officer, who held a public hearing at which several citizens objected to the permit on the ground that the treatment plant was a source of odors. After the close of the hearing, one or more of the citizens filed a petition for intervention pursuant to General Statutes § 22a–19, asserting that the odors from the treatment plant constituted unreasonable pollution under the [Connecticut Environmental Protection Act (act)]. The petition was granted, and the hearing officer considered the substantive allegations therein.

"In his proposed final decision, the hearing officer found that the evidence in the record did not support the conclusion that the odors constituted unreasonable pollution. The hearing officer also determined that there was no reasonable or prudent alternative to the continued operation of the treatment plant. Accordingly, the hearing officer recommended the renewal of the permit. * * *

"In his final decision, the [commissioner] did not accept the hearing officer's proposed finding that the odors did not constitute unreasonable pollution under the act. The [commissioner], instead, determined that the testimony at the public hearing supported a finding of unreasonable pollution. The [commissioner] nevertheless issued the permit, with a condition addressing the odor problems, because there was no feasible and prudent alternative to the continued operation of the plant. Subsequently, after the [water pollution control authority] had agreed to undertake certain measures to address the odors, an administrative consent order was substituted for that condition and the permit was reissued without any condition relevant to the odor problem." Water Pollution Control Authority v. Keeney, 234 Conn. 488, 490–91, 662 A.2d 124 (1995).

At trial, evidence was presented including, inter alia, the testimony of the four plaintiffs that, at various times, the plant emitted sewage odors, a rotten egg-like odor, diesel odors, a sweet odor and a chlorine odor. The presence of these odors caused symptoms such as coughing, vomiting, headaches, and a burning sensation to the lips and eyes. According to the complaint, the odors became intolerable by the summer of 1990. The case went to trial in September, 1997.

After a trial, the jury returned a verdict for the plaintiffs. In accordance with that verdict, the trial court ordered the defendants to pay damages to the plaintiffs in the amount of $675,000. * * *

I

The defendants first contend that the trial court improperly instructed the jury on the "unreasonable use" element of common-law private nuisance. Specifically, the defendants argue that the charge was improper because the trial court failed to instruct the jury expressly that, in determining the reasonableness or unreasonableness of the defendants' use of the land, the jury was required to balance the harm to the plaintiffs against such factors as the social utility of the defendants' use of the land in conformity with the mandate of the department. We disagree with the defendants' argument.

The trial court gave the following instruction to the jury concerning unreasonable use. "To establish a nuisance, the plaintiffs must prove certain things. The first is that the condition was such that in its very nature was likely to inflict harm by producing odors or insects in such a manner as to unreasonably interfere with [the] plaintiffs' enjoyment of each of their properties.

"The second requirement is that the condition was a continuing one. By that, I mean simply that it must be more than a temporary condition springing from a particular or isolated act or failure to act on the part of the defendants, that it has to have continued in existence for some appreciable length of time, continuing as opposed to temporary, is what this element is about.

"A third requirement which must be met is that the use made of the property by the defendants was unreasonable or unlawful. Now there's no doubt that the [defendants were] making a lawful use of the property. You need give no thought to that requirement, but you must decide whether the use the town was making of the property was a reasonable use. You must consider the location of the condition and any other circumstances that you find proven which indicate whether the defendants [were] making a reasonable use of the property. Now, that's not to suggest that the mere use of the property for a sewer treatment plant is reasonable or unreasonable. Clearly, that's a reasonable use of property and the plaintiffs don't claim otherwise. So although this is phrased in our law as a separate and third requirement, if you don't find that the plant is producing odors or insects in such a manner as to unreasonably interfere with the plaintiffs' enjoyment of their property, then you don't really need to worry about the third [burden]. If you find that the plant is producing odors—or was or is producing odors or insects, that is the use of the property that you will find that is either reasonable or unreasonable. [The][p]laintiffs must prove that the use of the property as they have proven the property to be used was—to have been used was unreasonable, and that's [the] plaintiffs' third burden. . . ."

The defendants take issue with [several] particular statements of the trial court made over the course of the instructions to the jury. The defendants first cite to the statement as to whether "the mere use of the property for a sewer treatment plant is reasonable or unreasonable," when the court noted that "[c]learly, that's a reasonable use of property and the plaintiffs don't claim otherwise." The second statement to which the defendants point in support of their claim is that "[i]f you find that the plant is producing odors—or was or is producing odors or insects, that is the use of the property that you will find is either reasonable or unreasonable." * * *

The defendants assert that in light of these statements, the trial court failed to inform the jury of the necessity of balancing the benefits of the activity against the harm complained of by the plaintiffs. Instead, according to the defendants, the instruction suggested to the jury that it should consider only the alleged harm in determining whether the defendants' use of the land was reasonable. As a consequence, the defendants claim that the need for the plant to control water pollution was not a factor before the jury in determining the reasonableness of the defendants' use of the land.

Moreover, the defendants contend that a proper instruction as to the unreasonable use element of a nuisance claim must include a balancing between the benefits or social utility of the plant for the health and welfare of town residents against the alleged harm suffered by the plaintiffs. * * *

An analysis of the defendants' claims requires us to review the contours of the unreasonable use element of a common-law private nuisance cause of action. As we previously have stated, "the law will not interfere with a use that is reasonable. It is the duty of every person to make a reasonable use of his own property so as to occasion no unnecessary damage or annoyance to his neighbor. *A fair test of whether a proposed use constitutes a nuisance is the reasonableness of the use of the property in the particular locality under the circumstances of the case.*" Nicholson v. Connecticut Half–Way House, Inc., 153 Conn. 507, 510, 218 A.2d 383 (1966) (emphasis added). The test of unreasonableness is "essentially a weighing process, involving a comparative evaluation of conflicting interests in various situations according to objective legal standards." O'Neill v. Carolina Freight Carriers Corp., 156 Conn. 613, 617–18, 244 A.2d 372 (1968). * * *

The charge to the jury in the present case was consistent with our prior holdings on the element of unreasonable use. When viewed in the context of the charge as a whole, the jury instructions concerning unreasonable use conveyed to the jury that it was to take into consideration and weigh the conflicting interests involved. The trial court stated at the outset of the explanation of the unreasonable use element of the claim that the jury "must consider the location of the condition and any other circumstances that you find proven which indicate whether the defendants [were] making a reasonable use of the property." This statement indicates that the jury must take into account a multiplicity of factors. Reference to the fact that the use of the property for a plant is a reasonable use makes clear that the use of the defendants' land to operate a plant is reasonable *in and of itself*. By then noting that the determination of reasonableness is to be made in the context of odors produced by the plant, the trial court underscored that the weighing process for the jury to conduct is of the reasonableness of use *in light of the production of unreasonable odors* that the jury had determined existed * * *.

Moreover, the defendants' arguments regarding the impropriety of the jury instructions necessarily are unpersuasive because they are based on an inaccurate construction of the concept of unreasonable use. * * * [T]he fact that operating a plant is permissible, or even necessary, on the land in question does not necessarily shield the defendants from liability for harm to the land of others that may result from that use. * * *

The defendants also place much emphasis on our prior statement in *Cyr* [v. Brookfield, 153 Conn. 261, 265, 216 A.2d 198 (1965)] that "[a]n intentional invasion of another's interest in the use and enjoyment of land is unreasonable under the rule stated in § 822 [of the Restatement (Second) of Torts], unless the utility of the actor's conduct outweighs the gravity of the harm." On the basis of this statement, the defendants assert that the element of unreasonable use cannot be met in this case unless the harm to the plaintiffs outweighs the social utility of a plant, that is, the harm outweighs the benefit to the residents of the town as a whole. The comments in the Restatement (Second) of Torts on utility versus gravity of harm do not, however, support the interpretation asserted by the defendants. The Restatement (Second) provides the example that "[e]ven though the noise and smoke from a factory cannot feasibly be eliminated, the utility of the factory is not weighed in the abstract. In a suit for damages, the legal utility of the activity may also be greatly reduced by the fact that the actor is operating the factory and producing the noise and smoke without compensating his neighbors for the harm done to them. The conduct for which the utility is being weighed includes both the general activity and what is done about its consequences." 4 Restatement (Second), Torts § 826, comment (e) (1979). The defendants' understanding of the balancing requirement does not involve simply the weighing of factors to determine reasonableness as the law requires. Instead, application of the defendants' approach would result in an all-or-nothing scenario wherein the plaintiffs could never prove unreasonable use because their harm could never trump the undisputed need for a town plant. In other words, the plaintiffs would be expected to bear all of the harm without compensation for their damages, while receiving no greater benefits from the continued operation of the plant than any other resident of the town. Such an interpretation goes far beyond the necessary weighing process to be undertaken by the jury. * * *

II

The defendants next claim that the trial court improperly refused to direct a verdict for them on the grounds of collateral estoppel. Specifically, the defendants contend that the nuisance claim was barred by collateral estoppel because: (1) the department previously had found that there was no "feasible and prudent alternative" use to which the defendants could put the land; (2) this finding is equivalent to a finding that the use was not "unreasonable"; and (3) one of the plaintiffs intervened in the department hearings in question but did not appeal its decision. We disagree. * * *

The determination of whether there is a feasible and prudent alternative to the continued operation of the plant is made pursuant to § 22a–19(b), which provides that "the agency shall consider the alleged unreasonable pollution, impairment or destruction of the public trust in the air, water or other natural resources of the state and *no conduct shall be authorized or approved which does, or is reasonably likely to, have such effect so long as*, considering all relevant surrounding circumstances and factors, *there is a feasible and prudent alternative* consistent with the reasonable requirements of the public health, safety and welfare." (Emphasis added.)

In other words, § 22a–19(b) explicitly provides that a permit will not be renewed in the face of unreasonable pollution *if there is a feasible and prudent alternative.* In this case, the commissioner determined that there was *no* feasible and prudent alternative to continued operation of the plant. The determination that there was no such alternative is not, however, preclusive of a concurrent finding that such operation nevertheless causes unreasonable pollution. Indeed, the commissioner in this instance concomitantly found that "the testimony at the public hearing supported a finding of unreasonable pollution." Therefore, the commissioner's determination that there was no other feasible and prudent alternative does not resolve the question of whether the operation of the plant constituted unreasonable use for purposes of a private nuisance claim. * * *

III

The defendants' third claim is that the trial court improperly failed to dismiss the action because the defendants should be protected from common-law nuisance actions when they engage in conduct mandated by law and approved by a department permit. This argument is without merit. * * *

In the present case, the defendants place great emphasis on the fact that they have been granted a permit from the department to operate the plant. We are also mindful that the operation of such plants generally is consistent with the state policy "to conserve, improve and protect its natural resources and environment and to control air, land and water pollution in order to enhance the health, safety and welfare of the people of the state. * * * " General Statutes § 22a–1. That the defendants have been authorized to operate a plant does not, however, mean that they are therefore free from liability when, as the jury found in the present case, the operation of the plant created a private nuisance from which the plaintiffs suffered damages. Such a conclusion would conflict with * * * the plain language of § 22a–430–3 (d)(1)(B) of the Regulations of Connecticut State

Agencies concerning water treatment permits, which unambiguously provides that "[t]he issuance of a permit does not * * * authorize any injury to persons or property or invasion of other private rights. * * * " Accordingly, we affirm the trial court's dismissal of the defendants' motion to dismiss.

NOTES AND QUESTIONS

1. *Economic Welfare Analysis.* As Ronald Coase demonstrated in his landmark paper, The Problem of Social Cost, 3 J.L. & Econ. 1 (1960), from an economic welfare standpoint nuisance cases present a reciprocal conflict. Neighbors of a pulp mill are hurt if the mill is permitted to pollute the surrounding air and water. But the mill is hurt if the neighbors are given the right to block its polluting activities. The ultimate question is which of the conflicting activities should prevail. Economists typically answer that the efficient result, in which the more valuable activity prevails, should be preferred.

Coase demonstrated that private bargaining against a background of clear legal rules will produce the economically efficient result, provided there are no barriers to a voluntary transaction between the parties. Economists call the costs of surmounting these barriers, which can include the costs of gathering information, making contact with the other affected parties, conducting negotiations, and enforcing the negotiated result, "transaction costs." If transaction costs are zero, the Coase theorem predicts that the efficient outcome will be achieved no matter which party is assigned the legal entitlement.

Consider a conflict between a sewage treatment plant and nearby residences, like that in *Walsh v. Stonington*. Suppose odors from the plant affect 25 homes, lowering the value of each by $20,000. Suppose also that the plant could eliminate those odors through use of a new treatment method at a cost of $450,000. If the law gives neighbors an entitlement to be free of unpleasant odors, how will the conflict be resolved? The plant's operators will either have to eliminate the odor or pay the neighbors enough so that they will choose not to complain. Since in our example it is cheaper to control the odors ($450,000) than to compensate the neighbors (25 x $20,000 = $500,000), the efficient solution is for the plant to adopt the new treatment method. Assuming the plant is managed by economically rational actors, it will choose to do so.

If instead the law permits the plant to vent its odors without liability, the Coase theorem predicts that the same outcome will result, provided there are no transaction costs. In this case, the neighbors will have to pay the plant to control its odors. Operators of the plant will agree to adopt the new treatment method if the neighbors together can pay a total of at least $450,000. That would require a contribution of $18,000 from each neighbor ($450,000 / 25 = $18,000). Since each neighbor suffers $20,000 worth of harm from the odors, each should be willing to make that contribution.

Will the plant actually adopt the new method in this second example? Coase recognized that, in the real world, transaction costs are frequently significant. What transaction costs might prevent bargaining in this example? Aside from transaction costs, can you see any other possible barriers to achieving the efficient result?

Even if transaction costs are sufficiently low for the Coase theorem to apply, society may not be indifferent to the choice of entitlements, which can have powerful distributional consequences. In the example above, assigning the entitlement to either the plant or the neighbors may result in adoption of the new odor control technology, the efficient solution. But placement of the entitlement will determine who bears the costs of resolving the conflict.

Furthermore, the Coase theorem (and economic efficiency analysis in general) does not effectively account for costs and benefits that are not readily translated into monetary terms. Expert testimony from a real estate appraiser can establish the effect of the plant on the market value of neighboring homes. But does that value capture the full effect on the neighbors? Would a neighbor who does not wish to leave the community be indifferent between the plant eliminating its odors and giving her $20,000? Or suppose the dispute is over water pollution rather than odors, and the neighbors are concerned not only with their property values, but with the health of their children and the ecological integrity of the river. Can and should those values be monetized to determine the preferred outcome? Cost-benefit analysis is discussed in more detail in Chapter 1, Section 3(C).

2. *Interstate Disputes.* In the discussion problem, the pollution from the mill crossed state boundaries. What law should govern such disputes?

In two important cases early in the twentieth century, the Supreme Court recognized a federal common law of nuisance, which could be invoked by states against interstate pollution. In Missouri v. Illinois, 200 U.S. 496 (1906), Missouri complained that the city of Chicago had polluted the Mississippi River. Chicago's sewer system had originally been designed to empty into Lake Michigan, which was also the source of the city's water. Pollution from the sewer outfall soon threatened the city's water supply. To solve this problem, Chicago's engineers devised a plan to reverse the flow of the Chicago River away from Lake Michigan to the Des Plaines River, which eventually flowed to the Mississippi River. Some 357 miles downstream of Chicago, St. Louis drew its drinking water from the Mississippi. Justice Holmes, writing for the Court, observed that, in a case of "serious magnitude, clearly and fully proved," nuisance might provide a remedy for a downstream state. The Court concluded, however, that Missouri, which allowed its own cities to discharge sewage into the river, had failed to prove that Chicago's discharges had caused any harm to St. Louis.

The next year, in Georgia v. Tennessee Copper Co., 206 U.S. 230 (1907), the Court held that Georgia was entitled to an injunction against the operation of two copper smelters located just across the border in Tennessee, fumes from which were damaging forests and crops in Georgia. Justice Holmes again wrote for the Court:

> It is a fair and reasonable demand on the part of a sovereign that the air over its territory should not be polluted on a great scale by sulphurous acid gas, that the forests on its mountains, be they better or worse, and whatever domestic destruction they have suffered, should not be further destroyed or threatened by the act of persons beyond its control, that the crops and orchards on its hills should not be endangered from the same source.

Id. at 238. The parties agreed to postpone entry of a final decree while they attempted to settle the dispute. The state reached a settlement with one of the two smelters, but in 1914 applied for a permanent injunction against the other. In the interim, operators of the smelter had spent more than $600,000, and managed to reduce sulfur emissions by more than half. Nonetheless, the Court concluded that the remaining emissions, which averaged more than 30 tons of sulfur per day, continued to cause damage in Georgia. It therefore imposed emissions limitations, ordering the smelter to limit emissions to no more than 20 tons per day during the summer months, and 40 tons per day at other times. Georgia v. Tennessee Copper Co., 237 U.S. 474 (1915).

In the modern era, the Supreme Court has effectively nullified the federal common law of nuisance. In City of Milwaukee v. Illinois, 451 U.S. 304 (1981), the Court concluded that the federal common law of nuisance had been preempted by the Clean Water Act:

> We conclude that, at least so far as concerns the claims of respondents, Congress has not left the formulation of appropriate federal standards to the courts through the application of often vague and indeterminate nuisance concepts of maxims of equity jurisprudence, but rather has occupied the field through the establishment of a comprehensive regulation program supervised by an expert administrative agency.

It applied the same rationale to ocean pollution in Middlesex County Sewerage Authority v. National Sea Clammers Association, 453 U.S. 1 (1981). Although the Supreme Court has not directly addressed the issue, the same reasoning would seem to apply to the Clean Air Act. See United States v. Kin–Buc, Inc., 532 F.Supp. 699 (D.N.J.1982).

The Clean Water Act contains a "savings clause" providing that its citizen suit provision does not "restrict any right which any person (or class of persons) may have under any statute or common law * * *." 33 U.S.C. § 1365(e). Most federal environmental statutes include similar provisions. Courts have read that clause as evidence of a Congressional intent not to preempt state law nuisance actions. In interstate nuisance cases, the Supreme Court has held that the law of the source state, rather than of the receiving state, applies. In International Paper v. Ouellette, 479 U.S. 481 (1987), a nuisance suit filed by property owners on the Vermont side of Lake Champlain against a paper mill on the New York side, the Court explained:

> After examining the [Clean Water Act] as a whole, its purposes and history, we are convinced that if affected States were allowed to

impose separate discharge standards on a single point source, the inevitable result would be a serious interference with the achievement of the full purposes and objectives of Congress. Because we do not believe Congress intended to undermine this carefully drawn statute, we conclude that the CWA precludes a court from applying the law of an affected State against an out-of-state source.

Our conclusion that Vermont nuisance law is inapplicable to a New York point source does not leave respondents without a remedy. The CWA precludes only those suits that may require standards of effluent control that are incompatible with those established by the procedures set forth in the Act. The saving clause specifically preserves other state actions, and therefore nothing in the Act bars aggrieved individuals from bringing a nuisance claim pursuant to the law of the source State. * * *

An action brought against [International Paper Co.] would not frustrate the goals of the CWA as would a suit governed by Vermont law. First, application of the source State's law does not disturb the balance among federal, source-state, and affected-state interests. Because the Act specifically allows source States to impose stricter standards, the imposition of source-state law does not disrupt the regulatory partnership established by the permit system. Second, the restriction of suits to those brought under source-state nuisance law prevents a source from being subject to an indeterminate number of potential regulations. Although New York nuisance law may impose separate standards and thus create some tension with the permit system, a source only is required to look to a single additional authority, whose rules should be relatively predictable. Moreover, States can be expected to take into account their own nuisance laws in setting permit requirements.

3. *The Interplay of Statutes and Common Law.* As we shall see, federal pollution laws (and their state analogues) impose substantive standards and require permits for polluting sources. Violation of a standard or permit may be a nuisance or negligence per se, automatically subjecting the violator to common-law liability, as well as whatever consequences are imposed by statute. See, e.g., Gill v. LDI, 19 F.Supp.2d 1188, 1198–99 (W.D.Wash.1998) (holding that violation of Clean Water Act permit amounts to nuisance per se under Washington law).

Compliance with statutory and regulatory standards, on the other hand, is not an automatic bar to a tort action. See, e.g., Galaxy Carpet Mills v. Massengill, 255 Ga. 360, 338 S.E.2d 428 (1986) (polluting boilers could be declared a nuisance even though operated in accordance with state permit); Village of Wilsonville v. SCA Servs., 86 Ill.2d 1, 55 Ill.Dec. 499, 426 N.E.2d 824 (1981) (enjoining operation of hazardous waste disposal as public and private nuisance notwithstanding state permit). Compliance may, however, be evidence of reasonableness or of the expected standard of care.

Whether a defendant who is in compliance with a permit will nonetheless be liable in nuisance may depend upon a variety of factors, including whether the permit directly addresses the alleged nuisance, and the extent to which the concerns of neighbors were accounted for in permit proceedings. See New England Legal Found'n v. Costle, 666 F.2d 30 (2d Cir.1981) (holding nuisance claim precluded where EPA had specifically authorized use of high-sulfur coals); Twitty v. North Carolina, 527 F.Supp. 778 (E.D.N.C.1981) (rejecting nuisance suit against state for storing PCBs in landfill and against EPA for authorizing storage). In addition, statutes sometimes explicitly or implicitly preempt tort claims.

Should regulatory compliance protect against a tort action? Will allowing such a defense encourage defendants to ignore hazards not recognized by the regulations? On the other hand, without such a defense might defendants be found liable even when their actions were reasonable at the time? Psychologists have found that people who know the outcome tend to overestimate the predictability of past events, a phenomenon known as "hindsight bias." Where a defendant's actions have proven insufficient, in retrospect, to prevent harm, hindsight bias makes it more difficult for judges and juries to view those precautions as reasonable. See Jeffrey Rachlinski, Regulating in Foresight Versus Judging Liability in Hindsight: The Case of Tobacco, 33 Ga. L. Rev. 813 (1999).

4. *Remedies in Nuisance Actions.* Historically, a plaintiff who proved a nuisance was entitled to injunctive relief. Since the industrial revolution, however, courts have been reluctant to enjoin economically valuable polluting activities. In the famous case of Boomer v. Atlantic Cement Co., 26 N.Y.2d 219, 309 N.Y.S.2d 312, 257 N.E.2d 870 (1970), the court found that air pollution from a cement plant constituted a nuisance, but allowed the operator to escape an injunction by paying compensatory damages. Today, American courts typically "balance the equities" to determine if injunctive relief is justified in a nuisance case.

It is important to keep in mind that an injunction need not be a simple command to stop all pollution, and that injunctive and monetary relief are not mutually exclusive. Courts enjoy considerable discretion to combine compensatory and injunctive remedies, and to tailor injunctions to the circumstances of the particular case. A court can retain jurisdiction or appoint a special master to oversee long-term compliance with an injunction.

How might the *Boomer* court have structured an injunction, taking into account both the value of the plant's operations and the plaintiffs' interest in being free of pollution? What difficulties would the court face in crafting and implementing such an injunction? What advantages would a carefully-tailored injunction offer over compensatory damages alone?

5. *The Scope of Monetary Damages.* Suppose Acme Chemical spills a toxic compound into the Swift River just upstream from Cold Bay, contaminating downstream property and killing fish and other aquatic life in both river and bay. Which of the following plaintiffs, if any, should be able to recover?

- Aaron, a downstream property owner
- Betty, who operates a commercial fishing boat on Cold Bay

- Chris, the owner of a local seafood restaurant
- Dorothy, the owner of a charter recreational fishing boat
- Elliot, who enjoys canoeing on Swift River to observe fish and wildlife
- Florence, a Native American who regards consumption of fish from Swift River as an important aspect of a subsistence lifestyle

Direct damage to real property, such as that suffered by Aaron, is always compensable. If the injury is permanent, for example if a toxin cannot be removed from the soil, the measure of damages is the diminution in property value due to contamination. If the injury is remediable, restoration or cleanup costs may be a more appropriate measure. See, e.g., Restatement (2d) of Torts, § 929(a); Davey Compressor Co. v. City of Delray Beach, 639 So.2d 595 (Fla.1994). "Stigma" damages may also be awarded if negative market perceptions leave the value of the property diminished even after complete remediation. See Walker Drug Co. v. La Sal Oil Co., 972 P.2d 1238 (Utah 1998); In re Paoli R.R. Yard PCB Litigation, 35 F.3d 717, 797–98 (3d Cir.1994). In addition to lost property value, Aaron may recover "hedonic" damages for discomfort, annoyance, and inconvenience caused by the spill. See, e.g., Weinhold v. Wolff, 555 N.W.2d 454 (Iowa 1996); Branch v. Western Petroleum, 657 P.2d 267 (Utah 1982)).

Courts have struggled to find principled bases for addressing the claims of fishermen and others who are economically dependent upon a natural resource but lack a proprietary interest. One approach is to distinguish compensable "direct" harm to fishing interests from non-compensable "indirect" harm to processors, restaurateurs, and others. See Pruitt v. Allied Chemical, 523 F.Supp. 975 (E.D.Va.1981); Union Oil Co. v. Oppen, 501 F.2d 558 (9th Cir.1974). Can this distinction be defended? Can you think of any other line that might be drawn to limit the class of potential plaintiffs?

Common law historically limited tort recovery to economic damages. Statutes, including the Clean Water Act and CERCLA, have broadened the scope of recovery in some circumstances. These provisions allow recovery by government trustees for damages to natural resources, including lost existence and option values.

Punitive damages may also be awarded if the defendant's conduct is sufficiently wrongful. After finding that Exxon had recklessly caused the 1989 grounding of the Exxon Valdez, which spilled 11,000,000 gallons of oil into Alaska's Prince William Sound, a jury awarded commercial fishermen and native Alaskans $5 billion in punitive damages. See In re Exxon Valdez, 229 F.3d 790, 794 (9th Cir.2000).

SECTION 2. TOXIC TORTS

Toxic torts are personal injury actions based on exposure to substances that present an unusually high risk to human health or the environment.

Toxic tort actions arise in a variety of contexts, including occupational and environmental exposure.

As the excerpt from *Leaf River* suggests, toxic tort actions generally present difficult issues of causation. To prevail, plaintiffs must show: 1) that they were exposed to chemicals released by the defendants; 2) that those chemicals can cause the types of harm they suffered; and 3) that the chemicals in fact did cause the harm. In re Paoli R.R. Yard PCB Litigation, 35 F.3d 717, 752 (3d Cir.1994).

Each of these elements may require expert testimony and expensive tests, making toxic tort cases expensive and time-consuming to litigate. Plaintiffs in *Leaf River* failed to satisfy the first element, because they did not offer tests showing dioxin contamination of their property. In a later case involving the same mill, plaintiffs provided proof of exposure, but were unable to trace the dioxins to defendant's mill. Anglado v. Leaf River Forest Products, 716 So.2d 543 (Miss.1998). As the following excerpt illustrates, however, often the most difficult hurdle for toxic tort plaintiffs is proof that exposure has caused their injury.

In re "Agent Orange" Product Liability Litigation
United States District Court, Eastern District of New York, 1985.
611 F.Supp. 1223.

[More than 15,000 named plaintiffs, representing 24 million Vietnam veterans filed a class action alleging that exposure to "Agent Orange," manufactured by the chemical company defendants, had caused them various health problems. Agent Orange, a mix of the herbicides 2,4–D and 2,4,5–T, which contained dioxin as a contaminant, was used as a defoliant during the war. It got its nickname from the bright label on its containers.

The case was assigned to Chief Judge Jack Weinstein, who generally is regarded as among the most brilliant members of the federal judiciary. Judge Weinstein brokered a $180 million settlement, the largest tort recovery to that date in the United States. The settlement authorized recovery by all service persons and their biological children without any showing of causation. Judge Weinstein approved the settlement in a lengthy opinion, 597 F.Supp. 740 (E.D.N.Y.1984), despite expressing reservations about the causation issue. Id. at 745–46.

Many veterans groups opposed the settlement, however, because it limited each member of the extremely large class to a maximum recovery of $12,700. Several hundred claimants elected to opt out of the class action to pursue their individual claims. In the following opinion, Judge Weinstein rejected their claims.]

■ WEINSTEIN, DISTRICT JUDGE.

Defendants, seven chemical companies, have moved to dismiss or in the alternative for summary judgment. Plaintiffs are Vietnam veterans and members of their families who have opted out of the class previously certified by the court * * *. They allege that as a result of the veterans' exposure to Agent Orange, a herbicide manufactured by the defendants, they suffer from various health problems. * * *

Plaintiff Vietnam veterans do suffer. Many deserve help from the government. They cannot obtain aid through this suit against private corporations. * * *

The most serious deficiency in plaintiffs' case is their failure to present credible evidence of a causal link between exposure to Agent Orange and the various diseases from which they are allegedly suffering. * * *

In support of their contention that Agent Orange did not cause the various ailments that allegedly afflict the veteran plaintiffs, defendants rest upon a number of epidemiological studies. As this court has indicated in extensive and repeated recorded colloquy with counsel and in prior opinions, all reliable studies of the effect of Agent Orange on members of the class so far published provide no support for plaintiffs' claims of causation.

Epidemiological studies rely on "statistical methods to detect abnormally high incidences of disease in a study population and to associate these incidences with unusual exposures to suspect environmental factors." Dore, "A Commentary on the Use of Epidemiological Evidence in Demonstrating Cause-in-Fact," 7 Harv. Envtl. L. Rev. 429, 431 (1983). In their study of diseases in human populations, epidemiologists use data from surveys, death certificates, and medical and clinical observations. Id.

A number of sound epidemiological studies have been conducted on the health effects of exposure to Agent Orange. These are the only useful studies having any bearing on causation.

All the other data supplied by the parties rests on surmise and inapposite extrapolations from animal studies and industrial accidents. It is hypothesized that, predicated on this experience, adverse effects of Agent Orange on plaintiffs might at some time in the future be shown to some degree of probability.

The available relevant studies have addressed the direct effects of exposure on servicepersons and the indirect effects of exposure on spouses and children of servicepersons. No acceptable study to date of Vietnam veterans and their families concludes that there is a causal connection between exposure to Agent Orange and the serious adverse health effects claimed by plaintiffs. * * *

Plaintiffs cite a number of studies conducted on animals and industrial workers as evidence of a causal link between exposure to [dioxin] and the development of various hepatotoxic, hematotoxic, genotoxic, and enzymatic responses. None of these studies do more than show that there may be a causal connection between dioxin and disease. None show such a connection between plaintiffs and Agent Orange. * * *

Even most of plaintiffs' experts express doubt about causation, except for some ill-defined possible "association" as compared with associations with any specific other products or natural carcinogens; none supports the conclusion that present evidence permits a scientifically acceptable conclusion that Agent Orange did cause a specific plaintiff's specific disease. * * *

Plaintiffs offer the opinion of two experts who conclude that in the cases of the specific opt-out plaintiffs before the court, exposure to Agent Orange caused adverse health effects. One is Dr. Singer's submission. The other is Dr. Epstein's. * * *

Dr. Singer, who is board certified in internal medicine, hematology, and oncology, reaches a number of conclusions based on his review of the numerous form affidavits with their attached checklists. He bases his opinion on his medical background, a review of the literature on the biomedical effects of Agent Orange, and an examination of the individual affidavits. He apparently did not examine any medical records or any plaintiffs. * * *

Dr. Singer notes at the outset that 2,4–D, 2,4,5–T, and 2,3,7,8–tetra-chlorodibenzo-p-dioxin ("dioxin") "are potent and toxic agents capable of inducing a wide variety of adverse effects both in animals and in man." Dr. Singer then analyzes the various ailments suffered by the individual affiants. * * *

As a review of Dr. Singer's affidavit reveals, he attributes some 37 separate diseases, disorders, and symptoms—including baldness and diarrhea—to exposure to Agent Orange. * * *

Stripped of its verbiage, Dr. Singer summarizes his overall conclusion by stating that *if* the affiants are telling the truth and *if* there is no cause for their complaints other than Agent Orange, then Agent Orange must have caused their problems. Dr. Singer states:

> *Assuming the truth of the affidavits submitted, and absent any evidence of pre-existing, intervening, or superseding causes for the symptoms and diseases* complained of in these affidavits, it is my opinion to a reasonable degree of medical probability (that is, more likely than not) that the medical difficulties described by the affiants were proximately caused by exposure to Agent Orange. (Emphasis supplied.)

Put differently, Dr. Singer's analysis amounts to this: the affiants complain of various medical problems; animals and workers exposed to extensive dosages of [dioxin] have suffered from related difficulties; therefore, assuming nothing else caused the affiants' afflictions, Agent Orange caused them. One need hardly be a doctor of medicine to make the statement that if X is a possible cause of Y, and if there is no other possible cause of Y, X must have caused Y. Dr. Singer's formulation avoids the problem before us: which of myriad possible causes of Y created a particular veteran's problems. To take just one of the diseases reported by plaintiffs in an undifferentiated form, and relied upon by Dr. Singer, hepatitis: this is a disease common in the civilian population and there is not the slightest evidence that its incidence is greater among those exposed to Agent Orange than those not exposed. * * *

Plaintiffs belatedly submitted affidavits by Dr. Samuel S. Epstein. He has been specially trained in the fields of pathology, bacteriology, and public health. * * *

* * * Dr. Epstein attributes some fourteen different diseases and afflictions to exposure to Agent Orange of fifteen plaintiffs. Dr. Epstein's affidavits, even if considered timely, are insufficient to oppose the motion for summary judgment. All the diseases in the cases he relies upon are found in the general population of those who were never exposed to Agent Orange. There is no showing that the incidence of the diseases relied upon are greater in the Agent Orange-exposed population than in the population generally. * * *

Central to the inadequacy of plaintiffs' case is their inability to exclude other possible causes of plaintiffs' illnesses—those arising out of their service in Vietnam as well as those that all of us face in military and civilian life. For example, the largest number of plaintiffs considered by Dr. Singer suffer from symptoms such as exhaustion, depression, sleep disturbances, anxiety and anger. He concludes that these symptoms are "compatible with" exposure to dioxin. As scientific literature establishes, such symptoms are also frequently identified with Vietnam stress syndrome due to battle and other military stresses. Dr. Singer in no way rules out stress syndrome as the cause of plaintiffs' neurological symptoms. * * *

After careful scrutiny of all available evidence in this protracted litigation, there is no doubt that a directed verdict at the close of each of plaintiffs' cases would be required. Such careful scrutiny of proposed evidence is especially appropriate in the toxic tort area. * * *

Having voluntarily given up the advantages of the class action, each plaintiff is in the position of being unable to prove either (1) that his disease is due to Agent Orange, or (2) that any particular defendant produced the Agent Orange to which he may have been exposed. No case has ever permitted recovery in such a situation. There is no possible theory of law on which these individual opt-out plaintiffs can recover. * * *

The cases of the veterans and any other members of the class who opted out of the class are dismissed.

NOTES AND QUESTIONS

1. *Causation.* Proving causation is often exceedingly difficult in toxic tort cases. As the New Jersey Supreme Court has explained:

> In toxic tort cases, the task of proving causation is invariably more complex because of the long latency period of illness caused by carcinogens or other toxic chemicals. The fact that ten or twenty years or more may intervene between the exposure and the manifestation of the disease highlights the practical difficulties encountered in the effort to prove causation. Moreover, the fact that segments of the entire population are afflicted by cancer and other toxically-induced diseases requires plaintiffs, years after their exposure, to counter the argument

that other intervening exposures or forces were the "cause" of their injury.

Ayers v. Jackson, 106 N.J. 557, 585, 525 A.2d 287, 301 (1987).

Plaintiffs must prove both "general causation," i.e., that the substance to which they were exposed is capable of causing the type of injury they suffered, and "specific causation," i.e., that the substance caused their specific injury. Scientific uncertainty complicates both tasks.

For obvious reasons, controlled tests of the effects of deliberate exposure of humans to substances suspected of toxicity are hardly ever available. Plaintiffs therefore must rely on other types of evidence to prove causation. They commonly offer one or more of the following, listed in order of increasing probative value: 1) expert testimony about structure-activity relationships (predictions about the toxicity of a given substance based on information about the effects of chemically related compounds); 2) experimental studies using isolated animal tissues ("in vitro" studies); 3) experimental studies on live animals ("in vivo" studies); and 4) epidemiological studies of human disease.

Structure-activity evidence rests on educated guesses that similar compounds will produce similar types and levels of harm. In vitro studies can illuminate biological pathways of harm. Effects produced in a test tube, however, may not occur in live animals. Because human beings are biologically similar in many respects to other mammals, in vivo tests on animals such as rats or mice often provide useful models for medical research. Nonetheless, it is difficult to extrapolate from animal toxicity tests, which are often performed using high doses and animal strains known to be especially susceptible to disease, to low dose exposure of human beings.

Epidemiological studies compare the incidence of disease in an exposed human population to the background incidence without exposure. Because they directly relate human exposure to disease, epidemiological studies provide the strongest evidence that a substance does or does not produce a particular disease. When available, they are often given more weight by courts than other evidence. But the results of these studies are also difficult to interpret, for several reasons. The scope of epidemiological studies is limited by cost and the chance occurrence of exposure. Studies of a small exposed population may miss a weak, but real, association. Studies of the effects of high exposure, as often occurs in occupational settings, may be difficult to apply to lower environmental doses. Often, epidemiological studies are not undertaken until litigation draws attention to a potential effect. As a result, they are necessarily short term, and may not reveal an effect with a long latent period.

Well-designed and implemented epidemiological studies generate relative risk factors that can be used to prove causation. Suppose 10 of every 10,000 persons in the general population develops chronic myelogenous leukemia, a rare form of cancer. If 21 of 10,000 persons exposed to substance X develop chronic myelogenous leukemia, the relative risk factor (incidence in the exposed population divided by incidence in the control population) for substance X would be 2.1 (21/10). Since the risk of leukemia is more than twice as high in the exposed group, there is a better than 50% probability (i.e., it is more likely than not), that any leukemia in the exposed group is attributable to exposure.

On the other hand, if only 16 of 10,000 exposed persons develop chronic myelogenous leukemia, the relative risk factor is 1.6. In this group, only six of 16 leukemias would be attributable to substance X, and the probability that any individual case is due to substance X would be 37.5%. In the absense of additional evidence implicating substance X or ruling out other possible leukemia causes, ordinary legal standards would not allow a finding that any leukemia in this group was due to substance X.

In these circumstances, application of ordinary tort principles leads to either over- or under-compensation. In the first example above, all twenty-one plaintiffs would recover, although only eleven leukemias were caused by substance X. On the other hand, in the second example, no plaintiff would recover, although six have been harmed by substance X. Faced with the probabilistic nature of toxic tort cases, courts have struggled to find a balance between excessive generosity to plaintiffs, which discourages socially valuable activities that require or produce toxic substances, and excessive generosity to defendants, which leaves injured plaintiffs uncompensated and provides too little deterrence.

Can the choice between over- and under-deterrence be avoided? Some observers have suggested that each member of the exposed group be compensated in proportion to the increased risk of disease. See Richard Delgado, Beyond Sindell: Relaxation of Cause–In–Fact Rules for Indeterminate Plaintiffs, 70 Calif. L. Rev. 881 (1982); Glen O. Robinson, Probabilistic Causation and Compensation for Tortious Risk, 14 J. Legal Stud. 779, 787 (1985); Christopher H. Schroeder, Corrective Justice and Liability for Increasing Risks, 37 UCLA L. Rev. 439 (1990). In the first example above, each plaintiff would recover 11/21 (the proportion of cancers attributable to substance X) of the damages attributable to a cancer. In the second case, each would recover 6/16 of that amount. What advantages would this approach have over the traditional requirement that each plaintiff individually prove harm? What disadvantages? Should it apply in a lawsuit brought not as a class action but by an individual plaintiff? Should some minimum level of increased risk be required before liability is imposed?

2. *Statistical Significance.* There is still another complication to consider. In any study, the observed incidence of disease will include chance variation within the population as well as the effects of exposure to the substance at issue. By convention, epidemiologists regard an effect as proven only if statistical tests show a very low probability (typically 5% or less) that the observed outcome resulted from chance variation. The power of studies to distinguish real from chance variation goes up as the number of test subjects goes up. If the exposed population is small or the background rate high, it may be impossible to obtain statistically significant results. Should courts allow plaintiffs to bring in evidence of epidemiologic studies which suggest an effect but do not meet conventional scientific standards for statistical significance? Should such evidence ever be sufficient to establish causation? Compare Brock v. Merrell Dow Pharmaceuticals, Inc., 884 F.2d 166, 167 (5th Cir.1989) (finding plaintiffs' failure to present statistically significant epidemiological evidence fatal to their case) with DeLuca v. Merrell Dow Pharmaceuticals, Inc., 911 F.2d 941, 955 (3d Cir.1990) (describing statistical significance as only one factor in the evaluation of epidemiological evidence).

3. *The Substantial Factor Test.* Some courts have loosened the causation requirements for toxic tort plaintiffs by applying the "substantial factor" test, originally developed for multiple tort-feasor situations. Under this test, a plaintiff can prevail on a showing that the defendant's action was a substantial factor in the injury, without having to prove that the injury would not have occurred absent defendant's action. See Elam v. Alcolac, Inc., 765 S.W.2d 42, 174 (Mo.App.1988). A toxic substance may be considered a substantial factor in the injury if it contributes more than a negligible amount to the risk of harm. In Kennedy v. Southern California Edison, 219 F.3d 988 (9th Cir.2000), the Ninth Circuit, applying California law, held that a jury could reasonably find that radiation exposure was a "substantial factor" in plaintiff's disease in the face of uncontroverted expert testimony that there was only a 1 in 100,000 chance that the exposure caused the disease. The court explained:

> Presented perhaps more concretely, if the entire U.S. population were exposed to the amount of radiation in appellee's hypothetical upon which its expert based his statistical opinion, then approximately 2,500 people would contract [plaintiff's disease]. While this number is relatively small, it is more than "negligible."

Id. at 999.

Do you agree with the court's interpretation of what constitutes a negligible risk? Critics of the substantial factor test argue that focusing on risk alone is inappropriate. "[R]isk does not equate with cause. If ten people shoot at a deer, each contributes to the risk that the deer will be hit, but if a single bullet strikes the animal, only one person caused its death." Bert Black and David H. Hollander Jr., Unravelling Causation: Back to the Basics, 3 U. Balt. L. Rev. 1, 21 (1993). Is this an apt analogy to toxic exposure cases?

4. *Eliminating Cause-in-Fact?* Should standard causation analysis be relaxed more radically in toxic tort cases? Professor Margaret Berger argues that requiring proof that defendant's substance caused plaintiff's harm encourages defendants to avoid developing or disclosing information about potential health risks. She suggests imposing liability instead for failure to provide the public with information about the risks posed by a substance, subject to an affirmative defense that the adverse health reactions could not plausibly have been caused by exposure to defendant's product or substance. She would protect defendants who release sufficient information from liability. Margaret A. Berger, Eliminating General Causation: Notes Towards a New Theory of Justice and Toxic Torts, 97 Columbia L. Rev. 2117 (1997). Is this proposal appealing? Does it rest on unproven assumptions that most chemicals are harmful? That most cancers are attributable to artificial chemicals? In light of the difficulties of obtaining clear scientific proof that a substance is or is not toxic, how would courts define the standards for testing? How should they factor in the dose to which defendant exposes plaintiffs? The ability or inability of a plaintiff to avoid exposure? Would this proposal over-deter the use of relatively safe substances?

5. *Expert Witness Testimony under the Federal Rules of Evidence.* Concerned that juries may not be able to evaluate scientific evidence and may be improperly swayed by the emotional appeals of injured plaintiffs, courts have devised special admissibility tests for expert witness testimony. For many years the federal courts used the *Frye* test, so called after the case in which it was first enunciated, Frye v. United States, 293 F. 1013 (D.C.Cir. 1923), to determine admissibility. *Frye* allowed expert testimony only if the technique concerned was generally accepted in the relevant scientific community.

In Daubert v. Merrell Dow Pharmaceuticals, 509 U.S. 579 (1993), the Supreme Court ruled that adoption of the Federal Rules of Evidence in 1975 had superseded the *Frye* test. Under the Federal Rules, the Court explained, the trial judge must determine whether expert testimony will assist the trier of fact. "This entails a preliminary assessment of whether the reasoning or methodology underlying the testimony is scientifically valid and of whether that reasoning or methodology properly can be applied to the facts in issue. * * * The focus, of course, must be solely on principles and methodology, not on the conclusions that they generate." Id. at 592–95. Factors to be considered include whether the theory or technique has been tested; whether it has been subjected to peer review; the known or potential error rate; and general acceptance in the relevant scientific community. Id. at 593–94.

Daubert offered a partial victory to both plaintiffs and defendants. Plaintiffs at least nominally won relief from *Frye*'s general acceptance test, which the Supreme Court described as "rigid," and "at odds with the liberal thrust" of the Federal Rules of Evidence. Id at 588. Defendants, on the other hand, gained a strong endorsement of the role of the trial judge as evidentiary gatekeeper, shielding the jury from unreliable expert evidence. Surveys of federal judges and attorneys before and after *Daubert* suggest that *Daubert* has led to closer scrutiny and more frequent exclusion of expert testimony. See Molly Treadwell Johnson et al., Expert Testimony in Federal Civil Trials: A Preliminary Analysis (Federal Judicial Center 2000).

State courts have split on *Daubert*. A 1999 study reported that the highest courts of seventeen states had explicitly endorsed *Daubert*, while seven had explicitly rejected *Daubert* in favor of *Frye*. Other states apply their own, unique, tests. See Bert Black, Expert Evidence in the Wake of the Daubert–Jones–Kumho Tire Trilogy (ALI–ABA Course of Study 1999).

6. *Accrual of the Cause of Action.* Virtually all jurisdictions now apply the "discovery rule" to claims based on development of disease long after exposure. The statute of limitations runs not from the time of exposure but from the time when the plaintiff knew or should have known of the injury. Determining that date may not be easy.

Suppose a train derails near the construction site at which Alicia is working outdoors. The derailment releases "toxiphene," a substance which can cause lung cancer. Three years later, Alicia develops shortness of breath, but attributes her symptoms to the general effects of aging, a new sedentary job, and recent weight gain. Two years after that, a physical exam reveals that Alicia has a lung tumor. The statute of limitations in this jurisdiction for negligence is 1 year. Can Alicia bring suit? Does it matter whether the derailment and resulting release were widely reported in the local media? Whether Alicia actually knew of the derailment or the release?

7. *Defining Compensable Injury.* Suppose Brad works at the train yard where the derailment occurs, exposing him to toxiphene. Aware of the exposure, Brad consults his doctor, who opines that the exposure has increased Brad's risk of lung cancer from 1 in 1,000 to roughly 1 in 100. The doctor suggests annual chest X-rays to ensure that the disease, if it develops, will be caught early. Brad is not suffering any current symptoms. Does he have a present claim for the increased risk of cancer? For his fear that he will become a cancer victim? For the costs of medical monitoring?

Courts have generally refused to allow recovery solely on the basis of an increased risk of developing cancer or other diseases in the future. Many courts, however, have allowed recovery on a slightly different theory for fear of future disease, which is recognized as a form of emotional distress. For a claim of negligent infliction of emotional distress, many jurisdictions require proof of some present physical impact or injury other than mere exposure to the toxic substance. See, e.g., Ball v. Joy Technologies, 958 F.2d 36, 38 (4th Cir.1991). A few have done away with the need for physical injury or allowed recovery based on the impact of exposure alone. See Hagerty v. L & L Marine Serv., 788 F.2d 315, 318, *modified on denial of rehearing en banc,* 797 F.2d 256 (5th Cir.1986); Herber v. Johns–Manville Corp., 785 F.2d 79, 85 (3d Cir.1986).

Which is the better approach? Is the answer different for toxic torts than traditional ones? Consider another hypothetical. C buys a container of defendant's yogurt which, due to defendant's negligence, contains broken glass. C discovers the glass when she puts the first spoonful in her mouth. She is not cut but is upset, and fears that she may have swallowed some of the glass. Cf. Restatement (2d) of Torts, § 436A, illus. 1. Is C's emotional distress claim equivalent to B's? If not, which is stronger and why?

Fear of future disease must be "reasonable" to support recovery. Is B's fear reasonable? Should reasonableness depend on the extent to which exposure has increased the risk, or only on the absolute magnitude of the risk? Is it relevant that surveys show that cancer is a particularly "dread" disease? The California Supreme Court has limited recovery for fear of future disease to plaintiffs who can show that they are more likely than not to develop disease in the future. The Court explained:

We cannot say that it would never be reasonable for a person who has ingested toxic substances to harbor a genuine and serious fear of cancer where reliable medical or scientific opinion indicates that such ingestion has significantly increased his or her risk of cancer, but not to a probable likelihood. Indeed, we would be very hard pressed to find that, as a matter of law, a plaintiff faced with a 20 percent or 30 percent chance of developing cancer cannot genuinely, seriously, and reasonably fear the prospect of cancer. Nonetheless, we conclude * * * that emotional distress caused by the fear of cancer that is not probable should generally not be compensable in a negligence action.

As a starting point in our analysis, we recognize the indisputable fact that all of us are exposed to carcinogens every day. * * *

Thus, all of us are potential fear of cancer plaintiffs, provided we are sufficiently aware of and worried about the possibility of developing cancer from exposure to or ingestion of a carcinogenic exposure. The enormity of the class of potential plaintiffs cannot be overstated * * *.

Potter v. Firestone Tire & Rubber Co., 6 Cal.4th 965, 25 Cal.Rptr.2d 550, 863 P.2d 795 (1993).

Some, but not all, courts have allowed recovery of the costs of medical monitoring following toxic exposure. What arguments can you think of for and against awards of medical monitoring costs? Do the concerns about a potential flood of litigation expressed in the excerpt from *Potter* apply equally to medical monitoring claims? Does it matter whether the plaintiff has medical insurance which would pay for the tests? Might a medical monitoring award reduce the potential future damages, should plaintiff develop disease? Where medical monitoring costs are recoverable, plaintiffs typically are required to show a significantly increased risk of contracting a serious latent disease, and that early detection and treatment of the disease is beneficial. See In re Paoli R.R. Yard PCB Litigation, 916 F.2d 829, 852 (3d Cir.1990); *Potter*, 863 P.2d at 821.

SECTION 3.   COMMON LAW VERSUS PUBLIC LAW

As we shall see in more detail in later chapters, statutes and regulations have overtaken the common law as the primary mechanism for controlling environmental harm. Common law liability can substitute for, supplement, or be pre-empted by prescriptive (sometimes called "command and control") regulation. The appropriate role of private and public law in the environmental context, both generally and in specific circumstances, remains a subject of intense debate.

Steven Shavell, Liability for Harm Versus Regulation of Safety

13 J. Legal Stud. 357, 357–65 (1984).

Liability in tort and the regulation of safety represent two very different approaches for controlling activities that create risks of harm to others. Tort liability is private in nature and works not by social command but rather indirectly, through the deterrent effect of damage actions that may be brought once harm occurs. Standards, prohibitions, and other forms of safety regulation, in contrast, are public in character and modify behavior in an immediate way through requirements that are imposed before, or at least independently of, the actual occurrence of harm. * * *

To identify and assess the factors determining the social desirability of liability and regulation, it is necessary to set out a measure of social welfare; and here that measure is assumed to equal the benefits parties derive from engaging in their activities, less the sum of the costs of precautions, the harms done, and the administrative expenses associated with the means of social control. The formal problem is to employ the means of control to maximize the measure of welfare.

We can now examine four determinants that influence the solution to this problem. The first determinant is the possibility of a *difference in knowledge about risky activities* as between private parties and a regulatory authority. This difference could relate to the benefits of activities, the costs of reducing risks, or the probability or severity of the risks.

Where private parties have superior knowledge of these elements, it would be better for them to decide about the control of risks, indicating an advantage of liability rules, other things being equal. * * *

The second of the determinants of the relative desirability of liability and regulation is that *private parties might be incapable of paying for the full magnitude of the harm done.* Where this is the case, liability would not furnish adequate incentives to control risk, because private parties would treat losses caused that exceeded their assets as imposing liabilities only equal to their assets. But under regulation inability to pay for harm done would be irrelevant, assuming that parties would be made to take steps to reduce risk as a precondition for engaging in their activities. * * *

Let us turn next to the third of the four general determinants, the chance that *parties would not face the threat of suit for harm done.* Like incapacity to pay for harm, such a possibility results in a dilution of the incentives to reduce risk created by liability, but is of no import under regulation.

* * * One reason that a defendant can escape tort liability is that the harms he generates are widely dispersed, making it unattractive for any victim individually to initiate legal action. This danger can be offset to a degree if victims are allowed to maintain class actions * * *. A second cause of failure to sue is the passage of a long period of time before harm manifests itself. This raises the possibility that by the time suit is contemplated, the evidence necessary for a successful action will be stale or the responsible parties out of business. A third reason for failure to sue is difficulty in attributing harm to the parties who are in fact responsible for producing it. This problem could arise from simple ignorance that a given harm or disease was caused by a human agency (as opposed to being

"natural" in origin) or from inability to identify which one or several out of many parties was the cause of the harm. * * *

The last of the determinants is the magnitude of the *administrative costs incurred by private parties and by the public* in using the tort system or direct regulation. Of course, the costs of the tort system must be broadly defined to include the time, effort, and legal expenses borne by private parties in the course of litigation or in coming to settlements, as well as the public expenses of conducting trials, employing judges, empaneling juries, and the like. Similarly, the administrative costs of regulation include the public expense of maintaining the regulatory establishment and the private costs of compliance.

[Professor Shavell concludes that two of these factors—differential knowledge and administrative costs—will generally favor liability approaches whereas the other two—incapacity to pay for harm done and likelihood of escaping suit—favor regulation.] This suggests not only that neither tort liability nor regulation could uniformly dominate the other as a solution to the problem of controlling risks, but also that they should not be viewed as mutually exclusive solutions to it. A complete solution to the problem of the control of risk evidently should involve the joint use of liability and regulation, with the balance between them reflecting the importance of the determinants.

Roger Meiners & Bruce Yandle, Common Law and the Conceit of Modern Environmental Policy

7 Geo. Mason L. Rev. 923, 946–59 (1999).

The standard economic justification for federal intervention is based on the notion of externality. Under this classification, pollution is a spillover from otherwise beneficial activities that imposes costs on people who did not agree to incur those costs. Since the polluter does not take the spillover costs into account when producing and pricing products, the outcome leads to an inefficient allocation of resources. It is then the business of the state to correct the mispricing of environmental assets. While elegant models can be constructed to illuminate the problem, the difficulty comes in identifying actual situations where state intervention can be justified on economic grounds. How much pollution (or anything else that irritates someone) is too much? Economic literature provides little operational guidance as to when the state should intervene to "internalize" a perceived externality. A sharp theoretical focus provides ways of thinking about benefits and costs, and there is a suggestion, at least, that taking regulatory actions to deal with externalities may be more costly than the gains obtained from doing so. We note that evidence to the contrary notwithstanding, these discussions implicitly assume that politicians are driven primarily by a desire to make the world more efficient.

In recent years, a competing line of inquiry has focused on property rights, which yields a logical framework where the common law tort of nuisance converges with the economic concept of unpaid opportunity cost. Pollution that has meaning in law and economics occurs when property rights are not well specified or effectively enforced. It is then the state's responsibility to enforce property rights and related agreements. When property rights are defined and enforced, economic agents who seek to use an environmental asset must deal with holders of the related rights. Bargaining between parties allows for the transfer of rights, and at common law, contracting around the common law rule. Contracting allows for activities that might otherwise provide a cause of action against a polluter, and the contracting parties bear the cost of their actions. Common law and property rights convert a commons to a managed asset that is treated with owner-like concern. * * *

Critics of the common law approach to solving environmental problems deride the process as unworkable. It is a quaint historical relic that could be better replaced by bright people putting their minds to devising rules, enforced by the EPA and its minions in the states, that would protect us against a host of environmental ills. If correct, there is no reason why that logic should not apply to other areas largely governed by the common law. * * *

We presume that many truly believed that the pre–1970 legal structure regarding the environment, a combination of common law, state and local rules, and a few federal rules, was simply inadequate. Horror stories of pre-EPA environmental ruin, ranging from the burning of the Cuyahoga River to the tragedy at Love Canal seemingly support this presumption, as does the parade of horribles trotted out by political leaders seeking to expand federal environmental programs. * * *

In 1969, the sight of flames leaping from the Cuyahoga River in Ohio shocked many Americans, but it was not big news in Cleveland. An oil slick on the river caught fire and that fire lit wooden train trusses. There had been fires in the river before; the Cuyahoga, an industrial sewer, was biologically dead. A few years before the fire, Bar Realty Corporation sued the city of Cleveland for allowing the river to deteriorate to such a condition. The trial court ordered the city to investigate the causes of the pollution and ordered "such nuisances * * * to be abated." The Supreme Court of Ohio reversed, holding that the river was under the control of state authorities. The Ohio Water Pollution Control Board erased common law protections by granting various industries permissions to discharge wastes into the Cuyahoga and, thereby, Lake Erie. When regulation takes precedent [sic] over common law rights, the result can be destructive to the environment. * * *

The erection of a massive federal environmental bureaucracy came at significant cost. By the EPA's own estimates, federal environmental regulations cost as much as $200 billion per year in current dollars. Yet the cost of federal regulations is not only one of dollars and cents. Federal regulations have also curtailed traditional common law remedies for pollution.

In general, the various federal statutes did not eliminate the right to bring common law actions; they created an alternative that is, in general, much easier to bring (and win). One advantage for defendants is that if they can show compliance with statutory standards, whether the standards are related to likelihood of injury or not, that presents strong evidence to the jury that the defendant must be complying with "the law." * * *

The various federal regulatory schemes have had a clear impact on common law, especially in its application to interstate pollution cases. As early as 1981, courts held that federal acts preempted federal common law with respect to water discharge effluent standards. These decisions held that federal courts lacked the authority to impose more stringent effluent limitation standards than those imposed by the federal agencies responsible for determining appropriate standards. * * *

* * * Perhaps the greatest effect that regulatory standards (either state or federal) may have on common law claims is on the plaintiffs' ability to establish the element of their tort claim related to harm or damage. Arguably, if an agency has blessed the quantity and quality of a discharge either to air or water (i.e., a permit stipulates release of specific pollutants), it may be more difficult for a plaintiff to successfully prove damage. Thus, even if the courts in a jurisdiction do not hold that statutory standards preempt common law claims, decision-makers hearing such actions (e.g., juries, judges) may, nonetheless, reach decisions that give that effect. * * *

Statute law displaced common law for precisely the opposite reasons generally offered by those who extol statute law's virtues. Critics of common law argue that common law protection is unreliable in that bad consequences still happen despite the law, that evidence of cause and effect is difficult to provide, and that enforcement is subject to unpredictable whims of common law judges and juries. Without asking "Relative to What?" common law is seen as providing uneasy and unreliable environmental protection, making it possible for polluters to impose environmental costs with impunity. We contend that common law environmental protection was, if anything, too strict for those who wanted to generate pollution with greater impunity. At common law, there were no EPA permits or uniform technology requirements that sanctioned the actions of the polluter.

Common law remedies varied across the states. That is, common law judges reflected on the customs and traditions of their communities. No "one suit fits all" could evolve from common law courts. And no group of nationally organized rent seekers could ever simultaneously obtain cartel-forming judge-made law. Common law does not fit in a rent-seeking world. Common law evolved to protect rights, not to protect interest groups.

Statute law, on the other hand, provides an escape for polluters. One is hard pressed to find a single instance where a major industrial polluter who violated EPA permits was shut down under statute law. Fines are levied instead (and the fines are often trivial compared to jury verdicts), and the polluters are given more time, under a sternly worded consent decree, to reduce discharges to levels permitted by statute.

* * * [Friedrich Hayek's] *The Fatal Conceit* reminds us that centralized decision makers who seek homogeneous solutions for heterogeneous problems face a severe information problem that expands as decisions are taken from communities to higher levels of governments.

When elected or appointed to office, bright people armed with enough information can build an improved society. Such belief is common but is simply not consistent with our theoretical understanding of how governments work, nor with thousands of years of human experience. * * *

Those plagued with the fatal conceit believe that national governments are always better equipped to gather more and better information than the unfettered forces of markets constrained by rules of law. Yet, even if central authorities solve the information problem, statute writing is a batch process where information is assembled periodically and durable statutes are written and implemented. As the world evolves and changes, the informational underpinnings of statutes still in force become obsolete. On the other hand, the common law process is continuous; it draws together information on controversies as they occur; and evolves as the world changes. While errors may be made in either case, in statute writing the cost of error is logically higher, because statutes are all-encompassing and more costly to change.

Frank B. Cross, Common Law Conceits: A Comment on Meiners & Yandle

7 Geo. Mason L. Rev. 965, 966–81 (1999).

Meiners and Yandle claim that the effectiveness of the common law was destroyed or at least undermined significantly by the intervention of federal environmental legislation and regulation. The most obvious problem with this theory is that common law has not generally been preempted by such legislation. Virtually every major piece of federal environmental legislation contains a savings clause stating that the statute would not "restrict any right that any person (or class of persons) may have under any statute or common law." Because of such savings clauses, common law actions remain much as they did before the passage of the environmental protection statutes. * * *

Perhaps recognizing the limitations of their preemption claims, Meiners and Yandle suggest that federal regulation makes it harder to win common law claims. Thus, they suggest the common law, insofar as it survives at all, is frail. They must concede that compliance with federal regulation is generally not a recognized defense to a common law action, but contend that compliance must be a "strong evidence to the jury" or that courts would "defer to administrative agencies'" determinations or that plaintiffs would be unable to prove damages. These claims, however, are unsupported by so much as a single citation and thus appear wrong. * * *

While regulatory compliance is not an effective defense to common law liability, regulatory noncompliance is a powerful tool for common law plaintiffs. Meiners and Yandle overlook this key point. A violation of environmental regulations is commonly regarded as proof of negligence or nuisance per se, thus easing considerably a plaintiff's burden of proof in a tort action. Therefore, rather than weakening the common law, statutory requirements may actually strengthen its application.

Any vitality that the common law ever had is still present. The four billion dollar judgment in the Exxon Valdez oil spill is but the most obvious example of the continuance of common law remedies. * * * A quick check of litigation records demonstrates the continued vitality of the common law, particularly the nuisance remedy favored by Meiners and Yandle. A Westlaw survey found that the number of nuisance actions associated with pollution or hazardous substances has grown since the passage of federal environmental legislation [from a total of 259 environmental nuisance cases reported in federal and state courts for the period 1965–70 to 1,114 for the period 1990–95]. * * *

Meiners and Yandle's theoretical claim is readily amenable to empirical testing. If, as they say, a less effective public law system supplanted a more effective common law system of environmental protection in the 1970s, one would expect the environment to have deteriorated as a result. In fact, the vast majority of environmental problems have been alleviated, while most national pollution problems were at their peak in the common law era.

The common law era saw some of the most dramatic pollution episodes. It was during this time that the Cuyahoga River caught fire and that Donora, Pennsylvania and New York City suffered from "killer smogs." The era before federal legislation was marked by "massive oil spills, killer smogs, rivers burning, fish kills, the impending death of Lake Erie." A historical analysis of nuisance law in England found that it was "ineffectual" in dealing with "pollution of the air and water." * * *

The environment became considerably cleaner following the passage of federal environmental legislation. * * *

Reliance on the common law might be defended on economic efficiency grounds, though I am dubious of broad claims to this effect. The free market environmentalists want to capture the environment for themselves, though, and make expansive claims that the common law would be stricter or more protective of the environment than is current regulation. If they were right and sincere in these claims, greater reliance on the common law would probably be a bad thing—more strictness in environmental protection is not generally advisable. I suspect they are wrong, however. The evidence suggests that reliance on the common law would roll back environmental protection considerably, overshooting the mark and resulting in too little environmental protection. Even if the rollback proved desirable as a policy matter, its occurrence would certainly destroy the credibility of those who advocated the common law as a tool to strengthen environmental regulation.

Edward Brunet, Debunking Wholesale Private Enforcement of Environmental Rights

15 Harv. J. L. & Pub. Pol'y 311, 313–23 (1992).

A shift to a scheme of private enforcement of environmental rights in property, tort, or contract will face a number of obstacles. * * *

The high transaction costs of individual suits will often prevent necessary enforcement. Many environmental breaches of property and contract rights are likely to be modest property damage injuries, above the threshold of a small claims court but not large enough to interest a plaintiffs' attorney seeking a contingent fee. Such claims may cost more to enforce than damages or injunctive recovery would warrant. * * * Consequently, small injuries may go unremedied, because individual plaintiffs would not themselves have a sufficient economic stake in the litigation to incur the litigation costs.

Furthermore, even *de minimis* environmental claims will often raise complex issues of causation. It may be clear that fish in a private property owner's stream have been killed, but at the same time there may be uncertainty over the identity of the cause or water polluter. Resolution of such causation issues is complex and expensive. * * *

Private litigants funding their own environmental enforcement actions are likely to have difficulty proving that defendants have violated established substantive standards of environmental conduct. The necessity of proving on-going, site-specific violations of environmental standards is very difficult and costly [because] it often requires the alleged or suspected violator's cooperation, which is rarely forthcoming. Private citizens who suffer some type of environmental injury but lack litigation experience or resources will have difficulty overcoming these obstacles. * * *

[T]here are reasons to be skeptical of systematic use of even high-stakes personal injury suits as a means of environmental enforcement. * * * First, individual suits bring highly inconsistent judgments. * * * Second, a high percentage of damage recovery goes to attorneys rather than to victims. * * * Third, those fortunate enough to sue early often recover more than those unfortunate enough to suffer belated damages. * * *

One of the main reasons for the birth of the modern administrative agency was the inability of private individuals to protect themselves effectively when in conflict with more powerful and experienced opponents in the business world. Examination of the origin of New Deal agencies reveals that agency prosecution was partially premised on the notion that the vigorously managed, fully equipped, and experienced litigation unit of an administrative agency was a far superior litigant than victimized private individuals.

NOTES AND QUESTIONS

1. *Public and Private Law.* As Professor Shavell points out, public and private law can both play a role in addressing environmental (and other) problems. Furthermore, as we shall see, public law can take a wide variety of forms, and can be implemented at the local, state, or federal level. Shavell identifies several factors to consider in deciding whether liability or regulation should play the primary role, including the availability of information, ability to pay, likelihood that a private suit will be pursued, and administrative costs. Can you think of other factors important to the choice? What about the ability of the decisionmaker to evaluate the available information? The need for uniform decisions or local flexibility? Note that Shavell's stated goal is to determine the means of control that will maximize social welfare, in other words, to design the most efficient regulatory system. Is that the only relevant goal? Should distributional or other factors be considered?

Recall the characteristics of environmental problems identified in Chapter 1, Section 1. In light of those characteristics, how effective would you expect private law to be against environmental harms? Suppose you were asked to develop a legal response to the problem of global warming. Would you rely primarily on liability or regulation? Would both have a role to play? What would be the strengths and weaknesses of each? Should other strategies, such as incentives or subsidies be included?

2. *Free Market Environmentalism.* Professors Meiners and Yandle advocate a free market approach to environmental protection. Perhaps the best known defense of the free market position is the book *Free Market Environmentalism* by Terry L. Anderson and Donald R. Leal, published in 1991. Free market environmentalists believe the government's primary role in environmental protection should be the creation and enforcement of clear property rights in natural resources, rather than command and control regulation. Recall the discussion of the tragedy of the commons in Chapter 1. Individual property rights can solve the tragedy of the commons if the property owner internalizes all costs and benefits. Why did Hardin recommend coercion (i.e., government regulation) rather than private property interests as the solution to environmental pollution? Can property rights play a role in reducing pollution? How? Of the following environmental problems, which do you think would be most amenable to a free-market solution: a) global warming; b) loss of ocean fisheries; c) long-term nuclear waste disposal; d) disputes over the level of harvesting on national forests?

3. *Skepticism About Motivations.* Some critics charge that those who call themselves free market environmentalists are not always sincere about seeking to advance environmental protection. It has been pointed out, for example, that many of the same groups that profess to support free market environmentalism have called for tort reform measures that would reduce the ability of plaintiffs to recover in common law actions. See Andrew McFee Thompson, Free Market Environmentalism and the Common Law: Confusion, Nostalgia, and Inconsistency, 45 Emory L. J. 1329, 1363 (1996). Do Professors Meiners and Yandle regard environmental regulations as too lax or too stringent? Do you find their claim that the growth of statutory environmental law has actually harmed the environment persuasive? For very different views of history, see Joel Franklin Brenner, Nuisance Law and the Industrial Revolution, 3 J. Legal Stud. 403, 408–420 (1974) (concluding that the law of nuisance was ineffective against air and water pollution in 19th-century England); J.R. McNeill, Something New Under the Sun: An Environmental History of the Twentieth–Century World 58–72 (2000) (concluding that only with the rise of statutes did the law begin to effectively address the air pollution problems of the early 20th century).

CHAPTER THREE

THE ADMINISTRATIVE LAW OF THE ENVIRONMENT

SECTION 1. THE ADMINISTRATIVE DECISIONMAKING PROCESS

A. INTRODUCTION

The practice and understanding of Environmental Law is inextricably intertwined with Administrative Law. While common law doctrines retain some vitality in this area, environmental law is substantially a statutory subject implemented by state and federal governmental agencies. Environmental statutes on both the federal and state levels typically set general norms and standards while delegating the details of the policymaking to administrative agencies. Administrative Law is the body of law that governs agency decisionmaking, orders the relationships between the three branches of government, and ensures that private parties affected by agency decisions receive the protection of constitutional and statutory standards.

Administrative agencies can affect the environment in the following three ways:

- by undertaking actions themselves that have environmental effects,

- by licensing or permitting activities undertaken by individuals, private firms or breaches of government; and

- by adopting regulations or other policies that impact environmental quality.

The primary environmental agency at the federal level is the United States Environmental Protection Agency (EPA), which was created in 1970. However, many other federal agencies have important environmental responsibilities, and under the National Environmental Policy Act (NEPA), 42 U.S.C. §§ 4321–4370a, all federal agencies have an environmental mandate or responsibility. Thus, important environmental policy decisions may be made by almost any federal agency, including the Department of Defense, or the Department of Commerce. Most states have a department of environmental quality or natural resources that functions in a manner similar to the federal EPA. In addition, many different state agencies also affect state environmental decisionmaking.

Federal agencies in the United States can trace their roots to the (now eliminated) Interstate Commerce Commission which was established in 1887. From this nineteenth century origin, the federal bureaucracy got its start and developed into the extensive network of agencies and governmental organizations that we have today. With the evolution of the federal administrative state came the development of the field of administrative law which arose to regulate the exercise of authority by government instrumentalities. There are four principal sources of administrative law; 1) constitutional principle, 2) the common law, 3) specific agency enabling or organic statutes and 4) the Administrative Procedure Act. At the state level, agencies are subject to analogous procedural and substantive rules based upon state law.

B.   AGENCY POWER AND ITS LIMITS

The law pertaining to administrative agencies touches a wide variety of fundamental legal and public policy questions many of which have significant environmental implications. Some issues pertain to governmental structure and the relationship of administrative agencies to the Congress and to the President. Four other large and important questions must be understood:

1) What are the procedural requirements for agency action?

2) When is judicial review of agency behavior available?

3) If available, what is the scope of judicial review of agency conduct?

4) How can agency policies be carried out and enforced?

The material which follows presents some of the main administrative law themes and administrative practices within an environmental law context. Observe the administrative law principle and appreciate its significance in a range of factual scenarios.

1.   THE NONDELEGATION DOCTRINE

How do agencies obtain the authority to make environmental decisions? Although Article I of the United States Constitution provides that "all legislative powers shall be vested in a Congress of the United States," Congress (as well as state legislatures) routinely delegates wide powers to administrative agencies, including the Environmental Protections Agency. This is constitutionally permissible as long as the legislation prescribes basic policy and contains criteria that are sufficiently clear to enable Congress, the courts, and the public to ascertain whether the agency has conformed with those standards. Mills v. United States, 36 F.3d 1052 (11th Cir.1994). This is known as the nondelegation doctrine and it bars the excessive delegation of discretionary authority from Congress to administrative agencies. This doctrine is believed to implement separation of powers values preventing Congress from shifting untethered, legislative power to executive agencies. During the nineteenth and the early-twentieth century, the nondelegation principle has been used to test various legislative grants including those to the President, to the federal courts and to cabinet agencies. They have all been upheld as permissible delegations of power which merely allowed executive branch actions to "fill up the details" once Congress had set the legislative policy.

During the twentieth century the Supreme Court has employed the nondelegation doctrine in a changing way with leniency when broad transfers of discretionary power were to be upheld, and later, with stringency when Congress had transferred too much legislative power to either government agencies or private organizations. Beginning in 1928, the Court set forth a loose standard in J. W. Hampton, Jr. & Co. v. United States, 276 U.S. 394 (1928), announcing what is known as the "intelligible principle" test for nondelegation. In the *J.W. Hampton* case, a legislative delegation is said to be acceptable when Congress establishes "by legislative act an intelligible principle to which the person or body authorized [to act] is directed to conform." After this decision, a number of Depression Era New Deal congressional statutes giving the President broad economic authority were stricken for failure to provide sufficient standards to constrain executive power. See Panama Refining Co. v. Ryan, 293 U.S. 388 (1935); Schechter Poultry Corp. v. United States, 295 U.S. 495 (1935) and Carter v. Carter Coal, 298 U.S. 238 (1936).

Following this period of active judicial review restricting Congressional efforts to grant broad power to the President and to federal agencies, the Supreme Court reversed itself again and embarked upon a lengthy period of non-intervention. With the holding in Yakus v. United States, 321 U.S. 414 (1944), upholding World War II era rent and price controls, the Court recognized the need for agency discretion as long as some limit existed. In this post-World War II period, the courts generally found "intelligible principles" in legislation and upheld a series of statutes against nondelegation challenges. Recent examples include: Mistretta v. United States, 488 U.S. 361 (1989) (upholding the Sentencing Reform Act delegation to U.S. Sentencing Commission to develop mandatory sentencing guidelines) and Touby v. United States, 500 U.S. 160 (1991) (Attorney General's power to place drugs on the list of controlled substances and thereby creating federal criminal liability). In the 1970s–1980s, law has de-emphasized the nondelegation doctrine by finding sufficient legislative guidance in general legislative purposes or agency directives.

Beginning with Justice Rehnquist's concurring opinion in Industrial Union Dept., AFL–CIO v. American Petroleum Institute, 448 U.S. 607 (1980) (known as the "Benzene Cases"), though, the nondelegation principle has received renewed interest. Justice Rehnquist acknowledged that Congress need not do more than lay down the general policy and standards, leaving the agency to fill in the blanks. But he opined that section 6(b)(5) of the Occupational Safety and Health Act, which directed the Secretary of Labor to set health and safety standards which would "most adequately assure[], to the extent feasible, on the basis of the best available evidence, that no employee will suffer material impairment of health or functional capacity," did not provide sufficient standards to survive constitutional scrutiny.

That concurrence emboldened a new round of nondelegation claims. Recently, however, in Whitman v. American Trucking Associations, Inc., 531 U.S. 457 (2001) the Court reaffirmed its broad interpretation of the nondelegation clause. A panel of the D.C. Circuit had ruled that section 109 of the Clean Air Act, which directs EPA to determine national ambient air quality standards (NAAQS), delegated too much legislative power to EPA. The appellate court reasoned that the statute failed to provide an "intelligible principle" to guide the agency's exercise of its authority. Writing for a unanimous Supreme Court, Justice Scalia rejected this interpretation. Reiterating a "repeated" adherence to the "intelligible principle" standard of the *J.W. Hampton* case, he found section 109 (b)(1) of the Clean Air Act to be "in fact well within the outer limits of our nondelegation precedents." Id. at 474. He reviewed a long list of twentieth century Supreme Court opinions considering the nondelegation principle and concluded that the Court had never required that legislation provide agencies with a "determinative criterion" for setting specific standards. The Court easily upheld the Clean Air Act's rather vague delegation as being within the permissible range, stating that:

> requiring EPA to set such standards at a level that is "requisite"—that is, not lower or higher than is necessary—to protect the public health with an adequate margin of safety, fits comfortably within the scope of discretion permitted by our precedent.

Id. at 475. With this sweeping language, Justice Scalia reaffirmed the "intelligible principle" concept and broad agency discretion in implementing protective environmental and public health policy. In his concurrence, Justice Stevens addressed an issue of judicial realism by stating that the Court would have been "wiser and more faithful to [prior nondelegation case holdings]" to frankly acknowledge that the power delegated to EPA was "legislative" but adequately limited by the terms of the CAA. He wrote,

> It seems clear that an executive agency's exercise of rulemaking authority pursuant to a valid delegation from Congress is "legislative." As long as the delegation provides a sufficiently intelligible principle, there is nothing inherently unconstitutional about it.

Id. at 472. Whether based upon constitutional theory or not, the judicial focus will continue to be on finding an "intelligible principle" in Congress' guidance. After the decision in *American Trucking* are any federal environmental statutes in jeopardy?

2. CONGRESSIONAL SUPERVISION OF ADMINISTRATIVE AGENCIES

Congress has a great variety of ways to supervise and influence agency conduct. Initially, Congress controls the way agencies are structured, their statutory mandates, and how they are governed. Congress, acting as individual members or as committees, possesses both indirect and direct means of affecting agency behavior. Congressional members may have informal contacts with agencies in hopes of influencing an agency's specific decision (i.e. funding a local project) or developing a set of regulations of importance to an industry or local government (i.e. coal mining reclamation rules). Members of Congress may also use informal channels to support or to block certain executive appointments to agencies.

On the direct side, Congress has many powers over agencies including control over statutory design of an agency's mandate and appropriations for agency activities. Major federal agency rules may also be reviewed and overruled by Congress within sixty days of issuance under the Contract with America Advancement Act of 1996. Under 5 U.S.C. § 801, enacted as part of the Small Business Regulatory Enforcement Fairness Act of 1996, Pub. L. No. 104–121, § 251 (1996), agencies must submit major rules and the cost-benefit analyses prepared for those rules to Congress before the rules may take effect. The rule must be withdrawn if Congress passes a joint resolution disapproving it and the President signs the resolution (overcoming constitutional limitations derived from INS v. Chadha, 462 U.S. 919 (1983)).

Congress also can pass statutes designed to shape the way agencies make decisions. In order to mandate that agencies consider the environmental impact of their actions, Congress passed the National Environmental Policy Act of 1969, 42 U.S.C. § 4321 *et seq.* Similarly, Congress passed the National Historic Preservation Act, 16 U.S.C. § 470, to require federal agencies to take into account the effect of their decisions on historic sites. The Endangered Species Act, 16 U.S.C. §§ 1531–1539, prohibits federal agencies from taking action that would jeopardize the continued existence of any endangered or threatened species of wildlife.

Congress also has passed statutes out of concern for the economic impact of agency regulations. The Regulatory Flexibility Act of 1980, 5 U.S.C. § 601, requires that agencies determine the effects of their actions on small businesses. The Paperwork Reduction Act of 1980, 44 U.S.C. § 3501 *et seq.* is an attempt to reduce the burdens of government-mandated record keeping.

3. EXECUTIVE SUPERVISION OF AGENCY DECISIONS

Article II of the U.S. Constitution vests executive power in the President, but the term "executive power" is undefined. As the chief administrator of the executive branch of government, the President can influence policy through his appointment and removal of agency officials. The appointment of these officials must be done in conformity with the procedures set out in the Appointments Clause, Art. II, sec. 2, of the U. S. Constitution. All Presidents, however, seek direct influence over agency policy as well. The chief method of doing this is by using the Office of Management and Budget (OMB) to review and coordinate the exercise of agency powers.

In 1981, President Ronald Reagan initiated a new era of executive control over the federal bureaucracy by issuing Executive Order 12,291, which required that agencies justify their "major" rules (those with an impact of $100 million or more) with a Regulatory Impact Analysis (RIA). Executive Order 12,291, 3 C.F.R Pt. § 128 (1981) (reprinted at 5 USCA § 601 at 432). The RIA, which describes the potential costs and benefits of the proposed rule, must be forwarded to the OMB, an arm of the Executive Office of the President. Executive Order 12,291 further provided that regulatory actions should not be undertaken unless the potential benefits outweighed the potential costs to society. In 1993, President Bill Clinton issued Executive Order 12,866 to replace the Reagan Era Executive Order 12,291. Like its predecessor, Executive Order 12,866 allows OMB to review "significant regulatory actions." If OMB returns a rule, it must put its reasons in writing in a public document. Conflicting views are worked out between the agency head and the OMB as well as by the President or Vice President. The Clinton order lessened the amount of executive control exerted over agencies. It reduced by about 50% the number of EPA rules that were previously routinely reviewed by OMB.

How extensive is OMB's substantive power? In Associated Builders and Contractors Inc. v. Brock, 862 F.2d 63, 69 (3d Cir.1988), the court ruled that "OMB cannot in the guise of reducing paperwork substitute its judgment for that of any agency having substantive rulemaking responsibility." This decision was affirmed by the U.S. Supreme Court in Dole v. United Steelworkers of America, 494 U.S. 26 (1990). Federal law has increasingly required federal agencies to analyze the impact of their regulatory and programmatic action. Beyond costs analysis, federal law requires 1) environmental impact analysis; 2) constitutional "takings" analysis; 3) federalism impact analysis; and 4) unfunded mandate analysis.

C.   AGENCY POLICYMAKING ALTERNATIVES

Administrative agencies such as the Environmental Protection Agency make policy in two principal ways: 1) by rulemaking, issuing general, forward-looking rules which announce policy applicable to a range of individual circumstances and 2) by adjudication, making individual decisions applying policy to particular situations. Congress often specifies which method the agency must follow in enabling statutes; in the absence of such specific authority, the Administrative Procedure Act (APA). Sometimes the choice of which way to proceed is dictated by constitutional due process values which may require adjudicatory procedures. See Londoner v. City of Denver, 210 U.S. 373 (1908).

1.   AGENCY RULEMAKING

An important way in which agencies act is by making rules. Under the Administrative Procedure Act ("APA"), a rule is "the whole or a part of an agency statement of general or particular applicability and future effect designed to implement, interpret, or prescribe law or policy" or to establish rules of practice. 5 U.S.C. § 551(4). There are a number of advantages for agencies setting their policies by rules or regulations. The agency can announce a coherent and comprehensive policy response to an area under its authority. Through the notice and comment methodology, to be discussed below, it can receive a wide and diverse range of public opinion concerning the subject matter of the regulation. Developing the regulation in this way allows the agency to establish a complex rule in a unified fashion not relying upon incremental or case-by-case policymaking through adjudication. Once the rule is established, regulated parties know of their legal responsibilities and the potential sanctions for non-compliance.

There are several different kinds of rulemaking:

a. *Informal or Notice and Comment Rulemaking*

Excerpts from the Administrative Procedure Act

5 U.S.C. § 553.

Sec. 533. **Rulemaking**

(b) General notice of proposed rulemaking shall be published in the Federal Register, unless persons subject thereto are named and either personally served or otherwise have actual notice thereof in accordance with law. The notice shall include—

> (1) a statement of the time, place, and nature of public rulemaking proceedings;

> (2) reference to the legal authority under which the rule is proposed; and

> (3) either the terms or substance of the proposed rule or a description of the subjects and issues involved.

* * *

(c) After notice required by this section, the agency shall give interested persons an opportunity to participate in the rulemaking through submission of written data, views, or arguments with or without opportunity for oral presentation. After consideration of the relevant matter presented, the agency shall incorporate in the rules adopted a concise general statement of their basis and purpose.

* * *

(d) The required publication or service of a substantive rule shall be made not less than 30 days before its effective date, except

> (1) a substantive rule which grants or recognizes an exemption or relieves a restriction;

> (2) interpretive rules and statements of policy; or

> (3) as otherwise provided by the agency for good cause found and published with the rule.

(e) Each agency shall give an interested person the right to petition for the issuance, amendment, or repeal of a rule.

Most agency rules, including many of those adopted pursuant to federal environmental statutes, are promulgated informally. APA § 553 prescribes the procedure for informal rulemaking as "notice and comment." This should be compared to "formal" rulemaking carried out under the adjudicatory process of APA §§ 556–57. Under the informal method, the agency must publish a general notice of the proposed rule in the Federal Register. This is followed by a reasonable time period during which the agency receives and considers written comments from all interested parties. After giving consideration to the comments presented, the agency must publish the final rule adopted along with a "concise general statement of its basis and purpose" in the Federal Register.

The question of what constitutes adequate notice presents an interesting legal problem since the APA does not demand a very detailed form of notice. The key seems to be sufficient information to provide interested parties an opportunity to comment effectively and in a timely manner. What if the final regulation issued deviates, in a significant way, from the original notice? Courts have adopted a "logical outgrowth" test to determine the adequacy of the APA notice. See Fertilizer Institute v. EPA, 935 F.2d 1303 (D.C.Cir.1991). Challenges to EPA rulemaking have been unsuccessful when the agency had given commenters information about various rule alternatives that might be adopted in the final regulation. See Arizona Public Service Co. v. EPA, 211 F.3d 1280 (D.C.Cir.2000).

Agencies also generally must disclose the studies, tests or other methods they rely upon in developing their final regulation. For instance, Portland Cement Ass'n v. Ruckelshaus, 486 F.2d 375 (D.C.Cir.1973), reversed a Clean Air Act emission standard promulgated by EPA because the agency had not released adequate source testing data during the rulemaking period. This position reflects a judicial gloss on APA § 553 (c), that the ability to participate in rulemaking must be meaningful.

Final rules must be published in the Federal Register with a concise general statement of their basis and purpose. 5 U.S.C. § 553(c). The idea behind this requirement is that regulations should be supported by an explanation of how they were selected from alternatives. In Automotive Parts and Accessories v. Boyd, 407 F.2d 330, 335 (D.C.Cir.1968), the court emphasized the need to "see what major issues of policy were ventilated by the informal proceedings and why the agency reacted to them as it did."

As this discussion shows, the APA prescribes only minimal procedural requirements for informal rulemaking. One question that has arisen is whether courts can order agency procedures in addition to those required by the APA such as additional comment opportunities, cross examination rights and the chance to challenge with experts evidence in the record. In the celebrated *Vermont Yankee* decision, the U.S. Supreme Court ruled that while such "hybrid" procedures could be voluntarily adopted by an agency, they could not be judicially required in addition to those set out in the APA or in agency statutes. 405 U.S. at 519.

b. *Formal Rulemaking*

Informal rulemaking is the norm in modern administrative practice. However, in a limited range of circumstances, an agency's authorizing statute will require that rules be made "on the record" following a hearing. That language invokes APA § 553(c) which provides that "[w]hen rules are required by statute to be made on the record after opportunity for an agency hearing," the agency must follow sections 556 and 557 of the APA. Formal rulemaking is similar to adjudication and the agency must conduct a trial-type hearing and provide interested persons an opportunity to testify and cross examine adverse witnesses in advance of issuing the rule. These elements convert rulemaking into an adjudicatory process. Formal rulemaking is relatively rare in environmental law.

c.   *Exempt Rulemaking*

Section 553 of the APA exempts certain types of rules from even the minimal notice and comment requirements of informal rulemaking. Exemptions exist for (a) interpretive rules, (b) general policy statements, (c) procedural rules, and (d) when the agency finds for "good cause" that notice and public procedures are "impractical unnecessary or contrary to the public interest". These are usually described as "non-legislative rules."

There are also exemptions in APA § 553(a) for a military or foreign function of the United States and agency management of personnel or public property, loans, grants, benefits, or contracts.

d.   *Negotiated Rulemaking*

An agency also may use a negotiation process to develop a rule. In 1990, Congress enacted the Negotiated Rulemaking Act permitting federal agencies to conduct negotiations among interested parties to develop regulatory proposals. See 5 U.S.C. §§ 561–570. This practice is commonly referred to as "regulatory negotiation," or "Reg. Neg." Regulatory negotiation is a recognition of the fact that because a rule is often a compromise among interest groups, it may be desirable to enter into a structured bargaining process to develop certain rules. The negotiation involves the rulemaking agency conducting a thorough examination and revision of a proposed rule with interest groups that will be affected directly by the rule. In this way both sides can benefit from this process, as *interests* have greater control over the content of agency rules and *agencies* obtain a more accurate picture of the costs and benefits of policy alternatives. If and when the negotiation process results in an agreement, the agency issues the agreed-upon language as a proposed rule, and then follows the usual procedure for notice and comment rulemaking.

In today's lawsuit-happy atmosphere, regulatory negotiation is an extremely attractive option for agencies and interest groups. This process allows for greater participation of the interests involved and keeps the overall costs at a minimum. Agencies hope that groups given the opportunity to participate in the rulemaking will be less inclined to challenge the final rule. Regulatory negotiation is, however, an exceptionally political process, not to be undertaken unless a party is prepared to do battle over issues of science and policy under the glaring heat of the media spotlight. Regulatory negotiation is discussed in more detail in Section 4, at the end of this chapter.

D.   FORMAL AGENCY ADJUDICATION

In addition to making rules, agencies adjudicate individual cases and decide whether a person's conduct complies with the laws and rules they administer. Agencies also impose sanctions when a person has committed a violation. Adjudication, therefore, is very diverse and occurs in numerous situations. Adjudication differs from rulemaking in two significant ways. First, adjudication resolves disputes among specific individuals in specific cases, whereas rulemaking affects the rights of broad classes of unspecified individuals. Second, because adjudication involves concrete disputes, its an immediate impact on specific entities.

The APA sets standards for "formal" adjudication, which applies when adjudication is "required by statute to be determined on the record after opportunity for an agency hearing." APA § 554(a). The requirement of a formal agency adjudication triggers minimum procedural standards set out in the APA, sections 554, 556, and 557, which deal comprehensively with such matters as notice, right to a hearing, and the standards for presenting evidence and making a decision. The jurisprudence on these matters is extensive, but, in general, the form of formal adjudication resembles a court trial in which there is testimony, the introduction of documents, and cross-examination of witnesses. There are special standards for the evaluation of evidence. The process of decisionmaking in an agency is often hierarchical: the hearing may be conducted by an officer known as an administrative law judge, who prepares an initial decision. The final decision may be made by an agency head or board. A formal adjudication concludes with a written decision that "shall include * * * findings and conclusions, and the reason or basis therefor, on all the material issues of fact, law, or discretion presented on the record." APA § 557(c).

E.   INFORMAL AGENCY ADJUDICATION

Many agency decisions are made by what are termed "informal" means. These may be quite important decisions: processing claims, issuing licenses or permits, awarding contracts or grants, releasing entitlement funds to states or individuals, or deciding on the method of implementing a government program. Probably most agency decisions affecting the environment fall into this category.

Such decisions do not constitute rulemaking since they apply only to a particular individual or case. Under the APA, any action that is not a rule is, by definition, an order, which is a residual category under the statute. APA § 551; Yesler Terrace Community Council v. Cisneros, 37 F.3d 442 (9th Cir.1994). *Orders* are the result of an *adjudication*, but many such decisions are not required by statute to be made "on the record after opportunity for a hearing" as specified by APA § 554.

Thus, many agency actions are termed "informal agency adjudication." Although the APA does not explicitly cover this category of agency actions, the courts have imposed certain minimum standards of due process to enable them to exercise their function of judicial review: an administrative record and a contemporaneous explanation of the decision. See Citizens to Preserve Overton Park v. Volpe, 401 U.S. 402 (1971).

SECTION 2. JUDICIAL REVIEW OF AGENCY ACTION

Not only the legislative and executive branches of government exercise control over agencies decisionmaking. The courts also play an important role. However, important legal and policy questions are implicated by the question of whether judicial review of agency decisions is available. The concepts of 1) jurisdiction; 2) reviewability; 3) standing; and 4) ripeness, exhaustion, and mootness are crucial to the availability of judicial review.

A. JURISDICTION

A litigant wishing to challenge an agency's action (or non-action) in court must locate a court which has jurisdiction over the disputed claim. Jurisdiction is a matter involving the power of a court to hear a petition for review and with regard to federal agency behavior, jurisdiction is usually found in the federal courts. The jurisdictional source may be found in one of two ways; 1) agency-specific enabling acts (i.e. Clean Air Act, RCRA, or CERCLA) which provide for judicial review actions taken under the statute and create federal court jurisdiction over requests for review and 2) federal question or "arising under" jurisdiction providing a party with sufficient legal standing with the ability to obtain judicial review of a civil claim in the U.S. district courts pursuant to 28 U.S.C. § 1331. Most environmental statutes explicitly provide federal court jurisdiction and allocate review responsibility between the district courts and the courts of appeal.

B. REVIEWABILITY

Excerpts from the Administrative Procedure Act
5 U.S.C. §§ 701–704.

Sec. 701. **Application: Definitions**

(a) This chapter applies according to the provisions thereof except to the extent that—

(1) statutes preclude judicial review; or

(2) agency action is committed to agency discretion by law.

* * *

Sec. 702. **Right of Review**

A person suffering legal wrong because of agency action, or adversely affected or aggrieved by agency action within the meaning of a relevant statute, is entitled to judicial review thereof.

Sec. 703. **Form and Venue of Proceedings**

"The form of proceeding for judicial review is the special statutory review proceeding relevant to the subject matter in a court specified by statute or in the absence or inadequacy thereof any applicable form of legal action, including actions for declaratory judgements or writs of prohibitory or mandatory injunction or habeas corpus in a court of competent jurisdiction.

Sec. 704. **Actions Reviewable**

"Agency action made reviewable by statute and final agency action for which there is no other adequate remedy in a court are subject to judicial review.

The Administrative Procedure Act provides for judicial review of "[a]gency action made reviewable by statute and final agency action for which there is no other adequate remedy in a court." APA § 704. This section has been read to create a presumption in favor of judicial review and, as a result, courts with appropriate jurisdiction, hear many administrative agency challenges.

The APA does identify two instances when APA judicial review is not authorized: 1) when statutes preclude judicial review, and 2) when agency action is committed to agency discretion by law. See APA § 701 (a) (1) & (2). In the first example, there is no right to court review when a statute has expressly or implicitly precluded review. In the second situation, the APA denies judicial review of agency action when that action has been "committed to agency discretion by law." The meaning of this exception to the general policy allowing review has not always been clear but the traditional understanding has been that judicial review is not allowed when "statutes are drawn in such broad terms that in a given case there is no law to apply." Look for this issue in the *Citizens to Preserve Overton Park, Inc. v. Volpe* case which follows. Finding that a statute commits an agency action to "agency discretion" requires a statutory analysis resulting in the conclusion that Congress implicitly intended to preclude judicial review.

C. STANDING

Only a party with standing to sue may challenge agency action in federal court. State courts have developed their own standing concepts which may be more lenient or more restrictive than the federal standing rules. Some commentators have written that the emerging law of standing is more a reflection of the political viewpoints of individual judges than a matter of constitutional theory. See Richard J. Pierce, Is Standing Law or Politics? 77 N.C.L. Rev. 1741 (1999). While the law of standing is complicated and constantly subject to revision and reinterpretation, it can be said that the basic rule structure for the law of standing originates from two sources: 1) the "case or controversy" requirement of Article III, and 2) additional judicial concerns often deemed "prudential."

Since Article III, § 2 limits federal judicial power to "cases or controversies," standing law has been viewed as having a constitutional basis. The essential structure of standing gives only certain litigants access to the federal courts for the resolution of their grievances. In general, in order to establish standing a plaintiff must demonstrate that: 1) the plaintiff has suffered an "injury-in-fact," 2) the injury must be "fairly traceable" to the challenged action and, 3) the plaintiff's injury can be "redressed" by a judicial remedy. Each of these three constitutionally—mandated requirements deserves attention.

1. INJURY–IN–FACT

At the most fundamental minimum, the plaintiff must have suffered some form of injury to establish standing to sue. Early cases required that the plaintiff show that a legal right had been violated by the government agency's action. Modern law provides a much broader conception of harm or injury-in-fact which includes common law injuries and harm to environmental, recreational, and aesthetic, as well as economic interests. Congress may also create "rights" the deprivation of which can also serve as an injury-in-fact. See Havens Realty Corp. v. Coleman, 455 U.S. 363 (1982). However, the injury must be one which has "significantly affected" the particular plaintiff and as the *Sierra Club v. Morton* decision below indicates, a "mere interest in a problem" will not be sufficient to cause a specific injury on which standing can be grounded. An interesting question is presented by the citizen suit provisions of most federal environmental laws which create a legal right of action in "any person" to enforce the law regardless of whether that person is "aggrieved" or can demonstrate specific injury-in-fact. Can a statute eliminate or replace the constitutionally-based injury-in-fact requirement?

With standing law requiring an individualized injury-in-fact, how could an organization such as an environmental group satisfy the harm requirement? Such an organization might wish to sue to vindicate its own interest or those interests of its individual members. Organizations can demonstrate injury-in-fact in two distinct ways. First, an environmental group might sue to vindicate its own interests. See Ecological Rights Found. v. Pacific Lumber Co., 61 F.Supp.2d 1042 (N.D.Cal.1999) (group's ability to educate the public about environmental compliance issues harmed by defendants' failure to comply with (CWA monitoring and reporting rules)).

Second, groups can vindicate the interests of their members if they can show organizational standing to raise their members' interests. In Hunt v. Washington State Apple Adv. Comm'n, 432 U.S. 333 (1977), the Supreme Court set forth a three-part test establishing when an organization has standing to sue on behalf of its members. The Court ruled that an association has standing to bring suit on behalf of its members when: (a) its members would otherwise have standing to sue in their own right; (b) the interests it seeks to protect are germane to the organization's purpose; and (c) neither the claim asserted nor the relief requested requires the participation of individual members in the lawsuit.

In a suit where the group is representative of its members' interests, commonly, the focus is on the first factor—whether the group's members themselves would have standing to sue. Often, as in Friends of the Earth, Inc. v. Laidlaw Environmental Services, Inc., 528 U.S. 167 (2000), the environmental group was found to establish injury-in-fact based on affidavits of its individual members stating that unlawful discharges into the river had adversely affected their use and enjoyment of it. However, the second *Hunt* prong can also be important, as in Wyoming Timber Industry Ass'n v. U.S. Forest Service, 80 F.Supp.2d 1245 (D.Wyo.2000), where logging companies were found not have standing to contest a suspension of road construction in national forests because the alleged recreational or aesthetic injuries were not germane to the group's purposes.

2.   "FAIRLY TRACEABLE" OR THE CAUSATION REQUIREMENT

A plaintiff must also establish that the harm it suffers is "fairly traceable" to the challenged agency conduct. The Supreme Court has ruled inconsistently in a number of cases requiring a tight causal link in some cases while accepting a much looser connection in others. For a more relaxed view of the "fairly traceable" standing requirement see United States v. Students Challenging Regulatory Agency Procedures (SCRAP), 412 U.S. 669 (1973) and Northeastern Florida Chapter of Associated General Contractors v. Jacksonville, 508 U.S. 656 (1993). For a more restrictive view, see Warth v. Seldin, 422 U.S. 490 (1975).

3.   REDRESSABILITY

The final constitutional element of standing is redressability. The plaintiff must demonstrate a "substantial likelihood" that a favorable court ruling would actually redress the harm said to result from the challenged action. This element of standing law has erected a barrier to some plaintiffs by requiring that they demonstrate a "substantial likelihood" that a governmental agency is causing them harm and that a favorable court ruling would actually redress that harm. In Simon v. Eastern Kentucky Welfare Rights Organization, 426 U.S. 26 (1976), an organization representing indigents sought to challenge an IRS ruling reducing the amount of indigent care hospitals were required to provide in order to qualify for charitable, tax exempt status. The organization sought to establish standing by submitting affidavits of indigents who asserted they had been denied hospital care. The Court held that the plaintiffs lacked standing because a court ruling overturning the IRS interpretation would not necessarily lead to greater indigent care. Hospitals might simply choose to forego the tax exemption rather than increasing services to indigents. Redressability therefore would depend on the choices of third parties not before the Court; those choices would not be legally constrained, although they might as a practical matter be affected, by any judicial remedy. See also Allen v. Wright, 468 U.S. 737 (1984) (tax exempt status for racially discriminatory private school). It is worth noting that more recent Supreme Court decision have concluded that an injury is not redressable when a court cannot issue an enforceable order against the parties involved in illegal activity. Similar issues are raised in Lujan v. Defenders of Wildlife, 504 U.S. 555 (1992), discussed below.

Steel Company v. Citizens for a Better Environment, 523 U.S. 83 (1998), also rested on the redressability concept. In that case, the Court held that the plaintiffs lacked standing because neither prospective injunctive relief nor civil penalties payable to the U.S. Treasury, the only remedies available under the statute, would redress the injury caused by the defendant's past statutory violations. *Steel Company* was limited to wholly past violations while Friends of the Earth v. Laidlaw, 528 U.S. 167 (2000), which held that the deterrent effect of civil penalties could provide standing if the alleged violation was ongoing or could recur.

4. NON–CONSTITUTIONAL OR PRUDENTIAL STANDING CONSIDERATIONS

In addition to the elements of standing law required to satisfy Article III constitutional considerations, the Court has imposed other requirements to advance values important to the federal judiciary. These come generally under the heading of prudential considerations affecting the law of standing. Because they are not dictated by the constitution, they can be changed by legislation.

One important prudential concern for plaintiffs seeking to raise claims under environmental statutes is the zone of interests test. Section 702 of the Administrative Procedure Act provides for judicial review at the behest of "[a] person suffering legal wrong because of agency action or adversely affected or aggrieved by agency action within the meaning of a relevant statute. . . ." In Association of Data Processing Service Organizations, Inc. v. Camp, 397 U.S. 150 (1970), the Court interpreted that provision to require that the plaintiff's asserted injury fall arguably within the zone of interests to be protected by the statute under which the claim was asserted. This became known as the "zone of interest" test and it has become a method for limiting challenges to federal agency action based upon the scope of legislative intent. In 1991, the Court used the doctrine to deny standing to postal workers suing to challenge the U.S. Postal Service's decision to relinquish its monopoly over international remailing services. It concluded that the workers' employment concerns were not in the congressional "zone of interest" in the postal legislation which focused upon the efficiency of the mails. See Air Courier Conference of America v. American Postal Workers Union, 498 U.S. 517 (1991). Environmental cases sometimes turn on this issue. Compare Grand Council of the Crees v. FERC, 198 F.3d 950 (D.C.Cir.2000) (native groups challenge to a FERC decision allowing a Quebec utility to sell electricity in the U.S. at higher rates not within the zone of interest of the Federal Power Act) and Central South Dakota Cooperative Grazing Dist. v. Secretary, 266 F.3d 889 (8th Cir.2001) (grazing district whose only interest in grazing lands was economic not within zone of interest of NEPA) with New Mexico Cattle Growers Ass'n v. U.S. Fish and Wildlife Service, 81 F.Supp.2d 1141 (D.N.M.1999), reversed on other grounds, 248 F.3d 1277 (10th Cir.2001) (organization of cattle and sheep ranchers and farmers fell within zone of interests of NEPA because it sought to protect members' consumptive interests in the land and water at issue, to prevent environmental damage on other lands, and to preserve aesthetic aspects, and the health and safety of the environment in which they lived).

There are two other potential standing barriers to environmental plaintiffs. First, litigants may not use the federal courts as a forum to air their "generalized grievances" about the conduct of government. Denial of standing in these situations, under this theory, is supposed to lead to a more appropriate resolution by the "politically-responsive" branches of government. Taxpayers suits are frequently blocked by the "generalized grievance" doctrine under rules set out in the case of Flast v. Cohen, 392 U.S. 83 (1968) and Frothingham v. Mellon, 262 U.S. 447 (1923). Second, a party must represent her own rights and not those of a third person. This prudential rule is, of course, subject to the principles allowing organizational standing and also to certain exceptions when the plaintiff is in close relationship with the harmed person or if that person suffers from some impediment limiting or discouraging their own action to protect their rights.

5.   LITIGATED QUESTIONS

Sierra Club v. Morton

United States Supreme Court, 1972.
405 U.S. 727, 92 S.Ct. 1361, 31 L.Ed.2d 636.

■ MR. JUSTICE STEWART delivered the opinion of the Court.

The Mineral King Valley is an area of great natural beauty nestled in the Sierra Nevada Mountains in Tulare County, California, adjacent to Sequoia National Park. It has been part of the Sequoia National Forest since 1926, and is designated as a national game refuge by special Act of Congress. Though once the site of extensive mining activity, Mineral King is now used almost exclusively for recreational purposes. Its relative inaccessibility and lack of development have limited the number of visitors each year, and at the same time have preserved the valley's quality as a quasi-wilderness area largely uncluttered by the products of civilization.

The United States Forest Service, which is entrusted with the maintenance and administration of national forests, began in the late 1940's to give consideration to Mineral King as a potential site for recreational development. Prodded by a rapidly increasing demand for skiing facilities, the Forest Service published a prospectus in 1965, inviting bids from private developers for the construction and operation of a ski resort that would also serve as a summer recreation area. The proposal of Walt Disney Enterprises, Inc., was chosen from those of six bidders, and Disney received a three-year permit to conduct surveys and explorations in the valley in connection with its preparation of a complete master plan for the resort.

The final Disney plan, approved by the Forest Service in January 1969, outlines a $35 million complex of motels, restaurants, swimming pools, parking lots, and other structures designed to accommodate 14,000 visitors daily. This complex is to be constructed on 80 acres of the valley floor under a 30–year use permit from the Forest Service. Other facilities, including ski lifts, ski trails, a cog-assisted railway, and utility installations, are to be constructed on the mountain slopes and in other parts of the valley under a revocable special-use permit. To provide access to the resort, the State of California proposes to construct a highway 20 miles in length. A section of this road would traverse Sequoia National Park, as would a proposed high-voltage power line needed to provide electricity for the resort. Both the highway and the power line require the approval of the Department of the Interior, which is entrusted with the preservation and maintenance of the national parks.

Representatives of the Sierra Club, who favor maintaining Mineral King largely in its present state, followed the progress of recreational planning for the valley with close attention and increasing dismay. They unsuccessfully sought a public hearing on the proposed development in 1965, and in subsequent correspondence with officials of the Forest Service and the Department of the Interior, they expressed the Club's objections to Disney's plan as a whole and to particular features included in it. In June 1969 the Club filed the present suit in the United States District Court for the Northern District of California, seeking a declaratory judgment that various aspects of the proposed development contravene federal laws and regulations governing the preservation of national parks, forests, and game refuges, and also seeking preliminary and permanent injunctions restraining the federal officials involved from granting their approval or issuing permits in connection with the Mineral King project. The petitioner Sierra Club sued as a membership corporation with "a special interest in the conservation and the sound maintenance of the national parks, game refuges and forests of the country," and invoked the judicial-review provisions of the Administrative Procedure Act, 6 U.S.C. § 701 et seq.

After two days of hearings, the District Court granted the requested preliminary injunction. It rejected the respondents' challenge to the Sierra Club's standing to sue, and determined that the hearing had raised questions "concerning possible excess of statutory authority, sufficiently substantial and serious to justify a preliminary injunction...." The respondents appealed, and the Court of Appeals for the Ninth Circuit reversed, 433 F.2d 24. With respect to the petitioner's standing, the court noted that there was "no allegation in the complaint that members of the Sierra Club would be affected by the actions of [the respondents] other than the fact that the actions are personally displeasing or distasteful to them," id. at 33, and concluded:

"We do not believe such club concern without a showing of more direct interest can constitute standing in the legal sense sufficient to challenge the exercise of responsibilities on behalf of all the citizens by two cabinet level officials of the government acting under Congressional and Constitutional authority." Id. at 30.

Alternatively, the Court of Appeals held that the Sierra Club had not made an adequate showing of irreparable injury and likelihood of success on the merits to justify issuance of a preliminary injunction. The court thus vacated the injunction. The Sierra Club filed a petition for a writ of certiorari which we granted to review the questions of federal law presented.

II

The first question presented is whether the Sierra Club has alleged facts that entitle it to obtain judicial review of the challenged action. Whether a party has a sufficient stake in an otherwise justiciable controversy to obtain judicial resolution of that controversy is what has traditionally been referred to as the question of standing to sue. Where the party does not rely on any specific statute authorizing invocation of the judicial process, the question of standing depends upon whether the party has alleged such a "personal stake in the outcome of the controversy," Baker v. Carr, 369 U.S. 186, 204, as to ensure that "the dispute sought to be adjudicated will be presented in an adversary context and in a form historically viewed as capable of judicial resolution." Flast v. Cohen, 392 U.S. 83, 101,[3] Where, however, Congress has authorized public officials to perform certain functions according to law, and has provided by statute for judicial review of those actions under certain circumstances, the inquiry as to standing must begin with a determination of whether the statute in question authorizes review at the behest of the plaintiff.

The Sierra Club relies upon § 10 of the Administrative Procedure Act (APA), 5 U.S.C. § 702, which provides:

> "A person suffering legal wrong because of agency action, or adversely affected or aggrieved by agency action within the meaning of a relevant statute, is entitled to judicial review thereof."

Early decisions under this statute interpreted the language as adopting the various formulations of "legal interest" and "legal wrong" then prevailing as constitutional requirements of standing. But, in Association of Data Processing Service Organizations, Inc. v. Camp, 397 U.S. 150, and Barlow v. Collins, 397 U.S. 159, decided the same day, we held more broadly that persons had standing to obtain judicial review of federal agency action under § 10 of the APA where they had alleged that the challenged action had caused them "injury-in-fact," and where the alleged injury was to an

---

3. Congress may not confer jurisdiction on Art. III federal courts to render advisory opinions, *Muskrat v. United States*, 219 U.S. 346, 31 S.Ct. 250, 55 L.Ed. 246, or to entertain "friendly" suits, *United States v. Johnson*, 319 U.S. 302, 63 S.Ct. 1075, 87 L.Ed. 1413, or to resolve "political questions," *Luther v. Borden*, 7 How. 1, 12 L.Ed. 581, because suits of this character are inconsistent with the judicial function under Art. III. But where a dispute is otherwise justiciable, the question whether the litigant is a "proper party to request an adjudication of a particular issue," *Flast v. Cohen*, 392 U.S. 83, 100, 88 S.Ct. 1942, 1952, 20 L.Ed.2d 947, is one within the power of Congress to determine.

interest "arguably within the zone of interests to be protected or regulated" by the statutes that the agencies were claimed to have violated.[5]

In *Data Processing,* the injury claimed by the petitioners consisted of harm to their competitive position in the computer-servicing market through a ruling by the Comptroller of the Currency that national banks might perform data-processing services for their customers. In *Barlow,* the petitioners were tenant farmers who claimed that certain regulations of the Secretary of Agriculture adversely affected their economic position vis-a-vis their landlords. These palpable economic injuries have long been recognized as sufficient to lay the basis for standing, with or without a specific statutory provision for judicial review. Thus, neither *Data Processing nor Barlow* addressed itself to the question, which has arisen with increasing frequency in federal courts in recent years, as to what must be alleged by persons who claim injury of a noneconomic nature to interests that are widely shared. That question is presented in this case.

III

The injury alleged by the Sierra Club will be incurred entirely by reason of the change in the uses to which Mineral King will be put, and the attendant change in the aesthetics and ecology of the area. Thus, in referring to the road to be built through Sequoia National Park, the complaint alleged that the development "would destroy or otherwise adversely affect the scenery, natural and historic objects and wildlife of the park and would impair the enjoyment of the park for future generations." We do not question that this type of harm may amount to an "injury in fact" sufficient to lay the basis for standing under § 10 of the APA. Aesthetic and environmental well-being, like economic well-being, are important ingredients of the quality of life in our society, and the fact that particular environmental interests are shared by the many rather than the few does not make them less deserving of legal protection through the judicial process. But the "injury in fact" test requires more than an injury to a cognizable interest. It requires that the party seeking review be himself among the injured.

The impact of the proposed changes in the environment of Mineral King will not fall indiscriminately upon every citizen. The alleged injury will be felt directly only by those who use Mineral King and Sequoia National Park, and for whom the aesthetic and recreational values of the area will be lessened by the highway and ski resort. The Sierra Club failed to allege that it or its members would be affected in any of their activities or pastimes, by the Disney development. Nowhere in the pleadings or affidavits did the Club state that its members use Mineral King for any purpose, much less that they use it in any way that would be significantly affected by the proposed actions of the respondents.[8]

---

5. In deciding this case we do not reach any questions concerning the meaning of the "zone of interests" test or its possible application to the facts here presented.

8. The only reference in the pleadings

The Club apparently regarded any allegations of individualized injury as superfluous, on the theory that this was a "public" action involving questions as to the use of natural resources, and that the Club's longstanding concern with and expertise in such matters were sufficient to give it standing as a "representative of the public." This theory reflects a misunderstanding of our cases involving so-called "public actions" in the area of administrative law.

The origin of the theory advanced by the Sierra Club may be traced to a dictum in Scripps–Howard Radio v. FCC, 316 U.S. 4, in which the licensee of a radio station in Cincinnati, Ohio, sought a stay of an order of the FCC allowing another radio station in a nearby city to change its frequency and increase its range. In, discussing its power to grant a stay, the Court noted that "these private litigants have standing only as representatives of the public interest." id., at 14. But that observation did not describe the basis upon which the appellant was allowed to obtain judicial review as a "person aggrieved" within the meaning of the statute involved in that case, since *Scripps-Howard* was clearly "aggrieved" by reason of the economic injury that it would suffer as a result of the Commission's action. The Court's statement was, rather, directed to the theory upon which Congress had authorized judicial review of the Commission's actions. That theory had been described earlier in FCC v. Sanders Bros. Radio Station, 309 U.S. 470, 477, as follows:

> Congress had some purpose in enacting section 402(b)(2). It may have been of opinion that one likely to be financially injured by the issue of a license would be the only person having a sufficient interest to bring to the attention of the appellate court errors of law in the action of the Commission in granting the license. It is within the power of Congress to confer such standing to prosecute an appeal.

to the Sierra Club's interest in the dispute is contained in paragraph 3 of the complaint, which reads in its entirety as follows:

> "Plaintiff Sierra Club is a non-profit corporation organized and operating under the laws of the State of California, with its principal place of business in San Francisco, California since 1892. Membership of the club is approximately 78,000 nationally, with approximately 27,000 members residing in the San Francisco Bay Area. For many years the Sierra Club by its activities and conduct has exhibited a special interest in the conservation and the sound maintenance of the national parks, game refuges and forests of the country, regularly serving as a responsible representative of persons similar interested. One of the principal purposes of the Sierra Club is to protect and conserve the national resources of the Sierra Nevada Mountains.

> Its interests would be vitally affected by the acts hereinafter described and would be aggrieved by those acts of the defendants as hereinafter more fully appears."

In an *amici curiae* brief filed in this Court by the Wilderness Society and others, it is asserted that the Sierra Club has conducted regular camping trips into the Mineral King area, and that various members of the Club have used and continue to use the area for recreational purposes. These allegations were not contained in the pleadings, nor were they brought to the attention of the Court of Appeals. Moreover, the Sierra Club in its reply brief specifically declines to rely on its individualized interest, as a basis for standing. Our decision does not, of course, bar the Sierra Club from seeking in the District Court to amend its complaint by a motion under Rule 15, Federal Rules of Civil Procedure.

Taken together, *Sanders* and *Scripps-Howard* thus established a dual proposition: the fact of economic injury is what gives a person standing to seek judicial review under the statute, but once review is properly invoked, that person may argue the public interest in support of his claim that the agency has failed to comply with its statutory mandate. It was in the latter sense that the "standing" of the appellant in *Scripps-Howard* existed only as a "representative of the public interest." It is in a similar sense that we have used the phrase "private attorney general" to describe that function performed by persons upon whom Congress has conferred the right to seek judicial review of agency action. See Data Processing, supra, 397 U.S., at 154.

The trend of cases arising under the APA and other statutes authorizing judicial review of federal agency action has been toward recognizing that injuries other than economic harm are sufficient to bring a person within the meaning of the statutory language, and toward discarding the notion that an injury that is widely shared is *ipso facto* not an injury sufficient to provide the basis for judicial review. We noted this development with approval in Data Processing, 397 U.S., at 154, in saying that the interest alleged to have been injured "may reflect 'aesthetic, conversational, and recreational' as well as economic values." But broadening the categories of injury that may be alleged in support of standing is a different matter from abandoning the requirement that the party seeking review must himself have suffered an injury.

Some courts have indicated a willingness to take this latter step by conferring standing upon organizations that have demonstrated "an organizational interest in the problem" of environmental or consumer protection. Environmental Defense Fund, Inc. v. Hardin, 428 F.2d 1093, 1097. It is clear that an organization whose members are injured may represent those members in a proceeding for judicial review. But a mere "interest in a problem," no matter how longstanding the interest and no matter how qualified the organization is in evaluating the problem, is not sufficient by itself to render the organization "adversely affected" or "aggrieved" within the meaning of the APA. The Sierra Club is a large and long-established organization, with a historic commitment to the cause of protecting our Nation's natural heritage from man's depredations. But if a "special interest" in this subject were enough to entitle the Sierra Club to commence this litigation, there would appear to be no objective basis upon which to disallow a suit by any other bona fide "special interest" organization however small or short-lived. And if any group with a bona fide "special interest" could initiate such litigation, it is difficult to perceive why any individual citizen with the same bona fide special interest would not also be entitled to do so.

The requirement that a party seeking review must allege facts showing that he is himself adversely affected does not insulate executive action from judicial review, nor does it prevent any public interests from being protected through the judicial process.[9] It does serve as at least a rough attempt to put the decision as to whether review will be sought in the hands of those who have a direct stake in the outcome. That goal would be undermined were we to construe the APA to authorize judicial review at the behest of organizations or individuals who seek to do no more than vindicate their own value preferences through the judicial process. The principle that the Sierra Club would have us establish in this case would do just that.

As we conclude that the Court of Appeals was correct in its holding that the Sierra Club lacked standing to maintain this action, we do not reach any other questions presented in the petition, and we intimate no view on the merits of the complaint. The judgment is Affirmed.

■ MR. JUSTICE DOUGLAS dissented in an opinion not reproduced here.

■ MR. JUSTICE POWELL and MR. JUSTICE REHNQUIST took no part in the consideration or decision of this case.

Lujan v. Defenders of Wildlife

United States Supreme Court, 1992.
504 U.S. 555, 112 S.Ct. 2130, 119 L.Ed.2d 351.

■ JUSTICE SCALIA delivered the opinion of the Court with respect to Parts I, II, III–A, and IV, and an opinion with respect to Part III–B in which the CHIEF JUSTICE, JUSTICE WHITE, and JUSTICE THOMAS join.

This case involves a challenge to a rule promulgated by the Secretary of the Interior interpreting § 7 of the Endangered Species Act of 1973 (ESA), 87 Stat. 884, 892, as amended, 16 U.S.C. § 1536, in such fashion as to render it applicable only to actions within the United States or on the high seas. The preliminary issue, and the only one we reach, is whether the respondents here, plaintiffs below, have standing to seek judicial review of the rule.

I

Section 7(a)(2) of the Act provides, in pertinent part:

"Each Federal agency shall, in consultation, with and with the assistance of the Secretary [of the Interior], insure that any action authorized, funded, or carried out by such agency.... is not likely to jeopardize the continued existence of any endangered species or threat-

---

9. In its reply brief, after noting the fact that it might have chosen to assert individualized injury to itself or to its members as a basis for standing, the Sierra Club states:

"The Government seeks to create a 'heads I win, tails you lose' situation in which either the courthouse door is barred for lack of assertion of a private, unique injury or a preliminary injunction is denied on the ground that the litigant has advanced private injury which does not warrant an injunction adverse to a competing public interest. Counsel have shaped their case to avoid this trap."

The short answer to this contention is that the "trap" does not exist. The test of injury in fact goes only to the question of standing to obtain judicial review. Once this standing is established, the party may assert the interests of the general public in support of his claims for equitable relief.

ened species or result in the destruction or adverse modification of habitat of such species which is determined by the Secretary, after consultation as appropriate with affected States, to be critical." 16 U.S.C. § 1536(a)(2).

In 1978, the Fish and Wildlife Service (FWS) and National Marine Fisheries Service (NMFS), on behalf of the Secretary of the Interior and the Secretary of Commerce respectively, promulgated a joint regulation stating that the obligations imposed by § 7(a)(2) extend to actions taken in foreign nations. 43 Fed.Reg. 874 (1978). The next year, however, the Interior Department began to reexamine its position. Letter from Leo Kuliz, Solicitor, Department of the Interior, to Assistant Secretary, Fish and Wildlife and Parks, Aug. 8, 1979. A revised joint regulation, reinterpreting § 7(a)(2) to require consultation only for actions taken in the United States or on the high seas, was proposed in 1983, 48 Fed.Reg. 29990 (1983), and promulgated in 1986, 51 Fed.Reg. 19926 (1986); 50 C.F.R. 402.01 (1991).

Shortly thereafter, respondents, organizations dedicated to wildlife conservation and other environmental causes, filed this action against the Secretary of the Interior, seeking a declaratory judgment that the new regulation is in error as to the geographic scope of § 7(a)(2), and an injunction requiring the Secretary to promulgate a new regulation restoring the initial interpretation.

II

Over the years, our cases have established that the irreducible constitutional minimum of standing contains three elements: *First*, the plaintiff must have suffered an "injury-in-fact"—an invasion of a legally-protected interest which is (a) concrete and particularized, and (b) actual or imminent, not conjectural or hypothetical. *Second*, there must be a causal connection between the injury and the conduct complained of—the injury has to be "fairly ... trace[able] to the challenged action of the defendant, and not ... th[e] result [of] the independent action of some third party not before the court." Simon v. Eastern Ky. Welfare Rights Org., 426 U.S. 26, 41–42 (1976). *Third*, it must be "likely," as opposed to merely "speculative," that the injury will be "redressed by a favorable decision." Id. at 38, 43.

When the suit is one challenging the legality of government action or inaction, the nature and extent of facts that must be averred (at the summary judgment stage) or proved (at the trial stage) in order to establish standing depends considerably upon whether the plaintiff is himself an object of the action (or foregone action) at issue. If he is, there is ordinarily little question that the action or inaction has caused him injury, and that a judgment preventing or requiring the action will redress it. When, however, as in this case, a plaintiff's asserted injury arises from the government's allegedly unlawful regulation (or lack of regulation) of *someone else*, much more is needed. In that circumstance, causation and redressability ordinarily hinge on the response of the regulated (or regulable) third party to the government action, or inaction—and perhaps on the response of others as well.

III

We think the Court of Appeals failed to apply the foregoing principles in denying the Secretary's motion for summary judgment. Respondents had not made the requisite demonstration of (at least) injury and redressability.

A

Respondents' claim to injury is that the lack of consultation with respect to certain funded activities abroad "increas[es] the rate of extinction of endangered and threatened species." Of course, the desire to use or observe an animal species, even for purely aesthetic purposes, is undeniably a cognizable interest for purpose of standing.

But the "injury in fact" test requires more than an injury to a cognizable interest. It requires that the party seeking review be himself among the injured. To survive the Secretary's summary judgment motion, respondents had to submit affidavits or other evidence showing, through specific facts, not only that listed species were in fact being threatened by funded activities abroad, but also that one or more of respondents' members would thereby be "directly" affected apart from their " 'special interest' in th[e] subject." Sierra Club v. Morton, 405 U.S. at 735.

With respect to this aspect of the case, the Court of Appeals focused on the affidavits of two Defenders' members—Joyce Kelly and Amy Skilbred. Ms. Kelly stated that she traveled to Egypt in 1986 and "observed the traditional habitat of the endangered nile crocodile there and intend[s] to do so again, and hope(s) to observe the crocodile directly," and that she "will suffer harm in fact as a result of [the] American . . . role . . . in overseeing the rehabilitation of the Aswan High Dam on the Nile . . . and [in] develop[ing] . . . Egypt's . . . Master Water Plan." Ms. Skilbred averred that she traveled to Sri Lanka in 1981 and "observed th[e] habitat" of "endangered species such as the Asian elephant and the leopard" at what is now the site of the Mahaweli Project funded by the Agency for International Development (AID), although she "was unable to see any of the endangered species;" "this development project," she continued, "will seriously reduce endangered, threatened, and endemic species habitat including areas that I visited . . . [which] may severely shorten the future of these species;" that threat, she concluded, harmed her because she "intend[s] to return to Sri Lanka in the future and hope[s] to be more fortunate in spotting at least the endangered elephant and leopard." When Ms. Skilbred was asked at a subsequent deposition if and when she had any plans to return to Sri Lanka, she reiterated that "I intend to go back to Sri Lanka," but confessed that she had no current plans: "I don't know [when]. There is a civil war going on right now. I don't know. Not next year, I will say. In the future."

We shall assume for the sake of argument that these affidavits contain facts showing that certain agency-funded projects threaten listed species—

though that is questionable. They plainly contain no facts, however, showing how damage to the species will produce "imminent" injury to Ms. Kelly and Skilbred. That the women "had visited" the areas of the projects before the projects commenced proves nothing. As we have said in a related context, "[p]ast exposure to illegal conduct does not in itself show a present case or controversy regarding injunctive relief . . . if unaccompanied by any continuing, present adverse effects." Lyons, 461 U.S. at 102.

And the affiants' profession of an "inten[t]" to return to the places they had visited before—where they will presumably, this time, be deprived of the opportunity to observe animals of the endangered species—is simply not enough. Such "some day" intentions—without any description of concrete plans, or indeed even any specification of *when* the some day will be—do not support a finding of the "actual or imminent" injury that our cases require.

Besides relying upon the Kelly and Skilbred affidavits, respondents propose a series of novel standing theories. The first, inelegantly styled "ecosystem nexus," proposes that any person who uses *any part* of a "contiguous ecosystem" adversely affected by a funded activity has standing even if the activity is located a great distance away. This approach, as the Court of Appeals correctly observed, is inconsistent with our opinion in *National Wildlife Federation*, which held that a plaintiff claiming injury from environmental damage must use the area affected by the challenged activity and not an area roughly "in the vicinity" of it. 497 U.S., at 887–889. It makes no difference that the general-purpose section of the ESA states that the Act was intended in part "to provide a means whereby the ecosystems upon which endangered species and threatened species depend may be conserved," 16 U.S.C. § 1531(b). To say that the Act protects ecosystems is not to say that the Act creates (if it were possible) rights of action in persons who have not been injured in fact, that is, persons who use portions of an ecosystem not perceptibly affected by the unlawful action in question.

Respondents' other theories are called, alas, the "animal nexus" approach, whereby anyone who has an interest in studying or seeing the endangered animals anywhere on the globe has standing; and the "vocational nexus" approach, under which anyone with a professional interest in such animals can sue. Under these theories, anyone who goes to see Asian elephants in the Bronx Zoo, and anyone who is a keeper of Asian elephants in the Bronx Zoo, has standing to sue because the Director of AID did not consult with the Secretary regarding the AID-funded project in Sri Lanka. This is beyond all reason. Standing is not "an ingenious academic exercise in the conceivable," United States v. Students Challenging Regulatory Agency Procedures (SCRAP), 412 U.S. 669, 688, (1973), but as we have said requires, at the summary judgment stage, a factual showing of perceptible harm. It is clear that the person who observes or works with a particular animal threatened by a federal decision is facing perceptible harm, since the very subject of his interest will no longer exist. It is even plausible—though it goes to the outermost limit of plausibility—to think that a person who observes or works with animals of a particular species in the very area of the world where that species is threatened by a federal decision is facing such harm, since some animals that might have been the subject of his interest will no longer exist see Japan Whaling Assn. v. American Cetacean Soc., 478 U.S. 221, 231, n. 4, (1986). It goes beyond the limit, however, and into pure speculation and fantasy, to say that anyone who observes or works with an endangered species, anywhere in the world, is appreciably harmed by a single project affecting some portion of that species with which he has no more specific connections.

B

The most obvious problem in the present case is redressability. Since the agencies funding the projects were not parties to the case, the District Court could accord relief only against the Secretary: He could be ordered to revise his regulation to require consultation for foreign projects. But this would not remedy respondents' alleged injury unless the funding agencies were bound by the Secretary's regulation, which is very much an open question. Whereas in other contexts the ESA is quite explicit as to the Secretary's controlling authority, see, e.g., 16 U.S.C. § 1533(a)(1) ("The Secretary shall" promulgate regulations determining endangered species); § 1535(d)(1) ("The Secretary is authorized to provide financial assistance to any State"), with respect to consultation the initiative, and hence arguably the initial responsibility for determining statutory necessity, lies with the agencies, see § 1536(a)(2) *("Each Federal agency shall*, in consultation with and with the assistance of the Secretary, insure that any" funded action is not likely to jeopardize endangered or threatened species) (emphasis added). When the Secretary promulgated the regulation at issue here, he thought it was binding on the agencies, see 51 Fed.Reg., at 19928 (1986). The Solicitor General, however, has repudiated that position here, and the agencies themselves apparently deny the Secretary's authority. (During the period when the Secretary took the view that § 7(a)(2) did apply abroad, AID and FWS engaged in a running controversy over whether consultation was required with respect to the Mahaweli project, AID insisting that consultation applied only to domestic actions.)

Respondents assert that this legal uncertainty did not affect redressability (and hence standing) because the District Court itself could resolve the issue of the Secretary's authority as a necessary part of its standing inquiry. Assuming that it is appropriate to resolve an issue of law such as this in connection with a threshold standing inquiry, resolution by the District Court would not have remedied respondents' alleged injury anyway, because it would not have been binding upon the agencies. They were not parties to the suit, and there is no reason they should be obliged to honor an incidental legal determination the suit produced.

A further impediment to redressability is the fact that the agencies generally supply only a fraction of the funding for a foreign project. AID, for example, has provided less than 10% of the funding for the Mahaweli Project. Respondents have produced nothing to indicate that the projects they have named will either be suspended, or do less harm to listed species, if that fraction is eliminated. [I]t is entirely conjectural whether the nonagency activity that affects respondents will be altered or affected by the agency activity they seek to achieve. There is no standing.

IV

The Court of Appeals found that respondents had standing for an additional reason: because they had suffered a procedural injury. The so-called "citizen suit" provision of the ESA provides, in pertinent part, that "any person may commence a civil suit on his own behalf (A) to enjoin any person, including the United States and any other governmental instrumentality or agency . . . who is alleged to be in violation of any provision of this chapter." 16 U.S.C. § 1540(g). The court held that because § 7(a)(2) requires interagency consultation, the citizen-suit provision creates a "procedural righ[t]" to consultation in all "persons"—so that *anyone* can file suit in federal court to challenge the Secretary's (or presumably any other official's) failure to follow the assertedly correct consultative procedure, notwithstanding their inability to allege any discrete injury flowing from that failure. To understand the remarkable nature of this holding one must be clear about what it does *not* rest upon: This is not a case where plaintiffs are seeking to enforce a procedural requirement the disregard of which could impair a separate concrete interest of theirs (e.g., the procedural requirement for a hearing prior to denial of their license application, or the procedural requirement for an environmental impact statement before a federal facility is constructed next door to them).[7] Nor is it simply a case where concrete injury has been suffered by many persons, as in mass fraud or mass tort situations. Nor, finally, is it the unusual case in which Congress has created a concrete private interest in the outcome of a suit against a private party for the government's benefit, by providing a cash bounty for the victorious plaintiff. Rather, the court held that the injury-in-fact requirement had been satisfied by congressional conferral upon all persons of an abstract, self-contained, noninstrumental "right" to have the Executive observe the procedures required by law. We reject this view.

We have consistently held that a plaintiff raising only a generally available grievance about government—claiming only harm to his and every citizen's interest in proper application of the Constitution and laws,

---

7. There is this much truth to the assertion that "procedural rights" are special: The person who has been accorded a procedural right to protect his concrete interests can assert that right without meeting all the normal standards for redressability and immediacy. Thus, under our case law, one living adjacent to the site for proposed construction of a federally licensed dam has standing to challenge the licensing agency's failure to prepare an environmental impact statement, even though he cannot establish with any certainty that the statement will cause the license to be withheld or altered, and even though the dam will not be completed for many years. (That is why we do not rely, in the present case, upon the Government's argument that, even if the other agencies were obliged to consult with the Secretary, they might not have followed his advice.) What respondents' "procedural rights" argument seeks, however, is quite different from this: standing for persons who have no concrete interests affected—persons who live (and propose to live) at the other end of the country from the dam.

and seeking relief that no more directly and tangibly benefits him than it does the public at large does not state an Article III, case or controversy.

* * *

We hold that respondents lack standing to bring this action and that the Court of Appeals erred in denying the summary judgment motion filed by the United States. The opinion of the Court of Appeals is hereby reversed, and the cause remanded for proceedings consistent with this opinion.

It is so ordered.

■ JUSTICE KENNEDY, with whom JUSTICE SOUTER joins, concurring in part and concurring in the judgment.

Although I agree with the essential parts of the Court's analysis, I write separately to make several observations.

In my view, Congress has the power to define injuries and articulate chains of causation that will give rise to a case or controversy where none existed before, and I do not read the Court's opinion to suggest a contrary view. In exercising this power, however, Congress must at the very least identify the injury it seeks to vindicate and relate the injury to the class of persons entitled to bring suit. The citizen-suit provision of the Endangered Species Act does not meet these minimal requirements, because while the statute purports to confer a right on "any person ... to enjoin ... the United States, and any other governmental instrumentality or agency ... who is alleged to be in violation of any provision of this chapter," it does not of its own force establish that there is an injury in "any person" by virtue of any "violation." 16 U.S.C. § 1540(g)(1)(A).

The Court's holding that there is an outer limit to the power of Congress to confer rights of action is a direct and necessary consequence of the case and controversy limitations found in Article III. I agree, that it would exceed those limitations if, at the behest of Congress and in the absence of any showing of concrete injury, we were to entertain citizen-suits to vindicate the public's nonconcrete interest in the proper administration of the laws. While it does not matter how may persons have been injured by the challenged action, the party bringing suit must show that the action injures him in a concrete and personal way. This requirement is not just an empty formality. It preserves the vitality of the adversarial process by assuring both that the parties before the court have an actual, as opposed to professed, stake in the outcome and that "the legal questions presented ... will be resolved, not in the refined atmosphere of a debating society, but in a concrete factual context conducive to a realistic appreciation of the consequence of judicial action."

■ JUSTICE STEVENS, concurring in the judgment.

I

In my opinion a person who has visited the critical habitat of an endangered species, has a professional interest in preserving the species and its habitat, and intends to revisit them in the future has standing to challenge agency action that threatens their destruction. Congress has found that a wide variety of endangered species of fish, wildlife, and plants are of "aesthetic, ecological, educational, historical, recreational, and scientific value to the Nation and its people." 16 U.S.C. § 1531(a)(8). Given that finding, we have no license to demean the importance of the interest that particular individuals may have in observing any species or its habitat, whether those individuals are motivated by aesthetic enjoyment, an interest in professional research, or an economic interest in preservation of the species. Indeed, this Court has often held that injuries to such interests are sufficient to confer standing, and the Court reiterates that holding today.

The Court nevertheless concludes that respondents have not suffered "injury in fact" because they have not shown that the harm to the endangered species will produce "imminent" injury to them. I disagree. An injury to an individual's interest in studying or enjoying a species and its natural habitat occurs when someone (whether it be the government or a private party) takes action that harms that species and habitat. In my judgment therefore, the "imminence" of such an injury would be measured by the timing and likelihood of the threatened environmental harm, rather than—as the Court seems to suggest by the time that might elapse between the present and the time when the individuals would visit the area if no such injury should occur.

In this case the likelihood that respondents will be injured by the destruction of the endangered species is not speculative. If respondents are genuinely interested in the preservation of the endangered species and intend to study or observe these animals in the future, their injury will occur as soon as the animals are destroyed. Thus the only potential source of "speculation" in this case is whether respondents' intent to study or observe the animals is genuine.[2] In my view, Joyce Kelly and Amy Skilbred have introduced sufficient evidence to negate petitioner's contention that their claims of injury are "speculative" or "conjectural."

The plurality also concludes that respondents' injuries are not redressable in this litigation for two reasons. First, respondents have sought only a declaratory judgment that the Secretary of the Interior's regulation inter-

---

2. As were recognized in *Sierra Club v. Morton*, 405 U.S. at 735, the impact of changes in the aesthetics or ecology of a particular area does "not fall indiscriminately upon every citizen". The alleged injury will be felt directly only by those who use [the area], and for whom the aesthetic and recreational values of the area will be lessened.... Thus respondents would not be injured by the challenged projects if they had not visited the sites or studied the threatened species and habitat. But, as discussed above, respondents did visit the sites; moreover, they have expressed an intent to do it again. This intent to revisit the area is significant evidence tending to confirm the genuine character of respondents' interests but I am not at all sure that an intent to revisit would be indispensable in every case. The interest that confers standing in a case of this kind is comparable, though by no means equivalent, to the interest in a relationship among family members that can be immediately harmed by the death of an absent member, regardless of when, if ever, a family reunion is planned to occur. Thus, if the facts of this case had shown repeated and regular visits by the respondents, proof of an intent to revisit might well be superfluous.

preting § 7(a)(2) to require consultation only for agency actions in the United States or on the high seas is invalid and an injunction requiring him to promulgate a new regulation requiring consultation for agency actions abroad as well. But the plurality opines, even if respondents succeed and a new regulation is promulgated, there is no guarantee that federal agencies that are not parties to this case will actually consult with the Secretary. Furthermore, the plurality continues, respondents have not demonstrated that federal agencies can influence the behavior of the foreign governments where the affected projects are located. Thus, even if the agencies consult with the Secretary and terminate funding for foreign projects, the foreign governments might nonetheless pursue the projects and jeopardize the endangered species. Neither of these reasons is persuasive.

We must presume that if this Court holds that § 7(a)(2) requires consultation, all affected agencies would abide by that interpretation and engage in the requisite consultations. Certainly the Executive Branch cannot be heard to argue that an authoritative construction of the governing statute by this Court may simply be ignored by any agency head. Moreover, if Congress has required consultation between agencies, we must presume that such consultation will have a serious purpose that is likely to produce tangible results. As Justice Blackmun explains, it is not mere speculation to think that foreign governments, when faced with the threatened withdrawal of United States assistance, will modify their projects to mitigate the harm to endangered species.

II

Although I believe that respondents have standing, I nevertheless concur in the judgment of reversal because I am persuaded that the Government is correct in its submission that § 7(a)(2) does not apply to activities in foreign countries. * * *

■ JUSTICE BLACKMUN, with whom JUSTICE O'CONNOR joins, dissenting.

I part company with the Court in this case in two respects. First, I believe that respondents have raised genuine issues of fact—sufficient to survive summary judgment—both as to injury and as to redressability. Second, I question the Court's breadth of language in rejecting standing for "procedural" injuries. I fear the Court seeks to impose fresh limitations on the constitutional authority of Congress to allow citizen-suits in the federal courts for injuries deemed "procedural" in nature. I dissent.

I think a reasonable finder of fact could conclude from the information in the affidavits and deposition testimony that either Kelly or Skilbred will soon return to the project sites, thereby satisfying the "actual or imminent" injury standard. The Court dismisses Kelly's and Skilbred's general statements that they intended to revisit the project sites as "simply not enough." But those statements did not stand alone. A reasonable finder of fact could conclude, based not only upon their statements of intent to return, but upon their past visits to the project sites, as well as their professional backgrounds, that it was likely that Kelly and Skilbred would make a return trip to the project areas.

By requiring a "description of concrete plans" or "specification of *when* the some day [for a return visit] will be," the Court, in my view, demands what is likely an empty formality. No substantial barriers prevent Kelly or Skilbred from simply purchasing plane tickets to return to the Aswan and Mahaweli projects. This case differs from other cases in which the imminence of harm turned largely on the affirmative actions of third parties beyond a plaintiff's control.

The Court also concludes that injury is lacking, because respondents' allegations of "ecosystem nexus" failed to demonstrate sufficient proximity to the site of the environmental harm. To support that conclusion, the Court mischaracterizes our decision in Lujan v. National Wildlife Federation, 497 U.S. 871 (1990), as establishing a general rule that "a plaintiff claiming injury from environmental damage must use the area affected by the challenged activity." In *National Wildlife Federation* the Court required specific geographical proximity because of the particular type of harm alleged in that case: harm to the plaintiff's visual enjoyment of nature from mining activities. One cannot suffer from the sight of a ruined landscape without being close enough to see the sites actually being mined. Many environmental injuries, however, cause harm distant from the immediately affected by the challenged action. Environmental destruction may affect animals traveling over vast geographical ranges, see, e.g., Japan Whaling Assn. v. American Cetacean Soc., 478 U.S. 221 (1986) (harm to American whale watchers from Japanese whaling activities), or rivers running long geographical courses, see, e.g., Arkansas v. Oklahoma, 503 U.S. 91 (1992) (harm to Oklahoma residents from wastewater treatment plant 39 miles from border). It cannot seriously be contended that a litigant's failure to use the precise or exact site where animals are slaughtered or where toxic waste is dumped into a river means he or she cannot show injury.

The Court also rejects respondents' claim of vocational or professional injury. The Court says that it is "beyond all reason" that a zoo "keeper" of Asian elephants would have standing to contest his government's participation in the eradication of all the Asian elephants in another part of the world. I am unable to see how the distant location of the destruction *necessarily* (for purposes of ruling at summary judgment) mitigates the harm to the elephant keeper. If there is no more access to a future supply of the animal that sustains a keeper's livelihood, surely there is harm.

The Court concludes that any "procedural injury" suffered by respondents is insufficient to confer standing. It rejects the view that the "injury-in-fact requirement ... [is] satisfied by congressional conferral upon *all* person of an abstract, self-contained, noninstrumental 'right' to have the Executive observe the procedures required by law." Whatever the Court might mean with that very broad language it cannot be saying that "procedural injuries" *as a class* are necessarily insufficient for purposes of Article III standing.

It is to be hoped that over time the Court will acknowledge that some classes of procedural duties are so enmeshed with the prevention of a substantive, concrete harm that an individual plaintiff may be able to demonstrate a sufficient likelihood of injury just through the breach of that procedural duty. For example, in the context of the NEPA requirement of environmental impact statements, this Court has acknowledged "it is now well settled that NEPA itself does not mandate particular results [and] simply prescribes the necessary process," but "these procedures are almost certain to affect the agency's substantive decision." Robertson v. Methow Valley Citizens Council, 490 U.S., 332, 350 (1989) (emphasis added). This acknowledgment of an inextricable link between procedural and substantive harm does not reflect improper appellate fact-finding. It reflects nothing more than the proper deference owed to the judgment of a coordinate branch—Congress—that certain procedures are directly tied to protection against a substantive harm.

In conclusion, I cannot join the Court on what amounts to a slash-and-burn expedition through the law of environmental standing.

I dissent.

D.   RIPENESS, EXHAUSTION AND MOOTNESS

There are three important concepts related to the timing of judicial review: 1) ripeness, 2) exhaustion of administrative remedies, and 3) mootness.

1.   RIPENESS

The ripeness and mootness doctrines spring from the Article III "case or controversy" requirement focusing on the existence or non-existence of the plaintiff's alleged injury-in-fact. A claim brought too early is not ripe for review. The ripeness principle is incorporated into the APA's § 704 which limits judicial review to "final agency action for which there is no other adequate remedy in court" unless otherwise provided for by statute.

Certain agency acts are clearly final, such as agency adjudications where there is no further right of internal agency appeal. Also, promulgation of a final regulation at the conclusion of the agency rulemaking process would also seem to be final. However, absent special statutory authorization, the courts have held that regulations generally cannot be judicially reviewed until they are enforced against a party. This rule means that, in general, pre-enforcement review of agency regulations *is not* allowed. Most environmental statutes run counter to this general rule by making specific provision for pre-enforcement judicial review of agency regulations but only for a limited time period 60 or 120 days after their issuance or promulgation. The Clean Air Act § 307(b) and the Clean Water Act § 509(b) are good examples. Why do you suppose these statutes are designed in this way? However, these laws also contain the proviso that regulations cannot be challenged during individual enforcement proceedings. Why is that?

What about the wide range of actions not resulting from formal agency rulemaking or adjudicatory procedures? Are they final action and consequently, ripe for judicial review? A wide range of cases have treated this issue including the highway funding decision in the *Overton Park* case discussed below. Another case, Bennett v. Spear, 520 U.S. 154 (1997), the Supreme Court unanimously held that a biological opinion issued by the U.S. Fish and Wildlife Service pursuant to the Endangered Species Act was a final agency action subject to review. It noted two conditions required for such a finding: 1) the action must mark the consummation of the agency's decisionmaking process, that is it must not be merely tentative; and 2) the action must be one by which rights or obligations have been determined or from which legal consequences will flow. Courts of Appeal have since implemented this view. See Park Lake Resources L.L.C. v. U.S. Dept. of Agriculture, 197 F.3d 448, 452–53 (10th Cir.1999).

Even if an agency action is final, it may not be ripe for judicial review. In Ohio Forestry Association v. Sierra Club, 523 U.S. 726 (1998), the Sierra Club challenged the forest management plan developed for the Wayne National Forest. The Club alleged that the plan permitted excessive timber harvest and excessive clear-cutting. The plan had been formally adopted, and it had legal consequences because all forest management actions would have to be consistent with it. Nonetheless, a unanimous Court held that the challenge was not ripe. In doing so, it considered: "1) whether delayed review would cause hardship to the plaintiffs; 2) whether judicial intervention would inappropriately interfere with further administrative action; and (3) whether the courts would benefit from further factual development of the issues presented." *Id.* at 733. The Court noted that the Sierra Club would have the opportunity to challenge site-specific timber harvest plans before any trees could be cut, and that judicial review would be aided by the focus that a particular logging proposal could provide. The Court also pointed out that Congress had not specifically provided for pre-implementation review of forest plans.

2.   EXHAUSTION OF ADMINISTRATIVE REMEDIES

A second doctrine affecting the timing of judicial review is the principle that the litigant must exhaust administrative remedies prior to seeking court review. There are several policy justifications for the exhaustion doctrine including limiting unnecessary judicial intervention into agency matters, clarifying legal and factual issues prior to court review and allowing agencies the opportunity to correct their errors. See McCarthy v. Madigan, 503 U.S. 140 (1992). Nonetheless as a general matter, the Supreme Court held in Darby v. Cisneros, 509 U.S. 137 (1993), that there is no general exhaustion element beyond the Administrative Procedure Act § 704 requirement of "finality" unless the agency's authorizing statute or regulations require it. The focus is often upon whether the agency action is final and in some cases that issue may be in dispute. Most environmental statutes do not specifically require intra-agency appeal as a pre-condition of obtaining judicial review. See e.g. Clean Water Act § 509(b)(1) (review of EPA action under the CWA). Recent environmental decisions have rein-forced the *Darby* position but identified clear statutory exhaustion provisions precluding judicial review at that point. There are situations, however, in which exhaustion is required. See Shawnee Trail Conservancy v. U.S. Dept. of Agriculture, 222 F.3d 383 (7th Cir.2000). (Forest Service regulations required that plaintiff pursue agency appeal before seeking judicial review).

3.   MOOTNESS

If it is too late to obtain judicial review, the case is said to be moot. A case is moot when there is no live or active controversy between the parties. Whereas the plaintiff must prove each element of standing, the defendant bears the burden of proving that a case is moot. If a case becomes moot, it is therefore, non-justiciable. The Supreme Court noted in Hall v. Beals, 396 U.S. 45, 48 (1969), that if a case is moot, "it loses its character as a present, live controversy of the kind that must exist if [the Court is] to avoid advisory opinions on abstract propositions of law." The key concept is that a case becomes moot when the issues presented to the court are no longer alive. The mootness concept would, therefore, appear to be grounded in the Article III "case or controversy" requirement rather than to be considered a prudential doctrine. However, the Court has debated this question on occasion. Yet, it has found it difficult to justify the mootness doctrine in at least one exception circumstance—the exception to strict mootness theory for conduct "capable of repetition, yet evading review."

There is an important exception to the mootness doctrine for conduct "capable of repetition, yet evading review." If a the challenged action does not remain in effect long enough to be fully litigated prior to its cessation or expiration, and there is a reasonable expectation that the same complaining party will be subjected to the same action again, litigation may proceed after the action ceases or expires. Weinstein v. Bradford, 423 U.S. 147, 149 (1975). Thus, for example, a challenge to an annual catch limit for a commercial fishery does not become moot when the limit expires. See Greenpeace Action v. Franklin, 14 F.3d 1324 (9th Cir.1992).

This death of the live controversy could occur at any moment after the litigation is initiated by the plaintiff and it is especially problematic for plaintiffs in environmental enforcement citizen suits. Claims can become moot if the underlying legal rules change in a way which make plaintiff's claims irrelevant. For instance, if EPA repealed or amended an air pollution control regulation which had previously applied to an industry, the industry's challenge to the rule would be moot. A number of other circumstances might also moot a case, for example: 1) the defendant provides the plaintiff with the full relief requested of 2) the condition that is the subject of the suit is of a finite duration and ceases to exist before judicial review.

Mootness could be a significant legal issue in a pollution standard violation case and especially, in an environmental citizen's suit action. For instance, what if a water pollution discharger out of compliance with its permit, was sued under CWA § 505 for violating its CWA permit. What if after filing the action, the discharger came into compliance with its permit?

If the violative conduct has been permanently ceased, the discharger should be able to obtain a dismissal of the suit on the grounds of mootness. The courts have not given this view a broad reading when a defendant voluntarily terminates illegal conduct as in the water pollution example. Placing the burden on the defendant, the Supreme Court in the *Gwaltney* decision stated that in order for such a case to be moot, it must be " 'absolutely clear' that the allegedly wrongful behavior could not reasonably be expected to reoccur." 484 U.S. at 66. This position does not mean that there is no conceivable chance of a future violation, just that it is not reasonable to anticipate that the wrongful conduct will be repeated in the future. Is it virtually impossible for the water pollution to reoccur? The Court reiterated this view in Friends of the Earth v. Laidlaw Environmental Services, Inc., 528 U.S. 167 (2000), noting that the defendant bears a "heavy burden" of convincing a court that the polluting conduct "cannot reasonably be expected to recur." In *Laidlaw*, despite the fact that the facility had been closed, the court concluded that the dispute was not moot because the defendant retained its water discharge permit. This fact indicated to the Court that the potential for future water discharges and future violations still existed.

CLASS DISCUSSION PROBLEM: A FREEWAY IN DULUTH

In Duluth, Minnesota a proposed new highway is generating great controversy. In order to relieve the extremely heavy traffic demand in the downtown area, state and city officials have proposed the construction of a two-lane freeway from 10th Avenue East through 26th Avenue East. At its beginning point near 10th Avenue East the freeway will enter a tunnel and pass beneath Leif Erikson Park, for which it will be necessary to utilize 0.2 acres of parkland. After passing through the park, the freeway will follow the shore of Lake Superior to its terminus at 26th Avenue East.

Because the freeway is to be constructed with federal funds, the proposal calls into play the decision-making process under the Federal–Aid Highway Act, 23 U.S.C. §§ 101–156. Under this law the U.S. Secretary of Transportation cannot approve any state or local highway project for federal funding unless she finds that "such projects are based upon a continuing and comprehensive transportation planning process carried on cooperatively by States and local communities * * *." 23 U.S.C. § 134. The state and local sponsors must develop transportation improvement plans which consider social, economic, environmental, and energy conservation goals as well as the probable effect on land use and future development. In addition, 23 U.S.C. § 138 of the Federal–Aid Highway Act states that before the Secretary of Transportation can approve any project involving the use of any publicly owned park, recreation area, wildlife refuge, or historic site, she must find that there is "no feasible or prudent alternative" to such use and that "all possible planning" has been carried out to minimize harm to the site.

The Secretary of Transportation has determined that the National Environmental Policy Act (NEPA) also applies to the freeway project, and to comply with both section 138 and NEPA a composite final environmental impact/section 4(f) statement (EIS) has been prepared (the origin of the section 138 requirements was section 4(f) of the Department of Transportation Act of 1966).

The EIS gives a detailed description of the affected parkland and lists seven alternative routes that avoid the park and explains why each of those was either infeasible or imprudent. The EIS also describes mitigation measures that are planned: when construction is completed, vegetation in and around the park will be replanted, and the Minnesota Department of Transportation has agreed to acquire an additional 2.3 acres of usable parkland from private owners, thus increasing the park's total size by 2.1 acres. The EIS also discusses plans for noise reduction and additional pedestrian' and bicycle trails.

Leif Erikson Park is also a historic site that is listed on the National Register of Historic Places pursuant to the National Historic Preservation Act (NHPA), 16 U.S.C. §§ 470 et seq.

In addition to the environmental review provided by NEPA, § 106 of the National Historic Preservation Act requires federal agencies, "prior to the approval of any Federal funds" for any project, to take into account sites and properties eligible for or included in the National Register and to ask for comment from the Advisory Council on Historic Preservation. 16 U.S.C. § 470f. Federal agencies are under an express obligation to locate, all possible eligible sites that may be affected by any "undertaking." To fulfill this requirement they are to consult with the State Historic Preservation Officer. Section 110(f) of the NHPA requires that agencies, to the maximum extent possible, undertake such planning and actions as may be necessary to minimize harm to any National Historic Landmark that may be adversely affected by a project and to provide the Council with an opportunity for comment. 16 U.S.C. § 470f. An agency, however, is not legally required to follow the Council's advice. 36 C.F.R. § 800.6(c)(2). See also Waterford Citizens' Association v. Reilly, 970 F.2d 1287 (4th Cir.1992). Section 106 does not indicate what action agency should take.

Several individuals and groups still oppose the new freeway. First, the Northern Bell Telephone Company is protesting that the proposed tunnel will result in damage to its telephone equipment, leading to severe service disruptions to customers during and after construction. Second, the Minnesota Conservation Club (MCC), which has 856 members who live within a 100–mile radius of Leif Erikson Park, opposes both the tunnel under the park and the use of the city-owned shoreline of Lake Superior, which constitutes the last significant stretch of vacant shore lands within the city limits. The MCC argues that although the EIS/4(f) statement discusses alternatives to the use of 0.2 acres of parkland, there is no consideration of the impact of building the highway along the shore of Lake Superior, which will have a much greater adverse impact on the environment.

Northern Bell and MCC plan to file suit to ask for injunctive relief from the building of the freeway. What are their chances of success?

Suppose you represent either the Northern Bell Telephone Company or Minnesota Conservation Club. Consider the issues raised by the material in Section 2.

E. THE SCOPE OF REVIEW

Citizens to Preserve Overton Park, Inc. v. Volpe

United States Supreme Court, 1971.
401 U.S. 402, 91 S.Ct. 814, 28 L.Ed.2d 136.

■ Opinion of the Court by MR. JUSTICE MARSHALL, announced by MR. JUSTICE STEWART.

The growing public concern about the quality of our natural environment has prompted Congress in recent years to enact legislation designed to curb the accelerating destruction of our country's natural beauty. We are concerned in this case with § 4(f) of the Department of Transportation Act of 1966, as amended, and § 18(a) of the Federal–Aid Highway Act of 1968, 82 Stat. 823, 23 U.S.C. § 138 (1964 ed. Supp. V) (hereafter, § 138). These statutes prohibit the Secretary of Transportation from authorizing the use of federal funds to finance the construction of highways through public parks if a "feasible and prudent" alternative route exists. If no such route is available, the statutes allow him to approve construction through parks only if there has been "all possible planning to minimize harm" to the park.

Petitioners, private citizens as well as local and national conservation organizations, contend that the Secretary has violated these statutes by authorizing the expenditure of federal funds for the construction of a six-lane interstate highway through a public park in Memphis, Tennessee. Their claim was rejected by the District Court, which granted the Secretary's motion for summary judgment, and the Court of Appeals for the Sixth Circuit affirmed. After oral argument, this Court granted a stay that halted construction and, treating the application for the stay as a petition for certiorari, granted review. We now reverse the judgment below and remand for further proceedings in the District Court.

Overton Park is a 342 acre city park located near the center of Memphis. The park contains a zoo, a nine-hole municipal golf course, an outdoor theater, nature trails, a bridle path, an art academy, picnic areas, and 170 acres of forest. The proposed highway, which is to be a six-lane, high-speed, expressway, will sever the zoo from the rest of the park. Although the roadway will be depressed below ground level except where it crosses a small creek, 26 acres of the park will be destroyed. The highway is to be a segment of Interstate Highway I–40, part of the National System of Interstate and Defense Highways. I–40 will provide Memphis with a major east-west expressway which will allow easier access to downtown Memphis from the residential areas on the eastern edge of the city.

Although the route through the park was approved by the Bureau of Public Roads in 1956 and by the Federal Highway Administrator in 1966, the enactment of § 4(f) of the Department of Transportation Act prevented distribution of federal funds for the section of the highway designated to go through Overton Park until the Secretary of Transportation determined whether the requirements of § 4(f) had been met. Federal funding for the rest of the project was, however, available; and the state acquired a right-of-way on both sides of the park. In April 1968, the Secretary announced that he concurred in the judgment of local officials that I–40 should be built through the park. And in September 1969 the state acquired the right-of-way inside Overton Park from the city. Final approval for the project—the route as well as the design—was not announced until November 1969, after Congress had reiterated in § 138 of the Federal–Aid Highway Act that highway construction through public parks was to be restricted. Neither announcement approving the route and design of I–40 was accompanied by a statement of the Secretary's factual findings. He did not indicate why he believed there were no feasible and prudent alternative routes or why design changes could not be made to reduce the harm to the park.

Petitioners contend that the Secretary's action is invalid without such formal findings and that the Secretary did not make an independent determination but merely relied on the judgment of the Memphis City Council. They also contend that it would be "feasible and prudent" to route I–40 around Overton Park either to the north or to the south. And they argue that if these alternative routes are not "feasible and prudent," the present plan does not include "all possible" methods for reducing harm to the park. Petitioners claim that I–40 could be built under the park by using either of two possible tunneling methods, and they claim that, at a minimum, by using advanced drainage techniques the expressway could be depressed below ground level along the entire route through the park including the section that crosses the small creek.

Respondents argue that it was unnecessary for the Secretary to make formal findings, and that he did, in fact, exercise his own independent judgment which was supported by the facts. In the District Court, respondents introduced affidavits, prepared specifically for this litigation, which indicated that the Secretary had made the decision and that the decision was supportable. These affidavits were contradicted by affidavits introduced by petitioners, who also sought to take the deposition of a former Federal Highway Administrator who had participated in the decision to route I–40 through Overton Park.

The District Court and the Court of Appeals found that formal findings by the Secretary were not necessary and refused to order the deposition of the former Federal Highway Administrator because those courts believed that probing of the mental processes of an administrative decisionmaker was prohibited. And, believing that the Secretary's authority was wide and reviewing courts' authority narrow in the approval of highway routes, the lower courts held that the affidavits contained no basis for a determination that the Secretary had exceeded his authority.

We agree that formal findings were not required. But we do not believe that in this case judicial review based solely on litigation affidavits was adequate.

A threshold question—whether petitioners are entitled to any judicial review—is easily answered. Section 701 of the Administrative Procedure Act, 5 U.S.C. § 701 (1964 ed. Supp. V), provides that the action of "each authority of the government of the United States," which includes the Department of Transportation, is subject to judicial review except where there is a statutory prohibition on review or where "agency action is committed to agency discretion by law." In this case, there is no indication that Congress sought to prohibit judicial review and there is most certainly no "showing of 'clear and convincing evidence' of a . . . legislative intent" to restrict access to judicial review. Abbott Laboratories v. Gardner, 387 U.S. 136, 141 (1967). * * *

Similarly, the Secretary's decision here does not fall within the exception for action "committed to agency discretion." This is a very narrow exception. Berger, Administrative Arbitrariness and Judicial Review, 65 Col.L.Rev. 55 (1965). The legislative history of the Administrative Procedure Act indicates that it is applicable in those rare instances where "statutes are drawn in such broad terms that in a given case there is no law to apply." S.Rep. No. 752, 79th Cong., 1st Sess., at 26 (1945).

Section 4(f) of the Department of Transportation Act and § 138 of the Federal–Aid Highway Act are clear and specific directives. Both the Department of Transportation Act and the Federal–Aid to Highway Act provide that the Secretary "shall not approve any program or project" that requires the use of any public parkland "unless (1) there is no feasible and prudent alternative to the use of such land, and (2) such program includes all possible planning to minimize harm to such park. . . ." This language is a plain and explicit bar to the use of federal funds for construction of highways through parks—only the most unusual situations are exempted.

Despite the clarity of the statutory language, respondents argue that the Secretary has wide discretion. They recognize that the requirement that there be no "feasible" alternative route admits of little administrative discretion. For this exemption to apply the Secretary must find that as a matter of sound engineering it would not be feasible to build the highway along any other route. Respondents argue, however, that the requirement that there be no other "prudent" route requires the Secretary to engage in a wide-ranging balancing of competing interests. They contend that the Secretary should weigh the detriment resulting from the destruction of parkland against the cost of other routes, safety considerations, and other factors, and determine on the basis of the importance that he attaches to these other factors whether, on balance, alternative feasible routes, would be "prudent."

But no such wide-ranging endeavor was intended. It is obvious, that in most cases considerations of cost, directness of route, and community disruption will indicate that parkland should be used for highway construction whenever possible. Although it may be necessary to transfer funds from one jurisdiction to another, there will always be a smaller outlay required from the public purse when parkland is used since the public already owns the land and there will be no need to pay for right-of-way. And since people do not live or work in parks, if a highway is built on parkland no one will have to leave his home or give up his business. Such factors are common to substantially all highway construction. Thus, if Congress intended these factors to be on an equal footing with preservation of parkland there would have been no need for the statutes.

Congress clearly did not intend that cost and disruption of the community were to be ignored by the Secretary. But the very existence of the statutes indicates that protection of parkland was to be given paramount importance. The few green havens that are public parks were not to be lost unless there were truly unusual factors present in a particular case or the cost or community disruption resulting from alternative routes reached extraordinary magnitudes. If the statutes are to have any meaning, the Secretary cannot approve the destruction of parkland unless he finds that alternative routes present unique problems.

Plainly, there is "law to apply" and thus the exemption for action "committed to agency discretion" is inapplicable. But the existence of judicial review is only the start: the standard for review must also be determined. For that we must look to § 706 of the Administrative Procedure Act, 5 U.S.C. § 706. A "reviewing court shall . . . hold unlawful and set aside agency action, findings, and conclusions found" not to meet six separate standards. In all cases agency action must be set aside if the action was "arbitrary, capricious, an abuse of discretion, or otherwise not in accordance with law" or if the action failed to meet statutory, procedural, or constitutional requirements. In certain narrow, specifically limited situations, the agency action is to be set aside if the action was not supported by "substantial evidence." And in other equally narrow circumstances the reviewing court is to engage in a de novo review of the action and set it aside if it was "unwarranted by the facts."

Petitioners argue that the Secretary's approval of the construction of I–40 through Overton Park is subject to one or the other of these latter two standards of limited applicability. First, they contend that the "substantial evidence" standard of § 706(2)(E) must be applied. In the alternative, they claim that § 706(2)(F) applies and that there must be a de novo review to determine if the Secretary's action was "unwarranted by the facts." Neither of these standards is, however, applicable.

Review under the substantial-evidence test is authorized only when the agency action is taken pursuant to a rulemaking provision of the Administrative Procedure Act itself, 5 U.S.C. § 553, or when the agency action is based on a public adjudicatory hearing. See 5 U.S.C. §§ 556, 557. The Secretary's decision to allow the expenditure of federal funds to build I–40 through Overton Park was plainly not an exercise of a rulemaking function. And the only hearing that is required by either the Administrative Procedure Act or the statutes regulating the distribution of federal funds for highway construction is a public hearing conducted by local officials for the purpose of informing the community about the proposed project and eliciting community views on the design and route. The hearing is nonadjudicatory, quasi-legislative in nature. It is not designed to produce a record that is to be the basis of agency action—the basic requirement for substantial-evidence review.

Petitioner's alternative argument also fails. De novo review of whether the Secretary's decision was "unwarranted by the facts" is authorized by § 706(2)(F) in only two circumstances. First, such de novo review is authorized when the action is adjudicatory in nature and the agency fact-finding procedures are inadequate. And, there may be independent judicial fact-finding when issues that were not before the agency are raised in a proceeding to enforce nonadjudicatory agency action. Neither situation exists here.

Even though there is no de novo review in this case and the Secretary's approval of the route of I–40 does not have ultimately to meet the substantial-evidence test, the generally applicable standards of § 706 require the reviewing court to engage in a substantial inquiry. Certainly, the Secretary's decision is entitled to a presumption of regularity. But that presumption is not to shield his action from a thorough, probing, in-depth review.

The court is first required to decide whether the Secretary acted within the scope of his authority. This determination naturally begins with a delineation of the scope of the Secretary's authority and discretion. As has been shown, Congress has specified only a small range of choices that the Secretary can make. Also involved in this initial inquiry is a determination of whether on the facts the Secretary's decision can reasonably be said to be within that range. The reviewing court must consider whether the Secretary properly construed his authority to approve the use of parkland as limited to situations where there are no feasible alternative routes or where feasible alternative routes involve uniquely difficult problems. And the reviewing court must be able to find that the Secretary could have reasonably believed that in this case there are no feasible alternatives or that alternatives do involve unique problems.

Scrutiny of the facts does not end, however, with the determination that the Secretary has acted within the scope of his statutory authority. Section 706(2)(A) requires a finding that the actual choice made was not "arbitrary, capricious, an abuse of discretion, or otherwise not in accordance with law." To make this finding the court must consider whether the decision was based on a consideration of the relevant factors and whether there has been a clear error of judgment. Although this inquiry into the facts is to be searching and careful, the ultimate standard of review is a narrow one. The court is not empowered to substitute its judgment for that of the agency.

The final inquiry is whether the Secretary's action followed the necessary procedural requirements. Here the only procedural error alleged is the failure of the Secretary to make formal findings and state his reason for allowing the highway to be built through the park.

Undoubtedly, review of the Secretary's action is hampered by his failure to make such findings, but the absence of formal findings does not necessarily require that the case be remanded to the Secretary. Neither the Department of Transportation Act nor the Federal–Aid Highway Act requires such formal findings. Moreover, the Administrative Procedure Act requirements that there be formal findings in certain rulemaking and adjudicatory proceedings do not apply to the Secretary's action here. See 5 U.S.C. §§ 553(a)(2), 554(a). And, although formal findings may be required in some cases in the absence of statutory directives when the nature of the agency action is ambiguous, those situations are rare. Plainly, there is no ambiguity here; the Secretary has approved the construction of I–40 through Overton Park and has approved a specific design for the project.

Thus it is necessary to remand this case to the District Court for plenary review of the Secretary's decision. That review is to be based on the full administrative record that was before the Secretary at the time he made his decision. But since the bare record may not disclose the factors that were considered or the Secretary's construction of the evidence it may be necessary for the District Court to require some explanation in order to determine if the Secretary acted within the scope of his authority and if the Secretary's action was justifiable under the applicable standard.

The court may require the administrative officials who participated in the decision to give testimony explaining their action. Of course, such inquiry into the mental processes of administrative decisionmakers is usually to be avoided. And where there are administrative findings that were made at the same time as the decision, there must be a strong showing of bad faith or improper behavior before such inquiry may be made. But here there are no such formal findings and it may be that the only way there can be effective judicial review is by examining the decisionmakers themselves.

The District Court is not, however, required to make such an inquiry. It may be that the Secretary can prepare formal findings that will provide an adequate explanation for his action. Such an explanation will, to some extent, be a *"post hoc* rationalization" and thus must be viewed critically. If the District Court decides that additional explanation is necessary, that court should consider which method will prove the most expeditious so that full review may be had as soon as possible.

Reversed and remanded.

NOTES AND QUESTIONS

1. *Overton Park* involved the type of agency decisionmaking known as "informal agency adjudication." Such decisions are generally reviewable.— Under what circumstances is judicial review unavailable? When, if ever, should court review be entirely precluded

Overton Park is interpreted to require the courts to engage in a three-part inquiry to perform their function of judicial review. What is this three-part inquiry?

The District Court, on remand in *Overton Park*, after a 25–day trial that involved affidavits of the Secretary of Transportation and the testimony of his subordinates, reversed the Secretary's decision and remanded the case to the agency for yet another determination. The Secretary was ultimately unable to show that there was no prudent or feasible alternative, and the road was not built.

2. *The Administrative Record.* For a court to exercise judicial review, there must be some kind of administrative record. In formal agency decisionmaking, whether rulemaking or adjudicatory, there will be an administrative record consisting of all the transcripts, exhibits, and papers filed in the proceeding. However. this will not be the case in informal agency decisionmaking.

Did an administrative record exist in *Overton Park*? Read carefully the Supreme Court's instruction that the District Court exercise "plenary review" of the Secretary's decision. Upon what is this "plenary review" to be based?

Overton Park is authority that agencies must compile an administrative record even in informal adjudicatory and informal rule-making proceedings. What is the required content of this administrative record?

Suppose the agency gathers *post hoc* rationalizations and statements of support for the decision. Will this be sufficient?

Must the agency compile formal and contemporaneous Findings of Fact and Conclusions of Law? In Camp v. Pitts, 411 U.S. 138 (1973), the Supreme Court answered this question by accepting a very brief explanation by the Comptroller of Currency for denying a branch bank application. The denial was based upon facts showing no need for additional banking services in the particular community. The Court noted that "[u]nlike *Overton Park*, in the present case there was a contemporaneous explanation of the agency decision. The explanation may have been curt, but it surely indicated the determinative reason for the final action taken: the finding that a new bank was an uneconomic venture * * *." (*Id.* at 143).

3. *Standards of judicial review.* Consider again the different standards of judicial review discussed in the *Overton Park* case. The court quotes from APA § 706, which contains the following six standards:

(A) arbitrary, capricious, an abuse of discretion, or otherwise not in accordance with law;

(B) contrary to constitutional right, power, privilege, or immunity;

(C) in excess of statutory jurisdiction, authority, or limitations, or short of statutory right;

(D) without observance of procedure required by law;

(E) unsupported by substantial evidence in a case subject to sections 556 and 557 of this title or otherwise reviewed on the record of an agency hearing provided by statute; or

(F) unwarranted by the facts to the extent that the facts are subject to trial de novo by the reviewing court.

Note that "substantial evidence review" is tied to sections 556 and 557 of the APA, which means that it is applicable if the agency decision was made after a trial-type hearing on the record, characteristic of both formal adjudication and formal "on the record" rulemaking. Substantial evidence review means that the court should not assess the facts of the matter itself, but should evaluate the *reasonableness* of the agency's fact finding. A court should consider the "whole record," which means it should evaluate not only evidence that supports the agency but also the relevant evidence both for and against the decision. Universal Camera Corp. v. NLRB, 340 U.S. 474 (1951).

A second important standard of review is "abuse of discretion" review under APA § 706(A). This standard of review is applied both to informal rulemaking under APA § 553 and informal adjudication such as the *Overton Park* decision. Under this standard of review the courts will demand a clear statement of the basis and purpose of the agency action. A spin-off of "abuse of discretion" review is the "hard look" or "reasoned decisionmaking" approach under which a court will demand that the agency's decision fall within the bounds of reasoned decisionmaking and will engage in a relatively close judicial analysis of the issues involved. See e.g., Baltimore Gas and Elec. Co. v. Natural Resources Defense Council, 462 U.S. 87 (1983) (upholding a Nuclear Regulatory Commission rule which did not place any negative environmental weight on the risks of long-term spent fuel storage in connection with the licensing of nuclear power plants.)

A third standard is de novo judicial review. Since *Overton Park*, de novo review has limited application. In what two instances is it still viable according to the Supreme Court?

F.   INTERPRETATION OF AGENCY AUTHORITY

Chevron, U.S.A., Inc. v. Natural Resources Defense Council

United States Supreme Court, 1984.
467 U.S. 837, 104 S.Ct. 2778, 81 L.Ed.2d 694.

■ Justice Stevens delivered the opinion of the Court.

In the Clean Air Act Amendments of 1977, Congress enacted certain requirements applicable to States that had not achieved the national air quality standards established by the Environmental Protection Agency (EPA) pursuant to earlier legislation. The amended Clean Air Act required these "nonattainment" States to establish a permit program regulating "new or modified major stationary sources" of air pollution. Generally, a permit may not be issued for a new or modified major stationary source unless several stringent conditions are met. The EPA regulation promulgated to implement this permit requirement allows a State to adopt a plantwide definition of the term "stationary source." Under this definition, an existing plant that contains several pollution-emitting devices may install or modify one piece of equipment without meeting the permit conditions if the alteration will not increase the total emissions from the plant. The question presented by these cases is whether EPA's decision to allow States to treat all of the pollution-emitting devices within the same industrial grouping as though they were encased within a single "bubble" is based on a reasonable construction of the statutory term "stationary source."

I

The EPA regulations containing the plantwide definition of the term stationary source were promulgated on October 14, 1981. Respondents filed a timely petition for review in the United States Court of Appeals for the District of Columbia Circuit. The Court of Appeals set aside the regulations. . . .

II

When a court reviews an agency's construction of the statute which it administers, it is confronted with two questions. First, always, is the question whether Congress has directly spoken to the precise question at issue. If the intent of Congress is clear, that is the end of the matter; for the court, as well as the agency, must give effect to the unambiguously expressed intent of Congress. If, however, the court determines Congress has not directly addressed the precise question at issue, the court does not simply impose its own construction on the statute, as would be necessary in the absence of an administrative interpretation. Rather, if the statute is silent or ambiguous with respect to the specific issue, the question for the court is whether the agency's answer is based on a permissible construction of the statute.[11]

"The power of an administrative agency to administer a congressionally created ... program necessarily requires the formulation of policy and the making of rules to fill any gap left, implicitly or explicitly, by Congress." Morton v. Ruiz, 415 U.S. 199, 231 (1974). If Congress has explicitly left a gap for the agency to fill, there is an express delegation of authority to the agency to elucidate a specific provision of the statute by regulation. Such legislative regulations are given controlling weight unless they are arbitrary, capricious, or manifestly contrary to the statute. Sometimes the legislative delegation to an agency on a particular question is implicit rather than explicit. In such a case, a court may not substitute its own construction of a statutory provision for a reasonable interpretation made by the administrator of an agency.

We have long recognized that considerable weight should be accorded to an executive department's construction of a statutory scheme it is

---

11. The court need not conclude that the agency construction was the only one it permissibly could have adopted to uphold the construction, or even the reading the court would have reached if the question initially had arisen in a judicial proceeding.

entrusted to administer, and the principle of deference to administrative interpretations

"has been consistently followed by this Court whenever decision as to the meaning or reach of a statute has involved reconciling conflicting policies, and a full understanding of the force of the statutory policy in the given situation has depended upon more than ordinary knowledge respecting the matters subjected to agency regulations.

" . . . If this choice represents a reasonable accommodation of conflicting policies that were committed to the agency's care by the statute, we should not disturb it unless it appears from the statute or its legislative history that the accommodation is not one that Congress would have sanctioned." United States v. Shimer, 367 U.S. 374, 382, 383 (1961).

In light of these well-settled principles it is clear that the Court of Appeals misconceived the nature of its role in reviewing the regulations at issue. Once it determined, after its own examination of the legislation, that Congress did not actually have an intent regarding the applicability of the bubble concept to the permit program, the question before it was not whether in its view the concept is "inappropriate" in the general context of a program designed to improve air quality, but whether the Administrator's view that it is appropriate in the context of this particular program is a reasonable one. Based on the examination of the legislation and its history which follows, we agree with the Court of Appeals that Congress did not have a specific intention on the applicability of the bubble concept in these cases, and conclude that the EPA's use of that concept here is a reasonable policy choice for the agency to make.

* * *

IV

The Clean Air Act Amendments of 1977 are a lengthy, detailed, technical, complex, and comprehensive response to a major social issue. A small portion of the statute expressly deals with nonattainment areas. The focal point of this controversy is one phrase in that portion of the Amendments [i.e., the meaning of the terms "major stationary source"—Eds.]

Basically, the statute required each State in a nonattainment area to prepare and obtain approval of a new SIP by July 1, 1979. In the interim those States were required to comply with the EPA's interpretative Ruling of December 21, 1976. The deadline for attainment of the primary NAAQS's was extended until December 31, 1982, and in some cases until December 31, 1987, but the SIP's were required to contain a number of provisions designed to achieve the goals as expeditiously as possible.

Most significantly for our purposes, the statute provided that each plan shall

"(6) require permits for the construction and operation of new or modified major stationary sources in accordance with section 173. . . ."

Before issuing a permit, § 173 requires (1) the state agency to determine that there will be sufficient emissions reductions in the region to offset the emissions from the new source and also to allow for reasonable further progress toward attainment, or that the increased emissions will not exceed an allowance for growth, (2) the applicant to certify that his other sources in the State are in compliance with the SIP, (3) the agency must determine that the applicable SIP is otherwise being implemented, and (4) the proposed source to comply with the lowest achievable emission rate (LAER).

The 1977 Amendments contain no specific reference to the "bubble concept." Nor do they contain a specific definition of the term "stationary source," though they did not disturb the definition of "stationary source" applicable by the terms of the Act to the NSPS [new source performance standard] program.

VI

As previously noted, prior to the 1977 Amendments, the EPA had adhered to a plantwide definition of the term "source" under a NSPS program. [After the Amendments, EPA considered changing its plantwide definition, but decided against it.]

In August 1980, however, the EPA adopted a regulation that, in essence, applied the basic reasoning of the Court of Appeals in these cases. The EPA took particular note of the two then-recent Court of Appeals decisions, which had created the bright-line rule that the "bubble concept" should be employed in a program designed to maintain air quality but not in one designed to enhance air quality. Relying heavily on those cases, EPA adopted a dual definition of "source" for nonattainment areas that required a permit whenever a change in either the entire plant, or one of its components, would result in a significant increase in emissions even if the increase was completely offset by reductions elsewhere in the plant. The EPA expressed the opinion that this interpretation was "more consistent with congressional intent" than the plantwide definition because it "would bring in more sources or modifications for review," 45 Fed. Reg. 52697 (1980), but its primary legal analysis was predicated on the two Court of Appeals decisions.

In 1981 a new administration took office and initiated a "Government-wide reexamination of regulatory burdens and complexities." In the context of that review, the EPA reevaluated the various arguments that had been advanced in connection with the proper definition of the term "source" and concluded that the term should be given the same definition in both nonattainment areas and PSD areas.

In explaining its conclusion, the EPA first noted that the definitional issue was not squarely addressed in either the statute or its legislative history and therefore that the issue involved an agency "judgment as how to best carry out the Act." It then set forth several reasons for concluding that the plantwide definition was more appropriate. It pointed out that the dual definition "can act as a disincentive to new investment and modernization by discouraging modifications to existing facilities" and "can actually retard progress in air pollution control by discouraging replacement of older, dirtier processes or pieces of equipment with new, cleaner ones." Moreover, the new definition "would simplify EPA's rules by using the same definition of 'source' for PSD, nonattainment new source review and the construction moratorium. This reduces confusion and inconsistency." Finally, the agency explained that additional requirements that remained in place would accomplish the fundamental purposes of achieving attainment with NAAQS's as expeditiously as possible. These conclusions were expressed in a proposed rulemaking in August 1981 that was formally promulgated in October.

VII

In this Court respondents expressly reject the basic rationale of the Court of Appeals' decision. That court viewed the statutory definition of the term "source" as sufficiently flexible to cover either a plantwide definition, a narrower definition covering each unit within a plant, or a dual definition that could apply to both the entire "bubble" and its components. It interpreted the policies of the statute, however, to mandate the plantwide definition in programs designed to maintain clean air and to forbid it in programs designed to improve air quality. Respondents place a fundamentally different construction on the statute. They contend that the text of the Act requires the EPA to use a dual definition—if either a component of a plant, or the plant as a whole, emits over 100 tons of pollutant, it is a major stationary source. They thus contend that the EPA rules adopted in 1980, insofar as they apply to the maintenance of the quality of clean air, as well as the 1981 rules which apply to nonattainment areas, violate the statute.

Statutory Language

The definition of the term "stationary source" in § 111(a)(3) refers to "any building, structure, facility, or installation" which emits air pollution. This definition is applicable only to the NSPS program by the express terms of the statute; the text of the statute does not make this definition applicable to the permit program. * * *

* * * Although the definition in that section is not literally applicable to the permit program, it sheds as much light on the meaning of the word "source" as anything in the statute. As respondents point out, use of the words "building, structure, facility, or installation," as the definition of source, could be read to impose the permit conditions on an individual building that is a part of a plant. A "word may have a character of its own not to be submerged by its association." Russell Motor Car Co. v. United States, 261 U.S. 514, 519 (1923). On the other hand, the meaning of a word must be ascertained in the context of achieving particular objectives, and the words associated with it may indicate that the true meaning of a word must be ascertained in the context of achieving particular objectives, and the words associated with it may indicate that the true meaning of the series is to convey a common idea. The language may reasonably be interpreted to impose the requirement on any discrete, but integrated, operation which pollutes. This gives meaning to all of the terms—a single

building, not part of a larger operation, would be covered if it emits more than 100 tons of pollution, as would any facility, structure, or installation. Indeed, the language itself implies a "bubble concept" of sorts: each enumerated item would seem to be treated as if it were encased in a bubble. * * *

We are not persuaded that parsing of general terms in the text of the statute will reveal an actual intent of Congress. We know full well that this language is not dispositive; the terms are overlapping and the language is not precisely directed to the question of the applicability of a given term in the context of a larger operation. To the extent any congressional "intent" can be discerned from this language, it would appear that the listing of overlapping, illustrative terms was intended to enlarge, rather than to confine, the scope of the agency's power to regulate particular sources in order to effectuate the policies of the Act.

Legislative History

In addition, respondents argue that the legislative history and policies of the Act foreclose the plantwide definition, and that the EPA's interpretation is not entitled to deference because it represents a sharp break with prior interpretations of the Act.

Based on our examination of the legislative history, we agree with the Court of Appeals that it is unilluminating. * * * We find that the legislative history as a whole is silent on the precise issue before us. It is, however, consistent with the view that the EPA should have broad discretion in implementing the policies of the 1977 Amendments.

More importantly, that history plainly identifies the policy concerns that motivated the enactment; the plantwide definition is fully consistent with one of those concerns—the allowance of reasonable economic growth—and, whether or not we believe it most effectively implements the other, we must recognize that the EPA has advanced a reasonable explanation for its conclusion that the regulations serve the environmental objectives as well. Indeed, its reasoning is supported by the public record developed in the rulemaking process, as well as by certain private studies.

Our review of the EPA's varying interpretations of the word "source"—both before and after the 1977 Amendments—convinces us that the agency primarily responsible for administering this important legislation has consistently interpreted it flexibly—not in a sterile textual vacuum, but in the context of implementing policy decisions in a technical and complex arena. The fact that the agency has from time to time changed its interpretation of the term "source" does not, as respondents argue, lead us to conclude that no deference should be accorded the agency's interpretation of the statute. An initial agency interpretation is not instantly carved in stone. On the contrary, the agency, to engage in informed rulemaking, must consider varying interpretations and the wisdom of its policy on a continuing basis. Moreover, the fact that the agency has adopted different definitions in different contexts adds force to the argument that the definition itself is flexible, particularly since Congress has never indicated any disapproval of a flexible reading of the statute.

Significantly, it was not the agency in 1980, but rather the Court of Appeals that read the statute inflexibly to command a plantwide definition for programs designed to maintain clean air and to forbid such a definition for programs designed to improve air quality. The distinction the court drew may well be a sensible one, but our labored review of the problem has surely disclosed that it is not a distinction that Congress ever articulated itself, or one that the EPA found in the statute before the courts began to review the legislative work product. We conclude that it was the Court of Appeals, rather than Congress or any of the decision-makers who are authorized by Congress to administer this legislation, that was primarily responsible for the 1980 position taken by the agency.

The arguments over policy that are advanced in the parties' briefs create the impression that respondents are now waging in a judicial forum a specific policy battle which they ultimately lost in the agency and in the 32 jurisdictions opting for the "bubble concept," but one which was never waged in the Congress. Such policy arguments are more properly addressed to legislators or administrators, not to judges.

In these cases the Administrator's interpretation represents a reasonable accommodation of manifestly competing interests and is entitled to deference: the regulatory scheme is technical and complex, the agency considered the matter in a detailed and reasoned fashion, and the decision involves reconciling conflicting policies. Congress intended to accommodate both interests, but did not do so itself on the level of specificity presented by these cases. Perhaps that body consciously desired the Administrator to strike the balance at this level, thinking that those with great expertise and charged with responsibility for administering the provision would be in a better position to do so; perhaps it simply did not consider the question at this level; and perhaps Congress was unable to forge a coalition on either side of the question, and those on each side decided to take their chances with the scheme devised by the agency. For judicial purposes, it matters not which of these things occurred.

Judges are not experts in the field, and are not part of either political branch of the Government. Courts must, in some cases, reconcile competing political interests, but not on the basis of the judges' personal policy preferences. In contrast, an agency to which Congress has delegated policy making responsibilities may, within the limits of that delegation, properly rely upon the incumbent administration's views of wise policy to inform its judgments. While agencies are not directly accountable to the people, the Chief Executive is, and it is entirely appropriate for this political branch of the Government to snake such policy choices—resolving the competing interests which Congress itself either inadvertently did not resolve, or intentionally left to be resolved by the agency charged with the administration of the statute in light of everyday realities.

When a challenge to an agency construction of a statutory provision, fairly conceptualized, really centers on the wisdom of the agency's policy, rather than whether it is a reasonable choice within a gap left open by

Congress, the challenge must fail. In such a case, federal judges—who have no constituency—have a duty to respect legitimate policy choices made by those who do. The responsibilities for assessing the wisdom of such policy choices and resolving the struggle between competing views of the public interest are not judicial ones: "Our Constitution vests such responsibilities in the political branches."

We hold that the EPA's definition of the term "source" is a permissible construction of the statute which seeks to accommodate progress in reducing air pollution with economic growth. "The Regulations which the Administrator has adopted provide what the agency could allowably view as . . . [an] effective reconciliation of these twofold ends. . . ."

NOTES AND QUESTIONS

1. *Judicial Review of Questions of Law. Chevron* is one of the most frequently cited administrative law cases. There is good reason for this fact—agencies frequently must find statutory support for the things they do and for the ways they do them. Those adversely affected by agency action often challenge agency legal interpretations to delay or block the action. *Chevron* analysis is common because it provides a framework for this judicial review. Should courts, as generalists, be reluctant to intrude into the complex and controversial policy making of specialized, expert agencies? Does the Supreme Court's test allow a court to refuse deference to an agency's interpretation of the law? Under what circumstances? Cutting through the legal verbiage, what policies support judicial review of agency actions, and to what extent do those policies justify or permit deference to the agency on matters of statutory interpretation? Does judicial review improve the rationality of government decisionmaking? Do the courts exercise a "quality control" function? Is such review worth the cost in terms of administrative efficiency? Consider the following possible benefits:

1. Preventing agencies from ignoring their statutory mandate.
2. Ensuring that all required procedures are followed.
3. Protecting against undue political influence or other bias.
4. Ensuring the openness ("transparency") of agency decisions.
5. Improving the quality of an agency's technical judgments.

Is strong judicial review of agency action more or less appropriate for environmental than for other agency decisions? Why?

2. *The Scope of Chevron.* A series of cases have reached the U.S. Supreme Court focusing upon the question of identifying the limits of *Chevron* deference owed to administrative practice in applying a statute. These cases contain a great deal of importance for EPA and other environmental agencies because they issue a large number of formal regulations, guidance documents, and interpretations of their many authorities.

In U.S. v. Mead Corp., 121 S.Ct. 2164 (2001), the Court considered the challenge brought by an importer of day planners over the tariff classification given the product by the U.S. Customs Services. The tariff ruling was issued by way of a "ruling letter" to Mead which had the effect of reclassifying imported day planners and making them subject to a 4% tariff when previously there had been none. Mead challenged the tariff classification and found federal judges to be receptive to their argument that the Customs Service ruling deserved no judicial deference. *Chevron* deference now appears to represent a high degree of insulation from intrusive judicial review of agency interpretations. Following the *Mead Corporation* case, this status will be accorded in a more limited range of circumstances. Justice Souter wrote that:

> Administrative implementation of a particular statutory provision qualifies for *Chevron* deference when it appears that Congress delegated authority to the agency generally to make rules carrying the force of law, and that the agency interpretation claiming deference was promulgated in the exercise of that authority.

Id. at 2171. How could an agency demonstrate this congressional intent? The Court mentioned the nature of the power granted to the agency— specifically mentioning adjudication, notice-and-comment rulemaking or "some other indication of comparable congressional intent." *Id.* It seems then, that this highest degree of judicial deference carrying with it the "effect of law" stems from express congressional authorizations providing for relatively formal administrative procedure "tending to foster fairness and deliberation...." *Id.* at 2172. To reinforce the Court's conclusion, Justice Souter also found a lack of precedential impact and a non-binding effect of the action on third parties as additional grounds for denying *Chevron* deference.

The *Mead Corporation* decision emphasized that there were several levels of judicial deference to administrative interpretation of authority with *Chevron* deference being the highest level. This spectrum contains other levels of deference including "some deference" as specified in Skidmore v. Swift & Co., 323 U.S. 134 (1944). Less deference, but still "some" is granted when "the regulatory scheme is highly detailed, and [the agency] can bring the benefit of specialized experience to bear on the subtle question...." *Id.* at 2175–6. Skidmore v. Swift & Co., 323 U.S. 134 (1944). The degree of deference under *Skidmore* depends upon the "power to persuade" or the respect accorded to it on judicial review would be reflected in "the [agency] writer's thoroughness, logic and expertise, its fit with prior interpretations, and other sources of weight." Mead, 121 S.Ct. at 2176. How would EPA defend an attack on an interpretive guidance document if *Skidmore* deference was all that would be accorded to it?

G.   REVIEWING AGENCY PROCEDURAL CHOICES

Portland Audubon Society v. The Endangered Species Committee

United States Court of Appeals, Ninth Circuit, 1993.
984 F.2d 1534.

■ REINHARDT, CIRCUIT JUDGE.

The Endangered Species Act requires that "[e]ach Federal agency shall ... insure that any action authorized, funded or carried out by such agency

... is not likely to jeopardize the continued existence of any endangered species ... or result in the destruction or adverse modification of [critical] habitat of such species." However, if the Secretary of the Interior ("Secretary") finds that a proposed agency action would violate § 1536(a)(2), an agency may apply to the Committee for an exemption from the Endangered Species Act. The Committee was created by the Endangered Species Act for the sole purpose of making final decisions on applications for exemptions from the Act, § 1536(e), and it is composed of high level officials. Because it is the ultimate arbiter of the fate of an endangered species, the Committee is known as "The God Squad."

The Secretary must initially consider any exemption application, publish a notice and summary of the application in the *Federal Register,* and determine whether certain threshold requirements have been met. If so, the Secretary shall, in consultation with the other members of the Committee, hold a hearing on the application ... and prepare a written report to the Committee. Within thirty days of receiving the Secretary's report, the Committee shall make a final determination whether or not to grant the exemption from the Endangered Species Act based on the report, the record of the Secretary's hearing, and any additional hearings or written submissions for which the Committee itself may call. An exemption requires the approval of five of the seven members of the Committee.

On May 15, 1992, the Committee approved an exemption for the Bureau of Land Management for thirteen of forty-four timber sales. It was only the second exemption ever granted by the Committee. [Pursuant to 16 U.S.C. § 1536 (n)] the environmental groups filed a timely petition for review in this court on June 10, 1992. The environmental groups have Article III standing if for no other reason than that they allege procedural violations in an agency process in which they participated.

Both in their petition and in this motion the environmental groups contend that improper ex parte contacts between the White House and members of the Committee tainted the decision-making process. They base their charges on two press reports, one by Associated Press ("AP") and one by Reuters, and on the facts stated in the declaration of Victor Sher, lead counsel for the environmental groups. Published on May 6, 1992, the AP and Reuters accounts reported that, according to two anonymous administration sources, at least three Committee members had been "summoned" to the White House and pressured to vote for the exemption. In his declaration filed August 25, 1992, Sher stated that his conversations with "several sources within the Administration," who asked for anonymity, revealed that the media reports were accurate, and further that the pressure exerted by the White House may have changed the vote of at least one Committee member. Sher declared that his sources indicated that, in addition to in person meetings, at least one Committee member had "substantial on-going contacts with White House staff concerning the substance of his decision on the application for exemption by telephone and facsimile, as well as through staff intermediaries.'' He also declared that he had learned from his sources that White House staff members had made substantial comments and recommendations on draft versions of the ''Endangered Species Committee Amendment,'' a part of the Committee's final decision. For the purposes of the present motion, the Committee neither admits nor denies that these communications occurred.

* * *

The environmental groups contend that the Endangered Species Act incorporates by reference the ex parte communications ban of the APA and forbids ex parte contacts with members of the Committee regarding an exemption application. The ex parte prohibition is set forth at 5 U.S.C. § 557(d)(1). Section 557(d)(*l*) is a broad provision that prohibits any ex parte communications relevant to the merits of an agency proceeding between ''any member of the body comprising the agency'' or any agency employee who ''is or may reasonably be expected to be involved in the decisional process'' and any ''interested person outside the agency.'' 5 U.S.C. §§ 557(d)(1)(A)–(B). The purpose of the ex parte communications prohibition is to ensure that '' 'agency decisions required to be made on a public record are not influenced by private, off-the-record communications from those personally interested in the outcome.' ''

It is of no consequence that the sections of the Endangered Species Act governing the operations of the Committee fail to mention the APA. The APA itself mandates that its provisions govern certain administrative proceedings. By its terms, section 554 of the APA, which pertains to formal adjudications, applies to ''every case of adjudication required by statute to be determined on the record after [the] opportunity for an agency hearing.'' 5 U.S.C. § 554(a). That section also provides that any hearing conducted and any decision made in connection with such an adjudication shall be ''in accordance with sections 556 and 557 of this title.'' 5 U.S.C. § 554(c)(2).

In other words, by virtue of the terms of APA § 554, sections 556 and 557 are applicable whenever that section applies. Accordingly, the ex parte communications prohibition applies whenever the three requirements set forth in APA § 554(a) are satisfied: The administrative proceeding must be 1) an adjudication; 2) determined on the record; and 3) after the opportunity for an agency, hearing.[13] The question is, therefore, are those three conditions met here? We find our answer primarily in the language of section 1536(h)(1)(A) of the Endangered Species Act.

We conclude that the first requirement of APA § 554(a) is satisfied. Certain administrative decisions closely resemble judicial determinations

---

13. Section 553(c) of the APA makes the ex parte communications prohibition applicable formal rulemaking proceedings as well. Under § 553(c), where rules are required by statute to be made on the record after opportunity for agency hearing (formal rulemaking), §§ 556 and 557 apply. In its brief the government contends that Committee decisions are formal rulemaking. While we do not agree, we note that even if the Committee's argument were correct, the ex parte communications prohibition would still apply via § 553(c). Thus, for practical purposes the government all but concedes the applicability of the ex parte communications prohibition to Committee proceedings.

and, in the interests of fairness, require similar procedural protections. Where an agency's task is "to adjudicate disputed facts in particular cases," an administrative determination is quasi-judicial. By contrast, rulemaking concerns policy judgments to be applied generally in cases that may arise in the future; it is *sometimes* guided by more informal procedures.[15] Under the Endangered Species Act the Committee decides whether to grant or deny specific requests for exemptions based upon specific factual showings. Thus, the Committee's determinations are quasi judicial. Accordingly, they constitute "adjudications" within the meaning of § 554(a).

The legislative history of the Endangered Species Act confirms our conclusion in this respect. The Senate committee report accompanying the 1982 amendments to the Endangered Species Act stated that "the Endangered Species Committee is designed to function as an *administrative court of last resort.*" (emphasis added). The Report states that the Committee's decision will be based, in part, upon a "formal adjudicatory hearing." The Report also makes clear that the Committee's duty is to be the ultimate arbiter of conflicts that the parties involved have been unable to resolve.

The language of the Endangered Species Act explicitly meets the second requirement of section 554(a). Section 1536(h)(1)(A) of the Act mandates that the Committee make its final determination of an exemption application "on the record." No further discussion is required on this point.

It is equally clear that the third requirement of APA § 554(a) is satisfied here. Section 1536(h)(1)(A) of the Endangered Species Act also requires that the Committee's final decision be "based on the report of the Secretary, *the hearing* held under (g)(4) of this section [(the Secretary's hearing)] and on such other testimony or evidence as it may receive." Wherever the outer bounds of the "after opportunity for an agency hearing" requirement may lie, we hold that where, as here, a statute provides that an adjudication be determined at least is part *based on* an agency hearing, that requirement is fulfilled.

Because Committee decisions are adjudicatory in nature, are required to be on the record, and are made after an opportunity for an agency hearing, we conclude that the APA's ex parte communication prohibition is applicable. This result is similar to the one we reached in a case involving formal rulemaking, Central Lincoln Peoples' Util. Dist. v. Johnson (9th Cir.1984). There we held that because Congress required rate decisions under the Pacific Northwest Electric Power Conservation Act to be made on the record after a hearing, the procedural protections of the APA were triggered, including the ban on ex parte communications. In that case the applicable provision was APA § 553(c), which, in language almost identical to that contained in § 554(c)(2), provides that "[w]hen *rules* are required by statute to be made on the record after opportunity for an agency hearing, sections 556 and 557 of this title apply." (emphasis added). Similarly, the pertinent language of the Endangered Species Act, section

---

15. There are two types of rulemaking proceedings—formal and informal. The APA does not bar ex parte communications in informal rulemaking proceedings.

1536(h)(1)(A), parallels the language of the statute that we considered in *Central Lincoln.* Thus, the statutory language of the Endangered Species Act, like that of the Pacific Northwest Electric Power Conservation Act, is sufficient to trigger the APA's ex parte communication prohibition.

Conclusion

In sum, we hold that the Committee's proceedings regarding an application for exemption from the Endangered Species Act are governed by those provisions of the APA applicable to formal adjudications and, in particular, by the prohibition on ex parte communications.... Therefore, the environmental groups' motion for discovery is DENIED but the matter is REMANDED to the Committee for further proceedings.

NOTES AND QUESTIONS

1. *The Portland Audubon Society* case considers the adequacy of a government agency's procedures. Both agency procedure and agency action are subject to judicial review. In fact, APA § 706(2)(D) specifically provides that courts may set aside agency actions that are "without observance of procedure required by law." 5 U.S.C. § 706(2)(D). Agency failure to follow the procedural requirements of its own authorizing statute, its own agency rules or the APA, can result in a court remand. Should an agency's substantive decision be reversed and remanded for every possible procedural violation including minor, non-prejudicial ones? Should judicial intervention depend on the nature of the agency's action?

Why was it significant that the *Portland Audubon Society* court categorized the exemption procedure of the Endangered Species Committee as "adjudication" rather than rulemaking? Does the answer reflect the APA's view of procedural fairness within the context of agency quasi-judicial behavior determining individual rights and duties? Why should fairness have a different meaning in agency rulemaking or other forms of informal action? As the losing party in the *Portland Audubon Society* case, would you feel fairly treated by the exemption decision process if the White House contacts to the committee had been allowed? How should the damage of such illicit contacts be remedied after the fact?

2. Much of environmental law focuses upon the activities of administrative agencies such as EPA in developing and applying environmental protection policies by way of congressional authorization. Often, the study of environmental law concentrates on the growth of regulatory policy and the review of agency rulemaking in the courts. Increasingly, however, EPA undertakes agency adjudication in the enforcement and implementation of the environmental laws for which it has responsibility. EPA's system of adjudication applies to two important aspects of its environmental programs: 1) permitting appeals and 2) challenges to administratively-imposed penalties. In addition, the agency conducts administrative hearings for a broad range of other decisions including debarment from government contracting, ocean dumping permits and RCRA Corrective Action Orders.

EPA's administrative judicial system has two levels: 1) Administrative Law Judges (ALJs) and 2) an Environmental Appeals Board (EAB). There are 12 ALJs who preside over matters which are required by the Administrative Procedure Act § 554(a) to be "determined on the record after an opportunity for an agency hearing." The ALJs, called Presiding Officers, act as trial judges making findings of fact, drawing conclusions of law and issuing judgments in the form of decisions. One important function they serve is to rule on EPA requests for civil penalties to be imposed against polluters under at least 10 environmental statutes. Environmental enforcement has recently stressed administrative action. A good example of this increased emphasis on agency-administered penalties is Clean Water Act § 309(g) [33 U.S.C. § 1319(g)]. While EPA annually refers some 200 to 300 cases to the Department of Justice for civil enforcement, it brings 5,000 to 6,000 administrative enforcement actions each year.

Following EPA's Consolidated Rules of Practice, the ALJ conducts a quasi-judicial proceeding that contains the government's complaint, settlement negotiations, answers, discovery, motions, hearings and decisions. See 40 C.F.R. Part 22. The government must prove its case by "a preponderance of the evidence." *Id.* at § 22.24. Appeals from an ALJ decision may be taken to EPA's Environmental Appeals Board which is the agency's final decisionmaker in administrative appeals. The EAB was formed in 1992 in a desire to better deal with an expanding administrative docket. It conducts *de novo* review of ALJ decisions and may reverse, modify or affirm that penalty determination. Appeal from the EAB to the federal courts is determined by the specific environmental statute involved.

As in the *Portland Audubon Society* case, EPA's Consolidated Rules take a strong stand against *ex parte* discussions regarding the merits of a proceeding. The impartiality of the decisionmaker is important. Any such communication made during the proceeding "shall be served upon all other parties." 40 C.F.R. § 22.8. Why take this disclosure-based approach to such actions? What type of ex parte contacts are more likely to occur, contact by EPA or by the defendant? Is disclosure sufficient to deter or cure the effects of such contacts? If the proceedings are intended to be "efficient, fair and impartial," as the EPA rules declare, should the sanctions for *ex parte* contacts be greater?

H. MAKING "REASONABLE" REGULATORY CHOICES

Safe Buildings Alliance v. Environmental Protection Agency

United States Court of Appeals, District of Columbia Circuit, 1988.
846 F.2d 79.

■ EDWARDS, CIRCUIT JUDGE.

Since 1979, the Environmental Protection Agency ("EPA") has provided technical assistance to elementary and secondary school officials in identifying and controlling asbestos in school buildings. Although EPA required that school buildings be inspected for asbestos-containing material ("ACM") and that the results of those inspections be reported to school officials and parents, it supplied only imprecise nonbinding advice concerning the repair or removal of ACM. EPA also declined to say what ambient concentrations of asbestos posed a danger to the health of a teachers, administrators and maintenance workers. As a result, some school officials did nothing, perhaps endangering the health of school building occupants. Others harkened to the self-interested advice of newly created asbestos removal firms and ordered removal of all ACM. Those removals were sometimes unnecessary, at times even detrimental, since slipshod work may increase ambient concentrations of asbestos.

Congress enacted the Asbestos Hazard Emergency Response Act of 1986 ("AHERA"), Pub. L. No. 99–519, 100 Stat. 2970 (codified at 15 U.S.C. §§ 2641–2654 (Supp. IV 1986)), in an attempt to right this highly confused and potentially dangerous state of affairs. Bemoaning "the lack of regulatory guidance" from EPA, 15 U.S.C.§ 2641(a)(l), Congress commanded the agency to issue regulations *within 360 days* covering school inspections, the accreditation of inspectors and management planners, and the determination and implementation of appropriate response actions. 15 U.S.C. § 2643(a).

EPA promulgated regulations prior to the statutory deadline. The petitioners in this case, former manufacturers of ACM, contend that these regulations fail in several ways to fulfill AHERA's mandate. For reasons stated herein, we deny their petitions for review.

I. Background

AHERA is an admittedly hasty response to a widespread and pressing problem. Given the nature of the assignment, there was no way for EPA to achieve absolute precision in regulations dealing with asbestos hazards. Indeed, the statute does not even appear to contemplate regulatory *precision*. It requires EPA to "promulgate regulations describing a response action in a school building under the authority of a local educational agency, using the least burdensome methods which protect human health and the environment." 15 U.S.C. § 2643(d)(l). At first blush, this crucial provision appears to demand nothing more than a list of appropriate responses to ACM in various circumstances. Moreover, AHERA contains incorporating references to EPA's existing guidelines, which merely describe different possible responses, see 15 U.S.C. § 2643(d)(2)–(5), and only requires that local educational agencies, not EPA itself, develop asbestos management plans for buildings under their control. See 15 U.S.C. § 2643(i)(l).

Other aspects of the statute, however, suggest that more specific advice is required. The legislative "findings" in AHERA openly criticize EPA for offering inadequate guidance. See 15 U.S.C. § 2641(a). Moreover, AHERA states explicitly that, "[i]n determining the least burdensome methods, the Administrator shall take into account local circumstances, including occupancy and use patterns within the school building and short-and long-term costs." 15 U.S.C. § 2643(d)(1). How EPA is to make such determinations and how specific they are to be, given that AHERA covers over 30,000 schools across the country in divergent circumstances, Congress neglected to say.

Complicating EPA's job further is the uncertainty concerning the dangers of exposure to low levels of asbestos. Senator Stafford, one of AHERA's chief sponsors, noted that "[t]he American Cancer Society, reflecting prevailing scientific opinion, testified that there is no known safe level of asbestos exposure and that efforts should be made to avoid even low-level exposure." 132 CONG. REC. at S15,064 (daily ed. Oct. 3, 1986). He went on to emphasize that AHERA only requires EPA to identify response actions that are *sufficient* to protect human health; it need not prove that a particular response action is absolutely *necessary* to protect human health. *Id.* at S15,066. "Doubt," he said, "should be resolved in favor of affording greater protection." *Id.* Senator Stafford further emphasized that EPA need not establish a quantitative measure of safety before it permitted or required certain response actions.

Given Congress' awareness of the dearth of precise information about the hazards of exposure to asbestos, the tight timetable it imposed on EPA, its requirement that EPA conduct further studies to ascertain "whether there is a need to establish standards for, and regulate asbestos exposure in, public and commercial buildings," 15 U.S.C. § 2653; see 15 U.S.C. § 2641(b)(3), and its short-term focus on the sufficiency rather than the necessity of certain response actions to protect human health, AHERA was plainly intended as the framework for an evolving administrative response to the perils posed by ACM in schools. Congress impelled EPA to act quickly to address existing hazards. In doing so, it accorded EPA considerable leeway in determining adequate methods of dealing with extant problems. Congress expected EPA to improve on the guidelines it had hitherto offered to school officials, but it did not—because it could not—say exactly how fast or how far EPA should go in rendering its counsel more precise. Congress contemplated, however, that EPA would refine its initial regulatory approaches over time, as more information about the dangers of asbestos became available, as the relative merits of different abatement techniques became known, and as the costs of various responses became clearer. See Joint Explanatory Statement, 132 CONG. REC. at S15,065. It is against the backcloth of this legislative design that we must assess the petitioners' objections to EPA's attempt to embody AHERA's aims in detailed regulations.

II. Analysis

A. *EPA's Alleged Failure to Define The Least Burdensome Response Action*

The petitioners fault EPA for failing to specify a single least burdensome response action in the various situations described in 15 U.S.C. § 2643(d)(2)–(5). In addition, they contend that EPA abdicated its responsibility by leaving it to school officials to ascertain the least burdensome abatement methods in the unique circumstances of their schools, following their receipt of reports from accredited inspectors and management planners.

We reject these contentions. Indeed, it is highly ironic that industry representatives assail EPA for supplying inadequate guidance to school officials when their counsel have assured us that those officials are now thoroughly satisfied with the regulatory guidance provided by EPA. Confronted by the Sisyphean task of reconciling Congress' general demand that it describe "a response action ... using the least burdensome methods which protect human health and the environment," 15 U.S.C. § 2643(d)(*l*), with Congress' injunction to "take into account local circumstances, including occupancy and use patterns within the school building and short-and long-term costs" in over 30,000 cases, *id.*, EPA reasonably concluded that some compromises were necessary. In the preamble to its final rule, EPA stated that "a rigid response action decision structure is not appropriate for this rule, primarily because many asbestos hazard situations are too circumstantial and appropriate response actions are too 'hazard specific' to fit neatly into a discrete set of prescriptive categories." 52 Fed. Reg. at 41,838 (1987). Instead, EPA offered a list of specific responses that it adjudged sufficient to protect human health, along with a *method* by which school officials should be able to determine the least burdensome response in the buildings they supervise.

We find that EPA's regulations effect a reasonable, faithful interpretation of AHERA's somewhat contradictory commands.[3] As the petitioners concede, "Congress understood that EPA could not visit thousands of schools and write a specific plan for managing [ACM] in each one." What EPA could—and did—do was require that schools be searched for ACM by inspectors accredited in conformity with EPA regulations; that officials of schools containing ACM obtain a report detailing abatement options and recommendations by a management planner (also accredited in accordance with EPA regulations); that those officials, in formulating a management plan, choose from among the set of response actions found by EPA to be sufficient to protect human health and the environment; and that their plan be approved by the state governor, thereby assuring further oversight. This seems to us a careful, intelligent attempt to meet Congress' confusing demands. In light of the deference due EPA in these circumstances, we cannot but reject the petitioners' objection.

B. *EPA's Failure to Establish Safe Levels of Asbestos Exposure*

The petitioners argue that, even if EPA need only define response actions sufficient to protect human health and the environment in a variety of situations, it cannot do so without first determining what levels of

---

3. The rigid "time limits set by Congress indicate that a reviewing court should accord the [EPA] an extra dollop of deference." *Puerto Rico Maritime Shipping Auth.* *v. Federal Maritime Comm'n,* 678 F.2d 327, 336 (D.C.Cir.) (1982). We have done so in reviewing this case.

asbestos exposure are safe. Yet, EPA has not pronounced any ambient concentrations safe or unsafe. Hence, they contend, EPA's regulations lack a rational basis, and must be set aside as arbitrary and capricious.

This argument is meritless. Congress explicitly recognized that experts presently disagree over what levels of exposure are safe. See 132 Cong. Rec. at S15,064–66. Nevertheless, it stated that EPA's existing guidelines should serve as minimum standards in devising appropriate response actions. Congress nowhere said that EPA need rely exclusively or even mainly on air monitoring techniques in selecting response actions, or that it need establish a quantitative measure that it deems safe. Indeed, the legislative history affirmatively suggests an intent not to impose such requirements. See id. Congress left these matters for EPA to decide, and commissioned further studies of the hazards of asbestos exposure. Congress envisioned growing precision in EPA's regulations over time, as more information becomes available, but it did not intend that EPA do nothing until scientific experts agreed on a quantitative measure of safety. Indeed, the petitioners' insistence that EPA construct a quantitative model before it do anything else offends common sense as well as congressional intent, for the *potential* hazards posed by presently undamaged ACM obviously could not be quantified or measured by air monitoring techniques.

It should also be borne in mind that EPA's regulations were framed against the backdrop of past proceedings to establish safe levels of asbestos. This is not a case where an agency, confronted by conflicting evidence, merely threw up its hands and declined to act. Rather, EPA conducted hearings in an attempt to determine the dangers associated with different concentrations of asbestos. Because Congress required it to define response actions that are sufficient to protect human health (erring on the side of caution), not to find the absolute minimum responses necessary to accomplish that end, EPA considered it unnecessary to resolve prevailing disagreements among scientific experts. Instead, it selected response actions that Congress and most experts deemed sufficient to protect those who study or work in school buildings. In view of the special deference owed to an agency's expert judgment on matters at the frontiers of science, . . . we can hardly brand EPA's failure to establish a safe level of exposure or to require the use of air monitoring arbitrary and capricious.

C. *EPA's Decision to Permit Removal of ACM in All Cases*

Section 763.90(a) of EPA's regulations reads in part: "Nothing in this section shall be construed to prohibit removal of [ACM] from a school building at any time, should removal be the preferred response action of the local education agency."

The petitioners advance two objections to this provision. They argue, first, that EPA possesses no evidence showing that the removal of ACM is *ever* beneficial. The available evidence, they say, reveals that even properly conducted removals *raise* asbestos levels, and that EPA should therefore have forbidden removals. Second, they argue that, even if their first point is unsound, EPA should not have permitted removals when current asbestos levels are below the "clearance level" that must be attained whenever an abatement action is performed, or when they are not the least burdensome method of curing a school's asbestos problem.

EPA considered and reasonably rejected the first of these arguments. See 52 Fed. Reg. at 41,844. It noted that studies showing increases in asbestos levels following removal were based on a small sample of cases, in at least some of which abatement actions were *not* done properly. EPA's regulations covering removal were intended to prevent this occurrence in the future. To the extent that the petitioners have a quarrel with EPA's regulations, their dissatisfaction should be directed at those provisions that were designed to preclude unsafe and incomplete removals, not at the clause permitting removals in circumstances where school officials consider removals prudent. The petitioners, however, have not challenged those provisions.

The conclusion that EPA acted properly in not banning removals appears inescapable in light of the fact that Congress apparently assumed that removal would always be an option. For example, Congress set as a minimum the response actions described in EPA's existing guidelines and those response actions include removal in almost every case. See 15 U.S.C. § 2643(d)(2)–(5). Senators Stafford and Moynihan also mentioned removal as an option for local educational agencies. See 132 CONG. REC. at S15,066, S15,068. The petitioners' broadside attack on the permissibility of removal, based in part on studies involving removal techniques that are not now authorized and despite contrary indications in the legislative history, is unavailing.

The petitioners' second argument is patently mistaken. It may be the case that in some instances well-performed removal is merely innocuous rather than beneficial. But that fact, although a sound reason for school officials not to waste money on needless removals, is not an adequate reason for EPA to proscribe removals in some or all cases. The legislative history renders it abundantly clear that EPA, as Senator Baucus said, "should not discourage a school from going ahead and eliminating their long-term asbestos problem if school officials should decide that is the best course of action." 132 CONG. REC. at S15,067; see id. at S15,066 (remarks of Senator Stafford). Moreover, Congress stated clearly that AHERA does not constrain school officials to use the least burdensome method found by EPA to be sufficient to protect human health and the environment. EPA's regulation permitting removal in all cases is thus fully in accord with congressional intent.

III.   Conclusion

EPA's regulations defining least burdensome response actions, establishing a method by which management plans are to be formulated and implemented, and permitting removal of ACM if school officials so desire represent a reasonable interpretation of AHERA's less than pellucid demands. Accordingly, we deny the petitions for review.

NOTES AND QUESTIONS

1. Agencies, such as EPA, are often asked to act in the face of incomplete or contradictory data. Administrative agencies do not exist in a world of perfect information and they must make judgements based upon, among other things, their expertise, external pressure and partial data. The *Safe Buildings Alliance* case presents an example of a situation where EPA was asked to fashion a regulatory response to a perceived health and safety problem affecting school buildings and students across the nation. While operating under a short, defined time limit, the agency chose to adopt a flexible strategy of offering a list of responses sufficient to protect public health and a method for local use to determine the "least burdensome" method of response. How could EPA intelligently set asbestos response requirements without first determining "safe" ambient concentrations for the substance? Why wasn't EPA's approach found to be arbitrary and capricious? Why was the D.C. Circuit so accepting of this flexibility? Why wasn't the court more demanding of EPA's choice and its justification?

2. Many EPA decisions involve the analysis of scientific and engineering information and result in the making of important regulatory decisions based upon these analyses. When these technically complex and economically expensive judgements are later challenged in court, judges must evaluate both the agency's procedure and substantive choices. The substantive review of EPA decisions asks federal judges, who are legal generalists by training and experience, to evaluate expert agency choices. This deep judicial involvement in highly technical matters has been the source of controversy throughout the modern history of environmental law. During the first decade of EPA's Clean Air Act regulation, two respected appellate judges—Harold Leventhal and David Bazelon—debated this issue in Ethyl Corp. v. EPA, 541 F.2d 1 (D.C.Cir.1976). Summarized, the debate went this way:

> Judge Bazelon argued that "technically illiterate" judges should not get involved in the substance of agency decisions. His solution to the need for courts to supervise agency decisionmaking was purely procedural: "in cases of great technological complexity, the best way for courts to guard against unreasonable or erroneous administrative decisions is not for the judges themselves to scrutinize the technical merits of each decision. Rather, it is to establish a decisionmaking process that assures a reasoned decision that can be held up to the scrutiny of the scientific community."

> Judge Leventhal disagreed. He argued that substantive review was, in fact, necessary if judges were to carry out their statutory and constitutional duties: "The substantive review of administrative action is modest, but it cannot be carried out in a vacuum of understanding. Better no judicial review at all than a charade that gives the imprimatur without the substance of judicial confirmation that the agency is not acting unreasonably." Judge Leventhal went on to emphasize that he was not advocating wholesale substitution of judicial judgements for that of the agency. He concluded, however, that: "on issues of substan-

tive review, on conformance to statutory standards and requirements of rationality, the judges must act with restraint. Restraint, yes, abdication, no."

Alfred C. Aman & William T. Mayton, Administrative Law 492 (1993). Should judges focus on agency processes to assure a "reasoned decision" as Judge Bazelon suggested? Or, should judges employ the "modest" substantive review of administrative action recommended by Judge Leventhal? Should judges "second-guess" technical choices made by agencies following modern administrative procedures and practices? Should special, technically-trained judges serve on a Science and Technology Court to consider theses cases? How can a legal generalist determine the "rationality" of a scientifically-based agency choice?

SECTION 3. INNOVATIONS IN ADMINISTRATIVE PRACTICE: NEGOTIATED RULEMAKING

A. INTRODUCTION

The functions of administrative agencies are varied. In the area of environmental law, agencies such as the Environmental Protection Agency (EPA) often implement congressional environmental policy through the issuance of administrative regulations or other rules. After their issuance following a lengthy process of informal rulemaking, detailed above, such rules become the subject of judicial review of the agency's action. Since government regulations often require expensive or time-consuming responses by firms and individuals, they are frequently targeted for attack in court. These rulemaking challenges are brought to contest EPA or another agency's method of developing the regulation or the substance of the regulation itself. Litigation can extend the regulatory development period for years and can impose substantial costs both on the government in defending itself and on the regulated industry or interest group in challenging the regulation.

Negotiated rulemaking emerged in the 1980s as an alternative to the standard notice and comment method informal rulemaking authorized by federal environmental statutes and by the APA. It was hoped that negotiated rulemaking, also known as regulatory negotiation, would reduce the time and expense of rulemaking as well as the conflict that often produced litigation. The concept of involving interested parties in agency policy development had been recognized as early as 1919 by the Federal Trade Commission and New Deal industrial association codes. Later in the mid–1970s the idea was given modern attention by Secretary of Labor John Dunlop but it is a 1982 report authored by Philip J. Harter for the Administrative Conference of the United States that is credited with promoting the concept. See Philip J. Harter, Negotiating Regulations: A Cure for Malaise, 71 Geo. L.J. 1, 30 (1982). The Harter idea built on the notion that establishing a process of consensus building would limit later conflict and law suits. This was considered to be a significant advantage since it had been frequently asserted that during the 1980s nearly 80% of the 300 regulations issued by EPA each year ended up in court. A consensus-based process was thought to be one way to expedite necessary and legitimate administrative regulations.

During the 1980s, eight federal agencies, including EPA, the Department of the Interior and the Nuclear Regulatory Commission, initiated or completed a regulatory negotiation without specific statutory authority. In 1990, Congress enacted the Negotiated Rulemaking Act (NRA) 5 U.S.C. § 561–570, which authorized, yet did not require, the use of the negotiated rulemaking process. It remains an option for agencies to take in the rulemaking process. In addition to the NRA, since 1990 Congress has passed legislation in over ten instances mandating the use of regulatory negotiation in specific applications for HUD, the NRC, the Department of Health and Human Services, and the Department of the Interior. In the Clinton Administration, the negotiated rulemaking process was strongly emphasized as a way of improving federal agency practices, initially in Vice President Gore's 1993 National Performance Review and later in President Clinton's Executive Order 12,866 and related memoranda. In 1995, as part of the Clinton administration's effort to "reinvent" federal environmental regulation, EPA was directed to review its regulations in order to determine appropriate candidates for regulatory negotiation. Nonetheless, one academic study determined that during the period from 1983–1996, agency use of negotiated rulemaking had actually been slight, finding that,

1. Seventeen federal agencies had initiated at least one negotiated rulemaking.

2. Each of these agencies had announced an average of 4 proceedings.

3. EPA was the leading agency with 18 such procedures including 12 final rules.

4. There were 35 final rules issued using negotiated rulemaking out of a total of 47,603 federal rules or .07%.

5. Nearly 20% of negotiated rulemaking procedures were abandoned prior to reaching any consensus.

Cary Coglianese, Assessing Consensus: The Promise and Performance of Negotiated Rulemaking, 46 Duke L.J. 1255, 1277 (1997).

B.   NEGOTIATED RULEMAKING PRACTICE

Negotiated rulemaking supplements the notice-and-comment procedures of the APA with a negotiation process that takes place before an agency issues a proposed regulation. The agency establishes a negotiated rulemaking committee comprised of representatives from regulated firms, trade associations, citizen groups, and other affected organizations, as well as members of the agency staff. The committee meets publicly to negotiate a proposed rule. The services of outside conveners or facilitators are also provided for in the statute. If the committee reaches consensus, the agency will then adopt the consensus rule as its proposed rule and proceeds according to the usual notice-and-comment procedures specified in the APA. Proponents of negotiated rulemaking claim that these procedures— which encourage affected parties to reach an agreement at the outset—will decrease the amount of time it takes to develop regulations and, more notably, reduce or eliminate subsequent litigation.

Whether or not to pursue the development of a regulation by way of negotiated rulemaking is a discretionary judgment for each agency. The NRA sets out a list of factors to guide an agency in deciding whether the use of the negotiated rulemaking procedure is "in the public interest." Section 563 states that the agency shall consider whether,

(1) there is a need for a rule;

(2) there are a limited number of identifiable interests that will be significantly affected by the rule;

(3) there is a reasonable likelihood that a committee can be convened with a balanced representation of persons who

   (A) can adequately represent the interests identified under paragraph (2); and

   (B) are willing to negotiate in good faith to reach a consensus on the proposed rule;

(4) there is a reasonable likelihood that a committee will reach a consensus on the proposed rule within a fixed period of time;

(5) the negotiated rulemaking procedure will not unreasonably delay the notice of proposed rulemaking and the issuance of the final rule;

(6) the agency has adequate resources and is willing to commit such resources, including technical assistance, to the committee; and

(7) the agency, to the maximum extent possible consistent with the legal obligations of the agency, will use the consensus of the committee with respect to the proposed rule as the basis for the rule proposed by the agency for notice and comment.

5 U.S.C. § 563. What policies seem to be reflected in the selection of a topic worthy of negotiated rulemaking treatment?

Section 564 requires that public notice of planned negotiated rulemaking proceedings be placed in the *Federal Register* and appropriate trade and specialized publications. Persons or interest groups believing that they have not been adequately represented on the negotiating committee must be given the opportunity to apply for membership. However, the final composition of the committee still remains within the discretion of the agency. The overarching duty of the committee is to reach "a consensus" concerning the proposed rule and if such a consensus is reached, it must be communicated to the agency in the form of a report containing the proposed rule.

The committee may adopt procedures for its operation without regard to the requirements of APA § 553. The NRA concludes with § 570,

Any agency action relating to establishing, assisting, or terminating a negotiated rulemaking committee under this subchapter shall not be subject to judicial review. Nothing in this section shall bar judicial review of a rule if such judicial review is otherwise provided by law. A rule which is the product of negotiated rulemaking and is subject to judicial review shall not be accorded any greater deference by a court than a rule which is the product of other rulemaking procedures.

What are the multiple goals of § 570? Why was it necessary for Congress to specifically set these goals out in statutory language?

Has the use of regulatory negotiation reduced the rate of "rule litigation" as proponents claimed it would? The Clinton Administration's National Performance Review claimed that it had brought the rate down from 80% to 20% although this statistic has been disputed in the academic literature. Several of the rules developed with negotiated rulemaking have been challenged in court but so far only one judicial opinion has discussed the process used to adopt the regulation. See USA Group Loan Services, Inc. v. Riley, 82 F.3d 708 (7th Cir.1996) (rule upheld).

C. DIFFERING VIEWS OF REGULATORY NEGOTIATION

Philip J. Harter, Fear of Commitment: An Affliction of Adolescents
46 Duke L.J. 1398–1404 (1997).

III. The Use of Consensus in Policymaking

* * * Fifteen years ago, when the theory of negotiated rulemaking was just emerging, I predicted a number of major benefits from the practice. Among them was the fact that the parties would be able to participate directly and immediately in the decision, thereby providing a legitimacy that is missing from hybrid rulemaking. In addition, the costs of developing the rule may be lower since the parties would not have to engage in as much adversarial research and positioning. The parties could focus on the issues that actually separate them and on the issues of importance to them. "Rulemaking by negotiation can reduce the time and cost of developing regulations by emphasizing practical and empirical concerns rather than theoretical predictions." The parties have the experience and ability to focus on the details necessary to make a rule work day-to-day in the field. Interestingly, the lack of judicial review was *not* advocated as a prime benefit. It would be a likely ancillary benefit of the parties' mutual acceptance of the rule and its ensuing legitimacy, but was not an end in itself.

Such were the predictions before any reg negs were actually undertaken. Formal evaluations are extraordinarily expensive and face the difficulties inherent in making counter-factual predictions (i.e., what would have happened if some other process were used to develop the rule), or finding a suitably analogous rule with which to compare a given proceeding. As a result, few formal evaluations have been conducted, so that it is difficult to determine in a rigorous way the extent to which the theory has been borne out.

One major evaluation has been undertaken to compare negotiated rules at the EPA with those developed by the traditional notice-and-comment process. The study is currently being conducted for the EPA by Cornelius M. Kerwin, Dean of the School of Public Affairs at American University and Professor Laura I. Langbein. They have released a draft report of their analysis of the reg neg portion of their study. Their initial conclusions include:

> Based on the data presented above, negotiated rulemaking is successful on several critical dimensions. It is widely perceived by participants as an effective means for developing regulations on virtually all important qualitative dimensions. The criteria established in literature and law for the selection of candidates for reg neg appear to be relevant in the selection process used by EPA, although their importance appears to vary from case to case and the discretion exercised by key Agency officials in the use of techniques is obviously considerable. The opportunity to participate in the process appears to be extended broadly, albeit not universally, and EPA or the facilitator it secured were frequently identified as an initiator of participation.

> The process of negotiation itself emerges as a very powerful vehicle for learning what the participants in the process value highly, and there are many types of information that is exchanged. The interviews suggest further that what is learned has long-term value and is not confined to a particular rulemaking.... The negotiation process employs a number of devices to subdivide issues, such as working groups and caucuses, that were viewed as effective by a substantial number of respondents. And the use of non-committee observers serves as a device to expand participation without inflating the negotiating groups past workable limits. Facilitators were generally viewed as competent, unbiased and providing a number of services that promoted consensus.

> Most participants believe their participation had a substantial effect on the agreement that was produced and report that the opportunity to have an impact on the outcome was one of the aspects of the process they considered most valuable. Moreover, a careful review of the experience with negotiated rulemakings indicates that those predictions have, indeed, been realized in diverse settings. Negotiated rulemakings have been used by agencies to develop rules they knew would be controversial but which were required by statute to be issued in a very short period and for rules for which the customary notice-and-comment process simply had not worked. * * * In some instances, the reg neg committees have been able to develop rules in a relatively expeditious time when the issues have been languishing on the agency's dockets for years—precisely because the agency has not been able to resolve the underlying controversies. And, in one of the few instances in which a negotiated rule was closely analogous to a rule developed

by traditional means, the negotiated rulemaking took only half as long to draft the rule and cost only half as much.

The rules that emerge through reg neg reflect a shop-floor insight and expertise. Hence, they can develop considerable innovation and take account of issues that would likely escape the attention of an agency in a traditional rulemaking. EPA's equipment leak standard is such an example. So is the steel erection standard: the committee identified a vast number of issues that would greatly improve safety beyond the relatively narrow set of issues initially foreseen by the Occupational Safety and Health Administration (OSHA).

Interestingly, there is some indication that rules that emerge from reg negs are more stringent than those the agency would have been able to issue on its own; nevertheless, these rules are cheaper to implement precisely because the committee can focus on ways to get the greatest return. As for judicial review, there has *never* been a judicial challenge to a negotiated rule where the agency issued the rule as negotiated and the parties agreed not to challenge it.

Unlike other forms of administrative procedure, reg negs and other means of consensus building have few fixed rules. Their hallmark is their flexibility: they are highly adaptive and can be modified to take account of changing circumstances. While pliable, they are not formless. The benefits of negotiated rulemaking have resulted from a careful attention to detail and a few fundamental precepts. Since both the integrity of the process and its success turn on their observance, it is worth emphasizing them here.

William Funk, Bargaining Toward the New Millennium: Regulatory Negotiation and the Subversion of the Public Interest

46 Duke L.J. 1351–1374 (1997).

IV. Negotiated Rulemaking And The Perversion Of The Administrative Process

The above discussion concludes that negotiated rulemaking can be employed consistently with all formal legal requirements and restrictions applicable to agency rulemaking. To say this, however, is not to say that negotiated rulemaking is consistent with the norms of the administrative process. To the contrary, the theory and principles of regulatory negotiation are inconsistent with the theory and principles of the APA.

A. *The Rule of Law*

First, consider the theory and principles of the APA. Implicit in the APA is the notion of the rule of law. Agencies exist to carry out the law. Their statutory directions may be specific or general, but the agencies' actions are justified and legitimized by their service to those directions. Even under the doctrine announced in *Chevron U.S.A., Inc., v. Natural*

Resources Defense Council, Inc., requiring judicial deference to an agency's reasonable interpretations of ambiguous statutes, the agency's actions proceed from an implicit delegation from Congress to make law, consistent with the agency's authorizing statute. The statute is not just a brake or anchor on agency autonomy; it is the source and reason for the agency's actions.

Now consider regulatory negotiation. The law still exists, but the law is now merely a limitation on the range of bargaining. The parties to the negotiation are not serving the law, and the outcome of the negotiation is not legitimized by its service to the law. The regulation that emerges from negotiated rulemaking is, as Harter said, legitimized by the agreement of the parties. Accordingly, Harter argued, if the parties agree that a rule should contain a particular provision, the legality of that provision should not be determined by traditional methods. Instead, the courts should defer to an agreement of the parties that is not manifestly inconsistent with the purpose of the authorizing statute. Harter explains why:

> The parties are typically better able [than courts] to determine "what works" within the theory of the statute and hence what is the best way of achieving its overall goal. Or, a provision may be included in a statute to benefit a particular interest. If that interest does not insist on its full exercise as part of the agreement, ... [the fact] [t]hat they agreed indicates the interest achieved the protection sought in the statute. . . .

In short, law becomes nothing more than the expression of private interests mediated through some governmental body. Public choice theory changes from a descriptive to a normative theory.

Of course, supporters of negotiated rulemaking do not encourage or even sanction negotiations that bargain for outcomes beyond statutory authority. Nevertheless, as the above language suggests, and the actual practice confirms there is a subtle (and sometimes not so subtle) dynamic in the negotiation process that diminishes the sanctity of the law as both the source of agency authority and its limit.

In an article I wrote in 1987, I described how in one negotiated rulemaking the dynamics of the negotiating process resulted in substantial deviations from the law. Not only did the agency fail to police the negotiations in this regard, it was an active participant in the violation of the law. This occurred because it was in the agency's interest to achieve consensus. The agency's desire and need for consensus to achieve a rule that would not be contested made it willing to bargain for unauthorized provisions, so long as it furthered the goal of consensus. Prior to the regulatory negotiation, the agency had exercised its independent judgement as to certain legal requirements and had withstood contrary pleas by interested groups. In the context of the negotiations, however, the role of the agency had changed. In the new context, the agency's goal was to achieve consensus.

B.   *The Agency as Responsible Actor*

A second principle central to the APA is the role of the agency as the responsible actor. The agency is not a broker or mediation service. In the famous words of a classic administrative law case, the agency's "role does not permit it to act as an umpire blandly calling balls and strikes for adversaries appearing before it; the right of the public must receive active and affirmative protection." Nor is the agency merely an enforcer of private agreements. Rather the agency is the authority responsible for and empowered to achieve the statutory design.

This is not, however, the role of the agency in regulatory negotiation. To the contrary, negotiated rulemaking reduces the agency to the level of a mere participant in the formulation of the rule and essentially denies the agency any responsibility beyond effectuating the consensus achieved by the group. This is reflected in ACUS's recommendation, based upon Harter's study, that the agency representative should participate in the negotiation. This is not because the agency is responsible for the rulemaking, but because "[t]he agency is indisputably a party in interest and ... would be eligible for participation in negotiations." Harter conceded that "[a]gency participation can be viewed as inconsistent with the agency's role as the sovereign decisionmaker because participation may cloud its ability to determine independently what is the best regulation."

The agency, however, should not let this inconsistency persuade it to act in negotiations in a manner that reflects its sovereign decisionmaking capacity. ACUS cautioned that an agency should not be able to dominate the negotiations by virtue of its power to promulgate the final rule. As Harter explains, if the agency is able to issue edicts or specify acceptable outcomes, its role "is inconsistent with the concept of negotiations, in which the parties define issues and agree on acceptable [solutions]." Accordingly, the agency's participation should not differ in kind from that of the other parties in interest. In other words, it should bargain and trade its "interests" (the public interest) in the same way the other participants may trade their interests. It is likely that Judge Posner shared this perception of the process in *USA Group Loan Services v. Riley*, when he indicated that he doubted the propriety of the agency's agreement to abide by the consensus.

Harter recognizes the possible objection to this role as inconsistent with the concept of the agency as sovereign decisionmaker. "Under a view of the agency as the decisionmaker, as in the New Deal vision of the agency, it would be illegitimate for the agency to negotiate with the parties in interest." His answer to this is two-fold. First, the agency's representative, Harter says (and ACUS recommends), should not be allowed to bind the agency. Second, the agency would retain the authority to assess whether the consensus rule reflected the agency's policies sufficiently to merit publication. These answers, however, are disingenuous at best. As to the first response, the fact that the agency's representative cannot bind the agency does not distinguish the agency's representative from any other participant in the regulatory negotiation. Harter himself recognizes that no "single constituency would be bound irrevocably by the position taken by its representative." Instead, each participant must constantly keep his principals informed as to the direction he and the group are taking. Thus, the agency participant is no different from the non-agency participants.

As to Harter's second response, the agency's formal power not to propose the consensus rule does not change the fact that the agency *agrees* to publish the consensus rule before the negotiations begin. Certainly the agency has the power to reject a consensus rule which it agreed beforehand to publish, which it participated in developing, and to which its representative agreed to—a representative who is supposed to be a "senior official" of the agency who was keeping his principals abreast of the group's actions. However, unless an agency acts in bad faith and violates a written undertaking made at the beginning of the negotiation, it is bound to publish the consensus rule as its proposed rule, a rule adopted by a group in which the agency was a mere participant—bargaining, negotiating, and compromising just like all the other participants to achieve a rule agreed to by all.

Again, the formalities remain in place; the agency is titularly acting in a sovereign capacity. But the dynamics of the process all run in the opposite direction. The incentives that suggest regulatory negotiation in the first instance undermine any serious attempt by the agency to retain the role of agency-as-responsible-actor. If it rejects or blocks consensus by invoking its "authority," it engenders bad will among those it has induced to come to the table; it largely negates any benefit of the negotiation and may have wasted valuable time and resources on a futile endeavor; and it is back to "square one" with its rulemaking. In short, the dynamics of "getting to yes" pervert the role of the agency as sovereign.

C.   *Rulemaking as an Undertaking of Instrumental Rationality*

The APA as drafted, but even more as construed by the courts over its half century of experience, requires agencies to engage in a process designed to elicit solutions to problems. Originally, there was a perhaps naive view that expert, non-political agencies could find finite solutions to real world problems. Indeed, lack of confidence in this vision formed the basis for the passage of the APA itself, a compromise piece of legislation designed to constrain the discretion of agencies through procedural regularity and judicial oversight. The formal rulemaking procedures rather clearly embody a structure for the rational determination of facts and their application to legal requirements in a reasoned manner: the use of instrumental rationality.

* * *

Here, a practice, if not theory, of regulatory negotiation has managed to accommodate the requirements of the APA and judicial review for instrumental rationality, but it has done so in an insidious way, by having agency preamble writers make up rationalizations for decisions made on other grounds. The subversion of the principles of the APA is manifest when the outward and visible rationale masks the reality of bargained for exchanges.

D.   *The Search for the Public Interest*

Underlying the APA and all other statutes directing or authorizing agencies to adopt regulations is the notion that the agency will be acting in the public interest. In some cases the public interest may be largely undefined, as in the charge to the Federal Trade Commission to protect against "[u]nfair methods of competition" or to the Federal Communications Commission to regulate the broadcast spectrum as required by the "public convenience, interest, or necessity." In other cases it may be relatively better defined, as when a statute requires an agency to set an air emission standard as "the best system of emission reduction which (taking into account the cost of achieving such reduction and any nonair quality health and environmental impact and energy requirements) the Administrator determines has been adequately demonstrated." Nevertheless, in all cases much is left to the discretion and judgment of the agency to determine how to best achieve the statutory goals. Congress presumes that the exercise of that discretion and judgment will aim to further the public interest. Today we might interpret the oath required of all officers to support the Constitution as nothing less than an oath to serve the public interest pursuant to the statutes and Constitution of the United States.

What is meant by the public interest is not always clear. I mean it to be the best interests of the nation, the people, the body politic. So expressed, it is clear that determining the public interest is not a task one achieves; it is a goal one strives for. It encompasses the ideal notions of a James Landis as well as the more modern notions of civic republicans. Whatever it is, it is to be distinguished from the public choice or interest representation models of the administrative state.

Public choice theory arose out of studies of legislative and administrative processes to explain why the outcomes of those processes did not seem to achieve the public interest, but rather to reflect the capture of government processes, by special interests. The answer was that legislators and bureaucrats would act in their own self-interest (to get reelected or to enhance their agency's power and responsibility) and therefore would ally themselves with whatever special interest would further that end. In this sense, public choice theory is a descriptive, not a normative theory, although it has been used to argue for deregulation on the grounds that the unregulated market will be more efficient than government regulation and at least as moral. The conflict between public choice theory and a public interest concept of regulation is obvious.

Interest representation theory, on the other hand, is both descriptive and normative. It starts from the proposition that there is no "objective public interest," no "ascertainable national welfare as a meaningful guide to administrative decision." This assumption implies that agencies are adrift in their discretion, and the means traditionally employed to control their discretion are merely illusory. To supplant those traditional means of control, the interest representation model suggests that organized interests can themselves constrain agency discretion through expansive participation in agency processes. The courts play an important role in administrative decisionmaking by protecting all parties' rights to adequate, participation and directing agencies to attend to the interests of those participating. Interest representation theory implies that the true metal of regulation will emerge out of the fire of clashing interests. The agency is merely the filter through which this process operates. The relationship between interest representation theory and the theory of negotiated rulemaking is obvious. How interest representation theory could lead to public choice theory also seems obvious: the clash of interests results in one interest capturing the regulatory process.

It is not the place of this Article to address the descriptive validity of either public choice or interest representation models of the administrative state. This Article does maintain, however, that modern regulatory systems and statutes do not reflect a conscious embrace of the cynicism of public choice theory or an endorsement of the normative values of interest representation theory. This conclusion with respect to public choice theory should be self evident. If public choice theory were both accepted and consciously acknowledged by lawmakers it would destroy any legitimacy their laws would otherwise have. This conclusion with respect to interest representation is less obvious.

Many laws besides the Negotiated Rulemaking Act encourage and support methods to provide a voice for affected interests in developing rules that affect them. The APA's notice-and-comment requirement is an obvious beginning; the National Environmental Policy Act's notice-and-comment procedure for environmental impact statements is another. The various substantive statutes including hybrid rulemaking provisions are other examples. Moreover, the generic requirements beyond the APA for rule-makings of various types, such as the Regulatory Flexibility Act, the Unfunded Mandates Reform Act, and the Paperwork Reduction Act are still other examples. Nevertheless, an inspection of all these laws rebuts any suggestion that these enhanced public participation requirements substi-tute for the agency's responsibility to engage in reasoned decisionmaking in search of the public interest. For example, environmental impact statement requirements are consistently described as intended to improve the *agen-cy's* decisionmaking. The substantive statutes with hybrid procedures like-wise are laden with requirements to assure the *agency* is making a rational decision, not just adding up the votes of the interested parties. And the primary focus of generic rulemaking requirements beyond the APA is cost/benefit or risk assessment analysis to assure that the rules adopted are plainly adapted to their purpose—the public interest. Thus, while modern rulemaking seeks full participation by interested persons, the agency still determines the public interest. Modern rulemaking has not substituted interest representation theory for traditional notions of administrative rulemaking.

The same could be said for negotiated rulemaking. After all, the process has been carefully crafted to fit within traditional rulemaking requirements. Here, again, however, no matter how faithful negotiated rulemaking may be to the formalities of traditional rulemaking, its effect is to subvert the principles of that rulemaking. This is reflected once again in Harter's revealing statement that the legitimacy of the regulation "would lie in the overall agreement of the parties." Note the use of the word "parties." The rulemaking has "parties" who make the agreement. They make the agreement among and for themselves. They bargain and deal to achieve their own interests. There is no mention of the "public." The wisdom and fairness of the rule is equated with the satisfaction of the parties. Public law has been subtly transformed into private law relationships.

Moreover, negotiated rulemaking succeeds if the parties reach consensus. To the extent that agencies are taught that regulatory negotiation is a process to be used in the place of conventional notice-and-comment rulemaking, agencies learn that achieving consensus of the parties is the measure of success. The statistics in Professor Coglianese's article further confirm this lesson—if the consensus is not reached, or if the agency does not abide by the consensus, the likelihood of lawsuits increases, and the "benefits" of negotiated rulemaking evaporate. Thus, agencies are influenced to see their role not as serving the public interest, but as generating a consensus among the parties to the negotiation. Public choice theory is not resisted; it is adopted with a vengeance.

The effect on the culture and identification of the agency may outlive the particular negotiation. That is, when the negotiation is over, the consensus is obtained, and the rule is promulgated, where is the agency's interest in assuring compliance with the rule, in assuring that the rule continues to serve its purposes? The agency does not have the same sense of responsibility for the rule, because it does not reflect the agency's considered determination as serving the public interest; instead, it reflects the bargain of the parties. It is the parties' rule, not the agency's.

NOTES AND QUESTIONS

1. *Reg-Neg by the Numbers.* EPA has been the federal agency most actively utilizing the regulatory negotiation technique having employed it to produce 16 negotiated rulemakings since 1983. U.S. EPA, Negotiated Rulemaking at the EPA 4 (1998). This represents nearly 1/3 of all federal agency reg-negs. Although not heavily used, it does seem that EPA's use of regulatory negotiation is here to stay.

2. *To Join or Not to Join?* Assume that you represent an industry group or an environmental organization and that EPA has just announced in the *Federal Register* notice its intent to convene a negotiated rulemaking committee on a regulatory topic of interest to your group. The agency has informally discussed participation in the reg-neg process with your organization. Assume that the board of directors of your group wishes to discuss participation. How would you respond to the many questions that might be raised? Consider the following examples:

1) A question has been raised about the time and resource commitments needed for the reg-neg process. How much data and analysis would be needed for the process and how much time would be consumed in committee meetings? How would the resource drains compare to those commitments needed for participation in a conventional notice and comment rulemaking?

2) If the group participates in the reg-neg, can it later challenge in court the final rule that emerges from the committee assuming that EPA adopts it formally? What if the reg-neg committee develops a rule that significantly diverges from our group's interests? Can the group block adoption of such a rule by the committee? If not, can it withdraw from the committee so as not to be associated with a rule with which it disagrees?

3) Will other committee members negotiate in good faith? Should the group be wary that other interests may "gang up" against it? If the group joins the reg-neg committee, will it be able to form effective, working coalitions with other, like-minded committee members? If the group participates, will it have to take negotiating positions that will alienate other committee member allies and jeopardize future organizational relationships?

4) What other issues might be raised at this preliminary stage by members of the board of directors?

3. *Regulatory Negotiation and the Public Interest.* Do you agree with Professor Funk that EPA (and other agencies employing regulatory negotiation) abdicated its responsibilities as a servant of the public interest? Is there something inherently wrong with allowing parties who have an interest in a regulatory outcome to actually serve on the working committee that drafts the regulation? Does the assurance that committees will be balanced make the procedure truly reflective of the public interest? Does the fact that EPA can reject or ignore the reg-neg committee's report adequately protect the public interest?

CHAPTER FOUR

WHO'S IN CHARGE OF ENVIRONMENTAL DECISIONS?

In our federal system, responsibility for and control over decisions affecting the environment are shared among federal, state and local governments and private parties. This chapter examines the contours and controversies over that distribution of power. The federal government obtains its regulatory power from the federal constitution. States possess, as an attribute of sovereignty, a generalized police power that supports environmental regulation in the absence of countervailing federal law. Local governments obtain their authority from the states. They often have primary responsibility for land use decisions.

Of course, not all decisions affecting the environment are made by government at any level. Many are made by private actors in the marketplace. Government authority over these decisions is limited by practical considerations, may be theoretically undesirable, and may be effectively precluded in some circumstances by the takings clause of the federal constitution.

SECTION 1. FEDERALISM: NATIONAL AND STATE POWERS

A. HISTORICAL AND THEORETICAL BACKGROUND

The appropriate division of power over environmental policy between national and state or local governments has long been debated. Environmental problems were once virtually the exclusive province of state and local law. Despite judicial expansion of federal powers in the early to mid-twentieth century, not until the 1970s did federal environmental regulation become pervasive. The explosion of federal environmental law in the 1970s was driven by growing recognition of the interstate effects of pollution, coupled with the widespread perception that states were not adequately controlling environmental harms. Although they imposed federal minimum environmental requirements and erected a substantial federal regulatory structure, the federal environmental laws of the 1970s retained an important role for the states. Many of them, including the Clean Air Act, Clean Water Act, and Resource Conservation and Recovery Act, relied on "cooperative federalism," setting minimum environmental standards but allowing states to assume responsibility for implementing those standards.

In the 1990s, the tides of federalism reversed. Beginning in 1995, the Supreme Court decided a series of cases cutting back on the scope of federal power. At the same time, political pressures for "devolution" of environmental authority to the states increased. These pressures helped drive the Republican takeover of Congress in 1994, and the "Contract with America" Republican agenda, centered on reducing the federal regulatory presence. Although the "Contract" did not produce any major environmental legislation, devolution of environmental power remains a major political issue, played out not only in the legislature but in the environmental agencies.

Richard B. Stewart, Pyramids of Sacrifice? Problems of Federalism in Mandating State Implementation of National Environmental Policy

86 Yale L.J. 1196, 1210–22 (1977).

As a nation, we have traditionally favored noncentralized decisions regarding the use and development of the physical environment. This presumption serves utilitarian values because decisionmaking by state and local governments can better reflect geographical variations in preferences for collective goods like environmental quality and similar variations in the costs of providing such goods. Noncentralized decisions also facilitate experimentation with differing governmental policies, and enhance individuals' capacities to satisfy their different tastes in conditions of work and residence by fostering environmental diversity.

Important nonutilitarian values are also served by noncentralized decisionmaking. It encourages self-determination by fragmenting governmental power into local units of a scale conducive to active participation in or vicarious identification with the processes of public choice. This stimulus to individual and collective education and self-development is enriched by the wide range of social, cultural and physical environments which noncentralized decisionmaking encourages. * * * [T]he moral virtues of diversity have special force in the realm of environmental policy, for the condition of the natural environment and the corresponding nature and extent of commercial and industrial development profoundly shape patterns of life and perception.

In our nation, the factors favoring noncentralized decisionmaking have been powerfully reinforced by geography, history, and the structure of our politics. Nonetheless, the presumption in favor of decentralization has in recent years been repeatedly overridden by congressional legislation imposing federal standards and federal measures to control environmental degradation. * * *

A.   *The Rationales for Centralization*

* * *

1. *The Tragedy of the Commons and National Economies of Scale*

The Tragedy of the Commons arises in noncentralized decisionmaking under conditions in which the rational but independent pursuit by each decisionmaker of its own self-interest leads to results that leave all decisionmakers worse off than they would have been had they been able to agree collectively on a different set of policies. States and local communities whose citizens desire environmental quality are also concerned with employment and economic growth. Given the mobility of industry and commerce, any individual state or community may rationally decline unilaterally to adopt high environmental standards that entail substantial costs for industry and obstacles to economic development for fear that the resulting environmental gains will be more than offset by movement of capital to other areas with lower standards. If each locality reasons in the same way, all will adopt lower standards of environmental quality than they would prefer if there were some binding mechanism that enabled them simultaneously to enact higher standards, thus eliminating the threatened loss of industry or development. * * *

The characteristic insistence in federal environmental legislation upon geographically uniform standards and controls strongly suggests that escape from the Tragedy of the Commons by reduction of transactions [sic] costs has been an important reason for such legislation. The statutory structure of federal environmental programs also reflects other economies of scale that help explain centralizing tendencies. Collection of data and analysis of environmental problems, standard setting, and (in some instances) selection of control measures involve recurring, technically complex issues; such steps can often be taken far more cheaply once on the national level than repeatedly at the state and local level.

2. *Disparities in Effective Representation*

* * *

Industrial firms, developers, unions and others with incentives to avoid environmental controls are typically well-organized economic units with a large stake in particular decisions. The countervailing interest in environmental quality is shared by individuals whose personal stake is small and who face formidable transaction costs in organizing for concerted action. These factors tend to produce more effective and informed representation before legislative and administrative decisionmakers of interests favoring economic development as opposed to those favoring environmental quality. The technical complexity of environmental issues exacerbates this disparity by placing a premium on access to scarce and expensive scientific, economic, and other technical information and analytical skill.

The comparative disadvantage of environmental groups will often be reduced, however, if policy decisions are made at the national level. In order to have effective influence with respect to state and local decisions, environmental interests would be required to organize on a multiple basis, incurring overwhelming transaction costs. Given such barriers, environmental interests can exert far more leverage by organizing into one or a few units at the national level.

Centralized decisionmaking may imply similar scale economies for industrial firms, but these are likely to be of lesser magnitude—particularly if such firms are already national in scope. Moreover, effective representation may be less a function of comparative resources than of attainment of a critical mass of skills, resources, and experience. Industry and development interests can probably deploy these requisites regardless of whether decision is local or national. But a national forum for decision may greatly lessen the barriers to environmental interests' achievement of organizational critical mass, sharply reducing the disparity in effective representation.

* * *

3. *Spillovers*

Even if the "commons" problem were eliminated, decentralized environmental decisionmaking would remain flawed because spillover impacts of decisions in one jurisdiction on well-being in other jurisdictions generate conflicts and welfare losses not easily remedied under a decentralized regime.

The most obvious form of spillover is physical pollution. Prevailing winds or river flows may transport pollution generated in one state to another and visit damage there. These spillovers are in many instances pervasive and far-reaching. For example, a significant percentage of sulfate pollution in the eastern states is attributable to emissions originating hundreds of miles westward. Spillovers can also be psychic and economic. Environmental degradation in pristine areas often imposes substantial welfare losses on individuals in other states who value the option of visiting such areas or who take ideological satisfaction in their preservation. * * *

4. *Moral Ideals and the Politics of Sacrifice*

The groundswell of public concern with environmental quality that arose in the late 1960s had undeniable aspects of a moral crusade with powerful emotional, even religious, undercurrents. This development cannot be fully explained by utilitarian models that explain individual behavior in terms of calculated preference satisfaction. On the contrary, it partially reflects the sacrifice of preference-satisfaction in order to fulfill duties to others, or to transform existing preference structures in the direction of lessened dependence upon consumption of material goods and greater harmony with the natural environment. * * * The preservation of pristine areas may be understood in part as reflecting a special obligation to future generations (despite the fact that they may, in economic terms, be wealthier than we) to prevent the potentially irreversible loss of important categories of human experience. These measures to preserve natural environments, together with programs to protect endangered species, could also be viewed as an assumption of duties to nature. Alternatively, they could be understood as a deliberate renunciation of maximum economic progress in order to affirm a different view of the ends of human life to which the society should aspire.

National mechanisms for determining environmental policies facilitate, to a greater degree than their state and local counterparts, the achievement of commitments entailing material sacrifice; the moral content of rising environmental concern thus helps explain the increasing resort to centralized decision. Communities no less than individuals may be far more willing to undertake sacrifices for a common ideal if there are effective assurances that others are making sacrifices too. National policies can provide such assurances and also facilitate appeals to sublimate parochial interests in an embracing national crusade. * * *

B.   *The Antithetical Rationales: Local Resistance to National Environmental Policies*

* * * Having catalogued the reasons favoring centralized determination of environmental policies, we are now in a position to understand more precisely the corresponding grounds of state and local resistance to such policies. For the virtues of federal dictation are matched by corresponding vices.

1.   *Diseconomies of Scale*

While centralized decisionmaking may be necessary in order to overcome the commons problem and deal with spillovers, it also often generates burdens that are or will appear to be unjustified in particular localities. Federal environmental programs typically place heavy reliance on nationally uniform standards or controls. These uniformities, which reflect both political and administrative constraints in federal decisionmaking, impose economic and social costs on certain areas that are unnecessary or excessive in relation to the benefits obtained. For example, * * * [t]he nationally uniform technology-based discharge limitations in the [Clean Water Act] create regulatory "overkill" in many areas. Although the aggregate advantages of federal environmental measures may exceed the costs, particular localities will be loathe to enforce such measures when they involve local burdens that are not offset by local gains.

* * *

2.   *The Impairment of Self–Determination*

Environmental interests may well enjoy relatively more influence if environmental decisions are shifted from the state and local to the national level. But this shift is accomplished at the expense of local political self-determination. Decisions about environmental quality have far-reaching implications for economic activity, transportation patterns, land use, and other matters of profound concern to local citizens. Federal dictation of environmental policies depreciates the opportunity for and value of participation in local decisions on such matters. The impairment of local self-determination is considerably aggravated when * * * local fiscal resources and governmental powers are conscripted by federal agencies. Nor is it clear that this loss of self-determination always purchases a net gain in social welfare. Even if unorganized interests (such as environmentalists) are underrepresented at the local level, they may well be * * * overrepresented at the national level.

3.   *National Ideals as "Pyramids of Sacrifice"*

Moral crusades enjoy little credit with the nonbelievers who are taxed to underwrite such ventures. * * * Resistance and resentment may be heightened by the fact that many environmental programs distribute the costs of controls in a regressive pattern while providing disproportionate benefits for the educated and wealthy, who can better afford to indulge an acquired taste for environmental quality than the poor, who have more pressing needs and fewer resources with which to satisfy them. These circumstances may foster, and in part justify, a cynical attitude towards the moral justifications advanced by upper-middle class advocates for environmental programs which benefit that class disproportionately. The impairment of local political mechanisms of self-determination and official accountability involved in federally dictated environmental programs affords further grounds for resentment.

* * * Aspects of national environmental policy might * * * be viewed as the insensitive imposition of sacrifices on local communities * * * (in particular the poor communities), for the sake of a national elite's vision of a better society. * * *

NOTES AND QUESTIONS

1. *National Versus Local Regulation.* What rationales does Professor Stewart offer in favor of national environmental regulation? What counterarguments does he recognize in favor of local regulation? Which do you find more persuasive? Does it depend upon the problem? For which of the following environmental problems would you regard regulation at the national level as appropriate: drinking water quality; air quality; endangered species protection (does the answer depend upon the species?); preservation of open space; drilling for oil on the outer continental shelf, several miles offshore of the Gulf Coast states?

2. *Race to the bottom or healthy competition?* Professor Stewart describes the competition among states that may result in inefficiently low environmental standards as a tragedy of the commons. Others have dubbed this kind of destructive competition a "race to the bottom." Is the competition among states for economic development a "prisoners' dilemma," in which all states would be better off if they could cooperate, but each individually faces incentives to defect, reducing environmental and perhaps other standards to undesirably low levels? If so, one way to solve the dilemma would be to take away the defection option by imposing national minimum environmental standards.

Although the race-to-the-bottom rationale is a common justification for national regulation, not everyone agrees that the states are locked into a prisoners' dilemma. Professor Richard Revesz argues that states set environmental standards on the basis of their citizens' willingness to trade environmental quality for changes in wages, taxes, and other goods. If that competition results in lower environmental standards in particular states, Revesz concludes, it does so not because of an inefficient race to the bottom but rather because the citizens are unwilling to bear the costs of higher standards. Richard L. Revesz, Rehabilitating Interstate Competition: Rethinking the "Race-to-the-Bottom" Rationale for Federal Environmental Regulation, 67 N.Y.U. L. Rev. 1210 (1992). Even if there is a race to the bottom, Professor Revesz contends that federal environmental regulation will only shift that race to another venue, such as taxes or worker safety.

Neither Stewart nor Revesz offers any empirical evidence to support their conflicting views about the likelihood that states will engage in a detrimental race to the environmental bottom. What factors might contribute to such a race? Is there competition among states for industrial facilities and other forms of development? Are developers in a position to bargain strategically, hiding from the states their willingness to comply with environmental regulations in order to induce the states to under-regulate? Based on a survey of regulators, Professor Kirsten Engel argues that policymakers overestimate the effect of environmental standards on industries' choices of location. Consequently, she contends, states may relax their standards more than necessary in their effort to attract industrial facilities. Kirsten H. Engel, State Environmental Standard–Setting: Is There a "Race" and Is It "to the Bottom"?, 48 Hastings L.J. 271 (1997).

One other piece of data is available. Although most federal environmental laws allow the states to adopt more protective standards, few have chosen to do so. Does that suggest that there is a race to the bottom, or that the federal standards are too stringent?

3. *Uneven Political Power.* Professor Stewart argues that environmental groups may have more political clout at the national than at the local level. What accounts for this difference? One possibility is that local decisions underestimate the environmental interest because the environmentally concerned public is unable to effectively organize at the local level. Another possibility, however, is that the electorate in some localities simply has less interest in the environment relative to other goods than the national electorate. A small logging community in Oregon, for example, may not value old-growth forests and their associated species as highly as the national population does. In the latter case, is it legitimate for the national electorate to impose its views on the locality? Under what circumstances?

4. *Spillovers.* It is widely agreed that interstate environmental externalities, such as air or water pollution that physically spills over state borders, justify national intervention. Stewart suggests that economic spillovers also play a role, through the race to the bottom. Further, he points out that there may be psychic spillovers from intrastate actions. Extensive development of Alaska's coastal plain, for example, would upset many people who have never visited Alaska. Is it legitimate to impose federal environmental standards on Alaska to prevent that sort of harm?

What about intra-state externalities? Suppose, for example, that prevailing winds carry air pollutants from a heavily populated coastal portion of a state to a less populous area, but not across a state border (something like this happens in California, where the winds carry pollution east from the San Francisco Bay Area to the Central Valley, but not beyond the Sierra Nevada mountains). Would federal intervention be justified to aid the citizens of the less populous area? What other avenues of relief might be open to them?

B.   SOURCES OF FEDERAL POWER

Federal regulatory power must be grounded in the federal constitution. In the early years of the twentieth century, concerns about lack of constitutional authority inhibited robust federal regulation. Beginning with the New Deal, however, judicial decisions greatly expanded federal powers, allowing the expansion of federal environmental law in the 1960s and 1970s. By the 1980s, it was widely perceived that the constitution imposed virtually no limits on federal power to protect the environment, but that changed in the 1990s.

CLASS DISCUSSION PROBLEM: PLEASANTVILLE SCHOOL

The city of Pleasantville wishes to construct a new high school to accommodate recent population growth. Pleasantville has identified only one suitable site, a 40–acre vacant parcel close to the population to be served, and has succeeded in passing a bond issue to fund construction.

A few days before the scheduled groundbreaking ceremony, Pleasantville learned that the school site harbors two rare birds, the jewel-necked hummingbird and the drab flycatcher. The hummingbird, which is found only within a twenty-mile region in and around Pleasantville, is tiny but visually spectacular, with iridescent blue, red, and purple markings on its head and neck. It draws birders from across the country and beyond to the nearby Hummingbird National Wildlife Refuge. Scientists have been studying the hummingbird's distinctive coloration, hoping to duplicate the unusual iridescence for paints. The flycatcher, as its name suggests, is nondescript. Only a very small number of highly dedicated birders have any interest in seeing it. So far as Pleasantville is aware, there are no ongoing scientific studies of the flycatcher. But its range is not as limited as the hummingbird's. The flycatcher is sparsely distributed across several states. It is believed that at least a few birds each year migrate from one population to another, crossing state lines to do so.

As the City Attorney for Pleasantville, you are in a difficult situation. The U.S. Fish and Wildlife Service asserts that the school cannot be built on this site without illegally "taking" the hummingbird and flycatcher, both of which are listed as endangered under the federal Endangered Species Act. The Mayor and City Council insist that a new high school is desperately needed, and this is the only available site. Can you successfully argue that the United States lacks authority to protect the birds against this project?

1. THE COMMERCE CLAUSE

Among the powers of Congress enumerated in the federal constitution is the power "[t]o regulate Commerce * * * among the several States." Art. I, § 8, cl. 3. In the late 19th and early 20th centuries, the Supreme Court resisted congressional efforts to expand federal regulatory authority under the commerce clause. The battle came to a head over New Deal statutes governing wages and working hours of intrastate businesses. The Court at first held those statutes unconstitutional, ruling that Congress could only regulate activities with a direct effect on interstate commerce. A.L.A. Schechter Poultry Corp. v. United States, 295 U.S. 495 (1935). Shortly thereafter, however, faced with Roosevelt's Court-packing threat, the Court sharply reversed course. See, e.g., National Labor Relations Bd. v. Jones & Laughlin Steel Corp., 301 U.S. 1 (1937) (upholding the National Labor Relations Act against a commerce clause challenge). For sixty years after *Schechter Poultry*, the Court interpreted the commerce clause expansively.

In 1995, the Court reversed course, surprising many observers by ruling, for the first time since *Schechter Poultry*, that a federal statute exceeded the commerce power. A 5–4 majority struck down the Gun–Free School Zones Act of 1990, which had made it a federal crime knowingly to possess a gun near a school. United States v. Lopez, 514 U.S. 549 (1995). The Court emphasized the need to find some judicially-enforceable limit to the commerce power. Id. at 567.

Five years later, in *United States v. Morrison*, 529 U.S. 598 (2000), the Court issued another 5–4 decision striking down a federal statute under the commerce clause. *Morrison* dealt with the Violence Against Women Act, which created a federal cause of action for victims of crimes of violence motivated by gender. Noting that "[g]ender-motivated crimes of violence are not, in any sense of the phrase, economic activity," the Court rejected the claim that their aggregate effect on interstate commerce supported federal intervention. Again the Court emphasized the need to impose limits on the commerce power, lest it "completely obliterate the Constitution's distinction between national and local authority." Id. at 615.

There has been much speculation that the Supreme Court's narrowed view of the commerce clause could undermine federal environmental regulation. Much federal environmental law remains on solid constitutional foundations. Operations that produce goods for interstate commerce, or that produce air or water pollution that spills over across state lines, are clearly subject to federal regulation under the commerce clause. See Hodel v. Virginia Surface Mining and Reclamation Ass'n, 452 U.S. 264 (1981) (upholding federal Surface Mining Control and Reclamation Act on grounds that surface mining of coal diminishes usefulness of land and causes pollution and other environmental impacts that affect interstate commerce). Laws which extend to non-commercial activities and more local environmental impacts, however, may be more vulnerable to constitutional challenge.

Gibbs v. Babbitt

United States Court of Appeals, Fourth Circuit, 2000.
214 F.3d 483.

■ WILKINSON, CHIEF JUDGE.

In this case we ask whether the national government can act to conserve scarce natural resources of value to our entire country. Appellants challenge the constitutionality of a Fish and Wildlife Service regulation that limits the taking of red wolves on private land. The district court upheld the regulation as a valid exercise of federal power under the Commerce Clause. We now affirm because the regulated activity substantially affects interstate commerce and because the regulation is part of a comprehensive federal program for the protection of endangered species. Judicial deference to the judgment of the democratic branches is therefore appropriate.

I.

* * *

The red wolf, *Canis rufus,* is an endangered species whose protection is at issue in this case. The red wolf was originally found throughout the southeastern United States. It was once abundant in the "riverine habitats of the southeast," and was especially numerous near the "canebrakes" that harbored large populations of swamp and marsh rabbits, the primary prey of the red wolf. 51 Fed. Reg. 41,790, 41,791 (1986). The FWS found that "the demise of the red wolf was directly related to man's activities, especially land changes, such as the drainage of vast wetland areas for agricultural purposes . . . and predator control efforts at the private, State, and Federal levels." *Id.*

* * *

In 1986, the FWS issued a final rule outlining a reintroduction plan for red wolves in the 120,000–acre Alligator River National Wildlife Refuge in eastern North Carolina. This area was judged the ideal habitat within the red wolf's historic range. Between 1987 and 1992, a total of 42 wolves were released in the Refuge. In 1993, the reintroduction program was expanded to include the release of red wolves in the Pocosin Lakes National Wildlife Refuge in Tennessee. Since reintroduction, some red wolves have wandered from federal refuges onto private property. From available data, as of February 1998 it was estimated that about 41 of the approximately 75 wolves in the wild may now reside on private land.

This case raises a challenge to 50 C.F.R. § 17.84(c), a regulation governing the experimental populations of red wolves reintroduced into North Carolina and Tennessee pursuant to [Endangered Species Act] section 10(j). * * *

Section 17.84(c) allows a person to take red wolves on private land "*[p]rovided* that such taking is not intentional or willful, or is in defense of that person's own life or the lives of others." Private landowners may also take red wolves on their property "when the wolves are in the act of killing livestock or pets, *Provided* that freshly wounded or killed livestock or pets are evident." A landowner may also "harass red wolves found on his or her property ... *Provided* that all such harassment is by methods that are not lethal or injurious to the red wolf." Finally, landowners may take red wolves after efforts by Service personnel to capture such animals have been abandoned, and such taking has been approved in writing. * * *

In October 1990, plaintiff Richard Lee Mann shot a red wolf that he feared might threaten his cattle. The federal government prosecuted Mann under § 17.84(c), and Mann pled guilty. Mann's prosecution triggered some opposition to the red wolf program in the surrounding communities. * * *

In response to discontent with the reintroduction program, the North Carolina General Assembly passed a bill entitled "An Act to Allow the Trapping and Killing of Red Wolves by Owners of Private Land." The Act makes it lawful to kill a red wolf on private property if the landowner has previously requested the FWS to remove the red wolves from the property. This law facially conflicts with the federal regulation. * * *

Appellants Charles Gibbs, Richard Mann, Hyde County, and Washington County filed the instant action challenging the federal government's authority to protect red wolves on private land. They seek a declaration that the anti-taking regulation, as applied to the red wolves occupying private land in eastern North Carolina, exceeds Congress's power under the interstate Commerce Clause, U.S. Const. art. I, § 8, cl. 3. * * *

II.

We consider this case under the framework articulated by the Supreme Court in *United States v. Lopez*, 514 U.S. 549 (1995), and *United States v. Morrison*, 529 U.S. 598 (2000). While Congress's power to pass laws under the Commerce Clause has been interpreted broadly, both *Lopez* and *Morrison* reestablish that the commerce power contains "judicially enforceable outer limits." See *Lopez*, 514 U.S. at 566; *Morrison*, 120 S.Ct. at 1748–49. It is essential to our system of government that the commerce power not extend to effects on interstate commerce that are so remote that we "would effectually obliterate the distinction between what is national and what is local." *National Labor Relations Board v. Jones & Laughlin Steel Corp.*, 301 U.S. 1, 37 (1937). Indeed, the judiciary has the duty to ensure that federal statutes and regulations are promulgated under one of the enumerated grants of constitutional authority. It is our further duty to independently evaluate whether "a rational basis exist[s] for concluding that a regulated activity sufficiently affect[s] interstate commerce." *Lopez*, 514 U.S. at 557.

While this is rational basis review with teeth, the courts may not simply tear through the considered judgments of Congress. Judicial restraint is a long and honored tradition and this restraint applies to Commerce Clause adjudications. "Due respect for the decisions of a coordinate branch of Government demands that we invalidate a congressional enactment only upon a plain showing that Congress has exceeded its constitutional bounds." *Morrison,* 120 S.Ct. at 1748. * * *

The *Lopez* Court recognized three broad categories of activity that Congress may regulate under its commerce power. 514 U.S. at 558. "First, Congress may regulate the use of the channels of interstate commerce. Second, Congress is empowered to regulate and protect the instrumentalities of interstate commerce, or persons or things in interstate commerce, even though the threat may come only from intrastate activities. Finally, Congress' commerce authority includes the power to regulate those activities having a substantial relation to interstate commerce, *i.e.,* those activities that substantially affect interstate commerce." *Id.* at 558–59.

Section 17.84(c) is "not a regulation of the use of the channels of interstate commerce, nor is it an attempt to prohibit the interstate transportation of a commodity through the channels of commerce." *Lopez,* 514 U.S. at 559. The term "channel of interstate commerce" refers to, *inter alia,* "navigable rivers, lakes, and canals of the United States; the interstate railroad track system; the interstate highway system; ... interstate telephone and telegraph lines; air traffic routes; television and radio broadcast frequencies." *United States v. Miles,* 122 F.3d 235, 245 (5th Cir.1997). * * *

This case also does not implicate *Lopez*'s second prong, which protects things in interstate commerce. Although the Service has transported the red wolves interstate for the purposes of study and the reintroduction programs, this is not sufficient to make the red wolf a "thing" in interstate commerce. Therefore, if 50 C.F.R. § 17.84(c) is within the commerce power, it must be sustained under the third prong of *Lopez.*

Under the third *Lopez* test, regulations have been upheld when the regulated activities "arise out of or are connected with a commercial transaction, which viewed in the aggregate, substantially affects interstate commerce." *Lopez,* 514 U.S. at 561. In *Morrison,* the Supreme Court noted, "In every case where we have sustained federal regulation under *Wickard*'s aggregation principle, the regulated activity was of an apparent commercial character." *Morrison,* 120 S.Ct. at 1750 n. 4. The Court in *Lopez* likewise placed great emphasis on the "commercial concerns that are central to the Commerce Clause." *Lopez,* 514 U.S. at 583 (Kennedy, J., concurring).

Although the connection to economic or commercial activity plays a central role in whether a regulation will be upheld under the Commerce Clause, economic activity must be understood in broad terms. Indeed, a cramped view of commerce would cripple a foremost federal power and in so doing would eviscerate national authority. The *Lopez* Court's characterization of the regulation of homegrown wheat in *Wickard v. Filburn,** 317 U.S. 111 (1942), as a case involving economic activity makes clear the breadth of this concept. * * *

---

* *Wickard* upheld the imposition of a federal quota on production of wheat, including wheat grown for personal consumption on the farm. Eds.

Lopez and *Morrison* rest on the principle that where a federal statute has only a tenuous connection to commerce and infringes on areas of traditional state concern, the courts should not hesitate to exercise their constitutional obligation to hold that the statute exceeds an enumerated federal power. Respect for our federal system of government was integral to those decisions. Yet *Lopez* also counsels that "[w]here economic activity substantially affects interstate commerce, legislation regulating that activity will be sustained." 514 U.S. at 560. In enforcing limits on the Congress, we must be careful not to overstep the judicial role. * * *

With these basic principles in mind, we consider appellants' challenge to § 17.84(c).

III.

* * * The Supreme Court recently emphasized that "in those cases where we have sustained federal regulation of intrastate activity based upon the activity's substantial effects on interstate commerce, the activity in question has been some sort of economic endeavor." *Morrison,* 120 S.Ct. at 1750–51. * * * We therefore must consider whether the taking of red wolves on private land is "in any sense of the phrase, economic activity." *Morrison,* 120 S.Ct. at 1751–52.

Unlike the Violence Against Women Act (VAWA) in *Morrison* and the Gun–Free School Zones Act (GFSZA) in *Lopez,* § 17.84(c) regulates what is in a meaningful sense economic activity. * * * The protection of commercial and economic assets is a primary reason for taking the wolves. Farmers and ranchers take wolves mainly because they are concerned that the animals pose a risk to commercially valuable livestock and crops. Indeed, appellants' arguments focus quite explicitly on these economic concerns—they want freer rein to protect their property and investments in the land.

* * *

Because the taking of red wolves can be seen as economic activity in the sense considered by *Lopez* and *Morrison,* the individual takings may be aggregated for the purpose of Commerce Clause analysis. While the taking of one red wolf on private land may not be "substantial," the takings of red wolves in the aggregate have a sufficient impact on interstate commerce to uphold this regulation. This is especially so where, as here, the regulation is but one part of the broader scheme of endangered species legislation.

Further, § 17.84(c) is closely connected to a variety of interstate economic activities. Whether the impact of red wolf takings on any one of these activities qualifies as a substantial effect on interstate commerce is something we need not address. We have no doubt that the effect of the takings on these varied activities in combination qualifies as a substantial one. The first nexus between the challenged regulation and interstate commerce is tourism. The red wolves are part of a $29.2 billion national wildlife-related recreational industry that involves tourism and interstate travel. Many tourists travel to North Carolina from throughout the country for "howling events"—evenings of listening to wolf howls accompanied by educational programs. These howlings are a regular occurrence at the Alligator River National Wildlife Refuge. According to a study conducted by Dr. William E. Rosen of Cornell University, the recovery of the red wolf and increased visitor activities could result in a significant regional economic impact. Rosen estimates that northeastern North Carolina could see an increase of between $39.61 and $183.65 million per year in tourism-related activities, and that the Great Smoky Mountains National Park could see an increase of between $132.09 and $354.50 million per year. This is hardly a trivial impact on interstate commerce. Appellants understandably seek to criticize the Rosen study, but concede that the howling events attract interstate tourism and that red wolf program volunteers come from all around the country.

Appellants argue that the tourism rationale relates only to howling events on national park land or wildlife refuges because people do not travel to private land. They reason that without tourism on private land the regulated activity does not substantially affect interstate commerce. Yet this argument misses the mark. Since reintroduction, red wolves have strayed from federal lands onto private lands. * * * Because so many members of this threatened species wander on private land, the regulation of takings on private land is essential to the entire program of reintroduction and eventual restoration of the species. Such regulation is necessary to conserve enough red wolves to sustain tourism. * * *

Tourism, however, is not the only interstate commercial activity affected by the taking of red wolves. The regulation of red wolf takings is also closely connected to a second interstate market—scientific research. Scientific research generates jobs. It also deepens our knowledge of the world in which we live. The red wolf reintroduction program has already generated numerous scientific studies. * * *

The anti-taking regulation is also connected to a third market—the possibility of a renewed trade in fur pelts. Wolves have historically been hunted for their pelts. Congress had the renewal of trade in mind when it enacted the ESA. The Senate Report noted that the protection of an endangered species "may permit the regeneration of that species to a level where controlled exploitation of that species can be resumed. In such a case businessmen may profit from the trading and marketing of that species for an indefinite number of years, where otherwise it would have been completely eliminated from commercial channels." S. Rep. No. 91–526, at 3 (1969), *reprinted in* 1969 U.S.C.C.A.N. 1413, 1415. * * *

Finally, the taking of red wolves is connected to interstate markets for agricultural products and livestock. For instance, appellant landowners find red wolves a menace because they threaten livestock and other animals of economic and commercial value. By restricting the taking of red wolves, § 17.84(c) is said to impede economic development and commercial activities such as ranching and farming. This effect on commerce, however, still qualifies as a legitimate subject for regulation. It is well-settled under Commerce Clause cases that a regulation can involve the promotion or the restriction of commercial enterprises and development. * * *

This regulation is also sustainable as "an essential part of a larger regulation of economic activity, in which the regulatory scheme could be undercut unless the intrastate activity were regulated." *Lopez,* 514 U.S. at 561. The Supreme Court in *Hodel v. Indiana* stated: "A complex regulatory program ... can survive a Commerce Clause challenge without a showing that every single facet of the program is independently and directly related to a valid congressional goal. It is enough that the challenged provisions are an integral part of the regulatory program and that the regulatory scheme when considered as a whole satisfies this test." 452 U.S. 314, 329 n. 17 (1981).

The FWS issued this regulation pursuant to the provisions of the Endangered Species Act, a comprehensive and far-reaching piece of legislation that aims to conserve the health of our national environment. Congress undoubtedly has the constitutional authority to pass legislation for the conservation of endangered species.

Appellants repeatedly argue that individual takings of red wolves have only an insubstantial effect on interstate commerce and therefore that the application of the regulation to private landowners is invalid. But we emphasize that the effect on commerce must be viewed not from the taking of one wolf, but from the potential commercial differential between an extinct and a recovered species. A single red wolf taking may be insubstantial by some measures, but that does not invalidate a regulation that is part of the ESA and that seeks conservation not only of any single animal, but also recovery of the species as a whole. * * *

* * *

IV.

* * * *Lopez* and *Morrison* properly emphasize that we must carefully evaluate legislation in light of our federal system of government. "The Constitution requires a distinction between what is truly national and what is truly local." *Morrison,* 120 S.Ct. at 1754–55. We must particularly scrutinize regulated activity that "falls within an area of the law where States historically have been sovereign and countenance of the asserted federal power would blur the boundaries between the spheres of federal and state authority." Brzonkala, 169 F.3d at 837.

* * *

In contrast to gender-motivated violence or guns in school yards, the conservation of scarce natural resources is an appropriate and well-recognized area of federal regulation. The federal government has been involved in a variety of conservation efforts since the beginning of this century. In 1900, Congress passed the Lacey Act, which provided penalties for the taking of wildlife in violation of state laws. The Migratory Bird Treaty Act of 1918 forbade all takings of numerous bird species and explicitly preempted state laws. Furthermore, Congress has regulated wildlife on nonfederal property through numerous statutes * * *.

The Supreme Court has repeatedly upheld these statutes and the conservation efforts of Congress with regard to a variety of animal species. In *Missouri v. Holland,* the Court upheld the Migratory Bird Treaty Act as a necessary and proper means of executing Congress's treaty power. The conservation of endangered wildlife, Justice Holmes stated, was a "matter[] of the sharpest exigency for national well being." 252 U.S. 416, 432–33, (1920). * * * Later in *Andrus v. Allard,* the Court emphasized that the "assumption that the national commerce power does not reach migratory wildlife is clearly flawed." 444 U.S. 51, 63 n. 19 (1979).

* * *

The Supreme Court has recognized that protection of natural resources may require action from Congress. This general point holds true where endangered species are concerned. Species conservation may unfortunately impose additional costs on private concerns. States may decide to forego or limit conservation efforts in order to lower these costs, and other states may be forced to follow suit in order to compete. The Supreme Court has held that Congress may take cognizance of this dynamic and arrest the "race to the bottom" in order to prevent interstate competition whose overall effect would damage the quality of the national environment. In *Hodel v. Virginia Surface Mining and Reclamation Ass'n,* the Court upheld provisions of the Surface Mining Control and Reclamation Act of 1977 that regulated intrastate mining activities. 452 U.S. 264 (1981). The Court deferred to a congressional finding that nationwide standards were "essential" to insuring that competition in interstate commerce among sellers of coal would not be used to undermine environmental standards. * * * The Court emphasized, "The prevention of this sort of destructive interstate competition is a traditional role for congressional action under the Commerce Clause." *Id.* at 282.

* * * § 17.84(c) can be upheld while observing principled limitations on federal power. The regulation applies only to a single limited area— endangered species. It does not in any way grant Congress "an unlimited police power inconsistent with a Constitution of enumerated and limited federal powers." *Brzonkala,* 169 F.3d at 852. * * *

* * * Rather, the ESA and this regulation in particular permit the exercise of federal power only to conserve those species that are "endangered" or "threatened." * * * The rationale for upholding § 17.84(c), and the ESA generally, is restricted to the special relationship between endangered species and interstate commerce as drawn in Part III. It is not a connection that can be drawn outside of the endangered species context to support federal regulation of just any local or intrastate object with a medical, scientific, or economic value.

The rationale for this regulation thus stops far short of conferring upon Congress a broad police power. It is instead appellants' arguments for invalidating this regulation that go too far. If the federal government cannot regulate the taking of an endangered or threatened species on private land, its conservation and preservation efforts would be limited to only federal lands. A ruling to this effect would place in peril the entire federal regulatory scheme for wildlife and natural resource conservation.

* * *

■ LUTTIG, CIRCUIT JUDGE, dissenting.

* * *

* * * The killing of even all 41 of the estimated red wolves that live on private property in North Carolina would not constitute an economic activity of the kind held by the Court in *Lopez* and in *Morrison* to be of central concern to the Commerce Clause, if it could be said to constitute an economic activity at all. But even assuming that such is an economic activity, it certainly is not an activity that has a substantial effect on interstate commerce. The number of inferences (not even to mention the amount of speculation) necessary to discern in this activity a substantial effect on interstate commerce is exponentially greater than the number necessary in *Lopez* to show a substantial effect on interstate commerce from the sale of guns near schools or in *Morrison* to show a substantial effect on interstate commerce from domestic assault. * * *

NOTES AND QUESTIONS

1. *Scope of the Commerce Power.* What three categories of activities does the commerce clause permit Congress to regulate? Which of these categories is most likely to support environmental regulation?

2. *Aggregation of Individually Small Effects.* Under what circumstances may activities whose individual effect on commerce is small be aggregated to find a substantial effect justifying federal intervention? Do you agree with the majority in *Gibbs* that aggregation was permissible in that case? If aggregation is permissible, what is its scope? Should a court look at the effects on commerce of the extinction of only a single species, in this case the red wolf, or can the impacts of losing all endangered species be aggregated? While the difference might not seem important with respect to the red wolf, it may be crucial for less charismatic species. For example, the Delhi sands flower-loving fly is found only within an area about 20 miles in diameter near San Bernardino, California. Unlike the red wolf, it does not attract tourists. It had been the subject of a small amount of trade among insect collectors prior to its listing as endangered, and a few specimens are exhibited at museums outside California. Is federal protection of the fly valid under the commerce clause? See National Ass'n of Home Builders v. Babbitt, 130 F.3d 1041 (D.C.Cir.1997).

3. *Causal Chains and Attenuation.* According to the majority, how would the killing of one or more red wolves on private land affect commerce? Why does the dissent reject that conclusion? How attenuated is the causal chain between the activity regulated and interstate commerce, compared to those in *Lopez* or *Morrison*? Is the possibility of future interstate trade sufficient to justify federal protection of all limited natural resources? Would scientific study of the wolf alone have been sufficient to sustain the regulation?

4. *Wetlands Regulation and the Commerce Power.* Most commentators agree that endangered species and wetlands protection are the federal environmental programs most vulnerable under the commerce clause. Regulations adopted by the Army Corps of Engineers and Environmental Protection Agency under section 404 of the Clean Water Act assert federal jurisdiction over all wetlands "the use, degradation or destruction of which could affect interstate or foreign commerce." 33 C.F.R. § 328.3(a)(3) (1999). In a 1986 interpretation referred to as the "migratory bird rule," the agencies explained that federal jurisdiction extended to wetlands used as habitat by birds which migrate across state lines, or by any endangered species. Is the migratory bird rule constitutional? Before *Lopez* and *Morrison*, two federal circuits upheld it. See Hoffman Homes, Inc. v. Administrator, 999 F.2d 256 (7th Cir.1993); Leslie Salt Co. v. United States, 896 F.2d 354 (9th Cir.1990). In Solid Waste Agency of Northern Cook County v. U.S. Army Corps of Engineers, 531 U.S. 159 (2001), the Supreme Court avoided the constitutional question, ruling as a matter of statutory interpretation that the Clean Water Act did not authorize the migratory bird rule. See Chapter 6, Section 4.

5. *Justifications for Federal Intervention.* Assuming that Congress *can* regulate to protect wholly interstate species or wetlands, what principled ground is there for arguing that it *should* do so? Are there any circumstances in which the decision to protect interstate resources should be left to the states? If Congress does mandate protection, who should bear the costs, including the opportunity costs of foregone development?

6. *Other Environmental Laws and the Commerce Power.* To date, no federal court has struck down any federal environmental law under the commerce clause. Post-*Lopez* decisions include United States v. Olin Corp., 107 F.3d 1506 (11th Cir.1997) (upholding Comprehensive Environmental Response, Compensation, and Liability Act (CERCLA), which makes owners and operators of facilities contaminated with hazardous substances responsible for cleanup costs), and Allied Local and Regional Manufacturers Caucus v. U.S. EPA, 215 F.3d 61 (D.C.Cir.2000) (upholding regulations under the Clean Air Act limiting the content of volatile organic compounds in paint and other architectural coatings).

2. OTHER SOURCES OF FEDERAL POWER

The commerce clause has been the primary constitutional basis for most federal environmental regulation. Several other enumerated federal powers support environmental regulation, however. If the Supreme Court continues to restrict the commerce power, these other powers may become increasingly important.

The Treaty Power. The federal constitution grants the President, with the advice and consent of the Senate, power to make treaties. Art. II, § 2, cl. 1. Under the necessary and proper clause, Art. I, § 8, cl. 18, Congress has the power to make laws implementing treaties. The treaty power has long been thought to be above federalism concerns, such that legislation implementing treaties can extend into areas that otherwise would be beyond federal power. See Missouri v. Holland, 252 U.S. 416 (1920) (upholding the Migratory Bird Treaty Act under the treaty power, notwithstanding lack of federal authority to protect migratory birds before execution of the treaty). The treaty power is often cited in support of the Endangered Species Act, which was enacted in part to implement several international agreements. See 16 U.S.C. § 1531(a)(4); Gavin R. Villareal, Comment, One Leg to Stand On: The Treaty Power and Congressional Authority for the Endangered Species Act After *United States v. Lopez*, 76 Tex. L. Rev. 1125 (1998); Omar N. White, Comment, The Endangered Species Act's Precarious Perch: A Constitutional Analysis Under the Commerce Clause and the Treaty Power, 27 Ecology L.Q. 215 (2000).

The Property Power. Congress enjoys plenary power to "make all needful Rules and Regulations respecting the Territory or other Property belonging to the United States." Art. IV, § 3, cl. 2. This power allows Congress to protect natural resources, including wildlife, on federal lands. Kleppe v. New Mexico, 426 U.S. 529 (1976). For further discussion of the property clause and management of public lands, see Chapter 6, Section 2(B).

The Spending Power. The spending clause, Art. I, § 8, cl. 1, may be the broadest alternative to the commerce power. It gives Congress great discretion to expend funds to advance the general welfare, and permits it to impose conditions on the use of those funds. Conditions need not be within Congress' other powers, but they must be related to the purposes for which funds are expended. South Dakota v. Dole, 483 U.S. 203 (1987). Congress provides substantial funding to the states for a variety of environmental programs. It could couple that funding with environmental protection conditions, giving the states the choice of accepting the conditions or declining the funds. Offers of funding are often difficult to decline. The spending power has proven quite effective, for example, in persuading states to adopt coastal zone management programs meeting the requirements of the Coastal Zone Management Act, 16 U.S.C. §§ 1451–1464.

C. LIMITS ON FEDERAL POWER

New York v. United States

United States Supreme Court, 1992.
505 U.S. 144, 112 S.Ct. 2408, 120 L.Ed.2d 120.

■ JUSTICE O'CONNOR delivered the opinion of the Court.

* * *

I

We live in a world full of low level radioactive waste. Radioactive material is present in luminous watch dials, smoke alarms, measurement devices, medical fluids, research materials, and the protective gear and construction materials used by workers at nuclear power plants. Low level radioactive waste is generated by the Government, by hospitals, by research institutions, and by various industries. The waste must be isolated from humans for long periods of time, often for hundreds of years. Millions of cubic feet of low level radioactive waste must be disposed of each year.

Our Nation's first site for the land disposal of commercial low level radioactive waste opened in 1962 in Beatty, Nevada. Five more sites opened in the following decade: Maxey Flats, Kentucky (1963), West Valley, New York (1963), Hanford, Washington (1965), Sheffield, Illinois (1967), and Barnwell, South Carolina (1971). Between 1975 and 1978, the Illinois site closed because it was full, and water management problems caused the closure of the sites in Kentucky and New York. As a result, since 1979 only three disposal sites—those in Nevada, Washington, and South Carolina— have been in operation. Waste generated in the rest of the country must be shipped to one of these three sites for disposal.

In 1979, both the Washington and Nevada sites were forced to shut down temporarily, leaving South Carolina to shoulder the responsibility of storing low level radioactive waste produced in every part of the country. The Governor of South Carolina, understandably perturbed, ordered a 50% reduction in the quantity of waste accepted at the Barnwell site. The Governors of Washington and Nevada announced plans to shut their sites permanently.

Faced with the possibility that the Nation would be left with no disposal sites for low level radioactive waste, Congress responded by enacting the Low–Level Radioactive Waste Policy Act. Relying largely on a report submitted by the National Governors' Association, Congress declared a federal policy of holding each State "responsible for providing for the availability of capacity either within or outside the State for the disposal of low-level radioactive waste generated within its borders," and found that such waste could be disposed of "most safely and efficiently . . . on a regional basis." § 4(a)(1), 94 Stat. 3348. The 1980 Act authorized States to enter into regional compacts that, once ratified by Congress, would have the authority beginning in 1986 to restrict the use of their disposal facilities to waste generated within member States. The 1980 Act included no penalties for States that failed to participate in this plan.

By 1985, only three approved regional compacts had operational disposal facilities; not surprisingly, these were the compacts formed around South Carolina, Nevada, and Washington, the three sited States. The following year, the 1980 Act would have given these three compacts the ability to exclude waste from nonmembers, and the remaining 31 States would have had no assured outlet for their low level radioactive waste. With this prospect looming, Congress once again took up the issue of waste disposal. The result was the legislation challenged here, the Low–Level Radioactive Waste Policy Amendments Act of 1985.

The 1985 Act was * * * based largely on a proposal submitted by the National Governors' Association. In broad outline, the Act embodies a compromise among the sited and unsited States. The sited States agreed to extend for seven years the period in which they would accept low level radioactive waste from other States. In exchange, the unsited States agreed to end their reliance on the sited States by 1992.

* * *

The Act provides three types of incentives to encourage the States to comply with their statutory obligation to provide for the disposal of waste generated within their borders.

1. *Monetary incentives.* One quarter of the surcharges collected by the sited States must be transferred to an escrow account held by the Secretary of Energy. The Secretary then makes payments from this account to each State that has complied with a series of deadlines. * * *

2. *Access incentives.* The second type of incentive involves the denial of access to disposal sites. States that fail to meet the [progressive deadlines established by the Act may be assessed increasing surcharges and eventually denied access].

3. *The take title provision.* The third type of incentive is the most severe. The Act provides:

"If a State (or, where applicable, a compact region) in which low-level radioactive waste is generated is unable to provide for the disposal of all such waste generated within such State or compact region by January 1, 1996, each State in which such waste is generated, upon the request of the generator or owner of the waste, shall take title to the waste, be obligated to take possession of the waste, and shall be liable for all damages directly or indirectly incurred by such generator or owner as a consequence of the failure of the State to take possession of the waste as soon after January 1, 1996, as the generator or owner notifies the State that the waste is available for shipment." 42 U.S.C. § 2021e(d)(2)(C).

* * *

II

* * *

Petitioners do not contend that Congress lacks the power to regulate the disposal of low level radioactive waste. Space in radioactive waste disposal sites is frequently sold by residents of one State to residents of another. Regulation of the resulting interstate market in waste disposal is therefore well within Congress' authority under the Commerce Clause. Petitioners likewise do not dispute that under the Supremacy Clause Congress could, if it wished, pre-empt State radioactive waste regulation. Petitioners contend only that the Tenth Amendment limits the power of Congress to regulate in the way it has chosen. Rather than addressing the problem of waste disposal by directly regulating the generators and disposers of waste, petitioners argue, Congress has impermissibly directed the States to regulate in this field.

* * *

As an initial matter, Congress may not simply "commandee[r] the legislative processes of the States by directly compelling them to enact and enforce a federal regulatory program." Hodel v. Virginia Surface Mining & Reclamation Assn., Inc., 452 U.S. 264, 288 (1981). * * *

* * * We have always understood that even where Congress has the authority under the Constitution to pass laws requiring or prohibiting certain acts, it lacks the power directly to compel the States to require or prohibit those acts. The allocation of power contained in the Commerce Clause, for example, authorizes Congress to regulate interstate commerce directly; it does not authorize Congress to regulate state governments' regulation of interstate commerce.

This is not to say that Congress lacks the ability to encourage a State to regulate in a particular way, or that Congress may not hold out incentives to the States as a method of influencing a State's policy choices. Our cases have identified a variety of methods, short of outright coercion, by which Congress may urge a State to adopt a legislative program consistent with federal interests. Two of these methods are of particular relevance here.

First, under Congress' spending power, "Congress may attach conditions on the receipt of federal funds." South Dakota v. Dole, 483 U.S. 203, 206 (1987). Such conditions must (among other requirements) bear some relationship to the purpose of the federal spending; otherwise, of course, the spending power could render academic the Constitution's other grants and limits of federal authority. Where the recipient of federal funds is a State, as is not unusual today, the conditions attached to the funds by Congress may influence a State's legislative choices. * * *

Second, where Congress has the authority to regulate private activity under the Commerce Clause, we have recognized Congress' power to offer States the choice of regulating that activity according to federal standards or having state law pre-empted by federal regulation. Hodel v. Virginia Surface Mining & Reclamation Assn., Inc., supra, 452 U.S., at 288. This arrangement, which has been termed "a program of cooperative federalism," Hodel, supra, 452 U.S. at 289, is replicated in numerous federal statutory schemes.

By either of these two methods, as by any other permissible method of encouraging a State to conform to federal policy choices, the residents of the State retain the ultimate decision as to whether or not the State will comply. * * * Where Congress encourages state regulation rather than compelling it, state governments remain responsive to the local electorate's preferences; state officials remain accountable to the people.

By contrast, where the Federal Government compels States to regulate, the accountability of both state and federal officials is diminished. If the citizens of New York, for example, do not consider that making provision for the disposal of radioactive waste is in their best interest, they may elect state officials who share their view. That view can always be preempted under the Supremacy Clause if it is contrary to the national view, but in such a case it is the Federal Government that makes the decision in full view of the public, and it will be federal officials that suffer the consequences if the decision turns out to be detrimental or unpopular. But where the Federal Government directs the States to regulate, it may be state officials who will bear the brunt of public disapproval, while the federal officials who devised the regulatory program may remain insulated from the electoral ramifications of their decision. Accountability is thus diminished when, due to federal coercion, elected state officials cannot regulate in accordance with the views of the local electorate in matters not pre-empted by federal regulation.

* * *

III

* * * Construed as a whole, the Act comprises three sets of "incentives" for the States to provide for the disposal of low level radioactive waste generated within their borders. We consider each in turn.

* * *

The Act's first set of incentives, in which Congress has conditioned grants to the States upon the States' attainment of a series of milestones, is thus well within the authority of Congress under the Commerce and Spending Clauses. Because the first set of incentives is supported by affirmative constitutional grants of power to Congress, it is not inconsistent with the Tenth Amendment.

In the second set of incentives, Congress has authorized States and regional compacts with disposal sites gradually to increase the cost of access to the sites, and then to deny access altogether, to radioactive waste generated in States that do not meet federal deadlines. As a simple regulation, this provision would be within the power of Congress to authorize the States to discriminate against interstate commerce. Where federal regulation of private activity is within the scope of the Commerce Clause, we have recognized the ability of Congress to offer states the choice of regulating that activity according to federal standards or having state law pre-empted by federal regulation.

* * *

The Act's second set of incentives thus represents a conditional exercise of Congress' commerce power, along the lines of those we have held to be within Congress' authority. As a result, the second set of incentives does not intrude on the sovereignty reserved to the States by the Tenth Amendment.

The take title provision is of a different character. This third so-called "incentive" offers States, as an alternative to regulating pursuant to Congress' direction, the option of taking title to and possession of the low level radioactive waste generated within their borders and becoming liable for all damages waste generators suffer as a result of the States' failure to do so promptly. In this provision, Congress has crossed the line distinguishing encouragement from coercion.

* * *

The take title provision offers state governments a "choice" of either accepting ownership of waste or regulating according to the instructions of Congress. Respondents do not claim that the Constitution would authorize Congress to impose either option as a freestanding requirement. On one hand, the Constitution would not permit Congress simply to transfer radioactive waste from generators to state governments. Such a forced transfer, standing alone, would in principle be no different than a congressionally compelled subsidy from state governments to radioactive waste producers. The same is true of the provision requiring the States to become liable for the generators' damages. Standing alone, this provision would be indistinguishable from an Act of Congress directing the States to assume the liabilities of certain state residents. Either type of federal action would "commandeer" state governments into the service of federal regulatory purposes, and would for this reason be inconsistent with the Constitution's division of authority between federal and state governments. On the other hand, the second alternative held out to state governments—regulating pursuant to Congress' direction—would, standing alone, present a simple command to state governments to implement legislation enacted by Congress. As we have seen, the Constitution does not empower Congress to subject state governments to this type of instruction.

Because an instruction to state governments to take title to waste, standing alone, would be beyond the authority of Congress, and because a direct order to regulate, standing alone, would also be beyond the authority of Congress, it follows that Congress lacks the power to offer the States a choice between the two. * * *

Respondents emphasize the latitude given to the States to implement Congress' plan. The Act enables the States to regulate pursuant to Congress' instructions in any number of different ways. States may avoid taking title by contracting with sited regional compacts, by building a disposal site alone or as part of a compact, or by permitting private parties to build a disposal site. States that host sites may employ a wide range of designs and disposal methods, subject only to broad federal regulatory limits. This line of reasoning, however, only underscores the critical alternative a State lacks: A State may not decline to administer the federal program. No matter which path the State chooses, it must follow the direction of Congress.

* * * Whether one views the take title provision as lying outside Congress' enumerated powers, or as infringing upon the core of state sovereignty reserved by the Tenth Amendment, the provision is inconsistent with the federal structure of our Government established by the Constitution.

IV

* * * [T]he United States argues that the Constitution's prohibition of congressional directives to state governments can be overcome where the federal interest is sufficiently important to justify state submission. * * * [But n]o matter how powerful the federal interest involved, the Constitution simply does not give Congress the authority to require the States to regulate. The Constitution instead gives Congress the authority to regulate matters directly and to pre-empt contrary state regulation. Where a federal interest is sufficiently strong to cause Congress to legislate, it must do so directly; it may not conscript state governments as its agents.

* * *

The sited State respondents focus their attention on the process by which the Act was formulated. They correctly observe that public officials representing the State of New York lent their support to the Act's enactment. Respondents note that the Act embodies a bargain among the sited and unsited States, a compromise to which New York was a willing participant and from which New York has reaped much benefit. Respondents then pose what appears at first to be a troubling question: How can a federal statute be found an unconstitutional infringement of State sovereignty when state officials consented to the statute's enactment?

The answer follows from an understanding of the fundamental purpose served by our Government's federal structure. The Constitution does not protect the sovereignty of States for the benefit of the States or state governments as abstract political entities, or even for the benefit of the public officials governing the States. To the contrary, the Constitution divides authority between federal and state governments for the protection of individuals. * * *

[T]he facts of these cases raise the possibility that powerful incentives might lead both federal and state officials to view departures from the federal structure to be in their personal interests. Most citizens recognize the need for radioactive waste disposal sites, but few want sites near their homes. As a result, while it would be well within the authority of either federal or state officials to choose where the disposal sites will be, it is likely to be in the political interest of each individual official to avoid being held accountable to the voters for the choice of location. If a federal official is faced with the alternatives of choosing a location or directing the States to do it, the official may well prefer the latter, as a means of shifting responsibility for the eventual decision. If a state official is faced with the same set of alternatives—choosing a location or having Congress direct the choice of a location—the state official may also prefer the latter, as it may permit the avoidance of personal responsibility. The interests of public officials thus may not coincide with the Constitution's intergovernmental allocation of authority. Where state officials purport to submit to the direction of Congress in this manner, federalism is hardly being advanced.

* * *

■ JUSTICE WHITE, with whom JUSTICE BLACKMUN and JUSTICE STEVENS join, concurring in part and dissenting in part.

* * *

My disagreement with the Court's analysis begins at the basic descriptive level of how the legislation at issue in this case came to be enacted. * * * The Low–Level Radioactive Waste Policy Act of 1980 (1980 Act) and its amendatory Act of 1985 resulted from the efforts of state leaders to achieve a state-based set of remedies to the waste problem. They sought not federal pre-emption or intervention, but rather congressional sanction of interstate compromises they had reached.

* * *

Ultimately, I suppose, the entire structure of our federal constitutional government can be traced to an interest in establishing checks and balances to prevent the exercise of tyranny against individuals. But these fears seem extremely far distant to me in a situation such as this. We face a crisis of national proportions in the disposal of low-level radioactive waste, and Congress has acceded to the wishes of the States by permitting local decisionmaking rather than imposing a solution from Washington. New York itself participated and supported passage of this legislation at both the gubernatorial and federal representative levels, and then enacted state laws specifically to comply with the deadlines and timetables agreed upon by the States in the 1985 Act. For me, the Court's civics lecture has a decidedly hollow ring at a time when action, rather than rhetoric, is needed to solve a national problem.

* * *

■ JUSTICE STEVENS, concurring in part and dissenting in part.

* * *

The notion that Congress does not have the power to issue "a simple command to state governments to implement legislation enacted by Congress," is incorrect and unsound. There is no such limitation in the Constitution. * * * To the contrary, the Federal Government directs state governments in many realms. The Government regulates state-operated railroads, state school systems, state prisons, state elections, and a host of other state functions. I see no reason why Congress may not also command the States to enforce federal water and air quality standards or federal standards for the disposition of low-level radioactive wastes.

NOTES AND QUESTIONS

1. *A National Problem?* Is the problem of low-level radioactive waste disposal one that demands a national solution? Why? Does it pose a prisoners' dilemma for the states?

2. *Finding a Solution.* What options did Congress have to solve this problem? Why do you think the Low Level Radioactive Waste Policy Act and the 1985 amendments to the Act took the particular form they did? *New York* upheld the Act's monetary incentives for siting, as well as the provision allowing sited states to deny unsited states access to disposal facilities, but invalidated the take title provision. Will the Act be effective without its heaviest regulatory "stick"? Does Congress have any other sticks it might use to apply pressure on unsited states?

3. *Political Accountability and the Tenth Amendment.* In *New York*, the Court wrote that allowing the federal government to compel state regulation diminishes the accountability of both state and federal officials. Do you agree that state officials "will bear the brunt of public disapproval" under those circumstances, while federal officials "remain insulated from the electoral ramifications of their decision"? Does use of the spending power to "encourage" state legislation create the same accountability problems?

4. *Enforcing State Compromises.* The majority concedes that New York supported enactment of the statute it challenged in this case. Why doesn't that bar the Tenth Amendment claim? Could the Court have distinguished "compromise" legislation imposed at the request of the states from legislation imposed by the federal government contrary to the wishes of the states, or imposed at the request of some states over the objection of others?

5. *Encouragement Versus Coercion.* The Tenth Amendment permits federal "encouragement" of state regulation but prohibits federal "coercion." How does the *New York* majority distinguish coercion from encouragement? Do you find the distinction persuasive? Could withdrawal of federal funds ever amount to "coercion"? See South Dakota v. Dole, 483 U.S. 203, 211 (1987).

6. *Co-Opting State Actors.* In Printz v. United States, 521 U.S. 898 (1997), a 5–4 majority of the Court invalidated a federal statute requiring local law enforcement officers to perform background checks on prospective handgun purchasers. The Court rejected the government's argument that although states could not be compelled to make policy (under *New York*), they could be compelled to undertake ministerial acts to implement federal policy.

7. *The Tenth Amendment and Other Environmental Statutes.* Can Congress require that states establish a program for detecting and remedying lead contamination in water coolers in schools and day-care centers? See ACORN v. Edwards, 81 F.3d 1387 (5th Cir.1996) (no). That they relax their general rules of judicial standing in air pollution cases, on pain of loss of federal highway funds, limitations on construction of new pollution sources, and federal assumption of the state's air pollution control program? See Commonwealth of Virginia v. Browner, 80 F.3d 869 (4th Cir.1996) (yes). That, if they regulate fishing activity within their boundaries, they prohibit fishing methods harmful to endangered species or themselves face liability under of the Endangered Species Act? See Strahan v. Coxe, 127 F.3d 155 (1st Cir.1997) (yes).

D.   LIMITS ON STATE POWER

Fort Gratiot Sanitary Landfill, Inc. v. Michigan Department of Natural Resources

United States Supreme Court, 1992.
504 U.S. 353, 112 S.Ct. 2019, 119 L.Ed.2d 139.

■ JUSTICE STEVENS delivered the opinion of the Court.

In *Philadelphia v. New Jersey*, 437 U.S. 617, 618 (1978), we held that a New Jersey law prohibiting the importation of most "solid or liquid waste which originated or was collected outside the territorial limits of the State" violated the Commerce Clause of the United States Constitution. In this case petitioner challenges a Michigan law that prohibits private landfill operators from accepting solid waste that originates outside the county in which their facilities are located. Adhering to our holding in the *New Jersey* case, we conclude that this Michigan statute is also unconstitutional.

I

In 1978, Michigan enacted its Solid Waste Management Act (SWMA). That Act required every Michigan county to estimate the amount of solid waste that would be generated in the county in the next 20 years and to adopt a plan providing for its disposal at facilities that comply with state health standards. After holding public hearings and obtaining the necessary approval of municipalities in the county, as well as the approval of the Director of the Michigan Department of Natural Resources, the County Board of Commissioners adopted a solid waste management plan for St. Clair County. In 1987, the Michigan Department of Natural Resources issued a permit to petitioner to operate a sanitary landfill as a solid waste disposal area in St. Clair County.

On December 28, 1988, the Michigan Legislature amended the SWMA by adopting two provisions concerning the "acceptance of waste or ash generated outside the county of disposal area." Those amendments (Waste Import Restrictions), which became effective immediately, provide:

"A person shall not accept for disposal solid waste ... that is not generated in the county in which the disposal area is located unless the acceptance of solid waste ... that is not generated in the county is explicitly authorized in the approved county solid waste management plan." [Mich. Comp. Laws] § 299.413a.

* * *

In February 1989, petitioner submitted an application to the St. Clair County Solid Waste Planning Committee for authority to accept up to 1,750 tons per day of out-of-state waste at its landfill. In that application petitioner promised to reserve sufficient capacity to dispose of all solid waste generated in the county in the next 20 years. The planning commit-tee denied the application. In view of the fact that the county's management plan does not authorize the acceptance of any out-of-county waste, the Waste Import Restrictions in the 1988 statute effectively prevent petitioner from receiving any solid waste that does not originate in St. Clair County.

Petitioner therefore commenced this action seeking a judgment declaring the Waste Import Restrictions unconstitutional and enjoining their enforcement. * * *

II

* * * Solid waste, even if it has no value, is an article of commerce. Whether the business arrangements between out-of-state generators of waste and the Michigan operator of a waste disposal site are viewed as "sales" of garbage or "purchases" of transportation and disposal services, the commercial transactions unquestionably have an interstate character. The Commerce Clause thus imposes some constraints on Michigan's ability to regulate these transactions.

As we have long recognized, the "negative" or "dormant" aspect of the Commerce Clause prohibits States from "advanc[ing] their own commercial interests by curtailing the movement of articles of commerce, either into or out of the state." H.P. Hood & Sons, Inc. v. Du Mond, 336 U.S. 525, 535 (1949). A state statute that clearly discriminates against interstate commerce is therefore unconstitutional "unless the discrimination is demonstrably justified by a valid factor unrelated to economic protectionism." New Energy Co. of Ind. v. Limbach, 486 U.S. 269, 274 (1988).

* * *

The Waste Import Restrictions enacted by Michigan authorize each of the State's 83 counties to isolate itself from the national economy. Indeed, unless a county acts affirmatively to permit other waste to enter its jurisdiction, the statute affords local waste producers complete protection from competition from out-of-state waste producers who seek to use local waste disposal areas. In view of the fact that Michigan has not identified any reason, apart from its origin, why solid waste coming from outside the county should be treated differently from solid waste within the county, the foregoing reasoning would appear to control the disposition of this case.

III

Respondents Michigan and St. Clair County argue, however, that the Waste Import Restrictions * * * do not discriminate against interstate commerce on their face or in effect because they treat waste from other Michigan counties no differently than waste from other States. Instead, respondents maintain, the statute regulates evenhandedly to effectuate local interests and should be upheld because the burden on interstate commerce is not clearly excessive in relation to the local benefits. We disagree, for our prior cases teach that a State (or one of its political subdivisions) may not avoid the strictures of the Commerce Clause by curtailing the movement of articles of commerce through subdivisions of the State, rather than through the State itself.

* * *

Nor does the fact that the Michigan statute allows individual counties to accept solid waste from out of state qualify its discriminatory character. In [*Philadelphia v. New Jersey*], the statute authorized a state agency to promulgate regulations permitting certain categories of waste to enter the State. See 437 U.S., at 618–619. The limited exception covered by those regulations—like the fact that several Michigan counties accept out-of-state waste—merely reduced the scope of the discrimination; for all categories of waste not excepted by the regulations, the discriminatory ban remained in place. Similarly, in this case St. Clair County's total ban on out-of-state waste is unaffected by the fact that some other counties have adopted a different policy.

* * *

IV

Michigan and St. Clair County also argue that this case is different from *Philadelphia v. New Jersey* because the SWMA constitutes a comprehensive health and safety regulation rather than "economic protectionism" of the State's limited landfill capacity. * * *

* * * We may assume that all of the provisions of Michigan's SWMA prior to the 1988 amendments adding the Waste Import Restrictions could fairly be characterized as health and safety regulations with no protectionist purpose, but we cannot make that same assumption with respect to the Waste Import Restrictions themselves. Because those provisions unambiguously discriminate against interstate commerce, the State bears the burden of proving that they further health and safety concerns that cannot be adequately served by nondiscriminatory alternatives. Michigan and St. Clair County have not met this burden.

Michigan and St. Clair County assert that the Waste Import Restrictions are necessary because they enable individual counties to make adequate plans for the safe disposal of future waste. Although accurate forecasts about the volume and composition of future waste flows may be an indispensable part of a comprehensive waste disposal plan, Michigan could attain that objective without discriminating between in- and out-of-state waste. Michigan could, for example, limit the amount of waste that landfill operators may accept each year. There is, however, no valid health and safety reason for limiting the amount of waste that a landfill operator may accept from outside the State, but not the amount that the operator may accept from inside the State.

Of course, our conclusion would be different if the imported waste raised health or other concerns not presented by Michigan waste. In *Maine v. Taylor*, 477 U.S. 131 (1986), for example, we upheld the State's prohibition against the importation of live baitfish because parasites and other characteristics of nonnative species posed a serious threat to native fish that could not be avoided by available inspection techniques. * * *

In this case, in contrast, the lower courts did not find—and respondents have not provided—any legitimate reason for allowing petitioner to accept waste from inside the county but not waste from outside the county.

For the foregoing reasons, the Waste Import Restrictions unambiguously discriminate against interstate commerce and are appropriately characterized as protectionist measures that cannot withstand scrutiny under the Commerce Clause. The judgment of the Court of Appeals is therefore reversed.

■ CHIEF JUSTICE REHNQUIST, with whom JUSTICE BLACKMUN joins, dissenting.

When confronted with a dormant Commerce Clause challenge "[t]he crucial inquiry ... must be directed to determining whether [the challenged statute] is basically a protectionist measure, or whether it can fairly be viewed as a law directed to legitimate local concerns, with effects upon interstate commerce that are only incidental." Philadelphia v. New Jersey, 437 U.S. 617 (1978). Because I think the Michigan statute is at least arguably directed to legitimate local concerns, rather than improper economic protectionism, I would remand this case for further proceedings.

The substantial environmental, esthetic, health, and safety problems flowing from this country's waste piles were already apparent at the time we decided *Philadelphia*. Those problems have only risen in the intervening years. In part this is due to increased waste volumes, volumes that are expected to continue rising for the foreseeable future. In part it is due to exhaustion of existing capacity. It is no secret why capacity is not expanding sufficiently to meet demand—the substantial risks attendant to waste sites make them extraordinarily unattractive neighbors. The result, of course, is that while many are willing to generate waste—indeed, it is a practical impossibility to solve the waste problem by banning waste production—few are willing to help dispose of it. Those locales that do provide disposal capacity to serve foreign waste effectively are affording reduced environmental and safety risks to the States that will not take charge of their own waste.

The State of Michigan has stepped into this quagmire in order to address waste problems generated by its own populace. It has done so by adopting a comprehensive approach to the disposal of solid wastes generated within its borders. The legislation challenged today is simply one part of a broad package that includes a number of features: a state-mandated statewide effort to control and plan for waste disposal, requirements that local units of government participate in the planning process, restrictions to assure safe transport, a ban on the operation of waste disposal facilities unless various design and technical requirements are satisfied and appropriate permits obtained, and commitments to promote source separation, composting, and recycling. The Michigan legislation is thus quite unlike the simple outright ban that we confronted in *Philadelphia*.

In adopting this legislation, the Michigan Legislature also appears to have concluded that, like the State, counties should reap as they have sown—hardly a novel proposition. It has required counties within the State to be responsible for the waste created within the county. It has accomplished this by prohibiting waste facilities from accepting waste generated from outside the county, unless special permits are obtained. In the process, of course, this facially neutral restriction (*i.e.,* it applies equally to both interstate and intrastate waste) also works to ban disposal from out-of-state sources unless appropriate permits are procured. But I cannot agree that such a requirement, when imposed as one part of a comprehensive approach to regulating in this difficult field, is the stuff of which economic protectionism is made.

If anything, the challenged regulation seems likely to work to Michigan's economic disadvantage. This is because, by limiting potential disposal volumes for any particular site, various fixed costs will have to be recovered across smaller volumes, increasing disposal costs per unit for Michigan consumers. The regulation also will require some Michigan counties—those that until now have been exporting their waste to other locations in the State—to confront environmental and other risks that they previously have avoided. Commerce Clause concerns are at their nadir when a state Act works in this fashion—raising prices for all the State's consumers, and working to the substantial disadvantage of other segments of the State's population—because in these circumstances "a State's own political processes will serve as a check against unduly burdensome regulations." Kassel v. Consolidated Freightways Corp. of Del., 450 U.S. 662, 675 (1981). In sum, the law simply incorporates the commonsense notion that those responsible for a problem should be responsible for its solution *to the degree they are responsible for the problem but not further.* At a minimum, I think the facts just outlined suggest the State must be allowed to present evidence on the economic, environmental, and other effects of its legislation.

* * *

NOTES AND QUESTIONS

1. *The Dormant Commerce Clause.* In addition to serving as an affirmative grant of federal power, the commerce clause has been interpreted to restrict state power. The "dormant" commerce clause prohibits state interference with interstate commerce absent congressional authorization. Two different tests apply, depending upon whether the state or local law treats interstate and intrastate commerce differently. Discriminatory laws are presumptively invalid; they will be upheld only if the state or locality shows that no less discriminatory strategy could achieve its legitimate goal. C & A Carbone, Inc. v. Town of Clarkstown, 511 U.S. 383, 392 (1994). By contrast, laws which treat interstate and intrastate commerce evenhandedly will be upheld, unless the burdens they place on interstate commerce are clearly excessive compared to the local benefits. Pike v. Bruce Church, Inc.,

397 U.S. 137, 142 (1970). Sometimes it is difficult to tell the two apart? Which test did the Supreme Court apply in *Fort Gratiot*?

2. *Commerce and Garbage.* The flow of solid and hazardous waste across state lines has become one of the primary dormant commerce clause litigation battlegrounds. The Supreme Court has addressed the topic five times since 1978, in Philadelphia v. New Jersey, 437 U.S. 617 (1978); Chemical Waste Mgmt. v. Hunt, 504 U.S. 334 (1992); *Fort Gratiot*; Oregon Waste Sys. v. Department of Envtl. Quality, 511 U.S. 93 (1994); and C & A Carbone, Inc. v. Town of Clarkstown, 511 U.S. 383 (1994). Lower federal courts have been virtually swamped with litigation over garbage import and export. For a few recent examples, see Waste Mgmt. Holdings v. Gilmore, 252 F.3d 316 (4th Cir.2001); Huish Detergents, Inc. v. Warren County, 214 F.3d 707 (6th Cir.2000); U & I Sanitation v. City of Columbus, 205 F.3d 1063 (8th Cir.2000); Houlton Citizens' Coalition v. Town of Houlton, 175 F.3d 178 (1st Cir.1999).

What accounts for this abundance of disputes about interstate shipment of waste? State and local governments can face pressures to restrict the flow of solid waste either into or out of the jurisdiction. Providing for waste disposal is a traditional local police power function. Jurisdictions concerned about preserving scarce landfill space, minimizing the environmental and economic externalities their citizens experience near landfills, or simply not appearing to be available as dumping grounds for wealthier states may seek to restrict the import of waste. On the other hand, municipalities which have financed the construction of expensive incinerators, landfills, or transfer stations may restrict export by enacting "flow control" measures requiring disposal of locally-generated waste at local facilities in order to ensure the flow of sufficient waste to pay for those facilities. Are those legitimate local goals? Do they conflict with national needs?

3. *State and Local Options.* In *Fort Gratiot*, what could the state and county have done to achieve their goals without running afoul of the dormant commerce clause? Are you persuaded by the Court's suggestion that Michigan could cap the total amount of waste accepted at landfills? Would that serve the goal of ensuring solid waste self-sufficiency within the state? Are facially neutral caps necessarily constitutional? See Waste Mgmt. Holdings v. Gilmore, 252 F.3d 316 (4th Cir.2001) (holding invalid cap that affected only large regional landfills which relied almost entirely on out-of-state waste). Could Michigan constitutionally ban the import of waste from states lacking effective source reduction or recycling programs? See National Solid Wastes Mgmt. Ass'n v. Meyer, 165 F.3d 1151 (7th Cir.1999) (invalidating a Wisconsin statute prohibiting disposal of solid waste unless source community had a recycling ordinance meeting Wisconsin specifications). Could Michigan ban waste from states lacking some threshold level of landfill space per capita, on the grounds that those states have failed to shoulder their fair share of the landfill burden?

4. *The "Market Participant" Exception.* State and local governments are not subject to the strictures of the dormant commerce clause when they act as participants in the ordinary marketplace, rather than as regulators. Accordingly, a state or local government which owns a landfill can refuse to accept non-local waste. However, the exemption can be lost if the state acts both as market participant and as regulator. The federal courts have divided over whether municipalities can evade dormant commerce clause limits on export restrictions through franchise agreements, contracts under which a single hauler has the exclusive right to collect and process all municipal solid waste in the jurisdiction, and agrees to dispose of that waste at the local facility. See, e.g., USA Recycling v. Town of Babylon, 66 F.3d 1272 (2d Cir.1995); Houlton Citizens' Coalition v. Town of Houlton, 175 F.3d 178 (1st Cir.1999); Huish Detergents, Inc. v. Warren County, 214 F.3d 707 (6th Cir.2000).

5. *Is Federal Legislation Desirable?* Congress can authorize states to regulate in ways that interfere with interstate commerce. In recent years, states have unsuccessfully sought legislation authorizing import restrictions and flow control requirements. In light of the concerns identified by Professor Stewart, is this an area where federal regulation is appropriate? Why do you suppose Congress has so far declined to legislate in this area? Are decisions about *where* solid waste generated within a jurisdiction should be processed and disposed of appropriately left to local decisionmakers? Are those decisions separable from decisions about *how* solid waste generated within the jurisdiction should be treated?

6. *Acid Rain and the Dormant Commerce Clause.* Although garbage is a frequent subject of commerce clause disputes, it is not the only commodity whose interstate trade implicates environmental concerns. The Clean Air Act creates tradable permits for emissions of SO_2, a primary component of acid rain, between utilities, with the goal of encouraging economically efficient reductions in SO_2 emissions. The state of New York is convinced that SO_2 emissions in upwind states are contributing to acid rain harmful to New York's environment. Recently, New York enacted a statute requiring any New York utility that sells SO_2 allowances to an upwind state to pay the state a fee equal to the price of the allowances. N.Y. Pub. Serv. Law § 66–k. A utility industry group has challenged the statute on dormant commerce clause grounds. Is the legislation valid?

7. *Federal Supremacy and Preemption.* Valid federal law prevails over conflicting state or local law under the supremacy clause of the federal Constitution, Art. VI, cl. 2. Congress can expressly preempt state regulation, as it has in the Federal Insecticide, Fungicide, and Rodenticide Act, which explicitly precludes state regulation of pesticide labeling. 7 U.S.C. § 136v(b). The Supreme Court also recognizes two forms of implied preemption. Field preemption occurs when Congress intends to fully occupy a particular regulatory field. Conflict preemption occurs where compliance with both federal and state standards is impossible, or where a state law stands in the way of fulfillment of congressional objectives. See Paul S. Weiland, Comment, Federal and State Preemption of Environmental Law: A Critical Analysis, 24 Harv. Envtl. L. Rev. 237, 252–55 (2000).

By contrast to its recent decisions narrowly interpreting the scope of federal power, the Supreme Court has applied preemption rules broadly in several environmental cases. For example, in United States v. Locke, 529 U.S. 89 (2000), the Court held that federal law preempted Washington state regulations governing operation of oil tankers in Washington waters. While some commentators see the Court's recent preemption cases as inconsistent with its federalism jurisprudence, others point out that broad preemption may be preferred by business interests operating in multiple jurisdictions. See Stephen R. McAllister and Robert L. Glicksman, Federal Environmental Law in the "New" Federalism Era, 30 Envtl. L. Rep. 11122, 11143 (2000).

8. *Preemption at the State Level.* Because local governments are creatures of state law, states enjoy broad power to preempt local legislation. Most states recognize both express and implied preemption. Constitutional or legislative "home rule" provisions may limit the state's preemptive power by giving some or all local governments primary authority over local matters. The details of state and local powers vary from state to state. For detailed discussion of the extent and limits of state control over municipal governments, see Osborne M. Reynolds, Local Government Law 76–137 (2d ed. 2001).

SECTION 2. FORCING GOVERNMENT INTO THE MARKETPLACE: THE TAKINGS CLAUSE

Individuals influence government decisions through votes and political action. Individual decisions in the marketplace, such as which car to purchase and how much to drive, also directly impact the environment.

The role of the market in environmental decisions was discussed in Chapter 1, Section 3. Generally, if the market is functioning smoothly, it should facilitate transfer of resources, including environmental resources, to their highest-valued uses. One advantage of market transactions is that they force market participants to recognize the value of competing uses. The government, however, stands outside the market when it regulates, in the sense that it can compel or forbid devotion of resources to specific uses without paying a market price (of course, government decisions are always subject to the political market, and decisionmakers will pay the price in votes if they make an unpopular decision).

This freedom from market discipline allows government to use regulation to solve market imperfections, increasing the efficiency of market distribution of resources. But it can also interfere with efficient market operation. If it does not have to pay the economic costs imposed by its regulations, the government may not fully consider those costs, and may make decisions that do not maximize societal welfare. The government may, for example, demand that more land be left in open space than the people would be willing to pay for.

When it applies, the takings clause of the federal constitution forces the government into the market. By forbidding the taking of private property "for public use without just compensation," U.S. Const. Amend. V, the takings clause requires the government to pay the market price for property it "takes." Of course, identifying when property has been taken is not an easy task. Not surprisingly, those who view economic efficiency as the cornerstone goal of public policy, and believe the market generally works well to achieve that goal, favor a broad interpretation of the takings clause. Market skeptics and those who consider efficiency only one of many important public goals, tend to favor a narrower approach. The U.S. Supreme Court has struggled to find a viable balance.

CLASS DISCUSSION PROBLEM: DEVELOPMENT AT BLUE LAKE

Situated high in the granitic Snowy Mountains, Blue Lake is deep and remarkably clear. Its beauty has made it a popular vacation spot, and over the past several decades many second homes have sprouted along its shoreline. Unfortunately, this development pressure threatens the very beauty that triggered it. Blue Lake's clarity comes from its historically low nutrient levels, which severely limit algal growth. Erosion and increased impervious surfaces (chiefly roads and roofs) greatly accelerate the flow of nutrients from the surrounding basin into the lake. As development along the lakeshore has increased, the lake's waters have become measurably less clear and blue.

Before the 1960s, development pressure at Blue Lake was low, the environmental impacts of development had not yet been recognized, and the local government imposed few restrictions on lakeshore building. Beginning in 1968, the County (which is responsible for regulating development around the lake) adopted zoning regulations limiting development to one residence per lakefront parcel, and requiring setbacks from streams. These regulations were gradually tightened over the ensuing twenty-five years, with minimum lot sizes increasing to one-half acre and stream setbacks increasing to fifty feet by the early 1990s.

Nonetheless, the lake continued to lose clarity. After amassing considerable evidence that the lake's troubles were tied directly to increasing lake- and stream-side development, and that the economic future of the region depended upon maintaining the lake as a tourist attraction, in 1995 the County adopted an entirely new, much more restrictive, zoning system. For purposes of this problem, assume that state law explicitly permits this type of zoning.

Under the new system, planning officials assign points to individual vacant parcels based on specific environmental qualities, including erodibility, soil composition, existing vegetation, and distance from the lake. Only lots achieving a minimum score qualify for issuance of a building permit. Lots near streams and wetlands, natural nutrient filters whose disturbance could rapidly release large quantities of stored nutrients into the lake, are classified as Stream Environment Zone (SEZ), and automatically assigned a score of zero. No building or land disturbance is permitted on SEZ lots. All lot owners, including the owners of SEZ lots, receive "land coverage rights" (LCRs) authorizing creation of impervious surface in an amount equal to 1% of the surface area of their lot. LCRs are freely transferable. In order to build, lot owners must not only obtain a building permit but amass sufficient LCRs for the amount of impervious surface their project includes. They must also comply with all other applicable zoning restrictions, including a three-story height limitation in residential zones which prevents the construction of extremely tall structures with small footprints.

Oscar Simpson bought an undeveloped one-quarter acre (10,890 square foot) lot at Blue Lake for $6,000 in 1970, with the idea that he would build a cabin there when he retired. In 1996, he applied for a building permit to construct an 800–square foot cabin. Because his lot is classified SEZ the permit was denied. Based on the size of his lot, Simpson has been allocated LCRs for 108.9 square feet. LCRs in the area are currently selling for about $10 per square foot, so Simpson's allocation is worth roughly $1,000. An appraiser estimates that Simpson's lot would be worth $150,000 if he could build the cabin on it, and that it could be sold for between $5,000 and $8,000 undeveloped. Does Simpson have a valid taking claim against the county? Would your answer be different if Simpson had inherited the lot from his father in 1996, after imposition of the SEZ classification? Suppose that, rather than litigate his claim, Simpson sold the lot for $5,000 to Nathan Flanders in 1996. Would Flanders have a valid taking claim?

Lucas v. South Carolina Coastal Council

United States Supreme Court, 1992.
505 U.S. 1003, 112 S.Ct. 2886, 120 L.Ed.2d 798.

■ JUSTICE SCALIA delivered the opinion of the Court.

In 1986, petitioner David H. Lucas paid $975,000 for two residential lots on the Isle of Palms in Charleston County, South Carolina, on which he intended to build single-family homes. In 1988, however, the South Carolina Legislature enacted the Beachfront Management Act, which had the direct effect of barring petitioner from erecting any permanent habitable structures on his two parcels. A state trial court found that this prohibition rendered Lucas's parcels "valueless." * * *

I

South Carolina's expressed interest in intensively managing development activities in the so-called "coastal zone" dates from 1977 when, in the aftermath of Congress's passage of the federal Coastal Zone Management Act of 1972, 86 Stat. 1280, as amended, 16 U.S.C. § 1451 *et seq.*, the legislature enacted a Coastal Zone Management Act of its own. In its original form, the South Carolina Act required owners of coastal zone land that qualified as a "critical area" (defined in the legislation to include beaches and immediately adjacent sand dunes) to obtain a permit from the newly created South Carolina Coastal Council (Council) (respondent here) prior to committing the land to a "use other than the use the critical area was devoted to on [September 28, 1977]."

In the late 1970s, Lucas and others began extensive residential development of the Isle of Palms, a barrier island situated eastward of the city of Charleston. Toward the close of the development cycle for one residential subdivision known as "Beachwood East," Lucas in 1986 purchased the two lots at issue in this litigation for his own account. No portion of the lots, which were located approximately 300 feet from the beach, qualified as a "critical area" under the 1977 Act; accordingly, at the time Lucas acquired these parcels, he was not legally obliged to obtain a permit from the Council in advance of any development activity. His intention with respect to the lots was to do what the owners of the immediately adjacent parcels had already done: erect single-family residences. He commissioned architectural drawings for this purpose.

The Beachfront Management Act brought Lucas's plans to an abrupt end. Under that 1988 legislation, the Council was directed to establish a "baseline" connecting the landward-most "point[s] of erosion . . . during the past forty years" in the region of the Isle of Palms that includes Lucas's lots. S.C. Code Ann. § 48–39–280(A)(2) (Supp. 1988). In action not challenged here, the Council fixed this baseline landward of Lucas's parcels. That was significant, for under the Act construction of occupiable improvements was flatly prohibited seaward of a line drawn 20 feet landward of, and parallel to, the baseline. § 48–39–290(A). The Act provided no exceptions.

* * *

III

Prior to Justice Holmes' exposition in *Pennsylvania Coal Co. v. Mahon*, 260 U.S. 393 (1922), it was generally thought that the Takings Clause reached only a "direct appropriation" of property or the functional equivalent of a "practical ouster of [the owner's] possession." Transportation Co. v. Chicago, 99 U.S. 635, 642 (1879). Justice Holmes recognized in *Mahon*, however, that if the protection against physical appropriations of private property was to be meaningfully enforced, the government's power to redefine the range of interests included in the ownership of property was necessarily constrained by constitutional limits. If, instead, the uses of private property were subject to unbridled, uncompensated qualification under the police power, "the natural tendency of human nature [would be] to extend the qualification more and more until at last private property disappear[ed]." Id., at 415. These considerations gave birth in that case to the oft-cited maxim that, "while property may be regulated to a certain extent, if regulation goes too far it will be recognized as a taking." Ibid.

Nevertheless, our decision in *Mahon* offered little insight into when, and under what circumstances, a given regulation would be seen as going "too far" for purposes of the Fifth Amendment. In 70-odd years of succeeding "regulatory takings" jurisprudence, we have generally eschewed any "set formula" for determining how far is too far, preferring to "engag[e] in ... essentially ad hoc, factual inquiries," Penn Central Transportation Co. v. New York City, 438 U.S. 104, 124 (1978). We have, however, described at least two discrete categories of regulatory action as compensable without case-specific inquiry into the public interest advanced in support of the restraint. The first encompasses regulations that compel the property owner to suffer a physical "invasion" of his property. In general (at least with regard to permanent invasions), no matter how minute the intrusion, and no matter how weighty the public purpose behind it, we have required compensation. * * *

The second situation in which we have found categorical treatment appropriate is where regulation denies all economically beneficial or productive use of land. As we have said on numerous occasions, the Fifth Amendment is violated when land-use regulation "does not substantially advance legitimate state interests *or denies an owner economically viable use of his land.*"[7]

We have never set forth the justification for this rule. Perhaps it is simply, as Justice Brennan suggested, that total deprivation of beneficial use is, from the landowner's point of view, the equivalent of a physical appropriation. See San Diego Gas & Electric Co. v. San Diego, 450 U.S., at 652 (Brennan, J., dissenting). * * * Surely, at least, in the extraordinary circumstance when *no* productive or economically beneficial use of land is permitted, it is less realistic to indulge our usual assumption that the legislature is simply "adjusting the benefits and burdens of economic life," Penn Central Transportation Co., 438 U.S., at 124, in a manner that secures an "average reciprocity of advantage" to everyone concerned, Pennsylvania Coal Co. v. Mahon, 260 U.S. at 415. And the *functional* basis for permitting the government, by regulation, to affect property values without compensation—that "Government hardly could go on if to some extent values incident to property could not be diminished without paying for every such change in the general law," id., at 413—does not apply to the relatively rare situations where the government has deprived a landowner of all economically beneficial uses.

On the other side of the balance, affirmatively supporting a compensation requirement, is the fact that regulations that leave the owner of land

---

7. Regrettably, the rhetorical force of our "deprivation of all economically feasible use" rule is greater than its precision, since the rule does not make clear the "property interest" against which the loss of value is to be measured. When, for example, a regulation requires a developer to leave 90% of a rural tract in its natural state, it is unclear whether we would analyze the situation as one in which the owner has been deprived of all economically beneficial use of the burdened portion of the tract, or as one in which the owner has suffered a mere diminution in value of the tract as a whole. * * * The answer to this difficult question may lie in how the owner's reasonable expectations have been shaped by the State's law of property—*i.e.*, whether and to what degree the State's law has accorded legal recognition and protection to the particular interest in land with respect to which the takings claimant alleges a diminution in (or elimination of) value. In any event, we avoid this difficulty in the present case, since the "interest in land" that Lucas has pleaded (a fee simple interest) is an estate with a rich tradition of protection at common law, and since the South Carolina Court of Common Pleas found that the Beachfront Management Act left each of Lucas's beachfront lots without economic value.

without economically beneficial or productive options for its use—typically, as here, by requiring land to be left substantially in its natural state—carry with them a heightened risk that private property is being pressed into some form of public service under the guise of mitigating serious public harm. * * *

We think, in short, that there are good reasons for our frequently expressed belief that when the owner of real property has been called upon to sacrifice *all* economically beneficial uses in the name of the common good, that is, to leave his property economically idle, he has suffered a taking.[8]

The trial court found Lucas's two beachfront lots to have been rendered valueless by respondent's enforcement of the coastal-zone construction ban. Under Lucas's theory of the case, which rested upon our "no economically viable use" statements, that finding entitled him to compensation. Lucas believed it unnecessary to take issue with either the purposes behind the Beachfront Management Act, or the means chosen by the South Carolina Legislature to effectuate those purposes. The South Carolina Supreme Court, however, thought otherwise. In its view, the Beachfront Management Act was no ordinary enactment, but involved an exercise of South Carolina's "police powers" to mitigate the harm to the public interest that petitioner's use of his land might occasion. * * *

It is correct that many of our prior opinions have suggested that "harmful or noxious uses" of property may be proscribed by government regulation without the requirement of compensation. For a number of reasons, however, we think the South Carolina Supreme Court was too quick to conclude that that principle decides the present case. The "harmful or noxious uses" principle was the Court's early attempt to describe in theoretical terms why government may, consistent with the Takings Clause, affect property values by regulation without incurring an obligation to compensate—a reality we nowadays acknowledge explicitly with respect to the full scope of the State's police power. * * *

The transition from our early focus on control of "noxious" uses to our contemporary understanding of the broad realm within which government may regulate without compensation was an easy one, since the distinction between "harm-preventing" and "benefit-conferring" regulation is often in the eye of the beholder. It is quite possible, for example, to describe in *either* fashion the ecological, economic, and aesthetic concerns that inspired the South Carolina legislature in the present case. One could say that

---

8. Justice Stevens criticizes the "deprivation of all economically beneficial use" rule as "wholly arbitrary," in that "[the] landowner whose property is diminished in value 95% recovers nothing," while the landowner who suffers a complete elimination of value "recovers the land's full value." This analysis errs in its assumption that the landowner whose deprivation is one step short of complete is not entitled to compensation. Such an owner might not be able to claim the benefit of our categorical formulation, but, as we have acknowledged time and again, "[t]he economic impact of the regulation on the claimant and ... the extent to which the regulation has interfered with distinct investment-backed expectations" are keenly relevant to takings analysis generally. Penn Central Transportation Co. v. New York City, 438 U.S. 104, 124 (1978). * * *

imposing a servitude on Lucas's land is necessary in order to prevent his use of it from "harming" South Carolina's ecological resources; or, instead, in order to achieve the "benefits" of an ecological preserve. Whether one or the other of the competing characterizations will come to one's lips in a particular case depends primarily upon one's evaluation of the worth of competing uses of real estate. * * *

When it is understood that "prevention of harmful use" was merely our early formulation of the police power justification necessary to sustain (without compensation) *any* regulatory diminution in value; and that the distinction between regulation that "prevents harmful use" and that which "confers benefits" is difficult, if not impossible, to discern on an objective, value-free basis; it becomes self-evident that noxious-use logic cannot serve as a touchstone to distinguish regulatory "takings"—which require compensation—from regulatory deprivations that do not require compensation. A *fortiori* the legislature's recitation of a noxious-use justification cannot be the basis for departing from our categorical rule that total regulatory takings must be compensated. If it were, departure would virtually always be allowed. * * *

Where the State seeks to sustain regulation that deprives land of all economically beneficial use, we think it may resist compensation only if the logically antecedent inquiry into the nature of the owner's estate shows that the proscribed use interests were not part of his title to begin with. This accords, we think, with our "takings" jurisprudence, which has traditionally been guided by the understandings of our citizens regarding the content of, and the State's power over, the "bundle of rights" that they acquire when they obtain title to property. It seems to us that the property owner necessarily expects the uses of his property to be restricted, from time to time, by various measures newly enacted by the State in legitimate exercise of its police powers; "[a]s long recognized, some values are enjoyed under an implied limitation and must yield to the police power." Pennsylvania Coal Co. v. Mahon, 260 U.S., at 413. And in the case of personal property, by reason of the State's traditionally high degree of control over commercial dealings, he ought to be aware of the possibility that new regulation might even render his property economically worthless. In the case of land, however, we think the notion pressed by the Council that title is somehow held subject to the "implied limitation" that the State may subsequently eliminate all economically valuable use is inconsistent with the historical compact recorded in the Takings Clause that has become part of our constitutional culture.

Where "permanent physical occupation" of land is concerned, we have refused to allow the government to decree it anew (without compensation), no matter how weighty the asserted "public interests" involved—though we assuredly *would* permit the government to assert a permanent easement that was a pre-existing limitation upon the landowner's title. We believe similar treatment must be accorded confiscatory regulations, *i.e.*, regulations that prohibit all economically beneficial use of land: Any limitation so severe cannot be newly legislated or decreed (without compensation), but must inhere in the title itself, in the restrictions that background principles of the State's law of property and nuisance already place upon land ownership. A law or decree with such an effect must, in other words, do no more than duplicate the result that could have been achieved in the courts—by adjacent landowners (or other uniquely affected persons) under the State's law of private nuisance, or by the State under its complementary power to abate nuisances that affect the public generally, or otherwise.

On this analysis, the owner of a lake-bed, for example, would not be entitled to compensation when he is denied the requisite permit to engage in a landfilling operation that would have the effect of flooding others' land. Nor the corporate owner of a nuclear generating plant, when it is directed to remove all improvements from its land upon discovery that the plant sits astride an earthquake fault. Such regulatory action may well have the effect of eliminating the land's only economically productive use, but it does not proscribe a productive use that was previously permissible under relevant property and nuisance principles. * * *

It seems unlikely that common-law principles would have prevented the erection of any habitable or productive improvements on petitioner's land; they rarely support prohibition of the "essential use" of land, Curtin v. Benson, 222 U.S. 78, 86 (1911). The question, however, is one of state law to be dealt with on remand. We emphasize that to win its case South Carolina must do more than proffer the legislature's declaration that the uses Lucas desires are inconsistent with the public interest, or the conclusory assertion that they violate a common-law maxim such as *sic utere tuo ut alienum non laedas.* As we have said, a "State, by *ipse dixit,* may not transform private property into public property without compensation. . . ." Webb's Fabulous Pharmacies, Inc. v. Beckwith, 449 U.S. 155, 164 (1980). Instead, as it would be required to do if it sought to restrain Lucas in a common-law action for public nuisance, South Carolina must identify background principles of nuisance and property law that prohibit the uses he now intends in the circumstances in which the property is presently found. Only on this showing can the State fairly claim that, in proscribing all such beneficial uses, the Beachfront Management Act is taking nothing.

* * *

■ JUSTICE KENNEDY, concurring in the judgment.

* * *

In my view, reasonable expectations must be understood in light of the whole of our legal tradition. The common law of nuisance is too narrow a confine for the exercise of regulatory power in a complex and interdependent society. The State should not be prevented from enacting new regulatory initiatives in response to changing conditions, and courts must consider all reasonable expectations whatever their source. The Takings Clause does not require a static body of state property law; it protects private expectations to ensure private investment. I agree with the Court that nuisance prevention accords with the most common expectations of property owners who face regulation, but I do not believe this can be the sole source of state authority to impose severe restrictions. Coastal property may present such unique concerns for a fragile land system that the State can go further in regulating its development and use than the common law of nuisance might otherwise permit.

* * *

■ JUSTICE BLACKMUN, dissenting.

Today the Court launches a missile to kill a mouse.

* * *

The Beachfront Management Act includes a finding by the South Carolina General Assembly that the beach/dune system serves the purpose of "protect[ing] life and property by serving as a storm barrier which dissipates wave energy and contributes to shoreline stability in an economical and effective manner." S.C. Code Ann. § 48–39–250(1)(a) (Supp. 1990). The General Assembly also found that "development unwisely has been sited too close to the [beach/dune] system. This type of development has jeopardized the stability of the beach/dune system, accelerated erosion, and endangered adjacent property." § 48–39–250(4).

If the state legislature is correct that the prohibition on building in front of the setback line prevents serious harm, then, under this Court's prior cases, the Act is constitutional. * * * The Court consistently has upheld regulations imposed to arrest a significant threat to the common welfare, whatever their economic effect on the owner.

* * *

The Court does not reject the South Carolina Supreme Court's decision simply on the basis of its disbelief and distrust of the legislature's findings. It also takes the opportunity to create a new scheme for regulations that eliminate all economic value. From now on, there is a categorical rule finding these regulations to be a taking unless the use they prohibit is a background common-law nuisance or property principle.

I first question the Court's rationale in creating a category that obviates a "case-specific inquiry into the public interest advanced," if all economic value has been lost. If one fact about the Court's takings jurisprudence can be stated without contradiction, it is that "the particular circumstances of each case" determine whether a specific restriction will be rendered invalid by the government's failure to pay compensation. *United States v. Central Eureka Mining Co.*, 357 U.S. 155, 168 (1958). This is so because although we have articulated certain factors to be considered, including the economic impact on the property owner, the ultimate conclusion "necessarily requires a weighing of private and public interests." *Agins,* 447 U.S., at 261. When the government regulation prevents the owner from any economically valuable use of his property, the private interest is unquestionably substantial, but we have never before held that no public interest can outweigh it. * * *

Ultimately even the Court cannot embrace the full implications of its *per se* rule: It eventually agrees that there cannot be a categorical rule for a taking based on economic value that wholly disregards the public need asserted. Instead, the Court decides that it will permit a State to regulate all economic value only if the State prohibits uses that would not be permitted under "background principles of nuisance and property law."

* * *

The Court rejects the notion that the State always can prohibit uses it deems a harm to the public without granting compensation because "the distinction between 'harm-preventing' and 'benefit-conferring' regulation is often in the eye of the beholder." Since the characterization will depend "primarily upon one's evaluation of the worth of competing uses of real estate," the Court decides a legislative judgment of this kind no longer can provide the desired "objective, value-free basis" for upholding a regulation. The Court, however, fails to explain how its proposed common-law alternative escapes the same trap.

* * *

* * * In determining what is a nuisance at common law, state courts make exactly the decision that the Court finds so troubling when made by the South Carolina General Assembly today: They determine whether the use is harmful. * * * There simply is no reason to believe that new interpretations of the hoary common-law nuisance doctrine will be particularly "objective" or "value free." Once one abandons the level of generality of *sic utere tuo ut alienum non laedas,* one searches in vain, I think, for anything resembling a principle in the common law of nuisance.

* * *

[Justice Stevens dissented separately. Justice Souter would have dismissed the writ of certiorari as improvidently granted because the Court could not review the lower court's "questionable conclusion of total deprivation" of value.]

Palazzolo v. Rhode Island

United States Supreme Court, 2001.
533 U.S. 606, 121 S.Ct. 2448, 150 L.Ed.2d 592.

■ JUSTICE KENNEDY delivered the opinion of the Court.

* * *

I

The town of Westerly is on an edge of the Rhode Island coastline. * * * Westerly today has about 20,000 year-round residents, and thousands of summer visitors come to enjoy its beaches and coastal advantages.

One of the more popular attractions is Misquamicut State Beach, a lengthy expanse of coastline facing Block Island Sound and beyond to the

Atlantic Ocean. The primary point of access to the beach is Atlantic Avenue, a well-traveled 3–mile stretch of road running along the coastline within the town's limits. At its western end, Atlantic Avenue is something of a commercial strip, with restaurants, hotels, arcades, and other typical seashore businesses. The pattern of development becomes more residential as the road winds eastward onto a narrow spine of land bordered to the south by the beach and the ocean, and to the north by Winnapaug Pond, an intertidal inlet often used by residents for boating, fishing, and shellfishing.

In 1959 petitioner, a lifelong Westerly resident, decided to invest in three undeveloped, adjoining parcels along this eastern stretch of Atlantic Avenue. * * * To purchase and hold the property, petitioner and associates formed Shore Gardens, Inc. (SGI). After SGI purchased the property petitioner bought out his associates and became the sole shareholder. * * * Most of the property was then, as it is now, salt marsh subject to tidal flooding. The wet ground and permeable soil would require considerable fill—as much as six feet in some places—before significant structures could be built. * * *

[Between 1962 and 1966, SGI submitted three applications to fill and develop the property. The first was denied for lack of information. The others were denied based on their environmental impacts.] No further attempts to develop the property were made for over a decade. Two intervening events, however, become important to the issues presented. First, in 1971, Rhode Island enacted legislation creating the Council, an agency charged with the duty of protecting the State's coastal properties. Regulations promulgated by the Council designated salt marshes like those on SGI's property as protected "coastal wetlands," on which development is limited to a great extent. Second, in 1978 SGI's corporate charter was revoked for failure to pay corporate income taxes; and title to the property passed, by operation of state law, to petitioner as the corporation's sole shareholder.

In 1983 petitioner, now the owner, renewed the efforts to develop the property. An application to the Council, resembling the 1962 submission, requested permission to construct a wooden bulkhead along the shore of Winnapaug Pond and to fill the entire marsh land area. The Council rejected the application, noting it was "vague and inadequate for a project of this size and nature." The agency also found that "the proposed activities will have significant impacts upon the waters and wetlands of Winnapaug Pond," and concluded that "the proposed alteration ... will conflict with the Coastal Resources Management Plan presently in effect." Petitioner did not appeal the agency's determination.

Petitioner went back to the drawing board, this time hiring counsel and preparing a more specific and limited proposal for use of the property. The new application, submitted to the Council in 1985, echoed the 1966 request to build a private beach club. The details do not tend to inspire the reader with an idyllic coastal image, for the proposal was to fill 11 acres of the property with gravel to accommodate "50 cars with boat trailers, a dumpster, port-a-johns, picnic tables, barbecue pits of concrete, and other trash receptacles."

The application fared no better with the Council than previous ones. Under the agency's regulations, a landowner wishing to fill salt marsh on Winnapaug Pond needed a "special exception" from the Council. In a short opinion the Council said the beach club proposal conflicted with the regulatory standard for a special exception. To secure a special exception the proposed activity must serve "a compelling public purpose which provides benefits to the public as a whole as opposed to individual or private interests." * * *

II

The Takings Clause of the Fifth Amendment, applicable to the States through the Fourteenth Amendment, prohibits the government from taking private property for public use without just compensation. The clearest sort of taking occurs when the government encroaches upon or occupies private land for its own proposed use. Our cases establish that even a minimal "permanent physical occupation of real property" requires compensation under the Clause. In *Pennsylvania Coal Co. v. Mahon*, 260 U.S. 393 (1922), the Court recognized that there will be instances when government actions do not encroach upon or occupy the property yet still affect and limit its use to such an extent that a taking occurs. In Justice Holmes' well-known, if less than self-defining, formulation, "while property may be regulated to a certain extent, if a regulation goes too far it will be recognized as a taking." Id., at 415.

Since *Mahon*, we have given some, but not too specific, guidance to courts confronted with deciding whether a particular government action goes too far and effects a regulatory taking. First, we have observed, with certain qualifications, that a regulation which "denies all economically beneficial or productive use of land" will require compensation under the Takings Clause. Lucas, 505 U.S., at 1015. Where a regulation places limitations on land that fall short of eliminating all economically beneficial use, a taking nonetheless may have occurred, depending on a complex of factors including the regulation's economic effect on the landowner, the extent to which the regulation interferes with reasonable investment-backed expectations, and the character of the government action. These inquiries are informed by the purpose of the Takings Clause, which is to prevent the government from "forcing some people alone to bear public burdens which, in all fairness and justice, should be borne by the public as a whole." Armstrong v. United States, 364 U.S. 40, 49 (1960).

* * * When the Council promulgated its wetlands regulations, the disputed parcel was owned not by petitioner but by the corporation of which he was sole shareholder. When title was transferred to petitioner by operation of law, the wetlands regulations were in force. The state court held the postregulation acquisition of title was fatal to the claim for deprivation of all economic use, and to the *Penn Central* claim. While the first holding was couched in terms of background principles of state

property law and the second in terms of petitioner's reasonable investment-backed expectations, the two holdings together amount to a single, sweeping, rule: A purchaser or a successive title holder like petitioner is deemed to have notice of an earlier-enacted restriction and is barred from claiming that it effects a taking.

* * * Were we to accept the State's rule, the postenactment transfer of title would absolve the State of its obligation to defend any action restricting land use, no matter how extreme or unreasonable. A State would be allowed, in effect, to put an expiration date on the Takings Clause. This ought not to be the rule. Future generations, too, have a right to challenge unreasonable limitations on the use and value of land.

Nor does the justification of notice take into account the effect on owners at the time of enactment, who are prejudiced as well. Should an owner attempt to challenge a new regulation, but not survive the process of ripening his or her claim (which, as this case demonstrates, will often take years), under the proposed rule the right to compensation may not by asserted by an heir or successor, and so may not be asserted at all. The State's rule would work a critical alteration to the nature of property, as the newly regulated landowner is stripped of the ability to transfer the interest which was possessed prior to the regulation. The State may not by this means secure a windfall for itself. The proposed rule is, furthermore, capricious in effect. The young owner contrasted with the older owner, the owner with the resources to hold contrasted with the owner with the need to sell, would be in different positions. The Takings Clause is not so quixotic. * * *

We have no occasion to consider the precise circumstances when a legislative enactment can be deemed a background principle of state law or whether those circumstances are present here. It suffices to say that a regulation that otherwise would be unconstitutional absent compensation is not transformed into a background principle of the State's law by mere virtue of the passage of title. * * * A regulation or common-law rule cannot be a background principle for some owners but not for others. The determination whether an existing, general law can limit all economic use of property must turn on objective factors, such as the nature of the land use proscribed. A law does not become a background principle for subsequent owners by enactment itself. * * *

* * * [W]e have before us the alternative ground relied upon by the Rhode Island Supreme Court in ruling upon the merits of the takings claims. It held that all economically beneficial use was not deprived because the uplands portion of the property can still be improved. On this point, we agree with the court's decision. Petitioner accepts the Council's contention and the state trial court's finding that his parcel retains $200,000 in development value under the State's wetlands regulations. He asserts, nonetheless, that he has suffered a total taking * * *.

Assuming a taking is otherwise established, a State may not evade the duty to compensate on the premise that the landowner is left with a token interest. This is not the situation of the landowner in this case, however. A regulation permitting a landowner to build a substantial residence on an 18–acre parcel does not leave the property "economically idle." Lucas, supra, at 1019.

In his brief submitted to us petitioner attempts to revive this part of his claim by reframing it. He argues, for the first time, that the upland parcel is distinct from the wetlands portions, so he should be permitted to assert a deprivation limited to the latter. This contention asks us to examine the difficult, persisting question of what is the proper denominator in the takings fraction. Some of our cases indicate that the extent of deprivation effected by a regulatory action is measured against the value of the parcel as a whole; but we have at times expressed discomfort with the logic of this rule, a sentiment echoed by some commentators. Whatever the merits of these criticisms, we will not explore the point here. Petitioner did not press the argument in the state courts, and the issue was not presented in the petition for certiorari. The case comes to us on the premise that petitioner's entire parcel serves as the basis for his takings claim, and, so framed, the total deprivation argument fails.

For the reasons we have discussed, the State Supreme Court erred in * * * ruling that acquisition of title after the effective date of the regulations barred the takings claims. The court did not err in finding that petitioner failed to establish a deprivation of all economic value, for it is undisputed that the parcel retains significant worth for construction of a residence. The claims under the *Penn Central* analysis were not examined, and for this purpose the case should be remanded.

* * *

■ JUSTICE O'CONNOR, concurring.

* * * As the Court holds, the Rhode Island Supreme Court erred in effectively adopting the sweeping rule that the preacquisition enactment of the use restriction *ipso facto* defeats any takings claim based on that use restriction. * * *

The more difficult question is what role the temporal relationship between regulatory enactment and title acquisition plays in a proper *Penn Central* analysis. Today's holding does not mean that the timing of the regulation's enactment relative to the acquisition of title is immaterial to the *Penn Central* analysis. Indeed, it would be just as much error to expunge this consideration from the takings inquiry as it would be to accord it exclusive significance. Our polestar instead remains the principles set forth in *Penn Central* itself and our other cases that govern partial regulatory takings. Under these cases, interference with investment-backed expectations is one of a number of factors that a court must examine. Further, the regulatory regime in place at the time the claimant acquires the property at issue helps to shape the reasonableness of those expectations.

* * * Courts properly consider the effect of existing regulations under the rubric of investment-backed expectations in determining whether a compensable taking has occurred. As before, the salience of these facts

cannot be reduced to any "set formula." Penn Central, 438 U.S., at 124. The temptation to adopt what amount to *per se* rules in either direction must be resisted. The Takings Clause requires careful examination and weighing of all the relevant circumstances in this context. * * *

■ JUSTICE SCALIA, concurring.

* * *

In my view, the fact that a restriction existed at the time the purchaser took title (other than a restriction forming part of the "background principles of the State's law of property and nuisance," Lucas v. South Carolina Coastal Council, 505 U.S. 1003, 1029 (1992)) should have no bearing upon the determination of whether the restriction is so substantial as to constitute a taking. The "investment-backed expectations" that the law will take into account do not include the assumed validity of a restriction that in fact deprives property of so much of its value as to be unconstitutional. Which is to say that a *Penn Central* taking, no less than a total taking, is not absolved by the transfer of title.

■ JUSTICE STEVENS, concurring in part and dissenting in part.

* * *

Though the majority leaves open the possibility that the scope of today's holding may prove limited, the extension of the right to compensation to individuals other than the direct victim of an illegal taking admits of no obvious limiting principle. If the existence of valid land-use regulations does not limit the title that the first postenactment purchaser of the property inherits, then there is no reason why such regulations should limit the rights of the second, the third, or the thirtieth purchaser. Perhaps my concern is unwarranted, but today's decision does raise the specter of a tremendous—and tremendously capricious—one-time transfer of wealth from society at large to those individuals who happen to hold title to large tracts of land at the moment this legal question is permanently resolved.

■ JUSTICE BREYER, dissenting.

* * * [G]iven this Court's precedents, I would agree with Justice O'Connor that the simple fact that a piece of property has changed hands (for example, by inheritance) does not always and *automatically* bar a takings claim. Here, for example, without in any way suggesting that Palazzolo has any valid takings claim, I believe his postregulatory acquisition of the property (through automatic operation of law) by itself should not prove dispositive.

As Justice O'Connor explains, under *Penn Central Transp. Co. v. New York City*, 438 U.S. 104 (1978), much depends upon whether, or how, the timing and circumstances of a change of ownership affect whatever reasonable investment-backed expectations might otherwise exist. Ordinarily, such expectations will diminish in force and significance—rapidly and dramatically—as property continues to change hands over time. I believe that such factors can adequately be taken into account within the *Penn Central* framework.

Several amici have warned that to allow complete regulatory takings claims to survive changes in land ownership could allow property owners to manufacture such claims by strategically transferring property until only a nonusable portion remains. But I do not see how a constitutional provision concerned with fairness and justice could reward any such strategic behavior.

[Justice Ginsburg, joined by Justices Souter and Breyer, dissented on the grounds that Palazzolo's claim was not yet ripe for decision.]

NOTES AND QUESTIONS

1. *The Recent Revival of Interest in Regulatory Takings.* The Supreme Court first held that the takings clause applied to regulations in 1922. In *Pennsylvania Coal Co. v. Mahon*, 260 U.S. 393 (1922), the Court ruled that compensation was required for a Pennsylvania statute requiring a coal mining company to leave sufficient coal in place to support the surface. The company had conveyed the surface for residential use but expressly reserved the right to take all the underlying coal, with no liability for any resulting damage to the surface. The next major takings case dealing with land use regulations came more than fifty years later. In *Penn Central Transportation Co. v. New York City*, 438 U.S. 104 (1978), a 6–3 majority of the Court upheld restrictions imposed on remodeling of Grand Central Station, which had been declared a historic landmark.

Since *Penn Central*, the Court has been remarkably active in this area. Although the Court has often been sharply divided, landowners have enjoyed increasing success in takings cases in recent years. In 1987, the Court held, by a 6–3 vote, that a statute virtually identical to that in *Pennsylvania Coal* did not unconstitutionally take property because it protected public health and safety against subsidence. Keystone Bituminous Coal v. DeBenedictis, 480 U.S. 470 (1987). That same year, though, the Court signaled increasing sympathy for takings claims in two other cases. *First English Evangelical Lutheran Church v. County of Los Angeles*, 482 U.S. 304, held that compensation must be paid for the period during which a statute or ordinance that worked an unconstitutional taking was in effect. *Nollan v. California Coastal Commission*, 483 U.S. 825 (1987), held that a state agency could not constitutionally demand dedication to the public of an easement along the beach in return for a permit to build a beachfront home.

The 1987 trio was followed in the 1990s by two big wins for property rights advocates—*Lucas* in 1992, and *Dolan v. City of Tigard*, 512 U.S. 374 (1994), which prescribed closer judicial review of conditions imposed on development approvals. More recently, the Court has decided procedural issues in favor of property owners in *Suitum v. Tahoe Regional Planning Agency*, 520 U.S. 725 (1997) (holding takings claim ripe for review), and *City of Monterey v. Del Monte Dunes*, 526 U.S. 687 (1999) (holding that question of whether city's repeated rejection of development proposals amounted to a taking was properly submitted to jury).

2. *The Takings Clause and the Role of the Courts*. What is the purpose of the takings clause, particularly in the regulatory context? Would legislatures not constrained by the clause pay insufficient heed to the concerns of property owners? Do you agree with Justice Holmes' assertion in *Pennsylvania Coal v. Mahon* that, absent the takings clause, "the natural tendency of human nature" would be to regulate more and more restrictively "until at last private property disappears"? Would any political forces restrain that tendency?

3. *Takings Doctrine*. The basic principles of the Court's recent takings doctrine are easily stated, but far less easily applied. There are two classes of *per se* takings, in which compensation is required no matter how minimal the intrusion or how strong the public purpose behind it. The first includes physical takings, in which the government permanently physically occupies land. See Loretto v. Teleprompter Manhattan CATV Corp., 458 U.S. 419, 426 (1982). The second covers total takings, in which the government regulates away all economically viable use. As explained in *Lucas*, total takings require compensation unless the challenged regulation simply implements a pre-existing background principle of law. Since these tests were articulated, it has proven surprisingly difficult to determine whether a physical occupation has occurred, and even more difficult to determine whether all economically viable use has been lost.

The task becomes far more difficult if neither of the *per se* takings rules apply. In that case, regulations are evaluated under a general fairness test based primarily on three factors: the economic impact of the regulation, the extent to which it interferes with investment-backed expectations, and its character. Penn Central Transp. Co. v. New York City, 438 U.S. 104 (1978). None of the factors takes primacy over the others. The inquiry is *ad hoc*, and intensely fact-specific. Although the Court has not expressly said so, it appears to apply a presumption of validity, refusing to find a taking in the absence of "extreme circumstances." See United States v. Riverside Bayview Homes, 474 U.S. 121, 126. "[M]ere diminution in the value of property, however serious, is insufficient to demonstrate a taking." Concrete Pipe & Prod. of Cal., Inc. v. Construction Laborers Pension Trust for S. Cal., 508 U.S. 602, 645 (1993).

Why is the Court, in *Lucas* and *Palazzolo*, so anxious to articulate "objective, value-neutral" criteria for regulatory takings analysis? Can there be any such test for determining whether regulations "go too far"? Might the Court articulate clearer principles if it spoke openly of the competing values implicated by takings cases?

4. *The Denominator Problem*. In footnote 7, the *Lucas* majority acknowledged what has become known as the "denominator problem"—a court cannot determine whether all economically viable use has been lost without first determining what is the relevant parcel. Even if there is not a total taking, the denominator problem is relevant to the extent of interference with investment-backed expectations, one of the factors in the *ad hoc* fairness inquiry.

Lacking clearer assistance from the Supreme Court, the lower courts have struggled to solve the denominator problem. The lines of legal parcels are plainly not determinative.

The District of Columbia Circuit has explained:

> The definition of the relevant parcel profoundly influences the outcome of a takings analysis. Above all, the parcel should be functionally coherent. In other words, more should unite the property than common ownership by the claimant. Thus, a court must also consider how both the property-owner and the government treat (and have treated) the property.

District Intown Props. v. District of Columbia, 198 F.3d 874, 880 (1999). In *District Intown*, the plaintiff had purchased a single lot developed with an apartment building and landscaped lawns in 1961. In 1988, it subdivided the property into nine lots, one containing the apartment building, the other eight constituting the grounds. District Intown then applied for permits to build a single townhouse on each of the eight undeveloped lots. Before it received approval, neighbors filed a petition to designate the property a historic landmark. The petition was granted, District Intown's development request was denied as inconsistent with historic landmark status, and District Intown filed a takings action. Considering the degree of spatial and functional contiguity, the dates of acquisition, the extent to which the land had been treated as a single unit, and the extent to which the unregulated lot was benefitted by the restricted ones, the court ruled that all nine lots must be treated as a single parcel for purposes of the takings claim.

Do you agree with the *District Intown* decision? Are the factors it articulates relevant to the denominator determination? Should other factors be considered? How should courts deal with property that is gradually developed over a long period of time? Should the denominator include portions developed many years before the challenged regulation becomes effective, or only the remaining portions? See Loveladies Harbor, Inc. v. United States, 28 F.3d 1171 (Fed.Cir.1994) (holding that relevant parcel included only 51 acres, not additional 199 acres purchased at same time but developed before the challenged regulatory action).

5. *Temporary Takings.* What test should courts apply to development restrictions that are limited in time, such as building moratoria? Is a moratorium that prevents any building for a time a *per se* taking under *Lucas*, with only the compensation required affected by its duration? Or is it subject to the multi-factor fairness analysis of *Penn Central*? In First English Evangelical Lutheran Church v. County of Los Angeles, 482 U.S. 304 (1987), the Court held that if a regulation that unconstitutionally takes property is later rescinded, the government must nonetheless pay compensation for the time during which the taking was in effect. *First English* did not, however, address the question of how to determine whether a temporally limited regulation amounts to a taking. The Supreme Court has granted certiorari in Tahoe–Sierra Preservation Council v. Tahoe Regional Planning Agency, 216 F.3d 764 (9th Cir.2000) to decide that question.

6. *The Property Transfer Problem*. *Palazzolo* addresses another persistent takings puzzle, the effect of transfer of the property after a change in the regulatory regime. On the one hand, the Court has consistently recognized the importance of expectations, and a person who acquires property after a regulation is in effect cannot expect, at the time of acquisition, to use the property in a way that is inconsistent with the regulation. It seems that the buyer has lost nothing. On the other hand, if the buyer is barred from raising a takings claim, the seller will have lost something. The buyer will pay only the regulated price. The seller who acquired the property before regulation will lose her investment-backed expectations. Such a rule may greatly disadvantage owners without the time or financial resources to pursue a takings action.

What precisely does *Palazzolo* hold with respect to postregulation acquisition? What weight should the state court give on remand to the fact that Palazzolo acquired his interest after promulgation of Rhode Island's coastal wetlands regulations? Is it relevant that Palazzolo acquired by operation of law rather than by purchase? That he could have prevented the transfer by paying his company's income taxes?

7. *Exactions*. Local governments often require that developers dedicate a portion of their land to public uses (including roadways, schools, parks, and other infrastructure) in return for development approval. These requirements are called "exactions." In Nollan v. California Coastal Comm'n, 483 U.S. 825 (1987), the Court held that property exactions must bear an "essential nexus" to the governmental purpose they are intended to serve. *Nollan* struck down exaction of a lateral easement along the beachfront as insufficiently related to the Coastal Commission's stated concern that construction of a new house on the coastal lot would impair the public's view of the ocean. The Court addressed exactions again in Dolan v. City of Tigard, 512 U.S. 374 (1994). Striking down the required dedication of land for storm drainage and a bicycle path in connection with expansion of a plumbing supply store, the Court ruled that exactions must not only have a nexus to the government purpose, they must be roughly proportional in extent to the harm attributable to the proposed development.

The *Nollan/Dolan* exaction test does not apply to outright denials of development permission, which continue to be tested by the *Lucas* and *Penn Central* standards. See City of Monterey v. Del Monte Dunes, 526 U.S. 687 (1999). It is unclear whether it applies to exactions in the form of fees (such as school or park impact fees) rather than land dedication. The argument that it does not rests on the unique status of physical invasions as *per se* takings. As the Court noted in *Dolan*, 512 U.S. at 384:

> Without question, had the city simply required petitioner to dedicate a strip of land along Fanno Creek for public use, rather than conditioning the grant of her permit to redevelop her property on such a dedication, a taking would have occurred.

Unlike land exactions, fees imposed on landowners are not automatically takings. On the other hand, fees can have exactly the same economic impact as land dedications. They may threaten precisely the same "out-

and-out plan of extortion" the Supreme Court detected in *Nollan*, 483 U.S. at 837. For attempts to untangle this problem, see Garneau v. City of Seattle, 147 F.3d 802 (9th Cir.1998) (rejecting takings challenge to ordinance requiring that landlords provide relocation assistance to tenants displaced by property redevelopment); id. at 813 (O'Scannlain, J., dissenting) (arguing that the ordinance works a taking under the Nollan/Dolan test); Ehrlich v. City of Culver City, 12 Cal.4th 854, 50 Cal.Rptr.2d 242, 911 P.2d 429 (1996) (plurality opinion) (concluding that *Nollan* and *Dolan* apply to some, but not all, fee exactions).

8. *Transferable Development Rights.* What role do transferable development rights (TDRs), such as the land coverage rights in the Class Discussion Problem, play in takings analysis? In *Penn Central*, noting that the landowner could transfer building rights to other parcels in the vicinity, the Supreme Court stated:

> Although appellants and others have argued that New York City's transferable development-rights program is far from ideal, the New York courts here supportably found that, at least in the case of the Terminal, the rights afforded are valuable. While these rights may well not have constituted "just compensation" if a "taking" had occurred, the rights nevertheless undoubtedly mitigate whatever financial burdens the law has imposed on appellants and, for that reason, are to be taken into account in considering the impact of regulation.

438 U.S. at 137.

Three members of the Court signaled their disagreement with this analysis in Suitum v. Tahoe Regional Planning Agency, 520 U.S. 725 (1997). In *Suitum*, whose facts form the basis for the Class Discussion Problem, the Court decided only that the dispute was ripe for review. Justice Scalia, joined in his concurrence by Justices Thomas and O'Connor, criticized the argument that TDRs might be used to avoid a ruling that property had been taken:

> TDRs, of course, have nothing to do with the use or development of the land to which they are (by regulatory decree) "attached." The right to use and develop one's own land is quite distinct from the right to confer upon someone else an increased power to use and develop *his* land. The latter is valuable, to be sure, but it is a *new* right conferred upon the landowner in exchange for the taking, rather than a *reduction* of the taking. In essence, the TDR permits the landowner whose right to use and develop his property has been restricted or extinguished to extract money from others. Just as a cash payment from the government would not relate to whether the regulation "goes too far" (*i.e.*, restricts use of the land so severely as to constitute a taking), but rather to whether there has been adequate compensation for the taking; and just as a chit or coupon from the government, redeemable by and hence marketable to third parties, would relate not to the question of taking but to the question of compensation; so also the marketable TDR, a peculiar type of chit which enables a third party not to get cash from the government but to use his land in ways the

government would otherwise not permit, relates not to taking but to compensation.

520 U.S. at 747.

Which is the more persuasive analysis? Are TDRs equivalent to a cash payment after use of land is denied? Or must they be considered in evaluating the extent of the restriction imposed? Lower courts, relying on *Penn Central*, have continued to factor TDRs into the analysis of whether a taking has occurred. See Good v. United States, 39 Fed.Cl. 81, 108 (Fed.Cl. 1997).

9. *Takings Legislation*. Driven by the conviction that constitutional takings relief is too uncertain and the path to it too difficult, property rights proponents have sought legislation defining circumstances under which landowners must be compensated for the impacts of government regulation. Are legislatures or judges better situated to resolve disputes over compensation? Is takings analysis so fact-specific that it demands case-by-case, judicial resolution?

So far, the drive for takings legislation has not succeeded at the federal level, but has had some success in the states. During the 1990s, a large number of states enacted some form of takings legislation. See, e.g., Frank A. Vickory and Barry A. Diskin, Advances in Private Property Protection Rights: The States in the Vanguard, 34 Am. Bus. L. J. 561 (1997); Carl P. Marcellino, Note, The Evolution of State Takings Legislation and the Proposals Considered During the 1997–98 Legislative Session, 2 N.Y.U. J. Legis. & Pub. Pol'y 143 (1998–99). Many of these laws are procedural, requiring a formal assessment of the impacts on property values of all or a subset of government regulations. See, e.g., Del. Code Ann. tit. 29, § 605. Another procedural approach is to provide a special non-judicial forum for the resolution of takings claims, in the hope of easing litigation burdens on landowners. See, e.g., Me. Rev. Stat. Ann. tit. 5, § 3341 (providing for mediation of land use disputes).

A small number of state laws impose compensation requirements. Several of these rely on a threshold level of economic loss. Texas, for example, requires compensation when regulations reduce the market value of property at least 25%. Tex. Gov't Code Ann. § 2007.002(5)(B). Florida takes a more flexible approach, requiring compensation for regulations imposing an "inordinate burden" on landowners. Fla. Stat. Ann. § 70.001(2).

The compensation statutes have various limitations and exceptions. Most deny compensation if the regulated use would constitute a nuisance. See, e.g., Tex. Gov't Ann. § 2007.003(b)(6). Other exceptions are more idiosyncratic. Texas, for example, exempts regulations governing hunting and fishing. Tex. Gov't Ann. 2007.003(b)(10). Most state takings legislation applies across the board, but some federal proposals have been limited to particularly controversial areas of regulation, such as endangered species and wetlands protection.

Would you favor national takings legislation? If so, what form should it take? Should it apply to all regulations, or only a subset? What exceptions would you permit? Should it apply to regulations in effect before it is passed? Should it require compensation based on threshold loss or a more flexible standard? If you favor a threshold, how would you define the denominator?

*

PART II

NATURAL RESOURCES

A recurring theme of environmental law is the conflict between economic pressures to use and develop natural resources and the urge to preserve their ecological integrity and scenic beauty. Environmental law imposes both procedural requirements and substantive limits on decisions to alter the environmental status quo. Chapter 5 explores the National Environmental Policy Act, which requires that federal agencies consider environmental impacts before taking action, and other informational strategies. Chapter 6 looks at substantive limits on decisions affecting public resources, as well as privately-owned resources with a public dimension.

CHAPTER FIVE

NEPA and the Power of Information

Section 1. Introduction to NEPA

Excerpts from the National Environmental Policy Act

42 U.S.C. §§ 4321–4335.

Sec. 2 Congressional declaration of purpose

The purposes of this chapter are: To declare a national policy which will encourage productive and enjoyable harmony between man and his environment; to promote efforts which will prevent or eliminate damage to the environment and biosphere and stimulate the health and welfare of man; to enrich the understanding of the ecological systems and natural resources important to the Nation; and to establish a Council on Environmental Quality.

Sec. 101 Congressional declaration of national environmental policy

(a) The Congress, recognizing the profound impact of man's activity on the interrelations of all components of the natural environment, particularly the profound influences of population growth, high-density urbanization, industrial expansion, resource exploitation, and new and expanding technological advances and recognizing further the critical importance of restoring and maintaining environmental quality to the overall welfare and development of man, declares that it is the continuing policy of the Federal Government, in cooperation with State and local governments, and other concerned public and private organizations, to use all practicable means and measures, including financial and technical assistance, in a manner calculated to foster and promote the general welfare, to create and maintain conditions under which man and nature can exist in productive harmony, and fulfill the social, economic, and other requirements of present and future generations of Americans.

(b) In order to carry out the policy set forth in this chapter, it is the continuing responsibility of the Federal Government to use all practicable means, consistent with other essential considerations of national policy, to improve and coordinate Federal plans, functions, programs, and resources to the end that the Nation may—

(1) fulfill the responsibilities of each generation as trustee of the environment for succeeding generations;

(2) assure for all Americans safe, healthful, productive, and aesthetically and culturally pleasing surroundings;

(3) attain the widest range of beneficial uses of the environment without degradation, risk to health or safety, or other undesirable and unintended consequences;

(4) preserve important historic, cultural, and natural aspects of our national heritage, and maintain, wherever possible, an environment which supports diversity, and variety of individual choice;

(5) achieve a balance between population and resource use which will permit high standards of living and a wide sharing of life's amenities; and

(6) enhance the quality of renewable resources and approach the maximum attainable recycling of depletable resources.

(c) The Congress recognizes that each person should enjoy a healthful environment and that each person has a responsibility to contribute to the preservation and enhancement of the environment.

Sec. 102 Cooperation of agencies; reports * * *

The Congress authorizes and directs that, to the fullest extent possible: (1) the policies, regulations, and public laws of the United States shall be interpreted and administered in accordance with the policies set forth in this chapter, and (2) all agencies of the Federal Government shall—

(A) utilize a systematic, interdisciplinary approach which will insure the integrated use of the natural and social sciences and the environmental design arts in planning and in decisionmaking which may have an impact on man's environment;

(B) identify and develop methods and procedures, in consultation with the Council on Environmental Quality established by title II of this Act, which will insure that presently unquantified environmental amenities and values may be given appropriate consideration in decisionmaking along with economic and technical considerations;

(C) include in every recommendation or report on proposals for legislation and other major Federal actions significantly affecting the quality of the human environment, a detailed statement by the responsible official on—

(i) the environmental impact of the proposed action;

(ii) any adverse environmental effects which cannot be avoided should the proposal be implemented;

(iii) alternatives to the proposed action;

(iv) the relationship between local short-term uses of man's environment and the maintenance and enhancement of long-term productivity; and

(v) any irreversible and irretrievable commitments of resources which would be involved in the proposed action should it be implemented.

Prior to making any detailed statement, the responsible Federal official shall consult with and obtain the comments of any Federal agency which has jurisdiction by law or special expertise with respect to any environmental impact involved. Copies of such statement and the comments and views of the appropriate Federal, State, and local agencies, which are authorized to develop and enforce environmental standards, shall be made available to the President, the Council on Environmental Quality and to the public * * *, and shall accompany the proposal through the existing agency review processes;

* * *

(E) study, develop, and describe appropriate alternatives to recommended courses of action in any proposal which involves unresolved conflicts concerning alternative uses of available resources;

(F) recognize the worldwide and long-range character of environmental problems and, where consistent with the foreign policy of the United States, lend appropriate support to initiatives, resolutions, and programs designed to maximize international cooperation in anticipating and preventing a decline in the quality of mankind's world environment;

(G) make available to States, counties, municipalities, institutions, and individuals, advice and information useful in restoring, maintaining, and enhancing the quality of the environment;

(H) initiate and utilize ecological information in the planning and development of resource-oriented projects; and

(I) assist the Council on Environmental Quality established by subchapter II of this chapter.

* * *

Sec. 104 Other statutory obligations of agencies

Nothing in section [102 or 103] shall in any way affect the specific statutory obligations of any Federal agency (1) to comply with criteria or standards of environmental quality, (2) to coordinate or consult with any other Federal or State agency, or (3) to act, or refrain from acting contingent upon the recommendations or certification of any other Federal or State agency.

Sec. 105 Efforts supplemental to existing authorizations

The policies and goals set forth in this chapter are supplementary to those set forth in existing authorizations of Federal agencies.

Dinah Bear, NEPA at 19: A Primer on an "Old" Law with Solutions to New Problems

19 Envtl. L. Rep. 10060, 10061–65 (1989).

Title II of NEPA created the Council on Environmental Quality (CEQ) in the Executive Office of the President, composed of three Members appointed by the President with the advice and consent of the Senate. CEQ has a number of responsibilities, including preparation of an annual report on environmental quality, developing and recommending to the President national environmental policies, and documenting and defining environmental trends.

CEQ Guidance and Regulations

Shortly after NEPA was signed into law, President Nixon issued Executive Order 11514 which, among other things, directed CEQ to issue guidelines on preparation of environmental impact statements. Beginning in 1970, CEQ issued a series of these guidelines, which addressed the basic requirements of environmental impact assessment and administratively interpreted the thrust of the considerable case law that was occurring throughout the 1970s.

While the guidelines were useful, the environmental impact assessment process, or "NEPA process," as it frequently is referred to in the federal establishment, acquired some unfortunate "barnacles" during the mid-1970s. The most frequent complaints were the length of EISs and the delays that the NEPA process was perceived to cause in the decisionmaking process. Observers believed that the lack of uniformity throughout the government and uncertainty about what was required accounted to a large degree for these problems. Consequently, in 1977 President Carter issued Executive Order 11991, directing CEQ to issue binding regulations to federal agencies in an effort to make the process more uniform and efficient. * * *

Regulatory Structure

The CEQ regulations implementing the procedural provisions of NEPA [found at 40 C.F.R. Parts 1500–1508] apply to all agencies of the federal government, excluding Congress and any of its institutions, the judiciary, and the President, including the performance of staff functions for the President. The CEQ regulations are generic in nature, and do not address the applicability of the various procedural requirements to specific agency actions. Instead, each federal department and agency is required to prepare its own NEPA procedures that address that agency's compliance in relation to its particular mission. CEQ reviews and approves all agency procedures and amendments to those procedures.

The agency procedures are required to establish specific criteria for and identification of three classes of actions: those that require preparation of an environmental impact statement; those that require preparation of an environmental assessment; and those that are categorically excluded from further NEPA review. * * *

Categorical Exclusions

"Categorical exclusions" refer to acts falling within a predesignated category of actions that do not individually or cumulatively have a significant effect on the human environment. Thus, no documentation of environmental analysis is required. Agencies may list either very specific actions, or a broader class of actions with criteria and examples for guidance. However, federal officials must be alert to extraordinary circumstances in which a normally excluded action may have a significant environmental effect. A categorical exclusion is *not* an exemption from compliance with NEPA, but merely an administrative tool to avoid paperwork for those actions without significant environmental effects.

Environmental Assessments

An environmental assessment (EA) is supposed to be a concise public document that may be prepared to achieve any of the following purposes: to provide sufficient evidence and analysis for determining whether to prepare an EIS; to aid an agency's compliance with NEPA when no EIS is necessary; and to facilitate preparation of an EIS if one is necessary. An EA should include a brief discussion of the need for the proposal, of alternatives as required by NEPA § 102(2)(E), and of the environmental impacts of the proposed action and alternatives. * * * An EA is followed by one of two conclusions: either a Finding of No Significant Impact (FONSI) or a decision to prepare an EIS. A FONSI briefly presents the reasons why an action, not otherwise categorically excluded, will not have a significant effect on the human environment. * * *

While the EA and FONSI process is a valuable and even essential tool, it has been subjected, far too often, to two types of abuse. On the one hand, some compliance has reduced the EA analysis to a one-page form that is so cursory that it is questionable whether the underlying decision about whether to prepare an EIS is sound. On the other hand, an EA all too frequently takes on the look, feel, and form of an EIS, complete with the same qualitative contents and volume and weight. There can be several reasons for this, but certainly one unfortunate rationale has been to avoid as much public involvement as an EIS would stimulate, while being prepared to turn the EA into an EIS rapidly if a court would so order. * * *

Environmental Impact Statements

The primary purpose of an EIS is to serve as an action-forcing device to ensure that the policies and goals defined in NEPA are infused into the ongoing programs and actions of the federal government. It must provide full and fair discussion of significant environmental impacts and shall inform decisionmakers and the public of the reasonable alternatives that would avoid or minimize adverse impacts or enhance the quality of the human environment. In preparing EISs, *agencies should focus on significant environmental issues and alternatives and reduce paperwork and the accumulation of extraneous background data.* Texts should be concise, clear, and to the point, and should be supported by evidence that the agency has made the necessary environmental analyses. An EIS is *more* than a disclosure document; it should be used by federal officials to plan actions and make decisions.

* * *

Once the decision is made to prepare an EIS of any type, the proponent federal agency publishes a Notice of Intent (NOI) in the Federal Register. The NOI should describe the proper action and possible alternatives, the agency's intent to prepare an EIS, the agency's proposed scoping process, and any planned scoping meetings and the name and address of a contact person in the agency.

The agency must then engage in the "scoping process," a process to determine the scope of issues to be addressed in the EIS and for identifying the significant issues related to a proposed action. Scoping may or may not include meetings, but the process should involve interested parties at all levels of government, and all interested private citizens and organizations. Scoping is also the appropriate point to allocate responsibilities among lead and cooperating agencies, identify other environmental requirements that are applicable to the proposal, set any time and page limits, and, in general, structure the process in such a way that all identifiable participants are informed and involved at appropriate points. A well designed scoping process can have an extremely positive ripple effect throughout the rest of the NEPA process.

The next step is preparation of a draft EIS. The EIS may be prepared either by the lead agency, with assistance from any cooperating agencies, or by a contractor. * * * The agency may accept information from any party, including the applicant, but it *always* has the duty to independently evaluate such information.

* * *

Once the draft EIS is prepared, it must be circulated for at least 45 days for public comment and review. Federal agencies with jurisdiction by law or special expertise with respect to any of the relevant environmental impacts are expected to comment, although this may take the form of a "no comment" letter. At the conclusion of the comment period, the agency must evaluate the comment letters and respond to the substantive comments in the final EIS. The final EIS is sent to all parties who commented on the draft EIS. No decision may be made concerning the proposed action until at least 30 days after the Notice of Availability of the final EIS or 90 days after the publication of the Notice of Availability of the draft EIS, whichever is later.

At the time of decision, the decisionmaker must sign a Record of Decision (ROD). The ROD states what the decision is, identifies which alternatives were considered by the agency in making the decision, specifies which alternatives were considered to be environmentally preferable, and discusses factors that were balanced by the decisionmaker. Further, the ROD states whether all practical methods to avoid or minimize environmental harm are being adopted, and if not, why not. The ROD also includes a description of any applicable enforcement and monitoring programs.

Calvert Cliffs' Coordinating Committee, Inc. v. United States Atomic Energy Commission

United States Court of Appeals, District of Columbia Circuit, 1971.
449 F.2d 1109.

[This case involved judicial review of several rules of the Atomic Energy Commission. The discussion of the rules themselves is now of largely historical interest. The case is still noteworthy, however, as the first important judicial interpretation of NEPA.]

■ J. SKELLY WRIGHT, CIRCUIT JUDGE.

* * *

We begin our analysis with an examination of NEPA's structure and approach and of the Atomic Energy Commission rules which are said to conflict with the requirements of the Act. The relevant portion of NEPA is Title I, consisting of five sections. Section 101 sets forth the Act's basic substantive policy: that the federal government "use all practicable means and measures" to protect environmental values. Congress did not establish environmental protection as an exclusive goal; rather, it desired a reordering of priorities, so that environmental costs and benefits will assume their proper place along with other considerations. In Section 101(b), imposing an explicit duty on federal officials, the Act provides that "it is the continuing responsibility of the Federal Government to use all practicable means, consistent with other essential considerations of national policy," to avoid environmental degradation, preserve "historic, cultural, and natural" resources, and promote "the widest range of beneficial uses of the environment without ... undesirable and unintended consequences."

Thus the general substantive policy of the Act is a flexible one. It leaves room for a responsible exercise of discretion and may not require particular substantive results in particular problematic instances. However, the Act also contains very important "procedural" provisions—provisions which are designed to see that all federal agencies do in fact exercise the substantive discretion given them. These provisions are not highly flexible. Indeed, they establish a strict standard of compliance.

NEPA, first of all, makes environmental protection a part of the mandate of every federal agency and department. The Atomic Energy Commission, for example, had continually asserted, prior to NEPA, that it had no statutory authority to concern itself with the adverse environmental effects of its actions. Now, however, its hands are no longer tied. It is not only permitted, but compelled, to take environmental values into account. Perhaps the greatest importance of NEPA is to require the Atomic Energy Commission and other agencies to *consider* environmental issues just as they consider other matters within their mandates. This compulsion is most plainly stated in Section 102. There, "Congress authorizes and directs that, to the fullest extent possible: (1) the policies, regulations, and public laws of the United States shall be interpreted and administered in accordance with the policies set forth in this Act...." * * *

The sort of consideration of environmental values which NEPA compels is clarified in Section 102(2)(A) and (B). In general, all agencies must use a "systematic, interdisciplinary approach" to environmental planning and evaluation "in decisionmaking which may have an impact on man's environment." In order to include all possible environmental factors in the decisional equation, agencies must "identify and develop methods and procedures ... which will insure that presently unquantified environmental amenities and values may be given appropriate consideration in decisionmaking along with economic and technical considerations." "Environmental amenities" will often be in conflict with "economic and technical considerations." To "consider" the former "along with" the latter must involve a balancing process. In some instances environmental costs may outweigh economic and technical benefits and in other instances they may not. But NEPA mandates a rather finely tuned and "systematic" balancing analysis in each instance.

To ensure that the balancing analysis is carried out and given full effect, Section 102(2)(C) requires that responsible officials of all agencies prepare a "detailed statement" covering the impact of particular actions on the environment, the environmental costs which might be avoided, and alternative measures which might alter the cost-benefit equation. The apparent purpose of the "detailed statement" is to aid in the agencies' own decision making processes and to advise other interested agencies and the public of the environmental consequences of planned federal action. Beyond the "detailed statement," Section 102(2)(D)* requires all agencies specifically to "study, develop, and describe appropriate alternatives to recommended courses of action in any proposal which involves unresolved conflicts concerning alternative uses of available resources." This requirement, like the "detailed statement" requirement, seeks to ensure that each agency decision maker has before him and takes into proper account all possible approaches to a particular project (including total abandonment of the project) which would alter the environmental impact and the cost-benefit balance. Only in that fashion is it likely that the most intelligent, optimally beneficial decision will ultimately be made. Moreover, by compelling a formal "detailed statement" and a description of alternatives, NEPA provides evidence that the mandated decision making process has in fact taken place and, most importantly, allows those removed from the initial process to evaluate and balance the factors on their own.

Of course, all of these § 102 duties are qualified by the phrase "to the fullest extent possible." We must stress as forcefully as possible that this language does not provide an escape hatch for footdragging agencies; it does not make NEPA's procedural requirements somehow "discretionary." Congress did not intend the Act to be such a paper tiger. Indeed, the requirement of environmental consideration "to the fullest extent possible" sets a high standard for the agencies, a standard which must be rigorously enforced by the reviewing courts.

* * *

Thus the Section 102 duties are not inherently flexible. They must be complied with to the fullest extent, unless there is a clear conflict of *statutory* authority. Considerations of administrative difficulty, delay or economic cost will not suffice to strip the section of its fundamental importance.

* Now section 102(2)(E)—Eds.

We conclude, then, that Section 102 of NEPA mandates a particular sort of careful and informed decisionmaking process and creates judicially enforceable duties. The reviewing courts probably cannot reverse a substantive decision on its merits, under Section 101, unless it be shown that the actual balance of costs and benefits that was struck was arbitrary or clearly gave insufficient weight to environmental values. But if the decision was reached procedurally without individualized consideration and balancing of environmental factors—conducted fully and in good faith—it is the responsibility of the courts to reverse. As one District Court has said of Section 102 requirements: "It is hard to imagine a clearer or stronger mandate to the Courts."

Strycker's Bay Neighborhood Council, Inc. v. Karlen

United States Supreme Court, 1980.
444 U.S. 223, 100 S.Ct. 497, 62 L.Ed.2d 433.

■ PER CURIAM.

[The New York City Planning Commission, together with the United States Department of Housing and Urban Development planned a joint redevelopment project in Manhattan. The project was originally envisioned as a mix of 70% middle-income and 30% low-income housing, but later revised to 100% low-income. Trinity Episcopal School, which had built a combination school and middle-income housing development nearby, and a group of neighbors sued in federal court to enjoin the construction of low-income housing on a portion of the project known as Site 30. In the first round of litigation, the District Court found no violation of NEPA, but the Second Circuit reversed, holding that HUD had not adequately studied alternatives to the project.]

On remand, HUD prepared a lengthy report entitled Special Environmental Clearance (1977). After marshaling the data, the report asserted that, "while the choice of Site 30 for development as a 100 percent low-income project has raised valid questions about the potential social environmental impacts involved, the problems associated with the impact on social fabric and community structures are not considered so serious as to require that this component be rated as unacceptable." The last portion of the report incorporated a study wherein the Commission evaluated nine alternative locations for the project and found none of them acceptable. While HUD's report conceded that this study may not have considered all possible alternatives, it credited the Commission's conclusion that any relocation of the units would entail an unacceptable delay of two years or more. According to HUD, "[m]easured against the environmental costs associated with the minimum two-year delay, the benefits seem insufficient to justify a mandated substitution of sites."

[The District Court again ruled in favor of HUD, and the Second Circuit again reversed.] The appellate court focused upon that part of HUD's report where the agency considered and rejected alternative sites, and in particular upon HUD's reliance on the delay such a relocation would entail. The Court of Appeals purported to recognize that its role in reviewing HUD's decision was defined by the Administrative Procedure Act (APA), 5 U.S.C. § 706(2)(A), which provides that agency actions should be set aside if found to be "arbitrary, capricious, an abuse of discretion, or otherwise not in accordance with law...." Additionally, however, the Court of Appeals looked to "[t]he provisions of NEPA" for "the substantive standards necessary to review the merits of agency decisions...." The Court of Appeals conceded that HUD had "given 'consideration' to alternatives" to redesignating the site. Nevertheless, the court believed that " 'consideration' is not an end in itself." Concentrating on HUD's finding that development of an alternative location would entail an unacceptable delay, the appellate court held that such delay could not be "an overriding factor" in HUD's decision to proceed with the development. According to the court, when HUD considers such projects, "environmental factors, such as crowding low-income housing into a concentrated area, should be given determinative weight." The Court of Appeals therefore remanded the case to the District Court, instructing HUD to attack the shortage of low-income housing in a manner that would avoid the "concentration" of such housing on Site 30.

In *Vermont Yankee Nuclear Power Corp. v. NRDC*, 435 U.S. 519, 558 (1978), we stated that NEPA, while establishing "significant substantive goals for the Nation," imposes upon agencies duties that are "essentially procedural." As we stressed in that case, NEPA was designed "to insure a fully informed and well-considered decision," but not necessarily "a decision the judges of the Court of Appeals or of this Court would have reached had they been members of the decisionmaking unit of the agency." *Vermont Yankee* cuts sharply against the Court of Appeals' conclusion that an agency, in selecting a course of action, must elevate environmental concerns over other appropriate considerations. On the contrary, once an agency has made a decision subject to NEPA's procedural requirements, the only role for a court is to insure that the agency has considered the environmental consequences; it cannot " 'interject itself within the area of discretion of the executive as to the choice of the action to be taken.' " Kleppe v. Sierra Club, 427 U.S. 390, 410 n. 21 (1976).[2]

In the present litigation there is no doubt that HUD considered the environmental consequences of its decision to redesignate the proposed site for low-income housing. NEPA requires no more. The petitions for certiorari are granted, and the judgment of the Court of Appeals is therefore

Reversed.

---

2. If we could agree with the dissent that the Court of Appeals held that HUD had acted "arbitrarily" in redesignating the site for low-income housing, we might also agree that plenary review is warranted. But the District Court expressly concluded that HUD had not acted arbitrarily or capriciously and our reading of the opinion of the Court of Appeals satisfies us that it did not overturn that finding. Instead, the appellate court required HUD to elevate environmental concerns over other, admittedly legitimate, considerations. Neither NEPA nor the APA provides any support for such a reordering of priorities by a reviewing court.

■ JUSTICE MARSHALL, dissenting.

The issue raised by these cases is far more difficult than the *per curiam* opinion suggests. The Court of Appeals held that the Secretary of Housing and Urban Development (HUD) had acted arbitrarily in concluding that prevention of a delay in the construction process justified the selection of a housing site which could produce adverse social environmental effects, including racial and economic concentration. * * *

In the present case, the Court of Appeals did not "substitute its judgment for that of the agency as to the environmental consequences of its actions," for HUD in its Special Environmental Clearance Report acknowledged the adverse environmental consequences of its proposed action: "the choice of Site 30 for development as a 100 percent low-income project has raised valid questions about the potential social environmental impacts involved." These valid questions arise from the fact that 68% of all public housing units would be sited on only one crosstown axis in this area of New York City. * * * The environmental "impact ... on social fabric and community structures" was given a B rating in the report, indicating that from this perspective the project is "questionable" and ameliorative measures are "mandated." * * * The report also discusses two alternatives, Sites 9 and 41, both of which are the appropriate size for the project and require "only minimal" amounts of relocation and clearance. Concerning Site 9 the report explicitly concludes that "[f]rom the standpoint of social environmental impact, this location would be superior to Site 30 for the development of low-rent public housing." The sole reason for rejecting the environmentally superior site was the fact that if the location were shifted to Site 9, there would be a projected delay of two years in the construction of the housing.

The issue before the Court of Appeals, therefore, was whether HUD was free under NEPA to reject an alternative acknowledged to be environmentally preferable solely on the ground that any change in sites would cause delay. * * * Whether NEPA, which sets forth "significant substantive goals," *Vermont Yankee*, 435 U.S., at 558, permits a projected two-year time difference to be controlling over environmental superiority is by no means clear. Resolution of the issue, however, is certainly within the normal scope of review of agency action to determine if it is arbitrary, capricious, or an abuse of discretion. * * *

NOTES AND QUESTIONS

1. *The Role of the Courts.* Because NEPA does not contain a judicial review provision, review is conducted under the Administrative Procedure Act provisions discussed in Chapter 3. The Supreme Court, beginning with the *Strycker's Bay* decision, has consistently refused to permit substantive judicial review of agency decisions under NEPA. In *Robertson v. Methow Valley Citizens Council*, 490 U.S. 332, 350–51 (1989), the Court stated:

> [I]t is now well settled that NEPA itself does not mandate particular results, but simply prescribes the necessary process. If the adverse

environmental effects of the proposed action are adequately identified and evaluated, the agency is not constrained by NEPA from deciding that other values outweigh the environmental costs. * * * Other statutes may impose substantive environmental obligations on federal agencies, but NEPA merely prohibits uninformed—rather than unwise—agency action.

Does that conclusion follow from *Strycker's Bay*? Note that *Calvert Cliffs* mentions Section 101 of NEPA. Does that section provide any basis for substantive judicial review? How would a court determine whether an agency decision, for example to construct a ski resort on national forest land (the issue in *Robertson*), was arbitrary or capricious under NEPA?

2. *The Value of Process.* In the absence of substantive judicial review of agency decisions, what purpose(s) does NEPA serve? Does the preparation of an EIS alone improve the likelihood that environmental impacts will receive appropriate consideration? That the agency will become more sensitive to environmental concerns? Is there any point to public disclosure other than to assure the public that the agency is aware of the impacts? Might the EIS serve as a rallying point for the public to bring political pressure to bear to change the decision?

3. *NEPA and Agency Authority.* Does NEPA expand agency authority to take environmentally protective action? In Natural Resources Defense Council v. U.S. EPA, 859 F.2d 156 (D.C.Cir.1988), the court held that it does not. Do you agree? Even if it does not provide an additional grant of authority, might § 101 provide the justification for a more environmentally-protective interpretation of agency organic statutes?

SECTION 2.   THE DUTY TO PREPARE AN EIS

Whether and when an EIS must be prepared are often highly contentious issues. The problem and materials that follow are intended to help you explore those issues.

CLASS DISCUSSION PROBLEM: BELLA VISTA DEVELOPMENT

Southwest Development Corp. (SDC) wants to develop Bella Vista, a parcel it owns northwest of the City of Los Angeles. Bella Vista is the largest undeveloped parcel in this heavily urbanized area of Los Angeles County. SDC envisions a development covering roughly 1,000 acres, to be developed in two phases. Phase I, to be accomplished over the next 5 years, would include a hotel and entertainment complex, 2 million square feet of office space, and 5000 residential units. Phase II, planned for 10 years in the future, would add 5000 more residential units, a retail shopping area, and another 3 million square feet of office space.

Scattered across the Bella Vista property are approximately 70 acres of degraded wetlands. Over the past half century, loss of wetlands throughout not only southern California but along the Pacific flyway from Canada to Mexico has reduced the populations of several species of migratory waterfowl. SDC wants to place the hotel and entertainment complex, the center-piece of its proposed development, in a location that would require the filling of 19.5 wetland acres. No wetland filling would be required for Phase II.

SDC's project managers met informally on several occasions with officials from the regional office of the U.S. Army Corps of Engineers, the agency responsible for issuing wetland fill permits. Corps officials indicated that the proposal as it stood was unlikely to be approved, and suggested that SDC consider restoring at least some of the wetlands its project would not fill. Responding to that suggestion, SDC drafted a restoration plan for 52 acres of freshwater marsh on the Bella Vista property. After Corps officials indicated they thought this restoration plan would make the development proposal acceptable, SDC submitted a formal application to fill the 19.5 acres.

The county road that serves Bella Vista is already congested with commuters traveling from outlying suburbs to the city. Los Angeles County transportation officials have begun talks with state and federal officials about funding and routes for a wider road. The most likely route would cross a small wetlands area about five miles from Bella Vista. The County would like the widened road to serve both current traffic and what it views as the inevitable future development of Bella Vista.

The Corps prepared an Environmental Assessment on the SDC application, considering only the impacts of the proposed filling and restoration, and concluded that the environmental impacts were not significant because the wetlands were already significantly degraded. The Corps further concluded that even if the filling, taken alone, would have significant environmental effects, those effects would be mitigated to insignificance by the beneficial effects of the restoration project. The Corps issued the permit.

Friends of Bella Vista, a local environmental group, immediately filed suit, contending the Corps had violated NEPA by: (1) making its decision before studying the environmental impacts; (2) failing to consider the impacts of the entire proposed SDC development; (3) failing to consider other projects proposed or contemplated throughout the Pacific flyway, including but not limited to the County road widening; and (4) failing to produce an EIS.

Using the materials that follow, evaluate Friends' claims, and any remedies that may be available should they prevail on the merits.

Excerpts from Council on Environmental Quality Regulations
40 C.F.R. Parts 1500–1517.

Sec. 1502.4 Major Federal actions requiring the preparation of environmental impact statements

(a) Agencies shall make sure the proposal which is the subject of an environmental impact statement is properly defined. Agencies shall use the criteria for scope (§ 1508.25) to determine which proposal(s) shall be the subject of a particular statement. Proposals or parts of proposals which are related to each other closely enough to be, in effect, a single course of action shall be evaluated in a single impact statement. * * *

Sec. 1502.5   Timing

An agency shall commence preparation of an environmental impact statement as close as possible to the time the agency is developing or is presented with a proposal so that preparation can be completed in time for the final statement to be included in any recommendation or report on the proposal. The statement shall be prepared early enough so that it can serve practically as an important contribution to the decisionmaking process and will not be used to rationalize or justify decisions already made. For instance:

(a) For projects directly undertaken by Federal agencies the environmental impact statement shall be prepared at the feasibility analysis (go-no go) stage and may be supplemented at a later stage if necessary.

(b) For applications to the agency appropriate environmental assessments or statements shall be commenced no later than immediately after the application is received. Federal agencies are encouraged to begin preparation of such assessments or statements earlier, preferably jointly with applicable State or local agencies.

* * *

Sec. 1508.8   Effects

"Effects" include:

(a) Direct effects, which are caused by the action and occur at the same time and place.

(b) Indirect effects, which are caused by the action and are later in time or farther removed in distance, but are still reasonably foreseeable. Indirect effects may include growth inducing effects and other effects related to induced changes in the pattern of land use, population density or growth rate, and related effects on air and water and other natural systems, including ecosystems.

Effects and impacts as used in these regulations are synonymous. Effects includes ecological (such as the effects on natural resources and on the components, structures, and functioning of affected ecosystems), aesthetic, historic, cultural, economic, social, or health, whether direct, indirect, or cumulative. Effects may also include those resulting from actions which may have both beneficial and detrimental effects, even if on balance the agency believes that the effect will be beneficial.

Sec. 1508.18   Major Federal action

Major Federal action includes actions with effects that may be major and which are potentially subject to Federal control and responsibility.

Major reinforces but does not have a meaning independent of significantly (§ 1508.27). Actions include the circumstance where the responsible officials fail to act and that failure to act is reviewable by courts or administrative tribunals under the Administrative Procedure Act or other applicable law as agency action. * * *

Sec. 1508.23   Proposal

Proposal exists at that stage in the development of an action when an agency subject to the Act has a goal and is actively preparing to make a decision on one or more alternative means of accomplishing that goal and the effects can be meaningfully evaluated. Preparation of an environmental impact statement should be timed (§ 1502.5) so that the final statement may be completed in time for the statement to be included in any recommendation or report on the proposal. A proposal may exist in fact as well as by agency declaration that one exists.

Sec. 1508.25   Scope

Scope consists of the range of actions, alternatives, and impacts to be considered in an environmental impact statement. * * * To determine the scope of environmental impact statements, agencies shall consider 3 types of actions, 3 types of alternatives, and 3 types of impacts. They include:

(a) Actions * * * which may be:

   (1) Connected actions, which means that they are closely related and therefore should be discussed in the same impact statement. Actions are connected if they:

      (i) Automatically trigger other actions which may require environmental impact statements.

      (ii) Cannot or will not proceed unless other actions are taken previously or simultaneously.

      (iii) Are interdependent parts of a larger action and depend on the larger action for their justification.

   (2) Cumulative actions, which when viewed with other proposed actions have cumulatively significant impacts and should therefore be discussed in the same impact statement.

   (3) Similar actions, which when viewed with other reasonably foreseeable or proposed agency actions, have similarities that provide a basis for evaluating their environmental consequences together, such as common timing or geography. An agency may wish to analyze these actions in the same impact statement. It should do so when the best way to assess adequately the combined impacts of similar actions or reasonable alternatives to such actions is to treat them in a single impact statement.

(b) Alternatives, which include:

   (1) No action alternative.

(2) Other reasonable courses of actions.

(3) Mitigation measures (not in the proposed action).

(c) Impacts, which may be:

(1) Direct;

(2) indirect;

(3) cumulative.

Sec. 1508.27 Significantly

Significantly as used in NEPA requires considerations of both context and intensity:

(a) *Context.* This means that the significance of an action must be analyzed in several contexts such as society as a whole (human, national), the affected region, the affected interests, and the locality. * * * Both short-and long-term effects are relevant.

(b) *Intensity.* This refers to the severity of impact. * * * The following should be considered in evaluating intensity:

(1) Impacts that may be both beneficial and adverse. A significant effect may exist even if the Federal agency believes that on balance the effect will be beneficial.

(2) The degree to which the proposed action affects public health or safety.

(3) Unique characteristics of the geographic area such as proximity to historic or cultural resources, park lands, prime farmlands, wetlands, wild and scenic rivers, or ecologically critical areas.

(4) The degree to which the effects on the quality of the human environment are likely to be highly controversial.

(5) The degree to which the possible effects on the human environment are highly uncertain or involve unique or unknown risks.

(6) The degree to which the action may establish a precedent for future actions with significant effects or represents a decision in principle about a future consideration.

(7) Whether the action is related to other actions with individually insignificant but cumulatively significant impacts. Significance exists if it is reasonable to anticipate a cumulatively significant impact on the environment. Significance cannot be avoided by terming an action temporary or by breaking it down into small component parts.

* * *

A. "RECOMMENDATION OR REPORT ON PROPOSALS"

Kleppe v. Sierra Club

United States Supreme Court, 1976.
427 U.S. 390, 96 S.Ct. 2718, 49 L.Ed.2d 576.

■ JUSTICE POWELL delivered the opinion of the Court.

[This controversy involved actions of the Department of Interior regarding coal development on public lands. Plaintiff environmental groups contended that federal officials were required to prepare a comprehensive environmental impact statement on coal development in the Northern Great Plains region. The Department was in the process of completing a nationwide programmatic EIS on coal-related activities. During that process, the Department had committed to limiting new leasing activities, and preparing project-specific environmental analyses as required by NEPA.

Justice Powell first explained that plaintiffs had failed to produce any evidence of an action of regional scope. He then went on to address the Court of Appeals' conclusion that an EIS was required because the Department "contemplated" a regional program.]

We conclude that the Court of Appeals erred in both its factual assumptions and its interpretation of NEPA. We think the court was mistaken in concluding, on the record before it, that the petitioners were "contemplating" a regional development plan or program. * * *

Even had the record justified a finding that a regional program was contemplated by the petitioners, the legal conclusion drawn by the Court of Appeals cannot be squared with the Act. The court recognized that the mere "contemplation" of certain action is not sufficient to require an impact statement. But it believed the statute nevertheless empowers a court to require the preparation of an impact statement to begin at some point prior to the formal recommendation or report on a proposal. The Court of Appeals accordingly devised its own four-part "balancing" test for determining when during the contemplation of a plan or other type of federal action, an agency must begin a statement. The factors to be considered were identified as the likelihood and imminence of the program's coming to fruition, the extent to which information is available on the effects of implementing the expected program and on alternatives thereto, the extent to which irretrievable commitments are being made and options precluded "as refinement of the proposal progresses," and the severity of the environmental effects should the action be implemented.

* * *

The Court's reasoning and action find no support in the language or legislative history of NEPA. The statute clearly states when an impact statement is required, and mentions nothing about a balancing of factors. Rather, as we noted last Term, under the first sentence of § 102(2)(C) the moment at which an agency must have a final statement ready "is the time at which it makes a recommendation or report on a *proposal* for federal action." Aberdeen & Rockfish R. Co. v. SCRAP, 422 U.S. 289, 320 (1975) (emphasis in original). The procedural duty imposed upon agencies by this section is quite precise, and the role of the courts in enforcing that duty is similarly precise. A court has no authority to depart from the statutory language and, by a balancing of court-devised factors, determine a point during the germination process of a potential proposal at which an impact statement *should be prepared.* Such an assertion of judicial authority would leave the agencies uncertain as to their procedural duties under NEPA, would invite judicial involvement in the day-to-day decisionmaking process of the agencies, and would invite litigation. As the contemplation of a project and the accompanying study thereof do not necessarily result in a proposal for major federal action, it may be assumed that the balancing process devised by the Court of Appeals also would result in the preparation of a good many unnecessary impact statements.[15]

* * *

Our discussion thus far has been addressed primarily to the decision of the Court of Appeals. It remains, however, to consider the contention now urged by respondents. They have not attempted to support the Court of Appeals' decision. Instead, respondents renew an argument they appear to have made to the Court of Appeals, but which that court did not reach. Respondents insist that, even without a comprehensive federal plan for the development of the Northern Great Plains, a "regional" impact statement nevertheless is required on all coal-related projects in the region because they are intimately related.

* * *

We begin by stating our general agreement with respondents' basic premise that § 102(2)(C) may require a comprehensive impact statement in certain situations where several proposed actions are pending at the same time. * * * Thus, when several proposals for coal-related actions that will have cumulative or synergistic environmental impact upon a region are pending concurrently before an agency, their environmental consequences must be considered together. Only through comprehensive consideration of pending proposals can the agency evaluate different courses of action.

Agreement to this extent with respondents' premise, however, does not require acceptance of their conclusion that all proposed coal-related actions

---

15. This is not to say that § 102(2)(C) imposes no duties upon an agency prior to its making a report or recommendation on a proposal for action. This section states that prior to preparing the impact statement the responsible official "shall consult with and obtain the comments of any Federal agency which has jurisdiction by law or special expertise with respect to any environmental impact involved." Thus, the section contemplates a consideration of environmental factors by agencies during the evolution of a report or recommendation on a proposal. But the time at which a court enters the process is when the report or recommendation on the proposal is made, and someone protests either the absence or the adequacy of the final impact statement. This is the point at which an agency's action has reached sufficient maturity to assure that judicial intervention will not hazard unnecessary disruption.

in the Northern Great Plains region are so "related" as to require their analysis in a single comprehensive impact statement. * * *

Respondents conceded at oral argument that to prevail they must show that petitioners have acted arbitrarily in refusing to prepare one comprehensive statement on this entire region, and we agree. The determination of the region, if any, with respect to which a comprehensive statement is necessary requires the weighing of a number of relevant factors, including the extent of the interrelationship among proposed actions and practical considerations of feasibility. Resolving these issues requires a high level of technical expertise and is properly left to the informed discretion of the responsible federal agencies. Absent a showing of arbitrary action, we must assume that the agencies have exercised this discretion appropriately. Respondents have made no showing to the contrary.

* * *

In sum, respondents' contention as to the relationships between all proposed coal-related projects in the Northern Great Plains region does not require that petitioners prepare one comprehensive impact statement covering all before proceeding to approve specific pending applications. As we already have determined that there exists no proposal for regionwide action that could require a regional impact statement, the judgment of the Court of Appeals must be reversed, and the judgment of the District Court reinstated and affirmed. The case is remanded for proceedings consistent with this opinion.

■ JUSTICE MARSHALL, with whom JUSTICE BRENNAN joins, concurring in part and dissenting in part.

While I agree with much of the Court's opinion, I must dissent from Part IV, which holds that the federal courts may not remedy violations of the National Environmental Policy Act of 1969 (NEPA)—no matter how blatant—until it is too late for an adequate remedy to be formulated. As the Court today recognizes, NEPA contemplates agency consideration of environmental factors throughout the decisionmaking process. Since NEPA's enactment, however, litigation has been brought primarily at the end of that process—challenging agency decisions to act made without adequate environmental impact statements or without any statements at all. In such situations, the courts have had to content themselves with the largely unsatisfactory remedy of enjoining the proposed federal action and ordering the preparation of an adequate impact statement. This remedy is insufficient because, except by deterrence, it does nothing to further early consideration of environmental factors. And, as with all after-the-fact remedies, a remand for preparation of an impact statement after the basic decision to act has been made invites *post hoc* rationalizations, rather than the candid and balanced environmental assessments envisioned by NEPA. Moreover, the remedy is wasteful of resources and time, causing fully developed plans for action to be laid aside while an impact statement is prepared.

Nonetheless, until this lawsuit, such belated remedies were all the federal courts had had the opportunity to impose under NEPA. In this case, confronted with a situation in which, according to respondents' allegations, federal agencies were violating NEPA prior to their basic decision to act, the Court of Appeals for the District of Columbia Circuit seized the opportunity to devise a different and effective remedy. It recognized a narrow class of cases, essentially those where both the likelihood of eventual agency action and the danger posed by nonpreparation of an environmental impact statement were great, in which it would allow judicial intervention prior to the time at which an impact statement must be ready. The Court today loses sight of the inadequacy of other remedies and the narrowness of the category constructed by the Court of Appeals, and construes NEPA so as to preclude a court from ever intervening prior to a formal agency proposal. This decision, which unnecessarily limits the ability of the federal courts to effectuate the intent of NEPA, is mandated neither by the statute nor by the various equitable considerations upon which the Court relies.

* * *

Metcalf v. Daley

United States Court of Appeals, Ninth Circuit, 2000.
214 F.3d 1135.

■ Trott, Circuit Judge.

* * *

I   FACTUAL BACKGROUND

The Makah, who reside in Washington state on the northwestern Olympic Peninsula, have a 1500 year tradition of hunting whales. In particular, the Makah target the California gray whale ("gray whale"), which annually migrates between the North Pacific and the coast of Mexico. * * *

In 1855, the United States and the Makah entered into the Treaty of Neah Bay, whereby the Makah ceded most of their land on the Olympic Peninsula to the United States in exchange for "[t]he right of taking fish and of whaling or sealing at usual and accustomed grounds and stations...." Treaty of Neah Bay, 12 Stat. 939, 940 (1855). Despite their long history of whaling and the Treaty of Neah Bay, however, the Makah ceased whaling in the 1920s because widespread commercial whaling had devastated the population of gray whales almost to extinction. * * *

Because the gray whale had become virtually extinct, the United States signed in 1946 the International Convention for the Regulation of Whaling * * *. The International Convention for the Regulation of Whaling enacted a schedule of whaling regulations ("Schedule") and established the International Whaling Commission ("IWC"), which was to be composed of one member from each signatory nation. * * *

Subsequently, in 1949, Congress passed the Whaling Convention Act to implement domestically the International Convention for the Regulation of Whaling. See 16 U.S.C.A. § 916 et seq. (1985). The Whaling Convention Act prohibits whaling in violation of the International Convention for the Regulation of Whaling, the Schedule, or any whaling regulation adopted by the Secretary of Commerce. * * *

When the IWC was established on December 2, 1946, it took immediate action to protect the beleaguered mammal. Specifically, the IWC amended the Schedule to impose a complete ban on the taking or killing of gray whales. However, the IWC included an exception to the ban "when the meat and products of such whales are to be used exclusively for local consumption by the aborigines." This qualification is referred to as the "aboriginal subsistence exception."

In addition to being shielded from commercial whaling under international law, the gray whale received increased protection in 1970 when the United States designated the species as endangered under the Endangered Species Conservation Act of 1969, the predecessor to the Endangered Species Act of 1973 ("ESA"). In 1993, however, NMFS determined that the eastern North Pacific stock of gray whales had recovered to near its estimated original population size and was no longer in danger of extinction. As such, this stock of gray whales was removed from the endangered species list in 1994. * * *

After these gray whales were removed from the endangered species list, the Makah decided to resume the hunting of whales * * *. The Tribe asked representatives from the Department of Commerce to represent it in seeking approval from the IWC for an annual quota of up to five gray whales.

As evidenced in an internal e-mail message written by an NMFS representative, the United States agreed in 1995 to "work with" the Makah in obtaining an aboriginal subsistence quota from the IWC. * * *

In January 1996, Will Martin, an NOAA representative, sent an e-mail message to his colleagues informing them that "we now have interagency agreement to support the Makah's application in IWC for a whaling quota of 5 grey whales." Shortly thereafter, on March 22, 1996, NOAA entered into a formal written Agreement with the Tribe, which provided that "[a]fter an adequate statement of need is prepared [by the Makah], NOAA, through the U.S. Commissioner to the IWC, will make a formal proposal to the IWC for a quota of gray whales for subsistence and ceremonial use by the Makah Tribe." * * * [T]he Agreement provided that within thirty days of IWC approval of a quota, "NOAA will revise its regulations to address subsistence whaling by the Makah Tribe, and the Council will adopt a management plan and regulations to govern the harvest. . . ." * * *

Pursuant to the Agreement, the Makah prepared an adequate statement of need, and the United States presented a formal proposal to the IWC for a quota of gray whales for the Tribe at the IWC annual meeting in June 1996. * * * Ultimately, the United States realized that it did not have the three-quarters majority required to approve it. Thus, after consulting with the Makah, the United States withdrew the proposal * * *.

In June 1997, an attorney representing the organizations Australians for Animals and BEACH Marine Protection wrote a letter to NOAA and NMFS alleging that the United States Government had violated NEPA by authorizing and promoting the Makah whaling proposal without preparing an EA or an EIS. In response, the Administrator for NOAA wrote to Australians for Animals and BEACH Marine Protection on July 25, 1997, informing them that an EA would be prepared. Twenty-eight days later, on August 22, 1997, a draft EA was distributed for public comment.

On October 13, 1997, NOAA and the Makah entered into a new written Agreement, which, in most respects, was identical to the Agreement signed in 1996. * * * Four days later, and after the signing of this new Agreement, NOAA/NMFS issued, on October 17, 1997, a final EA and a Finding of No Significant Impact ("FONSI").

The 1997 IWC annual meeting was held on October 18, 1997, one day after the final EA had been issued. Before this meeting, however, the United States (representing the Makah) and the Russian Federation (representing a Siberian aboriginal group called the Chukotka) had met to discuss the possibility of submitting a joint proposal for a gray whale quota, as the IWC previously had granted a gray whale quota for the benefit of the Chukotka. After conferring, the United States and the Russian Federation decided to submit a joint proposal for a five-year block quota of 620 whales. The total quota of 620 assumed an average annual harvest of 120 whales by the Chukotka and an average annual harvest of four whales by the Makah. We note in passing that because "not every gray whale struck will be landed," the EA eventually concluded that the cumulative impact of the removal of injured gray whales by the Makah would total not just twenty whales over a five-year period, but forty-one. * * *

At the meeting * * * the quota was approved by consensus with no objections.

On April 6, 1998, NOAA issued a Federal Register Notice setting the domestic subsistence whaling quotas for 1998. [T]he Notice allowed the Makah to engage in whaling pursuant to the IWC-approved quota * * *.

IV   NEPA CLAIM

NEPA sets forth a "national policy which will encourage productive and enjoyable harmony between man and his environment ... [and] promote efforts which will prevent or eliminate damage to the environment and biosphere and stimulate the health and welfare of man." 42 U.S.C.A. § 4321 (1994). NEPA does not set out substantive environmental standards, but instead establishes "action-forcing" procedures that require agencies to take a "hard look" at environmental consequences. We have characterized the statute as "primarily procedural," and held that "agency action taken without observance of the procedure required by law will be set aside." Save the Yaak [Comm. v. Block, 840 F.2d 714,] 717 [(9th

Cir.1988)]. In this respect, we have observed in connection with the preparation of an EA that "[p]roper timing is one of NEPA's central themes. An assessment must be 'prepared early enough so that it can serve practically as an important contribution to the decisionmaking process and will not be used to rationalize or justify decisions already made.' " *Id.* at 718.

The phrase "early enough" means "at the earliest possible time to insure that planning and decisions reflect environmental values." Andrus v. Sierra Club, 442 U.S. 347, 351 (1979). The Supreme Court in referring to NEPA's requirements as "action forcing" has embraced the rule that for projects directly undertaken by Federal agencies, environmental impact statements "shall be prepared at the feasibility analysis (go-no go) stage and may be supplemented at a later stage if necessary." *Id.* at 351 n. 3.

All of these rules notwithstanding, NEPA does not require that agency officials be "subjectively impartial." Environmental Defense Fund v. Corps of Eng'rs of the U.S. Army, 470 F.2d 289, 295 (8th Cir.1972). The statute does require, however, that projects be objectively evaluated.

> NEPA assumes as inevitable an institutional bias within an agency proposing a project and erects the procedural requirements of § 102 to insure that there is no way [the decision-maker] can fail to note the facts and understand the very serious arguments advanced by the plaintiff if he carefully reviews the entire environmental impact statement.

Id.

In summary, the comprehensive "hard look" mandated by Congress and required by the statute must be timely, and it must be taken objectively and in good faith, not as an exercise in form over substance, and not as a subterfuge designed to rationalize a decision already made. * * *

* * * In the case at bar, the Makah first asked the Federal Defendants to help them secure IWC approval for a gray whale quota in 1995; however, NOAA/NMFS did not prepare an EA until 1997. During these two years, the United States and the Makah worked together toward obtaining a gray whale quota from the IWC. * * *

The Federal Defendants did not engage the NEPA process "at the earliest possible time." Instead, the record makes clear that the Federal Defendants did not even consider the potential environmental effects of the proposed action until long after they had already committed in writing to support the Makah whaling proposal. The "point of commitment" in this case came when NOAA signed the contract with the Makah in March 1996 and then worked to effectuate the agreement. It was at this juncture that it made an "irreversible and irretrievable commitment of resources." * * * Although it could have, NOAA did not make its promise to seek a quota from the IWC and to participate in the harvest conditional upon a NEPA determination that the Makah whaling proposal would not significantly affect the environment.

* * *

It is highly likely that because of the Federal Defendants' prior written commitment to the Makah and concrete efforts on their behalf, the EA was slanted in favor of finding that the Makah whaling proposal would not significantly affect the environment. * * *

We want to make clear, however, that this case does not stand for the general proposition that an agency cannot begin preliminary consideration of an action without first preparing an EA, or that an agency must always prepare an EA before it can lend support to any proposal. * * * Rather, our holding here is limited to the unusual facts and circumstances of this case where the defendants already had made an "irreversible and irretrievable commitment of resources"—i.e., by entering into a contract with the Makah before they considered its environmental consequences and prepared the EA.

V REMEDY

Appellees argue that, even if the Federal Defendants did violate NEPA by preparing the EA after deciding to support Makah whaling, the issue is moot because the only relief that the court could order is the preparation of an adequate EA, which, appellees contend, already has been done. In making this argument, appellees rely on Realty Income Trust v. Eckerd, 564 F.2d 447 (D.C.Cir.1977), in which the court refused to remand to the district court because an adequate EIS had been prepared before any action was taken that might harm the environment. Id. at 457. The *Eckerd* court explained:

> The problem here, to repeat, was simply one of timing, that is, that there was not a timely filing of an EIS with Congress. No complaint remains on appeal that the statements in substance were inadequate in any way.

Id.

We conclude that the case at bar is distinguishable from *Eckerd* and, therefore, appellees' reliance on that case is misplaced. Unlike in *Eckerd*, appellants do not concede that the EA that ultimately was prepared is adequate. To the contrary, appellants contend that the EA is demonstrably suspect because the process under which the EA was prepared was fatally defective—i.e., the Federal Defendants were predisposed to finding that the Makah whaling proposal would not significantly affect the environment. We agree. Moreover, appellants vigorously maintain that the EA is deficient with respect to its content and conclusions.

Our conclusions about the EA in this case raise an obvious question: Having already committed in writing to support the Makah's whaling proposal, can the Federal Defendants now be trusted to take the clear-eyed hard look at the whaling proposal's consequences required by the law, or will a new EA be a classic Wonderland case of first-the-verdict, then-the-trial? In order to avoid this problem and to ensure that the law is respected, must we—and can we—set aside the FONSI and require the Federal Defendants to proceed directly to the preparation of an Environmental Impact Statement? On reflection, and in consideration of our limited role in this process, we have decided that it is appropriate only to require a new EA, but to require that it be done under circumstances that ensure an objective evaluation free of the previous taint. * * *

■ KLEINFELD, CIRCUIT JUDGE, dissenting.

* * * The majority opinion errs in three respects: (1) it imposes a novel version of the "objectivity" requirement that cannot be applied in a predictable, consistent manner by other panels in other cases; (2) it misconstrues the regulation that controls the time when an environmental assessment ought to be prepared; (3) it requires that a new environmental assessment be prepared without finding anything wrong with the old one. Obviously the agency did not prepare the environmental assessment until its officials had already decided that they wanted to let the Makah Indians hunt whales. Why else would they have gone to the trouble of preparing an environmental assessment? But without identifying something wrong with the environmental assessment (and we have not), we have no warrant for setting it aside.

First, "objectivity." * * * All the majority shows is that the agency knew the answer it wanted before it asked the question. But * * * that "institutional bias" does not vitiate the environmental assessment's "objectivity". To show that the environmental assessment is not objective, an objector must show that there is something wrong with the assessment, not just that the agency that prepared it wanted a particular result.

* * *

Second, timing. The majority holds that the "at the earliest possible time" requirement in the regulations means before "making an irreversible and irretrievable commitment of resources." I agree with that proposition of law. But then the majority goes on to say that because the agency's commitment to the Makah tribe preceded the environmental assessment, the environmental assessment came too late. I respectfully disagree with the application of law to facts, though the issue is close.

The commitment to allow the Makah tribe to hunt whales was not an "irreversible and irretrievable commitment," despite the contract. * * * [T]here was a subsequent regulatory process before the first harpoon could be fired, so the environmental assessment was not untimely. * * * The timing requirement of the statute and regulations required that the agency prepare an environmental assessment before the Makah tribe was allowed to hunt whales. It did. * * *

Preparation of an environmental assessment, and, if necessary, an environmental impact statement, is itself a major commitment of resources, and it does not make practical sense to require that these resources be wasted where the agency is not yet in a position to implement a policy choice requiring that expenditure. * * *

Third, remedy. The majority's remedy brings us into conflict with the only other circuit to have considered the issue. In *Realty Income Trust v.*

Eckerd, the agency made a proposal to Congress, which involved moving a stream, before preparing its environmental impact statement. * * * The District of Columbia Circuit held that construction could proceed without a second environmental impact statement, despite the unlawful timing, because "equity should not require the doing of a vain or useless thing." That is to say, even if the environmental impact statement was prepared too late, the agency would not be required to prepare a new one in the absence of a showing that the statement was substantively inadequate.

The majority purports to distinguish *Eckerd* on the basis that in the case at bar, the environmental advocacy groups contend that the environmental assessment was "demonstrably suspect because the process under which the EA was prepared was fatally defective—i.e., the federal defendants were predisposed to finding that the Makah whaling proposal would not significantly affect the environment." But that does not distinguish *Eckerd* at all. * * * True, there is a challenge to the substantive adequacy of the environmental assessment in this case and not in *Eckerd*. But we do not rule upon the challenge. * * * In the absence of a judicial determination that the environmental assessment really *was* inadequate. * * * we cannot conclude that preparing another environmental assessment would be other than what *Eckerd* terms "a vain or useless thing."

* * *

The value of the environmental assessments and impact statements comes mostly after the agency has settled on a policy choice. The process of preparing them mobilizes groups that may generate political pressure sufficient to defeat the executive initiative. Exploration of the alternatives, and the facts brought out in preparation, may educate the agency, so that the initiative is modified in a useful way. * * * The quality of the statement may persuade Congress or others who must pass on the agency proposal that the agency was wrong in its policy choice. The statement also stands as an archive with which the public may evaluate the correctness of the agency's policy choices after implementation, to decide whether the agency has done what it promised during implementation, and whether to repose more or less confidence in the agency's policy choices in the future. Preparation and publication of the statements eliminate the agency's monopoly of information, thus enabling other participants in the political process to use the information to overcome the agency's policy choice. None of these values were subverted in this case by the agency's commitment to the Makah Tribe. * * * We have no warrant in this case to interfere.

NOTES AND QUESTIONS

1. *Timing.* The question of when an EIS must be prepared goes to the heart of the NEPA process. Does the holding in *Kleppe* mean that environmental factors need not be considered before a final proposal is made? Is there statutory authority for review of the environmental factors prior to the proposal stage? If so, what mechanism is to be employed? When do the

CEQ regulations (promulgated after *Kleppe*) require that an EIS be prepared? Are the regulations consistent with *Kleppe*?

Is it either practical or useful to demand that an agency prepare an EIS before it has decided whether to take action and what action to take? Do you agree with Judge Kleinfeld's assertion that the "value of the environmental assessments and impact statements comes mostly after the agency has settled on a policy choice"? If so, is that what Congress intended? Is there any way to insure that environmental study informs the policy choice, rather than follows it?

2. *Irreversible Commitment.* The majority and dissent in *Metcalf* agree that NEPA environmental analysis must be undertaken prior to "any irreversible and irretrievable commitment of resources." Where does that standard come from? Is it an appropriate test? What does the majority conclude amounted to an irreversible commitment? Why does the dissent disagree? Who has the better argument?

3. *Remedies.* Plaintiffs bringing a NEPA challenge normally seek an injunction against agency action pending preparation of an adequate EA or EIS. In light of the inability to substantively review decisions, is injunctive relief particularly necessary in NEPA cases? Alternatively, how likely is that relief to affect the ultimate decision? Are there circumstances under which you would expect a substantive impact? Failing that, might delay itself benefit environmental plaintiffs, and if so how?

Although injunctive relief is commonly granted when a court finds a NEPA violation, it is not automatic. The court must weigh "the degree to which the NEPA interest would, in fact, be served by an injunction, the efficacy of other forms of relief, and the harm" to countervailing interests before granting an injunction. State of Wisconsin v. Weinberger, 745 F.2d 412, 428 (7th Cir.1984).

4. *Exemptions from NEPA.*

(a) *Statutory conflict.* Because section 104 of NEPA preserves the specific statutory obligations of federal agencies, NEPA duties are not applicable where there is a clear and unavoidable statutory conflict. Strict statutory deadlines can create such a conflict. See Flint Ridge Development Co. v. Scenic Rivers Association, 426 U.S. 776 (1976).

(b) *Statutory exemptions.* Congress has exempted actions taken by EPA under the Clean Air Act and most EPA actions under the Clean Water Act from the EIS requirement by declaring that those actions shall not be deemed major federal actions significantly affecting the environment. See 15 U.S.C. § 793(c)(1); 33 U.S.C. § 1371(c)(1). What might justify those exemptions?

(c) *Functional equivalence.* In Portland Cement Ass'n v. Ruckelshaus, 486 F.2d 375 (D.C.Cir.1973), decided before enactment of the statutory exemption under the Clean Air Act, the court held that no EIS was required for an EPA regulation setting air pollution performance standards for new cement plants. According to the court, the legislative history and purposes of NEPA raised serious questions about the applicability of NEPA to "environmentally protective regulatory agencies" such as EPA. The EIS requirement might delay environmentally beneficial actions. But applying NEPA would assure consideration of effects on other resources, provide an opportunity for input by other federal agencies, and open the decision to the public. Unwilling to grant EPA a blanket exemption from NEPA, the court determined that this particular action was exempt because it provided for "the functional equivalent of a NEPA impact statement." In reaching that conclusion, the court noted that EPA was required to consider counter-productive environmental effects as well as the economic costs of regulation; that other agencies and the public had the opportunity to comment on the regulation; and that the decision was subject to judicial review.

The functional equivalence doctrine has since been applied to relieve EPA of the EIS mandate with respect to such actions as: an exemption from the Safe Drinking Water Act, Western Nebraska Resources Council v. U.S. EPA, 943 F.2d 867 (8th Cir.1991); a Resource Conservation and Recovery Act permit for "the nation's largest hazardous waste facility," State of Alabama ex rel. Siegelman v. U.S. EPA, 911 F.2d 499 (11th Cir.1990); registration of a pesticide under the Federal Insecticide, Fungicide and Rodenticide Act (FIFRA), permitting its marketing and use, Merrell v. Thomas, 807 F.2d 776 (9th Cir.1986); and deregistration under the FIFRA, taking a pesticide off the market, State of Wyoming v. Hathaway, 525 F.2d 66 (10th Cir.1975). Should this exemption apply only when the action being taken unequivocally strengthens environmental protections? Should it be limited to EPA, or extended to other agencies when they are acting to protect the environment? To what extent should it depend on the details of procedural correspondence with NEPA?

(d) *Ministerial acts*. NEPA does not apply when the federal agency has no discretion to take environmental effects into account. See, e.g., American Airlines v. Department of Transportation, 202 F.3d 788 (5th Cir.2000); Sugarloaf Citizens Ass'n v. FERC, 959 F.2d 508 (4th Cir.1992).

B.   "MAJOR FEDERAL ACTIONS"

South Carolina ex rel. Campbell v. O'Leary

United States Court of Appeals, Fourth Circuit, 1995.
64 F.3d 892.

■ NIEMEYER, CIRCUIT JUDGE.

* * *

As an important aspect of the United States' longstanding policy for the nonproliferation of nuclear weapons, the United States has sought to convert foreign nuclear reactors from using highly-enriched uranium, which may readily be employed in the construction of nuclear weapons, to low-enriched uranium, which cannot be so employed. Adopting a formal program to encourage that conversion, known as the Reduced Enrichment for Research and Test Reactors program (the "Reduced Enrichment program"), the United States has committed to accept highly-enriched spent nuclear fuel rods from European research reactors for storage in facilities in the United States. * * *

Because recently enacted statutes and regulations require that the modified Reduced Enrichment program receive environmental review before the Department of Energy can officially implement the policy, foreign nuclear reactors have been forced to retain spent fuel rods at their sites. Over time, storage space for spent fuel rods at foreign reactor sites began to run out, creating the risk that the foreign reactors would transfer their spent fuel rods to other countries for reprocessing, thus perpetuating the use of highly-enriched uranium in nuclear fuel in contravention of the United States' nonproliferation policy. A market in highly-enriched uranium would promote the fabrication of nuclear weapons.

In July 1993, * * * the Department of Energy recommended: (1) the preparation of an Environmental Impact Statement in connection with a long term plan of selecting a site and constructing a facility to receive 24,000 spent fuel rods from European research reactors; [and] (2) the preparation of an Environmental Assessment in connection with the immediate receipt of a few hundred spent fuel rods in urgent need of shipment for storage at the Department of Energy's existing storage facility at the Savannah River Site * * *.

[T]he Department of Energy released a final Environmental Assessment in April 1994, determining that 409 spent fuel rods were in urgent need of shipment and that there would be no significant environmental impact if these rods were shipped to the Savannah River Site. * * *

In September 1994, South Carolina filed this action, seeking an injunction to prohibit receipt of the 409 fuel rods. [The district court granted the injunction.]

South Carolina does not argue, nor can it, that the Department of Energy is dividing the importation of European spent fuel rods into several minor shipments in order to avoid the preparation of any Environmental Impact Statement, for the Department of Energy is already conducting an Environmental Impact Statement for the importation of the 24,000 spent fuel rods. Instead, South Carolina argues that there is no meaningful distinction between the urgent relief shipments of 409 rods and the total proposed shipment of 24,000 rods and that if an Environmental Impact Statement is required for the total shipment, the Department of Energy should likewise be required to prepare an Environmental Impact Statement for the "segmented" urgent relief shipments.

However, South Carolina apparently fails to appreciate the significance of the fact that there is no site or facility in the United States to receive the 24,000 rods and that an Environmental Impact Statement must be prepared for such a major endeavor. With respect to the 409 rods in need of urgent relief, however, the plan is to store them at existing and approved facilities at the Department of Energy's Savannah River Site. That site is currently being used on a continuing basis to receive spent nuclear fuel rods from U.S. research reactors, and no Environmental Assessment or Environmental Impact Statement is demanded for each domestic shipment of those rods to the Savannah River Site. The fact that the 409 rods under consideration originate in Europe, instead of the United States, has not been shown to impose a meaningfully different environmental impact. * * *

Furthermore, as we held in State of North Carolina v. City of Virginia Beach, 951 F.2d 596 (4th Cir.1991), the segmentation of one phase of a larger project prior to the completion of the environmental review of the entire project constitutes impermissible segmentation only if the component action has a "direct and substantial probability of influencing [the agency's] decision" on the larger project. Id. at 603. These urgent relief shipments fail to pose such an influence; they do not in any way commit the government to accepting the larger shipment of 24,000 rods nor do they determine the outcome of the Environmental Impact Statement that is currently being prepared for the larger shipment.

Finally, the district court held that the urgent relief shipments of 409 rods and the larger, proposed 24,000–rod shipments qualify as "connected actions," "cumulative actions," and "similar actions" within the meaning of 40 C.F.R. § 1508.25(a). If the district court were correct, then the applicable NEPA regulations would require that such related actions be considered in the same Environmental Impact Statement. However, a careful reading of the regulations fails to support the district court's conclusion.

Separate actions are considered "connected" if they (1) "[a]utomatically trigger other actions which may require Environmental Impact Statements"; (2) "[c]annot or will not proceed unless other actions are taken previously or simultaneously"; or (3) "[a]re interdependent parts of a larger action and depend on the larger action for their justification." See 40 C.F.R. § 1508.25(a)(1). The urgent relief shipments of 409 rods do not qualify as "connected actions" under any of these three definitions. The shipments involving 409 rods do not "automatically trigger" the acceptance of the larger 24,000–rod shipments, nor does their utility depend upon the viability of the larger shipment. The urgent relief shipments are independent and separable, and merely preserve the Department of Energy's option to accept the larger shipments.

The urgent relief shipments of 409 rods and the larger proposed shipments of 24,000 rods also do not qualify as "cumulative actions," which are defined as actions "which when viewed with other proposed actions have cumulatively significant impacts." 40 C.F.R. § 1508.25(a)(2). By itself, the proposed shipment of 24,000 spent fuel rods has a significant impact requiring an Environmental Impact Statement. Such a shipment will necessitate the construction of a new domestic storage facility regardless of whether the Department of Energy is permitted to accept the urgent relief shipments. Furthermore, the cumulative impact of accepting the urgent relief shipments is not "significant," in that it does not require the construction of a new facility or even materially deprive the United States of existing storage facilities. The Department of Energy has projected that it will run out of storage spaces at the Savannah River Site in May 1999 if it does not receive the urgent relief shipments, and in January 1999 if it does receive them.

We also disagree with the district court's characterization of the two separate projects as "similar actions." Similar actions are defined as having "similarities that provide a basis for evaluating their environmental consequences together, such as common timing or geography." 40 C.F.R. § 1508.25(a)(3). Other than the fact that both the urgent relief shipments and the larger 24,000–rod shipments involve spent nuclear fuel, the two shipments are dissimilar. The timing of the shipments is different, since the urgent relief shipments are scheduled to conclude within the next few months and the larger shipments will not begin for several years, if ever. Moreover, since a site for the larger facility has not been selected, it may be constructed at an entirely different area of the country with no geographic similarity to the Savannah River Site.

Accordingly, we conclude that the district court's segmentation argument is not supported in fact or by law.

■ Donald Russell, Circuit Judge, dissenting:

* * *

I continue to adhere to my position that the shipment of 409 spent nuclear fuel elements, or any portion of that amount, constitutes an improper segmentation from the Department of Energy's larger plan to accept 24,000 spent fuel elements from foreign research reactors over the next ten to thirteen years.

* * *

[T]he EIS studies three different alternatives for managing the spent nuclear fuel from foreign research reactors. The most ambitious management alternative, Management Alternative 1, would involve the acceptance of roughly 24,000 spent nuclear fuel elements over a ten to thirteen year period. Management Alternative 2 would involve the management of spent nuclear fuel overseas either by providing assistance, incentives, and coordination for the storage of spent fuel at one or more locations overseas, or by providing nontechnical assistance, incentives, and coordination for the reprocessing of spent nuclear fuel at overseas reprocessing facilities. Management Alternative 3, the hybrid alternative, would involve a combination of accepting spent fuel elements for storage in the United States and providing assistance for the management of spent fuel overseas. The Draft EIS also considers the alternative of taking no action.

The EIS does not propose a permanent solution to the storage of the 24,000 spent fuel elements that would be accepted under Management Alternative 1. Instead, the EIS proposes a two-phase storage plan for managing the accepted spent fuel for a 40–year period. In phase 1, spent nuclear fuel elements would be shipped to existing facilities for interim storage while the Department of Energy constructs a more permanent storage facility. The EIS explains that only two facilities could serve as potential phase 1 sites: the Savannah River Site and the Idaho National Engineering Laboratory. Phase 2 would begin when the DOE constructs a new facility or refurbishes an existing facility for the 40–year storage of the spent fuel elements. The Draft EIS considers five possible sites for such a phase 2 storage facility: the Savannah River Site, the Idaho National Engineering Laboratory, the Hanford Site, the Oak Ridge Reservation, and the Nevada Test Site.

* * *

The DOE insists that it will not select a management alternative until it issues the final EIS, which it claims will be completed in September 1995. In fact, the DOE has already begun implementation of Management Alternative 1. In September 1994, this Court allowed the government to accept a shipment of 153 spent nuclear fuel elements from foreign research reactors for storage at the Savannah River Site. In lifting the district court's injunction in this case, this Court authorizes the government to accept a second shipment of 157 rods to be stored at Savannah River. Although the DOE insists that these "urgent" shipments are part of a separate program, the fact remains that under Management Alternative 1, the government proposes to import the same type of spent fuel elements from the same set of research reactors and to store them at the same facility. The only difference between these "urgent" shipments and the shipments under Management Alternative 1 is the timing. By segmenting the "urgent" shipments from its larger plan to accept 24,000 rods, the DOE has begun implementing Management Alternative 1 before it has completed the EIS.

* * * It undermines the purposes of NEPA, and is a bit unseemly, for the DOE to begin implementation of its proposed action while it claims to be studying the environmental impacts and considering other alternatives. The EIS should be more than a formality. Before the DOE begins importing large amounts of spent nuclear fuel, which rank among the most dangerous material that humanity has ever tried to control, we should require the DOE to complete its environmental review.

* * *

Winnebago Tribe v. Ray

United States Court of Appeals, Eighth Circuit, 1980.
621 F.2d 269.

■ Bright, Circuit Judge.

Winnebago Tribe of Nebraska (the Tribe) appeals an order of the district court denying its request for a permanent injunction to bar construction of a proposed power line running from Raun, Iowa, to Hoskins, Nebraska. * * *

On July 13, 1978, appellee Iowa Public Service Company (IPS) * * * applied to the Corps for a permit to cross the Missouri River, as required by 33 U.S.C. § 403 (1976) (originally enacted as Rivers and Harbors Appropriation Act of March 3, 1899, § 10) (hereinafter section 10). Before granting the permit, the Corps prepared an environmental impact assessment on the impact of the river-crossing portion of the line (approximately 1.25 miles out of 67 miles). The assessment concluded that an environmental impact statement was not required because "[t]here are no significant environmental impacts associated with this project." * * * The Corps granted the section 10 permit on January 10, 1979.

* * *

The Tribe alleges that the administrative record should have considered environmental impacts posed by the entire transmission line, rather than just the river-crossing portion. Appellant's claim presents two related issues: (a) whether the Corps wields such control and responsibility over the entire project that nonfederal segments must be included in the assessment; and (b) assuming limited federal involvement, whether the Corps nevertheless must consider the impacts of nonfederal segments as secondary effects of the proposed action.

The Tribe notes initially that the power line will not be constructed without the section 10 permit. In light of "but for" veto power, the Tribe argues, the Corps wields sufficient control over the entire project to require project-wide environmental analysis. Factual or veto control, however, must be distinguished from legal control or "enablement." See NAACP v. Medical Center, Inc., 584 F.2d 619 (3d Cir.1978).

In "enablement" cases federal action is a legal condition precedent to accomplishment of an entire nonfederal project. Thus, for example, the federal statute at issue in Greene County Planning Board v. FPC, 455 F.2d 412 (2d Cir.1972), required the Federal Power Commission to assure that the entire project was "best adapted" to a comprehensive environmental plan before licensing construction of a power line. The statute at issue in this case is far narrower and cannot be construed as a grant of legal control over the entire project.[3]

The court in *Medical Center* identified three factors helpful in determining whether "but for" or factual control requires project-wide analysis: (1) the degree of discretion exercised by the agency over the federal portion of the project; (2) whether the federal government has given any direct financial aid to the project; and (3) whether "the overall federal involvement with the project [is] sufficient to turn essentially private action into federal action." * * *

---

3. Section 10 does not contain the type of broad mandate present in the Federal Power Commission Act. The Corps' jurisdiction under section 10 governs nonfederal actions only to the extent they "affect the course, condition, capacity or location of [navigable waters]...." United States v. Sexton Cove Estates, Inc., 526 F.2d 1293, 1299 (5th Cir.1976).

In the present suit, while the Corps has broad discretion to consider environmental impacts, that discretion must be exercised within the scope of the agency's authority. As noted above, the Corps' jurisdiction under section 10 extends only to areas in and affecting navigable waters. As the Third Circuit observed in United States v. Stoeco Homes, Inc., 498 F.2d 597, 607 (3d Cir.1974):

> The federal environmental protection statutes did not ... by their terms enlarge the jurisdiction of the Army Corps of Engineers under the Rivers and Harbors Appropriation Act of 1899. If there is no such jurisdiction environmental protection is still a matter primarily of state concern.

Thus, the Corps' discretion under section 10 does not dictate project-wide review.

The factors remaining for consideration under *Medical Center* are the presence of direct federal funding and the degree of federal involvement. There has been no direct or even indirect federal funding for this project. As for federal involvement, the fact that part of the line will cross the Winnebago Reservation does not suffice to turn this essentially private action into federal action. Federal law allows the state to condemn this land for any public purpose in the same manner as land owned in fee. 25 U.S.C. § 357 (1976). Thus, we conclude that the Corps did not have sufficient control and responsibility to require it to study the entire project.

The Tribe also notes that an agency must consider secondary or indirect impacts in determining whether there are any significant impacts upon the environment. Appellant argues that the administrative record does not reflect consideration of a secondary effect of granting the permit— namely, building the remainder of the line. If, however, appellant's position were correct, then an EIS for a properly segmented portion of highway would have to consider impacts of subsequent segments as well. A careful reading of the Council on Environmental Quality Guidelines leads us to reject appellant's contention as erroneous. Completion of the non-federal aspects of this single project does not constitute a secondary or indirect effect of the federal action.

NOTES AND QUESTIONS

1. In the Class Discussion Problem, does NEPA require the Corps of Engineers to consider the environmental effects of SDC's entire proposed development? Of the county's road widening? Of other projects or potential projects within the Pacific flyway? What test should a court apply in answering those questions?

2. *Segmentation.* Narrowly defining a project may allow an agency to avoid preparing an EIS for any part of the project, or may result in a series of separate environmental documents, none of which considers all the environmental impacts of the project. What guidance do the CEQ regulations offer for determining whether actions must be considered together in a single environmental document? What test did the Fourth Circuit apply in *South Carolina v. O'Leary*? Why does the dissent disagree? Will the shipment of 409 fuel rods to Savannah River affect the agency's decision on the larger question of what to do in the future about spent fuel from foreign reactors? Is that the right question to ask? Would the dissent have allowed the shipment of twenty fuel rods, or two, without preparation of an EIS?

3. *Small Handles*. A closely related problem, sometimes referred to as the "small handles" problem, arises when federal permission is required or federal funding is sought for one portion of a larger non-federal project. Should small handles cases be treated differently than claims (such as that in *O'Leary*) that a federal agency is segmenting an entirely federal project? Why? Are additional concerns important in the small handles situation? According to the *Winnebago* court, what test determines whether the federal agency must consider the environmental effects of non-federal aspects of the project? Is its approach consistent with the CEQ regulations? Is it sensible?

Consider two hypothetical situations: 1) A private firm proposes to build an aluminum processing plant in Oregon. No federal approvals are required. The Bonneville Power Administration (BPA), a federal agency, contracts with the firm to construct a power transmission line and supply power to the plant. Must BPA consider the environmental impacts of plant construction and operation, as well as those of the power transmission line? 2) A state transportation agency proposes to construct a new, 250–mile-long state highway. No federal funds will be used. The project includes an interchange with an existing interstate highway, which must be approved by the Federal Highway Administration (FHA). Must the FHA consider the environmental impacts of the entire highway?

4. *Highway Projects*. Courts are reluctant to allow state or local governments to determine the route of a highway prior to NEPA analysis by building the nonfederal segments before seeking federal approval or funding. See, e.g., Maryland Conservation Council, Inc. v. Gilchrist, 808 F.2d 1039 (4th Cir.1986). However, a portion of a larger highway project may be considered in isolation if it has independent utility and logical termini. See 23 C.F.R. § 771.111(f) (Federal Highway Administration NEPA guidelines); Preserve Endangered Areas of Cobb's History, Inc. v. U.S. Army Corps of Engineers, 87 F.3d 1242 (11th Cir.1996). Is this an appropriate test? Is it consistent with that applied in other segmentation and small handles cases?

5. *NEPA and Agency Inaction*. Is NEPA compliance ever required when an agency declines to take action? How do the CEQ regulations treat that question? What accounts for the different treatment of action and inaction? Does NEPA apply to: (a) a decision by the U.S. Forest Service not to use herbicides in a national forest (see Minnesota Pesticide Information & Education, Inc. v. Espy, 29 F.3d 442 (8th Cir.1994)); (b) U.S. refusal to regulate transport of nuclear waste through the waters of the U.S. Exclusive Economic Zone, where the scope of U.S. authority over those waters is uncertain (see Mayaguezanos por la Salud y el Ambiente v. United States,

198 F.3d 297 (1st Cir.1999)); (c) a decision by the Food and Drug Administration not to issue blanket regulations regarding genetically modified food crops (see Alliance for Bio–Integrity v. Shalala, 116 F.Supp.2d 166 (D.D.C. 2000))?

C.   "SIGNIFICANTLY AFFECTING THE QUALITY OF THE HUMAN ENVIRONMENT"

Sierra Club v. Peterson

United States Court of Appeals, District of Columbia Circuit, 1983.
717 F.2d 1409.

■ MacKINNON, SENIOR CIRCUIT JUDGE.

* * *

In 1980, the Forest Service received applications for oil and gas leases in the Palisades Further Planning Area [a 247,000 acre roadless area]. After conducting an Environmental Assessment (EA), the Forest Service recommended granting the lease applications, but with various stipulations attached to the leases. Because the Forest Service determined that issuance of the leases with the recommended stipulations would not result in significant adverse impacts to the environment, it decided that, with respect to the *entire* area, no Environmental Impact Statement was required at the leasing stage.

The leasing program approved by the Forest Service divides the land within the Palisades Further Planning Area into two categories—"highly environmentally sensitive"[3] lands and non-highly environmentally sensitive lands. * * *

[A] No Surface Occupancy Stipulation (NSO Stipulation) is attached to the leases for lands designated as "highly environmentally sensitive." This NSO Stipulation *precludes* surface occupancy unless and until such activity is specifically approved by the Forest Service.

For leases *without* a No Surface Occupancy Stipulation, the lessee must file an application for a permit to drill prior to initiating exploratory drilling activities. The application must contain a surface use and operating plan which details the proposed operations including access roads, well site locations, and other planned facilities. On land leased without a No Surface Occupancy Stipulation the Department *cannot* deny the permit to drill; it can only impose "reasonable" conditions which are designed to mitigate the environmental impacts of the drilling operations.

---

3. "Highly environmentally sensitive" areas are defined in the Environmental Assessment as those areas "with definable environmental characteristics which would be irreversibly altered by exploration activities." These areas include lands necessary for the protection of threatened or endangered wildlife species; lands with slope gradients of more than 40%; lands with regionally unique plant or animal species; and lands with significant cultural resources.

Following an unsuccessful administrative challenge to the decision to issue all the leases in accord with the Forest Service's plan, the Sierra Club sought declaratory and injunctive relief in the United States District Court for the District of Columbia. * * *

The district court upheld the finding of "no significant impact" and the decision to lease without preparing an EIS. The court based its decision upon the conclusion that the lease stipulations were valid and that the government could thereby "preclude any development under the leases." The court granted the federal defendants' motion for summary judgment, stating that "[t]he stipulations included in the leases ... will effectively insure that the environment will not be significantly affected until further analysis pursuant to NEPA."

The Sierra Club appeals only that portion of the district court's judgment which involves lands leased without a No Surface Occupancy Stipulation. The Sierra Club concedes that the Department retains the authority to preclude all surface disturbing activities on land leased with a NSO Stipulation until further site-specific environmental studies are made. By retaining this authority, the Department has insured that no significant environmental impacts can occur from the act of leasing lands subject to the NSO Stipulation.

Approximately 80% of the Palisades was designated as highly environmentally sensitive and, therefore, leased with the NSO Stipulation. Only the remainder, approximately 28,000 acres, is at issue in this appeal. As to this smaller area, the Sierra Club contends that the Department cannot preclude surface disturbing activities, including drilling, on lands leased without the NSO Stipulation. The Department has only retained, Sierra Club asserts, the authority to "condition" surface disturbing activities in an effort to "mitigate" any environmental harm which might result from the activities.

Thus, some surface disturbing activities may result from the act of issuing leases without NSO Stipulations on lands within the 28,000 acres. Appellant asserts, therefore, that the finding of "no significant impact" and the decision not to prepare an EIS, insofar as land leased within this smaller area is concerned, was improper. Because on these leases the Secretary cannot preclude surface disturbing activity, including drilling, the Sierra Club argues that the decision to lease is itself the point of irreversible, irretrievable commitment of resources—the point at which NEPA mandates that an environmental impact statement be prepared. We agree.

* * *

The finding of "no significant impact" is premised upon the conclusion that the lease stipulations will prevent any significant environmental impacts until a site-specific plan for exploration and development is submitted by the lessee. At that time, the federal appellees explain, an appropriate environmental analysis, either an Environmental Assessment or an EIS, will be prepared. In bifurcating its environmental analysis, however, the agency has taken a foreshortened view of the impacts which could result from the act of *leasing*. The agency has essentially assumed that leasing is a discrete transaction which will not result in any "physical or biological impacts." The Environmental Assessment concludes

> that there will be no significant adverse effects on the human environment due to oil and gas lease issuance. Therefore, no environmental impact statement will be prepared. The determination was based upon consideration of the following factors ... (a) few issued leases result in active exploration operations and still fewer result in discovery or production of oil or gas; (b) the act of issuing a lease involves no physical or biological impacts; (c) the cumulative environmental effect of lease issuance on an area-wide basis is very small; (d) effects of lease activities once permitted will be mitigated to protect areas of critical environmental concern by appropriate stipulations including no-surface occupancy; (e) if unacceptable environmental impacts cannot be corrected, activities will not be permitted; and (f) the action will not have a significant effect on the human environment.

The conclusion that no significant impact will occur is improperly based on a prophecy that exploration activity on these lands will be insignificant and generally fruitless.

While it may well be true that the majority of these leases will never reach the drilling stage and that the environmental impacts of exploration are dependent upon the nature of the activity, nevertheless NEPA requires that federal agencies determine at the outset whether their major actions can result in "significant" environmental impacts. Here, the Forest Service concluded that any impacts which might result from the act of leasing would either be insignificant or, if significant, could be mitigated by exercising the controls provided in the lease stipulations.

Even assuming, *arguendo,* that all lease stipulations are fully enforceable, once the land is leased the Department no longer has the authority to *preclude* surface disturbing activities even if the environmental impact of such activity is significant. The Department can only impose "mitigation" measures upon a lessee who pursues surface disturbing exploration and/or drilling activities. None of the stipulations expressly provides that the Department or the Forest Service can *prevent* a lessee from conducting surface disturbing activities. Thus, with respect to the smaller area with which we are here concerned, the decision to allow surface disturbing activities has been made at the *leasing stage* and, under NEPA, this is the point at which the environmental impacts of such activities must be evaluated.

* * *

The Department asserts that it cannot accurately evaluate the consequences of drilling and other surface disturbing activities until site-specific plans are submitted. If, however, the Department is in fact concerned that it cannot foresee and evaluate the environmental consequences of leasing without site-specific proposals, then it may delay preparation of an EIS provided that it reserves both the authority to *preclude* all activities pending submission of site-specific proposals and the authority to *prevent* proposed activities if the environmental consequences are unacceptable. If the Department chooses not to retain the authority to *preclude* all surface disturbing activities, then an EIS assessing the full environmental consequences of leasing must be prepared at the point of commitment—when the leases are issued. The Department can decide, in the first instance, by which route it will proceed.

* * *

Sierra Club v. Marsh

United States Court of Appeals, First Circuit, 1985.
769 F.2d 868.

■ BREYER, CIRCUIT JUDGE.

This case embodies an argument about whether a cargo port and a causeway that Maine plans to build at Sears Island will significantly affect the environment. * * *

The record shows that Sears Island is an undeveloped, wooded 940–acre island in upper Penobscot Bay. The island is connected to the mainland by a gravel bar exposed only at low tide. The mainland area adjacent to the island has been developed for industrial use: a chemical plant and a petroleum storage area sit on either side of the point leading to the gravel bar. Indeed, Searsport (where the island is located) is one of the busiest ports in Maine. * * * The most recent proposal for Sears Island consists of three parts: (1) a 1,200–foot solid-fill causeway that would connect Sears Island to the mainland with a railroad line and a two-lane road; (2) a dry-cargo marine terminal designed principally for the shipping of lumber and agricultural products, containerized cargo, and, possibly at a later stage in the project, coal; and (3) an industrial park in an area adjacent to the cargo port. * * *

[In 1981 the Maine DOT prepared an EA focused only on the causeway. The Federal Highway Administration adopted this EA], issued a FONSI, and approved federal funding for the causeway. At this point, at least four federal agencies objected—three "environmental" agencies (the Fish and Wildlife Service, EPA, the National Marine Fisheries Service) and the Coast Guard. These four agencies said that the EA was inadequate and that all three parts of the proposed development (causeway, port, and industrial development) should be considered together in an EIS.

Maine DOT then prepared another EA, this time on the port facility alone; the Federal Highway Administration adopted this EA and then issued another FONSI. Again, the three federal environmental agencies objected * * *. Responding to this criticism, the Federal Highway Administration adopted a new document, prepared by Maine DOT, called an "Environmental Assessment Summary." The new document considered both causeway and port, but it expressly disclaimed any need for consideration of "development on Sears Island outside of the current marine terminal project." On December 16, 1983 the Federal Highway Administration issued yet another FONSI for the causeway/port project.

On the same day, the Army Corps of Engineers (the agency responsible for issuing permits for the project) released its own EA, in respect to port and causeway, and, on the basis of that EA, issued a FONSI. * * * Then, without preparing an EIS, it issued a permit allowing causeway and port construction to begin. At that point, the Sierra Club filed suit.

* * *

The EAs before us concern the likely environmental effects of building the causeway and the port. Our reading of the record indicates that the major environmental bones of contention have included the following:

1. *Clam flats.* Building the causeway will eliminate 1.5 to 2 acres of clam flats; construction of the port will eliminate another 1.5 to 2 acres. Maine's DOT, however, will replace 2.14 acres of this habitat by seeding an area east of the causeway. * * *

2. *Lobsters, scallops, and other marine animals.* Building the marine terminal will require dredging and filling 90 acres now inhabited by lobsters, scallops, and other marine animals. * * * Maine's DOT, however, noted that many of the lobsters can move elsewhere and the scallop grounds are not very productive. * * *

3. *Waterfowl.* The appellants and several environmental agencies said the project would adversely affect certain birds by encroaching on their current habitat. Maine's DOT, after consulting with Maine wildlife agencies, concluded that it would not do so because the birds' winter feeding on the island is limited to areas that do not freeze, and the project will not deprive them of a significant amount of such habitat.

4. *Seals.* One of the federal environmental agencies argued that the project would drive seals from the area. Maine's DOT, however, concluded that the harbor seals are already accustomed to the shipping traffic and would not be significantly disturbed.

5. *Upland habitat.* The parties agree that the port terminal would eliminate at least 40 acres of wooded upland habitat which supports several kinds of mammals and birds (including foxes, whitetailed deer, osprey, and woodcock). Maine's DOT and the Corps concluded, however, that the loss was not significant because the 40 acres represent only 4 percent of the island's total "upland habitat"; displaced animals could go elsewhere; and the area has an abundance of such resources.

* * *

8. *Dredging and "spoil" disposal.* Construction of the port will require the disposal of over 2 million cubic yards of dredged material (called "spoils")—1.3 million in the initial phases of the project; 750,000 in the later stages. The Fish and Wildlife Service feared that Maine's plan to dump the spoils at a special ocean dump site would destroy a "benthic community"—organisms on which fish and other sea animals feed. The

Corps concluded that this possibility was not environmentally significant because the dredged material would cover only 65 acres, the "communities" could reestablish themselves, and Maine agreed to consider other ways of disposing of some of the material.

Whether or not these environmental effects, when considered together, do, or do not, show a "significant impact" is arguable. We note that the federal agencies, including the project's agency sponsors, differ among themselves about the significance of some of these effects. * * * [T]he Corps evidently believes that *promises* to mitigate certain environmental impacts in the future mean that these impacts lack significance. The CEQ, however, has written:

> Mitigation measures may be relied upon to make a finding of no significant impact only if they are imposed by statute or regulation, or submitted by an applicant or agency as part of the original proposal. As a general rule, the regulations contemplate that agencies ... should not rely on the possibility of mitigation to avoid the EIS requirement.
>
> If a proposal appears to have adverse effects which would be significant, and certain mitigation measures are then developed during the scoping or EA stages, the existence of such *possible* mitigation does not obviate the need for an EIS.... [Preparation of an EIS] is essential to ensure that the final decision is based on all the relevant factors and that the full NEPA process will result in enforceable mitigation measures through the Record of Decision.

Forty Most Asked Questions, 46 Fed. Reg. 18028, 18038 (1981) (emphasis in original). Regardless, were *only* the above-mentioned impacts at issue, we doubt that we could say that the "FONSI" conclusions of the Corps and the Federal Highway Administration were "arbitrary, capricious, an abuse of discretion." 5 U.S.C. § 706(2)(A).

The problems just noted become significant, however, when combined with a more serious omission by the Corps and the Federal Highway Administration—their failure to consider adequately the fact that building a port and causeway may lead to the further industrial development of Sears Island, and that further development will significantly affect the environment. The CEQ says that agencies must take account of such "indirect effects," which it defines as those that are

> caused by the action and are later in time or farther removed in distance, but are still reasonably foreseeable. Indirect effects may include *growth inducing effects* and other effects related to *induced changes in the pattern of land use, population density, or growth rate,* and related effects on air and water and other natural systems, including ecosystems.

40 C.F.R. § 1508.8 (emphasis added). Of course, agencies need not consider highly speculative or indefinite impacts. But, here the "impacts" seem neither speculative nor indefinite.

Whether a particular set of impacts is definite enough to take into account, or too speculative to warrant consideration, reflects several different factors. With what confidence can one say that the impacts are likely to occur? Can one describe them "now" with sufficient specificity to make their consideration useful? If the decisionmaker does not take them into account "now," will the decisionmaker be able to take account of them before the agency is so firmly committed to the project that further environmental knowledge, as a practical matter, will prove irrelevant to the government's decision?

In this case, the record contains clear answers to these questions. And those answers show that the agencies should have taken account of the "secondary impacts." First, the record makes it nearly impossible to doubt that building the causeway and port will lead to further development of Sears Island. Local planners have considered the port, causeway, and industrial park to be components of an integrated plan. * * *

Second, the plans for further development are precise enough for an EIS usefully to take them into account. The record contains, for example, a 35–page "Land Use Plan/Industrial Marketing Study" prepared for the owner of the southern half of the island, and the town's 50–page "Municipal Response Plan for the Industrial Development of Sears Island." * * *

Third, once Maine completes the causeway and port, pressure to develop the rest of the island could well prove irreversible. * * *

In sum, given the likely secondary effects of the Sears Island project and the other effects previously described, the record in this case cannot support a FONSI, and therefore an EIS must be prepared. We reach this conclusion not because preparation of an EIS is merely a technical requirement which, under NEPA and its implementing regulations, we must here enforce. Rather, this requirement reflects NEPA's underlying purpose in requiring agencies to determine and assess environmental effects in a systematic way—namely, having decisionmakers focus on these effects when they make major decisions. That is to say, the requirement flows not only from the letter, but also from the spirit, of NEPA.

* * *

NOTES AND QUESTIONS

1. *"Significantly."* How do the CEQ regulations define the term "significantly"? What tests did the courts apply in *Sierra Club v. Peterson* and *Sierra Club v. Marsh*? In the latter case, setting aside the possibility that development of the port and causeway would encourage further industrial development of Sears Island, would the direct effects have been sufficient to require an EIS?

2. *The Environmental Baseline or Status Quo.* An action that does not change the environmental status quo does not require an EIS. Does transfer out of federal ownership, without an immediate change in use, alter the status quo? Suppose the federal government acquires a cattle ranch by foreclosure. Can it sell the ranch without an EIS? See National Wildlife Fed'n v. Espy, 45 F.3d 1337 (9th Cir.1995). Must the National

Park Service complete an EIS before transferring land to a local government which intends to develop an amusement park? Does it matter whether additional federal approvals will be required before the park can be built? See Anacostia Watershed Soc'y v. Babbitt, 871 F.Supp. 475 (D.D.C.1994).

3. *Judicial Review.* What standard governs judicial review of an agency decision not to prepare an EIS? In Marsh v. Oregon Natural Resources Council, 490 U.S. 360, 375–77 (1989), the Supreme Court explained:

> In determining the proper standard of review, we look to § 10(e) of the Administrative Procedure Act (APA), 5 U.S.C. § 706, which empowers federal courts to "hold unlawful and set aside agency action, findings, and conclusions" if they fail to conform with any of six specified standards. We conclude that review of the narrow question before us of whether the Corps' determination that the FEIS need not be supplemented should be set aside is controlled by the "arbitrary and capricious" standard of § 706(2)(A).

> Respondents contend that the determination of whether the new information suffices to establish a "significant" effect is either a question of law or, at a minimum, a question of ultimate fact and, as such, "deserves no deference" on review. Apparently, respondents maintain that the question for review centers on the legal meaning of the term "significant" or, in the alternative, the predominantly legal question of whether established and uncontested historical facts presented by the administrative record satisfy this standard. Characterizing the dispute in this manner, they posit that strict review is appropriate under the "in accordance with law" clause of § 706(2)(A) or the "without observance of procedure required by law" provision of § 706(2)(D). We disagree.

> The question presented for review in this case is a classic example of a factual dispute the resolution of which implicates substantial agency expertise. The dispute thus does not turn on the meaning of the term "significant" or on an application of this legal standard to settled facts. Rather, resolution of this dispute involves primarily issues of fact. Because analysis of the relevant documents "requires a high level of technical expertise," we must defer to "the informed discretion of the responsible federal agencies." Kleppe v. Sierra Club, 427 U.S. 390, 412 (1976).

Is this decision consistent with the purposes of the EIS requirement? Should the same standards apply when the issue is whether an EIS is required at all, rather then whether it must be supplemented? See Sabine River Authority v. U.S. Dep't of Interior, 951 F.2d 669 (5th Cir.1992) (arbitrary and capricious standard applies after *Marsh v. ONRC*); Goos v. Interstate Commerce Comm'n, 911 F.2d 1283 (8th Cir.1990) (reasonableness standard continues to govern threshold question of NEPA application).

4. *Mitigation and Significance.* Can mitigation measures be used to justify a FONSI? If the answer is no, will substantial time and resources be wasted in the preparation of environmental documents for actions that ultimately will not have a significant effect? Could allowing the use of mitigation to support a FONSI encourage agencies to undertake mitigation? But recall that the environmental assessment process is less visible to the public than the EIS process. Will agencies tend to overestimate the effectiveness of mitigation measures? What assurance does the public have that such measures will actually be implemented?

5. *Indirect Impacts.* On what basis did the court in *Sierra Club v. Marsh* conclude that the agency was required to consider the effects of future industrial development on Sears Island? Is the court's treatment of this issue consistent with *South Carolina v. O'Leary* and *Winnebago Tribe v. Ray*? Does it impermissibly expand the scope of federal control?

SECTION 3.   CONTENTS OF THE EIS

Excerpts from Council on Environmental Quality Regulations

40 C.F.R. Parts 1500–1517.

Sec. 1502.14   Alternatives including the proposed action

This section is the heart of the environmental impact statement. * * * In this section agencies shall:

(a) Rigorously explore and objectively evaluate all reasonable alternatives, and for alternatives which were eliminated from detailed study, briefly discuss the reasons for their having been eliminated.

(b) Devote substantial treatment to each alternative considered in detail including the proposed action so that reviewers may evaluate their comparative merits.

(c) Include reasonable alternatives not within the jurisdiction of the lead agency.

(d) Include the alternative of no action.

* * *

Sec. 1502.15   Affected environment

The environmental impact statement shall succinctly describe the environment of the area(s) to be affected or created by the alternatives under consideration. The descriptions shall be no longer than is necessary to understand the effects of the alternatives. * * *

Sec. 1508.7   Cumulative impact

Cumulative impact is the impact on the environment which results from the incremental impact of the action when added to other past, present, and reasonably foreseeable future actions regardless of what agency (Federal or non-Federal) or person undertakes such other actions. Cumulative impacts can result from individually minor but collectively significant actions taking place over a period of time.

Sec. 1508.8   Effects

Effects include:

(a) Direct effects, which are caused by the action and occur at the same time and place.

(b) Indirect effects, which are caused by the action and are later in time or farther removed in distance, but are still reasonably foreseeable. Indirect effects may include growth inducing effects and other effects related to induced changes in the pattern of land use, population density or growth rate, and related effects on air and water and other natural systems, including ecosystems.

* * *

Citizens Against Burlington, Inc. v. Busey

United States Court of Appeals, District of Columbia Circuit, 1991.
938 F.2d 190.

■ Clarence Thomas, Circuit Judge.

The city of Toledo decided to expand one of its airports, and the Federal Aviation Administration decided to approve the city's plan. In this petition for review of the FAA's order, an alliance of people who live near the airport contends that the FAA has violated several environmental statutes and regulations. * * *

The Toledo Express Airport, object of the controversy in this case, lies about twenty-five miles to the west of downtown Toledo. * * *

Citizens Against Burlington first materialized about a year after the [Toledo–Lucas County] Port Authority * * * began to consider the possibility of the airport's expansion. The Port Authority soon heard from Burlington Air Express, which had been flying its planes out of an old World War II hangar at Baer Field, an Air National Guard airport in Fort Wayne. After looking at seventeen sites in four midwestern states, Burlington chose the Toledo Express Airport. Among Burlington's reasons were the quality of Toledo's work force and the airport's prior operating record, zoning advantages, and location (near major highways and close to Detroit and Chicago). For its part, the Port Authority expects the new hub to create one thousand new jobs in metropolitan Toledo and to contribute almost $68 million per year to the local economy after three years of the hub's operation. * * *

* * * This case concerns the most important responsibility that NEPA demands—that an agency reviewing proposals for action prepare an environmental impact statement, and, more specifically, that the agency discuss in its statement alternatives to the action proposed. We consider here whether the FAA has complied with NEPA in publishing an environmental impact statement that discussed in depth two alternatives: approving the expansion of the Toledo Express Airport, and not approving the expansion of the Toledo Express Airport.

Federal agencies must prepare environmental impact statements when they contemplate "major Federal actions significantly affecting the quality of the human environment." NEPA § 102(2)(C). An EIS must discuss, among other things, "alternatives to the proposed action," NEPA § 102(2)(C)(iii), and the discussion of alternatives forms "the heart of the environmental impact statement." 40 C.F.R. § 1502.14.

The problem for agencies is that "the term 'alternatives' is not self-defining." Vermont Yankee Nuclear Power Corp. v. Natural Resources Defense Council, Inc., 435 U.S. 519, 551 (1978). Suppose, for example, that a utility applies for permission to build a nuclear reactor in Vernon, Vermont. Free-floating "alternatives" to the proposal for federal action might conceivably include everything from licensing a reactor in Pecos, Texas, to promoting imports of hydropower from Quebec. If the Nuclear Regulatory Commission had to discuss these and other imaginable courses of action, its statement would wither into "frivolous boilerplate" * * *. If, therefore, the consideration of alternatives is to inform both the public and the agency decisionmaker, the discussion must be moored to "some notion of feasibility." Id., 435 U.S. at 551.

Recognizing the harm that an unbounded understanding of alternatives might cause, CEQ regulations oblige agencies to discuss only alternatives that are feasible, or (much the same thing) reasonable. 40 C.F.R. §§ 1502.14(a)–(c), 1508.25(b)(2). But the adjective "reasonable" is no more self-defining than the noun that it modifies. Consider two possible alternatives to our nuclear reactor in Vernon. Funding research in cold fusion might be an unreasonable alternative by virtue of the theory's scientific implausibility. But licensing a reactor in Lake Placid, New York might also be unreasonable, even though it passes some objective test of scientific worth. In either case, the proposed alternative is reasonable only if it will bring about the ends of the federal action—only if it will do what the licensing of the reactor in Vernon is meant to do. If licensing the Vernon reactor is meant to help supply energy to New England, licensing a reactor in northern New York might make equal sense. If licensing the Vernon reactor is meant as well to stimulate the Vernon job market, licensing a reactor in Lake Placid would be far less effective. * * *

* * * When an agency is asked to sanction a specific plan, the agency should take into account the needs and goals of the parties involved in the application. Perhaps more importantly, an agency should always consider the views of Congress, expressed, to the extent that the agency can determine them, in the agency's statutory authorization to act, as well as in other congressional directives.

* * *

In the first chapter of its environmental impact statement, the FAA begins by noting that the Port Authority had requested the agency's approval of the plan to develop Toledo Express. The agency then explains that "[t]he purpose and need for this action lies in [the] FAA's responsibility to review the airport design and runway configuration with respect to its safety, efficiency and utility within the national airspace system and its environmental impact on the surrounding area." After surveying the engineering reasons that justify an extended runway and new facilities, the FAA concludes by stating that the agency "has a statutory mandate to facilitate the establishment of air cargo hubs under Section 502(a)(7) [of the Airport and Airway Improvement Act of 1982 (AAIA), 49 U.S.C. app. § 2201(a)(7)] and to undertake capacity enhancement projects under Section 502(a)(11) [of the AAIA, 49 U.S.C. app. § 2201(a)(11)]."

In the second chapter of the environmental impact statement, the FAA begins by stating:

> The scope of alternatives considered by the sponsoring Federal agency, where the Federal government acts as a proprietor, is wide ranging and comprehensive. Where the Federal government acts, not as a proprietor, but to approve and support a project being sponsored by a local government or private applicant, the Federal agency is necessarily more limited. In the latter instance, the Federal government's consideration of alternatives may accord substantial weight to the preferences of the applicant and/or sponsor in the siting and design of the project.

The agency goes on to explain:

> In the present system of federalism, the FAA does not determine where to build and develop civilian airports, as an owner/operator. Rather, the FAA facilitates airport development by providing Federal financial assistance, and reviews and approves or disapproves revisions to Airport Layout Plans at Federally funded airports.... Similarly, under the Airline Deregulation Act of 1978, the FAA does not regulate rates, routes, and services of air carriers or cargo operators. Airline managements are free to decide which cities to serve based on market forces.

The EIS then describes five alternatives: approving the Port Authority's plan for expanding Toledo Express, approving other geometric configurations for expanding Toledo Express, approving other ways of channelling airplane traffic at Toledo Express, no action by the agency at all, and approving plans for other airports both in the Toledo metropolitan area and out of it, including Baer Field in Fort Wayne. Finally, the EIS briefly explains why the agency eliminated all the alternatives but the first and the fourth. See 40 C.F.R. § 1502.14(a).

The FAA's reasoning fully supports its decision to evaluate only the preferred and do-nothing alternatives. The agency first examined Congress's views on how this country is to build its civilian airports. As the agency explained, Congress has told the FAA to nurture aspiring cargo hubs. See AAIA § 502(a)(7), (11), 49 U.S.C. app. § 2201(a)(7), (11). At the same time, however, Congress has also said that the free market, not an ersatz Gosplan for aviation, should determine the siting of the nation's airports. See Airline Deregulation Act of 1978, Pub.L. No. 95–504, 92 Stat. 1705. Congress has expressed its intent by statute, and the FAA took both of Congress's messages seriously.

The FAA also took into account the Port Authority's reasons for wanting a cargo hub in Toledo. In recent years, more than fifty major companies have left the Toledo metropolitan area, and with them, over seven thousand jobs. The Port Authority expects the cargo hub at Toledo Express to create immediately more than two hundred permanent and six hundred part-time jobs with a total payroll value of more than $10 million. After three years, according to the Port Authority, the hub should create directly more than one thousand permanent jobs at the airport and one hundred and fifty other, airport-related jobs. The University of Toledo estimates that the new Toledo Express will contribute at least $42 million to the local economy after one full year of operation and nearly $68 million per year after three. In addition, the Port Authority expects the expanded airport, and Burlington's presence there, to attract other companies to Toledo. All of those factors, the Port Authority hopes, will lead to a renaissance in the Toledo metropolitan region.

Having thought hard about these appropriate factors, the FAA defined the goal for its action as helping to launch a new cargo hub in Toledo and thereby helping to fuel the Toledo economy. The agency then eliminated from detailed discussion the alternatives that would not accomplish this goal. Each of the different geometric configurations would mean technological problems and extravagant costs. So would plans to route traffic differently at Toledo Express, or to build a hub at one of the other airports in the city of Toledo. None of the airports outside of the Toledo area would serve the purpose of the agency's action. The FAA thus evaluated the environmental impacts of the only proposal that might reasonably accomplish that goal—approving the construction and operation of a cargo hub at Toledo Express. It did so with the thoroughness required by law.

We conclude that the FAA acted reasonably in defining the purpose of its action, in eliminating alternatives that would not achieve it, and in discussing (with the required do-nothing option) the proposal that would. The agency has therefore complied with NEPA.

Citizens agree that the FAA need only discuss reasonable, not all, alternatives to Toledo Express. Relying on Van Abbema v. Fornell, 807 F.2d 633 (7th Cir.1986), however, Citizens argues that "the evaluation of 'alternatives' mandated by NEPA is to be an evaluation of alternative means to accomplish the *general* goal of an action; it is not an evaluation of the alternative means by which a particular applicant can reach his goals."

Id. at 638. According to Citizens, the "general goal" of the Port Authority's proposal is to build a permanent cargo hub for Burlington [Air Express, Inc.]. Since, in Citizens' view, Fort Wayne (and perhaps Peoria) will accomplish this general goal just as well as Toledo, if not better, Baer Field is a reasonable alternative to Toledo Express, and the FAA should have discussed it in depth. * * *

We see two critical flaws in *Van Abbema*, and therefore in Citizens' argument. The first is that the *Van Abbema* court misconstrued the language of NEPA. *Van Abbema* involved a private businessman who had applied to the Army Corps of Engineers for permission to build a place to "transload" coal from trucks to barges. The panel decided that the Corps had to survey "feasible alternatives . . . to the applicant's proposal," or alternative ways of accomplishing "the general goal [of] deliver[ing] coal from mine to utility." In commanding agencies to discuss "alternatives to the proposed action," however, NEPA plainly refers to alternatives to the "major *Federal* actions significantly affecting the quality of the human environment," and not to alternatives to the applicant's proposal. NEPA § 102(2)(C) (emphasis added). An agency cannot redefine the goals of the proposal that arouses the call for action; it must evaluate alternative ways of achieving *its* goals, shaped by the application at issue and by the function that the agency plays in the decisional process. Congress did expect agencies to consider an applicant's wants when the agency formulates the goals of its own proposed action. Congress did not expect agencies to determine for the applicant what the goals of the applicant's proposal should be.

The second problem with *Van Abbema* lies in the court's assertion that an agency must evaluate "alternative means to accomplish the general goal of an action," 807 F.2d at 638—a statement that troubles us even if we assume that the panel was alluding to the general goals of the federal action instead of to the goals of the private proposal. Left unanswered in *Van Abbema* and Citizens' brief (and at oral argument) is why and how to distinguish general goals from specific ones and just who does the distinguishing. *Someone* has to define the purpose of the agency action. Implicit in *Van Abbema* is that the body responsible is the reviewing court. As we explained, however, NEPA and binding case law provide otherwise.

■ Buckley, Circuit Judge, dissenting in part.

* * *

I cannot fault the FAA for the attention given Burlington and its preferences. While both Toledo and Burlington are indispensable to the enterprise, Burlington is plainly the dominant partner; its requirements and desires shaped the project from the start. As the agency points out in its Record of Decision ("ROD"), "[t]he demand for this project is clearly based on a business decision by Burlington Air Express and the interest of a local airport sponsor, the Toledo–Lucas County Port Authority, in accommodating and facilitating this decision."

I do fault the agency for failing to attend to its own business, which is to examine all alternatives "that are practical or feasible from the technical and economic standpoint . . . rather than simply desirable from the standpoint of the applicant." Forty Most Asked Questions Concerning CEQ's National Environmental Policy Act Regulations, 46 Fed. Reg. 18,026, 18,027 (1981). As far as I can tell, the FAA never questioned Burlington's assertions that of the ones considered, Toledo Express is the only airport suitable to its purposes. * * *

I do not suggest that Burlington is untrustworthy, only that the FAA had the duty under NEPA to exercise a degree of skepticism in dealing with self-serving statements from a prime beneficiary of the project. It may well be that none of the sixteen other alternatives examined by Burlington and its consultants could be converted into a viable air cargo hub at acceptable cost. That, however, was something that the FAA should have determined for itself instead of accepting as a given. Under NEPA, "the federal agency must itself determine what is reasonably available." Trinity Episcopal School Corp. v. Romney, 523 F.2d 88, 94 (2d Cir.1975); see Van Abbema v. Fornell, 807 F.2d 633, 642 (7th Cir.1986) (condemning agency's "blind reliance on material prepared by the applicant"). By allowing the FAA to abandon this requirement, the majority establishes a precedent that will permit an applicant and a third-party beneficiary of federal action to define the limits of the EIS inquiry and thus to frustrate one of the principal safeguards of the NEPA process, the mandatory consideration of reasonable alternatives.

* * *

NOTES AND QUESTIONS

1. *Consideration of Alternatives.* NEPA's requirement that a federal agency consider alternatives to its proposed actions is somewhat broader than the EIS requirement. NEPA § 102(2)(E) requires that all agencies "study, develop, and describe appropriate alternatives to recommended courses of action in any proposal which involves unresolved conflicts concerning alternative uses of available resources."

What legal standard must the agency fulfill in considering alternatives under NEPA? Must alternatives be within the power of the action agency? Must each alternative fully achieve all goals of the proposed action? In Natural Resources Defense Council v. Morton, 458 F.2d 827 (D.C.Cir.1972), the proposed action was the sale of off-shore oil and gas leases. The D.C. Circuit found the EIS inadequate, in part because it did not consider alternatives that would supply less energy than the proposed leases. More recently, however, the same court ruled that the Federal Highway Administration need not consider a ten-lane alternative to a proposed twelve-lane highway bridge because ten lanes would not accommodate the traffic expected over the next twenty years. City of Alexandria v. Slater, 198 F.3d 862 (D.C.Cir.1999). Are these two decisions reconcilable? If not, which is more consistent with the purposes of NEPA?

2. *Defining Goals.* As *Citizens Against Burlington* illustrates, delineation of the goals of the project determines the scope of the required alternative discussion. Should goals be more broadly construed for fully federal actions than for federal approvals of non-federal activities? Is this issue similar to the "small handles" problem discussed in Section 2? To what extent should the federal agency (and reviewing courts) defer to the applicant's goals? How much practical difference does it make? In *Citizens Against Burlington*, how would the EIS have been different if the FAA had fully considered alternative sites such as Fort Wayne? Would the ultimate decision have been different? Would public understanding of, and reaction to, the decision have been altered?

3. In the Class Discussion Problem, suppose the Corps of Engineers conceded that it must prepare an EIS. Must that EIS consider redesign of the development to entirely avoid the wetlands on the site? Elimination of the hotel and entertainment complex? Development of a different site, not currently owned by Southwest Development? Redeveloping existing housing and office space in downtown Los Angeles?

4. *Mitigation.* In Robertson v. Methow Valley Citizens Council, 490 U.S. 332 (1989), the Supreme Court held that NEPA requires a discussion of the extent to which adverse effects can be mitigated or avoided, but that it does not mandate adoption of a mitigation plan. If an agency promises in an EIS to take mitigation actions, is that promise subsequently enforceable in court? Consider the following excerpt from William L. Andreen, In Pursuit of NEPA's Promise: The Role of Executive Oversight in the Implementation of Environmental Policy, 64 Ind. L.J. 205, 245–47 (1989):

> It should come as no surprise, considering the judicial reluctance to review an agency's substantive decision, that the courts have refused to enforce "commitments" found in an EIS. However misleading representations contained in an EIS may seem when viewed in light of actual agency performance,[281] the fact remains that those representations do not amount to enforceable duties. As the CEQ regulations amply demonstrate, an EIS is simply a planning document which is intended to inform the ultimate decisionmaker. Therefore, any attempt to enforce a mitigation measure or any other condition found in an EIS is, in reality, an effort to force a particular decision upon an agency by transforming a planning tool into a final decision. If any document generated during the NEPA process could give rise to such an action for enforcement, it would have to be an agency's ROD.
>
> While CEQ has expressed its belief that "the terms of a ROD are enforceable by * * * private parties," the regulations promulgated by

---

281. *City of Blue Ash v. McLucas*, 596 F.2d 709 (6th Cir.1979), involved an especially egregious example of an agency turning its back on an impact-reducing representation contained in its EIS. The Federal Aviation Administration (FAA) had prepared an EIS for its funding of an airport expansion in suburban Cincinnati. The EIS indicated that, due to public opposition, jet aircraft would be barred from using the renovated facility. Soon after the project was completed, however, the FAA reversed itself and declared that certain types of jets would, in fact, be granted access to the airport. Id. at 710–11.

CEQ reveal that the enforceable duties arising from a record of decision are more circumscribed. The regulations do not direct an agency to implement every aspect of a decision. Rather, CEQ chose only to require an agency to perform the "mitigation * * * and other conditions" identified during the EIS process and adopted in the agency's decision.[284] A court, consequently, could find a failure to implement such mitigation a breach of an agency's legal duty and order the agency to comply.

An agency, however, has no duty to adopt mitigation measures or other impact reducing conditions in its ROD. As a result, a potential litigant may find little to enforce. Moreover, a citizen will likely be unaware of whether an agency has ever performed its obligations to mitigate environmental damage. And even if one becomes aware of an implementation failure, the discovery may come so late in the process that a suit cannot be brought until after the project has been completed. In such a case, a court might be inclined to dismiss the action for mootness or to deny injunctive relief on account of laches.

SECTION 4. EVALUATING NEPA

Perhaps the strongest evidence of NEPA's success is the progeny it has spawned. At least 15 states and the District of Columbia have some form of environmental policy act modeled after NEPA, as do many foreign nations. Some commentators now recognize environmental impact assessment as an emerging principle of international law. See William L. Andreen, Environmental Law and International Assistance: The Challenge of Strengthening Environmental Law in the Developing World, 25 Columbia J. Envtl. L. 17, 40–41 (2000); 1 Phillippe Sands, Principles of International Environmental Law 579–95 (1995).

NEPA has also shown remarkable political stability. Title I (sections 2–105) has been amended only once. (Section 102(D), which allows states to take the lead in preparing EISs for certain actions, was added in 1975.) CEQ's implementing regulations have shown similar durability.

Of course, imitation and durability do not necessarily equate with success. Here are some possible yardsticks for evaluating NEPA:

1) Has it produced decisions that are substantively more environmentally protective than they otherwise would have been?

2) Has it ensured that agencies make decisions with better understanding of their environmental consequences?

3) Has it changed the culture of single-minded, mission-oriented federal agencies, making them more sensitive to environmental concerns?

4) Has it increased public awareness of, and involvement in, agency decisions with environmental consequences?

---

284. CEQ Regulations, 40 C.F.R. § 1505.3 (1987) * * *.

5) Are the costs of NEPA compliance justified by its benefits?

It is difficult to obtain reliable answers to any of these questions. Lynton Caldwell, a political scientist who was the primary architect of NEPA, believes the law has been successful in "forcing government agencies to ascertain the probable environmental consequences of their actions," but has failed to induce those agencies to act in accordance with the principles set forth in § 101(b). Lynton K. Caldwell, A Constitutional Law for the Environment: 20 Years with NEPA Indicates the Need, Environment, Dec. 1989, at 6, 10. Many observers agree that NEPA has forced mission-oriented agencies to diversify their staffs, bringing in environmental specialists or assigning their core staff to understand and communicate environmental concerns. That increased diversity, in turn, is thought to have produced greater environmental sensitivity. See, e.g., Paul J. Culhane, NEPA's Impacts on Federal Agencies, Anticipated and Unanticipated, 20 Envtl. L. 681, 690–91 (1990). Nonetheless, Culhane concludes that NEPA has not led to truly "rational" decisionmaking because agencies do not consider alternatives antithetical to their primary mission, EISs often do not reflect state-of-the-art scientific understanding, and the forecasts of impacts made in EISs are often wrong. Id. at 693–94.

Some commentators believe the openness required by NEPA has led to substantively better decisions:

> NEPA, and its requirement of an environmental impact statement open to public view and comment, ventilated the planning processes of federal agencies in a way that had never occurred before. The citizen, once only a nosy intruder, became a legitimate participant. [L]egitimating public participation, and demanding openness in planning and decisionmaking, has been indispensable to a permanent and powerful increase in environmental protection * * *.

Joseph Sax, Introduction to Symposium: Environmental Law: More Than Just a Passing Fad, 19 U. Mich. J. L. Ref. 797, 804 (1986).

Others, however, are more skeptical. In the absence of substantive requirements, solicitation of public input may be cynically viewed as a ploy to defuse public opposition. Furthermore, NEPA may be geared toward a one-way exchange of information from the government to the public, rather than a truly deliberative exchange. Jonathan Poisner, A Civic Republican Perspective on the National Environmental Policy Act's Process for Citizen Participation, 26 Envtl. L. 53 (1996). Does NEPA adequately encourage public input? Does it force agencies to take that input seriously? Poisner suggests the use of lay "juries," randomly selected from the community, to oversee the preparation of EISs. What do you think of that proposal? Is it feasible? Would it be desirable?

NEPA (and its state analogues) can play an important role in achieving environmental justice, which depends in large part upon providing members of the relevant community with reasonable access to the decisionmaking process. In 1994, President Clinton issued Executive Order 12898, requiring each federal agency to make environmental justice a part of its mission. A memorandum accompanying Executive Order 12898 specifically directed federal agencies to examine environmental effects on minority and low-income communities in their NEPA documents. Failure to adequately consider those impacts led the Nuclear Regulatory Commission to overturn a preliminary decision to permit a uranium enrichment plant in Louisiana. In the Matter of Louisiana Energy Services, L.P., LBP–97–8, 45 N.R.C. 367 (May 1, 1997).

NEPA alone does not ensure environmental justice, however. Wealthy communities are far more likely to be able to make effective use of NEPA's participatory avenues than others. Indeed, NEPA may amplify NIMBY (not in my backyard) reactions in wealthy communities, pushing environmentally undesirable facilities toward lower-income, often minority, communities.

NOTES AND QUESTIONS

1. *The Forest and the Trees.* Does NEPA as currently implemented focus too much on the details of individual projects, and too little on articulating a true national environmental policy? Richard Andrews suggests that NEPA has been least effective at the broadest policy levels, such as the determination of overall energy, logging, and appropriation decisions, where the most pervasive environmental impacts are set in motion. Richard N.L. Andrews, The Unfinished Business of National Environmental Policy, in Environmental Policy and NEPA: Past, Present, and Future 85 (Ray Clark and Larry Canter eds., 1997). Andrews attributes this failure to two aspects of NEPA. First, the EIS requirement is not readily applied to this most fundamental level of decisionmaking. Second, the lofty-sounding principles articulated in NEPA sections 2 and 101 do not constitute a true environmental policy that might guide these decisions because they

> require unspecified trade-offs against other "essential considerations of national policy," and they contain no specific objectives, criteria, or benchmarks by which their achievement might be measured.

Id. at 93.

How could greater substantive guidance be provided? Andrews suggests defining a set of specific environmental "benchmarks" or indicators with deadlines for their achievement. Several substantive federal environmental laws set benchmarks. The Clean Air Act, for example, calls for achievement of national ambient air quality standards that protect the public health and welfare with an adequate margin of safety.

Should EPA (or some other body) be directed to draft detailed operational benchmarks for the condition of the nation's air, water, and land that would fulfill NEPA's directives to assure safe, healthful, productive, and aesthetically and culturally pleasing surroundings; attain the widest range of beneficial uses of the environment without degradation; and achieve a balance between population and resource use? Suppose you were the EPA administrator charged with that task. How would you begin to approach it?

2. *Avoiding Environmental Impairment Where Feasible.* In the absence of comprehensively rational benchmarks, are there other ways to give NEPA greater substantive content? Many state NEPA analogs require that adverse environmental impacts be avoided if possible. Minnesota's, for example, forbids state action "likely to cause pollution, impairment, or destruction of the air, water, land or other natural resources located within the state, so long as there is a feasible and prudent alternative * * *." Minn. Stat. Ann. § 116D.04(6). California's requires that significant adverse impacts be avoided or mitigated if feasible, and any remaining significant impacts be justified by "[s]pecific overriding economic, legal, social, technological, or other benefits." Cal. Pub. Res. Code § 21081(a)(3). Should NEPA be amended to impose this type of requirement?

3. *The Interplay of NEPA and Substantive Environmental Laws.* A complex web of federal environmental statutes post-dating NEPA regulate such things as air pollution, water pollution, hazardous waste disposal, and harm to endangered species. NEPA can help make those laws effective by exposing the potential for federal actions to lead to violations of their standards. Does the existence of background standards obviate the need for NEPA to play a substantive role? Should environmental changes within the boundaries permitted by those substantive laws be deemed "insignificant" for NEPA purposes? In the *Calvert Cliffs* decision, Judge Wright argued against that interpretation:

> Certification by another agency that its own environmental standards are satisfied involves an entirely different kind of judgment. Such agencies, without overall responsibility for the particular federal action in question, attend only to one aspect of the problem: the magnitude of certain environmental costs. They simply determine whether those costs exceed an allowable amount. Their certification does not mean that they found no environmental damage whatever. In fact, there may be significant environmental damage (e.g., water pollution), but not quite enough to violate applicable (e.g., water quality) standards. Certifying agencies do not attempt to weigh that damage against the opposing benefits. Thus the balancing analysis remains to be done. It may be that the environmental costs, though passing prescribed standards, are nonetheless great enough to outweigh the particular economic and technical benefits involved in the planned action. The only agency in a position to make such a judgment is the agency with overall responsibility for the proposed federal action—the agency to which NEPA is specifically directed.

Calvert Cliffs' Coordinating Comm. v. U.S. Atomic Energy Comm'n, 449 F.2d 1109, 1123 (D.C.Cir.1971).

By contrast, under the California Environmental Quality Act, an environmental change is not considered a significant impact if it complies with a legal standard of general application adopted for the purpose of environmental protection through a public process. 14 Cal. Code Regs. § 15064(h). What arguments could you make in favor of this policy choice?

Ultimately do you agree with Judge Wright or with the California regulation?

4. *Limiting Reliance on Outside Consultants.* NEPA documents are often prepared by environmental consultants under contract. Should that practice be forbidden? Does reliance on outsiders decrease the probability that environmental concerns will play an important role in the actual decision process? Does it reduce the "agency culture-forcing" effect of NEPA? See Ray Clark, The National Environmental Policy Act and the Role of the President's Council on Environmental Quality, 15 Envtl. Prof. 4 (1993).

5. *Monitoring Project Impacts.* Should agencies be required to monitor project impacts subsequent to EIS approval and project implementation? If those impacts exceed estimates in the EIS, should the project be halted? Should the agency be required to keep a record comparing projected with actual impacts? See Council on Environmental Quality, The National Environmental Policy Act: A Study of Its Effectiveness after Twenty–Five Years 31–33 (1997).

6. *A Constitutional Right to Environmental Protection?* Several state constitutions include environmental rights in some form. The Illinois Constitution, for example, provides:

> Each person has the right to a healthful environment. Each person may enforce this right against any party, governmental or private, through appropriate legal proceedings subject to reasonable limitation and regulation as the General Assembly may provide by law.

Ill. Const. art. XI, § 2. Would you support a similar amendment to the federal constitution? To what extent does the Illinois provision permit or require courts to determine what is a "healthful environment"? Are the courts in a position to make that determination?

SECTION 5.   OTHER INFORMATION-BASED STRATEGIES

NEPA rests on the assumption (or at least hope) that requiring federal agencies to gather and make public information about the environmental impacts of their actions will encourage more environmentally responsible decisions. Information disclosure might have similar effects in private settings. Consumers, for example, might want to base their purchasing decisions on environmental impacts, but lack the information necessary to do so.

A variety of information disclosure strategies have been employed in efforts to reduce pollution, inform consumer choices, and facilitate political pressures. They include:

- **Publicly accessible databases.** The best known example is the Toxic Release Inventory (TRI) prescribed by the Emergency Planning and Community Right-to-Know Act of 1986 (EPCRA). Section 313 of EPCRA, codified at 42 U.S.C. § 11023, requires certain industrial facilities to annually report releases to air, water, and soil of listed chemicals they manufactured, processed, or used in quantities exceeding a threshold amount. EPA must make those reports available to the public through a computer database.

- **Warnings of hazardous exposures.** Perhaps the broadest warning requirement is found in California's Safe Drinking Water and Toxic Enforcement Act, popularly known as Proposition 65. It requires that businesses with more than 10 employees provide "clear and reasonable" warning before exposing individuals to chemicals listed by the state as carcinogens or reproductive toxicants. Cal. Health & Safety Code § 25249.6.

- **Environmental labeling.** A variety of voluntary or required labeling programs provide consumers with environmental information. Examples include: the use of terms such as "recycled" or "organic," or logos such as the "dolphin-friendly tuna" seal; environmental certification or seals of approval such as Germany's Blue Angel; and "report cards" such as the Energy Guide energy efficiency ratings on new household appliances.

Bradley C. Karkkainen, Information as Environmental Regulation: TRI and Performance Benchmarking, Precursor to a New Paradigm?

89 Georgetown L. J. 257, 287–333 (2000).

Mandatory production and disclosure of TRI information has prompted many firms to undertake ambitious voluntary emission reduction programs, often far beyond the levels required under current regulations. * * * Since TRI reporting began in 1988, reported releases of TRI-listed pollutants have dropped by nearly half, with the sharp downward trend continuing steadily year after year. * * * According to one EPA survey, some seventy percent of TRI reporting facilities indicate that they have intensified their waste reduction efforts under the influence of TRI.

* * *

TRI places information in the hands of corporate managers in the first instance. Consequently, it might be analogized to a private sector version of the National Environmental Policy Act, requiring a process—the production and disclosure of environmental information relevant to decisionmaking—rather than substantive outcomes. In neither case does the regulatory approach require that anything in particular be done with the information once it is produced. But by compelling managers to examine environmental outcomes, it may influence their decisionmaking. * * *

Many top corporate managers, previously unaware of the volumes of toxic pollutants their firms were generating, were indeed surprised by the information produced in the first rounds of TRI. In many cases, that knowledge prompted a swift and decisive response, as firms adopted ambitious improvement targets far above the levels required for compliance with regulatory requirements, often in the range of fifty, seventy, or even ninety percent reductions from initial TRI-reported levels. * * *

TRI-generated performance data are readily available to regulators, as well as to environmentalists and other citizen-critics of regulatory policy. Regulators can use TRI data to establish baselines, profiles, and trends in the pollution performance of facilities, firms, industrial sectors, communities, and states, and to make benchmarking comparisons among them. Moreover, the data provide some indication of the effectiveness of regulatory and non-regulatory environmental policies, providing the basis for comparative analysis and benchmarking of program outcomes. TRI data thus help regulators identify regulatory gaps and shortcomings, set research priorities, and identify the most effective programs so as to replicate or expand them. * * *

Simultaneously, citizen-critics of governmental policies can use TRI-derived information to criticize or support current policies and programs, propose new ones, and benchmark and evaluate the achievements of regulated entities and regulators alike. Thus, TRI-generated information holds great potential to alter the level of political demand for environmental regulation, and to redirect that demand toward perceived "problem" firms, industries, pollutants or communities as identified by TRI-generated criteria.

Adverse facility-, firm-, or industry-level TRI data thus carry the implicit threat that regulatory action may follow, whether at the initiative of regulators themselves or in response to rising political demand for regulatory action. But precisely because forward-thinking firms and investors anticipate that additional regulatory requirements may prove burdensome and costly, firms may come under self-imposed and market-driven pressures to undertake cost-effective, voluntary, pollution prevention measures. According to the CEO of a leading chemical manufacturer, pollution prevention becomes a matter of "hard, cold, economics . . . pay now or pay a whole lot more later."

* * *

In the absence of a broader and more comprehensive set of metrics, many users of TRI information are tempted to use it as a proxy for the overall environmental performance of a facility or firm simply because it is the most visible and accessible source of comparable, quantifiable data. But TRI information provides, at best, one narrow and potentially highly misleading indicator of environmental performance, measuring releases from major point sources of substances on a short and far-from-complete EPA-compiled list of toxic pollutants.

A firm with superior TRI data might nonetheless produce large volumes of conventional pollutants or solid waste, or recklessly despoil valuable wildlife habitats—all beyond TRI's purview—while a firm with poor TRI data could nonetheless be a superior environmental performer along these other dimensions. Nor can we safely assume that every improvement in TRI data counts as an environmental gain because, in some cases, it might reflect a shift to activities that cause equal or greater environmental harm that is not reflected in TRI data. To that extent, TRI's very power to drive performance improvements *as measured by the TRI metric* makes it potentially misleading and possibly counterproductive if it is not matched and counterbalanced by a set of equally powerful metrics for other important dimensions of environmental performance.

Similarly, because all reported TRI releases are measured uniformly in pounds, regardless of the relative toxicity of the pollutant, a firm or facility might cut its reported emissions and transfers without reducing—and possibly even while increasing—health and environmental risks by substituting lower-volume, higher-toxicity pollutants. * * *

In addition, because TRI measures only the quantity of the pollutant released without factoring in proximity to population, exposure route, dispersion, persistence, sensitivity of exposed populations, or other important risk-related factors, it does not provide a very good guide to actual human and environmental risks. While TRI data may be combined with other information to provide a richer and more nuanced picture of risk, such information is often not available, and is rarely provided in a form readily accessible to non-expert users. Many users are tempted to rely on TRI data as a handy proxy for the environmental and health risks associated with toxic pollutants. In short, they use TRI as an indicator of environmental *quality* (which it is not), rather than as an indicator of the environmental *performance* of a limited class of sources (the only use the data can fairly support). But to do so may lead to serious overestimation or underestimation of risk.

Clifford Rechtschaffen, The Warning Game: Evaluating Warnings Under California's Proposition 65

23 Ecology L.Q. 303, 313–48 (1996).

Laws utilizing information disclosure requirements—warnings, informational labeling, worker training and notification, and community reporting and disclosure—are based on several important, albeit diverse, rationales. The most common rationale is that such laws improve the efficient functioning of the market. Traditional microeconomic theory assumes consumers have perfect information. Where such information is lacking and will not be produced by the market, disclosure laws help insure that the market functions properly by bridging the information gap. * * * Relying on the power of the market, economists tout information disclosure laws as more efficient and less constraining than direct regulation, imposing lower costs on both business and regulators.

In addition, information disclosure laws are also premised on an entitlement rationale, as reflected in the title of recent "right-to-know" laws. The underlying notion is that members of the public have a "fundamental right to know" what chemicals are "out there" and the chemicals to which they are being exposed. Information promotes individual autonomy by providing individuals with knowledge of the risks involved in their choices and allowing them to decide whether or not to encounter these risks.

Information disclosure laws also promote citizen power and advance democratic decisionmaking. * * * Armed with more information, citizens can make better-informed decisions and are thus in a better position to bargain with private corporations and government.

* * * Information disclosure laws have inherent limitations as well. The marketplace model assumes markets in which there is an elastic demand for products and there are readily available product substitutes. It is also premised on the existence of perfectly rational consumers who seek information regarding alternatives when making decisions, make trade-offs that allow them to compute utilities for every alternative, and select the alternatives that maximize utility. However, these conditions are often not satisfied. Consumers may lack the time or interest to seek out information. Many may have difficulty understanding certain information, especially information about risks. In particular, less educated and limited-English speaking individuals are less likely to be able to read, understand, and use warning information. Even when individuals read and comprehend warnings, they often do not change their behavior in response to the information they receive. * * *

[Most consumer product warnings under Proposition 65] have been located on product labels. * * * Although the regulations state that warnings must be presented with "such conspicuousness as to render them likely to be read and understood by an ordinary individual under customary conditions of purchase or use," in practice this general requirement has imposed few limitations on businesses and has done little to insure that warnings are noticed. Many Proposition 65 warnings are inadequately designed to attract attention. * * *

Research shows that numerous design features can make warnings more conspicuous, such as using a high color contrast relative to the background; using large, legible, bold-face characters; placing warnings prominently; using symbols or icons; and using signal words. However, except for employing the signal word "WARNING," the great majority of Proposition 65 warnings have none of these characteristics. * * *

Proposition 65 warnings have appeared on the back of product labels, on the underside of product cans, or on the inside of lids covering product cans and boxes. Some have been in small print and dull type, sometimes squeezed onto labels already crowded with information. * * *

Proposition 65 does not require any specific warning language, but the regulations do set forth "safe harbor" warning messages, which have been used on virtually all consumer product warnings. The basic safe harbor message for a consumer product warning states: "WARNING: This product contains a chemical known to the State of California to cause cancer [birth defects or other reproductive harm]." The warning message does not use symbols, despite a great deal of evidence that in addition to increasing the attractiveness of a warning, symbols facilitate the ability of consumers to process warning information. Symbols are especially desirable given the substantial portion of the population that cannot read, is functionally illiterate, or cannot read English.

The safe harbor warning statement also does not inform individuals that use of the product will expose them to a listed chemical. Rather, it simply contains the less informative message that the product *contains* a listed chemical. This inadequacy directly hinders communication of the statute's central message. It also makes the warning less personally relevant to recipients and more likely to be overlooked, since, not surprisingly, consumers are more likely to attend to warnings that they find personally relevant.

* * *

A Proposition 65 warning essentially warns that there is some level of risk associated with a product. However, the safe harbor warning message does not provide the consumer with any basis for evaluating the level or nature of the risk posed by individual exposures. The consumer knows only that the product contains a chemical known to cause cancer or reproductive toxicity. * * *

Despite the prevalence of poor warnings, Proposition 65's warning requirement has stimulated significant consumer-product reformulation, due to a combination of industry concerns about liability and consumer reaction to warnings. In some instances, the reformulations have been close to industry-wide, reflecting the competitive pressures that arise once a portion of the industry alters its products. Almost all the reformulated products are being sold nationwide, giving the statute national effect. * * *

Enforcement actions have triggered many product reformulations. Nearly forty manufacturers of glazed ceramicware (china) have agreed to reduce lead levels in their flatware by fifty percent and in their hollowware by twenty-five percent within five years. Two companies have become entirely lead-free. * * *

A large segment of the nail polish industry agreed to remove toluene from dozens of consumer and professional nail polish products. Manufacturers have agreed to reformulate dozens of automobile paints, coatings, adhesives, and related products. Approximately three hundred wineries, representing a large share of the domestic wine industry, agreed to phase out their use of lead foil caps on wine bottles. * * *

Other reported instances of product reformulation have occurred absent direct enforcement. Old El Paso canned foods eliminated its use of lead-soldered cans, as did a Mexican canner/importer. Major Paint removed methylene chloride from forty-five of its Xynolyte Brand products. Sunoco reformulated the inks in plastic grocery bags to eliminate listed chemicals. Sara Lee's Kiwi Brand Products reformulated its shoe-waterproofing sprays to remove listed chemicals. Sears Roebuck & Company reported that its supplier reformulated dozens of products, including car wax and carburetor cleaner. An herbicide manufacturer altered its products to remove arsenic, a listed chemical.

The extraordinary steps taken by businesses to avoid consumer product warnings can be partially explained by liability concerns. In Proposition 65 enforcement suits, the California Attorney General's Office and private parties have been willing to forego imposing civil fines on defendant companies in exchange for product reformulation, and indeed have made this a goal of their enforcement policies. Facing statutory fines that can be enormous, many companies have consented to reformulate their products in order to reduce their potential liability. Other companies have reformulated as a prophylactic measure to avoid the possibility of a lawsuit entirely, given the statute's large penalties and the relatively unpredictable nature of citizen enforcement. * * *

More significant than the desire to minimize liability is corporate concern over consumer reaction to product warnings, and the power of green consumerism in the marketplace. Consumer demand can be extremely sensitive to the disclosure of adverse health and safety product information, particularly in food products. Businesses perceive the possibility of significant sales losses by disclosing toxic chemical presence in certain consumer products, and warnings for these products have, consequently, become anathema to business. * * *

Proposition 65 has had notable success in reducing toxics in consumer products, although two caveats should be noted. First, reformulation may not always be completely beneficial. Products that are reformulated may substitute chemicals that pose other risks of equal or greater dimension than the Proposition 65 chemicals they replace. Likewise, a product may pose risks marginally above the warning threshold yet have important benefits that would be impaired by removing a listed chemical. From a risk/benefit perspective, reformulation in this instance would not be desirable. Second, reformulation may constrain the choices of consumers who would otherwise be willing to incur the added risk posed by a product.

From a policy perspective, these examples are most troubling if driven by exaggerated consumer fears of the risks posed by products, rather than consumers' deliberate and well-informed decisionmaking. If the latter mechanism is responsible, then businesses are simply responding, appropriately, to the collectively expressed preferences of the market.

The above discussion has focused on products for which substitutes exist. Where there are no available substitutes, the marketplace has fared poorly as a mechanism for achieving toxics reductions. In these situations, businesses have provided warnings that exact little or no cost in terms of reduced consumer demand. Thus, gas stations throughout California contain warnings that "chemicals known to the state to cause cancer, birth defects, or other reproductive harm are found in gasoline, crude oil and many other petroleum products, and ether vapors, or result from their use." Consumers do not have the option of using a "safer" gasoline, since all brands contain benzene, a listed carcinogen. Similarly, all mothball deodorizers sold contain paradichlorobenzene, a listed carcinogen. Without the availability of alternative products, consumers most likely "filter out [these warnings] from their field of vision."[243]

NOTES AND QUESTIONS

1. *Information and Regulation.* What advantages do information mandates enjoy over command-and-control regulation? What disadvantages? How much environmental protection will they produce? How efficient will that protection be? Are disclosure mandates likely to be less politically controversial than substantive mandates? Could disclosure requirements such as the TRI help overcome some of the difficulties with toxic tort suits described in Chapter 2?

2. *Simplifying Without Over-Simplifying.* What are the shortcomings of TRI disclosures and Proposition 65 warnings? Can consumers be provided with enough information to help them make sound environmental decisions without swamping them with data? Will consumers correctly interpret the information they are given? What consequences might misinterpretation have? Are labels likely to be helpful where alternative products are characterized by complex environmental trade-offs, as in the case of cloth versus disposable diapers? Consider electricity generation. Several suppliers are now marketing "green" electricity. The environmental impacts of electricity production, however, take many forms. Nuclear power creates radioactive waste. Fossil fuel combustion causes air pollution and accelerates global warming. Hydropower dams are a major threat to certain fish species, and even wind turbines kill birds. How should "green" power be defined? Should consumers control the trade-offs between global warming, nuclear waste production, and endangered fish, or should those trade-offs be made through the political process?

243. See [John P.] Dwyer, [Innovative Risk Regulation Under Proposition 65, Prop 65 News, Feb. 1992], at 31. * * *

CHAPTER SIX

PUBLIC AND QUASI-PUBLIC RESOURCES

Many natural resources have traditionally been fully available for private ownership and trading in ordinary markets. Most land falls in that category, as do oil and other minerals. Some resources, however, have long been considered unsuitable for ordinary private ownership due to special public importance or special obstacles to exclusive possession. This chapter examines the treatment of several resources subject to such public claims, including water, wildlife, and federal lands.

SECTION 1. WATER ALLOCATION

Water is essential to natural ecosystems and many human activities. Management of water resources includes both the maintenance of water quality through pollution control (considered in detail in Chapter 11) and allocation of water to various uses. The two are obviously not completely separable. Water quality depends on the quantity of water as well as the amount of pollution. However, because the law of water allocation and water quality have different origins, and the two are managed through distinct institutions, we consider them separately here.

A. THE BASICS OF STATE WATER LAW

The law of water allocation is essentially a property doctrine, delineating and distributing private rights to withdraw water from natural sources. Like other property doctrines, water allocation is primarily a matter of state law, although the federal government holds regulatory power over interstate and international waterways, navigable waterways, and other waters with connections to interstate commerce.

Two major common law regimes govern the allocation of surface waters. Eastern states, which generally expect abundant rainfall, employ riparian rights, while the arid western states use prior appropriation. Mixed systems are found on the Pacific coast and Great Plains, which contain both humid and arid regions.

1. RIPARIAN RIGHTS

In the riparian system, water allocation is tied to ownership of land abutting or underlying natural waterways. The owners of riparian land enjoy exclusive rights to use the adjacent waters.

The common law rule was once said to be that all riparians had the right to receive the "natural flow" of the stream without diminution in quality or quantity. If rigorously applied, the natural flow rule could essentially eliminate consumptive uses, those that materially diminish the amount or quality of water. Not surprisingly, American courts long ago softened the natural flow rule, declaring that riparian owners had the right to make "reasonable" consumptive uses of abutting waters, consistent with the rights of other riparians to their own reasonable uses. Tyler v. Wilkinson, 24 F.Cas. 472 (D.R.I.1827).

Reasonable uses include agriculture, industry, mining, and recreation in addition to household use. Domestic uses, those necessary to supply household needs (historically including production of livestock for household consumption), are preferred over commercial or recreational uses. Evans v. Merriweather, 4 Ill. 492 (1842). Other conflicts are resolved on the basis of the reasonableness of the competing uses. The Restatement (2d) of Torts (1979) offers the following test:

§ 850A. Reasonableness of the Use of Water

The determination of the reasonableness of a use of water depends upon a consideration of the interests of the riparian proprietor making the use, of any riparian proprietor harmed by it and of society as a whole. Factors that affect the determination include the following:

(a) the purpose of the use,

(b) the suitability of the use to the watercourse or lake,

(c) the economic value of the use,

(d) the social value of the use,

(e) the extent and amount of the harm it causes,

(f) the practicality of avoiding the harm by adjusting the use or method of use of one proprietor or the other,

(g) the practicality of adjusting the quantity of water used by each proprietor,

(h) the protection of existing values of water uses, land, investments and enterprises, and

(i) the justice of requiring the user causing harm to bear the loss.

Most riparian states now supplement the common law system with permit requirements, often exempting domestic or small-volume uses. Typically permits are issued only for "reasonable" uses, in effect transferring the reasonableness determination from the courts to the permitting agency, and ensuring that it precedes establishment of the use.

2. PRIOR APPROPRIATION

In the arid west, riparianism was ill-suited to the need to move water. To facilitate mining and irrigation distant from the widely separated natural streams, western states developed the doctrine of prior appropriation.

Priority in time rather than ownership of land determines allocation in the prior appropriation system. The water right claimant need not own any riparian land, but must put water to "beneficial" use. Beneficial uses generally include domestic, agricultural, industrial, municipal and recreational uses. Today all western states except Colorado rely upon an administrative permit system to allocate water rights.

In times of shortage, users who acquired their rights later in time, known as "juniors," lose their water first. The last person to perfect an appropriative right is the first required to terminate use in drought years, and the first to perfect a right is the last cut off. Because they are quantified and prioritized, appropriative rights afford their holders greater certainty than riparian rights. Unlike riparian rights, however, appropriative rights can be lost by non-use. They are forfeited if not put to beneficial use for a specified number of years, typically five.

3. GROUNDWATER

Even though groundwater is an integral part of the hydrologic cycle and, in nature, surface and groundwater are interrelated, the law maintains a somewhat artificial distinction between those two different water sources. Four major doctrines govern groundwater allocation:

Absolute Ownership. The English common law applied a simple rule of capture to groundwater, allowing each owner of overlying land an absolute right to withdraw groundwater, regardless of the consequences for surrounding owners. This rule is still followed in Texas and a few eastern states, subject in many cases to liability for negligent or intentional injury and other limitations.

The Reasonable Use Doctrine. Many American states have modified the rule of capture with a reasonable use limitation, requiring that extracted groundwater be used for beneficial purposes and only on overlying land. Several states have adopted the standard of the Restatement (2d) of Torts § 858, which limits overlying owners to their reasonable share of the groundwater supply.

Correlative Rights. California and several other states apply a correlative rights doctrine similar to the riparian system for surface waters, requiring that owners of overlying land share the available groundwater.

Prior Appropriation. Several western states apply the doctrine of prior appropriation to at least some underground waters.

Most states, even in the east, have permit systems to administer groundwater extraction. Groundwater permits may be separate from or integrated with surface water permits.

B. WATER RIGHTS TRANSFERS AND MARKETS

Markets for water rights appeal to economists, who see them as an efficient mechanism for allocating scarce water resources; to urban water suppliers, who can afford to buy out agricultural users; and to environmentalists, who prefer transfers of existing water rights to new withdrawals. Although enthusiasm for water markets is widespread, it is not universal. Professor Eric Freyfogle questions whether markets can function efficiently, given the many external effects of water allocation, particularly effects on ecosystems and future human generations. He questions whether any market will adequately account for those effects. Eric T. Freyfogle, Water Rights and the Common Wealth, 26 Envtl. L. 27, 30–34 (1996). While those problems could be addressed by limiting or regulating water markets, Freyfogle also contends that water markets send the erroneous, and dangerous, message that water is a commodity like any other, to be used and discarded as people see fit. Id. at 34–36.

For better or worse, the utilization of water markets is growing, although a series of practical, legal, and political barriers have slowed that growth. As a practical matter, long-distance transfers of water are limited by high costs and losses by evaporation or seepage. Existing pricing systems also tend to discourage transfers. Many water users, both agricultural and domestic, pay highly subsidized rates. As a result, they have little incentive to conserve in ways that might free water for transfer to other users.

Legal barriers are found in both riparian and appropriative systems. Traditionally, riparian systems forbade severance of water rights from riparian lands. There appears to be a growing trend, however, toward permitting water use on non-riparian lands, provided the use is otherwise reasonable. A. Dan Tarlock, Law of Water Rights and Resources § 3.87 (2000 Release). Nonetheless, the inherent uncertainty of riparian rights remains a barrier to transfers.

Many prior appropriation states once prohibited the severance of water rights from the land upon which they were being exercised, but all now permit trading of water rights separately from land. Barton H. Thompson, Jr., Institutional Perspectives on Water Policy and Markets, 81 Cal. L. Rev. 671, 703 (1993). Transfers must not injure other water users, including downstream users who rely on return flows. Accordingly, appropriators may transfer only the water they consume. Quantifying that amount may be difficult, as return flows are difficult to estimate. Administrative transfer proceedings can also impose high transaction costs. Id. at 704.

In addition, some states impose "area-of-origin" restrictions, limiting out-of-basin transfers. Even without statutory restrictions, out-of-basin transfers may face substantial political resistance. See A. Dan Tarlock and Sarah B. Van de Wetering, Growth Management and Western Water Law: From Urban Oases to Archipelagoes, 5 Hastings W–NW J. Envtl. L. & Pol'y 163, 183–85 (1999); Thompson, supra, at 728–35. Opponents of such transfers frequently cite the Owens Valley experience, memorialized in the movie *Chinatown*, as a cautionary tale. Early in the 20th century, Los Angeles developers secretly acquired much of the land and water rights in the Owens Valley. When they diverted the water to Los Angeles, the Owens Valley was left dry, desolate, and economically devastated. Rural communities contend such social disruption outweighs the economic efficiencies of water transfers.

C. ENVIRONMENTAL AND PUBLIC RIGHTS TO WATER RESOURCES

1. NAVIGABILITY

Protection of the right of access to streams and the ocean for navigation has a long history. Roman law declared the sea, the seashore, and "running water" to be the common property of mankind. Institutes of Justinian 2.1.1. English law protected a public navigation right even against the King. See Arnold v. Mundy, 6 N.J.L. 1, 10 Am. Dec. 356 (N.J.1821). In the United States, the obvious link between navigation and interstate commerce led to the recognition of federal power over navigation long before the expansion of federal powers in other areas. Gibbons v. Ogden, 22 U.S. 1 (1824).

Many states have developed common law doctrines safeguarding public recreational use of navigable rivers and streams. The test for navigability is not stringent; waters are generally deemed navigable if deep enough to float logs to mills or markets, or suitable for recreational use by canoes or kayaks. See, e.g., Adirondack League Club v. Sierra Club, 92 N.Y.2d 591, 684 N.Y.S.2d 168, 706 N.E.2d 1192 (1998); State of Arkansas v. McIlroy, 268 Ark. 227, 595 S.W.2d 659 (1980). Landowners who hold title to the riverbed and banks cannot exclude boaters from streams that meet the navigability test.

2. THE PUBLIC TRUST DOCTRINE

In Martin v. Waddell, 41 U.S. (16 Pet.) 367 (1842), Chief Justice Taney declared that with the American Revolution, each state became sovereign and succeeded to the title of the English crown in their tidelands and the submerged lands underlying coastal waters. Three years later, in Pollard's Lessee v. Hagan, 44 U.S. (3 How.) 212 (1845), the Court held that the equal footing clause of the U.S. Constitution entitled all later-admitted states to ownership of their submerged lands. Although state sovereignty was originally understood to cover only waters under tidal influence, by the end of the nineteenth century it had been extended to navigable fresh waters. Barney v. Keokuk, 94 U.S. (4 Otto) 324 (1877). Navigability for this purpose requires only that the waterway could physically have been used for local trade or travel at the time of statehood.

The state holds these submerged lands for the benefit of the people. In Illinois Central Railroad v. Illinois, 146 U.S. 387, 452–53 (1892), the Supreme Court explained that title to these lands is:

> different in character from that which the State holds in lands intended for sale. It is different from the title which the United States hold in the public lands which are open to pre-emption and sale. It is a title held in trust for the people of the State that they may enjoy the navigation of the waters, carry on commerce over them, and have

liberty of fishing therein freed from the obstruction or interference of private parties. The interest of the people in the navigation of the waters and in commerce over them may be improved in many instances by the erection of wharves, docks and piers therein, for which purpose the State may grant parcels of the submerged lands; and, so long as their disposition is made for such purpose, no valid objections can be made to the grants.... But that is a very different doctrine from the one which would sanction the abdication of the general control of the State over lands under the navigable waters of an entire harbor or bay, or of a sea or lake. Such abdication is not consistent with the exercise of that trust which requires the government of the State to preserve such waters for the use of the public. The trust devolving upon the State for the public, and which can only be discharged by the management and control of property in which the public has an interest, cannot be relinquished by a transfer of the property. The control of the State for the purposes of the trust can never be lost, except as to such parcels as are used in promoting the interests of the public therein, or can be disposed of without any substantial impairment of the public interest in the lands and waters remaining.

Although it is intimately linked with the federal law giving states title to their submerged lands, the public trust doctrine has developed as state law, subject to considerable variation. Some courts will not permit any grant of state trust resources to private parties. See, e.g., Lake Michigan Fed'n v. U.S. Army Corps of Engineers, 742 F.Supp. 441 (N.D.Ill.1990). Many others allow transfer, but hold that the private owner takes subject to continuing public rights. It is often unclear whether public trust rights may be extinguished, and if so under what circumstances. Many states permit development in furtherance of public trust interests such as navigation, even at the expense of other trust values. Even in these circumstances, however, courts may demand an explicit and considered decision to impair trust values.

The public trust, at a minimum, confers public rights to use the waters for navigation, commerce, and fishing. It typically extends to other water-related activities such as swimming and recreational boating. In some states it goes considerably further, permitting access to the waters over private lands, and even reasonable use of the banks or shores incident to trust activities. Swimmers, for example, may have the right to rest and relax on the dry sand above the high-water mark that marks the boundary of public trust lands. See Matthews v. Bay Head Improvement Ass'n, 95 N.J. 306, 471 A.2d 355 (1984).

In the 1970s and 1980s, environmental activists began to seek protection of ecological as well as direct use values through the public trust doctrine. Consider the following cases from California, the state which has most aggressively interpreted the public trust as an environmental protection doctrine.

Marks v. Whitney

Supreme Court of California, 1971.
6 Cal.3d 251, 98 Cal.Rptr. 790, 491 P.2d 374.

■ McComb, Justice.

This is a quiet title action to settle a boundary line dispute caused by overlapping and defective surveys and to enjoin defendants (herein "Whitney") from asserting any claim or right in or to the property of plaintiff Marks. The unique feature here is that a part of Marks' property is tidelands acquired [from the state in 1874]; a small portion of these tidelands adjoins almost the entire shoreline of Whitney's upland property. Marks asserted complete ownership of the tidelands and the right to fill and develop them. Whitney opposed on the ground that this would cut off his rights as a littoral owner and as a member of the public in these tidelands and the navigable waters covering them. He requested a declaration in the decree that Marks' title was burdened with a public trust easement; also that it was burdened with certain prescriptive rights claimed by Whitney.

* * *

Questions: First. *Are these tidelands subject to the public trust; if so, should the judgment so declare?*

Yes. Regardless of the issue of Whitney's standing to raise this issue the court may take judicial notice of public trust burdens in quieting title to tidelands. This matter is of great public importance, particularly in view of population pressures, demands for recreational property, and the increasing development of seashore and waterfront property. A present declaration that the title of Marks in these tidelands is burdened with a public easement may avoid needless future litigation.

Tidelands are properly those lands lying between the lines of mean high and low tide covered and uncovered successively by the ebb and flow thereof. The trial court found that the portion of Marks' lands here under consideration constitutes a part of the Tidelands of Tomales Bay, that at all times it has been, and now is, subject to the daily ebb and flow of the tides in Tomales Bay, that the ordinary high tides in the bay overflow and submerge this portion of his lands, and that Tomales Bay is a navigable body of water and an arm of the Pacific Ocean.

* * * Prior to the issuance of this patent it was held that a patent to tidelands conveyed no title; or a voidable title. It was not until 1913 that this court decided in *People v. California Fish Co.*, 166 Cal. 576, 596, that:

> The only practicable theory is to hold that all tide land is included, but that the public right was not intended to be divested or affected by a sale of tide lands under these general laws relating alike both to swamp land and tide lands. Our opinion is that ... the buyer of land under these statutes receives the title to the soil, the *jus privatum*, subject to the public right of navigation, and in subordination to the right of the state to take possession and use and improve it for that

purpose, as it may deem necessary. In this way the public right will be preserved and the private right of the purchaser will be given as full effect as the public interests will permit.

* * *

Public trust easements are traditionally defined in terms of navigation, commerce and fisheries. They have been held to include the right to fish, hunt, bathe, swim, to use for boating and general recreation purposes the navigable waters of the state, and to use the bottom of the navigable waters for anchoring, standing, or other purposes. The public has the same rights in and to tidelands.

The public uses to which tidelands are subject are sufficiently flexible to encompass changing public needs. In administering the trust the state is not burdened with an outmoded classification favoring one mode of utilization over another. There is a growing public recognition that one of the most important public uses of the tidelands—a use encompassed within the tidelands trust—is the preservation of those lands in their natural state, so that they may serve as ecological units for scientific study, as open space, and as environments which provide food and habitat for birds and marine life, and which favorably affect the scenery and climate of the area. It is not necessary to here define precisely all the public uses which encumber tidelands.

"[T]he state in its proper administration of the trust may find it necessary or advisable to cut off certain tidelands from water access and render them useless for trust purposes. In such a case the state through the Legislature may find and determine that such lands are no longer useful for trust purposes and free them from the trust. When tidelands have been so freed from the trust—and if they are not subject to the constitutional prohibition forbidding alienation—they may be irrevocably conveyed into absolute private ownership." (City of Long Beach v. Mansell, 3 Cal. 3d 462, 482, 91 Cal. Rptr. 23, 37, 476 P.2d 423, 437.)

* * * We are not here presented with any action by the state or the federal government modifying, terminating, altering or relinquishing the *jus publicum* in these tidelands or in the navigable waters covering them. Neither sovereignty is a party to this action. This court takes judicial notice, however, that there has been no official act of either sovereignty to modify or extinguish the public trust servitude upon Marks' tidelands. The State Attorney General, as amicus curiae, has advised this court that no such action or determination has been made by the state.

We are confronted with the issue, however, whether the trial court may restrain or bar a private party, namely, Whitney, "from claiming or asserting any estate, right, title, interest in or claim or lien upon" the tidelands quieted in Marks. The injunction so made, without any limitation expressing the public servitude, is broad enough to prohibit Whitney from asserting or in any way exercising public trust uses in these tidelands and the navigable waters covering them in his capacity as a member of the public. This is beyond the jurisdiction of the court. It is within the province of the trier of fact to determine whether any particular use made or asserted by Whitney in or over these tidelands would constitute an infringement either upon the *jus privatum* of Marks or upon the *jus publicum* of the people. It is also within the province of the trier of fact to determine whether any particular use to which Marks wishes to devote his tidelands constitutes an unlawful infringement upon the *jus publicum* therein. It is a political question, within the wisdom and power of the Legislature, acting within the scope of its duties as trustee, to determine whether public trust uses should be modified or extinguished and to take the necessary steps to free them from such burden. In the absence of state or federal action the court may not bar members of the public from lawfully asserting or exercising public trust rights on these privately owned tidelands.

There is absolutely no merit in Marks' contention that as the owner of the *jus privatum* under this patent he may fill and develop his property, whether for navigational purposes or not; nor in his contention that his past and present plan for development of these tidelands as a marina have caused the extinguishment of the public easement. Reclamation with or without prior authorization from the state does not ipso facto terminate the public trust nor render the issue moot.

A proper judgment for a patentee of tidelands was determined by this court in *People v. California Fish Co., supra,* 166 Cal. at pp. 598–599, to be that he owns "the soil, subject to the easement of the public for the public uses of navigation and commerce, and to the right of the state, as administrator and controller of these public uses and the public trust thereof, to enter upon and possess the same for the preservation and advancement of the public uses and to make such changes and improvements as may be deemed advisable for those purposes."

National Audubon Society v. Superior Court of Alpine County

Supreme Court of California, 1983.
33 Cal.3d 419, 189 Cal.Rptr. 346, 658 P.2d 709.

■ BROUSSARD, JUSTICE.

Mono Lake, the second largest lake in California, sits at the base of the Sierra Nevada escarpment near the eastern entrance to Yosemite National Park. The lake is saline; it contains no fish but supports a large population of brine shrimp which feed vast numbers of nesting and migratory birds. Islands in the lake protect a large breeding colony of California gulls, and the lake itself serves as a haven on the migration route for thousands of Northern Phalarope, Wilson's Phalarope, and Eared Grebe. Towers and spires of tufa on the north and south shores are matters of geological interest and a tourist attraction.

Although Mono Lake receives some water from rain and snow on the lake surface, historically most of its supply came from snowmelt in the

Sierra Nevada. Five freshwater streams—Mill, Lee Vining, Walker, Parker and Rush Creeks—arise near the crest of the range and carry the annual runoff to the west shore of the lake. In 1940, however, the Division of Water Resources, the predecessor to the present California Water Resources Board, granted the Department of Water and Power of the City of Los Angeles (hereafter DWP) a permit to appropriate virtually the entire flow of four of the five streams flowing into the lake. DWP promptly constructed facilities to divert about half the flow of these streams into DWP's Owens Valley aqueduct. In 1970 DWP completed a second diversion tunnel, and since that time has taken virtually the entire flow of these streams.

As a result of these diversions, the level of the lake has dropped; the surface area has diminished by one-third; one of the two principal islands in the lake has become a peninsula, exposing the gull rookery there to coyotes and other predators and causing the gulls to abandon the former island. The ultimate effect of continued diversions is a matter of intense dispute, but there seems little doubt that both the scenic beauty and the ecological values of Mono Lake are imperiled.

Plaintiffs filed suit in superior court to enjoin the DWP diversions on the theory that the shores, bed and waters of Mono Lake are protected by a public trust. Plaintiffs' suit was transferred to the federal district court, which requested that the state courts determine the relationship between the public trust doctrine and the water rights system. * * *

This case brings together for the first time two systems of legal thought: the appropriative water rights system which since the days of the gold rush has dominated California water law, and the public trust doctrine which, after evolving as a shield for the protection of tidelands, now extends its protective scope to navigable lakes. Ever since we first recognized that the public trust protects environmental and recreational values (Marks v. Whitney (1971) 6 Cal. 3d 251 [98 Cal. Rptr. 790, 491 P.2d 374]), the two systems of legal thought have been on a collision course. They meet in a unique and dramatic setting which highlights the clash of values. Mono Lake is a scenic and ecological treasure of national significance, imperiled by continued diversions of water; yet, the need of Los Angeles for water is apparent, its reliance on rights granted by the board evident, the cost of curtailing diversions substantial.

Attempting to integrate the teachings and values of both the public trust and the appropriative water rights system, we have arrived at certain conclusions which we briefly summarize here. In our opinion, the core of the public trust doctrine is the state's authority as sovereign to exercise a continuous supervision and control over the navigable waters of the state and the lands underlying those waters. This authority applies to the waters tributary to Mono Lake and bars DWP or any other party from claiming a vested right to divert waters once it becomes clear that such diversions harm the interests protected by the public trust. The corollary rule which evolved in tideland and lakeshore cases barring conveyance of rights free of the trust except to serve trust purposes cannot, however, apply without modification to flowing waters. The prosperity and habitability of much of this state requires the diversion of great quantities of water from its streams for purposes unconnected to any navigation, commerce, fishing, recreation, or ecological use relating to the source stream. The state must have the power to grant nonvested usufructuary rights to appropriate water even if diversions harm public trust uses. Approval of such diversion without considering public trust values, however, may result in needless destruction of those values. Accordingly, we believe that before state courts and agencies approve water diversions they should consider the effect of such diversions upon interests protected by the public trust, and attempt, so far as feasible, to avoid or minimize any harm to those interests.

The water rights enjoyed by DWP were granted, the diversion was commenced, and has continued to the present without any consideration of the impact upon the public trust. An objective study and reconsideration of the water rights in the Mono Basin is long overdue. The water law of California—which we conceive to be an integration including both the public trust doctrine and the board-administered appropriative rights system—permits such a reconsideration; the values underlying that integration require it. * * *

1. *Background And History Of The Mono Lake Litigation.*

DWP supplies water to the City of Los Angeles. Early in this century, it became clear that the city's anticipated needs would exceed the water available from local sources, and so in 1913 the city constructed an aqueduct to carry water from the Owens River 233 miles over the Antelope–Mojave plateau into the coastal plain and thirsty city.

The city's attempt to acquire rights to water needed by local farmers met with fierce, and at times violent, opposition. But when the "Owens Valley War" was over, virtually all the waters of the Owens River and its tributaries flowed south to Los Angeles. Owens Lake was transformed into an alkali flat.

The city's rapid expansion soon strained this new supply, too, and prompted a search for water from other regions. The Mono Basin was a predictable object of this extension, since it lay within 50 miles of the natural origin of Owens River, and thus could easily be integrated into the existing aqueduct system.

After purchasing the riparian rights incident to Lee Vining, Walker, Parker and Rush Creeks, as well as the riparian rights pertaining to Mono Lake, the city applied to the Water Board in 1940 for permits to appropriate the waters of the four tributaries. At hearings before the board, various interested individuals protested that the city's proposed appropriations would lower the surface level of Mono Lake and thereby impair its commercial, recreational and scenic uses.

The board's primary authority to reject that application lay in a 1921 amendment to the Water Commission Act of 1913, which authorized the board to reject an application "when in its judgment the proposed appropriation would not best conserve the public interest." (Stats. 1921, ch. 329, § 1, p. 443 now codified as Wat. Code, § 1255). The 1921 enactment, however, also "declared to be the established policy of this state that the use of water for domestic purposes is the highest use of water" (*id.*, now codified as Wat. Code, § 1254), and directed the Water Board to be guided by this declaration of policy. Since DWP sought water for domestic use, the board concluded that it had to grant the application notwithstanding the harm to public trust uses of Mono Lake.

* * *

The scope of the public trust

Early English decisions generally assumed the public trust was limited to tidal waters and the lands exposed and covered by the daily tides; many American decisions, including the leading California cases, also concern tidelands. It is, however, well settled in the United States generally and in California that the public trust is not limited by the reach of the tides, but encompasses all navigable lakes and streams.

Mono Lake is, as we have said, a navigable waterway. The beds, shores and waters of the lake are without question protected by the public trust. The streams diverted by DWP, however, are not themselves navigable. * * * We conclude that the public trust doctrine, as recognized and developed in California decisions, protects navigable waters from harm caused by diversion of nonnavigable tributaries.

Duties and powers of the state as trustee

* * * [P]arties acquiring rights in trust property generally hold those rights subject to the trust, and can assert no vested right to use those rights in a manner harmful to the trust. * * *

[I]n our recent decision in City of Berkeley v. Superior Court, 26 Cal. 3d 515, 162 Cal. Rptr. 327, 606 P.2d 362, we considered whether deeds executed by the Board of Tidelands Commissioners pursuant to an 1870 act conferred title free of the trust. Applying the principles of earlier decisions, we held that the grantees' title was subject to the trust, both because the Legislature had not made clear its intention to authorize a conveyance free of the trust and because the 1870 act and the conveyances under it were not intended to further trust purposes. * * *

In summary, the foregoing cases amply demonstrate the continuing power of the state as administrator of the public trust, a power which extends to the revocation of previously granted rights or to the enforcement of the trust against lands long thought free of the trust. Except for those rare instances in which a grantee may acquire a right to use former trust property free of trust restrictions, the grantee holds subject to the trust, and while he may assert a vested right to the servient estate (the right of use subject to the trust) and to any improvements he erects, he can claim no vested right to bar recognition of the trust or state action to carry out its purposes.

Since the public trust doctrine does not prevent the state from choosing between trust uses, the Attorney General of California, seeking to maximize state power under the trust, argues for a broad concept of trust uses. In his view, "trust uses" encompass all public uses, so that in practical effect the doctrine would impose no restrictions on the state's ability to allocate trust property. We know of no authority which supports this view of the public trust. * * * Most decisions and commentators assume that "trust uses" relate to uses and activities in the vicinity of the lake, stream, or tidal reach at issue. The tideland cases make this point clear; after *City of Berkeley v. Superior Court*, no one could contend that the state could grant tidelands free of the trust merely because the grant served some public purpose, such as increasing tax revenues, or because the grantee might put the property to a commercial use.

Thus, the public trust is more than an affirmation of state power to use public property for public purposes. It is an affirmation of the duty of the state to protect the people's common heritage of streams, lakes, marshlands and tidelands, surrendering that right of protection only in rare cases when the abandonment of that right is consistent with the purposes of the trust.

* * *

4. The Relationship Between The Public Trust Doctrine And The California Water Rights System.

As we have seen, the public trust doctrine and the appropriate water rights system administered by the Water Board developed independently of each other. Each developed comprehensive rules and principles which, if applied to the full extent of their scope, would occupy the field of allocation of stream waters to the exclusion of any competing system of legal thought. Plaintiffs, for example, argue that the public trust is antecedent to and thus limits all appropriative water rights, an argument which implies that most appropriative water rights in California were acquired and are presently being used unlawfully. Defendant DWP, on the other hand, argues that the public trust doctrine as to stream waters has been "subsumed" into the appropriative water rights system and, absorbed by that body of law, quietly disappeared; according to DWP, the recipient of a board license enjoys a vested right in perpetuity to take water without concern for the consequences to the trust.

We are unable to accept either position. In our opinion, both the public trust doctrine and the water rights system embody important precepts which make the law more responsive to the diverse needs and interests involved in the planning and allocation of water resources. To embrace one system of thought and reject the other would lead to an unbalanced structure, one which would either decry as a breach of trust appropriations essential to the economic development of this state, or deny any duty to protect or even consider the values promoted by the public trust. Therefore, seeking an accommodation which will make use of the pertinent principles of both the public trust doctrine and the appropriative water rights system, and drawing upon the history of the public trust and the water rights system, the body of judicial precedent, and the views of expert commentators, we reach the following conclusions:

a.   The state as sovereign retains continuing supervisory control over its navigable waters and the lands beneath those waters. This principle, fundamental to the concept of the public trust, applies to rights in flowing waters as well as to rights in tidelands and lakeshores; it prevents any party from acquiring a vested right to appropriate water in a manner harmful to the interests protected by the public trust.

b.   As a matter of current and historical necessity, the Legislature, acting directly or through an authorized agency such as the Water Board, has the power to grant usufructuary licenses that will permit an appropriator to take water from flowing streams and use that water in a distant part of the state, even though this taking does not promote, and may unavoidably harm, the trust uses at the source stream. The population and economy of this state depend upon the appropriation of vast quantities of water for uses unrelated to in-stream trust values. California's Constitution, its statutes, decisions and commentators all emphasize the need to make efficient use of California's limited water resources: all recognize, at least implicitly, that efficient use requires diverting water from in-stream uses. Now that the economy and population centers of this state have developed in reliance upon appropriated water, it would be disingenuous to hold that such appropriations are and have always been improper to the extent that they harm public trust uses, and can be justified only upon theories of reliance or estoppel.

c.   The state has an affirmative duty to take the public trust into account in the planning and allocation of water resources, and to protect public trust uses whenever feasible. Just as the history of this state shows that appropriation may be necessary for efficient use of water despite unavoidable harm to public trust values, it demonstrates that an appropriative water rights system administered without consideration of the public trust may cause unnecessary and unjustified harm to trust interests. As a matter of practical necessity the state may have to approve appropriations despite foreseeable harm to public trust uses. In so doing, however, the state must bear in mind its duty as trustee to consider the effect of the taking on the public trust, and to preserve, so far as consistent with the public interest, the uses protected by the trust.

Once the state has approved an appropriation, the public trust imposes a duty of continuing supervision over the taking and use of the appropriated water. In exercising its sovereign power to allocate water resources in the public interest, the state is not confined by past allocation decisions which may be incorrect in light of current knowledge or inconsistent with current needs.

The state accordingly has the power to reconsider allocation decisions even though those decisions were made after due consideration of their effect on the public trust. The case for reconsidering a particular decision, however, is even stronger when that decision failed to weigh and consider public trust uses. In the case before us, the salient fact is that no responsible body has ever determined the impact of diverting the entire flow of the Mono Lake tributaries into the Los Angeles Aqueduct. This is not a case in which the Legislature, the Water Board, or any judicial body has determined that the needs of Los Angeles outweigh the needs of the Mono Basin, that the benefit gained is worth the price. Neither has any responsible body determined whether some lesser taking would better balance the diverse interests. Instead, DWP acquired rights to the entire flow in 1940 from a water board which believed it lacked both the power and the duty to protect the Mono Lake environment, and continues to exercise those rights in apparent disregard for the resulting damage to the scenery, ecology, and human uses of Mono Lake.

It is clear that some responsible body ought to reconsider the allocation of the waters of the Mono Basin. No vested rights bar such reconsideration. We recognize the substantial concerns voiced by Los Angeles—the city's need for water, its reliance upon the 1940 board decision, the cost both in terms of money and environmental impact of obtaining water elsewhere. Such concerns must enter into any allocation decision. We hold only that they do not preclude a reconsideration and reallocation which also takes into account the impact of water diversion on the Mono Lake environment.

* * *

Conclusion

This has been a long and involved answer to the two questions posed by the federal district court. In summarizing our opinion, we will essay a shorter version of our response.

The federal court inquired first of the interrelationship between the public trust doctrine and the California water rights system, asking whether the "public trust doctrine in this context [is] subsumed in the California water rights system, or . . . function[s] independently of that system?" Our answer is "neither." The public trust doctrine and the appropriative water rights system are parts of an integrated system of water law. The public trust doctrine serves the function in that integrated system of preserving the continuing sovereign power of the state to protect public trust uses, a power which precludes anyone from acquiring a vested right to harm the public trust, and imposes a continuing duty on the state to take such uses into account in allocating water resources.

* * *

This opinion is but one step in the eventual resolution of the Mono Lake controversy. We do not dictate any particular allocation of water. Our objective is to resolve a legal conundrum in which two competing systems of thought—the public trust doctrine and the appropriative water rights system—existed independently of each other, espousing principles which seemingly suggested opposite results. We hope by integrating these two doctrines to clear away the legal barriers which have so far prevented either the Water Board or the courts from taking a new and objective look at the water resources of the Mono Basin. The human and environmental uses of Mono Lake—uses protected by the public trust doctrine—deserve to be taken into account. Such uses should not be destroyed because the state mistakenly thought itself powerless to protect them. * * *

3. IN–STREAM FLOWS

Rising interest in environmental protection, as well as water-based recreation, has increased pressures to maintain minimum in-stream flow levels. The flexible reasonableness test, and perhaps the historic natural flow doctrine, provide riparian systems with a foundation for recognizing in-stream rights to serve evolving environmental values. Most riparian states now protect some minimum flows by statute. Nonetheless, the system's focus on private, rather than public, rights and the uncertainty and high costs of litigation remain substantial barriers to effective flow protection. Lynda Butler, Environmental Water Rights: An Evolving Concept of Public Property, 9 Va. Envtl. L.J. 323, 327–29 (1990).

In-stream flow protection has faced even higher barriers in the prior appropriation states. In recent years, however, the plight of aquatic ecosystems and demands for recreational uses have produced some progress. Traditionally, prior appropriation required physical diversion from the stream to perfect a water right. Today, many prior appropriation states have statutes permitting the government to appropriate water for in-stream uses. These statutes have survived legal challenges. See, e.g., Colorado River Water Conservation Dist. v. Colorado Water Conservation Bd., 197 Colo. 469, 594 P.2d 570 (1979); Idaho Dep't of Parks v. Idaho Dep't of Water Admin., 96 Idaho 440, 530 P.2d 924 (1974).

The ability to appropriate new in-stream water rights has limited utility for streams that are already over-appropriated. Recognition of in-stream rights, however, allows transfer of existing water rights to in-stream uses. Such transfers face significant transaction costs, as willing sellers may be difficult to locate and water rights are difficult to value. Nonetheless, in-stream flow statutes can allow private non-profit organizations to "retire" consumptive uses in favor of ecosystem protection. See Janet Neuman and Cheyenne Chapman, Wading Into the Water Market: The First Five Years of the Oregon Water Trust, 14 J. Envtl. L. & Litig. 135 (1999).

In both riparian and prior appropriation states, general environmental quality legislation and wild and scenic rivers statutes may also preclude or restrict new diversions to protect environmental and esthetic values.

NOTES AND QUESTIONS

1. *Rediscovering the Public Trust.* The public trust doctrine was virtually unknown, even to specialists, until it was uncovered by two enterprising scholars in 1970. See Sax, The Public Trust Doctrine in Natural Resource Law: Effective Judicial Intervention, 68 Mich. L. Rev. 471 (1970); Note, The Public Trust Doctrine, 79 Yale L.J. 769 (1970). Since then, the public trust doctrine has inspired a flood of scholarly writing. Early articles promoted the doctrine as a foundation for all manner of environmental protections. While that enthusiasm continues among some environmentalists, other scholars have begun to question the desirability, efficacy, and equity of broad application of the public trust.

2. *Justifications for the Public Trust Doctrine.* What justifies imposing judicial restrictions on the ability of the legislature to alienate public trust resources? According to Professor Joseph Sax, the "central idea of the public trust is preventing the destabilizing disappointment of expectations held in common but without formal recognition such as title." Joseph L. Sax, Liberating the Public Trust Doctrine from Its Historic Shackles, 14 U.C. Davis L. Rev. 185, 188 (1980). Do you agree? Do such public expectations merit protection? How should they be balanced with the private expectations of water rights holders? Why doesn't Professor Sax trust the legislature to protect public trust resources? Will requiring a clear statement of intent to extinguish trust values provide adequate protection, or should alienation of trust resources be prohibited? How should competing trust values, such as commerce, recreation, and ecosystem protection, be compared to one another? Should the legislature or the courts be responsible for that balancing?

Professor Carol Rose takes a slightly different view of the public trust. She argues that some resources, including roads and waterways, are "inherently public." In part, familiar economic arguments explain the importance of public ownership, since roads and waterways in private hands could be subject to holdouts and monopolies that might interfere with commerce. But Rose explains that the value of inherently public property increases with public use. The more people engage in commerce, the better, not only because commerce increases wealth but because it provides opportunities for socializing human interaction. Recreation can have a similar socializing effect, particularly in public spaces where people from all walks of life mingle. Perhaps even contemplation of nature can fall in this class, supporting public trust rights to nature protection. Carol Rose, The Comedy of the Commons: Custom, Commerce, and Inherently Public Property, 53 U. Chi. L. Rev. 711 (1986). Do you agree that recreational uses of certain lands and waters have special value to society if widely shared? How can those uses be identified? What consequences does this view have for alienability of trust resources? For evolution of the public trust doctrine?

3. *Expansion of the Doctrine.* Courts have expanded the scope of the public trust doctrine beyond the traditional triad of navigation, commerce, and fishing to encompass a wide variety of recreational uses of waters and in some cases ecological values. They have applied it beyond its traditional geographic scope as well, encompassing dry sands and the waters of non-navigable streams. Is this expansion justified? Should the public trust be extended to other ecologically sensitive lands, such as wetlands or old-growth forests? Should it protect the public interest in aesthetic or historic uses? What arguments could you make for or against broad expansion of the public trust doctrine?

4. *Allocating Costs.* Who should bear the costs of newly-recognized needs to restrict diversions to protect in-stream resources? Did the California Supreme Court appropriately balance the interests of the public and the City of Los Angeles in the Mono Lake case? Is imposition of the public trust in this context inconsistent with the basic assumptions of the prior appropriation system? Should water rights holders in California have anticipated the decision? If not, should they be compensated for the costs of finding substitute water sources? Are water markets preferable to the public trust doctrine as a mechanism of reallocating water to newly recognized uses? Can the barriers to markets be overcome?

5. *The Rescue of Mono Lake.* When Mark Twain visited Mono Lake, the isolation and harshness of the surroundings made him uneasy. In Roughing It (1899), Twain described Mono Lake as "this solemn, silent, sailless sea— this lonely tenant of the loneliest spot on earth." The lake is surrounded by barren, volcanic hillsides and its surface is fringed with outcroppings of tufa, some of them thousands of years old. They change in hue with the weather and the mountain sunlight, from delicate lavender to a pearl gray. These limestone spires have been left stranded in the surrounding sagebrush by the shrinking of the lake, which by 1982 had contracted to about half its historic volume.

In October 1994, the Los Angeles Department of Water and Power, State Water Resources Board, National Audubon Society, and Federal Bureau of Reclamation reached an accord that limits the city's diversions until the lake reaches a level twenty feet above its low, but still some twenty-five feet short of its historic level. Aided by a series of wet years, Mono Lake has risen rapidly, drowning land bridges which had been exposed to nesting islands. Migratory bird populations have already increased noticeably.

The Mono Lake accord was made possible in part by the allocation of state funds to help Los Angeles obtain alternative supplies of water. Mono Lake had supplied about fifteen percent of the city's water supply. The City has made up for the loss of its Mono Lake water through conservation efforts and purchases from other agencies.

SECTION 2.   PUBLIC LANDS MANAGEMENT

The United States owns some 660 million acres, nearly thirty percent of the nation's land. These lands, particularly the large undeveloped tracts, are referred to as the "public lands." For much of the nation's history, the federal government considered itself a temporary caretaker of those lands, holding them only until they could be conveyed into private hands to promote their development. In the late 19th century, however, the government began to reserve some parcels for long-term federal ownership as national parks and national forests. By the second half of the 20th century, the dominant theme had become retention and management, rather than disposal.

Many states apply the public trust doctrine to some state- and locally-owned lands, particularly public parks, holding that they may not be transferred into private hands or out of public use without, at a minimum, a clear statement of intent to transfer and a finding that the transfer serves a public purpose. See, e.g., Gould v. Greylock Reservation Commission, 350 Mass. 410, 419, 215 N.E.2d 114 (1966); Paepcke v. Public Bldg. Comm'n, 46 Ill.2d 330, 263 N.E.2d 11 (1970). Although trust language is often used to describe federal lands, their diversity, the long-held policy of disposal, and the detailed modern statutory schemes for their management have led courts to defer to the Congress. Nonetheless, the federal land management statutes protect an array of public and private claims to those lands.

This section provides a sense of those claims, and the conflicts that may arise among them. In so doing, it provides a glimpse of the complex field of public land law. For more comprehensive introductions to that field, see George C. Coggins and Robert L. Glicksman, Public Natural Resources Law (1990, supplemented annually), and George C. Coggins, Charles F. Wilkinson & John D. Leshy, Federal Public Land and Resources Law (3d ed. 1993) (the leading casebook).

A.   A BRIEF SURVEY OF THE PUBLIC LANDS

Four agencies, the Forest Service (in the Department of Agriculture), Bureau of Land Management, Fish and Wildlife Service, and National Park Service (all in the Department of Interior) manage the bulk of the public lands. Although all fifty states contain some federal land, the distribution of public lands is highly uneven, with the vast majority in the far western states and Alaska. The proportion of land in federal ownership ranges from less than 1% in Iowa and several east coast states to more than 80% in Nevada.

1.   THE FOREST SERVICE

In 1891, concerned by the rapid rate at which the nation's forests were being liquidated, Congress authorized the withdrawal of federal lands from entry and disposal to create the national forest system. By 1897, nearly 40 million acres had been withdrawn. The forest reserves, as they were then known, originally had only two purposes: watershed protection and provision of a continuous supply of timber.

Today the Forest Service manages 192 million acres which, in addition to supplying timber and other products, host an estimated 885 million visitors annually. U.S. General Accounting Office, Recreation Fees: Demonstration Fee Program Successful in Raising Revenues But Could Be Improved 15 (GAO/RCED–99–7) (1998). The majority of forest service lands are dedicated to multiple-use management under the National Forest

Management Act (NFMA), 16 U.S.C. §§ 1600–1614, and Multiple Use Sustained Yield Act (MUSYA), 16 U.S.C. §§ 528–531.

2. THE BUREAU OF LAND MANAGEMENT

The Bureau of Land Management (BLM) oversees the remnants of the old public domain. For many years, the public domain which had not yet been distributed into private hands served as a grazing commons on which ranchers freely pastured their livestock. As the population grew a "tragedy of the commons" ensued, and by the 1930s it was apparent that the public lands were badly overgrazed. In 1934, the Taylor Grazing Act, 43 U.S.C. § 315–316o, established the Grazing Service in the Department of Interior. Merger of the Grazing Service and General Land Office, the agency that had overseen disposal of the public domain, created the BLM in 1946.

Currently, the BLM is responsible for 264 million acres, much of it the arid rangelands that were never thought suitable for homesteading. The BLM lacked a comprehensive governing statute until 1976, when Congress passed the Federal Land Policy and Management Act (FLPMA), 43 U.S.C. §§ 1701–1785. FLPMA declared a federal policy of retaining these lands indefinitely unless "it is determined that disposal of a particular parcel will serve the national interest." 43 U.S.C. § 1701(a)(1). Like the Forest Service, the BLM manages the vast majority of its lands under a multiple-use mandate.

3. THE FISH AND WILDLIFE SERVICE

In addition to administering the Endangered Species Act and other federal wildlife protection laws (see Section 3 below), the Fish and Wildlife Service (FWS) manages the National Wildlife Refuge system, containing more than 92 million acres. National Wildlife Refuges are found in all fifty states, although more than 80% of the system's land area is in Alaska. Bradley C. Karkkainen, Biodiversity and Land, 83 Cornell L. Rev. 1, 32–33 (1997). Refuges may be created by legislation or executive order. Although many have been carved out of the public domain, many others have been created by acquisition of lands from private or state ownership.

Refuge lands are administered for the primary purpose of conserving fish, wildlife, and plant resources under the National Wildlife Refuge System Administration Act, 16 U.S.C. § 688dd–ee. Refuges have traditionally also been open to hunting and sport fishing. Recent amendments to the Refuge System Administration Act explicitly provide that wildlife-dependent recreation is a "legitimate and appropriate general public use" of refuge lands provided it is "compatible" with the mission of the refuge system and the purposes of the particular refuge. 16 U.S.C. §§ 668dd(a)(3), 668ee(1).

4. THE NATIONAL PARK SERVICE

Yellowstone, the first National Park in the world, was reserved in 1872. More than forty years later, the National Park Service (NPS) was created to govern the growing park system. National Parks can only be created by legislation, but the NPS also manages national monuments and other areas which can be established by executive order. The National Park System Organic Act, 16 U.S.C. § 1–20g, applies to all of these areas, except as otherwise provided by their individual enabling legislation.

The Organic Act directs NPS to "promote and regulate" the use of these lands in accordance with their fundamental purpose, which is:

> to conserve the scenery and the natural and historic objects and the wild life therein and to provide for the enjoyment of the same in such manner and by such means as will leave them unimpaired for the enjoyment of future generations.

16 U.S.C. § 1. The park system currently encompasses 83 million acres, much of that in Alaska, and hosts about 275 million annual visits. General Accounting Office, supra, at 15.

5. WILDERNESS AREAS

The wilderness system overlays the categories listed above, such that each of the four land management agencies administers wilderness areas. The Wilderness Act of 1964, 16 U.S.C. §§ 1131–1136, directs each land management agency to evaluate the large roadless areas under its jurisdiction for potential wilderness designation by Congress. These areas receive some protection pending the final determination. Roughly 96 million acres have been congressionally classified as wilderness, and millions more are still classified as "wilderness study areas."

The Wilderness Act defines a wilderness as "an area where the earth and its community of life are untrammeled by man, where man himself is a visitor who does not remain." 16 U.S.C. § 1131(c). Wilderness areas are managed:

> for the use and enjoyment of the American people in such manner as will leave them unimpaired for future use and enjoyment as wilderness * * *.

16 U.S.C. § 1131(a). The enabling legislation for specific wilderness areas can set out exceptions to this general non-impairment scheme. Absent such exceptions, the Wilderness Act forbids commercial uses, roads, and motorized vehicles, subject to existing rights such as rights of access to inholdings. 16 U.S.C. § 1133(c). Livestock grazing may continue where it was established prior to designation. 16 U.S.C. § 1133(d)(4).

B. FEDERALISM ON THE PUBLIC LANDS

With the limited exception of federal enclaves, over which the states have ceded exclusive jurisdiction to the United States, state law applies on federal land. Congress and the federal land management agencies often explicitly defer to state law, particularly with respect to water rights allocation and wildlife management.

Nonetheless, the federal government enjoys wide latitude to preempt state law and enact its own regulations with respect to the public lands. The property clause of the federal constitution, art. IV, § 3, cl. 2, provides that "Congress shall have Power to dispose of and make all needful Rules and Regulations respecting the Territory or other Property belonging to the United States." In Kleppe v. New Mexico, 426 U.S. 529 (1976), which involved the authority of the federal government over wild horses on the public lands, the Supreme Court adopted a broad interpretation of federal authority under the property clause, explaining that Congress enjoys complete power over the public lands.

This authority extends to regulation of activities outside federal land that threaten to interfere with the purpose for which the federal lands are designated. In Camfield v. United States, 167 U.S. 518 (1897), the Court concluded that Congress could prohibit the owner of several sections of private land which were "checkerboarded," alternating with federally-owned sections, from fencing his lands in such a way as to enclose the abutting public lands. Thirty years later, the Court concluded that the United States could prohibit leaving fires unextinguished "in or near" the national forests. United States v. Alford, 274 U.S. 264 (1927). More recently, the lower courts have upheld: a ban on hunting over state waters within the boundaries of a national park (recall that the states hold title to the beds of navigable waterways), U.S. v. Brown, 552 F.2d 817 (8th Cir.1977); a ban on motorboats on state waters within a wilderness area, State of Minnesota v. Block, 660 F.2d 1240 (8th Cir.1981); and a prohibition on the use of pesticides on private land within the New River Gorge National River, Stupak–Thrall v. United States, 89 F.3d 1269 (6th Cir. 1996) (en banc, district court affirmed by an equally divided court). The extent to which this power supports administrative, rather than direct congressional, regulation beyond the bounds of federal property remains somewhat unclear. Responding to local political pressures, federal land management agencies remain reluctant to extend their authority beyond the land under their care.

The commerce clause, art. I, § 8 cl. 3, provides additional authority for Congress to regulate activities on the public lands. For example, the Surface Mining Control and Reclamation Act, 30 U.S.C.A. §§ 1201–1328, which applies to mining on both public and private lands, is authorized under the commerce clause, Hodel v. Indiana, 452 U.S. 314, 324 (1981), as is restrictive zoning of private lands within the Columbia River Gorge National Scenic Area, Columbia River Gorge United–PPP v. Yeutter, 960 F.2d 110 (9th Cir.1992). The recent reinvigoration of the commerce clause by the Supreme Court is unlikely to challenge this authority, since most of the activities regulated on the public lands are commercial in nature.

C.   THE BALANCE OF LEGISLATIVE AND EXECUTIVE POWERS

Although the Constitution gives Congress plenary authority over federal property, as a practical matter the executive branch also enjoys substantial powers over the public lands. In recent years, those powers have proven quite controversial.

The executive branch cannot ignore legislation, but can fill in gaps where Congress has not spoken or has not spoken clearly. Congress has traditionally left the executive branch a great deal of discretion in legislation respecting the public lands. Moreover, in the absence of any relevant statute, Presidents have acted as if they had inherent power to withdraw federal lands for various purposes. Because Congress has by and large acquiesced in those withdrawals, the courts have not directly confronted the existence or scope of that inherent power. George Cameron Coggins and Robert L. Glicksman, Public Natural Resources Law, § 3.04(1) (2000 release).

Today the major issue is the extent to which the public land management statutes leave discretion to the executive branch. Congress always retains the authority to overrule executive actions. Enacting legislation is difficult, however, and a determined President can exercise the veto power. As a result, executive actions within statutory boundaries are likely to stand until altered by a new President. The extent of agency discretion is discussed below with respect to the multiple use and dominant-use lands.

Congress has also explicitly conferred on the President substantial power to withdraw public lands for preservation. When it passed FLPMA, Congress repealed or severely constrained many delegations of withdrawal power to the President. The most sweeping, however, remains. The Antiquities Act authorizes the President to:

> declare by public proclamation historic landmarks, historic and prehistoric structures, and other objects of historic or scientific interest that are situated upon the lands owned or controlled by the Government of the United States to be national monuments, and * * * reserve as a part thereof parcels of land, the limits of which in all cases shall be confined to the smallest area compatible with the proper care and management of the objects to be protected. * * *

16 U.S.C. § 431. Presidents began using the Antiquities Act to make large withdrawals for conservation purposes in 1908, when Theodore Roosevelt withdrew the Grand Canyon. In 1978, Jimmy Carter relied on the Antiquities Act to set aside 56 million acres in Alaska. Bill Clinton used it to protect some 6 million acres, including the 1.7 million acre Grand Staircase–Escalante National Monument. One prominent complaint about the Antiquities Act is that it imposes no procedural limitations on withdrawals. The President need not consult with anyone or provide advance notice before acting. Nor does NEPA apply, since the President is not subject to its requirements. James Rasband argues that public participation should play a more prominent role in withdrawals that effectively create de facto wilderness areas. James R. Rasband, Utah's Grand Staircase: The Right Path to Wilderness Preservation?, 70 U. Colo. L. Rev. 483 (1999).

NOTES AND QUESTIONS

1. *Permanent Retention or Ultimate Disposal?* Nearly seventy years after the Taylor Grazing Act ended large-scale disposal of public lands in the continental United States, federal land ownership remains a subject of enduring controversy, particularly in the western states where federal land ownership is concentrated. Several economists have argued that at least some public lands would be used more efficiently if they were sold into private ownership. See, e.g., Robert H. Nelson, Public Lands and Private Rights: The Failure of Scientific Management (1995); Dale A. Oesterle, Public Land: How Much is Enough?, 23 Ecology L.Q. 521 (1996); for arguments against privatization, see Scott Lehmann, Privatizing Public Lands (1995). Do you agree that privatization would improve efficiency? Would high transaction costs inhibit formation of "wilderness coalitions" which might buy lands for preservation? Is the goal of efficiency out-weighed by others, such as equitable access or preservation of non-market resources? For all the public lands, or only some?

2. *The Sagebrush Rebellion and its Progeny.* In the late 1970s, leaders of a western movement known as the Sagebrush Rebellion argued that title to the public lands should be turned over to the states. In 1979, Nevada's legislature asserted the right to control and dispose of public lands within its borders. Several other western states followed suit. See Bruce Babbitt, Federalism and the Environment: An Intergovernmental Perspective of the Sagebrush Rebellion, 12 Envtl. L. 847, 848 (1982).

Although the legal arguments behind the Sagebrush Rebellion were uniformly rejected, western resentment of federal land ownership did not disappear. In the 1990s, it resurfaced as the County Supremacy movement, in which western counties enacted ordinances purporting to take control of public lands. Again the legal claims were quickly rejected, but the ordi-nances encouraged civil disobedience and intimidation of federal officials. Elizabeth M. Osenbaugh & Nancy K. Stoner, The County Supremacy Movement, 28 Urb. Law. 497 (1996).

Disputes over control of the federal lands continue, although they ebb and flow with the changes of political administrations. On July 4, 2000, 500 local citizens calling themselves the Jarbridge Shovel Brigade forcibly reopened a washed-out forest road in Elko County, Nevada that the Forest Service had planned to replace with a trail in order to protect the endan-gered bull trout. Shortly thereafter, the local forest supervisor resigned in protest after the district attorney called for federal employees to be barred from buying goods and services in the county. By February 2001, county officials claimed they were near a settlement which would reopen the road in return for some county improvements to protect the river. Jim Carlton, Bitter Battle Over Rural West, Wall St. J., Feb. 16, 2001, at B1.

3. *Federal Financial Support of Local Communities.* Because federal lands are immune from state and local taxation, extensive federal holdings could place a heavy fiscal burden on states and local communities dependent on property taxes. However, through a series of statutory revenue sharing programs, the United States shares the receipts of resource development on those lands with the states. In addition, under the Payment in Lieu of Taxes (PILT) Act, 31 U.S.C. §§ 6901–6907, the United States makes annual payments to the states for every federally-owned acre. Critics of these programs note that the federal PILT payments typically far exceed the tax rates for private property, and that resource-development-based revenue sharing exacerbates local political pressures in favor of development. See George C. Coggins and Robert L. Glicksman, Public Natural Resources law § 5.04(5) (2000 Release).

4. *Limiting Executive Discretion.* Should Congressional action be required before severe limitations are imposed on resource extraction, such as the ban on new roads imposed by the Clinton administration on 58.5 million national forest acres eight days before George W. Bush was inaugurated as President? Before resources that are difficult to replace, such as old growth forests, are liquidated? Is the executive branch insufficiently or excessively responsive to political pressures in its management of the public lands? Do the Administrative Procedure Act and public lands legislation provide sufficient opportunities for public input? Would you support amendment of the Antiquities Act to limit withdrawals without Congressional action to no more than 50,000 acres?

D.   MULTIPLE-USE LANDS

The Forest Service and BLM have been directed to manage the bulk of their lands for multiple use. For the Forest Service,

> "Multiple use" means: The management of all the various renewable surface resources of the national forests so that they are utilized in the combination that will best meet the needs of the American people; making the most judicious use of the land for some or all of these resources or related services over areas large enough to provide sufficient latitude for periodic adjustments in use to conform to changing needs and conditions; that some land will be used for less than all of the resources; and harmonious and coordinated management of the various resources, each with the other, without impairment of the productivity of the land, with consideration being given to the relative values of the various resources, and not necessarily the combination of uses that will give the greatest dollar return or the greatest unit output.

16 U.S.C. § 531(a). BLM operates under a nearly identical definition. 43 U.S.C. § 1702(c).

Perkins v. Bergland

United States Court of Appeals, Ninth Circuit, 1979.
608 F.2d 803.

■ GOODWIN, CIRCUIT JUDGE.

Two brothers, who grazed cattle on public land, sued the Department of Agriculture to challenge a reduction in their grazing permits. They appeal a summary judgment for the government.

Thomas and David Perkins hold permits entitling each of them to graze cattle within the Prescott National Forest. The permits are issued by the United States Forest Service, an arm of the Department of Agriculture, as authorized by 16 U.S.C. § 580l (1976). In 1972, the Forest Supervisor, on recommendation of the local District Ranger, reduced Thomas's permit from 517 to 250 head of cattle (subsequently corrected to 266). The following year, the Supervisor similarly reduced David's permit from 158 to 50 head (later corrected to 58).

The agency based the reduction decisions on its finding that the public land involved had been damaged by overgrazing. The decisions were finally upheld by the Secretary of Agriculture in 1977. After exhausting administrative remedies, Thomas and David brought separate actions in district court, seeking judicial review and an injunction against enforcement of the reductions. The cases were consolidated in district court, and are considered together on appeal.

* * *

The Perkins brothers argued * * * that the Secretary's decisions * * * were * * * subject to judicial review. The government responded, and the district court agreed, that further review was unavailable because the decisions were "committed to agency discretion by law." 5 U.S.C. § 701(a)(2) (1976). * * *

FLPMA empowers the Secretaries of the Interior and Agriculture, each of whom grants grazing privileges on public lands within departmental jurisdictions, to incorporate in grazing permits and leases "such terms and conditions as [the Secretary] deems appropriate for management of the ... lands." 43 U.S.C. § 1752(e). The same section further provides that the Secretary must specify in the agreement "the numbers of animals to be grazed ... and that ... [the Secretary] may reexamine the condition of the range at any time and, if he finds on reexamination that the condition of the range requires adjustment in the amount or other aspect of grazing use, that the permittee or lessee shall adjust his use to the extent the Secretary concerned deems necessary."

If we were confronted with the quoted language alone, we would have to consider the government's argument that the Secretary's discretion is so broad in determining grazing capacity—necessarily exercised in accord with expert judgments—as to preclude all judicial review under *Overton Park*. Elsewhere, however, FLPMA explicitly provides that "it is the policy of the United States that ... judicial review of public land adjudication decisions be provided by law." 43 U.S.C. § 1701(a)(6) (1976). This declaration of policy at the outset of FLPMA removes any doubt Congress might otherwise have allowed to obscure the reviewability of grazing reduction decisions made subsequent to the law's enactment. * * * [T]he Secretary's decision is reviewable.

The remaining issue thus requires us to define the scope of review appropriate to the Secretary's decisions here.

Appellants assert for the first time in this court that certain sections of the Multiple–Use Sustained–Yield Act of 1960 (MUSYA), 16 U.S.C. §§ 528 *et seq.*, supply standards which a court can apply on judicial review to the highly technical assessment of the proper carrying capacity of grazing land. These statutory expressions give the appellants scant support. It must be presumed, at least initially, that those so-called standards were properly considered by the agency. These sections of MUSYA contain the most general clauses and phrases. For example, the agency is "directed" in section 529 to administer the national forests "for multiple use and sustained yield of the several products and services obtained therefrom," with "due consideration [to] be given to the relative values of the various resources in particular areas." This language, partially defined in section 531 in such terms as "that [which] will best meet the needs of the American people" and "making the most judicious use of the land", can hardly be considered concrete limits upon agency discretion. Rather, it is language which "breathe[s] discretion at every pore." Strickland v. Morton, 519 F.2d 467, 469 (9th Cir.1975). What appellants really seem to be saying when they rely on the multiple-use legislation is that they do not agree with the Secretary on how best to administer the forest land on which their cattle graze. While this disagreement is understandable, the courts are not at liberty to break the tie by choosing one theory of range management as superior to another.

Thus, we conclude that only very narrow review is appropriate here. The district court should ascertain whether the agency's factual findings as to range conditions and carrying capacity are arbitrary and capricious. If not, the matter ends there. In making that inquiry, the court may consider the Perkins brothers' contention that the methods utilized by the Forest Service in determining capacity were irrational. But their charge that the agency decision was "unrelated to reality" sheds no light on the subject. We find nothing in the statutes authorizing courts to choose between battling experts on the definition of "reality". Consequently, the trial court must refrain from entering that fray if it turns out that the appellants' position would require a choice between experts.

Sierra Club v. Espy

United States Court of Appeal, Fifth Circuit, 1994.
38 F.3d 792.

■ PATRICK E. HIGGINBOTHAM, CIRCUIT JUDGE

The district court issued a preliminary injunction barring the Forest Service from conducting even-aged management in any of the four Texas national forests. The injunction was based on the district court's finding of probable success on plaintiffs' claims under two statutes: the National Forest Management Act, 16 U.S.C. §§ 1600–1614, and the National Environmental Policy Act, 42 U.S.C. §§ 4321–4347. The government and the timber industry intervenors bring this interlocutory appeal challenging the district court's order.

We disagree with the district court's insistence that NFMA restricts even-aged management to exceptional circumstances. We are persuaded that the district court erected too high a barrier to even-aged management. The standard that even-aged management may be used only in exceptional circumstances goes to the heart of the finding by the district court of a likelihood of success on the merits and upsets the delicate balance struck by Congress between friends and foes of this harvesting method. We must vacate the preliminary injunction and remand.

The Forest Service of the Department of Agriculture is charged with administering the resources of this country's national forests "for outdoor recreation, range, timber, watershed, and wildlife and fish purposes." Multiple–Use Sustained–Yield Act of 1960, 16 U.S.C. § 528. The principles of MUSYA were expressly incorporated into the statutory and regulatory scheme of NFMA. The pressures to enact NFMA came from many sources. On the one hand, there was increasing national concern over the Forest Service's use of clearcutting. On the other hand, Congress felt it necessary to counteract a Fourth Circuit decision which strictly construed the Organic Act of 1897 to effectively prohibit the practice of clearcutting in the national forests. See *West Va. Div. of the Izaak Walton League of Am., Inc. v. Butz,* 522 F.2d 945 (4th Cir.1975) (the *Monongahela* decision). The result was a compromise expressed in a statute repealing the portion of the Organic Act interpreted in the *Monongahela* decision, yet imposing new procedural and substantive restraints on the Forest Service.

Specifically, NFMA sets forth requirements for Land and Resource Management Plans under which the national forests are managed. The national forests are divided into management units, and the Forest Service must prepare an LRMP for each unit. An LRMP must "provide for multiple use and sustained yield of the products and services obtained [from units of the National Forest System] ..., and, in particular, include coordination of outdoor recreation, range, timber, watershed, wildlife and fish, and wilderness...." 16 U.S.C. § 1604(e)(1). Once an LRMP is in place, the Forest Service can decide to sell timber only after analyzing timber management alternatives and the sale's particular environmental consequences. Site-specific analysis, sometimes referred to as compartment-level analysis, must be consistent with the LRMP. *Id.* § 1604(i).

Broadly stated, there are two ways to manage a forest's timber resources. The first method is even-aged management. Even-aged management includes clearcutting, where all the trees are cut down; seed tree cutting, where most of the trees are cut down, leaving only a few to naturally seed the cut area; and shelterwood cutting, where about double the number of trees are left standing as would be under the seed tree method. Even under the least intrusive even-aged management technique, shelterwood cutting, only about sixteen trees per acre remain after a cut. Moreover, under seed tree cutting, the older trees left to naturally seed the cut area are later removed. Even-aged management results in stands of trees that are essentially the same age. Before choosing to clearcut a portion of the forest, the Forest Service must find that clearcutting is the "optimum method" for achieving the objectives and requirements of the LRMP. 16 U.S.C. § 1604(g)(3)(F)(i). Similarly, before choosing to seed tree cut or shelterwood cut, the Forest Service must find that those methods are "appropriate" for achieving the objectives and requirements of the LRMP. *Id.*

The second method of timber resource management is uneven-aged management, also known as selection management. Uneven-aged management encompasses both single tree selection and group selection. Group selection involves cutting small patches of trees, while single tree selection involves selecting particular trees for cutting. Uneven-aged management maintains a continuous high-forest cover, and the stands are characterized by a number of differently aged trees.

* * *

On May 20, 1987, the Forest Service's Regional Forester signed the Record of Decision approving the LRMP and the Final EIS for the Texas national forests. The FEIS examined thirteen alternatives for managing the forests. Two of the alternatives provided for uneven-aged management of the forests' timber resources and the remainder for even-aged management. The Forest Service selected an alternative that provided for even-aged management. * * *

[Plaintiffs challenged the LRMP and FEIS through an administrative appeal and litigation. After a lengthy administrative and judicial process, the district court issued a preliminary injunction, which the Court of Appeals read as applicable only to nine pending timber sales.]

* * *

The government challenges the district court's interpretation of NFMA. Specifically, the government argues that the district court erred when it held that even-aged logging practices could only be used in exceptional circumstances. * * *

The district court's holding that NFMA requires even-aged management be used only in exceptional circumstances is in tension with *Texas Comm. on Natural Resources v. Bergland,* 573 F.2d 201 (5th Cir.), *cert. denied,* 439 U.S. 966 (1978) (*TCONR I*). There we found that Congress, after hearing testimony on both sides of the clearcutting issue, struck a delicate balance between the benefits of clearcutting and the benefits of preserving the ecosystems and scenic quality of natural forests. Specifically, NFMA "was an effort to place the initial technical, management responsibility for the application of NFMA guidelines on the responsible government agency, in this case the Forest Service. The NFMA is a set of outer boundaries within which the Forest Service must work." *Id.* We then cautioned the Forest Service that clearcutting could not be justified merely on the basis that it provided the greatest dollar return per unit output; "[r]ather[,] clearcutting must be used only where it is essential to accomplish the relevant forest management objectives." *Id.* at 212. We concluded by noting that "[a] decision to pursue even-aged management as the overall management plan under the NFMA is subject to the narrow arbitrary and capricious standard of review." *Id.*

TCONR I recognized that the Forest Service may use even-aged management as an overall management strategy. That even-aged management must be the optimum or appropriate method to accomplish the objectives and requirements set forth in an LRMP does not mean that even-aged management is the exception to a rule that purportedly favors selection management. Similarly, the requirement that even-aged logging protect forest resources does not in itself limit its use. Rather, these provisions mean that the Forest Service must proceed cautiously in implementing an even-aged management alternative and only after a close examination of the effects that such management will have on other forest resources.

The conclusion that even-aged management is not the "exception" to the "rule" of uneven-aged management is supported by NFMA's legislative history. On three separate occasions, Congress rejected amendments that would have made uneven-aged management the preferred forest management technique. * * *

TCONR points out that since the Randolph amendments would have *required* the use of uneven-aged management, they are not relevant on the issue of whether uneven-aged management is *preferred*. While TCONR correctly distinguishes the district court's holding from Senator Randolph's attempts to bar even-aged management, TCONR fails to persuade on the issue of whether rejection of congressional efforts to restrict even-aged logging sends a legislative message. That no amendment was specifically offered and rejected that proposed a preference for uneven-aged logging does not change the fact that legislators were loath to deprive the Forest Service of the option to select even-aged management. The final outcome of NFMA reflects those concerns.

Thus, NFMA does not bar even-aged management or require that it be undertaken only in exceptional circumstances; it requires that the Forest Service meet certain substantive restrictions before it selects even-aged management. To be sure, these restrictions reflect a congressional wariness towards even-aged management, constraining resort to its use. The sluicing effect of the required inquiries might be described as making a decision to employ even-aged management more difficult. However, it is not a description or characterization of the effects of the required decisional process that we face. The district court used "exceptional" as a decisional standard— and hence it upset the balance struck. In fairness, this distinction was far more subtle in the presentation to the district court.

The next issue is whether the Forest Service's timber sale EAs meet NFMA's substantive requirements. The district court held that since the EAs failed to protect forest diversity and resources, TCONR was likely to succeed on its claim that the Forest Service had impermissibly exceeded the outer boundaries of NFMA. * * *

The directive that national forests are subject to multiple uses, including timber uses, suggests that the mix of forest resources will change according to a given use. Maintenance of a pristine environment where no species' numbers are threatened runs counter to the notion that NFMA contemplates both even-and uneven-aged timber management. Indeed, NFMA regulations anticipate the possibility of change and provide that "[r]eductions in diversity of plant and animal communities and tree species from that which would be expected in a natural forest, or from that similar to the existing diversity in the planning area, may be prescribed only where needed to meet overall multiple-use objectives." 36 C.F.R. § 219.27(g); see also 16 U.S.C. § 1604(g)(3)(C) (LRMP must ensure research and evaluation of effects of each management system to assure no *"substantial and permanent* impairment" of land productivity) (emphasis added); 16 U.S.C. § 1604(g)(3)(E)(i) (LRMP must provide that timber be harvested only where "soil, slope, or other watershed conditions will not be *irreversibly* damaged") (emphasis added). That protection means something less than preservation of the status quo but something more than eradication of species suggests that this is just the type of policy-oriented decision Congress wisely left to the discretion of the experts—here, the Forest Service.

The Forest Service's discretion, however, is not unbridled. The regulations implementing NFMA provide a minimum level of protection by mandating that the Forest Service manage fish and wildlife habitats to insure viable populations of species in planning areas. 36 C.F.R. § 219.19. In addition, the statute requires the Forest Service to "provide for diversity of plant and animal communities." 16 U.S.C. § 1604(g)(3)(B). This diversity mandate itself has been the subject of considerable debate. The regulations define diversity as "[t]he distribution and abundance of different plant and animal communities and species within the area covered by a land and resource management plan." 36 C.F.R. § 219.3. At least one court has recognized the difficulty in requiring a precise level of diversity: "The agency's judgment in assessing issues requiring a high level of technical expertise, such as diversity, must ... be accorded the considerable respect that matters within the agency's expertise deserve." *Sierra Club v. Robertson,* 810 F.Supp. 1021, 1028 (W.D.Ark.1992), *aff'd in part, vacated in part on other grounds,* 28 F.3d 753 (8th Cir.1994).

We need not take this opportunity to define precisely the "outer boundaries" of NFMA's protection and diversity requirements, because we find that the timber sale EAs fall clearly within such boundaries. Each EA considered no action, even-aged management, and uneven-aged management alternatives. Although it is true that when all nine sales are taken together even-aged management emerges as the preferred alternative, each sale varies as to the extent of its usage. For instance, in Compartment 32, forty-six percent of the acres scheduled to be harvested will be harvested using selection management. The remaining acres will be harvested by seed tree cutting. In Compartment 98, twenty-three percent of the acres scheduled to be harvested will be harvested using selection cutting. The remaining acres will be harvested using the seed tree method. Finally, in Compartment 57, the Forest Service chose to harvest sixty acres of timber using group selection, an uneven-aged management method. Even this limited interspersing of even-and uneven-aged management helps assure a mix of early and late successional habitats.

Moreover, the EAs do not ignore old growth ecosystems. The Compartment 32 EA, for example, discusses the old growth component of the forest. Compartment 32 contains 964 acres of federal land and approximately 2,000 acres of privately owned land. The EA notes that no stands in the compartment were selected for old growth designation because of the fragmented ownership of the compartment. This determination cannot be said to be arbitrary or capricious.

The EAs also address wildlife habitat concerns. Each EA states that all existing wildlife populations will remain at viable levels, no matter which timber management alternative the Forest Service selects. * * *

The Forest Service is charged with managing the ever-changing resources of the national forests. In the absence of forest management, trees would grow older, the character of plant and animal diversity would change, and some wildlife species would decline in numbers. Harvesting trees using even-aged management techniques necessarily results in younger stands. Wildlife dependent on younger stands would flourish at the expense of species dependent on older growth forests. Harvesting trees using uneven-aged management techniques results in denser forests. Wildlife dependent on such cover would flourish at the expense of wildlife dependent on forest clearings. These forest dynamics make clear that protecting forest resources involves making trade-offs. We may believe that protection afforded by selection management is more desirable than that afforded by even-aged management; however, in the nine sales before the court, the agency's determination as to the appropriate level of protection was not unreasonable. We therefore defer to the agency's determination.

NOTES AND QUESTIONS

1. *Administrative Discretion and Identification of the Public Interest.* Do the multiple use mandates of NFMA and FLPMA provide sufficient guidance for the land management agencies? Do they delegate too much power? How should the agencies identify the mix of uses "that will best meet the needs of the American people"? What standard of judicial review applies to those determinations?

2. *Criticisms of Multiple Use.* Many commentators have been critical of the basic assumption of the multiple use statutes, that the land management agencies can be relied upon to identify, and continuously refine, the appropriate mix of public land uses. Michael Blumm explains:

> Multiple use management purportedly allows simultaneous production of compatible resources through sound land use planning. Multiple use has not delivered on this promise. Moreover, it has become clear that it cannot. Since multiple use is founded upon a standardless delegation of authority to managers of public lands and

waters, congressional endorsement of multiple use has created the archetypal "special interest" legislation. Exposed to sustained pressure from local commodity interest groups, federal agencies frequently capitulate to these forces because of the lack of standards governing land and water decisionmaking. For example, because of pressure from stockmen's associations, multiple use on the public rangelands has produced overgrazing; because of pressure from timber mills and timber-dependent communities, multiple use in the national forests has produced below-cost timber sales; because of pressure from electric utilities and the aluminum industry, multiple use of Columbia Basin streamflows has made the Snake River salmon an endangered species.

The power of these local interest groups should not be surprising. "Public choice" theory predicts that small, well-organized special interest groups will exert a disproportionate influence on policymaking. This prediction is particularly relevant in the case of public lands, where the interests of disorganized, distant public owners are regularly overshadowed by the opposing interests of locally concentrated commodity interests.

Michael C. Blumm, Public Choice Theory and the Public Lands: Why "Multiple Use" Failed, 18 Harv. Envtl. L. Rev. 405, 406–08 (1994).

As the *Perkins* decision shows, the agencies can also use their multiple-use discretion to limit extractive uses of the public lands. Recreational uses of the public lands have greatly increased in recent years, and the economic value of recreation and tourism now dominates that of timber and grazing in many western states. See Jan G. Laitos and Thomas A. Carr, The Transformation on Public Lands, 26 Ecology L.Q. 140 (1999). Is this shift likely to change the balance of power Blumm describes?

Even if multiple use is an imperfect method of managing the public lands, is it inevitable? Could Congress draft statutes that more tightly constrain agency discretion, yet leave enough flexibility to apply to the great diversity of public lands?

3. *Substantive Constraints on Agency Discretion.* In addition to its multiple-use mandate, NFMA does provide some apparently substantive standards for management of the national forests. Timber is to be harvested "only where . . . soil, slope, or other watershed conditions will not be irreversibly damaged," 16 U.S.C. § 1604(g)(3)(E)(i), and the lands "can be adequately restocked within five years after harvest," 16 U.S.C. § 1604(g)(3)(E)(ii). Clearcutting is to be used "only where . . . it is determined to be the optimum method . . . to meet the objectives and requirements of the relevant land management plan." 16 U.S.C. § 1604(g)(3)(F)(i). However, as the *Espy* decision illustrates, these standards have not significantly increased the intensity of judicial review of agency timber harvest practices. See Federico Cheever, Four Failed Forest Standards: What We Can Learn from the History of the National Forest Management Act's Substantive Timber Management Provisions, 77 Or. L. Rev. 601 (1998). NFMA also requires that the Forest Service "provide for diversity of plant and animal communities," within the multiple-use scheme. 16 U.S.C.

§ 1604(g)(3)(B). This standard too has proven difficult to turn into a tool for strong judicial review of forest management.

Extensive Forest Service regulations implement NFMA. Until recently, those regulations included the diversity provisions quoted in the *Espy* opinion. Although environmentalists widely regarded those provisions as strongly substantive, they also proved slippery as handles on the timber management program. The regulations were extensively revised in 2000. See National Forest System Land and Resource Management Planning, 65 Fed. Reg. 67514 (Nov. 9, 2000); 36 C.F.R. Part 219. They now proclaim ecological sustainability as the fundamental goal of national forest management. Not surprisingly, however, they still appear to leave the agency substantial discretion in determining what constitutes ecological sustainability and how it will be factored into individual decisions.

4. *Clearcutting on the National Forests.* The practice of clearcutting has been particularly controversial on the national forests. *Sierra Club v. Espy* is just one battle in a long-standing war over that practice. As the *Espy* opinion points out, NFMA was enacted in response to the Fourth Circuit's 1975 *Monongahela* decision, which held that the Organic Act of 1897 prohibited clearcutting. (The issue had not arisen until the 1960s because clearcutting had not been widely practiced earlier.)

In 1997, the Sixth Circuit struck down the management plan for the Wayne National Forest, concluding that the plan, which called for 7.5 million board feet of timber harvest annually, nearly eighty percent of it by clearcutting, "was improperly predisposed toward clearcutting." Sierra Club v. Thomas, 105 F.3d 248 (6th Cir.1997). The Sixth Circuit's decision, however, was reversed by the Supreme Court, which held that the challenge was not ripe for review in the absence of a site-specific logging plan. Ohio Forestry Ass'n v. Sierra Club, 523 U.S. 726 (1998).

Did the Fifth Circuit in *Espy* correctly interpret NFMA's treatment of clearcutting? Should legislation or regulations limit clearcutting more stringently? Under what circumstances, if any, should clearcutting be permitted?

5. *Land use Planning on the Public Lands.* Both NFMA and FLPMA mandate a land use planning process as the primary method of assuring balanced use of public resources. NFMA, for example, directs the Forest Service to prepare and periodically revise a Land and Resource Management Plan (LRMP) for each national forest. 16 U.S.C. § 1604. LRMPs, which are to be developed through an interdisciplinary process, 16 U.S.C. § 1604(b), with public participation, 16 U.S.C. § 1604(d), establish the framework for subsequent site-specific management decisions. All "permits, contracts, and other instruments for the use and occupancy of National Forest System lands shall be consistent with" the LRMP. 16 U.S.C. § 1604(i).

Forest plans, as well as individual project decisions implementing those plans, can be appealed through an administrative process by any interested person. 36 C.F.R. Part 215. Before 1998, the federal circuits had split on the question of whether LRMPs could be challenged in court. That year, the Supreme Court decided Ohio Forestry Association v. Sierra Club, 523 U.S. 726. The Court rejected a challenge to clearcutting provisions in an LRMP as unripe because the plan itself did not authorize any logging. The Court noted that Sierra Club remained free to challenge subsequent site-specific decisions implementing the plan, and left open the possibility of judicial review at the plan stage in the case of activities not requiring further site-specific decisions. Why did Sierra Club mount its challenge at the plan stage? The Court rejected the idea that the expense or practical difficulty of site-specific litigation could justify plan-based review. Id. at 734–35.

6. *The Role of Local Communities.* In its influential 1970 report, the Public Land Law Review Commission recommended that federal land management agencies give considerable weight to local community needs, and seek to preserve community stability and economic expectations. One method the Commission recommended was consultation with local governments during the planning process. Public Land Law Review Commission, One third of the Nation's Land at 61. NFMA and its implementing regulations require that the Forest Service notify local governments of its intent to draft or revise a LRMP, meet with local government representatives at several stages of the planning process, and consider local government comments and concerns. 16 U.S.C. § 1604(a); 36 C.F.R. 219.7.

In addition to these procedural duties, should the Forest Service give special weight to local concerns in its planning efforts? Note that forest plans are drafted locally. Is it likely that they will take local concerns into account even without specific legislative direction to that effect? Might attention to local concerns, particularly local economic concerns, lead the agency to ignore or underestimate risks to the ecological health of its lands?

7. *Grazing Permits and Private Rights.* The *Perkins* decision excerpted above is one in a long line of challenges to decisions reducing grazing on public lands. Grazing permits have been required on national forest lands since 1906, and on BLM lands since the 1934 enactment of the Taylor Grazing Act. The latter gives preferences to owners of land within the grazing district and to holders of current permits. Historically, permits have been routinely renewed. The expectation that they will be renewed indefinitely can add tremendously to the value of ranch properties. Not surprisingly, permit non-renewals or reductions in permitted grazing have sparked considerable litigation.

The courts have uniformly held that grazing permits are not "property," so that the government need not compensate ranchers for non-renewals or changes in terms. See, e.g., United States v. Fuller, 409 U.S. 488 (1973); Alves v. United States, 133 F.3d 1454 (Fed.Cir.1998); see also Public Lands Council v. Babbitt, 529 U.S. 728 (2000) (holding that amended regulations increasing the possibility that limitations will be imposed on grazing were authorized by the Taylor Grazing Act); Federal Lands Legal Consortium v. United States, 195 F.3d 1190 (10th Cir.1999) (ruling that permit holders had no property interest protected against deprivation without due process).

8. *Costs and Benefits.* Should some or all uses of the public lands be cost effective? The Forest Service has long been criticized for selling timber far below cost, but the red ink continues to flow. A Forest Service report issued in February 2001 reveals that timber sales nationwide generated revenues of $546.1 million in fiscal year 1998, compared to costs of $672 million, for a net loss of $125.9 million. U.S. Dep't of Agriculture, Forest Service, National Summary: Forest Management Program Annual Report, Fiscal Year 1998 at 59 (preliminary version 2001). The single worst performer was the Tongass National Forest in Alaska, where timber costs were over $45 million and revenues less than $6 million, for a return of only twelve cents per dollar spent. Id. at 119.

Nearly 40% of the gross revenues, over $212 million, was transferred to states and counties under timber revenue-sharing programs. Much of that money went to the Pacific northwest under a special program designed to ease the local economic burden of logging restrictions in the federal forests attributable to spotted owl protection. These transfer payments are not considered costs of the timber program; with them the federal revenue shortfall from national forest timber harvests is well over $300 million.

Many factors contribute to timber sale revenue shortfalls. The General Accounting Office has identified both agency practices, such as not using sealed bids, and the legislatively established accounting structure, which allows the Forest Service to retain timber sale revenues while relying on appropriated funds to pay the costs, as contributing to the persistence of below-cost timber sales. General Accounting Office, Forest Service: Barriers to Generating Revenue or Reducing Costs 5–6 (GAO/RCED–98–58) (1998). The Forest Service attributes recent nationwide losses in part to a decline in timber sale volume, from 12 billion board feet in 1988 to 3.3 billion board feet in 1998, raising per-unit management costs. The Service also points out that in recent years the majority of timber sales have been conducted primarily for forest management, rather than timber commodity, purposes. Nonetheless, even within the commodity sale category, sixty-six national forests, accounting for thirty-six percent of the total commodity harvest, showed negative financial balances. U.S. Dep't of Agriculture, Forest Service, supra, at 65.

Grazing on public lands is also heavily subsidized. FLPMA declares it to be federal policy that "the United States receive fair market value of the use of the public lands and their resources." 43 U.S.C. § 1701(a)(9). FLPMA has done little to achieve that goal, however. In 1995 grazing fees on public lands were pegged at roughly one-fourth their market value. Joseph M. Feller, 'Til the Cows Come Home: The Fatal Flaw in the Clinton Administration's Public Lands Grazing Policy, 25 Envtl. L. 703, 712 (1995). The Clinton administration floated a plan to double grazing fees, but quickly abandoned it in the face of vigorous opposition.

Underpricing of public land goods and services is not limited to resource extraction. Recreation is also subsidized. Federal law limits recreational fees and requires that they be deposited in the U.S. Treasury, subject to future congressional appropriation, rather than returned to the agency or unit generating them. 16 U.S.C. § 460l–6. In 1996, Congress authorized a fee demonstration program allowing the agencies to raise fees at certain sites, and directing that 80% of the revenues return to the local unit, with the remainder going to the agency. Pub. L. No. 104–134, § 315. Proceeds could only be spent on activities to improve visitor experiences and protection of the resources. A year into the program, the General Accounting Office concluded that it had raised substantial revenues without discouraging visitation, although concerns remained that low income visitors might be displaced. General Accounting Office, Recreation Fees: Demonstration Fee Program Successful in Raising Revenues But Could Be Improved (GAO/RCED–99–7) (1998). The demonstration program expires in September, 2001. As of the end of 2000 it had not been renewed. The National Park Service has been given blanket authorization to retain all its entrance and recreation fees. Pub. L. 106–176, § 310 (2000).

Can you think of any arguments in favor of subsidies for extractive or recreational uses of the public lands? Do you find them persuasive? Does your answer depend upon whether fees are returned to the unit generating them or not? Whether their use is limited to management activities connected to the fee-generating use?

E. PRESERVATION LANDS

Federal lands managed for the dominant purpose of resource preservation, including the National Parks, National Wildlife Refuges, and wilderness areas, are not subject to the same open-ended balancing as multiple-use lands. Nonetheless, they too experience management conflicts, the most common pitting recreational use against resource protection.

Southern Utah Wilderness Alliance v. Dabney

United States Court of Appeals, Tenth Circuit, 2000.
222 F.3d 819.

■ EBEL, CIRCUIT JUDGE.

Plaintiff–Appellee Southern Utah Wilderness Alliance ("Wilderness Alliance") challenged portions of a National Park Service ("NPS") backcountry management plan ("BMP") that affected access to areas of Canyonlands National Park in Utah. * * * Utah Shared Access Alliance ("Utah Shared Access"), a combination of groups supporting four-wheel drive vehicle recreation, intervened as defendants. On cross motions for summary judgment by Wilderness Alliance and the federal defendants, the district court upheld most of the BMP, but found in favor of Wilderness Alliance on its claim that the BMP's continued allowance of motorized vehicles on a ten-mile portion of the Salt Creek Jeep Road from Peekaboo Spring to Angel Arch was inconsistent with a clear legislative directive of Congress. * * *

In 1992, the NPS began developing a BMP for Canyonlands National Park and the Orange Cliffs Unit of Glen Canyon National Recreation Area in Utah. The goal of that plan as articulated by the NPS was "to develop backcountry management strategies to protect park resources, provide for high quality visitor experiences, and be flexible to deal with changing conditions." The plan was being developed in response to growing visitation to the areas, which had increased the impact on resources and diminished the quality of visitor experience.

One of the areas on which the plan was to focus was the area that is the subject of this appeal, a portion of Salt Creek Canyon. According to the NPS, the Salt Creek Road is a vehicle trail that runs in and out of Salt Creek, the only year-round, fresh water creek in Canyonlands National Park other than the Colorado and Green Rivers. There is no practical way to reroute the road to avoid the water course. To navigate this road safely, a high clearance four-wheel-drive vehicle and some experience in four-wheel driving, or the participation in a commercially guided tour, is necessary. The NPS found that it was receiving numerous requests every year for assistance in removing vehicles that broke down or became stuck on the Salt Creek Road. In addition, there were several instances every year of vehicles losing transmission, engine, or crankcase fluids in the water. The NPS became concerned with the adverse impacts inherent in the existence of a road and vehicle traffic in this narrow riparian corridor. A Notice of Intent to prepare a BMP was printed in the Federal Register. The NPS solicited possible solutions to the problems in the area, and hosted public discussions in Utah and Colorado in late 1992 and early 1993.

On December 18, 1993, the NPS released a draft environmental assessment ("EA") that described NPS's current policies, alternatives for change, and the environmental consequences of the alternatives described, including the alternative of taking no action. The EA identified the NPS's preferred alternative for each of the various problems. With respect to the problems on the trail in Salt Creek Canyon, the preferred alternative was to close the Salt Creek Road to vehicles after a particular landmark, Peekaboo Spring, leaving ten miles to be traversed by foot before reaching Angel Arch, a well-known landmark and popular destination among four-wheel drivers. During the EA's review period, the NPS held numerous public meetings. At the close of the review period in March 1994, the NPS noted that the proposal sparking the most debate was the closure of the ten-mile portion of the Salt Creek Road.

The final BMP, released on January 6, 1995, adopted an alternative that did not close the ten-mile portion of the Salt Creek Road; instead, it closed a one-half mile segment of the road and left the rest open to vehicles on a limited permit system. * * *

The provision of the Organic Act relating to the creation of the NPS and the purpose of the national parks it oversees provides:

> The service thus established shall promote and regulate the use of the Federal areas known as national parks ... by such means and measures as conform to the fundamental purpose of the said parks ...

which purpose is to conserve the scenery and the natural and historic objects and the wild life therein and to provide for the enjoyment of the same in such manner and by such means as will leave them unimpaired for the enjoyment of future generations.

16 U.S.C. § 1. Another provision of the Organic Act prohibits authorization of activities that derogate park values:

The authorization of activities shall be construed and the protection, management, and administration of these areas shall be conducted in light of the high public value and integrity of the National Park System and shall not be exercised in derogation of the values and purposes for which these various areas have been established, except as may have been or shall be directly and specifically provided by Congress.

16 U.S.C. § 1a–1. The enabling legislation creating Canyonlands National Park provides: "In order to preserve an area in the State of Utah possessing superlative scenic, scientific, and archeologic features for the inspiration, benefit, and use of the public, there is hereby established the Canyonlands National Park ..." 16 U.S.C. § 271. That legislation also mandates that Canyonlands be administered, protected, and developed in accordance with the purposes of the Organic Act. See 16 U.S.C. § 271d.

In the district court, the NPS asserted that the Organic Act and the enabling legislation creating Canyonlands National Park authorized a balancing between competing mandates of resource conservation and visitor enjoyment, and that its BMP represented a reasonable accommodation of conflicting mandates that should be afforded considerable deference. The district court reviewed the agency's interpretation in accordance with the analysis set forth in *Chevron,* where the Supreme Court stated:

First, always, is the question whether Congress has directly spoken to the precise question at issue. If the intent of Congress is clear, that is the end of the matter; for the court, as well as the agency, must give effect to the unambiguously expressed intent of Congress. If, however, the court determines Congress has not directly addressed the precise question at issue, the court does not simply impose its own construction on the statute, as would be necessary in the absence of an administrative interpretation. Rather, if the statute is silent or ambiguous with respect to the specific issue, the question for the court is whether the agency's answer is based on a permissible construction of the statute.

Chevron, 467 U.S. at 842–43. According to the district court, the first *Chevron* inquiry was determinative on the issue of continued vehicle access to the ten-mile portion of the Salt Creek Road. The court stated:

Congress has issued a clear answer to the question of whether the Park Service is authorized to permit activities within national parks that permanently impair unique park resources. The answer is no. As set out in the statutes discussed above, the Park Service's mandate is to permit forms of enjoyment and access that are *consistent* with preservation and *inconsistent* with significant, permanent impairment.

Finding that the evidence in the administrative record showed that "the riparian areas in Salt Creek Canyon are unique and that the effects of vehicular traffic beyond Peekaboo Spring are inherently and fundamentally inimical to their continued existence," the district court held that the BMP was inconsistent with the "clear legislative directive" of Congress.

On appeal, Utah Shared Access argues that the district court erred in resolving the issue under the first *Chevron* inquiry. Utah Shared Access argues that the district court should have reached the second *Chevron* inquiry because of ambiguities inherent in the relevant statutes and their application to the issue of vehicular access. We agree.

We first note that the district court erred in its framing of the question at issue for purposes of *Chevron* analysis. The district court characterized the question as whether the NPS is authorized to permit activities within national parks that permanently impair unique park resources. Stating the question that way predetermines the answer. We believe the precise question at issue is whether the BMP, in particular the portion of the BMP allowing vehicle use on the ten-mile segment of the Salt Creek Road from Peekaboo Spring to Angel Arch, is inconsistent with a clear intent of Congress expressed in the Organic Act and the Canyonlands enabling legislation. Framing the question in terms of "permanent impairment" might not necessarily be erroneous if the administrative record clearly showed that such permanent impairment would occur; however, we find that the record is not clear on that issue.

The Organic Act mandates that the NPS provide for the conservation and enjoyment of the scenery and natural historic objects and the wildlife therein "*in such manner and by such means as will leave them unimpaired for the enjoyment of future generations.*" 16 U.S.C. § 1 (emphasis added). Neither the word "unimpaired" nor the phrase "unimpaired for the enjoyment of future generations" is defined in the Act. It is unclear from the statute itself what constitutes impairment, and how both the duration and severity of the impairment are to be evaluated or weighed against the other value of public use of the park.

Although the Act and the Canyonlands enabling legislation place an overarching concern on preservation of resources, we read the Act as permitting the NPS to balance the sometimes conflicting policies of resource conservation and visitor enjoyment in determining what activities should be permitted or prohibited. The test for whether the NPS has performed its balancing properly is whether the resulting action leaves the resources "unimpaired for the enjoyment of future generations." Because of the ambiguity inherent in that phrase, we cannot resolve the issue before us under step one of *Chevron;* instead we must reach step two.

The question for the court under step two of *Chevron* is "whether the agency's answer is based on a permissible construction of the statute." *Chevron,* 467 U.S. at 843. To resolve this question, we must first determine what the agency's position is. In its brief to this court and at oral argument, the NPS has advised us that the Department of the Interior "has conducted a substantive reassessment of the proper construction of the Organic Act." On the basis of that reassessment, the Department took the position in its brief to this court that the Act prohibits "permanent impairment of those resources whose conservation is essential to the fundamental purposes and values for which an individual park has been established." The Department also took the position that the NPS has discretion under the Act to determine what resources are essential to the values and purposes of a particular national park, and what constitutes the impairment of those resources. In supplemental authority provided to this court just prior to oral argument, the Department submitted Draft NPS Management Policies (the "Draft Policies"), which clarify its position further. The Draft Policies address impairment of resources in terms of the duration, extent, timing, and cumulative effect of various impacts on park resources and values. They also are based on a premise that the Organic Act forbids broader categories of impairment in addition to those considered as permanent. In addition, the Draft Policies provide definitions for various terms in the Organic Act.

The Draft Policies propose to define "impairment of park resources and values" as "an adverse impact on one or more park resources or values that interferes with the integrity of the park's resources or values, or with the opportunities that otherwise would exist for the enjoyment of them by a present or future generation." The Draft Policies also propose to define "park resources and values" as "all the resources and values of a park whose conservation is essential to the purposes for which the area was included in the national park system ... and any additional purposes stated in a park's establishing legislation or proclamation."

The interpretation of the Act now offered by the Department and the NPS in this court and in the Draft Policies varies from the interpretation previously offered by the NPS in the district court. We must determine what weight to give the new interpretation. We conclude that there is currently no valid agency position worthy of deference.

An agency is free to change the meaning it attaches to ambiguous statutory language, and the new interpretation may still be accorded *Chevron* deference. * * * A position taken by an agency during litigation, however, is not sufficiently formal that it is deserving of *Chevron* deference. The agency's litigation position in this court thus lacks the requisite formality for *Chevron* deference under step two.

Similarly, agency policy statements, like litigation positions, do not usually warrant deference under step two of *Chevron*. Policy statements do not normally receive *Chevron* deference because they are usually expressed in an informal format and are not subject to rulemaking procedures.

A notice of availability of the Draft Policies, however, was published in the Federal Register and the public was given an opportunity to comment on them. Thus, the Draft Policies are unlike typical informal agency policy manuals. The fact that a notice regarding the Draft Policies appeared in the Federal Register and that they were subjected to comment procedures does not, however, automatically make them deserving of *Chevron* deference. The comments must still be considered and a rule must be properly adopted with a statement of its basis and purpose to complete the notice and comment rulemaking procedures. See 5 U.S.C. § 553(c). If the Draft Policies are finalized and adopted pursuant to the requisite rulemaking procedures, and then construed as substantive or legislative rules, they should be accorded *Chevron* deference; however, if, when ultimately finalized, they lack the requisite formality and are construed merely as interpretative rules, they should be examined under a less deferential standard that asks whether the agency's interpretation is "well reasoned" and "has the power to persuade."

At this time, the agency's Policies are still only in draft form and have not yet been finalized or adopted by the agency; therefore, we cannot accord either *Chevron* deference or the lesser deference applicable to interpretative rules to the agency's interpretation of the Act. Having no current interpretation in front of us that has been formally adopted by the agency, we examine the Act and the district court's disposition without giving deference to any agency interpretation.

The district court's legal interpretation of the Act was that the NPS is prohibited from permitting activities that result in "significant, permanent impairment." We agree that permitting "significant, permanent impairment" would violate the Act's mandate that the NPS provide for the enjoyment of the parks "in such manner and by such means as will leave them unimpaired for the enjoyment of future generations." 16 U.S.C. § 1. Although "significant, permanent impairment" may not be coterminous with what is prohibited by the Act because other negative impacts may also be prohibited, we find that it is within the range of prohibitions contemplated by Congress.

The district court determined that the administrative record demonstrated that permanent impairment would occur; however, the parties continue to dispute whether the impairment caused by vehicles would be permanent and how serious it would be. The administrative record includes the NPS's FONSI, which stated that any impairment would be temporary and minor. * * * Given the conflicting views regarding the level of impairment that vehicles would cause to the ten-mile segment of the Salt Creek Road, we remand for the district court to re-examine the evidence in the record regarding impairment, applying the appropriate standard to the NPS finding of temporary impairment.

On remand, the district court should not limit its analysis under step two of *Chevron* to whether the evidence demonstrates significant, permanent impairment. Rather, it should assess whether the evidence demonstrates the level of impairment prohibited by the Act. Moreover, by the time of trial, the Department of the Interior may have finalized and adopted its new NPS Management Policies. If the district court determines that those policies have been expressed in a binding format through the agency's congressionally delegated power, they should be considered legislative rules worthy of *Chevron* deference. If, however, the district court determines that they are merely interpretative rules, they should be evaluated pursuant to the less deferential standard articulated [above].

Because we find error in the district court's conclusion that the activity at issue is explicitly prohibited by the relevant statutes, we find the district court abused its discretion in granting an injunction. We therefore vacate the district court's order enjoining the BMP's allowance of continued motorized vehicle use on the Salt Creek Road in Salt Creek Canyon above Peekaboo Spring. * * *

NOTES AND QUESTIONS

1. *Balancing Conservation and Enjoyment.* Commentators have described the two-pronged mandate of the National Park System Organic Act as not only ambiguous but paradoxical. See, e.g., Richard West Sellars, Preserving Nature in the National Parks: A History (1997); Federico Cheever, The United States Forest Service and National Park Service: Paradoxical Mandates, Powerful Founders, and the Rise and Fall of Agency Discretion, 74 Denv. U. L. Rev. 625, 628–29 (1997); Robert L. Fischman, The Problem of Statutory Detail in National Park Establishment Legislation and Its Relationship to Pollution Control Law, 74 Denv. U. L. Rev. 779, 800 (1997). How did the National Park Service (NPS) describe the balance between its mandates for resource conservation and enjoyment in the District Court? In its Draft Policies? How different are the two positions?

2. *Standard of Review.* Did the Court of Appeal grant the appropriate degree of deference to the NPS's interpretation? Would the position announced in the Draft Policies survive ordinary *Chevron* review?

3. *How much Impairment is Permitted?* How should the District Court evaluate this dispute on remand? Must Wilderness Alliance prove that limited vehicle traffic will permanently impair Salt Creek to prevail? Must the NPS prove that it will not? What would constitute "permanent impairment"? What effects, if any, short of permanent impairment would justify banning vehicles? If on remand the court determines that the limited access alternative selected by the NPS will result in two to three instances of small amounts of engine fluids polluting the stream, should it rule for Wilderness Alliance?

4. *Concessions Contracts.* The NPS contracts with private entities known as concessionaires for the provision of a variety of services, including food, lodging, transportation, and recreation, for the 270 million people who annually visit the parks. Critics have charged that the NPS demands too little return on its concession contracts, and that concessions policy in the parks leads to overdevelopment. See George Cameron Coggins and Robert L. Glicksman, Concessions Law and Policy in the National Park System, 74 Denv. U. L. Rev. 729 (1997). "In 1996, concessionaires grossed more than $714 million, and pursuant to their lucrative contracts, paid the parks, on average, only 2% of their overall returns." Richard J. Ansson, Jr., Funding Our National Parks in the 21st Century: Will We Be Able to Preserve and Protect Our Embattled National Parks?, 11 Ford. Envtl. L. J. 1, 15 (1999). In 1998, concession reform legislation shortened the term of concession contracts, raised concession fees, and opened the process to increased competition. See 16 U.S.C. §§ 5951–5966. Although it provides the national parks with a source of additional funds, the new legislation does little to reduce the pressures to expand concession development.

5. *Commercial Uses.* With the exception of concessions, which are considered essential to visitor accommodation, commercial exploitation of park resources is generally forbidden. How should the NPS treat non-consumptive, or minimally consumptive, commercial activities, such as commercial photography or bioprospecting, the search for commercially valuable microorganisms? See Holly Doremus, Nature, Knowledge and Profit: The Yellowstone Bioprospecting Controversy and the Core Purposes of America's National Parks, 26 Ecology L.Q. 401 (1999).

6. *Wildlife Management.* Another source of controversy in the national parks is the management of wildlife, particularly near park boundaries. One long-running dispute involves the bison herd in Yellowstone National Park. In 1967, NPS discontinued a long-standing policy of ranching the bison like livestock. Thereafter, the herd was largely left unmanaged and free-roaming. The animals tend to range widely in search of food during the winter months; many cross park boundaries onto adjoining federal and non-federal lands. Montana officials, concerned about property damage and the possibility that the bison might spread disease to cattle herds, sued to compel NPS to prevent bison from wandering out of the park. That litigation was settled with the preparation of a joint bison management plan, under which NPS agreed to capture and slaughter bison migrating onto private land. Does the Organic Act permit NPS to destroy bison under these circumstances, provided that the slaughter does not threaten to eliminate the park herd? See Intertribal Bison Cooperative v. Babbitt, 25 F.Supp.2d 1135 (D.Mont.1998), *aff'd sub nom* Greater Yellowstone Coalition v. Babbitt, 175 F.3d 1149 (9th Cir.1999).

F. Ecosystem Management

Federal land management agencies experimented with ecosystem management in the 1980s, particularly in the area around Yellowstone National Park. In 1992, the Forest Service endorsed ecosystem management as a general approach to land management. With the backing of the newly-installed Clinton administration, the idea spread rapidly. By 1994, each of the major federal land management agencies claimed to be performing ecosystem management. In 1995, an interagency task force created by the White House issued a report urging all federal agencies to adopt the ecosystem approach.

Interagency Ecosystem Management Task Force, The Ecosystem Approach: Healthy Ecosystems and Sustainable Economies

3–4, 6–8 (Volume I 1995).

An ecosystem is an interconnected community of living things, including humans, and the physical environment within which they interact.

The ecosystem approach is a method for sustaining or restoring natural systems and their functions and values. It is goal driven, and it is based on a collaboratively developed vision of desired future conditions that integrates ecological, economic, and social factors. It is applied within a geographic framework defined primarily by ecological boundaries.

The goal of the ecosystem approach is to restore and sustain the health, productivity, and biological diversity of ecosystems and the overall quality of life through a natural resource management approach that is fully integrated with social and economic goals. This is essential to maintain the air we breath, the water we drink, the food we eat, and to sustain natural resources for future populations.

* * *

The ecosystem approach recognizes the interrelationship between natural systems and healthy, sustainable economies. It is a common sense way for public and private managers to carry out their mandates with greater efficiency. The approach emphasizes:

- Ensuring that all relevant and identifiable ecological and economic consequences (long term as well as short term) are considered.
- Improving coordination among federal agencies.
- Forming partnerships between federal, state, and local governments, Indian tribes, landowners, and other stakeholders.
- Improving communication with the general public.
- Carrying out federal responsibilities more efficiently and cost-effectively.
- Using the best science.
- Improving information and data management.
- Adjusting management direction as new information becomes available.

* * *

The survey teams and issue groups identified several recurring barriers that agencies face in implementing the ecosystem approach.

1. **Federal agency coordination**. A coordinated and comprehensive framework is essential to implement the ecosystem approach. Federal resource management has traditionally been characterized by specific missions, rigidly stratified and specialized organizational structures, and the subdivision of problems into narrowly defined tasks.

2. **Partnerships with nonfederal stakeholders**. The ecosystem approach requires active partnerships and collaboration with nonfederal parties, particularly state, local, and tribal governments, neighboring landowners, nongovernmental organizations, and universities. Although partnerships between the federal government and nonfederal entities are not uncommon, agencies need to strengthen their own outreach programs and improve the ability of nonfederal entities to participate. Together, they

must also project and articulate a desired ecosystem outcome with a shared vision for the future.

* * *

3. **Communication between federal agencies and the public**. Current outreach activities must be strengthened. Coordination with the public is generally perceived to be *secondary* to normal work of the agencies. Regional offices typically lack specialized staff with experience in working with the public. Most federal employees who should be interacting with the public are not trained in the skills needed for public participation aspects of the ecosystem approach—educating the public, motivating people to become involved, facilitating public discussions, building consensus, and resolving conflict.

* * *

4. **Resource allocation and management**. Agency coordination in ecosystem efforts can be improved by recognizing the interdependency of agency budgets. The ability of each agency to take an ecosystem approach is affected by its ability to budget for long-term goals, organize around and fund interdisciplinary activities, and quickly modify programs in response to new information. Agency budget priorities and structures, however, often reflect narrow, program-specific perspectives, are driven by immediate concerns, and are sometimes linked primarily to the production of tangible outputs such as commodities. Furthermore, Congress makes funding decisions on an agency by agency basis, making it difficult to coordinate the funding of interagency programs.

5. **Knowledge base and the role of science**. The existing *information* base—what we know about what exists in a place—and the existing *knowledge* base—how well we understand how ecological and economic components function—are both inadequate for many system-wide ecosystem analyses. The linkage between scientists and managers, and between natural resource agencies and other agencies and entities, is essential in establishing a shared vision of desired ecosystem conditions, for specifying how the vision can be achieved, and for monitoring and measuring progress toward goals.

6. **Information and data management**. No single entity has the resources or mandate to develop all relevant information on any ecosystem, or even the capability for locating and accessing information pertinent to an ecosystem that is available from other sources. Some agencies are sources for ecological data, others for social and economic data. Managers must have coherent and complete information from all of the sources in order to make reasonable decisions on their actions that affect the ecosystem.

7. **Flexibility for adaptive management**. Adaptive management requires a willingness to undertake prudent experimentation, consistent with sound scientific and economic principles, and to accept occasional failures. This contrasts with the strongly risk-averse nature of most agen-

cies and managers. Agencies are hampered in their efforts to adapt management practices in accordance with new circumstances. As a result, innovation is discouraged, new knowledge is applied too slowly, and inefficiencies persist to the detriment of both resources and communities.

RECOMMENDATIONS

As a matter of policy, the federal government should provide leadership in and cooperate with activities that foster the ecosystem approach to natural resource management, regulation, and assistance. Federal agencies should ensure that they utilize their authorities in a way that facilitates, and does not pose barriers to, the ecosystem approach. In administering their programs, federal agencies should be sensitive to the needs and rights of landowners, local communities, and the public, and should work with them toward common goals.

* * *

The Task Force further recommends that member agencies adopt the following management strategies. *First, agencies should attempt to focus their activities on the issues faced by particular ecosystems, the people who live in them, and the economies founded upon the ecosystem resources.* This will require agency programs that respond to the needs of specific geographic areas, not simply to statutory mandates.

Second, agencies should make every effort to engage in coordinated, integrated action. The ecosystem approach involves not only natural resource and land management agencies, but also the efforts of agencies whose missions are environmental, technical assistance, research, commerce, trade, or economic development. Ecological problems are almost always beyond the purview of any one agency, program or organization.

Third, agencies should strive toward open information flow. While respecting private property rights, agencies should improve and integrate the information they gather, make it broadly accessible, and forge strong links between the scientific community, the information technology community, and the information user community.

NOTES AND QUESTIONS

1. *The Definition Problem.* Ecosystem management is so vaguely defined that it has come to represent very different things to different people. While this malleability has helped build political support, it has led to considerable confusion. See Steven L. Yaffee, Three Faces of Ecosystem Management, 13 Conservation Biology 713 (1999). In the federal government, because the idea developed largely on an agency-by-agency basis, ecosystem management has not been uniformly defined. The major land management agencies define it as follows:

Forest Service: Using an ecological approach to achieve the management of national forests and grasslands by blending the needs of people and environmental values in such a way that national forests and grasslands represent diverse, healthy, productive, and sustainable ecosystems.

Bureau of Land Management: The integration of ecological, economic and social principles to manage biological and physical systems in a manner that safeguards the long-term ecological sustainability, natural diversity and productivity of the landscape.

Fish and Wildlife Service: Protecting or restoring the function, structure, and species composition of an ecosystem, recognizing that all components are interrelated.

National Park Service: A philosophical approach that respects all living things and seeks to sustain natural processes and the dignity of all species and to ensure that common interests flourish.

Richard Haeuber, Ecosystem Management and Environmental Policy in the United States: Open Window or Closed Door?, 40 Landscape & Urban Planning 221, 224 (1998). A large number of other definitions have been proposed by scientists, industry groups, and others. See Norman L. Christensen et al., The Report of the Ecological Society of America Committee on the Scientific Basis for Ecosystem Management, 6 Ecological Applications 665, 668 (1996).

In what ways do the various agency definitions diverge? How important are those differences? How closely do they track the interagency task force definition? Are the differences appropriate, given the different missions of the agencies, or is a uniform definition needed?

2. *New Paradigm Meets Old.* How is ecosystem management different from traditional land management strategies? Is it primarily about process or substance? Can it be integrated successfully into the existing framework of multiple use management? Preservation management? Will an ecosystem approach help land managers resolve the conflicts posed by, for example, timber harvest methods on the national forests or recreation in the national parks?

3. *Ecosystem Management in the Courts.* Do the statutes governing public land management allow adoption of ecosystem approaches? Given the broad discretion granted federal land managers, the answer would seem to be yes. Several courts, including the Supreme Court, have upheld regulations and actions taken for ecosystem management purposes. See, e.g., Public Lands Council v. Babbitt, 529 U.S. 728 (2000); Seattle Audubon Soc. v. Moseley, 80 F.3d 1401 (9th Cir.1996). In Communities for a Great Northwest v. Clinton, 112 F.Supp.2d 29 (D.D.C.2000), the district court ruled that plaintiff farm and livestock groups lacked standing to challenge the Interior Columbia Basin Ecosystem Management Program, covering 75 million acres in the Pacific Northwest. Plaintiffs had asserted that ecosystem-based management violated FLPMA, NFMA, and the Multiple–Use Sustained Yield Act.

4. *Ecosystems and People.* What place does ecosystem management assign human beings? How, if at all, does the shift to an ecosystem approach change that role? Should people be considered components of public land ecosystems? Which people? How should social, economic, and ecological considerations be integrated in management of the public lands? See Oliver A. Houck, Are Humans Part of Ecosystems?, 28 Envtl. L. 1 (1998), for an argument that physical and biological conditions, rather than human satisfaction, should be the measure of management success.

5. *Public Participation.* Ecosystem management is generally defined to include a strong role for public participation in management decisions. Why is that considered important? Is it consistent with another fundamental principle of ecosystem management, that decisions must rest on the best available scientific information? Will agencies voluntarily surrender their exclusive management authority to collaborative processes? Does the law permit them to do so? Should they?

6. *Experience to Date.* The ecosystem management initiative is too new to draw firm conclusions about its impact. Broadly defining ecosystem management as extending management across political or property boundaries to ecological boundaries or shifting the management focus from single resources to landscapes and ecological processes, a 1996 study identified more than 600 sites where ecosystem management was being practiced. Steven L. Yaffee et al., Ecosystem Management in the United States: An Assessment of Current Experience (Island Press, 1996). The authors concluded:

> The image these efforts provide of the experience to date is hopeful. Clearly, implementing ecosystem management projects is challenging, since it involves collaboration, complex systems, problematic policies, and a skeptical public. But people are dealing with these challenges effectively. Their successes can be enhanced by increasing the understanding and skills of the people involved in ecosystem management projects, renewing policies and programs that influence the environment in which projects take place, and recognizing that ecosystem management is both a set of goals and a long term process of change. Nevertheless, participants in these projects are excited about the promise of these approaches to achieving sustainable resource management in the future.

7. *The Future.* The federal ecosystem management initiatives of the 1990s were accomplished entirely by administrative action, without any explicit legislative mandate. The property rights movement, and other conservative western interests, have expressed considerable skepticism about ecosystem management, fearing that it might become a justification for greater restrictions on resource extraction as well as more intensive regulation of nonfederal lands.

It is unclear whether ecosystem management will persist under the administration of George W. Bush. On one hand, ecosystem management seems to run counter to the boundary-oriented nature of both public and private law, and to the law's preference for certainty and stability. See Robert B. Keiter, Ecosystems and the Law: Toward and Integrated Approach, 8 Ecological Applications 332 (1998). On the other hand, the pressures that produced the ecosystem management initiative, including the need to protect species whose range crosses property boundaries, are unlikely to disappear. Enthusiasm among agency personnel for the experiments in ecosystem management to date may also bode well for its future. See Yaffee et al., supra, at 40; Haeuber, supra, at 229–33.

SECTION 3.   BIODIVERSITY PROTECTION

The term biodiversity refers to the entire range of living creatures, from microscopic bacteria to enormous whales. Estimates of the number of species on earth range from 3 million to 100 million. Bruce A. Stein et al., A Remarkable Array: Species Diversity in the United States, in Precious Heritage: The Status of Biodiversity in the United States 58 (Stein et al. eds. 2000). The United States harbors a substantial portion of the world's biotic diversity, including ten percent of the world's mammal species, and seven percent of its flowering plants. Id. at 67.

Worldwide, biodiversity is disappearing at an unprecedented rate. The International Union for the Conservation of Nature reported in 2000 that one in every four mammal species and one in eight bird species face significant risk of extinction. In the United States, as much as one-third of the native flora and fauna may be at risk. See Lawrence L. Master et al., Vanishing Assets: Conservation Status of U.S. Species, in Precious Heritage, supra at 101–04.

As you read the materials that follow, consider not only why we should care about threats to biodiversity, but to what extent those threats can and should be addressed by law. If law is not the entire answer, what else should we do, individually and as a society, to improve future prospects for biodiversity?

A.   HISTORICAL BACKGROUND

In Roman law, wild animals were unowned until captured or killed by human enterprise. The only restriction on hunting was that landowners had the exclusive right to take wildlife on their property.

English law was quite different. The Crown held complete authority over hunting and wildlife management, even on private lands. The Crown, and later Parliament, jealously guarded the right to hunt, reserving it to landed gentry in part to restrict the spread of weapons among the lower classes but also as a signal of elite status.

In the United States, the states succeeded to the sovereign's broad authority to regulate with respect to wildlife management. See Martin v. Waddell's Lessee, 41 U.S. (16 Pet.) 367 (1842). Nonetheless, until the middle of the 19th century, free taking of wildlife was the general rule. The apparent inexhaustibility of wildlife resources, coupled with resistance to the English class structure, discouraged states from using their authority aggressively to protect wildlife. Instead, early colonial and state laws facilitated the capture of wildlife by opening private lands to public hunting and fishing. See Hope M. Babcock, Should *Lucas v. South Carolina Coastal Council* Protect Where the Wild Things Are? Of Beavers, Bob–O–Links, and Other Things That Go Bump in the Night, 85 Iowa L. Rev. 849, 883 (2000). Many states also offered bounties to encourage killing of predators such as wolves. See Dale D. Goble, Of Wolves and Welfare Ranching, 16 Harv. Envtl. L. Rev. 101, 104 (1992).

Restrictions on the taking of wildlife gained importance in the second half of the 19th century, as the mammals and birds that once dominated the continent fell to the guns of market hunters. In the 1850s, states began to enact bag limits and restrict hunting seasons. Karin P. Sheldon, Overview of Wildlife Law, *in* Environmental Law: From Resources to Recovery 204 (1993). It soon became clear, however, that state action alone was insufficient to stem the rapid decline of wildlife populations. Poachers could effectively evade state restrictions by removing their illegally-taken bounty from the state or claiming to have caught it legally in another state. Robert S. Anderson, The Lacey Act: America's Premier Weapon in the Fight Against Unlawful Wildlife Trafficking, 16 Pub. Land L. Rev. 27, 38 (1995).

The cautious first federal foray into wildlife law, the Lacey Act, currently codified at 16 U.S.C. §§ 3371–3378, addressed both of these problems, making it a federal crime to transport wildlife taken in violation of state law across state lines and subjecting imported game to state law as if it had been killed there.

At the time the Lacey Act was passed, it was widely believed that federal power did not extend to direct wildlife management. Judicial interpretation of state power over wildlife had given rise to a fiction of state "ownership" which seemed to preclude federal intervention. See Geer v. Connecticut, 161 U.S. 519 (1896); The Vessel 'Abby Dodge' v. United States, 223 U.S. 166 (1912).

The Supreme Court finally repudiated the state ownership doctrine as a special limitation on federal power over wildlife in Hughes v. Oklahoma, 441 U.S. 322, 326 n. 2 (1979). Long before then, however, Congress, relying on the treaty power and the New Deal-era expansion of the commerce power, had greatly expanded federal wildlife law.

In 1913, the Migratory Bird Act imposed federal restrictions on hunting of migratory birds. After two federal courts declared the Act unconstitutional, the executive branch quickly negotiated a migratory bird treaty with Great Britain (acting for Canada). Congress then re-enacted essentially the same provisions as the Migratory Bird Treaty Act (currently codified at 16 U.S.C. §§ 703–712). The Supreme Court upheld the new law under the treaty power. Missouri v. Holland, 252 U.S. 416 (1920).

Emboldened by the Supreme Court's clear declaration that state power over wildlife did not exclude federal authority, Congress expanded federal regulation from hunting restrictions designed to ensure continuing availability of game for harvest to conservation for esthetic and other noneconomic purposes. By 1973, federal regulation had reached its zenith with passage of the Endangered Species Act (ESA), 16 U.S.C. §§ 1531–1544, which prohibits the taking of any animal species federally designated as endangered.

Legal protection of plants remains far weaker than legal protection of animals. At common law, ownership of plants followed ownership of the soil in which they grew. With the exception of scattered limitations on timber harvest, the law provided virtually no protection for plants until the second half of the 20th century. Today, the ESA and the Convention on International Trade in Endangered Species restrict commerce in declining plant species, and the ESA prohibits removal or destruction of listed plants on federal property.

Despite the great expansion of federal wildlife regulation since 1900, state law remains important and, in light of the judicial trend toward a narrower interpretation of federal power, may become more so. States provide the primary source of hunting and fishing regulations, even on federal lands. Although the state ownership doctrine has been discredited, states are still considered trustees of fish and wildlife resources on behalf of their citizens, giving them broad power to impose regulations consistent with, or more protective than, federal law. See, e.g., Babcock, *supra*, at 886–89. Many states have statutes protecting species recognized as endangered or threatened within the state, although most lack at least some of the protections of the federal law. See Dale D. Goble et al., Local and National Protection of Endangered Species: An Assessment, 2 Envtl. Sci. & Pol'y 43, 50 (1999). These laws are particularly crucial to protection of endangered plants. The federal ESA prohibits the taking of listed plants on private property "in knowing violation of any law or regulation of any State or in the course of any violation of a State criminal trespass law." 16 U.S.C. § 1538(a)(2)(B). Thus, landowners can legally destroy federally listed plants on their property unless forbidden to do so by state law. According to a recent study, only seven states and two federal territories prohibit the killing of protected plants on private property. Jeffrey J. Rachlinski, Protecting Endangered Species Without Regulating Private Landowners: The Case of Endangered Plants, 8 Cornell J.L. & Pub. Pol'y 1, 12 (1998).

Native American rights play a special role in wildlife law. Traditional tribal cultures were heavily dependent on local wildlife resources. See United States v. Winans, 198 U.S. 371, 381 (1905) ("Salmon were not much less necessary to the existence of the Indians than the atmosphere they breathed."). Consequently, numerous treaties between tribes and the United States include provisions protecting tribal hunting and fishing practices, both on and off reservations. Exercise of these rights remains important, both economically and culturally, to many tribes. States can impose conservation restrictions on Indian hunting and fishing, but those restrictions must not have the effect of discriminating against Indians. Any available harvest must be "fairly apportioned" between Indians and non-Indians. Department of Game v. Puyallup Tribe, 414 U.S. 44, 48 (1973). In a long-running dispute over salmon fishing rights in the state of Washington, the Supreme Court eventually held that the tribe was entitled to roughly half the harvest. Washington v. Washington State Commercial Passenger Fishing Vessel Ass'n, 443 U.S. 658 (1979).

Congress retains the power to abrogate Indian treaties. Subsequent federal law, therefore, can change established Indian treaty rights to wildlife if the legislation clearly shows congressional intent to do so. In United States v. Dion, 476 U.S. 734 (1986), the Supreme Court held that the Bald Eagle Protection Act abrogated treaty rights to hunt eagles on a reservation. Lower courts have split on whether the Endangered Species Act applies to non-commercial hunting by Native Americans. Compare United States v. Billie, 667 F.Supp. 1485 (S.D.Fla.1987), with United States v. Dion, 752 F.2d 1261 (8th Cir.1985) (en banc), *rev'd on other grounds*, 476 U.S. 734 (1986).

Wildlife and wildlife parts are associated with many Native American religious practices. The free exercise clause is sometimes asserted as a defense to prosecution for wildlife violations. Although that defense has occasionally proven successful, it has typically been rejected. See United States v. Abeyta, 632 F.Supp. 1301 (D.N.M.1986) (dismissing prosecution of Indian who killed golden eagle for religious purposes); United States v. Jim, 888 F.Supp. 1058 (D.Or.1995) (upholding restrictions on hunting of bald and golden eagles, despite substantial burden on religious freedom).

B. JUSTIFICATIONS FOR BIODIVERSITY PROTECTION

Holly Doremus, Patching the Ark: Improving Legal Protection of Biological Diversity

18 Ecology L. Q. 265, 269–81 (1991).

* * * [T]he arguments for preservation of biological diversity can be divided into three categories: utilitarian, esthetic, and moral. * * *

The Utilitarian Basis for Preservation of Diversity

* * * Individual species provide us with a number of direct benefits. For example, we have domesticated our food crops, both plant and animal, from wild species. Other species might provide new crops. Wild relatives of current crop species can also provide a source of useful genetic traits. * * *

Biological diversity is also a useful source of new medicinal drugs. Chemicals derived from higher plants form the major ingredient in about a quarter of all prescriptions written in the United States; chemicals derived from lower plants and microbes account for another eighth. Many of these drugs can be produced more cheaply by extraction than by chemical synthesis. Numerous species have yet to be examined for their medicinal properties. Thus, many undiscovered medicinally useful chemicals may exist in the natural world.

A number of animal species serve another important function in medicine as model systems for the study of human diseases. For obvious reasons, researchers cannot deliberately infect human subjects to facilitate laboratory study of the progress and properties of a disease. However, they can and do use animals as laboratory subjects. Examples include the use of desert pupfish to study kidney disease and of armadillos to study leprosy. * * *

Besides the direct benefits described above, ecosystems provide a number of indirect benefits to humanity. These "ecosystem services" include climate control, oxygen production, removal of carbon dioxide from the atmosphere, soil generation, nutrient cycling, and purification of fresh-water supplies. Some of these functions could probably be performed by managed systems, at least on a small scale, but management of such systems on a global scale is presently beyond our technological capability. Moreover, some of these processes, such as nutrient cycling, are highly complex and not yet fully understood.

* * *

The Esthetic Basis for Preservation of Diversity

Many people find beauty in the natural world, viewing natural objects, both living and nonliving, with a sense of admiration, wonder, or awe. Esthetic interest in nature is demonstrated in a variety of ways. For example, millions of Americans visit national parks and wildlife refuges every year. Some sixty million Americans participate in bird watching, and millions more engage in other forms of wildlife-related recreation. * * *

Individual species and specific natural areas may also come, over time, to be imbued with powerful symbolic value. They may embody the cultural or political identity of a people. The bald eagle is one such symbolic species * * *.

The interest that the biota holds for scientists and natural historians also has esthetic overtones. For example, one may appreciate the beauty of the interactions among species, or of the construction of an organism to function optimally in its environment. * * *

The esthetic value of diversity extends to ecosystem, species, and genetic diversity. * * * Ecosystems have esthetic value beyond that of the species they contain because the interactions that occur among species, and the way the system as a whole responds to perturbations, are themselves interesting. And genetic diversity is esthetically valuable both because the differences among individuals may fascinate us (as in the case of our own species), and because it provides the building blocks from which new manifestations of nature's wonder can be constructed. * * *

The Ethical Basis for Preservation of Diversity

In 1949, Aldo Leopold advocated the extension of ethical obligations to the relations between man and nature, calling for the development of an "ecological conscience" reflecting "a conviction of individual responsibility for the health of the land." Since then, several commentators have argued that nonhuman organisms, and even nonliving natural objects, have or should have rights based on their intrinsic value. Under such a view, human beings have an ethical obligation not to destroy these creatures and objects, at least in the absence of a strong countervailing value.

An ethical obligation to "nature" could conceivably be directed primarily to individuals, species, ecosystems, or the global environment as a whole. Human beings find it easiest to empathize and identify with individual beings and with vertebrate animals * * *. Therefore, people may most readily accept a moral obligation toward individual "higher" animals. Animal liberation philosophers have proposed ethical obligations toward all creatures able to experience pain, or capable of valuing their lives. * * *

Taking a different approach than animal rights proponents, a number of philosophers have expressed the view that man's ethical obligation to nature extends not primarily to individuals but to species or natural systems. This view echoes Leopold's famous statement: "A thing is right when it tends to preserve the integrity, stability, and beauty of the biotic community. It is wrong when it tends otherwise." Those espousing this view have emphasized the importance of the continuation of the biotic community, and the moral considerability of ecosystems and species. Some commentators have argued that species have a right to function normally in their ecosystems * * *.

Ethical obligations to nature need not rest on such a nonanthropocentric foundation. Several philosophers and theologians, while not granting "rights" similar to those held by human beings to other species or to natural systems, have appealed to a tradition of human responsibility for stewardship of the Earth. The theological argument for stewardship proceeds from the premise that God created nature in part for his own enjoyment. The nature of the creation gives rise to a three-fold role for man with respect to nature: man is both overlord, wondering onlooker, and caretaker. The combination of these roles requires that man, insofar as possible, allow nature to flourish and to continue in its place. This duty to nature is not absolute, however; it occupies a position secondary to man's duty to his fellow man. * * *

Public Policy Consequences of the Various Arguments For Preservation

Acceptance of any of the arguments given above for the preservation of biological diversity leads to the conclusion that preservation of some part of our biota is desirable as a matter of public policy. The different bases for preservation do not, however, necessarily justify protection of the same proportion of the total, nor of the same resources. * * *

Utilitarian grounds have been most often cited in and to Congress as justifying a national policy of protection of biological resources, although esthetic and ethical arguments have also been made. Utilitarian appeals may be most common because the people seeking protection of plants and animals believe that these justifications will have a greater appeal to the public than will other arguments. * * *

Although the utilitarian argument may be the easiest to sell to the public, it does not, by itself, provide a basis for preservation of the full spectrum of biological diversity. One common utilitarian argument is that, since most species have not been investigated with an eye to their exploitability, it would be foolhardy to allow them to become extinct before such an investigation has been made. This argument provides a solid basis for preservation of tropical systems, where little or nothing is known about a vast number of species, but is less applicable to developed countries like the United States, where, although large gaps in our knowledge remain, much of the flora and fauna has been at least cursorily investigated. Many species may have little or no utilitarian value, either individually or as components of an ecosystem. If utilitarian reasons are the only basis for preservation, we need not preserve these species. * * *

A strict utilitarian view would also justify extermination of a species or an ecosystem to serve a human purpose, even a fairly limited purpose. Although few would argue that a starving man might not maintain his life by eating the only available food source even if it was the last example of an endangered species, many choices are less stark. As an example, the bark of the Pacific yew (*Taxus brevifolia*), a tree found in oldgrowth forests of the Pacific Northwest, contains taxol, a chemical which can act as an anticancer drug. The tree is rare and slow-growing, the bark contains only a low concentration of the chemical, and high doses are needed to inhibit the growth of cancer cells. A utilitarian view might sanction the use of all specimens of the Pacific yew in destructive experiments if there were a good chance that such a course would allow scientists to develop a synthesis for taxol.

* * *

The esthetic argument * * * could allow the extermination of species and ecosystems which most people do not find appealing. For example, although many biologists would disagree, most people find swamps esthetically distasteful. Unless a scientific elite is made the arbiter of esthetic value, swamps might properly be turned into esthetically preferable meadows.

Similarly, if the purpose of preservation is primarily esthetic, people may demand that their esthetic experience be given first priority even when it conflicts with the health of the species or ecosystem. Such conflicts currently occur, for example, with respect to whale watching off the California coast. Because tourists demand the best possible view of the sounding whales, tour boats endeavor to get as close as possible. Some marine scientists believe that these intrusions have caused the whales to alter their migratory path significantly. If the primary basis for preservation of biological wonders such as whales is esthetic, perhaps they are not worth preserving unless they can be viewed at close range during their migration.

* * *

By contrast, nonanthropocentric moral arguments provide a basis for preservation of the entire range of biological diversity, at least if the ethical obligation runs primarily to species or natural systems rather than to individual creatures. An ethical obligation directed at individual organisms might lead indirectly to the protection of genetic diversity, but would not, in principle, allow one to distinguish between individuals of rare and abundant species. For example, under a view that primarily values individual creatures, it would be difficult to justify removal of feral goats or sheep from an island where they are eating the last examples of a rare plant.

Other factors also limit the reach of an ethical obligation running to individual organisms. Many (probably most) of the current threats to nonhuman species come from indirect causes, such as elimination of habitat, rather than from direct exploitation. Human activities causing these indirect threats are morally ambiguous compared to actions such as the clubbing of baby seals, as they often do not result in immediately apparent harm to individual animals. * * *

Only a moral obligation extending to ecosystems or even to the global biota as a whole provides a reason to preserve the full range of biological diversity. Such an obligation could be based on the rareness of life in the universe, the complexity of the systems which have evolved on the Earth, and the unique nature of human consciousness. Leopold and others have viewed the diversity of natural systems as a good in itself; the apparent rarity of life beyond our planet may enhance the value of that diversity.

Furthermore, *Homo sapiens*, as a species uniquely capable of appreciating the effects of its actions, may have a special obligation to see that those actions do not unnecessarily impinge on the biota. Humans are capable both of appreciating the range of life that has developed on Earth, and of modifying the environment in ways that threaten much of that range. This combination of awareness and power may carry with it a special responsibility to preserve, to the extent compatible with human survival, the other biological resources of the planet.

NOTES AND QUESTIONS

1. *Why Protect Biodiversity?* Should we strive to protect biodiversity, and if so to what extent? Which arguments do you find most persuasive, utilitarian, esthetic, or moral? What level should be the focus of our concern? Should we be concerned about old-growth forest as a community or about the individual plant and animal species that make up that community? If the community, how should we decide how much to protect? If the species, should we be satisfied to save a gene bank if we believed frozen embryos or cells could regenerate those plants and animals long into the future? Or should we seek to reintroduce species to areas from which they have been lost? Wolves, for example, once roamed much of North America. They have been successfully returned to a few areas, including Yellowstone National Park, and seem to be relatively tolerant of human impacts. Should we also try to bring wolves back to metropolitan Denver or the northeast corridor?

2. *The Value of Ecosystem Services.* Much of the utilitarian value provided by nature lies outside the market system, and is therefore difficult to measure. No one currently pays for plants to replace carbon dioxide in the atmosphere with oxygen, for example, or for wetlands to filter water. Concerned that these services are not adequately considered in public and private decisions, economists have tried to estimate their monetary value. Based on willingness-to-pay studies and other data, one widely-circulated report places the global value of ecosystem services somewhere between $16 and $54 trillion annually (in 1994 dollars), compared to global gross national product totals of $18 trillion per year. Robert Costanza et al., The Value of the World's Ecosystem Services and Natural Capital, 387 Nature 252 (1997).

3. *The Precautionary Principle and Burdens of Proof.* Because extinction is irreversible, many commentators urge application of the "precautionary principle," which, in the spirit of "better safe than sorry," calls for action to protect the environment to precede certainty of harm. Developed to insure that scientific uncertainty does not unduly stall protective efforts, the precautionary principle essentially places the burden of proof on those who would change the environmental status quo.

The precautionary principle, in one form or another, has been incorporated into several recent international agreements. The 1992 Rio Declaration on Environment and Development, for example, provides:

> In order to protect the environment, the precautionary approach shall be widely applied by States according to their capabilities. Where there are threats of serious or irreversible damage, lack of full scientific certainty shall not be used as a reason for postponing cost-effective measures to prevent environmental degradation.

Preamble, Principle 15. Some observers argue that the precautionary principle has become a general principle of international law, although others disagree. See James Cameron & Juli Abouchar, The Status of the Precautionary Principle in International Law, *in* The Precautionary Principle and International Law: The Challenge of Implementation 29, 36–50 (David Freestone & Ellen Hey, eds. 1996).

Should the precautionary principle apply to biodiversity protection, either internationally or within the United States? How should it be operationalized? In other words, how strong a suspicion of potential harm should be sufficient to halt development, and how certain must it be that harm will not be serious or irreversible before development is permitted?

4. *Taxol Update.* Demand for taxol no longer threatens the Pacific yew. Taxol and several closely related compounds can now be synthesized starting with needles of various common yew species. Hedge clippings which were once a disposal problem for gardeners now provide a renewable and economical source of these useful drugs. See Sarah Lonsdale, Shoots of Recovery, Daily Telegraph (London), May 13, 2000, at 17.

C.   THE ENDANGERED SPECIES ACT: THE FLAGSHIP BIODIVERSITY STATUTE

The most celebrated and controversial biodiversity protection measure in the United States is the federal Endangered Species Act (ESA). This section begins with a brief overview of the law, then considers listing, the prohibition on take, and the incidental take permit provision in greater detail.

1. OVERVIEW

The U.S. Fish & Wildlife Service (FWS) of the Department of Interior is primarily responsible for implementing the ESA, although the National Marine Fisheries Service, an agency of the Department of Commerce, is responsible for protection of marine species and anadromous fish (fish that migrate from fresh water to the ocean during their life cycle). FWS maintains a list of species determined by regulation to be endangered or threatened. ESA § 4, 16 U.S.C. § 1533. The Services are supposed to designate "critical habitat" concurrent with species listing. Id.

Listed species are protected by two key regulatory provisions. Section 7 applies only to federal agencies. It imposes a duty to carry out programs for the conservation of listed species. ESA § 7(a)(1), 16 U.S.C. § 1536(a)(1). This provision allows agencies to use their existing authorities to assist listed species, but leaves them considerable discretion in choosing how to do so. See Carson–Truckee Water Conservancy Dist. v. Clark, 741 F.2d 257 (9th Cir.1984); Pyramid Lake Paiute Tribe v. United States Dept. of the Navy, 898 F.2d 1410 (9th Cir.1990).

Section 7 also requires federal agencies to ensure that actions they carry out, authorize, or fund are not likely to jeopardize the continued existence of any listed species or adversely modify or destroy its critical habitat. ESA § 7(a)(2), 16 U.S.C. § 1536(a)(2). This duty is fulfilled through a three-step process. First, the agency asks the appropriate Service whether any listed species are in the project area. Next, the agency undertakes a "biological assessment" to determine if the project is likely to affect any of those species. If so, the agency initiates formal consultation with the Service on the impacts of the project. Formal consultation culminates in issuance by the Service of a biological opinion as to whether the proposed action is likely to jeopardize the species or adversely modify its critical habitat. 16 U.S.C. § 1536(b)(3)(A). An action fails the jeopardy test if it "reasonably would be expected, directly or indirectly, to reduce appreciably the likelihood of both the survival and recovery of a listed species in the wild by reducing the reproduction, numbers, or distribution of that species." 50 C.F.R. § 402.02. It has impermissible impacts on critical habitat if it would appreciably diminish the value of that habitat for survival and recovery. Id. If the Service finds jeopardy or adverse modification of critical habitat, it must suggest "reasonable and prudent alternatives" that would allow the project to proceed without impermissibly harming the species. 16 U.S.C. § 1536(b)(3)(A). "No jeopardy" biological opinions are accompanied by incidental take statements which protect the action agency against liability under section 9.

In practice, section 7 consultation rarely halts projects. One study found that FWS conducted more than 94,000 informal and 2,700 formal consultations between 1987 and 1992. Those consultations produced 352 jeopardy opinions and actually blocked only 54 actions. World Wildlife Fund, For Conserving Listed Species, Talk is Cheaper than We Think: The Consultation Process Under the Endangered Species Act (Nov. 1994).

The other important regulatory provision of the ESA is section 9, which imposes a series of prohibitions applicable to all persons. With respect to endangered plants, section 9 forbids shipment or receipt in interstate or foreign commerce; removal from or malicious destruction on federal land; and removal or destruction from other lands in knowing violation of state law or in the course of a violation of state criminal trespass law. ESA § 9(a)(2), 16 U.S.C. § 1538(a)(2). Endangered animals receive stronger protection; no person may "take" an endangered animal within the United States or on the high seas. ESA § 9(a)(1), 16 U.S.C. § 1538(a)(1).

Knowing violation of the ESA is punishable by civil penalties of up to $25,000 per violation or criminal penalties of up to $50,000 per violation and imprisonment for up to one year. ESA § 11(a), (b), 16 U.S.C. § 1540(a), (b). Citizen suits are available to enjoin violations, and successful citizen plaintiffs can recover attorney fees. ESA § 11(g), 16 U.S.C. § 1540(g).

The first important judicial test of the ESA came shortly after its passage. In 1973, the snail darter, a 3–inch fish, was discovered in a stretch of the Little Tennessee River slated for impoundment behind the Tellico Dam, a federal project authorized in 1967. In 1975, in response to petitions submitted by opponents of the dam project, among others, FWS listed the snail darter as endangered. The Supreme Court subsequently ruled that the ESA required an injunction halting construction of the dam, which was more than 80% complete, because closing of the dam gates would "either eradicate the known population of snail darters or destroy their critical habitat." Tennessee Valley Auth. v. Hill, 437 U.S. 153, 171 (1978). In the course of its opinion, the Court explained that "examination of the language, history, and structure of the legislation under review here indicates beyond doubt that Congress intended endangered species to be afforded the highest of priorities." Id. at 174.

Congress reacted to the *TVA* decision by creating a narrow exception from the "no jeopardy" provision of section 7. The Endangered Species Committee, made up of seven cabinet-level officials, can grant an exemption if it finds by a super-majority vote that: there are no reasonable and prudent alternatives to the proposed action; the benefits of the action clearly outweigh those of alternatives consistent with conserving the species; the action is of regional or national significance; and there has been no irreversible commitment of resources pending the application for an exemption. ESA § 7(h); 16 U.S.C. § 1536(h). The Committee does not necessarily have the last word, however. After it refused to grant an exemption for Tellico Dam, Congress passed an appropriations rider exempting the dam from the ESA. After the dam was completed, the snail darter was found in a handful of other streams in the region and was downlisted to threatened. See Zygmunt J ⁿ Plater, The Embattled Social Utilities of the Endangered

Species Act: A Noah Presumption and Caution Against Putting Gasmasks on the Canaries in the Coalmine, 27 Envtl. L. 845, 860–61 (1997).

2.   LISTING

Excerpts from the Endangered Species Act

16 U.S.C. §§ 1531–1544.

Sec. 3   Definitions

* * *

(6) The term "endangered species" means any species which is in danger of extinction throughout all or a significant portion of its range other than a species of the Class Insecta determined by the Secretary to constitute a pest whose protection under the provisions of this chapter would present an overwhelming and overriding risk to man.

* * *

(16) The term "species" includes any subspecies of fish or wildlife or plants, and any distinct population segment of any species of vertebrate fish or wildlife which interbreeds when mature.

* * *

(20) The term "threatened species" means any species which is likely to become an endangered species within the foreseeable future throughout all or a significant portion of its range.

Sec. 4   Determination of endangered species and threatened species

(a) Generally

(1) The Secretary shall by regulation * * * determine whether any species is an endangered or a threatened species because of any of the following factors:

(A) the present or threatened destruction, modification, or curtailment of its habitat or range;

(B) overutilization for commercial, recreational, scientific, or educational purposes;

(C) disease or predation;

(D) the inadequacy of existing regulatory mechanisms;

(E) other natural or manmade factors affecting its continued existence.

* * *

(b) Basis for determinations

(1)(A) The Secretary shall make determinations required by subsection (a)(1) of this section solely on the basis of the best scientific and commercial data available to him after conducting a review of the status of the species and after taking into account those efforts, if any, being made by any State or foreign nation, or any political subdivision of a State or foreign nation, to protect such species, whether by predator control, protection of habitat and food supply, or other conservation practices, within any area under its jurisdiction, or on the high seas.

* * *

Oregon Natural Resources Council v. Daley

6 F.Supp.2d 1139 (D.Or.1998).

■ STEWART, UNITED STATES MAGISTRATE JUDGE.

Plaintiffs, a group of environmental organizations, challenge the determination by defendants William M. Daley, the Secretary of Commerce, and Rolland A. Schmitten, the Director of the National Marine Fisheries Service ("NMFS"), that the Oregon Coast evolutionarily significant unit of coho (silver) salmon (*Oncorhynchus kisutch*) ("Oregon Coast ESU") did not warrant listing as a threatened or endangered species under the Endangered Species Act ("ESA"), 16 USC §§ 1531–1544. This determination was based, among other reasons, on the expectation that the recently adopted Oregon Coastal Salmon Restoration Initiative ("OCSRI") would reverse the decline of the Oregon Coast ESU.

* * * All parties have consented to allow a Magistrate Judge to enter final orders and judgment in this case in accordance with FRCP 73 and 28 USC § 636(c).

* * *

On October 20, 1993, several organizations submitted a petition asking the Secretary of Commerce, acting through the NMFS, to add the west coast populations of coho salmon to the endangered or threatened species list. The NMFS subsequently identified six coho salmon evolutionarily significant units ("ESU")[3] that include populations in southern British Columbia, Washington, Oregon, and California. The Oregon Coast ESU includes coho salmon from Oregon coastal drainages between Cape Blanco and the Columbia River. * * *

---

3. The ESA defines "species" to include subspecies and any "distinct population segment of any species of vertebrate fish ... which interbreeds when mature." 16 USC § 1532(16). In 1991, the NMFS issued a policy stating that a Pacific salmonid population would be considered a distinct population segment if it represented an ESU of the biological species. 56 Fed. Reg. 58,612 (Nov 20, 1991). To be considered an ESU, the population must be "substantially reproductively isolated from other conspecific population units," and it must "represent an important component in the evolutionary legacy of the biological species." Id.

On July 25, 1995, the NMFS issued a proposed rule listing three coho salmon ESUs, including the Oregon Coast ESU, as endangered or threatened. * * *

[Subsequently, the NMFS published final rules listing the Central California and Transboundary ESUs as threatened, but determined that the Oregon Coast ESU did not warrant listing. Plaintiffs challenged] the legality of the NMFS's final determination not to list the Oregon Coast ESU as threatened.

* * *

UNDISPUTED FACTS

I. *Status of West Coast Coho Salmon*

During this century, indigenous, naturally reproducing populations of coho salmon "have been extirpated in nearly all Columbia River tributaries and they are in decline in numerous coastal streams throughout Washington, Oregon, and California." 62 Fed. Reg. at 24,588. Natural coho runs in all six ESUs identified by the NMFS on the west coast "are substantially below historic levels." *Id.* For example, Oregon Coast ESU spawning escapements[7] dropped from an estimated 1.0–1.4 million fish in the early 1900s to between 16,500–37,688 fish in 1991–92. However, after 1992, spawner numbers began to increase until they reached 78,343 fish in 1996. * * *

In response to the 1993 petition to list the west coast coho salmon, the NMFS formed the Biological Review Team ("BRT"), a team of 16 scientists, to review the scientific data and conduct a coast-wide status review of this species. On July 5, 1994, the BRT released a report reviewing the status of the coho salmon populations in Oregon * * *. The BRT concluded that the coho salmon populations in the Oregon Coast ESU "are severely depressed relative to historic levels" and ultimately "that a listing is warranted for this ESU." However, the BRT did not consider the effectiveness of any existing or proposed conservation measures.

Two months later on September 2, 1994, the BRT issued another report * * *. The BRT again noted the drastic decline in coho salmon populations within the Oregon Coast ESU and stated that the species "is likely to become endangered in the foreseeable future if present conditions continue."

* * *

II. *The Northwest Forest Plan*

Federal forest lands within the range of the Oregon Coast ESU are managed under the Northwest Forest Plan ("NFP"). The NFP was adopted by the Secretary of Interior and Agriculture on April 13, 1994, as

---

7. "Escapements" are adult salmon leaving the ocean to return to their natal streams to spawn.

Option 9 from the report by the Federal Ecosystem Management Team ("FEMAT").

According to the NMFS, the NFP contains measures * * * that significantly benefit coho salmon on federal lands. However, "the overall effectiveness of the NFP in conserving Oregon and California coho salmon is limited by the extent of Federal land and the fact that Federal land ownership is not uniformly distributed in watersheds within the affected ESUs." In the Oregon Coast ESU, "[f]ederal lands managed under the NFP comprise about 35 percent of the total area."

III. *OCSRI*

In response to the NMFS's proposal to list the Oregon Coast ESU, Oregon's Governor John Kitzhaber launched the OCSRI in October 1995. * * *

* * * [T]he OCSRI contains numerous conservation measures that are designed to improve coho salmon habitat. Some of these had already been implemented, while others had not. Many measures are voluntary, such as the Watershed Councils. * * *

IV. *March 28, 1997 BRT Status Review*

On March 28, 1997, the BRT issued an updated status review in which it evaluated the most recent data and information, excluding "the potential effects of numerous measures in the [Oregon] Plan that may influence freshwater habitat conditions." * * *

The BRT concluded that "[w]hile harvest and hatchery reforms may substantially reduce short-term risk of extinction, habitat protection and restoration were viewed as key to ensuring long-term survival of the ESU...." However, the BRT did not evaluate the freshwater habitat protection measures in the OCSRI.

V. *Memorandum of Agreement*

In April 1997, shortly before the court-ordered deadline for a final listing decision, the NMFS entered into a Memorandum of Agreement ("MOA") with Governor Kitzhaber. The MOA states that "[t]he NMFS has evaluated the OCSRI and believes that some portions will require adjustments early in implementation to ensure that Oregon coastal coho will be sustained, particularly with respect to habitat protection and restoration."

The MOA can be terminated unilaterally by either the NMFS or Oregon at any time "upon 30 days' notice in writing." * * *

VI. *NMFS Staff Recommendations*

On April 1, 1997, Hilda Diaz–Soltero, the Acting Director of NMFS's Office of Protected Resources ("OPR"), wrote to defendant Rolland Schmitten, advising him that NMFS's Northwest and Southwest Regional Directors were considering recommending that the NMFS not list the Oregon Coast ESU in deference to the OCSRI. Ms. Diaz–Soltero expressed OPR's concern "about the biological, policy, and legal implications of" such a decision. She stated that "[i]f the [NMFS] follows these recommendations from the region[ ], it will be setting a bad precedent for future listing actions. NMFS is likely to lose a lawsuit if it follows the regions' likely recommendations because they will be difficult to defend in court."

According to Ms. Diaz–Soltero "[t]he Administrative Record points clearly to the need to list . . . the Oregon Coast ESU[ ] as threatened." She also stated that "[t]he BRT's most recent conclusion should be taken as reason for caution. NMFS should err on the side of the conservation of the species and list it."

The April 1, 1997 memorandum concluded by stating that the OPR "believes that it is unlikely that the [O]CSRI, even if implemented through an MOA, will be sufficient to change the status of coho salmon from 'threatened' to 'not warranted'," and that:

> In all of our conference calls, [the OPR] has heard nothing compelling, including harvest/hatchery provisions of Oregon's CSRI, that would cause it to recommend against listing the Oregon Coast ESU. This stock will not stabilize through harvest and hatchery measures. We must also address freshwater habitat, and to do that, we must list.

* * *

Next, on April 24, 1997, Elizabeth Gaar, Director of the NMFS's Northwest Regional Habitat Conservation Program, transmitted to Jacqueline Wyland, Northwest Regional Protected Species Program Director, an 85–page analysis of the OCSRI's habitat protection measures * * *. That memorandum evaluated and rated each of the OCSRI's habitat protection measures with respect to the 17 habitat factors for decline ("FFD") of the Oregon Coast ESU. The memorandum concluded that 11 FFD have a low likelihood of being reversed by OCSRI measures, six FFD have a moderate likelihood of being reversed, and no FFD has a high likelihood of being reversed. Evaluating whether the "NMFS can determine today that the OCSRI will halt or reverse the downward habitat trend by addressing what NMFS has determined to be the factors for this habitat decline," it concluded that "[i]n many cases . . . based upon what we can determine today, [the OCSRI] does not successfully achieve this goal."

VII.   *The Final Rule*

The next day, on April 25, 1997, the NMFS withdrew its proposed rule issued 20 months earlier to list the Oregon Coast ESU as threatened, and instead determined that the Oregon Coast ESU is not threatened. * * * [T]he final rule concludes that the Oregon Coast ESU "does not warrant listing at this time," explaining:

> The OCSRI contains the tools necessary to ensure that adequate habitat measures are ultimately adopted and implemented: a comprehensive monitoring program, scientific review, and an adaptive management program. Natural escapement has been increasing markedly in recent years and reached 80,000 fish in 1996. *On the basis of the*

harvest and hatchery improvements together with the habitat protections in the NFP and given the improving trends in escapement, the Oregon Coast Coho is not likely to become endangered in the interval between this decision and the adoption of improved habitat measures by the State of Oregon. Under the April 1997 MOA between NMFS and the Governor of Oregon, described in the previous section, NMFS will propose to Oregon additional forest practices modifications necessary to provide adequate habitat conditions for coho. If these or other comparable protections are not adopted within 2 years, NMFS will act promptly to change the ESA status of this ESU to whatever extent may be warranted (emphasis added).

* * *

DISCUSSION

* * * [T]his court concludes that the final rule is based upon an erroneous legal standard and therefore must be set aside. This court also finds that the explanation for the final rule is contrary to the evidence currently available to the NMFS and therefore was arbitrary and capricious.

I. *NMFS Applied the Wrong Legal Standard*

The fatal flaw in the final rule is that the NMFS failed to use the proper legal standard for determining whether the Oregon Coast ESU is threatened. As already noted, a species is threatened if it is "likely to become an endangered species *within the foreseeable future* throughout all or a significant portion of its range." 16 USC § 1532(20) (emphasis added). In concluding that the Oregon Coast ESU is not likely to become endangered, the final rule does not use the words "within the foreseeable future." Instead, it states that "the Oregon Coast coho is not likely to become endangered *in the interval between* this decision and the adoption of improved habitat measures by the State of Oregon."

The ESA does not define the term "foreseeable future." As the appropriate definition for the "foreseeable future," plaintiffs urge this court to require the NMFS to analyze the survival chances of a species over the long term, possibly up to 100 years. The federal defendants disagree with plaintiffs' proposed length of time, but concede that a reasonable time frame for the "foreseeable future" in this case would be the one used in the NFP. That time frame is ten coho life cycles. Since each coho life cycle is three years, this means a total of 30 years.

This court need not decide whether the "foreseeable future" for coho salmon is 30 or 100 years because it is clear that the NMFS only determined that the Oregon Coast ESU would not become endangered within the next two years, falling far short of any reasonable definition of the "foreseeable future." The reference to "the adoption of improved habitat measures by the State of Oregon" means the possible amendments to the State of Oregon's forest practices regulations which may occur in 1999.
* * *

Thus, the NMFS concluded only that the Oregon Coast ESU likely will not become endangered in the two years after issuance of the final rule in May 1997 while the State of Oregon attempts to provide adequate habitat protections. The NMFS reached no conclusion concerning endangerment in the foreseeable future. * * *

The ESA requires a determination as to the likelihood—rather than merely the prospect—that a species will not become endangered in the foreseeable future. In addition, as discussed below, that determination must be based on the current regulatory structure. It is not enough for the NMFS to merely hope that the Oregon Legislature will in fact adopt the requisite forest practices amendments within two years and hope that they may prove to be sufficient to protect the Oregon Coast ESU. * * *

It is incongruous for the NMFS to defer listing a species as "threatened" because the agency is hoping for a significant alteration in the conditions or practices presently threatening the long-term viability of the species, which in turn might prevent the species from actually reaching the "endangered" level. The whole purpose of listing species as "threatened" or "endangered" is not simply to memorialize species that are on the path to extinction, but also to compel those changes needed to save these species from extinction. By definition, a "threatened" species is one that is likely to become endangered in the foreseeable future *barring significant changes in the conditions or practices that are threatening the long-term viability of that species*. A listing decision is intended to cause those significant changes. Accordingly, if the Oregon ESU is likely to become endangered in the foreseeable future unless Oregon implements significant changes in its environmental laws and policies (and even then success is by no means assured), then by definition the Oregon ESU *is* presently a threatened species. At most, the OCSRI may prevent the Oregon Coast ESU from actually reaching the "endangered" level and may ultimately allow the NMFS to delist the species once recovery efforts are far enough along.

* * *

II.   *The Final Rule is Arbitrary and Capricious*

Even if the NMFS had applied the correct legal standard, it acted arbitrarily and capriciously by relying on improper factors and offering an explanation for its decision that runs contrary to the administrative record. * * *

As previously noted, one section of the ESA requires the Secretary to consider five factors in a listing decision; the fourth factor is "the adequacy of existing regulatory mechanisms." 16 USC § 1533(a)(1)(D). The next section of the ESA requires the Secretary to consider these five factors based upon the best available data "after taking into account those efforts, if any, being made by any State ... to protect such species, whether by predator control, protection of habitat and food supply, or other conservation practices." 16 USC § 1533(b)(1)(B). Plaintiffs argue that the two sections read together permit the Secretary to consider only state protective efforts that are regulatory and currently operational, and not state protective efforts that are voluntary in nature and rely on future action. Defendants respond that § 1533(b)(1)(B) does not state that state conservation efforts have to be existing, and only refers to protective measures, not regulatory measures. Thus, defendants conclude that the Secretary may consider state protective efforts even if they are to be taken in the future and rely on voluntary action.

The statutory reference to "existing regulatory mechanisms" in § 1533(a)(1)(D) is precise and unambiguous and, if standing alone, would preclude consideration of any future or voluntary conservation efforts which, by definition, are not "existing" or "regulatory." However, the language of § 1533(b)(1)(B) concerning "efforts" and "other conservation practices" is much broader and, if standing alone, would permit the Secretary to consider non-regulatory efforts. The question is whether § 1533(b)(1)(B) should be read merely to clarify what types of "existing regulatory mechanisms" may be considered as the fourth factor in § 1533(a)(1)(D) or whether it should be interpreted to expand upon the five factors by, in effect, adding yet another factor.

First, with respect to future actions, the answer is straightforward. Even the broad language of § 1533(b)(1)(B) cannot reasonably be interpreted to include future efforts, whether regulatory or non-regulatory. It speaks only in the present tense in terms of "efforts, if any, being made," and not future efforts which have yet to be made. * * *

The more difficult issue is whether the ESA permits consideration of voluntary actions, as opposed to regulatory actions. Since the reference to "regulatory mechanisms" in § 1533(a)(1)(D) could easily include conservation efforts embodied in state regulations, it is difficult to understand why § 1533(b)(1)(B) specifically refers to "efforts" by states to "protect such species, whether by predator control, protection of habitat and food supply, or other conservation practices." Such efforts could be regulatory and, hence, properly considered as "regulatory mechanisms" under § 1533(a)(1)(D). The parties have failed to shed any light on Congressional intent through the use of this language.

* * *

Nevertheless, for the same reason that the Secretary may not rely on future actions, he should not be able to rely on unenforceable efforts. Absent some method of enforcing compliance, protection of a species can never be assured. Voluntary actions, like those planned in the future, are necessarily speculative. * * *

Therefore, voluntary or future conservation efforts by a state should be given no weight in the listing decision. Instead, the NMFS must base its decision on current, enforceable measures. As discussed below, the final rule improperly relied on future and voluntary measures contained in the OCSRI.

* * *

Based upon the concerns of the BRT about the long-term risks to the Oregon Coast ESU from habitat degradation, even assuming that harvest and hatchery measures are fully implemented, habitat measures were critical to the listing decision. * * *

With respect to habitat management, the final rule relied in part upon the NFP * * *. A viability panel established as part of the FEMAT process estimated an 80% likelihood that the measures in the NFP would be sufficient to allow coho salmon to stabilize on federal land. The NMFS Habitat Conservation Program evaluated the NFP and found that many of the FFD of coho salmon have a high to moderate likelihood of being reversed on federal land. Thus, the administrative record supports the adequacy of the habitat measures in the NFP.

Nevertheless, as previously noted, federal lands comprise only 35% of the total land within the Oregon Coast ESU. Given the large quantity of habitat on non-federal lands, the NMFS concedes in the final rule that the effectiveness of the NFP is inherently limited * * *.

[The NMFS relied on the OCSRI for habitat protection outside federal land. However] the NMFS explicitly recognized that the habitat measures of the OCSRI are not currently adequate, although they might prove to be adequate in the future:

> Overall, however, the habitat measures of the OCSRI *do not currently provide* the protections NMFS considers essential to creating and maintaining the high quality habitat needed to sustain Oregon Coast coho over the long term across a range of environmental conditions. The OCSRI contains the tools necessary to ensure that adequate habitat measures are ultimately adopted and implemented (emphasis added).

This is very faint praise for the OCSRI. Even the tools in the OCSRI for ensuring future habitat protection did not provide a high level of assurance to the NMFS. * * *

Therefore, the NMFS entered into the MOA with Governor Kitzhaber. However, as already noted, the problem of future and voluntary action extends to the entire MOA, which not only requires future action by the State of Oregon, but also can be terminated by either party with 30 days notice. Although the NMFS has no incentive to terminate the MOA, Oregon might. If the political winds change, and Governor Kitzhaber is replaced by a governor who does not support the OCSRI or MOA, nothing would prevent Oregon from terminating the MOA and not adopting improved habitat measures.

The final rule itself admits that "the determination not to list the Oregon Coast ESU relies heavily on continued implementation of the OCSRI (in accordance with the MOA), including the enactment of improved habitat measures." Thus, the final rule is premised upon promises of future, as well as voluntary actions, the ability of which to protect and restore the Oregon Coast ESU is necessarily speculative and uncertain. This court declines to tie the fate of the Oregon Coast ESU to the whim of politics and promises of future state conservation actions that may be years or decades away from implementation.

* * *

Even more telling are the recommendations of the OPR, as encompassed by Ms. Diaz–Soltero's letters, that the habitat measures are insufficient to support a "no list" decision. While this court declines plaintiffs' invitation to delve into the structure of the NMFS and determine to which staff members the Secretary should defer regarding ESA matters, the memoranda highlight the dissatisfaction with the OCSRI among NMFS staff members. Indeed, the administrative record is replete with documents from the NMFS that are critical of the OCSRI. Although this factor alone does not render the NMFS's decision arbitrary and capricious, it serves to cast doubt on the legitimacy of its reasons for failing to list the Oregon Coast ESU as threatened.

However laudable Oregon's efforts to employ new management techniques to try to restore the Oregon Coast ESU, such future, voluntary conservation efforts cannot be a legal substitute for listing. There is simply no rational basis for the NMFS to assume that Oregon will adopt any, much less adequate, habitat measures. Further, at this point the NMFS cannot possibly judge the effectiveness of any voluntary measures that Oregon does implement because they have not been tested. In short, whether the OCSRI's and MOA's habitat measures can succeed over the long term is currently unknown and unknowable. Any rational listing decision requires the testing of conservation measures to determine their effectiveness in protecting a species. Should the OCSRI ultimately achieve the results its proponents predict, the Oregon Coast ESU may be delisted.

Regardless of the adequacy of habitat measures, defendants argue that the NMFS's decision was reasonable due to the harvest and hatchery measures. They note that the BRT was evenly split as to whether full implementation of the harvest and hatchery measures would be sufficient to move the Oregon Coast ESU out of the threatened category and that most of the harvest and hatchery measures are already implemented. Thus, they conclude that based on the conflicting scientific evidence, the NMFS could reasonably decide not to list the Oregon Coast ESU as threatened.

This court accepts the proposition that in the event of a scientific disagreement between experts, the Secretary is free to rely on the expert opinion of his choice. Nonetheless, defendants' argument fails for two reasons.

First, even though many of the harvest reforms have already been implemented, their future is uncertain. The harvest measures contained in the OCSRI are "only a 4–year (1997–2000) interim proposal, and [have] no guarantee beyond 2000." The MOA was implemented partly as a response to concern that these measures would not continue past the year 2000. In the MOA, Oregon commits to continue the harvest measures beyond 2000 unless the NMFS approves any proposed changes. However, the ability of

Oregon to terminate the MOA with 30 days notice hardly constitutes a reasonable assurance that the measures will continue.

Second, the opinion by half of the BRT that the OCSRI's harvest and hatchery measures were sufficient to move the Oregon Coast ESU out of the threatened category was premised on full implementation of the harvest and hatchery measures. However, an overarching "strong concern" of the BRT was "[u]ncertainty regarding the true extent of hatchery influence on natural populations." In the final rule, the NMFS itself cautions that while Oregon's Wild Fish Management Policy, adopted in 1994, has improved hatchery operations in Oregon, "full and prompt implementation of the policy has not occurred." 62 Fed. Reg. at 24,598. In any event, many of the hatchery measures were already in place by July 1995 when the NMFS issued its proposed rule listing the Oregon Coast ESU as threatened. The final rule fails to explain what happened after July 1995 that turned the hatchery measures into a basis to not list the Oregon Coast ESU.

In fact, the final rule in general appears to be very pessimistic regarding the status of the Oregon Coast ESU. It accepts the conclusions regarding the general decline of the Oregon Coast ESU, emphasizes the importance of habitat measures, and finds the OSCRI to be inadequate. Thus, to say that the NMFS merely resolved a conflict between conflicting conclusions of BRT scientists is disingenuous at best.

* * *

CONCLUSION

The NMFS's ultimate conclusion not to list the Oregon Coast ESU flies in the face of its express concerns regarding the OCSRI. The wait-and-see stance of the NMFS has no support in the ESA or case law. Instead of placing the risk on the future and voluntary conservation measures proposed by the OCSRI, the NMFS unlawfully placed the risk of failure squarely on the species. Thus, this court finds the NMFS's final rule regarding the Oregon Coast ESU was arbitrary and capricious and remands this matter back to the NMFS for further consideration consistent with this Opinion.

NOTES AND QUESTIONS

1. *Numbers of Endangered Species.* As of February 2001, 971 U.S. species were listed as endangered and 273 as threatened. (The "box-score" of listed species, updated monthly, is available on the FWS web site, at http://endangered.fws.gov/boxscore.html.) The listing of more than 200 additional species has been found to be "warranted but precluded" by work on higher priority species. See 16 U.S.C. § 1533(b)(3)(B)(iii). This backlog persists because the Services are chronically short of funds for listing activities. Many other species may be at significant risk but are not listed either because of lack of information or because of political opposition to listing.

2. *Science and Listing Decisions.* ESA section 4(b)(1) requires that listing decisions be made "solely on the basis of the best scientific and commercial information available." Commercial information in this context refers to scientific data supplied by industry sources. Congress intended listing decisions to be entirely scientific and objective. Is that possible, though? Listing requires two major determinations: 1) delineation of a group meeting the statutory definition of "species;" and 2) determination that the group is at sufficient risk of extinction to qualify as "endangered" or "threatened." Neither is entirely scientific. The first requires identification of the purposes for which species should be saved, and evaluation of the extent to which individual groups serve those purposes. The second requires choices about acceptable extinction risk. For an argument that hiding these policy choices behind a curtain of scientific objectivity has undesirable consequences, see Holly Doremus, Listing Decisions Under the Endangered Species Act: Why Better Science Isn't Always Better Policy, 75 Wash. U. L.Q. 1029 (1997). How scientific were the judgments made by NMFS in the coho salmon listing decisions reviewed in *ONRC v. Daley*? How much did the scientific expertise of the agency or nature of the decisions affect the standard of judicial review?

3. *Coho Salmon and the Oregon Salmon Plan.* According to the district court, what precisely was wrong with NMFS's decision not to list the Oregon coastal coho? Under what circumstances can state, local, or federal regulations designed to protect the species justify refusal to list? Does it matter that regulations can always be changed by the agency or legislature that created them? Must the Services offer evidence that any regulatory measures they rely on will remain in effect for the foreseeable future? Can the Services ever consider protective measures that have not yet been implemented? Can they give any weight to measures that are not regulatory, such as economic incentives to conserve habitat? The Services recently issued a draft policy explaining that they will consider both future and non-regulatory conservation efforts in listing decisions. In deciding what weight to give those efforts, the Services will take into account the likelihood that they will be implemented and the likelihood that they will prove effective. 65 Fed. Reg. 37102, 3710–05 (June 13, 2000). Is this policy legal? Is it desirable?

4. *Endangered Versus Threatened.* According to the statutory definition, what is the difference between an endangered and a threatened species? Does it matter to which category a species is assigned? While the prohibitions of section 9 apply by their terms only to endangered species, section 4(d) directs the Services to issue such regulations as they deem "necessary and advisable to provide for the conservation" of threatened species. Under this provision, the Services can relax some of the prohibitions in section 9 with respect to threatened species, provided they find that those prohibitions are not needed for the species to make progress toward recovery. FWS has generally given threatened species the full protection of section 9. See 50 C.F.R. § 17.31. NMFS, which has far fewer listings to deal with, commonly issues detailed special rules for threatened species.

5. *Critical Habitat.* Concurrent with listing, to the maximum extent prudent and determinable, the ESA directs the Services to designate critical habitat. ESA § 4(a)(3), 16 U.S.C. § 1533(a)(3). Critical habitat includes areas containing physical or biological features essential to the conservation of the species which may require special management protection. ESA § 3(5), 16 U.S.C. § 1532(5). Areas outside the species' range at the time of listing may be included only if the Services determine they are essential for the conservation of the species. Id. In determining critical habitat, the Services must consider economic and other impacts. ESA § 4(b)(2), 16 U.S.C. § 1533(b)(2).

Despite the strong wording of the law, the Services have designated critical habitat for less than 10% of listed species. Critical habitat designation has proven to be a flashpoint for political controversy, and the Services contend that the costs of determining critical habitat far outweigh its conservation benefits. In 1996, the Services issued a listing priority guidance placing critical habitat designation behind all other listing actions. For the next several years, they made virtually no critical habitat designations. A steady stream of lawsuits and judicial orders to designate critical habitat followed. FWS then declared that court orders to designate critical habitat would preclude any action on new listing petitions for fiscal year 2001.

The Services believe destruction or adverse modification of critical habitat will almost always violate the no jeopardy prong of section 7. Based on the statutory definition of critical habitat, do you agree? Might critical habitat designation have other potential benefits? Do its benefits justify the costs? For a thoughtful discussion of the critical habitat problem, see Jason M. Patlis, Paying Tribute to Joseph Heller with the Endangered Species Act: When Critical Habitat Isn't, 20 Stan. Envtl. L. J. 133 (2001).

CLASS DISCUSSION PROBLEM: SONAR AND WHALES

The United States Navy has spent more than ten years and $350 million developing a highly sensitive submarine detection system using low frequency active sonar (LFAS) technology. The system uses underwater speakers towed behind ships to generate extremely loud low frequency sound waves, which travel great distances underwater, bouncing back from objects in their path. By sweeping the ocean with intense, low frequency sonar, the Navy can detect modern quiet submarines over vast areas.

The Navy is now ready to deploy up to four ships towing LFAS arrays, but the proposal has run into considerable controversy. A recent test of a mid-frequency sonar near the Bahamas coincided with a rash of whale beachings. Autopsies on several whales revealed inner ear damage which could have been caused by exposure to high-intensity underwater sound. The Navy proposes to deploy the LFAS system world-wide; several endangered whale and sea turtle species live in waters where LFAS might be used.

If the Navy simply deploys the LFAS system, will it violate the ESA? What, if anything, must it do to satisfy the ESA? Who could challenge deployment? What would a plaintiff have to prove? What relief would be available?

Under the Coastal Zone Management Act, federal actions affecting the coastal zone of a state with an approved coastal zone management plan must be consistent with that approved plan. The federal agency must submit a consistency determination to the state coastal management body. See 16 U.S.C. § 1456. If the state body does not respond within 60 days, it is presumed to concur with the consistency determination. If the state objects, the federal agency may proceed at risk of a judicial finding of inconsistency, enter into mediation of the disagreement, or seek a presidential exemption.

The Navy has submitted a consistency determination to the California Coastal Commission for LFAS operations off the California coast. If the Commission concurs with that determination, does it risk ESA liability?

3.　THE PROHIBITION ON TAKE

Excerpts from the Endangered Species Act

16 U.S.C. § 1531–1544.

Sec. 3　Definitions

* * *

(19) The term "take" means to harass, harm, pursue, hunt, shoot, wound, kill, trap, capture, or collect, or to attempt to engage in any such conduct.

* * *

Sec. 9　Prohibited Acts

(a)(1) Except as provided in [section 10], with respect to any endangered species of fish or wildlife * * * it is unlawful for any person subject to the jurisdiction of the United States to—

* * *

(B) take any such species within the United States or the territorial sea of the United States;

* * *

(g) It is unlawful for any person subject to the jurisdiction of the United States to attempt to commit, solicit another to commit or cause to be committed, any offense defined in this section.

Excerpts from Fish and Wildlife Service regulations

50 C.F.R. Part 17.

Sec. 17.3　Definitions

* * *

Harm in the definition of "take" in the Act means an act which actually kills or injures wildlife. Such act may include significant habitat modification or degradation where it actually kills or injures wildlife by significantly impairing essential behavioral patterns, including breeding, feeding or sheltering.

* * *

Babbitt v. Sweet Home Chapter of Communities for a Great Oregon

United States Supreme Court, 1995.
515 U.S. 687, 115 S.Ct. 2407, 132 L.Ed.2d 597.

■ JUSTICE STEVENS delivered the opinion of the Court.

The Endangered Species Act of 1973 (ESA or Act) contains a variety of protections designed to save from extinction species that the Secretary of the Interior designates as endangered or threatened. Section 9 of the Act makes it unlawful for any person to "take" any endangered or threatened species. The Secretary has promulgated a regulation that defines the statute's prohibition on takings to include "significant habitat modification or degradation where it actually kills or injures wildlife." This case presents the question whether the Secretary exceeded his authority under the Act by promulgating that regulation.

I

* * *

Respondents in this action are small landowners, logging companies, and families dependent on the forest products industries in the Pacific Northwest and in the Southeast, and organizations that represent their interests. They brought this declaratory judgment action against petitioners, the Secretary of the Interior and the Director of the Fish and Wildlife Service, in the United States District Court for the District of Columbia to challenge the statutory validity of the Secretary's regulation defining "harm," particularly the inclusion of habitat modification and degradation in the definition. Respondents challenged the regulation on its face. Their complaint alleged that application of the "harm" regulation to the red-cockaded woodpecker, an endangered species, and the northern spotted owl, a threatened species, had injured them economically.

Respondents advanced three arguments to support their submission that Congress did not intend the word "take" in § 9 to include habitat modification, as the Secretary's "harm" regulation provides. First, they correctly noted that language in the Senate's original version of the ESA would have defined "take" to include "destruction, modification, or curtailment of [the] habitat or range" of fish or wildlife, but the Senate deleted that language from the bill before enacting it. Second, respondents argued that Congress intended the Act's express authorization for the Federal

Government to buy private land in order to prevent habitat degradation in § 5 to be the exclusive check against habitat modification on private property. Third, because the Senate added the term "harm" to the definition of "take" in a floor amendment without debate, respondents argued that the court should not interpret the term so expansively as to include habitat modification.

The District Court considered and rejected each of respondents' arguments, finding "that Congress intended an expansive interpretation of the word 'take,' an interpretation that encompasses habitat modification." The court noted that in 1982, when Congress was aware of a judicial decision that had applied the Secretary's regulation, it amended the Act without using the opportunity to change the definition of "take." The court stated that, even had it found the ESA "silent or ambiguous" as to the authority for the Secretary's definition of "harm," it would nevertheless have upheld the regulation as a reasonable interpretation of the statute. The District Court therefore entered summary judgment for petitioners and dismissed respondents' complaint.

A divided panel of the Court of Appeals initially affirmed the judgment of the District Court. After granting a petition for rehearing, however, the panel reversed. Although acknowledging that "[t]he potential breadth of the word 'harm' is indisputable," the majority concluded that the immediate statutory context in which "harm" appeared counseled against a broad reading; like the other words in the definition of "take," the word "harm" should be read as applying only to "the perpetrator's direct application of force against the animal taken." * * *

The Court of Appeals' decision created a square conflict with a 1988 decision of the Ninth Circuit that had upheld the Secretary's definition of "harm." See Palila v. Hawaii Dept. of Land and Natural Resources, 852 F.2d 1106 (1988) (*Palila II*). The Court of Appeals neither cited nor distinguished *Palila II*, despite the stark contrast between the Ninth Circuit's holding and its own. We granted certiorari to resolve the conflict. Our consideration of the text and structure of the Act, its legislative history, and the significance of the 1982 amendment persuades us that the Court of Appeals' judgment should be reversed.

II

* * *

The text of the Act provides three reasons for concluding that the Secretary's interpretation is reasonable. First, an ordinary understanding of the word "harm" supports it. The dictionary definition of the verb form of "harm" is "to cause hurt or damage to: injure." In the context of the ESA, that definition naturally encompasses habitat modification that results in actual injury or death to members of an endangered or threatened species.

Respondents argue that the Secretary should have limited the purview of "harm" to direct applications of force against protected species, but the dictionary definition does not include the word "directly" or suggest in any way that only direct or willful action that leads to injury constitutes "harm." Moreover, unless the statutory term "harm" encompasses indirect as well as direct injuries, the word has no meaning that does not duplicate the meaning of other words that § 3 uses to define "take." A reluctance to treat statutory terms as surplusage supports the reasonableness of the Secretary's interpretation.

Second, the broad purpose of the ESA supports the Secretary's decision to extend protection against activities that cause the precise harms Congress enacted the statute to avoid. In *TVA v. Hill*, 437 U.S. 153 (1978), we described the Act as "the most comprehensive legislation for the preservation of endangered species ever enacted by any nation." Whereas predecessor statutes enacted in 1966 and 1969 had not contained any sweeping prohibition against the taking of endangered species except on federal lands, the 1973 Act applied to all land in the United States and to the Nation's territorial seas. As stated in § 2 of the Act, among its central purposes is "to provide a means whereby the ecosystems upon which endangered species and threatened species depend may be conserved...." 16 U.S.C. § 1531(b).

In *Hill*, we construed § 7 as precluding the completion of the Tellico Dam because of its predicted impact on the survival of the snail darter. Both our holding and the language in our opinion stressed the importance of the statutory policy. "The plain intent of Congress in enacting this statute," we recognized, "was to halt and reverse the trend toward species extinction, whatever the cost. This is reflected not only in the stated policies of the Act, but in literally every section of the statute." Although the § 9 "take" prohibition was not at issue in *Hill*, we took note of that prohibition, placing particular emphasis on the Secretary's inclusion of habitat modification in his definition of "harm." In light of that provision for habitat protection, we could "not understand how TVA intends to operate Tellico Dam without 'harming' the snail darter." Congress' intent to provide comprehensive protection for endangered and threatened species supports the permissibility of the Secretary's "harm" regulation.

Respondents advance strong arguments that activities that cause minimal or unforeseeable harm will not violate the Act as construed in the "harm" regulation. Respondents, however, present a facial challenge to the regulation. Thus, they ask us to invalidate the Secretary's understanding of "harm" in every circumstance, even when an actor knows that an activity, such as draining a pond, would actually result in the extinction of a listed species by destroying its habitat. Given Congress' clear expression of the ESA's broad purpose to protect endangered and threatened wildlife, the Secretary's definition of "harm" is reasonable.[13]

---

13. The dissent incorrectly assets that the Secretary's regulation "dispenses with the foreseeability of harm" * * *. [T]he regulation merely implements the statute, and it is therefore subject to the statute's "knowingly violates" language and ordinary requirements of proximate causation and foreseeability. * * *

Third, the fact that Congress in 1982 authorized the Secretary to issue permits for takings that § 9(a)(1)(B) would otherwise prohibit, "if such taking is incidental to, and not the purpose of, the carrying out of an otherwise lawful activity," strongly suggests that Congress understood § 9(a)(1)(B) to prohibit indirect as well as deliberate takings. * * * No one could seriously request an "incidental" take permit to avert § 9 liability for direct, deliberate action against a member of an endangered or threatened species, but respondents would read "harm" so narrowly that the permit procedure would have little more than that absurd purpose. "When Congress acts to amend a statute, we presume it intends its amendment to have real and substantial effect." Congress' addition of the § 10 permit provision supports the Secretary's conclusion that activities not intended to harm an endangered species, such as habitat modification, may constitute unlawful takings under the ESA unless the Secretary permits them.

* * *

We need not decide whether the statutory definition of "take" compels the Secretary's interpretation of "harm," because our conclusions that Congress did not unambiguously manifest its intent to adopt respondents' view and that the Secretary's interpretation is reasonable suffice to decide this case. See generally Chevron U.S.A. Inc. v. Natural Resources Defense Council, Inc., 467 U.S. 837 (1984). The latitude the ESA gives the Secretary in enforcing the statute, together with the degree of regulatory expertise necessary to its enforcement, establishes that we owe some degree of deference to the Secretary's reasonable interpretation.

III

Our conclusion that the Secretary's definition of "harm" rests on a permissible construction of the ESA gains further support from the legislative history of the statute. The Committee Reports accompanying the bills that became the ESA do not specifically discuss the meaning of "harm," but they make clear that Congress intended "take" to apply broadly to cover indirect as well as purposeful actions. The Senate Report stressed that " '[t]ake' is defined . . . in the broadest possible manner to include every conceivable way in which a person can 'take' or attempt to 'take' any fish or wildlife." The House Report stated that "the broadest possible terms" were used to define restrictions on takings. The House Report underscored the breadth of the "take" definition by noting that it included "harassment, *whether intentional or not*." (emphasis added) The Report explained that the definition "would allow, for example, the Secretary to regulate or prohibit the activities of birdwatchers where the effect of those activities might disturb the birds and make it difficult for them to hatch or raise their young." These comments, ignored in the dissent's welcome but selective foray into legislative history, support the Secretary's interpretation that the term "take" in § 9 reached far more than the deliberate actions of hunters and trappers.

* * *

The definition of "take" that originally appeared in S. 1983 differed from the definition as ultimately enacted in one other significant respect: It included "the destruction, modification, or curtailment of [the] habitat or range" of fish and wildlife. Respondents make much of the fact that the Commerce Committee removed this phrase from the "take" definition before S. 1983 went to the floor. We do not find that fact especially significant. The legislative materials contain no indication why the habitat protection provision was deleted. That provision differed greatly from the regulation at issue today. Most notably, the habitat protection in S. 1983 would have applied far more broadly than the regulation does because it made adverse habitat modification a categorical violation of the "take" prohibition, unbounded by the regulation's limitation to habitat modifications that actually kill or injure wildlife. The S. 1983 language also failed to qualify "modification" with the regulation's limiting adjective "significant." We do not believe the Senate's unelaborated disavowal of the provision in S. 1983 undermines the reasonableness of the more moderate habitat protection in the Secretary's "harm" regulation.

* * *

IV

When it enacted the ESA, Congress delegated broad administrative and interpretive power to the Secretary. The task of defining and listing endangered and threatened species requires an expertise and attention to detail that exceeds the normal province of Congress. Fashioning appropriate standards for issuing permits under § 10 for takings that would otherwise violate § 9 necessarily requires the exercise of broad discretion. The proper interpretation of a term such as "harm" involves a complex policy choice. When Congress has entrusted the Secretary with broad discretion, we are especially reluctant to substitute our views of wise policy for his. See *Chevron*, 467 U.S. at 865–866. In this case, that reluctance accords with our conclusion, based on the text, structure, and legislative history of the ESA, that the Secretary reasonably construed the intent of Congress when he defined "harm" to include "significant habitat modification or degradation that actually kills or injures wildlife."

In the elaboration and enforcement of the ESA, the Secretary and all persons who must comply with the law will confront difficult questions of proximity and degree; for, as all recognize, the Act encompasses a vast range of economic and social enterprises and endeavors. These questions must be addressed in the usual course of the law, through case-by-case resolution and adjudication.

The judgment of the Court of Appeals is reversed.

■ JUSTICE O'CONNOR, concurring.

My agreement with the Court is founded on two understandings. First, the challenged regulation is limited to significant habitat modification that causes actual, as opposed to hypothetical or speculative, death or injury to identifiable protected animals. Second, even setting aside difficult questions of scienter, the regulation's application is limited by ordinary principles of proximate causation, which introduce notions of foreseeability. These limitations, in my view, call into question Palila v. Hawaii Dept. of Land and Natural Resources, 852 F.2d 1106 (C.A.9 1988) (*Palila II*), and with it, many of the applications derided by the dissent. Because there is no need to strike a regulation on a facial challenge out of concern that it is susceptible of erroneous application, however, and because there are many habitat-related circumstances in which the regulation might validly apply, I join the opinion of the Court.

* * *

As an initial matter, I do not find it as easy as Justice Scalia does to dismiss the notion that significant impairment of breeding injures living creatures. To raze the last remaining ground on which the piping plover currently breeds, thereby making it impossible for any piping plovers to reproduce, would obviously injure the population (causing the species' extinction in a generation). But by completely preventing breeding, it would also injure the individual living bird, in the same way that sterilizing the creature injures the individual living bird. To "injure" is, among other things, "to impair." One need not subscribe to theories of "psychic harm" to recognize that to make it impossible for an animal to reproduce is to impair its most essential physical functions and to render that animal, and its genetic material, biologically obsolete. This, in my view, is actual injury.

* * *

In my view, then, the "harm" regulation applies where significant habitat modification, by impairing essential behaviors, proximately (foreseeably) causes actual death or injury to identifiable animals that are protected under the Endangered Species Act. Pursuant to my interpretation, *Palila II*—under which the Court of Appeals held that a state agency committed a "taking" by permitting mouflon sheep to eat mamane-naio seedlings that, when full-grown, might have fed and sheltered endangered palila—was wrongly decided according to the regulation's own terms. Destruction of the seedlings did not proximately cause actual death or injury to identifiable birds; it merely prevented the regeneration of forest land not currently sustaining actual birds.

This case, of course, comes to us as a facial challenge. We are charged with deciding whether the regulation on its face exceeds the agency's statutory mandate. I have identified at least one application of the regulation (*Palila II*) that is, in my view, inconsistent with the regulation's *own* limitations. That misapplication does not, however, call into question the validity of the regulation itself. One can doubtless imagine questionable applications of the regulation that test the limits of the agency's authority. However, it seems to me clear that the regulation does not on its terms exceed the agency's mandate, and that the regulation has innumerable valid habitat-related applications. Congress may, of course, see fit to revisit this issue. And nothing the Court says today prevents the agency itself from narrowing the scope of its regulation at a later date.

With this understanding, I join the Court's opinion.

■ JUSTICE SCALIA, with whom THE CHIEF JUSTICE and JUSTICE THOMAS join, dissenting.

I think it unmistakably clear that the legislation at issue here (1) forbade the hunting and killing of endangered animals, and (2) provided federal lands and federal funds *for the acquisition of private lands*, to preserve the habitat of endangered animals. The Court's holding that the hunting and killing prohibition incidentally preserves habitat on private lands imposes unfairness to the point of financial ruin—not just upon the rich, but upon the simplest farmer who finds his land conscripted to national zoological use. I respectfully dissent.

* * *

The Endangered Species Act is a carefully considered piece of legislation that forbids all persons to hunt or harm endangered animals, but places upon the public at large, rather than upon fortuitously accountable individual landowners, the cost of preserving the habitat of endangered species. There is neither textual support for, nor even evidence of congressional consideration of, the radically different disposition contained in the regulation that the Court sustains. For these reasons, I respectfully dissent.

Strahan v. Coxe

United States Court of Appeals, First Circuit, 1997.
127 F.3d 155.

■ TORRUELLA, CHIEF JUDGE.

In April 1995, Richard Strahan ("Strahan") filed suit against Trudy Coxe, Secretary of the Massachusetts Executive Office of Environmental Affairs, John Phillips, Commissioner of the Massachusetts Department of Fisheries, Wildlife, and Environmental Law Enforcement, and Philip Coates, Director of the Massachusetts Division of Marine Fisheries (together "defendants"), claiming that these Massachusetts state officers were violating the federal Endangered Species Act ("ESA") * * *. Strahan sought a preliminary injunction ordering the Commonwealth to revoke licenses and permits it had issued authorizing gillnet and lobster pot fishing and barring the Commonwealth from issuing such licenses and permits in the future unless it received "incidental take" * * * permits from the National Marine Fisheries Service ("NMFS") under the ESA * * *. Defendants moved to dismiss Strahan's complaint and, in the alternative, for summary judgment.

On September 24, 1996, the district court: (1) denied defendants' motion for summary judgment on Strahan's ESA claims; * * * and (3) granted summary judgment on Strahan's ESA claims * * *. In this ruling, the district court declined to grant the preliminary injunctive measures sought by Strahan. Instead, the court issued a preliminary injunction ordering defendants to: (1) "apply for an incidental take permit [under the ESA] from NMFS ... for Northern Right whales"; * * * (3) "develop and prepare a proposal ... to restrict, modify or eliminate the use of fixed-fishing gear in coastal waters of Massachusetts listed as critical habitat for Northern Right whales in order to minimize the likelihood additional whales will actually be harmed by such gear"; and (4) "convene an Endangered Whale Working Group and to engage in substantive discussions with the Plaintiff [Strahan], or his representative, as well as with other interested parties, regarding modifications of fixed-fishing gear and other measures to minimize harm to the Northern Right whales." Defendants appeal the district court's preliminary injunction order. Plaintiff Strahan cross-appeals the district court's: (1) refusal to grant him the precise injunctive relief sought * * *.

BACKGROUND

I.   Status of the Northern Right whale

* * * Northern Right whales are the most endangered of the large whales, presently numbering around 300. Entanglement with commercial fishing gear has been recognized as a major source of human-caused injury or death to the Northern Right whale. Collision with ships is also a significant cause of Northern Right whale death.

The majority of Northern Right whales are present in Massachusetts waters only during spring feeding. The district court found, based on statements made by defendants as well as on affidavits from three scientists, that Northern Right whales have been entangled in fixed fishing gear in Massachusetts coastal waters at least nine times. Moreover, a Northern Right whale mortality was reported off Cape Cod, Massachusetts in May 1996.

* * *

II.   Massachusetts' regulatory authority scheme

The Massachusetts Division of Marine Fisheries ("DMF") is vested with broad authority to regulate fishing in Massachusetts's coastal waters, which extend three nautical miles from the shoreline. Nearly all commercial fishing vessels must receive a permit from DMF in order to take fish, including shellfish, from Massachusetts coastal waters. * * *

STANDARD OF REVIEW

In ruling on a motion for preliminary injunction, a district court is charged with considering:

(1) the likelihood of success on the merits; (2) the potential for irreparable harm if the injunction is denied; (3) the balance of relevant impositions, i.e., the hardship to the nonmovant if enjoined as contrasted with the hardship to the movant if no injunction issues; and (4) the effect (if any) of the court's ruling on the public interest.

Ross–Simons of Warwick, Inc. v. Baccarat, Inc., 102 F.3d 12, 15 (1st Cir.1996). Under the ESA, however, the balancing and public interest prongs have been answered by Congress' determination that the "balance of hardships and the public interest tips heavily in favor of protected species." National Wildlife Fed'n v. Burlington Northern R.R., 23 F.3d 1508, 1510 (9th Cir.1994). Our review of the district court's ruling on a motion for preliminary injunction is deferential and, "unless the appellant can show that the lower court misapprehended the law or committed a palpable abuse of discretion, the court of appeals will not intervene." Ross–Simons of Warwick, Inc., 102 F.3d at 16.

DISCUSSION

* * *

II.   Endangered Species Act

A.   Statutory and regulatory background

The Endangered Species Act was enacted with the purpose of conserving endangered and threatened species and the ecosystems on which they depend. See 16 U.S.C. § 1531. The ESA is "the most comprehensive legislation for the preservation of endangered species ever enacted by any nation." TVA v. Hill, 437 U.S. 153, 180, 98 S.Ct. 2279, 2294, 57 L.Ed.2d 117 (1978). * * * The Northern Right whale has been listed as endangered pursuant to the ESA.

* * *

B.   Legal challenges

The district court's reasoning, in finding that Massachusetts' commercial fishing regulatory scheme likely exacted a taking in violation of the ESA, was founded on two provisions of the ESA read in conjunction. The first relates to the definition of the prohibited activity of a "taking," see § 1538(a)(1)(B), and the second relates to the solicitation or causation by a third party of a prohibited activity, such as a taking, see § 1538(g). The district court viewed these provisions, when read together, to apply to acts by third parties that allow or authorize acts that exact a taking and that, but for the permitting process, could not take place. Indeed, the district court cited several opinions that have also so held. See, e.g., Sierra Club v. Yeutter, 926 F.2d 429, 438–39 (5th Cir.1991) (finding Forest Service's management of timber stands was a taking of the red-cockaded woodpecker in violation of the ESA); Defenders of Wildlife v. EPA, 882 F.2d 1294, 1301 (8th Cir.1989) (holding that the EPA's registration of pesticides containing strychnine violated the ESA, both because endangered species had died from ingesting strychnine bait and because that strychnine could only be distributed pursuant to the EPA's registration scheme); Palila v. Hawaii Dep't of Land and Nat. Resources, 639 F.2d 495, 497–98 (9th Cir.1981) (holding state's practice of maintaining feral goats and sheep in palila's habitat constituted a taking and ordering state to remove goats and sheep); Loggerhead Turtle v. County Council of Volusia County, 896 F.Supp. 1170, 1180–81 (M.D.Fla.1995) (holding that county's authorization of vehicular beach access during turtle mating season exacted a taking of the turtles in violation of the ESA). The statute not only prohibits the acts of those parties that directly exact the taking, but also bans those acts of a third party that bring about the acts exacting a taking. We believe that, contrary to the defendants' argument on appeal, the district court properly found that a governmental third party pursuant to whose authority an actor directly exacts a taking of an endangered species may be deemed to have violated the provisions of the ESA.

The defendants argue that the statute was not intended to prohibit state licensure activity because such activity cannot be a "proximate cause" of the taking. The defendants direct our attention to long-standing principles of common law tort in arguing that the district court improperly found that its regulatory scheme "indirectly causes" these takings. Specifically, the defendants contend that to construe the proper meaning of "cause" under the ESA, this court should look to common law principles of causation and further contend that proximate cause is lacking here. The defendants are correct that when interpreting a term in a statute which is, like "cause" here, well-known to the common law, the court is to presume that Congress intended the meaning to be interpreted as in the common law. We do not believe, however, that an interpretation of "cause" that includes the "indirect causation" of a taking by the Commonwealth through its licensing scheme falls without the normal boundaries.

The defendants protest this interpretation. Their first argument is that the Commonwealth's licensure of a generally permitted activity does not cause the taking any more than its licensure of automobiles and drivers solicits or causes federal crimes, even though automobiles it licenses are surely used to violate federal drug laws, rob federally insured banks, or cross state lines for the purpose of violating state and federal laws. The answer to this argument is that, whereas it is possible for a person licensed by Massachusetts to use a car in a manner that does not risk the violations of federal law suggested by the defendants, it is not possible for a licensed commercial fishing operation to use its gillnets or lobster pots in the manner permitted by the Commonwealth without risk of violating the ESA by exacting a taking. Thus, the state's licensure of gillnet and lobster pot fishing does not involve the intervening independent actor that is a necessary component of the other licensure schemes which it argues are comparable. Where the state has licensed an automobile driver to use that automobile and her license in a manner consistent with both state and federal law, the violation of federal law is caused only by the actor's conscious and independent decision to disregard or go beyond the licensed purposes of her automobile use and instead to violate federal, and possibly state, law. The situation is simply not the same here. In this instance, the state has licensed commercial fishing operations to use gillnets and lobster pots in specifically the manner that is likely to result in a violation of federal law. The causation here, while indirect, is not so removed that it extends outside the realm of causation as it is understood in the common law.

The defendants' next argument need only detain us momentarily. They contend that the statutory structure of the ESA does not envision utilizing the regulatory structures of the states in order to implement its provisions, but that it instead leaves that implementing authority to NMFS. The point that the defendants miss is that the district court's ruling does not impose positive obligations on the Commonwealth by converting its regulation of commercial fishing operations into a tool of the federal ESA regulatory scheme. The Commonwealth is not being compelled to enforce the provisions of the ESA. Instead, the district court's ruling seeks to end the Commonwealth's continuing violation of the Act.[3]

Defendants also contend that the district court's ruling is erroneous because it fails to give deference to the position of NMFS, the federal agency charged with enforcing the ESA. The defendants' position is flawed for two reasons. First, the ESA gives NMFS, through the Secretary, discretion in authorizing takings incidental to certain commercial activity; the Act does not give a federal court, having determined that a taking has occurred, the same discretion in determining whether to grant injunctive relief. Second, the fact that NMFS has expressly declined to ban gillnet or lobster pot fishing in Cape Cod Bay does not reflect a policy determination by NMFS that such a ban is unnecessary. For these two reasons, we find the defendants' deference arguments without merit.

C. Factual challenges

We review the district court's findings of fact for clear error. The district court found that entanglement with fishing gear in Massachusetts waters caused injury or death to Northern Right whales. Indeed, the district court cited several of the Commonwealth's documents in support of this finding, including its statement that "[f]ive right whales have been found entangled in fixed fishing gear in Massachusetts waters; three in gillnets and two in lobster lines." The court further cited to affidavits of three scientists that suggested that entanglement of Northern Right whales had harmed, injured, or killed those whales. The court cited eleven occasions on which Northern Right whales had been found entangled in fishing gear in Massachusetts waters between 1978 and 1995. The court also indicated that at least fifty-seven percent of all Northern right whales have scars indicating prior entanglement with fishing gear and noted that, even where the whale survives, the entanglement still wounds the whale. Although these findings indicate only that entanglements have occurred in Massachusetts waters, the district court determined that three whales had been found entangled in gear deployed in Massachusetts waters.

The defendants contend that the factual evidence before the district court did not support a finding that the Commonwealth has perpetrated a taking. The defendants' main contention is that the "District Court made

---

3. We note that the defendants' concerns about the authority of the district court to force the Commonwealth to ban gillnet and lobster pot fishing where the federal administering agency, NMFS, has chosen not to do so are misplaced. Had the district court actually ordered such a ban, we might consider these concerns, but indeed the district court has not required the Commonwealth in its injunction to impose such a ban. The situation complained of by the defendants is simply not before us.

its 'taking' determination ... based on speculation that Northern Right whales have become entangled in fishing gear: (1) deployed in Massachusetts coastal waters; and (2) licensed by the Commonwealth." The defendants first state that they submitted affidavit evidence indicating that no deaths of Northern Right whales had occurred in Massachusetts coastal waters. While this may be true, it answers only half the taking question, which bars not only killings of, but also injuries to, Northern Right whales. Because the district court need not have made a determination as to whale deaths in determining whether the Commonwealth exacted a taking, we find no error.

The defendants acknowledge that the district court relied on a scientist's affidavit that was supplied by amicus curiae Conservation Law Foundation. The defendants do not challenge the factual statements asserted in the affidavit, including the one relied upon by the district court that "[t]hree of the entanglements of endangered whales ... clearly involved fishing gear that was deployed in Massachusetts waters." Despite the defendants' protests that the district court was engaging in speculation when it found that whales have become entangled in fishing gear deployed in Commonwealth's waters, in fact the district court relied on the unchallenged factual assertion in the scientific affidavit. Thus, the defendants' first challenge to the district court's fact-finding speculation is not valid.

With respect to the district court's determination that these entanglements involved gear licensed by the Commonwealth, the district court relied on the affidavit regarding the three entanglements that occurred in Massachusetts waters. The affidavit explained that the whales were found entangled in gear "fixed" in Massachusetts waters such that the whale could not escape because it could not break free of the gear. The district court's inference that gear fixed in Massachusetts waters was licensed by the Commonwealth, and was not set illegally or brought into Massachusetts waters from another area by the whale, was reasonable and we find no clear error in that inference.

The defendants next contend that the district court ignored evidence of the significant efforts made by the Commonwealth to "minimize Northern Right Whale entanglements in fishing gear," and evidence of other causes of takings of Northern Right whales. With respect to the determination of whether a taking has occurred, the district court quite rightly disregarded such evidence. Given that there was evidence that any entanglement with fishing gear injures a Northern Right whale and given that a single injury to one whale is a taking under the ESA, efforts to minimize such entanglements are irrelevant. For the same reasons, the existence of other means by which takings of Northern Right whales occur is irrelevant to the determination of whether the Commonwealth has engaged in a taking.

Finding neither any error of law nor any clear error with respect to the factual findings, we believe that the district court properly applied the ESA to the facts presented and was correct in enjoining the Commonwealth so as to prevent the taking of Northern Right whales in violation of the ESA.

III.   Scope of injunctive relief

Defendants claim that the injunctive relief granted by the district court goes beyond the scope of remedies available in an action against state officials. Specifically, defendants claim that, although the district court could have ordered an injunction barring all Commonwealth licensing activity, it could not require the Commonwealth to implement measures designed to accord Northern Right whales greater regulatory protection. * * *

[The court concluded that the injunction did not violate the Tenth Amendment.]

We believe that the district court acted within the scope of its equitable powers. The ESA governs the relief available in a citizen suit and authorizes citizen suits to enjoin acts in violation of the ESA. See 16 U.S.C. § 1540(g)(1)(A).

> [T]he comprehensiveness of this equitable jurisdiction is not to be denied or limited in the absence of a clear and valid legislative command. Unless a statute in so many words, or by a necessary and inescapable inference, restricts the court's jurisdiction in equity, the full scope of that jurisdiction is to be recognized and applied.

Weinberger v. Romero–Barcelo, 456 U.S. 305, 313 (1982). The ESA does not limit the injunctive power available in a citizen suit, and, thus, we understand the Act to grant a district court the full scope of its traditional equitable injunctive powers. * * *

Strahan contends that the district court committed reversible error by refusing to grant the injunctive relief he sought. He contends that the Court in *TVA* ruled that injunctive relief is mandatory upon a finding of a violation of the ESA. In fact, the *TVA* Court specifically rejected this proposition, stating "[i]t is correct, of course, that a federal judge sitting as a chancellor is not mechanically obligated to grant an injunction for every violation of law." *TVA*, 437 U.S. at 193. The Court recognized, however, that in the instance presented, in which the activity at issue would have caused eradication of an entire endangered species if not enjoined, the only remedy that could prevent that outcome was a permanent injunction halting the activity. *Id.* at 194–95.

The district court, having determined that the Commonwealth's probable violation of the ESA could be curtailed without such extreme measures, declined to impose the injunction Strahan sought. The district court was not required to go any farther than ensuring that any violation would end. We are satisfied that the district court was aware of the need to curtail any violation and bring about the Commonwealth's compliance with the ESA and that its order adequately achieves those ends.

* * *

NOTES AND QUESTIONS

1.   *Meaning of "Harm."* In *Sweet Home*, the majority expressly declined to decide whether the term "harm" within the statutory definition of "take" must be construed to include any significant habitat modification that kills or injures wildlife. Suppose the Department of Interior were to revise the definition of harm to include only direct application of force against an animal. Would that definition survive judicial review? How would *Chevron* apply?

2. *Habitat Acquisition.* Habitat loss is widely agreed to be the single greatest current threat to dwindling species. See, e.g., David S. Wilcove et al., Quantifying Threats to Imperiled Species in the United States, 48 BioScience 607 (1998). Much of the habitat those species need is found on privately-owned lands. See General Accounting Office, Endangered Species Act: Information on Species Protection on Nonfederal Lands (1995).

Although plaintiffs in *Sweet Home* agreed that habitat protection plays a key role in species conservation, they argued that Congress intended to protect habitat primarily by purchasing it under authority granted in ESA section 5. What should be the relative roles of regulation and habitat acquisition in endangered species policy? Is it unfair to prohibit development of property occupied by endangered species without compensating the landowner? On the other hand, is it unfair for landowners to assume that title to land carries with it the right to exterminate a species? Will regulations without compensation encourage landowners to conceal the presence of endangered species on their property or surreptitiously eliminate those species? See, e.g., Robert Innes et al, Takings, Compensation, and Endangered Species Protection on Private Lands, 12 J. Econ. Persp. 35 (1998); Barton H. Thompson, Jr., The Endangered Species Act: A Case Study in Takings and Incentives, 49 Stan. L. Rev. 305 (1997). Will political barriers to taxation prevent acquisition of sufficient habitat even if there is strong support for endangered species protection?

3. *Proving Take.* What evidence is needed to establish a take? Do you agree that Strahan adequately proved take by Massachusetts? In a habitat destruction case, must the government show injury to an identifiable individual animal, or is it sufficient to produce expert testimony of the presence of listed species and likelihood of harm? Must plaintiff show that the landowner knew or should have known of occupancy and the potential for harm?

As a landowner, how carefully would you investigate your property for endangered species before beginning your project? If you suspected listed species might be present, would you contact the Services? What are the possible consequences of either choice? See J.B. Ruhl, How to Kill Endangered Species, Legally: The Nuts and Bolts of Endangered Species Act "HCP" Permits for Real Estate Development, 5 Envtl. Law. 345 (1999).

4. *Third-Party Take.* Do you agree with the *Strahan* court that Massachusetts violated the ESA by failing to more stringently regulate gillnetting and lobster pots? Does it matter that NMFS could have imposed the regulations Strahan sought? Was NMFS also guilty of take?

Assuming Massachusetts adopts satisfactory regulations following this decision, does the ESA regulate its enforcement of those regulations? Could Massachusetts be liable for take if whales become entangled in illegally set gear? Under what circumstances? See Loggerhead Turtle v. County Council of Volusia County, 92 F.Supp.2d 1296 (M.D.Fla.2000) (holding county which had adopted ordinance forbidding harmful beach lighting not liable for take of endangered turtles by lighting which violated the ordinance).

5. *Remedies*. Once a court has found a violation of the take prohibition, is an injunction automatic? Does it matter how likely the take is to recur? See National Wildlife Fed'n v. Burlington Northern R.R., 23 F.3d 1508 (9th Cir.1994). How much of a threat the take poses to survival of the species?

6. *Hypotheticals*. In each of the following hypothetical situations, has a take been committed? If so, by whom? How likely is an enforcement action by the government or a citizen suit to be effective?

(a) Jane Doe is driving 45 mph in a 35 mph zone on a county road in the Florida keys, when a Key deer (an endangered species) leaps in front of her car. Unable to stop, Jane hits and kills the deer. County officials, who are responsible for setting and enforcing the speed limit, are aware that dozens of Key deer have been killed in recent years by speeding cars.

(b) John Farmer owns land along a creek in the northwest. John maintains a small dam to divert water for irrigation purposes. The dam, constructed in 1955 with all required permits, has no fish passage facilities. Chinook salmon once spawned in the creek both above and below the dam, but because of John's dam and others like it, only a handful now return each year. In 1998, fourteen chinook were seen at the base of John's dam. None were counted above the dam. The next year, state and federal officials removed four dams downstream from John's. In 2000, the creek below John's dam teemed with thousands of chinook. Experts concluded that many of these salmon were unable to spawn because there was insufficient spawning habitat for the large number of fish. Is John liable for take in 1998? In 2000? Does your answer depend upon the condition of upstream spawning habitat?

(c) The threatened red-cockaded woodpecker hollows out nests in live pine trees. It prefers trees at least 60 years old, in stands relatively clear of hardwoods. Historically, periodic fire maintained southern pine forests in a state suitable for the red-cockaded woodpecker. Fire suppression and even-aged timber management together have caused its decline. Southern Timber Corp. owns thousands of acres of pine plantations inhabited by a handful of red-cockaded woodpeckers. It refuses to institute a program of prescribed burning, fearing that doing so will increase the population of woodpeckers, leading to tighter restrictions on timber harvest.

4. PERMITTING TAKE: HABITAT CONSERVATION PLANS

Excerpts from the Endangered Species Act

16 U.S.C. § 1531–1544.

Sec. 10. Exceptions

(a)(1) The Secretary may permit, under such terms and conditions as he shall prescribe—

* * *

(B) any taking otherwise prohibited by section 1538(a)(1)(B) of this title if such taking is incidental to, and not the purpose of, the carrying out of an otherwise lawful activity.

(2)(A) No permit may be issued by the Secretary authorizing any taking referred to in paragraph (1)(B) unless the applicant therefor submits to the Secretary a conservation plan that specifies—

(i) the impact which will likely result from such taking;

(ii) what steps the applicant will take to minimize and mitigate such impacts, and the funding that will be available to implement such steps;

(iii) what alternative actions to such taking the applicant considered and the reasons why such alternatives are not being utilized; and

(iv) such other measures that the Secretary may require as being necessary or appropriate for purposes of the plan.

(B) If the Secretary finds, after opportunity for public comment, with respect to a permit application and the related conservation plan that—

(i) the taking will be incidental;

(ii) the applicant will, to the maximum extent practicable, minimize and mitigate the impacts of such taking;

(iii) the applicant will ensure that adequate funding for the plan will be provided;

(iv) the taking will not appreciably reduce the likelihood of the survival and recovery of the species in the wild; and

(v) the measures, if any, required under subparagraph (A)(iv) will be met;

and he has received such other assurances as he may require that the plan will be implemented, the Secretary shall issue the permit. The permit shall contain such terms and conditions as the Secretary deems necessary or appropriate to carry out the purposes of this paragraph, including, but not limited to, such reporting requirements as the Secretary deems necessary for determining whether such terms and conditions are being complied with.

(C) The Secretary shall revoke a permit issued under this paragraph if he finds that the permittee is not complying with the terms and conditions of the permit.

Robert D. Thornton, Searching for Consensus and Predictability: Habitat Conservation Planning Under the Endangered Species Act of 1973

21 Envtl. L. 605, 621–24 (1991).

Section 10(a) of the ESA grew out of a multi-year conflict between a proposed development project and two species of endangered butterflies. In early 1976, the local board of supervisors ended a decade-long dispute over the appropriate level of development at San Bruno Mountain on the San Francisco Peninsula in Northern California by requiring the landowner to dedicate two-thirds of the mountain as a park. Two weeks after the final conveyance of the property to the state parks foundation, the FWS proposed to list the Callippe Silverspot butterfly as an endangered species and to designate critical habitat on the mountain. The critical habitat proposal substantially overlapped all of the remaining areas on the mountain designated for development by the County.

The proposed listing initiated a three-year planning process involving the environmental community, the landowners and developers, and local, state and federal agencies. After two years of intensive negotiation, the parties agreed on a habitat conservation plan which allowed the proposed development to proceed, but which also established a long-term program for the protection of the butterflies and several other species of concern.

The San Bruno Mountain plan addresses the ecological community on the mountain as a single unit. Although the plan focused on the conflict between development and the preservation of the butterflies, the plan also sought to preserve the diversity of species and their habitat on the mountain. The plan reflected a conscious attempt by its drafters to anticipate and resolve any conflicts that might develop over other biological resources on the mountain.

Under the plan, private development becomes a source of funds for acquiring habitat and for funding the needed habitat management measures. The plan's drafters carefully selected sites for private development using criteria reflecting the biological requirements of the species on the mountain. The plan establishes rigorous procedures to ensure that any land development occurs in conformity with the plan.

Two of the participants in the plan's development described its significant elements as follows:

1. *Protection of Open Space.* The plan preserves in open space 80 percent of the mountain; all but 2.7 percent of this total is preserved in an undisturbed condition. Approximately 90 percent of the habitat of the Mission Blue and Callippe Silverspot butterflies is protected under the plan.

2. *Diversity of Habitat Protected.* An essential feature of the plan is the preservation of the diversity of habitat on the mountain, including hilltops and valleys, north-and south-facing slopes, grasslands, brush, and other habitats. The effort was to protect the butterflies by protecting the diversity of the mountain's ecological community.

* * *

4. *Funding of Plan Activities.* The plan provides a source of permanent funding to carry out conservation activities through assessments (which will be imposed through recorded covenants and restrictions) that will raise approximately $60,000 per year, which is in addition to substan-

tial, interim funding provided by the developers. The agreement provides that the permanent funding will be adjusted annually for inflation to insure an inflation-free source of funding. The level of ongoing private support for endangered species conservation is unprecedented.

5. *Ongoing Management of Public and Private Habitat.* The plan establishes the County as the ongoing manager of the habitat throughout the mountain and insures a uniformity of management within the various jurisdictional areas on the mountain. One of the key components of the plan is that it subjects both public and private activities within conserved habitat areas to the conservation principles enunciated in the plan. Thus, county and state parklands on the mountain are required to be managed in the interest of habitat conservation to the same extent as privately held habitat.

6. *Assurances to Private Sector.* The implementing agreement includes unprecedented provisions that assure the private sector landowners and developers that, except as specifically set forth in the agreement, no further mitigation or compensation will be required in the interest of wildlife or their habitat on the mountain.

* * *

Despite the consensus between the developer and the leading environmental group concerning the plan's terms, the plan suffered from the absence of any specific ESA provision authorizing the FWS to permit the incidental taking contemplated by the conservation plan. As a result, the plan's proponents sought, and in 1982 Congress adopted, an amendment authorizing the FWS to issue incidental take permits in accordance with the terms of an HCP. Section 10(a)'s legislative history indicates that the San Bruno Mountain HCP is the model for the ESA's new provision and is also the standard against which similar conservation plans will be measured. * * *

National Wildlife Federation v. Babbitt

United States District Court, Eastern District of California, 2000.
128 F.Supp.2d 1274.

■ LEVI, DISTRICT JUDGE.

Plaintiffs challenge the United States Fish and Wildlife Service's issuance of an incidental take permit [to the City of Sacramento] to allow development in the Natomas Basin, a 53,000 acre tract of largely undeveloped land * * *.

The Natomas Basin HCP is intended "to promote biological conservation along with economic development and the continuation of agriculture within the Natomas Basin." The HCP lists 26 species that are "potentially subject to take," and which are to "be included in the state and federal permits issued in accordance with the Plan." The proposed permit authorizes incidental take resulting from urban development, as well as any incidental take that may occur through rice-farming or result from management of the Plan's reserve lands. The HCP was developed as a regional conservation plan for the entire Natomas Basin, and was intended for use in connection with [Incidental Take Permit (ITP)] applications for each of the municipalities and water companies with interests in the Basin * * *. [Relying on the plan, FWS issued a permit to the City of Sacramento. No other permit applications had yet been filed.]

The Plan is administered by the Natomas Basin Conservancy ("NBC") which has the responsibility to establish and oversee "a concerted Basin-wide program for acquiring and managing mitigation lands on behalf of the permittees." * * *

The Plan calls upon the NBC to assemble connected 400 acre blocks of reserve lands—with one block of at least 2500 acres—for the benefit of the Giant Garter Snake and to protect Swainson's hawk habitat and nesting areas. The HCP states that "to the maximum extent practicable, the [Natomas Basin] HCP will ensure that habitat acquisition will be provided *in advance* of habitat conversion resulting from urban development in the Natomas Basin." Funding for land acquisition, however, is derived from the collection of mitigation fees for development. Thus, with regard to the phasing of land acquisition, the HCP actually requires only that, after an initial acquisition of 400 acres, which is to be made "as soon as possible," "no more than one year shall elapse between receipt of a fee and expenditure of that fee in the purchase or other acquisition of mitigation land."

The Plan is based on certain key principles and assumptions. First, the Plan assumes that only 17,500 acres of Basin land will be developed over the 50 year life of the permit, and that a substantial proportion of the undeveloped land will remain in agriculture, particularly rice, which is believed to have unique value as habitat for the [Giant Garter Snake (GGS)]. The Plan's conclusion that a ratio of .5 acres of reserve lands for each 1 acre of developed land will ensure the biological needs of the protected species is based on the assumption that a considerable portion of the undeveloped and agricultural lands in the Basin will remain undeveloped, thereby augmenting the habitat value of the reserve lands.

Second, the Plan pursues a regional approach to conservation. Whereas without the Plan, individual landowners could pursue separate permit applications, or develop their land without securing an ITP, the HCP is intended to provide a consolidated approach under which resources may be pooled and conservation lands may be purchased throughout the Basin. Third, the HCP treats all Basin lands as fungible, as equally valuable habitat. Thus, the HCP requires developers to "mitigate" for the anticipated take of individuals or habitat by payment of a fee for each acre developed. Rather than differentiating among lands according to their value as habitat for protected species, the HCP requires all landowners within the Permit area to pay a mitigation fee for developing their land, regardless of whether any particular parcel has or lacks habitat value. Depending on one's point of view, this uniform treatment is either a strength or a weakness of the Plan. It is a strength because mitigation fees are to be collected on all acreage and are used "to set aside 0.5 acres of habitat land for each 1.0 acres of gross development that occurs in the Basin." It is a potential weakness because the Plan does not attempt to identify, prior to intensified development under the ITP, particular parcels for acquisition as reserves, based upon the importance of those parcels as habitat, but simply specifies acquisition criteria, and leaves specific reserve acquisition to the future decisionmaking of the NBC.

* * *

IV. Endangered Species Act Claims

* * * [P]laintiffs' ESA claims fall into two categories. First, plaintiffs challenge as arbitrary the Service's findings as to the adequacy of the Plan's provisions, particularly those related to funding and mitigation; second, plaintiffs contend that the Service's findings regarding the biological effects of the Plan on covered species are arbitrary and capricious. As explained below, under the APA's deferential standard of review, the Service's findings largely pass muster with respect to the Plan as a whole; however, with respect to the City's Permit, the Service's findings do not. * * *

A. ESA § 10(a)(2)(A)—minimum criteria for a habitat conservation plan

Plaintiffs argue that the Service's approval of the HCP is improper because the HCP does not adequately disclose its impacts on covered species and their habitat. ESA § 10(a)(2)(A) states that no incidental take permit may be issued unless the applicant submits an HCP that meets certain requirements. One such requirement is that the HCP specify "the impact which will likely result from such taking." * * * [T]he HCP does discuss the impact that will likely result from development activities, rice farming, and operation of water conveyance systems in the Natomas Basin. While the Plan and associated supporting documents do not make specific quantitative estimates of take, they do make general assessments of the effect of development under the Plan as to the various species affected, particularly the GGS and the Swainson's hawk. Plaintiffs argue, however, that the ESA requires precise quantitative measures of take. According to plaintiffs, the HCP must estimate the number of individual members of a species within the Permit area and must then estimate the number of members of the species that will be taken. Plaintiffs cite no authority for this interpretation of the ESA. The Secretary's contrary interpretation of the statute is entitled to deference. The court finds that the HCP meets the minimum requirements for a habitat conservation plan.

B. ESA § 10(a)(2)(B)(ii)—minimize and mitigate the impact of permitted takings "to the maximum extent practicable"

Plaintiffs argue that the Service's (B)(ii) finding, that the Plan will minimize and mitigate takings to the maximum extent practicable, is arbitrary and capricious because the Service failed to consider any alternatives involving greater mitigation measures. * * * The linchpin of the HCP is the .5 to 1 preserved to developed acre ratio and the mitigation fee that is based on this ratio. Thus, to consider an alternative providing greater mitigation, in the context of this HCP, the record should provide some basis for concluding, not just that the chosen mitigation fee and land preservation ratio are practicable, but that a higher fee and ratio would be impracticable.

The Secretary does not appear to disagree with the above analysis but rather argues that the record does adequately demonstrate that the HCP provides for the maximum practicable mitigation fee and reserve land ratio. However, the record is nearly non-existent on this matter. There are conclusory statements in the record to the effect that "the common and local wisdom is that a fee in the range from $2000 to $2500 per acre is practicable," but the record is devoid of evidence that the Service subjected this assumption to any examination or attempted to determine if a higher base fee would also be practicable. There is no economic analysis, discussion of mitigation fees in similar plans and circumstances, or even representations from particular landowners. * * * The plain language of the statutory provision requiring that the Plan minimize and mitigate its effects "to the maximum extent practicable" is not satisfied by a fee set, as here, at the minimum amount necessary to meet the minimum biological necessities of the covered species. The record lacks adequate evidence and analysis of whether a fee higher than that initially proposed by the working group would be economically practicable.

The Secretary finds support for the (B)(ii) finding in part in the Plan's provision allowing increases in the mitigation fee as necessary to cover increased costs. But increases over the life of the Plan are capped at 50% of the initial base fee for most, although not all, types of expenditures.[18] Moreover, because fee increases are not applied retroactively, the Plan's provisions for fee increases can be expected to produce revenue only if and to the extent that future developers are willing to participate in the HCP. The problem that this mitigation structure presents is particularly acute for the City's Permit, given the relatively small portion of the Basin within the City and the pace at which development of the City's land is expected. Thus, it is possible, even likely, that City developers will avoid the future substantial increases in the mitigation fee that will be borne by out of City developers. While this structure may make sense, at least without analysis and explanation, it is not obvious how the Secretary concluded that City developers would pay a fee that is the maximum practicable, particularly when later developers are expected to pay a much larger fee. In short, the Secretary's conclusion that $2240 per acre is the maximum practicable initial base mitigation fee is unsupported by substantial evidence in the record, and therefore is arbitrary and capricious.

* * *

18. Most significantly, the cap does not apply to fee increases necessitated by increased land acquisition costs.

For these reasons, the Service's (B)(ii) finding is arbitrary and capricious considering the HCP as a whole and the City's Permit in particular.

C. ESA § 10(a)(2)(B)(iii)—adequate funding

Plaintiffs argue that the Service's finding that the City would "ensure" adequate funding for the Plan is arbitrary, for two reasons. First, plaintiffs contend that the initial mitigation fee, even in light of the Plan's provisions for fee increases, is inadequate to cover the costs of the various components of the mitigation program. The record, however, provides an adequate basis for the Secretary's conclusion to the contrary. The initial fee was set based on the estimated needs of the NBC prepared by experts * * *. Although plaintiffs point to evidence in the record suggesting that the fee was deemed inadequate by some, the Service's decision to rely on [expert] analysis is entitled to deference.

Second, plaintiffs argue that the (B)(iii) finding was arbitrary and capricious with respect to the City's permit, in light of the City's explicit refusal to "ensure" funding in the event of a shortfall. This argument has merit. Plaintiffs argue that nothing in the record supports the HCP's assertion * * * that:

> The [Natomas Basin] HCP can be implemented independently by some individual permittees, but not by others, without adversely affecting the conservation program as a whole. This is because each land use agency is responsible under the Plan for mitigating the effects of urban development occurring within its respective permit area, regardless of the actions of other agencies.

Indeed, the record suggests a much more complicated picture than the Plan depicts concerning the consequences of nonparticipation by the other land-use agencies with jurisdiction over parts of the Basin. Given that the Plan does not permit retroactive fee increases, increases in the mitigation fee will be applied only to land developed after the need for a greater fee becomes apparent and the fee increase is approved. Thus, the Plan's funding mechanism depends on continual infusions of new developable land to provide funding for mitigation necessitated by previous development. Regardless of the City's incentives, if most or all of the City's land has been developed by the time the need for additional mitigation funding becomes apparent—a likelihood if the City lands are rapidly developed under the current fee—there may simply be no land left to which an increased fee could be applied. Given the Plan's acknowledgment that it is uncertain whether land-use agencies other than the City will submit applications, the statement that "each land use agency is *responsible* under the Plan for mitigating the effects of urban development occurring within its respective permit area," is not accurate with respect to the City, which refused to "ensure" funding for the mitigation necessitated by development under its permit.

* * *

It is not clear that a funding mechanism that is not backed by the applicant's guarantee could ever satisfy the requirement of § 1539(a)(2)(B)(iii) that the applicant "ensure" funding for the Plan. Assuming, however, that a cost shifting mechanism "ensures" funding within the meaning of § 1539(a)(2)(B)(iii), in these circumstances, where the adequacy of funding depends on whether third parties decide to participate in the Plan, the statute requires the applicant's guarantee.

* * * [W]hile the Service's (B)(iii) finding is not arbitrary with respect to the Plan as a whole, it is arbitrary and capricious with respect to the City's Permit.

D.   ESA § 10(a)(2)(B)(iv)—Survival and Recovery, and § 7(a)(2)—No Jeopardy

Plaintiffs argue that in making the findings required by ESA §§ 10(a)(2)(B)(iv) and 7(a)(2) (collectively, the "no jeopardy" findings), the Service failed adequately to explain how habitat loss authorized by the HCP would avoid jeopardizing the continued survival of the Giant Garter Snake, Swainson's hawk, and other covered species. * * * The no jeopardy findings, like the (B)(ii) and (B)(iii) findings, are undermined by the administrative record's focus on the regional HCP. Although the no jeopardy findings are adequately supported by the record if the Service's assumption that Sacramento and Sutter Counties will seek ITPs under the Plan is valid, the Service failed adequately to consider whether the findings could be made with respect to the issuance of an ITP to the City alone. In short, while the no jeopardy findings are not arbitrary with respect to the Plan, they are arbitrary with respect to the Permit.

(1)   The Plan

Plaintiffs argue that the Service's no jeopardy findings are arbitrary and capricious for five reasons: (1) The Service "failed to articulate a rational connection between [the findings] and the fact that tens of thousands of acres of habitat will be destroyed and degraded under the HCP"; (2) the Service failed to explain its change in policy position on the habitat protections needed by covered species; (3) the Service "improperly ignored, and failed to explain its departure from, uncontradicted expert evidence regarding the survival and recovery needs of the imperiled species"; (4) the Service's no jeopardy findings are based on improper speculation; and (5) the Service failed to articulate a rational connection between the no jeopardy findings and the "admitted fact that the HCP's initial conservation strategy is highly uncertain to succeed."

As to plaintiffs' first argument, plaintiffs' principal contention is that the Service's reliance on the HCP's forecast of 17,500 acres of development over the 50 year term of the ITP is arbitrary. Plaintiffs argue that "up to 32,000 acres of habitat in the Natomas Basin" will be destroyed under the HCP. Plaintiffs have not established, however, that the Service's reliance on the 17,500 acre figure is unreasonable, and the Service adequately articulated its basis for the estimate.[24] Moreover, there are two important safeguards that justify reliance on the 17,500 acre figure. First, the HCP calls for a review at 9,000 acres, with a moratorium on development past 12,000 acres pending completion of the review. If the pace of development at that point exceeds expectations, various modifications may be requested or required, including a revocation of the permit. And second, because the 17,500 acre assumption is so central to the HCP, any significant departure from that figure would require reinitiation of consultation, again possibly leading to revocation or substantial modification of the permit. Based on the forecast of 17,500 acres, and using the 1:.5 development to preservation ratio, the Service concurred with the HCP's estimate that 8750 acres of reserve land would be protected under the Plan, and that most of the remainder of the Basin would be in agricultural lands, which frequently provide excellent habitat. The Service concluded that the reserve lands, together with undeveloped land kept in agriculture, would suffice to maintain, and in some cases increase, the Basin's populations of covered species.

Plaintiffs argue, in addition, that the Service's failure to include "basic information," such as the baseline condition and conservation needs of the species, and the effects of the HCP, undermines the "rational connection" between the no jeopardy findings and the record. * * * Plaintiffs' contention appears to be that the ESA requires detailed quantitative information as to each of these factors prior to the issuance of a permit, but plaintiffs cite no authority for such a requirement, and such a requirement would not be reasonable. For the Giant Garter Snake, for example, a reclusive species, it would be extraordinarily difficult to count the number of individual snakes, determine their habitat and habits, and reach conclusions as to their genetic makeup and variability. Instead, the 1997 Biological Opinion makes certain assumptions about the species based upon potential loss of habitat, which is a reasonable approach. Moreover, the Plan overprotects by assuming that any acre lost to development is potential habitat requiring the 1:.5 mitigation.

* * *

Plaintiffs' fourth contention is that the Service improperly speculated as to the likely success of the Plan's conservation measures. The subjects of "speculation" that plaintiffs identify include: (1) that habitat areas will be available for acquisition; [and] (2) that local governments and landowners will cooperate in the NBC's efforts to acquire reserve lands * * *.

The uncertainties to which plaintiffs object do not undermine the "rational connection" between the no jeopardy findings and the evidence in the record. Plaintiffs' first, second, and fifth charges of "speculation" are concerned with the uncertainties inherent in the market-based mitigation mechanism employed by the HCP. The NBC is given funds and acquisition criteria, and permitted to compete in the marketplace for land and for

---

24. The 1997 Biological Opinion explains that the 17,500 acre figure is a prediction based on the City's and Counties' General Plans, which the Service deemed to provide "a reasonable basis for predicting the extent and location of future urban development."

water rights. In the absence of any identified "critical habitat" in the Basin, or substantial evidence in the record that the market for land and water rights will not function—that is, that land and water rights will be unavailable to the NBC even if the Plan provides adequate funding—the adoption of such a market-based mitigation structure is not an arbitrary or otherwise impermissible exercise of the Secretary's discretion. * * *

As to plaintiffs' final challenge to the no jeopardy findings, which concerns the allegedly uncertain success of the HCP's initial conservation strategy, plaintiffs appear to contend that, in the face of incomplete data as to species' recovery needs and uncertainty as to the efficacy of the HCP, the Service's issuance of the ITP is arbitrary and capricious. Plaintiffs provide no authority for the duty they seek to impose on the Secretary, the resolution of all uncertainties before proceeding with a Plan, nor is any such duty apparent from the text of the ESA or case law. A certain degree of what plaintiffs label "speculation" and "uncertainty" is inevitable in any decisionmaking process, particularly one as complicated as that which led to the issuance of the ITP. The law does not require that the Secretary achieve certainty before acting.

(2) The Permit

Although the Service's no jeopardy findings are not arbitrary and capricious with respect to the Plan as a whole—that is, assuming that Sacramento and Sutter Counties will seek permits under the Plan—the record is startlingly devoid of support for the findings with respect to the possibility that only the City would participate in the Plan. This is understandable, perhaps, given the regional approach of the HCP which is its greatest strength. But the court does not have before it what the drafters of the Plan apparently envisioned, a permit or permits for all of the jurisdictions within the Basin; rather, the court has for review only a permit for the City, and may not assume that other jurisdictions will also join in the HCP.

The Service's expert analysis of the likely impacts of the Plan assumes that all Basin development occurs under the HCP subject to the mitigation fee. As discussed above, the record provides insufficient consideration by the Service of whether funding for mitigation would be adequate if only the City's lands were developed under the Plan. Moreover, the record contains little or no analysis of the effect on the species of the City's permit considered on its own. Thus, there is no analysis of the importance of the City's lands as habitat for covered species. At oral argument, counsel for the Secretary asserted that the court could assume that the City's lands were less valuable habitat than other Basin lands, but the court cannot so assume; it must rely on the considered judgment of the Service and the record. * * *

Furthermore, there is little discussion of the effect on the GGS if the Plan's goal of large connected blocks of reserve lands cannot be met because only the City participates in the Plan. Such a fundamental change in the Plan's conservation strategy requires discussion. Yet the Service merely acknowledges the problem without explaining how the reserves set aside by the City's development will be adequate to protect the GGS and the other affected species.

The problem of the reserve lands is just an example of a larger problem when the Plan is applied only to the City's Basin lands. The Secretary concedes that the ITP will result in take of threatened species, including between 14 and 37% of the Basin population of the GGS, but relies on certain features of the Plan, including the monitoring, adaptive management, and 9,000 acre review provisions, to adequately mitigate the impact of the take. The Secretary's emphasis on these provisions, however, only underscores the tension between the HCP's regional nature and the local focus of the ITP and the Service's biological findings. Based on the projected development in City's area of the Basin, the midcourse review will come too late to result in any change with respect to the City's permit. The record shows that the portion of the Basin with approved development plans, most of which is in the City, is expected to be developed quickly, while the pace of development in the Counties is largely unknown. Thus, the halfway point moratorium and opportunity for mid-course correction, so important to the HCP, are irrelevant to the City's permit, which contains no analogous features for correction and reconsideration. Similarly, the record does not suggest that the Service considered whether the monitoring and adaptive management provisions of the regional Plan could be effective if the City is the sole permittee. Given the evidence that the City's lands will be developed quite quickly, the Service's failure to consider whether the survival of the species will be put at risk by the City's permit, if the regional mitigation approach of the HCP is not available, is arbitrary and capricious.

* * *

NOTES AND QUESTIONS

1. What precisely is the holding of *National Wildlife Federation v. Babbitt*? On remand, what changes or additional analysis must FWS do to reissue the permit? Would participation by neighboring jurisdictions necessarily remedy the problems?

2. Do you agree that the Plan itself met the requirements of section 10, with the exception of the funding mechanism? Were the "no jeopardy" findings adequately supported? Who bears the burden of proof on that issue? Does section 10 permit "market-based" HCP approaches, relying on acquisition of reserves from willing sellers as development proceeds? What evidence is required to support those findings? Must FWS evaluate the importance of specific lands to the species?

3. *HCPs by the Numbers.* By 1992, a decade after enactment of the incidental take provision, only fourteen HCPs had been approved, and by the end of 1994 there were only 25 more. At that point, however, the program took off. By February 2001, 341 HCPs covering 30 million acres had been approved and many more were in the development process. The early HCPs typically covered relatively small areas, and involved only one or a small number of landowners. Recently, however, regional HCPs have become more common. By early 1996, 25 HCPs exceeded 100,000 acres and 18 more exceeded 500,000 (about 750 square miles). FWS, Habitat Conservation Planning Is Streamlined Under New Guidelines Announced by Two Services (Sept. 16, 1996). Local governments are often the permit holders under these large regional HCPs, as in the Natomas plan.

4. *Pros and Cons of HCPs.* Advocates of the HCP provision contend that it offers the opportunity to move away from reactive, species-specific conservation toward a more efficient and effective forward-looking, ecosystem-based approach. In some respects, HCPs effectively expand the protections of section 9. HCPs can cover species not listed, and because issuance of an incidental take permit is a federal action subject to section 7 they must protect against the possibility of jeopardy to listed plants. Large-scale plans can produce large contiguous reserves more likely to protect species in the long run but impossible or exceedingly difficult to create in response to piece-meal individual development projects. Finally, proponents claim, the program reduces political pressure on the ESA itself by accommodating some development while protecting species.

Not everyone is enthusiastic about HCPs, however. Many environmentalists are concerned that development may not turn out to be compatible with conservation. They assert that incidental take should be permitted only if the plan will provide a net benefit to the species, helping it move toward recovery and eventual delisting. Even those who support the concept of HCPs are concerned about its implementation, fearing that development pressure will encourage the Services to approve plans supported by insufficient data. Barriers to public participation at the early stages of plan drafting and judicial inclinations toward deference to agency decisions feed these fears.

Does the Natomas experience counsel optimism or pessimism about the prospects for HCPs?

5. *No Surprises.* Of particular concern to HCP critics is a policy first adopted by FWS in 1994, and subsequently formalized as a regulation, that limits the responsibility of permittees for unforeseen shortcomings of HCPs. The "no surprises" rule provides that a permittee who is in compliance with a plan that adequately covered a species will not be required to provide additional financing or land for conservation if additional measures are subsequently deemed necessary to protect the species. 50 C.F.R. § 17.22(b). FWS regards these assurances as central to the recent increase in permit applications.

Is this policy consistent with the ESA? A pending lawsuit alleges that it is not. Spirit of the Sage Council v. Babbitt, Civ. No. 1:98CV01873 (D.D.C., filed 1998).

D. OTHER BIODIVERSITY PROVISIONS

Many other federal and state laws protect biodiversity in one way or another. Economic incentives and market mechanisms form one part of the biodiversity protection picture. Habitat acquisition and management for wildlife purposes are authorized under several federal laws, and supported by federal taxes under the Pittman–Robertson Wildlife Restoration Act, 16 U.S.C. §§ 669–669k, and Migratory Bird Hunting and Conservation Stamp Act, 16 U.S.C. §§ 718–718k. Several programs provide subsidies to farmers who manage their lands for wildlife, or deny subsidies to farmers whose practices are harmful. See J.B. Ruhl, Farms, Their Environmental Harms, and Environmental Law, 27 Ecology L.Q. 325–27 (2000).

A large number of state and federal regulatory statutes also contribute to biodiversity protection. Some of the most important federal provisions include the Migratory Bird Treaty Act, 16 U.S.C. §§ 703–712; Bald and Golden Eagle Protection Act, 16 U.S.C. §§ 668–668d; Wild Free–Roaming Horses and Burros Act, 16 U.S.C. §§ 1331–1340; Marine Mammal Protection Act, 16 U.S.C. §§ 1371–1389; and Magnuson–Stevens Fishery Conservation and Management Act, 16 U.S.C. §§ 1802–1883. For comprehensive discussions of federal biodiversity law, see Bradley C. Karkkainen, Biodiversity and Land, 83 Cornell L. Rev. 1 (1997) and J.B. Ruhl, Biodiversity Conservation and the Ever–Expanding Web of Federal Laws Regulating Non–Federal Lands: Time for Something Completely Different?, 66 U. Colo. L. Rev. 555 (1995).

A number of international agreements are also relevant to biodiversity protection. There are treaties specifically focused on wildlife protection, such as the Convention for the Protection of Migratory Birds, Aug. 16–Dec. 8, 1916, U.S.-Gr. Brit., 39 Stat. 1702, and the International Convention for the Regulation of Whaling, Dec. 2, 1946, 62 Stat. 1716, 161 U.N.T.S. 72. There are also many agreements on habitat protection, including the Ramsar Convention on Wetlands Protection, Convention on Wetlands of International Importance Especially as Waterfowl Habitat, Feb. 2, 1971, 996 U.N.T.S. 245, 11 I.L.M. 969, and the Convention for the Protection of the World Cultural and Natural Heritage, Nov. 23, 1972, 27 U.S.T. 37, 1037 U.N.T.S. 151. The 1992 Convention on Biological Diversity, 31 I.L.M. 818 (1992), sets the international framework for protection and exploitation of biotic resources. See, e.g., Michael A. Bowman and Catherine Redgwell, eds., International Law and the Conservation of Biological Diversity (1996); Lakshman Guruswamy & Jeffrey A. McNeely, eds., Protection of Global Biodiversity: Converging Strategies (1998). The United States is one of the few major nations not to have ratified this convention.

Section 4. Wetlands Protection

A. Introduction

Wetlands form the interface between terrestrial and aquatic habitats. They include such diverse areas as bogs, marshes, wet meadows, playa lakes, prairie potholes and, in Alaska, tundra wetlands. Wetlands may be tidal or freshwater, seasonal or year-round, and inundated from above through flooding or rain, or from below through a high groundwater table.

Wetlands were once regarded as places to avoid or eliminate. Nearly ten percent of the land area of the continental United States, over 220 million acres, was wetlands at the time of European colonization. By the 1980s, more than half of these wetlands acres had been destroyed, primarily by drainage, and converted to agriculture. National Research Council, Wetlands: Characteristics and Boundaries 16 (1995). California and the farm belt of the midwest suffered especially high losses. See Thomas E. Dahl, Wetlands Losses in the United States, 1780s to 1980s, at 6 (1991).

We now recognize that wetlands perform many ecological functions. They are highly productive ecosystems, harboring a wide variety of plant and animal species. More than one-third of the threatened and endangered species in the U.S. live only in wetlands. Many commercially-harvested fish and shellfish breed in wetlands. A large number of migratory bird species, including many popular with hunters and birdwatchers, rest, forage or nest in wetlands. These areas also serve crucial hydrologic functions, moderating floods and reducing their erosive impact by slowing surface waters. In addition, they filter wastes from surface waters, contribute to nutrient cycling, and can remove the greenhouse gas carbon dioxide from the atmosphere. See U.S. Environmental Protection Agency, Office of Water, Office of Wetlands, Oceans and Watersheds, America's Wetlands: Our Vital Link Between Land and Water (undated) (available at http://www.epa.gov/owow/wetlands/vital/toc.html).

Federal efforts to protect wetlands began in 1934 with the Duck Stamp Program, which imposed a tax on migratory bird hunting to support acquisition of waterfowl habitat. Nonetheless, the Department of Agriculture continued to subsidize wetland conversion, and wetland losses accelerated. By the 1960s, growing awareness of the ecological importance of wetlands and of their rapid disappearance created pressure for regulatory wetlands protection. A few states and localities began to require permits for wetland destruction. Finally, in 1972, Congress passed the Clean Water Act, section 404 of which authorized the issuance of permits for the discharge of fill to "navigable waters," defined elsewhere in the Act as "waters of the United States." The Army Corps of Engineers, which historically had been responsible for preventing obstructions to navigation under the Rivers and Harbors Act, 33 U.S.C. §§ 401–418, was given responsibility for this permitting program. Not entirely trusting the Corps to give proper weight to environmental values, however, Congress also gave EPA a significant role in the section 404 program.

Initially, the Corps narrowly construed its section 404 authority. By 1975, however, several courts had ruled that the Clean Water Act applied well beyond navigable waters as traditionally defined. See United States v. Holland, 373 F.Supp. 665 (M.D.Fla.1974); Natural Resources Defense Council v. Callaway, 392 F.Supp. 685 (D.D.C.1975); Conservation Council of North Carolina v. Costanzo, 398 F.Supp. 653 (E.D.N.C.1975). In response to these decisions, the Corps issued new regulations extending section 404 to wetlands.

Today, the section 404 program is the centerpiece of federal wetlands policy, but both land acquisition and economic incentives also play a role. Federal acquisition of wetlands continues, particularly for National Wildlife Refuges. Federal agricultural law includes both positive economic incentives for wetlands protection, under the Wetlands Reserve Program, and penalties for wetlands destruction, under the "Swampbuster" program. See 16 U.S.C. § 3801–3824.

Loss of wetlands has slowed in recent years, but the United States has yet to achieve the goal of "no net loss" set by President George H.W. Bush in 1989. Between 1986 and 1997, annual wetland losses in the continental United States averaged 58,500 acres, eighty percent less than the average annual loss in the preceding decade. Urban development is now the primary threat to wetlands, accounting for thirty percent of losses between 1986 and 1997, but agriculture, silviculture, and rural development are also key threats. Thomas E. Dahl, Status and Trends of Wetlands in the Conterminous United States 1986 to 1997, at 9–11 (2000).

CLASS DISCUSSION PROBLEM: THE LOVELY HARBOR COMPANY DEVELOPS WETLANDS

In 1963 the Lovely Harbor Company (LHC) purchased approximately 350 acres of vacant land on the shores of Folly Beach Sound for $300,000. Sheltered by Folly Beach Island from the storm waves of the Atlantic Ocean, Folly Beach Sound is a beautiful, quiet area of tidal marshes and wetlands, teeming with aquatic life and water birds. LHC's land is the last large, privately-owned undeveloped parcel on Folly Beach sound. There are other large coastal parcels nearby, but they do not enjoy the same favorable weather conditions.

LHC plans to develop a golf course and housing complex on 250 acres of its Folly Beach Sound land. LHC does not plan to develop the remaining 100 acres of land immediately, but would like to clear it and plant it with soybeans to bring in some immediate income. LHC expects to develop this remaining land for single family residential use in a few years, assuming market conditions remain favorable.

In preparation for its contemplated development, LHC hired consultants to survey its remaining land for wetlands. Twenty-five acres bordering Folly Beach Sound are regularly subject to shallow flooding by the tides. Another 6–acre parcel, well back from the coast, contains several depressions in which water pools following heavy rains. This area is surrounded by low hills, and there is no obvious surface drainage from it to the sound. Although the rest of the land is usually dry, a biologist has warned the company that as many as 125 acres are covered with "hydrophytic plants" capable of growing in wetland areas.

An appraisal by a reputable expert has determined that the twenty-five tideland acres would be worth as much as $250,000 per acre as waterfront lots for residential dwelling. If they cannot be filled for development, however, these tidelands would be worth no more than a few hundred dollars per acre. Furthermore, LHC's plans for the entire 250–acre tract hinge on gaining permission to dredge and fill in the tidelands. LHC plans an upscale, water-oriented development with a series of canals providing each lot with water access to Folly Beach Sound. If the company cannot dredge and fill in the tidelands, it will have to abandon its canal project, substantially reducing the value of the entire parcel for residential development. The six-acre ponding area is also important to LHC's plans; it happens to lie precisely where LHC would like to put the clubhouse for its golf course.

In preliminary discussions, state and federal officials indicated that they would not grant a permit for any dredging or filling on LHC's land. They explained that LHC's tidelands include the "most important salt water marsh area remaining in Folly Beach Sound." They also cited the presence of a rare 20–acre coastal woodlot on the uplands portion of LHC's land, which would be destroyed if LHC's development proceeds as planned. LHC believes its development would provide substantial economic benefits to the region without disrupting the local ecology. Consequently, the company has strongly objected to the suggestion that it might not qualify for a permit.

Federal and state authorities now propose a compromise. They will issue a permit allowing dredging and filling on thirty of the 125 acres that support hydrophytic plants if LHC agrees to transfer the twenty-five tideland acres to the state by quitclaim deed (the state claims it already holds title to these lands under the public trust doctrine), and to preserve both the ponding area and the coastal woodlot in their natural state.

As you read the following materials, try to determine what legal rights LHC has in this situation. Should the company accept the offered deal?

B.   SCOPE OF FEDERAL WETLANDS AUTHORITY

Excerpts from the Clean Water Act

33 U.S.C. §§ 1251–1387.

Sec. 404   Permits for dredged or fill material

(a) The Secretary [of the Army] may issue permits, after notice and opportunity for public hearings for the discharge of dredged or fill material into the navigable waters at specified disposal sites * * *.

(b) Subject to subsection (c) of this section, each such disposal site shall be specified for each such permit by the Secretary (1) through the application of guidelines developed by the Administrator [of the Environmental Protection Agency], in conjunction with the Secretary * * *, and (2) in any case where such guidelines under clause (1) alone would prohibit the specification of a site, through the application additionally of the economic impact of the site on navigation and anchorage.

(c) The Administrator is authorized to prohibit the specification (including the withdrawal of specification) of any defined area as a disposal site, and he is authorized to deny or restrict the use of any defined area for specification (including the withdrawal of specification) as a disposal site, whenever he determines, after notice and opportunity for public hearings, that the discharge of such materials into such area will have an unacceptable adverse effect on municipal water supplies, shellfish beds and fishery areas (including spawning and breeding areas), wildlife, or recreational areas.

* * *

(f)(1) Except as provided in paragraph (2) of this subsection, the discharge of dredged or fill material—

(A) from normal farming, silviculture, and ranching activities such as plowing, seeding, cultivating, minor drainage, harvesting for the production of food, fiber, and forest products, or upland soil and water conservation practices;

* * *

is not prohibited by or otherwise subject to regulation under this section * * *.

(2) Any discharge of dredged or fill material into the navigable waters incidental to any activity having as its purpose bringing an area of the navigable waters into a use to which it was not previously subject, where the flow or circulation of navigable waters may be impaired or the reach of such waters be reduced, shall be required to have a permit under this section.

Sec. 502   Definitions

* * *

(7) The term "navigable waters" means the waters of the United States, including the territorial seas.

Excerpts from Corps of Engineers Regulations
33 C.F.R. Part 328.

Sec. 328.3 Definitions

(a) The term *waters of the United States* means

(1) All waters which are currently used, or were used in the past, or may be susceptible to use in interstate or foreign commerce, including all waters which are subject to the ebb and flow of the tide;

(2) All interstate waters including interstate wetlands;

(3) All other waters such as intrastate lakes, rivers, streams (including intermittent streams), mudflats, sandflats, wetlands, sloughs, prairie potholes, wet meadows, playa lakes, or natural ponds, the use, degradation or destruction of which could affect interstate or foreign commerce including any such waters:

(i) Which are or could be used by interstate or foreign travelers for recreational or other purposes; or

(ii) From which fish or shellfish are or could be taken and sold in interstate or foreign commerce; or

(iii) Which are used or could be used for industrial purpose by industries in interstate commerce;

(4) All impoundments of waters otherwise defined as waters of the United States under the definition;

(5) Tributaries of waters identified in paragraphs (a)(1) through (4) of this section;

(6) The territorial seas;

(7) Wetlands adjacent to waters (other than waters that are themselves wetlands) identified in paragraphs (a)(1) through (6) of this section.

* * *

(b) The term *wetlands* means those areas that are inundated or saturated by surface or ground water at a frequency and duration sufficient to support, and that under normal circumstances do support, a prevalence of vegetation typically adapted for life in saturated soil conditions. Wetlands generally include swamps, marshes, bogs, and similar areas.

(c) The term *adjacent* means bordering, contiguous, or neighboring. Wetlands separated from other waters of the United States by man-made dikes or barriers, natural river berms, beach dunes and the like are "adjacent wetlands."

United States v. Riverside Bayview Homes, Inc.

United States Supreme Court, 1985.
474 U.S. 121, 106 S.Ct. 455, 88 L.Ed.2d 419.

■ JUSTICE WHITE delivered the opinion of the Court.

This case presents the question whether the Clean Water Act (CWA), 33 U.S.C. § 1251 et seq., together with certain regulations promulgated under its authority by the Army Corps of Engineers, authorizes the Corps to require landowners to obtain permits from the Corps before discharging fill material into wetlands adjacent to navigable bodies of water and their tributaries.

The relevant provisions of the Clean Water Act originated in the Federal Water Pollution Control Act Amendments of 1972, 86 Stat. 816, and have remained essentially unchanged since that time. Under §§ 301 and 502 of the Act, 33 U.S.C. §§ 1311 and 1362, any discharge of dredged or fill materials into "navigable waters"—defined as the "waters of the United States"—is forbidden unless authorized by a permit issued by the Corps of Engineers pursuant to § 404, 33 U.S.C. § 1344. After initially construing the Act to cover only waters navigable in fact, in 1975 the Corps issued interim final regulations redefining "the waters of the United

States" to include not only actually navigable waters but also tributaries of such waters, interstate waters and their tributaries, and nonnavigable intrastate waters whose use or misuse could affect interstate commerce. 40 Fed. Reg. 31320 (1975). More importantly for present purposes, the Corps construed the Act to cover all "freshwater wetlands" that were adjacent to other covered waters. * * *

Respondent Riverside Bayview Homes, Inc. (hereafter respondent), owns 80 acres of low-lying, marshy land near the shores of Lake St. Clair in Macomb County, Michigan. In 1976, respondent began to place fill materials on its property as part of its preparations for construction of a housing development. The Corps of Engineers, believing that the property was an "adjacent wetland" under the 1975 regulation defining "waters of the United States," filed suit in the United States District Court for the Eastern District of Michigan, seeking to enjoin respondent from filling the property without the permission of the Corps.

* * *

The question whether the Corps of Engineers may demand that respondent obtain a permit before placing fill material on its property is primarily one of regulatory and statutory interpretation: we must determine whether respondent's property is an "adjacent wetland" within the meaning of the applicable regulation, and, if so, whether the Corps' jurisdiction over "navigable waters" gives it statutory authority to regulate discharges of fill material into such a wetland. * * *

[T]he question whether the regulation at issue requires respondent to obtain a permit before filling its property is an easy one. The regulation extends the Corps' authority under § 404 to all wetlands adjacent to navigable or interstate waters and their tributaries. Wetlands, in turn, are defined as lands that are "inundated *or saturated* by surface *or ground water* at a frequency and duration sufficient to support, and that under normal circumstances do support, a prevalence of vegetation typically adapted for life in saturated soil conditions." The plain language of the regulation refutes the Court of Appeals' conclusion that inundation or "frequent flooding" by the adjacent body of water is a *sine qua non* of a wetland under the regulation. Indeed, the regulation could hardly state more clearly that saturation by either surface or ground water is sufficient to bring an area within the category of wetlands, provided that the saturation is sufficient to and does support wetland vegetation.

* * *

Without the nonexistent requirement of frequent flooding, the regulatory definition of adjacent wetlands covers the property here. The District Court found that respondent's property was "characterized by the presence of vegetation that requires saturated soil conditions for growth and reproduction," and that the source of the saturated soil conditions on the property was ground water. There is no plausible suggestion that these findings are clearly erroneous, and they plainly bring the property within the category of wetlands as defined by the current regulation. In addition, the court found that the wetland located on respondent's property was adjacent to a body of navigable water, since the area characterized by saturated soil conditions and wetland vegetation extended beyond the boundary of respondent's property to Black Creek, a navigable waterway. Again, the court's finding is not clearly erroneous. Together, these findings establish that respondent's property is a wetland adjacent to a navigable waterway. * * *

An agency's construction of a statute it is charged with enforcing is entitled to deference if it is reasonable and not in conflict with the expressed intent of Congress. Accordingly, our review is limited to the question whether it is reasonable, in light of the language, policies, and legislative history of the Act for the Corps to exercise jurisdiction over wetlands adjacent to but not regularly flooded by rivers, streams, and other hydrographic features more conventionally identifiable as "waters."[8]

On a purely linguistic level, it may appear unreasonable to classify "lands," wet or otherwise, as "waters." Such a simplistic response, however, does justice neither to the problem faced by the Corps in defining the scope of its authority under § 404(a) nor to the realities of the problem of water pollution that the Clean Water Act was intended to combat. In determining the limits of its power to regulate discharges under the Act, the Corps must necessarily choose some point at which water ends and land begins. Our common experience tells us that this is often no easy task: the transition from water to solid ground is not necessarily or even typically an abrupt one. Rather, between open waters and dry land may lie shallows, marshes, mudflats, swamps, bogs—in short, a huge array of areas that are not wholly aquatic but nevertheless fall far short of being dry land. Where on this continuum to find the limit of "waters" is far from obvious.

Faced with such a problem of defining the bounds of its regulatory authority, an agency may appropriately look to the legislative history and underlying policies of its statutory grants of authority. Neither of these sources provides unambiguous guidance for the Corps in this case, but together they do support the reasonableness of the Corps' approach of defining adjacent wetlands as "waters" within the meaning of § 404(a). Section 404 originated as part of the Federal Water Pollution Control Act Amendments of 1972, which constituted a comprehensive legislative attempt "to restore and maintain the chemical, physical, and biological integrity of the Nation's waters." 33 U.S.C. § 1251. This objective incorporated a broad, systemic view of the goal of maintaining and improving water quality: as the House Report on the legislation put it, "the word 'integrity' ... refers to a condition in which the natural structure and function of ecosystems [are] maintained." H.R. Rep. No. 92–911, p. 76 (1972). * * *

8. We are not called upon to address the question of the authority of the Corps to regulate discharges of fill material into wet- lands that are not adjacent to bodies of open water and we do not express any opinion on that question.

In keeping with these views, Congress chose to define the waters covered by the Act broadly. Although the Act prohibits discharges into "navigable waters," the Act's definition of "navigable waters" as "the waters of the United States" makes it clear that the term "navigable" as used in the Act is of limited import. In adopting this definition of "navigable waters," Congress evidently intended to repudiate limits that had been placed on federal regulation by earlier water pollution control statutes and to exercise its powers under the Commerce Clause to regulate at least some waters that would not be deemed "navigable" under the classical understanding of that term.

Of course, it is one thing to recognize that Congress intended to allow regulation of waters that might not satisfy traditional tests of navigability; it is another to assert that Congress intended to abandon traditional notions of "waters" and include in that term "wetlands" as well. Nonetheless, the evident breadth of congressional concern for protection of water quality and aquatic ecosystems suggests that it is reasonable for the Corps to interpret the term "waters" to encompass wetlands adjacent to waters as more conventionally defined. Following the lead of the Environmental Protection Agency, the Corps has determined that wetlands adjacent to navigable waters do as a general matter play a key role in protecting and enhancing water quality:

> "The regulation of activities that cause water pollution cannot rely on ... artificial lines ... but must focus on all waters that together form the entire aquatic system. Water moves in hydrologic cycles, and the pollution of this part of the aquatic system, regardless of whether it is above or below an ordinary high water mark, or mean high tide line, will affect the water quality of the other waters within that aquatic system.

> "For this reason, the landward limit of Federal jurisdiction under Section 404 must include any adjacent wetlands that form the border of or are in reasonable proximity to other waters of the United States, as these wetlands are part of this aquatic system." 42 Fed. Reg. 37128 (1977).

We cannot say that the Corps' conclusion that adjacent wetlands are inseparably bound up with the "waters" of the United States—based as it is on the Corps' and EPA's technical expertise—is unreasonable. In view of the breadth of federal regulatory authority contemplated by the Act itself and the inherent difficulties of defining precise bounds to regulable waters, the Corps' ecological judgment about the relationship between waters and their adjacent wetlands provides an adequate basis for a legal judgment that adjacent wetlands may be defined as waters under the Act.

This holds true even for wetlands that are not the result of flooding or permeation by water having its source in adjacent bodies of open water. The Corps has concluded that wetlands may affect the water quality of adjacent lakes, rivers, and streams even when the waters of those bodies do not actually inundate the wetlands. For example, wetlands that are not flooded by adjacent waters may still tend to drain into those waters. In such circumstances, the Corps has concluded that wetlands may serve to filter and purify water draining into adjacent bodies of water, and to slow the flow of surface runoff into lakes, rivers, and streams and thus prevent flooding and erosion. In addition, adjacent wetlands may "serve significant natural biological functions, including food chain production, general habitat, and nesting, spawning, rearing and resting sites for aquatic ... species." In short, the Corps has concluded that wetlands adjacent to lakes, rivers, streams, and other bodies of water may function as integral parts of the aquatic environment even when the moisture creating the wetlands does not find its source in the adjacent bodies of water. Again, we cannot say that the Corps' judgment on these matters is unreasonable, and we therefore conclude that a definition of "waters of the United States" encompassing all wetlands adjacent to other bodies of water over which the Corps has jurisdiction is a permissible interpretation of the Act. Because respondent's property is part of a wetland that actually abuts on a navigable waterway, respondent was required to have a permit in this case.[9]

Following promulgation of the Corps' interim final regulations in 1975, the Corps' assertion of authority under § 404 over waters not actually navigable engendered some congressional opposition. The controversy came to a head during Congress' consideration of the Clean Water Act of 1977 * * *. In the end, however, as we shall explain, Congress acquiesced in the administrative construction.

Critics of the Corps' permit program attempted to insert limitations on the Corps' § 404 jurisdiction into the 1977 legislation: the House bill as reported out of committee proposed a redefinition of "navigable waters" that would have limited the Corps' authority under § 404 to waters navigable in fact and their adjacent wetlands (defined as wetlands periodically inundated by contiguous navigable waters). H.R. 3199, 95th Cong., 1st Sess., § 16 (1977). The bill reported by the Senate Committee on Environment and Public Works, by contrast, contained no redefinition of the scope of the "navigable waters" covered by § 404 * * *.

The Conference Committee adopted the Senate's approach: efforts to narrow the definition of "waters" were abandoned * * *.

The significance of Congress' treatment of the Corps' § 404 jurisdiction in its consideration of the Clean Water Act of 1977 is twofold. First, the scope of the Corps' asserted jurisdiction over wetlands was specifically

---

9. Of course, it may well be that not every adjacent wetland is of great importance to the environment of adjoining bodies of water. But the existence of such cases does not seriously undermine the Corps' decision to define all adjacent wetlands as "waters." If it is reasonable for the Corps to conclude that in the majority of cases, adjacent wetlands have significant effects on water quality and the aquatic ecosystem, its definition can stand. That the definition may include some wetlands that are not significantly intertwined with the ecosystem of adjacent waterways is of little moment, for where it appears that a wetland covered by the Corps' definition is in fact lacking in importance to the aquatic environment—or where its importance is outweighed by other values—the Corps may always allow development of the wetland for other uses simply by issuing a permit.

brought to Congress' attention, and Congress rejected measures designed to curb the Corps' jurisdiction in large part because of its concern that protection of wetlands would be unduly hampered by a narrowed definition of "navigable waters." Although we are chary of attributing significance to Congress' failure to act, a refusal by Congress to overrule an agency's construction of legislation is at least some evidence of the reasonableness of that construction, particularly where the administrative construction has been brought to Congress' attention through legislation specifically designed to supplant it.

Second, it is notable that even those who would have restricted the reach of the Corps' jurisdiction would have done so not by removing wetlands altogether from the definition of "waters of the United States," but only by restricting the scope of "navigable waters" under § 404 to waters navigable in fact *and their adjacent wetlands.* * * * These views provide additional support for a conclusion that Congress in 1977 acquiesced in the Corps' definition of waters as including adjacent wetlands.

* * *

We are thus persuaded that the language, policies, and history of the Clean Water Act compel a finding that the Corps has acted reasonably in interpreting the Act to require permits for the discharge of fill material into wetlands adjacent to the "waters of the United States." The regulation in which the Corps has embodied this interpretation by its terms includes the wetlands on respondent's property within the class of waters that may not be filled without a permit; and, as we have seen, there is no reason to interpret the regulation more narrowly than its terms would indicate. Accordingly, the judgment of the Court of Appeals is

Reversed.

Solid Waste Agency of Northern Cook County v. United States Army Corps of Engineers

United States Supreme Court, 2001.
531 U.S. 159, 121 S.Ct. 675, 148 L.Ed.2d 576.

■ CHIEF JUSTICE REHNQUIST delivered the opinion of the Court.

Section 404(a) of the Clean Water Act (CWA or Act) 33 U.S.C. § 1344(a), regulates the discharge of dredged or fill material into "navigable waters." The United States Army Corps of Engineers (Corps), has interpreted § 404(a) to confer federal authority over an abandoned sand and gravel pit in northern Illinois which provides habitat for migratory birds. We are asked to decide whether the provisions of § 404(a) may be fairly extended to these waters, and, if so, whether Congress could exercise such authority consistent with the Commerce Clause, U.S. Const., Art. I, § 8, cl. 3. We answer the first question in the negative and therefore do not reach the second.

Petitioner, the Solid Waste Agency of Northern Cook County (SWANCC), is a consortium of 23 suburban Chicago cities and villages that united in an effort to locate and develop a disposal site for baled nonhazardous solid waste. The Chicago Gravel Company informed the municipalities of the availability of a 533–acre parcel, bestriding the Illinois counties Cook and Kane, which had been the site of a sand and gravel pit mining operation for three decades up until about 1960. Long since abandoned, the old mining site eventually gave way to a successional stage forest, with its remnant excavation trenches evolving into a scattering of permanent and seasonal ponds of varying size (from under one-tenth of an acre to several acres) and depth (from several inches to several feet).

The municipalities decided to purchase the site for disposal of their baled nonhazardous solid waste. By law, SWANCC was required to file for various permits from Cook County and the State of Illinois before it could begin operation of its balefill project. In addition, because the operation called for the filling of some of the permanent and seasonal ponds, SWANCC contacted federal respondents (hereinafter respondents), including the Corps, to determine if a federal landfill permit was required under § 404(a) of the CWA, 33 U.S.C. § 1344(a).

Section 404(a) grants the Corps authority to issue permits "for the discharge of dredged or fill material into the navigable waters at specified disposal sites." *Ibid*. The term "navigable waters" is defined under the Act as "the waters of the United States, including the territorial seas." § 1362(7). The Corps has issued regulations defining the term "waters of the United States" to include

"waters such as intrastate lakes, rivers, streams (including intermittent streams), mudflats, sandflats, wetlands, sloughs, prairie potholes, wet meadows, playa lakes, or natural ponds, the use, degradation or destruction of which could affect interstate or foreign commerce...." 33 CFR § 328.3(a)(3) (1999).

In 1986, in an attempt to "clarify" the reach of its jurisdiction, the Corps stated that § 404(a) extends to intrastate waters:

"a. Which are or would be used as habitat by birds protected by Migratory Bird Treaties; or

"b. Which are or would be used as habitat by other migratory birds which cross state lines; or

"c. Which are or would be used as habitat for endangered species; or

"d. Used to irrigate crops sold in interstate commerce."

51 Fed. Reg. 41217. This last promulgation has been dubbed the "Migratory Bird Rule."

The Corps initially concluded that it had no jurisdiction over the site because it contained no "wetlands," or areas which support "vegetation typically adapted for life in saturated soil conditions," 33 CFR § 328.3(b) (1999). However, after the Illinois Nature Preserves Commission informed the Corps that a number of migratory bird species had been observed at the site, the Corps reconsidered and ultimately asserted jurisdiction over the balefill site pursuant to subpart (b) of the "Migratory Bird Rule." The Corps found that approximately 121 bird species had been observed at the site, including several known to depend upon aquatic environments for a significant portion of their life requirements. Thus, on November 16, 1987, the Corps formally "determined that the seasonally ponded, abandoned gravel mining depressions located on the project site, while not wetlands, did qualify as 'waters of the United States' ... based upon the following criteria: (1) the proposed site had been abandoned as a gravel mining operation; (2) the water areas and spoil piles had developed a natural character; and (3) the water areas are used as habitat by migratory bird [sic] which cross state lines."

During the application process, SWANCC made several proposals to mitigate the likely displacement of the migratory birds and to preserve a great blue heron rookery located on the site. Its balefill project ultimately received the necessary local and state approval. By 1993, SWANCC had received a special use planned development permit from the Cook County Board of Appeals, a landfill development permit from the Illinois Environmental Protection Agency, and approval from the Illinois Department of Conservation.

Despite SWANCC's securing the required water quality certification from the Illinois Environmental Protection Agency, the Corps refused to issue a § 404(a) permit. * * *

Petitioner filed suit under the Administrative Procedure Act in the Northern District of Illinois challenging both the Corps' jurisdiction over the site and the merits of its denial of the § 404(a) permit. The District Court granted summary judgment to respondents on the jurisdictional issue, and petitioner abandoned its challenge to the Corps' permit decision. On appeal to the Court of Appeals for the Seventh Circuit, petitioner renewed its attack on respondents' use of the "Migratory Bird Rule" to assert jurisdiction over the site. Petitioner argued that respondents had exceeded their statutory authority in interpreting the CWA to cover non-navigable, isolated, intrastate waters based upon the presence of migratory birds and, in the alternative, that Congress lacked the power under the Commerce Clause to grant such regulatory jurisdiction.

* * *

This is not the first time we have been called upon to evaluate the meaning of § 404(a). In *United States v. Riverside Bayview Homes, Inc.,* 474 U.S. 121 (1985), we held that the Corps had § 404(a) jurisdiction over wetlands that actually abutted on a navigable waterway. In so doing, we noted that the term "navigable" is of "limited import" and that Congress evidenced its intent to "regulate at least some waters that would not be deemed 'navigable' under the classical understanding of that term." *Id.,* at 133. But our holding was based in large measure upon Congress' unequivocal acquiescence to, and approval of, the Corps' regulations interpreting the CWA to cover wetlands adjacent to navigable waters. We found that

Congress' concern for the protection of water quality and aquatic ecosystems indicated its intent to regulate wetlands "inseparably bound up with the 'waters' of the United States." *Id.*, at 134.

It was the significant nexus between the wetlands and "navigable waters" that informed our reading of the CWA in *Riverside Bayview Homes*. Indeed, we did not "express any opinion" on the "question of the authority of the Corps to regulate discharges of fill material into wetlands that are not adjacent to bodies of open water...." *Id.*, at 131–132, n. 8. In order to rule for respondents here, we would have to hold that the jurisdiction of the Corps extends to ponds that are *not* adjacent to open water. But we conclude that the text of the statute will not allow this.
* * * 3

Respondents next contend that whatever its original aim in 1972, Congress charted a new course five years later when it approved the more expansive definition of "navigable waters" found in the Corps' 1977 regulations. In July 1977, the Corps formally * * * defined "waters of the United States" to include "isolated wetlands and lakes, intermittent streams, prairie potholes, and other waters that are not part of a tributary system to interstate waters or to navigable waters of the United States, the degradation or destruction of which could affect interstate commerce." Respondents argue that Congress was aware of this more expansive interpretation during its 1977 amendments to the CWA. Specifically, respondents point to a failed House bill, H.R. 3199, that would have defined "navigable waters" as "all waters which are presently used, or are susceptible to use in their natural condition or by reasonable improvement as a means to transport interstate or foreign commerce." 123 Cong. Rec. 10420, 10434 (1977). * * *

Although we have recognized congressional acquiescence to administrative interpretations of a statute in some situations, we have done so with extreme care. "[F]ailed legislative proposals are a particularly dangerous ground on which to rest an interpretation of a prior statute." *Central Bank of Denver, N.A. v. First Interstate Bank of Denver, N.A.*, 511 U.S. 164, 187 (1994). A bill can be proposed for any number of reasons, and it can be rejected for just as many others. The relationship between the actions and inactions of the 95th Congress and the intent of the 92d Congress in passing § 404(a) is also considerably attenuated. Because "subsequent history is less illuminating than the contemporaneous evidence," *Hagen v. Utah*, 510 U.S. 399, 420 (1994), respondents face a difficult task in overcoming the plain text and import of § 404(a).

We conclude that respondents have failed to make the necessary showing that the failure of the 1977 House bill demonstrates Congress'

---

3. Respondents refer us to portions of the legislative history that they believe indicate Congress' intent to expand the definition of "navigable waters." Although the Conference Report includes the statement that the conferees "intend that the term 'navigable waters' be given the broadest possible constitutional interpretation," S. Conf. Rep. No. 92–1236, p. 144 (1972), neither this, nor anything else in the legislative history to which respondents point, signifies that Congress intended to exert anything more than its commerce power over navigation. * * *

acquiescence to the Corps' regulations or the "Migratory Bird Rule," which, of course, did not first appear until 1986. Although respondents cite some legislative history showing Congress' recognition of the Corps' assertion of jurisdiction over "isolated waters," as we explained in *Riverside Bayview Homes,* "[i]n both Chambers, debate on the proposals to narrow the definition of navigable waters centered largely on the issue of wetlands preservation." 474 U.S., at 136. Beyond Congress' desire to regulate wetlands adjacent to "navigable waters," respondents point us to no persuasive evidence that the House bill was proposed in response to the Corps' claim of jurisdiction over nonnavigable, isolated, intrastate waters or that its failure indicated congressional acquiescence to such jurisdiction.

* * *

We thus decline respondents' invitation to take what they see as the next ineluctable step after *Riverside Bayview Homes*: holding that isolated ponds, some only seasonal, wholly located within two Illinois counties, fall under § 404(a)'s definition of "navigable waters" because they serve as habitat for migratory birds. As counsel for respondents conceded at oral argument, such a ruling would assume that "the use of the word navigable in the statute . . . does not have any independent significance." We cannot agree that Congress' separate definitional use of the phrase "waters of the United States" constitutes a basis for reading the term "navigable waters" out of the statute. We said in *Riverside Bayview Homes* that the word "navigable" in the statute was of "limited import" and went on to hold that § 404(a) extended to nonnavigable wetlands adjacent to open waters. But it is one thing to give a word limited effect and quite another to give it no effect whatever. The term "navigable" has at least the import of showing us what Congress had in mind as its authority for enacting the CWA: its traditional jurisdiction over waters that were or had been navigable in fact or which could reasonably be so made.

Respondents—relying upon all of the arguments addressed above—contend that, at the very least, it must be said that Congress did not address the precise question of § 404(a)'s scope with regard to nonnavigable, isolated, intrastate waters, and that, therefore, we should give deference to the "Migratory Bird Rule." We find § 404(a) to be clear, but even were we to agree with respondents, we would not extend *Chevron* deference here.

Where an administrative interpretation of a statute invokes the outer limits of Congress' power, we expect a clear indication that Congress intended that result. See Edward J. DeBartolo Corp. v. Florida Gulf Coast Building & Constr. Trades Council, 485 U.S. 568, 575 (1988). This requirement stems from our prudential desire not to needlessly reach constitutional issues and our assumption that Congress does not casually authorize administrative agencies to interpret a statute to push the limit of congressional authority. This concern is heightened where the administrative interpretation alters the federal-state framework by permitting federal encroachment upon a traditional state power. Thus, "where an otherwise acceptable construction of a statute would raise serious constitutional problems, the Court will construe the statute to avoid such problems unless such construction is plainly contrary to the intent of Congress." *DeBartolo, supra,* at 575.

Twice in the past six years we have reaffirmed the proposition that the grant of authority to Congress under the Commerce Clause, though broad, is not unlimited. See United States v. Morrison, 529 U.S. 598 (2000); *United States v. Lopez,* 514 U.S. 549 (1995). Respondents argue that the "Migratory Bird Rule" falls within Congress' power to regulate intrastate activities that "substantially affect" interstate commerce. They note that the protection of migratory birds is a "national interest of very nearly the first magnitude," *Missouri v. Holland,* 252 U.S. 416, 435 (1920), and that, as the Court of Appeals found, millions of people spend over a billion dollars annually on recreational pursuits relating to migratory birds. These arguments raise significant constitutional questions. For example, we would have to evaluate the precise object or activity that, in the aggregate, substantially affects interstate commerce. This is not clear, for although the Corps has claimed jurisdiction over petitioner's land because it contains water areas used as habitat by migratory birds, respondents now, *post litem motam,* focus upon the fact that the regulated activity is petitioner's municipal landfill, which is "plainly of a commercial nature." But this is a far cry, indeed, from the "navigable waters" and "waters of the United States" to which the statute by its terms extends.

These are significant constitutional questions raised by respondents' application of their regulations, and yet we find nothing approaching a clear statement from Congress that it intended § 404(a) to reach an abandoned sand and gravel pit such as we have here. Permitting respondents to claim federal jurisdiction over ponds and mudflats falling within the "Migratory Bird Rule" would result in a significant impingement of the States' traditional and primary power over land and water use. Rather than expressing a desire to readjust the federal-state balance in this manner, Congress chose to "recognize, preserve, and protect the primary responsibilities and rights of States . . . to plan the development and use . . . of land and water resources. . . ." 33 U.S.C. § 1251(b). We thus read the statute as written to avoid the significant constitutional and federalism questions raised by respondents' interpretation, and therefore reject the request for administrative deference.

We hold that 33 CFR § 328.3(a)(3) (1999), as clarified and applied to petitioner's balefill site pursuant to the "Migratory Bird Rule," 51 Fed. Reg. 41217 (1986), exceeds the authority granted to respondents under § 404(a) of the CWA. The judgment of the Court of Appeals for the Seventh Circuit is therefore

Reversed.

■ JUSTICE STEVENS, with whom JUSTICE SOUTER, JUSTICE GINSBURG, and JUSTICE BREYER join, dissenting.

* * *

The Court has previously held that the Corps' broadened jurisdiction under the CWA properly included an 80–acre parcel of low-lying marshy land that was not itself navigable, directly adjacent to navigable water, or even hydrologically connected to navigable water, but which was part of a larger area, characterized by poor drainage, that ultimately abutted a navigable creek. *United States v. Riverside Bayview Homes, Inc.,* 474 U.S. 121 (1985).[2] Our broad finding in *Riverside Bayview* that the 1977 Congress had acquiesced in the Corps' understanding of its jurisdiction applies equally to the 410–acre parcel at issue here. Moreover, once Congress crossed the legal watershed that separates navigable streams of commerce from marshes and inland lakes, there is no principled reason for limiting the statute's protection to those waters or wetlands that happen to lie near a navigable stream.

In its decision today, the Court draws a new jurisdictional line, one that invalidates the 1986 migratory bird regulation as well as the Corps' assertion of jurisdiction over all waters except for actually navigable waters, their tributaries, and wetlands adjacent to each. Its holding rests on two equally untenable premises: (1) that when Congress passed the 1972 CWA, it did not intend "to exert anything more than its commerce power over navigation," *ante,* at 680, n. 3; and (2) that in 1972 Congress drew the boundary defining the Corps' jurisdiction at the odd line on which the Court today settles.

* * *

As we recognized in *Riverside Bayview,* the interests served by the statute embrace the protection of "significant natural biological functions, including food chain production, general habitat, and nesting, spawning, rearing and resting sites" for various species of aquatic wildlife. 474 U.S., at 134–135. For wetlands and "isolated" inland lakes, that interest is equally powerful, regardless of the proximity of the swamp or the water to a navigable stream. Nothing in the text, the stated purposes, or the legislative history of the CWA supports the conclusion that in 1972 Congress contemplated—much less commanded—the odd jurisdictional line that the Court has drawn today.

* * *

2. The District Court in *Riverside Bayview* found that there was no direct "hydrological" connection between the parcel at issue and any nearby navigable waters. The wetlands characteristics of the parcel were due, not to a surface or groundwater connection to any actually navigable water, but to "poor drainage" resulting from "the Lamson soil that underlay the property." Nevertheless, this Court found occasional surface run-off from the property into nearby waters to constitute a meaningful connection. *Riverside Bayview,* 474 U.S., at 134. Of course, the *ecological* connection between the wetlands and the nearby waters also played a central role in this Court's decision. *Riverside Bayview,* 474 U.S., at 134–135. Both types of connection are also present in many, and possibly most, "isolated" waters. Indeed, although the majority and petitioner both refer to the waters on petitioner's site as "isolated," their role as habitat for migratory birds, birds that serve important functions in the ecosystems of other waters throughout North America, suggests that—ecologically speaking—the waters at issue in this case are anything but isolated.

Although it might have appeared problematic on a "linguistic" level for the Corps to classify "lands" as "waters" in *Riverside Bayview,* 474 U.S., at 131–132 we squarely held that the agency's construction of the statute that it was charged with enforcing was entitled to deference * * *. Today, however, the majority refuses to extend such deference to the same agency's construction of the same statute. This refusal is unfaithful to both *Riverside Bayview* and *Chevron.* For it is the majority's reading, not the agency's, that does violence to the scheme Congress chose to put into place.

Contrary to the Court's suggestion, the Corps' interpretation of the statute does not "encroac[h]" upon "traditional state power" over land use. "Land use planning in essence chooses particular uses for the land; environmental regulation, at its core, does not mandate particular uses of the land but requires only that, however the land is used, damage to the environment is kept within prescribed limits." *California Coastal Comm'n v. Granite Rock Co.,* 480 U.S. 572, 587 (1987). The CWA is not a land-use code; it is a paradigm of environmental regulation. Such regulation is an accepted exercise of federal power.

It is particularly ironic for the Court to raise the specter of federalism while construing a statute that makes explicit efforts to foster local control over water regulation. Faced with calls to cut back on federal jurisdiction over water pollution, Congress rejected attempts to narrow the scope of that jurisdiction and, by incorporating § 404(g), opted instead for a scheme that encouraged States to supplant federal control with their own regulatory programs. Because Illinois could have taken advantage of the opportunities offered to it through § 404(g), the federalism concerns to which the majority adverts are misplaced. * * *

NOTES AND QUESTIONS

1. Is *Solid Waste Agency* consistent with *Riverside Bayview*? What inconsistencies do the dissenters see? How does the majority respond?

2. *Effect of Solid Waste Agency.* What is the extent of the Corps' regulatory jurisdiction following *Solid Waste Agency*? Does the decision affect the regulatory definition of "waters of the United States," or only the interpretive "migratory bird rule"? Would the Corps have prevailed if it had shown not only that birds used the ponds but that birdwatchers came from many states to observe the birds? As the Court points out in *Solid Waste Agency,* the migratory bird rule also described wetlands "[w]hich are or would be used as habitat for endangered species" as subject to federal jurisdiction. Does that portion of the rule survive? Could the Corps re-issue the migratory bird rule through notice and comment rulemaking on the theory that migratory birds form an ecological connection between isolated wetlands and navigable waterways?

3. *Adjacent Wetlands.* What does it mean for wetlands to be "adjacent" to waters of the United States? Must there be a surface hydrologic connection, or is a connection through groundwater sufficient? Is a seasonal marsh from which overflow runs to a navigable waterway during occasional flood periods an "adjacent" wetland? See United States v. Banks, 115 F.3d 916 (11th Cir.1997) (holding that wetlands were adjacent based on hydrological connection through groundwater and through surface water during storm events).

4. *Wetlands and the Commerce Clause.* If Congress enacted the migratory bird rule as an amendment to the Clean Water Act, would it be constitutional? Two circuits have upheld the rule's constitutionality, but both decisions predate the Supreme Court's recent restriction of the commerce power. See Hoffman Homes, Inc. v. Administrator, 999 F.2d 256 (7th Cir.1993); Leslie Salt Co. v. United States, 896 F.2d 354 (9th Cir.1990).

5. *Delineating Wetlands.* The regulatory definition of wetlands as "areas that are inundated or saturated . . . at a frequency and duration sufficient to support . . . vegetation typically adapted for life in saturated soil conditions" leaves many details unresolved. In practice, wetland delineation is carried out by examination of the vegetation, soils, and hydrology of the area, under the guidance of a Wetlands Delineation Manual produced in 1987 by the Corps of Engineers. The manual defines as diagnostic features of wetlands vegetation in which more than half the dominant species of plants are obligate wetland species, species found primarily in wetlands, or species which grow equally well in both wetlands and uplands; soils which are classified as hydric or show reducing (anaerobic) conditions; and inundation or soil saturation for about one-eighth or more of the growing season.

In 1989, the Corps, together with the other three agencies with some responsibility for identifying wetlands under federal law (EPA, the Fish and Wildlife Service, and the Natural Resources Conservation Service), produced a Joint Manual intended to provide a unified standard for wetlands delineation. Critics charged that the Joint Manual would greatly expand federal wetlands jurisdiction, and Congress barred its use, or the use of any subsequent manual not produced through notice and comment rulemaking. See Energy and Water Development Appropriations Act of 1992, Pub. L. No. 102–104, 105 Stat. 510 (1991). As a result, all four agencies now rely on the 1987 Corps of Engineers Manual.

6. *Regulated Activities.* Section 404 regulates only the discharge of dredged or fill material. It does not, by its terms, address the draining of wetlands. In Save Our Community v. EPA, 971 F.2d 1155 (5th Cir.1992), the Fifth Circuit agreed with EPA and the Corps that section 404 does not prohibit the removal of water from wetlands by pumping. Most wetland draining, however, is accomplished by dredging drainage ditches, a process that generally produces at least "incidental fallback," that is the redeposit of small quantities of dirt disturbed by a shovel or backhoe to approximately the same location. Ditching may also be accompanied by "sidecasting," the piling of removed soil alongside the ditch.

The Corps and EPA have always asserted that sidecasting is discharge of dredged material, and subject to section 404. They have waffled on incidental fallback. Regulations adopted in 1977 covered "any addition of dredged material into the waters of the United States." 42 Fed. Reg. 37,145 (July 19, 1977). In 1986, however, new regulations exempted "*de minimis,* incidental soil movement during normal dredging operations." 51 Fed. Reg. 41,232 (Nov. 13, 1986). In 1993, prompted by a lawsuit over development of more than 700 acres of wetlands using sophisticated techniques, such as welding shut openings in backhoe buckets, to minimize fallback, the agencies reversed course again, defining the "discharge of dredged material" to include "any addition of dredged material into, including any redeposit of dredged material within, the waters of the United States" 58 Fed. Reg. 45,008, 45,035 (Aug. 25, 1993). In the preamble to the 1993 rule, known as the Tulloch Rule after the litigation that inspired it, the agencies explained that "it is virtually impossible to conduct mechanized landclearing, ditching, channelization, or excavation in waters of the United States without causing incidental redeposition of dredged material (however small or temporary) in the process." 58 Fed. Reg. 45,017. The Tulloch Rule did exempt activities that would not destroy or degrade the waters of the United States, but placed the burden of proof on that issue on the person engaged in the activity.

The D.C. Circuit invalidated the Tulloch Rule in National Mining Association v. U.S. Army Corps of Engineers, 145 F.3d 1399 (D.C.Cir.1998). The court explained:

> We agree with the plaintiffs, and with the district court, that the straightforward statutory term "addition" cannot reasonably be said to encompass the situation in which material is removed from the waters of the United States and a small portion of it happens to fall back. Because incidental fallback represents a net withdrawal, not an addition, of material, it cannot be a discharge. * * * The agencies' primary counterargument—that fallback constitutes an "addition of any pollutant" because material becomes a pollutant only upon being dredged— is ingenious but unconvincing. Regardless of any legal metamorphosis that may occur at the moment of dredging, we fail to see how there can be an addition of dredged material when there is no addition of material. Although the Act includes "dredged spoil" in its list of pollutants, 33 U.S.C. § 1362(6), Congress could not have contemplated that the attempted removal of 100 tons of that substance could constitute an addition simply because only 99 tons of it were actually taken away. * * *

> [The National Wildlife Federation] complains that our understanding of "addition" reads the regulation of dredged material out of the statute. They correctly note that since dredged material comes from the waters of the United States, any discharge of such material into those waters could technically be described as a "redeposit," at least on a broad construction of that term. * * * But we do not hold that the Corps may not legally regulate some forms of redeposit under its § 404 permitting authority. We hold only that by asserting jurisdiction over "any redeposit," including incidental fallback, the Tulloch Rule outruns the Corps's statutory authority. Since the Act sets out no bright line between incidental fallback on the one hand and regulable redeposits on the other, a reasoned attempt by the agencies to draw such a line would merit considerable deference. But the Tulloch Rule makes no effort to draw such a line, and indeed its overriding purpose appears

to be to expand the Corps's permitting authority to encompass incidental fallback and, as a result, a wide range of activities that cannot
remotely be said to "add" anything to the waters of the United States.

Id. at 1404–05.

Did the D.C. Circuit correctly interpret the Clean Water Act? If
dredging stirs up the mud, making materials that once were bound up in
the soil biologically available, why isn't that the "addition" of dredged
material to the waters of the United States? On the other hand, do you
agree that the agencies can regulate sidecasting? Is the movement of soil a
small distance within a wetland the addition of dredged material?

Three days before the inauguration of George W. Bush, the Corps and
EPA issued a new regulation responding to *National Mining Association*.
The new regulation provides:

> The Corps and EPA regard the use of mechanized earth-moving
> equipment to conduct landclearing, ditching, channelization, in-stream
> mining or other earth-moving activity in waters of the United States as
> resulting in a discharge of dredged material unless project-specific
> evidence shows that the activity results in only incidental fallback.
> This paragraph does not and is not intended to shift any burden in any
> administrative or judicial proceeding under the CWA.
>
> *Incidental fallback* is the redeposit of small volumes of dredged
> material that is incidental to excavation activity in waters of the
> United States when such material falls back to substantially the same
> place as the initial removal. Examples of incidental fallback include soil
> that is disturbed when dirt is shoveled and the back-spill that comes
> off a bucket when such small volume of soil or dirt falls into substan-
> tially the same place from which it was initially removed.

66 Fed. Reg. 4550, 4575 (Jan. 17, 2001) (to be codified at 33 C.F.R.
§ 323.2(d)(2)). Is this new regulation valid?

Did Congress intend to regulate the types of activities that produce
fallback when it enacted section 404? If so, why didn't it explicitly require a
permit for dredging or draining as well as filling? Might legislators have
assumed, as the regulatory agencies now assert, that such activities almost
always add dredged material to the waters? Or did Congress intend only to
regulate wetlands alteration to the extent it threatens water quality and
assume that draining did not pose such a threat? What can (and should)
regulatory agencies do when technological advances create what seem to be
"loopholes" in the law they implement?

7. *State Wetland Programs.* Section 404 authorizes delegation to state
authorities of responsibility for permits "for the discharge of dredged or fill
material into the navigable waters (other than those waters which are
presently used, or are susceptible to use in their natural condition or by
reasonable improvement as a means to transport interstate or foreign
commerce * * *)" within their jurisdiction. 33 U.S.C. § 1344(g). To date
only Michigan and New Jersey have assumed section 404 authority.

Even without delegated authority, states have considerable leverage
over the section 404 permit process. Section 401 of the Clean Water Act,

discussed in more detail in Chapter 11, allows states to veto or impose conditions on federally-permitted activities involving discharges to the waters of the United States that are inconsistent with state water quality standards. According to EPA, "Some States rely on Section 401 certification as their primary mechanism to protect wetlands in the State." U.S. Environmental Protection Agency, Section 401 Certification and Wetlands (revised May 25, 1999) <http://www.epa.gov/OWOW/wetlands/facts /fact24. html>.

Many states do have some form of state or local regulatory wetland protection, overlapping to various degrees with section 404. Virtually all coastal states, for example, regulate the dredging and filling of coastal wetlands. A number of states also regulate activities in some or all freshwater wetlands. However, according to one analysis, only fourteen states protect isolated freshwater wetlands to any significant extent. See Jon Kusler, The SWANCC Decision and State Regulation of Wetlands 9 (2001). Many states are considering adopting or strengthening protection in the wake of the *Solid Waste Agency* decision. In states requiring wetland permits, obtaining federal authorization under section 404 does not obviate the requirement of a separate state permit. See 33 U.S.C. § 1344(t) ("Nothing in this section shall preclude or deny the right of any State or interstate agency to control the discharge of dredged or fill material in any portion of the navigable waters within the jurisdiction of such State.").

C.   WETLANDS PERMIT DECISIONS

The Army Corps of Engineers and EPA share responsibility for implementing the § 404 program. The Corps bears the primary responsibility for evaluating permit applications. It must ensure that the action permitted complies with regulatory Guidelines (excerpted below) developed primarily by EPA, in consultation with the Corps. Even if the application meets the requirements of the Guidelines, the Corps may still deny a permit if, following consideration of a wide range of factors, it concludes that the proposed activity would be contrary to the public interest. 33 C.F.R. § 320.4(a)(1).

Although receipt of a Corps permit is necessary for a regulated project to proceed, it is not sufficient to ensure that the project can go ahead. EPA may veto any Corps-issued permit that would cause "an unacceptable adverse effect" on water supplies, fisheries, wildlife, or recreation. 33 U.S.C. § 1344(c).

Excerpts from Environmental Protection Agency Regulations

40 C.F.R. Part 230.

Sec. 230.10   Restrictions on Discharge

(a) Except as provided under section 404(b)(2), no discharge of dredged or fill material shall be permitted if there is a practicable alternative to the proposed discharge which would have less adverse impact on the aquatic ecosystem, so long as the alternative does not have other significant adverse environmental consequences.

(1) For the purpose of this requirement, practicable alternatives include, but are not limited to:

(i) Activities which do not involve a discharge of dredged or fill material into the waters of the United States or ocean waters;

(ii) Discharges of dredged or fill material at other locations in waters of the United States or ocean waters;

(2) An alternative is practicable if it is available and capable of being done after taking into consideration cost, existing technology, and logistics in light of overall project purposes. If it is otherwise a practicable alternative, an area not presently owned by the applicant which could reasonably be obtained, utilized, expanded or managed in order to fulfill the basic purpose of the proposed activity may be considered.

(3) Where the activity associated with a discharge which is proposed for a special aquatic site* does not require access or proximity to or siting within the special aquatic site in question to fulfill its basic purpose (i.e., is not "water dependent"), practicable alternatives that do not involve special aquatic sites are presumed to be available, unless clearly demonstrated otherwise. In addition, where a discharge is proposed for a special aquatic site, all practicable alternatives to the proposed discharge which do not involve a discharge into a special aquatic site are presumed to have less adverse impact on the aquatic ecosystem, unless clearly demonstrated otherwise.

* * *

(b) No discharge of dredged or fill material shall be permitted if it:

(1) Causes or contributes, after consideration of disposal site dilution and dispersion, to violations of any applicable State water quality standard;

(2) Violates any applicable toxic effluent standard or prohibition under section 307 of the Act;

(3) Jeopardizes the continued existence of species listed as endangered or threatened under the Endangered Species Act, or results in likelihood of the destruction or adverse modification of a habitat which is determined by the Secretary of Interior or Commerce, as appropriate, to be a critical habitat under the Endangered Species Act. If an exemption has been granted by the Endangered Species Committee, the terms of such exemption shall apply in lieu of this subparagraph;

* * *

---

* [Wetlands are among the areas considered "special aquatic sites." See 40 C.F.R. §§ 230.3(q–1); 230.41.—Eds.]

(c) Except as provided under section 404(b)(2), no discharge of dredged or fill material shall be permitted which will cause or contribute to significant degradation of the waters of the United States. * * *

(d) Except as provided under section 404(b)(2), no discharge of dredged or fill material shall be permitted unless appropriate and practicable steps have been taken which will minimize potential adverse impacts of the discharge on the aquatic ecosystem.

National Wildlife Federation v. Whistler

United States Court of Appeals, Eighth Circuit, 1994.
27 F.3d 1341.

■ JOHN R. GIBSON, SENIOR CIRCUIT JUDGE.

The Turnbow Development Corporation sought permission from the United States Corps of Engineers to make several changes necessary to provide water access to a planned residential development. The Corps issued the permit * * *. The National Wildlife Federation and Michael Donahue, a Federation member and an owner of property adjacent to the mitigation area, brought this action before the district court seeking to suspend the permit. The district court denied the requested relief and granted summary judgment for the defendants. Donahue appeals from the district court's judgment. We affirm.

The planned housing development is located just south of Bismarck, North Dakota, on uplands on the east side of the Missouri River. The requested permit would allow Turnbow to provide these lots with boat access to the Missouri River by re-opening an old river channel adjacent to the planned development, thereby destroying the channel's existing wetlands status. * * * In total, approximately 14.5 acres of wetlands would be converted to deep water habitat.

As required by 33 C.F.R. § 325.2–.3, the Corps gave public notice of the application and solicited comments from several state and federal agencies. These agencies suggested that the Corps condition the permit on a mitigation plan to offset the loss of wetlands, but lodged no further objections. Turnbow responded with a plan to enhance an existing twenty-acre wetlands area by providing it with year-round water and saturated soil conditions. After additional public notice and comment, the Corps issued an environmental assessment and decision document containing the agency's determination that the permit should be issued. The Corps concluded that the project's purpose was to provide boat access to the Missouri River from Turnbow's planned development. Given this purpose, the Corps considered the project water-dependent and site-specific. No other alternative, the Corps stated, would serve Turnbow's purpose. "A boat access area located elsewhere," the agency reasoned, "would not be functional for the applicant's needs." The Corps concluded that the permit did not conflict with the public interest and satisfied the Clean Water Act section 404(b)(1) guidelines. The agency further found that the project involved no significant impact on the quality of the human environment, and therefore did not require an environmental impact statement under the National Environmental Policy Act, 42 U.S.C. § 4321–4370a (1988). The agency issued the permit subject to forty-two conditions, including the requirement that Turnbow complete the enhancements to the mitigation area prior to any construction on the wetlands.

Donahue and the Federation sought a temporary restraining order and preliminary injunction to suspend the permit. The court denied the request for a temporary order and, after a two-day evidentiary hearing on the preliminary injunction issue, granted the Corps' motion for summary judgment. The court determined that "the Corps did not act in an arbitrary and capricious manner in processing and issuing the permit involved here." The court also stated that "no other properties are available to Turnbow which are suitable for residential lots with boat access to the river." This appeal followed.

Donahue argues on appeal that the Corps failed to perform an adequate alternatives analysis, as required by 40 C.F.R. § 230.10, before issuing the permit. In particular, Donahue argues that the Corps completely failed to consider the feasibility of a nearby public boat ramp as a means of water access to residents. * * *

* * * "It would hardly be putting the case too strongly to say that the Clean Water Act and the applicable regulations do not contemplate that wetlands will be destroyed simply because it is more convenient than not to do so." *Buttrey v. United States,* 690 F.2d 1170, 1180 (5th Cir.1982). Thus, where "there is a *practicable alternative* . . . which would have less adverse impact on the aquatic ecosystem," the Corps cannot issue a dredge or fill permit. 40 C.F.R. § 230.10(a) (1993) (emphasis added). Moreover, if a dredge or fill permit application does not concern a water-dependent project, the Corps assumes that practicable alternatives exist unless the applicant "clearly demonstrated otherwise." 40 C.F.R. § 230.10(a)(3). This presumption of practicable alternatives "is *very* strong," *Buttrey,* 690 F.2d at 1180 (emphasis in original), "creat[ing] an incentive for developers to avoid choosing wetlands when they could choose an alternative upland site," *Bersani v. Robichaud,* 850 F.2d 36, 44 (2d Cir.1988).

Despite these protections, Donahue faces an uphill road. When the Corps has followed the proper procedure, as here, a court may reverse only if the Corps' decision to issue the permit was an abuse of discretion, contrary to law, or arbitrary and capricious. 5 U.S.C. § 706(2)(A) (1988). * * *

Donahue argues that the Corps failed to even consider the availability of a local public boat ramp as an adequate alternative to Turnbow's proposal. The Corps explicitly acknowledged the existence of the boat ramp in its decision document, concluding that this access area was not "functional for the applicant's needs." In light of the Corps' determination of the project's purpose, the boat dock was, at best, an alternative. Our review of the record convinces us that the Corps considered the boat dock, but dismissed it as inadequate.

Donahue also argues that to the extent that the Corps did conduct an alternatives analysis, it reached an arbitrary and capricious result. Central to evaluating practicable alternatives is the determination of a project's purpose. Donahue suggests that the project's purpose is to build a residential or "high-end" residential development. Donahue relies on decisions by other courts that have rejected attempts by developers to build housing developments and adjacent boat docks on wetlands. In *Shoreline Associates v. Marsh*, 555 F.Supp. 169 (D.Md.1983), *aff'd*, 725 F.2d 677 (4th Cir.1984), for example, the court rejected one such attempt, stating that the "primary aspect of the proposed project is the construction of a townhouse community, not the construction of a boat storage facility and launch, which are incidental to it." *Id.* at 179. Similarly, in *Korteweg v. Corps of Engineers of the United States Army*, 650 F.Supp. 603, 606 (D.Conn.1986), the court also upheld the denial of a permit for a riverside residential development. Although "the ability to tie one's boat at an adjacent dock would make the [lots] more valuable . . . , the docks are neither essential to the [lots] nor are they integral to their residential use." *Id.* at 605. Thus, each of these courts concluded that the housing project was not water-dependent and applied the regulatory presumption that practicable alternatives exist.

The Corps, however, began its analysis of Turnbow's application by stating that the planned housing development site was located on uplands and therefore could proceed without a permit. The Corps limited its alternatives analysis to the boat access area. This exclusion of the residential portion of the project led the Corps to conclude that the "project's purpose is to provide boat access to the Missouri River from lots Mr. Turnbow proposes to develop adjacent to the project area." The Corps did not consider the uplands housing development to be part of the project for which Turnbow requested a permit. The project, so defined, is clearly water-dependent. Moreover, insofar as the project contemplated immediate boat access to Turnbow's residential development, it was also site-specific. Turnbow's locating of the planned residential buildings on the surrounding uplands distinguishes this case from both *Shoreline* and *Korteweg*, where the developers sought to build their planned residential buildings on the wetlands. In those cases, the developers could have presumably relocated the entire developments to other locations. Here, the Corps found that Turnbow's development would proceed on the uplands residences even if the Corps denied the permit.

* * *

Donahue argues that the Corps mistakenly defined the purpose of Turnbow's project. * * * The Corps found that the project, as modified to include the mitigation site, resulted in little or no net loss to the nation's wetlands. Moreover, the Corps found that Turnbow's uplands housing development would proceed even without the creation of water access. Donahue does not specifically contest either of these findings, and we cannot conclude that they are arbitrary and capricious. In light of these findings, and after conducting a thorough review, the Corps accepted Turnbow's characterization of the overall project as encompassing two severable projects, a conclusion that is not without support. "Obviously, an applicant cannot define a project in order to preclude the existence of any alternative sites and thus make what is practicable appear impracticable." *Sylvester II,* 882 F.2d at 409. The cumulative destruction of our nation's wetlands that would result if developers were permitted to artificially constrain the Corps' alternatives analysis by defining the projects' purpose in an overly narrow manner would frustrate the statute and its accompanying regulatory scheme. We do not believe the case before us raises these concerns. Moreover, our standard of review is a limited one. We conclude that neither the Corps' project definition nor its decision that no practicable alternatives existed was arbitrary and capricious.

Accordingly, we affirm.

Bersani v. Robichaud

United States Court of Appeals, Second Circuit, 1988.
850 F.2d 36.

■ Timbers, Circuit Judge.

Appellants John A. Bersani, the Pyramid Companies, Newport Galleria Group and Robert J. Congel ("Pyramid", collectively) appeal from a judgment * * * granting summary judgment in favor of appellees, the United States Environmental Protection Agency ("EPA"), [and] the United States Army Corps of Engineers (the "Corps") * * *.

I.

* * * Sweedens Swamp is a 49.5 acre wetland which is part of an 80 acre site near Interstate 95 in South Attleboro, Massachusetts. Although some illegal dumping and motorbike intrusions have occurred, these activities have been found to have had little impact on the site which remains a "high-quality red maple swamp" providing wildlife habitat and protecting the area from flooding and pollution.

The effort to build a mall on Sweedens Swamp was initiated by Pyramid's predecessor, the Edward J. DeBartolo Corporation ("DeBartolo"). DeBartolo purchased the Swamp some time before April 1982. At the time of this purchase an alternative site was available in North Attleboro (the "North Attleboro site"). * * *

Pyramid took over the project in 1983 * * *.

One of the key issues in dispute in the instant case is just when did Pyramid begin searching for a suitable site for its mall. EPA asserts that Pyramid began to search in the Spring of 1983. Pyramid asserts that it began to search several months later, in September 1983. The difference is crucial because on July 1, 1983—a date between the starting dates claimed by EPA and Pyramid—a competitor of Pyramid, the New England Development Co. ("NED"), purchased options to buy the North Attleboro site. This site was located upland and could have served as a "practicable alterna-

tive" to Sweedens Swamp, *if* it had been "available" at the relevant time.
* * *

In December 1983, Pyramid purchased Sweedens Swamp from DeBartolo. In August 1984, Pyramid applied under § 404(a) to the New England regional division of the Corps (the "NE Corps") for a permit. It sought to fill or alter 32 of the 49.6 acres of the Swamp; to excavate nine acres of uplands to create artificial wetlands; and to alter 13.3 acres of existing wetlands to improve its environmental quality. Later Pyramid proposed to mitigate the adverse impact on the wetlands by creating 36 acres of replacement wetlands in an off-site gravel pit.

* * *

In January 1985, the NE Corps hired a consultant to investigate the feasibility of Sweedens Swamp and the North Attleboro site. The consultant reported that either site was feasible but that from a commercial standpoint only one mall could survive in the area. On February 19, 1985, the NE Corps advised Pyramid that denial of its permit was imminent. On May 2, 1985, the NE Corps sent its recommendation to deny the permit to the national headquarters of the Corps. Although the NE Corps ordinarily makes the final decision on whether to grant a permit, in the instant case, because of widespread publicity, General John F. Wall, the Director of Civil Works at the national headquarters of the Corps, decided to review the NE Corps' decision. Wall reached a different conclusion. He decided to grant the permit after finding that Pyramid's offsite mitigation proposal would reduce the adverse impacts sufficiently to allow the "practicable alternative" test to be deemed satisfied. * * *

Although he did not explicitly address the issue, Wall apparently assumed that the relevant time to determine whether there was a practicable alternative was the time of the application, not the time the applicant entered the market. In other words, Wall appears to have assumed that the market entry theory was not the correct approach. For example, while addressing the traditional "practicable alternatives" analysis as an alternative ground for his decision, Wall found that the North Attleboro site was unavailable "because it has been optioned by another developer." Since the site was not optioned at the time EPA argues Pyramid entered the market, this language suggests (to Pyramid at least) that Wall could not have been employing the market entry approach.

On May 31, 1985, Wall ordered the NE Corps to send Pyramid, EPA and FWS a notice of its intent to grant the permit. The NE Corps complied on June 28, 1985.

[Following notice and two public hearings, EPA vetoed the Corps' decision.] It found (1) that the filling of the Swamp would adversely affect wildlife; (2) that the North Attleboro site could have been available to Pyramid at the time Pyramid investigated the area to search for a site; (3) that considering Pyramid's failure or unwillingness to provide further materials about its investigation of alternative sites, it was uncontested that, at best, Pyramid never checked the availability of the North Attleboro site as an alternative; (4) that the North Attleboro site was feasible and would have a less adverse impact on the wetland environment; and (5) that the mitigation proposal did not make the project preferable to other alternatives because of scientific uncertainty of success. In the second of these findings, EPA used what Pyramid calls the "market entry" approach.

On July 1, 1986, Pyramid commenced the instant action in the district court to vacate EPA's final determination as arbitrary and capricious. * * *

II.

One of Pyramid's principal contentions is that the market entry approach is inconsistent with [the 404(b)(1) guidelines].

* * * Pyramid reasons that the 404(b)(1) guidelines are framed in the present tense, while the market entry approach focuses on the *past* by considering whether a practicable alternative *was* available at the time the applicant entered the market to search for a site. To support its argument that the 404(b)(1) guidelines are framed in the present tense, Pyramid quotes the following language:

> "An alternative is practicable if it *is* available.... If it is otherwise a practicable alternative, an area not *presently* owned by the applicant which *could* reasonably *be* obtained, utilized, expanded or managed in order to fulfill the basic purpose of the proposed activity *may be* considered."

40 C.F.R. § 230.10(a)(2). It then argues that EPA says "is" means "was." * * *

While this argument has a certain surface appeal, we are persuaded that it is contrary to a common sense reading of the regulations; that it entails an overly literal and narrow interpretation of the language; and that it creates requirements not intended by Congress.

First, while it is true that the language is in the present tense, it does not follow that the most natural reading of the regulations would create a time-of-application rule. As EPA points out, "the regulations do not indicate *when* it is to be determined whether an alternative 'is' available," i.e., the "present" of the regulations might be the time the application is submitted; the time it is reviewed; or any number of other times. Based upon a reading of the language in the context of the controlling statute and the regulations as a whole, moreover, we conclude that when the agencies drafted the language in question they simply were not thinking of the specific issues raised by the instant case, in which an applicant had available alternatives at the time it was selecting its site but these alternatives had evaporated by the time it applied for a permit. We therefore agree with the district court that the regulations are essentially silent on the issue of timing and that it would be appropriate to consider the objectives of the Act and the intent underlying the promulgation of the regulations.

Second, as EPA has pointed out, the preamble to the 404(b)(1) guidelines states that the purpose of the "practicable alternatives" analysis is to * * * create an incentive for developers to avoid choosing wetlands when they could choose an alternative upland site. Pyramid's reading of the regulations would thwart this purpose because it would remove the incentive for a developer to search for an alternative site at the time such an incentive is needed, i.e., at the time it is making the decision to select a particular site. If the practicable alternatives analysis were applied to the time of the application for a permit, the developer would have little incentive to search for alternatives, especially if it were confident that alternatives soon would disappear. Conversely, in a case in which alternatives were not available at the time the developer made its selection, but became available by the time of application, the developer's application would be denied even though it could not have explored the alternative site at the time of its decision.

* * *

IV.

[Pyramid argues that the market entry theory is too vague to provide adequate notice to the regulated community, because] any number of points in time could constitute "entry" into the market. It speculates whether market entry occurs "from the time the first internal memorandum is written," or the time "the first consultant [is] hired," or the time the "first negotiation for a site [is] conducted." We are persuaded, however, that EPA is correct in asserting that it is unnecessary to pin down the standard to such a degree and that it would confuse things further to attempt to do so. Since the point of "entry" necessarily will vary from case to case, we believe the concept of "market entry" is the best method and is specific enough to put a developer on notice of when it should be considering alternative sites.

* * *

[W]e believe the extensive administrative record supports a finding that the North Attleboro site was available to Pyramid when it entered the market. Even if Pyramid were found not to have entered the market until September 1983, after NED had acquired options to purchase the North Attleboro site, it does not necessarily follow that the site was unavailable. Aside from the fact that NED did not acquire all the options for the North Attleboro site until June 1984, it also was possible for Pyramid to attempt to purchase the options from NED. The record shows no such attempts to purchase the site, or even to investigate its availability. Alternatively, even though the district court apparently was not persuaded by it, there also is evidence in the record to show that Pyramid actually entered the market in the Spring of 1983, before NED had purchased its options. Finally, the evidence shows that the North Attleboro site had been available to DeBartolo, Pyramid's predecessor. EPA could reasonably have determined that Pyramid should be held to "stand in the shoes" of DeBartolo * * *.

■ GEORGE C. PRATT, CIRCUIT JUDGE, dissenting.

* * * In this case I have no problem with EPA's basic approach. It conscientiously attempted to weigh the economic advantages against the

ecological disadvantages of developing Sweedens Swamp and, in approaching this determination, it properly looked to alternate available sites. However, EPA went wrong—seriously wrong—when it adopted the market entry theory to decide whether an alternate site was available. By focusing on the decisionmaking techniques and tactics of a particular developer, instead of the actual alternatives to disturbing the wetland, EPA ignored the statute's central purpose.

The market entry theory in effect taints a particular developer with respect to a particular site, while ignoring the crucial question of whether the site itself should be preserved. Under the market entry theory, developer A would be denied a permit on a specific site because when he entered the market alternatives were available, but latecomer developer B, who entered the market after those alternatives had become unavailable, would be entitled to a permit for developing the same site. In such a case, the theory no longer protects the land, but instead becomes a distorted punitive device: it punishes developer A by denying him a permit, but grants developer B a permit for the same property—and the only difference between them is when they "entered the market."

* * *

Furthermore, in a business that needs as much predictability as possible, the market entry theory will regrettably inject exquisite vagueness. When does a developer enter the market? When he first contemplates a development in the area? If so, in what area—the neighborhood, the village, the town, the state or the region? Does he enter the market when he first takes some affirmative action? If so, is that when he instructs his staff to research possible sites, when he commits money for more intensive study of those sites, when he contacts a real estate broker, when he first visits a site, or when he makes his first offer to purchase? Without answers to these questions a developer can never know whether to proceed through the expense of contracts, zoning proceedings, and EPA applications. * * *

Since congress delegated to EPA the responsibility for striking a difficult and sensitive balance among economic and ecological concerns, EPA should do so only after considering the circumstances which exist, not when the developer first conceived of his idea, nor when he entered the market, nor even when he submitted his application; rather, EPA, like a court of equity, should have the full benefit of, and should be required to consider, the circumstances which exist at the time it makes its decision. This is the only method which would allow EPA to make a fully informed decision—as congress intended—based on whether, at the moment, there is available a site which can provide needed economic and social benefits to the public, without unnecessarily disturbing valuable wetlands.

NOTES AND QUESTIONS

1. *Practicable Alternatives Analysis.* The § 404 guidelines prohibit the issuance of a permit to fill wetlands unless there is no practicable alternative that would have less adverse impact. The Corps adjusts the stringency of the practicable alternatives test based on the expected impact of the proposed project. Regulatory Guidance Letter 93–02. The First Circuit endorsed this approach in Norfolk v. United States Army Corps of Engineers, 968 F.2d 1438, 1447–48 (1st Cir.1992).

What is the purpose of the practicable alternatives test? What constitutes a practicable alternative? Does it depend on the resources of the individual developer seeking a permit? See Regulatory Guidance Letter 93–02 ("[T]he nature of the applicant may also be a relevant consideration in determining what constitutes a practicable alternative. It is important to emphasize, however, that it is not a particular applicant's financial standing that is the primary consideration for determining practicability, but rather characteristics of the project and what constitutes a reasonable expense for these projects that are most relevant to practicability determinations.").

Does it depend on who owns land that might offer a practicable alternative? Consider a hypothetical. Suppose Mall Development, Inc. proposes to build a mall on Dismal Swamp, a wetland. Five miles away, Supermalls Co. owns Dry Meadow, a site that contains no wetlands. Both companies acknowledge that Dry Meadow is suitable for a mall. Indeed, Supermalls has begun the preliminary process of planning one. Mall Development offers to purchase Dry Meadow, but Supermalls refuses to sell at the price offered. Shortly thereafter, Mall Development applies for a section 404 permit to fill Dismal Swamp in order to construct a mall. Is Dry Meadow a practicable alternative? Does it matter whether the area can support more than one mall?

2. *Timing.* At what point in time is the alternatives analysis conducted? The Corps has never endorsed the market entry approach, and continues to evaluate the existence of practicable alternatives as of the time the permit application is processed. Which is the better approach? What impact would the "market entry" approach have on developers' future choices of sites for non-water-dependent activities? Would it allow a subsequent developer to obtain a permit to develop Sweedens Swamp after Bersani had been denied a permit? If so, is that appropriate or not?

3. *Project Purposes and the § 404 Guidelines.* Identification of the purposes of the proposed project affects evaluation under the guidelines in two ways. First, if the project is not water-dependent, the Corps must presume that less damaging alternatives are available. Second, the project purpose strongly affects the identification of alternatives.

Was the project in *Whistler* water-dependent? How did the court distinguish other decisions holding that water-oriented housing developments were not water-dependent? Is some or all of the project proposed by Lovely Harbor Company in the Class Discussion Problem water-dependent? What alternatives must the Corps consider in evaluating LHC's permit application?

4. *General Permits.* Section 404(e) authorizes the Corps of Engineers to issue "general" permits on a nationwide, regional, or statewide basis for categories of activities it finds will have minimal individual and cumulative adverse effects on the environment. Notice and an opportunity for comment must be provided before general permits, which must be re-issued every five years, can become effective. The Corps has issued 44 nationwide permits. See 65 Fed. Reg. 12818 (March 9, 2000). No individual permit is needed for activities covered by a general permit; the discharger must simply comply with the general permit regulations. Many, but not all, of the nationwide permits allow landowners to undertake the authorized activity without notifying the Corps.

Until recently, the most controversial nationwide permit was NWP 26, which authorized discharges affecting up to ten acres of headwaters or isolated wetlands. NWP 26 became controversial because, although each permitted project affected only a small area, cumulative losses could be large. In 1996, the Corps limited NWP 26 to projects affecting no more than three acres, and announced that it would phase NWP 26 out entirely. 61 Fed. Reg. 65,874 (Dec. 13, 1996). In 2000, the Corps issued a series of activity-specific NWPs to replace NWP 26. 65 Fed. Reg. 12,818 (March 9, 2000). The new permits are limited to activities affecting no more than one-half acre of wetlands, and most set a predischarge notice threshold of one-tenth acre. The National Association of Home Builders and other regulated groups have challenged the new permits.

In 1995, in part to compensate for the restrictions on NWP 26, the Corps issued a new permit, NWP 29, covering fill of up to one-half acre of non-tidal wetlands for the purpose of constructing a single-family home. 60 Fed. Reg. 38,650 (July 27, 1995). In Alaska Center for the Environment v. West, 31 F.Supp.2d 714 (D.Alaska 1998), the District Court ruled that the environmental assessment accompanying NWP 29 had not adequately considered the alternatives of a smaller acreage ceiling and exclusion of high-value waters. In 1999, the Corps reissued NWP 29 with a new limit of one-quarter acre. 64 Fed. Reg. 47,175 (Aug. 30, 1999).

5. *EPA's Veto Power.* Why do you think Congress gave EPA veto power over Corps-issued permits? On what basis did the EPA justify its veto in *Bersani*? Can EPA veto a permit if it concedes that no practicable alternative exists? See James City County v. Environmental Protection Agency, 12 F.3d 1330 (4th Cir.1993) (upholding veto of permit for construction of a dam and reservoir based on environmental consequences alone).

6. *Penalties.* Under Clean Water Act section 309, 33 U.S.C. § 1319, violations of section 404 are punishable by civil penalties of up to $25,000 per day of violation. Is each day that illegal fill remains in a wetland a separate day of violation? See, e.g., United States v. Ciampitti, 669 F.Supp. 684 (D.N.J.1987). In addition to penalties, the government often seeks an order requiring restoration of the wetlands to its original condition, or as near that condition as feasible. See, e.g., United States v. Cumberland Farms, 826 F.2d 1151 (1st Cir.1987). Where restoration is not possible, the government may seek alternative environmental benefits, such as dedication of wildlife habitat.

Criminal penalties are also available. 33 U.S.C. § 1319(c). Criminal prosecution of wetlands cases has aroused considerable political controversy. In general, the government does not seek criminal sanctions unless the defendants have been notified of the violation and persisted.

In one highly-publicized case, the defendant desired to expand his truck repair business onto an adjoining site. Before purchasing the site, he was told by three different consultants that it was a protected wetland. After the purchase, he began filling the site without a permit. He was informed personally by a Corps inspector that a permit was required to fill the site, and twice notified by letter that his activities violated section 404. He continued to place truckloads of fill on the site even after the United States obtained a temporary restraining order against him. Defendant was subsequently convicted of 40 separate violations of CWA § 309(c)(2), and sentenced to three years imprisonment, followed by five years probation, and a fine of $200,000. United States v. Pozsgai, 757 F.Supp. 21 (E.D.Pa.), aff'd in part, rev'd in part, 947 F.2d 938 (3d Cir.1991). The fine was later reduced to $5,000 based on Mr. Pozsgai's inability to pay. United States v. Pozsgai, 22 E.L.R. 20772 (E.D.Pa.1992). In a parallel civil action, Mr. Pozsgai and his wife were ordered to restore the property. United States v. Pozsgai, 999 F.2d 719 (3d Cir.1993).

Are criminal penalties ever an appropriate sanction for violation of section 404? If so, under what circumstances?

7. *Section 404 and NEPA.* Issuance of a section 404 permit is a major federal action requiring environmental analysis under NEPA. The Corps' NEPA regulations require consideration of the impacts of the specific activity requiring the permit "and those portions of the entire project over which the district engineer has sufficient control and responsibility to warrant Federal review." 33 C.F.R. Part 325, Appendix B § 7(b). In Sylvester v. U.S. Army Corps of Engineers, 884 F.2d 394 (9th Cir.1989), the Corps issued a permit to fill eleven acres of wetlands to construct a golf course as part of a larger resort complex. The Ninth Circuit upheld the Corps' decision to limit its NEPA review to the impacts of the golf course, despite the conclusion that there was no practicable alternative to the fill because the golf course was essential to the success of the resort. Can these two determinations be reconciled? Is *Sylvester* consistent with the NEPA segmentation rulings discussed in Chapter 5, Section 2(B)? More recently, the Ninth Circuit held that the NEPA analysis for a proposal to fill 21 acres of wetlands need not consider the environmental impacts of the entire 1,000 acre development associated with the fill. See Wetlands Action Network v. U.S. Army Corps of Engineers, 222 F.3d 1105 (9th Cir.2000).

D. MITIGATION

The Section 404 Guidelines prohibit any discharge of fill "unless appropriate and practicable steps have been taken which will minimize potential adverse impacts of the discharge on the aquatic ecosystem." 40 C.F.R. § 230.10(d). The Guidelines have been construed to require mitigation of impacts, not only through proper management of the permitted project, but also by compensating for destroyed wetlands.

The Guidelines do not make clear, however, to what extent mitigation can be used as a justification for approving a permit which otherwise would not be granted. EPA and the Corps long disagreed on the appropriate role of mitigation in permit decisions. In *Bersani*, for example, the Corps decided to grant the permit in part on the theory that creation of replacement wetlands in an abandoned gravel pit would reduce the adverse impacts of the project to or below those of the alternative uplands site. EPA's disagreement with that conclusion was one reason for its veto.

In 1990, EPA and the Corps reached an agreement on mitigation, memorialized in the following Memorandum.

Memorandum Of Agreement Between the Environmental Protection Agency and the Department of the Army Concerning the Determination of Mitigation Under the Clean Water Act Section 404(b)(1) Guidelines

55 Fed. Reg. 9210 (Mar. 12, 1990).

* * *

II. Policy

A. The Council on Environmental Quality (CEQ) has defined mitigation in its regulations at 40 CFR 1508.20 to include: avoiding impacts, minimizing impacts, rectifying impacts, reducing impacts over time, and compensating for impacts. The Guidelines establish environmental criteria which must be met for activities to be permitted under Section 404. The types of mitigation enumerated by CEQ are compatible with the requirements of the Guidelines; however, as a practical matter, they can be combined to form three general types: avoidance, minimization and compensatory mitigation. The remainder of this MOA will speak in terms of these more general types of mitigation.

B. The Clean Water Act and the Guidelines set forth a goal of restoring and maintaining existing aquatic resources. The Corps will strive to avoid adverse impacts and offset unavoidable adverse impacts to existing aquatic resources, and for wetlands, will strive to achieve a goal of no overall net loss of values and functions. * * * However, the level of mitigation determined to be appropriate and practicable under Section 230.10(d) may lead to individual permit decisions which do not fully meet this goal because the mitigation measures necessary to meet this goal are not feasible, not practicable, or would accomplish only inconsequential reductions in impacts. Consequently, it is recognized that no net loss of wetlands functions and values may not be achieved in each and every permit action. * * *

C. * * * The Corps, except as indicated below, first makes a determination that potential impacts have been avoided to the maximum extent practicable; remaining unavoidable impacts will then be mitigated to the extent appropriate and practicable by requiring steps to minimize impacts, and, finally, compensate for aquatic resource values. * * * It may be appropriate to deviate from the sequence when EPA and the Corps agree the proposed discharge is necessary to avoid environmental harm (e.g., to protect a natural aquatic community from saltwater intrusion, chemical contamination, or other deleterious physical or chemical impacts), or EPA and the Corps agree that the proposed discharge can reasonably be expected to result in environmental gain or insignificant environmental losses.

* * *

1. *Avoidance.* Section 230.10(a) allows permit issuance for only the least environmentally damaging practicable alternative. The thrust of this section on alternatives is avoidance of impacts. Section 230.10(a) requires that no discharge shall be permitted if there is a practicable alternative to the proposed discharge which would have less adverse impact to the aquatic ecosystem, so long as the alternative does not have other significant adverse environmental consequences. In addition, Section 230.10(a)(3) sets forth rebuttable presumptions that 1) alternatives for non-water dependent activities that do not involve special aquatic sites are available and 2) alternatives that do not involve special aquatic sites have less adverse impact on the aquatic environment. Compensatory mitigation may not be used as a method to reduce environmental impacts in the evaluation of the least environmentally damaging practicable alternatives for the purposes of requirements under Section 230.10(a).

2. *Minimization.* Section 230.10(d) states that appropriate and practicable steps to minimize the adverse impacts will be required through project modifications and permit conditions. * * *

3. *Compensatory Mitigation.* Appropriate and practicable compensatory mitigation is required for unavoidable adverse impacts which remain after all appropriate and practicable minimization has been required. Compensatory actions (e.g., restoration of existing degraded wetlands or creation of man-made wetlands) should be undertaken, when practicable, in areas adjacent or contiguous to the discharge site (on-site compensatory mitigation). If on-site compensatory mitigation is not practicable, off-site compensatory mitigation should be undertaken in the same geographic area if practicable (i.e., in close physical proximity and, to the extent possible, the same watershed). In determining compensatory mitigation, the functional values lost by the resource to be impacted must be considered. Generally, in-kind compensatory mitigation is preferable to out-of-kind. There is continued uncertainty regarding the success of wetland creation or other habitat development. Therefore, in determining the nature and extent of habitat development of this type careful consideration should be given to its likelihood of success. Because the likelihood of success is greater and the impacts to potentially valuable uplands are reduced, restoration should be the first option considered.

In the situation where the Corps is evaluating a project where a permit issued by another agency requires compensatory mitigation, the Corps may consider that mitigation as part of the overall application for purposes of public notice, but avoidance and minimization shall still be sought.

Mitigation banking may be an acceptable form of compensatory mitigation under specific criteria designed to ensure an environmentally successful bank. * * * Simple purchase or "preservation" of existing wetlands resources may in only exceptional circumstances be accepted as compensatory mitigation. * * *

III. Other Procedures

* * *

B. In achieving the goals of the CWA, the Corps will strive to avoid adverse impacts and offset unavoidable adverse impacts to existing aquatic resources. Measures which can accomplish this can be identified only through resource assessments tailored to the site performed by qualified professionals because ecological characteristics of each aquatic site are unique. Functional values should be assessed by applying aquatic site assessment techniques generally recognized by experts in the field and/or the best professional judgment of Federal and State agency representatives, provided such assessments fully consider ecological functions included in the Guidelines. The objective of mitigation for unavoidable impacts is to offset environmental losses. Additionally for wetlands, such mitigation should provide, at a minimum, one for one functional replacement (i.e., no net loss of values), with an adequate margin of safety to reflect the expected degree of success associated with the mitigation plan, recognizing that this minimum requirement may not be appropriate and practicable, and thus may not be relevant in all cases, as discussed in Section II.B of this MOA.[7] In the absence of more definitive information on the functions and values of specific wetlands sites, a minimum of 1 to 1 acreage replacement may be used as a reasonable surrogate for no net loss of functions and values. However, this ratio may be greater where the functional values of the area being impacted are demonstrably high and the replacement wetlands are of lower functional value or the likelihood of success of the mitigation project is low. Conversely, the ratio may be less than 1 to 1 for areas where the functional values associated with the area being impacted are demonstrably low and the likelihood of success associated with the mitigation proposal is high.

* * *

D. Monitoring is an important aspect of mitigation, especially in areas of scientific uncertainty. Monitoring should be directed toward determining

---

7. For example, there are certain areas where, due to hydrological conditions, the technology for restoration or creation of wetlands may not be available at present, or may otherwise be impracticable. In addition, avoidance, minimization, and compensatory mitigation may not be practicable where there is a high proportion of land which is wetlands. * * *

whether permit conditions are complied with and whether the purpose intended to be served by the condition is actually achieved. * * * Monitoring should not be required for purposes other than these, although information for other uses may accrue from the monitoring requirements. For projects to be permitted involving mitigation with higher levels of scientific uncertainty, such as some forms of compensatory mitigation, long term monitoring, reporting and potential remedial action should be required. * * *

E. Mitigation requirements shall be conditions of standard Section 404 permits. * * * This ensures legal enforceability of the mitigation conditions and enhances the level of compliance. If the mitigation plan necessary to ensure compliance with the Guidelines is not reasonably implementable or enforceable, the permit shall be denied.

U.S. Army Corps of Engineers, Environmental Protection Agency, Natural Resources Conservation Service, Fish and Wildlife Service, National Oceanic and Atmospheric Administration, Federal Guidance for the Establishment, Use and Operation of Mitigation Banks

60 Fed. Reg. 58605 (Nov. 28, 1995).

I. Introduction

For purposes of this guidance, mitigation banking means the restoration, creation, enhancement and, in exceptional circumstances, preservation of wetlands and/or other aquatic resources expressly for the purpose of providing compensatory mitigation in advance of authorized impacts to similar resources.

The objective of a mitigation bank is to provide for the replacement of the chemical, physical and biological functions of wetlands and other aquatic resources which are lost as a result of authorized impacts. Using appropriate methods, the newly established functions are quantified as mitigation "credits" which are available for use by the bank sponsor or by other parties to compensate for adverse impacts (i.e., "debits"). [T]he use of credits may only be authorized * * * when adverse impacts are unavoidable. In addition * * * credits may only be authorized when on-site compensation is either not practicable or use of a mitigation bank is environmentally preferable to on-site compensation. * * *

Mitigation banks provide greater flexibility to applicants needing to comply with mitigation requirements and can have several advantages over individual mitigation projects, some of which are listed below:

1. It may be more advantageous for maintaining the integrity of the aquatic ecosystem to consolidate compensatory mitigation into a single large parcel or contiguous parcels when ecologically appropriate;

2. Establishment of a mitigation bank can bring together financial resources, planning and scientific expertise not practicable to many project-specific compensatory mitigation proposals. This consolidation of resources can increase the potential for the establishment and long-term management of successful mitigation that maximizes opportunities for contributing to biodiversity and/or watershed function;

3. Use of mitigation banks may reduce permit processing times and provide more cost-effective compensatory mitigation opportunities for projects that qualify;

4. Compensatory mitigation is typically implemented and functioning in advance of project impacts, thereby reducing temporal losses of aquatic functions and uncertainty over whether the mitigation will be successful in offsetting project impacts;

5. Consolidation of compensatory mitigation within a mitigation bank increases the efficiency of limited agency resources in the review and compliance monitoring of mitigation projects, and thus improves the reliability of efforts to restore, create or enhance wetlands for mitigation purposes.

6. The existence of mitigation banks can contribute towards attainment of the goal for no overall net loss of the Nation's wetlands by providing opportunities to compensate for authorized impacts when mitigation might not otherwise be appropriate or practicable.

II.   Policy Considerations

* * *

1. *Goal Setting*

The overall goal of a mitigation bank is to provide economically efficient and flexible mitigation opportunities, while fully compensating for wetland and other aquatic resource losses in a manner that contributes to the long-term ecological functioning of the watershed within which the bank is to be located. * * *

2. *Site Selection*

The agencies will give careful consideration to the ecological suitability of a site for achieving the goal and objectives of a bank, i.e., that it posses [sic] the physical, chemical and biological characteristics to support establishment of the desired aquatic resources and functions. * * *

3. *Technical Feasibility*

Mitigation banks should be planned and designed to be self-sustaining over time to the extent possible. The techniques for establishing wetlands and/or other aquatic resources must be carefully selected, since this science is constantly evolving. The restoration of historic or substantially-degraded wetlands and/or other aquatic resources (e.g., prior-converted cropland, farmed wetlands) utilizing proven techniques increases the likelihood of success and typically does not result in the loss of other valuable resources. Thus, restoration should be the first option considered when siting a bank. Because of the difficulty in establishing the correct hydrologic conditions associated with many creation projects and the tradeoff in wetland functions involved with certain enhancement activities, these methods should only be considered where there are adequate assurances to ensure success and that the project will result in an overall environmental benefit.

* * *

Proposed mitigation techniques should be well-understood and reliable. When uncertainties surrounding the technical feasibility of a proposed mitigation technique exist, appropriate arrangements (e.g., financial assurances, contingency plans, additional monitoring requirements) should be in place to increase the likelihood of success. Such arrangements may be phased-out or reduced once the attainment of prescribed performance standards is demonstrated.

4.   *Role of Preservation*

Credit may be given when existing wetlands and/or other aquatic resources are preserved in conjunction with restoration, creation or enhancement activities, and when it is demonstrated that the preservation will augment the functions of the restored, created or enhanced aquatic resource. Such augmentation may be reflected in the total number of credits available from the bank.

In addition, the preservation of existing wetlands and/or other aquatic resources in perpetuity may be authorized as the sole basis for generating credits in mitigation banks only in exceptional circumstances, consistent with existing regulations, policies and guidance. Under such circumstances, preservation may be accomplished through the implementation of appropriate legal mechanisms (e.g., transfer of deed, deed restrictions, conservation easement) to protect wetlands and/or other aquatic resources, accompanied by implementation of appropriate changes in land use or other physical changes as necessary (e.g., installation of restrictive fencing).

Determining whether preservation is appropriate as the sole basis for generating credits at a mitigation bank requires careful judgment regarding a number of factors. Consideration must be given to whether wetlands and/or other aquatic resources proposed for preservation (1) perform physical or biological functions, the preservation of which is important to the region in which the aquatic resources are located, and (2) are under demonstrable threat of loss or substantial degradation due to human activities that might not otherwise be expected to be restricted. * * *

Criteria for Use of a Mitigation Bank

* * *

2.   *Relationship to Mitigation Requirements*

Under the existing requirements of Section 404, all appropriate and practicable steps must be undertaken by the applicant to first avoid and then minimize adverse impacts to aquatic resources, prior to authorization to use a particular mitigation bank. Remaining unavoidable impacts must be compensated to the extent appropriate and practicable. [R]equirements for compensatory mitigation may be satisfied through the use of mitigation banks when either on-site compensation is not practicable or use of the mitigation bank is environmentally preferable to on-site compensation.

It is important to emphasize that applicants should not expect that establishment of, or purchasing credits from, a mitigation bank will necessarily lead to a determination of compliance with applicable mitigation requirements, or as excepting projects from any applicable requirements.

3.   *Geographic Limits of Applicability*

The service area of a mitigation bank is the area (e.g., watershed, county) wherein a bank can reasonably be expected to provide appropriate compensation for impacts to wetlands and/or other aquatic resources. * * * Designation of the service area should be based on consideration of hydrologic and biotic criteria, and be stipulated in the banking instrument. Use of a mitigation bank to compensate for impacts beyond the designated service area may be authorized, on a case-by-case basis, where it is determined to be practicable and environmentally desirable.

* * *

4.   *Use of a Mitigation Bank vs. On–Site Mitigation*

The agencies' preference for on-site mitigation, indicated in the 1990 Memorandum of Agreement on mitigation between the EPA and the Department of the Army, should not preclude the use of a mitigation bank when there is no practicable opportunity for on-site compensation, or when use of a bank is environmentally preferable to on-site compensation. On-site mitigation may be preferable where there is a practicable opportunity to compensate for important local functions including local flood control functions, habitat for a species or population with a very limited geographic range or narrow environmental requirements, or where local water quality concerns dominate.

In choosing between on-site mitigation and use of a mitigation bank, careful consideration should be given to the likelihood for successfully establishing the desired habitat type, the compatibility of the mitigation project with adjacent land uses, and the practicability of long-term monitoring and maintenance to determine whether the effort will be ecologically sustainable, as well as the relative cost of mitigation alternatives. In general, use of a mitigation bank to compensate for minor aquatic resource impacts (e.g., numerous, small impacts associated with linear projects; impacts authorized under nationwide permits) is preferable to on-site mitigation. With respect to larger aquatic resource impacts, use of a bank may be appropriate if it is capable of replacing essential physical and/or biological functions of the aquatic resources which are expected to be lost or degraded. Finally, there may be circumstances warranting a combination of on-site and off-site mitigation to compensate for losses.

* * *

6. *Timing of Credit Withdrawal*

The number of credits available for withdrawal (i.e., debiting) should generally be commensurate with the level of aquatic functions attained at a bank at the time of debiting. The level of function may be determined through the application of performance standards tailored to the specific restoration, creation or enhancement activity at the bank site or through the use of an appropriate functional assessment methodology.

The success of a mitigation bank with regard to its capacity to establish a healthy and fully functional aquatic system relates directly to both the ecological and financial stability of the bank. Since financial considerations are particularly critical in early stages of bank development, it is generally appropriate, in cases where there is adequate financial assurance and where the likelihood of the success of the bank is high, to allow limited debiting of a percentage of the total credits projected for the bank at maturity. Such determinations should take into consideration the initial capital costs needed to establish the bank, and the likelihood of its success. However, it is the intent of this policy to ensure that those actions necessary for the long-term viability of a mitigation bank be accomplished prior to any debiting of the bank. In this regard, the following minimum requirements should be satisfied prior to debiting: (1) banking instrument and mitigation plans have been approved; (2) bank site has been secured; and (3) appropriate financial assurances have been established. In addition, initial physical and biological improvements should be completed no later than the first full growing season following initial debiting of a bank. The temporal loss of functions associated with the debiting of projected credits may justify the need for requiring higher compensation ratios in such cases.
* * *

7. *Crediting/Debiting/Accounting Procedures*

Credits and debits are the terms used to designate the units of trade (i.e., currency) in mitigation banking. Credits represent the accrual or attainment of aquatic functions at a bank; debits represent the loss of aquatic functions at an impact or project site. Credits are debited from a bank when they are used to offset aquatic resource impacts.

An appropriate functional assessment methodology * * * acceptable to all signatories should be used to assess wetland and/or other aquatic resource restoration, creation and enhancement activities within a mitigation bank, and to quantify the amount of available credits. The range of functions to be assessed will depend upon the assessment methodology identified in the banking instrument. The same methodology should be used to assess both credits and debits. If an appropriate functional assessment methodology is impractical to employ, acreage may be used as a surrogate for measuring function. Regardless of the method employed, the number of credits should reflect the difference between site conditions under the with- and without-bank scenarios. * * *

NOTES AND QUESTIONS

1.   *Mitigation and "No Net Loss."* Is the policy on mitigation announced in the 1990 Memorandum of Agreement consistent with the goal of "no net loss" of wetlands? Under what circumstances does it permit net loss? Many observers have been critical of compensatory mitigation, particularly off-site. Critics cite concerns with loss of site specific wetland values, technical difficulties in creating certain types of wetlands, and the temptation to rely on wetlands creation rather than rigorously requiring avoidance and minimization of impacts. See, e.g., Michael C. Blumm, The Clinton Wetlands Plan: No Net Gain in Wetlands Protection, 9 J. Land Use Envtl. L. 203, 226–28 (1994). How well does the 1990 Memorandum of Agreement address these concerns? A National Academy of Sciences panel recently reported that created wetlands often do not effectively replace the ecological functions of natural wetlands. The panel concluded that the "no net loss" goal is not being met. See Andrew C. Revkin, Efforts to Save Wetlands are Inadequate, Study Says, New York Times, June 27, 2001, at A14.

2.   *Preservation as Compensatory Mitigation.* Is it ever appropriate to allow preservation of an existing wetland, through purchase or a conservation easement, to serve as mitigation for a project that will destroy wetlands? Is the use of preservation as mitigation consistent with the goal of "no net loss"? How effectively does section 404 alone protect wetlands? Can the added security of a formal preservation agreement compensate for losses at other sites? What ratio of preserved to destroyed wetlands would you consider adequate? How does the Federal Guidance on mitigation banking treat the issue of preservation as compensation?

3.   *Mitigation Banks.* Mitigation banking offers several potential advantages over individual mitigation at each project site. Banks may be well developed before credits are sold, providing greater assurance of long-term success. They can produce larger, more biologically valuable, mitigation sites. Mitigation banks may also be economically preferable to project-by-project mitigation. They offer economies of scale, decreasing per-acre costs and thereby increasing the extent of "practicable" mitigation. Where active management may be necessary, banks can offer greater assurance of long-term financial viability. Over the past decade, mitigation banking has become a popular tool for wetlands protection, as well as a profitable business enterprise. "In 1992, there were only forty-six existing mitigation banks, only one of which was an entrepreneurial bank. As of March 1999, more than 200 banks were operating and several hundred more were in the planning stages. Of the existing banks, approximately ninety are entrepreneurial banks." Royal C. Gardner, Money for Nothing? The Rise of Wetland Fee Mitigation, 19 Va. Envtl. L. J. 1, 11–12 (2000). Does mitigation banking, under the terms of the Federal Guidance, answer concerns about compensatory mitigation?

4. *Fee Mitigation and Valuing Wetlands.* If a local mitigation bank is not available, and on-site mitigation is impractical, should payment of a fee to a non-profit or public fund for the purpose of creating, restoring, or preserving wetlands be acceptable as mitigation? Should fee mitigation ever be permitted when a local mitigation bank is available? See generally Gardner, *supra.*

5. *Mitigation Banking and Takings.* Does the potential for private, for-profit mitigation banks reduce the possibility that government regulations which preclude development of a wetland area will be deemed an unconstitutional taking?

*

PART III

TOXICS AND WASTE

CHAPTER SEVEN

TOXIC SUBSTANCES

SECTION 1. RISK ASSESSMENT AND MANAGEMENT

A. SETTING POLICY ON ENVIRONMENTAL RISKS

Toxins are the best known and among the most degrading stresses that mankind applies to the environment. Environmental toxins present both a threat to human health and the well-being of ecosystems. Although there is broad agreement that toxins are dangerous both to human health and the environment, there is disagreement as to the dangerousness of specific chemicals and products as well as the degree to which various toxins are harmful. The bewildering complexity of the scientific and policy problems presented by toxins has led to the development of "Environmental Risk Analysis" as a tool of legal and policy decision making. Risk analysis has evolved as a way to order and simplify the choices that must be made about chemical exposure.

The term "risk" has many meanings. A commonly invoked definition of "risk" is "the probability of an adverse event." In environmental law, risk usually refers either to the probability that an individual will suffer some adverse consequence as a result of exposure to a pollutant or the consequences of such exposure to an entire population. Risk is commonly analyzed both in terms of the probability of a harm occurring and the perceived magnitude of that harm.

Risk and the Environment, Improving Regulatory Decisionmaking, A Report of the Carnegie Commission on Science, Technology, and Government

76–79 (1993).

Risk assessment is a composite of established disciplines, including toxicology, biostatistics, epidemiology, economics, and demography. The goals of risk assessment are to characterize the nature of the adverse effects and to produce quantitative estimates of one or both of the following fundamental quantities: (1) the *probability* that an individual (a hypothetical or identified person) will suffer disease or death as a result of a specified exposure to a pollutant or pollutants; and (2) the *consequences* of such an exposure to an entire population (i.e., the number of cases of disease or death).

Risk assessment can be either generic (e.g., an estimate of the number of excess annual cancers caused by all 189 hazardous air pollutants identified in the 1990 Clean Air Act Amendments) or site—and/or chemical-specific (e.g., the probability that a specified child will suffer neurological impairment as a result of exposure to lead in his household drinking water).

Numerical estimates derived from risk assessment serve as inputs to several very different kinds of decisions, including (1) "acceptable risk" determinations (wherein action is taken if the risk exceeds some "bright line," which can be zero); (2) "cost-benefit" determinations, where the risks reduced by a proposed action are translated into benefits (e.g., lives saved, life-years extended), expressed in dollar amounts, and compared to the estimated costs of implementing the action and some rule of thumb regarding how much cost it is wise to incur to achieve a given level of benefit (e.g., $10 million to save one additional life); and (3) cost-effectiveness determinations, where the action that maximizes the amount of risk reduction (not necessarily expressed in dollar terms) per unit cost is favored.

Since at least 1983 (with the publication of the National Research Council's "Redbook"), the dominant paradigm for risk assessment has been a sequential, four-step process:

■ *Hazard identification*—in which a qualitative determination is made of what kinds of adverse health or ecological effects a substance can cause. Typically, agencies have focused on cancer as the effect that drives further analysis and regulation. So, for example, a typical hazard identification for vinyl chloride released from industrial facilities would involve the collection and critical analysis of short-term test-tube assays (for mutagenicity, etc.), of long-term animal assays (typically two-year rodent carcinogenicity tests), and of human epidemiologic data—either cohort studies (in which populations exposed to vinyl chloride are followed to assess whether their rates of any disease were significantly greater than those of unexposed or less-exposed populations) or case-control studies (which focus on victims of a particular disease to see whether they were significantly more likely to have been exposed to vinyl chloride than similar but disease-free individuals).

■ *Exposure assessment*—in which a determination is made of the amounts of a substance to which a hypothetical person (usually the "maximally exposed individual") and/or the total population are exposed. To return to the vinyl chloride example, this part of risk assessment would bring to bear techniques of emissions characterization (how much vinyl chloride leaves the plant in a given time?), fate—and transport analysis (how is the chemical dispersed in the atmosphere and transformed into other compounds?), uptake analysis (how much air do people breathe, both outdoors and indoors?), and demographic analysis (how many hours per day do people spend in various locations near the plant, and how long do they reside in one locale before moving away?).

■ *Dose-response assessment*—in which an estimate is made of the probability or extent of injury at the exposure levels determined above, by quantifying the "potency" of the chemical in question. For vinyl chloride again, scientists would determine its carcinogenic potency by fitting the animal bioassay data (number of tumors produced at different exposure levels) to a mathematical model (usually one that is linear at low doses), and then transforming the resultant potency estimate for rodents into a human potency estimate through the use of a "scaling factor" (usually, a ratio of the body surface areas of the two species). Additionally, human epidemiologic data could be used to validate or supplant the animal-based potency estimate.

■ *Risk characterization*—in which the results of the above steps are integrated to describe the nature of the adverse effects and the strength of the evidence and to present one or more "risk numbers." For example, EPA might say, "This vinyl chloride plant is estimated to produce up to 3 excess cases of liver cancer every 70 years among the 100,000 people living within 1 mile of the facility" or "the maximally exposed individual faces an excess lifetime liver cancer risk of 5.4×10^{-4}."

Risk assessment is essentially a tool for extrapolating from scientific data to a risk number. The tool is made up of a host of assumptions, which are an admixture of science and policy. Sometimes either science or policy predominates, but it is often difficult to get a broad consensus that this is so.

A view among some in industry and elsewhere is that risk assessment systematically overestimates risk and frightens the public: as they see it, the typical risk assessment takes a trivial emission source, pretends that people are pressed up against the fenceline of the source 24 hours a day for 70 years, gauges the toxicity of the pollutant released by exposing ultrasensitive rodents to huge doses in the laboratory, and then uses the most "conservative" dose-response model to estimate a risk to humans at the low ambient exposures of interest. The view of some in environmental and public interest groups, and elsewhere, is that risk assessment may often inherently underestimate the true magnitude of the problem, by ignoring complicating but salient factors, including synergies among exposures, vast variations in susceptibility among humans, and unusual exposure pathways (e.g., inhalation of steam in showers containing volatilized chemicals from contaminated water).

Because the science underlying most risk assessment assumptions is inconclusive, arguments over whether or not an assumption is scientifically valid often distill down to debates about whether it is better to err on the side of "false positives" (if there is an error, it will more likely be a false indication of danger) or "false negatives" (if there is an error, it will more likely be a false indication of safety). Those who might be harmed by the substance being assessed will generally favor false positives; those who would gain from the substance will generally favor false negatives.

Two practical consequences of risk assessments reliance on poorly substantiated assumptions are that numerical risk estimates tend to be highly uncertain and highly variable. Uncertainty refers to how likely a given estimate (expressed as a range of values) is to be true. However close a number is to being correct, it is correct only for a particular scenario—for example, average exposure level, or average individual susceptibility to the adverse effect at issue. Yet we know that exposures typically vary across space and time, and individuals probably vary widely in their susceptibility to different toxicants. Thus, any statement that "the risk is $A \times 10^{-B}$" is really a shorthand for the general truth that "we are Y percent sure that the risk is no more than $A \times 10^{-B}$ for Z percent of the population." If Y and Z were both very close to 100 percent, EPA and other agencies would not be seriously misleading themselves and the public with these shorthand statements, but that assumption is highly speculative in many cases.

Risk assessment can be most useful when those who rely on it to inform the risk management process understand its nature and its limitations, and use it accordingly. This means that decision makers must at least understand that the process is assumption and value-laden; that they understand what assumptions were used in the assessment in question, and what values they reflect; that the risk estimate with which they work is expressed as a range, with the level of certainty that the true average is in that range quantified; and, that variability is expressed to the degree that it is known, i.e., how many and what kind of persons (e.g., children) will likely be at significantly higher or lower risk than the hypothetical average individual. Risk managers must take all these factors into account in making a decision, along with political and economic factors extrinsic to the risk assessment.

John M. Stonehouse and John D. Mumford, Science, Risk Analysis, and Environmental Policy Decisions
39–42 (UNEP 1994).

The central conclusion is that risk perception is multidimensional, perceptions differing between individuals and contexts, so that for policy purposes "risk" as rated by the public is not reducible to a single value such as a function, albeit a subjective one, of probability x damage (Pidgeon et al., 1992). As a result, risk policy making inevitably involves confrontation, balance and compromise. People also differ in their willingness to take risks, apparently as part of inherent personality diversity.

Risk may not be "accepted" and therefore "acceptable" in the sense that it is consciously balanced against a perceived good, but "tolerated" where necessary: in general people are risk averse, which has led to caution in the acceptance of risk in policy making. This, together with the imprecision of the safety factors by which it is commonly expressed, has led to frustration among many scientists that overcautious risk avoidance is leading to losses of social benefits through worthwhile risks not being taken, and some predictions that "*de minimis*" risk analyses are losing credibility and will not be sustainable. However, the view that the public "fails" to appreciate true risk levels and that public intolerance of "small" risks, that scientists consider to be worth taking, may be addressed by education and explanation of real risk levels in rational terms, is currently losing ground to the view that risk perceptions are deeply seated. Therefore, public confrontations may be better averted if these perceptions are not treated as "problems" to be "rectified" by education but as, in themselves, valid elements of the background to the public management of risk, which should be addressed and incorporated from the beginning in risk analyses. The "acceptability" of risk is therefore widely estimated using entirely political processes, being subjectively set by politically accountable bodies such as parliaments.

A well known finding about risk perception is that several factors, other than the absolute probabilistic risk level, influence peoples' perceptions of risk as intolerable. These "outrage factors" have been extensively researched for safety risks, and reasons for some of them investigated. In general, risks are less tolerable if they are:

- with *inadequate, unclear or selective corresponding benefits*;
- *imposed*, not being undertaken voluntarily by the risk bearer;
- *outside personal control*, the risk bearer having to trust to others the management of risk;
- seen as *unethical or unfair* in the distribution of the risk burden;
- publicly managed by *untrustworthy information sources*;
- *artificial* as opposed to natural;
- *insidious*, with damage happening in unseen ways (e.g. poisoning);
- of *unknown time duration*, particularly slow-acting damage which may affect subsequent generations;
- *unfamiliar*;
- *associated with memorable events* such as disasters. (People appear to have a peculiar dread of mass-scale disasters); also it appears that an event is conceived as "probable" if it is easily imagined or remembered, due to a convenient internal "rule of thumb" to facilitate the building of mental models of the world, known as the "availability heuristic"—memorable events such as disasters are by definition mentally "available" in this way.

Increasing understanding of the way in which risk perception is modified by psychological and social factors has accelerated developments in *Risk Communication*. The importance of this field is being increasingly recognized, due in part to the increase of legal requirements of the practitioners of risky activities to inform the public of risk levels, but also of the manifest political problems encountered by policy makers in the social tolerance of risk. The latter are amply illustrated by the widespread failure over the years of campaigns by authorities to convince the public of the acceptability of risks, and the analysis of the deep seated roots of outrage factors has illuminated the failings of the conventional approach of risk comparisons, for example, by comparing the risks of living near a nuclear reactor with that of walking across the road, to have much effect on public risk tolerance. * * *

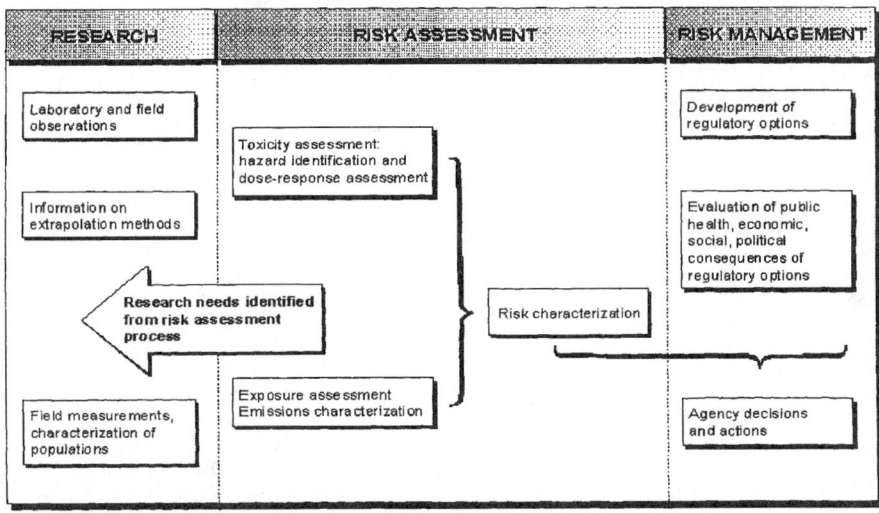

NAS/NRC risk assessment/management paradigm.

NOTES AND QUESTIONS

1. There are about 60,000 chemicals in common use. Reasonably complete toxicology data exist for only about 1000 chemical substances because such data are very costly to obtain. The lack of complete information regarding the vast number of chemical substances often makes accurate risk assessment difficult. The Food and Drug Administration uses a standard criterion for the assessment of risk. If a substance causes more than one cancer per million lifetimes among those exposed, the risk is "non trivial"; less than one cancer per million lifetimes is a "trivial risk." This one-in-a-million risk reduces the life expectancy of the average exposed person by $\frac{1}{100}$ of a day.

Although precise and accurate data is often hard to find, other common "life expectancy reduction" (LER) risks have been estimated as follows:

ESTIMATED LIFE EXPECTANCY REDUCTION
FROM RISKS AND ACTIVITIES*

Activity or risk	Days LER
Heart disease	2100
Being unmarried	2000
Cigarette smoking	1600
Cancer	980
Being 30 lbs. overweight	900
Grade school dropout	800
Unskilled laborer	700
Stroke	520

* SOURCE: *Nuclear Energy: A Sensible Alternative*, 322 (Ott & Spinrad eds. 1985).

Activity or risk	Days LER
Vietnam army duty	400
Mining or construction work (due to accidents only)	300
Motor vehicle accidents	200
Pneumonia, influenza	130
Homicide	90
Drowning	40
Poison + suffocation + asphyxiation	37
Energy production and use	25
Diet drinks	2
Hurricanes, tornadoes	1
Airline crashes	1
All-nuclear electricity	0.04–2[a]
Harrisburg area residents (from TMI accident)	0.001
Radioactive waste burial ground leaks, risk to nearest neighbors	0.0001
Sky–Lab fall	0.000002

Thus, this estimate proposes that drinking a can of diet cola each day may kill 2 people in 100,000 each year, while cigarette smoking is 800 times as dangerous. Do we tend to overestimate the risks of toxic waste sites and nuclear power plants? Is there a significant difference between people's perception and reality? How can this discrepancy harm public policymaking? See Stephen Breyer, *Breaking the Vicious Circle* (1990) [arguing our regulatory priorities are random and irrational]. Does it make sense to control risks of 1 in one million? The background risk of cancer today is 250,000 in 1 million. An added risk of 1 would amount to 250,001 in 1 million.

2. Uncertainties exist at each phase of the risk assessment process: hazard identification, exposure assessment, and risk characterization. The following excerpt summarizes the problems of the exposure assessment stage:

There are at least four major pitfalls in the exposure assessment process to which one should be sensitive. First, the typical or average person, rather than the theoretical maximum exposed individual (MEI), should be the focus of a health risk assessment. Although the risk for those potentially exposed to particularly high levels needs to be understood, too much emphasis has been placed on the (MEI). Instead, the typical person should be the primary emphasis of the analyses even though the risk to others should also be understood. The distinction is important. If, for example, a regulatory agency bases its decision on the results of an assessment assuming that a person eats about 100 grams of fish every day of his or her lifetime (99th percentile), yet the average American eats only eighteen grams of fish per day (lifetime average), the analysis should reflect the fact that ninety-nine of 100 persons are not represented by the corresponding risk estimate. To help minimize the potential for misunderstanding, it is recommended that the number of exposed persons at each of the anticipated dose levels be presented, along with the most likely and upper estimates of exposure.

This has been done in only a limited number of assessments. Using an exhibit like Table 1, the risk manager or the court can readily understand the severity of the risk for each segment of the population. Provided with this information, it can then be decided whether large or small sums of money need to be expended to reduce the health risks.

The next pitfall is a variation of the first one. It involves the repeated use of conservative assumptions. Several published papers have discussed this issue and have demonstrated its importance. The problem can be illustrated in a recent attempt to assess the dioxin hazard posed by municipal waste incinerators. An agency evaluated the theoretical cancer risk for a child who lived within a short distance (0.8 km) from the hypothetical incinerator. At first review, the analysis seemed reasonable until one noted that the child ate about two teaspoons of dirt each day, that his house was down-wind of the stack, that he ate fish from a pond near the incinerator, his fish consumption was at the ninety-fifth percentile level, he drank contaminated water from the pond, he ate food grown primarily from the family garden, and he drank milk from a cow which grazed on forage at the farm. This is not quite the description of a typical person living near a municipal incinerator. Regrettably, the associated upper estimate of the risk was the only one reported in the press. Certainly, it would have been more appropriate to have studied and presented the number of persons likely to be exposed to this level, as well as the level of exposure for the typical person living within ten miles of the facility. It may also have been useful to note that few farms are located near incinerators due to the need to service large communities. Without such a presentation of the data, risk managers and the public can easily be misled and, as a result, make poor decisions.

The third pitfall is to conduct an exposure assessment without considering the environmental fate of the chemical. In general, many factors such as degradation by sunlight, soil and water microbes, and evaporation will influence the degree of human exposure. For instance, the public health hazard posed by the potential contamination of groundwater by ethanol (alcohol) washed down the sinks of taverns and restaurants was recently evaluated. It was alleged that the disposal of this listed carcinogen might place the restaurant in violation of one of California's new laws, Proposition 65. Consequently, a risk assessment was conducted. It was soon recognized that the environmental half-life of the chemical was a critical factor in this analysis. Specifically, chemicals such as methanol, ethanol, and phenol have relatively short half-lives in most waters; only about four to eight hours. This means that soon after release the ethanol would be degraded and rendered harmless by water-borne microbes or lost through volatilization, and that virtually none of the alcohol would reach the tap water of homeowners. What had been portrayed as a potentially serious hazard was shown to be insignificant when half-life was considered.

Another pitfall is to neglect to consider using biological monitoring to validate or confirm the degree of human exposure. Over the past five years, analytical chemists have increased their ability to detect very small quantities of non-natural chemicals in blood, urine, hair, feces, breath, and fat. For many chemicals, the results would be a direct indicator of either recent or lifetime exposure to a chemical. For example, the exposure to dioxin in 2,4,5–T (Agent Orange) of veterans who served in Vietnam was recently evaluated by analyzing the amount of dioxin in their blood. This study, conducted almost fifteen to twenty years after the last day of service in Vietnam, allowed epidemiologists to conclude that the vast majority of veterans had only a modest degree of exposure to dioxin; a contaminant which has been alleged to produce numerous adverse health effects in field soldiers.

The last trap is the failure to validate some of the assumptions used in the analysis or the reasonableness of the results. In an attempt to position themselves so as to be above the accusation that their assessments are not sufficiently health protective, many scientists have gone overboard in selecting certain parameters used in the calculations. One example of the problem of making assumptions without checking the reasonableness, occurred during an evaluation of the cancer hazard posed by dioxin-contaminated soot from an office building fire. The risk assessment assumed that the office workers might be exposed to the dioxin in the soot for the entire forty years that they might work in the building and that the dioxin would be released through volatilization at a particular rate. It was calculated that persons who worked forty years in the office building would be exposed to an increased cancer risk much greater than 1 in 1,000,000, and as a result, the building was not reoccupied. Even if one agreed with the assertion that an increased cancer risk of 1 in 1,000,000 is the maximum risk to which one should be exposed, something in the analysis seemed flawed. After some study, it was shown that the assumption regarding dioxin's volatility was too conservative. Apparently, no one checked to see if the volatilization rate was reasonable. Specifically, had this assumption been accurate, the dioxin would have all been volatilized and been removed via the ventilation system only four years after reoccupation. In short, the exposure assessment assumed exposure was to occur for forty-six years even though it would not have been present after four years. The moral is that in any assessment a validation should be performed to insure that the assumptions and results are reasonable.

Dennis J. Paustenback, Health Risk Assessments: Opportunities and Pitfalls, 14 Colum. J. Entl. L. 397, 402–05 (1989).

3. Another recent critique of risk assessment challenges the "linear model" correlating human exposure to toxic materials with the incurrence of health effects. The approach emphasizes the concept of hormesis which suggests that human exposure to a substance at low levels might be beneficial even if exposures at higher levels might be extremely hazardous.

Conceptually, the hormesis hypothesis assumes that as a human dose of a hazardous substance rises from zero there are initially positive or beneficial effects until a "tipping point" is reached and the additional exposures result in increasingly negative consequences. This counter-intuitive view point has been advanced by Professor Frank Cross who has drawn his conclusions from scientific studies involving exposures to radiation, chemical toxics and carcinogens. He writes to explain the phenomena,

> The theoretical reason for hormetic effects lies in the body's adaptive or stimulatory response to low levels of exposure. When the body senses such exposure, defensive mechanisms are activated. This biological response over-compensates for the threat posed by the very low levels of exposure and makes the defense mechanisms more robust than before the exposure. The theory is well known and established with respect to vaccines, which often involve introducing a small exposure to a pathogenic agent in order to activate defenses and prepare the body for the threat of a larger exposure. Indeed, this effect is true of most drugs. Aspirin, for example, is beneficial at low doses but can cause toxicity at high doses. At some exposure level, the toxicity overwhelms the body's defenses, whether or not they have been stimulated by low-level exposures. At these higher exposure levels, many substances are truly hazardous.

Frank B. Cross, Incorporating Hormesis in Risk Regulation, 30 ELR 10778 (2000). Although acknowledging that the evidence supporting the hormesis thesis is not conclusive, Cross nevertheless posits that "the scientific database is sufficient to incorporate hormesis into regulation, and the quantity of data is such that hormesis cold become a default assumption of risk assessment, presumed until disproven in a particular circumstance." This thesis has provoked an interesting debate among scholars of risk regulation. See Hormesis and Environmental Regulation: Views from the Legal Profession, BELLE Newsletter, Vol. 9, No. 2, January, 2001 at http://www.belleonline.com/home92.html How could the hormesis concept be significant in risk assessment and health and environmental regulation? How much information should EPA have before incorporating this idea into its regulatory standard setting practices?

4. In many cases the EPA's risk assessment methods and conclusions have been challenged by independent scientists. A case in point is dioxin, a ubiquitous and natural by-product of combustion, which is generated by automobiles, forest fires, wood stoves, and barbecues, as well as most incinerators and pulp and paper mills. In the fall of 1994, the EPA issued a three-volume report on dioxin, the result of four years of agency study and several million dollars in cost. The report sought to justify lower dioxin emissions from paper mills, incinerators, and other regulated sources. The report was peer-reviewed by 39 scientists drawn largely from academia, who were asked to respond to 43 questions submitted by the agency. The independent panel found that the EPA had overstated the risks of dioxins, that its conclusions were not scientifically defensible, and that it could not agree with the EPA's characterization of risk to humans.

Kathryn Kelly, a toxicologist who was a member of the panel, stated as follows in a letter to the Wall Street Journal, June 5, 1995:

... The firmness with which scientists rejected EPA's claims clearly shows why the politics of environmental management needs to be kept out of the scientific review process. And herein lies the problem: Regulators don't look at scientific data the same way scientists do.

Take 20 studies, 19 of which show negative results. In the scientific arena, the weight-of-evidence approach to evaluating data would tend to favor the 19 studies, all other things being equal. Not so in the regulatory arena, where one positive result is sufficient for policy making. "Regulatory agencies don't want to disprove anything; they just want to know if there is enough data to support a regulatory decision," explained a participant at the May 16–17 meeting of the scientific advisory panel. "If the data are ambiguous, a regulatory agency will simply pick and choose the data that support its position and ignore the rest."

Hence, EPA's frequent assertion of adverse effects of dioxins, despite the vast weight of evidence contradicting that position. "EPA's review highlights findings that demonstrate associations between dioxins and human cancers, while ignoring contradictory data," said panelists Michael Gough of Congress's Office of Technology Assessment. "That's not science, that's policy."

The dilemma is compounded by the inherent conflict of interest created when EPA conducts research on the very issues it regulates. Like asking a fox to design the building specifications for the chicken coop, asking EPA to conduct scientific research and then regulate objectively on the basis of those results creates a hopeless conflict of interest. "EPA is doing EPA's research in EPA labs with EPA employees under EPA oversight. How could they not have a vested interest in the outcome?" said another scientist who participated in the May meeting. "Scientific research needs to get out of EPA and out of agency oversight, and be brought back into the harsh light of peer review."

5. *The Varying Standards of Regulation.* How should the law respond to risk analysis and the need for controlling exposure to hazardous substances? While nonregulatory methods (such as labeling, traceable permits, emission taxes, deposit refunds) have been suggested, the main approach taken has been that of regulation. There is no uniform pattern of regulation of toxic substances. Statutes vary greatly in their description of the analysis that regulatory agencies must perform. In general, three regulatory approaches may be distinguished.

First, certain statutes such as the Delaney Clause; the Federal Food, Drug, and Cosmetic Act; and § 112 of the Clean Air Act require health-based controls of toxics. These are rigid laws that do not allow consideration of costs versus benefits (although in the case of the Clean Air Act, technology based controls must be tried first).

Second, some statutes regulate toxics in terms of what is technologically feasible. For example, the Clean Water Act sets toxic limits in terms of the "best available technology" (although health-based water quality standards also may apply in some cases). The Occupational Health and Safety Act includes a feasibility test: it sets limits on worker exposure to toxic substances in the work place and ensures that no worker suffer material impairment of health or functional capacity "to the extent feasible."

Third, the overwhelming majority of statutes employ a balancing test of some sort, requiring that regulations balance the economic and social costs of controls against the health and safety benefits of regulation.

The following cases explore the problems presented by some of these approaches.

Industrial Union Department, AFL–CIO v. American Petroleum Institute [The Benzene Case]

United States Supreme Court, 1980.
448 U.S. 607, 100 S.Ct. 2844, 65 L.Ed.2d 1010.

■ MR. JUSTICE STEVENS announced the judgment of the Court and delivered an opinion, in which THE CHIEF JUSTICE and MR. JUSTICE STEWART joined and in Parts I, II, III–A, III–B, III–C and III–E of which MR. JUSTICE POWELL joined.

The Occupational Safety and Health Act of 1970 (Act), 84 Stat. 1590, 29 U.S.C. § 651 et seq., was enacted for the purpose of ensuring safe and healthful working conditions for every working man and woman in the Nation. This litigation concerns a standard promulgated by the Secretary of Labor to regulate occupational exposure to benzene, a substance which has been shown to cause cancer at high exposure levels. The principal question is whether such a showing is a sufficient basis for a standard that places the most stringent limitation on exposure to benzene that is technologically and economically possible. * * *

Wherever the toxic material to be regulated is a carcinogen, the Secretary has taken the position that no safe exposure level can be determined and that § 6(b)(5) requires him to set an exposure limit at the lowest technologically feasible level that will not impair the viability of the industries regulated. In this case, after having determined that there is a causal connection between benzene and leukemia (a cancer of the white blood cells), the Secretary set an exposure limit on airborne concentrations of benzene of one part benzene per million parts of air (1 ppm), regulated dermal and eye contact with solutions containing benzene, and imposed complex monitoring and medical testing requirements on employers whose workplaces contain 0.5 ppm or more of benzene. * * *

I.

Benzene is a familiar and important commodity. * * * Benzene is used in manufacturing a variety of products including motor fuels (which may contain as much as 2 percent benzene), solvents, detergents, pesticides, and other organic chemicals.

The entire population of the United States is exposed to small quantities of benzene, ranging from a few parts per billion to 0.5 ppm, in the ambient air. Over one million workers are subject to additional low-level exposures as a consequence of their employment. The majority of these employees work in gasoline service stations, benzene production (petroleum refineries and cooking operations), chemical processing, benzene transportation, rubber manufacturing, and laboratory operations.

Benzene is a toxic substance. Although it could conceivably cause harm to a person who swallowed or touched it, the principal risk of harm comes from inhalation of benzene vapors. When these vapors are inhaled, the benzene diffuses through the lungs and is quickly absorbed into the blood. Exposure to high concentrations produces an almost immediate effect on the central nervous system. Inhalation of concentrations of 20,000 ppm can be fatal within minutes; exposures in the range of 250 to 500 ppm can cause vertigo, nausea, and other symptoms of mild poisoning. Persistent exposures at levels above 25–40 ppm may lead to blood deficiencies and diseases of the blood-forming organs, including aplastic anemia, which is generally fatal.

Industrial health experts have long been aware that exposure to benzene may lead to various types of nonmalignant diseases. * * *

Between 1974 and 1976 additional studies were published which tended to confirm the view that benzene can cause leukemia, at least when exposure levels are high. * * *

In its published statement giving notice of the proposed permanent standard, OSHA did not ask for comments as to whether or not benzene presented a significant health risk at exposures of 10 ppm or less. Rather, it asked for comments as to whether 1 ppm was the minimum feasible exposure limit. As OSHA's Deputy Director of Health Standards, Grover Wrenn, testified at the hearing, this formulation of the issue to be considered by the Agency was consistent with OSHA's general policy with respect to carcinogens. Whenever a carcinogen is involved, OSHA will presume that no safe level of exposure exists in the absence of clear proof establishing such a level and will accordingly set the exposure limit at the lowest level feasible. The proposed 1 ppm exposure limit in this case thus was established not on the basis of a proven hazard at 10 ppm, but rather on the basis of "OSHA's best judgement at the time of the proposal of the feasibility of compliance with the proposed standard by the [a]ffected industries." Given OSHA's cancer policy, it was in fact irrelevant whether there was any evidence at all of a leukemia risk at 10 ppm. The important point was that there was no evidence that there was not some risk, however small, at that level. The fact that OSHA did not ask for comments on whether there was a safe level of exposure for benzene was indicative of its further view that a demonstration of such absolute safety simply could not be made.

Whenever initial monitoring indicates that employees are subject to airborne concentrations of benzene above 1 ppm averaged over an 8–hour workday, with a ceiling of 5 ppm for any 15–minute period, employers are required to modify their plants or institute work practice controls to reduce exposures within permissible limits. Consistent with OSHA's general policy, the regulation does not allow respirators to be used if engineering modifications are technologically feasible. * * *

As presently formulated, the benzene standard is an expensive way of providing some additional protection for a relatively small number of employees. According to OSHA's figures, the standard will require capital investments in engineering controls of approximately $266 million, first-year operating costs * * * of $187 million to $205 million and recurring annual costs of approximately $34 million. The figures outlined in OSHA's explanation of the costs of compliance to various industries indicate that only 35,000 employees would gain any benefit from the regulation in terms of a reduction in their exposure to benzene. * * *

Although OSHA did not quantify the benefits to each category of worker in terms of decreased exposure to benzene, it appears from the economic impact study done at OSHA's direction that those benefits may be relatively small.

II.

Any discussion of the 1 ppm exposure limit must, of course, begin with the Agency's rationale for imposing that limit. The written explanation of the standard fills 184 pages of the printed appendix. Much of it is devoted to a discussion of the voluminous evidence of the adverse effects of exposure to benzene at levels of concentration well above 10 ppm. This discussion demonstrates that there is ample justification for regulating occupational exposure to benzene and that the prior limit of 10 ppm, with a ceiling of 25 ppm (or a peak of 50 ppm) was reasonable. It does not, however, provide direct support for the Agency's conclusion that the limit should be reduced from 10 ppm to 1 ppm.

* * * The Agency made no finding that * * * any * * * empirical evidence, or any opinion testimony demonstrated that exposure to benzene at or below the 10 ppm level had ever in fact caused leukemia. * * * [T] he Court of Appeals noted that OSHA was "unable to point to any empirical evidence documenting a leukemia risk at 10 ppm * * *."

In the end OSHA's rationale for lowering the permissible exposure limit to 1 ppm was based, not on any finding that leukemia has ever been caused by exposure to 10 ppm of benzene and that it will not be caused by exposure to 1 ppm, but rather on a series of assumptions indicating that some leukemias might result from exposure to 10 ppm and that the number of cases might be reduced by reducing the exposure level to 1 ppm. In reaching that result, the Agency first unequivocally concluded that benzene is a human carcinogen. Second, it concluded that industry had failed to prove that there is a safe threshold level of exposure to benzene below which no excess leukemia cases would occur. In reaching this conclusion OSHA rejected industry contentions that certain epidemiological studies indicating no excess risk of leukemia among workers exposed at levels below 10 ppm were sufficient to establish that the threshold level of safe exposure was at or above 10 ppm. It also rejected an industry witness' testimony that a dose-response curve could be constructed on the basis of the reported epidemiological studies and that this curve indicated that reducing the permissible exposure limit from 10 to 1 ppm would prevent at most one leukemia and one other cancer death every six years.[38]

Third, the Agency applied its standard policy with respect to carcinogens,[39] concluding that, in the absence of definitive proof of a safe level, it must be assumed that any level above zero presents some increased risk of cancer. As the federal parties point out in their brief, there are a number of scientists and public health specialists who subscribe to this view, theorizing that a susceptible person may contract cancer from the absorption of even one molecule of a carcinogen like benzene.

Fourth, the Agency reiterated its view of the Act, stating that it was required by § 6(b)(5) [of OSHA] to set the standard either at the level that has been demonstrated to be safe or at the lowest level feasible, whichever is higher. If no safe level is established, as in this case, the Secretary's interpretation of the statute automatically leads to the selection of an exposure limit that is the lowest feasible. Because of benzene's importance to the economy, no one has ever suggested that it would be feasible to eliminate its use entirely, or to try to limit exposures to the small amounts that are omnipresent. Rather, the Agency selected 1 ppm as a workable exposure level and then determined that compliance with that level was technologically feasible and that "the economic impact of . . . (compliance) will not be such as to threaten the financial welfare of the affected firms or the general economy." It therefore held that 1 ppm was the minimum feasible exposure level within the meaning of § 6(b)(5) of the Act.

III.

Our resolution of the issues in these cases turns, to a large extent, on the meaning of and the relationship between § 3(8), which defines a health

---

38. OSHA rejected this testimony in part because it believed the exposure data in the epidemiological studies to be inadequate to formulate a dose-response curve. It also indicated that even if the testimony was accepted—indeed as long as there was any increase in the risk of cancer—the Agency was under an obligation to "select the level of exposure which is most protective of exposed employees."

39. In his dissenting opinion, Mr. Justice Marshall states that the Agency did not rely "blindly on some Draconian carcinogen 'policy'" in setting a permissible exposure limit for benzene. He points to the large number of witnesses the Agency heard and the voluminous record it compiled as evidence that it relied instead on the particular facts concerning benzene. With all due respect, we disagree with Mr. Justice Marshall's interpretation of the Agency's ratio-

nale for its decision. After hearing the evidence, the Agency relied on the same policy view it had stated at the outset, namely, that, in the absence of clear evidence to the contrary, it must be assumed that no safe level exists for exposure to a carcinogen. The Agency also reached the entirely predictable conclusion that industry had not carried its concededly impossible burden of proving that a safe level of exposure exists for benzene. As the Agency made clear later in its proposed generic cancer policy it felt compelled to allow industry witnesses to go over the same ground in each regulation dealing with a carcinogen, despite its policy view. The generic policy, which has not yet gone in to effect, was specifically designed to eliminate this duplication of effort in each case by foreclosing industry from arguing that there is a safe level for the particular carcinogen being regulated.

and safety standard as a standard that is "reasonably necessary and appropriate to provide safe or healthful employment," and § 6(b)(5), which directs the Secretary in promulgating a health and safety standard for toxic materials to "set the standard which most adequately assures, to the extent feasible, on the basis of the best available evidence, that no employee will suffer material impairment of health or functional capacity * * *."

In the Government's view, § 3(8)'s definition of the term "standard" has no legal significance or at best merely requires that a standard not be totally irrational. It takes the position that § 6(b)(5) is controlling and that it requires OSHA to promulgate a standard that either gives an absolute assurance of safety for each and every worker or reduces exposures to the lowest level feasible. The Government interprets "feasible" as meaning technologically achievable at a cost that would not impair the viability of the industries subject to the regulation. The respondent industry representatives, on the other hand, argue that the Court of Appeals was correct in holding that the reasonably necessary and appropriate language of § 3(8), along with the feasibility requirement of § 6(b)(5), requires the Agency to quantify both the costs and the benefits of a proposed rule and to conclude that they are roughly commensurate.

In our view, it is not necessary to decide whether either the Government or industry is entirely correct. For we think it is clear that § 3(8) does apply to all permanent standards promulgated under the Act and that it requires the Secretary, before issuing any standard, to determine that it is reasonably necessary and appropriate to remedy a significant risk of material health impairment. Only after the Secretary has made the threshold determination that such a risk exists with respect to a toxic substance, would it be necessary to decide whether § 6(b)(5) requires him to select the most protective standard he can consistent with economic and technological feasibility, or whether, as respondents argue, the benefits of the regulation must be commensurate with the costs of its implementation. Because the Secretary did not make the required threshold finding in these cases, we have no occasion to determine whether costs must be weighed against benefits in an appropriate case.

A

Under the Government's view, § 3(8), if it has any substantive content at all, merely requires OSHA to issue standards that are reasonably calculated to produce a safer or more healthy work environment. Apart from this minimal requirement of rationality, the Government argues that § 3(8) imposes no limits on the Agency's power, and thus would not prevent it from requiring employers to do, whatever would be "reasonably necessary" to eliminate all risks of any harm from their workplaces. With respect to toxic substances and harmful physical agents, the Government takes an even more extreme position. Relying on § 6(b)(5)'s direction to set a standard "which most adequately assures ... that no employee will suffer material impairment of health or functional capacity," the Government contends that the Secretary is required to impose standards that either guarantee workplaces that are free from any risk of material health impairment, however small, or that come as close as possible to doing so without ruining entire industries.

If the purpose of the statute were to eliminate completely and with absolute certainty any risk of serious harm, we would agree that it would be proper for the Secretary to interpret §§ 3(8) and 6(b)(5) in this fashion. But we think it is clear that the statute was not designed to require employers to provide absolutely risk-free workplaces whenever it is technologically feasible to do so, so long as, the cost is not great enough to destroy an entire industry. Rather, both the language and structure of the Act, as well as its legislative history, indicate that it was intended to require the elimination, as far as feasible, of significant risks of harm.

By empowering the Secretary to promulgate standards that are "reasonably necessary or appropriate to provide safe or healthful employment and places of employment," the Act implies that, before promulgating any standard, the Secretary must make a finding that the workplaces in question are not safe. But "safe" is not the equivalent of "risk-free." There are many activities that we engage in every day—such as driving a car or even breathing city air—that entail some risk of accident or material health impairment; nevertheless, few people would consider these activities "unsafe." Similarly, a workplace can hardly be considered "unsafe" unless it threatens the workers with a significant risk of harm.

Therefore, before he can promulgate any permanent health or safety standard, the Secretary is required to make a threshold ruling that a place of employment is unsafe—in the sense that significant risks are present and can be eliminated or lessened by a change in practices. This requirement applies to permanent standards promulgated pursuant to § 6(b)(5), as well as to other types of permanent standards. For there is no reason why § 3(8)'s definition of a standard should not be deemed incorporated by reference into § 6(b)(5). The standards promulgated pursuant to § 6(b)(5) are just one species of the genus of standards governed by the basic requirement. That section repeatedly uses the term "standard" without suggesting any exception from, or qualification of, the general definition; on the contrary, it directs the Secretary to select "the standard"—that is to say, one of various possible alternatives that satisfy the basic definition in § 3(8)—that is most protective. Moreover, requiring the Secretary to make a threshold finding of significant risk is consistent with the scope of the, regulatory power granted to him by § 6(b)(5), which empowers the Secretary to promulgate standards, not for chemicals and physical agents generally, but for "toxic materials" and "harmful physical agents."

Mr. Justice Marshall states that our view of § 3(8) would make the first sentence in § 6(b)(5) superfluous. We disagree. The first sentence of § 6(b)(5) requires the Secretary to select a highly protective standard once he has determined that a standard should be promulgated. The threshold finding that there is a need for such a standard in the sense that there is a significant risk in the workplace is not unlike the threshold finding that a chemical is toxic or a physical agent is harmful. Once the Secretary has made the requisite threshold finding, § 6(b)(5) directs him to choose the most protective standard that still meets the definition of a standard under § 3(8), consistent with feasibility. * * *

In the absence of a clear mandate in the Act, it is unreasonable to assume that Congress intended to give the Secretary the unprecedented power over American industry that would result from the Government's view of §§ 3(8) and 6(b)(5), coupled with OSHA's cancer policy. Expert testimony that a substance is probably a human carcinogen either because it has caused cancer in animals or because individuals have contracted cancer following extremely high exposure would justify the conclusion that the substance poses some risk of serious harm no matter how minute the exposure and no matter how many experts testified that they regarded the risk as insignificant. That conclusion would in turn justify pervasive regulation limited only by the constraint of feasibility. In light of the fact that there are literally thousands of substances used in the workplace that have been identified as carcinogens or suspect carcinogens, the Government's theory would give OSHA power to impose enormous costs that might produce little, if any, discernible benefit.[51]

If the Government was correct in arguing that neither § 3(8) nor § 6(b)(5) requires that the risk from a toxic substance be quantified sufficiently to enable the Secretary to characterize it as significant in an understandable way, the statute would make such a "sweeping delegation of legislative power" that it might be unconstitutional under the Court's reasoning in A.L.A. Schechter Poultry Corp. v. United States, 295 U.S. 495, 539, 55 S.Ct. 837, 847, 79 L.Ed. 1570, and Panama Refining Co. v. Ryan 293 U.S. 388, 55 S.Ct. 241, 79 L.Ed. 446. A construction of the statute that avoids this kind of open-ended grant should certainly be favored.

* * *

Given the conclusion that the Act empowers the Secretary to promulgate health and safety standards only where a significant risk of harm exists, the critical issue becomes how to define and allocate the burden of proving the significance of the risk in a case such as this, where scientific knowledge is imperfect and the precise quantification of risks is therefore impossible. The Agency's position is that there is substantial evidence in the record to support its conclusion that there is no absolutely safe level for a carcinogen and that, therefore, the burden is properly on industry to prove, apparently beyond a shadow of a doubt, that there is a safe level for benzene exposure. The Agency argues that, because of the uncertainties in this area any other approach would render it helpless, forcing it to wait for

---

51. OSHA's proposed generic cancer policy indicates that this possibility is not merely hypothetical. Under its proposal whenever there is a certain quantum of proof—either from animal experiments, or, less frequently, from epidemiological studies—that a substance causes cancer at any exposure level, an emergency temporary standard would be promulgated immediately, requiring employers to provide monitoring and medical examinations and to reduce exposures to the lowest feasible level. A proposed rule would then be issued along the same lines with objecting employers effectively foreclosed from presenting evidence that there is little or no risk associated with current exposure levels. * * *

the leukemia deaths that it believes are likely to occur before taking any regulatory action.

We disagree. As we read the statute, the burden was on the Agency to show, on the basis of substantial evidence, that it is at least more likely than not that long-term exposure to 10 ppm of benzene presents a significant risk of material health impairment. Ordinarily, it is the proponent of a rule or order who has the burden of proof in administrative proceedings. See 5 U.S.C. § 556(d). In some cases involving toxic substances, Congress has shifted the burden of proving that a particular substance is safe onto the party opposing the proposed rule.[61] The fact that Congress did not follow this course in enacting the Occupational Safety and Health Act indicates that it intended the Agency to bear the normal burden of establishing the need for a proposed standard.

* * *

Contrary to the Government's contentions, imposing a burden on the Agency of demonstrating a significant risk of harm will not strip it of its ability to regulate carcinogens, nor will it require the Agency to wait for deaths to occur before taking any action. First, the requirement that a "significant" risk be identified is not a mathematical straitjacket. It is the Agency's responsibility to determine, in the first instance, what it considers to be a "significant" risk. Some risks are plainly acceptable and others are plainly unacceptable. If, for example, the odds are one in a billion that a person will die from cancer by taking a drink of chlorinated water, the risk clearly could not be considered significant. On the other hand, if the odds are one in a thousand that regular inhalation of gasoline vapors that are 2 percent benzene will be fatal, a reasonable person might well consider the risk significant and take appropriate steps to decrease or eliminate it. Although the Agency has no duty to calculate the exact probability of harm, it does have an obligation to find that a significant risk is present before it can characterize a place of employment as "unsafe."[62]

Second, OSHA is not required to support its finding that a significant risk exists with anything approaching scientific certainty. Although the

---

61. See Environmental Defense Fund Inc. v. EPA, 179 U.S. App.D.C. 43, 49, 57–63, 548 F.2d 998, 1004, 1012–1018 (1976), cert. denied, 431 U.S. 925, 97 S.Ct. 2199, 53 L.Ed.2d 239, where the court rejected the argument that the EPA has the burden of proving that a pesticide is unsafe in order to suspend its registration under the Federal Insecticide, Fungicide, and Rodenticide Act. The court noted that Congress had deliberately shifted the ordinary burden of proof under the Administrative Procedure Act, requiring manufacturers to establish the continued safety of their products.

62. In his dissenting opinion, post at 2896, Mr. Justice Marshall states: "(W)hen the question involves determination of the acceptable level of risk, the ultimate decision must necessarily be based on considerations of policy as well as empirically verifiable facts. Factual determinations can at most define the risk in some statistical way; the judgment whether that risk is tolerable cannot be based solely on a resolution of the facts." We agree. Thus, while the Agency must support its finding that a certain level of risk exists by substantial evidence, we recognize that its determination that a particular level of risk is "significant" will be based largely on policy considerations. At this point we have no need to reach the issue of what level of scrutiny a reviewing court should apply to the latter type of determination.

Agency's findings must be supported by substantial evidence, § 6(b)(5) specifically allows the Secretary to regulate on the basis of the "best available evidence." * * * [T]his provision requires a reviewing court to give OSHA some leeway where its findings must be made on the frontiers of scientific knowledge. Thus, so long as they are supported by a body of reputable scientific thought, the Agency is free to use conservative assumptions in interpreting the data with respect to carcinogens, risking error on the side of overprotection rather than underprotection.[63]

* * *

It should also be noted that, in setting a permissible exposure level in reliance on less-than-perfect methods, OSHA would have the benefit of a backstop in the form of monitoring and medical testing. Thus, if OSHA properly determined that the permissible exposure limit should be set at 5 ppm, it could still require monitoring and medical testing for employees exposed to lower levels. By doing so, it could keep a constant check on the validity of the assumptions made in developing the permissible exposure limit, giving it a sound evidentiary basis for decreasing the limit if it was initially set too high. Moreover, in this way it could ensure that workers who were unusually susceptible to benzene could be removed from exposure before they had suffered any permanent damage.

[Justice Powell concurred in all of the plurality's judgment except the part declining to decide whether OSHA was required to use cost-benefit analysis. Justice Powell was of the opinion that cost-benefit analysis was required.]

[Justice Rehnquist concurred, but would have held the first sentence of section 6(b)(5), with its requirement that OSHA regulate on the basis of what is "feasible," unconstitutional as constituting an unlawful delegation of legislative power to the executive.]

■ MR. JUSTICE MARSHALL with whom MR. JUSTICE BRENNAN, MR. JUSTICE WHITE, and MR. JUSTICE BLACKMUN join, dissenting.

American Textile Manufacturers Institute, Inc. v. Donovan [The Cotton Dust Case]

United States Supreme Court, 1981.
452 U.S. 490, 101 S.Ct. 2478, 69 L.Ed.2d 185.

■ JUSTICE BRENNAN delivered the opinion of the Court.

Congress enacted the Occupational Safety and Health Act of 1970 (Act) "to assure so far as possible every working man and woman in the Nation

---

63. Mr. Justice Marshall states that, under our approach, the Agency must either wait for deaths to occur or must "deceive the public" by making a basically meaningless determination of significance based on totally inadequate evidence. Mr. Justice Marshall's view, however, rests on the erroneous premise that the only reason OSHA did not attempt to quantify benefits in this case was because it could not do so in any reasonable manner. As the discussion of the Agency's rejection of an industry attempt at formulating a dose-response curve demonstrates, however, the Agency's rejection of methods such as dose-response curves was based at least in part on its view that nothing less than absolute safety would suffice.

safe and healthful working conditions...." 29 U.S.C. § 651(b). The Act authorizes the Secretary of Labor to establish, after notice and opportunity to comment, mandatory nationwide standards governing health and safety in the workplace. 29 U.S.C. §§ 655(a), (b). In 1978, the Secretary, acting through the Occupational Safety and Health Administration (OSHA), promulgated a standard limiting occupational exposure to cotton dust, an airborne particle byproduct of the preparation and manufacture of cotton products, exposure to which induces a "constellation of respiratory effects" known as "byssinosis." * * *

Petitioners in these consolidated cases, representing the interests of the cotton industry, challenged the validity of the "Cotton Dust Standard" in the Court of Appeals for the District of Columbia Circuit pursuant to § 6(f) of the Act. They contend in this Court, as they did below, that the Act requires OSHA to demonstrate that its Standard reflects a reasonable relationship between the costs and benefits associated with the Standard. Respondents, the Secretary of Labor and two labor organizations, counter that Congress balanced the costs and benefits in the Act itself, and that the Act should therefore be construed not to require OSHA to do so. They interpret the Act as mandating that OSHA enact the most protective standard possible to, eliminate a significant risk of material health impairment, subject to the constraints of economic and technological feasibility. The Court of Appeals held that the Act did not require OSHA to compare costs and benefits. We granted certiorari to resolve this important questioned which was presented but not decided in last Term's Industrial Union Dept. v. American Petroleum Institute, 448 U.S. 607, 100 S.Ct. 2844, 65 L.Ed.2d 1010 (1980), and to decide other issues related to the Cotton Dust Standard.

I.

Byssinosis, known in its more severe manifestations as "brownlung" disease, is a serious and potentially disabling respiratory disease primarily cause by the inhalation of cotton dust. Byssinosis is a "continuum ... disease," that has been categorized into four grades. In its least serious form, byssinosis produces both subjective symptoms, such as chest tightness, shortness of breath, coughing, and wheezing, and objective indications of loss of pulmonary functions. In its most serious form, byssinosis is a chronic and irreversible obstructive pulmonary disease, clinically similar to chronic bronchitis or emphysema, and can be severely disabling. At worst, as is true of other respiratory diseases including bronchitis, emphysema, and asthma, byssinosis can create an additional strain on cardiovascular functions and can contribute to death from heart failure. * * *

* * * The Cotton Dust Standard promulgated by OSHA establishes mandatory PEL's [permissible exposure limits] over an 8–hour period of 200 ug/m3 for yarn manufacturing, 750 ug/m3 [micrograms per cubic

meter] for slashing and weaving operations, and 500 ug/m3 for all other processes in the cotton industry.

* * *

On the basis of the evidence in the record as a whole, the Secretary determined that exposure to cotton dust represents a "significant health hazard to employees," and that "the prevalence of byssinosis should be significantly reduced" by the adoption of the Standard's PEL. In assessing the health risks from cotton dust and the risk reduction obtained from lowered exposure, OSHA relied particularly on data showing a strong linear relationship between the prevalence of byssinosis and the concentration of lint-free respirable cotton dust. Even at the 200 ug/m3 PEL, OSHA found that the prevalence of at least Grade 1/2 byssinosis [the lowest of the four] would be 13 percent of all employees in the yarn manufacturing sector.

In promulgating the Cotton Dust Standard, OSHA interpreted the Act to require adoption of the most stringent standard to protect against material health impairment, bounded only by technological and economic feasibility. OSHA therefore rejected the industry's alternative proposal for a PEL of 500 ug/m3 in yarn manufacturing, a proposal which would produce a 25 percent prevalence of at least Grade 1/2 byssinosis. The agency expressly found the Standard to be both technologically and economically feasible based on the evidence in the record as a whole. Although recognizing that permitted levels of exposure to cotton dust would still cause some byssinosis, OSHA nevertheless rejected the union proposal for a 100 ug/m3 PEL because it was not within the "technological capabilities of the industry." Similarly, OSHA set PEL's for some segments of the cotton industry at 500 ug/m3 in part because of limitations of technological feasibility. Finally, the Secretary found that "engineering dust controls in weaving may not be feasible even with massive expenditures by the industry," and for that and other reasons adopted a less stringent PEL of 750 ug/m3 for weaving and slashing.

The Court of Appeals upheld the Standard in all major respects. The court rejected the industry's claim that OSHA failed to consider its proposed alternative or give sufficient reasons for failing to adopt it. The court also held that the Standard was "reasonably necessary and appropriate" within the meaning of § 3(8) of the Act, because of the risk of material health impairment caused by exposure to cotton dust. * * *

We affirm in part, and vacate in part.

II.

The principal question presented in these cases is whether the Occupational Safety and Health Act requires the Secretary, in promulgating a standard pursuant to § 6(b)(5) of the Act, to determine that the costs of the standard bear a reasonable relationship to its benefits. Relying on §§ 6(b)(5) and 3(8) of the Act, petitioners urge not only that OSHA must show that a standard addresses a significant risk of material health impairment, see Industrial Union Dept. v. American Petroleum Institute,

448 U.S., at 639, 100 S.Ct., at 2863 (plurality opinion), but also that OSHA must demonstrate that the reduction in risk of material health impairment is significant in light of the costs of attaining that reduction. * * *[26]

A

* * *

Although their interpretations differ, all parties agree that the phrase "to the extent feasible" contains the critical language in § 6(b)(5) for purposes of these cases. The plain meaning of the word "feasible" supports respondents' interpretation of the statute. According to Webster's Third New International Dictionary of the English Language 831 (1976), "feasible" means "capable of being done, executed, or effected." In effect then, as the Court of Appeals held, Congress itself defined the basic relationship between costs and benefits, by placing the "benefit" of worker health above all other considerations save those making attainment of this "benefit" unachievable. Any standard based on a balancing of costs and benefits by the Secretary that strikes a different balance than that struck by Congress would be inconsistent with the command set forth in § 6(b)(5). Thus, cost-benefit analysis by OSHA is not required by the statute because feasibility analysis is.

When Congress has intended that an agency engage in cost-benefit analysis, it has clearly indicated such intent on the face of the statute. One early example is the Flood Control Act of 1936, 33 U.S.C. § 701a: "(T)he Federal Government should improve or participate in the improvement of navigable waters or their tributaries, including watersheds thereof, for flood-control purposes if *the benefits to whomsoever they may accrue are in excess of the estimated costs*, and if the lives and social security of people are otherwise adversely affected." (Emphasis added.)

A more recent example is the Outer Continental Shelf Lands Act Amendments of 1978, 43 U.S.C. § 1347(b) (1976 ed., Supp. III), providing that offshore drilling operations shall use "the best available and safest

---

26. Petitioners ATMI et al. express their position in several ways. They maintain that OSHA "is required to show that a reasonable relationship exists between the risk reduction benefits and the costs of its standards." Petitioners also suggest that OSHA must show that "the standard is expected to achieve a significant reduction in (the significant risk of material health impairment)" based on "an assessment of the costs of achieving it." * * * Respondent Secretary disputes petitioners' description of the exercise, claiming that any meaningful balancing must involve "placing a (dollar) value on human life and freedom from suffering," and that there is no other way but through formal cost-benefit analysis to accomplish petitioners' desired balancing. Cost-benefit analysis contemplates "systematic enumeration of all benefits and all costs, tangible and intangible, whether readily quantifiable or difficult to measure, that will accrue to all members of society if a particular project is adopted." E. Stokey & R. Zeckhauser, A Primer for Policy Analysis 134 (1978); see Commission on Natural Resources, National Research Council, Decision Making for Regulating Chemicals in the Environment 38 (1975). See generally E. Mishan, Cost–Benefit Analysis (1976), Prest & Turvey. Cost–Benefit Analysis, 300 Economic Journal 683 (1965). Whether petitioners' or respondent's characterization is correct, we will sometimes refer to petitioners' proposed exercise as "cost-benefit analysis."

technologies which the Secretary determines to be economically feasible, wherever failure of equipment would have significant effect on safety, health, or the environment, except where the Secretary determines that the incremental benefits are clearly insufficient to justify the incremental costs of using such technologies." These and other statutes demonstrate that Congress uses specific language when intending that an agency engage in cost-benefit analysis. Certainly in light of its ordinary meaning, the word "feasible" cannot be construed to articulate such congressional intent. We therefore reject the argument that Congress required cost-benefit analysis in § 6(b)(5).

B

Even though the plain language of § 6(b)(5) supports this construction, we must still decide whether § 3(8), the general definition of an occupational safety and health standard, either alone or in tandem with § 6(b)(5), incorporates a cost-benefit requirement for standards dealing with toxic materials or harmful physical agents. Section 3(8) of the Act, 29 U.S.C. § 652(8) (emphasis added), provides:

> The term "occupational safety and health standard" means a standard which requires conditions, or the adoption or use of one or more practices, means, methods, operations, or processes, reasonably necessary or appropriate to provide safe or healthful employment and places of employment.

Taken alone, the phrase "reasonably necessary or appropriate" might be construed to contemplate some balancing of the costs and benefits of a standard. Petitioners urge that, so construed, § 3(8) engrafts a cost-benefit analysis requirement on the issuance of § 6(b)(5) standards, even if § 6(b)(5) itself does not authorize such analysis. We need not decide whether § 3(8), standing alone, would contemplate some form of cost-benefit analysis. For even if it does, Congress specifically chose in § 6(b)(5) to impose separate and additional requirements for issuance of a subcategory of occupational safety and health standards dealing with toxic materials and harmful physical agents: it required that those standards be issued to prevent material impairment of health to the extent feasible. Congress could reasonably have concluded that health standards should be subject to different criteria than safety standards because of the special problems presented in regulating them.

Agreement with petitioners' argument that § 3(8) imposes an additional and overriding requirement of cost-benefit analysis on the issuance of § 6(b)(5) standards would eviscerate the "to the extent feasible" requirement. Standards would inevitably be set at the level indicated by cost-benefit analysis, and not at the level specified by § 6(b)(5). For example, if cost-benefit analysis indicated a protective standard of 1,000 ug/m3 PEL, while feasibility analysis indicated a 500 ug/m3 PEL, the agency would be forced by the cost-benefit requirement to choose the less stringent point. We cannot believe that Congress intended the general terms of § 3(8) to countermand the specific feasibility requirement of § 6(b)(5). Adoption of petitioners' interpretation would effectively write § 6(b)(5) out of the Act. We decline to render Congress' decision to include a feasibility requirement nugatory, thereby offending the well-settled rule that all parts of a statute, if possible, are to be given effect. * * *

The legislative history of the Act, while concededly not crystal clear, provides general support for respondents' interpretation of the Act. The congressional Reports and debates certainly confirm that Congress meant "feasible" and nothing else in using that term. Congress was concerned that the Act might be thought to require achievement of absolute safety, an impossible standard, and therefore insisted that health and safety goals be capable of economic and technological accomplishment. Perhaps most telling is the absence of any indication whatsoever that Congress intended OSHA to conduct its own cost-benefit analysis before promulgating a toxic material or harmful physical agent standard. The legislative history demonstrates conclusively that Congress was fully aware that the Act would impose real and substantial costs of compliance on industry, and believed that such costs were part of the cost of doing business. * * *

■ JUSTICE POWELL took no part in the decision of these cases.

NOTES AND QUESTIONS

1. Accurately assessing risks is a difficult, and often imprecise undertaking for administrative agencies. However, in most instances these agencies must also factor in cost or economic considerations into their regulatory decision making. The following excerpt, although written contemporaneously with the *Benzene* and *Cotton Dust* decisions addresses this issue.

Balancing

A critical question is the extent to which economic costs should be weighed against the benefits of risk reduction. Statutes dealing with the environment and energy differ in their approach to this issue, and the courts are wrestling with it. There are four types of statutory frameworks, as described below.

1) One class of statutes requires that the agency balance cost and benefits. Some statutes explicitly require cost-benefit analysis. The most important example is the National Environmental Policy Act (NEPA), which mandates "balancing of the environmental costs of a project against its economic and technological benefits"; a numerical, cost-benefit analysis is required in cases where other methods provide inadequate detail. * * * Similarly, FIFRA requires suspension of pesticides when there is "unreasonable risk to man or the environment, taking into account the economic, social, and environmental costs and benefits" of the pesticide. Similar language appears in the Toxic Substances Control Act.

When the "unreasonable risk" language appears, the courts have imposed balancing as a prerequisite to regulation. Under the Consumer Products Safety Act (CPSA) and the Federal Hazardous Substances Act

(FHSA), the courts have held that such language "necessarily involves a balancing test like that familiar in tort law." This balancing formula, called "Learned Hand's algebra" after the great jurist of the 1920's, has three components: the burden of the regulations, the probability of harm occurring from the product or conduct at issue, and the severity of the harm if it occurs. A regulation is valid if the severity of the injury, factored by its probability, outweighs the burden of regulation. This allows the courts to make a subjective assessment of the imposition on the consumer.

2) A second approach to balancing costs and benefits appears in the Clean Water Act. The EPA must consider costs, but they are much less central to the decision than under the first approach. In establishing phase I (1977) effluent standards, the agency must consider the total cost of standards, including potential unemployment and dislocation. It need not make a quantitative comparison of cost and benefit, and it is to impose the standard unless the marginal level of effluent reduction is "wholly out of proportion" to the cost. For phase II (1987) standards, the total cost need not be compared to benefit, but only considered. One court of appeal has required a cost-effectiveness analysis of alternative strategies to implement phase II controls.

When an individual polluter wishes a variance from the effluent standards, the result is different. The U.S. Supreme Court ruled in 1980 that the economic capability of an individual plant to bear the costs of a phase I standard may not be considered, EPA v. National Crushed Stone Association, 449 U.S. 64 (1980). But under phase II individual economic hardship will justify a variance. The reasoning is that phase I standards already incorporate costs, because they are calculated on the basis of the best control system now in use; segments of industry that have not attained this level should be required to do so. Individual consideration is appropriate for phase II because such cost analysis has not yet been performed.

3) A third approach is to ignore costs and focus on the issue of health risk. The Delaney clause of the federal Food, Drug, and Cosmetic Act, which provides that no additive can be approved "if it is found to induce cancer," is an example. In theory, once tests demonstrate the carcinogenicity of a substance, no consideration of its benefits or the costs of its removal is relevant; the additive is banned. This approach is used in other statutes, although not with the same clean-cut rejection of balancing. For instance, the Clean Air Act requires the establishment of primary national ambient air quality standards solely as a function of health risk. Considerations of economic or technological infeasibility cannot be used in formulating these standards, Union Electric Co. v. EPA, 427 U.S. 246 (1976).

4) It is the Occupational Safety and Health Act that has been the main focus of the debate over balancing. Regulation under this act raises very difficult questions about the assessment and acceptability of health risk, and the answers to the problems of low-level occupational

exposure to toxic substances will influence policies in many other areas. Section 6(b)(5) of the statute provides that standards must assure "to the extent feasible" that "no employee will suffer material impairment of health."

When the benzene case reached the Supreme Court in 1980, the main opinion avoided the issue of balancing. Then in 1981 the court ruled in *American Textile Manufacturers Institute (ATMI)* [v. Donovan] that balancing was inappropriate under its reading of the legislative history of the Occupational Safety and Health Act. The court held that Congress had performed balancing and intended to place "the 'benefit' of worker health above all other considerations save those making attainment of this 'benefit' unachievable. Any standard based on a balancing of costs and benefits by the Secretary that strikes a different balance than that struck by Congress would be inconsistent with the command set forth in § 6(b)(5)", 452 U.S. 490, 509 (1981). The court also held that interpretation of the phrase "reasonably necessary" to require balancing of costs and benefits "would eviscerate the to the extent feasible requirement." Id.

The court ruled that feasibility, not cost-benefit consideration, is the only factor that takes precedence over worker health. It defined feasible as "capable of being done." It refined the definition of economic feasibility, but still left some aspects uncertain. For instance, OSHA conducted studies to estimate the cost of complying with the new standards and concluded that the cost would not seriously threaten the textile industry and that the industry would maintain "long-term profitability and competitiveness." The court refused to decide whether a standard that threatens this status is feasible. * * *

The ATMI decision also implied that the "reasonably necessary" language might require cost-benefit balancing for other hazards. The feasibility principle of section 6(b)(5) only reflects the intent of Congress to regulate toxic materials as much as possible; it does not necessarily apply to safety or noise standards, for example. Therefore standards in those areas might require "some form of cost-benefit analysis." Again, the court did not decide this issue.

However the problems are resolved, if balancing is to play a role in environmental law, some attempt must be made to value human life and health. Society, either implicitly or explicitly, places a dollar value on the preservation or saving of a life. * * *

Human life is not the only aspect that is difficult to evaluate, and balancing under environmental statutes often involves comparing tangible costs and benefits. It is through balancing that the courts attempt to weigh such factors as scenic beauty, preservation of animal life, and quality of life.

Prospects for Risk Assessment

There is no doubt that agencies and courts will continue to be troubled by risk questions. The easiest administrative policy—eradication of risk to the greatest extent possible—has been declining in popularity as we have become aware of the finite nature of our resources. The costs of environmental regulation seemed less burdensome at a time when the United States had dealer economic advantages. Yet the calculus of risk involves basic values that will always be weighted differently by different individuals. Decision-makers select a policy that implicitly weighs health, quality of life, economic opportunity, and environmental amenities. Consensus is almost impossible, yet we have no alternative but to seek increasingly rational approaches.

Pacolo F. Ricci and Lawrence S. Molton, Risk and Benefit in Environmental Law, 214 Science 1096 (1981).

2. Justice Stevens' plurality opinion in the *Benzene* case (Industrial Union Department, AFL–CIO v. American Petroleum Institute) has been very influential. The Courts of Appeals have generally considered that the plurality opinion in *Benzene* was adopted by a majority of the Supreme Court in *American Textile Manufacturers Institute*. Do you agree?

A significant application of the *Benzene* case standard is AFL–CIO v. OSHA, 965 F.2d 962 (11th Cir.1992), which involved judicial review of OSHA's Air Contaminants Standard, a set of permissible exposure limits (PELs) for 428 toxic substances. The court vacated the Air Contaminants Standard and remanded to the agency. Consider the following excerpts from the decision.

Section 3(8) of the OSH Act defines "occupational health and safety standard" as "a standard which requires conditions, or the adoption or use of one or more practices, means, methods, operations, or processes, *reasonably necessary or appropriate* to provide safe or healthful employment and places of employment." 29 U.S.C. § 652(8) (emphasis added). The Supreme Court has interpreted this provision to require that, before the promulgation of any permanent health standard, OSHA make a threshold finding that a significant risk of material health impairment exists at the current levels of exposure to the toxic substance in question, Benzene, 448 U.S. at 614–15, 642, 100 S.Ct. at 2850–51, 2864; ATMI, 452 U.S. at 505–06, 101 S.Ct. at 2488–89, "and that a new, lower standard is therefore 'reasonably necessary or appropriate to provide safe or healthful employment and places of employment.'" Benzene, 448 U.S. at 615, 100 S.Ct. at 2850. OSHA is not entitled to regulate any risk, only those which present a "significant" risk of "material" health impairment. OSHA must therefore determine: (1) what health impairments are "material," and (2) what constitutes a "significant" risk of such impairment. Moreover, OSHA ultimately bears the burden of proving by substantial evidence that, such a risk exists and that the proposed standard is necessary. The agency "has no duty to calculate the exact probability of harm," *id.* at 655, 100 S.Ct. at 2871, or "to support its finding that a significant risk exists with anything approaching scientific certainty," *id.* at 656, 100 S.Ct. at 2871. However, OSHA must provide at least an estimate of the actual risk asserted with a particular toxic substance, and explain in an understandable way why that risk is significant. In past rulemakings, OSHA has satisfied this requirement by estimating either the number of workers likely to suffer the effects of exposure or the percentage of risk to any particular worker.

Although the court found that the Air Contaminants rule satisfied the "material impairments" test, the "significant risk" requirement was not met because OSHA did not quantify or explain to a reasonable degree the risk posed by *each* individual toxic substance regulated (*Id.* at 975). OSHA's generic finding that the Standard as a *whole* would prevent 55,000 occupational illnesses and 683 deaths annually was therefore insufficient. The court further stated (*Id.* at 976):

Moreover, a determination that the new standard is "reasonably necessary or appropriate," 29 U.S.C. § 652(8), and that it is the standard that "most adequately assures * * * that no employee will suffer material impairment of health or functional capacity," *id.* § 655(b)(5), necessarily requires some assessment of the level at which significant risk of harm is eliminated or substantially reduced. See Benzene, 448 U.S. at 653, 100 S.Ct. at 2869–70. Yet with rare exceptions, the individual substance discussions in the Air Contaminants Standard are virtually devoid of reasons for setting those individual standards. In most cages, OSHA cited a few studies and then established a PEL without explaining why the studies mandated the particular PEL chosen. For example, the PEL for bismuth telluride appears to be based on a single study that showed almost no effects of any kind in animals at several times that concentration. 54 Fed.Reg. at 2508. Similarly, the PEL for ferrovanadium dust was based on pulmonary changes at exposure levels many hundreds of times higher than OSHA's new standard. *Id.* at 2510. See also, e.g., iron pentacarbonyl, *id.* at 2412; cesium hydroxide, *id.* at 2455; iron salts, *id.* at 2466; ethylene dichloride, *id.* at 2484; sulfur tetrafluoride, *id.* at 2526. For some substances, OSHA merely repeated a boilerplate finding that the new limit would protect workers from significant risk of some material health impairment.

On the other hand, OSHA established PELs for carbon tetrachloride and vinyl bromide, both carcinogens, at levels where OSHA itself acknowledged that the risk of material health impairment remained significant. 54 Fed.Reg. at 2679–80, 2694. For carbon tetrachloride, OSHA stated that at the new level "residual risk" continues to be significant * * * 3.7 excess deaths per 1,000 workers exposed over their working lifetimes. *Id.* at 2680. For vinyl bromide, OSHA stated that the new PEL "will not eliminate this significant risk, because * * * residual risk [at the new level] is 40 excess deaths per 1,000 exposed workers * * * [and thus] is clearly significant." *Id.* at 2694. The only explanation given by OSHA in the final rule for setting its standard where a significant risk of material health impairment remains was that the time and resource constraints of attempting to promulgate an air contaminants standard of this magnitude prevented detailed analysis of these substances.

The court also criticized OSHA's use of safety factors (*Id.* at 978–979):

We find OSHA's use of safety factors in this rulemaking problematic. First, OSHA's use of safety factors in this rulemaking is very similar to the approach criticized by the Supreme Court in *Benzene*. Second, even assuming that the use of safety factors is permissible under the Act and *Benzene*, application of such factors without explaining the method by which they were determined, as was done in this case, is clearly not permitted.

From OSHA's description, safety factors are used to lower the standard below levels at which the available evidence shows no significant risk of material health impairment because of the possibility that the evidence is incorrect or incomplete; i.e., OSHA essentially makes an assumption that the existing evidence does not adequately show the extent of the risk. That may be a correct assumption, but beyond a general statement that the use of safety factors common in the scientific community, OSHA did not indicate how the existing evidence for individual substances was inadequate to show the extent of the risk from those substances.

The lesson of *Benzene* is clearly that OSHA may use assumptions, but only to the extent that those assumptions have some basis in reputable scientific evidence. If the agency is concerned that the standard should be more stringent than even a conservative interpretation of the existing evidence supports, monitoring and medical testing may be done to accumulate the additional evidence needed to support that more protective limit. *Benzene* does not provide support for setting standards below the level substantiated by the evidence. Nor may OSHA base a finding of significant risk at lower levels of exposure on unsupported assumptions using evidence of health impairments at significantly higher levels of exposure.

Finally, the court found OSHA's treatment of "feasibility" lacking (*Id.* at 980–985):

> The Supreme Court has defined "feasibility" as "capable of being done, executed, or effect." See ATMI, 452 U.S. at 513 n. 31, 101 S.Ct. at 2492 n. 31 ("[A]ny standard that was not *economically or technologically* feasible would a *fortiori* not be 'reasonably necessary or appropriate' under the Act." (Emphasis added.)). Again, the burden is on OSHA to show by substantial evidence that the standard is feasible, although OSHA need not prove feasibility with scientific certainty.

To show that a standard is technologically feasible, OSHA must demonstrate "that modern technology has at least conceived some industrial strategies or devices which are likely to be capable of meeting the PEL and which the industries are generally capable of adopting." *United Steelworkers*, 647 F.2d at 1266. Further, "the undisputed principle that feasibility is to be tested industry-by-industry demands that OSHA examine the technological feasibility of each industry individually." *Id.* at 1301.

In this rulemaking, OSHA first identified the primary air contaminant control methods: Engineering controls are methods such as ventilation, isolation, and substitution. 64 Fed.Reg. at 2789. Complementing the engineering controls are work practices and administrative reforms (e.g., housekeeping, material handling or transfer procedures, leak detection programs, training, and personal hygiene). *Id.* at 2789–90. Finally, personal protective equipment such as respirators and gloves may become necessary when these other controls are not fully effective. *Id.* at 2790.

However, OSHA made no attempt to show the ability of technology to meet specific exposure standards in specific industries. Except for an occasional specific conclusion as to whether a particular process control could meet a particular PEL, OSHA merely presented general conclusions as to the availability of these controls in a particular industry.

Nor has OSHA adequately demonstrated that the standard is economically feasible. OSHA must "provide a reasonable assessment of the likely range of costs of its standard, and the likely effects of those costs on the industry," *id.* at 1266, so as to "demonstrate a reasonable likelihood that these costs will not threaten the existence or competitive structure of an industry, even if it does portend disaster for some marginal firms," *id.* at 1272.

OSHA's economic feasibility determinations therefore suffer from the same faults as its technological feasibility findings. Indeed, it would seem particularly important not to aggregate, disparate industries when making a showing of economic feasibility. OSHA admits that its economic feasibility conclusions only "have a high degree of validity on a sector basis," *id.*, as opposed to a subsector or more industry-specific basis.

However, reliance on such tools as average estimates of cost can be extremely misleading in assessing the impact of particular standards on individual industries. Analyzing the economic impact for an entire sector could conceal particular industries laboring under special disabilities and likely to fail as a result of enforcement.

OSHA's analysis of perchloroethylene (perc) is a prime example of the problems with OSHA's approach to this rulemaking. Perc is a widely used solvent in the drycleaning and industrial degreasing industries. *Id.* at 2686.

Although OSHA stated that it "does not believe that information in the record at the present time demonstrates that it is feasible to reduce exposures to lower levels," OSHA's feasibility analysis for perc is grossly inadequate. For technological feasibility, OSHA limited its discussion to showing that its new PEL of 25 ppm was achievable. OSHA stated that 25 ppm can be achieved with newer equipment and engineering and work practice controls. OSHA also stated that "a significant percentage of operations, including smaller operations, have installed" the newer equipment, and that the industry as a whole "is gradually replacing older equipment with newer equipment." However, there is no explanation or evidence cited in the final rule to support the proposition that an even lower PEL is not technologically feasible.

On the other hand, OSHA's economic feasibility determination for perc cannot support either the new PEL of 25 ppm or the agency's decision not to set an even lower PEL. OSHA used the two-digit SIC code, SIC 72—Personal Services, to define the industries affected by the perc standard. This creates two problems. First, drycleaning is the only industry in SIC 72—affected by the perc standard. SIC 72 covers numerous other industries, including funeral services, shoe repair, barber and beauty shops, and photography studios. Nevertheless, OSHA took the costs of compliance with the new perc standard, which would be borne only by the drycleaning industry subsector, and compared those costs to the profits and sales of the entire personal services sector. As a result, OSHA must have significantly understated the costs of compliance for the drycleaning industry. Indeed, petitioners claim that the actual economic impact on this industry would be more than ten times OSHA's estimate.

Moreover, while the drycleaning industry received at least some feasibility analysis for perc the other major user of that chemical, industrial degreasing operations, received none. This industry is not in SIC 72, which was the only industry sector reviewed for technological or economic feasibility for the new perc standard. Therefore, OSHA clearly has not fulfilled its duty to examine the feasibility of its perc standard for each affected industry.

3. Following the *Benzene* decision, EPA confirmed through further epidemiological tests that benzene poses very serious risk to workers. The EPA compiled a 36,000–page record, held hearings, and promulgated a new PEL in December 1987. The new PEL lowered the eight-hour average exposure limit from 10 ppm to 1 ppm. The new PEL was based upon risk assessments that the old PEL of 10 ppm posed a risk of 95 additional leukemia deaths per 1000 workers, that this was significant, and that the new PEL would save many lives.

The new PEL is identical to that which the EPA promulgated in 1977 and that was struck down in 1980 by the *Benzene* decision. What was gained by forcing the EPA to carry out additional tests, compile a record, and hold public hearings? Is judicial review worth the cost? Does it merely contribute bureaucratic paperwork and complexity?

4. *Environmental Disclosure and Communication.*

a. *Securities Laws.* Regulation 5K promulgated by the Securities Exchange Commission (SEC) requires all publicly held companies to disclose material contingent on environmental-liabilities arising under federal, state, or local laws. Such disclosures must be made in a company's Annual Report (10K) or Quarterly Report (10Q) as well as other SEC filings.

b. *Emergency Planning and Community Right-to-Know Act (EPCRA)*, 42 U.S.C. § 11001 et seq. Section 313 of EPCRA, 42 U.S.C. § 1113, requires owners or operators of manufacturing facilities to submit annual reports on the amounts of listed toxic chemicals their facilities release into the environment, either routinely or as a result of an accident. This reporting requirement applies to owners and operators of facilities that are in Standard Industrial Classification (SIC) Codes 20–39:

Code Industry

• Food and Kindred Products

- Tobacco Products
- Textile Mill Products
- Apparel and Other Finished Products Made from Fabrics
- Lumber and Wood Products
- Furniture and Fixtures
- Paper and Allied Products
- Printing, Publishing and Allied Industries
- Chemicals and Allied Products
- Petroleum Refining and Related Industries
- Rubber and Miscellaneous Plastic Products
- Leather and Leather Products
- Stone, Clay, Glass and Concrete Products
- Primary Metal Industries
- Fabricated Metal Products
- Industrial and Commercial Machinery and Computer Equipment
- Electronic and Other Electrical Equipment and Components
- Transportation Equipment
- Measuring, Analyzing and Controlling Instruments; Photographic, Medical and Optical Goods; Watches and Clocks
- Miscellaneous Manufacturing

Facilities covered by § 313 must use Reporting Form R to report the following information:

1.   The name, location and principal business activities at the facility;

2.   Off-site locations to which any waste that contains the listed chemical is transferred;

3.   Whether the listed chemical is manufactured, imported, processed, or otherwise used and the general use categories of the chemical;

4.   An estimate (in ranges) of the maximum amounts of the listed chemical present at the facility at any time during the preceding year;

5.   The quantity of the listed chemical entering each environmental medium-air, water and land-annually;

6.   Waste treatment and disposal methods and the efficiency of such methods for each waste stream;

7.   Information on source reduction and recycling or pollution prevention; and

8.   A certification by a senior management official that the report is complete and accurate.

The reports under EPCRA are available to the public. It is therefore possible to compile a national inventory of toxic chemical releases. The reported data are listed in the EPA's annual Toxic Release Inventory (TRI), which is a powerful tool for pressuring factories to reduce pollution.

c. *Occupational Safety and Health Act (OSHA)*. The Hazard Communication Standard (HSI) under OSHA establishes uniform hazard communication standards for employers. Each employee working in a manufacturing facility who is or may be exposed to toxic chemicals must receive information and appropriate training on safety measures. Chemical manufacturers must evaluate the hazards of chemicals they produce or import and this information must be passed on to downstream employers through labels and Material Safety Data Sheets (MSDS).

5. Another non-regulatory approach to toxic substance control is EPA agreements with industries to set negotiated caps on their release of toxics. For example, on June 7, 2000, EPA reached an agreement with the manufacturers of a pesticide called chlorpyrifos. This chemical is the most commonly used pesticide in the home. EPA estimated that 21 to 24 million pounds of chlorpyrifos are applied on average per year, with half of that being applied around homes, schools, office buildings and parks. The agreement between the manufacturers and EPA uses a "phase out" approach that will completely eliminate several uses of the chemical. For a discussion of this agreement, see Elaine Bueschen, An Agreement Between EPA and Pesticide Manufacturers to Mitigate the Risks of Chlorpyrifos, 31 ELR 10452 (2001).

This agreement is a byproduct of the Food Quality Protection Act of 1996. What are the regulatory implications of such non-regulatory controls? What guidelines must EPA follow when negotiating these agreements? What guidelines should they follow? If the manufacturers of this chemical were willing to negotiate such an agreement, does this suggest that they were admitting the risk level presented by it was too high? If so, why wouldn't EPA employ a conventional "command and control" approach? What is EPA's remedy if industry fails to adhere to the agreement? What did EPA bargain away in making this agreement? See Memorandum of Agreement Between EPA and Signatory Registrants Regarding the Registration of Pesticides Containing Chlorpyrifos, June, 2000.

6. If you were EPA Administrator, how would you recommend dealing with the following issues?

a. *Electric and Magnetic Fields (EMF)*. Health questions recently have been raised concerning electric and magnetic fields. These fields are created whenever electric current passes through power lines or electrical equipment. Some EMF epidemiological studies have reported positive correlations between residential and occupational exposures to EMF and certain cancers, including lymphoma and breast cancer. Electric utility companies are aware of the problem and are spending over $1 billion per year in field management, "prudent avoidance, and research." Additional research studies indicate a "worst case" risk of EMF exposure is a modest increase in illness on the order of two to three times normal (as opposed to 40 times normal for cigarette smoking). All researchers agree that results so far are inconclusive.

What are the implications of EMF for (a) new regulatory standards; (b) toxic tort litigation; (c) workers' compensation claims; (d) eminent domain; and (e) litigation to block new construction or facility upgrades? See Roy W. Krieger and Michael E. Withey, EMF and the Public Health, 9 Nat. Resources & Env't. 3 (1994); C. Michelle Depew, Challenging the Fields: The Case for Electromagnetic Field Injury Tort Remedies Against Utilities, 36 S.Tex.L.Rev. 125 (1995); Roland A. Giroux, Daubert v. Merrell Dow: Is this Just What the EMF Doctor Ordered? 12 Pace Envt'l L.Rev. 393 (1995) ["In sum, research data to date indicate that there may be a link between EMF exposure and a small increase in the population's cancer rate. No cause-and-effect relationship, however, has yet been established, and no hazardous level of exposure has been determined. Researchers are not sure whether extremely low frequency non-ionizing EMF can produce adverse health effects, but most believe there is a chance that low-level fields could pose a health problem and continuing research is needed." Id. at 418.]

   b. *Radon.* Radon is a colorless, odorless, and tasteless radioactive gas emitted from naturally decaying uranium present in the Earth's crust. Radon may be emitted from rocks such as granite, shale, and limestone; it is found also in some soils contaminated with industrial waste. Radon emitted outdoors is harmless; indoors, however, it can build up concentrations that some studies have found to be harmful.

The EPA has estimated that 5,000 to 20,000 residential radon-induced lung cancer deaths occur each year. EPA has suggested that the upper limit of acceptable radon contamination is four pico Curies per liter (a pico Curie is equal to one-millionth of a Curie). Dr. Vernon J. Houk, then Assistant Surgeon General of the United States announced in 1988 that he would not buy or move into a home without knowing its radon level. However, many doctors and scientists disagree. A 1991 Report by the Natural Academy of Sciences found that radon risks may be overstated by 20–30 percent: "Direct extrapolation of risk estimates from mining to the home environment may overestimate the numbers of radon-caused lung cancer diseases."

Epidemiological data on radon illnesses is virtually unavailable, and several studies have found that homeowners typically are exposed to only one-third as much radon inside their homes as monitoring devices indicate.

What should be done? See Robert D. King, The Legal Implications of Residential Radon Contamination: The First Decade, 18 Wm. and Mary L. Rev. 107 (1993).

   c. *Endocrine Disruption.* In recent years, scientists have proposed that chemicals might be disrupting the endocrine(hormonal) systems of humans and wildlife. They have also hypothesized that endocrine disruption might result in cancer, harm to male and female reproductive systems, thyroid damage, or other adverse consequences. In response, EPA issued a Special Report on Environmental Endocrine Disruption. EPA has not yet attempted to directly regulate endocrine effects, but it has categorized much of the evidence as "credible." This lack of EPA action is due, in large part, to the challenge of elucidating cause and effect relationships for observed responses. EPA has expressed the need for further research. At what point does regulation become feasible or is it necessary?

SECTION 2. THE REGULATION OF TOXIC MATERIALS POSSESSING USEFUL CHARACTERISTICS—THE FEDERAL, INSECTICIDE, FUNGICIDE AND RODENTICIDE ACT (FIFRA)

A. INTRODUCTION TO PESTICIDE REGULATION

Certain substances are intended to have toxic effects—then purpose is to kill or retard the growth of living organism such as animals and plants. Pesticides and herbicides represent such a substance; designed to eradicate forms of life deemed unnecessary or objectionable by humans. In the past, these materials were known aptly as "economic poisons" due to their usefulness in maximizing economic ally related activities, notably agricultural production. However, pesticides and herbicides have also been considered beneficial in numerous household applications as well.

Federal pesticide law has its origins in the early 1900's when its focus was on preventing the manufacture sale or distribution of misbranded or adulterated pesticide presumably to assure that purchases received the expected product. Later amendments to the law in the 1940s emphasized proper labeling instructions to protect the consumer applicator from accidental over exposure and self-poisoning. The modern law, FIFRA, began with the 1972 Federal Environmental Pesticide Act which expanded the statutory focus to include the protection of both human health and the environment.

FIFRA, the federal law outlined below, is administered by EPA and is basically a product licensing statute providing in § 3(a) that no pesticide may be sold or distributed in the United States without first being "registered" with EPA. Through this registration process, the federal government controls pesticide use throughout the nation.

Under FIFRA § 3(c)(5) EPA "shall" register a pesticide if it determines that

(A) its composition is such as to warrant the proposed claims for it;

(B) its labeling and other material required to be submitted comply with the requirements of this subchapter;

(C) it will perform its intended function without unreasonable adverse effects on the environment; and

(D) when used in accordance with widespread and commonly recognized practice it will not generally cause unreasonable adverse effects on the environment.

Generally, EPA exercises its protective function by denying new pesticide registrations or by placing protective conditions on them. This happens slowly since EPA registers about 26 new pesticide active ingredients per year. Pesticides previously registered under the less-protective federal law in effect prior to November, 1984, must be "re-registered" under the current law. This process has made extremely slow progress to reexamine the over 20,000 pesticides already on the market. Besides controlling product registration FIFRA directs EPA to establish label and produce use requirements. The reach of EPA's is quite considerable extending to:

- 30 major pesticide producers plus another 100 small producers
- 2,500 pesticide formulators
- 29,000 distributors
- 40,000 commercial pest control firms
- 1 million farms
- 3.5   million farm users
- several million industry and government users
- 90 million households

Linda Jo Schierow, Describing FIFRA

(Cong. Research Service, 1997).

    i.   Introduction

    1.   The Federal Insecticide, Fungicide, and Rodenticide Act, as amended (FIFRA), requires EPA to regulate the sale and use of pesticides in the United States through registration and labeling of the estimated 21,000 pesticide products currently in use. The Act directs EPA to restrict the use of pesticides as necessary to prevent unreasonable adverse effects on people and the environment, taking into account the costs and benefits of various pesticide uses. FIFRA prohibits sale of any pesticide in the United States unless it is registered and labeled indicating approved uses and restrictions. It is a violation of the law to use a pesticide in a manner that is inconsistent with the label instructions. EPA registers each pesticide for each approved use, for example, to control boll weevils on cotton. In addition, FIFRA requires EPA to reregister older pesticides based on new data that meet current regulatory and scientific standards. Establishments that manufacture or sell pesticide products must register with EPA. Facility managers are required to keep certain records and to allow inspections by Agency or state regulatory representatives.

    ii. Definition of "Pesticide"

    1.   Pesticides are broadly defined in FIFRA Section 2(u) as chemicals and other products used to kill, repel. or control pests. Familiar examples include pesticides used to kill insects and weeds that can reduce the yield and sometimes harm the quality of agricultural commodities, ornamental plantings, forests, wooden structures. and pastures. But the broad definition of "pesticide" in FIFRA also applies to products with less familiar "pesticidal uses."

2. For example, substances used to control mold, mildew, algae, and other nuisance growths on equipment, in surface water, or on stored grains are pesticides. The term also applies to disinfectants and sterilants, insect repellents arid fumigants, rat poison, mothballs, and many other substances.

iii. History of Pesticide Law

1. Although federal pesticide legislation was first enacted in 1910, it aimed to reduce economic exploitation of farmers by manufacturers and distributors of adulterated or ineffective pesticides. Congress did not address the potential risks to human health posed by pesticide products until it enacted the original 1947 version of Fl FRf1. The U.S. Department of Agriculture (USDA) was responsible for administering the pesticide statutes during this period. However, responsibility was shifted to the EPA when that Agency was created in 1970. Broader congressional concerns about long-and short-term toxic effects of pesticide exposure to people who applied pesticides (applicators), wildlife, nontarget insects and birds, and on food consumers subsequently led to a complete revision of FIFRA in 1972.

2. The 1972 law is the basis of current federal policy. Substantial changes were made in 1988 (P.L. 100–532) to accelerate the reregistration process, and again in 1996 (P.L. 104–170). The 1996 amendments facilitate registration of pesticides for special (so-called "minor") uses, reauthorize collection of fees to support reregistration. and require coordination of regulations implementing FIFRA and the Federal Food, Drug, and Cosmetic Act (FFDCA) (P.L. 104–170).

iv. Registration of Pesticide Products

1. When pesticide manufacturers apply to register a pesticide active ingredient, pesticide product, or a new use of a registered pesticide under FIFRA Section 3, EPA requires them to submit scientific data on pesticide toxicity and behavior in the environment. EPA may require data from any combination of more than 100 different tests, depending on the toxicity and degree of exposure. To register a pesticide use on food, EPA also requires applicants to identify analytical methods that can be used to test food for pesticide residues and to determine the amount of pesticide residue that could remain on crops, as well as on (or in) food products, assuming that the pesticide is applied according to the manufacturers' recommended rates and methods. Based on the data submitted, EPA determines whether and under what conditions the proposed pesticide use presents an unreasonable risk to human health or the environment. If the pesticide is proposed for use on a food crop. EPA also determines whether a "safe" level of pesticide residue, called a "tolerance," can be established under the FFDCA. A tolerance must be established before a pesticide registration may be granted for use on food. If any registration is granted, the Agency specifies the approved uses and conditions of use, including safe methods of pesticide storage and disposal, which the registrant must explain on the product label. FIFRA requires that federal regulations for pesticide labels preempt state, local, and tribal regulations. Use of a pesticide product in a manner inconsistent with its label is prohibited.

2.   EPA may classify and register a pesticide product for general or restricted use. Products known as "restricted-use pesticides" are those judged to be more dangerous to the applicator or to the environment. Such pesticides can be applied only by people who have been trained and certified. Individual states and Indian tribes generally are responsible for training and certifying pesticide applicators.

3.   FIFRA Section 3 also allows "conditional," temporary registrations if 1) the proposed pesticide ingredients and uses are substantially similar to currently registered products and will not create additional significant environmental risks; 2) an amendment is proposed for additional uses of a registered pesticide and sufficient data are submitted indicating that there is no significant additional risk; or 3) data requirements for a new active ingredient require more time to generate than normally allowed, and use of the pesticide during the period will not cause any unreasonable adverse effect on the environment and will be in the public interest.

v.   Public Disclosure, Exclusive Use and Trade Secrets

1.   Section 3 directs EPA to make the data submitted by the applicant publicly available within 30 days after a registration is granted. However, applicants may claim certain data are protected as trade secrets under Section 10. If EPA agrees that the data are protected, the Agency must withhold that data from the public, unless the data pertain to the health effects or environmental fate or effects of the pesticide ingredients. Information may be protected if it qualifies as a trade secret and reveals 1) manufacturing processes; 2) details of methods for testing, detecting. or measuring amounts of inert ingredients; or 3) the identity or percentage quantity of inert ingredients.

2.   Companies sometimes seek to register a product based upon the registration of similar products. relying upon the data provided by the original registrant that is publicly released. This is allowed. However, Section 3 of FIFRA provides for a 10–year period of "exclusive use" by the registrant of data submitted in support of an original registration or a new use. In addition, an applicant who submits any new data in support of a registration or registration is entitled to compensation for the cost of data development by any subsequent applicant who supports an application with that data within 15 years of its submission. If compensation is not jointly agreed upon by the registrant and applicant, binding arbitration can be invoked.

vi. Reregistration

1.   Most pesticides currently registered in the United States are older pesticides and were not subject to modern safety reviews. Amendments to FIFRA in 1972 directed EPA to "reregister" approximately 35,000 older products. thereby assessing their safety in light of current standards. The task of reregistering older pesticides has been streamlined by reviewing groupings of products having the same active ingredients, on a generic instead of individual product basis. Many of the 35,000 products will not be reviewed and their registrations will be canceled, because registrants do not

wish to support reregistration. Nevertheless. the task for registrants and EPA remains immense and costly. To accelerate the process of reregistration, Congress, in 1988, imposed a 10–year reregistration schedule. To help pay for the additional costs of the accelerated process, Congress directed EPA to require registrants to pay reregistration and annual registration maintenance fees on pesticide ingredients and products. The 1996 amendments to FIFRA extended EPA's authority to collect maintenance fees through FY 2001. Exemptions from fees or reductions are allowed for minor-use pesticides, public health pesticides and small business registrants.

vii. Special Review

1.   EPA continues to evaluate the safety of pesticides after they are registered as new information becomes available. FIFRA requires registrants to report promptly any new evidence of adverse effects from pesticide exposure. If evidence indicates that a registered pesticide may pose an unreasonable risk, EPA may initiate a special review of available information to reevaluate the risks and benefits of each registered use. FIFRA also authorizes EPA to require registrants to conduct new studies to fill gaps in scientific understanding to assist risk assessments. As a result of a special review EPA may conclude that registration is adequate, needs amendment, or should be canceled.

viii. Canceling or Suspending Registration

1.   If a special review or reregistration evaluation finds that a registered use may cause "unreasonable adverse effects," EPA may amend or cancel the registration. FIFRA also allows registrants to request cancellation or amendment of a registration to terminate selected pesticide uses. Requesting voluntary cancellation sometimes reflects a registrant's conclusion that the cost of additional studies is not worth the expected benefit (that is, profit) from sales if the registration is maintained.

2.   If a registration is canceled for one or more LISCS of a pesticide, FIFRA does not permit it to be sold or distributed for those uses in the United States, although for a specified period of time, U.S. farmers may use remaining stocks and commerce may continue for commodities that were legally treated with the pesticide. FIFRA allows registrants to appeal an EPA decision to cancel a registration. Appeal initiates a lengthy review process during which their product may continue to be marketed. However, if there is threat of an "imminent hazard" during the time required to cancel a registration, FIFRA authorizes EPA to Suspend registration. Suspension orders, which also may be appealed, stop sales and use of the pesticide. In the event of suspension and cancellation, FIFRA section 15 directs EPA to request an appropriation from Congress to compensate anyone who owned any of the pesticide an suffered any loss due to the suspension or cancellation. The registrant of the suspended and canceled product is responsible, however, for all of the transportation and disposal costs, and most storage costs.

ix. Use of Unregistered Pesticides

1. FIFRA also allows for unregistered use of pesticide products in special circumstances. Section 5 allows experimental use permits for purposes of research and to collect data needed to register a pesticide. Section 18 allows "emergency exemptions" from the provisions of FIFRA to be granted to federal or state agencies for example, if there is a virulent outbreak of a disease that cannot be controlled by registered products. In addition. Section 24(c), permits states to allow additional uses of a federally registered product to meet "special local needs."

x. The Role of States

1. Generally, EPA enforces FIFRA requirements. However, FIFRA Section 26 gives states primary authority. including inspection authority, for enforcing FIFRA provisions related to pesticide use. In addition, the individual states are responsible for training programs to certify applicators of restricted use pesticides. States initially review and may give preliminary approval to applications for emergency exemptions and special local needs registrations (although under some conditions FIFRA allows EPA later to deny state approved applications).

xi. Export to Unregistered Pesticides

1. FIFRA does not give EPA the authority to regulate domestic production and export of unregistered pesticides, even if U.S. registration has been cancelled for health or environmental reasons. However, FIFRA does require exporters to prepare or pack pesticides as specified by the purchaser and in accord with some of the FIFRA labeling provisions. For example, exporters must translate warning information into the language of the destination. FIFRA also requires exporters of unregistered pesticides to obtain the purchaser's signature on a statement acknowledging that the pesticide is unregistered and cannot be sold in the United States. EPA is required to notify governments of other countries and international agencies whenever a registration, cancellation, or suspension of any pesticide becomes or ceases to be effective in the United States.

B. REMOVING PESTICIDES FROM THE MARKET

As the discussion above indicates, FIFRA requires that virtually all new pesticides be first registered with the EPA. This involves submitting the chemical formula, the proposed product labeling, and test results to EPA for scrutiny. Section 3 provides the regulatory standard for registration that the pesticide must perform its intended mission "without unreasonable adverse effects on the environment," which is defined in § 2 as *"any unreasonable risk to man and the environment, taking into account the economic, social, and environmental costs and benefits of the use of the pesticide."*(emphasis supplied) This process of registration requires the agency to weigh and balance a number of competing factors including the impact of the pesticide on public health and the environment.

Once registered under FIFRA, a pesticide may lose its registration by cancellation or suspension. For cancellation of registration, EPA must issue a notice of intent either to cancel a pesticide's registration or to hold a hearing to determine whether it should be canceled, if there appear to be "unreasonable adverse effects on the environment."§§ 6(b)(1) & (2). In the case of a § 6(b)(1) notice, the proposed action becomes final at the end of 30 days unless a request for a hearing is received "from a person adversely affected." Cancellation typically triggers a lengthy adjudicatory hearing and scientific review process during which the pesticide remains on the market. See § 6(d). In more compelling, emergency situations, EPA is also authorized under FIFRA § 6(c) to issue a suspension order for any pesticide found to be an "imminent hazard." An imminent hazard is defined to be "a situation which exists when the continued use of a pesticide during the time required for cancellation ... would be likely to result in unreasonable adverse effects on the environment or will involve unreasonable hazard to the survival of a species declared endangered or threatened ... pursuant to the Endangered Species Act...." § 2(1). Not surprisingly, every suspension order must be accompanied by a concurrent cancellation notice. § 6(c)(1).

Judicial review of "any order issued ... following a public hearing" is to be conducted in the U.S. Court of Appeals. § 16(b) Why would this court be selected rather than the federal district court? Review can be obtained by "any person who will be adversely affected by such order and who had been a party to the proceedings...." Under this statutory formulation, who can appeal a grant or denial of registration, suspension, or cancellation? Can an environmental group obtain judicial review? For a comprehensive, critical view of FIFRA, see Donald Hornstein, Lessons from Federal Pesticide Regulation and the Paradigms and Politics of Environmental Law Reform, 10 Yale J. on Reg. 369 (1993).

A highly publicized case study of registration cancellation can be observed with the pesticide Alar. Alar, whose trade name is daminozide, is a pesticide that is used primarily upon apples, grapes, cherries, and peanuts. When sprayed directly on growing fruit in early summer, Alar regulates growth and, in the case of apples, makes them redder and crunchier. Fruit producers considered that Alar enhanced the quality of the product that they sent to market. In the 1980s, the use of Alar became a matter of nationwide concern. A report issued by the Natural Resources Defense Council (NRDC) called the pesticide a dangerous chemical that posed a health risk 45 times higher than EPA's acceptable risk level of one chance in a million of causing cancer over a lifetime of exposure. The NRDC calculated that the risk to children was over 240 times the acceptable level. Consumers' Union, a consumer watchdog group, test 50 store samples of apple juice taken from store shelves in New York State and found that 3/4 of them contained Alar residues. As a measure of the extent of public awareness of the issue, the Alar controversy was also featured on the popular television program "60 Minutes." The following two excerpts describe the nature of the debate over Alar and the final EPA action canceling all food use registration for the pesticide.

Douglas Campt, Daminozide: A Case Study of a Pesticide Controversy

13 EPA Journal 32–34 (May 1987).

Like EDB, the pesticide daminozide, or Alar, has captured the American public's attention. When the evening television news shows sky rockets interspliced with baby foods on the assembly line, this conveys an alarming message to the viewer: "UDMH is a component of daminozide. UDMH is used in rocket fuel. UDMH is in your baby's food." This TV report was very effective in delivering a message to the public, but not very effective in expressing the complexities of known, and unknown, effects of pesticide residues in food.

A plant growth regulator used primarily on apples, daminozide offers important food production benefits. However, new data now indicate that it also may pose a potential cancer risk.

Like EDB also, the daminozide issue is plagued with scientific uncertainties. These unresolved questions have limited the Environmental Protection Agency's ability to act as quickly and definitively as would be necessary to lessen public confusion and calm public anxieties. * * *

EDB, daminozide, and numerous other pesticides recently in the news point to what has become for EPA an all-too-familiar regulatory dilemma should the Agency base its actions primarily on timeliness or on certainty? Often, when compelling new health and safety questions about a pesticide arise, studies that would help elucidate the pesticide's risks are missing or inadequate. That leaves us with a difficult decision. Do we move forward briskly with an aggressive regulatory proposal that may later prove to have been unreasonably stringent?

Our decision is influenced to an extent by the provisions of the Federal Insecticide, Fungicide and Rodenticide Act (FIFRA) which requires a weighing of the risks and benefits to determine whether or not a pesticide poses "unreasonable adverse effects" or an "imminent hazard" prior to cancelling a pesticide registration or suspending its registration. It is the responsibility of the license holder or registrant to provide data and to prove that the benefits of a pesticide outweigh the risk of that pesticide. Before we take action, however, we must have data showing the risks and benefits of the pesticide so that we may make the balancing test of whether or not the benefits in fact do outweigh the risks. The absence of such data is not a supportable basis for cancelling or suspending a pesticide product's registration. This means that EPA must have its ducks in a row and its data in hand if the Agency hopes to prevail in a cancellation or suspension proceeding.

In the case of daminozide, EPA received several toxicity studies in the early 1980s which indicated that unsymmetrical dimethylhydrazine, or UDMH, a metabolite and degradate of daminozide, causes tumors in mice. These oncogenicity studies and some mutagenicity data showing toxicity, along with studies indicating that daminozide and UDMH occurred in raw and processed foods and thus had a potential for human exposure, prompted EPA to initiate a Special Review of daminozide in 1984 to determine if its registration should be cancelled or otherwise restricted. In August 1985, EPA proposed an expedited cancellation of all food crop uses of daminozide, based on a finding that the potential cancer risks from dietary exposure to daminozide and UDMH outweighed the known benefits.

By law, EPA refers such regulatory proposals to the FIFRA Scientific Advisory Panel (SAP) for review. This independent panel of scientists convenes to review the scientific analyses leading to EPA's pesticide regulatory decisions. After a public meeting in late September 1985, the panel concluded that the daminozide cancer studies, while giving rise to concern about potential health effects, were flawed and not sufficient to predict cancer risks from exposure to daminozide and UDMH in food products. The SAP believed the existing studies were scientifically inadequate and could not support the Agency's daminozide risk assessment.

At the same time, the Department of Agriculture (USDA) argued that EPA underestimated the benefits of continued daminozide use, and submitted additional benefits information. USDA urged the Agency to reconsider its decision to cancel daminozide.

After several months of careful reconsideration, the Agency postponed a final regulatory decision on daminozide until new data could be developed by its producer. Meanwhile, however, we needed to balance our quest for scientific certainty with some action. Because scientists will virtually never reach a state of absolute certainty about a pesticide's hazards, some actions may be taken at a point short of knowing all the answers.

Fortunately, under FIFRA we have the option of taking interim risk reduction measures while we wait for data that we need to answer some of the larger questions about long-term risks. With daminozide, the Agency took a number of actions to ensure that exposure would be as low as possible until EPA has the data necessary to make a final determination on the chemical. We reduced the legal application rates; temporarily lowered the tolerance for apples; and limited application to grapes not intended to be processed into raisins. Meanwhile, the manufacturer, Uniroyal, has limited the amount of daminozide produced for use on grapes, and has agreed to include in every bag of daminozide a user advisory recommending that treated apples not be sold for processing into applesauce. These measures, taken together, will limit public exposure to daminozide during the next 18 months. By then, new studies better elucidating daminozide's cancer potential will be available, and a final regulatory decision can be reached.

The situation surrounding daminozide is still deeply controversial, illustrating the frustrations and polarized feelings that can result when EPA strives to achieve a balance between timeliness and scientific certainty. As Assistant Administrator John Moore has noted, the really unfortunate aspect of a case like daminozide is that nobody wins, now or in the end. EPA is blamed by all sides for not acting more quickly; the public loses faith in government as its protector; environmentalists become frustrated and sue EPA; apple growers, especially small growers, face an impossible marketing problem (they need daminozide and legally may use it, but their treated fruit may be rejected in some markets); food processors are caught in the middle since the market is so disrupted; retail food stores cannot sell daminozide-treated produce or products without appearing socially irresponsible; the states feel that they must step in and set their own reduced tolerances, further disrupting the market since standards then vary from state to state; and the producer of daminozide suffers because no matter what the data ultimately show, the product's reputation has been damaged and may never completely recover.

Environmental Protection Agency, Daminozide: Termination of Special Review

54 Fed.Reg. 47492 (Nov. 14, 1989).

A pesticide product may be sold or distributed in the United States only if it is registered or exempt from registration under the Federal Insecticide, Fungicide and Rodenticide Act (FIFRA) as amended (7 U.S.C. 136 et seq.). The standards for registration of a pesticide which are set forth in section 3 of FIFRA requires that a pesticide be able to accomplish its intended purpose without causing "unreasonable adverse effects on the environment," (7 U.S.C. 136a(c)(5)), that is, without causing "any unreasonable risk to man or the environment, taking into account the economic, social and environmental costs and benefits of the use of the pesticide." (FIFRA Section 2(bb)). If at any time, EPA determines that a pesticide no longer meets this standard for registration, then the Administrator may cancel this registration under section 6 of FIFRA.

Special Review is EPA's process for determining whether the use of a pesticide poses unreasonable effects to man or the environment; i.e., if continuation of the current registration is appropriate. If a pesticide meets or exceeds the risk criteria set forth in 40 CFR part 154, then a Special Review is initiated and information on the risks and benefits of the pesticide product use or uses in question is gathered and evaluated. If the use or uses in question are determined to pose unreasonable adverse effects to human health or the environment, then the registration of the product may be cancelled or modified as appropriate.

On May 24, 1989, EPA issued its preliminary determination to cancel all food use registrations of daminozide and retain non-food use registrations unmodified (51 FR 22558). EPA's decision was based on its conclusion that the carcinogenic risk from dietary exposure to daminozide exceeded the benefits of the food uses of daminozide, and thus cancellation was appropriate. For the non-food uses, it was determined that the benefits of the use of daminozide on ornamental and bedding plants outweighed the risks incurred during the application of daminozide.

On July 2, 1989, Uniroyal [Uniroyal Chemical Company, the sole registrant of daminozide in the United States] entered into an agreement with EPA that provided that Uniroyal would voluntarily halt domestic sales of daminozide for food use until the completion of the Special Review process, including any administrative hearings. The agreement also provided that Uniroyal would recall existing stocks of daminozide food use products and reimburse product holders who participate in the recall effort. Recalled product would be repackaged and relabeled as the non-food product.

On October 11, 1989, EPA received Uniroyal's request for voluntary cancellation of all food use registrations of daminozide. As indicated above, EPA intends to approve Uniroyal's request, making the cancellation effective November 17, 1989. The cancellation order prohibits continued sale, distribution and use of daminozide for food uses as of November 17,1989.

NOTES AND QUESTIONS

1. The EPA has acted to suspend, cancel, or restrict the use of over 60 pesticides, including DDT, aldrin, dieldrin, hephtaclor, chlordane, and EDB. Formerly, the EPA had to pay for the disposal of existing stocks of a canceled pesticide, but a 1988 amendment to FIFRA requires manufacturers to assume this responsibility. The registration of pesticides is financed by a fee system. Did the Alar affair end correctly?

The EPA originally proposed to cancel the registration of Alar for use on food in 1980, but a science advisory panel found flaws in the methodology used in animal studies of UDMH and Alar. Uniroyal undertook another two-year bioassay, and its first-year data were reported in January 1989. NRDC performed an analysis of this data and concluded that between 4700 and 6000 of the nation's 22 million preschool children will ultimately get cancer from exposure to Alar. NRDC's conclusion was based upon several assumptions: that preschool children were particularly at risk because (1) the risk of cancer is time-dependent and they are exposed for a greater period of time (their exposure will continue throughout their lives); (2) they weigh less than adults; and (3) they eat more apple products than adults. The NRDC analysis was widely publicized on the popular television program "Sixty Minutes" on February 26, 1989. EPA's analysis of the first-year data differed markedly from NRDC's. EPA first calculated the cancer risk to be 9 in 1 million, 25 times less than NRDC, and even this was revised downward to 4.5 in 1 million. See Marshall, A is for Apple, Alar, and ... Alarmist? 254 Science 20 (1991).

Consider the benefits of Alar. It is a plant growth regulator that keeps ripening apples on the trees and causes them to remain firm and red during storage. Alar penetrates an apple's skin and is not removed by washing. After Alar was banned, apple growers filed a product defamation suit against NRDC claiming $200 million in damages, but this was later dropped. EPA has continued to adhere to its conclusion that Alar should be banned for use on food. See Kimm, Alar's Risks, 254 Science 1276 (1991).

On the other hand, Dr. Elizabeth Whelan, the President of the American Council on Science and Health commented as follows on the Alar affair:

Americans don't know that naturally occurring chemicals that can be toxic or carcinogenic are in all foods. Though you and I may know it's the dose that makes the poison, the average person doesn't. Some may argue that it is too much to ask the general population to know this. But would it be too much to hope that Americans would at least know where food comes from and how it is produced? The answer, apparently, is yes.

What many Americans feel they know for sure is that we should ban pesticides "just in case." They don't understand how we benefit from the use of agricultural chemicals and that they are the reason we have the most plentiful and inexpensive food supply in the world.

We need to introduce a new type of risk to the consumer. The risk of not taking risks, and the risk of elevating theoretical risks to center stage. Just because a well-publicized band of nutrition terrorists scream "cancer" is no reason to dismantle our food-production system in a mindless search for a totally risk-free society. That's the lesson to be learned from the Great Apple Scare. 88 Successful Farming 30 (Feb. 1990).

2. *Preemption of State and Local Regulation of Pesticides.* Does FIFRA preempt state and local regulation of pesticides? In an effort to have uniform, federal pesticide product labeling, the statute provides that states "shall not impose or continue in effect any requirements for labeling or packaging in addition to or different from those required under this subchapter." § 136(v)(b). This express preemption on labeling is clear from the language of the statute. While this desire for uniformity may be necessary for producers of nationally-distributed pesticides, there could be indirect effects of such a rule that go beyond this rationale. Consider the impact of this labeling preemption on state law tort claims against pesticide manufacturers based upon a theory of failure of the duty to warn of potential environmental risks and hazards. In Arkansas–Platte & Gulf Partnership v. Van Waters & Rogers, Inc., 981 F.2d 1177 (10th Cir.1993), the appeals court concluded that,

> to the extent that state tort claims ... require a showing that defendants' labeling and packaging should have included additional, different, or alternatively stated warnings from those required under FIFRA, they would be expressly preempted.

Id. at 1179. This appears to be the common view of the preemptive effect of FIFRA on such actions. See MacDonald v. Monsanto Co., 27 F.3d 1021 (5th Cir.1994). Claims based on inadequate testing or breach of warranty may not be preempted. See Bingham v. Terminix Intl. Co., 850 F.Supp. 516 (S.D.Miss.1994).

What about non-labeling issues? FIFRA § 136v(a) provides that states "may regulate the sale or use of any federally registered pesticide or device in the State, but only if an to the extent the regulation does not permit any sale or use prohibited by this subchapter." The congressional intent behind this provision is to recognize state authority to impose stricter regulation on pesticide uses than required by FIFRA. But what about local governments? In Wisconsin Public Intervenor v. Mortier, 501 U.S. 597 (1991), the Supreme Court treated the local government as being encompassed by the word "state" and ruled that a town ordinance regulating pesticide application and precluding any aerial spraying was not preempted by § 136v(a) of FIFRA essentially because there was no actual conflict between the federal statute and the local ordinance. In the Court's view, it was up to the state to decide how police powers were to be allocated. Would it be possible for a locality to adopt an ordinance imposing onerous licensing requirements for pesticide application which effectively eliminated most lawful commercial pest control work?

3. As apparent from the discussion above, FIFRA adopts a premarket, licensing strategy in the regulation of pesticides. Theoretically, each active ingredient is evaluated by EPA under the standard set in FIFRA § 136a aimed at the prevention of "unreasonable adverse effects on the environment." This "unreasonable effects" test is further defined in FIFRA § 136(bb) as meaning "any unreasonable risk to man or the environment, taking into account the economic, social, and environmental costs and benefits." The licensing strategy assumes that EPA will collect and analyze sufficient accurate risk assessment and cost data to serve as an effective "gatekeeper," denying market access to new pesticides presenting such "unreasonable risks." Licensing is the legal prerequisite to marketing. This strategy takes an optimistic view of agency capacity to regulate a technically complex area in a case-by-case, substance-by-substance fashion. Notice that FIFRA requires EPA to act through adjudication rather than through rulemaking procedures. What are the costs associated with regulating in this way? Is this adjudicatory method well-suited to rapid action? Isn't there an inevitable conflict between the interests of EPA and industry—the desire for more extensive and reliable chemical effects information and the need to market a commercially useful product?

Consider the importance of technical information in the FIFRA registration process. Data contained in registration applications is submitted by the pesticide manufacturer not by EPA. What might be the impact of this fact on the licensing system? One commentator wrote,

> Another [data] quality issue is the source of the data, especially in the uncertain science of long-latency toxic illnesses in which inference and interpretation are always open to debate. The inevitably conflicting interests between EPA and the industries it regulates invite the withholding or slanting of data submissions. The conflict rarely results in outright concealment, falsification, or deliberate misstatement of results (though this unfortunately is not unknown). Rather, every stage of the investigation process, from experimental design to execution to interpretation of results, is subject to judgment and inference and to bias. A screening or approval system may magnify the bias problem by casting EPA and industry in more obviously adversarial roles. A National Academy of Sciences study of EPA decision making warned about dependence on regulated industries data and analysis

and suggested a number of remedial measures, including reduced use of consulting firms that also work for industry, peer review, review by other agencies, stringent guidelines and protocols, certification of laboratories, and a strong in-house research capability....

John S. Applegate, The Perils of Unreasonable Risk: Information, Regulatory Policy, and Toxic Substances Control, 91 Colum. L. Rev. 261, 310 (1991). Finally, what about the large number of older pesticides that were registered prior to 1984 under a more permissive regulatory regime? Would you suggest emphasizing the allocation of increased EPA resources to the reregistration of these substances since less may be known about their effects and they are already in commercial use? Why would EPA have focused attention on the registration of new pesticides?

C. Pesticides and Safe Food

Les v. Reilly

United States Court of Appeals, Ninth Circuit, 1992.
968 F.2d 985.

■ Schroeder, Circuit Judge:

Petitioners seek review of a final order of the Environmental Protection Agency permitting the use of four pesticides as food additives although they have been found to induce cancer. Petitioners challenge the final order on the ground that it violates the provisions of the Delaney clause, 21 U.S.C. § 348(c)(3), which prohibits the use of any food additive that is found to induce cancer.

Prior to 1988, EPA regulations promulgated in the absence of evidence of carcinogenicity permitted use of the four pesticides at issue here as food additives. In 1988, however, the EPA found these pesticides to be carcinogens. Notwithstanding the Delaney clause, the EPA refused to revoke the earlier regulations, reasoning that, although the chemicals posed a measurable risk of causing cancer, that risk was "de minimis."

We set aside the EPA's order because we agree with the petitioners that the language of the Delaney clause, its history and purpose all reflect that Congress intended the EPA to prohibit all additives that are carcinogens, regardless of the degree of risk involved.

Background

The Federal Food, Drug, and Cosmetic Act (FFDCA), 21 U.S.C. §§ 301–394 (West 1972 & Supp.1992), is designed to ensure the safety of the food we eat by prohibiting the sale of food that is "adulterated." 21 U.S.C. § 331(a). Adulterated food is in turn defined as food containing any unsafe food "additive." 21 U.S.C. § 342(a)(2)(C). A food "additive" is defined broadly as "any substance the intended use of which results or may reasonably be expected to result * * * in its becoming a component * * * of any food." 21 U.S.C. § 321(s). A food additive is considered unsafe unless there is a specific exemption for the substance if a regulation prescribing the conditions under which it may be used safely.

21 U.S.C. 348(a).

Before 1988, the four pesticide chemicals with which we are here concerned—benomyl, mancozeb, phosmet and trifluralin—were all the subject of regulations issued by the EPA permitting their use. In October 1988, however, the EPA published a list of substances, including the pesticides at issue here, that had been found to induce cancer. Regulation of Pesticides in Food: Addressing the Delaney Paradox Policy Statement, 53 Fed.Reg. 41,104, 41,119 (Oct. 19, 1988). As known carcinogens, the four pesticides ran afoul of a special provision of the FFDCA known as the Delaney clause, which prescribes that additives found to induce cancer can never be deemed "safe" for purposes of the FFDCA. The Delaney clause is found in FFDCA section 409, 21 U.S.C. § 348. That section limits the conditions under which the Secretary may issue regulations allowing a substance to be used as a food additive:

> No such regulation shall issue if a fair evaluation of the data before the Secretary—(A) fails to establish that the proposed use of the food additive, under the conditions of use to be specified in the regulation, will be safe: *Provided*, That no additive shall be deemed to be safe if it is found to induce cancer when ingested by man or animal, or if it is found, after tests which are appropriate for the evaluation of the safety of food additives, to induce cancer in man or animal * * *.

21 U.S.C. § 348(c)(3).

The FFDCA also contains special provisions which regulate the occurrence of pesticide residues on raw agricultural commodities. Section 402 of the FFDCA, 21 U.S.C. § 342(a)(2)(B), provides that a raw food containing a pesticide residue is deemed adulterated unless the residue is authorized under section 408 of the FFDCA, 21 U.S.C. § 346a, which allows tolerance regulations setting maximum permissible levels and also provides for exemption from tolerances under certain circumstances. When a tolerance or an exemption has been established for use of a pesticide on a raw agricultural commodity, then the FFDCA allows for the "flow-through" of such pesticide residue to processed foods, even when the pesticide may be a carcinogen. This flow-through is allowed, however, only to the extent that the concentration of the pesticide in the processed food does not exceed the concentration allowed in the raw food. The flow-through provisions are contained in section 402 which provides:

> That where a pesticide chemical has been used in or on a raw agricultural commodity in conformity with an exemption granted or a tolerance prescribed under section 346a of this title [FFDCA section 408] and such raw agricultural commodity has been subjected to processing such as canning, cooking, freezing, dehydrating, or milling, the residue of such pesticide chemical remaining in or on such processed food shall, notwithstanding the provisions of sections 346 and 348 of this title [FFDCA sections 406 and 409], not be deemed unsafe if

such residue in or on the raw agricultural commodity has been re-moved to the extent possible in good manufacturing practice and the concentration of such residue in the processed food when ready to eat is not greater than the tolerance prescribed for the raw agricultural commodity.

21 U.S.C. § 342(a)(2)(C).

It is undisputed that the EPA regulations at issue in this case allow for the concentration of cancer-causing pesticides during processing to levels in excess of those permitted in the raw foods.

The proceedings in this case had their genesis in October 1988 when the EPA published a list of substances, including these pesticides, that were found to induce cancer. 53 Fed.Reg. 41,104, App.B. Simultaneously, the EPA announced a new interpretation of the Delaney clause: the EPA proposed to permit concentrations of cancer-causing pesticide residues greater than that tolerated for raw foods so long as the particular sub-stances posed only a "de minimis" risk of actually causing cancer. 53 Fed.Reg. at 41,110. Finding that benomyl, mancozeb, phosmet and trifluralin (among others) posed only such a de minimis risk, the Agency an-nounced that it would not immediately revoke its previous regulations authorizing use of these substances as food additives. *Id*. at 41,105, 41,120–23.

Petitioners filed an administrative petition in May 1989 requesting the EPA to revoke those food additive regulations. Following public comment the EPA issued a Notice of Response refusing to revoke the regulations. Response to Petition Requesting Revocation of Food Additive Regulations, 55 Fed.Reg. 17,560, 17,567 (benomyl), 17,568 (mancozeb), 17,569 (trifluralin) (Apr. 25, 1990). After the petitioners filed objections to that response, the EPA published its final order denying the petition to revoke the food additive regulations. Order Responding to objections to EPA's Response, 56 Fed.Reg. 7750 (Feb. 25, 1991). This petition for review pursuant to 21 U.S.C. § 348(g)(1) followed.

Discussion

The issue before us is whether the EPA has violated section 409 of the FFDCA, the Delaney clause, by permitting the use of carcinogenic food additives which it finds to present only a de minimis or negligible risk of causing cancer. The Agency acknowledges that its interpretation of the law is a new and changed one. From the initial enactment of the Delaney clause in 1958 to the time of the rulings here in issue, the statute had been strictly and literally enforced. 56 Fed.Reg. at 7751–52. The EPA also acknowledges that the language of the statute itself appears, at first glance, to be clear on its face. *Id*. at 7751 ("[S]ection 409 mandates a zero risk standard for carcinogenic pesticides in processed foods in those instances where the pesticide concentrates during processing or is applied during or after processing.").

The language is clear and mandatory. The Delaney clause provides that no additive shall be deemed safe if it induces cancer. 21 U.S.C. § 348(c)(3). The EPA states in its final order that appropriate tests have established that the pesticides at issue here induce cancer in humans or animals. 56 Fed.Reg. at 7774–75. The statute provides that once the finding of carcinogenicity is made, the EPA has no discretion. As a leading work on food and drug regulation notes:

> [T]he Delaney Clause leaves the FDA room for scientific judgment in deciding whether its conditions are met by a food additive. But the clause affords no flexibility once FDA scientists determine that these conditions are satisfied. A food additive that has been found in an appropriate test to induce cancer in laboratory animals may not be approved for use in food for any purpose, at any level, regardless of any "benefits" that it might provide.

Richard A. Merrill and Peter B. Hutt, *Food and Drug Law*, 78 (1980).

This issue was litigated before the D.C. Circuit in connection with the virtually identical "color additive" prohibition of 21 U.S.C. § 376(b)(5)(B). The D.C. Circuit concluded that "[t]he natural—almost inescapable—reading of this language is that if the Secretary finds the additive to 'induce' cancer in animals, he must deny listing." Public Citizen v. Young, 831 F.2d 1108, 1112 (D.C.Cir.1987), *cert. denied*, 485 U.S. 1006 (1988). The court concluded that the EPA's de minimis interpretation of the Delaney clause in 21 U.S.C. § 376 was "contrary to law." 831 F.2d at 1123. The *Public Citizen* decision reserved comment on whether the result would be the same under the food additive provisions as it was under the food color provisions, 831 F.2d at 1120, but its reasoning with respect to the language of the statute is equally applicable to both.

The Agency asks us to look behind the language of the Delaney clause to the overall statutory scheme governing pesticides, which permits the use of carcinogenic pesticide's on raw food without regard to the Delaney clause. Yet section 402 of the FFDCA, 21 U.S.C. § 342(a)(2)(C), expressly harmonizes that scheme with the Delaney clause by providing that residues on processed foods may not exceed the tolerance level established for the raw food. The statute unambiguously provides that pesticides while concentrate in processed food are to be treated as food additives, and these are governed by the Delaney food additive provision contained in section 409. If pesticides which concentrate in processed foods induce cancer in humans or animals, they render the food adulterated and must be prohibited.

The legislative history, too, reflects that Congress intended the very rigidity that the language it chose commands.

The EPA contends that the legislative history shows that Congress never intended to regulate pesticides, as opposed to other additives, with extraordinary rigidity under the food additives provision. The Agency is indeed correct that the legislative history of the food additive provision does not focus on pesticides, and that pesticides are regulated more comprehensively under the Federal Insecticide, Fungicide, and Rodenticide Act (FI-

FRA), 7 U.S.C. §§ 136–136y (West 1980 & Supp.1992). Nevertheless, the EPA's contention that Congress never intended the food additive provision to encompass pesticide residues is belied by the events prompting passage of the provision into law: FDA approval of Aramite was the principal impetus for the food additive Delaney clause and Aramite was itself a regulated pesticide. Thus, Congress intended to regulate pesticides as food additives under section 409 of the FFDCA, at least to the extent that pesticide residues concentrate in processed foods and exceed the tolerances for raw foods.

Finally, the EPA argues that a de minimis exception to the Delaney clause is necessary in order to bring about a more sensible application of the regulatory scheme. It relies particularly on a recent study suggesting that the criterion of concentration level in processed foods may bear little or no relation to actual risk of cancer, and that some pesticides might be barred by rigid enforcement of the Delaney clause while others, with greater cancer-causing risk, may be permitted through the now through provisions because they do not concentrate in processed foods. See National Academy of Sciences, *Regulating Pesticides in Food: The Delaney Paradox* (1987). The EPA in effect asks us to approve what it deems to be a more enlightened system than that which Congress established. The EPA is not alone in criticizing the scheme established by the Delaney clause. See, e.g., Richard A. Merrill, FDA's Implementation of the Delaney Clause: Repudiation of Congressional Choice or Reasoned Adaptation to Scientific Progress, 5 Yale J. on Reg. 1, 87 (1988) (concluding that the Delaney clause is both unambiguous and unwise: "at once an explicit and imprudent expression of legislative will"). Revising the existing statutory scheme, however, is neither our function nor the function of the EPA.

The EPA's refusal to revoke regulations permitting the use of benomyl, mancozeb, phosmet and trifluralin as food additives on the ground the cancer risk they pose is de minimis is contrary to the provisions of the Delaney clause prohibiting food additives that induce cancer. The EPA's final order is set aside.

NOTES AND QUESTIONS

1. *Understanding the Delaney Paradox.* The Delaney Paradox involves the intersection between two federal statutory policies: FIFRA and the Food, Drug and Cosmetic Act(FDCA). The Delaney Clause was an amendment to the FDCA added in 1958. As you know, EPA's FIFRA pesticide registrations undergo a cost-benefit analysis considering and balancing a number of factors. The Delaney Clause pertaining to food additives specifically provided that "no additive shall be deemed to be safe if it is found to induce cancer when ingested by man or animal, or if it is found, after tests which are appropriate for the evaluation of the safety of food additives, to induce cancer in man or animal." FDCA § 409(21 U.S.C. § 348). While the language of the Delaney Clause seemingly prohibited all residues of cancer-causing pesticides in processed foods, § 408 directed EPA to set pesticide tolerances for raw agricultural commodities "to protect the public health" while also considering "the necessity for ... an adequate, wholesome and economical food supply." These raw food tolerances set under § 408 employ a risk/benefit balancing analysis which seems inconsistent with the total prohibition of § 409—the Delaney Clause. This is the paradox. In addition, the "flow through" elements of § 402 mentioned in *Les v. Reilly* compounds the confusion since,

> The combination of the section 402 "flow-through" provision and the different standards in sections 408 and 409 creates an anomalous situation whereby a potentially carcinogenic pesticide residue can become a lawful additive to food in spite of the Delaney Clause. As long as the residue does not exceed the section 408 tolerance, the pesticide need not meet the more exacting Delaney standard found in section 409.

James S. Turner, Delaney Lives! Reports of Delaney's Death Are Greatly Exaggerated, 28 Envtl. L. Rep. 10003 (1998). In the *Les v. Reilly* case, the EPA regulation at issue would have allowed for a pesticide concentration *in excess of* the raw food tolerance and therefore would have even violated the § 402 "flow-through" provision. Why was cancer accorded the preeminent position trumping all other concerns in the original Delaney Clause? What if a pesticide were found to cause a one extra case of cancer in 10 million people but actually prevented 1,000 people from contracting another life threatening illness. How should this balance be struck?

2. *Congressional Effort to Address Food Safety—The Food Quality Protection Act of 1996.* The battle over the regulation of pesticide residues in food has been a struggle lasting for many decades and at least since the 1958 passage of the Delaney Clause. The regulatory debate was significantly influenced by a 1987 report of the National Research Council of the National Academy of Sciences entitled "Regulating Pesticides in Food: the Delaney Paradox." The report made two important recommendations. First, it noted that "pesticide residues in food, whether marketed in raw or processed form or governed by old or new tolerances, should be regulated on the basis of consistent standards. Current law and regulations governing residues in raw and processed foods are inconsistent with this goal." Id. at 11. It added that "[a] negligible risk standard [of one-in-a-million lifetime mortality risk] for carcinogens in food, applied consistently to all pesticides and to all forms of food, could dramatically reduce total dietary exposure to oncogenic pesticides with modest reduction of benefits." Id. at 12.

In 1996, Congress enacted the Food Quality Protection Act, Pub. L. No. 104–170 (1996) (codified as amended in sections of 7 U.S.C. and 21 U.S.C.), to deal with issues of food safety. The most significant elements of this law which relate to the setting of food tolerances are as follows:

A. *General Standards for Tolerances.* The new law requires that pesticide tolerances for food be "safe," defined as "a reasonable certainty that no harm will result from aggregate exposure," including all exposure through the diet and other non-occupational exposures, including drinking water, for which there is reliable information. It also distinguishes between "threshold" and "non-threshold" effects, consistent with EPA practice.

Significance. The new law establishes a single, health-based standard for all pesticide residues in all types of food, replacing the sometimes conflicting standards in the old law. There are no differences in the standards applicable to tolerances set for raw and processed foods. Additional provisions ensure coordination with standards and actions under FIFRA for a more consistent regulatory scheme.

B. *Resolution of the "Delaney Paradox."* The new law provides that tolerances for pesticide residues in all types of food (raw or processed) will be set under the same provisions of law. The standards apply to all risks, not just cancer risks.

Significance. The legislation eliminates the Delaney Paradox. The Delaney clause no longer applies to any tolerances set for pesticide residues in food. Rather, the EPA must determine that tolerances are "safe," defined as "a reasonable certainty that no harm will result from aggregate exposure" to the pesticide. EPA and others will be able to devote resources that have been consumed by Delaney-related activities to higher priority public health and environmental protection issues.

C. *Consideration of Pesticide Benefits.* In certain narrow circumstances, the new law allows tolerances to remain in effect that would not otherwise meet the safety standard, based on the benefits afforded by the pesticide. Pesticide residues would only be "eligible" for such tolerances if use of the pesticide prevents even greater health risks to consumers or the lack of the pesticide would result in "a significant disruption in domestic production of an adequate, wholesome, and economical food supply." Tolerances based on benefits considerations would be subject to a number of limitations on risk and more frequent reassessment than other tolerances. All tolerances would have to be consistent with the special provisions for infants and children.

Significance. This provision narrows the range of circumstances in which benefits may be considered and places limits on the maximum level of risk that could be justified by benefits considerations. It would also apply only to "non-threshold" risks posed by pesticides, e.g. carcinogenic effects for which conservative quantitative risk assessment is appropriate.

D. *Other Factors to be Considered in Setting Tolerances.* The new law requires EPA to consider the validity, completeness and reliability of available study data; the nature of potential toxic effects and available information on the relationship of study results to human risk; dietary consumption patterns and variations in the sensitivities of major identifiable subpopulations; cumulative and aggregate(dietary and nondietary) effects of exposure to the pesticide and other substances with common mechanisms of toxicity; effects on the endocrine system; and scientifically recognized appropriate safety factors.

Significance. As scientific understanding of potential cumulative and aggregate effects advances, it is likely that additional data will be required for EPA decisions, along with more information on subpopulation exposure and risk. In most cases, EPA will be able to use existing FIFRA authority to require this information. The additional data will enhance the scientific basis and protectiveness of pesticide regulations.

For more on the Food Quality Protection Act see James Smart, All the Stars in the Heavens Were in the Right Places: The Passage of the Food Quality Protection Act of 1996, 17 Stan. Envt'l L. J. 273 (1998).

3. *Alternatives to Chemical Pesticides.* Opposition to chemical use in agriculture is growing. However, renunciation of pesticide use would require major changes in the way many farmers operate. According to EPA, between 800 million and 1 billion pounds of some 600 pesticide ingredients are used each year providing the pesticide industry with $6 billion in sales. The National Academy of Sciences has found that farmers who apply little or no chemicals to crops are usually as productive as those who use pesticides and synthetic fertilizers. The Academy's study found that federal agricultural subsidy programs, which pay a subsidy for every bushel farmers produce, provide the incentive for farmers to use ample amounts of chemical fertilizers and generous applications of pesticides to protect their harvest. Natural farming techniques, it was found, even if they were less productive, would bring supply into line with demand raising prices and making up for the subsidies. New York Times, Sept. 8, 1989, at A-1.

Are farmers locked into a cycle of chemical farming that is costly, allows weeds and insects to develop genetic resistance to farm chemicals, endangers the health of farm workers, but produces little or no economic benefits? Is it time to change the direction of American agriculture and wean farmers from chemical farming?

Consider the following elements of a federal farm program directed to foster sustainable agriculture: (1) reduction of farm subsidy programs; (2) encouragement of soil and water conservation; and (3) reduction of dependence on farm chemicals (for fertilizer and pesticides) by relying more on crop rotation, mechanical cultivation, and biological pest controls.

Is the best response to excessive pesticide use the development of superior technology? Consider the following two examples.

1) EPA granted, preliminary (FIFRA) registration approval to the Mycogen Corporation and Ciba Seeds to market the first genetically engineered corn seeds that make their own pesticides. The corn contains both natural genetic material and genes produced for Bt, a soil bacteria, added to lessen the chance that insects will develop a tolerance to the corn's own anti-insect characteristics. This new corn hybrid makes a protein designed to protect the corn plant from European corn borers, insects that cause $1 billion per year in crop damage throughout the U.S. farming areas. Mycogen claims that the use of the new hybrid will reduce or eliminate the need to use conventional pesticides against these insects and that the genes used are natural and harmless to humans and animals. See Washington Post, Aug. 13, 1995 A 16 col. 1.

2) Under an EPA permit, the Department of Agriculture will begin field tests in California, Hawaii and Texas on a light-activated dye in commercial citrus and some other crops. The targets for the new product—

called Sure Dye by its developers, PhotoDye International—are the highly damaging Mediterranean and Mexican fruit flies which has attacked U.S. crops in recent years. SureDye is composed of common red and yellow dyes used in products such as soap and cosmetics. When eaten by the flies, the dyes will use the insects own biological processes to kill them. As sunlight penetrates the fly's body covering called the cuticle, it is collected by the dye. The solar energy than changes to a form that excretes oxygen molecules within the fly which interferes with cell functions and within hours kills the insect. It is hoped that SureDye will enable farmer to substantially cut the use of the pesticide Malathion which is currently used to combat the pests. See Washington Post, Aug. 11, 1995 A 21 Col. 1.

4. EPA reports that increasingly new pesticide registrations have been granted for safer chemicals—either biological or reduced risk, conventional chemical products. For instance, in FY99 nineteen of the twenty-six active pesticide ingredients registered were considered to be "safer pesticides." Such safer pesticide ingredients are defined by EPA as having one or more of the following characteristics:

a. they have low risk to human health,

b. low toxicity to non-target organisms(birds, fish and plants),

c. low ground water contamination potential,

d. low use rates,

e. low pest resistance potential,

f. compatible with integrated pest management, or

g. are biopesticides.

Environmental Protection Agency, Office of Pesticide Programs FY98–99 Biennial Report 39. Why not require that all registered pesticides possess these characteristics?

5. *The Export of Unregistered Pesticides.* Pesticides manufactured in the United States may be exported to other nations regardless of whether they are registered or not. Estimates indicate that between 25–30% of American pesticide exports are unregistered. This means that there appears to be one standard for American domestic use and another for foreign use. Pesticides may be unregistered in the United States for reasons unrelated to the hazards presented by the chemical—for instance, the manufacturer may produces such a small quantity of the product that its total market value does not justify spending the costs needed for FIFRA registration. In more controversial cases, the exported pesticides have had their registrations denied or canceled for use in the United States and consequently, they are effectively banned from this country. Under FIFRA, EPA may not prohibit the export of pesticides unregistered for use in the United States. Consider the agency's rationale for opposing a ban on these exports.

> As a matter of policy, the agency opposes the institution of a general ban on exports of unregistered pesticides. First, the EPA believes that banning exports will not solve the pesticide problems of developing nations, since most if not all of the banned pesticides would

be available from other pesticide-exporting countries. Second, concentrating on controlling the use and management of all pesticides will be more effective than concentrating upon a few. Third, the agency's regulatory decisions are based upon risk-benefit evaluations specific to the United States. The risk-benefit balance in other countries may differ due to different growing conditions, pest control problems, and environmental and public health considerations. Fourth, pesticide manufacturers may choose not to register a pesticide in the United States simply because there is no market for it. Another concern is that a complete ban might violate the open market provisions of the General Agreement on Trade and Tariffs (GATT).

James H. Colopy, Poisoning the Developing World: The Exportation of Unregistered and Severely Restricted Pesticides from the United States, 13 UCLA J. Envtl. L. & Pol'y 167, 185 (1994/95). What do you think about these reasons justifying EPA's position? Selling this kind of pesticide abroad has proved controversial with critics charging not only that such exports endanger workers and consumers in the foreign country, but also that a "circle of poison" is created as imported pesticide-tainted agricultural and other products end up on American dinner tables and in the stream of commerce.

FIFRA § 136o does require that "prior to export, the foreign purchaser has signed a statement acknowledging that the purchaser understands the such pesticide is not registered for use in the United States and cannot be sold in the United States." Why does the statute require the buyer to make such an acknowledgment? What purpose does it serve? In addition, FIFRA requires that the statement must be "transmitted to an appropriate official of the government of the importing country." Why require the buyer to make this governmental notification? What would or should the importing nation's government do in this circumstance? Does this give the government of the importing country prior notice and, presumably, the ability to prevent the importation? Should FIFRA require that formal "consent" be obtained from the importing government? Why have less developed countries favored such an approach?

Section 3.   The Toxic Substances Control Act (TSCA)

A.   Introduction to Toxic Substances Regulation

The Toxic Substances Control Act (TSCA), 15 U.S.C. §§ 2601 et seq., was enacted in 1976 to fulfill a regulatory gap: the premarket scrutiny of chemical substances. TSCA was designed to allow the EPA to test chemicals for safety before they are manufactured or distributed to the public.

TSCA provides for a two-tier pattern of regulation. Section 6 permits the EPA to regulate a substance that "presents or will present an unreasonable risk of injury to health or the environment." Section 4 empowers the EPA to require the testing of a suspect substance to get the toxicological data in order to make the decision whether or not to regulate under section 6. Section 5 requires each manufacturer or importer of a new chemical to submit a notice to EPA at least 90 days before manufacture or importation. The EPA will review the chemical prior to market entry. Under section 6 the EPA can regulate the manufacturing, processing, or distribution of the chemical through any means from required labeling to an outright ban on importation or production.

TSCA establishes an Interagency Testing Committee comprised of scientists from various federal agencies. Under section 4, the Agency "shall by rule require that testing [of a particular chemical] be conducted" if three factors are present: (i) activities involving the chemical "may present an unreasonable risk of injury to health or the environment"; (ii) "insufficient data and experience" exist upon which to determine the effects of the chemical on health or environment; and (iii) testing is necessary to develop such data. The companies that manufacture and process the substance are to conduct the tests and submit the data to the agency. Costs of testing are to be shared among the companies, either by agreement or by EPA order in the absence of agreement.

A test rule promulgated under section 4 is subject to judicial review in a court of appeals, pursuant to section 19(a) of TSCA. A test rule may be set aside if it is not "supported by substantial evidence in the rulemaking record taken * * * as a whole." The standard for requiring testing is a finding of "unreasonable risk." The EPA can promulgate a test rule without direct evidence of human exposure and even where potential exposure is brief and non-recurrent. See Chemical Manufacturers Association v. U.S. Environmental Protection Agency, 859 F.2d 977 (D.C.Cir.1988).

The EPA has instituted bans on only three products under TSCA: polychlorinated biphenyls (PCBs), asbestos, and chlorofluorocarbons (CFCs). See Donna M. Suglia, Product Bans,and the Toxic Substances Control Act, 2 Buff. Envtl. L.J. 101 (1994).

The following case concerns the EPAs regulation of PCBs.

B.   Litigated Issues

Environmental Defense Fund, Inc. v. Environmental Protection Agency

United States Court of Appeals, District of Columbia Circuit, 1980.
636 F.2d 1267.

■ Edwards, Circuit Judge:

In this case the Environmental Defense Fund (EDF) petitions for review of regulations, issued by the U.S. Environmental Protection Agency (EPA), that implement section 6(e) of the Toxic Substances Control Act (TSCA). That section of the Act provides broad rules governing the disposal, marking, manufacture, processing, distribution, and use of a class of chemicals called polychlorinated biphenyls (PCBs).

EDF seeks review of three aspects of the regulations. First, it challenges the determination by EPA that certain commercial uses of PCBs are "totally enclosed," a designation that exempts those uses from regulation under the Act. Second, it claims that the EPA acted contrary to law when it limited the applicability of the regulations to materials containing concentrations of PCBs' greater than fifty parts per million (ppm). Third, EDF challenges the decision by EPA to authorize the continued use of eleven non-totally enclosed uses of PCBs.

Polychlorinated Biphenyls

Polychlorinated biphenyls (PCBs) have been manufactured and used commercially for fifty years for their chemical stability, fire resistance, and electrical resistance properties. They are frequently used in electrical transformers and capacitors. However, PCBs are extremely toxic to humans and wildlife. The extent of their toxicity is made clear in the EPA Support Document accompanying the final regulations, in which the EPA Office of Toxic Substances identified several adverse effects resulting from human and wildlife exposure to PCBs.

Epidemiological data and experiments on laboratory animals indicate that exposure to PCBs pose carcinogenic and other risks to humans. Experimental animals developed tumors after eating diets that included concentrations of PCBs as low as 100 parts per million (ppm). Experiments on monkeys indicate that diets with PCB concentrations of less than ten ppm reduce fertility and cause still births and birth defects. Other data show that PCBs may adversely affect enzyme production, thereby interfering with the treatment of diseases in humans.

Congressional Response

Responding to the dangers associated with the use of PCBs and other toxic chemicals, Congress in 1976 enacted the Toxic Substances Control Act (TSCA), Pub.L. No. 94469, 90 Stat. 2003 (1976). Although the Act is generally designed to cover the regulation of all chemical substances, section 6(e) refers solely to the disposal, manufacture, processing, distribution, and use of PCBs. No other section of the Act addresses the regulation of a single class of chemicals.

* * *

As enacted, section 6(e) of the Act sets forth a detailed scheme to dispose of PCB, to phase out the manufacture, processing, and distribution of PCB, and to limit the use of PCBs. Specifically, section 6(e) provides that, within six months of the effective date of the Act (January 1, 1977), EPA must prescribe methods to dispose of PCBs and to require that PCB containers be marked with appropriate warnings. 15 U.S.C. § 2605(e)(*l*). One year after the effective date of the Act, PCBs can be manufactured, processed, distributed, and used only in a "totally enclosed manner." *Id.* § 2605(e)(2)(A). One year later, all manufacture of PCBs is prohibited. *Id.* § 2605(e)(3)(A)(i). Six months after that (i.e. two and one-half years after the effective date of the Act), all processing and distribution of PCBs in commerce is prohibited. *Id.* § 2605(e)(3)(A)(ii). Thus, today, except for the specified authorizations and exemptions described below, the Act permits PCBs to be used only in a totally enclosed manner, and it completely prohibits the manufacture, processing, and distribution of PCBs.

The statute sets forth only limited exceptions to these broad prohibitions. Subsection 6(e)(2)(B) allows the Administrator of EPA to authorize by rule the continued use of PCBs in a non-totally enclosed manner if he finds that the proposed activity "will not present an unreasonable risk of injury to health or the environment." *Id.* § 2605(e)(2)(B). Under subsection 6(e)(3)(B), the Administrator may grant a case-by-case exemption to the prohibitions on manufacture, processing, and distribution of PCBs in subsection 6(e)(3). An exemption, which may be granted for one year subject to conditions set by the Administrator, id. § 2605(e)(3)(B), must be based on the Administrator's findings that "an unreasonable risk of injury to health or environment would not result, *and* * * * good faith efforts have been made to, develop a chemical [substitute] which does not present an unreasonable risk of injury to health or the environment." *Id.* (emphasis added).

* * *

Use Authorizations

The Act permits the Administrator to authorize "by rule" non-totally enclosed uses of PCBs if he finds that such uses "will not present an unreasonable risk of injury to health or the environment." 15 U.S.C. § 2605(e)(2)(B).[17] Using the criteria set forth in subsection 6(c)(*l*),[18] the

---

17. EDF argues that no use authorizations should be allowed since § 6(e) should be construed as a legislative finding that PCBs pose an unreasonable risk of injury to health and the environment. We reject this argument.

There can be no doubt, as both EDF and EPA point out in their briefs, that exposure to PCBs poses substantial risks to health and the environment. There is ample legislative history to demonstrate that Congress was aware of some of the serious risks posed by the continued manufacture and use of PCBs. This awareness, however, is a far cry from EDF's conclusion that Congress has made a specific finding that PCBs pose an unreasonable risk of injury to health or the environment. Moreover, were we to hold that Congress had made such a finding, § 6(e)(2)(B), permitting use authorizations, would have no meaning. * * *

18. Subsection 6(c)(*l*), which governs the promulgation of rules under § 6(a) for most chemical substances, provides in part that:

(1) In promulgating any rule under subsection (a) of this section with respect to a chemical substance or mixture, the Administrator shall consider and publish a statement with respect to—

(A) the effects of such substance or mixture on health and the magnitude of the exposure of human beings to such substance or mixture,

(B) the effects of such substance or mixture on the environment and the magnitude of the exposure of the environment to such substance or mixture,

(C) the benefits of such substance or mixture for various uses and the availability of substitutes for such uses, and

(D) the reasonably ascertainable economic consequences of the rule, after consideration of the effect on the national economy, small business, technological innovation, the environment, and public health.

15 U.S.C. § 2605(c)(*l*). Subsections 6(c)(2), (3), and (4) list the procedural requirements for promulgating a rule.

Administrator found that eleven non-totally enclosed uses did not present an unreasonable risk. On the basis of these findings, EPA authorized the continued use of the eleven non-totally enclosed uses here in dispute.

In attacking these use authorizations, EDF claims that the Administrator employed the wrong criteria in making his determinations concerning "unreasonable risk".[20] In particular, EDF argues that Congress intended to preclude the Administrator from using the subsection 6(c)(l) criteria in promulgating the PCB use authorization rules.

The basis for EDF's argument is found in subsection 6(e)(4), which requires the Administrator to promulgate rules in accordance with the procedural provisions in subsections 6(c)(2), (3), and (4); no reference to subsection 6(c)(1) is found in subsection 6(e)(4).[21] EDF claims that this omission evidences a congressional intent to preclude EPA from using the 6(c)(l) criteria in making "unreasonable risk" determinations pursuant to subsection 6(e)(2)(B). Because the Administrator used those criteria,[22] EDF argues, that the unreasonable risk determinations were "fatally flawed * * * [placing] disproportionate weight * * * on the adverse economic impact of a ban, [and seriously undermining] the Congressional objective of bringing about the development and use of substitutes in existing PCB activities * * *."

Without more, however, we find that the omission of a reference to subsection 6(c)(l) in 6(e)(4) does not imply that Congress meant to *prevent* EPA from considering the challenged criteria in making unreasonable risk determinations under 6(e)(2)(B). There is nothing in the wording of the statute or the legislative history that affirmatively supports the position of EDF.

Moreover, because the expression "unreasonable risk of injury to health or the environment" is left undefined in section 6(e), the Administrator was required to give some meaning to it. Since the 6(c)(l) criteria obviously pertain to factors of "unreasonable risk," it was entirely appropriate for EPA to consider such criteria in ascribing a meaning to the use authorization provision in 6(e)(2)(B). EDF has shown nothing to indicate

Section 6(a) of the Act, which governs the regulations of non-PCB substances, permits the Administrator to issue seven types of regulations whenever he finds that there is a reasonable basis to conclude that the manufacture, processing, distribution in commerce, use, or disposal of a chemical substance or mixture, or that any combination of such activities, presents or will present *an unreasonable risk of injury to health or the environment*.

15 U.S.C. § 2605(a) (emphasis added). Once he has made this finding, the Administrator is to choose the "least burdensome" regulation that will "protect adequately against such risk." Id.

20. The dispute over the proper criteria arises because § 6(e) offers no definition of the expression "unreasonable risk of injury to health or the environment."

21. Subsection 6(e)(4) provides: "Any rule under paragraph (1), (2)(B), or (3)(B) shall be promulgated in accordance with paragraphs (2), (3), and (4) of subsection (c) of this section."

22. "Although not subject to section 6(c)(l) of TSCA, EPA used the criteria in section 6(c)(l) to determine whether or not the risk from a non-totally enclosed activity is 'unreasonable.'" Preamble to Final Ban Regulations, 44 Fed.Reg. 31,529 (1979).

otherwise. In fact, EDF does not really contest use of the first three criteria in 6(c)(1)—i.e. the effects on health and on the environment, and the availability of substitutes. Rather, EDF's primary focus is on the fourth criterion in 6(c)(1), relating to the economic consequences of the authorization. Yet, EDF's objections to the "economic consequences" criterion cannot stand in the face of section 2(c) of the Act, which expressly requires the Administrator to consider such factors.[23]

Furthermore, the particular economic factors that EPA took into account were plainly reasonable. The Administrator did not simply propose to consider the effect of the ban on industry, but also the effects on "the national economy, small business, technological innovation, the environment, and public health." This formulation, which considers a broad range of benefits and costs of the ban and use authorization, is entirely consistent with the section 2(c) requirement that the Administrator consider the economic and social impact on his actions.

Because the 6(c)(1) criteria fulfill an express mandate of the statute and reflect a reasonable interpretation of an ambiguous phrase, we conclude that the Administrator did not err in choosing those criteria to make the unreasonable risk determinations under 6(e)(2)(B).

* * *

With these general guidelines in mind, we review EPA's PCB use authorizations.

In an attempt to reduce the costs of compliance and the risks associated with exposure to PCBs, the Administrator created two categories for transformers—PCB-contaminated transformers (containing PCB concentrations between fifty and 500 ppm) and PCB transformers (containing PCB concentrations greater than 500 ppm).

Because the Administrator found that proper protective clothing and good management practices should reduce PCB exposure to "very low levels," the regulations permit routine servicing of PCB transformers and electromagnets. Additionally, the administrator heard uncontradicted evidence that a prohibition of routine servicing would significantly increase the chances of catastrophic transformer failure, presenting "far greater risks to health and the environment than that associated with the minimal PCB exposure during routine servicing." However, the Administrator found that the rebuilding of PCB transformers and electromagnets (i.e. non-routine servicing) risks greater exposure to PCBs due to leaks, spillage, or volatilization of the dielectric. The Administrator also found that a prohibition against "any servicing (including rebuilding) of PCB transformers that involves removing the coils from the casing * * * will cost about $12 million the first year and steadily less each year thereafter." Applying these findings to the 6(c)(1) criteria, the Administrator ruled that contin-

23. Section 2(c) of the Act requires the Administrator to "consider the environmental, economic, and social impact of *any action* the Administrator takes or proposes to take under this chapter." 15 U.S.C. § 2601(c) (1976) (emphasis added).

ued routine servicing, without rebuilding, and not involving the removal of coils, would present no unreasonable risk of injury. The uncontradicted evidence and the explication of policy considerations in the present record is sufficient to uphold the use authorization for routine servicing of PCB transformers and electromagnets. . . .

It is clear that the Administrator has properly applied the 6(c)(*1*) criteria in making the unreasonable risk determinations. Where scientific knowledge is incomplete, EPA has set forth specific policy considerations explaining the final regulations. Finding substantial evidence in the record to support the Administrator's findings, we uphold the authorizations for railroad transformers.

The Fifty PPM Regulatory Cutoff

As a part of the regulatory scheme for PCBs under section 6(e), EPA limited application of the Disposal and Ban Regulations to materials containing concentrations of at least fifty ppm of PCBs. With one exception,[33] materials with lower concentrations remain unregulated under the TSCA regulations. EDF contends that this limitation contravenes the statutory command in subsections 6(e)(2)(A) and 6(e)(3)(A) to regulate "any polychlorinated biphenyl." While we do not adopt all of EDF's reasoning, we find that, under the applicable standard for judicial review, there is no substantial evidence in the record to support the Administrator's decision to establish a Regulatory Cutoff at fifty ppm.

Throughout the rulemaking proceeding for both the Disposal and Ban Regulations, EPA assumed that it would adopt some sort of regulatory cutoff. In the Disposal Regulations, EPA set the cutoff at 500 ppm, not because of health and environmental considerations, but in order to choose "a level at which regulated disposal of most PCB's can be implemented as soon as possible." Preamble to Final Disposal Regulations, 43 Fed.Reg. 7,151 (1978). EPA was reluctant to impose a lower cutoff since, from available information, the agency could not determine the "regulatory impact on commercial products" for lower levels. Subsequent to those proceedings, however, the agency acquired evidence that led it to believe that the "impact on commercial products of defining lower levels of contamination as 'PCB Mixtures' appears less than first believed * * * [As a result], the Agency plans to propose a lower concentration of PCB's, possibly in the range of 50 ppm or below, to define PCB mixture in the forthcoming" Ban Regulations. *Id.*

In the Proposed Ban Regulations, EPA listed four reasons for setting the regulatory cutoff at fifty ppm. First, EPA believed that a fifty ppm limit would "exclude from the rule municipal sludges and other mixtures containing low (less than 50 ppm) levels of PCB's whose presence is due to ambient levels of PCB present in the air or water." Preamble to Proposed Ban Regulations, 43 Fed.Reg. 24,804 (1978). As EPA develops in its brief,

---

33. EPA prohibited the use of waste oil, containing any detectable amount of PCBs, as a sealant, coating or dust control agent. See 44 Fed.Reg. 31,549 (1979) (to be codified in 40 C.F.R. § 761.30(d)).

Congress did not design section 6(e) to regulate ambient sources of PCBs. Second, EPA believed that some industrial chemical processes inevitably produce traces of PCBs, and that careful controls could reduce the concentrations of PCBs only to fifty ppm. Third, EPA felt that it was impractical to regulate the "diffuse and extremely numerous PCB sources" with concentrations below fifty ppm. *Id.* EPA believed that the proposed cutoff would ensure maximum effectiveness of the regulation by focusing "Agency attention under TSCA upon the most significant and controllable sources of PCB exposure." *Id.* Fourth, the agency believed that other statutes were available to regulate low concentrations of PCBs, particularly municipal sludges and dredge soils.

In the Final Ban Regulations, EPA adopted the proposed fifty ppm regulatory cutoff. Although industry favored a cutoff of 500 ppm in order to reduce the costs of complying with the regulations, EPA found that industry could comply with the more stringent standard. See Preamble to Final Ban Regulations, 44 Fed.Reg. 31,516 (1979). Furthermore, lowering the cutoff from 500 to fifty ppm would "result in substantially increased health and environmental protection." *Id.*

A cutoff below fifty ppm, on the other hand, would "provide an additional degree of environmental protection but would have a grossly disproportionate effect on the economic impact and would have a serious technological impact on the organic chemicals industry." *Id.* While it did not have firm data, EPA believed that for some chemical processes, it was technically impossible to eliminate the inadvertent production of PCBs. EPA also feared that because of limited disposal facilities, a lower cutoff would increase disposal requirements and interfere with the disposal of high concentration wastes. In short, EPA believed that the fifty ppm cutoff "provides adequate protection for human health and the environment while defining a program that EPA can effectively implement." *Id.*

* * *

Partly in order to incorporate congressional intent, the Administrator chose a regulatory cutoff at a level that he felt would exclude the ambient sources from regulation. We are troubled by this regulation, however, since the purpose of section 6(e) is to prevent the "introduction of additional PCB's into the environment." The selection of a cutoff undermines the congressional intent to regulate non-ambient sources of PCBs if non-ambient sources of contamination remain unregulated. It is equally troubling that the Administrator apparently is not aware of the amount of PCBs excluded from regulation by the fifty ppm or other possible cutoffs. Particularly because the Administrator has found that any exposure to PCBs may have adverse effects, the Administrator's flat exclusion of some industrial sources of contamination must undergo careful scrutiny. While some cutoff may be appropriate, we note that the Administrator did not explain why the regulation could not be designed expressly to exclude ambient sources, thus directly fulfilling congressional intent, rather than achieve that goal indirectly with a cutoff, thereby partly contravening congressional intent. Thus, a desire to exclude ambient sources of contamination, without more, cannot support the regulatory cutoff.

EPA also seeks to justify the regulatory cutoff on the basis of the serious impact a lower cutoff would have on industries that inadvertently produce PCBs during the manufacturing process. See Preamble to Final Ban Regulations, 44 Fed. Reg. 31,516 (1979). As EPA readily concedes, however, the inadvertent commercial production of PCBs is to be regulated under the Act. By providing a blanket exemption for concentrations below fifty ppm, the Administrator has circumvented the authorizations and exemptions requirements provided in the statute. EPA made no finding that the cutoff would involve no unreasonable risk to health or the environment.

* * *

We reemphasize that the Administrator has other, more appropriate means providing him with flexibility to avoid disproportionate impacts on industries or on health and the environment. Those tools are the authorization and exemption provisions in subsections 6(e)(2)(B) and 6(e)(3)(B). The standards enunciated therein, requiring findings of no "unreasonable risk of injury to health and the environment" and in the case of exemptions, good faith efforts to find substitutes, reflect a plain congressional intention that cannot be ignored. For if there is an unreasonable risk of injury, as there maybe given EPA's findings, surely Congress did not intend to permit the continued use, manufacture, processing or distribution of PCBs in concentrations below fifty ppm. EPA's *ad hoc* consideration of economic impact and disposal requirements, leading to a conclusion that the fifty ppm cutoff "provides adequate protection for human health and the environment," Preamble to Final Ban Regulations, 44 Fed.Reg. 31,516 (1979), is neither as rigorous nor as strict as the statutorily required unreasonable risk determination based on the subsection 6(c)(1) criteria.[47] Thus, we remand this part of the record to EPA for further proceedings.

Conclusion

* * *

We feel constrained to add one final note to emphasize our concern in this case. Human beings have finally come to recognize that they must eliminate or control life threatening chemicals, such as PCBs, if the miracle of life is to continue and if earth is to remain a living planet. This is precisely what Congress sought to do when it enacted section 6(e) of the Toxic Substances Control Act. Yet, we find that forty-six months after the effective date of an act designed to either totally ban or closely control the

---

47. So that there is no misunderstanding, we are not striking down the 50 ppm cutoff because EPA has failed to justify that particular level instead of a slightly lower level. "In reviewing a numerical standard, we must ask whether the agency's numbers are within a 'zone of reasonableness,' not whether its numbers are precisely right." Hercules, Inc. v. EPA, 598 F.2d 91, 106–07 (D.C.Cir. 1978). EPA has failed to adduce substantial evidence that 50 ppm is within the zone of reasonableness.

use of PCBs, 99 percent of the PCBs that were in use when the Act was passed are still in use in the United States.[53] With information such as this in hand, timid souls have good reason to question the prospects for our continued survival, and cynics have just cause to sneer at the effectiveness of governmental regulation.

The EPA regulations can hardly be viewed as a bold step forward in the battle against life threatening chemicals. There is no substantial evidence in the record to support certain of the EPA regulatory enactments, and portions of the regulations are plainly contrary to law. Thus, the effort by EPA has, in certain respects, fallen far short of the mark set by the congressional mandate found in section 6(e) of the Toxic Substances Control Act.

On remand, we trust that EPA will act with a sense of urgency to find effective solutions to enforce the Act. We are not so naive as to assume or suggest that hasty responses will ensure effective regulations. However, we are well able to see, from the plain text of the Act, that the deadlines for the enactment of regulations to enforce section 6(e) have passed. We therefore believe that EPA should act with expedition to complete the important task assigned to it by Congress.

So ordered.

NOTES AND QUESTIONS

1. *PCBs as a Target for TSCA.* Of the thousands of varieties of toxic chemicals, why were PCBs singled out for special treatment under TSCA? What are PCBs? They are polychlorinated biphenyls which are a class of chemical compounds that were manufactured for a variety of purposes, including cooling and lubricating transformers, capacitors, and other electrical equipment. PCBs are particularly useful for these purposes because they do not easily burn and they are excellent insulators. Monsanto Corporation, the only U.S. manufacturer of PCBs, produced them between 1930 and 1977. They are also produced as a byproduct of various organic chemicals. Perhaps it is due to foreign experience with the chemical as well as domestic factors. In Japan in the 1970s, great publicity was accorded to an incident in which PCBs contaminated cooking oil causing several deaths and severe illnesses. In the United States, there was a single manufacturer of PCBs which in 1976 was phasing out of the business. Thus, it was easy and popular for Congress to pass § 6(e) which provided a schedule for stopping the manufacture of PCBs and gradually curtailing their use. TSCA § 6(e)(2)(A), with limited exceptions, prohibited after 1977 the "*manufacture, process[ing], or distribut[ion] in commerce or use*" of PCBs except in a "totally enclosed manner." This is not surprising since EPA has determined that PCBs are carcinogenic and mutagenic material with a host of

---

53. A recent House committee report on the proposed Toxic Substances Control Act Amendment of 1980, H.R. 7126, lamented that the "EPA definition [of totally en- closed uses] exempted from the [§ 6(e)] ban approximately 99 percent of all PCBs found in the United States." H.R.Rep. No. 968, 96th Cong., 2d Sess. 6 (1980).

other serious human health impacts including immune system suppression, liver damage, endocrine disruption, and skin irritation.

2. What Prompted the Environmental Defense Fund (EDF) to pursue this Lawsuit? Does the court's interpretation of the "unreasonable risk" issue mean that EDF may have won the battle but lost the war? Following the EDF case, EPA issued a series of new regulations concerning PCBs. They may be found in 40 C.F.R. Part 761 and govern the use, manufacture, processing, and distribution of PCBs. Throughout the PCB regulations, the 50 ppm cutoff is used to demarcate the boundaries of many important regulatory requirements.

3. *The PCB "Mega Rule" of 1998.* In June, 1998, seven years after announcing its Advanced Notice of Proposed Rulemaking, EPA published its PCB Mega Rule, a comprehensive revision of TSCA regulations at 40 C. F.R. §§ 761.1–.398. Called the Mega Rule, it adopted significant amendments to existing rules affecting the use, manufacture, processing, distribution and disposal of PCBs. The rule was initially challenged in Central and South West Services, Inc. v. EPA, 220 F.3d 683 (5th Cir.2000), where the court upheld the concept that PCB use was generally prohibited subject to exceptions which EPA might establish. It also upheld the decontamination procedures specified in the Mega Rule which would permit the use of equipment or structures contaminated with PCBs in excess of 50 ppm. Interestingly, the court ruled that EPA restrictions on PCB use would be judged under an "arbitrary and capricious" standard of review while EPA actions expanding PCB use would have to be justified under a "substantial evidence" rationale. Why would the court have taken such a bifurcated approach to the standard of review question? See James A. Vroman, Disposal and Remediation Options Under the PCB Mega Rule, 29 ELR 10459 (1999).

Corrosion Proof Fittings v. Environmental Protection Agency

United States Court of Appeals, Fifth Circuit, 1991.
947 F.2d 1201.

■ JERRY E. SMITH, CIRCUIT JUDGE:

Facts and Procedural History.

Asbestos is a naturally occurring fibrous material that resists fire and most solvents. Its major uses include heat-resistant insulators, cements, building materials, fireproof gloves and clothing, and motor vehicle brake linings. Asbestos is a toxic material, and occupational exposure to asbestos dust can result in mesothelioma, asbestosis, and lung cancer.

The EPA began these proceedings in 1979, when it issued an Advanced Notice of Proposed Rulemaking announcing its intent to explore the use of TSCA "to reduce the risk to human health posed by exposure to asbestos." See 54 Fed.Reg. 29,460 (1989). While these proceedings were pending, other agencies continued their regulation of asbestos uses, in particular the Occupational Safety and Health Administration (OSHA), which in 1983 and 1984 involved itself with lowering standards for workplace asbestos exposure.[1]

An EPA-appointed panel reviewed over one hundred studies of asbestos and conducted several public meetings. Based upon its studies and the public comments, the EPA concluded that asbestos is a potential carcinogen at all levels of exposure, regardless of the type of asbestos or the size of the fiber. The EPA concluded in 1986 that exposure to asbestos "poses an unreasonable risk to human health" and thus proposed at least four regulatory options for prohibiting or restricting the use of asbestos, including a mixed ban and phase-out of asbestos over ten years; a two-stage ban of asbestos, depending upon product usage; a three-stage ban on all asbestos products leading to a total ban in ten years; and labeling of all products containing asbestos.

Over the next two years, the EPA updated its data, received further comments, and allowed cross-examination on the updated documents. In 1989, the EPA issued a final rule prohibiting the manufacture, importation, processing, and distribution in commerce of most asbestos-containing products. Finding that asbestos constituted an unreasonable risk to health and the environment, the EPA promulgated a staged ban of most commercial uses of asbestos. The EPA estimates that this rule will save either 202 or 148 lives, depending upon whether the benefits are discounted, at a cost of approximately $450–800 million, depending upon the price of substitutes.

The rule is to take effect in three stages, depending upon the EPA's assessment of how toxic each substance is and how soon adequate substitutes will be available.[2] The rule allows affected persons one more year at each stage to sell existing stocks of, prohibited products. The rule also

---

1. OSHA began to regulate asbestos in the workplace in 1971. At that time, the permissible exposure limit was 12 fibers per cubic centimeter (f/cc), which OSHA lowered several times until today it stands at 0.2 f/cc. OSHA currently is considering lowering the limit to 0.1 f/cc, following a challenge to the regulation in *Building & Constr. Trades Dep't v. Brock*, 838 F.2d 1258, 1267–69 (D.C.Cir.1988). The Mine Safety and Health Administration (MSHA) since 1976 has limited mine worker asbestos exposure to 2 f/cc. See 30 C.F.R. § 71.702 (1990).

The Consumer Product Safety Commission (CPSC) has banned consumer patching compounds containing respirable asbestos, see 16 C.F.R. §§ 1304–05 (1990), and also requires labeling for other products containing respirable asbestos. Similarly, the Food and Drug Administration has banned general-use garments containing asbestos unless used for protection against fire. See 16 C.F.R. § 1500.17 (1990).

2. The main products covered by each ban stage are as follows:

(1) Stage 1: August 27, 1990: ban on asbestos-containing floor materials, clothing, roofing felt, corrugated and flat sheet materials, pipeline wrap, and new asbestos uses;

(2) Stage 2: August 25, 1993: ban on asbestos-containing "friction products" and certain automotive products or uses;

(3) Stage 3: August 26, 1996: ban on other asbestos-containing automotive products or uses, asbestos-containing building materials including non-roof and roof coatings, and asbestos cement shingles.

See 54 Fed.Reg. at 29,461–62.

imposes labeling requirements on stage 2 or stage 3 products and allows for exemptions from the rule in certain cases.

A.   The Standard of Review

Contrary to the EPA's assertions, the arbitrary and capricious standard found in the APA and the substantial evidence standard found in TSCA are different standards, even in the context of an informal rulemaking. Congress specifically went out of its way to provide that "the standard of review prescribed by paragraph (2)(E) of section 706 [of the APA shall not apply and the court shall hold unlawful and set aside such rule if the court finds that the rule is not supported by substantial evidence in rulemaking record * * * taken as a whole."] 15 U.S.C. § 2618(c)(1)(B)(i). "The substantial evidence standard mandated by [TSCA] is generally considered to be more rigorous than the arbitrary and capricious standard normally applied to informal rulemaking," Environmental Defense Fund v. EPA, 636 F.2d 1267, 1277 (D.C.Cir.1980), and "afford[s] a considerably more generous judicial review" than the arbitrary and capricious test. The test "imposes a considerable burden on the agency and limits its discretion in arriving at a factual predicate."

"Under the substantial evidence standard, a reviewing court must give careful scrutiny to agency findings and, at the same time, accord appropriate deference to administrative decisions that are based on agency experience and expertise." Environmental Defense Fund, 636 F.2d at 1277. As with consumer product legislation, "Congress put the substantial evidence test in the statute because it wanted the courts to scrutinize the Commission's action more closely than an arbitrary and capricious standard would allow."

The recent case of Chemical Mfrs. Assn. v. EPA, 899 F.2d 344 (5th Cir.1990), provides our basic framework for reviewing the EPA's actions. In evaluating whether the EPA has presented substantial evidence, we examine (1) whether the quantities of the regulated chemical entering into the environment are "substantial" and (2) whether human exposure to the chemical is "substantial" or "significant." *Id.* at 359. An agency may exercise its judgment without strictly relying upon quantifiable risks, costs, and benefits, but it must "cogently explain why it has exercised its discretion in a given matter."

B.   The EPA's Burden Under TSCA

TSCA provides, in pertinent part, as follows:

(a) Scope of regulation. If the Administrator finds that there is a *reasonable basis* to conclude that the manufacture, processing, distribution in commerce, use, or disposal of a chemical substance or mixture, or that any combination of such activities, presents or will present an *unreasonable risk of injury* to health or the environment, the Administrator shall by rule apply one or more of the following requirements to such substance or mixture to the extent necessary *to protect adequately* against such risk using the *least burdensome* requirements. *Id.* (emphasis added). As the highlighted language shows, Congress did not enact TSCA as a zero-risk statute. The EPA, rather, was required to consider both alternatives to a ban and the costs of any proposed actions and to "carry out this chapter in a reasonable and prudent manner [after considering] the environmental, economic, and social impact of any action." 15 U.S.C. § 2601(c).

We conclude that the EPA has presented insufficient evidence to justify its asbestos ban. We base this conclusion upon two grounds: the failure of the EPA to consider all necessary evidence and its failure to give adequate weight to statutory language requiring it to promulgate the least burdensome, reasonable regulation required to protect the environment adequately. Because the EPA failed to address these concerns, and because the EPA is required to articulate a "reasoned basis" for its rules, we are compelled to return the regulation to the agency for reconsideration.

1.

Least Burdensome and Reasonable.

TSCA requires that the EPA use the least burdensome regulation to achieve its goal of minimum reasonable risk. This statutory requirement can create problems in evaluating just what is a "reasonable risk." Congress's rejection of a no-risk policy, however, also means that in certain cases, the least burdensome yet still adequate solution may entail somewhat more risk than would other, known regulations that are far more burdensome on the industry and the economy. The very language of TSCA requires that the EPA, once it has determined what an acceptable level of non-zero risk is, choose the least burdensome method of reaching that level.

In this case, the EPA banned, for all practical purposes, all present and future uses of asbestos—a position the petitioners characterize as the "death penalty alternative," as this is the *most* burdensome of all possible alternatives listed as open to the EPA under TSCA. TSCA not only provides the EPA with a list of alternative actions, but also provides those alternatives in order of how burdensome they are. The regulations thus provide for EPA regulation ranging from labeling the least toxic chemicals to limiting the total amount of chemicals an industry may use. Total bans head the list as the most burdensome regulatory option.

By choosing the harshest remedy given to it under TSCA, the EPA assigned to itself the toughest burden in satisfying TSCA's requirement that its alternative be the least burdensome of all those offered to it. Since, both by definition and by the terms of TSCA, the complete ban of manufacturing is the most burdensome alternative—for even stringent regulation at least allows a manufacturer the chance to invest and meet the new, higher standard—the EPA's regulation cannot stand if there is any other regulation that would achieve an acceptable level of risk as mandated by TSCA.

We reserve until a later part of the opinion a product-by-product review of the regulation. Before reaching this analysis, however, we lay down the inquiry that the EPA should undertake whenever it seeks total ban of a product.

The EPA considered, and rejected, such options as labeling asbestos products, thereby warning users and workers involved in the manufacture of asbestos-containing products of the chemical's dangers, and stricter workplace rules. EPA also rejected controlled use of asbestos in the workplace and deferral to other government agencies charged with worker and consumer exposure to industrial and product hazards, such as OSHA, the CPSC, and the MSHA. The EPA determined that deferral to these other agencies was inappropriate because no one other authority could address all the risks posed "throughout the life cycle" by asbestos, and any action by one or more of the other agencies still would leave an unacceptable residual risk.

Much of the EPA's analysis is correct, and the EPA's basic decision to use TSCA as a comprehensive statute designed to fight a multi-industry problem was a proper one that we uphold today on review. What concerns us, however, is the manner in which the EPA conducted some of its analysis. TSCA requires the EPA to consider, along with the effects of toxic substances on human health and the environment, "the benefits of such substance[s] or mixture[s] for various uses and the availability of substitutes for such uses," as well as "the reasonably ascertainable economic consequences of the rule, after consideration for the effect on the national economy, small business, technological innovation, the environment, and public health." *Id.* § 2605(c)(*l*)(C–D).

The EPA presented two comparisons in the record: a world with no further regulation under TSCA, and a world in which no manufacture of asbestos takes place. The EPA rejected calculating how many lives a less burdensome regulation would save, and at what costs. Furthermore the EPA, when calculating the benefits of its ban, explicitly refused to compare it to an improved workplace in which currently available control technology is utilized. This decision artificially inflated the purported benefits of the rule by using a baseline comparison substantially lower than what currently available technology could yield.

Under TSCA, the EPA was required to evaluate, rather than ignore, less burdensome regulatory alternatives. TSCA imposes a least-to-most-burdensome hierarchy. In order to impose a regulation at the top of the hierarchy—a total ban of asbestos—the EPA must show not only that its proposed action reduces the risk of the product to an adequate level, but also that the actions Congress identified as less burdensome also would not do the job. The failure of the EPA to do this constitutes a failure to meet its burden of showing that its actions not only reduce the risk but do so in the Congressionally-mandated *least burdensome* fashion.

Thus it was not enough for the EPA to show, as it did in this case, that banning some asbestos products might reduce the harm that could occur from the use of these products. If that were the standard, it would be no standard at all, for few indeed are the products that are so safe that a complete ban of them would not make the world still safer.

This comparison of two static worlds is insufficient to satisfy the dictates of TSCA. While the EPA may have shown that a world with a complete ban of asbestos might be preferable to one in which there is only the current amount of regulation, the EPA has failed to show that there is not some intermediate state of regulation that would be superior to both the currently regulated and the completely-banned world. Without showing that asbestos regulation would be ineffective, the EPA cannot discharge its TSCA burden of showing that its regulation is the least burdensome available to it. Upon an initial showing of product danger, the proper course for the EPA to follow is to consider each regulatory option, beginning with the least burdensome, and the costs and benefits of regulation under each option. The EPA cannot simply skip several rungs, as it did in this case, for in doing so, it may skip a less-burdensome alternative mandated by TSCA. Here, although the EPA mentions the problems posed by intermediate levels of regulation, it takes no steps to calculate the costs and benefits of these intermediate levels. See 54 Fed.Reg. at 29,462, 29,474. Without doing this it is impossible, both for the EPA and for this court on review, to know, that none of these alternatives was less burdensome than the ban in fact chosen by the agency.

2.

The EPA's Calculations

Furthermore, we are concerned about some of the methodology employed by the EPA in making various of the calculations that it did perform. In order to aid the EPA's reconsideration of this and other cases, we present our concerns here.

When the EPA does discount costs or benefits, however, it cannot choose an unreasonable time upon which to base its discount calculation. Instead of using the time of injury as the appropriate time from which to discount, as one might expect, the EPA instead used the time of exposure.

The difficulties inherent in the EPA's approach can be illustrated by an example. Suppose two workers will be exposed to asbestos in 1996, with worker X subjected to a tiny amount of asbestos that will have no adverse health effects, and worker Y exposed to massive amounts of asbestos that quickly will lead to an asbestos-related disease. Under the EPA's approach, which takes into account only the time of exposure rather than the time at which any injury manifests itself, both examples would be treated the same. The EPA's approach implicitly assumes that the day on which the risk of injury occurs is the same day the injury actually occurs. Such an approach might be proper when the exposure and injury are one and the same, such as when a person is exposed to an immediately fatal poison, but is inappropriate for discounting toxins in which exposure often is followed by a substantial lag time before manifestation of injuries.

Of more concern to us is the failure of the EPA to compute the costs and benefits of its proposed rule past the year 2000, and its double-counting of the costs of asbestos use. In performing its calculus, the EPA only included the number of lives saved over the next thirteen years, and counted any additional lives saved as simply "unquantified benefits."

Although various commentators dispute whether it ever is appropriate to discount benefits when they are measured in human lives, we note that it would skew the result to discount only costs without according similar treatment to the benefits side of the equation. Adopting the position of the commentators who advocate not discounting benefits would force the EPA similarly not to calculate costs in present discounted real terms, making comparisons difficult. Furthermore, in evaluating situations in which different options incur costs at varying time intervals, the EPA would not be able to take into account that soon-to-be-incurred costs are more harmful than postponable costs. Because the EPA must discount costs to perform its evaluations properly, the EPA also should discount benefits to preserve an apples-to-apples comparison, even if this entails discounting benefits of a non-monetary nature.

The EPA and intervenors now seek to use these unquantified lives saved to justify calculations as to which the benefits seem far outweighed by the astronomical costs. For example, the EPA plans to save about three lives with its ban of asbestos pipe, at a cost of $128–227 million (*i.e.,* approximately $43–76 million per life saved). Although the EPA admits that the price tag is high, it claims that the lives saved past the year 2000 justify the price.

Such calculations not only lessen the value of the EPA's cost analysis, but also make any meaningful judicial review impossible. While TSCA contemplates a useful place for unquantified benefits beyond the EPA's calculation, unquantified benefits never were intended as a trump card allowing the EPA to justify any cost calculus, no matter how high.

The concept of unquantified benefits, rather, is intended to allow the EPA to provide a rightful place for any remaining benefits that are impossible to quantify after the EPA's best attempt, but which still are of some concern. But the allowance for unquantified costs is not intended to allow the EPA to perform its calculations over an arbitrarily short period so as to preserve a large unquantified portion.

Unquantified benefits can, at times, permissibly tip the balance in close cases. They cannot, however, be used to effect a wholesale shift on the balance beam. Such a use makes a mockery of the requirements of TSCA that the EPA weigh the costs of its actions before it chooses the least burdensome alternative.

3.

Reasonable Basis

In addition to showing that its regulation is the least burdensome one necessary to protect the environment adequately, the EPA also must show that it has a reasonable basis for the regulation. 15 U.S.C. § 2605(a). To some extent, our inquiry in this area mirrors that used above, for many of the methodological problems we have noted also indicate that the EPA did not have a reasonable basis. We here take the opportunity to highlight some areas of additional concern.

Most problematical to us is the EPA's ban of products for which no substitutes presently are available. In these cases, the EPA bears a tough burden indeed to show that under TSCA a ban is the least burdensome alternative, as TSCA explicitly instructs the EPA to consider "the benefits of such substance or mixture for various uses and the availability of substitutes for such uses." *Id.* § 2605(c)(1)(C). These words are particularly appropriate where the EPA actually has decided to ban a product, rather than simply restrict its use, for it is in these cases that the lack of an adequate substitute is most troubling under TSCA.

As the EPA itself states, "[w]hen no information is available for a product indicating that cost-effective substitutes exist, the estimated cost of a product ban is very high." 54 Fed.Reg. at 29,468. Because of this, the EPA did not ban certain uses of asbestos, such as its use in rocket engines and battery separators. The EPA, however, in several other instances, ignores its own arguments and attempts to justify its ban by stating that the ban itself will cause the development of low-cost, adequate substitute products.

As a general matter, we agree with the EPA that a product ban can lead to great innovation, and it is true that an agency under TSCA, as under other regulatory statutes, "is empowered to issue safety standards which require improvements in existing technology or which require the development of new technology." *Chrysler v. Department of Transp.*, 472 F.2d 659, 673 (6th Cir.1972). As even the EPA acknowledges, however, when no adequate substitutes currently exist, the EPA cannot fail to consider this lack when formulating its own guidelines. Under TSCA, therefore, the EPA must present a stronger case to justify the ban, as opposed to regulation, of products with no substitutes.

We note that the EPA does provide a waiver provision for industries where the hoped-for substitutes fail to materialize in time. See 54 Fed.Reg. at 29,464. Under this provision, if no adequate substitutes develop, the EPA temporarily may extend the planned phaseout.

The EPA uses this provision to argue that it can ban any product, regardless of whether it has an adequate substitute, because inventive companies soon will develop good substitutes. The EPA contends that if they do not, the waiver provision will allow the continued use of asbestos in these areas, just as if the ban had not occurred at all.

The EPA errs, however, in asserting that the waiver provision will allow a continuation of the status quo in those cases in which no substitutes materialize. By its own terms, the exemption shifts the burden onto the waiver proponent to convince the EPA that the waiver is justified. See id. As even the EPA acknowledges, the waiver only "may be granted by [the] EPA in very limited circumstances." *Id.* at 29,460.

The EPA thus cannot use the waiver provision to lessen its burden when justifying banning products without existing substitutes. While TSCA gives the EPA the power to ban such products, the EPA must bear its heavier burden of justifying its total ban in the face of inadequate substitutes. Thus, the agency cannot use its waiver provision to argue that the ban of products with no substitutes should be treated the same as the ban of those for which adequate substitutes are available now.

We also are concerned with the EPA's evaluation of substitutes even in those instances in which the record shows that they are available. The EPA explicitly rejects considering the harm that may flow from the increased use of products designed to substitute for asbestos, even where the probable substitutes themselves are known carcinogens. The EPA justifies this by stating that it has "more concern about the continued use and exposure to asbestos than it has for the future replacement of asbestos in the products subject to this rule with other fibrous substitutes." The agency thus concludes that any "[r]egulatory decisions about asbestos which poses well-recognized, serious risks should not be delayed until the rise of all replacement materials are fully quantified."

This presents two problems. First, TSCA instructs the EPA to consider the relative merits of its ban, as compared to the economic effects of its actions. The EPA cannot make this calculation if it fails to consider the effects that alternate substitutes will pose after a ban.

Second, the EPA cannot say with any assurance that its regulation will increase workplace safety when it refuses to evaluate the harm that will result from the increased use of substitute products. While the EPA may be correct in its conclusion that the alternate materials pose less risk than asbestos, we cannot say with any more assurance than that flowing from an educated guess that this conclusion is true.

Considering that many of the substitutes that the EPA itself concedes will be used in the place of asbestos have known carcinogenic effects, the EPA not only cannot assure this court that it has taken the least burdensome alternative, but cannot even prove that its regulations will increase workplace safety. Eager to douse the dangers of asbestos, the agency inadvertently actually may increase the risk of injury Americans face. The EPA's explicit failure to consider the toxicity of likely substitutes thus deprives its order of a reasonable basis.

Our opinion should not be construed to state that the EPA has an affirmative duty to seek out and test every workplace substitute for any product it seeks to regulate. TSCA does not place such a burden upon the agency. We do not think it unreasonable, however, once interested parties introduce credible studies and evidence showing the toxicity of workplace substitutes, or the decreased effectiveness of safety alternatives such as non-asbestos brakes, that the EPA then consider whether its regulations are even increasing workplace safety, and whether the increased risk occasioned by dangerous substitutes makes the proposed regulation no longer reasonable. In the words of the EPA's own release that initiated the asbestos rulemaking, we direct that the agency consider the adverse health effects of asbestos substitute "for comparison with the known hazards of asbestos," so that it can conduct, as it promised in 1979, a "balanced consideration of the environmental, economic, and social impact of any action taken by the agency.''

In short, a death is a death, whether occasioned by asbestos or by a toxic substitute product, and the EPA's decision not to evaluate the toxicity of known carcinogenic substitutes is not a reasonable action under TSCA. Once an interested party brings forth credible evidence suggesting the toxicity of the probable or only alternatives to a substance, the EPA must consider the comparative toxic costs of each. Its failure to do so in this case thus deprived its regulation of a reasonable basis, at least in regard to those products as to which petitioners introduced credible evidence of the dangers of the likely substitutes.

4.

Unreasonable Risk of Injury

The final requirement the EPA must satisfy before engaging in any TSCA rulemaking is that it only take steps designed to prevent "unreasonable" risks. In evaluating what is "unreasonable," the EPA is required to consider the costs of any proposed actions and to "carry out this chapter in a reasonable and prudent manner (after considering) the environmental, economic, and social impact of any action." 15 U.S.C. § 2601(c).

As the District of Columbia Circuit stated when evaluating similar language governing the Federal Hazardous Substances Act, "[t]he requirement that the risk be 'unreasonable' necessarily involves a balancing test like that familiar in tort law: The regulation may issue if the severity of the injury that may result from the product, factored by the likelihood of the injury, offsets the harm the regulation itself imposes upon manufacturers and consumers." Forester v. CPSC, 559 F.2d 774, 789 (D.C.Cir.1977). We have quoted this language approvingly when evaluating other statutes using similar language. See, e.g., *Aqua Slide*, 569 F.2d at 839.

That the EPA must balance the costs of its regulations against their benefits further is reinforced by the requirement that it seek the least burdensome regulation. While Congress did not dictate that the EPA engage in an exhaustive, full-scale cost-benefit analysis, it did require the EPA to consider both sides of the regulatory equation, and it rejected the notion that the EPA should pursue the reduction of workplace risk at any cost. See American Textile Mfrs. Inst., 452 U.S. at 510 n. 30, 101 S.Ct. at 2491 n. 30 ("unreasonable risk" statutes require "a generalized balancing of costs and benefits" (citing Aqua Slide, 569 F.2d at 839)). Thus "Congress also plainly intended the EPA to consider the economic impact of any actions taken by it under * * * TSCA." Chemical Mfrs. Ass'n, 899 F.2d at 348.

Even taking all of the EPA's figures as true, and evaluating them in the light most favorable to the agency's decision (non-discounted benefits, discounted costs, analogous exposure estimates included), the agency's analysis results in figures as high as $74 million per life saved. For example, the EPA states that its ban of asbestos pipe will save three lives over the next thirteen years, at a cost of $128–227 million ($43–76 million per life saved), depending upon the price of substitutes; that its ban of asbestos shingles will cost $23–34 million to save 0.32 statistical lives ($72–106 million per life saved); that its ban of asbestos coatings will cost $46–181 million to save 3.33 lives ($14–54 million per life saved); and that its ban of asbestos paper products will save 0.60 lives at a cost of $4–5 million ($7–8 million per life saved). See 54 Fed.Reg. at 29,484–85. Were the analogous exposure estimates not included, the cancer risks from substitutes such as ductile iron pipe factored in, and the benefits of the ban appropriately discounted from the time of the manifestation of an injury rather than the time of exposure, the costs would shift even more sharply against the EPA's position.

While we do not sit as a regulatory agency that must make the difficult decision as to what an appropriate expenditure is to prevent someone from incurring the risk of an asbestos-related death, we do note that the EPA, in its zeal to ban any and all asbestos products, basically ignored the cost side of the TSCA equation. The EPA would have this court believe that Congress, when it enacted its requirement that the EPA consider the economic impacts of its regulations, thought that spending $200–300 million to save approximately seven lives (approximately $30–40 million per life) over thirteen years is reasonable.

As we stated in the OSHA context until an agency "can provide substantial evidence that the benefits to be achieved by [a regulation] bear a reasonable relationship to the costs imposed by the reduction, it cannot show that the standard is reasonably necessary to provide safe or healthful workplaces." *American Petroleum Inst.*, 581 F.2d at 504. Although the OSHA statute differs in major respects from TSCA, the statute does require substantial evidence to support the EPA's contentions that its regulations both have a reasonable basis and are the least burdensome means to a reasonably safe workplace.

The EPA's willingness to argue that spending $23.7 million to save less than one-third of a life reveals that its economic review of its regulations, as required by TSCA, was meaningless. As the petitioners' brief and our review of EPA caselaw reveals, such high costs are rarely, if ever, used to support a safety regulation. If we were to allow such cavalier treatment of the EPA's duty to consider the economic effects of its decisions, we would have to excise entire sections and phrases from the language of TSCA. Because we are judges, not surgeons, we decline to do so.

NOTES AND QUESTIONS

1. One of the most widely publicized environmental and public health hazards is asbestos. As the *Corrosion Proof Fittings* case indicates, in 1989 EPA banned the manufacture, importation, processing and distribution in commerce of most asbestos products. That case illustrates the difficulty in attempting to impose a categorical ban on substances widely used in commerce. When reflecting upon the language and structure of TSCA consider the following questions: a) why did Congress insert the "substantial evidence" test into the law? b) why was the usual "arbitrary and capricious" standard for reviewing administrative action insufficient? and c) what are the social costs and benefits of the "least burdensome regulation" and the " 'reasonable basis' requirements?" Also, why was this case litigated in the Fifth Circuit?

2. We live in an age of chemicals. There are literally thousands of chemicals and chemical compounds that are currently used for innumerable purposes. Some of these applications are benign and useful without presenting hazards while others pose significant risks to people and the environment. Section 6(a) of TSCA authorizes EPA to take a wide range of action when it finds that a chemical substance or mixture "presents or will present an unreasonable risk of injury to health or the environment." This provision authorizing EPA contains an explicit proviso that EPA may act "to the extent necessary to protect adequately against such risk suing the *least burdensome requirements.*" Considering this restriction, § 6(a) lists the following five possible EPA responses that will provide sufficient public and environmental protection:

A.   prohibiting or limiting the amount of the manufacture, processing or distribution of toxic substances,

B.   requiring warnings and instructions concerning use, distribution or disposal of toxic substances,

C.   prohibiting or regulating the commercial use of the toxic substance,

D.   prohibiting or regulating the methods of disposal of the toxic substance,

E.   requiring manufacturers or processors to give notice of unreasonable risk of injury to distributors, purchasers and to the public.

In making this choice under § 6(c), EPA must consider the effects and magnitude of exposure on health and the environment, the benefits of the substance including the availability of substitutes, and the reasonable ascertainable economic consequences of imposing the restriction. Considering this template for TSCA regulation, in the *Corrosion Proof Fittings* case, why wasn't EPA's study and analysis sufficient to support the staged ban on the use of asbestos? What does this decision say about the usefulness of TSCA § 6 to regulate toxic substances? Do you think that it would have mattered if EPA were proposing to regulate asbestos in a less severe way?

CHAPTER EIGHT

WASTES, RECYCLING, AND RESOURCE CONSERVATION

Until the 1940s, most solid waste generated in the United States consisted of food wastes and ashes from coal burning furnaces. Scrap metals and other materials were routinely recycled, in many cases by scavengers. There was relatively little chemical waste. With increasing urbanization and industrialization in the second half of the twentieth century, the situation has changed dramatically. Households in the United States generate about 220 million tons of solid waste each year. Industrial operations such as mining, manufacturing, and agriculture produce additional hundreds of millions of tons of waste. Carelessly discarded materials, especially hazardous wastes, can present major threats to human health and the environment. Discarding materials that could be reused or recycled also may unnecessarily waste resources.

The primary federal legislation dealing with waste management is the Resource Conservation and Recovery Act of 1976 (RCRA), which was enacted as a set of amendments to the federal Solid Waste Disposal Act. Radioactive wastes are treated separately, under a series of federal statutes. State and local law also plays an important role, particularly in regulating the disposal of non-hazardous wastes.

SECTION 1. MANAGEMENT OF MUNICIPAL SOLID WASTE

Excerpts from the Resource Conservation and Recovery Act

42 U.S.C. §§ 6901–6992k.

Sec. 1002 Congressional findings

(a) The Congress finds with respect to solid waste—

(1) that the continuing technological progress and improvement in methods of manufacture, packaging, and marketing of consumer products has resulted in an ever-mounting increase, and in a change in the characteristics, of the mass material discarded by the purchaser of such products;

(2) that the economic and population growth of our Nation, and the improvements in the standard of living enjoyed by our population, * * * have resulted in a rising tide of scrap, discarded, and waste materials;

* * *

(4) that while the collection and disposal of solid wastes should continue to be primarily the function of State, regional, and local agencies, the problems of waste disposal as set forth above have become a matter national in scope and in concern and necessitate Federal action through financial and technical assistance and leadership in the development, demonstration, and application of new and improved methods and processes to reduce the amount of waste and unsalvageable materials and to provide for proper and economical solid waste disposal practices.

(b) The Congress finds with respect to the environment and health, that—

(1) although land is too valuable a national resource to be needlessly polluted by discarded materials, most solid waste is disposed of on land in open dumps and sanitary landfills;

(2) disposal of solid waste and hazardous waste in or on the land without careful planning and management can present a danger to human health and the environment;

* * *

(4) open dumping is particularly harmful to health, contaminates drinking water from underground and surface supplies, and pollutes the air and the land;

* * *

(8) alternatives to existing methods of land disposal must be developed since many of the cities in the United States will be running out of suitable solid waste disposal sites within five years unless immediate action is taken.

(c) The Congress finds with respect to materials, that—

(1) millions of tons of recoverable material which could be used are needlessly buried each year;

* * *

(d) The Congress finds with respect to energy, that—

(1) solid waste represents a potential source of solid fuel, oil, or gas that can be converted into energy;

(2) the need exists to develop alternative energy sources for public and private consumption in order to reduce our dependence on such sources as petroleum products, natural gas, nuclear and hydroelectric generation; and

(3) technology exists to produce usable energy from solid waste.

———

Municipal solid waste is a fancy term for ordinary household garbage. It includes everything from grass clippings to furniture, clothing, food scraps, newspapers, appliances, and batteries. Municipal solid waste includes garbage from commercial facilities, schools, and other institutions, as well as individual households. It contains such potentially hazardous substances as paints, solvents, batteries, and pesticides. Although the proportion of hazardous materials is small, because of the large volumes of municipal solid waste the absolute quantities of hazardous substances are substantial. Improperly managed municipal solid waste can pose a serious threat to the environment. As of 1986, one-fifth of the sites on the Superfund list were former municipal landfills. See Kirsten Engel, Reconsidering the National Market in Solid Waste: Trade-offs in Equity, Efficiency, Environmental Protection, and State Autonomy, 73 N. Car. L. Rev. 1481, 1489 (1995).

Nationwide, the U.S. produced roughly 88 million tons of municipal solid waste in 1960. That number increased to over 200 tons by 1990. During the same period, per capita solid waste generation rates doubled, increasing from 2.7 pounds per day to 4.5 pounds per day. In the 1990s, however, the rate of growth slowed significantly; as of 1998 the per capita rate remained 4.5 pounds per day, for a total of 220 million tons of municipal solid waste nationwide. Environmental Protection Agency, Environmental Fact Sheet, Municipal Solid Waste Generation, Recycling and Disposal in the United States: Facts and Figures for 1998, at 2 (April 2000). Municipal solid waste is disposed of through landfilling, incineration, and recycling.

A.   LANDFILLS

Landfilling remains the primary disposal strategy, accounting for 55% of Municipal solid waste in 1998. Environmental Protection Agency, supra, at 12.

Subtitle D of the Resource Conservation and Recovery Act (RCRA) prescribes minimum standards for municipal solid waste disposal. For a detailed description of those standards, see John H. Turner, Off to a Good Start: The RCRA Subtitle D Program for Municipal Solid Waste Landfills, 15 Temple Envtl. L. & Tech. J. 1 (1996). RCRA prohibits open dumping of municipal waste, 42 U.S.C. § 6945(a), and sets minimum siting and design criteria for landfills, 42 U.S.C. § 6944, 40 C.F.R. Pt. 258. Those standards prescribe liners, leachate collection systems, and groundwater monitoring wells to minimize the possibility that toxic substances leached from a landfill might contaminate groundwater. Landfill owners and operators must demonstrate financial responsibility, assuring that landfills will be properly closed and adequately cared for after closure. 40 C.F.R. §§ 258.71 to 258.73.

The increased stringency of permitting requirements imposed by RCRA contributed to a nationwide decline in the number of landfills over

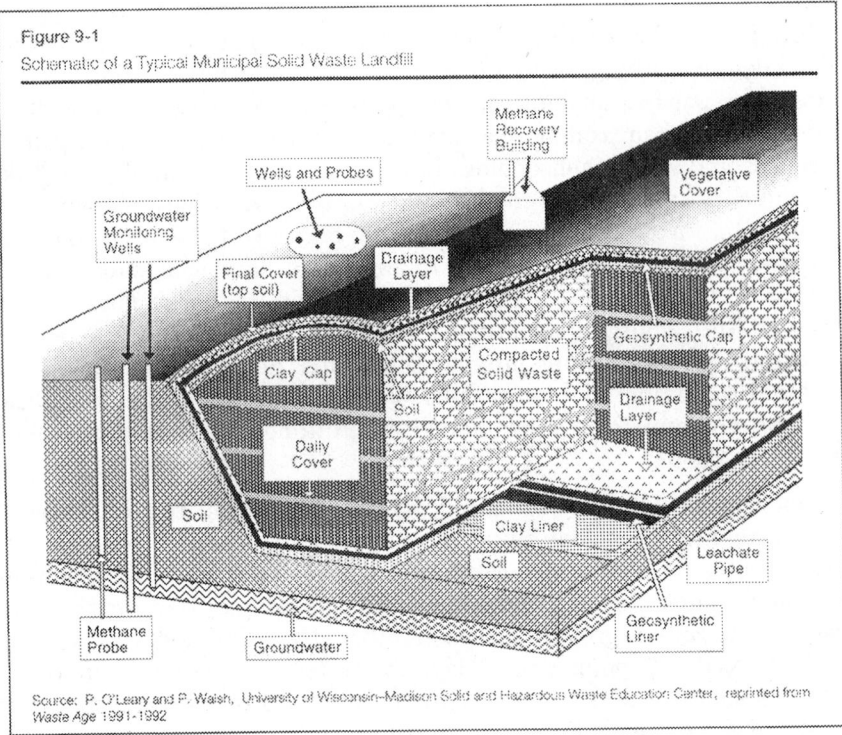

Figure 9-1

Schematic of a Typical Municipal Solid Waste Landfill

Source: P. O'Leary and P. Walsh, University of Wisconsin–Madison Solid and Hazardous Waste Education Center, reprinted from *Waste Age* 1991-1992

the last 10 to 15 years. In 1988, there were 8,000 sanitary landfills nationwide. By 1998, there were only 2,300. Environmental Protection Agency, supra, at 12.

B. INCINERATION

About 17% of the municipal solid waste in the United States is incinerated. Environmental Protection Agency, supra, at 2. Incineration greatly decreases the volume of waste, but it leaves a residue of ash that may be hazardous. Incineration also generates air pollutants that must be controlled to comply with the Clean Air Act.

Burning does offer a potential advantage. It can produce electricity while disposing of waste. In the late 1970s and early 1980s, the combination of the energy crisis and the search for landfill alternatives produced a wave of enthusiasm for garbage incineration. The Public Utility Regulatory Policies Act of 1978 required electric utilities to buy power generated by waste-to-energy facilities, Pub. L. No. 95–617, § 210(a) (codified at 16 U.S.C. § 824a–3), and EPA encouraged their construction. The enthusiasm for incineration proved short-lived, however. By 1990, low prices for oil and natural gas, combined with the high costs of controlling hazardous air emissions, made waste-to-energy facilities economically unattractive by comparison to landfilling in most locations. That may change again in the near future, if electricity costs continue their steep increase in the West and other locations.

C.   RECYCLING

Familiar recyclable materials in municipal solid waste include paper, some plastics, and yard waste, which can be composted to produce garden mulch. Before the industrial age, the high costs of many raw materials encouraged both recycling and source reduction. Until the mid–19th century, for example, paper was made from rags, that is, recycled fabric, rather than wood fibers. Recycling in the U.S. faded with industrialization, briefly rose again as a patriotic endeavor during World War II, then subsided once again.

Today, recycling is enjoying a renaissance, fueled by environmental rather than economic concerns. Recycling levels have risen steeply over the past forty years. In 1960, only six percent of the total municipal solid waste generated, less than six million tons, was recycled. Recycling efforts received a boost in the late 1980s from rising landfill tipping fees and the perception that landfill capacity would soon be exhausted. EPA adopted a national goal of reducing or recycling at least twenty-five percent of municipal solid waste. By 1994, forty-four states had announced similar or more stringent reduction and recycling targets. Frank Ackerman, Why Do We Recycle? 19 (1997). For example, California's Integrated Waste Management Act, Cal. Pub. Res. Code §§ 40000–49620, adopted in 1989, requires communities to divert at least twenty-five percent of their waste by 1995, and fifty percent by 2000.

The much-feared landfill crisis never materialized although landfill space remains limited in a few areas of the country, including the urban northeast. Diversion efforts are only partially responsible for the fading of the landfill crisis. The fear that landfill space was running out had always been exaggerated, fueled by statistics showing a rapid decline in the number of landfill facilities nationwide. Many small landfills did close, but they were replaced by a smaller number of much larger, facilities.

Nonetheless, efforts to increase recycling continue. By 1998, over twenty-eight percent of the nation's municipal waste stream, more than sixty million tons, was recycled, and EPA had raised its national recycling goal to thirty-five percent by 2005. California diverted forty-two percent of its municipal solid waste from disposal in 2000, and predicted that it would soon meet the fifty percent goal. Integrated Waste Management Board, Press Release, California Waste Diversion Up 51 Percent in Last Two Years (January 24, 2001).

The European Community has experimented with building the costs of recycling into the initial purchase price of consumer items. Germany has been a leader in these efforts. In 1991, Germany adopted a law requiring retailers to install bins where consumers could dispose of product packaging free of charge. The law allowed an alternative for "primary packaging," such as the tube that holds toothpaste, as opposed to "secondary packaging" that can be removed and discarded immediately after sale, such as the paper carton holding the toothpaste tube. Retailers did not have to take back primary packaging if effective industry-wide systems for collection and

recycling were available. As expected, retailers leaned on product manufacturers, who reduced secondary packaging and collaboratively established a
number of collection and recovery initiatives for primary packaging. The
best known is the "green dot" program run by a private company, Duales
System Deutschland (DSD). Product manufacturers pay a fee, which varies
with the type and extent of packaging, in return for the right to place a
green dot on their packaging. DSD provides curbside collection facilities for
green dot packaging, which is then sorted and recycled. Manufacturers pass
the green dot fee on to consumers in the price of the product. This system
has both increased recycling and decreased packaging waste. As one observer explains:

> If a company can manage the take-back and valorization of its
> product more cheaply than others through such innovations as packag-
> ing design, it gains a competitive advantage. As a result of this
> dynamic, a stroll through a German supermarket today shows a far
> different shelf than just five years ago. There are more concentrated
> products, lightweight bottles, refills, and far less outer packaging and
> plastic than before. Toothpaste, for example, is no longer sold with an
> outer carton.

James Salzman, Sustainable Consumption and the Law, 27 Envtl. L. 1243,
1273 (1997).

There are some difficulties with the green dot system, however.

DSD's waste management costs have exceeded estimates, partially
because the public puts non-recyclable material in the curbside recyclable bins. In addition, while 90 percent of the primary packages carried
the green dot, only 60 percent of the companies paid the required
licensing fee, leaving DSD in financial straits. Third, DSD does not
have the capacity to recycle all the materials collected, forcing the
company to store many recycled materials or export them for processing.

Germany's Polluter Pays Concept Could Be Applied to U.S. Industry, 17
Int'l Env't Rptr. (BNA) 368 (1994).

A few years after instituting packaging "take-back" requirements,
Germany extended the idea from packaging to a wide variety of products,
requiring that manufacturers provide for their recycling or incineration in
a waste-to-energy facility. The European Union recently adopted a requirement that auto makers take back cars that no longer have resale value, and
ensure that 85% of the material in the cars is recovered for future use. See
Carol J. Williams, EU Sees to It That When Cars Die, They Meet Their
Maker, L.A. Times, Feb. 26, 2000, at A2.

Enthusiasm for recycling is not universal. In a 1996 cover article in the
Sunday New York Times magazine, John Tierney argued that recycling was
economically nonsensical. "Recycling," he wrote, "may be the most wasteful activity in modern America: a waste of time and money, a waste of
human and natural resources." John Tierney, Recycling is Garbage, New
York Times, June 30, 1996, Sec. 6, at 24. Tierney argued primarily that the

economic costs of recycling exceeded its economic benefits. He pointed out that collecting recyclable items, at least in New York City, was more expensive than collecting garbage, and that the City often also had to pay recyclers to accept the material after collection. Tierney went so far as to calculate the costs to New Yorkers of recycling their garbage by multiplying the time it took a local college student to sort, rinse, and deliver his recyclables to a basement collection point—eight minutes per week—times the standard hourly wage for a janitor in New York City. His calculation yielded a whopping $792 in additional labor costs per ton of collected material, not counting the cost of the space in which recyclables are stored. He argued that the market should determine whether and to what extent recycling would occur. The easiest way to assure that, he suggested, would be to institute volume-based pricing for garbage collection (sometimes called "pay-as-you-throw") instead of covering waste disposal costs through property or other general taxes. If recycling proved more economically attractive than waste disposal for some or all wastes, consumers would naturally prefer it.

Tierney's article brought a spate of responses. Many critics pointed out that the economic costs of recyclables collection vary with the collection system and the amount collected. The more successful the recycling program, the less the per-unit collection costs tend to be. At least in large cities, diverting a high volume of material to recycling is likely to reduce the costs of garbage collection. Furthermore, where tipping fees are high, savings may more than cover any extra costs of collecting recyclables. Recycling advocates also questioned Tierney's claim that the time spent by homeowners in sorting recyclables should be counted as economic costs, noting that we do not pay people for performing other civic duties.

The economic and environmental benefits of recycling are often difficult to quantify. In part that is because they vary with the costs of disposal, by landfilling or incineration, in the local area. But there are other complications. Markets for recycled materials take time to develop, and may fluctuate widely even when mature. The environmental impacts of both virgin production and recycled production can be hidden.

How to achieve the optimum level of recycling is also a knotty issue. Although no one argues against the theory of unit-based pricing for disposal (pay-as-you-throw), even such a seemingly obvious step turns out to have significant drawbacks. One reason most communities in the U.S. have traditionally financed waste disposal from general taxes is to encourage appropriate disposal. Disposal charges, even at levels below the true costs of disposal, encourage significant quantities of illegal dumping, which may be quite costly to prevent or correct. See Don Fullerton and Thomas C. Kinnaman, Household Responses to Pricing Garbage by the Bag, 86 Am. Econ. Rev. 971 (1996).

D. WASTE MINIMIZATION

Another strategy to reduce disposal is waste minimization, also known as source reduction. The best way to handle waste may be not to produce it in the first place. Reducing packaging and consuming less are two ways to minimize waste production. Mandatory recycling schemes, such as the German green dot program, may encourage waste minimization if the costs of recycling are high.

The Pollution Prevention Act of 1990, 42 U.S.C. §§ 13101–13109, gives the force of federal law to waste reduction efforts. The Act authorizes the EPA to encourage pollution prevention efforts, requires companies to provide information on source reduction and recycling activities, and requires the EPA to review its regulations to determine their potential for encouraging source reduction.

NOTES AND QUESTIONS

1. *Federalism and Waste Disposal.* What, if anything, justifies federal regulation of solid waste disposal? Would federal imposition of recycling or waste minimization mandates be justifiable?

2. *Evaluating Recycling.* How should a community, state, or nation determine the appropriate level of recycling? Should recycling pay for itself in the short term? Why or why not? If recycling must be subsidized, what is the appropriate source of funds? A surcharge on landfill tipping fees? Increased property taxes?

Given the questionable economic justifications in many locations, what explains the high popularity of recycling among citizens? Does recycling simply provide a means of expiating our guilt for other environmental sins, perhaps allowing us to evade feelings of responsibility for more serious problems? Or does it provide indirect or non-monetary benefits that might justify financial subsidies?

A recent EPA publication states that recycling: provides jobs, reduces the need for landfilling and incineration, prevents pollution; saves energy, reduces greenhouse gas emissions (from landfills), conserves natural resources, and helps protect the environment for future generations. Environmental Protection Agency, Puzzled About Recycling's Value? Look Beyond the Bin, January 1998, at 1. Do you agree with these claims? Are any of these benefits likely to be missed by the market? Can you think of any other benefits from recycling? Might recycling increase awareness of wasteful consumption? Would that be valuable?

3. *Strategies to Encourage Recycling or Source Reduction.* If recycling is desirable, what strategy or combination of strategies should be used to encourage it? Considering equity, administrative costs, and feasibility, what role would you assign to: subsidies for recycled products; other positive economic incentives (one example is a contest in which waste management officials in Berkeley, California, periodically examine the garbage of volunteers, awarding cash prizes if the amount of recyclable material is below a certain threshold); surcharges on waste disposal; surcharges on consumption of virgin materials; or recycling mandates imposed on individuals or local governments?

If mandates are part of the strategy, how should they be enforced? California's Integrated Waste Management Act, for example, permits the imposition of fines up to $10,000 per day on communities which fail to meet the diversion goals, with the money used to boost diversion rates in the jurisdiction. Cal. Pub. Res. code § 41850(a). Are such penalties appropriate? Will they prove politically difficult to impose?

SECTION 2. MANAGEMENT OF HAZARDOUS WASTE

The Resource Conservation and Recovery Act (RCRA) sets up a "cradle-to-grave" system for regulation of hazardous wastes from their generation to their ultimate disposal. RCRA does not deal with the clean-up of inactive hazardous waste disposal sites, which is covered instead by the Comprehensive Environmental Response, Compensation and Liability Act (CERCLA, see Chapter 9). States remain primarily responsible for the difficult task of siting new hazardous waste facilities, and may regulate hazardous waste management more stringently than RCRA mandates.

A. SUBTITLE C OF THE RESOURCE CONSERVATION AND RECOVERY ACT

The amount of hazardous waste produced in the United States has grown continually since World War II, reaching 279 million tons in 1995. RCRA's principal thrust is tracking and regulation of these wastes from generation to disposal in order to protect human health and the environment. To that end, Subtitle C of RCRA, 42 U.S.C. §§ 6921–6939e, regulates the generation, transport, treatment, storage, and disposal of hazardous wastes. The Subtitle C program covers an enormous number of facilities and entities, including about 2,000 treatment, storage and disposal facilities (often referred to by the acronym TSDFs), 23,000 transporters, and 775,-000 generators of hazardous waste.

1. A BRIEF OVERVIEW OF SUBTITLE C

The requirements of Subtitle C apply only to "solid waste" identified as "hazardous." A preliminary, and highly contentious, issue is whether the material is a solid waste at all. If so, it is considered a hazardous waste if it has been specifically identified by EPA as hazardous or if it is ignitable, corrosive, reactive, or toxic under prescribed test conditions. See 40 C.F.R. Part 261. Radioactive wastes are excluded from RCRA's coverage. See 42 U.S.C. § 6903(27). Medical wastes are subject to the special regulations of Subtitle J, 42 U.S.C. §§ 6992–6992k.

Generators of hazardous waste are subject to RCRA section 3002, 42 U.S.C. § 6922. EPA defines as "generators" persons who produce hazardous waste or cause a hazardous waste to become subject to regulation. 40 C.F.R. § 260.10. Generators must keep accurate records of the waste they generate, prepare a manifest to accompany waste sent off-site for disposal, and submit periodic reports to EPA. Manifests for off-site treatment, storage, or disposal must certify that the generator has a waste minimization program in place, and that the proposed method of treatment, storage, or disposal minimizes present and future hazards to human health and the environment to the extent practicable. "Small" generators, who produce no more than 100 kilograms of hazardous waste per month, are exempt from many of these requirements. See 40 C.F.R. 261.5(b).

Transporters are regulated under RCRA section 3003, 42 U.S.C. § 6923. They must keep adequate records, accept only properly labeled waste, and comply with the manifest system by delivering the waste and its accompanying manifest to the designated facility. Hazardous waste transporters are also regulated by the Department of Transportation under the Hazardous Materials Transportation Act, 49 U.S.C. §§ 5101–5127.

Treatment, storage and disposal of hazardous wastes are regulated by RCRA sections 3004. Treatment, storage, and disposal facilities (TSDFs) must obtain a permit under RCRA section 3005, 42 U.S.C. § 6925, and meet detailed record-keeping, design, operation, and financial responsibility standards promulgated under RCRA section 3004, 42 U.S.C. § 6924. These standards are intended to assure that TSDFs are operated safely and eventually closed in a manner that protects public and environmental health. TSDFs must comply with limitations on the methods of disposal or treatment of specific hazardous wastes. RCRA established a conditional "land ban," prohibiting landfilling of hazardous wastes unless EPA finds that human health and the environment will be adequately protected. The standards for waiver of the land ban have been hotly contested.

RCRA allows EPA to delegate to the states authority to administer and enforce approved state hazardous waste programs in lieu of the federal program. RCRA § 3006, 42 U.S.C. § 6926(b). To gain approval, state programs must be equivalent to, consistent with, and no less stringent than the federal program. Id. As of March 31, 2000, 49 states and territories had gained approval to implement basic hazardous waste programs. Authority to implement programs added to satisfy the 1984 Hazardous and Solid Waste Amendments, including land disposal restrictions, corrective action, and toxicity characteristic testing, is delegated separately. As of March 31, 2000, only Vermont had received full delegation for all aspects of its hazardous waste program.

CLASS DISCUSSION PROBLEM: THE PHELPS–LEE FOUNDRY

The Phelps–Lee Foundry uses sand for mold liners and core butts in its casting operations. During use, the sand becomes contaminated with small amounts of copper, chromium, brass, tin, lead and other metals. According to EPA regulations, a solid waste exhibits the characteristic of toxicity if, under standard testing conditions, an extract of the waste contains chromium or lead at levels of 5 mg/l or above. Phelps–Lee has not tested its waste sand.

Phelps–Lee has developed a new process for reconditioning used sand for reuse and recovering the contaminating metals, which have significant commercial value. The process separates the metals from the sand at high efficiency. The products are clean sand, which Phelps–Lee returns to its process, and purified metals. Phelps–Lee reuses some of the metals in its foundry operations and sells others.

Phelps–Lee has patented this process and now uses it routinely. Prior to reclamation, the used sand is piled near the reclamation plant on a liner designed to protect the ground from contact with the sand or water leaching through the sand. All sand is reclaimed within a day or two of its use in casting.

The Phelps–Lee reclamation process uses large amounts of water and produces a large volume of effluent, which contains unspecified amounts of metals. Phelps–Lee pumps the effluent into a holding pond. The company contends that it is not necessary to treat the water, since it evaporates naturally or seeps down into the soil, which acts as a natural filter removing the metals from the water. Periodically, a metal reclamation company removes the residue or "sludge" that collects on the bottom of the pond, and hauls it away to a reclamation plant. Phelps–Lee does not charge for the sludge.

(a) Recently Phelps–Lee received a letter from the EPA stating that the company may be subject to RCRA's regulatory requirements as a waste treatment, storage, and disposal facility. Is Phelps–Lee in violation of RCRA? If so, what remedies would be appropriate?

(b) Suppose Phelps–Lee tested its used sand using EPA's prescribed toxicity characteristic leaching procedure, and determined that the extract contained only 0.4 mg/l chromium and 0.3 mg/l lead. Could EPA list the used sand as a hazardous waste? Must it do so?

2. IDENTIFYING "SOLID WASTE"

Excerpts from the Resource Conservation and Recovery Act

42 U.S.C. §§ 6901–6992k.

Sec. 1004 Definitions

(27) The term "solid waste" means any garbage, refuse, sludge from a waste treatment plant, water supply treatment plant, or air pollution control facility and other discarded material, including solid, liquid, semi-solid, or contained gaseous material resulting from industrial, commercial, mining, and agricultural operations, and from community activities, but does not include solid or dissolved material in domestic sewage, or solid or dissolved materials in irrigation return flows or industrial discharges which are point sources subject to permits under [section 402 of the Clean Water Act], or source, special nuclear, or byproduct material as defined by the Atomic Energy Act of 1954, as amended.

Excerpts from the Environmental Protection Agency Regulations

40 C.F.R. Part 261.

Sec. 261.2   Definition of solid waste

(a) (1) A *solid waste* is any discarded material that is not excluded by § 261.4(a) or that is not excluded by variance granted under §§ 260.30 and 260.31.

(2) A *discarded material* is any material which is:

    (i) *Abandoned*, as explained in paragraph (b) of this section; or

    (ii) *Recycled*, as explained in paragraph (c) of this section; or

    (iii) *Considered inherently waste-like*, as explained in paragraph (d) of this section; or

    (iv) A *military munition* identified as a solid waste in 40 CFR 266.202.

(b) Materials are solid waste if they are *abandoned* by being:

(1) Disposed of; or

(2) Burned or incinerated; or

(3) Accumulated, stored, or treated (but not recycled) before or in lieu of being abandoned by being disposed of, burned, or incinerated.

(c) Materials are solid wastes if they are *recycled*—or accumulated, stored, or treated before recycling—as specified in paragraphs (c)(1) through (4) of this section.

    (1) *Used in a manner constituting disposal.* (i) Materials noted with a " * " in Column 1 of Table I are solid wastes when they are:

        (A) Applied to or placed on the land in a manner that constitutes disposal; or

        (B) Used to produce products that are applied to or placed on the land or are otherwise contained in products that are applied to or placed on the land (in which cases the product itself remains a solid waste).

(ii) However, commercial chemical products listed in § 261.33 are not solid wastes if they are applied to the land and that is their ordinary manner of use.

    (2) *Burning for energy recovery.* (i) Materials noted with a " * " in column 2 of Table 1 are solid wastes when they are:

        (A) Burned to recover energy;

        (B) Used to produce a fuel or are otherwise contained in fuels (in which cases the fuel itself remains a solid waste).

(ii) However, commercial chemical products listed in § 261.33 are not solid wastes if they are themselves fuels.

(3) *Reclaimed.* Materials noted with a " * " in column 3 of Table 1 are solid wastes when reclaimed (except as provided under 40 CFR 261.4(a)(17)). Materials noted with a "——" in column 3 of Table 1 are not solid wastes when reclaimed (except as provided under 40 CFR 261.4(a)(17)).

(4) *Accumulated speculatively.* Materials noted with a " * " in column 4 of Table 1 are solid wastes when accumulated speculatively.

(d) *Inherently waste-like materials.* [Specified materials] are solid wastes when they are recycled in any manner * * *.

(3) The Administrator will use the following criteria to add wastes to that list:

(i)(A) The materials are ordinarily disposed of, burned or incinerated; or

(B) The materials contain toxic constituents listed in appendix VIII of part 261 and these constituents are not ordinarily found in raw materials or products for which the materials substitute (or are found in raw materials or products in smaller concentration) and are not used or reused during the recycling process; and

(ii) The material may pose a substantial hazard to human health and the environment when recycled.

(e) *Materials that are not solid waste when recycled.*

(1) Materials are not solid wastes when they can be shown to be recycled by being:

(i) Used or reused as ingredients in an industrial process to make a product, provided the materials are not being reclaimed; or

(ii) Used or reused as effective substitutes for commercial products; or

(iii) Returned to the original process from which they are generated, without first being reclaimed or land disposed. The material must be returned as a substitute for feedstock materials. * * *

(2) The following materials are solid wastes, even if the recycling involves use, reuse, or return to the original process (described in paragraphs (e)(1)(i) through (iii) of this section):

(i) Materials used in a manner constituting disposal, or used to produce products that are applied to the land; or

(ii) Materials burned for energy recovery, used to produce a fuel, or contained in fuels; or

(iii) Materials accumulated speculatively * * *.

TABLE 1

	Use constituting disposal (§ 261.2(c)(1)) (1)	Energy recovery/fuel (§ 261.2(c)(2)) (2)	Reclamation (§ 261.2(c) (except as provided in 261.4(a)(17) for mineral processing secondary materials)(3)) (3)	Speculative accumulation (§ 261.2(c)(4)) (4)
Spent Materials	(*)	(*)	(*)	(*)
Sludges (listed in 40 CFR part 261.31 or 261.32) . . .	(*)	(*)	(*)	(*)
Sludges exhibiting a characteristic of hazardous waste	(*)	(*)	. . . .	(*)
By-products (listed in 40 CFR part 261.31 or 261.32)	(*)	(*)	(*)	(*)
By-products exhibiting a characteristic of hazardous waste	(*)	(*)	. . . .	(*)
Commercial chemical products listed in 40 CFR part 261.33	(*)	(*)	. . . .	. . . .
Scrap metal	(*)	(*)	(*)	(*)

Note: The terms "spent materials," "sludges," "by-products," and "scrap metal" and "processed scrap metal" are defined in § 261.1.

Sec. 260.30 Variances from classification as a solid waste.

In accordance with the standards and criteria in § 260.31 and the procedures in § 260.33, the Administrator may determine on a case-by-case basis that the following recycled materials are not solid wastes:

(a) Materials that are accumulated speculatively without sufficient amounts being recycled (as defined in § 261.1(c)(8) of this chapter);

(b) Materials that are reclaimed and then reused within the original primary production process in which they were generated;

(c) Materials that have been reclaimed but must be reclaimed further before the materials are completely recovered.

* * *

American Petroleum Institute v. United States Environmental Protection Agency

United States Court of Appeals, District of Columbia Circuit, 2000.
216 F.3d 50.

■ Per Curiam:

* * *

RCRA is a comprehensive environmental statute granting EPA authority to regulate solid and hazardous wastes. "Solid wastes" are governed by Subtitle D of RCRA, and are generally subject to less stringent management standards than "hazardous wastes" which are regulated under Subtitle C. For purposes of RCRA, Congress defined solid waste as follows:

The term "solid waste" means any garbage, refuse, sludge from a

FIGURE 2
DEFINITION OF A SOLID WASTE

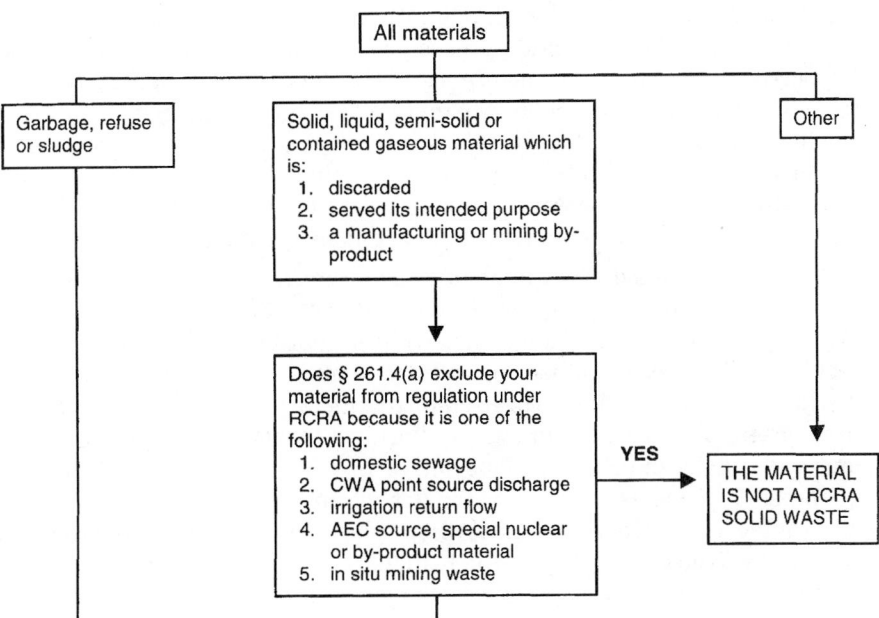

Adapted from 40 C.F.R. Part 260, App. 1.

waste treatment plant, water supply treatment plant, or air pollution control facility and other discarded material, including solid, liquid, semisolid, or contained gaseous material resulting from industrial, commercial, mining, and agricultural operations, and from community activities. . . .

42 U.S.C. § 6903(27).

In pursuit of its congressionally conferred duty and authority to regulate solid waste under RCRA, the EPA has adopted regulations defining solid waste for purposes of its hazardous waste regulations: "A solid waste is any discarded material," 40 C.F.R. § 261.2(a)(1) (1999), subject to a number of exclusions enumerated in § 261.4(a) and case-by-case variances under §§ 260.30 and 260.31. The term "discarded material" for purposes of the regulation means any material which is abandoned, recycled, or considered inherently wastelike. 40 C.F.R. § 261.2(a)(2).

In 1994 and 1998 rulemakings in pursuit of its RCRA obligations, the EPA examined the production processes of the petroleum refining industry. As pertinent to the issue before us, EPA considered whether to exclude from the definition of solid waste two secondary materials: oil-bearing wastewaters generated by the petroleum refining industry and recovered oil produced by the petrochemical manufacturing industry. EPA determined that oil-bearing wastewaters are solid waste for purposes of RCRA regulation * * *. Industry petitioners challenge [this conclusion].

In petroleum refining, impurities are removed and usable hydrocarbon fractions are isolated from crude oil feedstock. Large quantities of water are used, and the resulting wastewaters contain a small percentage of residual oil. These "oilbearing wastewaters" are destined for ultimate discharge, but only after a three-step treatment process is first applied. The first phase of treatment, known as "primary treatment," removes certain materials including the oil. This phase has at least two beneficial consequences: (1) it meets a Clean Water Act requirement that refineries remove oil from their wastewater, and (2) it allows refineries to recover a not insignificant quantity of oil (which industry claims can range up to 1,000 barrels a day at certain refineries) which is cycled back into the refinery production process.

Industry petitioners and EPA disagree over when these wastewaters become discarded for purposes of the solid waste definition. While no one disputes that discard has certainly occurred by the time the wastewaters move into the later phases of treatment, the question is whether discard happens before primary treatment, allowing regulation of wastewater as solid waste at that point, or not until primary treatment is complete and oil has been recovered for further processing.

EPA's initial proposal excluded oil-bearing wastewaters. However, it changed its mind in 1994 and concluded that even before the oil is recovered in primary treatment, "the wastewaters are discarded materials and hence solid wastes subject to regulation under RCRA." 59 Fed. Reg. 38,540/1. EPA stated: "Primary wastewater treatment operations exist to treat plant wastewaters." *Id.* at 38,539/3. It noted that the percentage of oil in the wastewater is very small and "not significant in the context of a refinery's overall production activities," and that the Clean Water Act mandates such treatment. *Id.* For these stated reasons, EPA concluded that "[c]learly, wastewater treatment is the main purpose of the systems in question, and any oil recovery is of secondary import." 59 Fed. Reg. at 38,539/3.

EPA restated its conclusion in its subsequent 1995 Proposed Rule and retained it in the Final Rule. See 63 Fed. Reg. at 42,184 (codified at 40 C.F.R. § 261.4(a)(12)(ii)). The actual regulation does not mention wastewaters. But by not being excluded, all wastewaters including oil-bearing wastewaters are considered to fall under EPA's general regulatory definition of solid waste.

Whether a material has been "discarded," subjecting it to RCRA regulation, is a question we have considered in four prior cases. First, in *American Mining Congress v. EPA,* 824 F.2d 1177 (D.C.Cir.1987) ("*AMC I*"), we held that the term "discarded" conforms to its plain meaning. Thus, items that are "disposed of, abandoned, or thrown away" are discarded. *AMC I* concluded that "in-process secondary materials," that is, materials "destined for immediate reuse in another phase of [an] industry's ongoing production process," are not discarded under RCRA. *Id.* at 1185, 1193. We recently reaffirmed that holding in *Association of Battery Recyclers, Inc. v. U.S. EPA,* 208 F.3d 1047 (D.C.Cir.2000), where we reiterated that EPA cannot regulate as solid waste secondary materials "destined for reuse as part of a continuous industrial process" that is therefore "not abandoned or thrown away." *Id.* at 1056.

At the other end of the spectrum we have held that a material that has been "indisputably 'discarded' " can, of course, be subjected to regulation as solid waste. *API v. EPA,* 906 F.2d 729, 741 (D.C.Cir.1990). Where a material was "delivered to [a metals reclamation] facility not as part of an '*ongoing* manufacturing or industrial process' within 'the generating industry,' but as part of a mandatory waste treatment plan prescribed by EPA," we concluded that a material was not precluded from being classified by EPA as a solid waste. *Id.*

A material somewhere between the extremes of ongoing production and indisputable discard was addressed in *American Mining Congress v. EPA,* 907 F.2d 1179 (D.C.Cir.1990) ("*AMC II*"). Industry petitioners claimed that sludges from wastewater stored in surface impoundments, which "may" later be reclaimed for treatment, could not be regulated. *Id.* at 1186. We disagreed and deferred to EPA's determination that such sludges have been discarded. Nothing, we reasoned, prevents EPA from regulating as "solid wastes" materials managed in land disposal units which are no longer part of an industrial process.

* * *

Industry petitioners * * * contend that * * * oil-bearing wastewaters cannot be regulated because they are unquestionably in-process materials not yet discarded. Alternately, even if the status of oil-bearing wastewaters is not so plain, petitioners assert that EPA's conclusion is arbitrary and capricious because it is not based on reasoned decisionmaking. Petitioners emphasize that primary treatment yields valuable oil that is reinserted into the refining processes in a continuous operation. They also claim that oil recovery operations began long before Clean Water Act regulations required it. In sum, they contend that oil recovery in primary treatment is a part of in-process oil production.

At bottom, the parties disagree over the proper characterization of primary treatment. Is it simply a step in the act of discarding? Or is it the last step in a production process before discard? Our prior cases have not had to draw a line for deciding when discard has occurred. While the issue was closest in *AMC II,* the sludges in dispute there were described as being stored in surface impoundments "that may at some time in the future be reclaimed." *AMC II,* 907 F.2d at 1186. We concluded that EPA's interpretation of "discarded" as including the sludges was reasonable and entitled to deference under Chevron U.S.A. Inc. v. Natural Resources Defense Council, Inc., 467 U.S. 837, 842–45 (1984). * * *

It may be permissible for EPA to determine that the predominant purpose of primary treatment is discard. Legal abandonment of property is premised on determining the intent to abandon, which requires an inquiry into facts and circumstances. Where an industrial by-product may be characterized as discarded or "in process" material, EPA's choice of characterization is entitled to deference. However, the record must reflect that EPA engaged in reasoned decisionmaking to decide which characterization is appropriate. The record in this case is deficient in that regard. EPA has noted two purposes of primary treatment and concludes, "[c]learly, wastewater treatment is the main purpose." 1994 Rule, 59 Fed. Reg. 38,539/3. As English teachers have long taught, a conclusion is not "clear" or "obvious" merely because one says so.

EPA points out that primary treatment only recovers a small amount of oil relative to the entire output of a typical refining facility. However, the oil is still valuable and usable, so that reason alone cannot show discard. The rock of a diamond mine may only contain a tiny portion of precious carbon, but that is enough to keep miners busy. According to claims by the refining industry, the net amount of oil recovered may reach 1,000 barrels a day for certain refineries. It is plausible to claim, as industry petitioners do, that refiners engage in primary treatment first and foremost to recover this usable resource. At the very least, EPA cannot merely rely on the small relative amount of oil recovered from primary treatment without further explanation.

EPA also notes that the Clean Water Act requires primary treatment before discharge. If refiners got nothing from primary treatment, this might be a compelling rationale because it would be hard to explain why, other than to discard, refiners would engage in a costly treatment activity with no economic benefits. However, petitioners claim they would engage in primary treatment regardless of the treatment standards in order to recover the desired oil. EPA does not explain why this possibly valid motivation is not compelling. EPA makes no attempt to balance the costs and benefits of primary treatment, or otherwise to explain why the Clean Water Act requirements are the real motivation behind primary treatment. Indeed, without further explanation, it is not inherently certain why a substance is definitively "discarded" if its possessor is continuing to process it, even though the possessor's decision to continue processing may have been influenced, or even predominantly motivated, by some external factor. Otherwise put, it is not so obvious as EPA would have us hold that if the industry petitioners conceded that their overriding motivation in further processing the wastewaters was compliance with Clean Water Act regulations that they would then conclusively be discarding the material in question even while further processing it. If the non-Clean Water Act benefits of the initial treatment are enough to justify firms' incurring the costs (petitioners point to material in the record that may support such a proposition), the EPA would have to reconcile that fact with any conclusion that the Clean Water Act purpose was primary.

In short, EPA has not set forth why it has concluded that the compliance motivation predominates over the reclamation motivation. Perhaps equally importantly it has not explained why that conclusion, even if validly reached, compels the further conclusion that the wastewater has been discarded. Therefore, because the agency has failed to provide a rational explanation for its decision, we hold the decision to be arbitrary and capricious. We therefore vacate the portion of EPA's decision declining to exclude oil-bearing wastewaters from the statutory definition of solid waste, and remand for further proceedings. We do not suggest any particular result on remand, only a reasoned one demonstrating when discard occurs if EPA wishes to assert jurisdiction.

NOTES AND QUESTIONS

1. *Identifying Solid Waste.* RCRA and its implementing regulations have been described as mind-numbingly complex. That complexity begins with the definition of "solid waste." Even experienced environmental lawyers struggle to understand whether a particular material is a solid waste for RCRA purposes. That question is crucial, because only solid wastes are potentially subject to the detailed requirements of Subtitle C.

How helpful is the flowchart EPA provides (reproduced at Figure 2)? Must the material be solid? Must it be waste, as that term is ordinarily understood? Are all wastes included?

Why is it so difficult to produce a simple definition of the term solid waste? What tensions do the statutory and regulatory definitions struggle to resolve? What do you suppose accounts for the statutory exemptions?

2. *Statutory and Regulatory Definitions.* The regulatory definition of "solid waste" in 40 C.F.R. § 261.2, excerpted above, "applies only to wastes that are also hazardous for purposes of the regulations implementing subtitle C of RCRA." 40 C.F.R. § 261.1(b)(1). Only materials meeting the regulatory definition of solid waste, which EPA considers somewhat narrower than the statutory definition, can be hazardous wastes subject to the cradle-to-grave regulatory and record-keeping requirements of subtitle C. The statutory definition governs actions to abate imminent and substantial endangerment to health or the environment caused by solid waste. Abatement actions are discussed further in Section A(5) below.

What materials might meet the statutory, but not the regulatory, definition of solid waste? EPA interprets the regulatory definition to require that a material be not only discarded, but abandoned. One place the agency has drawn a distinction between the two definitions is in the context of military munitions. The regulatory definition of solid waste, according to EPA, does not include unexploded ordinance and munition fragments left after firing at a range, although it does include ordinance recovered from the range or buried in place after firing. EPA concedes that the statutory definition of solid waste includes ordinance and munition fragments that land off range and are not promptly retrieved or rendered non-hazardous, so that a lawsuit could compel abatement of any imminent and substantial threat associated with those munitions. See 40 C.F.R. § 266.202. The agency contends that neither definition includes ordinance and fragments that remain on the range after firing.

Does it make sense to define "solid waste" differently for subtitle C than for imminent and substantial endangerment actions? Is EPA's application of the definition to munitions reasonable? Do you agree that spent bullets that fall to the ground on the firing range are not statutory solid waste, but those that fall off the range are? What justifies that distinction? Is it relevant that firing is a normal and expected use of munitions? The D.C. Circuit upheld EPA's military munitions rule in Military Toxics Project v. Environmental Protection Agency, 146 F.3d 948 (D.C.Cir.1998). On application of the statutory definition to a non-military firing range, see Connecticut Coastal Fishermen's Ass'n v. Remington Arms Co., 989 F.2d 1305 (2d Cir.1993).

3. *Recycling Versus Waste.* One of the most difficult aspects of identifying solid waste is distinguishing materials that are truly waste from those undergoing recycling or further processing for the extraction or production of useful materials. Early identification of waste materials serves RCRA's goal of tracking hazardous wastes from their production to their ultimate disposal in order to ensure appropriate treatment at every step in between. However, as the *American Petroleum Institute* excerpt demonstrates, it is not always easy to determine where processing, reprocessing or recycling end and disposal or treatment of waste begins. How did EPA attempt to draw that line for oil-bearing wastewaters? What flaws did the court find in EPA's analysis? What explanation would be required to convince the court that treatment was the predominant purpose of wastewater processing? If EPA could make that showing, would that automatically make the wastewaters "solid waste" for RCRA purposes? If not, what else would be required?

Can materials be both waste and raw materials? Suppose the Acme Corporation purchases lead plates which have been removed from used batteries, removes the lead from those plates and produces lead ingots, which it then sells. Are the plates Acme uses as its raw material "solid waste"? See United States v. ILCO, 996 F.2d 1126 (11th Cir.1993).

4. *Is Fine-Tuning Needed?* RCRA allows material falling outside the definition of "solid waste" to essentially escape regulation, while imposing requirements viewed by industry as extremely burdensome on those solid wastes that are also hazardous. RCRA therefore may under-regulate hazardous materials that are not "solid waste." On the other hand, imposition of additional regulations on materials that are destined for reuse, reclamation, or recycling may discourage practices that are environmentally desirable in the sense that they conserve natural resources. Would a regulatory scheme less dependent on whether the material is waste and more finely tuned to the hazards posed by the material in a particular process be preferable to the current scheme? Could such a scheme be designed and implemented, or would it be too complex to be practical?

3. IDENTIFYING "HAZARDOUS WASTE"

Excerpts from the Resource Conservation and Recovery Act

42 U.S.C. §§ 6901–6992k.

Sec. 1004 Definitions

(5) The term "hazardous waste" means a solid waste, or combination of solid wastes, which because of its quantity, concentration, or physical, chemical, or infectious characteristics may—

(A) cause, or significantly contribute to an increase in mortality or an increase in serious irreversible, or incapacitating reversible, illness; or

(B) pose a substantial present or potential hazard to human health or the environment when improperly treated, stored, transported, or disposed of, or otherwise managed.

* * *

Sec. 3001 Identification and listing of hazardous waste

(a) Not later than eighteen months after October 21, 1976, the Administrator shall, after notice and opportunity for public hearing, and after consultation with appropriate Federal and State agencies, develop and promulgate criteria for identifying the characteristics of hazardous waste, and for listing hazardous waste, which should be subject to the provisions of this subchapter, taking into account toxicity, persistence, and degradability in nature, potential for accumulation in tissue, and other related factors such as flammability, corrosiveness, and other hazardous characteristics. Such criteria shall be revised from time to time as may be appropriate.

(b)(1) Not later than eighteen months after October 21, 1976, and after notice and opportunity for public hearing, the Administrator shall promulgate regulations identifying the characteristics of hazardous waste, and listing particular hazardous wastes (within the meaning of section 6903(5) of this title), which shall be subject to the provisions of this subchapter. Such regulations shall be based on the criteria promulgated under subsection (a) of this section and shall be revised from time to time thereafter as may be appropriate. * * *

———

Under RCRA, only solid wastes can be hazardous wastes. EPA regulations specifically exclude some solid wastes, including household wastes, agricultural wastes used as fertilizers, and drilling wastes from oil and natural gas exploration, from hazardous waste classification. See 40 C.F.R. § 261.4(b). Solid wastes not excluded by § 261.4(b) are hazardous wastes if they qualify as either *characteristic wastes* or *listed wastes.*

Solid wastes are characteristic wastes if they exhibit any of four hazardous characteristics: ignitability, corrosivity, reactivity, or toxicity. Ignitable wastes burn easily, posing a threat of fire. Corrosive wastes are strong acids and bases, capable of eating through metals. Reactive wastes are unstable, with the potential to explode, react violently with water, or produce toxic fumes when exposed to water or strong acid or base. Toxic wastes have the potential to release toxic substances to the environment in toxic concentrations if handled improperly. EPA regulations further define these characteristics, and prescribe tests for determining if a particular solid waste exhibits them. See 40 C.F.R. Part 261, Subpart C.

Of the four characteristics, toxicity is the most important, and the most controversial. EPA has prescribed a test, known as the Toxicity Characteristic Leaching Procedure (TCLP), intended to simulate the leaching process in a landfill. See 40 C.F.R. § 261.24. The TCLP rule was upheld against an industry challenge in Edison Electric Institute v. U.S. EPA, 2 F.3d 438 (D.C.Cir.1993). In a 1996 study, EPA acknowledged some shortcomings of the TCLP. See U.S. Environmental Protection Agency, Hazardous Waste Characteristics Scoping Study (1996). But the agency has been unable to identify a better method for accurately predicting the toxicity characteristics of leachate.

Waste generators are responsible for determining if their wastes are characteristic hazardous wastes. EPA regulations give generators the option of undertaking the prescribed tests (or their functional equivalent) or "[a]pplying knowledge of the hazard characteristic of the waste in light of the materials or the processes used." 40 C.F.R. § 262.11(c).

Solid wastes are also hazardous for RCRA purposes if EPA has listed them as hazardous. The agency currently maintains three separate lists. The first includes hazardous wastes from non-specific sources (40 C.F.R. § 261.31). These wastes, known as "F wastes" because their EPA identification numbers begin with F, include spent solvents and wastes from chemical processes. The second list (40 C.F.R. § 261.32) is "K wastes," hazardous wastes from specific manufacturing processes, such as wood preserving and the chemical production. The third list (40 C.F.R. § 261.33) consists of discarded commercial chemicals or chemical intermediates that are hazardous ("U wastes") or acutely hazardous ("P wastes").

Generators of a listed waste who believe the waste from their facility is relatively innocuous can petition for exclusion of their waste from the list through a process known as "delisting." To obtain an exclusion, the generator must demonstrate that the facility's waste does not exhibit the criteria for which the waste category as a whole was listed. See 40 C.F.R. § 260.22. If a petition succeeds, the waste from that facility is no longer considered a listed waste. Waste generators view the delisting process as slow, expensive, and uncertain. See, e.g., Jeffrey M. Gaba, The Mixture and

Derived-from Rules Under RCRA: Once a Hazardous Waste Always a Hazardous Waste?, 21 Envtl. L. Rep. 10033 (1991).

Excerpts from Environmental Protection Agency Regulations

40 C.F.R. Part 261.

Sec. 261.11   Criteria for listing hazardous waste

(a) The Administrator shall list a solid waste as a hazardous waste only upon determining that the solid waste meets one of the following criteria:

(1) It exhibits any of the characteristics of hazardous waste identified in subpart C.

(2) It has been found to be fatal to humans in low doses or, in the absence of data on human toxicity, it has been shown in studies to have an oral LD 50 toxicity (rat) of less than 50 milligrams per kilogram, an inhalation LC 50 toxicity (rat) of less than 2 milligrams per liter, or a dermal LD 50 toxicity (rabbit) of less than 200 milligrams per kilogram or is otherwise capable of causing or significantly contributing to an increase in serious irreversible, or incapacitating reversible, illness.* (Waste listed in accordance with these criteria will be designated Acute Hazardous Waste.)

(3) It contains any of the toxic constituents listed on appendix VIII and, after considering the following factors, the Administrator concludes that the waste is capable of posing a substantial present or potential hazard to human health or the environment when improperly treated, stored, transported or disposed of, or otherwise managed:

(i) The nature of the toxicity presented by the constituent.

(ii) The concentration of the constituent in the waste.

(iii) The potential of the constituent or any toxic degradation product of the constituent to migrate from the waste into the environment under the types of improper management considered in paragraph (a)(3)(vii) of this section.

(iv) The persistence of the constituent or any toxic degradation product of the constituent.

(v) The potential for the constituent or any toxic degradation product of the constituent to degrade into non-harmful constituents and the rate of degradation.

(vi) The degree to which the constituent or any degradation product of the constituent bioaccumulates in ecosystems.

---

* LD 50 is the dose, expressed in weight toxin per body weight, that is lethal to 50% of the animals tested under standard conditions. LC 50 is the concentration lethal to 50% of test subjects.—Eds.

(vii) The plausible types of improper management to which the waste could be subjected.

(viii) The quantities of the waste generated at individual generation sites or on a regional or national basis.

(ix) The nature and severity of the human health and environmental damage that has occurred as a result of the improper management of wastes containing the constituent.

(x) Action taken by other governmental agencies or regulatory programs based on the health or environmental hazard posed by the waste or waste constituent.

(xi) Such other factors as may be appropriate.

Substances will be listed on Appendix VIII only if they have been shown in scientific studies to have toxic, carcinogenic, mutagenic or teratogenic effects on humans or other life forms. (Wastes listed in accordance with these criteria will be designated Toxic Wastes.)

(b) The Administrator may list classes or types of solid waste as hazardous waste if he has reason to believe that individual wastes, within the class or type of waste, typically or frequently are hazardous under the definition of hazardous waste found in Section 1004(5) of the Act.

* * *

Dithiocarbamate Task Force v. Environmental Protection Agency

United States Court of Appeals, District of Columbia Circuit, 1996.
98 F.3d 1394.

■ STEPHEN F. WILLIAMS, Circuit Judge.

This consolidated case concerns four classes of carbamate compounds—carbamates proper, carbamoyl oximes, thiocarbamates and dithiocarbamates (collectively "carbamates")—whose similar names reflect similarities in their chemical origins and structures. All are derivatives of carbamic acid. Carbamates and derivative products are used as pesticides, herbicides and fungicides; they are also used in various ways by the rubber, wood and textile industries. In the rulemaking giving rise to this lawsuit the Environmental Protection Agency listed many of these carbamate-based products, as well as waste streams generated in carbamate-based production processes, as hazardous wastes under the Resource Conservation and Recovery Act, 42 U.S.C. §§ 6901–6992k ("RCRA") (1994). Petitioners, the Dithiocarbamate Task Force (treated collectively with intervenor Uniroyal Chemical Co. as "DTF" or the "Task Force"), Zeneca Inc., and Troy Chemical Corp., are (or represent) manufacturers who make various carbamate-based products or use carbamates in their production processes. They challenge a portion of these listings as arbitrary and capricious.

Because we find that in promulgating some of the challenged rules EPA failed to meet the minimum standard required of it by the Administrative Procedure Act, see 5 U.S.C. § 706(2)(A) (1994), we vacate in part and affirm in part.

* * *

Once the EPA decides to list a waste as hazardous, the substance is assigned a particular code and included in the appropriate lists in Subpart D of Part 261. Wastes generated by manufacturing processes are listed as K wastes. Chemical products or manufacturing chemical intermediates that are hazardous if they are discarded or intended to be discarded are listed as P or U wastes, the P designation being reserved for "acute hazardous wastes" of this type. (EPA made 18 P listings in this rulemaking but none is disputed here.)

* * *

The Present Rulemaking: [In this rulemaking,] 40 carbamate industry products received U listings, 18 received P listings and all 58 were listed on Appendix VIII. In addition, manufacturers involved in each of the four classes of carbamates had at least one production waste stream listed as a K waste.

The U Listings: * * *

[P]etitioners argue that in making the determination necessary in the second step of a § 261.11(a)(3) listing—determining "that the waste is capable of posing a substantial present or potential hazard to human health or the environment when improperly treated, stored, transported or disposed of or otherwise managed"—EPA did not consider all of the 11 specified factors. (There are really only ten, since the final factor is a catch-all, allowing the Administrator to consider any other factor she finds relevant.) EPA argues both that § 261.11(a)(3) does not require the Administrator to consider all ten factors, and that in any event she did consider them.

The theory that § 261.11(a)(3) does not require consideration of the ten factors defies the language of the rule, which we have already quoted.
* * *

Accordingly, despite the great deference we owe an agency in the interpretation of its own regulations, see Udall v. Tallman, 380 U.S. 1, 4, 85 S.Ct. 792, 795, 13 L.Ed.2d 616 (1965), we must apply the regulation's specific language over the agency's current interpretation.

If EPA finds a factor to be irrelevant or unimportant in a particular listing, of course, that finding would be subject to very deferential review. But with no such finding, the court has no reason to suppose that the agency considered each factor, as required by its own regulation.

Almost as an afterthought, EPA argues in its brief that it did consider all the factors in § 261.11(a)(3). At oral argument, counsel for EPA acknowledged that EPA did not consider each factor for each of the products listed, but at most considered them in the aggregate, for each of the four classes of chemicals. Where it is reasonable to consider the factors in relation to a class of chemicals, EPA may do so. As we develop below in connection with the K wastes, that means essentially that if the known similarities of members of a class are such that it is reasonable to infer the presence of a disputed characteristic throughout the class (not just among members for which it has been shown), the EPA is free to draw that inference. * * *

EPA makes two generalizations in its analysis of the U wastes. For some of the § 261.11(a)(3) factors, EPA assumed that it could impute the character of some products to all other products. For other factors, it borrowed from the analysis of the K wastes, as it had conducted field studies relating to the latter but none directly applicable to the products.

Underlying all of EPA's generalizations is the premise that within the four groups, the chemicals have similar structures and therefore similar toxicological effects. At least at some level of generality, we do not understand petitioners to quarrel with the principle that structural similarities in chemicals imply at least some probability of similar attributes. What they do challenge is the legitimacy of the class-wide inferences that EPA makes in considering virtually every factor.

Initially EPA proposed not only individual U listings for identified substances but also a generic U listing for all four classes of chemicals, on the ground that such chemicals were "structurally similar" and "[a]s a group ... exhibit significant toxicity to a number of organisms." In the final rule, however, EPA concluded that its categories "may be overly broad," and abandoned its proposal for generic U listings * * *. Nonetheless, the EPA soldiered on with its class-based approach in making the specific U listings.

EPA's class-based approach allowed it successfully to consider two of the listed factors, "nature of the toxicity" and "concentration," factors (i) and (ii), and petitioners offer no convincing reason to doubt that these may be considered across all products, with the exception of IPBC, U375, discussed below in connection with K156, 157 & 158. As to quantities of U wastes generated, factor (viii), EPA addressed it only in a discussion of the economic impact of the rule, referring to a total quantity of 40 metric tons, which compares with 841,000 metric tons of waste generated as K wastes. Its discussion of other regulatory controls, factor (x), is exceptionally sketchy, considering that most of the substances listed as U wastes are extensively regulated under the Federal Insecticide Fungicide and Rodenticide Act ("FIFRA"), 7 U.S.C. § 136 (1995). Although EPA pointed out that RCRA regulation will not totally duplicate FIFRA regulation, since RCRA regulation exempts *household* users while FIFRA causes the issuance of disposal instructions "to *all* users," see Response to Comments at 66 (emphasis added), the agency's response leaves unclear what the advantage is in covering non-household users twice.

Foremost in our review, however, is EPA's consideration of mismanagement, the defects of which, as we shall see, interact with, and aggravate, the meagerness of the discussion of non-RCRA regulatory controls. Mismanagement is not only specifically listed among the numbered factors, "plausible types of improper management to which the waste could be subjected", factor (vii), but is also an aspect of two others: "[t]he potential of the constituent or any toxic degradation product . . . to migrate . . . into the environment" under improper management, factor (iii), and the "nature and severity of the human health and environmental damage . . . as a result of the improper management of wastes . . .," factor (ix). More important, the very question that the ten factors of § 261.11(a)(3) are supposed to help answer—the hazard posed by the substance—is explicitly phrased in terms of improper management. That language in turn echoes the statutory definition, which (in one of its aspects) looks to whether the substance will "pose a . . . substantial present or potential hazard to human health or the environment when *improperly* treated, stored, transported, or disposed of, or otherwise managed." 42 U.S.C. § 6903(5)(B) (emphasis added). EPA, in turn, said in promulgating § 261.11(a)(3) that it would not consider a substance to pose a "substantial" hazard unless the possibility of mismanagement were plausible. * * *

Most of what the EPA had to say on the subject of mismanagement regarding the U wastes seemed to amount to an assertion of the obvious: accidents will happen. Of course—but if that constituted "plausible mismanagement", see § 261.11(a)(3)(vii), it would be ubiquitous and therefore unnecessary to be considered in a listing, contrary to the express language of § 261.11(a)(3). For specifics, EPA relied heavily on a train wreck in California that spilled a dithiocarbamate (metam-sodium) into a river and so caused environmental destruction. DTF argues that listing would have no *direct* effect on the likelihood of such spills, because the train's handling would in any event have been governed by Department of Transportation regulations. EPA resists that claim, arguing that under § 261.11(a)(3), "[T]he proper inquiry is not whether Subtitle C or other regulatory controls would prevent environmental harm, but whether the substances are *capable* of posing a hazard *if* improperly treated, stored, transported, disposed of or otherwise managed." But even if that be the correct reading of the express reference to mismanagement in § 261.11(a)(3)(vii), DTF's argument would necessarily come back in through factor (x), which looks to the relationship between RCRA regulation and the existing regulatory matrix, presumably with the intention of assuring that products will be listed only where doing so will yield some incremental benefit.

EPA further argues that accidents such as the metam-sodium train spill are relevant to RCRA because listing a product as a hazardous waste is likely to make handlers more careful. Perhaps, but not necessarily. The EPA itself noted in another context that RCRA listing might actually result in a stigma, leading to subterfuge of regulations, see Hazardous Waste Treatment Council v. U.S. EPA, 861 F.2d 270, 272, 275–76 (D.C.Cir.1988), and a commenter in this rulemaking made the same point. As EPA never responded, we have no clue as to its official view of the matter. "[W]e may not supply a reasoned basis for the agency's action that the agency itself has not given." *Motor Vehicle Manufacturers Ass'n v. State Farm Mutual Insurance Co.*, 463 U.S. 29, 43 (1983).

* * *

EPA's effort to generalize from its best evidence of mismanagement, its discussion of bird kills resulting from the "use or possible misuse" of carbofuran, a carbamate proper, is more convincing. Most of these products are herbicides, fungicides and insecticides spread into the environment for agricultural purposes * * *. But EPA's own formulation here, alluding equally to "use or possible misuse," indicates that EPA has expanded the concept of mismanagement to embrace any uses of the chemical, such as spraying on crops. Again factor (x)'s reference to other regulatory measures is pertinent. Hazards from the proper use of such chemicals might justify a ban under FIFRA, 7 U.S.C. § 136a(c)(5)(D), but that is not the purpose of RCRA. Outside the area of increases in mortality or serious illnesses, see 42 U.S.C. § 6903(5)(A), which EPA does not appear to invoke here, the statute is concerned with the hazards of a substance when "*improperly* treated, stored, transported, or disposed of, or otherwise managed." *Id.* at § 6903(5)(B) (emphasis added).

To summarize: EPA's discussion of the quantities of waste is slight and oblique, but we need not consider whether such an inadequacy would require us to vacate the rule. Where EPA falls down completely is on the interlocked topics of other regulatory controls (factor (x)) and mismanagement (factor (vii)). It is tempting to say that the toxicity of these chemicals alone marks them as hazardous, and, of course, in one of the purely colloquial senses of the word, they are. But 40 CFR § 261.11(a)(2) gives explicit toxicity benchmarks that are not satisfied here. That relationship underscores what would be true anyway—that a failure on EPA's part to give serious consideration to the "softer" variables of § 261.11(a)(3) tends to turn its application of that section into an exercise in totally standardless discretion. Accordingly, we vacate the challenged U listings as arbitrary and capricious.

The K–Wastes: In analyzing EPA's approach to the K waste listing, we first note the operation of § 261.11(b), which allows the agency to list classes of wastes which "typically or frequently are hazardous under the definition of hazardous waste found in" RCRA. * * * At oral argument counsel for EPA conceded, correctly we think, that the section does not supply an independent basis for listing, but simply reiterates the truism that regulation by class of substance is appropriate in the cases where the evidence, including of course inferences from relevant similarities of members of the class, is strong enough. As EPA said in promulgating § 261.11(b), it would be appropriate to list as a class "those wastes which demonstrate a reasonable likelihood of hazard as a class," noting that the agency would have to demonstrate that "sufficient uniformity exists or is likely to exist." Identification of Hazardous Waste, 45 Fed.Reg. at 33,114/3. We reject petitioners' claims insofar as they contest this principle.

EPA gathered data for its analysis of the K wastes by sending questionnaires to all manufacturers in the carbamate industry and sampling the waste streams at the eight largest facilities (representing about 89% of the industry's total production). It divided the waste streams into ten groups, constructing a composite, or model, waste stream for each. After a Risk Assessment, it concluded that six of the ten should be listed. * * *

EPA conducted field studies of actual waste streams and performed a risk analysis specific to the waste streams. It pointed to similarities in production processes that support a class-based approach to the various segments of the industry. It also identified constituents of concern in each waste stream. This is a reasonable approach—up to a point. Where EPA is confronted with evidence challenging its classification, it must respond, either by altering the class or by reasonably defending its choices. * * *

K160: Zeneca, the only maker of thiocarbamates, challenges the K160 listing for solid thiocarbamate wastes. Zeneca's attack takes two forms. First, it objects to EPA's inclusion of its wastewater treatment sludge within the K160 listing. Second, it attacks the K160 listing as being based on an arbitrary mismanagement premise. In fact it is unclear whether Zeneca's wastewater treatment sludge is covered by the K160 listing, but we need not address that issue because we must vacate the listing.

EPA assumed that the solid thiocarbamate wastes would be dumped in unlined landfills, even though its understanding at the time was that Zeneca was putting its waste in lined landfills meeting the requirements of Subtitle C of RCRA. EPA defends this mismanagement scenario as plausible, arguing that unlined landfills had been used in the past and that it had no way of knowing if Zeneca would continue to ship its waste to lined landfills.

Of course complete certainty is not possible. But on a parallel issue, deciding not to list wastewaters from the production of thiocarbamates and dithiocarbamates, regardless of past disposal practices, EPA reasoned "that since the carbamate manufactures [sic] have already made a considerable investment in wastewater treatment systems using tanks, [EPA believes] they will continue to use them." Final Rule, 60 Fed. Reg. at 7831/3. The Agency also stated that the past management practice is unlikely to be repeated as "permitting authorities are strongly biased against" it. *Id*. EPA has sought to distinguish that reasoning, on the ground that here the use of high-quality landfills may not represent any capital investment by Zeneca. But the probative fact for the thiocarbamate and dithiocarbamate wastewater was surely not the sunk costs, which cannot properly guide a firm's future allocation of resources, but the fact that its behavior showed that, without a hazardous waste listing, the relevant firms had found it sensible, taking into account all relevant costs and benefits (including litigation risks averted), to adopt adequate disposal methods. The point is equally probative that Zeneca will continue in its practice, and that, if new firms enter the industry, they will follow suit. Because EPA failed to identify a plausible mismanagement scenario, we vacate the listing of K160.

NOTES AND QUESTIONS

1. *The Significance of Listing.* RCRA subtitle C applies to all solid wastes that exhibit the characteristics of ignitability, corrosivity, reactivity, or toxicity. In light of that background coverage, what is the purpose and significance of the regulatory lists of hazardous wastes?

2. *The Listing Decision.* What findings must EPA make in order to justify listing a solid waste, or class of solid wastes, as hazardous? Must EPA list any waste that generally exhibits one of the characteristics? Must a waste exhibit one or more characteristics in order to be listed? If not, is there a threshold level of hazard below which EPA may not list a waste?

With respect to wastes containing toxic constituents, how should the agency balance the various factors listed in 40 C.F.R. § 261.11? In particular, how should it identify "plausible types of improper management," and what weight should it give to other regulatory programs? In *Dithiocarbamate Task Force*, did the court hold that EPA could not base a listing on observed spills of carbamate materials in train accidents? What additional findings might support such a listing? Can EPA consider the extent to which listing as a hazardous waste might increase compliance with other legal requirements, such as Department of Transportation regulations? Must EPA provide data showing that increased compliance is likely? Why did petitioner Zeneca, which was disposing of its waste in landfills meeting Subtitle C requirements, object to listing of that waste as hazardous? Is EPA foreclosed from listing Zeneca's waste because Zeneca is currently managing that waste responsibly? Suppose Zeneca's profits fall in the future. Might it cut costs by disposing of its waste in a non-Subtitle C landfill? Must EPA constantly monitor the industry to ensure that proper management continues?

3. *The Mixture and Derived-From Rules.* Characteristic hazardous wastes remain hazardous only as long as they exhibit a hazardous characteristic. See 40 C.F.R. § 261.3(d)(1). Under the mixture and derived-from rules, however, listed hazardous wastes remain hazardous until they are explicitly delisted. The mixture rule states that a solid waste becomes a hazardous waste if it is mixed with a listed waste, unless the listing was based solely on a characteristic that the mixture no longer exhibits, 40 C.F.R. § 261.3(a)(2)(iii), or the mixture has been delisted, 40 C.F.R. § 261.3(a)(2)(iv). The derived-from rule provides that listed hazardous wastes remain hazardous, even after treatment, until they are specifically delisted. See 40 C.F.R. § 261.3(c). Under the derived-from rule, residues from treatment of hazardous wastes, such as ash from hazardous waste incinerators, must be treated and disposed of as a hazardous waste.

The mixture and derived-from rules were first promulgated in 1980. In response to an industry challenge, the D.C. Circuit vacated the rules, holding that they had been promulgated in violation of the procedural requirements of the APA. Shell Oil Co. v. EPA, 950 F.2d 741 (D.C.Cir. 1991). The court suggested that EPA might want to consider reinstating the rules on an interim basis pending full notice and comment. EPA took this suggestion, temporarily reissuing the rules in 1992. Significant controversy ensued, leading Congress to forbid the issuance of new rules before October 1, 1993 and require that the interim rule remain in effect until replaced. Pub. L. No. 102–389, 106 Stat. 1571. The legislation set a deadline of October 1, 1994. When EPA did not meet that deadline, industry groups filed suit to enforce it. The suit was settled by consent decree requiring issuance of a final rule by December 1996. Again EPA failed to meet the deadline, which the court extended. The agency finally issued a new Hazardous Waste Identification Rule in 2001. 66 Fed. Reg. 27266 (May 16, 2001). The new rule retains both the mixture and derived-from rules, excluding both mixtures and derivatives of wastes listed solely on the basis of ignitability, corrosivity, or reactivity which no longer exhibit those characteristics.

What justifies the mixture and derived-from rules? EPA has explained:

> The mixture and derived-from rules are necessary to regulate hazardous wastes in a way that protects human health and the environment. Mixtures and residuals of hazardous waste represent a large and varied universe. Many hazardous wastes continue to be toxic after they have been mixed with other waste or have been treated. * * *

> We believe that without the mixture and derived-from rules, some generators would alter their waste to the point it no longer meets the listing description without detoxifying, immobilizing, or otherwise actually treating the waste. For example, without a "mixture" rule, generators of hazardous wastes could escape regulatory requirements by mixing listed hazardous wastes with other hazardous wastes or nonhazardous solid wastes to create a "new" waste that arguably no longer meets the listing description, but continues to pose a serious hazard. Similarly, without a "derived-from" rule, hazardous waste generators could potentially evade regulation by minimally processing or managing a hazardous waste and claiming that the resulting residue is no longer the listed waste, despite the continued hazards of the residue. * * *

64 Fed. Reg. 63382, 63389 (Nov. 19, 1999). Is this reasoning persuasive? Won't truly hazardous mixtures be captured by the characteristic waste rules? Should mixing that dilutes a waste until it no longer exhibits any of the characteristics be discouraged? Why? Are toxic wastes different than ignitable, corrosive, or reactive wastes for this purpose?

4. *Conditional Exemptions.* RCRA draws a sharp line between ordinary solid waste and hazardous waste. The former is almost entirely left to state regulation, while the latter is subject to cradle-to-grave federal controls. In reality, however, the degree of hazard generally falls on a continuum, so that harmless wastes cannot be cleanly distinguished from potentially harmful ones. What should EPA do about materials that fall in the gray area? One approach, known as conditional exemption or contingent management, exempts solid wastes from hazardous classification if they are managed in compliance with specific regulatory requirements. Conditional exemption allows EPA to tailor management requirements to the realistic hazards associated with the waste. In its 1999 proposed Hazardous Waste Identification Rule, for example, EPA has suggested that it might exempt certain low-risk wastes on condition that they be disposed of in a solid waste landfill. See 64 Fed. Reg. 63382, 63405 (Nov. 19, 1999). In support of this approach, EPA relies on the listing criteria in 40 C.F.R. § 261.11, including the risk of plausible mismanagement and existence of other regulatory controls. Is conditional exemption lawful? Is it desirable? For a critical discussion, see Jeffrey M. Gaba, Regulation by Bootstrap: Contingent Management of Hazardous Wastes Under the Resource Conservation and Recovery Act, 18 Yale J. Reg. 85 (2001).

5. *The Household Waste Exclusion.* EPA's first RCRA regulations, issued in 1980, excluded a number of solid wastes, including household waste, from the definition of hazardous waste. See 40 C.F.R. § 261.4(b)(1). Household waste can contain small amounts of hazardous substances, such as cleaning fluids, pesticides, and discarded batteries. The preamble to the regulations declared that residues remaining after treatment, including incineration, of household wastes also would not be regulated as hazardous wastes. See 45 Fed. Reg. 33099 (May 19, 1980).

In 1984, Congress enacted RCRA § 3001(i), 42 U.S.C. § 6921(i), to "clarify" the household waste exclusion. Section 3001(i) provides that a "resource recovery facility recovering energy from the mass burning of municipal solid waste shall not be deemed to be treating, storing, disposing of, or otherwise managing hazardous wastes" provided it receives and burns only household waste and non-hazardous commercial or industrial waste. In City of Chicago v. Environmental Defense Fund, 511 U.S. 328 (1994), the Supreme Court ruled that this statute does not exempt the ash remaining after incineration of household wastes in waste-to-energy facilities from regulation as hazardous waste. The Court explained:

> The plain meaning of this language is that so long as a facility recovers energy by incineration of the appropriate wastes, *it* (*the facility*) is not subject to Subtitle C regulation as a facility that treats, stores, disposes of, or manages hazardous waste. The provision quite clearly does *not* contain any exclusion for the *ash itself*. Indeed, the waste the facility produces (as opposed to that which it receives) is not even mentioned.

Id. at 334–35.

Waste-to-energy operators were concerned that the *City of Chicago* decision would greatly increase the costs of managing ash. Subtitle C hazardous waste must be disposed of in licensed hazardous waste landfills with special design characteristics and operating procedures. Disposal of ash as hazardous waste can cost ten to fifteen times as much as disposal in a solid waste landfill. Some cities feared they might have to close their incinerators as a result of these increased costs. A study five years after the decision, however, found that most of the waste from incinerators passed the toxicity characteristic test, and therefore was not deemed hazardous. In part, that result is due to EPA's decision to allow combustors to combine relatively non-toxic "bottom ash," the larger unburned particles that remain on the grate after combustion, with "fly ash," the lighter particles that are suspended in the gas stream and collected in the air pollution control equipment, which tends to have higher concentrations of metals and organic materials. See Markus G. Puder, Trash, Ash, and the Phoenix: A Fifth Anniversary Review of the Supreme Court's *City of Chicago* Waste-to-Energy Combustion Ash Decision, 26 B.C. Envtl. Aff. L. Rev. 473, 510 (1999).

6. *A Way Out?* Currently, listed hazardous wastes remain subject to the burdensome requirements of subtitle C until they are delisted, a slow, expensive process which must be completed individually for each facility. Is a simpler exit procedure needed for low-risk wastes? EPA has been exploring the possibility of self-implementing (that is, not requiring individual EPA review or action) risk-based exemptions from subtitle C for years. So far, however, the agency has been stymied by its inability to assess the risks precisely enough to specify exemption levels. For a recent discussion of a framework under which low risk wastes could be exempted from subtitle C, see 64 Fed. Reg. 63382 (Nov. 19, 1999).

4. LAND DISPOSAL RESTRICTIONS

Excerpts from the Resource Conservation and Recovery Act

42 U.S.C. §§ 6901–6992k.

Sec. 1002   Congressional findings

* * *

(b) The Congress finds with respect to the environment and health, that—

* * *

(2) disposal of solid waste and hazardous waste in or on the land without careful planning and management can present a danger to human health and the environment;

* * *

(5) the placement of inadequate controls on hazardous waste management will result in substantial risks to human health and the environment;

(6) if hazardous waste management is improperly performed in the first instance, corrective action is likely to be expensive, complex, and time consuming;

(7) certain classes of land disposal facilities are not capable of assuring long-term containment of certain hazardous wastes, and to avoid substantial risk to human health and the environment, reliance on land disposal should be minimized or eliminated, and land disposal, particularly landfill and surface impoundment, should be the least favored method for managing hazardous wastes * * *.

Sec. 3004   Standards applicable to owners and operators of hazardous waste treatment, storage, and disposal facilities

* * *

(d) Prohibitions on land disposal of specified wastes

(1) Effective 32 months after November 8, 1984 * * *, the land disposal of the hazardous wastes referred to in paragraph (2) is prohibited unless the Administrator determines the prohibition on one or more methods of land disposal of such waste is not required in order to protect human health and the environment for as long as the waste remains hazardous, taking into account—

(A) the long-term uncertainties associated with land disposal,

(B) the goal of managing hazardous waste in an appropriate manner in the first instance, and

(C) the persistence, toxicity, mobility, and propensity to bioaccumulate of such hazardous wastes and their hazardous constituents. * * *

(e)(1) Effective twenty-four months after November 8, 1984 * * *, the land disposal of the hazardous wastes referred to in paragraph (2) is prohibited unless the Administrator determines the prohibition of one or more methods of land disposal of such waste is not required in order to protect human health and the environment for as long as the waste remains hazardous, taking into account the factors referred to in subparagraph (A) through (C) of subsection (d)(1) of this section. For the purposes of this paragraph, a method of land disposal may not be determined to be protective of human health and the environment for a hazardous waste referred to in paragraph (2) (other than a hazardous waste which has complied with the pretreatment regulations promulgated under subsection (m) of this section), unless upon application by an interested person it has been demonstrated to the Administrator, to a reasonable degree of certainty, that there will be no migration of hazardous constituents from the disposal unit or injection zone for as long as the wastes remain hazardous.

(2) The hazardous wastes to which the prohibition under paragraph (1) applies are as follows—

(A) dioxin-containing hazardous wastes numbered F020, F021, F022, and F023 (as referred to in the proposed rule published by the Administrator in the Federal Register for April 4, 1983) * * *

(g)(1) Not later than twenty-four months after November 8, 1984, the Administrator shall submit a schedule to Congress for—

(A) reviewing all hazardous wastes listed (as of November 8, 1984) under section 6921 of this title other than those wastes which are referred to in subsection (d) or (e) of this section; and

(B) taking action under paragraph (5) of this subsection with respect to each such hazardous waste.

(2) The Administrator shall base the schedule on a ranking of such listed wastes considering their intrinsic hazard and their volume * * *.

(4) The schedule under this subsection shall require that the Administrator shall promulgate regulations in accordance with paragraph (5) or make a determination under paragraph (5)—

(A) for at least one-third of all hazardous wastes referred to in paragraph (1) by the date forty-five months after November 8, 1984;

(B) for at least two-thirds of all such listed wastes by the date fifty-five months after November 8, 1984; and

(C) for all such listed wastes and for all hazardous wastes identified under [RCRA § 3001] by the date sixty-six months after November 8, 1984.

In the case of any hazardous waste identified or listed under section 6921 of this title after November 8, 1984, the Administrator shall determine whether such waste shall be prohibited from one or more methods of land disposal in accordance with paragraph (5) within six months after the date of such identification or listing.

(5) Not later than the date specified in the schedule published under this subsection, the Administrator shall promulgate final regulations prohibiting one or more methods of land disposal of the hazardous wastes listed on such schedule except for methods of land disposal which the Administrator determines will be protective of human health and the environment for as long as the waste remains hazardous, taking into account the factors referred to in subparagraphs (A) through (C) of subsection (d)(1) of this section. * * *

(6) * * * (C) If the Administrator fails to promulgate regulations, or make a determination under paragraph (5) for any hazardous waste referred to in paragraph (1) within 66 months after November 8, 1984, such hazardous waste shall be prohibited from land disposal.

* * *

(j) Storage of hazardous waste prohibited from land disposal

In the case of any hazardous waste which is prohibited from one or more methods of land disposal under this section (or under regulations promulgated by the Administrator under any provision of this section) the storage of such hazardous waste is prohibited unless such storage is solely for the purpose of the accumulation of such quantities of hazardous waste as are necessary to facilitate proper recovery, treatment or disposal.

(k) "Land disposal" defined

For the purposes of this section, the term "land disposal", when used with respect to a specified hazardous waste, shall be deemed to include, but not be limited to, any placement of such hazardous waste in a landfill, surface impoundment, waste pile, injection well, land treatment facility, salt dome formation, salt bed formation, or underground mine or cave.

* * *

(m) Treatment standards for wastes subject to land disposal prohibition

(1) Simultaneously with the promulgation of regulations under subsection (d), (e), (f), or (g) of this section prohibiting one or more methods of land disposal of a particular hazardous waste, and as appropriate thereafter, the Administrator shall, after notice and an opportunity for hearings and after consultation with appropriate Federal and State agencies, promulgate regulations specifying those levels or methods of treatment, if any, which substantially diminish the toxicity of the waste or substantially reduce the likelihood of migration of hazardous constituents from the waste so that short-term and long-term threats to human health and the environment are minimized.

(2) If such hazardous waste has been treated to the level or by a method specified in regulations promulgated under this subsection, such waste or residue thereof shall not be subject to any prohibition promulgated under subsection (d), (e), (f), or (g) of this section and may be disposed of in a land disposal facility which meets the requirements of this subchapter. Any regulation promulgated under this subsection for a particular hazardous waste shall become effective on the same date as any applicable prohibition promulgated under subsection (d), (e), (f), or (g) of this section.

Hazardous Waste Treatment Council v. United States Environmental Protection Agency

United States Court of Appeals, District of Columbia Circuit, 1989.
886 F.2d 355.

■ PER CURIAM.

In 1984, Congress amended the Resource Conservation and Recovery Act ("RCRA"), to prohibit land disposal of certain hazardous solvents and wastes containing dioxins except in narrow circumstances to be defined by Environmental Protection Agency ("EPA") regulations. See Hazardous and Solid Waste Amendments, § 201(a), 42 U.S.C. § 6924(e) (Supp. IV 1986). In these consolidated cases, petitioners seek review of EPA's final "solvents and dioxins" rule published pursuant to Congress' 1984 mandate. We conclude that the rule under review is consistent with RCRA, but remand one aspect of the rulemaking to the agency for further explanation.

I. A. Statutory Scheme

The Hazardous and Solid Waste Amendments of 1984 ("HSWA"), Pub. L. No. 98–616, 98 Stat. 3221 (1984), *inter alia,* substantially strengthened EPA's control over the land disposal of hazardous wastes regulated under RCRA's "cradle to grave" statutory scheme. In preambular language to the HSWA, Congress, believing that "land disposal facilities were not capable of assuring long-term containment of certain hazardous wastes," expressed the policy that "reliance on land disposal should be minimized or eliminated." 42 U.S.C. § 6901(b)(7). In order to effectuate this policy, HSWA amended section 3004 of RCRA to prohibit land disposal of hazardous waste unless the waste is "pretreated" in a manner that minimizes "short-term and long-term threats to human health and the environment," *id.*

§ 6924(m), or unless EPA can determine that the waste is to be disposed of in such a fashion as to ensure that "there will be no migration of hazardous constituents from the disposal [facility]...." *Id.* § 6924(d)(1), (e)(1), & (g)(5).

As amended, RCRA requires EPA to implement the land disposal prohibition in three phases, addressing the most hazardous "listed" wastes first. In accordance with strict statutory deadlines, the Administrator is obligated to specify those methods of land disposal of each listed hazardous waste which "will be protective of human health and the environment." In addition, "[s]imultaneously with the promulgation of regulations ... prohibiting ... land disposal of a particular hazardous waste, the Administrator" is required to

> promulgate regulations specifying those levels or methods of treatment, if any, which substantially diminish the toxicity of the waste or substantially reduce the likelihood of migration of hazardous constituents from the waste so that short-term and long-term threats to human health and the environment are minimized.

Id. § 6924(m).

Respecting two categories of hazardous wastes, including the solvents and dioxins at issue here Congress, however, declined to wait for phased EPA implementation of the land disposal prohibition. For these wastes, Congress imposed earlier restrictions, prohibiting land disposal after dates specified in the HSWA except in accordance with pretreatment standards or pursuant to regulations specifying "protective" methods of disposal. *Id.* § 6924(e)(1). These prohibitions, as applied to the solvents and dioxins listed in the HSWA, were to take effect November 8, 1986. *Id.*

* * *

1. *Section 3004(m) Treatment Standards.*

In the Proposed Rule, EPA announced its tentative support for a treatment regime embodying both risk-based and technology-based standards. The technology-based standards would be founded upon what EPA determined to be the Best Demonstrated Available Technology ("BDAT"); parallel risk-based or "screening" levels were to reflect "the maximum concentration [of a hazardous constituent] below which the Agency believes there is no regulatory concern for the land disposal program and which is protective of human health and the environment." The Proposed Rule provided that these two sets of standards would be melded in the following manner:

First, if BDAT standards were more rigorous than the relevant health-screening levels, the latter would be used to "cap the reductions in toxicity and/or mobility that otherwise would result from the application of BDAT treatment[.]" Thus, "treatment for treatment's sake" would be avoided. Second, if BDAT standards were less rigorous than health-screening levels, BDAT standards would govern and the screening level would be used as "a goal for future changes to the treatment standards as new and more efficient treatment technologies become available." Finally, when EPA determined that the use of BDAT would pose a greater risk to human health and the environment than land disposal, or would provide insufficient safeguards against the threats produced by land disposal, the screening level would actually become the 3004(m) treatment standard.

EPA invited public comment on alternative approaches as well. The first alternative identified in the Proposed Rule (and the one ultimately selected by EPA) was based purely on the capabilities of the "best demonstrated available technology." Capping treatment levels to avoid treatment for treatment's sake, according to EPA, could be accomplished under this technology-based scheme by "the petition process":

> Under this approach, if a prescribed level or method of treatment under section 3004(m) resulted in concentration levels that an owner/operator believed to be overly protective, the owner/operator could petition the Agency to allow the use of an alternative treatment level or method or no treatment at all by demonstrating that less treatment would still meet the petition standard of protecting human health and environment.

* * *

The Agency received comments supporting both approaches, but ultimately settled on the pure-technology alternative. Of particular importance to EPA's decision were the comments filed by eleven members of Congress, all of whom served as conferees on the 1984 RCRA amendments. As EPA recorded in the preamble to the Final Rule:

> [these] members of Congress argued strongly that [the health screening] approach did not fulfill the intent of the law. They asserted that because of the scientific uncertainty inherent in risk-based decisions, Congress expressly directed the Agency to set treatment standards based on the capabilities of existing technology.
>
> The Agency believes that the technology-based approach adopted in [the] final rule, although not the only approach allowable under the law, best responds to the above stated comments.

Final Rule at 40,578.

EPA also relied on passages in the legislative history supporting an approach under which owners and operator [sic] of hazardous waste facilities would be required to use "the best [technology] that has been demonstrated to be achievable." *Id.* (quoting 103 Cong. Rec. S9178) (daily ed. July 25, 1984) (statement of Senator Chaffee). And the agency reiterated that the chief advantage offered by the health-screening approach—avoiding "treatment for treatment's sake"—could "be better addressed through changes in other aspects of its regulatory program." *Id.* As an example of what parts of the program might be altered, EPA announced that it was "considering the use of its risk-based methodologies to characterize wastes as hazardous pursuant to section 3001 [of RCRA]." *Id.*

Petitioner CMA [Chemical Manufacturers Association] challenges this aspect of the rule as an unreasonable construction of section 3004(m)'s mandate to ensure that "short-term and long-term threats to human health and the environment are minimized." 42 U.S.C. § 6924(m) (1982 & Supp. IV 1986). In the alternative, CMA argues that EPA has failed to explain the basis—in terms of relevant human health and environmental considerations—for its BDAT regime, which allegedly requires treatment in some circumstances to levels far below the standards for human exposure under other statutes administered by EPA. Thus, CMA claims that EPA's action in promulgating a technology-based rule is arbitrary and capricious.

* * *

II.   *Section 3004(m) Treatment Standards*

CMA challenges EPA's adoption of BDAT treatment standards in preference to the approach it proposed initially primarily on the ground that the regulation is not a reasonable interpretation of the statute. CMA obliquely, and Intervenors Edison Electric and the American Petroleum Institute explicitly, argues in the alternative that the agency did not adequately explain its decision to take the course that it did. We conclude, as to CMA's primary challenge, that EPA's decision to reject the use of screening levels is a reasonable interpretation of the statute. We also find, however, that EPA's justification of its choice is so fatally flawed that we cannot, in conscience, affirm it. We therefore grant the petitions for review to the extent of remanding this issue to the agency for a fuller explanation.

A.   *The Consistency of EPA's Interpretation with RCRA.*

Our role in evaluating an agency's interpretation of its enabling statute is as strictly circumscribed as it is simply stated: We first examine the statute to ascertain whether it clearly forecloses the course that the agency has taken; if it is ambiguous with respect to that question, we go on to determine whether the agency's interpretation is a reasonable resolution of the ambiguity. *Chevron v. Natural Resources Defense Council*, 467 U.S. 837, 842–45 (1984).

1.   *Chevron Step I: Is the Statute Clear?*

We repeat the mandate of § 3004(m)(1): the Administrator is required to promulgate "regulations specifying those levels or methods of treatment, if any, which substantially diminish the toxicity of the waste or substantially reduce the likelihood of migration of hazardous constitutents from the waste so that short-term and long-term threats to human health and the environment are minimized." 42 U.S.C. § 6924(m)(1).

CMA reads the statute as requiring EPA to determine the levels of concentration in waste at which the various solvents here at issue are "safe" and to use those "screening levels" as floors below which treatment would not be required. CMA supports its interpretation with the observation that the statute directs EPA to set standards only to the extent that "threats to human health and the environment are minimized." We are unpersuaded, however, that Congress intended to compel EPA to rely upon screening levels in preference to the levels achievable by BDAT.

The statute directs EPA to set treatment standards based upon either "levels or methods" of treatment. Such a mandate makes clear that the choice whether to use "levels" (screening levels) or "methods" (BDAT) lies within the informed discretion of the agency, as long as the result is "that short-term and long-term threats to human health and the environment are minimized." To "minimize" something is, to quote the Oxford English Dictionary, to "reduce [it] to the smallest possible amount, extent, or degree." But Congress recognized, in the very amendments here at issue, that there are "long-term uncertainties associated with land disposal," 42 U.S.C. § 6924(d)(1)(A). In the face of such uncertainties, it cannot be said that a statute that requires that threats be minimized unambiguously requires EPA to set levels at which it is conclusively presumed that no threat to health or the environment exists.

* * *

This is not to say that EPA is free, under § 3004(m), to require generators to treat their waste beyond the point at which there is no "threat" to human health or to the environment. That Congress's concern in adopting § 3004(m) was with health and the environment would necessarily make it unreasonable for EPA to promulgate treatment standards wholly without regard to whether there might be a threat to man or nature. That concern is better dealt with, however, at *Chevron*'s second step; for, having concluded that the statute does not unambiguously and in all circumstances foreclose EPA from adopting treatment levels based upon the levels achievable by BDAT, we must now explore whether the particular levels established by the regulations supply a reasonable resolution of the statutory ambiguity.

2. *Chevron Step II: Is EPA's Interpretation Reasonable?*

The screening levels that EPA initially proposed were not those at which the wastes were thought to be entirely safe. Rather, EPA set the levels to reduce risks from the solvents to an "acceptable" level, and it explored, at great length, the manifest (and manifold) uncertainties inherent in any attempt to specify "safe" concentration levels. The agency discussed, for example, the lack of any safe level of exposure to carcinogenic solvents; the extent to which reference dose levels (from which it derived its screening levels) understate the dangers that hazardous solvents pose to particularly sensitive members of the population; the necessarily artificial assumptions that accompany any attempt to model the migration of hazardous wastes from a disposal site; and the lack of dependable data on the effects that solvents have on the liners that bound disposal facilities for the purpose of ensuring that the wastes disposed in a facility stay there. * * *

CMA suggests, despite these uncertainties, that the adoption of a BDAT treatment regime would result in treatment to "below established levels of hazard." It relies for this proposition almost entirely upon a chart in which it contrasts the BDAT levels with (1) levels EPA has defined as "Maximum Contaminant Levels" (MCLs) under the Safe Drinking Water Act; (2) EPA's proposed "Organic Toxicity Characteristics," threshold levels below which EPA will not list a waste as hazardous by reason of its having in it a particular toxin; and (3) levels at which EPA has recently granted petitions by waste generators to "delist" a particular waste, that is, to remove it from the list of wastes that are deemed hazardous. CMA points out that the BDAT standards would require treatment to levels that are, in many cases, significantly below these "established levels of hazard."

If indeed EPA had determined that wastes at any of the three levels pointed to by CMA posed no threat to human health or the environment, we would have little hesitation in concluding that it was unreasonable for EPA to mandate treatment to substantially lower levels. In fact, however, none of the levels to which CMA compares the BDAT standards purports to establish a level at which safety is assured or "threats to human health and the environment are minimized." Each is a level established for a different purpose and under a different set of statutory criteria than concern us here; each is therefore irrelevant to the inquiry we undertake today.

* * *

Finally, CMA points to the "delisting levels" as appropriate points of comparison. The term is a bit misleading, however. EPA delists particular wastes in response to individual petitions, see, e.g., 42 U.S.C. § 6921(f)(1), and it has not adopted formal, or even *de facto,* levels below which any waste will be delisted. That EPA has delisted, in particular circumstances, wastes containing concentrations of solvents higher than those called for by the BDAT standards adds nothing to CMA's argument. The treatment standards establish a generic approach, requiring that all wastes deemed to be hazardous be treated to a set level in order to minimize threats to health and to the environment. If a waste is listed as hazardous, and an individual generator wants to dispose of it without meeting the BDAT standards, it may petition to have its particular waste delisted. If the agency grants the delisting petition, only the petitioner is affected; the generally required level of treatment remains the same. Hence, there is no inconsistency between a "delisting level," accepted in particular circumstances, that permits a higher level of a particular contaminant then the BDAT level otherwise generally applicable.

* * *

B. *Was EPA's Explanation Adequate?*

[I]n order to determine whether we can affirm EPA's action here, we must parse the language of the Final Rule to see whether it can be interpreted to make a sensible argument for the approach EPA adopted. We find that it cannot.

As we have said, EPA, in its Proposed Rule, expressed a tentative preference for an approach that combined screening levels and BDAT. It indicated that it thought either that approach or BDAT alone was consistent with the statute, and recognized that there were myriad uncertainties inherent in any attempt to model the health and environmental effects of the land disposal of hazardous wastes. It initially concluded, however, that despite those uncertainties, the better approach was to adopt the combination of screening levels and BDAT. Nevertheless, in the Final Rule, it rejected its earlier approach, and adopted a regime of treatment levels defined by BDAT alone.

* * *

[A]fter EPA issued the Proposed Rule, some commenters, including eleven members of Congress, chastised the agency on the ground that the use of screening levels was inconsistent with the intent of the statute. They stated that because of the uncertainties involved, Congress had mandated that BDAT alone be used to set treatment standards. EPA determined that the "best respon[se]" to those comments was to adopt a BDAT standard. It emphasized, however, that either course was consistent with the statute (and that it was therefore not *required* to use BDAT alone). Finally, it asserted, without explanation, that its major purpose in initially proposing screening levels "may be better addressed through changes in other aspects of its regulatory program," and gave an example of one such aspect that might be changed.

This explanation is inadequate. It should go without saying that members of Congress have no power, once a statute has been passed, to alter its interpretation by post-hoc "explanations" of what it means * * *.

It is unclear whether EPA recognized this fundamental point. On the one hand, it suggested that the adoption of a BDAT-only regime "best-respond[ed]" to the comments suggesting that the statute required such a rule. On the other hand, EPA went on at some length to establish that the comments were in error, in that screening levels are permissible under the statute. * * *

Nor is anything added by EPA's bald assertion that its reason for initially preferring Result B (screening levels) "may be" better served by other changes in the statutory scheme. In its Proposed Rule, EPA had, after extensive analysis of the various alternatives, come to the opposite conclusion. It is insufficient, in that context, for EPA to proceed in a different direction simply on the basis of an unexplained and unelaborated statement that it might have been wrong when it earlier concluded otherwise.

* * *

V. Conclusion

We conclude that the solvents and dioxins rule is not arbitrary, capricious, or contrary to RCRA in any of the respects argued by petitioners, but remand the matter for the EPA to clarify its reasons for adopting the Final Rule in preference to the Proposed Rule. In order to avoid disrupting EPA's regulatory program, we will withhold issuance of our mandate for 90 days, during which the agency may either withdraw the Final Rule or publish an adequate statement of basis and purpose.

■ SILBERMAN, CIRCUIT JUDGE, concurring in part and concurring in the result.

I concur in all of the majority's *per curiam* opinion but its purported resolution of the *Chevron* "Step II" question concerning the reasonableness of BDAT treatment standards as a construction or application of RCRA. * * * I do not believe it proper for the court to have reached the Step II question as to whether the selection of BDAT treatment levels was "a reasonable policy choice for the agency to make." *Chevron U.S.A. Inc. v. Natural Res. Defense Council*, 467 U.S. 837, 845 (1984). In the absence of a valid *agency* explanation as to how it has attempted to accommodate the competing interests Congress has committed to its care via RCRA, it is in my view inappropriate (perhaps analytically impossible) even to address, much less resolve, CMA's challenge to the reasonableness of EPA's treatment regime under the statute. Because the court today remands for further EPA explanation of its adoption of BDAT standards, the majority's *Chevron* Step II discussion should be considered *dicta.*

* * *

Randolph L. Hill, An Overview of RCRA: The "Mind–Numbing" Provisions of the Most Complicated Environmental Statute

21 Envtl. L. Rep. 10254, 10268–69 (1991).

The land disposal restrictions (LDRs, or the land ban) are the centerpiece of the 1984 Amendments to RCRA. The land ban reflects a significant change in the focus of the subtitle C regulatory program: from one oriented toward preventing hazardous waste releases to one that encourages minimization and treatment of hazardous wastes. The land ban also incorporates the "hammer" concept.

"Land ban" is a misnomer for the program. The LDRs restrictions do not prohibit all hazardous wastes from land disposal. Rather, they represent a creative statutory method for ensuring that EPA establish standards for hazardous wastes destined for land disposal.

The LDR provisions do prohibit the land disposal of hazardous wastes pursuant to a five-phase statutory schedule. By November 1986, listed solvent-containing or dioxin-containing wastes were banned. In July 1987, the so-called California list* wastes were banned; these included any listed or characteristic wastes that fell into one of the following categories: (1) liquid wastes containing high concentrations of free cyanide, (2) liquid wastes containing high concentrations of certain heavy metals, (3) liquid wastes containing high concentrations of polychlorinated biphenyls (PCBs), (4) liquid wastes with low pH, or (5) other wastes containing high concen-

---

* So called because the list was taken from existing California regulations.—Eds.

trations of halogenated organic compounds. For the remaining listed or characteristic hazardous wastes, Congress instructed EPA to divide the wastes into three groups based on their relative degree of hazard. EPA banned the first third of the listed wastes in August 1988, the second third in June 1989, and the final third and any characteristic wastes in May 1990.

The statute provides four ways to avoid the prohibition against land disposal. First, under § 3004(m), EPA may establish treatment standards for the waste "which substantially diminish the toxicity of the waste or substantially reduce the likelihood of migration of hazardous constituents from the waste so that short-term and long-term threats to human health and the environment are minimized." Wastes that meet the treatment standards set by EPA under § 3004(m) may be disposed of in a land disposal unit. EPA sets § 3004(m) standards in one of two ways: (1) EPA establishes a maximum concentration level for hazardous constituents in the waste (for wastewaters) or the waste extract using the new TCLP (for nonwastewaters); or (2) EPA specifies a particular treatment technology to be used on the waste.

The relationship between § 3004(m) and the other LDR provisions is referred to as the statutory hammer in the LDR. It is so called because if EPA were to fail to promulgate § 3004(m) standards by the required date, all land disposal of that waste would be prohibited on that date (even wastes that had been treated to levels similar to those EPA might set). The hammers provide a strong incentive for EPA to develop and promulgate the required standards on time to avoid the serious disruptions in the economy that would result from an inability to legally dispose of any hazardous wastes. They were indeed effective; EPA issued all of its § 3004(m) regulations on time.

The second method for avoiding the land ban is through a "no-migration" petition. Hazardous wastes, whether treated or untreated, may by disposed of in any land disposal unit if "it has been demonstrated to [EPA], to a reasonable degree of certainty, that there will be no migration of hazardous constituents from the disposal unit or [for deep injection wells] injection zone for as long as the wastes remain hazardous."

Third, EPA may grant a "national capacity variance" for up to two years after the statutory ban would otherwise take effect based on when "adequate alternative treatment, recovery, or disposal capacity ... will be available." In other words, if the capacity does not exist to treat all the wastes to the § 3004(m) level using the § 3004(m) method at the time EPA issues the § 3004(m) standards, EPA can allow up to two additional years to allow that capacity to develop.

* * *

EPA must set § 3004(m) standards for newly identified or newly listed hazardous wastes within six months of when the wastes become hazardous; there is, however, no hammer or other prohibition on land disposal if EPA fails to do so. * * *

NOTES AND QUESTIONS

1. *Judicial Review and Agency Explanations.* Was it inconsistent for the *Hazardous Waste Treatment Council* majority to both uphold the agency's technology-based standards as a reasonable interpretation of the statute and remand them for further explanation? What purpose is served by the remand? Would you expect the agency to withdraw or significantly modify its rule? If you were general counsel for EPA, how would you draft the agency's response?

Shortly after the decision, EPA published a supplemental explanation for its adoption of standards based solely on the best demonstrated available technology (BDAT). The agency expressed its intention ultimately to use threshold levels of hazardous constituents to cap technology-based treatment requirements, but explained that it was "presently unable to promulgate such levels" because of the kinds of uncertainties noted by the *Hazardous Waste Treatment Council* majority. See 55 Fed. Reg. 6640, 6641 (Feb. 26, 1990). EPA concluded that it would "retain treatment standards that are based on performance of BDAT until it develops acceptably certain threshold concentration levels." Id. at 6642. EPA's efforts to identify risk-based threshold levels continue, but the goal is as elusive as ever.

2. *The "Land Ban".* To what extent does RCRA § 3004 prohibit land disposal of hazardous wastes? What routes does the statute offer for overcoming the prohibition?

3. *Treatment Standards Versus Hazardous Waste Identification.* EPA has consistently taken the position that it may require treatment to risk levels below those needed to justify identification as a hazardous waste. Compare the language and purposes of the relevant statutory provisions. Do you agree with EPA? The D.C. Circuit upheld EPA's authority to require treatment beyond the level needed to remove hazardous characteristics in Chemical Waste Management v. United States Environmental Protection Agency, 976 F.2d 2 (D.C.Cir.1992). In *Hazardous Waste Treatment Council*, the Chemical Manufactures Association argued that EPA could not set treatment standards more severe than the levels at which it had delisted certain wastes. Why did the court reject this argument?

4. *RCRA's "Hammer".* In the 1984 amendments to § 3004, Congress created a detailed scheme directing EPA to issue land disposal restrictions and accompanying treatment standards in phases, beginning with the most hazardous wastes. The amendments included a "hammer," § 3004(g)(6), providing that land disposal would be flatly prohibited if EPA failed to meet its deadlines. What effect would that prohibition have on generators? Could they simply store their waste pending development of treatment standards? Why do you suppose Congress included the hammer provision?

Does the hammer apply to wastes listed after November 1984? What happens if EPA fails to issue treatment standards and land disposal restrictions for such wastes within six months following listing? In Columbia Falls Aluminum Co. v. Environmental Protection Agency, 139 F.3d 914 (D.C.Cir.1998), the court vacated EPA's treatment standard for spent potliner from aluminum production, a waste listed in 1988. The treatment standards were predicated on the Toxicity Characteristic Leaching Procedure, which the court found grossly underpredicted leaching of fluoride from the waste. The court held that vacating the treatment standard also required it to vacate the prohibition on land disposal, lest that prohibition force the aluminum industry to a halt. It did, however, indicate willingness to stay its decision to allow EPA a reasonable time to develop a new standard. What is the effect of the court's decision, not only in this case, but on future rulemakings? Should the court have deferred to EPA's view that land disposal must be prohibited in the absence of valid treatment standards?

5. *"No Migration"*. Section 3004 allows EPA to permit land disposal, without pretreatment, by methods it determines are protective of human health and the environment. See § 3004(d), (e), (g). No land disposal method can be approved unless the person seeking approval demonstrates, "to a reasonable degree of certainty, that there will be no migration of hazardous constituents from the disposal unit or injection zone for as long as the wastes remain hazardous." Must the disposal method ensure containment of every single molecule of every hazardous material in the waste? In Natural Resources Defense Council v. United States Environmental Protection Agency, 907 F.2d 1146 (D.C.Cir.1990), a panel of the D.C. Circuit, over the vigorous dissent of Judge Wald, upheld EPA's reading of the "no migration" standard to bar only migration of hazardous constituents in sufficient concentration to qualify as hazardous wastes.

6. *RCRA and Cleanup of Contaminated Sites*. In general, RCRA is a forward-looking statute, requiring proper handling of newly generated hazardous wastes in order to prevent contamination. In order to minimize contamination threats, it takes a cautious approach. Besides ensuring environmental protection, that caution is intended to discourage the generation of hazardous wastes. But different incentives may be desirable in the context of remediation of existing contaminated sites. Under EPA's "contained-in" policy, soils containing hazardous wastes above certain minimum concentrations are themselves considered hazardous wastes. Faced with complaints that RCRAs regulations, particularly limitations on land disposal and burdensome permitting requirements for treatment, storage and disposal facilities, were delaying remediation efforts, EPA has developed special rules to streamline the permit process and permit on-site storage of remediation wastes. 63 Fed. Reg. 65874 (Nov. 30, 1998). The agency acknowledges that RCRA compliance continues to complicate many state remediation efforts.

5.   CORRECTIVE ACTION AND ENFORCEMENT

(a) *Corrective Action*. The EPA may issue a corrective action administrative order or file a civil suit for injunctive relief to require clean up of any release of hazardous waste at a permitted (or seeking to be permitted) treatment, storage or disposal facility. Corrective action orders can compel clean up of past as well as current releases, including releases of materials that were not considered hazardous at the time of release. The agency can even require corrective action beyond the boundary of the facility. See RCRA §§ 3004(u), (v) and 3008(h), 42 U.S.C. §§ 6924(u), (v), and 6928(h). Violation of a corrective action order may lead to suspension or revocation of authority to operate and a civil penalty of up to $25,000 per day.

The corrective action program is intended to prevent currently operating facilities from becoming Superfund sites that must be cleaned up at federal expense. The program has been criticized as slow, excessively bureaucratic, and ineffectual. Although the corrective action program was legislatively authorized in 1984, by 1997 cleanup had not yet begun at nearly one third of high priority corrective action sites. EPA has recently instituted a series of reforms intended to streamline the corrective action program. Although it remains to be seen how effective these measures will be, they seem to having a beneficial effect. By 2000, only 10% of the high priority sites were still awaiting the beginning of cleanup measures. See General Accounting Office, Hazardous Waste: EPA Has Removed Some Barriers to Cleanups (GAO/RCED–00–224) (2000).

(b) *Enforcement.* Like other environmental laws, RCRA authorizes administrative, civil, and criminal enforcement options, and allows citizen suits. See RCRA §§ 3008, 7002; 42 U.S.C. §§ 6928, 6972. The relationship between state and federal enforcement efforts in RCRA-authorized states is in some doubt. In Harmon Industries v. Browner, 191 F.3d 894 (8th Cir.1999), the Eighth Circuit held that EPA could not "overfile," bringing its own enforcement action after state enforcement has begun, in a state with an authorized RCRA program. According to *Harmon*, if EPA deems state enforcement efforts inadequate, for example because the state does not levy adequate fines, the only remedy is withdrawal of the state's authorization. Id. at 901.

The *Harmon* decision relied on the language of RCRA, which provides that authorized state programs operate "in lieu of the Federal program," 42 U.S.C. § 6926(b), and that "[a]ny action taken by a State under a hazardous waste program authorized under this section shall have the same force and effect as action taken by the Administrator under this subchapter," id. § 6926(d). The court also concluded that, given the statutory "in lieu of" language, EPA and the state were sufficiently linked that res judicata operated to bar the federal enforcement action. Id. at 903. Because other federal environmental statutes do not include this precise language, *Harmon*'s overfiling bar would not necessarily apply. Moreover, some other federal courts have declined to follow *Harmon* even with respect to RCRA. See, e.g., United States v. Power Engineering Co., 125 F.Supp.2d 1050 (D.Colo.2000) (holding that RCRA's "in lieu of" language does not govern enforcement actions). Should the federal government be permitted to enforce RCRA's provisions even when a state agency has already taken enforcement action? If the answer is no, might states under-enforce, taking "sham" enforcement action or entering into collusive settlements to protect violators against strict federal enforcement? On the other hand, if the answer is yes, might regulated parties face unfair over-enforcement, penalizing them twice for the same violation? Is a middle ground interpretation possible, allowing EPA to overfile only if state enforcement is inadequate? See Northside Sanitary Landfill v. Thomas, 804 F.2d 371, 382 (7th Cir.1986) ("Even if the EPA is dissatisfied with, for example, the enforcement action taken by a state against a specific hazardous waste disposal facility, or the settlement agreement reached between the state and the facility, so long as the state has exercised its judgment in a reasonable manner and within its statutory authority, the EPA is without authority to commence an independent enforcement action or to modify the agreement."). Over-filing is discussed further in Chapter 11, Section 5(B).

(c) *Imminent and Substantial Endangerment.* RCRA § 7003, 42 U.S.C. § 6973, gives EPA broad authority to issue an administrative order or file a judicial action against any person who has contributed to past or present handling, storage, treatment, transportation, or disposal of solid or hazardous waste which "may present an imminent and substantial endangerment to health or the environment." This authority provides the primary route for forcing cleanup of petroleum and other materials outside the reach of the Comprehensive Environmental Response, Compensation, and Liability Act.

Courts have interpreted § 7003 generously. "[A]n endangerment is substantial if there is reasonable cause for concern that someone or something may be exposed to a risk of harm by a release or a threatened release of a hazardous substance if remedial action is not taken, keeping in mind that protection of the public health, welfare and the environment is of primary importance." B.F. Goodrich Co. v. Murtha, 697 F.Supp. 89, 96 (D.Conn.1988). An endangerment may be imminent if conditions which could give rise to harm are present, even though the actual harm will not be realized for years. See, e.g., Price v. United States Navy, 39 F.3d 1011, 1018–1019 (9th Cir.1994). There must, however, be some necessity for action and the potential for substantial or serious harm if action is not taken. See *Price*, 39 F.3d at 1019; Foster v. United States, 922 F.Supp. 642 (D.D.C.1996).

Citizen suits are also available to remedy imminent and substantial endangerment. RCRA § 7002(A)(1)(B), 42 U.S.C. § 6972(a)(1)(B). This section further provides that the court shall have jurisdiction to restrain any person who has contributed to the imminent and substantial endangerment, or order them to take such other action as may be necessary. The Supreme Court has ruled that RCRA's citizen suits may not be used to recover the costs of a completed cleanup, stating:

> That RCRA's citizen suit provision was not intended to provide a remedy for past cleanup costs is further apparent from the harm at which it is directed. Section 6972(a)(1)(B) permits a private party to bring suit only upon a showing that the solid or hazardous waste at issue "may present an imminent and substantial endangerment to health or the environment." The meaning of this timing restriction is plain: An endangerment can only be "imminent" if it "threaten[s] to occur immediately," Webster's New International Dictionary of En-

glish Language 1245 (2d ed. 1934), and the reference to waste which "may present" imminent harm quite clearly excludes waste that no longer presents such a danger. * * * It follows that § 6972(a) was designed to provide a remedy that ameliorates present or obviates the risk of future "imminent" harms, not a remedy that compensates for past cleanup efforts.

Meghrig v. KFC Western, Inc., 516 U.S. 479, 485 (1996).

Does *Meghrig* bar recovery of costs incurred after a RCRA citizen suit has been filed? See Avondale Federal Savings Bank v. Amoco Oil Co., 170 F.3d 692 (7th Cir.1999) (holding that landowner who remediated property while awaiting ruling on request for injunction under RCRA could not recover remediation costs); see also id. at 695 (Wood, J., dissenting) ("No one would disagree that the result the majority feels constrained to reach today creates perverse incentives for landowners whose property has been contaminated by another party.").

Does *Meghrig* bar government recovery of cleanup costs under § 7003?

B.   SITING HAZARDOUS WASTE FACILITIES: ENVIRONMENTAL JUSTICE

Americans enjoy the benefits of a consumptive, resource-intensive lifestyle, but all too often object to dealing with the consequences of that lifestyle. This is particularly true of the siting of "locally undesirable land uses," or LULUs. Hazardous waste treatment and disposal facilities, which impose focused costs on near neighbors while spreading their benefits to the community at large, are classic LULUs.

Controversies over the siting of hazardous waste facilities sparked the modern environmental justice movement, which focuses on the vulnerability of poor and minority neighborhoods to concentration of environmental hazards. Environmental justice encompasses much more than siting decisions; environmental justice claims have been raised in connection with enforcement, cleanup of contaminated sites, and the setting of general environmental standards such as acceptable toxin levels in fish. See, e.g., Eileen Gauna, Fairness in Environmental Protection, 31 Envtl. L. Rep. 10528, 10530 (2001). Nonetheless, siting decisions provide a useful lens through which to examine the concerns for distributional equity that underlie the quest for environmental justice or, to put it in stronger terms, the battle against environmental racism.

CLASS DISCUSSION PROBLEM: AN INCINERATOR FOR SMALLVILLE?

Smallville is a poor rural community in southwestern Georgia. About 45% of the residents of Smallville are African–American, compared to 35% in the county, 27% statewide, and roughly 12% nationwide. Twenty percent of Smallville's population is unemployed.

American Waste Disposal, Inc. (AWD) has announced plans to site a hazardous waste incinerator in Smallville. The incinerator would accept waste from throughout the southeastern United States. AWD considers Smallville an ideal site because it is centrally located, sparsely populated, and has a large available unskilled labor force. AWD will need zoning approval from the county, a Clean Air Act permit and a RCRA permit to construct the incinerator. The latter two permits would be issued by the state under delegated authority.

Smallville residents are divided on the desirability of the incinerator. Some see it as a source of employment and economic growth. Construction of the facility will employ about 500 workers for three years. Operations thereafter will employ 200, most of them unskilled. Other residents worry about air emissions and possible spills of the toxic materials that will be brought to the incinerator for disposal.

As a resident of Smallville, would you support or oppose the AWD incinerator? Would your opinion change if AWD committed to hiring at least half its work force from the local area? If the state offered to provide funding for a new park or to modernize the local schools in return for the community accepting the incinerator? What steps might opponents take to block the facility?

1. DEVELOPMENT OF THE ENVIRONMENTAL JUSTICE MOVEMENT

As early as 1972, the Green Power Foundation issued a report on environmental conditions in Los Angeles, drawing attention to the special environmental problems of urban areas, and noting that those areas contained high proportions of non-white residents. Perhaps the first organized resistance to perceived environmental injustice occurred in 1982, when the Commission for Racial Justice of the United Church of Christ helped poor African–American residents of Warren County, North Carolina, mount protests against the siting of a hazardous waste landfill. Although unsuccessful in their immediate goal, these protests drew attention to the vulnerability of poor minority communities to LULU siting, and suggested that the techniques of the civil rights movement could help protect those communities.

The Warren County experience also led to demographic studies of hazardous waste sites. In 1983, the General Accounting Office found that three of the four largest hazardous waste facilities in the southeastern U.S. were in predominately African–American communities. In 1987, the Commission for Racial Justice released a national study on the racial and socioeconomic characteristics of areas near hazardous waste sites, concluding that community racial composition was closely correlated with the presence of toxic waste facilities, due to "an insidious form of racism." United Church of Christ, Commission for Racial Justice, Toxic Wastes and Race in the United States ix (1987).

The Commission for Racial Justice report triggered the environmental justice movement, which combines civil rights and environmental activism. In 1991, the First National People of Color Environmental Leadership

Summit, organized by the Commission for Racial Justice, produced a statement of Principles of Environmental Justice, including universal rights to clean air, land, water and food, safe workplaces, and equality of participation at all levels of decisionmaking. See Proceedings, First National People of Color Environmental Leadership Summit xiii-xiv (1991). By the mid–1990s, ensuring environmental justice had become official federal policy. EPA established an Office of Environmental Justice in 1992. In 1994, President Clinton issued Executive Order 12898, directing all federal agencies, "[t]o the greatest extent practicable and permitted by law," to "make achieving environmental justice part of its mission by identifying and addressing, as appropriate, disproportionately high and adverse human health or environmental effects of its programs, policies, and activities on minority populations and low-income populations in the United States."

2. DECIPHERING THE DATA

The extent and causes of inequities in the siting of hazardous waste facilities have been hotly debated. The nationwide study by the Commission for Racial Justice examined the racial and socioeconomic characteristics of communities, defined as 5–digit ZIP code areas, around all operating commercial hazardous waste treatment, storage and disposal facilities in the United States. Using 1980 census data, the Commission found that "the ZIP code areas with the highest number of commercial hazardous waste facilities also had the highest mean percentage of residents who belong to a [non-white] racial and ethnic group." Commission for Racial Justice, United Church of Christ, Toxic Wastes and Race in the United States 13 (1987).

> Specifically, in communities with one operating commercial hazardous waste facility, the mean minority percentage of the population was approximately twice that of communities without facilities (24 percent vs. 12 percent). In communities with two or more operating commercial hazardous waste facilities or one of the five largest landfills, the mean minority percentage of the population was more than three times that of communities without facilities (38 percent vs. 12 percent).

> The analysis also revealed that mean household income and the mean value of owner-occupied homes were not as significant as the mean minority percentage of the population in differentiating residential ZIP codes with lesser numbers of hazardous waste facilities versus those with greater numbers and the largest landfills. After controlling for regional differences and urbanization, the mean value of owner-occupied homes in a community was a significant discriminator, but less so than the minority percentage of the population.

Id. A subsequent update concluded that the situation remained much the same in 1993. As of that date, "people of color were 47 percent more likely than whites to live near a commercial hazardous waste facility." Benjamin A. Goldman & Laura Fitton, Toxic Wastes and Race Revisited 128 (1994).

There are few other nationwide studies. In one, researchers at the University of Massachusetts–Amherst reached strikingly different conclusions than the Commission on Racial Justice. Douglas L. Anderton et al., Environmental Equity: The Demographics of Dumping, 31 Demography 229, 243–44 (1994). The University of Massachusetts group compared African American and Latino/Latina population levels in census tracts with and without operating commercial hazardous waste treatment, storage and disposal facilities (TSDFs). They used as control tracts only those in metropolitan areas containing TSDFs. They found that the percentage of African Americans was not significantly different in tracts with and without TSDFs, although the percentage of Latinos/Latinas was slightly higher in tracts with at least one TSDF. Tracts near those with TSDFs did have higher minority populations than those more removed from TSDFs, bringing the results of this study closer to those of the ZIP code studies.

A team headed by Professor Vicki Been evaluated both the current demographics of host communities, and changes over time. Vicki Been & Francis Gupta, Coming to the Nuisance or Going to the Barrios? A Longitudinal Analysis of Environmental Justice Claims, 24 Ecology L.Q. 1 (1997). They concluded that the African–American population of host tracts at the time of siting, from the 1970s on, was not significantly different from that of non-host tracts, although tracts which had hosted a waste facility before 1970 had a significantly higher percentage of African Americans than other tracts. Recent siting decisions appeared to be correlated with the proportion of Latino/Latina residents. High poverty rates turned out to be a negative predictor of waste facility siting; working class and lower middle class neighborhoods appeared more vulnerable than extremely poor ones. These investigators were unable to find a post-siting effect of TSDFs on either the racial and ethnic mix or the socioeconomic status of the neighborhood.

The results of local siting studies have also been mixed. A study of the Detroit area, for example, found that the percentage of minorities rose sharply near commercial hazardous waste facilities. Considering the area as a whole, the population more than 1.5 miles away from any commercial hazardous waste facility was 18% minority. Within one mile of a facility, it was 48% minority. Paul Mohai & Bunyan Bryant, Environmental Racism: Reviewing the Evidence, in Bunyan Bryant & Paul Mohai, eds., Race and the Incidence of Environmental Hazards 163, 171–72 (1992). In the Los Angeles area, a recent study shows that TSDFs were sited in census tracts with higher than average proportions of poor and minority residents. Manuel Pastor, Jr., Racial/Ethnic Inequality in Environmental–Hazard Exposure in Metropolitan Los Angeles, California Policy Research Center Report (2001). Like the Been and Gupta study, this one found no evidence that market dynamics after siting caused an increase in minority or poor populations. Interestingly, Pastor's work demonstrated that mixed Latino/African–American communities were most vulnerable to TSDF siting, perhaps because such mixed communities were least capable of organizing to defend themselves.

On the other hand, another study found no significant difference in percentages of minority residents in census tracts with and without operating TSDFs in the St. Louis area. Thomas Lambert and Christopher Boerner, Environmental Inequity: Economic Causes, Economic Solutions, 14 Yale J. on Reg. 195, 203 (1997). Lambert and Boerner concluded that, after siting, minority populations grew faster in the host tracts than in the general area, suggesting that market dynamics were more important than targeted siting to any inequity in the distribution of TSDFs. Id. at 205.

NOTES AND QUESTIONS

1. *Terminology.* Various terms have been used to describe the inequitable distribution of environmental hazards. Dr. Benjamin Chavis, longtime civil rights activist, former executive director of the National Association for the Advancement of Colored People, and co-author of the 1987 Commission for Racial Justice report, coined the term "environmental racism" to describe the situation depicted by that report. Those who describe themselves as members of the movement also speak of environmental justice or injustice, terms they describe as broader, encompassing socioeconomic as well as racial disparities. Industries seeking permits sometimes prefer to talk about environmental equity, and seek to focus that term on demonstrable environmental risks. See Luke W. Cole & Sheila R. Foster, From the Ground Up: Environmental Racism and the Rise of the Environmental Justice Movement 15 (2001).

What term do you think best captures the problem? How does the choice of terms affect perceptions of the problem and the search for solutions? According to Professor Richard Lazarus, "If environmental justice had not been so cast in terms of race, it is quite doubtful that the movement would have enjoyed such a strong political half-life." Richard J. Lazarus, "Environmental Racism! That's What It Is.", 2000 U. Ill. L. Rev. 255, 259. Another commentator, more sympathetic to the nationwide need for facilities, suggests that the use of strong rhetoric on both sides of the siting debate poses an unnecessary barrier to effective resolution of the problem. Lisa A. Binder, Religion, Race and Rights: A Rhetorical Overview of Environmental Justice Disputes, 6 Wis. Envtl. L. J. 1 (1999).

2. *Identifying Environmental Racism.* Because resources are unequally distributed by race, operation of the market economy often has unequal racial impacts. Should those unintentional effects be classified as "environmental racism"? Does the extent to which that background distribution has been shaped by past intentional discrimination matter? Consider the views of Professor Gerald Torres:

> The term racism draws its contemporary moral strength by being clearly identified with the history of the structural oppression of African–American and other people of color in this society. * * * When seeking to determine whether an activity is racist, the one characteristic that must be present is one of domination and subordination. The

action need not necessarily be one of intention, but it may be both intentional and dominating.

In analyzing environmental policies and activities from the perspective of their subordinating impact on racial groups we are led inexorably to examine the distributional impacts of environmental rules. We can examine both the substantive distributional impact of those rules in practice and the substantive blindness in the production of rules that lead to racially subordinating activities. In short, when we label an environmental practice as an example of environmental racism we are saying that the predictable distributional impact of that decision contributes to the structure of racial subordination and domination that has similarly marked many of our public policies in this country. We might also be saying that excluding considerations of racial impact in constructing the substantive environmental rules contributes to the subordination of identifiable racial groups. In many cases, this subordinating impact will be the result of an unconscious process. Regardless of how unconscious the process may be, however, if the perception of the affected class is that the impact is fundamentally racially targeted then we must assume that the substantive effect is racist unless a better or different justification can be put forward.

Gerald Torres, Introduction: Understanding Environmental Racism, 63 U. Colo. L. Rev. 839, 839–40 (1992). Do you agree? Must the racial impact be objectively identifiable, or does it depend solely on the perception of the minority group? How significant must the impact be? What justifications, if any, can remove the taint of racism from a siting decision?

3.   *Defining Environmental Justice.* The Environmental Protection Agency defines environmental justice as "the fair treatment and meaningful involvement of all people regardless of race, color, national origin, or income with respect to the development, implementation, and enforcement of environmental laws, regulations, and policies. Fair treatment means that no group of people, including a racial, ethnic, or socioeconomic group, should bear a disproportionate share of the negative environmental consequences resulting from industrial, municipal, and commercial operations or the execution of federal, state, local, and tribal programs and policies."

Is this definition adequate to guide decisions? What is "meaningful involvement," and how can it be assured? Are affirmative efforts to build community political capacity a necessary element of environmental justice? Will those efforts simply expand the NIMBY (Not In My Back Yard) syndrome to include poor minority neighborhoods as well as wealthy white ones? Is opposition to TSDFs more justified in poor neighborhoods, which receive less benefit from the activities that generate hazardous waste?

What impacts are "disproportionate"? Should hazardous waste facilities and other LULUs be distributed evenly across the entire landscape? How should population density be factored in? Should some places be off-limits to hazardous waste facilities? How should those areas be identified? Should the calculation of proportionality include local economic benefits, such as jobs, provided by a facility? Do impacts resulting from market dynamics after siting count? Does the law have a role to play in remedying those impacts?

What consequences count as "environmental"? Do socioeconomic effects, such as depression of land values or destabilization of communities, matter?

4. *Understanding the Data.* The brief description above of the major studies illustrates the difficulties in determining whether and to what extent waste facility siting decisions are inequitable. One complication is the choice of study area. The Commission on Racial Justice Study and Goldman's follow-up used ZIP codes as proxies for communities. The University of Massachusetts group and Professor Been's team used census tracts instead. The use of proxies allows investigators to take advantage of the wealth of demographic data that has already been compiled. If proxies must be used, which is more appropriate for this type of study? Census tracts are generally smaller than ZIP codes, so their use may reveal more localized distributional patterns. They also have the advantages of being roughly comparable in population numbers, and drawn with the intention of reflecting neighborhood divisions. On the other hand, they may not fully capture the impacts of hazardous waste facilities. Because many waste facilities are located at the edge of a census tract, near the highways or rail lines that often form tract boundaries, their impacts may be felt more strongly in neighboring tracts than in the host tract. Been & Gupta, *supra*, at 13.

What other differences do you see among the studies described above? How might those differences affect the conclusions? Which study or studies do you find most persuasive?

5. *Facility Presence and Environmental Risk.* All of the studies described above relied entirely on the presence or absence of hazardous waste treatment, storage or disposal facilities as an indicator of environmental justice. While it is easy to measure, the presence of a facility does not necessarily correlate with environmental risk. The level of risk presumably depends upon the design and operation of the facility as well as the mix of materials it accepts. If a facility complies with all applicable state and federal regulations, does its siting raise no environmental equity concerns? Or are significant impacts, environmental or economic, not addressed by environmental laws?

6. *National Data and Local Decisions.* Much of the evidence of environmental racism rests on a limited number of nationwide and local studies. What role should this data play in a local siting dispute in an area that has not been closely studied? Should it matter to local decisionmakers in Smallville, or to a judge reviewing their decision, that siting decisions nationwide or in Detroit appear to be discriminatory? As an advocate for incinerator opponents in Smallville, what benefits and risks would you see in linking the local controversy to the broader environmental justice movement?

3. THE LAW OF ENVIRONMENTAL JUSTICE

A. *Civil Rights Litigation*

It is not surprising that the environmental justice movement, with its close ties to civil rights activism, looked to civil rights law for vindication. Early environmental justice litigation concentrated on allegations of racial discrimination in permitting decisions, seeking relief under the equal protection clause of the federal constitution. These claims face high evidentiary burdens. Establishing an equal protection violation requires proof of discriminatory intent. Washington v. Davis, 426 U.S. 229 (1976). Direct evidence of discriminatory purpose is extremely difficult to produce. Permitting bodies simply do not proclaim that racial animus motivates their decisions. Although the Supreme Court has made it clear that circumstantial evidence can be sufficient to establish discriminatory intent, see Village of Arlington Heights v. Metropolitan Housing Development Corp., 429 U.S. 252, 266–268 (1977), persuasive circumstantial evidence of discriminatory purpose is also difficult to find. Disparate impacts due to existing structural segregation or discrimination generally cannot be tied to current discriminatory intent. The number of siting decisions in any local jurisdiction is typically small, making it hard to obtain statistically significant data on disparate impacts and even harder to demonstrate a pattern suggesting racial animus. Moreover, permitting agencies react to applications brought forward by private parties, rather than initiating proposals. If the only applications for hazardous waste facilities are in areas with substantial minority populations, it is difficult to accuse the permitting body of targeting those neighborhoods.

So far, no environmental justice plaintiff has been able to surmount these barriers. Several suits alleging equal protection violations in landfill siting decisions have failed. See Bean v. Southwestern Waste Management Corp., 482 F.Supp. 673 (S.D.Tex.1979), aff'd without opinion, 782 F.2d 1038 (5th Cir.1986); East Bibb Twiggs Neighborhood Ass'n v. Macon–Bibb County Planning & Zoning Comm'n, 706 F.Supp. 880 (M.D.Ga.1989), *aff'd* 896 F.2d 1264 (11th Cir.1989); R.I.S.E., Inc.. v. Kay, 768 F.Supp. 1144 (E.D.Va.1991), aff'd without opinion, 977 F.2d 573 (4th Cir.1992).

Finding equal protection claims unpromising, environmental justice advocates turned to Title VI of the Civil Rights Act of 1964. Section 601 of Title VI provides:

> No person in the United States shall, on the ground of race, color or national origin, be excluded from participation in, be denied the benefits of, or be subjected to discrimination under any program or activity receiving Federal financial assistance.

42 U.S.C. § 2000d. Section 601 has been interpreted to proscribe only intentional discrimination. See Alexander v. Choate, 469 U.S. 287, 293 (1985). Section 602, however, which directs federal agencies to issue regulations to prevent discrimination, permits regulations covering disparate impacts as well as intentional discrimination. See 42 U.S.C. § 2000d–1; Alexander, 469 U.S. at 292–94.

EPA regulations implementing section 602 provide:

(b) A recipient [of federal funds] shall not use criteria or methods of administering its program which have the effect of subjecting individuals to discrimination because of their race, color, national origin or sex, or have the effect of defeating or substantially impairing accomplishment of the objectives of the program with respect to individuals of a particular race, color, national origin, or sex.

(c) A recipient shall not choose a site or location of a facility that has the purpose or effect of excluding individuals from, denying them the benefits of, or subjecting them to discrimination under any program to which this part applies on the grounds of race, color, or national origin or sex; or with the purpose or effect of defeating or substantially impairing the accomplishment of the objectives of this subpart.

40 C.F.R. § 7.35. Title VI and its implementing regulations apply only to programs receiving federal funding, but that includes many environmental permitting programs. The federal government provides significant funding to states under the majority of the federal environmental laws, including the Clean Air Act, Clean Water Act, and RCRA.

One significant hurdle to lawsuits under Title VI regulations has been uncertainty over whether private plaintiffs could enforce those regulations. Until recently, there were indications that a private right of action might be feasible. In 1997, the Third Circuit allowed a challenge to the siting of a contaminated soil remediation facility to proceed, holding that EPA's Title VI disparate impact regulations were privately enforceable. Chester Residents Concerned for Quality Living v. Seif, 132 F.3d 925 (3d Cir.1997). The Supreme Court granted certiorari, but before it could hear the case the state revoked the facility's permit, mooting the dispute. On April 19, 2001, a district court granted a preliminary injunction in a suit brought by local residents against the New Jersey Department of Environmental Protection over an air emission permit granted to an industrial facility, holding that plaintiffs had made out a prima facie case of disparate impact in violation of EPA's Title VI regulations. South Camden Citizens in Action v. New Jersey Dept. of Environmental Protection, 145 F.Supp.2d 446 (D.N.J.2001). Just five days later, however, the Supreme Court ruled, by a vote of 5–4, that no private right of action exists to enforce regulations issued under section 602. Alexander v. Sandoval, 532 U.S. 275 (2001).

There may be another route to private enforcement of disparate impact regulations under Title VI. Following the Supreme Court decision, the district court reinstated the injunction in *South Camden Citizens*, ruling that although plaintiffs could not bring their claim directly under Title VI, they could bring it under 42 U.S.C. § 1983. The court held that EPA's Title VI regulations created a federal right, enforceable through section 1983, to be free of discriminatory impacts caused by the actions of EPA funding recipients. Should this decision hold up, it could substantially reduce the barriers to environmental justice claims. It may not survive appellate review, however. The Third Circuit has stayed the decision, finding that the plaintiffs were not likely to prevail on appeal. See Environmental Justice: Third Circuit Should Reconsider Decision Lifting Ban on Camden Plant, Residents Say, 32 Env't Rep. (BNA) 1223 (2001).

Even if the *South Camden* decision survives, environmental justice plaintiffs will continue to face significant barriers. Proving disparate impact, although easier than proving discriminatory purpose, can be challenging. Connecting a disparate impact to the actions of the permitting agency (the recipient of federal funds), rather than the applicant, adds an additional complication. Moreover, Title VI suits cannot challenge federal permitting decisions.

B. Environmental Litigation

Environmental justice advocates have been understandably skeptical of the ability of environmental laws to advance their cause. Substantive environmental laws tend to set uniform acceptable levels of pollution or environmental hazards, disregarding the distribution of hazards across the landscape. Although they often provide avenues for public participation, effective use of those avenues requires sophistication, time, and money. Given the unequal distribution of those resources, opportunities for public input may exacerbate environmental injustices by enhancing the power of wealthy communities to engage in NIMBY politics.

Nonetheless, environmental laws have in some circumstances proven effective tools for combating environmental injustice. Perhaps the best known example comes from attempts to site a hazardous waste incinerator in Kettleman City, California. Although nearly 40% of the residents of Kettleman City spoke only Spanish, the County prepared the environmental review documents only in English. A state trial court ruled that the County had violated the California Environmental Quality Act (California's NEPA analogue) by effectively precluding meaningful community involvement. El Pueblo Para el Aire y Agua Limpio v. County of Kings, 22 Envtl.L.Rep. 20,357 (Cal.Super.Ct.1991). That may be an isolated success, however. No court has ever ruled that NEPA required translation of environmental review documents to facilitate local participation. Some states now mandate translation of information about certain hazards, see, e.g., N.J. Stat. Ann. 34:5A–4(c); Or. Rev. Stat. 654.770, but many others do not.

C. Administrative Remedies

The power of litigation under either civil rights or environmental laws to remedy environmental injustice faces two major limitations: difficulties of proof, and a poor fit between the aims of the environmental justice movement and legislation developed with other aims in mind. Federal legislation specific to environmental justice could reduce these barriers, but has not been forthcoming. In the 1990s, the Clinton administration sought to reduce the gap between environmental justice concerns and existing law through administrative initiatives.

Executive Order 12898: Federal Actions to Address Environmental Justice in Minority Populations and Low-income Populations

59 Fed. Reg. 7629 (Feb. 11, 1994).

Section 1–1.   Implementation

1–101.   *Agency Responsibilities.* To the greatest extent practicable and permitted by law * * * each Federal agency shall make achieving environmental justice part of its mission by identifying and addressing, as appropriate, disproportionately high and adverse human health or environmental effects of its programs, policies, and activities on minority populations and low-income populations in the United States * * *.

* * *

Section 2–2.   Federal Agency Responsibilities for Federal Programs

Each Federal agency shall conduct its programs, policies, and activities that substantially affect human health or the environment, in a manner that ensures that such programs, policies, and activities do not have the effect of excluding persons (including populations) from participation in, denying persons (including populations) the benefits of, or subjecting persons (including populations) to discrimination under, such programs, policies, and activities, because of their race, color, or national origin.

* * *

Section 6–6.   General Provisions

* * *

6–608.   *General.* Federal agencies shall implement this order consistent with, and to the extent permitted by, existing law.

6–609.   *Judicial Review.* This order is intended only to improve the internal management of the executive branch and is not intended to, nor does it create any right, benefit, or trust responsibility, substantive or procedural, enforceable at law or equity by a party against the United States, its agencies, its officers, or any person. This order shall not be construed to create any right to judicial review involving the compliance or noncompliance of the United States, its agencies, its officers, or any other person with this order.

William J. Clinton, Memorandum on Environmental Justice

30 Weekly Comp. Pres. Doc. 279 (1994).

Today I have issued an Executive Order on Federal Actions to Address Environmental Justice in Minority Populations and Low–Income Populations. * * *

The purpose of this separate memorandum is to underscore certain provisions of existing law that can help ensure that all communities and persons across this Nation live in a safe and healthful environment. Environmental and civil rights statutes provide many opportunities to address environmental hazards in minority communities and low-income communities. Application of these existing statutory provisions is an important part of this Administration's efforts to prevent those minority communities and low-income communities from being subject to disproportionately high and adverse environmental effects.

I am therefore today directing that all department and agency heads take appropriate and necessary steps to ensure that the following specific directives are implemented immediately:

In accordance with Title VI of the Civil Rights Act of 1964, each Federal agency shall ensure that all programs or activities receiving Federal financial assistance that affect human health or the environment do not directly, or through contractual or other arrangements, use criteria, methods, or other arrangements that discriminate on the basis of race, color, or national origin.

Each Federal agency shall analyze the environmental effects, including human health, economic and social effects, of Federal actions, including effects on minority communities and low-income communities, when such analysis is required by the National Environmental Policy Act of 1969. Mitigation measures outlined or analyzed in an environmental assessment, environmental impact statement, or record of decision, whenever feasible, should address significant and adverse environmental effects of proposed Federal actions on minority communities and low-income communities.

* * *

In re Chemical Waste Management of Indiana, Inc.

EPA Environmental Appeals Board, 1995.
6 E.A.D. 66.

■ Opinion of the Board by Judge Reich.

On March 1, 1995, U.S. EPA Region V issued a final permit decision approving the application of Chemical Waste Management of Indiana, Inc. ("CWMII") for the renewal of the federal portion[1] of a Resource Conservation and Recovery Act ("RCRA") permit and a Class 3 modification of the same permit for its Adams Center Landfill Facility in Fort Wayne, Indiana.
* * *

---

1. The State of Indiana has received authorization to administer its own RCRA program, pursuant to section 3006 of RCRA, 42 U.S.C. § 6926. Indiana has not, however, received authorization to administer the requirements contained in the Hazardous and Solid Waste Amendments to RCRA ("HSWA"). Consequently, when a RCRA permit is issued in Indiana, the State issues the part of the permit relating to the non-HSWA requirements and EPA issues the part of the permit relating to the HSWA requirements.

During the comment period * * *, Petitioners and other commenters raised what the parties refer to as "environmental justice" concerns. More specifically, issues were raised as to whether the operation of CWMII's facility will have a disproportionately adverse impact on the health, environment, or economic well-being of minority or low-income populations in the area surrounding the facility. * * *

During the pendency of CWMII's permit application, Executive Order 12898, relating to environmental justice, was issued. * * *

In response to the environmental justice concerns raised during the comment period on the draft modified permit, the Region held what was billed as an "informational" meeting in Fort Wayne, Indiana, on August 11, 1994. The meeting was attended by concerned citizens, and representatives of CWMII, the Indiana Department of Environmental Management, and the Region. The purpose of the meeting was to "allow representatives of all parties involved to freely discuss Environmental Justice and other key issues, answer questions and gain understanding of each party's concerns." The Region also performed a demographic analysis of census data on populations within a one-mile radius of the facility. The Region ultimately concluded that the operation of the facility would not have a disproportionately adverse health or environmental impact on minority or low-income populations living near the facility.

* * *

We believe it is useful to begin by considering the precise nature of Petitioners' environmental justice claim in the context of this RCRA proceeding and the effect, if any, the issuance of Executive Order 12898 should have on the way in which the Agency addresses such a claim.

"Environmental justice," at least as that term is used in the Executive Order, involves "identifying and addressing, as appropriate, disproportionately high and adverse human health or environmental effects of [Agency] programs, policies, and activities on minority populations and low-income populations...." 59 Fed. Reg. at 7629. Some of the commenters also believe that environmental justice is concerned with adverse effects on the *economic* well-being of such populations. Thus, when Petitioners couch their arguments in terms of environmental justice, they assert that the issuance of the permit and the concomitant operation of the facility will have a disproportionately adverse impact not only on the health and environment of minority or low-income people living near the facility but also on economic growth and property values.

* * *

Although it is not made explicit in the petitions, it is nevertheless clear that Petitioners do not believe that the threats posed by the facility can be addressed through revision of the permit. Rather, it is apparent that Petitioners believe that their concerns can be addressed only by permanently halting operation of the facility at its present location or, at a minimum, preventing the Phase IV Expansion of the facility. Thus, Petitioners challenge the permit decision, including the modification, in its entirety, rather than any specific permit conditions.

At the outset, it is important to determine how (if at all) the Executive Order changes the way a Region processes a permit application under RCRA. For the reasons set forth below, we conclude that the Executive Order does not purport to, and does not have the effect of, changing the substantive requirements for issuance of a permit under RCRA and its implementing regulations. We conclude, nevertheless, that there are areas where the Region has discretion to act within the constraints of the RCRA regulations and, in such areas, as a matter of policy, the Region should exercise that discretion to implement the Executive Order to the greatest extent practicable.

Permit Issuance Under RCRA: While, as is discussed later, there are some important opportunities to implement the Executive Order in the RCRA permitting context, there are substantial limitations as well. As the Region notes in its brief, the Executive Order by its express terms is to be implemented in a manner that is consistent with existing law. Section 6–608. The Region correctly points out that under the existing RCRA scheme, the Agency is required to issue a permit to any applicant who meets all the requirements of RCRA and its implementing regulations. The statute expressly provides that:

> Upon a determination by the Administrator (or a State, if applicable), of compliance by a facility for which a permit is applied for under this section with the requirements of this section and section 3004, the Administrator (or the State) *shall issue* a permit for such facilities.

RCRA § 3005(c)(1), 42 U.S.C. § 6925 (emphasis added). * * * Accordingly, if a permit applicant meets the requirements of RCRA and its implementing regulations, the Agency *must* issue the permit, regardless of the racial or socio-economic composition of the surrounding community and regardless of the economic effect of the facility on the surrounding community.

Implementing the Executive Order: Nevertheless, there are two areas in the RCRA permitting scheme in which the Region has significant discretion, within the constraints of RCRA, to implement the mandates of the Executive Order. The first of these areas is public participation. [40 C.F.R.] Part 124 already provides procedures for ensuring that the public is afforded an opportunity to participate in the processing of a permit application. The procedures required under part 124, however, do not preclude a Region from providing other opportunities for public involvement beyond those required under part 124. We hold, therefore, that when the Region has a basis to believe that operation of the facility may have a disproportionate impact on a minority or low-income segment of the affected community, the Region should, as a matter of policy, exercise its discretion to assure early and ongoing opportunities for public involvement in the permitting process.

A second area in which the Region has discretion to implement the Executive Order within the constraints of RCRA relates to the omnibus clause under section 3005(c)(3) of RCRA. The omnibus clause provides that:

> Each permit issued under this section shall contain such terms and conditions as the Administrator (or the State) determines necessary to protect human health and the environment.

42 U.S.C. § 6925(c)(3). Under the omnibus clause, if the operation of a facility would have an adverse impact on the health or environment of the surrounding community, the Agency would be required to include permit terms or conditions that would ensure that such impacts do not occur. Moreover, if the nature of the facility and its proximity to neighboring populations would make it impossible to craft a set of permit terms that would protect the health and environment of such populations, the Agency would have the authority to deny the permit. In that event, the facility would have to shut down entirely. Thus, under the omnibus clause, if the operation of a facility truly poses a threat to the health or environment of a low-income or minority community, the omnibus clause would require the Region to include in the permit whatever terms and conditions are necessary to prevent such impacts. This would be true even without a finding of disparate impact.

There is nothing in section 3005(c)(3) to prevent the Region from taking a more refined look at its health and environmental impacts assessment, in light of allegations that operation of the facility would have a disproportionately adverse effect on the health or environment of low-income or minority populations. Even under the omnibus clause some judgment is required as to what constitutes a threat to human health and the environment. It is certainly conceivable that, although analysis of a broad cross-section of the community may not suggest a threat to human health and the environment from the operation of a facility, such a broad analysis might mask the effects of the facility on a disparately affected minority or low-income segment of the community. (Moreover, such an analysis might have been based on assumptions that, though true for a broad cross-section of the community, are not true for the smaller minority or low-income segment of the community.) A Region should take this under consideration in defining the scope of its analysis for compliance with § 3005(c)(3).

Of course, an exercise of discretion under section 3005(c)(3) would be limited by the constraints that are inherent in the language of the omnibus clause. In other words, in response to an environmental justice claim, the Region would be limited to ensuring the protection of the health or environment of the minority or low-income populations. The Region would not have discretion to redress impacts that are unrelated or only tenuously related to human health and the environment, such as disproportionate impacts on the economic well-being of a minority or low-income community. With that qualification in mind, we hold that when a commenter submits at least a superficially plausible claim that operation of the facility will have a disproportionate impact on a minority or low-income segment of the affected community, the Region should, as a matter of policy, exercise its discretion under section 3005(c)(3) to include within its health and environmental impacts assessment an analysis focusing particularly on the minority or low-income community whose health or environment is alleged to be threatened by the facility. In this fashion, the Region may implement the Executive Order within the constraints of RCRA and its implementing regulations.

* * *

Reviewing Challenges Based on the Executive Order: As a threshold matter, the Region suggests that claims relating to the implementation of the Executive Order are not subject to review. In support of this argument, the Region points out that the Executive Order itself expressly provides that it does not create any substantive or procedural rights that could be enforced through litigation. * * * However, while the Region is correct that section 6–609 precludes judicial review of the Agency's efforts to comply with the Executive Order, it does not affect implementation of the Order *within* an agency. More specifically, it does not preclude the *Board*, in an appropriate circumstance, from reviewing a Region's compliance with the Executive Order as a matter of policy or exercise of discretion to the extent relevant under section 124.19(a). Section 124.19(a) authorizes the Board to review any condition of a permit decision (or as here, the permit decision in its entirety). Accordingly, the Board can review the Region's efforts to implement the Executive Order in the course of determining the validity or appropriateness of the permit decision at issue. With that in mind, we turn to the specific challenges raised by Petitioners in this case.

* * *

The Region's Demographic Study: Petitioners * * * question the Region's efforts to determine whether operation of the facility will have a disproportionate impact on a minority or low-income community. To assess whether there would indeed be a disproportionate impact on low-income or minority populations, the Region performed a demographic study, based on census figures, of the racial and socio-economic composition of the community surrounding the facility. The Region concluded that no minority or low-income communities will face a disproportionate impact from the facility. Petitioners argue that, in arriving at this conclusion, the Region erred by ignoring available census and other information submitted during the comment period that allegedly demonstrate a disproportionate impact of the facility on minority or low-income populations, particularly those at distances greater than one mile. Petitioners particularly criticize the Region's decision to restrict the focus of its study to the community living within a one-mile radius of the facility. Petitioners contend that the facility adversely affects citizens who live further than one mile away from the facility. * * *

As explained above, the Region can and should consider a claim of disproportionate impact in the context of its health and environmental impacts assessment under the omnibus clause at section 3005(c)(3) of

RCRA. The proper scope of a demographic study to consider such impacts is an issue calling for a highly technical judgment as to the probable dispersion of pollutants through various media into the surrounding community. This is precisely the kind of issue that the Region, with its technical expertise and experience, is best suited to decide. In recognition of this reality, the procedural rules governing Appeals of permitting decisions place a heavy burden on petitioners who seek Board review of such technical decisions. To carry that burden in this case, Petitioners would need to show either that the Region erred in concluding that the permit would be protective of populations within one mile of the facility, or that, even if it were protective of such close-in populations, it for some reason would not protect the health or environment of citizens who live at a greater distance from the facility. We believe that Petitioners have failed to demonstrate that the Region erred in either of these respects.

The petition mentions two parts of the administrative record in support of its claim. First, it refers to the comments of Fort Wayne City Councilman Cletus Edmonds, who contends that the facility will adversely affect the economic growth and housing of some 13,500 of his African–American constituents. As noted above, however, neither RCRA nor its implementing regulations requires the Agency to consider the economic effects of a facility.

Second, the petition mentions an environmental impact study submitted by the City of New Haven. That study indicates that particulates from the facility "could" affect an African–American community living as far as two miles away from the facility * * *. This conclusion, however, is stated in a very tentative fashion and provides no indication of the probabilities involved or the adverse effects, if any, increased exposure might cause. It does not show why the Region's conclusions as to the protectiveness of the permit were erroneous or why, if the population within one mile of the facility is protected (as the Region concludes), there would nonetheless be impacts beyond one mile cognizable under section 3005(c)(3). We conclude, therefore, that Petitioners have failed to carry their burden of demonstrating that the Region's technical judgment in this case does not deserve the same deference that the Board normally accords to such judgments. Review of this issue is therefore denied.

In the Matter of Louisiana Energy Services, L.P. (Claiborne Enrichment Center)

Nuclear Regulatory Commission, 1998.
47 N.R.C. 77.

This proceeding involves an application by Louisiana Energy Services (LES) for a license to construct and operate the Claiborne Enrichment Center (CEC) near Homer, Louisiana. The NRC Staff * * * support issuance of the license. A local group, the Citizens Against Nuclear Trash (CANT), opposes it on environmental and safety grounds.

On May 1, 1997, the Atomic Safety and Licensing Board issued a decision in CANT's favor on several "environmental justice" issues and denied the license * * *. We granted review to consider the environmental justice question. * * *

LES seeks an NRC license to construct and operate the CEC, which would be the first privately owned uranium enrichment facility in the United States. The 30–year license sought by LES would authorize it to possess and use byproduct, source, and special nuclear material to enrich uranium using a gas centrifuge process. * * *

If licensed, the CEC would be constructed on the central 70 acres of a wooded 442–acre site juxtaposed between two unincorporated African–American communities in Louisiana, Center Springs and Forest Grove. * * * Construction of the CEC would necessitate the closing and relocation of Parish Road 39, which currently bisects the LeSage site from North to South.

* * *

We turn now to the portion of our decision that presents the thorniest and most sensitive issues, with profound implications of both a legal and a policy nature: environmental justice. Resting its decision largely on President Clinton's executive order on environmental justice, E.O. 12898, the Board * * * found the NRC Staff's environmental review of the CEC inadequate on two grounds: (1) it failed to investigate thoroughly the possibility that "racial considerations" affected the facility's siting; and (2) it failed to account fully for the CEC's "disparate impact" on two nearby African–American communities. The Board called for a new and complete NRC Staff investigation into the racial discrimination issue and for a revised NEPA discussion of the CEC's disparate impact on the local communities. * * *

The Board decision reflects an earnest effort to apply and give meaning to the executive order in the case of the proposed LES facility. It declared, in words we fully endorse, that "racial discrimination [is] a persistent and enduring problem in American society." It therefore directed the NRC Staff to conduct an "objective, thorough, and professional investigation" of the site selection process that led to the choice of the LeSage site, an area with a population more than 97% African–American, to permit a determination whether "the selection process was tainted by racial bias." * * *

What the Board in this case seems to envision is a free-ranging NRC Staff inquiry into the motives of LES (and perhaps state and local) decisionmakers, with only the broad instruction that the Staff should "lift some rocks and look under them." With no clear legal basis or clearly discernible objective, the Board's approach cannot in our view be sustained, notwithstanding the worthy intentions that motivated it.

Under NEPA, agencies are required to consider not only strictly environmental impacts, but also social and economic impacts ancillary to them. But nothing in NEPA or in the cases interpreting it indicates that the statute is a tool for addressing problems of racial discrimination. * * *

For these and other reasons, which we detail below, we reverse the Board's requirement of a further NRC Staff investigation into racial discrimination.

1.   The Board apparently felt bound by President Clinton's executive order, and by a former NRC Chairman's commitment to abide by that order, to inquire on its own into racial discrimination, so as to "give meaning" to the executive order. But the Board's effort to enforce what it saw as a "nondiscrimination directive" in the executive order was misplaced. The executive order, by its own terms, established no new rights or remedies. Its purpose was merely to "*underscore* certain provision[s] of *existing* law that can help ensure that all communities and persons across this Nation live in a safe and healthful environment" (emphasis added). See Memorandum for the Heads of All Departments and Agencies, 30 Weekly Comp. Pres. Doc. 279 (Feb. 14, 1994).

The only "existing law" conceivably pertinent here is NEPA, a statute that centers on environmental impacts. The Board's proposed racial discrimination inquiry goes well beyond what NEPA has traditionally been interpreted to require. Despite nearly 30 years of extensive NEPA litigation on countless putative impacts and effects of federal actions we are unaware of a single judicial or agency decision that has invoked NEPA to consider a claim of racial discrimination. * * *

An agency inquiry into a license applicant's supposed discriminatory motives or acts would be far removed from NEPA's core interest: "the physical environment—the world around us, so to speak." Metropolitan Edison Co., 460 U.S. at 772. Were NEPA construed broadly to require a full examination of every conceivable aspect of federally licensed projects, "available resources may be spread so thin that agencies are unable adequately to pursue protection of the physical environment and natural resources." Id. at 776. * * *

Here, the Board would have the NRC Staff engage in a highly complex racial bias study with no obvious stopping point. To perform what the Board requires—an "objective, thorough, and professional investigation that looks beneath the surface"—Staff (among other tasks) presumably would have to retrace the CEC's entire history and determine, largely through inference and indirect evidence, whether an invidious racial animus infected the siting process or motivated any of the numerous federal, state, local, or corporate officials involved in it. The Board-ordered racial inquiry, in short, might in the end dwarf the core NEPA environmental inquiry. The effort would come with no guaranty of an accurate or useful result and would consume enormous NRC Staff resources.

The Commission process would not end with the new NRC Staff investigation. In this contested proceeding, resolving the racial discrimination issue fully and fairly, and completing the record, presumably would require the Commission to authorize a reopened discovery and hearing process on the results of the Staff study. This would lead ultimately to renewed Board proceedings to resolve what are likely to be disputed racial discrimination findings. In a nutshell, we would be embarking upon a second major litigation, possibly taking months or years to resolve, on an issue well outside NEPA's principal concern, the "physical environment," and far afield from the NRC's experience and expertise.

2. The Board's contemplated free-ranging inquiry into the site selection process would go well beyond what the CEQ has stated is required of an agency considering a license application. The site screening process is used by a license applicant to identify sites that may meet the stated goals of the proposed action. It is not uncommon for only one of many possible sites to be deemed reasonable. CEQ's implementing guidance provides that an EIS must "rigorously explore . . . all *reasonable* alternatives." 40 C.F.R. § 1502.14(a) (emphasis added). For those alternatives that have been eliminated from detailed study, the EIS is required merely to "briefly discuss" why they were ruled out. Id. Where (as here) "a federal agency is not the sponsor of a project, the federal government's consideration of alternatives may accord substantial weight to the preferences of the applicant and/or sponsor in the siting and design of the project." City of Grapevine v. DOT, 17 F.3d at 1506.

Here, the only site identified by the Licensee as suiting its stated goals was the LeSage site, and as a result, it was the only site rigorously examined by the NRC Staff in the FEIS. In accordance with NEPA, the Staff discussed the process used by LES to select a suitable site, and found it reasonable. Though required to do no more than "briefly discuss" why other sites were not chosen, the Staff in this case provided a detailed discussion, occupying 17 pages in the FEIS. It identified more than twenty-five facility and site characteristics used by LES. The Board did not find, and CANT did not contend, that the criteria discussed in the FEIS showed overt signs of racism. Nor did CANT "offer tangible evidence" of an "obviously superior site" sufficient to call for a more thorough site-by-site NEPA review. See Roosevelt Campobello International Park Commission v. EPA, 684 F.2d 1041, 1047 (1st Cir.1982).

Exploring whether the LES siting criteria might perpetuate institutional racism, as CANT has contended, or might have been manipulated purposefully to discriminate, as the Board suggests, would require the NRC Staff to do much more than "briefly discuss" the reasons for eliminating the many other sites (79) initially considered. We are aware of no NEPA principle, and the Board cites none, requiring an elaborate comparative site study to resolve allegations of racial discrimination.

* * *

As the Board quite correctly noted, racial discrimination has proved "a persistent and enduring problem in American society," "is rarely, if ever, admitted," and is "difficult to ferret out." For these reasons, Congress and the Supreme Court have crafted a carefully woven system of legal remedies, and modes of proof and rebuttal, for the fair and equitable resolution of racial discrimination claims. Here, the Board gleaned from the record various pieces of evidence that it viewed as creating an "inference" of racial discrimination, but did not consider or even mention the customary allocation of burdens or standards of proof for such claims. * * *

b. *Disparate Impact*

We turn now to an issue that lies close to the heart of NEPA: whether the CEC will have significant special impacts on the two nearby, overwhelmingly African–American, communities of Center Springs and Forest Grove. As President Clinton's executive order on environmental justice reminds us, adverse impacts that fall heavily on minority and impoverished citizens call for particularly close scrutiny.

The Board determined that the FEIS adequately considered all but two of the claimed local impacts: the need to relocate Parish Road 39 and diminution of property values. As to the former, it found that the discussion of relocating the road did not consider the interference with pedestrian traffic between Center Springs and Forest Grove. The Board also found that the FEIS failed to consider particularized adverse effects on property values in Forest Grove and Center Springs. We affirm the Board's findings.

i. RELOCATION OF PARISH ROAD 39

The FEIS states that closing and relocating Parish Road 39 will increase the length of the road between the two communities by 0.38 mile. The FEIS found that this extra distance will increase driving time and therefore "inconvenience" community residents traveling by car between the two communities. The FEIS does not mention the impact that the increased distance will have on pedestrians.

Despite LES's argument to the contrary, the record supports the Board's finding that Parish Road 39 is frequently used by pedestrians who would be adversely impacted by its relocation. CANT's expert witness, Dr. Bullard, testified that he interviewed residents of Forest Grove and Center Springs and was informed that Parish Road 39 is a vital and frequently used pedestrian link between the two communities. The Board found Dr. Bullard's testimony on this point to be supported by Bureau of Census statistics and unrebutted by other parties. The Board pointed out that many residents of the two impoverished communities have no choice but to travel by foot. Further, some of the residents whom Dr. Bullard interviewed are elderly. In these circumstances, the Board reasonably found that adding an extra 0.38 mile each way to a pedestrian commute would be more than a mere inconvenience, especially for elderly or infirm residents.

* * *

ii. IMPACT ON PROPERTY VALUES

We also agree with the Board that the NRC Staff should revise the FEIS to analyze local property-value effects more thoroughly.

The current FEIS gives only cursory attention to the property-values issue. It recognizes that "to the extent the CEC affects the environment, those living closest will be the most affected," and that the CEC will have "some negative" impact on property values. But it does not specify where, why, or to what extent the impacts on property values would be likely felt. Because Forest Grove and Center Springs are adjacent to the CEC's proposed site, the negative impact on property values predicted by the Staff would presumably fall heaviest on these two communities. CANT's expert witness, Dr. Bullard, whom the Board found "both credible and convincing," presented what the Board characterized as "a reasoned, persuasive, and unchallenged explanation why the CEC will negatively affect property values in these minority communities." * * *

To be sure, the Board also found that two or three parcels of property near the CEC may increase in value, as possible sites for new business ventures supporting LES (e.g., food service and equipment vendors). It found, however, that the new business ventures would not create an overall increase in property values in the adjacent communities. We believe the Board's finding was reasonable. Moreover, since Forest Grove and Center Springs receive almost no parish services, their property values would not necessarily benefit from the influx of new tax money into the parish from the CEC. In short, nothing we have identified in the record undermines the Board's finding that the CEC would likely affect property values in Forest Grove and Center Springs adversely.

* * *

The Board directed the NRC Staff to consider whether actions can be taken to mitigate the impacts of relocating Parish Road 39. We concur in that direction, and also direct the NRC Staff to consider whether actions can be taken to mitigate the impacts on property values. Dr. Bullard describes roads in Forest Grove and Center Springs as generally "either unpaved or poorly maintained." There may well be simple and relatively inexpensive measures that could be taken to improve existing driving and walking conditions (e.g., improving current roads and footpaths). This in turn could mitigate property devaluation in these communities by improving overall living conditions. It is also possible that enhancing other community amenities or addressing a general housing concern may be appropriate to mitigate further any devaluation in property values. The FEIS must be revised to include a discussion of possible mitigating measures. * * *

Chairman Jackson disapproved Section 5.a of the Commission order, titled Racial Discrimination in Siting. She would have affirmed in part and reversed in part the Board's requirement of a further NRC Staff investigation into the CEC's siting. In light of the alleged irregularities, gaps, and inconsistencies in the siting process, it was her preference that the NRC Staff should further investigate the siting process, without focusing on LES's alleged intentional racial motives, to ensure that the siting criteria were reasonable and were applied equitably.

IT IS SO ORDERED.

NOTES AND QUESTIONS

1. *Litigation and Political Action.* To date, environmental justice litigation, under either civil rights or environmental laws, has achieved few direct victories. It is important to keep in mind, however, that litigation is not pursued in isolation. Protests and political organizing have been crucial to the environmental justice movement, and frequently have succeeded in blocking siting. Indeed, a knowledgeable commentator argues that "taking environmental problems out of the streets and into the courts" is often "a tactical mistake." Luke W. Cole, Empowerment as the Key to Environmental Protection: The Need for Environmental Poverty Law, 19 Ecology L.Q. 619, 650 (1992). On the other hand, Richard Lazarus notes that civil rights suits have substantial symbolic value. Richard J. Lazarus, Pursuing 'Environmental Justice': The Distributional Effects of Environmental Protection, 87 Nw. U. L. Rev. 787, 829 (1993). What is the appropriate role of litigation (and lawyers) in the struggle for environmental justice? What can political action achieve that litigation cannot, and vice versa?

2. *Administrative Appeals.* Although they are generally not required to do so, many administrative agencies provide an internal appeal process for persons dissatisfied with decisions. Unless agency regulations or the applicable statute makes the agency appeal process mandatory, a dissatisfied party has the choice of seeking review through the agency process or resorting directly to federal court. See Darby v. Cisneros, 509 U.S. 137 (1993).

Details of agency appeals processes vary widely. At the Nuclear Regulatory Commission, licensing decisions are made initially by three-person licensing boards. Licensing board decisions may be appealed to the full commission by any party. See 10 C.F.R. § 2.760. The Commission is a five-member independent body; its members are appointed by the President, with the advice and consent of the Senate, for five-year terms.

EPA permit decisions under RCRA, and certain permit decisions under the Clean Water and Clean Air Acts are appealable to a specialized review body, the Environmental Appeals Board. See 40 C.F.R. § 124.19(a). The Board may also decide on its own initiative to review any condition in such permits. Id., § 124.19(b). Where available, appeal to the Board is mandatory prior to resort to federal court. Id., § 124.19(e). The Board consists of four career EPA employees appointed by the Administrator; it sits in panels of three, which decide cases by majority vote. See 40 C.F.R. § 1.25(e)(1). The Board cannot hear appeals from permits issued under authorized state RCRA programs. Where the state has partial authorization, the Board can hear appeals from conditions imposed under federal, but not state, authority. See In re Great Lakes Chemical Corp. Main Plant, 5 E.A.D. 395 (EAB 1994).

3. *Executive Order 12898.* Shortly after President Clinton issued Executive Order 12898, an observer derided it as "nothing but fluff." David Schoenbrod, Environmental 'Injustice' Is About Politics, Not Racism, Wall St. J., Feb. 23, 1994, at A21. Is that an accurate assessment? What, if anything, does the Executive Order add to the law of environmental justice? Note that the Executive Order does not provide grounds for judicial review. Are administrative appeals an effective mechanism to address environmental justice concerns?

4. *Environmental Justice Considerations in RCRA Permitting Decisions.* In *Chemical Waste Management*, precisely what did the Board hold with respect to the consideration of environmental justice in the RCRA permitting process? Can a permit be denied for environmental justice reasons alone? To what extent can or must socioeconomic impacts and equity considerations play a role in the permitting decision? Can EPA consider the aggregate effects of the facility in combination with other existing facilities? For a careful analysis of EPA's authority to include environmental justice considerations in a variety of permit decisions, see Richard J. Lazarus & Stephanie Tai, Integrating Environmental Justice into EPA Permitting Authority, 26 Ecology L.Q. 617 (1999).

5. *Siting and Racial Discrimination.* In *Louisiana Energy Services*, the licensing board had concluded that evidence presented by siting opponents, "the most significant portions of which are largely unrebutted or ineffectively rebutted, is more than sufficient to raise a reasonable inference that racial considerations played some part in the site selection process." In the Matter of Louisiana Energy Servs., L.P., LBP–97–8 (Atomic Safety and Licensing Board, May 1, 1997). The board concluded that "a thorough Staff investigation of the site selection process is needed in order to comply with the President's nondiscrimination directive in Executive Order 12898." On what basis did the Commission reach its very different conclusion? Who has the better argument?

6. *Federal Environmental Justice Legislation?* Is a new federal statute needed or desirable to combat environmental injustice? Or is environmental justice best addressed at the state or local level? If you would favor a federal statute, what form should it take? Should it be modeled on civil rights laws or environmental laws? What precisely would be the goals of such a law? What provisions should it include? Are procedural mandates sufficient, or is some substantive mandate necessary? Is it possible to frame a substantive mandate applicable to all federal actions that may raise environmental justice concerns?

SECTION 3.   MANAGEMENT OF RADIOACTIVE WASTE

Radioactive wastes present special disposal problems because they can be highly dangerous for extraordinarily long periods of time. For example, ten years after it is removed from a nuclear reactor, a spent fuel assembly emits sufficient radiation to kill a person in just a few minutes. Some of the radioactive components in spent fuel decay fairly rapidly, but others, such as plutonium–239 persist for thousands of years. There is no way to accelerate the decay process. Accordingly, these materials must be effectively isolated for periods many orders of magnitude longer than a human life span.

Uranium occurs in nature almost entirely in the form of U–238, which is not fissionable. The fissionable isotope, U–235, makes up less than one percent of the uranium in ores. Production of nuclear fuel begins with the mining of these ores, which are then crushed, converted to a gaseous state, and "enriched" to increase the concentration of U–235. The enriched gas is reconverted to a solid powder, shaped into pellets, and enclosed in metal tubes known as "cladding." The tubes are assembled into fuel rods to power a nuclear reactor. Controlled fission of the U–235 in the reactor core provides heat, which produces steam to drive the generators that in turn produce electricity.

Fresh fuel emits little radioactivity and requires no special handling. At the end of their useful life, however, the spent fuel rods are very hot and highly radioactive. They are removed from the reactor and stored in water to prevent overheating and protect against radiation. Spent fuel can be reprocessed by disassembly of the rods and chemical recovery of fissionable isotopes. In the United States, however, reprocessing of commercial fuel has been discouraged since the 1970s, largely because of the risk of terrorism and nuclear proliferation. Reprocessing isolates plutonium in a form suitable for weapons use. Reprocessing also produces substantial amounts of radioactive waste, so it is by no means a complete solution to the waste problem.

Concerns about reactor safety and waste disposal have long made nuclear power controversial in the United States. In the mid–1970s, the federal courts seemed receptive to these concerns. The D.C. Circuit overturned two Nuclear Regulatory Commission (NRC) licensing decisions, holding among other things that EISs for the plants had not adequately considered the problems of fuel disposal. The Supreme Court reversed in a famous decision. Vermont Yankee Nuclear Power v. Natural Resources Defense Council, 435 U.S. 519 (1978). The Court ruled that the agency had sufficiently considered fuel cycle issues and alternative energy sources. Justice Rehnquist, writing for the Court, concluded:

> Nuclear energy may some day be a cheap, safe source of power or it may not. But Congress has made a choice to at least try nuclear energy, establishing a reasonable review process in which courts are to play only a limited role. * * * Time may prove wrong the decision to develop nuclear energy, but it is Congress or the States within their appropriate agencies which must eventually make that judgment.

Id. at 556–58.

Ironically, *Vermont Yankee* came at the very end of U.S. nuclear power expansion. No new plants have been ordered since 1978, and all those ordered between 1973 and 1978 were subsequently canceled. See Michael B. Gerrard, Fear and Loathing in the Siting of Hazardous and Radioactive Waste Facilities: A Comprehensive Approach to a Misperceived Crisis, 68 Tul. L. Rev. 1047, 1074 (1994). High construction costs, public opposition, and licensing delays have all been blamed (or credited, depending upon one's point of view) for this informal, but effective, moratorium.

Despite the lack of new reactors, nuclear power currently provides about one-fifth of the nation's electricity, and appears to hold a strong position in the current market. See Mark Holt & Carl E. Behrens, Nuclear Energy Policy (CRS Brief for Congress) (2001). Although eight reactors closed during the decade, total electricity output from the nation's nuclear plants grew nearly twenty-five percent in the 1990s. Operating costs at existing nuclear plants are currently thought to be lower than for competing technologies. Id. Plants initially licensed for forty years are proving to have a longer lifespan. The Nuclear Regulatory Commission recently renewed the operating license of the Calvert Cliffs plant for an additional twenty years, and several other renewal applications are pending.

The lack of a permanent nuclear waste solution may be the biggest current impediment to renewed expansion of the nuclear power industry. RCRA does not apply to radioactive wastes. Instead, they are governed by two distinct regulatory systems, one for high level and the other for low level wastes. Both waste types present disposal problems.

High level radioactive wastes include the waste products from nuclear fission, such as spent fuel rods and assemblies, coolant fluids, and associated gases. Each of the 104 nuclear power plants operating in the United States produces 20 to 30 metric tons (a metric ton is 1000 kg, equal to 2,204 pounds) of spent fuel—ash-grey, button-sized pellets of radioactive waste—annually. There already are more than 40,000 metric tons of such material in temporary storage around the country. See Dept. of Energy, Office of Civilian Radioactive Waste Management, Annual Report to Congress FY 1999 at 15 (2000). High level waste also includes waste from government-owned research reactors, weapons production facilities, and naval nuclear submarines.

Under the Nuclear Waste Policy Act, 42 U.S.C. §§ 10101–10270, the federal government is responsible for selecting and developing a geological repository to permanently isolate high level wastes. The program is funded in part by fees imposed on commercial nuclear reactors. The challenges of developing a high level radioactive waste disposal site are detailed in the Class Discussion Problem on Yucca Mountain in Chapter 1.

Low level radioactive wastes include virtually all radioactive wastes other than spent fuel and reprocessing wastes. Although some types of low level waste can be highly radioactive, in general these wastes are less dangerous and decay more quickly than high level wastes. Low level waste represents the vast majority of the volume of radioactive waste, but only a small proportion of the radioactivity. It includes a wide variety of materials, including non-fuel wastes from nuclear power plants, used equipment and reagents from scientific laboratories and hospitals, and wastes from the production of consumer goods such as smoke detectors.

Responsibility for low level waste disposal is shared between the federal government and the states. About two-thirds of the low level waste in the United States is generated by the Department of Energy at its laboratories, and disposed of in Department of Energy facilities. Commercial operations produce the remaining waste; nuclear utilities are responsible for about two-thirds of the total commercial waste. See Mark Holt, Civilian Nuclear Waste Disposal (CRS Issue Brief) (2001). The Low Level Radioactive Waste Policy Act, codified as amended at 42 U.S.C. § 2021b– 2021j, declares that states are responsible for providing for the disposal of commercial low level waste generated within their borders. As originally enacted in 1980, the Act relied primarily on a "carrot" to encourage the creation of sufficient disposal facilities. It authorized states to enter into regional compacts providing for disposal, either through location of a facility in a compact state or by contract with another compact. Once a compact is ratified by Congress, it can exclude waste from non-member states. 42 U.S.C. § 2021e. Because this carrot did not produce any new sites, Congress added a "stick" in 1985—states that failed to provide for disposal would have to "take title" to the waste generated within their borders, becoming financially responsible for its disposal. The Supreme Court struck down the "take title" provision under the Tenth Amendment in *New York v. United States*, 505 U.S. 144 (1992), excerpted in Chapter 4, Section 1(C). Shorn of its primary enforcement mechanism, the law has not led to creation of new facilities. Several compacts have been formed, but none has yet located a new disposal site. The Southeastern Compact is currently trying to determine how to force North Carolina, which had agreed to be the compact's host state, to license a facility. See Supreme Court Rejects SE Compact Bid to Bring NC Suit Directly to High Court, Nuclear Waste News, June 28, 2001.

NOTES AND QUESTIONS

1. *Evaluating Nuclear Power*. What role should nuclear power play in the nation's energy strategy? Nuclear power generation, unlike the burning of coal, oil, or natural gas, does not produce CO_2, and therefore does not contribute to global warming. How should this advantage be weighed against the problem of nuclear waste disposal? How should reactor safety be evaluated? In the 1970s, industry and agency experts asserted that the probability of a major reactor accident was exceedingly low, ranging from 1in 100,000 to 1 in 1 billion per year per reactor. See Carolina Envtl. Study Group v. United States, 510 F.2d 796 (D.C.Cir.1975). The Chernobyl and Three Mile Island incidents called these estimates into question. Proponents of nuclear power, however, point out that Three Mile Island is the only commercial reactor incident in the United States that has ever threatened public health or safety. Although frightening, that incident turned out not to be disastrous. Experts estimate that exposure to radioactive materials released in that incident will ultimately cause no more than five cancer deaths, and may cause none. They also argue that modern reactors are even safer than those currently in operation.

2. *Liability for Nuclear Accidents*. The Price–Anderson Act, 42 U.S.C. § 2210, requires that each licensed reactor carry $200 million in liability insurance, and provides that in the event of a nuclear accident damages exceeding that amount will be assessed equally across the industry, up to a cap. At present licensing levels, the cap is about $9 billion per incident. The

Price–Anderson Act will not cover licenses issued after August 1, 2002, unless Congress extends it. See 42 U.S.C. § 2210(c). Would you favor or oppose its extension? What benefits does the Act offer? What are its shortcomings?

3. *The Siting Game.* Who should choose disposal sites for radioactive wastes (high or low level), and on what basis should those determinations be made? Is it appropriate for the federal government to select sites? How can the states be encouraged to do so? What role, if any, should the local public play in the decision?

CHAPTER NINE

Superfund and Hazardous Waste Liability

Section 1. Introduction

A. From Pollution Control to Remediation

The development of modern, federal environmental legislation began in the early 1970s with the passage of the National Environmental Policy Act (NEPA) and the Clean Air and Water Acts. By 1976, Congress had enacted the Resource Conservation and Recovery Act or RCRA which established an EPA-administered regulatory regime to combat land pollution. The approach taken during this formative period emphasized the vesting of EPA with principal responsibility for the design and implementation of pollution control programs which would govern air, water and land polluting activities. The focus of these programs was to be prospective-ensuring that environmental quality goals would be met over time as polluting conduct was abated. This regulatory structure has endured up to today and continues as a major emphasis of American environmental policy.

In 1978, another environmental problem—the cleanup of inadequate hazardous waste disposal—became an intense public issue demanding immediate attention. While it is difficult to attribute a single cause of congressional action, a highly-publicized emergency situation occurring in Love Canal, New York during the spring and summer of 1978 riveted public attention and was extremely influential in getting Congress to act. The Love Canal situation confronted the public and Congress with a different kind of environmental problem from that presented by air and water pollution control—one which emphasized cleanup of environmentally dangerous conditions. The Comprehensive Environmental Response, Compensation, and Liability Act (or CERCLA) enacted in 1980 represented a new federal policy adopted to reverse the legacy of haphazard industrial waste disposal practices which emphasized an "out of sight, out of mind" approach. In the media portrayal, Love Canal became synonymous with industrial carelessness in the disposal of highly dangerous waste materials, serving as a convincing testament to many of the callousness of industry and lurking chemical threats to public health and safety. It served as a prime example of the inadequacy of scientific knowledge and government policy during the first 80 years of the century and it called for remediation and cleanup of an industrially-contaminated site. With wide media coverage, the Love Canal episode created a striking scenario of contamination which influenced public opinion and galvanized legislative support for CERCLA nearly two years later.

B. Love Canal as an Example of Pervasive Environmental Hazard

The facts behind the Love Canal situation served as a model of improper industrial hazardous waste disposal practices and the need for responsive public policy to respond to the problems presented. In the Love Canal case, Hooker Chemicals & Plastics Corporation had begun chemical manufacturing operations at its Niagara Falls plant in 1905 and dramatically increased its production during World War II to satisfy the demands of the U.S. Government and defense contractors. As the company's production grew, so did its need to dispose of its toxic chemical wastes. Curiously, the serious problems at Love Canal arose because Hooker attempted to find new, less objectionable ways to dispose of production wastes. As a reviewing federal court wrote in 1994,

> Until Hooker began its wartime production, it was able to sewer and dispose of chemicals on-site. Increased volume of chemical waste, combined with growing opposition to open dumping in streams, forced Hooker to consider alternative means of waste disposal. Incineration could not handle the anticipated heavy waste disposal demands. In-ground disposal developed as a viable alternative.

> Hooker became interested in the nearby Love Canal site as a landfill for wastes from its Niagara Falls plant in 1941 and obtained permission from the owner ... to use the site without the expense of an outright purchase.

United States v. Hooker Chemicals & Plastics Corp., 850 F.Supp. 993 (W.D.N.Y.1994). In an area that was largely undeveloped at the time, Hooker created long rectangular disposal cells which were 60 feet wide and 10 feet deep out of an abandoned canal into which nearly 25,000 tons of chemical wastes and fly ash were deposited. The disposal practices last only 12 years. In 1954, Hooker ceased its waste disposal in Love Canal, placed a layer of clay cover over the disposal trenches, and deeded the 16 acre parcel to the Niagara Falls Board of Education for $1. Most of this land was then used for the construction of the Niagara Falls 99th Street Elementary School.

During the ensuing 24 years, the Love Canal neighborhood developed into an ordinary residential neighborhood with some rather extraordinary characteristics. The special problems included explosions occurring at the site which sometimes launched burning debris into adjacent property, chemicals surfacing at the school construction site, odor complaints, craters forming in the school playground, sludge collecting in construction trenches, acid holes forming in the area and common occurrence of eye irritation. Residents had complained to state and local governmental officials during this time period, yet little had been done. Complaints about surface exposure to chemical wastes increased during the mid–1970s and the complaints now asserted that toxic materials were actually seeping into the basements of homes in the Love Canal neighborhood. In the spring of 1978 conditions had deteriorated to the point that the State of New York formed an Interagency Task Force to decide on a course of remedial action. The Task Force visited Love Canal in April of 1978 and found the following situation.

> ... [A] rainfall left the area quite muddy. In the southern sector a heavy chemical odor pervaded, and pools of water containing a black, oily substance rested on the surface. Boards were placed across some of these puddles to permit walking in the area. There was very little vegetation. The surface area around the school "was relatively intact except for a number of drums that appeared to be surfacing through the underlying vegetation." In the center was a baseball diamond.

Id. at 1040. The government team also found nearly 50 pounds of the pesticide lindane and other toxic substances on the surface of the play area used by the elementary school children. On August 2, 1978, the New York State Health Commissioner, fearing possible carcinogenic effect and potential liver damage, declared a health emergency for Love Canal and asked the Niagara Falls School Board not to open the elementary school in September. In the end, numerous houses immediately adjacent to the canal were destroyed and the residents evacuated, relocated and compensated for their losses. The federal government ultimately received judgments for $68 million against Hooker Chemical and for $50 million against Hooker's parent corporation, Occidental Chemical Company.

C.   THE ENACTMENT OF CERCLA OR SUPERFUND LEGISLATION

Public reaction to the Love Canal episode focused national awareness and media attention on the problem of hazardous waste dumps across the nation. In the aftermath of Love Canal, EPA attempted to use two of its existing authorities to deal with hazardous waste dump cleanups. Many pre-CERCLA cases were filed by EPA under the "imminent and substantial endangerment" abatement authorities found in RCRA § 7003. While this section gave EPA the ability to seek a range of injunctive relief, it did not provide a government-administered fund for the cleanup of abandoned sites. In addition, § 311 of the Clean Water Act was used for other situation. Section 311 authorized the Coast Guard to respond to "spills" of oil and hazardous substances but only into navigable waters. This Clean Water Act enforcement power was of little help when the pollution only affected a site's soil and the underlying groundwater. Consequently, EPA considered these existing powers to be inadequate to deal with a pervasive and serious public health and environmental danger.

Recognizing the limitations inherent in both statutory sections, in 1979 the Carter Administration encouraged Congress to consider legislation authorizing federal cleanups of hazardous waste sites and the creation of a significant, federal fund to pay for the work. Legislative action finally came about in the fall of 1980 when the House adopted Superfund legislation in September. Following the 1980 Presidential and Congressional elections, the Senate reconvened a lame duck session and, with the support of the new Republican leadership, passed its own version of the Superfund legislation. The final legislative "horse trading" resulted in a number of significant changes in the prior bills including the reduction in the government administered Superfund from $4.1 billion to $1.6 billion and the elimination of a toxic tort compensation provision which would have created a federal tort cause of action for those injured by hazardous exposures. Acting hurriedly and with little, clear legislative history, the final CERCLA bill was signed into law by outgoing President Carter on December 11, 1980; a little more than a month before President Ronald Reagan's swearing in ceremony. The 1980 CERCLA or Superfund law has lasted for over 20 years with only a 1986 legislative fine tuning (known as SARA) and a number of 1990s, issue-specific modifications. It remains as the main component of federal law governing hazardous waste cleanup and it has encouraged states to adopt their own state law "Superfunds."

SECTION 2.   CERCLA's BASIC STRUCTURE AND POLICY PRINCIPLES

A.   ESSENTIAL STATUTORY FORM

CERCLA is a statute of broad scope and purpose. Best known for its substantial liability-creating features, the law also sets out a comprehensive federal policy governing the methods of site cleanup, the process of selecting remedies, the financing of removal and remedial work, and the collection and distribution of relevant site cleanup information. While viewed primarily as a remedial statute serving to cleanup the contaminated results of past practices, the act and its liability features can also be considered as compliance incentives for the current waste disposal regulations. By establishing broad and extensive liability for site cleanups, CERCLA encourages those presently involved with the disposal of hazardous waste to consistently observe modern waste handling rules mandated by RCRA and state law so as to avoid the situations giving rise to CERCLA liability. As such, the ongoing RCRA hazardous waste disposal regulatory program and the CERCLA cleanup liability program act to reinforce each other. The optimal result of a successful CERCLA program would be the elimination of public health and environmental damage from hazardous waste disposal sites as these facilities observe proper waste handling principles. Beyond this, CERCLA can be considered as an environmental policy which encourages waste reduction or the total elimination of hazardous wastes as industrial byproducts. Without the release of any hazardous waste, there would be no need for any remediation.

Viewing CERCLA from the broadest perspective, the statute establishes three major elements which can be summarized as follows:

- **Cleanup Authority**—federal authority to assess and clean up actual and potential releases of hazardous substances,

- **Financing Capacity**—the Hazardous Substance Response Trust Fund or Superfund to finance EPA site cleanups, and

- **Liability Assessment**—a liability system for those found to be "responsible parties" under the statute for releases or threats of releases of hazardous substances.

Each of these three elements will be examined in greater detail in later materials. As an overview of this complex statute consider the following summary of the Act. Codified sections are provided first followed by bracketed United States Code sections.

———

Significant Sections of CERCLA

§ 101[§ 9601]—Definitions section which includes such important terms as "release," "hazardous substance," "facility," "liable," and "owner or operator."

§ 103[§ 9603]—Requiring, upon penalty of fines and incarceration, the notification of the National Response Center of reportable quantities of hazardous substances.

§ 104[§ 9604]—Authorizing the federal government to undertake response actions including removals or remedial actions of hazardous substances in a manner consistent with the National Contingency Plan.

§ 105[§ 9605]—Authorizing the establishment and revision of the National Contingency Plan(NCP) to deal with hazardous substances releases and the creation of the National Priorities List(NPL) setting forth the facilities presenting the greatest risk to human health and the environment.

§ 106[§ 9606]—Authorizing abatement actions to be taken by way of judicially-imposed remedy and through the EPA's issuance of administrative orders.

§ 107[§ 9607]—Liability imposed for four categories of potentially responsible parties or PRPs for 1) all removal or remedial costs incurred by the federal government "not inconsistent" with the NCP, 2) any other necessary response costs incurred by any other person "consistent with the NCP," 3) damages affecting natural resources, and 4) the costs of health assessments.

§ 111[§ 9611]—Establishing the Superfund to finance government response actions and to reimburse private parties for their costs incurred while carrying out the NCP.

§ 113[§ 9613]—Prevents pre-enforcement judicial review of cleanup response actions and allows private parties to sue other PRPs for contribution for cleanup costs.

§ 116[§ 9616]—Creates a schedule for NPL site listing, remedial planning and execution.

§ 121[§ 9621]—Prescribes standards for CERCLA authorized site cleanups with a preference for remedial actions that are permanent, protective of health and the environment and cost effective attaining cleanup levels that meet a "legally applicable or relevant and appropriate standard, requirement, criteria or limitation" found in federal or more restrictive state law.

§ 122[§ 9622]—Sets forth standards for government settlements with PRPs.

B. THREE "JURISDICTIONAL" ELEMENTS OF CERCLA

However, the fundamental coverage of CERCLA's provisions must be understood as a threshold matter. CERCLA applies and its remedial features are triggered when three elements coexist. There must be:

- A release or a threat of a release of,
- A hazardous substance from,
- A facility or vessel.

Gaining an understanding of these three concepts is crucial to comprehending the scope of CERCLA and its potential application. Each element must be considered separately.

Release. This term represents a key feature of CERCLA since the statute is aimed at cleaning up contaminated sites and those places have received their pollution by way of a "release." What is a "release?" The statute provides a definition for this important term. It states in § 101(22) [§ 9601(22)] that a release means,

> any spilling, leaking, pumping, pouring, emitting, emptying, discharging, injecting, escaping, leaching, dumping, or disposing into the environment(including abandonment or discarding of barrels, containers, and other closed receptacles containing any hazardous substance or pollutant or contaminant).

How broad or narrow is this definition? Must a release be an intentional or willing act? Should a person be found to be releasing a hazardous substance in the absence of such knowing activity? Stated in another way, should a "release" require the active participation of an individual or an organization or should there be a passive "release" as well? What does this question suggest about assigning liability for cleanup costs and other damages?

This statutory definition of the term "release" would seemingly reach any discharge of hazardous substances. Read the section closely and notice that all of the defining terms are modified by the words "into the environment." Most of the time this element is satisfied as when the contaminant reaches the air, surface waters or groundwater. What if an outdoor industrial tank leaks toxic chemicals on to a concrete pad or into a lined lagoon? Should that be considered a release? EPA has claimed that a "release ... to the environment" includes such situations because the potential for further escape is always possible and courts have generally held that any uncontrolled movement of hazardous materials into the environment constitutes a release. See New York v. Shore Realty Corp., 759 F.2d 1032 (2d Cir.1985).

How far should this principle be extended? In State of Vermont v. Staco, Inc., 684 F.Supp. 822 (D.Vt.1988), the district court found a "release" when industrial workers unknowingly brought mercury wastes home on their work clothes, they washed their clothes sending the wastes to their septic tanks, the tanks were pumped out with the effluent taken to a treatment plant, and the mercury wastes were found in the treatment plant sludge. Is this taking CERCLA liability too far?

Section 107(a)(4) also imposes CERCLA liability for remedial actions taken in response to a "threatened release." The statute does not define this term. What could it mean? Should this term be defined in terms of risk? As a judge, how would you decide whether there was a "threatened release?" Some cases have interpreted this term broadly to include rusting and corroding drums, the site owner's inexperience in dealing with hazardous wastes, a lack of proper waste handling licensing, and plant floor spills not meeting the "release" definition. See Amland Properties Corp. v. ALCOA, 711 F.Supp. 784 (D.N.J.1989) and New York v. Shore Realty Corp., 759 F.2d 1032 (2d Cir.1985). Should the analysis consider only the "likelihood" of harm or should it also incorporate the "magnitude" of the harm as well?

CERCLA represents a prime example of political compromise. As such, the statute contains a number of exclusions and exceptions that can only be explained in a political way. Congress specifically excluded four kinds of activities from the definition of "release" and these include: 1) any release which results in exposure to persons solely in a workplace, with respect to a claim which such persons may assert against the employer(like workmen's compensation), 2) engine exhausts of a motor vehicle, rolling stock, aircraft, vessel, or pipeline pumping station engine, 3) any release of nuclear materials from a nuclear "incident" as defined in the Atomic Energy Act or the Uranium Mill Tailings Act, and 4) the normal application of fertilizer. Another area of exemption is § 107(j) which exempts "federally permitted releases" which are defined in CERCLA to include discharges authorized under most federal environmental protection statutes and certain fluid injection practices related to oil and natural gas production. Throughout the 1990s Congress was unable to comprehensively amend CERCLA but it did address industry-specific liability issues through legislation attached to other bills. See e.g., the Asset Conservation, Lender Liability, and Deposit Insurance Protection Act of 1996, P.L. 104–208, 110 Stat. 3009 and the Superfund Recycling Equity Act of 1999, Act of Nov. 29, 1999, Pub. L. 106–113, § 1000(a)(9).

Hazardous Substance. Once again, the statute defines this term and does so in an extremely broad way by making reference to a range of hazardous materials identified under a number of environmental statutes. Section 101(14) provides that a "hazardous substance" includes substances identified as hazardous or toxic under the Clean Water Act, RCRA, the Clean Air Act, the Toxic Substances Control Act, and any other substance specifically designated as hazardous under CERCLA § 102. Currently, EPA has recognized over 700 substances and mixtures as being "hazardous substances" under CERCLA and it is not hard to see how many releases could result in CERCLA liability. See 40 C.F.R. § 302.4. This "list of lists" approach to identifying hazardous wastes subject to cleanup is expansive but it also has express limitations built into the statutory definition of "hazardous substance." Consider the following part of § 101(14) which generally defines "hazardous substance." It states,

> The term does not include petroleum, including crude oil or any fraction thereof which is not otherwise specifically listed or designated as a hazardous substance under [the prior "list of lists"] and the term does not include natural gas, natural gas liquids, liquefied natural gas, or synthetic gas usable for fuel(or mixtures of natural gas and such synthetic gas).

Why does this exemption exist? Why would Congress remove these substances from CERCLA? The "petroleum exclusion" has given rise to a good deal of litigation with mixed results. In Two Rivers Terminal, L.P. v. Chevron USA, Inc., 96 F.Supp.2d 426 (M.D.Pa.2000), the court dismissed a CERCLA cost recovery claim against a former owner of contaminated land on the grounds that there was no evidence of a release or threatened release of a "hazardous substance" at the site. Since the only products stored at the site and detected there were fuel oil and leaded gasoline, the district court ruled that the petroleum exclusion applied. However, in Tosco Corp. v. Koch Industries, Inc., 216 F.3d 886 (10th Cir.2000), the appeals court upheld the liability of a former owner and operator of an oil refinery in a similar action. Examining the record in the case, the court found that "hazardous wastes have commingled with the petroleum products in the soil and floating on the groundwater beneath the refinery . . ." and that the mixture did not invoke the CERCLA exemption. Id. at 893.

Facility. A definition of a "facility" would seem to be the easiest component of CERCLA's three triggering elements. It is defined by the § 101(9) in both a specific, concrete way (including buildings, structures, pits, ponds and lagoons) and an open-ended way phrased in the following terms,

> any site or area where a hazardous substance has been deposited, stored, disposed of, or placed, or otherwise [has] come to be located. . . .

This language has been given extremely broad sweep by the courts to include places that would not be considered a "facility" in ordinary language. See e.g., Louisiana v. Braselman Corp., 78 F.Supp.2d 543 (E.D.La.1999) (railroad tracks constituted a "facility");U.S. v. Ward, 618 F.Supp. 884 (D.N.C.1985) (rural sides of roads where hazardous wastes had been sprayed); and New York v. General Electric Co., 592 F.Supp. 291 (N.D.N.Y.1984) (dragstrip where PCB-laced oil had been used as a dust suppressor). In the following case excerpt, see how these three CERCLA threshold elements are analyzed by the courts and what consequences follow a holding that they are met.

Amoco Oil Company v. Borden, Inc.

United States Court of Appeals, Fifth Circuit, 1989.
889 F.2d 664.

■ REAVLEY, CIRCUIT JUDGE.

In a private action brought under the [CERCLA], Amoco Oil Co. ("Amoco") sought a declaratory judgment for liability and response cost damages from Borden, Inc. ("Borden"), from which Amoco had purchased contaminated industrial property. Finding that Amoco had failed to establish CERCLA liability, the district court entered judgment for Borden. Holding that Amoco has met the liability requirements, we reverse and remand for determination of damages.

The property at issue is a 114–acre tract of land in Texas City, Texas. For many years, Borden operated a phosphate fertilizer plant on the site. As a by-product of the fertilizer manufacturing process, large quantities of phosphogypsum were produced. The site now contains a large inactive pile of phosphogypsum covering approximately 35 acres.

Phosphogypsum alone contains low levels of radioactivity. More highly radioactive sludges and scales from processing equipment, however, were dumped into the phosphogypsum pile, creating "hot" areas within the pile. Additionally, during processing, radioactive materials became concentrated in manufacturing equipment, pipe, and filter cloths used in production. These materials constitute "off-pile" wastes and were left primarily near a junkyard on the property and near the abandoned manufacturing buildings. Some of the off-pile sites contain over 500 times the background level of radiation.

In 1977 Amoco became interested in purchasing the property. The parties discussed two prices: $1.8 million for the site "as is," or $2.2 million if Borden would remove the phosphogypsum. Allegedly unaware of the site's radioactivity, Amoco accepted the "as is" option.

Amoco claims it had no knowledge of the radioactive nature of phosphogypsum until it was so informed by the Texas Department of Water Resources in 1978. Amoco then hired several consultants to measure the radioactivity, to determine geology and hydrology, and to characterize the data. The consultant's reports revealed the various elevated radiation levels throughout the site. The site is currently unused and is secured with fences and guards to prevent access. Amoco claims that permanent remedial action will cost between $11 million and $17 million.

Amoco continued to pursue its CERCLA cost recovery claim, which the district court bifurcated into liability and remedial phases. Borden's primary defenses against liability were: (1) that it had sold the property on an "as is" basis, and that this fact and the doctrine of caveat emptor should preclude a finding of liability; and (2) that the levels of radiation emanating from the site are not high enough to be considered a release of a hazardous substance within the meaning of CERCLA.

On February 2, 1987, the district court issued a Memorandum and Order denying Amoco's motion for entry of judgment on the CERCLA claim. In that order, the court rejected Borden's caveat emptor argument, holding that common-law defenses do not apply to CERCLA claims and that there can be no implied transfer of CERCLA liability. The court further held, however, that Amoco must prove that some threshold level of radioactivity exists at the site in order to establish CERCLA liability and selected the standards for remedial actions at inactive uranium processing sites, see 40 C.F.R. Part 192 (1988) ("Inactive Tailings Standards"), promulgated by the Environmental Protection Agency ("EPA") under the Uranium Mill Tailings Radiation Control Act, 42 U.S.C.A. §§ 7901–7942 (1983 & Supp. 1989), to determine hazardous radionuclide levels.

After hearing evidence at a later trial, the court used data that averaged radiation levels throughout the phosphogypsum pile and concluded that the property's radiation levels did not exceed the Inactive Tailings Standards. It then entered judgment for Borden. Amoco appeals the court's holding that a threshold level of radionuclides must be shown to exist at the site to establish CERCLA liability, the appropriateness of the Inactive Tailings Standards for defining that threshold, and the court's application of that standard.

II.   Discussion

A.   CERCLA

CERCLA substantially changed the legal machinery used to enforce environmental cleanup efforts and was enacted to fill gaps left in an earlier statute, the Resource Conservation and Recovery Act ("RCRA"). The RCRA left inactive sites largely unmonitored by the EPA unless they posed an imminent hazard. News at establishing a means of controlling and financing both governmental and private responses to hazardous releases at abandoned and inactive waste disposal sites. Bulk Distribution Centers, Inc. v. Monsanto Co., 589 F.Supp. 1437, 1441 (S.D.Fla.1984). Section 9607(a), one of CERCLA's key provisions for furthering this objective, permits both government and private plaintiffs to recover from responsible parties the costs incurred in cleaning up and responding to hazardous substances at those sites.

Because of the complexity of CERCLA cases, which often involve multiple defendants and difficult remedial questions, courts have bifurcated the liability and remedial, or damages, phases of CERCLA litigation.... In doing so, disputed factual and legal issues pertaining only to liability are resolved before deciding the more complicated and technical questions of appropriate cleanup measures and the proportionate fault of liable parties. Bifurcation and the use of summary judgment provide efficient approaches to these cases by narrowing the issues at each phase, by avoiding remedial questions if no liability attaches, and by potentially hastening remedial action or settlement discussions once liability is determined....

B.   Liability

To establish a prima facie case of liability in a CERCLA cost recovery action, a plaintiff must prove: (1) that the site in question is a "facility" as defined in § 9601(9); (2) that the defendant is a responsible person under § 9607(a); (3) that a release or a threatened release of a hazardous substance has occurred; and (4) that the release or threatened release has caused the plaintiff to incur response costs.... If the plaintiff establishes each of these elements and the defendant is unable to establish the applicability of one of the defenses listed in § 9607(b), the plaintiff is entitled to summary judgment on the liability issue. This is true even when "there is a genuine issue as to appropriate damages."

A plaintiff may recover those response costs that are necessary and consistent with the National Contingency Plan ("NCP"). § 9607(a)(4)(B); see 40 C.F.R. Part 300 (1988). Thus, once liability is established, the court must determine the appropriate remedy and which costs are recoverable. The court then must ascertain, under CERCLA's contribution provision, each responsible party's equitable share of the cleanup costs. § 9613(f).

It is undisputed that Amoco's property falls within the statutory definition of a "facility;" that Borden is a responsible party within the meaning of CERCLA; and that the statutory defenses to liability are inapplicable. The question of liability centers around the determination of whether a release of a hazardous substance has occurred. Amoco and the EPA, as *amicus curiae*, specifically claim that the district court erred in requiring Amoco to show that the property's radioactive emissions violated a quantitative threshold to establish the release of a hazardous substance within the meaning of § 9607(a)(4). That section provides in relevant part:

[A]ny person who accepts or accepted any hazardous substances for transport to disposal or treatment facilities, incineration vessels or sites selected by such person, from which there is a release, or a threatened release which causes the incurrence of response costs, of a hazardous substance, shall be liable for—....

(B) any other necessary costs of response incurred by any other person consistent with the national contingency plan;....

1.   Hazardous Substance

Radium–226, the primary radioactive waste on the property, decays to form a gas, radon–222, and solid "daughter products."[1] Radon and its daughter products are considered radionuclides, which are defined as "any nuclide that emits radiation." 40 C.F.R. § 61.91(c) (1988). The term hazardous substance includes "any element, compound, mixture, solution, or substance designated pursuant to section 9602 of [CERCLA], ... [and] any hazardous air pollutant listed under section 112 of the Clean Air Act...." § 9601(14). The EPA has designated radionuclides as hazardous

---

1. The new element resulting from the atomic disintegration of a radioactive element is called the daughter of the original element.

substances under § 9602(a) of CERCLA. See 40 C.F.R. § 302.4 (1988). Additionally, the regulations promulgated by the EPA under § 112 of the Clean Air Act, 42 U.S.C. § 7412, list radionuclides as a hazardous air pollutant. See 40 C.F.R. § 61.01(a) (1988).

The new element resulting from the atomic disintegration of a radioactive element is called the daughter of the original element. The plain statutory language fails to impose any quantitative requirement on the term hazardous substance and we decline to imply that any is necessary. Radionuclides meet the listing requirements and therefore the radioactive materials on Amoco's property are hazardous substances within the meaning of CERCLA.

This holding is supported by courts that have considered the definitional requirements of the term and congressional comments contained in the legislative history....

2. Release

The term "release" is defined to mean: "any spilling, leaking, pumping, pouring, emitting, emptying, discharging, injecting, escaping, leaching, dumping, or disposing into the environment (including the abandonment or discarding of barrels, containers, and other closed receptacles containing any hazardous substance or pollutant or contaminant)...." § 9601(22). As with "hazardous substance," the plain statutory language fails to impose any quantitative requirement on the term "release." We believe that the definition of "release" should be construed broadly,.... "to avoid frustrat[ing] the beneficial legislative purposes." *Dedham Water Co. v. Cumberland Farms Dairy, Inc.*, 805 F.2d 1074, 1081 (1st Cir.1986).

Borden's actions met the release requirement in two ways. First, it did so by disposing of the phosphogypsum and highly radioactive wastes on the property. See § 9601(22). Second, the gas emitting from the radionuclides constitutes a release within the meaning of the statute.

3. Response Costs

The statutory provision suggesting a threshold for liability is the requirement that a release or threatened release have "caused the incurrence of response costs." § 9607(a)(4). Response costs are generally and specifically defined to include a variety of actions designed to protect the public health or the environment. To justifiably incur response costs, one necessarily must have acted to contain a release threatening the public health or the environment.

In our interpretation of the requirement that a release "cause the incurrence of response costs," we are notably entering unexplored territory. As with many of CERCLA's provisions, the legislative history is bereft of discussion about the causal nexus between releases and response costs. Additionally, courts have not been faced with a scenario suggesting that a plaintiff's action was not justified by the hazard posed. Borden argues that this case presents such a situation.

Borden has pointed out that all matter is radioactive to some degree. While harmless at low concentrations, at some point on a continuum it poses an unacceptable risk to human life and the environment. Given CERCLA's broad liability provisions and the pervasive nature of radionuclides, Borden argues that without a quantitative limit CERCLA liability could attach to the release of any substance and theoretically could reach "everything in the United States." The district court was apparently persuaded by Borden's argument. In finding a standard essential, it noted that "most of the radionuclides in the atmosphere come from natural sources [and that] radionuclides are used or produced in thousands of locations throughout the United States."

Yet, concerns about the most extreme reach of liability—extending to naturally occurring hazardous substances—are misplaced. Remedial actions taken in response to hazardous substances as they occur naturally are specifically excluded from the NCP and are therefore not recoverable. § 9604(a)(3)(A). The only concern that should support the use of a quantitative measure at the liability phase is potential abuse of the broad provisions, which may subject some defendants to harassing litigation.

Amoco and the EPA argue that CERCLA liability attaches upon the release of any quantity of a hazardous substance and that the extent of a release should be considered only at the remedial phase. However, we must reject this approach because adherence to that view would permit CERCLA's reach to exceed its statutory purposes by holding parties liable who have not posed any threat to the public or the environment. Accordingly, we find use of a standard of justification acceptable for determining whether a release or threatened release of a hazardous substance has caused the incurrence of response costs. In the absence of any specific direction from Congress, we believe that the question of whether a release has caused the incurrence of response costs should rest upon a factual inquiry into the circumstances of a case and the relevant factual inquiry should focus on whether the particular hazard justified any response actions. CERCLA's provisions provide guidance for making this determination. Section 9621(d) governs the extent of cleanup, which is required "at a minimum [to] assure[] protection of human health and the environment." § 9621(d)(1). To attain that goal, the scope of remedial action may be established by any "legally applicable or relevant and appropriate . . . requirement" ("ARAR"). § 9621(d)(2)(A). ARARs include "any standard, requirement, criteria, or limitation under any Federal environmental law" or any more stringent "State environmental or facility siting law." *Id.* As these standards define the limits of appropriate response costs, and therefore recoverable expenses, they are also useful for establishing the limits of liability. While not the exclusive means of justifying response costs, we hold that a plaintiff who has incurred response costs meets the liability requirement as a matter of law if it is shown that *any* release violates, or any threatened release is likely to violate, *any* applicable state or federal standard, including the most stringent.

Amoco has clearly met this requirement by showing that the radioactive emissions exceeded the limits set in Subpart B of the Inactive Tailings Standards [the federal standard for inactive uranium mill tailings piles]. . . .

As there has been a release of a hazardous substance that justified the incurrence of response costs and the other elements of a prima facie case have been met, Amoco is entitled to summary judgment on the liability issue.

CLASS DISCUSSION PROBLEM

Mario has contacted you about the purchase of an 8 acre parcel of land he has recently purchased from Ted. Mario intends to use the land and the buildings on it to build and maintain Indy-style race cars. Ted had previously used the location as a commercial truck garage for 22 years and there was some evidence that the facility had been used by other owners continuously since the 1930s for the servicing of machinery and vehicles. After taking title to the property and inspecting the buildings on it, Mario has discovered of things including: 1) chipping, flaking and peeling paint on the interior walls of the structures which were painted before 1978 and might contain lead, 2) leaking barrels in a storage room containing a common solvent trichloroethylene or TCE which have spilled onto the floor, 3) above-ground oil and gasoline storage tanks which have leaked onto the pavement and adjacent soil, 4) excessive buildup of fertilizer on the rear part of the site resulting from an unsuccessful prior attempt to grow grass, and 5) soot and other particles on one part of the tarmac which were the residue of prior engine testing. How would you respond to the following questions?

1. Does the peeling paint on interior walls trigger any duties of notification or response under CERCLA? Assume that the paint does contain lead and that lead has been identified as an air toxic under the Clean Air Act. Would it matter that the paint was only used on interior surfaces? What if it was used to paint an outside wall sign?

2. What about the leaking barrels of TCE? Would it be significant to the analysis that the spill remained within the storage room? What if it seeped through an outside wall and soaked into the ground but still within the boundaries of the 8 acre site?

3. Is Mario exempt from liability because the garage was never considered to be nor used as a waste disposal "facility" under any state or federal regulatory scheme?

4. The leaking oil and gasoline represents an "automatic" CERCLA-triggering action. Right? What about the chemical fertilizer and the engine soot? Check CERCLA § 101(22) and 107(i) carefully.

5. What if one of the leaking oil storage tanks only contains waste oil that had been received from customers and left at the garage for recycling purposes? Examine §§ 114(c) and 101(37).

6.   What if the rear part of the parcel had previously been wetlands filled with waste auto batteries by Ted. Ted had filled the area in 1988 under a valid § 404 dredge and fill permit issued by the U.S. Army Corps of Engineers? What if the § 404 permit specified that the fill used not contain materials "inherently harmful to wetland flora and fauna?" See § 101(10).

SECTION 3.   HAZARDOUS WASTE CLEANUP MECHANISMS UNDER CERCLA

A.   REMEDIATING CONTAMINATED SITES—THE INTERPLAY OF STATE AND FEDERAL LAW

CERCLA's main focus is on the cleanup of contaminated sites where hazardous substances have been released or where there is a threat of release. In many ways, this federal statute represents a modern extension of state public and private nuisance law-attempting to remedy conditions which threaten the environment and public health. However, in § 302(d), Congress stated that Superfund was intended to coexist with state law. The law states that nothing in CERCLA "shall affect * * * the obligations or liabilities of any person under* * *State law, including common law, with respect to releases of hazardous substances or other pollutants or contaminants." It must be understood that CERCLA was not intended to displace state common law. In fact, many judicial actions are brought under the multi-faceted authorities of CERCLA as well as state common and statutory law. State common law will only be found to be preempted when its operation would interfere with CERCLA's functioning or the statute's objectives. See e.g., In re Pfohl Bros. Landfill Litigation, 68 F.Supp.2d 236 (W.D.N.Y.1999) (preemption found when state law would eliminated liability from PRPs otherwise liable under CERCLA). In some cases, state law goes beyond the reach of Superfund and provides for more extensive remedies than those provided by federal law.

B.   INFORMATION GATHERING—EPA'S AUTHORITY TO INVESTIGATE AND TO OBTAIN INFORMATION

As the material following will indicate, CERCLA provides EPA, states and private parties with tremendous power to undertake cleanup actions and to seek cost recovery from a wide range of other responsible parties. How does EPA know where to focus its attention under CERCLA? Which sites are deserving of response actions first? Where should the limited Superfund cleanup monies be spent? All of these questions depend upon information regarding contaminated site conditions. EPA learns about these locations through two principle means: a) site discovery by various parties including citizens, state agencies and EPA's regional offices and b) direct notification by PRPs of hazardous substance releases. The Love Canal episode, predating CERCLA, was characterized by a long term pattern of citizen complaints to state and federal environmental agencies which finally brought an aggressive governmental response when home basements were invaded by seeping pollutants and when the national media took notice.

CERCLA § 104(b) grants EPA broad powers to collect information through investigations, monitoring, surveys, and testing to "identify the existence and extent of the release or threat thereof, the source and nature of hazardous substances, pollutants or contaminants involved, and the extent of danger to the public health or welfare or to the environment." Even more sweeping authority exists in § 104(e) which allows EPA to a) make information requests of PRPs, b) undertake physical on-site inspections and c) to remove samples during an on-site inspection. EPA has been granted great latitude in exercising these powers. See U.S. v. M. Genzale Plating, Inc., 723 F.Supp. 877 (E.D.N.Y.1989) (EPA's is entitled to site access if its demand is reasonably based in the belief that there may be a release or threat of release of hazardous substances). But see U.S. v. Tarkowski, 248 F.3d 596 (7th Cir.2001) (site access orders to search and seize must comply with the Fourth Amendment). Any attempted defiance of EPA's requests under these statutes can be met by an EPA-issued administrative order enforceable in court with a $25,000 per day civil penalty for non-compliance. With all of these sources of information from citizens, state agencies and its own regional offices, EPA can identify hazardous waste sites in need of assessment and determine if a federal, state or private party response is the best course of action.

C. THE NATIONAL PRIORITIES LIST (NPL)—IDENTIFYING THE WORST FIRST

In its structure, CERCLA could only have provided EPA the authority for hazardous waste site cleanup and cost recovery. The statute did this but it also went one step further—Congress directed EPA to identify the highest priority facilities in each state in need of immediate attention. The act accomplishes this priority setting goal in § 105(a)(8)(B) by requiring EPA to establish and to annually revise a National Priorities List or NPL which would spot the worst hazardous waste locations and set them as the first priority for EPA, state or private party cleanup. This list, technically Appendix B of the National Contingency Plan which will be discussed below, is intended to guide EPA in:

a. determining which sites warrant further investigation to assess their threat to human health and the environment;

b. identifying what CERCLA-financed cleanups may be appropriate;

c. notifying the public of sites EPA believes need further investigation; and

d. serving notice to PRPs that EPA may begin a CERCLA-financed remedial action.

Inclusion on the NPL follows a process of EPA and/or state site nomination, a notice of the proposal published in the *Federal Register*, EPA's receipt of and response to public comments received following the notice, and final selection by EPA.

Since the enactment of CERCLA, EPA and the states assessed over 41,000 sites, determining that1509 sites would be added to the list when they were found to present a sufficient threat to human health or the environment. By November of 2001, over half (804) of the NPL sites had all cleanup construction completed. Most of these sites were actually cleaned up in the 1990s after the prior decade when "the CERCLA program was characterized by a burgeoning bureaucracy, extensive and expensive litigation, and a morale-sapping management scandal." Maxine I. Lipides, Hazardous Waste 278 (3d ed. 1997).

This acceleration in the cleaning up unremediated NPL sites was the result of heavy, early criticism regarding the pace of Superfund cleanups. In 1993, EPA responded by instituting the Superfund Accelerated Cleanup Model(SACM) to speed up site cleanups and to focus EPA's long term remedial actions only at NPL sites. In the absence of comprehensive CERCLA reform since 1986, the SACM has significantly improved the rate of site remediation. However, as the NPL list contracts with "construction completions," it also expands with new site additions. By June, 2001, another 67 sites had been proposed for inclusion on the NPL. It has been estimated that there could be as many as 3,000 more NPL sites that could be listed in the future. CERCLA cleanups will undoubtedly continue well into the future.

What is the significance of being included on the NPL list? It is clearly a status that many property owners and other PRPs have challenged, largely unsuccessfully, in court. See e.g., Mead Corp. v. Browner, 100 F.3d 152 (D.C.Cir.1996). Courts, not surprisingly, test EPA's NPL listing decision under the "arbitrary and capricious" test and rarely overturn the agency's decision. There are some exceptions such as Kent County v. EPA, 963 F.2d 391 (D.C.Cir.1992) and Anne Arundel County v. EPA, 963 F.2d 412 (D.C.Cir.1992), where the appeals court held that EPA had erroneously relied upon unfiltered water samples to establish a site score. It is not hard to understand why a property owner would not want its land to be on the NPL: looming liability for cleanup expenses, EPA's continuing involvement, bad publicity, required disclosure in securities law filings and devastating impact on the marketability of the parcel or business. As important as NPL listing is, there are several points which are worth considering:

    a.   NPL status *is* mainly an identification device indicating "priority" sites deserving EPA's first attention,

    b.   EPA may use the Superfund to finance both *removal* and *remedial* actions at *NPL* sites,

    c.   EPA may use the Superfund to finance only *removal* actions at *non-NPL* sites,

    d.   NPL listing does *not* determine CERCLA liability of PRPs,

e. NPL status is *not* a prerequisite for later cost recovery actions and contribution claims against PRPs under §§ 107 and 113 after they clean up a site.

NPL listing is a significant classification suggesting long-term EPA involvement in the planning, undertaking and financing of the response actions selected for the site. However, it is notable that many non-NPL site cleanups are governed by CERCLA's substantive and procedural elements and that litigation is often brought to contest liability or allocation decisions regarding these locations.

B & B Tritech, Inc. v. United States

United States Court of Appeals, District of Columbia Circuit, 1992.
957 F.2d 882.

OPINION

Per Curiam: Petitioners argue that the Environmental Protection Agency (the "EPA" or "Agency") should not have listed the B & B Chemical Company site on the National Priorities List of hazardous waste releases. We deny the petition, but urge the Agency to promptly consider delisting the site.

I. Background

The Comprehensive Environmental Response, Compensation, and Liability Act of 1980 ("CERCLA") requires the President to prepare a "national contingency plan for the removal of ... hazardous substances," and therein to list "national priorities among the known releases or threatened releases throughout the United States." 42 U.S.C. § 9605(a) (1988). The EPA has been delegated responsibility for the National Priorities List ("NPL"), and periodically updates the list through informal rulemaking. The Hazard Ranking System ("HRS"), a mathematical model, is used to evaluate proposed NPL sites. Our prior decisions have fully described the NPL and the HRS. See, e.g., Linemaster Switch Corp. v. EPA, 291 App. D.C. 40, 938 F.2d 1299 (D.C.Cir.1991)....

The B & B Chemical Company ("B & B") is a family-owned firm with a manufacturing facility in Hialeah, Florida. On June 24, 1988, the EPA proposed adding the Hialeah facility to the NPL. See 53 FR 23,988 (1988). Groundwater sampling had revealed a plume of contamination underneath the site, in the shallow layer of the so-called Biscayne Aquifer. This plume apparently stemmed in part from "soakage pits" that B & B had once used for its waste water. The site received a proposed HRS score of 35.35 (the NPL threshold is 28.50), based solely on the risk that contamination would migrate through the ground water.

The Ground Water Migration Route score in the HRS is composed of two different factors: "Waste Characteristics" and "Targets." The Targets factor measures the risk that contamination will spread to a substantial population, and has two components: "Distance to Nearest Well/Population

Served" and "Ground Water Use." See 40 C.F.R. pt. 300 app. A § 3.5 (1990). The distance to nearest well "is measured from the hazardous substance ... to the nearest well that draws water from the aquifer of concern." Id. at 105. Population served "includes residents as well as others who would regularly use the water" from wells within three miles of the site, but those "who do not use water from the aquifer of concern are not to be counted." Id. at 107. The HRS has formulas for quantifying and then combining these two components.

There are four public wellfields within three miles of the Hialeah site, and these connect to a regional distribution system serving some 750,000 people. However, the wellfields draw from deeper ground water, while the contamination underneath the site is largely confined to the shallow aquifer layer. Moreover, the regional water authority no longer uses the fields as a source of supply, and only pumps them for a short period each day, so as to keep the equipment operable. The EPA nonetheless counted the wellfields in B & B's Targets score: the B & B facility was scored as "serving" a population of 750,000, the "nearest well" was found to be within one mile of the site, and the Agency proposed a Distance to Nearest Well/Population Served score of 35 (out of 40).

B & B protested the proposed NPL listing, but the Agency refused to change its HRS score, and the Hialeah site was added to the NPL effective October 1, 1990, see 55 Fed. Reg. 35,502 (1990). The company and its owners now petition for review.

II.   Analysis

Congress' goal in SARA was to assure that the HRS "accurately assesses relative risks to human health and the environment ... within the context of the purpose for the National Priorities List; i.e., identifying for the States and the public those facilities and sites which appear to warrant remedial actions." H.R. Conf. Rep. No. 962, 99th Cong., 2d Sess. 199 (1986). The B & B site did not receive the benefit of SARA, but was scored under the original version of the HRS. This case shows why Congress required a new model.

Petitioners rightly argue that the EPA's calculation of the Distance to Nearest Well/Population Served subfactor was highly formulaic. The Agency made two crucial assumptions. First, the entire Biscayne Aquifer was treated as single "aquifer of concern," and thus the shallow plume of contamination underneath the B & B site was presumed accessible to the nearby wellfields, despite the fact that these fields drew from the deep aquifer layer. The EPA's justification was that "traces" of contamination had been found in the deep layer, and that the boundary between the deep and shallow layers was sufficiently permeable for vertical migration. See Response to Comments at 4–48 to 4–50, reprinted in Petitioners' Appendix 236, 252–54. Second, the EPA found that 750,000 people were "using" the wellfields, despite the fact that the wellfields had been taken out of service and were only pumped intermittently to keep the equipment operable. The justification, here, was that a "limited amount of water from these wellfields enters the distribution system daily." Id. at 4–54, reprinted in Petitioners' Appendix 236, 258.

Despite our concern over the seemingly unfair effects of the overly formalistic approach followed by EPA in this case, we are constrained to deny the petition. Our case law endorses the "Hazard Ranking System's preference for using formulas," Eagle–Picher III, 822 F.2d at 146, and emphasizes that "the NPL s simply a rough list of priorities, assembled quickly and inexpensively," Eagle–Picher II, 759 F.2d at 932. Specifically, we have held that the EPA can treat two separate ground water routes as a single "aquifer of concern" if the two are connected. "Where a contaminated aquifer spreads water to an aquifer supplying a target population, contamination to the first is hazard to the second and the 'Agency reasonably treats them as a unit for purposes of the Hazard Ranking System.'" City of Stoughton, 858 F.2d at 752 (quoting Eagle–Picher III, 822 F.2d at 139) (brackets omitted). The presence of trace contaminants in the deep aquifer layer, together with the direct evidence of vertical permeability, was sufficient to demonstrate a connection between the two layers of the Biscayne Aquifer. See also Eagle–Picher III, 822 F.2d at 150 (upholding NPL listing despite fact that "water naturally cleanses itself of contaminants as it moves [from the site] through geological formations to the wells from which the water is drawn").

We also have specifically permitted Agency imprecision in calculating the target population. In Eagle–Picher I, a general challenge to the HRS, we held that the EPA could "estimate the population within a certain radius of the release [instead of] utilizing actual population figures." 759 F.2d at 921. In City of Stoughton, we declared that the Agency need not divide the population into subgroups, even where subdivision would produce a more accurate score. See 858 F.2d 754 at 754–55. Finally, in the recent Linemaster Switch case, we again allowed a challenged Targets score and emphasized that the EPA "properly . . . included within its calculation all people who draw water from wells located within three miles of the hazardous substances." 938 F.2d at 1307. Given these precedents, we are constrained to find that the EPA could count the four wellfields proximate to B & B: a population of 750,000 did indeed "use" the water from these fields, if this word is formulaically interpreted to cover minimally-used wells.

However, the Agency's decision remains a troubling one. The record does not disclose whether the B & B site poses any real risk to the public, because the EPA did not address that question. We do not know whether dangerous quantities of contaminants flow from the site to the wellfields, or from the fields into the regional distribution system. Agency counsel conceded at oral argument that the site would not be dangerous, indeed would not be listed, if the wellfields were only pumped once a year: that would be equivalent to zero pumping. But the Agency has not yet examined whether minimal daily pumping creates a significantly higher risk than zero pumping, given the "trace" wastes that B & B has contributed to the deep aquifer layer.[5]

Despite the very real possibility that their facility does not endanger the population, petitioners must now bear the considerable costs that result from an NPL listing. Moreover, these costs might have been avoided if the Agency had more promptly complied with SARA. The ground water segment of the new HRS is quite sophisticated; inter alia, "populations served by wells whose water is blended with that from other drinking water sources are to be apportioned based on the well's relative contribution to the total blended system." 55 Fed. Reg. 51,532, 51,572 (1990) (promulgating new HRS); see 40 C.F.R. pt. 300 app. A § 3.3 (1991) (new Targets section). In Linemaster Switch, where a listed site might have benefitted from the new HRS, we acknowledged that the site would not need to be rescored. See 938 F.2d at 1307. But we also emphasized that the "EPA has broad discretion in determining what remedial actions are warranted." Id. Specifically, "releases may be deleted from or recategorized on the NPL where no further response is appropriate." 40 C.F.R.§ 300.425(e) (1991). We urge the EPA to move forward, quickly, to a remedial investigation to determine whether B & B poses any measurable or meaningful health risk; if not, the Agency should act with dispatch to delist the B & B site.[6]

III. Conclusion

The petition for review is denied. We uphold the EPA's decision to place the B & B facility on the National Priorities List.

D. DESIGNING AND CARRYING OUT HAZARDOUS WASTE SITE CLEANUPS

1. DEFINING CERCLA RESPONSE: REMOVAL AND REMEDIAL ACTIONS

CERCLA also provides guidance for planning and taking the necessary steps to respond to hazardous waste site conditions. The statute recognizes two forms of response action to a release or threat of release of hazardous substances: 1) removal actions and 2) remedial actions. Both terms are defined in the statute at §§ 101(23) and 101(24). These two categories should be viewed as a chronological sequence of cleanup activities although the exact boundary between the two concepts is not clear. A removal is a short term or emergency response activity "necessary to prevent, minimize, or mitigate damages to the public health or welfare or to the environment." CERCLA § 101(23). Examples of such actions include providing fences around a site, alternative water supplies, temporary evacuation and hous-

---

5. It also appears that the wellfield water passes through a treatment plant before reaching the public. Neither party mentions this fact.

6. Furthermore, if the EPA finds that sites with no measurable or meaningful health risk continue to receive high HRS scores under the new model, it would seem prudent for the EPA to consider exempting such sites from the NPL.

ing and the removal of leaking sources of contamination. A "remedial action" contemplates a long term, permanent remedy to neutralize the threat from the site and to protect the public health and the environment. The statute contains an extensive list of examples of "remedies" and these include removing and disposing of contaminated soil, pumping out polluted groundwater, building dikes or other barriers around the site, installing clay covers, and collecting leachate and runoff. These extensive and complex remedial responses usually takes many years and millions of dollars to accomplish.

The distinction between "removal" and "remedial" actions can have great financial and procedural significance. EPA can spend monies from the Superfund on *removal* actions on *any* site whether or not it is listed on the NPL, EPA may only undertake *remedial* action on NPL sites. See 40 C.F.R. § 300.425(b). This fact has led to the assertion that EPA has characterized cleanup responses as removals in order to access the Superfund for non-NPL cleanup work In addition, removal actions may be taken by EPA in a more expedited manner without lengthy, decision making process required of a CERCLA remedial action. It is noteworthy that once EPA has spent funds on either a removal or a remedial action, it may commence a § 107 cost recovery action against any PRPs who are liable under the act.

2. THE NATIONAL CONTINGENCY PLAN (NCP): THE BLUEPRINT FOR DESIGNING AND CARRYING OUT SITE CLEANUPS

Once a release or threat of release of hazardous substances is identified at a site, how is the cleanup response organized and what are its substantive features? Section 105(a) of CERCLA directs that these response activities be governed by a unified, national blueprint: the National Contingency Plan or the NCP. The National Contingency Plan was originally developed under § 311 of the Clean Water Act for oil and hazardous substance spills in American waterways but has now been expanded by CERCLA to deal with hazardous waste site cleanups as well. Section 105(a) of Superfund states, in general terms, that the NCP "shall specify procedures, techniques, materials, equipment, and methods to be employed in identifying, removing, or remedying releases of hazardous substances. . . ." The language of this section sets the framework for EPA's NCP development. It states,

(1) methods for discovering and investigating facilities at which hazardous substances have been disposed of or otherwise come to be located;

(2) methods for evaluating, including analyses of relative cost, and remedying any releases or threats of releases from facilities which pose substantial danger to the public health or the environment;

(3) methods and criteria for determining the appropriate extent of removal, remedy, and other measures authorized by this chapter;

(4) appropriate roles and responsibilities for the Federal, State, and local governments and for interstate and nongovernmental entities in effectuating the plan;

(5) provision for identification, procurement, maintenance, and storage of response equipment and supplies;

(6) a method for and assignment of responsibility for reporting the existence of such facilities which may be located on federally owned or controlled properties and any releases of hazardous substances from such facilities;

(7) means of assuring that remedial action measures are cost-effective over the period of potential exposure to the hazardous substances or contaminated materials;

(8) [criteria for establishing removal and remedial priorities and the NPL,]

(9) specified roles for private organizations and entities in preparation for response and in responding to releases of hazardous substances, including identification of appropriate qualifications and capacity therefor and including consideration of minority firms in accordance with subsection (f) of this section; and

(10) standards and testing procedures by which alternative or innovative treatment technologies can be determined to be appropriate for utilization in response actions authorized by this chapter.

EPA has taken this authority and developed its National Contingency Plan containing Subpart E, which specifically deals with hazardous waste cleanup and is called the "Hazardous Substance Response Plan." See 40 C.F.R. part 300. The NCP was revised in 1990 and it currently applies to CERCLA response actions both taken by the government and by private parties. This revision was challenged and upheld in State of Ohio v. EPA, 997 F.2d 1520 (D.C.Cir.1993).

The NCP is extremely important since CERCLA provides that response costs may only be recovered if they are for actions taken in compliance with the NCP. The statute expresses this policy in two slightly different ways for EPA and PRP-led cleanups. Governments undertaking cleanup efforts can only recover removal and remedial costs which are *"not inconsistent* with the [NCP]." CERCLA § 107(a)(4)(A). With a few exceptions, courts have generally tended to be deferential to EPA's remedial choices by applying an "arbitrary and capricious" standard of review to these decisions. However, private parties may only recover these response costs which are *"consistent with* the [NCP]." Section 107(a)(4)(B). While this slight difference in terminology might seem trivial, it has been contested in litigation with the plaintiff PRP bearing the burden of proof on the issue. See e.g., General Electric Co. v. Litton, Inc., 920 F.2d 1415 (8th Cir.1990).

But how strictly must a private party follow the NCP? To counteract a prior line of cases requiring "strict compliance" with the NCP as a predicate to a PRPs cost recovery, EPA's 1990 NCP revision partially adopted "substantial compliance" interpretation. It stated that in the context of a private party action, consistency with the NCP requires only "substantial compliance" with regard to the procedural and public participation requirements. However, the revision demands that there be a strict showing that the remedy provided a "CERCLA-quality cleanup." See 40 C.F.R. § 300.700(c)(3)(i). This would seem to de-emphasize process and place more focus on the substantive result of the cleanup. Unfortunately for private parties, the NCP revision does not specifically define what is meant by the term "CERCLA-quality cleanup" although its preamble briefly states that the remedy must 1) protect human health and the environment, 2) use permanent solutions and alternative treatment technologies or resource recovery techniques to the maximum extent practicable, 3) be cost-effective, 4) attain ARARs, and 5) provide for meaningful public participation. Consequently, observing the NCP has both remedial and financial implications to both EPA and to private PRPs seeking the recovery of cleanup costs.

What is the NCP? It is a planning document that specifies the procedures for identifying, evaluating and responding to sites having an actual or threatened release of a hazardous substance. The Hazardous Substance Response Plan or Subpart E of the NCP contains seven components concerned with: 1) discovery and notification, 2) removal site evaluation, 3)removals, 4) site evaluation, 5) NPL determination and the setting of remedial priorities, 6) remedial investigation and feasibility study, and 7) remedial design and action. The NCP's complexity goes far beyond the CERCLA's statutory language and the plan is supplemented by numerous EPA guidance documents dealing with cleanup efforts. Attorneys and others specializing in this area of environmental practice must be familiar with these extensive EPA policies as well as those of state environmental agencies. EPA maintains an information clearinghouse for its Superfund document center, the National Response Center, and Hazardous Waste Ombudsman Program at: www.epa.gov/epahome/clearing.html

Washington State Dept. of Transp. v. Washington Natural Gas Co.

United States Court of Appeals, Ninth Circuit, 1995.
59 F.3d 793.

■ Tang, Senior Circuit Judge.

This is a review of several judgments of the United States district court, western district of Washington. The Washington State Department of Transportation (WSDOT) initiated this action against Washington Natural Gas Company (WNG), Pacificorp, and Advance Ross Corporation [herafter "WNG"] seeking recovery costs due under the Comprehensive Environmental Response, Compensation, and Liability Act (CERCLA), 42 U.S.C. § 9601, et seq. On cross-motions for partial summary judgment, the district court concluded that the defendants were responsible parties under CERCLA § 107. The district court conducted a bench trial to determine damages and entered a judgment in favor of WNG et al. The district court concluded that WSDOT was not entitled to recover its response costs because WSDOT did not comply with the National Contingency Plan ("NCP") promulgated by the Environmental Protection Agency ("EPA") pursuant to CERCLA.

WSDOT appeals the district court's judgment that WSDOT failed to comply with the NCP and was, therefore, not entitled to recover fromWNG.

The overarching issue on this appeal is whether WSDOT can recover its response costs. To answer this question, we must address several related issues. First, under 42 U.S.C. § 9607(a), is a state entitled to a presumption that its actions are consistent with the NCP? The effect of this presumption is to shift the burden of proving inconsistency with the NCP. We conclude that states are entitled to the presumption of consistency. Second, is WSDOT the "State" under 42 U.S.C. § 9607(a)? We conclude that WSDOT is the "State," but further conclude that erroneously placing the burden of proof on WSDOT was harmless error. Third, were WSDOT's actions consistent with the relevant NCP, thereby entitling WSDOT to recovery of its response costs? We conclude that WSDOT's actions were inconsistent with the NCP and thus WSDOT is not entitled to recover its costs.

BACKGROUND

In 1982, WSDOT began construction of the Tacoma Spur, an interstate highway project designed to connect Interstate 5 to Schuster Parkway and downtown Tacoma, Washington. In late 1983 and early 1984, WSDOT's geotechnical consultant, the firm of Hart Crowser, discovered tar-like material in soil borings taken to gain information on the material that would support planned highway structures. WSDOT reported the contamination to the Washington State Department of Ecology ("WSDOE"). WSDOE tested soil samples using the persistence testing method, which tests for PAH compounds. Because these soil samples came from the geotechnical borings, they were not obtained utilizing protocol typically followed to gather environmental samples. WSDOE reported that the tarry material was contaminated with polycyclic aromatic hydrocarbons ("PAHs") at a level of greater than one percent. Under WSDOE's regulations, material with a concentration of PAHs greater than one percent is considered "extremely hazardous waste."

WSDOE advised WSDOT that it might try to get the site listed on the CERCLA National Priority List, to obtain funding through the Superfund program. According to Hart Crowser, WSDOT did not want to pursue that option because it involved extra time and effort. Neither Hart Crowser nor WSDOT referred to the CERCLA National Contingency Plan to determine how to proceed.

WSDOT hired Hart Crowser as an environmental consultant to investigate the site and determine the type and extent of subsurface contamination. Hart Crowser began its investigation in July, 1984. The firm discovered from historical records that a coal gasification plant had operated on the construction site from 1884 until 1924. Sanborn maps indicated the location of the gas holders used to store the manufactured gas. Hart Crowser assumed that the plant, along with any gas holders, had been removed because the plant was not visible.

Hart Crowser also learned that tar was a likely by-product of the coal gasification process and may have accumulated in gas holders. However, Hart Crowser expected that the tar had been removed because it had some commercial value. The firm also assumed that any remaining tar waste had been dumped on the extremities of the plant grounds. To avoid running into the foundations of the gas holders, Hart Crowser did not put borings into the area where the gas holders had been located.

In addition to conducting historical research, Hart Crowser drilled twenty-six borings and obtained 359 soil samples. Upon testing these samples, Hart Crowser identified two types of contaminated material: tar-like material, and oily silt and sand. Hart Crowser's tests indicated a PAH concentration under one percent in the tar-like material. The highest concentration of PAHs in one sample of tar-like material was .5 percent and the second highest was .15 percent. The concentration of PAHs in the oily silt and sand did not exceed .02 percent. Hart Crowser did not use the test WSDOE had used to identify PAHs—Hart Crowser's method did not test for the total PAH level. Therefore Hart Crowser's report relied on WSDOE's original tests to conclude that the tar may be classified as a hazardous waste by WSDOE standards. Hart Crowser estimated the volume of the sub-surface contaminants by interpolating between the borings. The calculations yielded estimates that the site contained 40 to 100 cubic yards, a maximum of 100 tons, of coal tar and 4,500 to 6,000 cubic yards of oily silt and sand, a maximum of 10,000 tons. Hart Crowser issued a report containing its findings in November, 1984.

While Hart Crowser conducted its investigation, WSDOT organized an interagency team, consisting of representatives of WSDOT, WSDOE, and Hart Crowser, to discuss the action that needed to be taken. At various times, the team also included representatives of the Federal Highway Administration and the Tacoma–Pierce County Health Department.

After Hart–Crowser concluded the investigation, the interagency team met for several months to determine the appropriate course of action. The team concluded that all of the material had to be removed because it contained varying amounts of contamination. WSDOT recognized that the characterization of each of the two materials would have a major impact on the remedy selected and, therefore, the cost of removal. WSDOE considered the tar extremely hazardous waste under WSDOE regulations, based on its initial tests indicating a PAH concentration of greater than one percent. The team concluded that the only feasible option was to dispose of the tar at a hazardous waste facility in Arlington, Oregon. For the oily silt and sand, which was not considered a dangerous waste, the team considered the alternatives of on-site disposal, reuse, disposal at a landfill, disposal at the Arlington hazardous waste facility, and chemical treatment. Eventually the team decided to encapsulate the oily silt and sand in vaults on the site, an option considerably cheaper than disposal at Arlington.

Construction on the site began in September, 1985. In December, 1985, WSDOT's construction contractor discovered the remains of a large gas holder filled with a mixture of tar and other material. In February, 1986, the contractor unearthed the remains of an even larger gas holder, which was also filled with tar and other material, and a small pit filled with tar. The gas holders appeared to have been cut off at some level and then filled over.

WSDOT halted construction of the highway. Hart Crowser tested samples of the material in the second gas holder and in the tar pit using the persistence testing method WSDOE had used on the original contaminated samples. Samples taken from the tar pit area contained a PAH level of greater than one percent. Samples from the second gas holder contained PAH levels under one percent. The contents of the first holder had already been shipped and were never tested.

The team met frequently during this period and concluded that WSDOT needed to dispose of the tar-like material at Arlington. The team concluded that the volume of material did not affect the disposal options and therefore decided not to reexamine the options available to it. Construction had proceeded to a point that realigning the spur was not feasible. In addition, WSDOT faced the potential of significant cost increases for delays.

WSDOT's cleanup of the site was substantially completed by October, 1986, except for ongoing monitoring. Ultimately, 15,900 tons of coal tar were shipped to the landfill in Oregon, and 26,450 tons of oily silt and sand were encapsulated in concrete vaults on site. Handling and disposal of the tar cost $4,000,000 while handling and containment of the oily silt and sand cost $550,000.

On August 4, 1989, WSDOT filed this action against the defendants to recover response costs under § 107 of CERCLA. WSDOT subsequently filed three motions for partial summary judgment, and WNG filed a joint motion for partial summary judgment.

The district court granted WSDOT's motion as to the liability of WNG under CERCLA on the ground that each defendant was a responsible "person" under 42 U.S.C. § 9607. The court stated that the defendants challenged liability only on the basis that WSDOT failed to comply with the NCP. However, failure to comply with the NCP is not a defense to liability, but rather a factual issue affecting damages. Cadillac Fairview/California Inc. v. Dow Chem. Co., 840 F.2d 691, 695 (9th Cir.1988). The district court concluded, therefore, that the defendants offered no valid reason to deny summary judgment on liability. In its order, the district court also clarified legal standards applicable to the determination of damages. The district court concluded that WSDOT failed to qualify as a "State" under 42 U.S.C. § 9607(a)(4)(A) and therefore carried the burden of proving that its actions were consistent with the NCP, pursuant to 42 U.S.C. § 9607(a)(4)(B). The court added that WSDOT's actions would be evaluated for "substantial compliance" with the NCP. The court also decided that WSDOT's actions would be reviewed for compliance with the 1985 CP, rather than the 1982

NCP, because WSDOT incurred over 95 percent of its response costs after publication of the 1985 NCP.

The district court reserved the issue of damages for a bench trial. On December 28, 1992, after the bench trial, the district court issued a memorandum opinion finding that WSDOT failed to substantially comply with the 1985 NCP. Accordingly, the court concluded that WSDOT was not entitled to damages.

WSDOT appeals the district court judgment denying it damages. WNG, Pacificorp, and Advance Ross also appeal the court's judgments denying each of them attorney's fees and deposition costs.

DISCUSSION

Congress enacted CERCLA, 42 U.S.C. §§ 9601–9675, in December, 1980, "to initiate and establish a comprehensive response and financing mechanism to abate and control the vast problems associated with abandoned and inactive hazardous waste disposal sites." H.R. Rep. No. 1016(I), 96th Cong., 2d Sess. 22, reprinted in, 1980 U.S. Code Cong. & Admin. News 6119, 6125. Congress intended that CERCLA "facilitate the prompt cleanup of hazardous waste sites by placing the ultimate financial responsibility for cleanup on those responsible for hazardous wastes." U.S. v. R.W. Meyer, Inc., 889 F.2d 1497, 1500 (6th Cir.1989) (internal quotation omitted).

The national contingency plan ("NCP"), promulgated by EPA as required by CERCLA § 105, guides federal and state response activities. The NCP "provides the organizational structure and procedures for preparing for and responding to ... releases of hazardous substances...." 40 C.F.R. § 300.1. It "identifies methods for investigating the environmental and health problems resulting from a release or threatened release and criteria for determining the appropriate extent of response activities." Matter of Bell Petroleum Servs., Inc., 3 F.3d at 894.

This appeal involves interpretation of CERCLA § 107, which provides for the recovery of costs that a government or private party incurs in responding to the release of hazardous substances. Four categories of "persons," including owners and operators of hazardous waste sites, and generators and transporters of hazardous waste, are liable for:(A) all costs of removal or remedial action incurred by the United States Government or a State or an Indian tribe not inconsistent with the national contingency plan; [and](B) any other necessary costs of response incurred by any other person consistent with the national contingency plan....

Section 9607(a) "functions to distinguish between government response costs in subsection (A) and private response costs in subsection (B)." Wickland Oil Terminals v. Asarco, Inc., 792 F.2d 887, 891 (9th Cir.1986). While the United States government, or a state or Indian tribe, can obtain "all costs of removal or remedial action ... not inconsistent with the [NCP]," any other person can obtain "other necessary costs of response ... consistent with the [NCP]." (emphasis added). The language difference indicates that, when the United States government, a state, or an Indian tribe is seeking recovery of response costs, consistency with the NCP is presumed. Therefore, the potentially responsible party has the burden of proving inconsistency with the NCP. In contrast, any "other person" seeking response costs under § 9607(a)(4)(B) must prove that its actions are consistent with the NCP.

I. Is WSDOT the "State" under § 9607(a)(4)(A)?

[In this part of the opinion, the appellate court held that, contrary to the district court's view, the WSDOT did fit the statutory definition of a "state" under CERCLA. This conclusion was significant in allocating the burden of proving the consistency of the response actions to the NCP. On this point the court concluded: that since WSDOT should have been considered a "state" under CERCLA, WNG would have borne the burden of proving that WSDOT's actions were *inconsistent* with the NCP. In spite of the district court's erroneous allocation of the burden of proving NCP consistency, the appeals court ruled that "ample evidence" existed to support the lower court's conclusion that WSDOT did not act "consistently" with the NCP under either assignment of the burden of proof.]

II. Were WSDOT's actions "not inconsistent" with the NCP?

We evaluate consistency with the NCP by reviewing the actions of the party seeking response costs. The NCP is designed to make the party seeking response costs choose a cost-effective course of action to protect public health and the environment. If that party follows the detailed process set forth in the NCP, then its costs are not inconsistent with the NCP.

We have explained that the defendants carry the burden of proving that WSDOT's actions were inconsistent with the NCP, but have not yet discussed what the defendants must establish to carry this burden. To prove that a response action of the EPA was inconsistent with the NCP, a defendant must prove that the EPA's response action was arbitrary and capricious. This legal standard is justified " 'because determining the appropriate removal and remedial action involves specialized knowledge and expertise, [and therefore] the choice of a particular cleanup method is a matter within the discretion of the [government].' " Hardage, 982 F.2d at 1442 (quoting NEPACCO, 810 F.2d at 748).... Even under the deferential arbitrary and capricious standard, we conclude that WSDOT's actions were inconsistent with the NCP.

A. Applicable Version of the NCP

[In this part of the opinion the court held that when determining NCP consistency, it is the NCP version in effect when the actor incurred response costs which serves as the requisite "yardstick" for CERCLA compliance. In this case, WSDOT's response actions were found to be inconsistent with both the1982 and the 1985 NCPs.]

B.   Consistency with the NCP

We now review WSDOT's action for compliance with the NCP, to determine whether WSDOT's actions were arbitrary and capricious. WSDOT and its consultant, Hart Crowser, did not refer to the NCP for guidance on how to handle the contaminants on the site. WSDOT's lead representative on the coordination team handling the contamination project was not even aware that the NCP existed. Hart Crowser's project manager had never implemented the NCP in a remedial action. WSDOT's compliance with regulations that it did not consult is questionable. Nonetheless, an environmental cleanup could conceivably follow a standard procedure consistent with the NCP, even if the NCP is not actually referenced. Therefore we will evaluate WSDOT's actions under the standards set forth in the NCP.

Both the 1982 and the 1985 NCP require a remedial investigation "to determine the nature and extent of the threat presented by the release." 40 C.F.R. § 300.68(d) (1986); 40 C.F.R. § 300.68(f) (1984) (emphasis added). "This includes sampling, monitoring, as necessary, and includes the gathering of sufficient information to determine the necessity for and proposed extent of remedial action." Id. WSDOT's initial investigation, conducted by Hart Crowser, failed to determine either the nature or the extent of the threat posed.

Hart Crowser made several mistaken assumptions about the extent of the threat. Hart Crowser obtained a Sanborn insurance site map that showed the previous uses of the site. The map showed the location of a coal gasification plant that had once been on the site, as well as the location of gas holders used to store the manufactured gas. Hart Crowser assumed that the plant, including the gas holders, had been removed because the plant was not visible. However, Hart Crowser knew that the site was underlaid by fill-material placed above the naturally occurring material. Hart Crowser did not consider the possibility that only a portion of the plant had been removed, while the rest, including the remainder of the gas holders, had been filled in.

Additional mistakes contributed to miscalculation of the extent of the threat. Although Hart Crowser learned that tar, a by-product of gas, accumulates in gas holders, Hart Crowser expected that the tar had been removed because tar had some commercial value. Hart Crowser also assumed that unsold tar waste had been dumped on the extremities of the plant grounds, rather than near the plant. Finally, Hart Crowser did not put borings into the area where the gas holders had been located because it wanted to avoid running into the gas holder foundations.

Based on the site investigation, Hart Crowser estimated that 100 tons of tar-like material needed to be excavated. However, WSDOT's contractor eventually uncovered the lower sections of the gas-holders, which contained more tar-like material, as well as the tar pit. The tar material removed increased from the original estimate of 100 tons to a total of 16,000 tons.

In sum, WSDOT's remedial investigation utterly failed to determine the nature or the extent of the threat posed by the tar-like material. Hart Crowser drastically underestimated the amount of tar-like material on the site. Further, much of the tar-like material was classified as hazardous waste even though tests did not support this determination. The investigation did not provide "sufficient information to determine the necessity for and proposed extent of remedial action."

After setting forth standards for remedial investigation, the NCP sets forth detailed requirements on development and analysis of alternative courses of action. The NCP requires the party conducting the clean-up to develop several alternative courses of action, based on analysis of a number of factors including population, environmental and welfare concerns at risk; routes of exposure; amount, concentration, hazardous properties, environmental fate and transport and form of the substances present; hydrogeological factors; current and potential ground water use; climate, etc. . . .

Next, the NCP requires an initial screening of alternatives, applying the criteria of cost, acceptable engineering practices, and effectiveness, to narrow the list of alternatives that will be subjected to a more detailed analysis. Rationale for eliminating alternatives must be documented. The NCP requires a much more detailed analysis of the remaining alternatives, including detailed specification of alternatives, detailed cost estimation, engineering evaluation, assessment of the extent to which the alternative will adequately protect public health and the environment, etc.

WSDOT failed to satisfy these requirements. In the first investigation, prior to discovery of the additional tar, the interagency team informally considered several alternatives. In regard to the tar, testimony indicates that in situ treatment, which would effectively keep the material in place on site, was rejected because the material would not be removed. Incineration was rejected because of the expense. The record does not indicate that WSDOT subjected these alternatives to the kind of thorough analysis that the NCP requires. Hart Crowser's report to WSDOT does not contain a discussion of any of these alternatives. WSDOT's summary analysis states that disposal of the tar at Arlington is the only "feasible option" and does not indicate that other alternatives were even considered.

WSDOE's summary report indicates that the team gave more consideration to disposal of the oily silt and sand. The report discusses reuse, on-site disposal, landfill disposal, disposal at Arlington, and treatment. Although each alternative is discussed briefly, the interagency team did not follow the thorough requirements set forth in the NCP.

The interagency team fell particularly short when it failed to reevaluate alternatives after discovery of the additional tar. Analysis of alternatives follows assessment of the nature and extent of the problem. Once it became clear that the initial assessment grossly underestimated the amount of tarry material on the site, the team should have reconsidered the available alternatives. Instead, the team continued to rely on an analysis of alternatives designed to address a much smaller problem. In the process of developing and screening alternatives, WSDOT also failed to address the import of tests indicating varying PAH levels in the tar-like material. Hart Crowser initially discovered the tar-like material during a geotechnical investigation, in soil borings taken to evaluate the type of material that would be supporting the Tacoma Spur. WSDOE tested samples of the tar using the persistence method, which tests for the total level of PAH compounds, and concluded that the tar contained a PAH level of greater than one percent. Under Washington regulations, this contamination level is classified as "extremely hazardous." However, the type of sampling protocol used in environmental investigations was not used for the samples removed during the geotechnical investigation. During the subsequent environmental investigation, Hart Crowser tested additional soil samples, measuring the existence of specific PAH compounds rather than the total PAH level. However, WSDOT and the interagency team relied solely on the initial WSDOE tests in deciding that the waste needed to be disposed of at the Arlington facility. Had WSDOT followed the detailed requirements in the NCP to develop and analyze alternatives, its analysis would have indicated whether the concentration of PAH compounds made a difference in determining how to dispose of the contaminated material. See 40 C.F.R. § 300.68(e)(2)(iii) (1986) (requiring that the concentration of the hazardous material be considered when developing alternatives); 40 C.F.R. § 300.68(e)(2)(i)(B) (1984) (requiring that the amount and form of the substance present be considered).

Even after the additional material was discovered, WSDOT failed to consider the import of varying degrees of contaminant concentration. After the WSDOT's construction contractor unearthed the gas holder and tar pit, Hart Crowser conducted additional tests, including the persistence test that WSDOE had originally conducted. Samples taken from the tar pit area contained a PAH level greater than one percent. Samples from the gas holder contained PAH levels less than one percent. The contents of another gas holder had already been shipped and were never tested. Thus materials with varying concentrations of contaminants, and untested materials, were disposed of in the same manner without analysis of whether the varying concentrations warranted consideration of alternative disposal methods.

Finally, WSDOT failed to provide an opportunity for public review and comment of the alternative remedial measures it was considering. Although the public comment provision was not part of the 1982 NCP, it is contained in the 1985 NCP. WSDOT discovered the additional material after publication of the 1985 NCP and should have provided public comment after reevaluating the alternatives available to it.

Looking at the situation as a whole, we have no difficulty concluding that WSDOT's actions were inconsistent with the NCP. WSDOT failed to assess accurately both the nature and the extent of the threat posed by the presence of PAHs in the soil, failed to evaluate alternatives in the matter prescribed in the NCP, and failed to provide opportunity for public comment. Given the high degree of inconsistency with the requirements set forth in the NCP, WSDOT's action is arbitrary and capricious. Therefore,

WSDOT is not entitled to recover its response costs under 42 U.S.C. § 9607.

CONCLUSION

We AFFIRM the district court's decision that WSDOT failed to prove its case for damages. We also AFFIRM the court's decisions as to the defendants' claims for attorney's fees and deposition costs.

NOTES AND QUESTIONS

1. The *Washington DOT* case involves cleanup cost recovery against a PRP by a state agency proceeding under § 107(a)(4)(A). This section, applicable to the federal and state government, generally has been viewed as given government response actions the presumption of NCP consistency and the burden of proving the "negative" on the PRP. Considering this presumption, why was the court so unsympathetic to the Washington Department of Transportation? What had the Washington DOT done wrong in this case and what would you recommend to your client contemplating a site cleanup?

2. Try to isolate the standard of review in the *Washington DOT* case. What is it? Most cases employ an "arbitrary and capricious" test for evaluating the "consistency" of response costs with the NCP. Considering the meaning of this term in administrative law, would you expect courts to be highly skeptical and demanding of cleanup decisions? Would they be more likely to accepting and deferential? Which approach would you recommend?

What does "arbitrary and capricious" mean in this context? In the case of In re Bell Petroleum Services, Inc., 3 F.3d 889, the Fifth Circuit held that EPA's decision to provide an alternate water supply for a part of Odessa, Texas as part of its remedy selection was arbitrary and capricious mainly because EPA could not adequately defend its decision. Judge Jolly noted,

> After thoroughly reviewing the administrative record, we conclude that the EPA's decision to furnish the AWS [alternate water supply] was arbitrary and capricious. In vain we have searched the over 5,000 pages of administrative record, and found not one shred of evidence that anyone in the area was actually drinking chromium-contaminated water. Amazingly, the EPA made no attempt to learn whether anyone was drinking the water, or whether anyone intended to utilize the AWS, until after it had made its decision to contract the AWS. One would think that surely such information was essential in order to reach an informed, rational decision as to whether an AWS was necessary, and whether it would reduce any significant threat to public health. The administrative record reveals that the chromium-contaminated wells in the area all served commercial establishments, which the EPA prohibited from connecting to the AWS. Moreover, the EPA did not require residents to connect to the system and did not prohibit

them from using contaminated water from their wells. . . . No technical expertise is necessary to discern that the EPA's implementation of the AWS was arbitrary and capricious, as well as a waste of money.

3. Consistency questions have become the subject of increasing challenge in both government and private party site cleanups. Parties who have cleaned up contaminated sites have been denied CERCLA reimbursement for failing the "consistency" requirement. Why does CERCLA require NCP consistency? What goals does the statute seek to achieve by imposing this requirement? Due to the remedial character of the statute, it would seem logical that the "consistency" requirement was intended to result in site cleanups which would adequately protect public health and the environment. Should the NCP be considered a "floor" or a "ceiling" for CERCLA cleanup cost liability? Is the NCP consistency element included merely to prevent less costly and less protective response actions from being undertaken which will ultimately fail to achieve CERCLA's remedial goals? Is the consistency factor inserted to restrain wasteful and extravagant cleanups which exceed anything necessary for public health and environmental protection?

4. Should consistency be measured solely in terms of a substantive cleanup technique selected and employed or should it have a procedural dimension? Recent cases have begun to challenge the procedures followed in choosing a cleanup remedy. What does following the NCP's decisionmaking process described above accomplish? Of special concern have been public notice and participation measures. Why should courts dwell on the "process" issue? Should they require "strict" or "substantial" compliance with procedure?

In United States v. Burlington Northern Railroad Co., 200 F.3d 679 (10th Cir.1999), the Tenth Circuit held that EPA had acted in an arbitrary and capricious fashion by not following NCP public participation procedures when it replaced a previously proposed response action with an option which altered the earlier choice in scope and cost. The court concluded that this failure had prevented the public and PRPs form participation in EPA's decisionmaking process. *Id.* at 694. Interesting, this failure to follow proper administrative procedure did *not* provide a complete defense to PRP liability. The PRP was charged with the responsibility of proving that the EPA's procedural error "resulted in avoidable and unnecessary remediation costs." *Id.* at 695. Other cases have denied all recovery in similar situations.

This theme of public participation *during* the development and selection of the cleanup remedy has been determinative in a number of cases. See Public Service Co. of Colorado v. Gates Rubber Co., 175 F.3d 1177 (10th Cir.1999) (involvement of state health agency did not satisfy the opportunity for public comment); Pierson Sand & Gravel, Inc. v. Pierson Township, 89 F.3d 835 (6th Cir.1996); City of Oakland v. Nestle USA Inc., 2000 WL 1130066 (N.D.Cal.) (inadequate public participation in selection of remedy); and VME Americas, Inc. v. Hein–Werner Corp., 946 F.Supp. 683 (E.D.Wis.1996). Other cases have been more accepting of procedural variation. See e.g., Sealy Connecticut, Inc. v. Litton Industries, Inc., 93 F.Supp.2d 177 (D.Conn.2000).

3.   THE CERCLA CLEANUP PROCESS

The CERCLA site cleanup process starts with the discovery of the location and EPA's notification of the release or threatened release of hazardous substances. As noted above, this kind of information reaches EPA through a variety of means. Once discovered, sites are entered into the Comprehensive Environmental Response, Compensation, and Liability Information System or CERCLIS which is EPA's computerized inventory of potential hazardous substance release sites. At this point a lengthy and complex procedure commences to evaluate the site and to determine whether a short term removal action, a long term remedial action, or if no action is needed. The NCP governs this process as well as the cleanup standards to be applied to the site remediations. The general structure of this process is as follows.

i.   Preliminary Assessment/Site Inspection(PA/SI)

The Preliminary Assessment(PA) is a limited scope investigation performed on every CERCLIS site and it is designed to distinguish, based on limited data, between sites that pose little or no threat to human health and the environment and those that may present a threat and require further investigation. The PA can result in one of three recommendations that: 1) an emergency response or removal assessment be prepared, 2) no further action is needed, or 3) a determination of whether a remedial action is required. If the PA results in a conclusion that a long term remedy may be warranted, EPA then performs an actual Site Inspection(SI) to collect samples to determine what hazardous substances are present at the site and whether they have or may be released. The SI develops the information that will be needed by EPA to evaluate the risk presented by the site for its possible inclusion on the NPL.

ii.   NPL Designation

With the information derived from the PA/SI and other data, EPA employs a numerically based screening mechanism called the Hazard Ranking System(HRS) to determine if a site should be listed on the NPL. The HRS uses a structured analytical approach and assigns numerical values to risk factors presented by each site under study. The factors are organized into three groups: 1) the likelihood that a site has released or has the potential to release hazardous substances into the environment, 2) the characteristics of the wastes (e.g. toxicity and quantity), and 3) the people or sensitive environments affected by the release. Analyzing the multiple "pathways" of human and environmental exposure to hazardous substances (e.g. water, soil and air), the HRS assigns a numerical value for each pathway and these pathway scores are combined using a mathematical model to obtain a total score. Under this model the scores can range from 0 to 100 and sites with a score of 28.5 or higher are eligible for the NPL. EPA retains discretion to list a site even if the required score is obtained.

iii.   Remedial Investigation/Feasibility Study(RI/FS)

If, following the PA/FI and the NPL listing, it appears likely that a removal and/or a remedial response action will be needed, EPA undertakes first a Remedial Investigation and later a Feasibility Study to select the appropriate site remedy. Throughout this process, EPA establishes an administrative record that will act as the foundation for the decisions on the selection of a remedy. A docket is maintained by EPA, both in its offices and at a location close to the site, containing all factual data, guidance documents, technical literature and site-specific policy memos that might serve as the basis for remedy selection. 40 C.F.R. § 300.810(a). Building on all prior information, an RI is an extensive investigation of the site and it usually includes the collection of data to:

a. characterize site conditions,

b. determine the nature of the waste,

c. assess risk to human health and the environment, and

d. conduct testing to evaluate the potential performance and cost of the various treatment technologies that are being considered.

The RI is essentially an advanced information collection process leading to the Feasibility Study(FS) which usually proposes several alternative remedies and it evaluates them in relation to NCP policies. While the FS does not select a remedial option, it does set forth a range of response choices that will protect human health and the environment, evaluates them based on nine remedy selection criteria established in the NCP. See 40 C.F.R. § 300.430(d)(4). These criteria will be examined below. Thereafter, EPA issues a proposed cleanup plan which describes the remedial alternatives and establishes its "preferred remedy." Section 117 requires that the proposed plan will not be adopted until EPA gives public notice providing a brief analysis of the plan and allowing for an opportunity for a public meeting near the cleanup site. Another prerequisite imposed by§ 104(c) is state consultation and state assurance of financial contribution and future maintenance of the response actions.

iv.   Record of Decision(ROD)

The final step in the remedy selection process is the issuance of the Record of Decision or ROD. After considering all of the comments submitted to it, EPA reassesses the range of remedial alternatives, including its preferred remedy. As the following example demonstrates, the document outlines, in brief form, the nature of the site and its contamination, the available remedial options, the reasons for selecting the preferred remedy and how it meets the NCP requirements, and finally, an outline of the post-cleanup site condition. RODs are public documents and they are available on EPA's web site organized in a state-by-state table. At this point, EPA has selected the response action to be implemented and this decision is memorialized in the ROD. Under CERCLA § 113(h), this choice is not to be subjected to pre-implementation judicial review. See e.g., Clinton County Comm'rs v. EPA, 116 F.3d 1018 (3d Cir.1997). This provision was motivated by the goal of obtaining prompt site cleanups to effectuate the main purpose of Superfund.

v.   Remedial Design/Remedial Action(RD/RA)

The Remedial Design(RD) is the phase in the CERCLA site cleanup where the technical specifications for cleanup remedies and technologies are set. The actual engineering is undertaken as the site-specific remedy is designed. The Remedial Action(RA) follows the remedial design phase of the cleanup and is based on the specifications described in the Record of Decision(ROD). This is the final stage in the process before a construction and cleanup agreement is reached with an engineering contractor to actually implement the plan of work.

vi.   Construction Completion

EPA has developed a construction completions list to simplify its system of categorizing sites and better communicating the successful completion of cleanup activities. Sites qualify for listing when:

   a.   any necessary physical construction is complete, whether or not final cleanup levels or other requirements have been achieved;

   b.   EPA has determined that the response action should be limited to measures that do not involve construction; and

   c.   the site qualifies for deletion from the NPL.

vii.   Operation and Maintenance Analysis

After the cleanup construction activities are complete, the remedial action must be doing the job it was designed to do and, technically, it must be determined to be "operational and functional." Remedies requiring such operation and maintenance measures include landfill caps, gas collection systems, ground water extraction treatment, ground water monitoring, and surface water treatment. Once the operation and maintenance obligations begin, the state or the PRPs must maintain the effectiveness of the cleanup remedy. To do this they must do operation and maintenance monitoring which includes: inspection, sampling and analysis, routine maintenance, and reporting.

viii.   NPL Site Deletion

EPA may delete a NPL site if it determines that no further response is required to protect human health or the environment. Under the NCP, a site may be deleted where no further response is appropriate if EPA determines that one of the following criteria has been met:

a. EPA, in conjunction with the state, has determined that PRPs or other parties have implemented all appropriate response actions or

b. EPA, in consultation with the state, has determined that all appropriate Superfund-financed response actions under CERCLA have been implemented and that no further response by PRPs is appropriate.

Since 1999, EPA has streamlined the administrative process of deleting NPL sites to expedite matters.

4. CRITIQUE OF THE CERCLA CLEANUP PROCESS

Commentators have criticized CERCLA on a number of grounds including the length of time needed to go from the identification of hazardous waste contamination to the point when the site can be said to be remediated to safe levels. By early 1997, only 11 percent of the sites on EPA's National Priorities List(NPL) had been sufficiently cleaned and removed from the NPL. Administrative reforms undertaken by EPA in the 1990s have accelerated the pace of waste site cleanup with the result that by November, 2001 just over 50 percent of the NPL sites were at the stage of construction completion. The question remains, "why does it take so long for EPA to move Superfund sites through the system?" More specifically, how does EPA allocate and prioritize its own resources with regard to CERCLA cleanups? The following excerpt analyzes these questions using empirical data which focuses upon the cleanup progress at over 1,100 sites from the initial NPL listing, to the signing of the ROD making the remedy selection, and finally to the construction completion stage. Notice the conclusions regarding what does and what does not affect the speed of Superfund site cleanups. Also, do you agree with the larger conclusion drawn concerning the desirability of a liability-based system of cleanup funding rather than the provision of "public goods" from diffuse sources such as general taxes or appropriations.

Hilary Sigman, The Pace of Progress at Superfund Sites: Policy Goals and Interest Group Influence

44 J. L. & Econ. 315 (2001).

Bureaucracies, like other organizations, must solve the problem of how to prioritize their workload. They may chose priorities that reflect social goals. However, concentrated private interest groups may also manage to manipulate agency agendas, as the capture theory articulated by George Stigler and Sam Peltzman suggests. In addition, bureaucracies may respond to pressures imposed by legislators.

To study bureaucratic priorities, this paper uses activities of the Environmental Protection Agency (EPA) under Superfund, the federal program for cleanup of abandoned contaminated sites. There are a few reasons to choose the Superfund to study these issues. First, Superfund requires the agency to make site-by-site decisions at each of over 1,000 sites. Thus, we have a large number of comparable observations of the agency's behavior to study econometrically. Second, one can easily connect private interest groups and political pressures to each site. At most sites, private parties pay the costs of the site through legal liability. This funding approach creates a concentrated interest group with a high stake in the agency's decisions. In addition, the benefits of cleanup at Superfund sites are local. Thus, it is possible to identify another important interest group, the local community, and to associate a congressional representative with each site.

As a measure of the EPA's priorities for its work, the paper studies the speed with which the EPA moves sites through the Superfund. There are both direct and indirect motivations for focusing on this particular aspect of Superfund decision making. The direct motivation is that the speed of Superfund is a perennial policy concern. By early 1997, 16 years after Congress enacted the legislation, only 11 percent of the sites on Superfund's National Priorities List (NPL) had been declared to be clean and therefore deleted from the NPL. President Clinton touted more rapid Superfund progress in his 1997 State of the Union Address, but the General Accounting Office assessed the program's recent pace as poor.

A focus on the speed with which the EPA moves sites through Superfund also has analytical advantages. Speed provides a measure of the bureaucratic output, rather than an input, so it is closely related to social and interest group goals. It also provides an indicator of the distribution of agency work effort that the agency cannot readily manipulate for the sake of appearances. In addition, the agency has considerable discretion in choosing which sites to expedite. The EPA has set targets for the number of sites to reach certain stages by various dates, but there is no official policy on which sites to prioritize.

This paper uses data on the record of progress at NPL sites through January 1997. I estimate an econometric model of the length of time for sites to complete various stages of the Superfund process, using a model of multiple sequential durations. The paper focuses on three transitions: (1) proposed listing of the site on the National Priorities List, which marks the selection the site for federal cleanup; (2) signing of a Record of Decision (ROD), which reflects the completion of decision making about a remedy; and (3) construction completion, which marks the end of most cleanup activities at the site. The model allows unobserved cross-site heterogeneity, perhaps associated with the complexity of the site. In the presence of unobserved heterogeneity, joint estimation of the duration of the various stages addresses the selection problem that arises because sites cannot make later transitions if they have not completed earlier stages.

The empirical results provide evidence that the EPA responds to interest groups in prioritizing its resources. Both the liable parties and the local communities get weight in the agency's priorities. Liable parties appear to delay progress at their sites. Sites without viable liable parties experienced 29 percent faster decision making than sites with viable liable parties. Sites with deep-pocketed liable parties (where the private financial stake in the site is likely to be large) have slower cleanup. Similarly, powerful communities manage to expedite progress. Sites in communities with higher voter turnout received faster cleanup of their sites, while higher-income communities receive faster listing.

This interest group influence may have a small but significant impact on social welfare. A rough calculation suggests that delays caused by liable parties may decrease Superfund's net benefits by 8 percent (about $.8 million per site or $1 billion in total). Thus, the results support current congressional proposals to reduce the role of liability financing, although other effects of liability funding also need to be taken into consideration for a full assessment (see the discussion in Section V below). More generally, the results provide an argument for funding provision of environmental quality and other public goods from diffuse sources, such as broad-based taxes or general appropriations, to avoid the detrimental effects of interest group politics.

The agency does not appear to use broader social goals, such as health risks, to prioritize its workload. Sites' rate of progress is not materially affected by their hazardousness. In addition, sites in densely populated areas, where there may be greater human exposure, do not progress faster than other sites. Although contrary to social welfare, the irrelevance of exposure is not surprising because Superfund policy generally focuses on individual risk levels.

Despite the direct influence of interest groups such as the liable parties and local communities, the legislature does not have observable influence on cleanup speeds. Little evidence supports the frequent contention that powerful legislators (identified either by seniority or by serving on the Superfund authorizing subcommittee) significantly speed sites in their districts. . . .

V. WELFARE IMPLICATIONS

The results have implications for the welfare effects of interest group politics, in particular, the cost of the delays imposed by PRPs. The evaluation of these costs must be inexact given the available data, but this section presents some rough calculations.

Congress is currently considering restricting or eliminating the liability funding of Superfund. How much would be gained if Superfund relied on taxes to finance cleanup rather than legal liability? The estimates suggest that the presence of PRPs delays progress by 1.8 years (based on 29 percent faster progress by orphan sites in the second stage). With a large publicly traded PRP, the net effect of PRP presence is a delay of .8 years in the second stage and 1.7 years in the third stage, for a total of 2.5 years. Assuming the net benefits of cleanup arise entirely at completion and using a 5 percent social discount rate, a delay of 1.8 years reduces the net benefits of cleanup by 8.4 percent and a delay of 2.5 years reduces them by 11.5 percent.

To get a sense of the magnitude of these costs requires an estimate of the net benefits of completing cleanup. Recent research by Hamilton and Viscusi on a sample of 150 Superfund sites finds that these sites yield a cost per cancer case avoided of $3 million in 1993 dollars. An average of 4.87 cancer cases was avoided per site at the sites they studied. If the value of a statistical life is $5 million, then the sites had an average net benefit of $9.7 million per site. Using this value, the presence of PRPs would cost an average $1.1 million per site and their presence with a large publicly traded PRP would cost $1.1 million per site. Thus, the costs could be on the order of $1 billion for the entire NPL.

These values presume delay is uncorrelated with the net benefit of cleanup across sites. Hamilton and Viscusi find great variation in the net benefits across sites. A very few sites in their study account for the positive mean net benefit; the median site would not pass a cost-benefit test. If sites with liable parties have negative net benefits, delays are actually welfare improving. However, research suggests that the EPA selects less costly remedies at sites with liable parties, so net benefits at these sites may tend to be more favorable than average.

Thus, eliminating liability funding and moving to tax financing (as at orphan sites) might result in small gains from increased cleanup speeds. The policy implications of this result depend upon how these costs stack up against other costs and benefits of liability financing. On one hand, there are potential advantages of liability financing. Liability can provide incentives for precaution in managing potential contaminants. Liability financing and resulting PRP participation may also help control cleanup costs, as suggested above. On the other hand, liability may involve high transactions costs from legal expenses. Lloyd Dixon estimates hat transactions costs will account for as much 30 percent of private spending on Superfund, so the delay costs would not loom large relative to these costs.

In summary, the empirical results suggest a few conclusions about bureaucratic priorities. First, although the EPA is widely viewed as being a highly ideological agency, it does not appear to prioritize resources on the basis of environmental goals. This evidence may weaken arguments for allowing bureaucracies discretion in setting their agendas. Second, the EPA is sensitive to concentrated private interests in its priorities, providing support for capture theories. Such responsiveness to private interests may be helpful if it encourages the agency to consider private costs and benefits in its calculations. However, it may also be harmful if it subverts broader social goals. Indeed, the empirical results presented here suggest that removing a set of concentrated interests by using a diffuse funding source (such as a broad-based tax) might increase welfare. Finally, however important legislators' interventions with bureaucracies may be to election outcomes, this study finds no empirical evidence that they affect bureaucratic priorities.

5.   CLEANING UP CONTAMINATED SITES—NCP STANDARDS

When originally enacted in 1980, CERCLA directed EPA to establish site cleanup standards. The agency amended the existing NCP in 1985 and adopted a two-pronged approach to setting cleanup standards emphasizing: 1) protection of human health and the environment and 2) attainment of "applicable or relevant and appropriate Federal public health and environmental requirements." By this time, Congress's frustration with and distrust of EPA's commitment and ability to complete effective site cleanups prompted it in 1986 to amend the statute and to adopt § 121. Section 121(a) gives EPA highly detailed guidance regarding the setting of cleanup standards carried out by the federal government under § 104 or "secured" from PRPs under the authority of § 106. This guidance emphasizes that the remedies must be in accordance with the NCP "to the extent practicable" and that they must provide for cost-effective response taking into account the total short and long term costs of such actions. Buried within the language of § 121 are three additional policies which affect remedial selection:

- they must assure protection of human health and the environment,

- they must use permanent solutions and alternative treatment and resource recovery technologies to the maximum extent practicable,

- when hazardous substances remain onsite after cleanup, they must meet all "applicable" and/or "relevant and appropriate" requirements under federal and state law(ARARs).

Are these statutory goals for CERCLA cleanups consistent or compatible with one another? EPA took this guidance and, in 1990 it revised the NCP by establishing nine criteria for evaluating proposed cleanup remedies. The NCP now reads as follows,

Nine criteria for evaluation. The analysis of alternatives under review shall reflect the scope and complexity of site problems and alternatives being evaluated and consider the relative significance of the factors within each criteria. The nine evaluation criteria are as follows:

(A) *Overall protection of human health and the environment.*

Alternatives shall be assessed to determine whether they can adequately protect human health and the environment, in both the short and long term, from unacceptable risks posed by hazardous substances, pollutants, or contaminants present a the site by eliminating, reducing, or controlling exposures to levels established during development of remedial goals. . . .

(B) *Compliance with ARARs.*

The alternatives shall be assessed to determine whether they attain applicable or relevant and appropriate requirements["ARARs"] under federal environmental laws and state environmental or facility siting laws or provide grounds for invoking one of the waivers. . . .

(C) *Long-term effectiveness and permanence.*

Alternatives shall be assessed for the long term effectiveness and permanence they afford, along with the degree of certain that the alternative will prove successful.

(D) *Reduction of toxicity, mobility, or volume through treatment.*

The degree to which alternatives employ recycling or treatment that reduces toxicity, mobility, or volume shall be assessed, including how treatment is used to address the principal threats posed by the site. . . .

(E) *Short-term effectiveness.*

The short term impacts of alternatives shall be assessed considering the following:

(1) Short term risks that might be posed to the community during implementation of an alternative;

(2) Potential impacts on workers during remedial action and the effectiveness and reliability of protective measures;

(3) Potential environmental impacts of the remedial action and the effectiveness and reliability of mitigative measures during implementation; and

(4) Time until protection is achieved.

(F) *Implementability.*

The ease or difficulty of implementing the alternatives shall be assessed by considering the [technical and administrative feasibility as well as the availability of services and materials, including adequate off-site treatment].

(G) *Cost.*

The types of costs that shall be assessed include [a) the capital costs, b) the annual operation and maintenance costs; and c) the present value of future costs.]

(H) *State acceptance.*

(I) *Community acceptance.*

This assessment includes determining which components of the alternatives interested persons in the community support, have reservations about, or oppose. . . .

40 C.F.R. § 300.430(e)(9)(iii).

How are these factors to be applied in choosing a particular remedy? Are all of the factors to be weighted equally or are some of them dominant? Should they be? The NCP sets out a three-tiered system for applying the nine factors which includes: *Tier 1*—Threshold Criteria (Factors #1 & 2), *Tier 2*—Primary Balancing Criteria (Factors #3–7) and *Tier 3*—Modifying Criteria (Factors #8 & 9). This would seem to create a hierarchy among the nine factors with *Tier 1* being the foundation or starting point. Where is the factor of economic cost placed in this hierarchy? How should the "cost effective" factor be considered when CERCLA § 121(b) explicitly expresses a preference for remedies emphasizing "treatment which permanently and significantly reduces the volume, toxicity or mobility of the hazardous substances."

6. CERCLA SITE CLEANUP REMEDIES

What does it mean to "cleanup" a hazardous waste site? How do environmental agencies or PRPs select the correct package of remedial techniques when they design a remedial response plan for a CERCLA cleanup? The remedy selection process often pits different interest groups against one another—each attempting to maximize their own interests. For instance, local community groups and the state government might press for a high degree of costly cleanup which would minimize the risk of health or safety harms. On the other hand, the PRPs might wish to choose those methods which would require the lowest capital cost for construction and ongoing maintenance costs. All of this suggests that there are a range of remedies available to the remedial designer. What are the methods that could be employed?

EPA provided a view of these questions in its 1996 analysis of the initial 410 completed cleanups undertaken pursuant to CERCLA. At these sites EPA used more than 25 different types of cleanup approaches that were tailored both to the types of contaminants present and the natural resource that was affected by the pollution. For contaminated soils, excavation and removal of hazardous soil and solid waste was the most common method used being employed at 45percent of all sites. This technique usually removes polluted soil and debris by trucking it away from the cleanup site and treating it at a licensed hazardous waste facility. In addition, covering the land with a protective cap or soil cover occurred at 39 percent of the locations. When contaminated ground water was at issue, the technology most frequently used was the "pump and treat" method being used at 34 percent of the sites. The "pump and treat" method pumps water out of the ground through a series of wells, cleans it by treating the contaminants and either reinjecting it back into the ground or sending it to a municipal water treatment plant. Finally, innovative technologies were beginning to be used during this period with soil vapor extraction(extracting and treating toxic gas) and bioremediation(using natural organisms to break down contaminants) being the two most commonly used innovative technique.

While the common containment and treatment techniques sound like straightforward engineering responses, most CERCLA sites contain more than one type of chemical and often both water and soil resources have been impacted by the pollution. When this is true, EPA may use a combination of approaches to remedy the problem. This combined strategy emphasizes: 1) containment of the contaminants(surface drainage control, soil capping), 2) separating harmful chemicals from the soil and/or the water(soil vapor extraction, soil flushing, thermal desorption), and/or 3) rendering the material less toxic(bioremediation, incineration). Finally, most remedial actions also include "other remedies" in their package of required responses. These include the installation and monitoring of ground water wells, institutional controls(zoning and deed restrictions on the use of land), and the provision of alternate drinking water supplies. To assist remedial designers in the development of specific site cleanup plans,

EPA has developed guidance materials suggesting "presumptive remedies" for several types of contaminated sites(i.e. municipal landfills, wood treaters, VOCs and metals in soils, and contaminated ground water). This guidance has come from EPA's experience at sites with consistent patterns of remedies. The use of these presumptive remedial techniques is intended by EPA to streamline the cleanup process, improve consistency, reduce costs and speed up remediation.

7.   STATE INVOLVEMENT IN CLEANUP REMEDY SELECTION

Does EPA have unilateral power to make the remedy selection for site cleanup without regard to the wishes of the state or the local communities in which the site is located? If not, what role should these parties have in deciding whether and to what extent a site will be remediated? These are important questions which affect the effectiveness of the CERCLA hazardous waste site cleanup policy. Think of how the concerns of the various parties interested in the remediation of a site might be different.

CERCLA addresses the issue of non-EPA participation in a number of ways. First, public access to relevant information is to be established by way of a docket containing the administrative record must be maintained in EPA offices and at a public location near the cleanup site. This docket should contain site-specific information concerning the remedial work to be done. See 40 C.F.R. § 300.805(a). Second, the NCP requires EPA to publish notice of the availability of the proposed cleanup plan in the local newspaper and to give at least 30 days for written or oral comment. Third, EPA must also provide an opportunity for a public meeting at which questions and comments would be recorded, and to prepare a "responsiveness summary" containing its responses to any significant comments made during the public meeting. See 40 C.F.R. § 300.430(f)(3)(i). Potentially, public comments made in writing or at the public meeting could affect EPA's remedy choice by alerting the agency to other health, safety or environmental issues that it had not previously considered. It could also make remedial designers aware of the public acceptance of their risk assessment and the proposed response.

E.   EPA's HAZARDOUS WASTE SITE RESPONSE AUTHORITIES

The heart of the CERCLA policy is the goal of site remediation to protect the human health and the environment. As mentioned previously, the statute conceives of this site cleanup to have two kinds of response activities: a) short term or emergency "removal" actions and b) long term and permanent "remedial" activities. The statute has triggered thousands of response actions and has resulted in the expenditure of billions of private and public dollars. As of 2000, EPA reports that there had been over 6,400 removal actions taken at hazardous waste sites with private estimates setting the average cost at $500,000 each. See J. Hamilton and W. Kip Viscusi, Calculating Risks: The Spatial and Political Dimensions of Hazardous Waste Policy 8 (1999). The more complex, time-consuming and expensive remedial actions have averaged at least $30 million per site and had been undertaken or was planned at nearly 1500 locations. Over the life of the Superfund program, EPA reached settlements with PRPs with an estimated value of over $16 billion by 1999 and this figure does not include the sums spent from the multi-billion dollar government-managed Superfund. Needless to say, CERCLA has had a significant financial impact resulting in billions spent for site remediation. But how does a site cleanup actually occur? There are three basic approaches.

Under CERCLA, response actions to cleanup hazardous waste sites may come about in the following ways:

- **EPA Led Cleanup** Direct EPA-led cleanup under the authority of § 104 and funded by the Superfund followed by a § 107 cost recovery action against any solvent PRP(s).

What is the legal authority for EPA to clean up hazardous wastes under CERCLA? The basic authority for the federal government(delegated to EPA) to act is set out in § 104(a)(1) which states:

Whenever (A)any *hazardous substance* is *released or there is a substantial threat* of such a release into the *environment*, or (B) there is a release or substantial threat of release into the environment of any pollutant or contaminant which may present an imminent and substantial danger to the public health or welfare, the President is authorized to act, *consistent with the national contingency plan*, to remove or arrange for the *removal* of, and provide for *remedial action* relating to such hazardous substance, pollutant, or contaminant at any time(including its removal from any contaminated natural resource), or take any other response measure consistent with the national contingency plan which the President deems necessary to protect the public health or welfare or the environment.... (emphasis supplied)

This broad authority permits EPA to cleanup hazardous waste sites but it also requires that a) the states will maintain and operate the remedial actions as long as it is necessary, b) secure adequate hazardous waste disposal facilities in-state and c) pay 10 percent of the response costs or 50 percent if the facility is state-owned. Previously, the Superfund had funded these EPA cleanups but the tax authority which replenished this account expired at the end of 1995 and EPA's financial resources have become much more limited. This has resulted in EPA seeking site remediation through the other two means which follow.

- **PRP "Voluntary" Cleanup** EPA-initiated informal negotiation with PRPs combined with the threat of EPA action resulting in PRP-led "voluntary" site cleanups confirmed by settlement agreement.

This kind of cleanup is likely to happen after EPA officials send a "notice letter" to all PRPs to determine whether they are willing and financially able to undertake the cleanup action. The purpose of the notice letter practice is to facilitate PRP settlements through a process of negotiated settlement with the government. Under § 122(a) which was added to CERCLA by the 1986 amendments, EPA has been granted specific authority to enter into settlements with PRPs to perform response actions if EPA decides that such actions will be properly conducted. Congressional policy as well as the inherent CERCLA funding limitations makes privately-performed cleanups more and more common. In addition, PRPs have a strong incentive to take over the remedial process from EPA in order to maintain a higher degree of control over the project design and execution. Of course, EPA can apply pressure by either issuing a § 106 order(with its potential monetary penalties) or spending Superfund monies and then recovering them in a § 107 action. The final point is that many response actions are "voluntarily" undertaken by PRPs pursuant to a settlement agreement or consent decrees negotiated with EPA.

EPA has developed model consent decrees and administrative orders to expedite and to encourage settlements Using these models, the PRPs will no longer need to negotiate every feature of the agreement and they will receive certain protections against later liability.

- **PRP Ordered Cleanup** EPA order to PRPs to abate the danger posed by the hazard by way of either a) a judicially-granted injunction under CERCLA § 106(a) and RCRA § 7003 or b) a unilateral EPA administrative order under § 106.

Under the first of these two options, EPA may proceed to federal district court pursuant to § 106(a) to combat an "imminent and substantial endangerment to the public health or welfare or the environment" due to an "actual or threatened release of a hazardous substance." The court is given wide remedial power to "grant such relief as the public interest and the equities of the case may require." This section, similar to RCRA § 7003, grants the district courts with jurisdiction to abate the nuisance-like condition posed by the release. The court ordered result involves the federal courts in the first instance and therefore, has inherent time and resource disadvantages to EPA. Under the second option, EPA is empowered to issue its own administrative orders enforceable by $25,000 per day of violation civil penalties in order "to protect public health and welfare and the environment." These compliance directives, sometimes called unilateral administrative orders, are issued directly by EPA usually without any prior hearing. Serious punitive penalties can result from a PRP's failure to comply with them "without sufficient cause." See § 107(c)(3).

F. JUDICIAL REVIEW OF CERCLA CLEANUP DECISIONS

Litigation involving administrative agency decision making is one of the hallmarks of environmental law. Congressional policy with the other regulatory statutes such as the Clean Air and Clean Water Acts, actually encouraged a practice of pre-enforcement judicial review of regulations. This policy restricted court challenges to new rules and regulations to a limited "window" of time immediately after their formal adoption. The Clean Water Act sets 120 days as the time limit on challenging administrative action while the Clean Air Act establishes 60 days as the end date. See e.g., Clean Water Act § 509(b)(1) and Clean Air Act § 307(b)(1). This policy funneled all controversy over the rule's legality, in an administrative law sense, to a short period of exposure. The Clean Air Act goes even farther by designating one court—the U.S. Court of Appeals for the District of Columbia—as the exclusive venue for litigation over nationally-significant regulations. Clean Air Act § 307(b)(1). Why would these statutes wish to accelerate judicial review of administrative action? Why would they also provide, as does § 307(b)(2), that "[A]ction of the Administrator with respect to which review could have been obtained [under the judicial review provisions of the Act] shall not be subject to judicial review in civil or criminal proceeding for enforcement?"

Considering this strong pre-enforcement judicial review policy in other environmental laws, it might be surprising to learn that CERCLA § 113(h) states that, "no Federal court shall have jurisdiction under Federal law ... to review *any challenges to removal or remedial actions*" selected by EPA under either § 104 or § 106(a) except in cost recovery or enforcement actions. Why would Congress have taken such a restrictive position in § 113(h) after encouraging early judicial review in other environmental statutes? Consider the tradeoffs that are involved and the serious public health background of the CERCLA statute. The legislative policy underlying § 113(h) has been described in the following terms:

> The logic behind barring PRPs from challenging EPA's cleanup decisions before EPA seeks cost recovery is straightforward enough: While the PRPs lose their chance to limit EPA's expenditures in advance, they retain the right to challenge them in any subsequent cost-recovery actions. To the extent they then can establish that EPA's costs were inconsistent with the NCP, they avoid liability for those costs. While the lack of preimplementation review occasionally may result in excessive and non-recoverable expenditures, Congress plainly was willing to run this risk in the interest of expeditious response. The dollars that might be saved by allowing judicial review were not thought to justify the delays such litigation would entail.

Jeffrey G. Miller & Craig N. Johnston, The Law of Hazardous Waste Disposal and Remediation 689 (1996). Notice the breadth of § 113(h). It also precludes court challenges by local citizens and environmental groups who believe that the remedial choice is not protective enough. In general, courts have denied review pending completion of the response action. But see United States v. Princeton Gamma–Tech, Inc., 31 F.3d 138 (3d Cir. 1994) and United States v. Akzo Coatings, Inc., 949 F.2d 1409 (6th Cir.1991).

Section 4. Liability Under CERCLA

A. Introduction

The idea of environmental liability has evolved significantly over the years. At common law, several legal theories existed which could be used to enjoin, compensate or punish conduct which was harmful to human health and to the value of real property. These concepts carried the familiar names of public and private nuisance, trespass and strict liability and their doctrines enabled common law judges to fashion wide ranging remedies for environmental and personal injuries. Liability sprang from violations of the social norms reflected in these legal theories. Over the last forty years, the meaning of the term "environmental liability" has changed and has become closely associated with the developing administrative system of environmental regulation. Firms and individuals now equate this liability with compliance with environmental regulations such as discharge or emission rules under the Clean Water and Clean Air Acts. Liability in this context signifies conforming with technical pollution control regulations which often entails capital construction, operation and maintenance, record keeping, monitoring, and reporting costs. Looming behind these expenses stand the additional costs contained in enforcement sanctions including civil and criminal penalties, injunctive relief and reputation damage. All of these liabilities arise from the demands of the environmental protection programs initiated over the last three decades.

CERCLA shares features from both the common law and the regulatory traditions. On one hand, the statute is dedicated to the achievement of important public health, safety and environmental protection purposes reflected in expansive hazardous waste site cleanup authority. These purposes, if accomplished, could have significant remedial impacts in reducing the risk of environmental and personal harm. On the other hand, CERCLA represents a compensatory system obtaining remedial funding through the assignment of legal liability to PRPs—those considered to be responsible for the cleanup. The CERCLA-generated environmental liabilities serve the dual purposes of imposing cleanup expenses on "responsible parties" while also creating a powerful incentive for future compliance with hazardous materials handling rules. Through its liability-assigning features, CERCLA establishes an elaborate statutory "tort" law closely connected with the attainment of significant public policy objectives. As you read the materials that follow, evaluate the wisdom of public policy that funds responses to hazardous substances releases to the environment with a broad, individualized liability scheme rather than a more centralized, social welfare system which would widely spread costs by way of taxes or other devices.

The key feature of CERCLA is its remedial focus on cleaning up hazardous waste disposal sites. This emphasis centers upon the concept of responsibility—who is responsible for funding (and occasionally, undertaking) the remedial action? CERCLA's cost allocation aspect assigns significant financial liability to parties identified as PRPs. The distribution of legal liability has proven to be one of the most controversial aspects of the Superfund law and has given rise to body of jurisprudence interpreting the statute's meaning in particular fact situations. CERCLA has resulted in the development of a rich and varied federal court body of law occasionally with inter-circuit interpretive differences.

B. STATUTORY ARTICULATION OF LIABILITY

Liability under CERCLA is based upon a two-step analysis asking two general questions:

1. Has there been a release or threatened release of hazardous substances from a facility that has caused the government or other parties to incur response costs [**the *Causative* factor**] and

2. Is the entity one of the four categories of potentially responsible parties (PRPs) specified in § 107(a)? [**the *Identity* factor**]

Section 107 is not a model of legislative clarity. Read § 107(a) carefully and try to identify the most important terms and operative provisions. What creates CERCLA liability? Is anything missing? How could you improve on the statutory drafting?

CERCLA § 107(a) [42 U.S.C.§ 9607(a)]

Notwithstanding any other provision or rule of law, and subject only to the defenses set forth in subsection (b) of this section—

(1) the owner and operator of a vessel or a facility,

(2) any person who at the time of disposal of any hazardous substance owned or operated any facility which such hazardous substances were disposed of,

(3) any person who by contract, agreement, or otherwise arranged for disposal or treatment, or arranged with a transporter for transport for disposal or treatment, of hazardous substances owned or possessed by such person, by any other party or entity, at any facility or incinerator vessel owned or operated by another party or entity and containing such hazardous substances, and

(4) any person who accepts or accepted any hazardous substances for transport to disposal or treatment facilities, incineration vessels or sites selected by such person, from which there is a release, or a threatened release which causes the incurrence of response costs, of a hazardous substance, shall be liable for—

(A) all costs of removal or remedial action incurred by the United States Government or a State or an Indian tribe not inconsistent with the national contingency plan;

(B) any other necessary costs of response incurred by any other person consistent with the national contingency plan;

(C) damages for injury to, destruction of, or loss of natural resources, including the reasonable costs of assessing such injury, destruction, or loss resulting from such a release; and

(D) the costs of any health assessment or health effects study carried out under [§ 104(i)] of this title.

Examine the structure of § 107(a):

WHO → SHALL BE LIABLE FOR → WHAT?

Notice that CERCLA § 107(a) does not set forth the necessary elements of a *prima facie* case of liability for the recovery cleanup costs or other enumerated damages. An elaborate corpus of case law has developed to construe each of these components. Return to the *Causative* and *Identity* factors listed above. The *Causative* element will generally be satisfied when 1) there has been a release or threat of a release of hazardous substances from a facility and 2) the plaintiff seeking recovery has incurred response costs because of the release or its threat. Notice that the causation relates primarily to triggering the costs of responding to the polluting situation. The *Identity* factor will be discussed more fully below in section 4 on Identifying Potentially Responsible Parties or PRPs.

C. STANDARD OF LIABILITY

The text of § 107(a) merely states that designated PRPs "shall be liable" for listed costs, damages and other expenses. But what does the term "liable" mean in this context of a federal hazardous waste site cleanup statute? Think about what the various interpretations of the term "liable" could have meant. The entire gamut of tort-based liability theories could have been adopted including intentional, negligent, or strict liability. Why might Congress, in the post-Love Canal social and political environment, have rejected a liability standard requiring that the plaintiff prove the defendant PRP's negligence in its earlier waste disposal practices? Imagine the range of defensive arguments that could have been raised if negligence were the standard for CERCLA liability? How might have CERCLA's policy premise of "making the polluter pay" affected the choice of a standard for finding liability?

1. STRICT LIABILITY

CERCLA's drafters understood the controversial nature of the liability issue and they attempted to "finesse" the question both by omission in § 107 and by indirection in § 101(32). Section 107 makes no mention of what Congress intended for this important word. The definition—providing § 101(32) defines the word "liability" by reference to its meaning under another statute altogether. It states that under CERCLA the term "shall be construed to be the standard of liability which obtains under [§ 311 of the Clean Water Act]." Section 311, dealing with oil and hazardous substance spills into the water, does not specify a definition for "liability" but most courts in the pre-CERCLA period had interpreted that section to impose strict liability, that is, liability without regard to proof of the defendant's negligent or unreasonable conduct. There is evidence that CERCLA's congressional sponsors intended to build the strict liability standard into the law but they were unwilling to highlight this fact with explicit statutory language. One of bill's sponsors, Senator Jennings Randolph, provided the following insight into the legislative intent when he stated,

> We have kept strict liability in the compromise, specifying the standard of liability under section 311 of the Clean Water Act, but we have deleted any reference to joint and several liability, relying on common law principles to determine when parties should be severally liable ... The changes were made in recognition of the difficulty in prescribing in statutory terms liability standards which will be applica-

ble in individual cases. The changes do not reflect a rejection of the standards in the earlier bill.

> Unless otherwise provided in this act, the standard of liability is intended to be the same as that provided in section 311 of the Federal Water Pollution Control Act(33 U.S.C. 1321). I understand this to be a standard of strict liability.

126 Cong. Rec. S14964 (Nov. 24, 1980). With this somewhat indirect reference to the prevailing liability standard under CWA § 311, CERCLA was enacted into law by a lame-duck Congress just before Christmas in December of 1980.

By adopting a strict liability standard, CERCLA simplified the plaintiff's case in a cost recovery action and thereby making it more likely that a PRP, and not the Superfund, would actually pay for the cleanup and other related expenses. Curiously, this has allowed significant recoveries against defendant PRPs even when they took every reasonable precaution at the time of the waste disposal. The defendant's due care was simply not an issue when the liability theory was strict liability.

In case decisions, CERCLA's version of strict liability completely relaxed the required causal nexus between the defendant PRP's conduct and the release or threat of release of hazardous substances. All that has been necessary to prove is that the release or threat caused the plaintiff to incur response costs. An early CERCLA case decision, United States v. Wade, 577 F.Supp. 1326, 1333 (E.D.Pa.1983), established the proposition that the plaintiff must only prove that the PRP disposed of a hazardous substance at the facility and that the plaintiff incurred response costs. The plaintiff does not need to prove a causal nexus between the cleanup costs and a particular PRP's hazardous waste. In U.S. v. Alcan Aluminum Corp., 990 F.2d 711, 721 (2d Cir.1993), the appeals court interpreted the meaning of "strict liability" in the following terms,

> The plain meaning of [§ 107(a)] dictates that the government need only prove: (1) that there was a release or threatened release, which (2) caused incurrence of response costs, and (3) that the defendant generated hazardous waste at the clean-up site. *What is not required is that the government show that a specific defendant's waste caused incurrence of clean-up costs.*

990 F.2d at 721 (emphasis supplied). Why would the courts have eliminated any sense of linear, causal connection from the plaintiff's *prima facie* case?

Consider the fact that most hazardous waste cleanup sites contain substances deposited by many PRPs over a potentially-long period of time. Often these materials have blended or commingled in a mass on the surface or in the ground water under the site and these chemicals can combine or transform themselves into a new chemical "soup." As Judge Coffin wrote describing what EPA found when it began to cleanup hazardous wastes at a pig farm in O'Neil v. Picillo,

What they found—were massive trenches and pits "filled with free—flowing, multi-colored, pungent liquid wastes" and thousands of "dented and corroded drums containing a veritable potpourri of toxic fluids."

883 F.2d 176 (1st Cir.1989). Considering this quote, would a plaintiff be able to satisfy a strict demand that they had incurred cleanup costs to remediate each PRP's discreet contribution to the toxic "soup?" Most courts follow the *Alcan* principle and perhaps they do so on a presumption of a nexus between any disposal of hazardous waste and general site cleanup expenses.

2. RETROACTIVITY

CERCLA applies to grant cleanup authority and cost recovery actions for hazardous waste sites regardless of when the materials were deposited or released. In fact, many of the waste sites received hazardous materials well before CERCLA's enactment in 1980. Some PRPs have even claimed that they have been subjected to cleanup liability for pre-CERCLA conduct that was lawful at the time it occurred. All of this has led to PRP defensive arguments that this interpretation constitutes the creation of retroactive liability either 1) that is contrary to the intent of the statute or 2) that is unconstitutional. These positions have been consistently rejected by the courts. See e.g., United States v. Monsanto, 858 F.2d 160, 173–74 (4th Cir.1988);United States v. Alcan Aluminum Corp., 49 F.Supp.2d 96 (N.D.N.Y.1999) and Combined Properties/Greenbriar Ltd. Partnership v. Morrow, 58 F.Supp.2d 675 (E.D.Va.1999). The illegal retroactivity arguments have generally been rejected by an analysis focusing upon the statute's impact to remedy current hazardous substance releases even though caused by prior activities. Most courts view current cleanup obligations and liabilities to remedy existing environmental and public health conditions regardless of when they were created. The bottom line is that CERCLA *is not* viewed by courts as belated and unjustified punishment for past, lawful conduct and consequently, the retroactivity argument has failed.

3. JOINT AND SEVERAL LIABILITY

Often there are many contributors of hazardous substances at one waste disposal site. This should not be surprising since, over the years, a landfill or waste dump may have received containers from numerous generators and transporters. As in the *O'Neil v. Picillo* case excerpt above, the wastes are frequently mixed together forming a complex mass of toxic materials. How should liability for cleanup and other costs be distributed when there are multiple contributors to the problem? Should all PRPs be liable but only according to their level of contribution or the discrete risks they created? Should one party be primarily liable for the entire cost and then seek contribution, at a later stage, from other PRPs according to some theory of allocation? How would this problem be solved under a common law tort approach to harms inflicted by joint tortfeasors?

As mentioned above, CERCLA § 107(a) does not explain much about the concept of liability for cleanup expenses. In fact, as part of political compromise leading to passage, the final version of the 1980 statute eliminated all references to the legal concept of joint and several liability which had existed in the Senate bill. However, from the beginning courts have interpreted "shall be liable" language of § 107(a) as allowing for joint and several liability. The excerpts from the *Chem-Dyne, Monsanto* and the *Alcan* cases presented below presents differing examples on the application of joint and several liability. The "joint and several" tort principle applies when there is no basis for dividing the responsibility for the harm among several responsible parties. When in such a case a "single and indivisible harm" is caused by multiple PRPs, the joint and several liability theory permits the plaintiff to recover the full value of the damages against one PRP leaving to that party the obligation of seeking reimbursement for part of the loss from other PRPs. This is true regardless of that single PRP's actual impact or contribution to the indivisible waste site. On the other hand, if the harm is found to be "divisible," then the individual PRPs will be found liable only for the portion of the harm attributable to the division. What might be the policy justifications for embracing joint and several liability in the CERCLA context? What are its advantages?

An early, broad application of this joint and several liability rule occurred in United States v. Chem–Dyne, 572 F.Supp. 802 (S.D.Ohio 1983), where the federal government sought cleanup reimbursement against 24 defendants who had generated or transported hazardous substances to the Chem–Dyne treatment facility. In this influential opinion, the court stated that the application of either joint and several liability or discrete allocation was to be "determined under common law principles, where a court performing a case by case evaluation of the complex factual scenarios associated with multiple-generator waste sites will assess the propriety of applying joint and several liability on an individual basis." Turning to the facts at hand, Judge Rubin evaluated the merits of the "divisibility" argument with the following discussion,

> The question of whether the defendants are jointly or severally liable for the clean-up costs turns on a fairly complex factual determination. Read in light most favorable to the plaintiff, the following facts illustrate the nature of the problem. The Chem–Dyne facility contains a variety of hazardous waste from 289 generators or transporters, consisting of about 608,000 pounds of material. Some of the wastes have commingled but the identities of the sources of these wastes remain unascertained. The fact of the mixing of the wastes raises an issue as to the divisibility of the harm. Further, a dispute exists over which of the wastes have contaminated the ground water, the degree of their migration and concomitant health hazard. Finally, the volume of waste of a particular generator is not an accurate predictor of the risk associated with the waste because the toxicity or migratory potential of a particular hazardous substance generally varies independently with the volume of the waste.

This case, as do most pollution cases, turns on the issue of whether the harm caused at Chem–Dyne is "divisible" or "indivisible." If the harm is divisible and if there is a reasonable basis for apportionment of damages, each defendant is liable only for the portion of harm he himself caused. Restatement (second) of Torts, § 433A, 881. In this situation, the burden of proof as to apportionment is upon each defendant. Id. at § 433 B. On the other hand, if the defendants caused an indivisible harm, each is subject to liability for the entire harm. Id. at § 875. The defendants have not carried their burden of demonstrating the divisibility of the harm and the degrees to which each defendant is responsible.

572 F.Supp. at 811. The general use of the joint and several liability principle in the first few years after CERCLA's enactment was controversial and it resulted in claims that the statute was unfair in its application, imposing large, unjustified liability on parties who were unable to establish a divisibility of the harm and who could not find other PRPs to shoulder part of the costs. These arguments were made more compelling by the fact that, in practice, courts have found it very difficult for a PRP to meet its burden of proving that the harm was, in fact, "divisible." See e.g., United States v. Township of Brighton, 153 F.3d 307 (6th Cir.1998) and United States v. Alcan Aluminum Corp., 97 F.Supp.2d 248 (N.D.N.Y.2000). But see Dent v. Beazer Materials and Services, Inc., 156 F.3d 523 (4th Cir.1998) (no chemicals similar to those found at the site were released during the PRP's ownership).

Consider situations where the application of this liability theory to concentrate all or most of the cleanup expenses on one actor might be unjust: a) an unsophisticated small business buyer of contaminated land, 2) a hazardous waste generator who contributes 1 percent of the waste to the polluted site, 3) a trust beneficiary who becomes an "owner" of contaminated property by gift. These, and other, imaginable, hypotheticals have put pressure on the courts to mitigate the harshness of the joint and several liability doctrine. The case excerpts which follow demonstrate the judicial developments which attempt to modify the harsh features of this liability doctrine.

United States v. Monsanto Co.

United States Court of Appeals, Fourth Circuit, 1988.
858 F.2d 160.

■ Sprouse, Circuit Judge.

Oscar Seidenberg and Harvey Hutchinson (the site-owners) and Allied Corporation, Monsanto Company, and EM Industries, Inc. (the generator defendants),[7] appeal from the district court's entry of summary judgment holding them liable to the United States and the State of South Carolina

---

7. Originally a named generator defendant in this case, Aquair Corporation has entered into a settlement agreement with the plaintiffs.

(the governments) under section 107(a) of the Comprehensive Environmental Response, Compensation, and Liability Act of 1980 (CERCLA). 42 U.S.C.A. § 9607(a) (West Supp. 1987). The court determined that the defendants were liable jointly and severally for $1,813,624 in response costs accrued from the partial removal of hazardous waste from a disposal facility located near Columbia, South Carolina. The court declined, however, to assess prejudgment interest: against the defendants. We affirm the district court's liability holdings, but we vacate and remand for reconsideration its denial of prejudgment interest.

I.

In 1972, Seidenberg and Hutchinson leased a four-acre tract of land they owned to the Columbia Organic Chemical Company (COCC), a South Carolina chemical manufacturing corporation. The property, located along Bluff Road near Columbia, South Carolina, consisted of a small warehouse and surrounding areas. The lease was verbal, on a month-to-month basis, and according to the site-owners' deposition testimony, was executed for the sole purpose of allowing COCC to store raw materials and finished products in the warehouse. Seidenberg and Hutchinson received monthly lease payments of $200, which increased to $350 by 1980.

In the mid–1970s, COCC expanded its business to include the brokering and recycling of chemical waste generated by third parties. It used the Bluff Road site as a waste storage and disposal facility for its new operations. In 1976, COCC's principals incorporated South Carolina Recycling and Disposal Inc. (SCRDI), for the purpose of assuming COCC's wastehandling business, and the site-owners began accepting lease payments from SCRDI.

SCRDI contracted with numerous off-site waste producers for the transport, recycling, and disposal of chemical and other waste. Among these producers were agencies of the federal government and South Carolina,[8] and various private entities including the three generator defendants in this litigation. Although SCRDI operated other disposal sites, it deposited much of the waste it received at the Bluff Road facility. The waste stored at Bluff Road contained many chemical substances that federal law defines as ''hazardous.''

Between 1976 and 1980, SCRDI haphazardly deposited more than 7,000 fifty-five gallon drums of chemical waste on the four-acre Bluff Road site. It placed waste laden drums and containers wherever there was space, often without pallets to protect them from the damp ground. It stacked drums on top of one another without regard to the chemical compatibility of their contents. It maintained no documented safety procedures and kept no inventory of the stored chemicals. Over time many of the drums rusted, rotted, and otherwise deteriorated. Hazardous substances leaked from the

---

8. The federal instrumentalities that contracted with SCRDI included the Environmental Protection Agency, the Army, the Air Force, and the Center for Disease Control. The South Carolina Department of Health and Environmental Control also contracted with SCRDI for waste disposal.

decaying drums and oozed into the ground. The substances commingled with incompatible chemicals that had escaped from other containers, generating noxious fumes, fires, and explosions.

On October 26, 1977, a toxic cloud formed when chemicals leaking from rusted drums reacted with rainwater. Twelve responding firemen were hospitalized.[9] Again, on July 24, 1979, an explosion and fire resulted when chemicals stored in glass jars leaked onto drums containing incompatible substances. SCRDI's site manager could not identify the substances that caused the explosion, making the fire difficult to extinguish.

In 1980, the Environmental Protection Agency (EPA) inspected the Bluff Road site. Its investigation revealed that the facility was filled well beyond its capacity with chemical waste. The number of drums and the reckless manner in which they were stacked precluded access to various areas in the site. Many of the drums observed were unlabeled, or their labels had become unreadable from exposure, rendering it impossible to identify their contents. The EPA concluded that the site posed "a major fire hazard."

Later that year, the United States filed suit under section 7003 of the Resource Conservation and Recovery Act, 42 U.S.C. § 6973, against SCRDI, COCC, and Oscar Seidenberg. The complaint was filed before the December 11, 1980, effective date of CERCLA, and it sought only injunctive relief. Thereafter, the State of South Carolina intervened as a plaintiff in the pending action.

This incident sparked substantial publicity, and the site-owners concede that as of June 1977 they were aware of hazardous waste disposal activities taking place on their Bluff Road property

In the course of discovery, the governments identified a number of waste generators, including the generator defendants in this appeal, that had contracted with SCRDI for waste disposal. The governments notified the generators that they were potentially responsible for the costs of cleanup at Bluff Road under section 107(a) of the newly-enacted CERCLA. As a result of these contracts, the governments executed individual settlement agreements with twelve of the identified off-site producers. The generator defendants, however, declined to settle.

Using funds received from the settlements, the governments contracted with Triangle Resource Industries (TRI) to conduct a partial surface cleanup at the site. The contract required RAD Services, Inc., a subsidiary of TRI, to remove 75 percent of the drums found there and to keep a log of the removed drums. RAD completed its partial cleanup operation in October 1982. The log it prepared documented that it had removed containers and drums bearing the labels or markings of each of the three generator defendants.

---

9. The federal instrumentalities that contracted with SCRDI included the Environmental Protection Agency, the Army, the Air Force, and the Center for Disease Control. The South Carolina Department of Health and Environmental Control also contracted with SCRDI for waste disposal.

The EPA reinspected the site after the first phase of the cleanup had been completed. The inspection revealed that closed drums and containers labeled with the insignia of each of the three generator defendants remained at the site. The EPA also collected samples of surface water, soil, and sediment from the site. Laboratory tests of the samples disclosed that several hazardous substances[10] contained in the waste the generator defendants had shipped to the site remained present at the sites.[11]

Thereafter, South Carolina completed the remaining 25 percent of the surface cleanup. It used federal funds from the Hazardous Substances Response Trust Fund (Superfund), 42 U.S.C. § 9631, as well as state money from the South Carolina Hazardous Waste Contingency Fund, S.C.Code Ann. § 44–56–160, and in-kind contribution of other state funds to match the federal contribution.

In 1982, the governments filed an amended complaint, adding the three generator defendants and site-owner Harvey Hutchinson, and including claims under section 107(a) of CERCLA against all of the nonsettling defendants. The governments alleged that the generator defendants and site-owners were jointly and severally liable under section 107(a) for the costs expended completing the surface cleanup at Bluff Road.

In response, the site-owners contended that they were innocent absentee landlords unaware of and unconnected to the waste disposal activities that took place on their land. They maintained that their lease with COCC did not allow COCC (or SCRDI) to store chemical waste on the premises, but they admitted that they became aware of waste storage in 1977 and accepted lease payments until 1980.

The generator defendants likewise denied liability for the governments' response costs. Among other defenses, they claimed that none of their specific waste materials contributed to the hazardous conditions at Bluff Road, and that retroactive imposition of CERCLA liability on them was unconstitutional. They also asserted that they could establish an affirmative defense to CERCLA liability under section 107(b)(3), 42 U.S.C. § 9607(b)(3), by showing that the harm at the site was caused solely through the conduct of unrelated third parties. All parties thereafter moved for summary judgment.

10. The term "hazardous substance" is defined in section 101(14) of CERCIA, 42 U.S.C.A. § 9601(14) (West Supp.1987). The definition incorporates by reference the substances listed as hazardous or toxic under the Clean Water Act, 33 U.S.C.A. §§ 1317(a), 1321(b)(2)(a) (West 1986), the Clean Air Act, 42 U.S.C. § 7412(b), the Resource Conservation and Recovery Act of 1976, 42 U.S.C.A. § 6921 (West 1983 & Supp.1987), and the Toxic Substances Control Act, 15 U.S.C. § 2606. Section 102(a) of CERCIA also authorizes EPA to list additional substances that "may present substantial danger to the public health or welfare or the environment." 42 U.S.C.A. § 9602(a) (West Supp.1987).

11. It is undisputed that hazardous substances of the sort contained in each of the generator defendants' waste materials were found at the site. These substances included 1,1,1Trichloroethane, acetone, phenol, cresol (methyl phenol), chlorophenol, and 2,4 dichlorophenol.

After an evidentiary hearing, the district court granted the governments' summary judgment motion on CERCLA liability. The court found that all of the defendants were responsible parties under section 107(a), and that none of them had presented sufficient evidence to support an affirmative defense under section 107(b). The court further concluded that the environmental harm at Bluff Road was "indivisible," and it held all of the defendants jointly and severally liable for the governments' response costs. United States v. South Carolina Recycling & Disposal, Inc., 653 F.Supp. 984 (D.S.C.1984) *(SCRDI)*.

As to the site-owners' liability, the court found it sufficient that they owned the Bluff Road site at the time hazardous substances were deposited there. Id. at 993 (interpreting 42 U.S.C.A. § 9607(a)(2)). It rejected their contentions that Congress did not intend to subject "innocent" landowners to CERCLA liability. The court similarly found summary judgment appropriate against the generator defendants because it was undisputed that (1) they shipped hazardous substances to the Bluff Road facility; (2) hazardous substances "like" those present in the generator defendants' waste were found at the facility; and (3) there had been a release of hazardous substances at the site. * * * In this context, the court rejected the generator defendants' arguments that the governments had to prove that their specific waste contributed to the harm at the site, and it found their constitutional contentions to be "without force." * * * Finally, since none of the defendants challenged the governments' itemized accounting of response costs, the court ordered them to pay the full $1,813,624 that had been requested. * * * It refused, however, to add prejudgment interest to the amount owed. * * * This appeal followed. * * *

III.

The appellants next challenge the district court's imposition of joint and several liability for the governments' response costs. The court concluded that joint and several liability was appropriate because the environmental harm at Bluff Road was "indivisible" and the appellants had "failed to meet their burden of proving otherwise." *SCRDI,* 653 F.Supp. at 994. We agree with its conclusion.

While CERCLA does not mandate the imposition of joint and several liability, it permits it in cases of indivisible harm. See Shore Realty, 759 F.2d at 1042 n. 13; United States v. Chem–Dyne, 572 F.Supp. 802, 810–11 (S.D.Ohio 1983). In each case, the court must consider traditional and evolving principles of federal common law, which Congress has left to the courts to supply interstitially.

Under common law rules, when two or more persons act independently to cause a single harm for which there is a reasonable basis of apportionment according to the contribution of each, each is held liable only for the portion of harm that he causes. * * * When such persons cause a single and indivisible harm, however, they are held liable jointly and severally for the entire harm. We think these principles, as reflected in the Restatement

(Second) of Torts, represent the correct and uniform federal rules applicable to CERCLA cases.

Section 433A of the Restatement provides:

(1) Damages for harm are to be apportioned among two or more causes where

(a) there are distinct harms, or

(b) there is a reasonable basis for determining the contribution of each cause to a single harm.

(2) Damages for any other harm cannot be apportioned among two or more causes.

Restatement (Second) of Torts § 433A (1965).

Placing their argument into the Restatement framework, the generator defendants concede that the environmental damage at Bluff Road constituted a "single harm," but contend that there was a reasonable basis for apportioning the harm. They observe that each of the off-site generators with whom SCRDI contracted sent a potentially identifiable volume of waste to the Bluff Road site, and they maintain that liability should have been apportioned according to the volume they deposited as compared to the total volume disposed of there by all parties. In light of the conditions at Bluff Road, we cannot accept this method as a basis for apportionment.

The generator defendants bore the burden of establishing a reasonable basis for apportioning liability among responsible parties. Chem–Dyne, 572 F. Supp at 810; Restatement (Second) of Torts § 433B (1965). To meet this burden, the generator defendants had to establish that the environmental harm at Bluff Road was divisible among responsible parties. They presented no evidence, however, showing a relationship between waste volume, the release of hazardous substances, and the harm at the site. Further, in light of the commingling of hazardous substances, the district court could not have reasonably apportioned liability without some evidence disclosing the individual and interactive qualities of the substances deposited there. Common sense counsels that a million gallons of certain substances could be mixed together without significant consequences, whereas a few pints of others improperly mixed could result in disastrous consequences. Under other circumstances proportionate volumes of hazardous substances may well be probative of contributory harm. In this case, however, volume could not establish the effective contribution of each waste generator to the harm at the Bluff Road site.

Although we find no error in the trial court's imposition of joint and several liability, we share the appellants' concern that they not be ultimately responsible for reimbursing more than their just portion of the governments' response costs.[28] In its refusal to apportion liability, the district

---

28. The final judgment holds the defendants liable for slightly less than half of the total costs incurred in the cleanup, while it appears that the generator defendants collectively produced approximately 22 percent of the waste that SCRDI handled. Other evi-

court likewise recognized the validity of their demand that they not be required to shoulder a disproportionate amount of the costs. It ruled, however, that making the governments whole for response costs was the primary consideration and that cost allocation was a matter "more appropriately considered in an action for contribution between responsible parties after plaintiff has been made whole." SCRDI, 653 F.Supp. at 995 & n. 8. Had we sat in place of the district court, we would have ruled as it did on the apportionment issue, but may well have retained the action to dispose of the contribution questions. See 42 U.S.C.A. § 9613(f) (West Supp. 1987). That procedural course, however, was committed to the trial court's discretion and we find no abuse of it. As we have stated, the defendants still have the right to sue responsible parties for contribution, and in that action they may assert both legal and equitable theories of cost allocation.

■ WIDENER, CIRCUIT JUDGE, concurring and dissenting.

I concur in the majority opinion in all respects save its decision not to require the district court to treat the issue of allocation of costs of cleanup among the various defendants, and, as to that, I respectfully dissent. While it may be true that a subsequent suit for contribution may adequately apportion the damages among the defendants, I am of opinion that the district court, as a court of equity, is required to retain jurisdiction and answer that question now.

I see great danger in postponing the ultimate apportioning of the damages to a later day. As an example, a small generator which deposited a few gallons of relatively innocuous waste liquid at a site is jointly and severally liable for the entire cost of cleanup under this decision. And with that I agree. If that generator were readily available and solvent, however, the government might well, and probably would, proceed against him first in collecting its judgment. The vagaries of and delays in his subsequent suit for contribution might result in needless financial disaster. I do not see this as a desired or even permissible result.

United States v. Alcan Aluminum Corp.

United States Court of Appeals, Third Circuit, 1992.
964 F.2d 252.

■ GREENBERG, CIRCUIT JUDGE.

[This case involved the Butler Tunnel Site, which consisted of a network of approximately five square miles of deep underground mines and related tunnels, caverns, pools and waterways bordering the east bank of

---

dence indicates that agencies of the federal government produced more waste than did generator defendant Monsanto, and suggests that the amounts contributed by the settling parties do not bear a strictly proportionate relationship to the total costs of cleaning the facility. We note, however, that a substantial portion of the final judgment is attributable to litigation costs. We also observe that the EPA has contributed upwards of $50,000 to the Bluff Road cleanup, and that any further claims against the EPA and other responsible government instrumentalities may be resolved in a contribution action pursuant to CERCLA section 113(f).

the Susquehanna River in Pittston, Pennsylvania. The mine workings at the Site were drained by the Butler Tunnel, a 7500–foot tunnel which fed directly into the Susquehanna River. The mines were accessible from the surface by numerous air shafts or boreholes. In the late 1970s, companies owned and controlled by Russell Mahler deposited approximately 2 million gallons of oily liquid waste containing hazardous substances from numerous industrial facilities into one of the boreholes leading into the tunnel.

Alcan was one of Russell Mahler's customers and its aluminum manufacturing process generated a waste emulsion containing aluminum fragments. These fragments also contained copper, chromium, cadmium, lead and zinc which are deemed "hazardous" under CERCLA. Alcan filtered the used emulsion prior to disposing it, but some fragments remained. According to Alcan, the level of these compounds in the post-filtered, used emulsion was "far below the EP toxic or TCLP toxic levels and, indeed, orders of magnitude below ambient or naturally occurring background levels." Between mid–1978 and 1979, Russell Mahler disposed of over 32,000 gallons of Alcan's liquid waste into the borehole.

In September 1985, the tunnel discharged approximately 100,000 gallons of water contaminated with hazardous substances into the Susquehanna River and it was determined that this discharge was composed of the wastes deposited into the borehole in the late 1970s. In 1989, the United States filed a cost-recovery case against twenty defendants, including Alcan, for costs incurred by EPA in responding to the release. Nineteen of the twenty defendants settle with EPA by way of consent decree. Ruling on cross-motions for summary judgment, the district court ruled in favor of EPA entering judgment against Alcan in the amount of $473,790.18, which was the difference between the full response costs the Government had incurred in cleaning the Susquehanna River and the amount the Government had recovered from settling defendants.] . . .

F.   Divisibility of Harm

The . . . conclusions that (1) there is no quantitative threshold in the definition of hazardous substances and (2) the plaintiff need not establish a causal connection between a given defendant's waste and the release or the incurrence of response costs would initially appear to lead to unfair imposition of liability. As Alcan asserts, this definition of "hazardous substances" effectively renders everything in the universe hazardous, including, for example, federally approved drinking water. When this definition is read in conjunction with the rule that specific causation is not required, CERCLA seemingly would impose liability on every generator of hazardous waste, although that generator could not, on its own, have caused any environmental harm.[25]

25. Dean Prosser's hornbook highlights the paradox of liability where acts harmless in themselves together cause damage, observing:

A very troublesome question arises where the acts of each of two or more parties, standing alone, would not be wrongful, but together they cause harm to the plaintiff. If several defendants in-

While Alcan's assertion is of considerable strength, the Government's rebuttal is equally forceful. It notes that individual defendants must be held responsible for environmental injury brought about by the actions of multiple defendants, even if no single defendant itself could have produced the harm, for otherwise "each defendant in a multidefendant case could avoid liability by relying on the low concentrations of hazardous substances in its waste, while the plaintiff is left with the substantial clean-up costs associated with the defendant's accumulated wastes." The Government reasons that this strong public interest in forcing polluters in the multi-generator context to pay outweighs a defendant's interest in avoiding liability even if that defendant has not acted in an environmentally un-sound fashion when its actions are viewed without regard to the actions of others. The court in *United States v. Western Processing Co.*, adopting the position advanced by the Government in this case, observed:

> it is entirely possible for a hazardous waste facility to be comprised of entirely small amounts from many contributors. If each PRP could make [Alcan's] argument, i.e., that its particular contribution did not warrant remediation and thus that it should not be liable for any costs, *no* party would be liable, despite the fact that the site, as a whole, needed to be cleaned up and the government incurred costs in doing so.

734 F.Supp. at 937 (emphasis in original).

We find some merit in the arguments advanced by both the Government and Alcan. Accordingly, in our view, the common law principles of joint and several liability provide the only means to achieve the proper balance between Alcan's and the Government's conflicting interests and to infuse fairness into the statutory scheme without distorting its plain meaning or disregarding congressional intent.

[The court then concluded, in accord with numerous other cases, that it should determine "in accordance with traditional common law principles" whether applying joint and several liability would be "proper" under the circumstances. It then looked to the Restatement (Second) of Torts for guidance.]

Section 433A of the Restatement provides that, when two or more joint tortfeasors acting independently cause a distinct or single harm for which there is a reasonable basis for division according to the contribution of each, each is subject to liability only for the portion of the harm that the individual tortfeasor has caused. It states,

(1) Damages for harm are to be apportioned among two or more causes where

(a) there are distinct harms, or

dependently pollute a stream, the impurities traceable to each may be negligible and harmless, but all together may render the water entirely unfit for use. The difficulty lies in the fact that each defendant alone would have committed no tort. There would have been no negligence, and no nuisance, since the individual use of the stream would have been a reasonable use, and no harm would have resulted. William L. Prosser, *Law of Torts*, § 52, at 322 (4th ed.1971).

(b) there is a reasonable basis for determining the contribution of each cause to a single harm.

(2) Damages for any other harm cannot be apportioned among two or more causes.

Similarly, section 881 sets forth the affirmative defense based upon the divisibility of harm rule in section 433A:

If two or more persons, acting independently, tortiously cause distinct harms or a single harm for which there is a reasonable basis for division according to the contribution of each, each is subject to liability only for the portion of the total harm that he has himself caused.

However, where joint tortfeasors cause a single and indivisible harm for which there is no reasonable basis for division according to the contribution of each, each tortfeasor is subject to liability for the entire harm. Section 875 recites:

Each of two or more persons whose tortious conduct is a legal cause of a single and indivisible harm to the injured party is subject to liability to the injured party for the entire harm.

Obviously, of critical importance in this analysis is whether a harm is divisible and reasonably capable of apportionment, or indivisible, thereby subjecting the tortfeasor to potentially far-reaching liability.[27]

Under the Restatement, where a joint tortfeasor seeks to apportion the full amount of a plaintiff's damages according to that tortfeasor's own contribution to the harm, it is the tortfeasor's burden to establish that the damages are capable of such apportionment. As the comments concerning this issue explain, the burden of proving that the harm is capable of apportionment is placed on the tortfeasor to avoid:

the injustice of allowing a proved wrongdoer who has in fact caused harm to the plaintiff to escape liability merely because the harm which he has inflicted has combined with similar harm inflicted by other wrongdoers, and the nature of the harm itself has made it necessary that evidence be produced before is can be apportioned. In such a case the defendant may justly be required to assume the burden of producing that evidence, or if he is not able to do so, of bearing full responsibility. As between the proved tortfeasor who has clearly caused some harm, and the entirely innocent plaintiff, any hardship due to

---

27. Interestingly, the drafters of the Restatement found that joint pollution of water is typically subject to the divisibility rule. They write:

There are other kinds of harm which, while not so clearly marked out as severable into distinct parts, are still capable of division upon a reasonable and rational basis, and of fair apportionment among the causes responsible.... *Such apportionment is commonly made in cases of private nuisance, where the pollution of a stream ... has interfered with the plaintiff's use and enjoyment of his land.*

Section 433 A, Comment d (emphasis supplied) See e.d., Somerset Villa Inc. v. Lee's Summit, 436 S.W. 2d 658 (Mo.1968).

lack of evidence as to the extent of the harm should fall upon the former.

Comment on Section 433 B subsection (2).

These provisions underscore the intensely factual nature of the "divisibility" issue and thus highlight the district court's error in granting summary judgment for the full claim in favor of EPA without conducting a hearing. For this reason, we will remand this case for the court to determine whether there is a reasonable basis for limiting Alcan's liability based on its personal contribution to the harm to the Susquehanna River.

Our conclusions on this point are completely consistent with our previous discussion on causation, as there we were concerned with the Government's burden in demonstrating liability in the first instance. Here we are dealing with Alcan's effort to avoid liability otherwise established. We observe in this regard that Alcan's burden in attempting to prove the divisibility of harm to the Susquehanna River is substantial, and the analysis will be factually complex as it will require an assessment of the relative toxicity, migratory potential and synergistic capacity of the hazardous waste at issue. [citing the *U.S. v. Monsanto Co.* and *Chem-Dyne* cases] But Alcan should be permitted this opportunity to limit or avoid liability. If Alcan succeeds in this endeavor, it should only be liable for that portion of the harm fairly attributable to it.

Alcan maintains that there is no need for a hearing because, not only is the harm divisible, but its relative contribution to the injury to the Susquehanna River is zero. According to Alcan, "[i]t is technically impossible to have a release or threatened release such that a clean-up would be authorized or justified under the National Contingency Plan as a result of the addition of the metal compounds in the Alcan emulsion to the Butler Site. When one adds two materials that have the same concentrations of an element or compound, the net result is the same concentration. It can never result in a higher concentration." Alcan [also] asserts that "below ambient levels of any substance can never cause or contribute to a release or response costs."

The district court did not specifically address this argument.... However, we are not the proper forum to consider Alcan's argument as we have no way of determining whether the trace levels of metallic compounds in Alcan's used emulsion became concentrated and thereby posed an environmental threat. Furthermore, there may be other circumstances bearing on this issue of which we are not even aware. Thus, the district court should reevaluate Alcan's contention in light of the facts developed in the hearing on this issue.[29]

---

29. In this vein, we also reject the Government's argument that a hearing is unnecessary because Alcan has admitted that its emulsion was "commingled" with the other generators' waste: "commingled" waste is not synonymous with "indivisible" harm. We observe that some courts have held that a generator may present evidence that it has paid more than its "fair share" in a contribution proceeding, expressly permitted under 42 U.S.C. § 9613(f)(2).... In a sense, the "contribution" inquiry involves an analysis

In sum, on remand, the district court must permit Alcan to attempt to prove that the harm is divisible and that the damages are capable of some reasonable apportionment. We note that the Government need not prove that Alcan's emulsion caused the release or the response costs. On the other hand, if Alcan proves that the emulsion did not or could not, *when mixed with other hazardous wastes,* contribute to the release and the resultant response costs, then Alcan should not be responsible for *any* response costs. In this sense, our result thus injects causation into the equation but, as we have already pointed out, places the burden of proof on the defendant instead of the plaintiff. We think that this result is consistent with the statutory scheme and yet recognizes that there must be some reason for the imposition of CERCLA liability. Our result seems particularly appropriate in light of the expansive meaning of "hazardous substance." Of course, if Alcan cannot prove that it should not be liable for any response costs or cannot prove that the harm is divisible and that the damages are capable of some reasonable apportionment, it will be liable for the full claim of $473,790.18.

NOTES AND QUESTIONS

1.   What is the defense that the *Alcan* holding has established for PRPs in CERCLA cases? First, the Third Circuit noted that Alcan had the opportunity to prove that it contributed only to a divisible part of the harm and that it was responsible for this allocable part. Second, the court concluded its opinion with the following language, "if Alcan proves that the emulsion did not or could not, *when mixed with other hazardous wastes,* contribute to the release and the resultant response costs, then Alcan should not be responsible for *any* response costs." This statement raises a number of issues.

similar to the "divisibility" inquiry, as both focus on what harm the defendant caused. However, we believe that this inquiry, to the extent that it is the same as that discussed in above-noted cases, is best resolved at the initial liability phase and not at the contribution phase since it involves precisely relative degrees of *liability*. Thus, if the defendant can prove that the harm is divisible and that it only caused some portion of the injury, it should only be held liable for that amount. In our view, the logical consequences of delaying apportionment determination may well be drastic, for it seems clear that a defendant could easily be strong-armed into settling where other defendants have settled in order to avoid being held liable for the remainder of the response costs. Indeed, in this case the court determined that Alcan, one of 20 defendants, was liable for $473,790.18 in response

costs, although the total response costs amounted to $1,302,290.18. Thus, although Alcan comprised only 5 percent of the defendant pool, it was required by the court to absorb over 36 percent of the costs. Furthermore, Alcan's share of the liability seems to be disproportionate on a volume basis as well. We also point out that contribution will probably not be available from a settling defendant in an action by the United States. 42 U.S.C. § 9613(f)(2).

We note, of course, that a determination in a given case that harm is indivisible will *not* negate a defendant's right to seek contribution from other non-settling defendants, as the contribution proceeding is an equitable one in which a court is permitted to allocate response costs based on factors it deems appropriate, whereas the court is not vested with such discretion in the divisibility determination.

A. What kind of information will the PRP need to prove either divisibility or non-liability under the *Alcan* test? Is this defense likely to be of much use to smaller, less technologically-sophisticated PRP? One view is that the defense is a rich company rule.

> If Alcan's holding becomes widely followed, EPA response actions will become more like private contribution actions. Potentially responsible parties will need to retain toxicologists, environmental chemists, and clean-up cost specialists to aid in proving the harm caused by a particular waste.

Harris & Milan, Avoiding Joint and Several Liability Under CERCLA, 23 Env. Rep. 1726, 1728 (1992). How much benefit will this defense really provide to PRPs? Will many PRPs be successful in mounting this defense?

B. Has this *Alcan* defense actually reintroduced the legal concept of causation into the CERCLA cleanup liability formulation? Remember that as part of its *prima facie* case, the government does not have to prove that the PRP's release of hazardous substances caused it to incur specific response costs related to that release; just that it incurred costs in responding to a release of hazardous materials. In another *Alcan* decision, the Second Circuit acknowledged this fact when it wrote,

> In so ruling we candidly admit that causation is being brought back into the case—through the backdoor, after being denied entry at the frontdoor [the *prima facie* liability stage]—at the apportionment stage. We hasten to add nonetheless that causation—with the burden on defendant—is reintroduced only to permit a defendant to escape payment where its pollutants did not contribute more than background contamination and also cannot concentrate. To state this standard in other words, we adopt a special exception to the usual absence of a causation requirement, but the exception is applicable only to claims, like Alcan's, where background levels are not exceeded. And, we recognize this limited exception only in the absence of any EPA threshold.

United States v. Alcan Aluminum Corp., 990 F.2d 711 (2d Cir.1993). Is there any principled reason why the *Alcan* defense should not be generally available, especially if then burden of proof rests with the PRP?

C. Will the *Alcan* defense ultimately become a high-stakes "battle of the technical experts" focusing on the causation of response costs with the PRP disputing whether those costs were attributable to its release? While this may seem to run counter to the general doctrine of *prima facie* liability, at least the Second Circuit has opened the door for such an argument. In *Alcan* it ruled that,

> Alcan declares that the response actions at [the site] were attributable to substances such as PCB's, nitro benzene, phenol, dichlonoethone, toluene, and benzene. It contends that no soil contamination due to heavy metals was found there, and insists that the metallic constituents of its oil emulsion are insoluble compounds, submitting an affidavit supporting this theory of divisibility. The government submit-

ted a declaration stating that metal contaminants like those found in Alcan's waste emulsion were present in the environmental media at [the site], that the commingling of metallic and organic hazardous substances resulted indivisible harm, and that though some forms of lead, cadmium, and chromium are insoluble, they may chemically react with other substances and become water-soluble. These differing contentions supported by expert affidavits raise sufficient questions of fact to preclude the granting of summary judgment on the divisibility issue.

990 F.2d at 711.

2. While "divisibility" of the harm may be difficult to establish, it is not an impossible task in all circumstances. In one case, the Fifth Circuit reversed a district court's summary judgment and it found that a PRP had met it's burden of establishing a reasonable basis for apportioning the harm caused by the disposal of wastewater from a chrome plating operation. In the Matter of Bell Petroleum Services, Inc., 3 F.3d 889 (5th Cir.1993), Judge Jolly wrote the following,

> Our review of the record convinces us that Sequa met its burden of proving that, as a matter of law, there is a reasonable basis for apportionment. This case is closely analogous to the *Restatement's* illustrations in which apportionment of liability is appropriate. For example, where cattle owned by two or more defendants destroy the plaintiff's crops, damages are apportioned according to the number of cattle owned by each defendant, based on the reasonable assumption that the respective harm done is proportionate to that number. Thus, the *Restatement* suggests that apportionment is appropriate even though the evidence does not establish with certainty, the specific amount of harm caused by each defendant's cattle, and even though there is a possibility that only one of the defendant's cattle caused all of the harm, while the other defendant's cattle idly stood by. Likewise, pollution of a stream by two or more factories may be treated as divisible in terms of degree, and apportioned among the defendants on the basis of evidence of the respective quantities of pollution charged by each.

> As is evident from our previous discussion of the jurisprudence, most CERCLA cost-recovery actions involve numerous, commingled hazardous substances with synergistic effects and unknown toxicity. In contrast, this case involves only one hazardous substance—chromium—and no synergistic effects. The chromium entered the groundwater as the result of similar operations by three parties who operated at mutually exclusive times. Here, it is reasonable to assume that the respective harm done by each of the defendants is proportionate to the volume of chromium-contaminated water each discharged into the environment.

> Even though, it is not possible to determine with absolute certainly the exact amount of chromium each defendant introduced into the groundwater, there is sufficient evidence from which a reasonable and rational approximation of each defendant's Individual contribution to

the contamination can be made. The evidence demonstrates that Leigh owned the real property at the site from 1967 though 1981, and conducted chrome-plating activities there in 1971 and 1972. In 1972, Bell purchased the assets of the shop and leased the property from Leigh. It continued to conduct similar, but more extensive, chrome-plating activities there until mid–1976. In August 1976, Sequa purchased the assets from Bell, leased the property from Leigh, and conducted similar chrome-plating activities at the site until late 1977. In response to the EPA's motion for summary judgment, Sequa introduced evidence regarding chrome flake purchases during each operator's tenure. It also introduced evidence with respect to the value of the chromeplating done by each, as well as summaries of sales. Given the number of years that had passed since the activities were conducted, the records of these activities were not complete. However, there was testimony from various witnesses regarding the rinsing and wastewater disposal practices of each defendant, and the amount of chrome-plating activity conducted by each.

During the Phase III hearing, Sequa introduced expert testimony regarding a volumetric approach to apportionment. The first expert, Henderson, calculated the total amount of chromium that had been introduced into the environment by Leigh, Bell, and Sequa, collectively and individually. The second expert, Mooney, calculated the amount of chromium that would have been introduced into the environment by each operator on the basis of electrical usage records.

In addition to rejecting apportionment because of competing theories, the district court also rejected volume as a basis for apportionment, because there was no method of dividing the liability among the defendants which would rise to any level of fairness above mere speculation. It stated that each of the proposed apportionment methods involved significant assumption factors, because records had been lost, and because the theories differed significantly.

The existence of competing theories of apportionment is insufficient reason to reject all of those theories. It is true, as the district court noted, that the records of chrome-plating activity were incomplete. However, under the facts and circumstances of case, and in the light of the other evidence that is available, that factor may be taken into account in apportioning Sequa's share of the liability. Finally, the fact that Sequa's experts relied on certain assumptions in forming their opinions is not fatal to Sequa's ability to prove that there is a reasonable basis for apportionment. Expert opinions frequently include assumptions. If those assumptions are well-founded and reasonable, and not inconsistent with the facts as established by other competent evidence, they may be sufficiently reliable to support a conclusion that a reasonable basis for apportionment exists.

In sum, we conclude that the district court erred in imposing joint and several liability, because Sequa met its burden of proving that there is a reasonable basis for apportioning liability among the defendants on a volumetric basis. We therefore remand the case to the district court for apportionment.

How compatible is the *Monsanto* case with the quoted language from *Bell Petroleum Services*? If Congress were to amend CERCLA, should it provide specific statutory guidance on the question of divisiblity of harm? What would you recommend the Congressional policy to be?

3.   *Joint and Several Liability as a Strategic Device.* Why would EPA use joint and several liability in its dealings with PRPs? What would be some of the advantages of this liability theory? First, consider the leverage that the theory gives EPA-settle with us or suffer the consequences of joint and several liability. How far could EPA really push this advantage in actual practice? Second, EPA may use this device to shift the costs of cleanup to one or a small group of PRPs and spare itself the effort of locating other hard-to-find PRPs who might be bankrupt or have ceased to exist. Third, EPA could streamline and simplify its cost recovery or injunctive order litigation by focusing upon a small number of PRPs who have been principally involved with the contaminated site.

4.   *Timing Issues.* When does the assignment of joint and several liability occur in a CERCLA case? Usually this happens in the following two ways: a) EPA brings a cleanup cost recovery action under §§ 106 or 107(a) against PRPs to obtain reimbursement or b) a PRP who has financed site cleanup brings a cost recovery action under § 107(a)(4)(B) against other PRPs. Even at this stage, apportionment of liability can occur if the harm is found to be "divisible" under the *Monsanto* and *Alcan* case analysis. However, even if certain PRPs are held to be jointly and severally liable under CERCLA, these PRPs may attempt to limit the amount of damages they must pay by obtaining contribution from other PRPs. This subject will be discussed below in the section on "allocation of costs" but it is notable, at this point, that Congress enacted § 113(f) in 1986 to provide for an explicit statutory right of contribution. This provision reads that "[I]n resolving contribution claims, the court may allocate response costs among liable parties using such *equitable factors* as the court determines are appropriate."(emphasis supplied). Some courts incorporate this allocation into the initial liability proceeding while others insist that the contribution action must follow.

5.   *The Ultimate Wisdom of Joint Liability.* This collective liability feature has engendered a great deal of opposition both from PRPs and from the companies that insure them. In arguing for the repeal of joint and several liability, the insurance companies have argued eliminating this form of liability would leave more money available for site cleanup work and less would be spent on litigation and administrative costs. Do you agree with this premise? Could joint and several liability actually have the unintended consequence of leading to *less careful* conduct by parties handling hazardous materials since the ultimate response liability will be spread over all of the PRPs and not concentrated on one negligent party? Would carelessness by one PRP be perversely encouraged since any losses would be shared by all? See Richard Epstein, Two Fallacies in the Law of Joint Torts, 73 Geo. L.J. 1377 (1985).

6.   *Softening the Blow of Joint and Several Liability.* Congress has amended CERCLA several times since its original enactment in 1980. The most recent legislative changes address two industry-specific examples and by their specificity, they represent Congress's inability to enact comprehensive CERCLA reform. See "Asset Conservation, Lender Liability, and Deposit Insurance Protection Act of 1996," 110 Stat. 3009, P.L. 104–208 (1996) and "Recycling Equity Act," 113 Stat. 1501, P.L. 106–113 (1999). In spite of this incremental approach, CERCLA has not been significantly amended since 1986. Those amendments did not overturn the evolving joint and several liability "divisibility" rule but it did mitigate some undesirable effects in § 122(g) by encouraging settlements of de minimus hazardous waste contributors and in § 113(f)(1) by recognizing an action for contribution based on courts allocating "response costs among liable parties using such equitable factors as the court determines are appropriate." These elements will be considered below.

D.   IDENTIFYING POTENTIALLY RESPONSIBLE PARTIES UNDER CERCLA

With deceptive simplicity, § 107(a) states that four categories of defendants "shall be liable for" enumerated hazardous waste site cleanup and response costs. These four groups have become known as potentially responsible parties or PRPs. Many reported case decisions have interpreted the statute to determine its application to individuals, firms and other entities that have been targeted by EPA and others as PRPs. Finding the law's meaning, especially in light of CERCLA's sparse legislative history, has often asked courts to be creative in giving common words special significance within the broad remedial purposes of the statute. At this point it is worth recalling this quotation from Through the Looking Glass by Lewis Carroll.

> "When I use a word," Humpty Dumpty said, in rather a scornful tone, "it means what I choose it to mean neither more, nor less."
>
> "The question is," said Alice, "whether you CAN make words mean so many different things."
>
> "The question is," said Humpty Dumpty, "which is to be master that's all."

Lewis Carroll, Through the Looking Glass & What Alice Found There 79 (1963). With regard to CERCLA, the courts have been allocated the power of determining statutory meaning within diverse contexts thereby making them "master" of the words. However, we must begin with the language of the statute. A PRP is:

a) the owner and operator of a vessel or a facility;

b) any person who at the time of disposal of any hazardous substance owned or operated any facility at which hazardous substances were disposed of;

c) any person who by contract, agreement, or otherwise arranged for disposal or treatment, or who arranged with a transporter for transport for disposal or treatment, of hazardous substances owned or possessed by such person, by any other party or entity, at any facility or incinerator vessel owned or operated by another party or entity and containing such hazardous substances, and

d) any person who accepts or accepted any hazardous substances for transport to disposal or treatment facilities, incineration vessels or sites selected y such person, from which there is a release, or a threatened release which causes the incurrence of response costs, of a hazardous substance.

These four categories of PRPs may be generally labeled as: a) current owners or operators, b) prior owners or operators, c) arrangers or generators of hazardous substances, and d) transporters of hazardous substances. What policy is reflected by the identification of these four groups of PRPs?

1.   CURRENT OWNER OR OPERATOR OF A FACILITY

The first category of PRP is that of the "owner and operator" of a facility or vessel. Notice what is missing from this language-specificity and clear meaning. Absent is the word "current" although courts have uniformly interpreted this phrase from § 107(a)(1) as applying to the *current* owner at the time that the CERCLA litigation was initiated. See e.g., United States v. Fleet Factors Corp., 901 F.2d 1550 (11th Cir.1990). As we know, CERCLA is not a model of statutory clarity. As a further example of this point, the language of § 107(a)(1) creates confusion over whether liability attaches to a person who is: 1) both an owner *and* an operator or 2) an owner *or* an operator. Think of how this threshold definition could make a difference in liability and how it suggests broader or narrow liability for those merely having "ownership" of a facility. Most courts have viewed § 107(a)(1) as applying as in the second example and consequently, both current owners *and* current operators have been captured within its net. See e.g., Redwing Carriers, Inc. v. Saraland Apartments, 94 F.3d 1489 (11th Cir.1996). What else is missing from the statute? No causal connection of the PRP to the release or threat from a hazardous substance is required-merely the status of being a current owner or operator of the facility. Why would CERCLA create liability for parties who, potentially, had no connection to disposal of hazardous materials? Can you think of a rationale?

Who, then, could be a current "owner" of a facility? As we know from our Property law courses, the concept of ownership is sometimes difficult to define. There are many ownership interests in real property. Surely, the CERCLA statute assists by defining its meaning for purposes of assigning cleanup liability. Section 101(20)(A) states that the term "owner or operator" means ... any person "owning or operating such facility." Does this help, at all? Once again, CERCLA's meaning has been provided through an extensive series of court adjudications in a modern form of statutory common law. Imagine what "ownership" of a facility could mean. The easiest case exists where the owner holds fee simple title to the site. What if the fee simple owner leases the site to a lessee who operates it as a business? Could the lessee be considered an "owner" under CERCLA? Lessees have been found liable as owners if they exercise substantial control over the site or if they are considered the *de facto* owner by others. See Servco Pacific Inc. v. Dods, 106 F.Supp.2d 1034 (D.Haw.2000) (lessee had sufficient control to be considered owner or operator) and Commander Oil Corp. v. Barlo Equipment Corp., 215 F.3d 321 (2d Cir.2000) (de facto ownership test announced). What if a party merely holds an easement over land or what about a future interest such as a remainder under a will? See Comment, Extending Liability Under CERCLA: Easement Holders and the Scope of Controls, 87 Nw. U. L. Rev. 992 (1993). What about a land installment contract purchaser? See United States v. Northeastern Pharmaceutical and Chemical Co., 579 F.Supp. 823 (W.D.Mo.1984) (yes, even after the contract is signed but before title passes).

Section 107(a)(1) also speaks of facility "operators" as being PRPs. What or who is an "operator?" As we know, CERCLA does not define this term in a useful way. Struggling with the indeterminacy of this term, in United States v. Bestfoods, 524 U.S. 51 (1998), the U.S. Supreme Court stated that

> "under CERCLA, an operator is simply someone who directs the workings of, manages, or conducts the affairs of a facility. To sharpen the definition for purposes of CERCLA's concern with environmental contamination, an operator must manage, direct, or conduct operations specifically related to pollution, that is, operations having to do with the leakage or disposal of hazardous waste, or decisions about compliance with environmental regulations."

Id. at 66. This explication of the term appears to focus upon the management, direction or conduct of operations; in something more than a purely mechanical fashion. Consider all of the possible arrangements where a party is not the owner of the site but can be said to be the "operator" of it. A host of cases have dealt with the question of determining who is an "operator" and they have split into two lines of decision: 1) the actual control theory and 2) the legal authority to control doctrine.

Under the first series of decisions, the operator must have the authority to make disposal decisions and must have actually exercised that power in a direct or indirect fashion. An example of this is found in Marriott Corp. v. Simkins Industries, Inc., 929 F.Supp. 396 (S.D.Fla.1996), where the president and controlling shareholder of a firm was held liable as a § 107(a)(1) "operator" because he exercised actual authority over the day-to-day company operations including the disposal of waste materials. Courts following this test require some active involvement in the disposal activity and, for instance, an actor who designs or constructs a facility will not be an "operator." See Edward Hines Lumber Co. v. Vulcan Materials

Co., 861 F.2d 155 (7th Cir.1988). The second thread of cases finds "opera-tor" status when an actor merely has the legal authority to control and make site-specific disposal decisions regardless of whether that authority has been used. See e.g., Nurad, Inc. v. William E. Hooper & Sons Co., 966 F.2d 837 (4th Cir.1992). The cases in this line usually punish a party who had the authority to abate or avoid a disposal problem but failed to act.

2.   PRIOR OWNER OR OPERATOR AT THE TIME OF DISPOSAL

The liability exposure under § 107(a)(2) of CERCLA reaches back from the present to "any person who *at the time of disposal* of any hazardous substance owned or operated any facility at which such hazardous sub-stances were disposed of." This awkward sentence assigns liability to a party who was a prior owner or operator "at the time of disposal" of hazardous substances. Initially, the policy premise for this PRP category appears straightforward-cleanup response costs allocated if you disposed of wastes during your prior ownership or operation of a site. This is nothing more than an application of the "polluter pays" principle. However, the scope of § 107(a)(2) turns upon the statutory meaning of the term "dispos-al," which, in turn, takes its definition by reference to RCRA § 1004(3). That section states that "disposal" means,

> "the discharge, deposit, injection, dumping, spilling, leaking, or placing of any solid waste or hazardous waste into or on any land or water so that such solid waste or hazardous waste or any constituent thereof may enter the environment...."

What could Congress have intended with this definition? Does it require affirmative or active conduct of the owner or operator or could it apply in more passive situations where the party did nothing except own or operate the facility? What arguments could be made to apply this definition to the passive fact patterns? See the discussion in the *CDMG Realty Company* case below.

3.   ARRANGER FOR DISPOSAL OR TREATMENT OF HAZARDOUS SUBSTANCES

The third liability section—§ 107(a)(3)—confers liability to the party who "arranged" for the disposal or treatment of hazardous substances which they owned or possessed. Who would likely be encompassed by such a definition? Logically, this would involve the generators of the waste or perhaps, an entity brought in to dispose of a generator's hazardous wastes. This section has been broadly interpreted to include those parties such as waste brokers who have possessed the wastes and arranged for its disposal elsewhere. See United States v. Parsons, 723 F.Supp. 757 (N.D.Ga.1989). Generally, there must be some connection with the disposal decision for arranger liability to exist; mere possession, by itself, is usually not enough. See South Florida Water Management Dist. v. Montalvo, 84 F.3d 402 (11th Cir.1996). After CERCLA's enactment, a generator can no longer disasso-ciate itself from the consequences of the disposal of its own waste products. Generator's responsibility for hazardous waste contamination continues and serves, prospectively, as an incentive encouraging safe disposal practices.

Determining "arranger" liability has been heavily litigated due, in part, to the wide scope of potential application. Consider the possible scope of arranger liability at a large waste disposal site with numerous generators depositing their wastes over time. There could be an extremely large number of firms or others who had hazardous substances brought to such a waste site and all could be found to be "arrangers" under CERCLA. One interesting question that has arisen is whether the sale of a "product" that could later be disposed of constituted the arranging of disposal of hazardous substances. This has created what has become known as the "useful product" exemption. But what is a legitimate sale and what is a disposal agreement disguised as a sale? Courts have struggled with this question and come up with various formulations. A common test is exemplified by Carter–Jones Lumber Co. v. Dixie Distributing Co., 166 F.3d 840 (6th Cir.1999), which focuses on whether there was a sale of a "useful product" rather than waste to be disposed of. In one case, a generator sold contaminated waste oil to an automobile drag strip for use as a dust suppressor and this was characterized as "disposal" since the court found this to be an arrangement to relieve the seller of the waste oil. See New York v. General Electric Co., 592 F.Supp. 291 (N.D.N.Y.1984).

4. TRANSPORTERS OF HAZARDOUS SUBSTANCES WHO SELECT DISPOSAL SITES

CERCLA's final category of PRP is "any person who accepts ... hazardous substances for transport to disposal or treatment facilities ... selected by such person ... from which there is a release, or a threatened release which causes the incurrence of response costs...." § 107(a)(4). Must the transporter PRP be the sole site selector? The congressional design of transporter liability appears also to reach situations when the defendant actually participated, usually in a substantial way, in the choice of the disposal site. As the Third Circuit noted in Tippins, Inc. v. USX Corp., 37 F.3d 87 (3d Cir.1994),

> § 107(a)(4) applies if the transporter's advice was a *substantial contributing factor* in the decisions to dispose of the hazardous waste at a particular facility. As we interpret that section, a transporter selects the disposal facility when it *actively and substantially participates in the decision-making process* which ultimately identifies a facility for disposal.(emphasis supplied)

This position suggests that liability does not attach until the transporter's level of involvement in the disposal site selection reaches the point of "substantial participation." Also, it must be established that the PRP transporter actually moved hazardous substances, and not less serious, materials, to the place of disposal. See Prisco v. A & D Carting Corp., 168 F.3d 593 (2d Cir.1999). Some cases have also shielded transporters from CERCLA liability when the release occurred during shipment from circumstances beyond the control of the transporter. See e.g., United States v.

M/V Santa Clara I, 887 F.Supp. 825 (D.S.C.1995). If the transporter does "select" the disposal site and there are response costs incurred in responding to a release or threat, then the general CERCLA strict liability applies.

CLASS DISCUSSION PROBLEM

James Belton has come to you for advice regarding potential CERCLA liability for the cleanup of land that his company owns in Williamstown. Several weeks ago, an EPA and a state environmental agency site inspection revealed the presence of surface and ground water contamination on land that Belton owned and on adjacent properties. Through the course of your interview with Mr. Belton you have learned the following information.

In 1998, James Belton and his business partner Anita Frohmeyer, purchased the assets of Williamstown Motors, a Toyota dealership, from the Elba Corporation ("Elba"). Elba, whose sole shareholder was Barney Harris, had owned Williamstown Motors for 13 years. The assets acquired by Belton and Frohmeyer included the Toyota franchise, the dealership building, a service garage, a five acre, asphalt-paved vehicle parking lot and six acres of fenced land situated behind the two structures. There were a total of 15 acres of land included in the transaction. Belton was familiar with the automobile sales business having bought and sold a number of dealerships over the last twenty years. When Belton and Frohmeyer purchased Williamstown Motors, they received financing from Everbright National Bank ("ENB") which, under the terms of a complex financing agreement, gave the bank a security interest (similar to a mortgage) in all of the real and personal property owned by the dealership. As a condition of financing the purchase, ENB required that Belton and Frohmeyer provide it with a "due diligence" report analyzing the environmental condition of the Williamstown Motors site. The report was prepared by a local Williamstown real estate agent who concluded that the site was apparently well-managed with no environmental problems. With this information, ENB provided the financing and Elba acquired Williamstown Motors. Elba has been operating the dealership ever since.

The ownership and use history Williamstown Motors tract was as follows. In 1985, the 15 acre parcel was purchased by Barney Harris (for Elba) from the City of Williamstown (the "City") which had acquired title to the land in 1983 by way of a tax foreclosure proceeding. The prior owner, Sidney Vareen, had owned the property since 1970 but had failed to pay the real estate taxes owing on the parcel and the City took over title when the property was sold at auction. Vareen, a wealthy, California investor, had originally acquired the parcel as a real estate investment but he had never visited Williamstown to see his purchase. By 1975, his local site manager, Bella Lugano, began to lease the land to various short-term lessees who, among other things, parked farm equipment, sold Christmas trees, and buried construction debris and other wastes. Lugano made these leases in order to generate a small amount of rental income to offset ongoing property holding expenses. She also contracted with Aphis McQuire, a waste disposal contractor who worked for construction companies and other businesses, to have the parcel used for McQuire's client's disposal needs. Jerry Parker, a truck driver, was often employed by McQuire to drive his rig from various pickup points to the Williamstown parcel. Jerry, who was an hourly employee generally followed McQuire's directions concerning waste pickup and disposal at the Williamstown Motors site. Prior to 1970, the land had been agricultural land owned by a series of corn and wheat farmers.

1. Considering the facts stated above, what is the potential PRP liability of: a) Belton and Frohmeyer, b) Everbright National Bank, c) Barney Harris, d) Elba Corporation, e) Sidney Vareen, f) Bella Lugano's lessees, g) the City of Williamstown, h) Aphis McQuire, and i) Jerry Parker? What theory would subject any of these actors to CERCLA liability?

2. What if companies sending their wastes to the Williamstown Motors site where told that the site was a properly licensed and operating hazardous waste disposal facility?

3. Is there any provision of CERCLA that prohibits Belton and Frohmeyer from selling the Williamstown Motors site to another party? Is there any advantage to being a *prior owner* versus the *current owner* of a "facility" subject to CERCLA? Compare § 107 (a)(1) with § 107 (a)(2).

4. Are any of the PRPs protected by a statute of limitations defense since many of their activities took place in the 1970s and 1980s?

Evidence collected from the site so far indicates the following: Above ground—1) waste oil leaking from a storage tank behind the garage, 2) used brake fluid leaking from another drum on to the ground behind the garage, Under the surface in a covered trench in the 6 fenced acres—3) corroded structural paint cans containing paint residues and solvents, 4) a number of cracked, PCB-filled heavy electrical transformers, 5) a number of medical waste hazard bags,

United States v. Cello–Foil Products, Inc.

United States Court of Appeals, Sixth Circuit, 1996.
100 F.3d 1227.

■ JONES, CIRCUIT JUDGE.

Plaintiffs, the United States, the Michigan Attorney General and the State of Michigan, appeal the district court's grant of summary judgment to Defendants Cello–Foil Products, Inc., Clark Equipment Company, General Foods Corporation, and Hoover Universal, Inc., in this action for environmental response costs brought pursuant to the Comprehensive Environmental Response, Compensation, and Liability Act (CERCLA). We conclude the district court erred in its application of the arranger liability portion of CERCLA and genuine issues of material fact exist that preclude summary judgment. Therefore, we reverse and remand this case for further proceedings.

I.

This case involves a major hazardous waste cleanup involving the Verona Well Field, which is the primary public water supply to over 35,000 residents of Battle Creek, Michigan. In 1981, Michigan authorities determined volatile organic chemicals were contaminating the well field. With the assistance of the United States Environmental Protection Agency, the State determined that two of Thomas Solvent Company's ("Thomas Solvent") facilities, known as the Raymond Road Facility and the Annex, were two of the sources of the contamination.

Thomas Solvent, a producer and seller of solvents, operated in Battle Creek from the time of its incorporation in 1963 until 1984, the year it filed for voluntary bankruptcy. During these years, Thomas Solvent sold virgin solvents to numerous customers, including Defendants. Thomas Solvent usually delivered the solvents in fifty-five gallon drums.

Thomas Solvent used the Raymond Road Facility for the storage, transfer, and packaging of solvents and for the cleaning of tanker trucks. Through a drum-deposit arrangement, Thomas Solvent shipped the solvents in its re-usable drums and charged its customers a deposit. Most often, the Thomas Solvent delivery person retrieved the used drums when delivering new, full drums. The returned drums were usually taken to the Raymond Road Facility. The customers were credited for the amount of the drum deposit, when they returned the old drums to Thomas Solvent.

The contents of the returned drums varied. Some of the drums' contents had been emptied as much as possible, some had been refilled with water, and some contained unused solvents of up to fifteen gallons. Thomas Solvent employees inspected the drums when the drums reached either the Raymond Road Facility or the Annex. Drums in need of reconditioning were sent to a reconditioner, often without being rinsed or cleaned. Drums not in need of reconditioning were emptied of any remaining contents, often, onto the ground. The emptied drums were either immediately refilled with solvent or cleaned with a rinseate solution. Prior to 1978, the used rinseate was usually dumped onto the ground. In later years, Thomas Solvent began to recycle the rinseate at off-site locations.

In 1992, the United States and the State each filed complaints against Defendants. The Defendants are four longstanding customers of Thomas Solvent, which returned drums to Thomas Solvent during the period when Thomas Solvent employees were rinsing drums and disposing of the rinseate on the ground. The complaints, brought pursuant to CERCLA § 107, collectively sought over $5 million in past response costs for cleanup activities at the Raymond Road Facility plus a declaratory judgment for future response costs. Plaintiffs alleged that Defendants had arranged for disposal of hazardous substances when they returned the drums to Thomas Solvent. * * *

[T]he district court granted Defendants' motions for summary judgment on the issue of arranger liability. [Plaintiffs appealed]

II.

In this case we are called upon to interpret the scope of CERCLA arranger liability. The relevant provision of CERCLA states that:

Notwithstanding any other provision or rule of law, and subject only to the defenses set forth in subsection (b) of this section—

(3) any person who by contract, agreement, or otherwise arranged for disposal or treatment, or arranged with a transporter for transport for disposal or treatment, of hazardous substances owned or possessed by such person, by any other party or entity, at any facility or incineration vessel owned or operated by another party or entity and containing such hazardous substances, . . . shall be liable. . . .

42 U.S.C. § 9607(a). The Plaintiffs do not contend that the Defendants arranged for disposal by contract or agreement; rather, they assert that the Defendants "otherwise arranged for disposal" of their unused hazardous solvents through the drum-deposit arrangement. The Plaintiffs claim that the Defendants entered into an arrangement, whereby Thomas Solvent would pick up the residue-containing drums, take them to its Raymond Road Facility, dispose of the residue, and then credit the Defendants with their drum deposit. The district court found that the Defendants could not be held liable because they lacked "intent" to dispose of the residual hazardous substances.

CERCLA does not define the phrase "arrange for." We conclude that the requisite inquiry is whether the party intended to enter into a transaction that included an "arrangement for" the disposal of hazardous substances. The intent need not be proven by direct evidence, but can be inferred from the totality of the circumstances.

At first blush, discussing state of mind in a CERCLA case appears inappropriate. After all, if the tortured history of CERCLA litigation has taught us one lesson, it is that CERCLA is a strict liability statute. Notwithstanding the strict liability nature of CERCLA, it would be error for us not to recognize the indispensable role that state of mind must play in determining whether a party has "otherwise arranged for disposal . . . of hazardous substances." 42 U.S.C. § 9607(a).

We derive the intent element from the canons of statutory construction.

"Otherwise arranged" is a general term following in a series two specific terms and embraces the concepts similar to those of "contract" and "agreement." All of these terms indicate that the court must inquire into what transpired between the parties and what the parties had in mind with regard to disposition of the hazardous substance. Therefore, including an intent requirement into the "otherwise arranged" concept logically follows the structure of the arranger liability provision.

The theory that intent is relevant in this context is no stranger to us. The district court correctly noted that this circuit has read an intent or state of mind requirement into the "otherwise arranged for disposal" concept. In AM Int'l, Inc. v. International Forging Equip. Corp., 982 F.2d 989 (6th Cir.1993), this circuit was called upon to decide the applicability of arranger liability to AM International (AMI), which entered into an agreement to sell a manufacturing facility to a realty company. The facility contained several types of machinery and fixtures necessary for the manufacture of component parts for offset duplicating machines. After ceasing their manufacturing process, AMI cleaned up the facility and cleared it of industrial wastes. Nevertheless, because the facility was sold on an "as is, where is" basis, certain manufacturing features, including electroplating baths, salt pots for heat-treating, and the waste water treatment plant, were left by AMI containing the appropriate solutions, so that the lines would be prepared for an immediate start-up of the facility by a new owner.

Following a long line of cases distinguishing the sale of a useful asset from an arrangement for disposal, the court held that AMI had not arranged for disposal of the hazardous substances that it left in the building. The court stated: "Liability only attaches to parties that have taken an affirmative act to dispose of a hazardous substance . . . as opposed to convey a useful substance for a useful purpose." Id. at 999. Therefore, in the absence of a contract or agreement, a court must look to the totality of the circumstances, including any "affirmative acts to dispose," to determine whether the Defendants intended to enter into an arrangement for disposal. We believe that this principle is in line with the Seventh Circuit's "intentional action" requirement for arranger liability announced in *Amcast Indus. Corp. v. Detrex Corp.*, wherein the court concluded that the term "arranged for" "impl[ies] intentional action." 2 F.3d 746, 751 (7th Cir.1993), *cert. denied*, 510 U.S. 1044 (1994).

As mentioned above, examining state of mind or ascertaining intent at the contract, agreement, or other type of arrangement stage does not undermine the strict liability nature of CERCLA. The intent inquiry is geared only towards determining whether the party in question is a potentially liable party. Once a party is determined to have the requisite intent to be an arranger, then strict liability takes effect. If an arrangement has been made, that party is liable for damages caused by the disposal regardless of the party's intent that the damages not occur. Moreover, a party can be responsible for "arranging for" disposal, even when it has no control over the process leading to the release of substances. Therefore, once it has been demonstrated that a party possessed the requisite intent to be an arranger, the party cannot escape liability by claiming that it had no intent to have the waste disposed in a particular manner or at a particular site.

III.

In reviewing this summary judgment, we must determine whether the district court overlooked any genuine and material issues concerning the Defendants intent to arrange or not to arrange for the disposal of any solvents returned with the drums. The district court "[found] compelling Defendants' argument that, because they lacked intent to dispose of hazardous substances, they may not be held liable as arrangers." Employing the dictionary definition of "arrange" the district court concluded that, in order to arrange, the parties must "make preparations" or "plan." The district court also relied heavily on the Seventh Circuit's decision in *Amcast Indus. Corp. v. Detrex Corp.,* in which the court concluded that the term "arranged for" "impl[ies] intentional action." 2 F.3d at 751. The district court ultimately concluded that "[w]hatever else 'otherwise arranged for disposal means' . . . it does not apply to situations where there was no intent to dispose of a hazardous substance."

Although the district court correctly incorporated a state of mind requirement into the otherwise arranged for disposal concept, the court erred by applying the standard to the facts of this case. The following language from the district court's opinion illustrates court's error:

> [T]he court concludes, therefore, that Defendants are not liable under section 107(a)(3) absent a showing that they intended to dispose of the residual amounts of the hazardous substances remaining in their returned drums. It is immediately clear that the Government's claim against Defendants fails to establish liability. The *purpose* of Defendants' returning of the drums was to recover the deposits that Defendants had paid; *the Government has absolutely no proof that Defendants' purpose was to dispose of residual amounts of hazardous substances remaining in those drums.* That Defendants incidentally got rid of these residues does not mean that it was Defendants' purposeful intent to dispose of the residues; rather, this was merely incidental to the drum return.

J.A. at 128 (Memorandum Opinion at 9) (second emphasis added). The primary purpose of the drum return arrangement was to regain the deposit; however, we conclude the district court erred when it concluded the Government offered *absolutely no proof* that Defendants' further purpose was to dispose of the residual wastes returned with the drums.

The district court employed an overly restrictive view on what is necessary to prove intent, state of mind, or purpose, by assuming that intent could not be inferred from the indirect action of the parties. In doing so, the district court overlooked genuine issues of material fact. * * *

In this case, summary judgment would have been appropriate only if no genuine issues regarding intent existed. Our review of the record, however, reveals genuine issues of material fact regarding whether the parties returned solvents to Thomas Solvent with the additional purpose of disposal of unused solvents. The volumes of deposition testimony create scenarios, some conflicting, from which a trier of fact could conclude that Defendants, without a contract or agreement, otherwise arranged for disposal of their hazardous substances by Thomas Solvent. Such a finding would preclude the district court's conclusion that any disposal was incidental to the primary drum return transaction. For example, deposition testimony elicited from employees of Thomas Solvent and Defendants creates an issue as

to whether the Defendants ever took "affirmative acts to dispose" of unused solvent, as required by *AM lnt'l,* 982 F.2d at 999. By leaving amounts of solvents in drums ranging from one-half to ten gallons, which Defendants knew Thomas Solvent would carry away, a trier of fact could infer that Defendants were taking affirmative acts to dispose. By the same token, the finder of fact could conclude that Defendants did not leave solvents in the drums or that their acts in leaving residual amounts of solvents in the drums does not support an inference of purposeful or intentional disposal, or find that the drums were filled with waste water and other debris. A finder of fact must resolve this issue, and thus, the district court acted too hastily in finding no showing of intent. The district court overlooked genuine issues of material fact that make the resolution of this issue inappropriate at the summary judgment stage.[6] * * *

United States v. CDMG Realty Co.

United States Court of Appeals, Third Circuit, 1996.
96 F.3d 706.

■ BECKER, CIRCUIT JUDGE.

This appeal requires us to determine the meaning of the word "disposal" in the Comprehensive Environmental Response, Compensation, and Liability Act (CERCLA). Plaintiff HMAT Associates, the current owner of contaminated property, was sued by the United States under CERCLA for the costs of cleaning up the site. HMAT sought contribution from Defendant Dowel Associates, the company that sold the land to HMAT, on the ground that Dowel was a prior owner "at the time of disposal," 42 U.S.C. § 9607(a)(2). HMAT concedes that no one dumped waste at the property during Dowel's ownership, but offers two reasons why "disposal" took place during Dowel's tenure. HMAT first advances a "passive" disposal theory: that "disposal" occurred because contamination dumped in the land prior to Dowel's purchase of the property spread during Dowel's ownership. HMAT also offers an "active" disposal theory: that a soil investigation conducted by Dowel to determine whether the land could support construction caused the dispersal of contaminants, and that this constitutes "disposal."

---

6. One of the difficult issues this case presents is how much must be left in a returned drum before CERCLA liability attaches. As the evidence in this case indicates, typical commercially employed methods for emptying solvent barrels leaves some residue, approximately a tea cup's worth, in the barrel If every party who left this amount of residue in a drum were liable, every drum return agreement or arrangement would be considered an arrangement for disposal. In light of the demonstrated physical problems in completely emptying these drums, we are not convinced that CERCLA is intended to reach all such transactions. Rather, whether a drum return arrangement is an arrangement for disposal should be determined on a case-by-case basis. Furthermore, there appear to be benefits of these agreements, such as the reuse and recycling of drums, which we do not wish our interpretation of the statute to discourage. Thus, at this point it is important to reiterate that whether an arrangement has been made is an issue to he determined viewing the totality of the circumstances.

On cross-motions for summary judgment, the district court ruled in favor of Dowel. The court rejected HMAT's argument that the spread of contamination unaided by human conduct can confer CERCLA liability and held that any disturbance of contaminants caused by Dowel's soil testing was too insignificant to amount to "disposal." HMAT appeals the court's grant of Dowel's summary judgment motion and the denial of its own motion.

We hold that the passive migration of contamination dumped in the land prior to Dowel's ownership does not constitute disposal. Finding it unnecessary to reach the question whether the movement of contaminants unaided by human conduct can ever constitute "disposal," we conclude that the language of CERCLA's "disposal" definition cannot encompass the spreading of waste at issue here. This conclusion is based on an examination of CERCLA's text, is supported by the structure of the statute, and is consistent with CERCLA's purposes.

Regarding Dowel's soil testing, we hold that there is no threshold level of disturbance required to constitute "disposal," and that HMAT has identified evidence that would justify a factfinder's conclusion that contaminants were spread in the testing. We also hold, however, that because CERCLA clearly contemplates that prospective purchasers be allowed to conduct soil investigations to determine whether property is contaminated, a plaintiff must show not only that a soil investigation has caused the spread of contaminants, but also that the investigation was conducted negligently.

Thus, although we agree with the district court that HMAT's passive theory is not viable, HMAT may be able to proceed on its active theory. Accordingly, we will vacate the district court's grant of summary judgment to Dowel and remand for further proceedings consistent with this opinion.

I. Facts and Procedural History

The property at issue in this case, a ten-acre parcel of land in Morris County, New Jersey, was once part of the Sharkey's Farm Landfill (Sharkey's Landfill). Sharkey's Landfill operated as a municipal landfill from 1945 until 1972. During its operation, the landfill received waste from several counties in northern New Jersey. In addition to accepting municipal solid waste, the landfill received approximately 750,000 pounds of hazardous chemical waste from Ciba–Geigy Company, a large pharmaceutical concern. Additional chemical waste from other sources may also have been deposited there. For example, Koppers Chemical Company allegedly disposed of about 3,000,000 gallons of wastewater of unknown composition in the landfill. Between 1966 and 1972, county and state agencies received steady complaints about odors, smoke from fires, lack of proper cover, and the presence of dead animals in the landfill. The landfill was closed to further disposal in 1972.

The Environmental Protection Agency (EPA) and the New Jersey Department of Environmental Protection and Energy (NJDEPE) began investigating Sharkey's Landfill in the mid to late 1970s. In 1982, the EPA placed Sharkey's Landfill on the National Priorities List of Hazardous Waste Sites.

In December 1981, Dowel purchased the property. The land was vacant at the time of purchase, and it remained vacant during Dowel's ownership. Neither Dowel nor any other person deposited waste at the site during Dowel's term of ownership. Dowel's only activity on the land was a soil investigation, conducted in September 1981 (three months prior to finalizing its purchase) to determine the land's ability to support construction. The soil investigation, which was performed by Thor Engineering, involved nine drill borings, each twelve to eighteen feet into the ground. Thor's logs show that its equipment bored through various waste materials and groundwater and that several of the boreholes "caved" during the testing.

In November 1983, the NJDEPE notified Dowel that it was investigating the property and that Dowel should cease any planned activities at the site. In 1984, the EPA notified Dowel that Dowel was potentially liable for the cleanup costs of the site and invited it to undertake voluntary cleanup.

In 1987, Dowel sold the property to HMAT. In the contract of sale, Dowel fully disclosed that the property was part of the Sharkey Landfill, that the landfill was under investigation by state and federal environmental authorities, and that the property was part of a possible Superfund site.

In October 1989, EPA and NJDEPE commenced actions against parties potentially liable for the costs of cleaning up the Sharkey Landfill and seeking a declaration of future liability. HMAT, as the current owner of the property, was named as a defendant under CERCLA § 107(a)(1). Dowel was not sued. However, HMAT filed a third-party suit against Dowel, seeking contribution from Dowel as a former owner of the property "at the time of disposal" pursuant to CERCLA §§ 107(a)(2) and 113(f). * * *

II.   Passive Spreading in a Landfill as Disposal

A.   Introduction

CERCLA is a broad and complex statute aimed at the dangers posed by hazardous waste sites. Among other things, CERCLA provides a cause of action to recover "response costs" incurred in remedying an environmental hazard, and allows those liable for response costs to seek contribution from other liable parties. A plaintiff must meet four elements to establish CERCLA liability: (1) that hazardous substances were disposed of at a "facility"; (2) that there has been a "release" or "threatened release" of hazardous substances from the facility into the environment; (3) that the release or threatened release has required or will require the expenditure of "response costs"; and (4) that the defendant falls within one of four categories of responsible parties. If these requirements are met, responsible parties are liable for response costs regardless of their intent. * * *

The parties agree that the first three requirements are met. Their dispute concerns whether Dowel is a responsible party. HMAT contends that Dowel is liable as a person who owned or operated the facility "at the time of disposal" of a hazardous substance. [42 U.S.C. § 9607(a)(2).]

CERCLA defines "disposal" by incorporating the definition used by the Resource Conservation and Recovery Act (RCRA). See 42 U.S.C. § 9601(29) ("The terms 'disposal', 'hazardous waste', and 'treatment' shall have the meaning provided in section 1004 of the Solid Waste Disposal Act."). Under RCRA,

> The term "disposal" means the discharge, deposit, injection, dumping, spilling, leaking, or placing of any solid waste or hazardous waste into or on any land or water so that such solid waste or hazardous waste or any constituent thereof may enter the environment or be emitted into the air or discharged into any waters, including ground waters.

42 U.S.C. § 6903(3). Focusing on the breadth of this definition, HMAT reads "disposal" to encompass the passive migration of contaminants. HMAT offers no evidence that any passive migration has occurred here but asks us to take judicial notice that waste tends to spread once it is put in the ground, See Office of Remedial Response, United States Environmental Protection Agency, *Superfund Exposure Assessment Manual* 8 (1988) [Hereinafter *Superfund Manual* (waste in landfills tends to migrate due to, inter alia, rain, groundwater movement, and wind) and waste therefore must have spread during the six years Dowel owned the property. Several courts have been sympathetic to this argument. * * *]

We are unpersuaded. A thorough examination of the text and structure of CERCLA convinces us that the passive migration of contaminants alleged here does not constitute disposal. Our conclusion is based on the plain meaning of the words used in the disposal definition and is supported by the structure of CERCLA's liability scheme. We also believe that our interpretation is consistent with CERCLA's purposes.

B.   The Language

1.   The Definition of "Disposal"

The definition of disposal begins with "the discharge, deposit, injection, dumping, spilling, leaking, or placing of any solid waste or hazardous waste into or on any land or water." 42 U.S.C. § 6903(3). Courts holding that passive migration can constitute disposal have focused on the words "leaking" and "spilling," terms that generally do not denote active conduct.

We think there is a strong argument, however, that in the context of this definition, "leaking" and "spilling" should be read to require affirmative human action. Both "leaking" and "spilling" also have meanings that require some active human conduct. "Leak" can be defined as "to permit to enter or escape through a leak." *Webster's Third New International Dictionary, Unabridged* 1285 (Philip Babcock Gove & the Mirriam–Webster Editorial Staff eds., 1986) [hereinafter *Webster's*]. Similarly, "spill" can mean "to cause or allow to pour, splash, or fall out." *Id.* at 2195. Meaning derives from context, hence the constructional canon *noscitur a sociis*, which states that one may infer meaning by examining the surrounding words. The words surrounding "leaking" and "spilling"—"discharge," "deposit," "injection," "dumping," and "placing"—all envision a human actor. In the context of these other words, then, Congress may have intended active meanings of "leaking" and "spilling."

But we need not address this question in the broad terms of whether disposal always requires active human conduct. Even if it does not, we conclude that the passive migration at issue in this case cannot constitute disposal. While "leaking" and "spilling" may not require affirmative human conduct, neither word denotes the gradual spreading of contamination alleged here. A common definition of "leak"—and the one most favorable to HMAT—is "to enter or escape through a hole, crevice, or other opening." *Webster's, supra* at 1285. This definition requires that a substance "leak" from some *opening*. For example, the definition would encompass the escape of waste through a hole in a drum. But HMAT has offered no evidence of leaking drums. Compare, e.g., Nurad, Inc. v. William E. Hooper & Sons Co., 966 F.2d 837, 846 (4th Cir.) (the plaintiff presented evidence showing that tanks had leaked), *cert. denied,* 506 U.S. 940 (1992). And there is no other evidence that waste escaped from any opening during Dowel's ownership.

The definition of "spilling" is also unavailing. Although "spilling" too sometimes denotes the movement of liquid in the absence of human action, such a definition does not cover the spreading of waste at issue here. Passive definitions of "spill" suggest a rapid torrent, not gradual passive migration over the course of several years. See *Webster's,* supra at 2195 (defining "spill" as, inter alia, "to flow, run, or fall out, over, or off with waste, loss, or scattering as the result" and as "to come, go, or pass with a turbulent rush[; to] pour in an unrestrained, profuse, or disorderly manner"). Consider, for example, an "oil spill."

2. A Comparison With "Release"

It is especially unjustified to stretch the meanings of "leaking" and "spilling" to encompass the passive migration that generally occurs in landfills in view of the fact that another word used in CERCLA, "release," shows that Congress knew precisely how to refer to this spreading of waste. A prior owner who "owned a waste site at the time of disposal" is only liable in the event of a "release" or "threatened release." 42 U.S.C. § 9607. CERCLA defines release in relevant part as follows:

> The term "release," means any spilling, leaking, pumping, pouring, emitting, emptying, discharging, injecting, escaping, leaching, dumping, or disposing into the environment (including the abandonment or discarding of barrels, containers, and other closed receptacles containing any hazardous substance or pollutant or contaminant). . . .

42 U.S.C. § 9601(22). The definition of "release" is thus broader than that of "disposal": "release" encompasses "disposing" and some elements of the "disposal" definition and also includes some additional terms.

Most importantly, the definition of "release" includes the term "leaching," which is not mentioned in the definition of "disposal." "Leaching" is "the process or an instance of separating the soluble components from some material by percolation." *Webster's, supra* at 1282. Leaching of contaminants from rain and groundwater movement is a principal cause of contaminant movement in landfills, and is the most predominant cause of groundwater contamination from landfills. * * * The word "leaching" is commonly used in the environmental context to describe this migration of contaminants. Congress's use of the term "leaching" in the definition of "release" demonstrates that it was aware of the concept of passive migration in landfills and that it knew how to explicitly refer to that concept.

Yet Congress made prior owners liable only if they owned land at the time of "disposal," not at the time of "release."

3. "At the Time of Disposal"

Our conclusion that the meaning of the words in the "disposal" definition cannot cover the passive migration alleged in this case is buttressed by the language of CERCLA's liability provision. If the spreading of contaminants is constant, as HMAT would have us assume, characterizing liable parties as "any person who at the time of disposal ... owned or operated any facility," 42 U.S.C. § 9607(a)(2), would be a rather complicated way of making liable all people who owned or operated a facility after the introduction of waste into the facility. Furthermore, there would be no need for the separate responsible party category of current owner or operator, § 9607(a)(1). Although CERCLA is not written with great clarity, we will not impute to Congress an intent to set up a simple liability scheme through a convoluted methodology.

C. Structure: The Innocent Owner Defense

Our conclusion that the language of CERCLA's definition of "disposal" does not include the passive migration alleged here is also supported by a significant aspect of CERCLA's liability scheme, the innocent owner defense. Since the 1986 Superfund Amendments and Reauthorization Act (SARA), CERCLA has exempted certain "innocent owners" from liability.

CERCLA provides a defense to liability if the defendant can prove that the release or threatened release was caused solely by an act or omission of a third party. 42 U.S.C. § 9607(b)(3). The defense is generally not available if the third party causing the release is in the chain of title with the defendant. See 42 U.S.C. § 9601(35)(A). However, the defense is available in such circumstances if the person claiming the defense is an "innocent owner." To establish the innocent owner defense the defendant must show that "the real property on which the facility is located was acquired by the defendant after the disposal or placement of the hazardous substance on, in, or at the facility" and that "[a]t the time the defendant acquired the facility the defendant did not know and had no reason to know that any hazardous substance which is the subject of the release or threatened release was disposed of on, in, or at the facility."

Because CERCLA conditions the innocent owner defense on the defendant's having purchased the property "after the disposal" of hazardous waste at the property, "disposal" cannot constitute the allegedly constant spreading of contaminants. Otherwise, the defense would almost never apply, as there would generally be no point "after disposal." We think it unlikely that Congress would create a basically useless defense.

The innocent owner defense's apparent limitation to current owners also supports the conclusion that "disposal" does not encompass the passive spreading alleged here. The provision establishing the innocent owner defense states: "Nothing in this paragraph or in section 9607(b)(3) of this title [, which provides the causation defenses including the third party defense,] shall diminish the liability of any previous owner or operator who would be otherwise liable under this chapter." 42 U.S.C. § 9601(35)(C). This language certainly suggests that the innocent owner defense is unavailable to prior owners or operators.

While the question whether the innocent owner defense is available only to present owners is not before us—and we do not decide the issue— we note that such a limitation makes sense only if passive spreading of waste in a landfill is not included in disposal. If passive migration is excluded from "disposal," past owners will generally only be liable as owners "at the time of disposal" when they have committed or allowed affirmative acts of disposal on their property. They would thus have little need for the innocent owner defense, which requires, inter alia, that a defendant did not "cause[ ] or contribute [ ] to the release or threatened release," 42 U.S.C. § 9601 (35)(D); "exercised due care with respect to the hazardous substance concerned," § 9607(b)(3)(a); and "took precautions against foreseeable acts or omissions of any such third party [causing the release] and the consequences that could foreseeably result from such acts or omissions," § 9607 (b)(3)(b). On the other hand, if prior owners were liable because waste spread during their tenure and the innocent owner defense is available only to current owners, prior owners would be in a significantly worse position than current owners: they would be liable for passive migration of waste even if they had no reason to know of the waste's presence. We do not believe that this was Congress's intent.

D.   CERCLA's Purposes

We have explained our confidence that the meaning of the words defining "disposal" does not encompass the gradual spreading of waste in a landfill and that this conclusion is supported by the structure of the innocent owner defense. We also conclude that this reading of "disposal" is consistent with CERCLA's purposes.

Congress enacted CERCLA with two principal goals in minds—to facilitate the cleanup of potentially dangerous hazardous waste sites, and to force polluters to pay the costs associated with their pollution. Our holding is clearly consistent with the latter purpose. Those who owned previously contaminated property where waste spread without their aid cannot reasonably be characterized as "polluters"; excluding them from liability will not let those who cause the pollution off the hook. And, many of these owners will pay for the pollution: if they disclose the fact that the land contains waste, their selling price will reflect the cost of CERCLA liability. If they have knowledge of contamination and do not disclose it to a transferee, they are liable for response costs even after the transfer. 42 U.S.C. § 9601(35)(C). The only prior owners who will not pay any cleanup costs are those who bought and sold the land with no knowledge that the land is contaminated.

And our holding will not undermine the goal of facilitating the cleanup of potentially dangerous hazardous waste sites. Even if owners of previously contaminated land can evade liability by transferring the land, ample incentives remain to promote cleanup. Present owners and operators remain strictly liable for the costs of cleanup, as do some prior owners, people who arranged for disposal, and transporters of hazardous substances. Moreover, a number of provisions ensure that contamination will be discovered and the fact of contamination disclosed if the land is transferred. CERCLA imposes criminal liability (including prison sentences) for failure to report a "release" of hazardous substances above a certain threshold. See 42 U.S.C. § 9603. As mentioned, if an owner transfers land that it knows to be contaminated without disclosing the contamination, it remains liable even after the transfer. In addition, the innocent owner defense encourages potential buyers to investigate the possibility of contamination before a purchase. See 42 U.S.C. § 9601(35)(B) (in order to claim the innocent owner defense, a defendant must have undertaken all appropriate inquiry).

Thus, for the reasons we have stated, we agree with the district court that HMAT cannot proceed on its "passive" theory of disposal: the movement of contaminants alleged here does not constitute "disposal." However, because we conclude that HMAT may proceed on its "active" theory of disposal, the issue to which we now turn, we will vacate the court's order granting summary judgment to Dowel on HMAT's CERCLA claim.

III. Soil Investigation as Disposal

Having concluded that passive migration does not constitute disposal, we now consider HMAT's other asserted basis of liability. HMAT argues that Dowel's soil investigation, which was meant to determine the land's ability to support construction, caused the mixing, shifting, and spreading of contaminants and that this constitutes disposal. Although the district court suggested that HMAT's evidence of spreading was "speculative," it did not resolve whether the evidence was sufficient to allow a factfinder to conclude that the drilling caused any subsurface mixing. Instead, the court concluded that even accepting HMAT's version of events, Dowel's drilling "fell short of that conduct accepted as being enough of a disturbance to constitute disposal." According to the district court, only "significant disturbance of already contaminated soil constitutes disposal."

[In this part of the opinion, the court ruled that a genuine issue of material fact remained as to whether Dowel's drilling caused the dispersal of contaminants which could be considered a "disposal" under CERCLA. It remanded this issue to the district court for a more complete consideration.]

IV. Conclusion

For the foregoing reasons, the passive spreading of contamination in a landfill does not constitute "disposal" under CERCLA. Soil testing that disperses contaminants, however, may constitute "disposal" and HMAT has identified evidence that would justify a factfinder's conclusion that contaminants were dispersed in Dowel's testing. Nevertheless, because CERCLA contemplates that some soil investigation be allowed, HMAT must show not only that the soil investigation caused the spread of contaminants but also that the investigation was conducted negligently. The judgment of the district court will therefore be vacated and the case remanded for further proceedings consistent with this opinion.

NOTES AND QUESTIONS

1.   In *United States v. CDMG Realty Co.*, Dowel, the prior landowner, sold the Sharkey's Landfill 10 acre parcel to HMAT in 1987 with disclosure that it was part of a landfill currently under investigation by state and federal environmental authorities and that the property was part of a possible Superfund site. Why would HMAT have taken the risks of becoming a PRP under CERCLA? How might HMAT have limited its exposure to financial loss in this transaction?

2.   The *CDMG Realty* case represents one position on the "passive migration" issue. More specifically, this issue relates to the crucial PRP definition contained in § 107(a)(2), "any person who at the time of disposal of any hazardous substance owned or operated any facility at which such hazardous substances were disposed of...." As a threshold matter these cases focus on the question of who is a PRP—a fundamental matter. Following the *CDMG Realty* view are United States v. 150 Acres of Land, 204 F.3d 698 (6th Cir.2000) and ABB Indus. Sys., Inc. v. Prime Technology, Inc., 120 F.3d 351 (2d Cir.1997). On the other hand, at least two circuits have held that the statutory definition of "disposal" includes passive migration of hazardous substances. See Carson Harbor Village, Ltd. v. Unocal Corp., 227 F.3d 1196 (9th Cir.2000) and Nurad, Inc. v. William E. Hooper & Sons Co., 966 F.2d 837 (4th Cir.1992). This view of the matter considers three principle arguments: 1) three of the terms included in the defendants of "disposal" have well recognized passive meanings; 2) the courts should reject a "strained reading" that would limit "disposal" to active human conduct to achieve CERCLA's broad remedial purpose and 3) the passive meaning is consistent with the structure and purpose of CERCLA's liability provisions. Judge Fletcher writing in the *Carson Harbor Village* case explained the essential rationale this way,

> Thus, while the statute was surely designed, as the district court noted, to impose the costs of cleanup on "responsible parties," the imperative

was to create a mechanism for prompt cleanup and Congress was well aware that many directly responsible parties were insolvent or no longer in existence. For that reason, traditional causation requirements were abandoned in favor of a strict liability regime. The categories of PRP's incorporated in the liability provisions are correspondingly broad, sweeping in parties who may have done nothing affirmatively to contribute to contamination at a site and forcing them to disprove causation as an affirmative defense. See 42 U.S.C. § 9607(b)(3). Including as PRP's owners who held land while waste passively migrated through the property is entirely consistent with this liability regime.

227 F.3d at 1207. Is this position unfair to property owners who have merely owned land yet done nothing to cause a release of hazardous substances? If so, what about current owners and operators who are considered PRPs regardless of disposal practices? So the "passive migration" form of disposal just a method for identifying solvent PRPs?

E.   Finding Liability Within the PRP Label

CERCLA has important remedial consequences. Site investigations, remedial design, remedial construction and operation all are significant steps towards the cleanup of contaminated facilities and the protection of public health and the environment. They are also costly ventures often imposing multi-million dollar financial obligations on PRPs. As the previous section explains, CERCLA § 107(a) identifies four categories of Potentially Responsible Parties. These categories state that enumerated "persons" and "owners and operator[s]" shall be liable for cleanup response costs. In § 101(21) the statute defines the term "person" in a broad, inclusive way, encompassing,

> An individual, firm, corporation, association, partnership, consortium, joint venture, commercial entity, United State Government, State, municipality, commission, political subdivision of a State, or any interstate body.

Clearly, 1) people, 2) business and other organizations and 3) governments were encompassed by this definition. But who actually can be liable under CERCLA as an owner or operator of a facility; an arranger for the disposal of hazardous substances; or a transporter of such materials? Answering these questions combines an understanding of CERCLA with the application of various doctrines of state law in a number of discrete contexts.

1.   BUSINESS ENTITIES

Many of the PRPs are business organizations. This is not surprising since much of the conduct in question is undertaken for business purposes. But business entities come in many different sizes and in a number of different legal forms: corporations, partnerships, joint ventures, sole proprietorships, etc. These business units themselves may be held liable under CERCLA for cleanup costs and damages subject, of course, to the continued existence of the corporate entity and the availability of its assets to pay court-imposed judgments. Corporations which have potentially infinite periods of existence, do come and go-being acquired by other firms and by just ceasing to exist and terminating through dissolution. Considering the limited assets and the potentially short life span of many business organizations, those wishing to recover site cleanup costs(i.e. EPA or other PRPs) have looked to extend CERCLA liability to other PRPs related in some way to the business entity. This effort has manifested itself in efforts to find corporate officials, employees and shareholders as PRPs. It has also been reflected in attempts to find CERCLA liability in parent corporations and successor corporations.

i. Corporate Officers, Employees and Shareholders

Business entities such as corporations are artificial legal constructs established to serve economic purposes under our system of law. Within this structure, a range of individuals contribute to the work of the business serving as employees, managers, corporate officials and shareholders. Sometimes these functions overlap in one person. There is no express, legal immunity for corporate officers, employees and shareholders under CERCLA. Review the definition of the term "person" and note that it includes both individuals as well as business entities. Consequently, people can be liable under CERCLA if they otherwise fit the PRP categories—they owned or operated a facility or arranged for the disposal of hazardous substances. Serious legal questions have arisen concerning the actual scope of CERCLA liability in the employment context and over the interplay of state corporate law with CERCLA.

What does CERCLA mean for employees who are involved, in one way or another, with the disposal of hazardous substances? Should they bear CERCLA liability? Would EPA or a PRP pursue an employee? Generally, following a tort law analogy, liability will follow if an employee can be shown to have personally *operated* the facility or *arranged for* the disposal of hazardous substances. In litigation, the focus has been placed on giving these § 107(a) operative terms meaning in specific cases. Courts have taken two approaches in determining when an employee or a corporate officer was "operating" a facility based on the concept of control. The case of United States v. Gurley, 43 F.3d 1188 (8th Cir.1994), addresses this issue in the context of an employee liability fact pattern. In an opinion adopting the majority view actual control position, Circuit Judge Hansen wrote,

> Federal courts have struggled with these two concepts when addressing the question of whether an individual may be found liable as an "operator" under § 9607(a)(2). In some circuits, a plaintiff must prove that an individual defendant had actual responsibility for, involvement in, or control over the disposal of hazardous waste at a facility. [citing cases from the 2nd, 5th, and 7th Circuits] . . .
>
> On the other hand, in one circuit, a plaintiff can succeed by proving less than this; an individual defendant " 'need not have exercised actual control in order to qualify as [an] operator[s] under

§ 9607(a)(2), so long as the *authority* to control the facility was present.'" United States v. Carolina Transformer Co., 978 F.2d 832, 836–37 (4th Cir.1992) (emphasis added) (quoting Nurad, Inc. v. Hooper & Sons Co., 966 F.2d 837, 842 (4th Cir.1992), cert. denied, 506 U.S. 940 (1992)).

The *Gurley* court ultimately chose the "actual control" versus the "authority to control" test for "operator" status and concluded that "we hold that an individual may not be held liable as an 'operator' under § 9607(a)(2) unless he or she (1) had authority to determine whether hazardous wastes would be disposed of and to determine the method of disposal and (2) actually exercised that authority, either by personally performing the tasks necessary to dispose of the hazardous wastes or by directing others to perform those tasks." 43 F.3d at 1193. Using this test, the court used a case-by-case approach and found that the defendant, the son of the principal shareholder, did have responsibility for the disposal of hazardous waste. How expansive is the Gurley test for employee liability? Who is it likely to catch in its liability net?

At least six appellate circuits follow an approach similar to the *Gurley* case although some phrase it in different terms with different levels of "actual control" and some reach more forms of operational conduct. For instance, in Redwing Carriers, Inc. v. Saraland Apts., 94 F.3d 1489 (11th Cir.1996), the appeals court stated that "an individual need not have actually controlled the specific decision to dispose of hazardous sub-stances." Rather, it is enough if the individual "actually participated in the operations of the facility ... [or] actually exercised control over, or was otherwise intimately involved in the operations of the corporation immedi-ately responsible for the operation of the facility." Would you work for a firm disposing of hazardous wastes in such a jurisdiction? Could a lawyer advising such a firm about general business matters run afoul of the *Redwing Carriers* rule?

A more difficult problem exists when corporate shareholders and officers are targeted in a CERCLA action. Usually, the "corporation" is selected as a business entity because of its limitation on personal liability for its shareholders. Under this general corporate law theory, while the corporation's assets are at risk, the shareholders' liability exposure is limited to their shares or equity in the corporation. Creditors of failed corporations with no or limited assets usually do not receive payment of the debts owed them. The barrier of limited shareholder liability can be breached in most circumstances only by satisfying a demanding corporate law test of "piercing the corporate veil." It has been said that "[p]iercing is an equitable remedy the court can impose in order to avoid injustice." Franklin A. Gevurtz, Corporation Law 70 (2000). The EPA or a PRP might wish to "pierce the corporate veil" in order to reach the assets of share-holders when the corporate PRP is defunct or insolvent.

The mainstream view with regard to the potential CERCLA liability of shareholders, directors and officers of a corporation does not focus on corporate law but rather on the familiar CERCLA concepts of being an "owner,""operator," or "arranger" under § 107(a). Direct, personal liability can exist under CERCLA for these persons regardless of the protections normally available under state corporate law doctrine. See Browning–Ferris Industries v. Ter Maat, 195 F.3d 953 (7th Cir.1999) and Sidney S. Arst Co. v. Pipefitters Welfare Education Fund, 25 F.3d 417, 420 (7th Cir.1994). Sometimes, the hardest question is not whether direct action of a defendant constitutes "operation," but rather whether corporate conduct can be imputed to the president or other corporate officer. Judge Posner's opinion in the *Ter Maat* case highlights this issue. He wrote,

> The line between a personal act and an act that is purely an act of the corporation(or of some other employee) and not so imputed to the president or to other corporate officers is sometimes a fine one, but often it is clear on which side of the line a particular act falls. If an individual is hit by a negligently operated train, the railroad is liable in tort to him but the president of the railroad is not. Or rather, not usually; had the president been driving the train when it hit the plaintiff, or had been sitting beside the driver and ordered him to exceed the speed limit, he would be jointly liable with the railroad. If *Ter Maat* did not merely direct the general operations of [the corporation], or specific operations unrelated to pollution, but supervised the day-to-day operation of the landfill—for example, negotiating waste-dumping contracts with the owners of the wastes or directing where the wastes were to be dumped or designing or directing measures for preventing toxic substances in the wastes from leeching into the ground and thence into the groundwater—then he would be deemed the operator, jointly with his companies, of the site itself.

195 F.3d at 956. The court concluded that the shareholder/officer was integrally involved in the daily operations at the site and that he had held himself out to the state EPA as being the site operator.

ii. Parent Corporations and Their Subsidiaries

A general proposition of American corporate law is that a parent corporation—one having control through ownership of another corporation's stock—is not liable for the acts of its subsidiaries. Therefore, the parent's control of the subsidiary by way of the election of directors, establishing corporate bylaws, etc. will not, under corporate law theory, establish liability beyond the assets of the subsidiary. If the subsidiary is responsible for owning or operating a polluting facility, CERCLA does not make the parent liable just by virtue of the parent/subsidiary relationship. An exception to this "no liability" principle exists and a corporate parent may be liable under CERCLA if the parent's corporate veil is pierced under traditional common law rules. See United States v. Jon–T. Chemicals, Inc., 768 F.2d 686 (5th Cir.1985) (list of factors). If this happens, then a parent corporation may be charged with derivative CERCLA liability for its subsidiary's actions.

It is also possible for a parent corporation to have direct CERCLA liability when it operates a facility owned by its subsidiary. In the decision in United States v. Bestfoods, 524 U.S. 51 (1998), Justice Souter expressed this direct form of responsibility in the following terms,

> Under the plain language of the statute, any person who operates a polluting facility is directly liable for the costs of cleaning up the pollution. . . . This is so regardless of whether that person is the facility's owner, the owner's parent corporation or business partner, or even a saboteur who sneaks into the facility at night to discharge its poisons out of malice. If any such act of operating a corporate subsidiary's facility is done on behalf of a parent corporation, the existence of the parent-subsidiary relationship under state corporate law is simply irrelevant to the issue of direct liability.

Id. at 65. But, what does "operate" mean in this context? The critical focus is on the relationship between the parent corporation and the facility. The key is distinguishing between "a parental officer's oversight of a subsidiary from such an officer's control over the operation of the subsidiary's facility." Id. at 72. Under the *Bestfoods* decision, general oversight functions within the "norms of corporate behavior" allow the parent to escape "operator" liability. Justice Souter's explanation of this point is that, "the critical question is whether, in degree and detail, actions directed to the facility by an agent of the parent alone are eccentric under accepted norms of parental oversight of a subsidiary's facility." Id. What "norms" are relevant to individual cases and what actions are "eccentric?"

iii.   Successor Corporations

Corporations are not static business entities, they change their form and sometimes their existence over time. Often, one corporation is succeeded by another. Important questions have arisen with regard to CERCLA liabilities and successor corporations. Do they flow through to burden the successor or do they remain fixed to the initial corporate PRP? Why should these liabilities ever pass through to another business entity? In United States v. Mexico Feed and Seed Co., 980 F.2d 478 (8th Cir.1992), the appellate court explained why corporate successors should remain liable under CERCLA. Judge Beam wrote,

> An examination of the context in which Congress used the word "corporation" confirms our determination that corporate successors are plainly within the meaning of "person" in 42 U.S. § 9607. CERCLA is a remedial environmental statute with two essential purposes: 1) to provide swift and effective response to hazardous waste sites; and 2) to place the cost of that response on those responsible for creating or maintaining the hazardous condition. When including corporations within that set of entities which must bear the cost of cleaning up the hazardous conditions they have created, Congress could not have intended that those corporations be enabled to evade their responsibility by dying paper deaths, only to rise phoenix-like from the ashes, transformed, but free of their former liabilities. It would serve little purpose to include corporations responsible for hazardous waste sites, but not their corporate successors, within the class of "covered per-

son." Even in cases of good faith, a bona-fide successor reaps the economic benefits of its predecessor's use of hazardous disposal methods, and, as the recipient of the benefits, is also responsible for the costs of those benefits. Thus, a review of the purpose of CERCLA further reinforces our initial determination that successor corporations are subsumed within the plain meaning of the term "corporation."

What do you think of this rationale? Isn't the court really emphasizing the accomplishment of CERCLA policies over all else including state corporate law? Why would a policy easily finding successor companies free from the CERCLA liabilities of their predecessors present an enormous potential loophole in CERCLA?

Changes in corporate ownership or the ownership of corporate assets usually occurs in one of three ways: 1) through the sale of stock to another corporation, 2) through a merger or consolidation with another corporation or 3) through the sale of corporate assets to another corporation. In the *first* situation—the stock sale to an acquiring firm—the corporate entity remains intact and retains its liabilities in spite of the change in ownership. Therefore, the acquiring firm takes no risk except the danger that the old company would have no continuing value due to its high liabilities. In the *second* example—the merger or consolidation of the old firm into the new—the acquiring firm *retains* the legal liabilities of the predecessor company. In the *third* context—the sale or transfer of corporate assets—the acquiring firm is *not* liable for the liabilities of the predecessor company. With this traditional corporate law rule structure, many corporate successions have been structured as stock or asset purchases.

There are four generally-recognized exceptions to the nonliability position of the third example—asset acquisition and these theories have been employed to find CERCLA liability against successor corporations. An acquiring firm is liable for the actions of its predecessor company in any of the following four situations:

- the purchaser expressly or impliedly agrees to assume such obligations,
- the transaction constitutes a *de facto* merger or consolidation,
- the purchasing firm is merely a continuation of the selling corporation, or
- the transaction is a fraudulent effort to escape liability.

Although courts have taken many approaches, recent decisions have emphasized an expanded "substantial continuity" test where the purchasing company may be held liable if there is a substantial continuation of the acquired company's business. See e.g., B.F. Goodrich v. Betkoski, 99 F.3d 505 (2d Cir.1996) and United States v. Mexico Feed and Seed Co., 980 F.2d 478 (8th Cir.1992). Courts have followed an 8 part test announced in United States v. Carolina Transformer Co., 978 F.2d 832 (4th Cir.1992), which identifies the following factors:

1. Retention of the same employees,

2.   Retention of the same supervisory personnel,

3.   Retention of the same production facilities and the same location,

4.   Production of the same product,

5.   Retention of the same name,

6.   Continuity of assets,

7.   Continuity of general business operations, and

8.   Whether the successor holds itself out as the continuation of the previous enterprise.

When a court considers the question of whether a successor corporation is responsible for the CERCLA liabilities of its predecessor, what is the role of state corporate law in the calculus? Should federal courts interpreting the application of CERCLA be bound by a narrow version of successor liability found in one state's law? See City Management Corp. v. U.S. Chemical Co., 43 F.3d 244 (6th Cir.1994) (applying Michigan law to a successorship case). What are the consequences of "substantial continuity" rule in the design and execution of corporate acquisitions?

2.   LENDER'S LIABILITY

When first enacted in 1980, CERCLA contained a provision— § 101(20)(A)—that attempt to insulate lenders from liability under the statute. As an exclusion from the definition of "owner or operator," it did not include "a person, who, without participation in the management of a vessel or facility, holds indicia of ownership primarily to protect his security interest in the vessel or facility." Lenders could have "indicia of ownership" when their loans were secured by the real and personal property of the debtor. One case decision—United States v. Fleet Factors Corp., 901 F.2d 1550 (11th Cir.1990)—disqualified the use of this lender exemption by finding that creditors had "participated in the management" of the debtor "by participating in the financial management of a facility to a degree indicating a *capacity to influence* the corporation's treatment of hazardous wastes." Id. at 1557. Other cases suggested that a lender could be liable if it acquired title to property through foreclosure of a security interest. See Guidice v. BFG Electroplating and Manufacturing Co., 732 F.Supp. 556 (W.D.Pa.1989). These cases created great uncertainty in lenders as to when their CERCLA liability would begin.

In response to these judicial developments expanding lender liability (or at least expanding the possibility of such liability), in 1992 EPA issued an interpretive rule as an amendment to the National Contingency Plan in an attempt to disavow the *Fleet Factors* position and to provide lenders with some clarity. The rule stated that "[p]articipation in the management of a facility means actual participation in the management or operation of the facility by the holder, and does not included the mere capacity or unexercised right or ability to influence facility operations." 57 Fed. Reg. 18375 (1992). In addition, the rule allowed lenders to foreclose and to purchase at the foreclosure sale as long as they moved quickly to divest themselves of the property. Unfortunately for lenders, in 1994 the lender liability rule was invalidated by an appeals court on the ground that CERCLA did not give EPA the power to issue an interpretive rule for § 107. See Kelley v. EPA, 15 F.3d 1100 (D.C.Cir.1994).

The last phase of this complicated scenario was legislative. Congress enacted the Asset Conservation, Lender Liability, and Deposit Insurance Protection Act of 1996 which amends the definition of the terms "owner and operator" to more precisely indicate the meaning of the important concept of "participation in the management of a vessel or facility." This statute negates the *Fleet Factors* "capacity to control" test and indicates that a lender will be liable only when it "actually participates in the management or operational affairs of a vessel or facility." § 101(20)(F)(i)(I)–(II).

3. TRUSTS, ESTATES AND FIDUCIARIES

As most students of Property Law know, legal title to land may exist in a person or an entity that holds it for the benefit of another. The most common form of this legal relationship is the trust where a trustee holds the legal title to the land or other assets for the benefit of beneficiaries who are viewed as having equitable title to the assets or corpus of the trust. The trustee is considered to be a fiduciary—that is, someone who.... Fiducia-ries serve numerous useful purposes for their beneficiaries and they are held to a high level of care in the activities. Section 107(n)(5)(A) recognizes this traditional role of fiduciaries who function as trustees, executors, administrators, custodians, guardians, receivers, and conservators and in § 107(n)(4), CERCLA establishes fiduciary protection from personal liabili-ty for listed conduct related to a CERCLA response action at a contaminat-ed site. There are statutory boundaries to this fiduciary "safe harbor" in § 107(n) with one of the most important being the fiduciary negligence contributing to the release of hazardous substances. See § 107(n)(1)(4). Sometimes trustees can be found liable. See Phoenix v. Garbage Services Co., 816 F.Supp. 564 (D.Ariz.1993).

It is also noteworthy that while the fiduciary may have protection from CERCLA liability, the trust, estate or assets do not. They may be subject to statutory liability. This point gives rise to the interesting question of whether CERCLA liabilities attach to the ownership of land and other assets derived through inheritance. As the discussion below indicates, Congress amended the statute by adding an "innocent purchaser" defense in § 107(b)(3) which protects those who gain title to property through inheritance under defined circumstances. Therefore, inheriting already-contaminated property does not necessarily result in CERCLA liability in the heir. See e.g., Norfolk Southern Ry. Co. v. Shulimson Bros. Co., 1 F.Supp.2d 553 (W.D.N.C.1998). Through the operation of the "innocent purchaser" defense, the heir may not be considered to be the current owner of the "facility" under § 107(a) and therefore not responsible as a PRP.

4. UNITS OF GOVERNMENT

As "owners," "operators" and "arrangers," units of government are included as "person[s]" under § 101(21). This should be expected when considering the roles of government at all levels and the many possibilities for creating and disposing of hazardous materials. At the federal level, CERCLA clearly waives the government's sovereign immunity. Section 120(a)(1) provides,

> Each department, agency, and instrumentality of the United States ... shall be subject to, and comply with, this act in the same manner, and to the same extent, both procedurally and substantively as any non-governmental entity, including liability under Section 107 of this Act.

This waiver puts the federal government on equal footing with private parties and extends liability whenever a private party would be liable in a similar situation. The federal government "owns" military bases and other federal facilities and in 1986 Congress added § 120 which makes cleanups of these sites a subject of EPA supervision with state consultation and public participation in remedy selection. Military procurement and waste disposal has resulted in findings of CERCLA liability in a number of cases. See Price v. United States, 818 F.Supp. 1326 (S.D.Cal.1992) (Navy liable for 1930s shipments of waste to a junkyard for disposal); Santa Fe Pac. Realty Corp. v. United States, 780 F.Supp. 687 (E.D.Cal.1991) (Defense department liable as an "arranger") and FMC Corp. v. Department of Commerce, 29 F.3d 833 (3d Cir.1994) (en banc) (federal oversight of rayon manufacturing plant during World War II triggers potential liability as an "operator").

State government was considered to be liable under CERCLA. In Pennsylvania v. Union Gas Co., 491 U.S. 1 (1989), the Supreme Court ruled that Congress intended to eliminate state sovereign immunity and that it could do so under the Commerce Clause. Seven years later, it reversed itself with its decision in Seminole Tribe of Florida v. Florida, 517 U.S. 44 (1996), which overruled the Union Gas decision and concludes that Congress may not abrogate the States' immunity from private suits in federal courts by enacting Commerce Clause-based laws. See Burnette v. Carothers, 192 F.3d 52 (2d Cir.1999). But what about local governments? Are they similarly protection by the Eleventh Amendment? The U.S. Constitution accords Eleventh Amendment immunity to "States" and this has been interpreted as not protecting local governments when they act as municipal corporations and consequently, these governments are fully exposed to CERCLA liability. Many cases have found municipal liability. See e.g., B.F. Goodrich v. Murtha, 958 F.2d 1192 (2d Cir.1992). Others holding have protected local governments under other CERCLA policies such as the secured creditor liability exemption of § 101(20)(A). See e.g., Monarch Tile, Inc. v. City of Florence, 212 F.3d 1219 (11th Cir.2000).

F. DEFENSES TO CERCLA LIABILITY

The material in this chapter has presented CERCLA as a hazardous waste cleanup law establishing a sweeping liability scheme for the four statutory PRP categories. This broad distribution of substantial legal liability has been adopted in order to accelerate and fund remedial efforts so as to protect public health, safety and the environment. As with any legal system, liability is assigned according to doctrinal elements reflecting policy choices. The avoidance of CERCLA cleanup liability can occur when a party does not fit into the parameters of the PRP definitions or some other aspect of the fundamental CERCLA doctrine. But how else may liability be escaped? When, as a matter of policy, should the weight of liability be avoided?

CERCLA's drafters did recognize that existence of three statutorily-based defenses which they wrote into § 107(b). Under the terms of this section, there would be no liability if "the release or threat of release of a hazardous substance and the damages resulting therefrom were *caused solely by*,"—1) an act of God, 2) an act of war, and/or 3) an act or omission of a third party not in contractual relationship with the defendant. Notice the sole causation feature of § 107(b). It suggests that if the PRP contributes, in any way, to the release or the damages incurred, the defense will be lost. A fourth statutory defense—shielding innocent purchasers or landowners—was added to CERCLA by way of the SARA amendments of 1986. Each of these four statutory defenses will be considered below.

1. ACT OF GOD DEFENSE

This defense to CERCLA liability suggests intervention of nearly biblical proportions. The definition provided in § 101(1) states that an act of God means "an unanticipated grave natural disaster or other natural phenomena of an exceptional, inevitable, and irresistible character, the effects of which could not have been prevented or avoided by the exercise of due care or oversight." There are two components of this definition: 1) the unanticipated nature of the "disaster" and 2) the unavoidability of its effects even with due care. The defense has been generally unavailable as courts have considered natural events such as windstorms, torrential rains and river floods as being "foreseeable" natural perils for which precautions could be taken. See United States v. Stringfellow, 661 F.Supp. 1053 (C.D.Cal.1987) and United States v. Poly–Carb, Inc., 951 F.Supp. 1518 (D.Nev.1996). The possibilities seem endless. What if a lightening bolt hits an industrial plant and sparks a fire that results in the release of hazardous substances. Should the defense protect the current owner? See Wagner Seed Co. v. Daggett, 800 F.2d 310 (2d Cir.1986).

2. ACT OF WAR DEFENSE

This defense conjures up visions of advancing armies smashing industrial facilities and leaving barrels of hazardous materials in their wake. CERCLA does not define the meaning of an "act of war" and the few cases considering the defense have given it a narrow interpretation. Government contractors producing materiel for a war effort have attempted to employ the defense; yet without success. As stated in United States v. Shell Oil Co., 841 F.Supp. 962 (C.D.Cal.1993), an act of war, for purposes of CERCLA, requires the use of force by one government against another government or the wartime destruction of private property so as to harm an enemy. Thus, the definition of "war" has been limited to traditional conflicts between nations and not cases of civil disorder, riot or vandalism. Should this defense be available to property owners when a release of hazardous substances occurs on their land as the result of an act of international terrorism? What about a riot or other civil disturbance where the release of hazardous substances is caused by the intervention of rampaging individuals who damage or destroy safe storage facilities? Consider the "act of God" and the "act of war" defenses in conjunction with the third party defense discussed below. What is the common policy theme?

3.   THIRD PARTY DEFENSE

There are limits to CERCLA's expansive liability system and the third party defense established by § 107(b)(3). Examine the elements of this section. No liability exists if the release or threat and "damages resulting therefrom were caused solely by,"

> an act or omission of a third party other than an employee or agent of the defendant, or than one whose act or omission occurs in connection with a contractual relationship ... with the defendant ..., if the defendant establishes by a preponderance of the evidence that (a) he exercised due care with respect to the hazardous substance concerned, taking into consideration the characteristics of such hazardous substance, in light of all relevant facts an circumstances, and (b) he took precautions against foreseeable acts or omissions of any such third party and the consequences that could foreseeably result from such acts or omissions. . . .

What was Congress attempting to do by creating this defense? Imagine a situation where a trucker deposits barrels of hazardous materials on a land owner's property surreptitiously during the middle of the night. What if a neighbor accidentally spills hazardous substances into a ditch which runs through another land owner's property? How broad is this defense? How broad should it be? Recall that the defendant bears the burden of proof on the issue of all CERCLA defenses. This defense breaks down into three components:

1) the release was *solely caused* by the third party,

2) the *absence of a contractual relationship* between the third party and the defendant,

3) the defendant exercised *due care* regarding the hazardous substance and took *precautions* against foreseeable conduct of the third party.

Examine these three components. Which of these elements would be most difficult to establish? There has been substantial litigation activity considering attempts at raising the third party defense and much of it has focused upon the question of whether a "contractual relationship" existed between a third party and the defendant PRP. The existence of any such relationship *bars* the use of the defense by the PRP. Why should that be so?

Two lines of case decisions have emerged. First, one series of holdings finds that *nearly* any relationship between the two actors blocks the use of the defense. See Carter–Jones Lumber Co. v. Dixie Distributing Co., 166 F.3d 840 (6th Cir.1999), United States v. Monsanto Co., 858 F.2d 160 (4th Cir.1988) and Shapiro v. Alexanderson, 743 F.Supp. 268 (S.D.N.Y.1990). Second, another line of decisions narrows the disqualification to those situations where the third party's acts or omissions occur "in connection with a contractual relationship," but "only if the contract between the landowner and the third party somehow is connected with the handling of hazardous substances." The idea being that the defendant should only be barred from raising this defense only when its contract related to the disposal or release of hazardous substances. See e.g., Westwood Pharmaceuticals, Inc. v. National Fuel Gas Dist. Corp., 964 F.2d 85, 89 (2d Cir.1992) and Reichhold Chemicals, Inc. v. Textron, Inc., 888 F.Supp. 1116 (N.D.Fla. 1995). Which of these two approaches would better serve the rapid and effective cleanup site goals of CERCLA? Which interpretation could be viewed as being more unfair to the defendant? The elements of due care and precautionary action have also been challenged in court. Regarding due care, the defendant must demonstrate that it if it had notice of the hazardous substance release, that steps were taken to prevent the situation from spreading or from getting worse. See Idylwoods Assocs. v. Mader Capital, Inc., 915 F.Supp. 1290 (W.D.N.Y.1996) and Redwing Carriers, Inc. v. Saraland Apts., Ltd., 875 F.Supp. 1545 (S.D.Ala.1995).

State of New York v. Lashins Arcade Co.

United States Court of Appeals, Second Circuit, 1996.
91 F.3d 353.

■ MAHONEY, CIRCUIT JUDGE.

[In this case, the State of New York brought a § 9607(a) cost recovery action against Lashins Arcade Co. to recover its investigation and cleanup expenses for ground water contamination at a Westchester County, New York shopping center. Lashins, the current owner, claimed that it had been unaware of the state's formal investigation of the site at the time of the purchase. The trial court had granted Lashin's summary judgment motion based upon the third party defense provided by CERCLA § 107(b)(3) This appeal followed.]

DISCUSSION

* * * As an initial matter, there is no dispute that New York has established a prima facie case against Lashins under § 9607(a) for recovery of expenses incurred investigating and cleaning up the release of PCE at the Arcade. * * *

Since Lashins is a current owner of the Shopping Arcade, it is a potentially responsible defendant under § 9607(a)(1) * * * withstanding the fact that it did not own the Arcade at the time of disposal of the hazardous substances. Thus, Lashins may be held strictly liable for New

York's response costs unless it can satisfy one of CERCLA's affirmative defenses. We now turn to Lashins' claim that it may avoid such liability under the third-party defense of § 9607(b)(3).

Section 9607(b)(3) provides an affirmative defense for a party who can establish that the offending "release . . . of a hazardous substance and the damages resulting therefrom were caused solely by . . . an act or omission of a third party," provided that: (1) the third party is not "one whose act or omission occurs in connection with a contractual relationship, existing directly or indirectly, with the defendant," (2) the defendant "took precautions against foreseeable acts or omissions of any such third patty and the consequences that could foreseeably result from such acts or omissions," and (3) the defendant "exercised due care with respect to the hazardous substance concerned, taking into consideration the characteristics of such hazardous substance, in light of all relevant facts and circumstances."

The offending release here was clearly caused by third parties (Tripodi, Bedford Village Cleaners, Inc., Astrologo, and (New York contends) Milton Baygell). Although paragraphs (1)–(3) of § 9607(b) speak exclusively in the singular, referring to events and damages "caused solely by—(1) *an* act of God; (2) *an* act of war; [or] (3) *an* act or omission of a third party," § 9607(b) (emphasis added), paragraph (4) of § 9607(b) refers to "any combination of the foregoing paragraphs." We read paragraph (4) as allowing consideration of multiple causes within, as well as among, the several preceding paragraphs. Thus, in our view, damage that resulted from an earthquake and a subsequent flood would fall within paragraph (1) of § 9607(b), and damages caused by a number of acts by a single third party (as typically occurs when pollution is caused by a course of conduct), or a number of acts by several third parties (as in this case), would fall within paragraph (3). * * *

In this case, the only one of the allegedly offending third parties with whom Lashins had a contractual relationship was Milton Baygell. Further, Baygell's allegedly offending conduct did not "occur in connection with a contractual relationship . . . with [Lashins]" within the meaning of § 9607(b)(3), and therefore Lashins may not be disqualified from the protection afforded by § 9607(b)(3) because of its contractual relationship with Baygell.

This conclusion is mandated by the following ruling in Westwood Pharmaceuticals, Inc. v. National Fuel Gas Distribution Corp., 964 F.2d 85 (2d Cir.1992). * * *

In Westwood, the seller of the contaminated site sought exoneration from the buyer's conduct, whereas in this case the buyer seeks exoneration from the seller's activities, but this is surely an immaterial distinction in terms of the *Westwood* rationale. ("[A] landowner is precluded from raising the third-party defense only if the contract between the landowner and the third party somehow is connected with the handling of hazardous substances."). The straightforward sale of the Arcade by Baygell to Lashins clearly did not "relate to hazardous substances" or vest Lashins with authority "to exert some element of control over [Baygell's] activities" within the contemplation of our ruling in Westwood.

The second requirement for the successful assertion of a third-party defense demands that the defendant shall have taken adequate precautions against actions by the third party that would lead to a release of hazardous waste. Given that the last release in the instant case happened more than fifteen years before Lashins' purchase of the Arcade, there was obviously nothing Lashins could have done to prevent actions leading to a release.

Thus, the resolution of this appeal turns upon the validity of the district court's ruling that Lashins was entitled to summary judgment on the question whether Lashins "exercised due care with respect to the hazardous substance concerned . . . in the light of all relevant facts and circumstances" within the meaning of § 9607(b)(3). This requirement is not defined in the statute. CERCLA's legislative history, however, provides some guidance: [T]he defendant must demonstrate that he took all precautions with respect to the particular waste that a similarly situated reasonable and prudent person would have taken in light of all relevant facts and circumstances." H.R.Rep. No. 1016, 96th Cong., 2d Sess., pt. 1, at 34 (1980). Further, "due care" would include those steps necessary to protect the public from a health or environmental threat." United States v. A & N Cleaners & Launderers, Inc., 854 F.Supp. 229, 238 (S.D.N.Y.1994) (quoting H.R.Rep. No. 253, 99th Cong., 2d Sess. 187 (1986) U.S.Code Cong. & Admin.News 1986, 2835); see also Kerr–McGee Chem. Corp., 14 F.3d at 325 & n. 3 (due care not established when no affirmative measures taken to control site); Lincoln Properties v. Higgins, 823 F.Supp. 1528, 1543–44 (E.D.Cal.1992) (due care exercised where defendant removed contaminated wells).

Against this background, New York contends that Lashins inadequately investigated the contamination problem before buying the Arcade despite being notified about it, and after its purchase: "did *nothing* to contain, control or clean up the pollution except to continue to maintain a filter on its own property." New York points to cases such as *A & N Cleaners* and *Kerr-McGee Chemical Corp.* where § 9607(a) liability was imposed because the defendant did not take active measures to address a hazardous waste problem, and adds that Kerr–McGee Chemical Corp. and United States v. DiBiase Salem Realty Trust, Civ. A. No. 91–11028Iv1A, 1993 WL 729662 (D.Mass. Nov.19, 1993), establish that the "due care" standard does not permit a landowner to remain passive simply because public environmental authorities are addressing a hazardous waste situation.

We are not persuaded by New York's arguments, nor by the authorities that New York cites to us. The pertinent language of § 9607(b)(3) focuses the "due care" inquiry upon "all relevant facts and circumstances" of the case at hand. In this case, the RI/FS by Dvirka and Bartilucci had been commissioned six months before Lashins purchased the Arcade, and before Lashins had even learned that the Arcade was for sale. It would have been pointless to require Lashins to commission a parallel investigation once it acquired the Arcade and became more fully aware of the environmental problem, Pressed at oral argument as to what Lashins might appropriately have been required to do at that juncture, New York contended that Lashins was obligated to pay some or all of the cost of the RI/FS undertaken at the behest of the EPA and the NYSDEC.

This is surely an anomalous proposal. Response costs are assessed when there is liability under § 9607(a). It is counterintuitive to suppose that a defendant is required to pay some or all of those response costs in order to establish the affirmative defense provided by § 9607(b)(3) to liability under § 9607(a), thereby rendering the affirmative defense partly or entirely academic.

Nor do we discern any policy reasons for imposing such a rule We agree with HRW Systems, Inc. v. Washington Gas Light Co., 823 F.Supp. 318 (D.Md.1993), that the "due care" mandate of § 9607(b)(3) does not "impose a duty on a purchaser of land to investigate prior to purchase, in order to determine whether there is pollution on the land caused by someone with whom the purchaser is not in contractual privity." Id. at 349. No claim is made that Lashins' purchase of the Arcade deprived New York of any remedy available to it against any predecessor owners or operators under § 9607(a); consent decrees were in fact entered against Tripodi and Astrologo. It is surely the policy of CERCLA to impose liability upon parties responsible for pollution, rather than the general taxpaying public, but this policy does not mandate precluding a "due care" defense by imposing a rule that is tantamount to absolute liability for ownership of a site containing hazardous waste.

Finally, the cases cited by New York do not require the negation of Lashins' "due care" defense. None involved a defendant who played no role in the events that led to the hazardous waste problem and came on the scene after public authorities were well along in a program of investigation and remediation. *Kerr-McGee Chemical Corp* involved a landowner who was aware of the environmental problem and made no attempt to address it after preliminary investigative efforts by federal and state authorities provided notice of the contamination. In A & N *Cleaners,* the defendant landowners' sublessee (who subsequently became a lessee) was operating the offending dry cleaning establishment throughout the entire period of the defendants' ownership. In *DiBiase Salem Realty Trust,* a portion of the pollution occurred after the landowner commenced ownership, and the landowner did nothing to address the problem after becoming aware of the hazardous wastes as a result of preliminary investigations by state authorities. * * *

In sum, we perceive no basis for reversal of the district court's award of summary judgment to Lashins on the basis that Lashins satisfied its obligation to "exercise[ ] due care" with respect to the Arcade within the meaning of § 9607(b)(3). In so ruling, we proclaim no broad rule of exemption from the liability imposed by § 9607(a). Rather, mindful of the mandate of § 9607(b)(3) that the "due care" inquiry focus upon "all relevant facts and circumstances" of the case presented for decision, we conclude that Lashins' "due care" obligation did not require it to go beyond the measures that it took to address the contamination problem at the Arcade, and to supplant, duplicate, or underwrite the RI/FS previously commissioned by the EPA and pollution that ensued from activities which occurred more than fifteen years before Lashins purchased the Arcade.

4. INNOCENT PURCHASER DEFENSE

During the pre-purchase negotiation process, a land buyer might ask his or her attorney, "what are the potential risks associated with the purchase of this tract?" In the past, the counselor might identify a range of factors including land market risks, the failure of obtaining necessary financing, title defects or uncertainties and zoning or land use controls as being among the buyer's possible concerns. With the enactment of CERCLA, potential hazardous waste cleanup liability joined the list of extremely serious concerns, often eclipsing the traditional list of buyer considerations. By virtue of becoming the fee simple owner, a land purchaser would become strictly liable under § 107(a)(1) as a "current owner" and usually, could only look to the § 107(b)(3) third person defense for possible relief. Unfortunately, this defense would not be available to the buyer since the purchase contract and deed would link the buyer to prior owners and operators in a contractual way. Such a contractual relationship with such a party who had actually disposed of the hazardous materials would invalidate the third person defense. The result would be that such an owner who had not contributed to the contamination of the site could be held responsible for cleanup costs.

In 1986, Congress addressed the "innocent purchaser" problem by adding § 101(35) to the statute. This section devised an innocent purchaser defense as a subset of the general third party defense contained in § 107(b)(3). It applies in three distinct situations:

a) government acquisition by escheat or other involuntary or by eminent domain/condemnation,

b) private acquisition by inheritance or bequest, and

c) voluntary acquisition.

The third category is generally the most common applying to voluntary site purchases for commercial, industrial or other purposes. Property owners in all three categories must show—1) that they acquired the real property *after* the hazardous substances were disposed or placed on site and 2) that they satisfied the twin requirements of the third party defense that they exercised due care over the hazardous substances and that they took precautions against foreseeable acts or omissions of third parties. However, under § 101(35)(A), voluntary purchasers must demonstrate that,

at the time the defendant acquired the facility the defendant *did not know and had no reason to know* that any hazardous substance which is the subject to the release or threatened release was disposed of on, in, or at the facility.(emphasis supplied)

What policy premise lies behind this provision? Why not protect a purchaser who *did* know about site contamination at the time of purchase? Notice the structure of this section—it grants a defense only if the defendant a) did not have *actual* knowledge and b) did not have "reason to know" or *imputed* knowledge about the presence of hazardous substances. How can it be established that a purchaser did *not* have "reason to know" of site contamination prior to purchase? Section 101(35)(B) states that the defendant must have taken *"all appropriate inquiry* into the previous ownership and uses of the property consistent with good *commercial or customary practice....*" (emphasis supplied) Does this language help the potential buyer to evaluate ownership risk? This section also provides more guidance for determining the "all appropriate inquiry" question in this section by providing that,

> the court shall take into account any specialized knowledge or experience on the part of the defendant, the relationship of the purchase price to the value of the property if uncontaminated, commonly known or reasonably ascertainable information about the property, the obviousness of the presence or likely presence of contamination at the property, and the ability to detect such contamination by appropriate inspection.

Does this give helpful guidance to a reviewing court or a party considering a transaction? Some cases, such as In re Hemingway Transport Inc., 993 F.2d 915, 933 (1st Cir.1993), have analyzed the legislative history underlying this section and following it, they have imposed a sliding scale of stringency—commercial acquisitions demand the highest level, residential purchases less, and inheritances accorded the most leniency. How would you expect that commercial land transactions have been restructured so as to avoid CERCLA liability and to maximize the chances of making a successful "innocent purchaser" argument? What would you advise your client to do prior to buying a commercial or industrial parcel?

Maxine I. Lipeles, 4 Environmental Law—Hazardous Waste

501 (3d ed. 1997).

The innocent landowner defense has encouraged many current purchasers to conduct pre-acquisition environmental audits of the property to be acquired. The audits are often performed in the hope of finding no contamination and therefore building a record for future invocation of the innocent landowner defense, should CERCLA problems develop. In practice, the principal effect of these audits has been to detect existing contamination, and enable the buyer and seller to negotiate revised terms and conditions of the acquisition (e.g., reduced purchase price, placement into escrow of [a] portion of [the] purchase price to cover cleanup by buyer, delayed closing with seller conducting cleanup, and additional representations, warranties, and indemnities).

Offering some guidance regarding the elements of an appropriate inquiry by a potential buyer into the environmental conditions of a site are two standards issued by the American Society for Testing and Materials(ASTM) in May1993. One standard, Transactional Screen Process, Standard E.50.02.01 (ASTM 1993), recommends steps to take to determine whether an environmental site assessment is warranted. The function of the transaction screen is to identify the existence of potentially contaminating circumstances, such that further inquiry would be inappropriate. The second standard, Phase I Environmental Site Assessment Process, Standard E.50.02.02 (ASTM 1993), calls for a review of records concerning the site, a physical inspection, interviews with current owners, occupants, and governmental officials, and a report by an environmental professional opining as to the existence of "recognized environmental conditions." Whether courts will deem the preparation of a Phase I Environmental Site Assessment in accordance with the ASTM standard to constitute "all appropriate inquiry" for purposes of the innocent landowner defense (assuming that no contamination is discovered in the assessment) remains to be seen. Will less suffice? Will more be required? Will the nature of the site and the sophistication of the purchaser affect the answer to those questions? See CERCLA § 101(35)(B).

5. OTHER DEFENSES TO CERCLA LIABILITY

Although some courts have interpreted § 107(b) as being the exclusive source of CERCLA liability defenses, most have recognized a series of other theories. See North Carolina ex rel. Howes v. W.R. Peele, Sr. Trust, 876 F.Supp. 733, 740 (E.D.N.C.1995). Statutes of limitations on cost recovery actions provide one possible defense. Section 107 cost recovery actions must be commenced within 3 years after "completion" of the removal action and within 6 years after the "initiation" of physical on-site construction of a remedial action. See § 113(g)(2). As is apparent, the characterization of the response action as either "removal" or "remedial" can be of enormous strategic importance. Investigation and site study are usually considered to be removal actions while remedial responses are physical on-site construction activities conducted over a lengthy time period. See Kelley ex rel. State of Michigan v. E.I. duPont de Nemours, 786 F.Supp. 1268 (E.D.Mich.1992) (removal action defined) and Advanced Micro Devices, Inc. v. National Semiconductor Corp., 38 F.Supp.2d 802 (N.D.Cal.1999) (remedial action defined). Finally, equitable defenses such as waiver, estoppel, laches, and unclean hands are occasionally recognized but usually in contribution actions between PRPs and not in initial assignments of CERCLA liability. See e.g., United States v. Martell, 887 F.Supp. 1183 (N.D.Ind.1995).

G. Allocating CERCLA Costs and Damages

1. DIVISIBILITY OF JOINT AND SEVERAL HARMS AS A FORM OF ALLOCATION

CERCLA cases are often quite complex; both legally and factually. Most often, they involve facilities which have been contaminated by the actions of many actors over an extended period of time. Unlike the simple tort case concerning one plaintiff and one defendant, hazardous waste remedial actions can implicate hundreds of potentially liable parties. As the *Monsanto, Bell Petroleum* and *Alcan* cases demonstrate, government cost recovery actions brought under § 107(a) seek cleanup costs and other damages under a strict liability theory. This is also true when a non-PRP private party seeks the recovery of incurred cleanup costs. In the common case, there are numerous PRPs who have contributed to the creation of the contaminated site. As we know from the material above, courts may, and usually do, apply principles of joint and several liability when there is such an "indivisible" harm. Joint and several liability makes each defendant legally liable for all of the damages and costs incurred and it places the burden on the defendant to seek contribution from other PRPs. However, courts have used § 433A of the Restatement(Second) Torts to allow a defendant to avoid joint and several liability by showing that the harm caused is "divisible" or allocable to individual actors. In this way, when the defendant can prove "divisibility," its liability becomes several, not joint and several, and responsibility is limited to its "share" of the problem. In addition, when PRPs enter into a negotiated settlement with EPA, they may accept a "nonbinding preliminary allocation of responsibility" or an NBAR which estimates and allocates their liability for cleanup costs.

2. ALLOCATION IN PRIVATE PARTY ACTIONS

i. *Cost Recovery or Contribution Action*

During the first decade of CERCLA much of the cleanup costs recovery litigation involved the government seeking to replenish Superfund resources after it spent money on response actions. At present, the emphasis of CERCLA enforcement appears to be the private party management of site cleanups followed by multi-PRP settlement or cost reimbursement litigation. How does a private party obtain recovery of its costs under CERCLA and how are they allocated between PRPs? Two avenues present themselves in the statute. First, under § 107(a)(4)(B), PRP liability exists for "any other necessary costs of response incurred by any other person consistent with the national contingency plan." Second, § 113(f)(1) allows any PRP to "seek contribution from any other person who is liable or potentially liable [under § 107(a)] during or following a civil action under [§ 106 or § 107(a)] of this title." A question has arisen concerning whether PRPs may proceed under both of these provisions. There are several reasons why this question is important and the strategic advantages of § 107(a) versus § 113(f) include: 6 year versus 3 year statutes of limitations, joint and several liability versus several liability, and the unavailability or availability of contribution protection to parties that settle with EPA. Virtually all courts of appeal have concluded that a PRP—that is, a party liable under CERCLA—may *only* proceed under § 113(f) in a federal action for equitable contribution against other PRPs. See e.g., Bedford Affiliates v. Sills, 156 F.3d 416 (2d Cir.1998), Centerior Service Co. v. Acme Scrap Iron & Metal Corp., 153 F.3d 344 (6th Cir.1998) and New Castle County v.

Halliburton NUS Corp., 111 F.3d 1116 (3d Cir.1997). Establishing the § 113(f)(1) contribution claim requires that the § 107(a) *prima facie* case be proved and the § 107(b) statutory defenses are also available. See Uniroyal Chemical Co. v. Deltech Corp., 160 F.3d 238 (5th Cir.1998).

ii. *Applying Equitable Factors in Contribution Actions*

Section 113(f)(1) specifically states that "in resolving contribution claims, the court may allocate response costs among liable parties using *such equitable factors as the court determines are appropriate.*"(emphasis supplied) How should a court allocate response costs using the "equitable factors" guidelines provided by § 113(f)(1)? A good way to analyze this problem is to use a simplified hypothetical which assumes that there is a known cleanup cost—$X—and there are a number—Y—of PRPs identified under § 107(a) with varied connections to the contaminated site as waste generators, site owners or operators, or transporters. Assuming further that all Y PRPs remain in existence and are solvent, how should the $X be allocated? The simplest and most potentially *unfair* method would be a numerical pro rata allocation method which would divide $X by Y to yield an average damage figure. In what sense is this method unfair?

The following case—United States v. R.W. Meyer, Inc.—illustrates the use of another technique called the "Gore Factors" which employs a six-element test to analyze the allocation problem. Although the origin of these 6 elements is not disclosed in the opinion, these factors are derived from an unsuccessful CERCLA amendment proposed by (then) Congressman Al Gore of Tennessee. They have been commonly used as a starting point for judges in the process of allocating CERCLA liability among PRPs. Notice the breadth of the equitable powers accorded to trial judges seeking to fashion "fair" remedies in these cases. Usually, appellate courts view the lower courts role as balancing the equities in light of the totality of the circumstances and consequently, they apply a deferential "abuse of discretion" standard of review to the allocation decision. See e.g., Tosco Corp. v. Koch Industries, Inc., 216 F.3d 886 (10th Cir.2000) (upholds a 15 percent share allocation rather than the PRPs suggested 1.5 percent share).

CLASS DISCUSSION PROBLEM

The Ajax Corporation has just purchased the 25 acre Dickerson Road manufacturing facility owned by the Arnold Bakery Company. Ajax had hoped to use the Dickerson Road facility as the site of its new product distribution warehouse for the Southern Atlantic sales division of its building materials firm. It had carefully scoured the entire region for a suitable site and had decided upon the Dickerson Road facility after considering its size, its proximity to interstate highways and Ajax stores, and the fact that it had been used as a commercial bakery factory for the prior 22 years. Ajax Corporation's acquisition had been preceded by a Phase I Environmental Assessment performed by Enviro–Tech Consulting Co. which had found no "recognized environmental conditions" on the Arnold Bakery site.

As it turned out, the Enviro–Tech assessment, had not identified the fact that a serious groundwater contamination problem existed in the back 5 acres of the Dickerson Road and that the state Department of Environmental Quality and the federal EPA were in the process of completing their RI/FS which would recommend a multi-faceted, $10 million "pump and treat" ground water remedy. Soon after closing the deal with Arnold Bakery and taking title to the property, Ajax was presented with an EPA letter asserting that it was a PRP under § 107(a)(1) and demanding that Ajax undertake the cleanup. Rather than fight EPA in court over the order and risk even a more expensive remedy, Ajax decided to settle with EPA and pay the $10 million and have an environmental engineering firm undertake the remedy.

Ajax Corporation now is considering its options for collecting either all or part of the $10 million spent on the Dickerson Road cleanup. Research has revealed the following information concerning the site:

A) Arnold Bakery Co. had been the prior owner since 1971 but it has recently been acquired by Continental Baking Co. and has ceased to exist as a separate corporate entity,

B) the contamination was caused by hazardous waste disposal during the 1970s and 1980s by companies #1 through #5 in the rear 5 acres,

C) the volume of waste deposited on the site varied(according to EPA estimates) in the following way:

    i. #1–18%

    ii. #2–25%

    iii. #3–50%

    iv. #4–5%

    v. #5–2%

D) Biff's Trucking Company was used to transport 1/3 of the waste to the site,

E) Arnold Bakery Co. had *not* contributed any of the hazardous wastes to the site.

If Ajax Corporation is in a jurisdiction which only allows PRPs to recover cleanup costs by way of a CERCLA § 113(f) contribution action against other PRPs, what answers would you provide to the following list of question for Ajax's CEO?

1. Can Ajax Corporation sue one of the five waste generators under a theory of joint and several liability and recover the entire $10 million cleanup expense?

2. What, if any, is the significance of § 107(a) to a plaintiff such as Ajax Corporation who brings a § 113(f) contribution action against PRPs?

3. Assuming that PRPs #1 through #5 are all currently in existence, solvent and available to sue, how should liability be allocated? Should Ajax Corporation be absolved from all liability if all PRPs are financial-

ly able to pay the $10 million response costs. How should Biff's Trucking Company be treated in the allocation?

4. What if PRP #3 is insolvent, bankrupt or no longer in existence? How should a court allocate this "orphan share" that Ajax Corporation has paid for?

5. What if PRP #3 had previously settled with EPA for $2 million? How should that prior settlement affect Ajax Corporation's recovery?

United States v. R.W. Meyer, Inc.

United States Court of Appeals, Sixth Circuit, 1991.
932 F.2d 568.

■ BERTELSMAN, DISTRICT JUDGE.

[This appeal arose from a district court decision allocating responsibility for EPA and state cleanup costs for a metal plating operation in Cadillac, Michigan. Northernaire Plating had leased the facility from R.W. Meyer, Inc. under a 10 year lease. The PRPs in this case were 1) Northernaire Plating Company, 2) Willard S. Garwood, Northeraire's president and sole shareholder, and 3) R.W. Meyer, Inc. the property owner and Northernaire's landlord. Northeraire had discharged electroplating wastes into a catch basin and the material seeped into the ground as it migrated through the basin finally entering into a defective sewer pipe installed by Meyer. The district court had found the contamination to have been "indivisible" and imposing joint and several liability on the three PRPs for response costs of $342,823. The two parties—Northeraire and Garwood moving as one party-brought cross claims for contribution. The trial court ruled that 2/3(or $228,548) of the liability should be borne by Northernaire/Garwood and the remaining 1/3(or $114,207) should be allocated to R.W. Meyer, Inc. Meyer appealed from this judgment.]

Analysis

The trial court held that it was within its discretion to apply certain factors found in the legislative history of CERCLA in making its contribution apportionment. Although these factors were originally intended as criteria for deciding whether a party could establish a right to an apportionment of several liability in the EPA's initial removal action, the trial court found "these criteria useful in determining the proportionate share each party is entitled to in contribution from the other."

The criteria mentioned are:

(1) the ability of the parties to demonstrate that their contribution to a discharge release or disposal of a hazardous waste can be distinguished;

(2) the amount of the hazardous waste involved;

(3) the degree of toxicity of the hazardous waste involved;

(4) the degree of involvement by the parties in the generation, transportation, treatment, storage, or disposal of the hazardous waste;

(5) the degree of care exercised by the parties with respect to the hazardous waste concerned, taking into account the characteristics of such hazardous waste; and

(6) the degree of cooperation by the parties with Federal, State, or local officials to prevent any harm to the public health or the environment.

(Citing H.R. No. 253(III), 99th Cong., 2d Sess. 19, (1985), *reprinted* in 1986 U.S. Code Cong. & Admin. News 2835, 3038, 3042).

The trial court recognized that the lessee was the primary actor in allowing this site to become contaminated. (Appellant argues that the lessee was the *only* actor.) The trial court found, however, that in addition to constructing the defective sewer line which contributed to the contamination, appellant bore significant responsibility "simply by virtue of being the landowner." The trial court observed further that appellant "neither assisted nor cooperated with the EPA officials during their investigation and eventual cleanup of the ... site."

Chief Judge Hillman concluded, "As it is well within the province of this court, I have balanced each of the defendants' behavior with respect to the equitable guidelines discussed." As a result of the balancing, he made the apportionment described above.

The trial judge was well within the broad discretion afforded by the statute in making the apportionment he did.

Congress intended to invest the district courts with this discretion in making CERCLA contribution allocations when it provided, "the court may allocate response costs among the liable parties using such *equitable factors as the court determines are appropriate*." 42 U.S.C. §§ 9613(f)(1) (emphasis added).

Essentially, appellant argues here that a narrow, technical construction must be given to the term "contribution," so that, as in common law contribution, contribution under the statute is limited to the percentage a party's improper conduct causally contributed to the toxicity of the site in a physical sense. This argument is without merit. On the contrary, by using the term "equitable factors" Congress intended to invoke the tradition of equity under which the court must construct a flexible decrees balancing all the equities in the light of the totality of the circumstances.

[U]nder § 9613(f)(1) the court may consider any factor it deems in the interest of justice in allocating contribution recovery. Certainly, the several factors listed by the trial court are appropriate, but as it recognized, it was not limited to them. No exhaustive list of criteria need or should be formulated. However, in addition to the criteria listed above, the court may consider the state of mind of the parties, their economic status, any contracts between them bearing on the subject, any traditional equitable defenses as mitigating factors and any other factors deemed appropriate to balance the equities in the totality of the circumstances.

Therefore, the trial court quite properly considered here not only the appellant's contribution to the toxic slough described above in the technical causative sense, but also its moral contribution as the owner of the site. Review of the trial court's equitable balancing process is limited to a review for "abuse of discretion." This is in accord with the principle of equity that the chancellor has broad discretion to frame a decree.

This case, even though it involves over $300,000, is but a pimple on the elephantine carcass of the CERCLA litigation now making its way through the court system. Some of these cases involve millions or even billions of dollars in cleanup costs and hundreds or even thousands of potentially responsible parties.

I do not believe that Congress intended to require meticulous findings of the precise causative contribution each of several hundred parties made to a hazardous site. In many cases, this would be literally impossible. Rather, by the expansive language used in § 9613(f)(1) Congress intended the court to deal with these situations by creative means, considering all the equities and balancing them in the interests of justice. . . .

Although such an approach cannot be applied with mathematical precision, it is the fairest and most workable approach for apportioning CERCLA liability. Such an approach furthers the legislative intent of encouraging the prompt cleanup of hazardous sites by those equitably responsible. The parties actually performing the cleanup can look for reimbursement from other potentially responsible parties without fear that their contribution actions will be bogged down by the impossibility of making meticulous factual determinations as to the causal contribution of each party. Chief Judge Hillman was well within the equitable discretion afforded him by Congress in the way he handled this CERCLA contribution action.

Affirmed.

Control Data Corp. v. S.C.S.C. Corp.

United States Court of Appeals, Eighth Circuit, 1995.
53 F.3d 930.

■ RICHARD S. ARNOLD, Chief Judge.

Control Data Corporation brought this suit under the Comprehensive Environmental Response, Compensation, and Liability Act of 1980 (CERCLA), and the Minnesota Environmental Response and Liability Act (MERLA). Following a bench trial, the District Court found the Schloff defendants—S.C.S.C. Corp., Schloff Chemical, and Irvin and Ruth Schloff—liable under CERCLA and allocated responsibility for 33 1/3 percent of Control Data's response costs, as defined by CERCLA, to those defendants. [Liability was also found under Minnesota Law] * * *

The Schloff defendants appeal. We affirm the judgment of the District Court finding the Schloff defendants liable under CERCLA and allocating 33 1/3 percent of Control Data's response costs to them. * * *

I. Factual Background

Control Data owns and operates a printed-circuit-board facility on Meadowbrook Road in St. Louis Park, Minnesota. Across Meadowbrook Road and Minnehaha Creek, the Schloff defendants owned and operated a dry-cleaning supply business, Schloff Chemical, from 1975 until 1989. Irvin Schloff was president of Schloff Chemical from 1963 to 1989, and exercised day-to-day control over its operations until 1985, when a General Manager was hired. Ruth Schloff has been the record owner of the real property where Schloff Chemical was located since 1974. S.C.S.C. Corp. is the current corporate incarnation of Schloff Chemical.

In 1987, Control Data discovered a leak in its sewer line. Fearing contamination, Control Data initiated an investigation, and, indeed, discovered the presence of volatile organic compounds in the groundwater underlying the Control Data site. Principal among these contaminants were 1,1,1 trichloroethane (TCA) and its degradation substances and tetrachloroethylene (PERC) and its degradation substances. A degradation substance is what a chemical becomes when it begins to break down. PERC and TCA degrade into many of the same substances.

After confirming that groundwater contamination existed, Control Data reported its findings to the Minnesota Pollution Control Agency (MPCA) and began cooperating with that agency in an effort to clean up the site. Control Data has admitted that it is the source of the TCA and its degradation substances. TCA has been spilled, or "released" in CERCLA terminology, many times by Control Data. But Control Data denied ever using, much less releasing, PERC, a circumstance which led the MPCA to search for other sources for the PERC contamination. It turns out that Schloff Chemical was that source.

Schloff Chemical released PERC several times between 1975 and 1989. The PERC released by Schloff Chemical formed a "plume," or discernible body of contaminants, that has migrated beneath Minnehaha Creek and joined with the TCA plume, created by Control Data's releases, on the Control Data site. It is now impossible to discern one plume from the other.

In April of 1988, Control Data entered into a consent decree with the MPCA that required it to investigate, monitor, and clean up the contamination. Pursuant to this agreement, Control Data has installed a remediation system which removes both the TCA and the PERC contaminants concurrently. This cleanup is ongoing and will proceed for an undetermined period of time.

Control Data brought this lawsuit in order to recover a portion of the costs it incurred as a result of the PERC contamination on its site. The District Court found that the Schloff defendants were all liable under CERCLA because they were responsible for releasing hazardous substances into the environment, and that release had caused Control Data to incur response costs. Important to the District Court's reasoning was its finding that PERC is more toxic and more difficult to clean up than TCA. Since the remediation system was designed and constructed around the need to clean up PERC, the release of PERC created additional response costs.

This greater level of toxicity was also central in the District Court's allocation of liability. Though the Schloff defendants were responsible for only 10 percent of the contamination on the site, the District Court allocated 33 1/3 percent of the cost of cleanup to them. It did so because PERC is more toxic, and thus more harmful and difficult to remove, than TCA. * * * [Attorneys' fees were also recovered under MERLA but not under CERCLA.]

II.   CERCLA Framework

We begin our discussion, as we must, with the language of the statute.

Recovery of response costs by aprivate party under CERCLA is a two-step process. Initially, a plaintiff must prove that the defendant is liable under CERCLA. Once that is accomplished, the defendant's share of liability is apportioned in an equitable manner.

CERCLA liability is established under 42 U.S.C. § 9607(a). * * * Thus, in order to prove liability, a plaintiff must show that a defendant is within one of the four classes of covered persons enumerated in subsections (1) through (4); that a release |or| threatened release from a facility has occurred; that the plaintiff incurred response costs as a result; and that the costs were necessary and consistent with the national contingency plan.

A problematic portion of this calculus is the causation element. At the outset, we note that CERCLA does not require the plaintiff to prove that the defendant caused actual harm to the environment at the liability stage. Harm to the environment is material only when allocating responsibility as we discuss *infra*. Instead, CERCLA focuses on whether the defendant's release or threatened release caused harm to the plaintiff in the form of response costs. If so, and if the other elements are established, the defendant is liable under CERCLA.

Once liability is established, the focus shifts to allocation. Here, the question is what portion of the plaintiff's response costs will the defendant be responsible for? Allocation is a contribution claim controlled by 42 U.S.C. § 9613(f) (CERCLA § 113(f)). . . .

Courts have considered various factors in resolving contribution claims, see Nagle, CERCLA, Causation, and Responsibility, 78 Minn. L. Rev. 1493, 1522–23, n. 135 (1994), but the "Gore factors," so called after one of the sponsors of CERCLA, are the most widely used. The Gore factors are:

1.   the ability of the parties to demonstrate that their contribution to a discharge, release, or disposal of a hazardous waste can be distinguished;

2. the amount of hazardous waste involved;

3. the degree of toxicity of the hazardous waste;

4. the degree of involvement by the parties in the generation, transportation, treatment, storage, or disposal of the hazardous waste;

5. the degree of care exercised by the parties with respect to the hazardous waste concerned, taking into account the characteristics of such hazardous waste; and

6. the degree of cooperation by the parties with Federal, State, or local officials to prevent any harm to the public health or the environment.

Id. at 1522 n. 133. A primary focus of these factors is the harm that each party causes the environment. Those parties who can show that their contribution to the harm is relatively small in terms of amount of waste, toxicity of the waste, involvement with the waste, and care, stand in a better position to be allocated a smaller portion of response costs.

One primary goal of this private cost-recovery framework is to "encourage timely cleanup of hazardous waste sites," Litton Industrial, 920 F.2d at 1418. Thus, this Court has consistently held that CERCLA is a strict-liability statute, imposing liability without regard to degree of care or motivation for the plaintiff's actions in initiating a cleanup. At the same time, CERCLA seeks "to place the cost of that response on those responsible for creating or maintaining the hazardous condition." Mexico Feed & Seed, 980 F.2d at 486. Therefore, in the allocation phase, harm to the environment and care on the part of the parties plays a more substantial role.

III. The Schloff Defendants' CERCLA Liability

The Schloff defendants argue that they should not be liable under CERCLA for that portion of the response costs which are attributable to the investigation of contamination on the Control Data site. They do not, however, challenge the District Court's determination that they are liable for a share of the cleanup costs. Simply put, the Schloff defendants argue that Control Data's release was the sole cause of the investigation. Thus, because the Schloff defendants' releases had nothing to do with initiating the investigation, they cannot be held liable. In order to accept the Schloff defendants' argument, we would have to hold that CERCLA imposes upon a plaintiff the requirement to prove that each type of response cost was separately caused by the defendant's release. [The court rejected the Schloff, defendants' argument on several grounds and concluding with the following.]

The reasoning of the Supreme Court [in Key Tronic Corp. v. United States, 511 U.S. 809 (1994)] is particularly applicable to the case before us. "Tracking down other responsible solvent polluters increases the probability that a cleanup will be effective and get paid for. Key Tronic is therefore quite right to claim that such efforts significantly benefited the entire cleanup effort apart ... from the reallocation of costs." Key Tronic, 114

S.Ct. at 1967. Likewise, Control Data's efforts to identify all of the contaminants on its property "significantly benefited" the entire effort. Without that effort, the full extent of the contamination, including contamination restricted to the Schloff site not at issue in this case, might not have been discovered and remedied. Perhaps it is fortuitous for Control Data that it happened on to the Schloff defendants' contamination, just as it was fortuitous for Key Tronic to happen on to the Air Force's. Both circumstances are more fortuitous, however, for the environment, which is the primary and decisive factor under CERCLA. We must affirm the judgment of the District Court imposing liability on the Schloff defendants for all response costs, including the costs of investigation.

IV. Allocating Liability

The Schloff defendants challenge the District Court's allocation of one third of the response costs to them when they contributed only 10 percent of the volume of pollution. Their challenge is two-fold, arguing first that insufficient evidence existed to find PERC more toxic than TCA, and second that even if PERC is more toxic, it is an insufficient basis to use to increase liability. We disagree on both points.

CERCLA's allocation scheme "is an equitable determination, in which the district court must make its own factual findings and legal conclusions." We review the District Court's factual findings under a clearly erroneous standard and its applications of law *de novo*.

In this case, the District Court based its finding that PERC is 'a more toxic chemical largely on the MPCA's requirement that it be cleaned up to a level of 7 parts per billion (ppb) existing in the groundwater supply, whereas TCA had to be cleaned up only to a level of 200ppb. Additionally, PERC is a carcinogen, whereas TCA is not. Finally, PERC is the more difficult substance to strip from the airstream in the remediation system. While the Schloff defendants correctly assert that no evidence was adduced from a licensed toxicologist, the evidence which was introduced was more than adequate to justify the District Court's finding that PERC is substantially more toxic than TCA.

The Schloff defendants also argue that toxicity should not be used to increase the allocation of liability without proof of additional costs associated with that toxicity. We first disagree with the assertion that the greater toxicity of PERC did not add to the cleanup costs. The District Court found that the presence of PERC influenced the design and construction of the remediation system, because it is harder to remove and must be removed to a lower level than TCA. The logical conclusion is that it will cost more to remove the pollution related to PERC than it will to remove an equal volume of TCA-related pollution.

In addition, the District Court justified its decision by noting that CERCLA seeks to remedy harm to the environment, and that the more toxic chemical causes the greater harm. We agree. Once again, CERCLA, in the allocation stage, places the costs of response on those responsible for creating the hazardous condition. Allocating responsibility based partially on toxicity does just that because those who release substances that are more toxic are more responsible for the hazardous condition. The District Court was fully justified in increasing the Schloff defendants' responsibility on the basis of toxicity. . . .

NOTES AND QUESTIONS

1. How did the district court apply the Gore factors in the *R.W. Meyer* case? Why was a landlord allocated a 1/3 share in the cleanup costs although it did not contribute any of the wastes to the site? Should such a land owner be allocated part of the cleanup expenses because, after remediation, it will have a better quality industrial site than it had prior to the contamination?

   If, as Judge Bertelsman states in the *R.W. Meyer* case, there is no need for "mathematical precision" or "meticulous findings of the precise causative distribution," how could a PRP ever prove, on appeal, that its allocation in the trial court represented an "abuse of discretion?" With trial courts having such wide discretion, what arguments should or could be made for a PRP to minimize the size of its share of cleanup costs?

2. Beyond the Gore factors, federal courts have identified other equitable considerations which have affected the allocation of cleanup costs in § 113(f) contribution actions. See Kerr–McGee Chemical Corp. v. Lefton Iron & Metal Co., 14 F.3d 321 (7th Cir.1994) (inter-party indemnity agreements) and Weyerhaeuser Corp. v. Koppers Co., 771 F.Supp. 1406 (D.Md.1991) (land owner's acquiescence in the manner of operation and activities of "operator").

3. Although the six Gore factors are commonly recognized in CERCLA apportionment cases, they do not represent the exclusive list of equitable considerations. The equitable discretion mentioned in both the *R.W. Meyer* and the *Control Data* cases is reflected in the far-ranging "fairness" calculations undertaken by trial judges. In Nashua Corp. v. Norton Co., 116 F.Supp.2d 330 (N.D.N.Y.2000), Judge Rosemary Pooler considered the allocation question in a case where the prior owner/operator of a manufacturing plant(Norton) resisted heavy legal liability when the present owner/operator of the facility (Nashua) cleaned up the solvent contamination in the soil and ground water under the plant. Evidence showed that Norton had replaced underground solvent lines yet pollution from the solvents persisted under the plant. After noting that the Second Circuit had not adopted a "mandatory list of factors for consideration," Judge Pooler reasoned as follows,

   I find eight factors relevant. First, by an order of many magnitudes, Norton contributed the major portion of the toxic substances released to the subsurface environment. Second, Norton apparently did nothing before January 1969 to ensure that its underground transfer lines were holding pressure despite the fact that these lines were a readily apparent source for the contamination noted within the Site and in neighboring areas. Third, although Norton's clean-up efforts may have been state-of-the-art at the time, they were largely ineffective. Fourth, Norton did not disclose its massive leaks at the time of sale [to Nashua]. Fifth, both Nashua and Norton are or have been owners of the Site. Sixth, Nashua contributed a very minor portion of the contamination at the Site. Seventh, upon discovering a significant amount toluene in the Empire B–1 boring, Nashua did not immediately undertake clean-up efforts or notify appropriate environmental authorities. Eighth, since notification by the EPA in 1989, Nashua's response has been appropriate. Based on these circumstances, I apportion both past response costs and future response costs 90 percent to Norton and 10 percent to Nashua.... These percentage allocations apply to all past and future response costs in compliance with the NCP. Nashua's attorney's fees for this litigation are not recoverable under CERCLA.

Id. at 352. How does the *Nashua* case's equitable factors compare with those used in the *R.W. Meyer* and *Control Data* decisions. To what extent does a comparison of relative fault come into play in the court's exercise of equitable discretion? Fault can also be found in the adequacy of the response once contamination has occurred. For example, in United States v. DiBiase, 45 F.3d 541 (1st Cir.1995), a land owner was allocated a 15 percent share of cleanup expenses even though it stopped the disposal of sewage sludge and placed gates on the entrance to the property. Reviewing and confirming this allocation the First Circuit wrote,

Despite being warned of a potentially dangerous condition, he twiddled his thumbs; he failed to safeguard the Site, thus permitting third parties to dump at will and exacerbate an already perilous situation; fiddled while the earthen berms deteriorated; and turned a blind eye to evolving public health and safety concerns. Allocating 15 percent of the historic removal costs as appellant's share seems commensurate with these shortcomings and with the quantum of comparative fault fairly ascribable to him.

Id. at 545.

4. In a contribution action, should it matter what kind of PRPs are involved in the allocation? Analyzing numerous allocation cases, one commentator has developed the following table of key factors used in cases involving particular types of PRPs.

Allocation	**Key Factors Include**
1) Successive Owners or Operators	(i) respective degree of involvement at the site; (ii) time spent on the site; and (iii) degree of care exercised in managing hazardous substances at the site.
2) Owner vs. Operators	(i) relevant contractual provisions between them (including indemnifications or assignments of responsibility); (ii) owner's acquiescence in

Allocation	Key Factors Include
	the operations that caused the problem; (iii) degree of involvement and responsibility for contamination; and (iv) benefits received by the owner or operator.
3) Generator	(i) volume; (ii) toxicity; (iii) degree of cooperation with a government agency; and (iv) degree or care.
4) Generators vs. Owner/Operators	(i) degree of involvement; (ii) degree of care; and (iii) cooperation with a government agency

Ridgway M. Hall, Jr. et al., Superfund Manual 4–19 (6th ed. 1997).

H.   EPILOGUE AND CRITIQUE

James T. Hamilton & W. Kip Viscusi, Calculating Risks: The Spatial and Political Dimensions of Hazardous Waste Policy

240–43 (The MIT Press, 1999).

Conclusions

The current policy approach used in the Superfund program is a peculiar halfway house. EPA devotes substantial effort to identifying chemicals at a site and ascertaining their potential risks. It also assesses costs of a range of remedies in considerable detail. However, many key elements are missing in the agency's analysis. There is no explicit consideration of the size of the population at risk in final remediation decisions. Risks to a single individual have the same weight as risks to a large exposed population. Actual and hypothetical exposures to chemicals receive equal weight so that risks to a person who, in the future, may choose to live near a currently uninhabited Superfund site receive the same weight as risks to large populations that are currently involuntarily exposed. EPA also reports the conservative risk assessment value for each site, without focusing its policy attention on the expected risk level or most likely risk scenarios. Finally, explicit trade-offs that balance benefits and costs do not enter remediation decisions. These problems arise in part because of decision-making constraints in the Superfund legislation and in part because of the way regulators have implemented the program.

The cleanup decisions analyzed here were made in 1991 and 1992. Since 1993 the EPA has undertaken three waves of administrative reforms of the Super-fund program, though none of them fully addresses the kinds of issues we have raised. Most of the reforms have focused on more expeditious cleanup efforts rather than incorporation of benefit-cost concerns or the role of exposed populations. According to the agency's 1997 assessment of these reforms, the changes in policy have resulted in a number of program improvements: increased the speed of cleanups so that construction has been completed at 498 NPL sites, authorized potentially responsible parties to conduct or pay for nearly 70 percent of long-term cleanups, taken more than 15,000 small contributors out of the Superfund liability disputes, engineered a reduction in future Superfund costs of over $900 million, and led to the evaluation and archiving of 30,454 sites in the national tracking system for hazardous waste sites. Reforms that focused explicitly on cleanup policies included the creation of a National Remedy Review Board (NRRB) to examine site decisions in order to "promote cost effectiveness and national consistency in remedy selection." the issuance of Guidance on remedy selection rules of thumb, the updating of remedy decisions when new information becomes available, and the ranking of sites based on risk. The agency also began to examine how the risk assessment process could be improved upon, identifying four major areas for improvement and study: "community involvement in the risk assessment process; land use considerations; establishing background for risk assessment purposes; and uncertainty/probabilistic analysis."

These changes may ultimately reduce the transaction costs of the cleanup process, and conceivably may target resources more effectively. Even if fully implemented, however, these changes in policy would not explicitly require the agency to calculate risks on a population basis, present risk estimates to the public based on a variety of parameter assumptions. and make cleanup decisions on the basis of cost-effectiveness considerations such as the cost per cancer case avoided. During the course of our research, which was funded by the agency, we had a series of presentations at the Superfund office and elsewhere at EPA. The officials there had strong beliefs that our policy proposals would require a fundamental shift in EPA policy, which they would not consider in the absence of the passage of regulatory reform legislation or a Superfund reform bill that mandated such an approach. A principal goal of this book is to demonstrate that such fundamental shifts in policy evaluation are feasible and to indicate how such changes will affect cleanup actions and their consequences.

Our data show that the core economic elements of the proposed regulatory reform bills would dramatically alter EPA's policy choices. Put simply, the reforms would require that agency regulations maximize the net gain to society (benefits less costs) using plausible risk assumptions. Sound risk analysis and benefit-cost analysis would force wiser spending and eliminate many of the problems that decrease the overall performance of those potentially desirable regulatory efforts such as hazardous waste cleanup.

Consider how benefit-cost analysis would help one answer how effectively EPA has targeted its expenditures to reduce risks. For the most effective 5 percent of cleanup expenditures, through remediation EPA eliminates 99.47 percent of the cancer risks averted. All expenditures beyond that level will have cleanup costs per discounted case of cancer averted in excess of $140 million. Potentially EPA can generate virtually all the wins in reduced risk at a fraction of the cleanup costs. *At present, 95 percent of the expenditures at Superfund sites are devoted to eliminating only 0.5 percent of the cancer risk*

Under risk assessment and risk management reforms, EPA would assess population risks, rather than simply individual risks, from contamination at Superfund sites. The agency would present central tendency estimates so that analysts could see the range of risks at a site. More flexible remedy decisions based on risk levels rather than ARARs would reduce the costs associated with cleanup goals based on standards from other environmental programs. and costs based on the preference for permanent remedies.

Risk reform is inevitably vulnerable to the fear that it will become a vehicle for ignoring environmental hazards rather than remediating them more efficiently. Our analysis shows, however, that there is a wide zone within which risk reforms can improve efficiency without sacrificing human health considerations. In our analysis the shift toward site cleanups based on risk levels alone—rather than ARARs and calculations that include on-site future residents—would drop the number of sites remediated from 145 to 86 and site expenditures from $2.2 billion to $1.6 billion, but would reduce the number of cancer cases averted by only 21 (from 731 to 710) and the number of individuals protected from noncancer exposures by 16,000 (from 113,000 to 97,000). Our analysis further indicates that calculation of risks based on central tendency would shift a substantial fraction of sites into the cleanup discretionary zone, where EPA site managers currently have the authority to decide whether or not to remediate a site. Removal of preference for permanence would also allow managers to consider more cost-effective alternatives.

The findings for minority populations are perhaps the most telling. Sites that pass a benefit-cost test have a much higher mean minority percentage than the average for the overall set of sites considered. These results help provide an efficiency rationale for the environmental equity movement. If current political pressures lead to neglect of environmental harms in minority communities, as the environmental justice critics note, such communities could benefit from decisions made on the merits of risks. Our data support this: Sites with large minority populations had stronger benefit-cost performance. By focusing on objective measures of risk, benefit-cost analysis will highlight the policy importance of addressing the real risks that minorities may face from hazardous waste sites.

To be more effective, agency risk assessments should include more information—such as calculations of population risks—than they do now. EPA must better document any potentially important natural resource damages, noncancer effects, and synergistic influences. The transaction costs of these new calculations would be vastly offset by the savings afforded by an efficient implementation of the program, not the least of which will be the greater number of lives saved through better targeted policies. Our analysis shows that the government has a tremendous opportunity in the Superfund program both to cut costs and to be more protective of human health. Somewhat paradoxically, EPA's current seemingly uncompromising approach is less protective of life and health than more targeted and balanced policies would be. Real populations now at risk would receive the preference that they should be accorded as compared to hypothetical future populations. At present, EPA has largely succumbed to a variety of irrational biases in terms of how people think about risk as well as to political pressures that force it further away from a cost-effective effort for reducing risk. EPA's neglect of the existence and size of populations now exposed to risk epitomizes the gaps in analytic thinking that could be addressed through a sounder policy analysis approach.

PART IV

POLLUTION CONTROL

INTRODUCTION

In this Part, we consider the complex statutes and regulations that exist to abate degradation of two important environmental media, the air and waters. The term "pollution" is a deceptively difficult concept. One hundred percent pollution abatement is not warranted by economic theory and is seldom required by law. In most situations the policy pursued is a rough balancing of abatement costs and benefits—the real world equivalent of the economist's goal of an optimum level of pollution—which leaves some residual environmental impact.

The two major anti-pollution statutes, the Clean Air Act and the Clean Water Act, are primarily "command and control" regimes under which government prescribes the level of pollution a facility may emit. The standards prescribed are either (1) performance based, setting ambient quality levels, or (2) technology based, depending on technological feasibility.

In recent years, however, statutory and regulatory amendments have sought to emphasize the use of economic incentives and instruments in pollution control, such as cost-benefit analysis, charges, and trading.

CHAPTER TEN

AIR POLLUTION CONTROL

SECTION 1. INTRODUCTION AND OVERVIEW

Air pollution presents one of the most serious environmental problems of the modern age. Rarely does a week pass without some published reference to some aspect of this form of atmospheric contamination. Exposure to polluted air cannot be easily avoided as the lyric from the "American tribal love rock" musical *Hair* states—

Welcome, sulphur dioxide

Hello, carbon monoxide

The air, the air

Is everywhere

Breathe deep

While you sleep

Breathe deep

While air is an indispensable component of human life, individuals generally cannot control the quality of the air they breathe. As Robert Arvill noted,

> [A]n average person requires over thirty pounds of air a day or about six pints every minute, and he has to take it as it comes. He would not readily stand in sewage or drink dirty water. Yet daily the individual draws 26,000 breaths, between 18 and 22 each minute, many of which—if not all in some cases—are of filthy air.

R. Arvill, *Man and Environment* 97 (1967). In recent years the condition of the air quality in urban, suburban, and rural areas of our nation has become an important public issue. Improving the nation's air has become an aspect of public policy that in actuality is directed at a number of related sub-issues. These include automobile-created smog, industrial facility pollution, indoor air pollution including residential radon exposures, acid rain, hazardous or toxic air pollutants, and long distance pollutant transport. As is apparent, threats to the quality of the air originate from a variety of sources both natural and manmade. While such naturally polluting events such as volcanoes, fires, and windstorms lie outside the scope of social control, the wide spectrum of human actions that pollute the air has been the subject of governmental regulation.

A. HISTORICAL BACKGROUND

While the problem of air pollution might be considered to be of recent origin, it is worth noting that throughout recorded history authors have identified poor air quality as at least a matter of personal discomfort. In 61 A.D. the Roman philosopher Seneca described his reaction to the condition of the air quality in contemporary Rome in the following terms,

> As soon as I had gotten out of the heavy air of Rome and from the stink of the smoky chimneys thereof, which, being stirred, poured forth whatever pestilential vapors and soot they had enclosed in them, I felt an alteration of my disposition.

The Greek geographer, Strabo, also recognized the danger of toxic industrial air pollution and described a control technique familiar to the modern observer. He noted, "[T]hey build their silver-smelting furnaces with high chimneys, so that the gas from the ore may be carried high into the air, for it is heavy and deadly." Hughes, "Early Greek and Roman Environmentalists" in Historical Ecology—Essays on Environment and Social Change 57 (L. Bilsky ed. 1980). Strabo would find the tall smokestacks of today's copper smelters and coal-fire electric powerplants entirely familiar.

Recent university researchers have identified large scale hemispheric lead pollution occurring during the Greco—Roman civilization. The use of silver coins during the period from 500 B.C. to 300 A.D. caused the emission of lead as a byproduct of the silver smelting process. These airborne lead particles traveled as far as Greenland where they fell and were trapped in the ice sheet. The dramatic increase in the lead levels discovered in ice core samples reflected to researchers an emission rate of 4,000 metric tons of lead per year. Fallout during this period amounted to approximately 15% of all the lead deposited by millions of cars burning leaded gasoline during the 20th century.

Wood and coal burning in England constituted the most significant cause of air pollution during the period prior to the Industrial Revolution. For example, it is reported that in 1157 Eleanor of Aquitaine, wife of King Henry II, found wood burning so "unendurable" that she moved from Tutbury Castle in Nottingham. The English have long been concerned with the products of combustion and they have adopted legal responses in an attempt to control atmospheric pollution. See generally Stern et al., Fundamentals of Air Pollution 4 (2d ed. 1984). Professor Stern has described the early English experience in the following way.

> [In 1273], coal burning was prohibited in London; and in 1306, Edward I issued a royal proclamation enjoining the use of "seacoal" in furnaces. Elizabeth I barred the burning of coal in London when Parliament was in session. The repeated necessity for such royal action would seem to indicate that coal continued to be burned despite these edicts. By 1661 the pollution of London had become bad enough to prompt John Evelyn to submit a brochure entitled "Fumifugium, or the Inconvenience of the Aer, and Smoake of London Dissipated (together with some remedies humbly proposed)" to King Charles II and Parliament.

See Stern supra at 3–5. Evelyn actually proposed an innovative solution involving locational and meteorological principles. He proposed to move all industry to the leeward side of the City of London and plant sweet smelling and aromatic flowers and trees in the city. Kennedy & Porter, Air Pollution: Its Control and Abatement, 8 Vand.L.Rev. 854 (1955).

With the growth of industry during the 1700s and 1800s air pollution increased in England due to the accelerating use of coal as an industrial fuel and also because of the development of new chemical processes. Coal powered the engines of steam locomotives and ships while continuing to serve as a common urban home heating fuel. The smoke, ash, odors and acidic wastes created by these combustion activities prompted Parliament as early as 1819 to appoint a series of investigating committees and later to adopt legislation aimed at controlling these polluting activities. The Public Health Acts of 1848, 1866, and 1875 confirmed the English approach to smoke and ash abatement as a matter for local public health authorities. Curiously English legislation during this period treated the developing chemical industry as a target for separate and specialized administrative control. In 1863 Parliament enacted the Alkali Act which authorized a newly established Alkali Inspectorate to regulate specified chemical facilities. Since this effort began in the nineteenth century, English statutory/administrative air pollution control law has considerably developed. See D. Hughes, Environmental Law 285 (1986). During this same period the English courts also granted abatement remedies and damages for air polluting conduct under the common law theory of private nuisance in a number of cases. Id.

B. THE AMERICAN EXPERIENCE

The arrival of the European colonists in North America had an irreversible impact upon many environmental resources including the quality of the air. However, air quality in pre-colonial America was not perfect. The daily activities of Native Americans had localized effects upon the nature of the atmosphere. More importantly, natural sources of air pollution served to make the quality of North American air less than pristine. The number and variety of these natural pollution sources is surprising and includes (1) volcanic eruptions, (2) accidental forest and prairie fires, (3) dust storms, (4) ocean emission of aerosols, (5) green plant emission of volatile organics and pollens, and (6) sulfurous releases from hot springs. The patterns of European settlement and the introduction of new manufacturing technologies would soon worsen pre-existing natural conditions. See R. Nash, Wilderness and the American Mind 23–55 (3d ed. 1982) and W. Cronon, Changes in the Land: Indians, Colonists, and the Ecology of New England (1983).

During the American colonial period concerns about noxious air pollution manifested themselves in early town planning and public nuisance regulations. Often objectionable activities were physically separated from residential and commercial areas as much for fire safety reasons as for concern over smoke pollution. Later in the nineteenth century cities increasingly exercised their governmental police powers by adopting local ordinances regulating or prohibiting a broad array of social and economic activities. Included within this exercise of governmental power were efforts to abate public nuisances. Air pollution, while not a *per se* nuisance at common law, was often found to adversely affect the public interest and therefore was a proper source for overall local control. The principal 19th and early 20th century air pollution problem resulted from the burning of coal in industrial and residential activities, with bituminous being the worst offender. During this period little or no state effort was expended upon air pollution control.

While litigation challenged numerous aspects of local government public nuisance regulation, the regulatory practice was generally upheld. See 7 E. McQuillin, The Law of Municipal Corporations §§ 24.495–.503 (3d Ed.Rev.1981). As early as 1859 the city of New Orleans' ordinance regulating "dense smoke" was upheld against charges of vagueness and unreasonableness. New Orleans v. Lambert, 14 La.Ann. 247 (1859). Furthermore, the constitutionality of smoke abatement ordinances was firmly established as against 14th Amendment due process and equal protection challenges by the U.S. Supreme Court in 1916. In Northwestern Laundry v. Des Moines, 239 U.S. 486 (1916), while validating the Des Moines ordinance, the Court held that,

> [t]he state may by itself or through authorized municipalities declare the emission of dense smoke in cities or populous neighborhoods a nuisance and subject to restraint as such; and that the harshness of such legislation, or its effect upon business interests, short of a merely arbitrary enactment, are not valid constitutional objections. Nor is there any valid federal constitutional objection in the fact that the regulation may require the discontinuance of the use of property or subject the occupant to large expense in complying with the terms of the law or ordinance.

Id. at 491. However, not all municipal ordinances were upheld. See City of St. Louis v. Heitzeberg Packing and Provision Co., 141 Mo. 375, 42 S.W. 954 (1897). Through the period of the late nineteenth century and early twentieth century, "smoke abatement" was considered to be a municipal function but the regulatory approach employed was not integrated into a coordinated system of uniform pollution control. In fact, the need for reducing industrial emissions was not a uniformly held value. Some industrial cities, like Pittsburgh, Pennsylvania, prided themselves for their polluted environment as a reflection of the material prosperity that existed within the jurisdiction.

C.   THE COMMON LAW AND AIR POLLUTION

While serious governmental intervention for the improvement of air quality would not occur until the second half of the twentieth century, the common law provided a mechanism for the control of pollution in individual cases. The common law also provided both private civil remedies and public criminal penalties for air polluting acts. Common law trespass theory was occasionally used to support civil actions against a neighbor's pollution if (1) it interfered with the right of exclusive possession to the plaintiff's land and (2) the pollution was the direct result of an act committed by the defendant. D. Dobbs, R. Keeton, & D. Owen, Prosser and Keeton on the Law of Torts 67 (5th ed. 1985). A major limitation to the use of this common law approach to pollution abatement was the absence of a physical trespassory invasion in many smoke, gas or noise cases. A more availing remedial theory was that of nuisance, both public and private.

Common law actions based upon nuisance and trespass have not been very effective tools in combating air pollution. The problems posed by bringing such actions may be seen in the case of Chicago v. Commonwealth Edison Co., 24 Ill.App.3d 624, 321 N.E.2d 412 (1974), a case in which the City of Chicago attempted to enjoin an electric generating facility on the grounds that it was a public nuisance:

> A public nuisance is an unreasonable interference with a right common to the general public. Earlier cases recognized that the public had a right to clean, unpolluted air and that any deprivation of that right was actionable as a private injury and indictable as a public wrong. However, the notion of pure air has come to mean clean air consistent with the character of the locality and the attending circumstances. Whether smoke, odors, dust or gaseous fumes constitute a nuisance depends on the peculiar facts presented by each case. As a result of industrial expansion, the courts have utilized several factors in determining whether an industrial operation is an unreasonable interference with the right to clean air. One of those factors is the extent of injury or harm incurred to the public health, safety, peace or comfort. Another is a comparison of the operation's methods or effects to proscribed standards outlined by applicable federal, state, or local regulations. A third factor is the suitability of the industry's location. A fourth factor involves balancing the gravity of the harm done to the public against the utility of the defendant's business to the community as a whole.

> Courts of equity have traditionally been reluctant to enjoin an industrial operation unless it is clearly and satisfactorily proven to be a nuisance. If the right to relief is doubtful, either as to the law or under the facts presented, equitable relief will not usually be granted.

> The City has failed to answer the threshold question of whether Edison's Indiana facility causes substantial harm so as to constitute an actionable invasion of a public right. In order to be entitled to injunctive relief, a substantial harm or injury must be clearly demonstrated. Edison's Indiana facility is located in a highly industrialized area. The character of the locality necessitates that unpleasant odors, smoke and film will exist. These conditions in an industrial area have generally not been considered to be public nuisances.

Compare Reserve Mining Co. v. E.P.A., 514 F.2d 492 (8th Cir.1975), in which the court upheld a claim of public nuisance where asbestos fibers were being discharged in violation of Minnesota's air quality standards and there was a severe health danger to people living nearby.

It is notable, however, that nuisance and trespass theories continue to be relied upon by courts in a variety of air pollution situations. See e.g. National Audubon Society v. Department of Water, 858 F.2d 1409 (9th Cir.1988) (public and private nuisance theories used to abate mud and dust created by reliction in Mono Lake); Galaxy Carpet Mills, Inc. v. Massengill, 255 Ga. 360, 338 S.E.2d 428 (1986) (carpet dying plant's coal fired boilers may be a nuisance even though a state operating permit issued); Baker v. Burbank–Glendale–Pasadena Airport Authority, 39 Cal.3d 862, 218 Cal. Rptr. 293, 705 P.2d 866 (1985) (airport noise nuisance case); and Bradley v. American Smelting & Refining Co., 104 Wn.2d 677, 709 P.2d 782 (1985) (copper smelter trespass and nuisance case where arsenic and cadmium particulates interfere with exclusive possession).

As you read the materials which follow consider the following questions. (1) Is it possible to maintain an action based upon the federal common law of nuisance or has this been preempted by the Clean Air Act? See United States v. Kin–Buc, Inc., 532 F.Supp. 699 (D.N.J.1982). (2) What effect does the Clean Air Act have on cases filed under the theory of state common law nuisance or trespass? See § 304(e) [§ 7604(e)]. (3) Does compliance with federal or state regulatory requirements act as a bar to common law nuisance or trespass action? See Galaxy Carpet Mills, Inc. v. Massengill, supra. How should a common law system of liability fit into a highly developed system of federal regulation?

D.   AIR QUALITY DATA

1.   NATIONAL AIR QUALITY AND EMISSIONS DATA

America has come a long way in the improvement of its air quality. Viewing the twentieth century in its entirety puts things in perspective. Between 1900 and 1970, emissions of the six principal air pollutants, mentioned below, increased dramatically, For example, estimated emissions of nitrogen oxides (NO_x) increased 690%, volatile organic compounds increased 260%, and sulfur dioxide increased 210%. In 1970, Congress enacted the Clean Air Act and over the decade of the 1970's EPA started to implement its provisions. In the current political environment so critical of government environmental regulation, frequently used rhetoric would lead the casual observer to concluded that the nation's effort to control air pollution during the last 30 years has been ineffective and wasteful. But what is really happening? Is progress being made? While broad national statistics may obscure local conditions, a partial answer to these questions can be derived from EPA's annual Air Quality and Emission Trends data. What follows provides one measurement of the nation's progress in improving its air quality since the passage of the Clean Air Act.

EPA tracks six principal air pollutants across the nation: 1) Carbon Monoxide (CO), 2) Lead (Pb), 3) Nitrogen Dioxide (NO_2), 4) Ozone (O_3)—formed by volatile organic compounds (VOCs) and nitrogen oxides (NO_x), 5)

Particulate Matter (PM), and 6) Sulfur Dioxide (SO_2). Overall, national air quality levels measured at thousands of monitoring stations across the country have shown improvement over the past 20 years for all six pollutants. These monitors are operated by state, tribal and local government agencies as well as some federal agencies including EPA. They sample pollutant concentrations in the ambient or outside air. Despite this progress, more than 150 million tons of air pollution were released into the air in 1999 and approximately 62 million Americans live in counties where monitoring data indicates an unhealthy air quality for one or more of the six principal pollutants.

Percent Change In Ambient Pollutant Concentrations

	1980-1999	1990-1999
CO	−57	−36
Pb	−94	−60
NO_2	−25	−10
O_3 1-hr	−20	−4
8-hr	−12	no change
PM_{10}	—	−18
SO_2	−50	−36

Percent Change in Emissions

	1980-1999	1990-1999
CO	−22	−7
Pb	−95	−23
NO_X	+1	+2
VOC	−33	−15
PM_{10}	−55	−16
SO_2	−28	−21

Note the trends in the two factors. Generally, the air quality chart shows that the air quality based on air pollutant concentrations has improved over the twenty year period with the most substantial national, air quality improvements being registered for Lead (94%), Carbon Monoxide (57%), and Sulfur Dioxide (50%). A comparison with the emissions of these pollutants also reveals a twenty year reduction in pollution emissions with the exception of NO_x which have actually increased 1 percent over the last 20 years and 2 percent during the decade of the 1990's. It should be apparent that ambient air quality does not share a linear correlation with nationwide air pollution emissions. EPA explains this discrepancy in the following way:

Because most monitors are located in or near urban areas, air quality trends are affected by urban emissions which are sometimes different than nationwide emissions. Year-to-year air quality trends can also be affected by atmospheric conditions and other factors.

It is important to note that these reported emission reductions have occurred during a period of substantial social and economic growth in America. Some numbers put this into proper perspective. Between 1970 and 1999, U.S. population increased 33%, vehicles miles traveled increased 140%, and gross domestic product increased 147%. With this expansion in population, energy use and production, the emission reductions obtained following the adoption of the Clean Air Act programs reveal a significant measure of success in the U.S. air pollution control program. In addition, beginning in the early 1990's, estimated emissions of 188 hazardous air pollutants began a gradual decline following the 1990 CAA amendments. Ironically, with all of this environmental progress over the last three decades, much of the American public does not perceive the improvement— in fact, they believe just the opposite. On Earth Day, 2000 it was reported that Americans were pessimistic about environmental conditions and they believed that the conditions were deteriorating.

> "In March [2000], Environmental Defense (formerly the Environmental Defense Fund) commissioned an Earth Day poll. A clear majority of the 1,000 adults surveyed, 57 percent, said that U.S. environmental conditions are worse today than 30 years ago; 67 percent agreed that "Despite the Clean Air Act and Water Act, air and water pollution seem to continue to get worse." "Younger people were even gloomier than older people."

Jonathan Rauch, *There's Smog in the Air, But It Isn't All Pollution,* Wash. Post, April 30, 2000, at B1. Perhaps this popular misperception can be relied upon to secure public support for future air pollution controls made necessary by the continually expanding American population and changing lifestyle. Hopefully, this concern can be focused upon the global environmental problems such as extinction and biodiversity, depleted stratospheric ozone, urban sprawl, rain forest destruction and global warming.

2.   ESTABLISHING AN AIR POLLUTION YARDSTICK: THE AIR QUALITY INDEX (AQI)

The data presented above provides a view of national air pollution conditions yet it does not reflect local or regional conditions. In an analogy with politics, all air pollution is local. EPA has provided another way to assess trends in metropolitan air pollution conditions in the U.S. by way of the Air Quality Index or AQI. This information, presented in a clear and easily-accessible format, allows a person to evaluate the air pollution situation where they live.

EPA Trends Report—Chapter 3 Criteria Pollutants— Metropolitan Area Trends 59–63 (1998)

The Air Quality Index.

The Air Quality Index (AQI) provides information on pollutant concentrations for ground-level ozone, particulate matter, carbon monoxide, sulfur dioxide, and nitrogen dioxide. The AQI is "normalized" across pollutants so that an AQI value of 100 represents the level of health protection associated with the national health-based standard for each pollutant and an AQI value of 500 represents the level at which the pollutant causes significant harm. This Index has been adopted internationally and is used around the world to provide the public with information on air pollutants.

EPA has revised its Air Quality Index to enhance the public's understanding of air pollution across the nation. Previously known as the Pollutant Standards Index (PSI), this uniform air quality index is used by state and local agencies for reporting on daily air quality to the public. The revised Index can also serve as a basis for programs that encourage the public to take action to reduce air pollution on days when levels are projected to be of concern to local communities. A new national Internet website, AIRNOW (www.epa.gov/airnow), which includes "real time" air quality data and forecasts of summertime smog levels in many states, uses the AQI categories, colors, and descriptors to communicate information about air quality.

AQI values are derived from pollutant concentrations. They are reported daily in all MSAs of the United States with populations exceeding 350,000. The AQI is reported as a value between zero and 500 and a descriptive name (e.g., "unhealthy for sensitive groups") and is featured on local television or radio news programs and in newspapers.

Based on the short-term NAAQS, Federal Episode Criteria, and Significant Harm Levels for each pollutant, the AQI is computed for PM_{10}, SO_2, CO, O_3, and NO_2. Lead is the only criteria pollutant not included in the index because it does not have a short-term NAAQS, a Federal Episode Criteria, or a Significant Harm Level.

The AQI integrates information on criteria pollutant concentrations across an entire monitoring network into a single number that represents the worst daily air quality experienced in an urban area. For each of the criteria pollutants, concentrations are converted into an index value between zero and 500. The pollutant with the highest index value is reported as the AQI for that day. Therefore, the AQI does not take into account the possible adverse effects associated with combinations of pollutants (i.e., synergism).

An AQI value greater than 100 indicates that at least one criteria pollutant (NO_2 has no short-term standard) exceeded the level of the standard, therefore, designating air quality to be in the "unhealthy for sensitive groups" range on that day. Relatively high AQI values activate public health warnings. For example, an AQI above 200 initiates a First Stage Alert at which time sensitive populations (e.g., the elderly and persons with respiratory illnesses) are advised to remain indoors and reduce physical activity. An AQI over 300 initiates a Second Stage Alert at which time the general public is advised to avoid outdoor activity.

When air quality is "unhealthy for sensitive groups," EPA has added a corresponding requirement to report a pollutant-specific statement indicating what specific groups in the population are most at risk. For example, when the AQI is above 100 for ozone the AQI report will contain the statement "Children and people with asthma are the groups most at risk." Some Examples of Air Pollution Trends in Twenty Selected U.S. Metropolitan Statistical Areas (MSAs) 1990–1999.

Table 6–2.   Number of Days with AQI Values Greater Than 100, 1990–1999.

MSA	# of trend sites	1990	1991	1992	1993	1994	1995	1996	1997	1998	1999
Akron, OH	5	9	30	8	10	8	12	11	6	14	20
Albuquerque, NM	21	8	5	0	0	1	0	0	0	0	1
Atlanta, GA	10	42	23	20	36	15	35	25	31	50	61
Bakersfield, CA	8	99	113	100	97	98	105	109	55	76	88
Boston, MA	24	7	13	9	6	10	8	2	8	7	5
Chicago, IL	45	4	22	4	3	8	21	6	9	7	12
Denver, CO	22	9	6	11	3	1	2	0	0	5	1
Detroit, MI	29	11	28	8	5	11	14	13	12	17	15
Fresno, CA	12	62	83	69	59	55	61	70	75	67	81
Honolulu, HI	10	0	0	0	0	0	0	0	0	0	0
Houston, TX	23	51	36	32	28	38	66	26	47	38	50
Los Angeles–Long Beach, CA	38	173	168	175	134	139	113	94	60	56	27
Miami, FL	12	1	1	3	6	1	2	1	3	8	5
Minneapolis, MN	20	4	2	1	0	2	5	0	0	1	0
Nashville, TN	16	29	12	6	18	21	26	22	20	30	33
New York, NY	29	36	49	10	19	21	19	15	23	17	24
Raleigh–Durham-Ch. Hill, NC	5	15	5	0	11	2	1	1	13	21	26
Riverside–San Bernardino, CA	36	159	154	174	168	149	124	119	105	95	93
Tampa, FL	26	6	1	2	1	3	2	3	4	11	9
Washington, DC	40	25	48	14	52	20	29	18	29	47	39

EPA National Air Quality and Emission Trends Report, 1999 Table A–18.

SECTION 2.   AIR QUALITY CRITERIA AND STANDARDS UNDER THE CLEAN AIR ACT

A.   THE IDEA OF AIR QUALITY STANDARDS UNDER THE CLEAN AIR ACT

A significant question to be considered at the beginning of the study of the federal Clean Air Act is "what is air pollution?" If government shall intervene to improve environmental conditions, we must understand the harm that such action seeks to cure. How should we define the subject of what has become a massive regulatory effort? A number of perplexing questions confront our initial approach to this subject. Think about each of these questions from the multiple perspectives of all groups affected by air pollution regulation. Should air pollution be thought of as any human alteration of the natural atmosphere? What is the "natural" atmosphere and what are the impurities worthy of control? Can we ignore substances that are introduced into the air by natural forces such as volcanos and high winds? Should air pollution be defined identically in every state or must there be local or regional designations of unacceptable air? Is air pollution an immutable, unchanging condition or is the term to be redefined over a period of time?

Consider each of these questions and suggest alternative approaches to the basic definitional question of what constitutes air pollution. What values and interests should guide the policy discussion surrounding this determination? What kinds of information would be helpful in addressing this threshold issue? As an initial step read sections 108 and 109 [§§ 7408 & 7409] of the Clean Air Act and try to explain the federal policy and procedure for deciding the nature of air pollution.

CLASS DISCUSSION PROBLEM: REGULATING AIR POLLUTANT CARBON TRIOXIDE (CO_3)

The American Heart and Lung Association (AHLA) is a nonprofit organization dedicated to medical research in the area of pulmonary and cardiovascular health. For many years it has funded scientific studies to examine and determine the correlation, if any, between human exposure to air contaminants and the occurrence of adverse health effects. During the 1970's and 1980's, the AHLA has also been active in educating the public about the health risks associated with air pollution.

Assume that you are the legal counsel to the AHLA and that you have learned that over the last two years research has been funded to investigate the potential health effects of long-term exposure to several airborne gases including carbon trioxide (CO_3). These studies have collected information from a variety of sources, including workplace and non-occupational exposure data, and have concluded that long-term inhalation of carbon trioxide (CO_3), at a range of levels, is positively associated with a significantly increased incidence of lung disease. Further inquiry has also disclosed that CO_3 is present, in varying concentrations, in the air over much of the United States. Although there is no unanimous scientific opinion on the subject, most researchers believe that CO_3 results from the incomplete combustion of organic materials. In fact, the highest CO_3 readings have been detected in six metropolitan areas where home woodstoves are widely in use. With the expected increase in fossil fuel prices, the AHLA technical staff has told you that woodstove home heating will likely become more prevalent with a resultant elevation of CO_3 concentrations in the air.

As legal counsel for AHLA you have been asked to consider whether and how CO_3 can be regulated as an air pollutant under the Clean Air Act. Consider the following questions in conjunction with the materials that follow.

1) What authority does EPA have under the CAA to establish air quality standards for a substance such as CO_3? What procedure must EPA follow in setting such a standard? See CAA §§ 108 & 109 [§ 7408 & 7409]. Are there other possibilities? What are the implications of EPA's listing of CO_3 under § 108(a)(1)? What is the connection between listing an air pollutant, issuing an air quality criterion for it under § 108(a)(2), and setting national primary and secondary air quality standards under § 109?

2) If you were the EPA official in charge of establishing new air quality standards, what factors must you consider under §§ 108 and 109 of the CAA in deciding whether to establish an NAAQS for CO_3? How would considerations of the cost of complying with any new CO_3 NAAQS affect your judgment? How would you organize the task of deciding whether or not to issue an NAAQS for CO_3?

3) If EPA refuses to take any action under its §§ 108 & 109 Clean Air Act authorities to regulate CO_3, can it be compelled by AHLA petition or by lawsuit? Would it be any different if a "weak" NAAQS existed for CO_3 and the AHLA wished to have it strengthened?

4) If EPA declined to list CO_3 or set an NAAQS for it under § 109, could AHLA prevail upon a single state or group of states to set air quality standards for CO_3?

B. THE NATIONAL AMBIENT AIR QUALITY STANDARD (NAAQS) CONCEPT UNDER THE CLEAN AIR ACT

1. NATIONWIDE AIR QUALITY STANDARDS

The Clean Air Act of 1970 established the concept of the National Ambient Air Quality Standard (NAAQS) as a central idea and organizing principle of the federal scheme of air pollution control. As the material in the chapter will reveal, the Clean Air Act sets the achievement of the NAAQS as an ultimate regulatory goal and a principal measure of programmatic success. This section of the chapter will focus upon the air quality standard idea. Each component of the term "NAAQS" must be briefly examined.

First, these standards were intended to be national in application and therefore deny regional variation. Under this premise, achievement of the essential Clean Air Act policy would occur when the air in both Los Angeles and North Dakota would at least be as clean as the NAAQS required. This position stood in contrast to the air quality standards authorized under the 1967 air pollution statute.

Second, these standards applied to the quality of the ambient or outdoor air and consequently were not concerned with the condition of air quality within buildings. This issue of impure indoor air has subsequently become the target of increased attention of the public and regulatory agencies and will be discussed later in the chapter.

Third, the NAAQS was designed as an air quality standard and not as a "performance standard" directly applicable to individual pollution sources. The drafters of this statute determined that the Environmental Protection Agency would set environmental standards for designated air pollutants at safe, socially acceptable concentrations. Consequently, the statutory emphasis was on a NAAQS designed to define air pollution from a human perspective. Section 109(b) [§ 7409(b)] requires EPA to establish "primary ambient air quality standards" necessary for the protection of public health and "secondary" standards for the protection of the public welfare. The primary standards are not only expected to protect public health but also to provide "an adequate margin of safety." The secondary standards were intended to protect the "general welfare." With the 1990 amendments this distinction has little meaning since a geographic area can be declared in "non-attainment" status if it violates either primary or secondary standards.

Fourth, the attainment of these air quality standards must occur by a statutorily defined target date. Designing a regulatory system with such a time constraint was believed necessary to convert the NAAQS from aspiration goals into reality. However, by enacting a program that sought the attainment of the initial NAAQS by the mid–1970's, Congress seriously underestimated the complexity and the impact of the task.

2. THE PROCESS OF SETTING NATIONAL AMBIENT AIR QUALITY STANDARDS

The main purpose of the Clean Air Act is to "protect and enhance the quality of the Nation's air resources." Although the act attaches a great deal of importance to the NAAQS, the statute does not by its own terms set forth air pollution concentration levels. Instead, it directs EPA to establish these important air quality standards by way of an administrative rulemaking process. EPA has taken the position that when setting or revising an NAAQS it should evaluate 1) the nature and severity of the health effects caused by the pollutant, 2) the types of health evidence that it has before it,

3) the nature and extent of uncertainty in the regulatory calculation and 4) the size and nature of the sensitive population at risk from the air pollutant. In sections 108 and 109 the Clean Air Act instructs EPA to set primary and secondary national ambient air quality standards for any air pollutant which has an adverse impact on the public health or welfare. The primary standards are intended to protect public health while the secondary standards must "specify a level of air quality that attainment and maintenance of which * * * [will] protect the public welfare from any known or anticipated adverse effects associated with the presence of such air pollutant in the ambient air." Clean Air Act § 109(b)(1). This secondary standard is quite expansive and could reach adverse effects to soils, water, crops, vegetation, animals, manmade materials, weather, visibility, or climate. Every five years both the section 108 criteria and the section 109 NAAQS must be reviewed and revised when appropriate.

The NAAQSs restrict allowable concentrations of air pollutants. Under the CAA. EPA must set these standards when, in the EPA's judgment, a pollutant can "cause or contribute to air pollution which may reasonably be anticipated to endanger public health or welfare" and it is emitted "from numerous or diverse" stationary or mobile sources. The NAAQS development is to be preceded by an agency information gathering exercise that is to culminate in the formal "listing" of the serious air pollutants and then within 12 months of the issuance of "air quality criteria" for that particular pollutant. The Lead Industries Assn. v. EPA, 647 F.2d 1130, 1136 (D.C.Cir.1980), explained this process;

> Section 108 makes it clear that the term "air quality criteria" means something different from the conventional meaning of "criterion;" such "criteria" do not constitute "standards" or "guidelines," but rather refer to a document to be prepared by EPA which is to provide the scientific basis for promulgation of air quality standards for the pollutant.

During the 1970s EPA adopted NAAQS for a total of six air pollutants: sulphur dioxide (SO_2), photochemical ozone (O_3), hydrocarbons, carbon monoxide (CO), lead (Pb), nitrogen dioxide (NO_2), and particulate matter (PM_{10}). Hydrocarbons were delisted in 1983 but a subcategory, reactive hydrocarbons continue to be regulated as chemical precursors to the formation of O_3. Oddly enough, for all air pollutants except (SO_2), EPA has set the primary and secondary NAAQS at exactly the same level. Why do you suppose that EPA refused to set two levels of increasing stringent ambient air quality standards?

3.   THE NATIONAL AMBIENT AIR QUALITY STANDARDS (NAAQS)

All of the NAAQS can be found at 40 C.F.R. Part 50. This three page statement of air quality standards underplays the critical importance of the NAAQS to the entire Clean Air Act effort. Following this brief section are a series of technical appendices (A through K) which set forth the methods for determining the precise measurement of air quality conditions. The NAAQS are expressed in terms of two elements: (a) concentration (micrograms per cubic meter or parts per million) and (b) averaging time (1, 3, 8, 24 hour, quarterly, or annual basis). What is the practical difference between setting an air quality standard for a hypothetical pollutant at 100 ug/m$_3$ measured on a one hour versus an annual average? The following chart summarizes the status of the NAAQS. Notice the presence of both long and short term standards for most pollutants.

NATIONAL AMBIENT AIR QUALITY STANDARDS (NAAQS)

POLLUTANT	PRIMARY (HEALTH RELATED)		SECONDARY (WELFARE RELATED)	
	AVERAGING TIME	STANDARD LEVEL CONCENTRATION[a]	AVERAGING TIME	CONCENTRATION
TSP[b]	Annual Geometric Mean	75 ug/m^3		
PM$_{10}$[c]	Annual Arithmetic Mean	50 ug/m^3	Same as Primary	
	24–hour	150 ug/m^3	Same as Primary	
SO$_3$	Annual Arithmetic Mean	(0.03 ppm) 80 ug/m^{3}s	3–hour	1300 ug/m^3 (0.50 ppm)
	24–hour	(0.14 ppm) 365 ug/m^3		
CO	8–hour	9 ppm (10 ug/m^3)	No Secondary Standard	
	1–hour	35 ppm (40 ug/m^3)	No Secondary Standard	
NO$_2$	Annual Arithmetic Mean	0.053 ppm (100 ug/m^3)	Same as Primary	
O$_2$	Maximum Daily 1–hour Average	0.12 ppm[d] (235 ug/m^3)	Same as Primary	
Pb	Maximum Quarterly Average	1.5 ug/m^3	Same as Primary	

[a] Parenthetical value is an approximately equivalent concentration.
[b] TSP was the indicator pollutant for the original particulate matter (PM) standards. This standard has been replaced with the new PM$_{10}$ standard and it is no longer in effect.
[c] New PM standards were promulgated in 1987, using PM$_{10}$ (particles less than 10u in diameter) as the new indicator pollutant. The 24–hour standard is attained when the expected number of days per calendar year above 150 ug/m^3 is equal to or less than 1, as determined in accordance with Appendix K of the PM NAAQS.
[d] The standard is attained when the expected number of days per calendar year with maximum hourly average concentrations above 0.12 ppm is equal to or less than 1, as determined in accordance with Appendix H of the Ozone NAAQS.

The Clean Air Act anticipated that new NAAQS would be issued and existing standards would be revised as updated technical information became available. However, little change has occurred since 1971. EPA has been slow to exercise this standard setting authority. In fact, it added lead to its list of NAAQS in 1978 following prompting from the Second Circuit. See NRDC, Inc. v. Train, 545 F.2d 320 (2d Cir.1976). These lead standards were upheld in Lead Industries Ass'n, Inc. v. EPA, 647 F.2d 1130 (D.C.Cir. 1980). In May, 1996, EPA stated that it would not revise the SO$_2$ NAAQS. This final administrative decision was challenged in an appeal to the D.C. Circuit. In 1998, the appellate court held, in American Lung Ass'n v. EPA, 134 F.3d 388 (D.C.Cir.1998), that EPA had not sufficiently explained its decision not to revise the standard and it remained the matter back to the agency.

4.   THE SOURCES AND EFFECTS OF NAAQS AIR POLLUTANTS

1) Ozone (O_3)

a) *Nature and Sources of the Pollutant*

Ozone occurs naturally in the stratosphere (6 to 30 miles above the surface) and provides a protective layer insulating living organisms from the harmful effects of ultraviolet radiation from the sun. The ozone NAAQS is not concerned with stratospheric ozone but rather surface or ground level ozone. Ozone is not emitted directly into the air but is formed by the reaction of VOCs (Volatile Organic Compound) and NO_x in the presence of heat and sunlight. Ground-level ozone forms readily in the atmosphere, usually during hot summer weather. VOCs are emitted from a variety of sources, including motor vehicles, chemical plants, refineries, factories, consumer and commercial products, and other industrial sources. Nitrogen oxides are emitted from motor vehicles, power plants, and other sources of combustion. Changing weather patterns contribute to yearly differences in ozone concentrations from region to region. Ozone and the precursor pollutants that cause ozone also can be transported into an area from pollution sources found hundreds of miles upwind.

b) *Health and Environmental Effects*

Short-term (1–3 hours) and prolonged (6–8 hours) exposures to ambient ozone have been linked to a number of health effects of concern. For example, increased hospital admissions and emergency room visits for respiratory causes have been associated with ambient ozone exposures. Exposures to ozone can make people more susceptible to respiratory infection, result in lung inflammation, and aggravate pre-existing respiratory diseases such as asthma. Other health effects attributed to ozone exposures include significant decreases in lung function and increased respiratory symptoms such as chest pain and cough. These effects generally occur while individuals are engaged in exertion. Children, active outdoors during the summer when ozone levels are at their highest, are most at risk of experiencing such effects. Other at-risk groups include adults who are active outdoors (e.g., some outdoor workers) and individuals with pre-existing respiratory disease such as asthma and chronic lung disease. In addition, longer-term exposures to moderate levels of ozone present the possibility of irreversible changes in the lung structure which could lead to premature aging of the lungs and worsen chronic respiratory illnesses.

Ozone also affects vegetation and ecosystems, leading to reductions in agricultural and commercial forest yields, reduced growth and survivability of tree seedlings, and increased plant susceptibility to disease, pests, and other environmental stresses (e.g., harsh weather). In long-lived species, these effects may become evident only after several years or even decades, thus having the potential for long-term effects on forest ecosystems. Ground-level ozone damage to the foliage of trees and other plants also can decrease the aesthetic value of ornamental species as well as the natural beauty of our national parks and recreation areas.

2) Particulate Matter

a) *Nature and Sources of the Pollutant*

Particulate matter (PM) is the general term used for a mixture of solid particles and liquid droplets found in the air. Some particles are large or dark enough to be seen as soot or smoke. Others are so small they can be detected only with an electron microscope. $PM_{2.5}$ describes the "fine" particles that are less than or equal to 2.5 micrometers in diameter. In 1997, EPA set new $PM_{2.5}$ NAAQS standards and began to collect monitoring data on ambient concentrations. "Coarse" particles refers to particles greater than 2.5, but less than or equal to 10 micrometers in diameter. PM_{10} refers to all particles less than or equal to 10 micrometers in diameter. Ten micrometers are about one seventh the diameter of human hair. These particles originate from many different stationary and mobile sources as well as from natural sources. Fine particles result from fuel combustion from motor vehicles, power generation, and industrial facilities, as well as from residential fireplaces and wood stoves. Coarse particles are generally emitted from sources such as vehicles traveling on unpaved roads, materials handling, crushing and grinding operations, and windblown dust. Some particles are emitted directly from their sources, such as smokestacks and cars. In other cases, gases such as SO_2 NO_X, and VOCs interact with other compounds in the air to form fine particles. Their chemical and physical compositions vary depending on location, time of year, and weather.

b) *Health and Environmental Effects*

Particulate matter includes both fine and larger coarse particles. When breathed, these particles can accumulate in the respiratory system and are associated with numerous health effects. Exposure to coarse particles is primarily associated with the aggravation of respiratory conditions, such as asthma. Fine particles are most closely associated with such health effects as increased hospital admissions and emergency room visits for heart and lung disease, increased respiratory symptoms and disease, decreased lung function, and even premature death. Sensitive groups that appear to be at greatest risk to such effects include the elderly, individuals with cardiopulmonary disease such as asthma, and children. In addition to health problems, PM is the major cause of reduced visibility in many parts of the United States. Airborne particles also can impact vegetation and ecosystems and can cause damage to paints and building materials.

3) Carbon Monoxide (CO)

a) *Nature and Sources of the Pollutant*

Carbon monoxide (CO) is a colorless, odorless and, at high levels, a poisonous gas, formed when carbon in fuel is not burned completely. It is a component of motor vehicle exhaust, which contributes about 60 percent of all CO emissions nationwide. Non-road vehicles account for the remaining

CO emissions from the transportation sources category. High concentrations of CO generally occur in areas with heavy traffic congestion. In cities, as much as 95 percent of all CO emissions may come from automobile exhaust. Other sources of CO emissions include industrial processes, non-transportation fuel combustion, and natural sources such as wildfires. Peak CO concentrations typically occur during the colder months of the year when CO automotive emissions are greater and nighttime inversion conditions (where air pollutants are trapped near the ground beneath a layer of warm air) are more frequent.

b) *Health and Environmental Effects*

Carbon monoxide enters the bloodstream through the lungs and reduces oxygen delivery to the body's organs and tissues. The health threat from lower levels of CO is most serious for those who suffer from cardiovascular disease, such as angina pectoris. At much higher levels of exposure, CO can be poisonous, and even healthy individuals may be affected. Visual impairment, reduced work capacity, reduced manual dexterity, poor learning ability, and difficulty in performing complex tasks are all associated with exposure to elevated CO levels.

4) Lead (Pb)

a) *Nature and Sources of the Pollutant*

In the past, automotive sources were the major contributor of lead emissions to the atmosphere. As a result of EPA's regulatory efforts to reduce the content of lead in gasoline, the contribution from the transportation sector has declined over the past decade. Today, industrial processes, primarily metals processing, are the major source of lead emissions to the atmosphere. The highest air concentrations of lead are found in the vicinity of nonferrous and ferrous smelters, and battery manufacturers.

b) *Health and Environmental Effects*

Exposure to lead occurs mainly through inhalation of air and ingestion of lead in food, water, soil, or dust. It accumulates in the blood, bones, and soft tissues. Lead can adversely affect the kidneys, liver, nervous system, and other organs. Excessive exposure to lead may cause neurological impairments such as seizures, mental retardation, and behavioral disorders. Even at low doses, lead exposure is associated with damage to the nervous systems of fetuses and young children, resulting in learning deficits and lowered IQ. Recent studies also show that lead may be a factor in high blood pressure and subsequent heart disease. Lead can also be deposited on the leaves of plants, presenting a hazard to grazing animals.

5) Nitrogen Dioxide (NO$_2$)

a) *Nature and Sources of the Pollutant*

Nitrogen dioxide (NO$_2$) is a reddish brown, highly reactive gas that is formed in the ambient air through the oxidation of nitric oxide (NO). Nitrogen oxides (NO$_X$), the term used to describe the sum of NO, NO$_2$ and other oxides of nitrogen, play a major role in the formation of ozone, particulate matter, and acid rain. The major sources of man-made NO_X emissions are high-temperature combustion processes, such as those occurring in automobiles and power plants. Home heaters and gas stoves also produce substantial amounts of NO_2 in indoor settings.

b) *Health and Environmental Effects*

Short-term exposures (e.g., less than 3 hours) to low levels of nitrogen dioxide (NO_2) may lead to changes in airway responsiveness and lung function in individuals with pre-existing respiratory illnesses and increases in respiratory illnesses in children (5–12 years old). Long-term exposures to NO_2 may lead to increased susceptibility to respiratory infection and may cause permanent alterations in the lung. Nitrogen oxides react in the air to form ground-level ozone and fine particle pollution which are both associated with adverse health effects.

Nitrogen oxides contribute to a wide range of environmental effects, including the formation of acid rain and potential changes in the composition and competition of some species of vegetation in wetland and terrestrial systems, visibility impairment, acidification of freshwater bodies, eutrophication (i.e., excessive algae growth leading to a depletion of oxygen in the water) of estuarine and coastal waters (e.g., Chesapeake Bay), and increases in levels of toxins harmful to fish and other aquatic life.

6) Sulfur Dioxide (SO_2)

a) *Nature and Sources of the Pollutant*

Sulfur dioxide belongs to the family of sulfur oxide gases. These gases are formed when fuel containing sulfur (mainly coal and oil) is burned and during metal smelting and other industrial processes. Most SO_2 monitoring stations are located in urban areas. The highest monitored concentrations of SO_2 are recorded in the vicinity of large industrial facilities. Fuel combustion, largely from coal fired power plants, accounts for most of the total SO_2 emissions.

b) *Health and Environmental Effects*

High concentrations of SO_2 can result in temporary breathing impairment for asthmatic children and adults who are active outdoors. Short-term exposures of asthmatic individuals to elevated SO_2 levels while at moderate exertion may result in breathing difficulties that may be accompanied by such symptoms as wheezing, chest tightness, or shortness of breath. Other effects that have been associated with longer-term exposures to high concentrations of SO_2 in conjunction with high levels of PM, include respiratory illness, alterations in the lungs' defenses, and aggravation of existing cardiovascular disease. The subgroups of the population that may be affected under these conditions include individuals with cardiovascular disease or chronic lung disease, as well as children and the elderly.

Together, SO_2 and NO_X are the major precursors to acidic deposition (acid rain), which is associated with the acidification of soils, lakes, and streams, accelerated corrosion of buildings and monuments. Sulfur dioxide also is a major precursor to $PM_{2.5}$, which is a significant health concern as well as a main pollutant that impairs visibility.

Excerpts from the Clean Air Act

42 U.S.C. §§ 7408–09.

§ 108.   (a)(1) For the purpose of establishing national primary and secondary ambient air quality standards, the Administrator shall within 30 days after the date of enactment of the Clean Air Amendments of 1970 publish, and shall from time to time thereafter revise, a list which includes each air pollutant—

   (A) emissions of which, in his judgment, cause or contribute to air pollution which may reasonably be anticipated to endanger public health or welfare;

   (B) the presence of which in the ambient air results from numerous or diverse mobile or stationary sources; and

   (C) for which air quality criteria had not been issued before the date of enactment of the Clean Air Amendments of 1970, but for which he plans to issue air quality criteria under this section.

(2) The Administrator shall issue air quality criteria for an air pollutant within 12 months after he has included such pollutant in a list under paragraph (1). Air quality criteria for an air pollutant shall accurately reflect the latest scientific knowledge useful in indicating the kind and extent of all identifiable effects on public health or welfare which may be expected from the presence of such pollutant in the ambient air, in varying quantities. The criteria for an air pollutant, to the extent practicable, shall include information on—

   (A) those variable factors (including atmospheric conditions) which of themselves or in combination with other factors may alter the effects on public health or welfare of such air pollutant;

   (B) the types of air pollutants which, when present in the atmosphere, may interact with such pollutant to produce an adverse effect on public health or welfare; and

   (C) any known or anticipated adverse effects on welfare.

(b)(1) Simultaneously with the issuance of criteria under subsection (a), the Administrator shall, after consultation with appropriate advisory committees and Federal departments and agencies, issue to the States and appropriate air pollution control agencies information on air pollution control techniques, which information shall include data relating to the cost of installation and operation, energy requirements, emission reduction benefits, and environmental impact of the emission control technology. Such information shall include such data as are available on available technology and alternative methods of prevention and control of air pollution. Such information shall also include data on alternative fuels, processes, and operating methods which will result in elimination or significant reduction of emissions.

(2) In order to assist in the development of information on pollution control techniques, the Administrator may establish a standing consulting committee for each air pollutant included in a list published pursuant to subsection (a)(1) which shall be comprised of technically qualified individuals representative of State and local governments, industry, and the economic community. Each such committee shall submit, as appropriate, to the Administrator information related to that required by paragraph (1).

(c) The Administrator shall from time to time review, and, as appropriate, modify, and reissue any criteria or information on control techniques issued pursuant to this section. Not later than six months after the date of the enactment of the Clean Air Act amendments of 1977, the Administrator shall revise and reissue criteria relating to concentrations of NO 2 over such period (not more than three hours) as he deems appropriate. Such criteria shall include a discussion of nitric and nitrous acids, nitrites, nitrates, nitrosamines, and other carcinogenic and potentially carcinogenic derivatives of oxides of nitrogen.

(d) The issuance of air quality criteria and information on air pollution control techniques shall be announced in the Federal Register and copies shall be made available to the general public.

§ 109.   (a)(1) The Administrator—

   (A) within 30 days after the date of enactment of the Clean Air Amendments of 1970, shall publish proposed regulations prescribing a national primary ambient air quality standard and a national secondary ambient air quality standard for each air pollutant for which air quality criteria have been issued prior to such date of enactment; and

   (B) after a reasonable time for interested persons to submit written comments thereon (but no later than 90 days after the initial publication of such proposed standards) shall by regulation promulgate such proposed national primary and secondary ambient air quality standards with such modifications as he deems appropriate.

(2) With respect to any air pollutant for which air quality criteria are issued after the date of enactment of the Clean Air Amendments of 1970, the Administrator shall publish, simultaneously with the issuance of such criteria and information, proposed national primary and secondary ambient air quality standards for any such pollutant. The procedure provided for in paragraph (1)(B) of this subsection shall apply to the promulgation of such standards.

(b)(1) National primary ambient air quality standards, prescribed, under subsection (a) shall be ambient air quality standards the attainment and maintenance of which in the judgment of the Administrator, based on such criteria and allowing an adequate margin of safety, are requisite to protect the public health. Such primary standards may be revised in the same manner as promulgated.

(2) Any national secondary ambient air quality standard prescribed, under subsection (a) shall specify a level of air quality the attainment and maintenance of which in the judgment of the Administrator, based on such criteria, is requisite to protect the public welfare from any known or anticipated adverse effects associated with the presence of such air pollutant in the ambient air. Such secondary standards may be revised in the same manner as promulgated.

(c) The Administrator shall, not later than one year after the date of the enactment of the Clean Air Act Amendments of 1977, promulgate a national primary ambient air quality standard for NO 2 concentrations over a period of not more than 3 hours unless, based on the criteria issued under section 108(c), he finds that there is no significant evidence that such a standard for such a period is requisite to protect public health.

(d)(1) Not later than December 31, 1980, and at five-year intervals thereafter, the Administrator shall complete a thorough review of the criteria published under section 108 and the national ambient air quality standards promulgated under this section and shall make such revisions in such criteria and standards and promulgate such new standards as may be appropriate in accordance with section 108 and subsection (b) of this section. The Administrator may review and revise criteria or promulgate new standards earlier or more frequently than required under this paragraph.

(2)(A) The Administrator shall appoint an independent scientific review committee composed of seven members including at least one member of the National Academy of Sciences, one physician, and one person representing State air pollution control agencies.

(B) Not later than January 1, 1980, and at five-year intervals thereafter, the committee referred to in subparagraph (A) shall complete a review of the criteria published under section 108 and the national primary and secondary ambient air quality standards promulgated under this section and shall recommend to the Administrator any new national ambient air quality standards and revisions of existing criteria and standards as may be appropriate under section 108 and subsection (b) of this section.

(C) Such committee shall also (i) advise the Administrator of areas in which additional knowledge is required to appraise the adequacy and basis of existing, new, or revised national ambient air quality standards, (ii) describe the research efforts necessary to provide the required information, (iii) advise the Administrator on the relative contribution to air pollution concentrations of natural as well as anthropogenic activity, and (iv) advise the Administrator of any adverse public health, welfare, social, economic, or energy effects which may result from various strategies for attainment and maintenance of such national ambient air quality standards.

C.   Revising the National Ambient Air Quality Standards

American Lung Association v. Environmental Protection Agency

United States Court of Appeals, District of Columbia Circuit, 1998.
134 F.3d 388.

■ Tatel, Circuit Judge.

On behalf of the nation's nearly nine million asthmatics, the American Lung Association and the Environmental Defense Fund challenge the Environmental Protection Agency's refusal to revise the primary national ambient air quality standards for sulfur dioxide (SO_2). Declining to promulgate a more stringent national standard, the EPA Administrator concluded that the substantial physical effects experienced by some asthmatics from exposure to short-term, high level SO_2 bursts do not amount to a public health problem. Because the Administrator failed adequately to explain this conclusion, we remand for further elucidation.I

Driven by its "deep concern for protection of the health of the American people," Sen. Rep. No. 91–1196, at 1 (1970) ("Senate Report"), Congress enacted the Clean Air Act Amendments of 1970, Pub.L. No. 91–604, 84 Stat. 1676 (1970) (codified as amended at 42 U.S.C. §§ 7401–7671q (1994)), mandating a "massive attack on air pollution," Senate Report at 1. As amended, the Clean Air Act erects a comprehensive system of national ambient air quality standards ("NAAQS") to regulate health-threatening air pollutants. The statute defines primary NAAQS as "ambient air quality standards the attainment and maintenance of which in the judgment of the Administrator, based on such criteria and allowing an adequate margin of safety, are requisite to protect the public health." 42 U.S.C. § 7409(b)(1).

Once the EPA Administrator concludes that a pollutant "may reasonably be anticipated to endanger public health or welfare" and that it comes from "numerous or diverse mobile or stationary sources," *id.* § 7408(a)(1)(A)–(B), the Act requires the Administrator to produce "criteria," defined as the latest scientific data on "all identifiable effects on public health" caused by that pollutant. *Id.* § 7408(a)(2). Based on these comprehensive criteria and taking account of the "preventative" and "precautionary" nature of the act, Legal Industries Ass'n, Inc. v. EPA, 647 F.2d 1130, 1155 (D.C.Cir.1980), the Administrator must then decide what margin of safety will protect the public health from the pollutant's adverse effects—not just known adverse effects, but those of scientific uncertainty or that "research has not yet uncovered." *Id.* at 1153. Then, and without reference to cost or technological feasibility, the Administrator must promulgate national standards that limit emissions sufficiently to establish that margin of safety. See 42 U.S.C. § 7409(b)(1); States bear primary responsibility for attaining, maintaining, and enforcing these standards. See 42 U.S.C. § 7410.

In its effort to reduce air pollution, Congress defined public health broadly. NAAQS must protect not only average healthy individuals, but also "sensitive citizens"—children, for example, or people with asthma, emphysema, or other conditions rendering them particularly vulnerable to air pollution. If a pollutant adversely affects the health of these sensitive individuals, EPA must strengthen the entire national standard. *Lead Industries,* 647 F.2d at 1153 (NAAQS "must be set at a level at which there is 'an absence of adverse effect' on [ ] sensitive individuals") (quoting SENATE REPORT at 10).

Sulfur Dioxide and Asthmatics

A highly reactive colorless gas smelling like rotten eggs, sulfur dioxide derives primarily from fossil fuel combustion. Best known for causing "acid rain," at elevated concentrations in the ambient air, SO_2 also directly impairs human health. As the Administrator explains in the Final Decision on review here, SO_2 can affect healthy nonasthmatic individuals at concentrations above 2.0 parts per million ("ppm"); below 2.0 ppm, it primarily affects people with asthma. National. Ambient Air Quality Standards for Sulfur Oxides (Sulfur Dioxide)—Final Decision, 61 Fed.Reg. 25,566, 25,570 (1996).

Following the passage of the Clean Air Act, EPA promulgated the SO_2 NAAQS in effect today. The primary standards consist of a 24–hour standard (0.14 ppm averaged over 24 hours not to be exceeded more than once a year) and an annual standard (0.03 ppm annual arithmetic mean). *Id.* at 25,568. EPA also established a "secondary" three-hour standard (0.50 ppm averaged over three hours not to be exceeded more than once a year), designed to protect the "public welfare" against non-health-related effects such as visibility impairment or environmental degradation, see 42 U.S.C. § 7409(b)(2). Petitioners do not challenge these existing standards.

Approximately four percent of the nation's population suffers from asthma. Characterized by broncho constriction—shortness of breath, coughing, wheezing, chest tightness, and sputum production—asthma is triggered by many different stimuli, including cold or dry air, exercise or pollen, as well as airborne pollutants. The effects of broncho constriction can vary from short-term discomfort, such as an hour-long reaction with no lasting after-effects, to asthma attacks requiring medication or hospitalization. Although rare, death can result.

Sulfur dioxide induces broncho constriction in asthmatics, but only under certain conditions. To experience adverse effects from SO_2 concentrations below 1.0 ppm, asthmatics must be exposed for five minutes or longer while breathing quickly and heavily through both nose and mouth, the sort of breathing induced by light exercise, shoveling snow, climbing several flights of stairs, or jogging to catch a bus. At concentrations above 2.0 ppm, SO_2 causes adverse effects even if the exposure lasts less than five minutes or the asthmatic breathes regularly. See Second Addendum to Air Quality Criteria for Particulate Matter and Sulfur Oxides (1982): Assessment of Newly Available Health Effects Information (1986).

The Challenged Final Decision

This case concerns the effect on asthmatics of what are known as high-level SO_2 bursts, defined as emissions of 0.50 ppm or more lasting at least five minutes. Occurring sporadically and from specific sources, SO_2 bursts come primarily from power utilities; the rest come from non-utility sources such as industrial boilers, petroleum refineries, pulp and paper mills, sulfuric acid plants, and aluminum smelters.

Citing the health concerns of asthmatics and relying on a 1977 amendment to the Clean Air Act, in which Congress ordered the Agency to review and revise all criteria and NAAQS by 1980 and at five-year intervals thereafter, 42 U.S.C. § 7409(d), petitioners urged EPA to issue a new NAAQS limiting short-term SO_2 bursts. Not until 1996, after petitioners sued twice to compel a decision . . . , and after two rounds of public notice and comment, did EPA issue its final decision regarding SO_2 NAAQS. . . . Rejecting petitioners' arguments, EPA concluded not only that. the annual and 24-hour primary standards needed no revision, but also that an addition al five-minute standard was unnecessary to protect asthmatics. See Final Decision at 25,575–76.

In arriving at her final decision, the Administrator reviewed a decade of data on the extent of high-level short-term SO_2 bursts and their effects on public health. . . . Based on clinical studies of mild to moderate asthmatics, she found that when such individuals breathe rapidly while exposed to SO_2 concentrations of 0.60 ppm for five minutes, "substantial percentages ($\geq$ 25 percent)" experience effects "distinctly exceeding [the] typical daily variation in lung function," that asthmatics routinely experience. Final Decision at 25,572. The severity of these atypical effects, she found, "is likely to be of sufficient concern to cause disruption of ongoing activities, use of bronchodilator medication, and/or possible seeking of medical attention." *Id.*

The scientific community disagreed about the medical significance of these effects and whether they should be considered "ad verse." Some experts took the position that such symptoms usually have no lasting impact, amounting at worst to a brief period of reversible discomfort; others argued that even a one-hour disruption of activity can amount to a worrisome adverse health effect. The Administrator left this dispute unresolved. Instead, she discerned in the medical debate a consensus, which she adopted, that "*repeated* occurrences of such effects should be regarded as significant from a public health standpoint." *Id.* at 25,573 (emphasis added).

The Administrator then discussed the three exposure analyses on which the 1994 version of the proposed rule rested. These studies estimated that from 180,000 to 395,000 "exposure events"—defined as a heavily breathing asthmatic exposed to an SO_2 burst—occur annually, affecting from 68,000 to 166,000 asthmatic individuals. *Id.* at 25,374. In view of the Administrator's previous finding, reiterated by agency counsel at oral argument, that at least 25 percent of asthmatics experience atypical effects from exposure events, these data suggest that as many as 41,500 ($\geq$ 25 percent of 166,000) asthmatics experience atypical effects from repeated SO_2 bursts each year. At the same time, the Administrator acknowledged that subsequent industry studies of four non-utility sources suggest that the 1994 studies may have overestimated exposure for certain SO_2 sources, *id.*, meaning that the number of affected asthmatics could be lower. The Administrator did not resolve the conflict between the studies.

Armed with all these data, the Administrator concluded that "the likelihood that asthmatic individuals will be exposed ... is very low when viewed from a national perspective," that "5–minute peak SO_2 levels do not pose a broad public health problem when viewed from a national perspective," and that "short-term peak concentrations of SO_2 do not constitute the type of ubiquitous public health problem for which establishing a NAAQS would be appropriate." *Id.* at 25,575. Describing SO_2 bursts as "localized, infrequent and site-specific," she concluded that a new national standard was unnecessary. *Id.* The Administrator nevertheless decided to encourage individual states to address short-term high-level SO_2 emissions, initiating a rulemaking to provide appropriate guidance. . . .

Petitioners now challenge the Administrator's decision declining to promulgate a new NAAQS. They assert that by failing to establish a five-minute NAAQS capping SO_2 emissions at 0.60 ppm, EPA has violated its statutory responsibility to protect the public health. We review the Administrator's decision pursuant to 42 U.S.C. § 7607(d)(9)(A)–(C) ("[C]ourt may reverse any such [agency] action found to be ... arbitrary, capricious, an abuse of discretion, or otherwise not in accordance with law; ... [or] in excess of statutory ... authority, or limitations. . . .").

II

Petitioners challenge much of the data the Administrator relied on, as well as the conclusions she drew. Generally speaking, we will not second-guess EPA in its area of special expertise. . . . Applying this deferential standard of review, we accept the Administrator's analysis of the exposure studies in the record, as well as the implication of her analysis—that thousands of asthmatics can be expected to react atypically to SO_2 bursts each year.

Petitioners contend that the Administrator's analysis amounts to a conclusive finding that SO_2 bursts adversely affect asthmatics' health, thus triggering her duty to promulgate a new NAAQS. . . . At oral argument, counsel for EPA vigorously disputed petitioners' contention that the Administrator "found" an adverse health effect. As we read the record, agency counsel appears to be correct: The Administrator did not decide whether asthmatic reaction to SO_2 bursts—"disruption of ongoing activities, use of bronchodilator medication, and/or possible seeking of medical attention"—amounts to an adverse health effect or merely, as some medical experts argued, run-of-the-mill asthma symptoms indistinguishable from bronchodilation due to cold air or exercise. Final Decision at 25,572–73. Skipping this disputed question, the Administrator concluded that, regardless of the impact of single occurrences, "repeated occurrences of such effects should be regarded as significant from a public health standpoint." *Id.* at 25,573.

Disagreeing with this approach, petitioners argue that the Administrator *had* to answer the subsidiary "adverse effects" question, pointing to her warning to all states in the subsequent rulemaking that "[a]lthough these episodes are few, it is clear that 5–minute SO_2 ambient concentration peaks pose a health threat to sensitive exposed populations," Proposed State Guidelines Rulemaking at 211. We need not decide that issue at this time, however, because we think the Administrator has failed to explain the answer she did give, *i.e.*, that SO_2 bursts do not amount to a "public health" problem within the meaning of the Act. The link between this conclusion and the factual record as interpreted by EPA—that "repeated" exposure is "significant" and that thousands of asthmatics are exposed more than once a year—is missing. Why is the fact that thousands of asthmatics can be expected to suffer atypical physical effects from repeated five-minute bursts of high-level sulfur dioxide not a public health problem? Why are from 180,000 to 395,000 annual "exposure events" (the range indicated by the 1994 studies) or some fewer number (as suggested by the industry studies) so "infrequent" as to warrant no regulatory action? Why are disruptions of ongoing activities, use of medication, and hospitalization not "adverse health effects" for asthmatics? Answers to these questions appear nowhere in the administrative record.

In her only statement resembling an explanation for her conclusion that peak SO_2 bursts present no public health hazard, the Administrator characterizes the bursts as "localized, infrequent and site-specific." Final Decision at 25,575. But nothing in the Final Decision explains away the possibility that "localized," "site-specific" or even "infrequent" events might nevertheless create a public health problem, particularly since, in some sense, all pollution is local and site-specific, whether spewing from the tailpipes of millions of cars or a few offending smoke stacks. From the record, we know that at least six communities experience "repeated high 5–minute peaks greater than 0.60 ppm SO_2," *id.*, and agency counsel told us at oral argument that these so-called "hot spots" are not the only places where repeated exposure occurs. Nowhere, however, does the Administrator explain why these data amount to no more than a "local" problem.

Without answers to these questions, the Administrator cannot fulfill her responsibility under the Clean Air Act to establish NAAQS "requisite to protect the public health," 42 U.S.C. § 7409(b)(1), nor can we review her decision. Judicial deference to decisions of administrative agencies like EPA rests on the fundamental premise that agencies engage in reasoned decision-making.... With its delicate balance of thorough record scrutiny and deference to agency expertise, judicial review can occur only when agencies explain their decisions with precision, for "[i]t will not do for a court to be compelled to guess at the theory underlying the agency's action...." SEC v. Chenery Corp., 332 U.S. at 196–97, 67 S.Ct. at 1577. Where, as here, Congress has delegated to an administrative agency the critical task of assessing the public health and the power to make decisions of national import in which individuals' lives and welfare hang in the balance, that agency has the heaviest of obligations to explain and expose every step of its reasoning. For these compelling reasons, we have always required the Administrator to "cogently explain why [she] has exercised [her] discretion in a given manner." Motor Vehicle Mfrs. Ass'n v. State Farm Mut. Auto. Ins., 463 U.S. 29, 48, 103 S.Ct. 2856, 2869, 77 L.Ed.2d 443 (1983).

In this case, the Administrator may well be within her authority to decide that 41,500 or some smaller number of exposed asthmatics do not amount to a public health problem warranting national protective regulation, or that three or six or twelve annual exposures present no cause for medical concern. But unless she describes the standard under which she has arrived at this conclusion, supported by a "[ ]plausible" explanation, *id.* at 43, 103 S.Ct. at 2866–67, we have no basis for exercising our responsibility to determine whether her decision is "arbitrary, capricious, an abuse of discretion, or otherwise not in accordance with law; . . . [or] in excess of statutory . . . authority, or limitations . . ." 42 U.S.C. § 7607(d)(9)(A)–(C).

Given the gaps in the Final Decision's reasoning, we must remand this case to permit the Administrator to explain her conclusions more fully. We therefore need not resolve the debate between the parties over whether the Clean Air Act authorizes the Administrator to decline to protect an identifiable group of asthmatics from a known adverse health effect. Although our cases make clear that the Administrator has broad discretion to establish an "adequate margin of safety" above and beyond what scientific certainty prescribes and to craft regulations that protect against unknown harms, see Lead Industries, 647 F.2d at 1153–55 (Administrator must "err on the side of caution" when establishing the margin of safety, even where the "medical significance [of the effects] is a matter of disagreement"), they do not necessarily establish the converse proposition—that the Administrator may decline to establish a margin of safety in the face of documented adverse health effects. Since in this case the Administrator has failed adequately to explain her conclusion that no public health threat exists, we can leave the issue of the scope of her authority for another day.

We remand this case to the agency for further proceedings consistent with this opinion.

So ordered

NOTE ON THE REVISIONS OF THE NAAQS

Under § 109(d), EPA is required to re-evaluate the adequacy of the air quality criteria and standards at least every five years in order to keep them consistent with the most current technical data. EPA has been reluctant to frequently change theses fundamental air quality standards and this reluctance has resulted in litigation. In Environmental Defense Fund v. Thomas, 870 F.2d 892 (2d Cir.1989), EPA was sued by environmental groups and states for failing to revise the SO$_x$ NAAQS. EPA has been sued with a degree of regularity over this statutory duty. Other cases have pushed for revisions of other NAAQS. In this case EPA confronted a demand to revise the SO_2 NAAQS and the court concluded that while the decision of whether to revise an air quality standard was discretionary with EPA, that after modifying the air quality criteria the agency must make some decision regarding the revision and that decision would be reviewable. See e.g., American Lung Ass'n v. EPA, 884 F.Supp. 345 (D.Ariz.1994) (particulate standard); American Lung Ass'n v. EPA, 144 F.R.D. 622 (E.D.N.Y.1992) (ozone standard); and NRDC v. Train, 545 F.2d 320 (2d Cir.1976) (lead standard). In certain situations, EPA has reviewed air quality criteria for certain NAAQS and concluded that revisions were not appropriate or required further study. The courts have largely deferred to EPA's administrative judgment as long as EPA gives an explanation for its regulatory conclusion—either to act or not to act. Also, the agency's decision cannot be found irrational or contrary to the CAA. The *American Lung Association* case provides a good example. This legal jousting will continue as long as EPA and interest groups disagree on the meaning of air pollution data. In what circumstances would an environmental or public health group successfully convince EPA or a court that a new or revised NAAQS should be set? But what if EPA refuses to do anything except continue funding research and "considering" regulatory action? What statutory and non-statutory factors might EPA consider when responding to an environmental group's request? Just how much information is necessary to show that an air pollutant may cause an "adverse health effect?"

In July, 1997 EPA promulgated a revised ozone NAAQS that replaced the previously existing 1–hour standard of 0.12 ppm with a new 0.08 ppm primary standard measured over 8 hours. At the same time new particulate NAAQS were also issued for PM_{10} (10 micron particles) and $PM_{2.5}$ (2.5 micron particles). This rulemaking was challenged in American Trucking Ass'n v. EPA, 195 F.3d 4 (D.C.Cir.1999) (per curiam), where the court remanded or vacated the standards. The U.S. Supreme Court ultimately upheld EPA's standard setting.

D. NOTES AND QUESTIONS

1. SCOPE OF THE NATIONAL AMBIENT AIR QUALITY STANDARDS

What could be the subject of a NAAQS? Section 302(g) [§ 7602(g)] of the Clean Air Act defines the term "air pollutant" as, any air pollutant agent or combination of such agents, including any physical, chemical, biological, radioactive (including source material, special nuclear material, and byproduct material) substance or matter which is emitted into or otherwise enters the ambient air. Would CO_3 in the class discussion problem be an "air pollutant" under this definition? This broad definition leaves a number of questions unanswered. Does this definition create a conflict with the regulatory jurisdiction of any other federal agency and if so, how would the conflict be resolved? The 1977 Clean Air Act Amendments added the definitional references in § 302(g) to radioactive materials. However, these amendments also created a new § 122 [§ 7422] which directed EPA consider radioactive pollutants (as well as cadmium, arsenic, and polycyclic organic matter) for regulation under either the NAAQS approach of § 108 or the hazardous air pollutant emission standard of § 112. Why give the agency this choice? What about the Nuclear Regulatory Commission's interest in this matter? Read § 122(c)(1)–(3). Is this interagency power-sharing wise? Compare this relationship to the relationship of EPA and the Department of Transportation under § 231 (pertaining to the establishment of aircraft emission standards). What other methods of interagency action could be designed for these kinds of regulatory tasks?

Could EPA set an NAAQS for heat, odors, light, noise, or microwave radiation? CAA section 108 [§ 7408] states that EPA can list emissions which (1) cause or contribute to air pollution which may reasonably be anticipated to endanger public health or welfare, and (2) are present in the ambient air as a result of discharge from numerous or diverse mobile or stationary sources. Why does the CAA contain these two definitional elements? Could EPA set a § 108 standard for indoor air quality? What other air pollutants might be regulated in this way? In addition, how high does the "ambient air" go? Could EPA issue an NAAQS for air emissions polluting the stratosphere? See § 157 [§ 7457].

2. EPA CONSIDERATION OF COSTS IN SETTING NATIONAL AMBIENT AIR QUALITY STANDARDS

In American Petroleum Institute v. Costle, 665 F.2d 1176 (D.C.Cir. 1981), the Court of Appeals upheld EPA's relaxation of the ozone NAAQS by 50% from .08 parts per million to .12 parts per million on an hourly average for both the primary and the secondary standard. Recall the language of § 109(b)(1) [§ 7409(b)(1)] which states that the primary NAAQS shall be the "standards the attainment and maintenance of which in the judgment of the Administrator, based on such criteria and allowing an adequate margin of safety, are requisite to protect the public health." What about a consideration of the costs of meeting this health protection standard? Can or should EPA take these economic impacts into account when setting a primary NAAQS? What might be the implications of not inserting any economic limit on the creation of a health-based environmental standard?

The Supreme Court interpreted the CAA in Whitman v. American Trucking Ass'n, 531 U.S. 457 (2001) and it left no doubt that the NAAQS setting process was to focus upon public health protection and not costs. Justice Scalia's majority opinion concentrated on the language of the Act to reach his conclusion. He wrote,

> Section 109(b)(1) instructs EPA to set primary air quality standard "the attainment and maintenance of which . . . are requisite to protect the public health" with "an adequate margin of safety." 42 U.S.C. § 7409(b)(1). Were it not for the hundreds of pages of briefing respondents have submitted on the issue, one would have thought it fairly clear that this text does not permit the EPA to consider costs in setting

the standards. The language, as one scholar has noted, "is absolute." D. Currie, Air Pollution—Federal Law and Analysis 4–15 (1981).

531 U.S. at 465. He concluded by writing that, "the text of § 109(b), interpreted in its statutory and historical context and with appreciation for the CAA as a whole, unambiguously bars cost considerations from the NAAQS-setting process, and thus ends the matter for us as well as the EPA." *Id.* at 471. This would seem to end judicial debate on this point.

Does this view entirely exclude a risk-benefit balancing approach? Is it better to insert these economic concerns in the determination of the "adequate margin of safety" or is this even inappropriate or unwise considering the Clean Air Act's mandate? Judge Robb in the *American Petroleum Institute* decision stated that "[w]here the Administrator bases his conclusion as to an adequate margin of safety on a reasoned analysis and evidence of risk, the court will not reverse." 665 F.2d at 1187. Does this kind of judicial sentiment give the agency too much independence or does it merely accord EPA the necessary freedom to make a complex judgment in an area lacking in precise, scientific data? In addition, the technological feasibility of air pollution control is also *not* to be considered in NAAQS setting.

3.   OBTAINING JUDICIAL REVIEW OF AIR QUALITY STANDARDS

How is judicial review of NAAQS obtained in the federal courts? Read Clean Air Act § 307(b) [§ 7607(b)] carefully. This statutory section establishes the ground rules for receiving judicial scrutiny over EPA's conduct in administering the Clean Air Act. Federal jurisdiction to review NAAQS promulgation is lodged solely in the United States Court of Appeals for the District of Columbia and not in any other federal court. Section 307(b)(1) lists a number of other Clean Air Act responsibilities limited to exclusive D.C. Circuit review. Why are these activities relegated to the appellate court in Washington, D.C. for consideration? Notice the range of other EPA actions that may be reviewed in the U.S. Court of Appeals "for the appropriate circuit." Why are these administrative actions better suited to regional appellate review?

In addition, § 307 also confines the opportunity for obtaining judicial review of NAAQS (and all other actions subject to it) to a brief "window of time." It provides that,

> [A]ny petition for review under this subsection shall be filed within sixty days from the date notice of such promulgation, approval, or action appears in the Federal Register, except that if such petition is based solely on grounds arising after the sixtieth day, then any petition for review under this subsection shall be filed within sixty days after such grounds arise.

A 1990 amendment to § 307(b)(1) provides that filing a petition for reconsideration of a final rule or action will not extend the 60 day appeal period nor postpone its effectiveness.

Why would the drafters of the Clean Air Act have inserted this durational limitation on judicial review? While pondering that question consider the purpose of § 307(b)(2) [§ 7607(b)(2)] which adds that "[A]ction of the Administrator with respect to which review could have been obtained under paragraph (1) shall not be subject to judicial review in civil or criminal proceedings for enforcement." Is this provision unreasonable or possibly even unconstitutional?

4.   LIMITS ON CHALLENGES TO PROCEDURAL RULEMAKING DEFECTS

Special procedural safeguards govern a broad range of rulemaking activities under the Act, largely supplanting the general requirements imposed by the Administrative Procedure Act, 5 U.S.C. § 551 et seq. Section 307(d)(1) expressly states that "[T]he provisions of section 553 through 557 and section 706 of Title 5 shall not, except as expressly provided in this subsection, apply to actions to which this subsection applies." Section 307(d) [§ 7607(d)] sets forth specific rulemaking procedures governing EPA Clean Air Act responsibilities yet it also narrowly confines judicial review of procedural irregularity. The statute states that,

> [I]n reviewing alleged procedural errors, the court may invalidate the rule only if the errors were so serious and related to matters of such central relevance to the rule that there is a substantial likelihood that the rule would have been significantly changed if such errors had not been made.

§ 307(d)(8) [§ 7607(d)(8)]. Read this section in conjunction with § 307(d)(9) which establishes judicial grounds for reversing EPA action under the Clean Air Act. Rulemaking may still be found to be invalid as "arbitrary and capricious" but now procedural arbitrariness is defined in part by its effect on the rulemaking end result. The combination of § 307(d)(8) and § 307(d)(9) creates a procedural "harmless error" doctrine limiting the grounds for reversal. Also, § 307(d)(9)(D) requires a challenger raising procedural issues to have participated in the rulemaking process by raising timely objections. For an example of § 307 judicial review consider Union Oil Co. v. United States EPA, 821 F.2d 678, 684 (D.C.Cir.1987) where the court found EPA's failure to include a brief document on lead banking in the rulemaking docket to be harmless error.

What must a reviewing court do when confronted with allegations of administrative impropriety in rulemaking? Will many promulgations of NAAQS or other Clean Air Act regulations be invalidated for procedural error? What impact will such a statutory provision have on the practices of environmental groups and industrial trade organizations as they oversee EPA rulemaking?

5.   FORCING EPA ACTION TO ESTABLISH NAAQS

Can EPA be compelled to list additional criteria pollutants? On what basis? See NRDC, Inc. v. Train, 545 F.2d 320 (2d Cir.1976), requiring EPA to develop ambient air quality standards for lead. In 1978 EPA adopted a lead standard of 1.5 micrograms per cubic meter, maximum arithmetic mean average over the calendar quarter. In Lead Industries Association, Inc. v. EPA, 647 F.2d 1130 (D.C.Cir.1980), this standard was upheld on judicial review. Within the context of the CO_3 problem, how far should AHLA be able to go in compelling EPA to act? What if EPA continued not to act? What else could AHLA do?

SECTION 3. STATE IMPLEMENTATION PLANS UNDER THE CLEAN AIR ACT

A. INTRODUCTION AND OVERVIEW

The establishment of the NAAQS for selected air pollutants does not purify the atmosphere. Congress needed to devise a method for achieving clean air goals that would make the NAAQS a reality. But how should this be done? As the previous discussion indicates, air pollution is caused by a variety of human and natural activities and occurrences and it may be local or regional in its causes and effects. Industrial facilities and motor vehicles all contribute to pollution in a chemically and meteorologically complex way. Who should decide the strategy for attaining and maintaining the NAAQS? What are the arguments, both legal, political and practical, for and against federal control of this daunting task? How would you organize such a centralized system of environmental quality achievement? Assuming that an appropriate governmental entity could be selected, what about the temporal element? When would the NAAQS be attained in practice? Should these standards be achieved by the same deadline in every state and locality or should the more polluted areas be permitted more time to reach these clean air standards?

Think about these problems and the questions posed above. Consider the fact that Congress did not vest exclusive planning or regulatory power in the federal government when it designed the mechanism for attaining the NAAQS and achieving the other significant Clean Air Act policy goals. The declaration of Congressional purpose in the Clean Air Act states that

> air pollution prevention (that is, the reduction or elimination, through any measures, of the amount of pollutants produced or created at the source) and air pollution control at the source is the primary responsibility of states and local governments; and * * * that Federal financial assistance and leadership is essential for the development of cooperative Federal, State, regional, and local programs to prevent and control air pollution.

§ 101(a)(3)–(4) [§ 7401(a)(3)–(4)]. Why would Congress develop federal air pollution policy emphasizing state and local government primacy? The discussion in this section will examine this exercise in cooperative federalism. As you contemplate these materials consider how the organizational structure of the Clean Air Act affects its ability to achieve the ultimate programmatic goals of attaining the NAAQS. How are political considerations built into the system?

State Implementation Plans (SIP) are required by the Clean Air Act, and they combine two major functions related to air pollution control. These two functions are continuously revised and updated over time. *First*, SIPs represent an air quality planning document that assesses the nature of the air quality problem within the state and then determines in general terms the character of improvement in air quality needed to meet or maintain the NAAQS. This assessment phase, therefore, requires a determination of existing air quality conditions and an identification of the pollution or emissions caused by stationary, mobile and other sources. *Second*, the SIP is a regulatory instrument assigning air pollution control responsibilities to the wide variety of sources within the state. The SIP constitutes a package of EPA-approved control strategies and regulations which could include state laws, regulations, transportation controls, emission inventories and local ordinances that are designed to maintain good air quality complying with the NAAQS or to improve poor air quality to bring them into compliance with these standards. Each state submits this collection of techniques to EPA for full or partial approval. The approved SIPs are published and updated as they change in state-by-state subparts of 40 C.F.R Part 52. Once approved by EPA, the SIP is enforceable under both state and federal law as well as by citizen suit.

The states establish their SIPs by way of their own administrative procedure with the Clean Air Act only directing that states adopt SIPs "after reasonable notice and public hearing." § 110(a)(1) [§ 7410(a)(1)]. The Act does not specifically identify the precise kind of procedure which the states must use with most jurisdictions employing a legislative hearing format. Is this fair and does it comply with the Due Process considerations when the SIP sets an emission limitation for one facility? See Anaconda Co. v. Ruckelshaus, 482 F.2d 1301 (10th Cir.1973). Should more adjudicatory procedures be required in that case?

The heart of the SIP concept is found in Clean Air Act § 110(a)(2) [§ 7410(a)(2)]. Section 110(a)(1) requires that within 3 years of the promulgation or revision of any NAAQS each state must, after notice and public hearings, adopt and submit to EPA a plan for the implementation and enforcement of the air quality standard. EPA is charged with the task of reviewing and approving (or disapproving) the SIP or its components. The 1990 Clean Air Act amendments continues pre-existing policy of imposing time limits on the achievement of the NAAQS. However, the required attainment dates vary depending upon whether the area is in attainment (3 or 5 years) or non-attainment (5 to 20 years) status. § 110(n)(2) [§ 7410(n)(2)]. As will become apparent, significant sanctions potentially follow the failure to meet these dates.

Excerpts from the Clean Air Act

42 U.S.C. § 7410(a)(2).

§ 110(a)(2) Each implementation plan submitted by a State under this Act shall be adopted by the State after reasonable notice and public hearing. Each such plan shall—

(A) include enforceable emission limitations and other control measures, means, or techniques (including economic incentives such as fees, marketable permits, and auctions of emissions rights), as well as schedules and timetables for compliance, as may be necessary or appropriate to meet the applicable requirements of this Act;

(B) provide for establishment and operation of appropriate devices, methods, systems, and procedures necessary to—

(i) monitor, compile, and analyze data on ambient air quality, and

(ii) upon request, make such data available to the Administrator;

(C) include a program to provide for the enforcement of the measures described in subparagraph (A), and regulation of the modification and construction of any stationary source within the areas covered by the plan as necessary to assure that national ambient air quality standards are achieved, including a permit program as required in parts C and D [42 USCS §§ 7470 et seq., 7501 et seq.];

(D) contain adequate provisions—

(i) prohibiting, consistent with the provisions of this title, any source or other type of emissions activity within the State from emitting any air pollutant in amounts which will—

(I) contribute significantly to non-attainment in, or interfere with maintenance by, any other State with respect to any such national primary or secondary ambient air quality standard, or

(II) interfere with measures required to be included in the applicable implementation plan for any other State under part C [42 USCS §§ 7470 et seq.] to prevent significant deterioration of air quality or to protect visibility,

(ii) insuring compliance with the applicable requirements of sections 126 and 115 [42 USCS §§ 7426, 7415] (relating to interstate and international pollution abatement);

(E) provide (i) necessary assurances that the State (or, except where the Administrator deems inappropriate, the general purpose local government or governments, or a regional agency designated by the State or general purpose local governments for such purpose) will have adequate personnel, funding, and authority under State (and, as appropriate, local) law to carry out such implementation plan (and is not prohibited by any provision of Federal or State law from carrying out such implementation plan or portion thereof), (ii) requirements that the State comply with the requirements respecting State boards under section 128 [42 USCS § 7428], and (iii) necessary assurances that, where the State has relied on a local or regional government, agency, or instrumentality for the implementation of any plan provision, the State has responsibility for ensuring adequate implementation of such plan provision;

(F) require, as may be prescribed by the Administrator—

(i) the installation, maintenance, and replacement of equipment, and the implementation of other necessary steps, by owners or operators of stationary sources to monitor emissions from such sources,

(ii) periodic reports on the nature and amounts of emissions and emissions-related data from such sources, and

(iii) correlation of such reports by the State agency with any emission limitations or standards established pursuant to this Act, which reports shall be available at reasonable times for public inspection;

(G) provide for authority comparable to that in section 303 [42 USCS § 7603] and adequate contingency plans to implement such authority;

(H) provide for revision of such plan—

(i) from time to time as may be necessary to take account of revisions of such national primary or secondary ambient air quality standard or the availability of improved or more expeditious methods of attaining such standard, and

(ii) except as provided in paragraph (3)(C), whenever the Administrator finds on the basis of information available to the Administrator that the plan is substantially inadequate to attain the national ambient air quality standard which it implements or to otherwise comply with any additional requirements established under this Act;

(I) in the case of a plan or plan revision for an area designated as a nonattainment area, meet the applicable requirements of part D [42 USCS §§ 7501 et seq.] (relating to non-attainment areas);

(J) meet the applicable requirements of section 121 [42 USCS § 7421] (relating to consultation), section 127 [42 USCS § 7427] (relating to public notification), and part C [42 USCS §§ 7470 et seq.] (relating to prevention of significant deterioration of air quality and visibility protection);

(K) provide for—

(i) the performance of such air quality modeling as the Administrator may prescribe for the purpose of predicting the effect on ambient air quality of any emissions of any air pollutant for which the Administrator has established a national ambient air quality standard, and

(ii) the submission, upon request, of data related to such air quality modeling to the Administrator;

(L) require the owner or operator of each major stationary source to pay to the permitting authority, as a condition of any permit required under this Act, a fee sufficient to cover—

(i) the reasonable costs of reviewing and acting upon any application for such a permit, and

(ii) if the owner or operator receives a permit for such source, the reasonable costs of implementing and enforcing the terms and conditions of any such permit (not including any court costs or other costs associated with any enforcement action), until such fee requirement is superseded with respect to such sources by the Administrator's approval of a fee program under title V [42 USCS §§ 7661 et seq.]; and

(M) provide for consultation and participation by local political subdivisions affected by the plan.

CLASS DISCUSSION PROBLEM: DESIGNING THE STATE IMPLEMENTATION PLAN FOR CO_3

Assume that EPA has issued a National Ambient Air Quality Standard (NAAQS) for CO_3 and that it is applicable in your state. The primary standard and the secondary standard have been set at the same level of 2 parts per million (ppm) in the ambient air with one exceedance permitted per year. Suppose further that you are the Director of Air Pollution Programs and it is your responsibility to prepare the State Implementation Plan (SIP) element for CO_3. Preliminary technical information indicates the following:

a.   the state's air quality varies with regard to the concentration of CO_3 and that pollutant is emitted from a range of industrial, automotive and consumer product sources.

b. CO_3 is a relatively immobile air pollutant that once emitted is not transported over great distances.

c.   Only one part of your state (the Jacksontown metropolitan area) is believed to be violating the new CO_3 standard with consistent monitoring data over a three-year period showing readings of 3 ppm on at least 18 days per year. Air Quality Monitoring in the rest of the state indicates CO_3 levels below the NAAQS reflecting general attainment conditions.

d.   Preliminary assessments of CO_3 pollution in your state reveal that *all sources* of CO_3 in the Jacksontown non-attainment area generate a total of 1 million pounds of CO_3 emissions per year.

Consider the following questions related to the facts above.

1.   How would you propose to organize the task of SIP preparation? What kinds of information would you need to complete this task? What kinds of technical assistance may be needed to prepare the CO_3 SIP?

2.   Your staff has proposed a number of CO_3 control strategies around which to structure the SIP. Consider each of the following approaches and evaluate them on the basis of information requirements, the enforceability of provisions, fairness concerns and any other factors you believe are significant.

a.   *Option 1: Linear Relationship Approach.* Since the Jacksontown air quality exceeds attainment of the CO_3 NAAQS by 50% (3 ppm rather than 2 ppm), staff has recommended that the SIP uniformly reduce emissions of CO_3 from all sources by 50%. The methodology to be employed would determine existing CO_3 emission sources, identify their emission rates, and then reduce them equally by 50%. Although applying equally to all CO_3 sources, the strategy would impose the 50% reduction to both state of the art facilities as well as older, largely uncontrolled sources.

b. *Option 2: Computer Dispersion Modeling Approach.* Using site-specific CO_3 emissions data, staff has recommended the use of a computerized mathematical modeling technique that considers source location, elevation, emission rates, meteorological data, and other factors to determine an optimal group of control measures which, if implemented, would result in attainment of the CO_3 standard. Based upon these assumptions, the computer program would allocate emission reduction obligations in a number of optional ways, each demonstrating attainment with the NAAQS.

c. Option 3: *Job Preservation Approach.* Staff has also prepared an option which responds to the requests of labor unions and major manufacturers for protection from costly pollution control requirements that would arguably make their products less competitive on world markets. This approach would consider the impact of a range of proposed CO_3 control measures on existing manufacturing jobs and it would attempt to assign CO_3 emission controls in such a way as to minimize any adverse economic impact on those industrial sources. This strategy would shift control requirements away from large firms emitting CO_3 and impose them more heavily upon firms with fewer employees and also to automobiles and consumer product sources. The main idea underlying this approach would be the insulation of large employers from higher operating costs imposed by the SIP's CO_3 control measures.

d. *Option 4: The "Green" Approach.* Assume that the citizens of your state have demonstrated a high degree of environmental consciousness and they have elected a governor whose platform reflects this sentiment. The governor has instructed your agency to design new air pollution SIP controls that would be the most protective of health of any in the nation. Consequently, staff has proposed the preparation of a CO_3 SIP element which will provide air quality with a CO_3 concentration of no more than 1 ½ ppm (½ ppm *under* the NAAQS). This approach would make the air cleaner but it would also cause more stringent CO_3 regulation than any other option.

3. What if the Jacksontown metropolitan area was projected to experience significant growth pressure over the next decade with population and land development expanding well above the average in the state. How should this information be factored into the development of the SIP?

4. Does the SIP need to make any provision for those areas that currently are in attainment status for CO_3 or must planning and regulatory action be taken only when and if the CO_3 NAAQS is violated?

B. DEVELOPING THE STATE IMPLEMENTATION PLAN

1. OVERVIEW OF SIP DESIGN

The chief legal means for attaining the ambient air quality standards is the state implementation plan (SIP). The following excerpt outlines the development of the SIP device in the law and describes, in a general fashion, the way that the SIP program provides the link between the establishment of the NAAQS and its actual attainment. As such, the SIP serves as the action instrument which translates scientifically derived air quality standards into individual air pollution control regulations. Although this excerpt describes the air quality planning process prior to the 1990 amendments, its general content continues to be an accurate description of all quality planning.

Philip D. Reed, *State Implementation Plans* 11–14.3 to 11–28 in *Law of Environmental Protection*

S. Novick et al., eds. 1995.
Footnotes omitted.

[b]   The Scope and Substance of a SIP

Under the 1970 Acts SIPs were required for all areas. EPA initially focused its attention on areas violating the NAAQS, but was forced to provide detailed guidance for clean areas as well. The thrust of section 110, the SIP section, was on cleaning up areas with more pollution than allowed by the primary NAAQS. All the SIPs had to do for clean areas, EPA concluded, was keep air quality from dropping below the secondary standards. Environmentalists sued and the Supreme Court eventually allowed to stand a district court ruling that the Act's purpose "to protect and enhance" air quality obligated EPA to do more in attainment areas, even though all the substantive provisions of the Act were directed toward enhancement. In response, EPA promulgated prevention of significant deterioration (PSD) rules limiting new sources, which formed the basis of a more complex PSD program established in the 1977 Amendments and subsequently a new set of PSD rules. The attention on attainment areas also resulted in an expanded EPA requirement for air quality maintenance projections and programs for attainment areas. Despite these considerations, most SIP attention focused on non-attainment areas. As such, the programs were like those envisioned by the 1967 Air Quality Act, focusing state regulatory attention on the heavily-polluted AQCRs, but with much stronger pressure on the states to actually develop plans.

Section 110 sets out a list of substantive and procedural requirements for SIPs. As enacted in 1970, the Act envisioned that states would rely on emission limitations for stationary sources, transportation control plans to cut pollution from cars and trucks, and land use control plans to ensure that the siting of new facilities did not jeopardize attainment. The Act gives the states some flexibility, allowing "other measures" as necessary. EPA has interpreted this language to allow a number of alternatives, including economic incentives. The SIP must also provide for necessary source and ambient monitoring, enforcement, and staffing. Under the 1970 Amendments, putting these pieces together for a SIP was a three-step process.

[i]   Defining the Problem

The first step, defining the air quality problem, was begun by determining how much more pollution was in the air than the standards allow. Fifty percent more? A hundred percent more? The state also had to project growth over the next ten years and identify areas projected to exceed the NAAQS in the future as a result. This exercise, performed by checking air quality monitoring data or using models to estimate air quality, told the state how big a job awaited.

The state next had to figure out where the excessive pollution came from. To do so, it made an "inventory" of sources by counting the big ones, such as power plants or smelters, and counting or estimating the number of little ones, like boilers in apartment buildings. Next, the state estimated the amount of emissions from all these sources, using any monitoring data that might be available and estimating the rest with various engineering calculations and rules of thumb.

[ii]   Emission Limitations

Once the pollutants and sources of concern were identified, the states next were to develop control strategies. As noted above, control strategies fall into three categories: emission limits for stationary sources, transportation control plans for motor vehicles, and new source review. The remainder of this section focuses principally on control strategies for existing stationary sources.

Although states are not limited to this strategy, emission limitations have been the basic building block of stationary source control strategies in the first twenty years of implementation. Emission limits typically are set for broad categories of sources. In theory, a state regulatory agency could tailor a package of emission limits for each criteria pollutant and each AQCR, designing the rules to just attain the NAAQS at the lowest aggregate cost. The Agency would have to have reams of data on the cost and feasibility of control at each of the hundreds or thousands of individual sources, however, that data is not readily available. The search for an administratively feasible method of setting emission limits usually leads to uniform standards for broad categories of sources, based on general notions of what is feasible technologically for those sources and not too costly. The broader the category, the easier the process which could follow either of two tracks.

The state might take an aggressive approach, setting the categorical standard at a level associated with highly efficient controls. Flexibility could be built into such a system by allowing the regulated community to make a case for lower standards for subcategories with special technological or economic difficulties during the standard-setting process or by allowing variances for hard-hit individual sources.

An alternative to the aggressive SIP approach was to set the categorical standard at the level of the least common denominator to ensure that it was "reasonable" across the board. So long as the emission reductions resulting from imposition of the standard would produce attainment of the NAAQS, the Act does not dictate either approach. The SIP also may vary the categorical standards from one AQCR to the next, imposing tighter standards where pollution is heaviest.

The 1970 Act could have been interpreted to allow individual source variances from categorical SIP standards only under the exacting standards of section 110(f). EPA, however, read section 110(a)(3) as requiring it to approve any SIP revision, whether for an individual source or an entire category, so long as the change would not cause a violation of the NAAQS. Section 110(f) was, in EPA's view, limited to variances extending beyond the attainment deadline. In one of the pivotal early Clean Air Act cases, the Supreme Court agreed with EPA. The result is a fundamental distinction between the Clean Air Act and the Federal Water Pollution Control Act.

The 1970 Act has been referred to as "technology-forcing." As to existing stationary sources, however, whether and how much to force technology was left largely up to the states. EPA invited a degree of consistency by publishing information on "reasonably available" control technologies for criteria pollutants, but states were free to use other standards. The result of the process has been development of a bewildering variety of stationary source SIP provisions.

Inherent in the concept of an emission limitation is the notion that the amount of pollutants emitted will be limited. Large emission sources cannot avoid violations of the air quality standards by cutting emissions only when meteorological conditions likely will direct the pollution toward air quality monitors or concentrate it under a temperature inversion. Nor may such sources rely on tall smokestacks to disperse pollution.

EPA came to this interpretation slowly. Initially, it deemed tall stacks and intermittent control strategies (ICS) acceptable as emission limitations. While that interpretation was in force (and in the years leading up to the 1970 Amendments) hundreds of powerplants and smelters had been equipped with very tall smokestacks to avoid the high cost of removing sulfur from their flue gas. After having its policy rejected by the courts in 1974, EPA adopted the principle that sources with post–1970 stacks taller than "good engineering practice" would normally dictate must be regulated as though they had shorter stacks, unless tall stacks were the best available technology or where alternative controls (i.e., scrubbers) were "economically unreasonable or technologically unsound." In 1977 Congress tightened the ban on tall stacks further, but the stack height issue was not put to rest.

[iii] Modeling

The last step in the SIP process is to use air quality models to demonstrate that the emission reduction produced by the control strategies will attain and maintain the air quality standards in each AQCR. The analysis also must demonstrate that projected growth will not cause the region to slip out of attainment. Air quality models perform this function. The simplest is the "roll-back" model, which assumes a linear relationship between emission volume and air quality: In simplified form, a 10 percent reduction in aggregate emissions in the AQCR will wipe out a 10 percent violation of the NAAQS. Computerized diffusion models are a more complex alternative. These complicated mathematical models can take into account the relative locations of air quality monitors and major sources, as well as prevailing weather conditions, to provide more precise estimates of the air quality impacts of the control strategies.

If emission limitations, transportation controls, and new source review are SIP building blocks, then air quality modeling is the engineering science that explains how to put them together into a viable structure. Some might argue, however, that modeling is more sorcery than science. Computer modeling is an extremely complex and imprecise tool whose accuracy diminishes with the number of sources, the distance between source and monitor, and the variation in the terrain. The use of modeling in designing and evaluating SIPs is an inviting target for criticism because of its unavoidable imprecision, but the courts generally have recognized that modeling is the only tool EPA and the states have to carry out the air quality analyses required by the Act and have deferred to the agencies' technical expertise on these issues.

The "scientific" approach for translating a general air quality standard into enforceable, source-specific emission limitations is riddled with imprecision. Each calculation requires major assumptions and can be well off the mark. Errors at different stages might cancel each other out, but also could be additive. Moreover, the system is so complex that it is easy to manipulate pieces of it to come up with any desired result. To make it work, EPA had to develop detailed planning and modeling guidance, whose own complexity is a bar to understanding the process and a barrier to innovation.

2. THE STATE IMPLEMENTATION PLAN AS AN AIR QUALITY PLANNING PROCESS

Federal SIP Regulations

In addition to specific directions for SIP development in the CAA, very detailed federal regulations govern state preparation and revision of a SIP. See 40 C.F.R. Part 51. Numerous other guidance documents also exist to aid the states in formulating an approvable SIP. States must demonstrate that they have established adequate legal authority to implement the SIP provisions. Id. at §§ 51.230–51.232. The adoption of specific "control strategies" is required, as described in the Reed excerpt, to attain the necessary emission reductions for NAAQS pollutants. Id. at §§ 51.110–51.119. Under these regulations, the SIPs must describe the control measures that are incorporated into the plan and also the administrative procedures and enforcement methods for each control measure. EPA also provides control technique guidelines or CTGs which provide state and local air pollution authorities with current information on the technology and costs of various emission control techniques. These CTGs can be used to determine reasonable available control techniques for emission sources.

SIP Development in California

In air pollution control terms, there is no place like Southern California. An example of a highly detailed SIP aimed at the reduction of air contaminants in the most heavily polluted area of the nation demonstrates the variety of measures employed for reaching attainment. As an effort to devise a SIP which will ultimately provide for attainment of ozone and carbon monoxide (CO) in Southern California (the South Coast Air Basin), that state's Air Resources Board has submitted a comprehensive and complex SIP which concentrates on the reduction of automotive pollution. The SIP projects attainment of the ozone standard by 2010 and the CO standard no later than by 2004. This plan would immediately impose a range of "core" measures including those dealing with oxygenated fuels, fuel volatility, reformulated fuels, a new car and truck cold CO emission standard, enhanced evaporative emissions controls for gas fueled motor vehicles and additional controls on marine vessel tanks.

However, what if these measures are not enough? Emission reductions can also be found in unconventional sources such as consumer products. For instance, in October, 1999 the California Air Resources Board set VOC standards for 16 categories of consumer products which use hydrocarbons as part of their chemical composition or have an aerosol propellant. These products include hair spray, room air fresheners, insect repellents, laundry pre-wash, oven cleaner, nail polish remover, shaving cream, floor polish, furniture wax, glass cleaners, hair gels, tile cleaners, and engine degreaser. Collectively, the control of these consumer products will reduce VOC emissions by 45 tons per day—an amount equal to the emissions from 1.4 million cars. Since Southern California possesses some of the most polluted air in the nation, it is not surprising that its SIP contain the broadest and most innovative features to obtain emissions reductions. These steps seem to be working. In 1999, the Los Angeles-Long Beach area only had 27 days of air quality exceeding 100–down from 175 days in 1993. The California SIP has been subjected to numerous legal challenges including one which attached SIP components which were made voluntary.

3.   AIR QUALITY MAINTENANCE PLANNING

Does the SIP for the state in the discussion problem need to make any provision for those areas that currently are in attainment status for CO_3 or must planning and regulatory action need to be taken only when, and if, the CO_3 NAAQS is violated?

What if an area has achieved the NAAQS? Is it exempt from SIP controls? If so, might future population growth or industrial expansion result in the violation of the NAAQS? How is this possibility handled under the Clean Air Act? Areas that have the potential for violating the national ambient air quality standards within a ten-year period—due to projected growth and development—must be designated Air Quality Maintenance Areas (AQMAs). Such an area must be the subject of special air quality maintenance analysis and planning. The AQMA plan, usually submitted to EPA as a SIP revision, shall include "control strategy revisions and other measures to ensure that emissions associated with projected growth and development will be compatible with maintenance of the national standards." 40 C.F.R. § 51.40(c). This specialized plan seeks to ensure that states consider the additional air emissions caused by economic and social expansion within a reasonable time frame. Without such attention to future conditions, air quality improvement achieved by general SIP regulations could be overtaken by growth factors. See generally 40 C.F.R. § 51.52 et seq.

The 1990 Clean Air Act amendments have imposed the maintenance plan requirement on all non-attainment areas which are later redesignated into attainment status. See § 175A. Once meeting the primary NAAQS, a state must submit a SIP revision providing for maintenance of the air quality for 10 years and renew it every 10 years. This plan must contain contingency measures to assure that a state will promptly correct any subsequent violation of the NAAQS. What kind of automatic contingency measures could be included in a maintenance plan?

C.   AUTOMOBILES AND THE SIP

1.   AUTOMOBILES AND SMOG

Air pollution problems are not only the result of stationary source emissions. The Clean Air Act strategy also focuses upon the second major component of atmospheric pollution—emissions from mobile sources (primarily automobiles and trucks). The automobile has had a powerful influence upon American society in a variety of ways. Cars provide Americans with unequaled personal mobility greatly affecting the ways they live and work. However, as beneficial as this form of transportation has been it has also been recognized as the cause of serious, adverse environmental impact. As early as 1950, Dr. Arlie Haagen–Smit, a California biochemist, determined that uncombusted hydrocarbons from car engines could react with nitrous oxides in the presence of sunlight to create a photochemical smog.

This relationship between automobile emissions and unhealthy air quality has made the automobile and fuel combustion a major focus of federal air pollution legislation since 1955. Subsequent statutes and federal agency attention have been concerned with the development of less polluting motor vehicle technology. This emphasis on a technological approach resulting in the improvement of combustion efficiency of automobile engines would continue through the landmark Clean Air Act of 1970. See

Ditlow, Federal Regulation of Motor Vehicle Emissions Under the Clean Air Act Amendments of 1970, 4 Ecol.L.Q. 523 (1975). The effort to make the American automobile a cleaner operating vehicle by way of EPA regulation implementing congressional policy has greatly improved vehicle performance.

Air pollution is generally divided into two major categories: stationary and mobile. Of mobile sources, automobiles constitute the largest single contributor of air emissions. Many American cities experience unhealthful air quality due in large part to the effects of automobile exhaust and fuel evaporation. This atmospheric pollution is a function of both (1) the polluting characteristics of each individual vehicle and (2) the aggregate number of miles traveled by all vehicles. The Clean Air Act tail pipe emission regulation has substantially improved the combustion efficiency of new motor vehicles since 1970 and reduced emissions. Unfortunately the installation of automobile emission controls alone has not achieved the NAAQS in heavily polluted cities. The increased number of vehicles and miles traveled account for this fact. For example, in a 1974 appellate decision it was stated that the imposition of federal auto emission standards in New York City would "only achieve about 40 percent of the reduction in pollutants necessary to fulfill the EPA's primary [NAAQS] standards." See Friends of the Earth v. United States EPA, 499 F.2d 1118, 1121 n. 2 (2d Cir.1974).

How could the NAAQS ever be attained in heavily polluted urban centers even with significant auto exhaust control? Could the Clean Air Act address the problem of automobile created air pollution through SIP development and enforcement process? Is it possible to reduce the number of vehicle miles traveled? Questions—Imagine that you are the director of your state's air pollution control agency. Suggest several controls on transportation activities in your polluted urban areas might you include in your SIP? How would you select them? How would you know if they were sufficient, in combination with stationary source controls, to reach or make progress towards attainment of the NAAQS? How might these techniques be received by people living in these areas, local politicians and businesses? The Clean Air Act of 1970 authorized the inclusion of "land use controls" in SIPs as part of § 110(a)(2)(B). This language was stricken by the 1977 amendments to the statute. Why do you think this occurred? Can you think of any constitutional problems which might be created by this system of transportation and land use control?

2.   TAILPIPE EMISSION STANDARDS

a.   The Beginning of Federal Controls

The automobile has served as a national symbol of independence and mobility throughout this century. It has also created tremendous air quality and land use problems which we have begun to address. The importance of the car as air polluter has been recognized in federal and state legislation for more than thirty years. In 1955, Congress undertook the initial action in this area by authorizing the Department of Health,

Education and Welfare to conduct research on the subject of air pollution control. Federal policy has consistently emphasized federal auto emission standards in order to foreclose the establishment of numerous inconsistent state regulations.

California had set their own auto rules as early as 1968. Things moved slowly until 1970 when subchapter II of the Clean Air Act of 1970 set into motion the federal scheme of automobile emissions regulation that exists today. The Congressional approach to pollution from new automobiles has been described as one of "technology-forcing" applying to newly-manufactured vehicles. Under this theory the statute established (1) a stringent performance standard of 90% emission reduction from existing levels and (2) a five or six year deadline for the automobile manufacturing companies to achieve this standard in practice. Congress did allow for some state independence. Although the CAA establishes minimum vehicle emission standards, it allows California to go below those minimum to set more restrictive rules and permits other states to choose either the federal or the California standards.

Consider the legislative policy of technology-forcing within the context of the automobile manufacturing industry. Think about the following questions. What are the assumptions underlying such an idea of technology forcing? How does it view the growth and improvement of industrial technology? What assumptions does it make about the ability of manufacturers to extend prototype development into mass production under serious time constraints? Why hadn't auto manufacturers sold non-polluting cars prior to the 1970 Clean Air Act? What does it say about the ability of the market to provide products with these desirable performance characteristics? What does it also have to say about the political power of industrial interests?

b.   Establishing Automobile Emission Standards Under the Clean Air Act

Comprehending the statute authorizing EPA's program for setting motor vehicle emission standards is no easy task. Title II of the 1990 Clean Air Act amendments added enormously to the detail of the mobile source provisions of the Act. The most important provisions regarding vehicle emission standards are to be found in § 202(g) (light duty trucks and cars), § 202(h) (light duty trucks > 6000 lbs), and § 202(a)(3) (heavy duty trucks). You should read these sections with a careful eye for language involving the basis for regulatory standard setting, the various times for compliance, the provisions for agency flexibility and delay (if any), and the specialized terminology of this engineering area.

The original structure of § 202 was to set strict performance objectives combined with stated achievement dates. Relief from the adverse effects of this system (the inability to sell non-conforming new vehicles) was provided by way of administratively-granted waivers. Due to the enormous economic implications of imposing these strict standards, Congress, EPA and the courts have all acted to extend the deadline for achieving final, 90% auto emission reductions. The result has been a gradual phase-down of automobile emissions. Emission standards for motor vehicles consider two types of emissions; 1) tailpipe or exhaust emissions and 2) evaporative emissions. For tailpipe emissions EPA sets standards based on vehicle weight, model year temperature and useful life of the vehicle. By 1990, tailpipe emissions from new cars had dropped 90% for hydrocarbons and carbon monoxide and 75% for NO_x emissions over uncontrolled levels. EPA certifies new models of cars as being in compliance with emission standards taking into account performance deterioration over the vehicle's useful life. EPA also selectively tests models when they come off of the assembly line. Actual "in use" performance has deviated from these new car standards necessitating I & M measures to keep performance up to expected levels and to counter-act intentional tampering or disabling of the emission controls.

The 1990 Clean Air Act amendments pushed auto and light duty truck emissions down even further: another 35% reduction for hydrocarbons and 60% for oxides of nitrogen. These are called "Tier 1" standards and they went into effect in 1996 setting standards for CO, NO_x, Particulate matter (PM), and hydrocarbons. In 2000, EPA issued a "Tier 2" regulation which will establish a new, single set of tailpipe emission standards applicable to all passenger cars, vans, light trucks and sport utility vehicles. These heavier vehicles had previously been subject to less strict standards but the Tier 2 rules seek to unify these emission requirements in the future. These Tier 2 standards are designed to employ cleaner vehicle emission controls and yield critical emission reductions needed to meet the ozone NAAQS. A good way to visualize the gradual tightening of vehicle emission controls is by way of a chart.

Exhaust Emission Standards (grams/mile)

Light Duty Vehicles	Year	THC	NMHC	CO	NO_x	PM_{10}
	1992 (Tier 0)	0.41	.034	3.4	1.0	0.20
	1996 (Tier 1)	0.41	0.25	3.4	0.4	0.08
	Beginning in-2004 (Tier 2)	Various		3.4	0.07	Various

In 2001, separate tailpipe emission standards were set to control exhausts from gas and diesel powered heavy duty highway engines and vehicles beginning with the 2007 model year.

Tailpipe emissions only represent a part of the CAA vehicle control strategy: in order to control vehicle hydrocarbon emissions, note fuel volatility and fuel system evaporative losses must be controlled. The 1990 amendments required EPA to issue rules applicable to evaporative emissions of hydrocarbons from gas-powered vehicles during these operation, refueling and non-use in the summertime. See CAA § 202(k). The Act requires regulations setting forth "the greatest degree of emission reduction achievable, giving appropriate consideration to fuel volatility and to cost, energy and safety factors associated with the application of appropriated technology." These "in use" standards were set in the early 1990s with phase-in completed by the 1999 model year. Refueling also results in emissions and pursuant to CAA § 202(a)(6) EPA required on-board refueling vapor recovery systems (canisters) for all cars by 2000 and for trucks by 2004.

What about the emission of toxic air pollutants from automobiles and other transportation sources? The House report on the Clean Air Act amendments identified this as a potentially serious problem. By April, 1993 EPA completed a study of the need for and the feasibility of controlling such pollutants from vehicles and motor fuels. Under the 1990 Act, emissions of benzene, formaldehyde and 1, 3 butadiene were specifically considered. Under the 1990 Act, by mid–1995 EPA must promulgate standards for vehicles and motor fuels which the Administrator,

> determines reflect the greatest degree of emission reduction achievable through the application of technology which will be available, taking into consideration the standards established under subsection (a), the availability and costs of the technology, and the noise, energy, and safety factors, and lead time. Such regulations shall not be inconsistent with standards under section 202(a). The regulations shall, at a minimum, apply to emissions of benzene and formaldehyde.

§ 202(k)(2). What regulatory options could be available to EPA? What if the imposition of any emission standard restricting formaldehyde made it technically difficult or impossible to reach the CO standard? How should this conflict be resolved in terms of EPA's regulatory choice? Should the formaldehyde standard be abandoned? EPA has yet to issue these rules.

c.   Regulating Fuels and Fuel Additives

The Clean Air Act also considers motor vehicle fuels as part of the air pollution program and in § 211 it provides EPA with broad power, 1) to regulate fuels and fuel additives and 2) to require the registration, testing and certification of these products. The overall goal of § 211 is to encourage the development and use of cleaner-burning and less polluting motor fuels. This fuels registration and testing program requires manufacturers to register a fuel or additive with EPA prior to selling it. In 1994, EPA began requiring health testing of fuels and additives with the intention of identifying those that present a significant risk to the public. Since that time EPA has registered over 2,300 fuels and 4,800 additives.

Section 211(k) of the Act takes a more specific approach by adopting a Reformulated Gasoline Program (RFG) to reduce vehicle emissions and ozone forming substances found in fuel (oxygen, benzene, aromatic hydrocarbon and metal). In 1994 EPA established RFG regulations by way of a negotiated rulemaking process. They are found at 40 C.F.R. § 80.40 et seq. These RFG rules specify both performance and composition requirements and they became effective in 1995 and apply to the ten worst ozone nonattainment areas including Chicago, Houston, Los Angeles, Milwaukee, New York City, Philadelphia, San Diego, most of Connecticut, and Sacramento. In addition, at least 18 states have had certain counties "opt into" the RFG Program. All of Massachusetts and Rhode Island have opted in while other states and counties have also "opted out". The exact scope of the RFG Program is usually in flux. It has been estimated that about 32% of all gasoline sold in the U.S. is reformulated. The CAA § 211(k) sets five RFG composition standards which include:

1) oxygen content of at least 2% by weight

2) benzene maximum of 1% by volume

3) heavy metals prohibited

4) prohibition on an increase in NO_x over 1990 baseline

5) summer season toxics and VOC reductions

These RFG standards apply year round in all of the worst ozone areas. Usually, refiners, importers or fuel-blenders will blend gasoline to ensure meeting the RFG standards. To meet the oxygenation requirement, "oxygenates" must be added to the gasoline. These include methyl tertiary butyl ether (MTBE), ethanol and ethyl tertiary butyl ether (ETBE). Most of California and the Mid–Atlantic through Northeast use MTBE. The use of MTBE has been controversial in that it has been accused of contaminating water supplies and that in California it has banned its use prospectively.

Ethanol originates in agricultural products such as corn while MTBE and ETBE are derived from conventional fossil fuels. Initially in 1994 EPA required that 30% of oxygenates come from ethanol since it represented a renewable feedstock and the agency wished to promote such renewable fuels. The petroleum industry attacked this rule and in American Petroleum Institute v. EPA, 52 F.3d 1113 (D.C.Cir.1995), the D.C. Circuit invalidated the requirement as being beyond EPA's statutory authority. The RFG program continues to be controversial and litigated. See American Petroleum Institute v. EPA, 198 F.3d 275 (D.C.Cir.2000) (EPA lacks statutory authority to require RFG in unclassified non-attainment areas).

3. SIP TRANSPORTATION RELATED POLLUTION CONTROL MEASURES

There are a wide variety of transportation controls that have been considered or adopted as part of SIPs. These strategies focus upon two related goals: (1) the reduction of exhaust emissions per mile of vehicle travel and (2) the reduction of the number of vehicle miles driven. Examples of the first category include inspection and maintenance of in-use vehicles, retrofitting of older cars with pollution control devices, service station vapor control, regulation of motor fuel content, and the improvement of traffic flow on urban streets. Techniques of the second classification include tolls, gas or parking taxes, limits on parking or auto use, carpooling inducements, employer transit incentives, bus/carpool lane preference rules, bicycle lanes, pedestrian or vehicle free zones, gas rationing, mass transit subsidies, and limits on driving licenses or vehicle ownership. The Clean Air Act requires EPA to make available detailed information to environmental and transportation agencies concerning at least 19 transportation control measures which can reduce pollution. See § 108(f)

[§ 7408(f)]. The 1990 amendment went even farther in non-attainment areas by requiring increasing stringent transportation related measures depending upon the severity of the pollution problem. See § 182(c) [§ 7511a(c)]. All states with either CO or ozone non-attainment states must have vehicle inspection and maintenance programs (I/M)s other areas with greater pollution must adopt enhanced I/M programs while "severe" and "extreme" ozone non-attainment areas must adopt and implement "transportation control measures" or TCMs designed to lessen vehicle emissions. Such TCMs could include programs to reduce work-related trips, to encourage the greater use of mass transit or carpooling. See § 182(d)(1) [§ 7511a(d)(1)].

4. INSPECTION AND MAINTENANCE CONTROL REQUIREMENTS

Additional consideration of the inspection and maintenance (I & M) technique is warranted. These programs are intended to supplement new vehicle auto emission standards by examining cars in use on the roads and identifying those in need of emission control device maintenance. I & M recognizes that the efficiency of emission controls is subject to natural deterioration and also to human tampering. The primary goal of an I & M program is to maintain a high level of performance of auto emission controls on existing vehicles until these autos are replaced by new cars which will be subject to more stringent emission standards.

In 1977 Congress viewed I & M programs as effective and helpful for improving fuel economy. It consequently took steps to ensure that I & M would continue as a component of SIPs in polluted urban areas. The 1977 amendments seemingly required all states with polluted urban areas to revise their SIPs and include all "reasonably available control measures as expeditiously as practicable" in order to demonstrate attainment of the NAAQS by December 31, 1987. § 172(b) [§ 7502(b)]. These revisions would include I & M programs. The 1990 act continued the emphasis on I & M as a required SIP element in most ozone non-attainment areas, and heavily polluted areas were required to adopt enhanced I & M programs. See § 181(b)(4) [§ 7511(b)(4)].

D. ENSURING THE DEVELOPMENT OF AN ADEQUATE SIP

1. EPA AND SANCTIONS TO ASSURE THE DEVELOPMENT OF ADEQUATE SIPs

The Clean Air Act anticipates that national air quality objectives will be accomplished through a system federal/state shared responsibility. If under the Act the states are accorded the major duty for designing and enforcing the State Implementation Plans (SIPs), what assurance is there that they will be aggressive in taking the necessary steps to achieve the NAAQS by statutory deadlines? What leverage does EPA have to obtain the state's cooperation and willingness to take locally unpopular steps? Since the Clean Air Act places substantial emphasis on state preparation of effective SIPs whose timely implementation will result in NAAQS achievement, what happens if states submit inadequate SIPs? What if the SIPs are on the right track but do not go far enough?

The 1990 Act also grants EPA the power to impose a range of sanctions against states upon EPA's making of a "finding, disapproval, or determination" under § 179(a)(1)–(4) that,

(1) finds that a State has failed, for an area designated non-attainment under section 107(d), to submit a plan, or to submit 1 or more of the elements (as determined by the Administrator) required by the provisions of this Act applicable to such an area, or has failed to make a submission for such an area that satisfies the minimum criteria established in relation to any such element under section 110(k),

(2) disapproves a submission under section 110(k), for an area designated non-attainment under section 107, based on the submission's failure to meet one or more of the elements required by the provisions of this Act applicable to such an area,

(3)(A) determines that a State has failed to make any submission as may be required under this Act, other than one described under paragraph (1) or (2), including an adequate maintenance plan, or has failed to make any submission, as may be required under this Act, other than one described under paragraph (1) or (2), that satisfies the minimum criteria established in relation to such submission under section 110(k)(1)(A), or

(B) disapproves in whole or in part a submission described under subparagraph (A), or

(4) finds that any requirement of an approved plan (or approved part of a plan) is not being implemented.

If the deficiency is not corrected within 18 months, at least one of the following two sanctions must be imposed on the state as well as withholding of all or part of the Clean Air Act § 105 state air pollution planning and control program grants. The sanctions specified in the 1990 act are as follows:

a. HIGHWAY FUNDS.—The Secretary of Transportation shall not approve any project or award any grant under title 23, United States Code, other than for safety or mass transit.

b. OFFSETS.—In applying the emissions offset requirements of section 173 to new or modified sources or emissions units for which a permit is required under part D, the ratio of emission reductions to increased emissions shall be at least 2 to 1.

§ 179(b)(1)–(2) [§ 7509(b)]. If EPA makes a "finding" under one of the four elements of § 179(a), it notifies the state of the deficiency which, in turn, starts EPA's "sanctions clock." Sanctions must be imposed 18 months after EPA makes this finding unless the deficiency has been corrected within the time period. Without this correction, EPA will impose the "2:1" offset sanction first and then if the deficiency has not been corrected within 6 months, both sanctions are applied. With regard to the highway funding sanction, not all funding is affected—safety improvement projects as well as several other categories are exempt. In 2000, the Congressional Research Service concluded the following:

> The threat of sanctions is a powerful tool; but, perhaps because the threat is powerful, the imposition of sanctions is a rare event. EPA has formally notified the states of its intent to use this tool 858 times since 1990. Actual imposition of sanctions . . . has occurred 18 times in that time period; in most of these cases, the issue was resolved after the imposition of offset sanctions. Only 2 area have had highway sanctions imposed. As of October 1999, they were in effect for one small area (East Helena, Montana).James E. McCarthy, Clean Air Issues for the 106th Congress, CRS Issue Brief (2000).

Other parts of the Clean Air Act allow EPA to veto major construction projects if a state fails to properly develop or implement its SIP. See §§ 173(a)(4) [§ 7503(a)(4)] and 113(a)(5) [§ 7413(a)(5)]. Why would Congress have inserted these sanctions into the law? Are these optional sanctions likely to be used by EPA and would they be expected to encourage states to cooperate in SIP design and implementation? How would you view these sanctions if you were the head of your state's air pollution control agency? The economic development agency?

Does this part of § 179 punish a state for failing to attain the NAAQS? The consequences of failing to attain are specifically set forth for ozone, CO, and PM–10. See §§ 181(b)(4), 187(g), and 189(d). These sanctions range in their severity. For instance, if a "severe" ozone non-attainment area fails to achieve the NAAQS by the applicable attainment date, stationary sources must pay VOC emissions fee of $5,000 per ton, continued 3% reasonable further progress improvements must be demonstrated, and broadened new source review requirements must be imposed. See § 181(b)(4). On the other hand failure to meet CO standards on time triggers a SIP revision including the following feature resulting in a 5% annual reduction in CO emissions. The SIP must include,

> An economic incentive program under this paragraph shall be consistent with rules published by the Administrator and sufficient, in combination with other elements of the State plan, to achieve the next milestone. The State program may include a nondiscriminatory system, consistent with applicable law regarding interstate commerce, of State established emissions fees or a system of marketable permits, or a system of State fees on sale, import, or manufacture of products the use of which contributes to ozone formation, or any combination of the foregoing or other similar measures. The program may also include incentive and requirements to reduce vehicle emissions and vehicle miles traveled in the area, including any of the transportation control measures identified in section 108(f).

§ 182(g)(4)(A) [§ 7511a(g)]. What specific features could such a program have?

2. THE FEDERAL IMPLEMENTATION PLAN (FIP)—THE ULTIMATE SANCTION FOR STATE NON-COOPERATION

It is one thing to penalize a state for its failure to properly prepare an adequate SIP with fiscal or programmatic sanctions and yet another for EPA to step in and directly take over these planning functions. Congress, believing that such EPA intervention had been successful in the past and could continue to be beneficial, redrafted the FIP provision. Regarding past use of this federal power the 1990 House Report noted that,

> Historically, the FIP process has been effective. In some instances, it has prompted States to take actions required under the Act. For example, recent proposed FIPs in Phoenix, Chicago, and Southern California succeeded, after court action, in producing State air quality planning efforts in areas which had previously failed to comply with the provisions of the Act. The FIP process has also been useful in enforcing the prevention of significant deterioration (PSD) program under Part C of the Act. More than 30 States currently have PSD programs established and implemented through the FIP process.

H.R.Rep. No. 101–490 Part 1, 101st Cong., 2d Sess. 229 (1990). The 1990 Clean Air Act amendments create a mandatory duty in EPA to promulgate a FIP within 2 years of finding that (a) a state has failed to make a required SIP submission, (b) its submission does not satisfy the minimum criteria of § 110(k)(1)(A) or (c) that a SIP is disapproved in whole or in part. See § 110(c)(1). Obviously, EPA's making these "findings" or "disapprovals" will be important. Could EPA be forced to prepare a FIP through litigation? The term "Federal Implementation Plan" is defined in new § 302(y) as,

> a plan * * * promulgated by the Administrator to fill all or a portion of a gap or otherwise correct all or a portion of an inadequacy in a [SIP], and which includes enforceable emission limitations or other control measures, means or techniques * * *, and provides for attainment of the relevant [NAAQS].

Is this provision truly automatic in effect? Why might EPA be reluctant to take on the responsibility of FIP preparation? What might be the political and intergovernmental ramifications of EPA's intervention by FIP? Who would enforce the FIP?

What should be done when EPA fails to respond affirmatively or negatively to a state's SIP proposal? Can or should EPA be forced to act? What if EPA has disapproved an important part of a state's SIP, should EPA be forced to propose a federal SIP in its place?

SECTION 4. FEDERAL EMISSION LIMITATIONS

A. INTRODUCTION AND OVERVIEW

While the Clean Air Act's SIP allots major responsibility for the development of a pollution control strategy to the states, the statute reserved federal authority over setting standards for new stationary air pollution sources and for emitters of hazardous or toxic air pollutants in Clean Air Act §§ 111 and 112. An important exception to the freedom of states to adopt emission limitations and to grant variances occurs in the area of new source and air toxic source control. The new source performance standard or NSPS concept assumed a major position in the 1970 Clean Air Act and the regulation of air toxics took a prominent place as Title III of the 1990 amendments.

Why would Congress emphasize a system of centralized nationally-applicable standard-setting for new source and air toxics control? Uniform standard development would be just that—uniform. This would have EPA set the NSPS or air toxics standard once thus obviating the need for each state to do so. Many states would not have the technical capacity to set sophisticated engineering standards for a variety of pollution sources. It would also give industry a single design standard for its new industrial facilities and therefore be cost-effective. The § 111 concept emphasized a view that under EPA "technology forcing" pressure, pollution control techniques would continue to improve over time and that overall air quality would improve as new sources replaced old ones. In addition, uniform national performance standards would eliminate the phenomena of states using lax pollution requirements as an inducement inducing new industrial location.

The concept of uniform pollution control performance standard is common in the field of environmental regulation. Are there disadvantages of having a governmental standard setting system for industrial design and operation? What incentives and disincentives does such a system foster? To better understand this Congressional motivation you must comprehend the structure and language of § 111 and some of the principle features of § 112. In addition, the new source and hazardous air pollutant standards are formally developed EPA regulations which must be applied to sources and ultimately enforced. The next problem addresses issues related to rulemaking and enforcement issues.

B. SECTION 111 NEW SOURCE PERFORMANCE STANDARDS

Under § 111(b) [§ 7411(b)], EPA is directed 1) to publish a list of new source categories and 2) to establish national performance standards for each one. These standards must then be incorporated into and implemented by the states' SIPs. In this way the federal NSPS is implemented on a national basis. It is worth noting that NSPS are to be set for industrial categories and not for individual pollutants. Therefore, § 111 seeks to control all of the harmful emissions from a new source and not solely the NAAQS pollutants. This policy has been implemented in a number of the NSPS including the standard for primary aluminum reduction plants which limits the non-NAAQS pollutant fluoride. See 40 C.F.R. § 60.192.

New sources are stationary sources, "the construction or modification of which is commenced after the publication of regulations (or, if earlier, proposed regulations) * * *." § 111(a)(2) [§ 7411(a)(2)]. The statute sets forth yet another verbal formulation for pollution control technology required by § 111. This definition was amended in 1990 to state that a NSPS,

> means a standard for emissions of air pollutants which reflects the degree of emission limitation achievable through application of the best system of emission reduction which (taking into account the cost of achieving such reduction and any non-air quality health and environmental impact and energy requirements) the Administration determines has been adequately demonstrated.

§ 111(a)(1) [§ 7411(a)(1)]. The NSPS may be a design, equipment, work practice or operational standard only if it is "not feasible" to prescribe a standard of performance. Why would the CAA create this preference for standards of performance? This statutory language has provided a multitude of regulatory and litigation problems.

New York v. Reilly

United States Court of Appeals, District of Columbia Circuit, 1992.
969 F.2d 1147.

■ KAREN LECRAFT HENDERSON, CIRCUIT JUDGE:

Petitioners State of New York and State of Florida challenge the decision of the Environmental Protection Agency to forgo promulgation of two provisions of two proposed rules. The relevant provisions would have required incinerator operators to separate a percentage of certain types of waste from their waste streams before incineration and would have placed a ban on the incineration of lead-acid vehicle batteries. Because our review of the record demonstrates that EPA adequately supported its decision to drop the waste separation provision, we uphold this portion of the Agency's action. On the other hand, because EPA did not adequately explain why a ban on lead-acid vehicle battery combustion does not represent the best demonstrated technology for reducing harmful incinerator emissions, we remand for further explication of this issue. Section 111 of the Clean Air Act authorizes EPA to regulate municipal incinerators (municipal waste combustors or MWCs) as sources of air pollution. Pursuant to section 111(b)(1)(B) of the CAA, EPA directly regulates new sources of air pollution. Under section 111(d) of the CAA, EPA is required to establish guidelines to be used by the states in regulating existing sources of air pollution. Although EPA proposed separate rules to meet the requirements of sections 111(b) and 111(d), the relevant portions of the rules are virtually indistinguishable for our purpose.

In general, subsection 111(a) of the CAA requires EPA to set "standards of performance" for sources of air pollution. It provides:

> a standard of performance shall reflect the degree of emission limitation * * * achievable through application of the best technological system of continuous emission reduction which (taking into consideration the cost of achieving such emission reduction, any non-air quality

health and environmental impact and energy requirements) the Administrator determines has been adequately demonstrated.

42 U.S.C. § 7411(a)(1). EPA has labeled its goal in setting a standard of performance as selection of the "best demonstrated technology" (BDT).

EPA's BDT analysis of MWCs resulted in proposed rules which focused primarily on limiting emissions from incinerator smokestacks. At issue in this appeal are three subparts of the proposed rules. Proposed rule 40 C.F.R. § 60.56a(d) would have required operators of new sources of air pollution to achieve a twenty-five percent reduction by weight of unprocessed waste by separating out some or all of the following recoverable/recyclable materials: paper and paperboard combined; ferrous materials; nonferrous metals; glass; plastics; household batteries; and yard waste. Proposed rule 40 C.F.R. § 60.56a(e) would have placed a total prohibition on the burning of lead-acid vehicle batteries by new sources. Proposed rule 40 C.F.R. § 60.36a would have incorporated the requirements of sections 60.56a(d) and (e) into the guidelines for existing sources.

On December 4, 1990, EPA submitted a package of final rules to the Office of Management and Budget (OMB) for review pursuant to Executive Order 12291. OMB did not approve the sections of the proposed rules covering materials separation and battery burning. EPA then appealed to the President's Council on Competitiveness (Council). In a "Fact Sheet," the Council rejected the proposed rules on materials separation as being inconsistent with "several of the Administration's regulatory principles," including their failure to "meet the benefit/cost requirements for regulatory policy laid out in Executive Order 12291." The Fact Sheet also noted the Council's opinion that the materials separation requirement did not constitute a "performance standard" and that it violated principles of federalism. EPA subsequently abandoned the materials separation and battery burning provisions when it promulgated its final rules.

II.

A. The Separation Requirements

In determining the BDT for limiting harmful emissions, the EPA Administrator must "take into consideration the cost of achieving such emission reduction, and any non-air quality health and environmental impact and energy requirements." 42 U.S.C. § 7411(a)(1)(C). Because Congress did not assign the specific weight the Administrator should accord each of these factors, the Administrator is free to exercise his discretion in this area. We must therefore uphold EPA's decision to abandon the separation requirements if such action is supported on either air or non-air (including economic) grounds.

Under the CAA, promulgated rules must be accompanied by "an explanation of the reasons for any major changes in the promulgated rule from the proposed rule." 42 U.S.C. § 7607(d)(6)(A). The Act also requires the court to sustain the Administrator's actions unless they are "arbitrary, capricious, an abuse of discretion, or otherwise not in accordance with law." 42 U.S.C. § 7607(d)(9)(A). The petitioners claim that EPA's decision to omit the proposed materials separation requirement from its final rules was arbitrary and capricious because the decision was not supported by substantial evidence, the Agency failed to explain why certain alternatives were not adopted, it improperly based its finding on the "worst case scenario" and it improperly relied on the views of the Council rather than its own expertise. We conclude that EPA's failure to promulgate the materials separation provision survives all of these attacks.

The petitioners first claim that EPA's explanations for excluding the materials separation requirement are not adequately supported by the administrative record. We will uphold an agency's conclusions if they are supported by "such relevant evidence as a reasonable mind might accept as adequate to support a conclusion." Universal Camera Corp. v. NLRB, 340 U.S. 474 (1951) (quoting Consolidated Edison Co. v. NLRB), 305 U.S. 197, 229, 83 L.Ed. 126, 59 S.Ct. 206 (1938); see also Consolidated Oil & Gas, Inc. v. FERC, 806 F.2d 275, 279 (D.C.Cir.1986). Furthermore, even if the evidence supports both sides of an issue, we will sustain the agency "if a reasonable person could come to either conclusion on that evidence." Public Citizen Health Research Group v. Tyson, 796 F.2d 1479, 1485 (D.C.Cir.1986). We are particularly deferential when reviewing agency actions involving policy decisions based on uncertain technical information. Id. at 1505 ("As long as Congress delegates power to an agency to regulate on the borders of the unknown, courts cannot interfere with reasonable interpretations of equivocal evidence.").

The petitioners attack the sufficiency of the evidence supporting EPA's conclusions regarding both air and non-air benefits. On the issue of air-related benefits, EPA's proposed rules noted that, due to the substantial reductions achieved by air pollution control devices, it was unable to reliably quantify the emission reductions attributable to materials separation. At the time it proposed the rules, however, EPA concluded: "It is simply common sense, and the Agency's expectation, that reductions in the amount of pollution-generating materials combusted in an MWC will reduce the amount of pollutants in its air emissions." When it omitted the separation requirements from its final rules, EPA concluded that emissions reductions resulting from materials separation were not only difficult to quantify but were in fact relatively small. This conclusion has adequate support in the record. See Emission Standards Division, Division of the Office of Air Quality Planning and Standards, U.S. Envtl. Protection Agency, Pub. No. EPA–450/3–021, Municipal Waste Combustion: Background Information for Materials Separation 5–15 to 5–16 (1991) (describing tests examining emissions from unseparated versus separated waste and concluding that efficacy of existing antipollution devices results in small emissions reduction from waste separation).

The petitioners next challenge whether EPA's conclusions regarding non-air benefits are adequately supported in the record. Both the proposed rules and the final rules note that requiring separation and recycling could lead to either a cost benefit or a cost detriment. While EPA initially forecast a likely benefit in promulgating its final rules it determined that the record was too inconclusive to justify a materials separation rule. We must therefore determine whether EPA adequately supported its change in position. The preamble to the final rules recites that the Agency, based in part on its own analysis, agreed with those comments suggesting that the uncertainty over costs associated with separation and recycling might be even greater than EPA had originally believed. See, e.g., Comments of The U.S. Conference of Mayors National Resource Recovery Association, JA 342 ("We estimate that, depending on the technology/program mix, total program costs are likely to range from $100 to more than $200 per ton of recycled product, including collecting, processing, and marketing the material"). We conclude that these comments, on which the Agency expressly relied to confirm its own views on cost uncertainty, provide sufficient evidence to support its changed view.

The petitioners further claim that EPA improperly relied solely on the "worst case scenario" in arriving at its final conclusion regarding the economics of materials separation. Our review of the record demonstrates that several commenters supported EPA's economic predictions. See Summary of Public Comments and Responses, supra, at 4–55 to 4–56. Moreover, even if EPA's prediction did take into account the worst case scenario, its action would be permissible. This court has held that in applying a uniform standard to an industry, the standard must "be capable of being met under most adverse conditions which can reasonably be expected to recur." National Lime Ass'n v. EPA, 627 F.2d 416, 431 n. 46 (D.C.Cir. 1980).

Lastly, the petitioners claim that EPA acted improperly in relying on the opinion of the Council rather than exercising its own expertise. After reviewing the record, we conclude that EPA did exercise its expertise in this case. The procedural history of the rules at issue demonstrates that the Council's views were important in formulating EPA's final policy decision regarding materials separation. The fact that EPA reevaluated its conclusions in light of the Council's advice, however, does not mean that EPA failed to exercise its own expertise in promulgating the final rules.

In sum, EPA's change of position on the materials separation issue was not improper. We are extremely deferential to administrative agencies in cases involving technical rulemaking decisions, and EPA has supported its new view of the materials separation policy with adequate evidence. Because the CAA allows EPA to balance air and non-air benefits and costs, which it did, EPA's decision not to promulgate materials separation rules was neither arbitrary nor capricious.

B.   The Battery Burning Prohibition

Despite its continued belief that "lead acid batteries are certainly a significant source of lead in MWC emissions," EPA decided not to include a ban on the burning of lead-acid vehicle batteries in its final rules. The Agency offered three reasons for its decision to omit the ban: (1) commenters questioned whether it would be possible to achieve 100 percent compliance; (2) the Resource Conservation and Recovery Act includes strict provisions against the burning of lead-acid batteries; and (3) EPA is considering a comprehensive approach to recycling lead-acid batteries under section 6 of the Toxic Substances Control Act. Because EPA's proffered reasons for omitting the battery ban do not adequately explain why the ban is not the BDT in this area, this portion of the proposed rules is remanded to the Agency for more reasoned decisionmaking.

The petitioners countered EPA's first rationale by suggesting that, if 100 percent compliance with a ban on burning lead-acid batteries is impossible, EPA could have adopted some lesser restriction (e.g., a 99 or 95 percent ban). EPA responded by stating that it was limited to a choice between a 100 percent ban or no ban at all. We disagree with EPA's position. We have held that EPA has the authority to deviate from a proposed rule as long as its final rule represents a "logical outgrowth" of the proposal. EPA cannot claim to have been unaware of the possibility of a less restrictive rule as at least one commenter suggested a "best efforts" or "reasonable efforts" standard.

EPA's next two rationales simply recognize that the matter of lead-acid battery incineration can be addressed under other statutes. Because EPA originally proposed the ban as the BDT for reducing emissions from batteries, and the CAA requires the Agency to explain why it changed its mind on this point, the mere existence of other statutory authority which might undergird EPA's final stance is insufficient to justify the omission of the battery ban. EPA has admitted that a ban would achieve air benefits. The final rules however, do not discuss non-air benefits or other economic benefits which would justify omitting the provision despite the air benefits. We therefore conclude that the rules must be remanded to EPA to explain why the BDT for reducing emissions resulting from lead-acid vehicle batteries is not a total or limited ban on their combustion.

Because EPA did not adequately explain its reasons for not imposing a ban of some degree on the burning of lead-acid vehicle batteries, we remand the rules to the Agency. We uphold EPA's decision not to promulgate blanket materials separation rules, however, because the Agency adequately articulated and supported its change in position.

The petitions for review are therefore granted in part and denied in part.

So ordered.

Excerpts from EPA Clean Air Act Regulations

40 C.F.R. Part 60.

§ 60.720 Applicability and designation of affected facility.

(a) The provisions of this subpart apply to each spray booth in which plastic parts for use in the manufacture of business machines receive prime coats, color coats, texture coats, or touch-up coats.

(b) This subpart applies to any affected facility for which construction, modification, or reconstruction begins after January 8, 1986.

§ 60.721 Definitions.

(a) As used in this subpart, all terms not defined herein shall have the meaning given them in the Act or in Subpart A of this part.

"Business machine" means a device that uses electronic or mechanical methods to process information, perform calculations, print or copy information, or convert sound into electrical impulses for transmission, such as:

[typewriters, computers, telephones, calculators, and photocopy machines]

* * *

§ 60.722 Standards for volatile organic compounds.

(a) Each owner or operator of any affected facility which is subject to the requirements of this subpart shall comply with the emission limitations set forth in this section on and after the date on which the initial performance test, required by §§ 60.8 and 60.723 is completed, but not later than 60 days after achieving the maximum production rate at which the affected facility will be operated, or 180 days after the initial startup, whichever date comes first. No affected facility shall cause the discharge into the atmosphere in excess of:

(1) 1.5 kilograms of VOC's per liter of coating solids applied from prime coating of plastic parts for business machines.

(2) 1.5 kilograms of VOC's per liter of coating solids applied from color coating of plastic parts for business machines.

(3) 2.3 kilograms of VOC's per liter of coating solids applied from texture coating of plastic parts for business machines.

(4) 2.3 kilograms of VOC's per liter of coatings solids applied from touch-up coating of plastic parts for business machines.

(b) All VOC emissions that are caused by coatings applied in each affected facility, regardless of the actual point of discharge of emissions into the atmosphere, shall be included in determining compliance with the emission limits in paragraph (a) of this section.

[Many of the terms used in this section were defined in § 60.271.]

§ 60.723 Performance tests and compliance provisions.

* * *

(b) The owner or operator of an affected facility shall conduct an initial performance test as required under § 60.8(a) and thereafter a performance test each nominal 1–month period for each affected facility according to the procedures in this section.

* * *

§ 60.724 Reporting and recordkeeping requirements.

(a) The reporting requirements of § 60.8(a) apply only to the initial performance test. Each owner or operator subject to the provisions of this subpart shall include the following data in the report of the initial performance test required under § 60.8(a):

    (1) Except as provided for in paragraph (a)(2) of this section, the volume-weighted average mass of VOC's emitted to the atmosphere per volume of applied coating solids (N) for the initial nominal 1–month period for each coating operation from each affected facility.

* * *

(b) Following the initial report, each owner or operator shall:

    (1) Report the volume-weighted average mass of VOC's per unit volume of coating solids applied for each coating operation for each affected facility during each nominal 1–month period in which the facility is not in compliance with the applicable emission limits specified in § 60.722. Reports of noncompliance shall be submitted on a quarterly basis, occurring every 3 months following the initial report; and

    (2) Submit statements that each affected facility has been in compliance with the applicable emission limits specified in § 60.722 during each nominal 1–month period. Statements of compliance shall be submitted on a semiannual basis.

(c) These reports shall be postmarked not later than 10 days after the end of the periods specified in § 60.724(b)(1) and § 60.724(b)(2).

(d) Each owner or operator subject to the provisions of this subpart shall maintain at the source, for a period of at least 2 years, records of all data and calculations used to determine monthly VOC emissions from each coating operation for each affected facility as specified in 40 CFR 60.7(d).

NOTES AND QUESTIONS

1. *Setting and Updating the NSPS.* Read § 111(a)(1) [§ 7411(a)(1)]. Consider the following questions. How do you interpret the § 111(a)(1) criteria for adopting NSPS? Are they health-based or technology-based? What is the meaning of "adequate demonstrated" technology? How is cost to be taken into consideration? What is an "achievable" limitation? Why have the requirements, added in 1977 and retained in 1990, to take into account "non-air quality environmental impact and energy?" Why the emphasis on "continuous controls?"

The § 111(a) judgment allows balancing based on a consideration of cost, energy requirements, non-air quality environmental impacts, and other environmental considerations. See Portland Cement Assn v. Ruckelshaus, 486 F.2d 375 (D.C.Cir.1973) (balance the potential impacts and does not harm other environmental interest more than the air benefits). Does EPA have discretion in selecting those categories of sources for which

NSPS must be promulgated? Section 111(b)(1)(A) [§ 7411(b)(1)(A)] states that "the Administrator shall * * * publish a list of"

> categories of stationary sources. He shall include a category of sources in each list if in his judgment it causes, or contributes significantly to, air pollution which may reasonably be anticipated to endanger public health or welfare.

However, § 111(f) was added in 1977 and it directs EPA to list within one year and adopt within four years new source standards for categories of "major stationary sources," defined in § 302(j) [§ 7602(j)] as those having the "potential to emit * * * one hundred tons per year or more of any air pollutant." Apparently this statutory command failed to move EPA to set new NSPS. The 1990 Clean Air Act amendments amended § 111(f) and directed EPA to set NSPS for all previously listed major stationary sources over a 6 year period ending in 1996. Why was amended § 111(f) adopted?

EPA has set NSPS for approximately 70 new source industrial categories including, for instance, whiskey distillers, nonmetallic mineral processing plants, residential wood heaters, beverage can surface coating plants, petroleum dry cleaners, primary zinc smelters, and kraft pulp mills. See 40 C.F.R. Part 60, Subpart D through Subpart YYY (1999). NSPS for new categories are periodically issued, although EPA has taken lengthy time periods to issue final NSPS regulations. For instance, in 1992 the agency issued a NSPS for calciners and dryers used in the mineral industry more than 6 years after proposing the standards. What implications flow from such a delay? What strategic issues are presented to source owners or trade associations by then attempting to delay the issuance of a final NSPS?

The NSPS are important to the regulated industries and environmental agencies since the CAA Title V operating permit program mandates that they be incorporated as terms in facility operating permits for major sources. Making the NSPS provisions—both the substantive and procedural parts—part of an operating permit could expose the source to government and citizen suit enforcement actions.

2. *Source Definition for NSPS.* Definitions really matter under the Clean Air Act. The operation of a new air pollution source in violation of an NSPS is unlawful and punishable by a host of enforcement remedies. Also, compliance with NSPS requires that the source owner pursue new source review (NSR) and ultimately commit itself to a greater capital outlay. Consequently, being a "new source" under the Act might be a status to avoid. Cases have been litigated over the question of whether a source is legally a "New Source." For example, in Star Enterprise v. EPA, 235 F.3d 139 (3d Cir.2000), EPA had determined that the NSPS applicable to petroleum refineries applied to stationary gas generators located at an electrical power plant adjacent to a petroleum refinery. Contrary to EPA's view, the Court of Appeals held that the NSPS applied only to turbines "in a petroleum refinery," and that since these turbines were not "in" the refinery, the NSPS did not apply. Why do you suppose congress chose to impose more demanding requirements on new solutions sources? Does this choice have any undesirable consequences?

a. Congress made the NSPS applicable to new sources and also to modifications that increase emissions or add a new pollutant. A "new source" is defined as one "commencing construction or modification" after the proposal of an applicable NSPS. But when does "construction" begin so as to escape the rigors of the NSPS? Does "construction" include planning, contracting, purchase of the land, or site preparation? See United States v. City of Painesville, 644 F.2d 1186 (6th Cir.1981) [holding that a contract for the purchase of a boiler after publication of regulations made it a new source despite planning activities prior to the regulation and that a subsequent judicial remand of the NSPS did not nullify the obligation to comply with the eventual standard]. See also Sierra Pacific Power v. United States EPA, 647 F.2d 60 (9th Cir.1981) and Potomac Electric Power Co. v. EPA, 650 F.2d 509 (4th Cir.1981).

b. What is a "source" for the purpose of determining whether the NSPS program applies? Section 111(a)(3) [§ 7411(a)(3)] defines "stationary source" as "any building, structure, facility, or installation which emits or may emit any air pollutant." Does this definition help with the following problem? If an industrial plant with multiple emission points constructs an additional emission point but offsets the increase by reducing emissions at existing points, can it successfully claim that there is no modification because the term "source" refers to the combination of facilities? In ASARCO, Inc. v. EPA, 578 F.2d 319 (D.C.Cir.1978) the court invalidated prior EPA regulations permitting plantwide determinations of whether NSPS apply. Following this case, EPA has adopted a dual definition for "source" encompassing both the individual emissions point and the entire facility. This attempt to treat an entire plant as a source has become known as the "bubble concept" and has been approved for Prevention of Significant Deterioration (PSD) and non-attainment use. Why not also apply it in the NSPS context?

c. What about modifications of existing facilities? Section 111(a)(4) identifies modifications subject to NSPS when an alteration in the existing plant "increases the amount of any air pollutant emitted" or "results in the emission of any air pollutant not previously emitted." Why does the statute equate these kinds of events with the construction of a new facility? The Act also expands the range of modifications to include both physical changes and a "change in the methods of operation." However, there are limits to this expansive policy. If a plant increases its hours of operation or its production rate without any capital expenditure, would this be a "modification" subject to the NSPS? See 40 C.F.R. § 60.14(e)(2) & (3)(no). What about a fuel change increasing sulfur content? See Hawaiian Electric Co. v. United States EPA, 723 F.2d 1440 (9th Cir.1984)(yes, a modification). What about routine maintenance and repair actions on an existing source? 40 C.F.R. § 60.14(e)(no).

What about a major or significant plant modification? When is a plant reconstructed? EPA's NSPS regulations consider "reconstructed" units as new sources. Pursuant to these rules, any change that costs at least 50% of the total cost of a comparable new facility may subject the plant to NSPS requirements even if the air emissions do not increase. Once the 50% cost threshold is passed, EPA considers a number of other factors prior to apply the NSPS rules. See 40 C.F.R. § 60.5.

What might the implications be of a policy that extends the NSPS requirements to a broad range of plant modifications? Is it necessarily good for air quality? Will it discourage investment in older facilities for incremental improvements to the productive capacity and emission control efficiency? Might it encourage the continued use of older, marginally-efficient plants in an effort to avoid the imposition of the more costly NSPS? The U.S. General Accounting Office reported in 1985 older (pre–1971), existing electric generating facilities were expected to remain in service and comprise an ever-increasing share (l/3 by the year 2000) of domestic electricity production due to utility "life extension" projects. The CAA had encouraged that result. See USGAO, Electric Supply Older Plants' Impact on Reliability and Air Quality (Sept. 1990) [GAO/RCED–90–200].

d.   Relationship of NSPS to other Clean Air Act New Source Programs. The Clean Air Act has created specialized new source review programs for facilities locating in very clean (Prevention of Significant Deterioration) and very dirty (Non-attainment) areas. These programs are discussed below in the text. Each program imposes technological control requirements through the permitting process on these new sources separate and apart from the NSPS which must be at least as stringent as the NSPS. So where does the NSPS apply? It must be remembered that the PSD and non-attainment have source size thresholds and NSPS applies below that level.

3. *Clean Air Act Rulemaking Procedure.* One of the EPA's major responsibilities under the Clean Air Act is the development of regulations governing many aspects of the air pollution control program. Establishing the NSPS provides one example. Special procedural safeguards govern a broad range of rulemaking activities under the Clean Air Act, largely supplanting the general requirements under the Administrative Procedure Act. Read § 307(d) carefully. For instance, the notice of a proposed rule must be accompanied by "a statement of its basis and purpose." This procedural element was inserted in the Act in 1977 and effectively codified portions of the holding in Portland Cement Ass'n. v. Ruckelshaus, 486 F.2d 375 (D.C.Cir.1973). This statement shall include a summary of "(A) the factual data on which the proposed rule is based; (B) the methodology used in obtaining the data; and (C) the major legal interpretations and policy considerations underlying the proposed rule." § 307(d)(3) [§ 7606(d)(3)]. How do these procedural requisites go beyond that which is ordinarily required in the notice and comment rulemaking process? Why impose such extensive disclosure requirements on the agency? How might this obligation affect the EPA rulemaking process?

Other portions of § 307 are worth considering. This section further provides:

§ 307(d)(5) [§ 7607(d)(5)]. In promulgating a rule to which this subsection applies (i) the Administrator shall allow any person to submit written comments, data, or documentary information; (ii) the Administrator shall give interested persons an opportunity for the oral presentation of data, views, or arguments, in addition to an opportunity to make written submissions; (iii) a transcript shall be kept of any oral presentation; and (iv) the Administrator shall keep the record of such proceeding to provide an opportunity for submission of rebuttal and supplementary information.

6(A) The promulgated rule shall be accompanied by (i) a statement of basis and purpose like that referred to in paragraph (3) with respect to a proposed rule and (ii) an explanation of the reasons for any major changes in the promulgated rule from the proposed rule.

(B) The promulgated rule shall also be accompanied by a response to each of the significant comments, criticisms, and new data submitted in written or oral presentations during the comment period.

(C) The promulgated rule may not be based (in part or whole) on any information or data which has not been placed in the docket as of the date of such promulgation.

7(A) The record for judicial review shall consist exclusively of the material referred to in [this section].

(B) Only an objection to a rule or procedure which was raised with reasonable specificity during the period for public comment (including any public hearing) may be raised during judicial review. * * * Why do you suppose the CAA contains these procedural provisions? What purpose(s) do they serve?

In 1990 Congress added § 307(h) to the Act which provides that,

[I]t is the intent of Congress that, consistent with the policy of the Administrative Procedure Act, the Administrator in promulgating any regulation under this Chapter, including a regulation subject to a deadline, shall ensure a reasonable period for public participation of at least 30 days, except as otherwise provided [in listed sections].

Consider the following questions pertaining to these provisions. How do these requirements affect public participation in the EPA rulemaking process? Do they strike a balance between broad range public participation and administrative necessity? What about the interchange of ideas between EPA and commentators? Should EPA officials be subject to "live" cross-examination during the rule development process? Would this improve the rulemaking process or make it unwieldy and unmanageable? What if EPA makes a procedural error in following this complex scheme? Should the resulting rule be set aside because of it?

C. HAZARDOUS AIR POLLUTANT CONTROL (AIR TOXICS)

The main focus of the Clean Air Act in its first twenty years was the attainment and maintenance of the NAAQS. As previously noted, these air quality standards were intended to achieve clean air for health and welfare purposes. However, studies have associated serious illnesses (including cancer and lung diseases) and mortality to the exposure to a range of environmental contaminants or toxic substances. The most prominent of these correlations has been to cancer where the General Accounting Office has estimated that airborne toxics caused 3,000 annual cancer deaths in addition to birth defects, lung ailments, liver damage, and nervous system injuries. See U.S. Gen. Accounting Office, Air Pollution, EPA's Strategy and Resources May Be Inadequate to Control Air Toxics 8–9 (June 1991). Furthermore, the deposition of these airborne toxics on the land or in water is now believed to damage fish, birds, wildlife, and other natural resources. As a result, the NAAQS approach has been reinforced with a new emphasis on the control of hazardous air pollutants or air toxics. The following material presents this issue with a special emphasis on the response of the 1990 Clean Air Act amendments. Evaluate the statutory policy and the priority accorded it in the air quality program.

1.   THE NATURE AND SCOPE OF THE AIR TOXICS PROBLEM

Report of the House Committee on Energy and Commerce on H.R. 3030 (The Clean Air Act Amendments of 1990)

H.R.Rep. No. 101–490 Part 1, 101st Cong., 2d Sess. 315–323 (1990).

Title III: Provisions for Control of Hazardous Air Pollution

INTRODUCTION

Title III amends section 112 of the Clean Air Act to establish a new program for the control of hazardous air pollutants. Pollutants controlled under this section tend to be less widespread than those regulated under the NAAQS established under section 109 of the Act, but are often associated with more serious health impacts, such as cancer, neurological disorders, and reproductive dysfunctions. Because of their serious impacts, hazardous air pollutants are subject nationally to uniform, source category and subcategory specific controls. * * *

Summary of Title III

"Hazardous air pollutants" versus "criteria air pollutants"

The Clean Air Act distinguishes between two categories of pollutants: hazardous air pollutants and criteria or conventional air pollutants. Criteria air pollutants, as noted earlier, are defined as pollutants that "endanger public health or welfare" and "result from numerous or diverse mobile or stationary sources." These pollutants tend to be more pervasive, but less potent, than hazardous air pollutants. Examples include ozone, CO, and PM–10. The Act requires EPA to set National Ambient Air Quality Standards (NAAQS) for these pollutants, which the States have responsibility for achieving through State Implementation Plans (SIPs).

Hazardous air pollutants are pollutants that pose especially serious health risks. Under existing law, they are pollutants that "cause or contribute to an increase in mortality or an increase in serious irreversible, or incapacitating reversible, illness." They may reasonably be anticipated to cause cancer, neurological disorders, reproductive dysfunctions, other chronic health effects, or adverse acute human health effects.

Health and environmental effects from toxic emissions

Cancer risks from toxic emissions.—EPA, in a September 1989 draft report, presented an analysis of cancer risks in the U.S. from outdoor exposure to airborne toxic pollutants. The document, according to EPA, provides "updated information to suggest priorities for air toxics control." It states:

> This analysis is based primarily on information derived from recent studies and reports. Results are expressed as cancer risks from individual pollutants and source categories in terms of excess lifetime individual cancer risks and nationwide annual cancer cases.

> Health risks due to indoor exposure and noncancer health effects resulting from outdoor exposure are not included in this analysis but are addressed in separate studies. Risks from indoor exposures to certain pollutants can be significant because of higher indoor concentrations and the fact that most people spend much of their time indoors. Noncancer risks from outdoor exposure also may be significant but more information is needed to adequately quantify these risks.

> About 90 toxic air pollutants and 60 source categories were addressed in one or more of the studies examined. Additional risks associated with other pollutants and sources are uncharacterized. Of particular concern is the absence of information on pollutants secondarily formed in the atmosphere. Only one (formaldehyde) is considered in this analysis.

> Significant uncertainties are associated with estimating risk. These are due to both data limitations and assumption inherent in our current risk assessment methodology and the methodology required to combine and extrapolate information from individual studies to develop national estimates.

> Assumptions about cancer potencies of various chemicals or chemical mixtures are generally considered to overestimate the risk, as do assumptions about exposures. Uncertainties such as those due to missing pollutants, uncharacterized sources, and pollutant transformation in the atmosphere will underestimate the risk.

> Major findings on national cancer incidence and lifetime individual risk, highlighted below, are subject to uncertainties and data limitations as noted above.

Cancer incidence

Total excess cancer cases were estimated to be between 1,700 and 2,700 per year nationwide. This is equivalent to between 7 to 11 cancer cases per year per million population.

Of the approximately 90 pollutants evaluated, 12 accounted for over 90% of total annual cancer incidence. Of these, PIC (products of incomplete combustion) was responsible for about 35% of the total. Other major contributors include, 1,3–butadiene, hexavalent chromium, benzene, formaldehyde, and chloroform.

Motor vehicles accounted for almost 60% of total cancer incidence. Other area sources and point sources each accounted for approximately 20% of the total.

Other serious illnesses from toxic emissions.—There have been no quantitative assessments of the non-cancer risks created by toxic emissions although it is believed that toxic emissions can cause an array of serious illnesses besides cancer. These include birth defects, damage to the brain or other parts of the nervous system, reproductive disorders, and genetic mutations. In the case of emissions of some neurotoxins, even small doses can be lethal.

In 1987, senior EPA officials ranked qualitatively the non-cancer risks created by 31 environmental problems within the agency's jurisdiction. This report, called *"Unfinished Business, A Comparative Assessment of Our Environmental Problems,"* ranked these problems according to how important the problems were viewed by the public and how important problems were deemed by expert judgment and risk estimate. One of the 31 on the list was "hazardous/toxic air pollutants." According to the study, air toxics ranked as the second worst non-cancer health risk (and the sixth worst cancer problem on the list). The public polling data showed "air pollution" which includes hazardous/toxic air pollutants and criteria air pollutants to be ranked the fourth highest cause of concern on the list of environmental problems.

Environmental effects of toxic emission.—Toxics can cause adverse impacts to the environment as well as to human health. The Great Lakes in particular have been adversely affected, because their huge surface area acts as a sink for toxics that may come from air sources, some of which may be from hundreds of miles away. This problem was discovered when researchers found significant levels of PCBs and pesticides on remote Isle Royale National Park, a wilderness island in the middle of Lake Superior.

Many Great Lakes fish species are no longer considered edible because of toxic contamination. State agencies in every Great Lake State have issued health advisories warning that consumption of certain sport fish is unsafe due to elevated levels of PCBs, mercury, and other toxic pollutants. Michigan's Department of Natural Resources, in a January 13, 1990 letter to the Committee, said the "presence of PCBs is the most common reason for fish consumption advisories in the region." Atmospheric deposition contributes more than 50 percent of PCB loading in the upper Great Lakes and a significant, but undermined, portion of the mercury loading. These chemicals enter the bottom of the food chain at low levels, but through a process called "bioaccumulation" their concentrations increase as the chemicals move up the food chain. The species most commonly affected include fatty fish like lake trout and salmon in the case of PCBs (the chemical accumulates in their fat tissues) and large predator species like pike, muskie, and bass in the case of mercury.

Because of their small body weight, young children and fetuses are especially vulnerable to exposure to PCB-contaminated fish. One study has found long-term learning disabilities in children who had eaten high-levels of Great Lakes fish. Adults are also seriously affected. A recent study has found that a person eating one lake trout a year from Lake Michigan over his or her lifetime faces a cancer risk of 1 in 10,000.

2. THE REGULATION OF HAZARDOUS AIR POLLUTANTS PRIOR TO THE 1990 CLEAN AIR ACT

Like NSPS, hazardous air pollutants have been the subject of direct federal regulation under the Clean Air Act. Under the 1970 Act, both new and existing sources were regulated by § 112 through the technique of the National Emission Standard for Hazardous Pollutants or NESHAPs. Section 112(a)(1) [§ 7412(a)(1)] defined a hazardous pollutant as one,

> to which no ambient air quality standards is applicable and which in the judgment of the Administrator causes, or contributes to, air pollution which may reasonably be anticipated to result in an increase in mortality or an increase in serious irreversible, or incapacitating reversible, illness.

Did this language confer discretion on the Administrator? How much certainty of harmful effects does this section seem to require of EPA prior to regulating? Is risk of serious harm enough?

The 1970 Act provided for a three-step sequential process of (a) listing hazardous air pollutants, (b) standard-setting, and (c) standards enforcement. Its principal focus was the elimination of public health risks. During the early 1970's, EPA took little action to list pollutants for treatment under § 112. Consequently few hazardous pollutants were regulated under that section. In 20 years, EPA only managed to list eight such pollutants and adopt regulations for seven of them. Under the pre–1990 law, once a hazardous pollutant was listed, the standard-setting process must move at a rapid pace. Section 112 required that the EPA must propose "emission standards" for listed pollutants within 180 days and then issue final standards 180 days later, unless EPA finds that the pollutant "clearly is not" hazardous. § 112(b)(1)(B) [§ 7412(b)(1)(B)]. The NESHAP was to be set after a non-adjudicatory public hearing and it is effective upon promulgation. A careful reading of § 112 reveals that a NESHAP (1) must be an emission or a design, equipment, work practice or operational standard and (2) must provide an ample margin of safety to protect public health. Is "ample" margin of safety higher than "adequate" margin? Does the cost of control pay any role in the standard-setting process? Compare and contrast the standard-setting authority of § 112 with that of §§ 109 and 111 on this question.

Throughout the 1970s the § 112 program was controversial and quite limited in scope. Its history during this period was described in the following terms,

> Section 112 saw limited use, but plenty of controversy. EPA listed no more than a handful of hazardous pollutants and was slow to regulate all those on the list. Old section 112 could be read to require EPA to impose draconian controls to completely eliminate the risks whenever EPA concluded that an air pollutant may be hazardous at any level of emission. During the 1970s, concern over the severity of the regulatory requirements, and the belief that greater public health gains were to be won through attainment of the NAAQS, discouraged EPA from pulling the section 112 listing trigger very often.

Philip D. Reed, Federal Emission Limitations in Law of Environmental Protection 11–109 (S. Novick eds. 1995). By 1990, EPA had only regulated seven hazardous air pollutants under § 112—asbestos, beryllium, mercury, radionuclides, inorganic arsenic, benzene and vinyl chloride—and often only in extremely limited circumstances. Even this slow agency response was the result of litigation forcing EPA to act. See Sierra Club v. Gorsuch, 551 F.Supp. 785 (N.D.Cal.1982) (radionuclides) and New York v. Gorsuch, 554 F.Supp. 1060 (S.D.N.Y.1983) (organic arsenic).

3. MODERN AIR TOXICS REGULATION

Roy S. Belden, Clean Air Act

63–72 (ABA Section of Envt., Energy and Resources, 2001).

Control of Hazardous Air

Pollutants 1990 Amendments

In the 1990 Amendments, Congress completely restructured the air toxics program, with the goal of developing and implementing new technology-based standards for all listed HAP [Hazardous Air Pollutant] source categories and subcategories by November 15, 2000, including all major HAP sources and specified nonmajor "area" HAP sources [CAA § 112(e)]. As noted at the beginning of this chapter, the 1990 Amendments contemplate a two-phase NESHAP program. In the first phase, technology-based MACT standards will be promulgated, followed by development of residual-risk standards in the second phase. These two facets of the current NESHAP program are discussed in this chapter.

The Clean Air Act now lists 188 HAPs and specifically defines a hazardous air pollutant as "any air pollutant listed pursuant to subsection (b)" of Section 112. The CAA directs EPA periodically to review the HAP list; EPA may add or delete substances provided there is adequate scientific data to support such a determination. [CAA § 112(b)(2)]. In addition, any person may petition the EPA administrator to request that a pollutant either be added to or deleted from the list. [CAA § 112(b)(3)]. The agency is currently considering several petitions both to remove pollutants from and to add pollutants to the HAP list. To date, only one substance has been removed from the HAP list and none have been added.

Applicability

Section 112 of the Clean Air Act requires categories and subcategories of "major sources" of listed HAPs to meet maximum achievable control technology (MALT) emission limitations. The CAA generally defines a major source as any stationary source or group of stationary sources located within a contiguous area and under common control that emits or has the potential to emit, considering controls, 10 tons per year of an HAP or 25 tons per year of any combination of HAPs [CAA § 112(a)(1)]. An area source is defined as any nonmajor stationary source of HAPs [CAA § 112(a)(2)]. * * *

MACT Standard Setting

Source Categories

EPA was required, pursuant to CAA Section 112(c), to develop categories and subcategories of all major sources by November 15, 1991. EPA is also authorized to list categories of area sources. EPA's initial source category list, promulgated on July 16, 1992, contained 166 major source categories and 8 area source categories. EPA may revise the source category list, either on the agency's own initiative or based on consideration of a petition filed by any person. EPA most recently revised the source category and subcategory listings in November 1999.

After the categories and subcategories are listed, the Act directs EPA to promulgate MACT standards pursuant to Section 112(d). The CAA requires the agency to promulgate standards for not less than 40 source categories or subcategories by November 1992, another 25 percent by November 1994, an additional 25 percent by November 1997, and the remaining amount by November 2000. [CAA § 112(e)(1)]. In a December 3, Federal Register notice, EPA committed itself to promulgating at least 50 percent of the MACT standards for the source categories and subcategories (i.e., 87 of 174) by November 15, 1997, with the remaining standards scheduled to be promulgated by November 15, 2000. For the most part, EPA has adhered to its regulatory timeframes for issuing MACT standards; however, there have been delays in meeting the act's promulgation targets. As of December 2000, EPA had promulgated all of the MACT standards meeting the two-year, four-year, and seven-year target dates. However, EPA has promulgated only two MACT standards and proposed 15 standards for the ten-year (i.e., November 15, 2000) categories and subcategories. EPA still needs to promulgate approximately 40 MACT standards by May 15, 2002 to avoid triggering the Section 112(j) "hammer" provision. If EPA fails to promulgate all MACT standards by May 15, 2002, then under Section 112(j) of the Act, the owner or operator of a major source not currently covered by an applicable MACT must file an application for a permit to set a plant-specific MACT standard. An up-to-date listing of the status of EPA's promulgation of MACT standards is available at EPA's

Unified Air Toxics Web site which can be accessed at http://www.EPA.gov/ttn/uatw/. * * *

Defining MACT

Section 112(d) of the Clean Air Act specifies that EPA shall establish HAP emission standards for existing and new sources based on the maximum degree of reduction achievable "taking into consideration the cost of achieving such emission reduction, and any non-air quality health and environmental impacts and energy requirements." [CAA § 112(d)(2)]. This process for setting technology-based standards is similar to the NSPS program, with a few unique twists as to establishing the minimum level of control. For new sources, the minimum level of control (the "MACT floor") shall be set at a level no less stringent than "the emission control that is achieved in practice by the best controlled similar source, as determined by the Administrator." [CAA § 112(d)(3)]. Under this provision, EPA has taken the position that it has little discretion to alter the new source standard. In

particular, EPA has concluded that it may not consider the costs of control in setting new source MACT standards.

The MACT floor for existing standards is somewhat less stringent and affords the agency more flexibility. CAA Section 112(d) provides that the MACT standards shall not be less stringent than "the average emission limitation achieved by the best performing 12 percent of existing sources (for which the Administrator has emissions information) . . . in the category or subcategory for categories and subcategories with 30 or more sources." [CAA § 112(d)(3)(A)]. For categories or subcategories with less than 30 sources, the average limitation shall be based on the five best performing existing sources. [CAA § 112(d)(3)(B)]. EPA has taken the position that the "average emission limitation" of the top 12 percent of best controlled sources should be set at the 94th percentile (i.e., midpoint of the top 12 percent). Industry, in contrast, has argued that the average limit should be set at the 88th percentile (i.e., the minimum "average" level achieved by all top 12 percent of sources). To date, EPA's use of the average emission limitation in its MACT standard-setting methodology for existing sources has not been interpreted by the courts. However, in Sierra Club v. EPA.,[167 F.3d 658 (D.C.Cir.1999)] the D.C. Circuit reviewed whether EPA could use available state permit and regulatory data and supplement the state data with data from EPA's own testing program rather than using performance data from the specific facilities to calculate the average emission limitation achieved by the best performing 12 percent of sources. The court concluded that the use of state regulatory data involving applicable state emissions limits was permissible, but that EPA had not adequately explained the reasonableness of using the agency's supplemental testing data in its calculation of the MACT floor for existing medical waste incinerators. The court remanded the existing source MACT standards to EPA for further explanation on why the combined regulatory/test data provides an accurate picture of the emission performance of the incinerators. The court also held that EPA could set new source MACT standards based on a reasonable estimate of the performance of the "best controlled similar source"; however, these standards were also remanded because EPA did not sufficiently explain its rationale. The D.C. Circuit has also held that the Clean Air Act requires EPA to establish MACT standards for major HAP sources even if there is no control technology currently used by the particular industry to restrict such HAPs. [National Lime Ass'n v. EPA, 233 F.3d 625 D.C.Cir.2000)]. In such situations, the Act requires EPA to consider "process changes, substitution of materials or other modifications."

EPA also has authority under CAA Section 112(d) to go "beyond the floor" for existing sources and set standards more stringent than suggested by a MACT floor analysis. In general, EPA must demonstrate that such beyond-the-floor costs of control are reasonable. In National Lime Association, the D.C. Circuit remanded EPA's MACT standard for portland cement manufacturing facilities, because the agency failed to consider non-air quality health and environmental impacts in rejecting the need for beyond-the-floor standards for HAP metals. [233 F.3d at 635].

Compliance Deadlines

For existing sources, MACT standards must generally be achieved within three years of issuance of the final rule. In some instances, a one-year extension of the deadline may be obtained so that the source can install the requisite control technology. New sources must comply with the MACT standards from the commencement of operations. MACT standards and other applicable Section 112 requirements will generally be incorporated into a major source's Title V operating permit.

Section 112(1) also provides an early reduction option under which an existing source can elect to meet a 90 percent HAP reduction limit (95 percent for HAP particulates) before the applicable MACT standard is proposed? [CAA § 112(i)(5)]. Sources meeting this alternative HAP limit will qualify for a six-year extension of compliance with the final MACT standard for the particular HAP source category or subcategory. Sources could also qualify for the extension if they achieve the alternative standards before January 1, 1994, even if the otherwise applicable MACT standard was already proposed.

In addition, Section 112(g)(2) states that after the effective date of a Title V permit program in any state, no person may construct any major source of HAPs unless EPA (or the state permitting agency) determines that MACT for new sources will be met. Such a determination will be made on a case-by-case basis if no applicable MACT emission limitations have been established by EPA. [CAA § 112(g)(2)].

GACT Standards

Section 112(d)(5) of the Clean Air Act authorizes EPA to set emission standards or work practices for area sources of HAP emissions (i.e., nonmajor HAP emitters). EPA may promulgate NESHAP standards for area sources based on generally available control technologies (GACT), and EPA has broad authority to set GACT standards at levels less stringent than MACT-type standards [CAA§ 112(d)(5)]. GACT does not involve a "floor" technology standard evaluation, and it is generally a less vigorous emission standard than a MACT standard; however, it is not necessarily always less stringent than a MACT standard. For example, in the NESHAP for hazardous waste combustors, EPA determined that the same emissions standards should apply to both major and area HAP sources. EPA concluded that GACT for certain hazardous waste combustors should be the same as MACT because the standards are generally achievable by both types of sources. EPA is not required to promulgate GACT standards for HAP area sources, and thus far, only a few GACT standards have been promulgated (e.g., perchloroethylene emissions from dry cleaners).

Residual Risk Standards

EPA prepared and submitted its "Residual Risk Report to Congress" in March 1999, pursuant to CAA Section 112(f), which required EPA to report on the methods to be used to assess the residual risks that might remain after MACT standards had been promulgated and applied [U.S. EPA office of Air Quality Planning and Standards, Residual Risk Report to Congress, EPA–453/R–99–001 (Mar. 1999)]. EPA's Residual Risk Report includes a discussion of the methodologies the agency will use to analyze potential residual risks, as well as a framework for addressing the requirements to promulgate standards if necessary. Section 112(f)(2) directs EPA to promulgate residual risk standards within eight years after promulgation of applicable MACT standards if such residual risk protections are required "to provide an ample margin of safety to protect public health" or to set more stringent standards, if necessary, "to prevent, taking into consideration costs, energy, safety, and other relevant factors, an adverse environmental effect." [CAA § 112(f)(2)]. In the report, EPA did not identify a need for any additional legislation to address residual risks, but generally concluded that it had the requisite authority to proceed. EPA intends to use a risk analysis framework to identify, assess, and manage any residual risks remaining following the implementation of the MACT standards for the various source categories and subcategories.

To date, EPA has not proposed any residual risk standards; however, under Section 112(f), it must begin issuing residual risk standards in November 2001, if necessary, for the source categories of MACT standards that were required to be promulgated by November 15, 1992. In general, EPA is required to make a decision on whether residual risk standards are warranted for each category or subcategory subject to MACT standards. [CAA § 112(f)(2)]. Residual risk standards must be promulgated if the MACT standards applicable to sources in a particular category or subcategory emitting a known, probable, or possible human carcinogen do not reduce lifetime excess cancer risks to less than one in one million. [CAA § 112(f)(2)].

SECTION 5.   CLEANING UP THE AIR—THE PROBLEM OF NON-ATTAINMENT OF THE NAAQS

A.   INTRODUCTION AND OVERVIEW

The Clean Air Act establishes an environmental quality approach to the problem of combating air pollution. EPA has set NAAQS for a number of problematic pollutants and the states have been charged with the responsibility of devising a system for achieving these standards. If this were all that the Act contained, it would not have the same force or effect that it does. The critical factor providing some discipline to the Clean Air Act scheme for air quality improvement is the element of time. The NAAQS are to be attained by statutorily prescribed dates. For instance, under the terms of § 110 of the 1970 Clean Air Act, the primary NAAQS were to be met as early as May 31, 1975. However, in 1975 EPA informed Congress that nearly one quarter of the nation's Air Quality Control Regions were projected not to meet one or more NAAQS on time. Why would Congress have established this sweeping clean air goal and ordained its achievement in five years? Why build a fixed attainment date into the statute at all? Did this regulatory structure reflect either the optimism or the naiveté of the statute's drafters? Soon, the Act's simplicity would collide with other harsh realities.

What is to happen if air quality does not reach the NAAQS on time? Surprisingly, the 1970 Act did not address this depressing issue of attainment failure although some commentators suggested draconian consequences. For instance, Professor William Rodgers noted that,

> [T]he predicted consequence of non-attainment under the 1970 amendments was a flat ban on new sources for the obvious reason, to put it starkly, that if prevailing air quality brought death and destruction, there was little to commend a move that would aggravate conditions already quite bad enough. The very real prospect, then, was a shutdown of industrial growth in many parts of the nation.

1 W. Rodgers, *Environmental Law—Air and Water* 273 (1986). Beyond this significant industrial impact, imagine the possible remedies that could be proposed for air pollution caused by automobiles? The nonattainment issue highlighted an explosive issue of environmental federalism. To what degree would federal air pollution policies conflict with state and local economic development and land use interests?

As it turned out, EPA was unwilling to administer such a devastating blow to the American economy and in 1976 it fashioned an "offset" or "tradeoff" policy which would permit limited new source growth in nonattainment areas. New facilities would be allowed to locate in such areas if their emissions would be offset by a reduction in source emissions resulting in a "positive net air quality benefit." See 41 Fed.Reg. 55528–29 (1976). But even this new EPA policy could not relieve existing sources operating in these areas after the passage of the attainment dates. Must they close down? Would major domestic economic and social policy be determined by the Clean Air Act?

In 1977 Congress dealt with this complex issue by extending the NAAQS attainment dates, adopting the structure of the tradeoff policy, and demanding SIP revisions in nonattainment areas as a pre-conditioned for the extension. The statutory provisions for nonattainment policy are primarily found in §§ 171–178 [§§ 7501–08] which is also referred to as Part D. Section 172 forced the states to undertake a new round of SIP development aimed achieving NAAQS compliance by specified dates. Section 172(a) provided that primary NAAQS must be attained by no later than December 31, 1982. In addition, those areas unable to meet this deadline for photo-chemical oxidants (ozone) or carbon monoxide were eligible for a further extension until December 31, 1987. Section 172(b) [§ 7502(b)] set out a list of eleven plan components that rivals § 110(a)(2) in detail. The 1977 Clean Air Act amendments required that these Part D SIPs were to be submitted to EPA by January 1, 1979 with the agency approving them by July 1, 1979. The 1977 amendments retained the Act's goal of uniform NAAQS achievement by statutorily-mandated deadlines. It also maintained faith in the efficacy of the SIP process as the means for ultimately reaching the air quality standards.

In the 1977–1987 period, states were slow to amend their SIP and not surprisingly non-attainment was a widespread problem affecting tens of millions of people. In fact, by 1988 EPA estimated that 112 million people lived in ozone nonattainment areas. Why had the Act failed? Professor Arnold Reitze has suggested seven reasons why the efforts to reach Clean Air Act air quality goals failed.

(1) The problems the CAA was attempting to correct were being exacerbated by increases in population and consumption. The U.S. population of 205.05 million in 1970 grew to 250.41 million in 1990. U.S. energy consumption, which is responsible for most air pollution, went from 66.43 quadrillion British thermal units (Btus) in 1970 to 85.4 quads in 1990. Electric power generation, the most significant stationary source of air pollution, grew from 1532 billion kilowatt hours (KWH) in 1970 to 2795 billion KWH in 1990. Energy consumed by the transportation sector grew from 16.04 quads in 1970 to 22.36 quads in 1990. The size of the automobile fleet in the United States grew from 89.2 million vehicles in 1970 to 139 million vehicles in 1987. The effect of this growth is to nullify much of the progress made under the CAA.

(2) Congress passed the 1990 CAA Amendments and the President signed them into law. However, those opposed to the statute continue to work to prevent its effective implementation. The CAA imposes its costs unevenly. Economic growth in some areas of the nation is restricted more than in other areas. Some industries have faced huge costs for compliance at a time when they faced stiff foreign competition. The many opponents to the CAA requirements translate their opposition into political action. The Reagan/Bush Administrations, acting through the Office of Management and Budget and through the Council on Competitiveness, slowed or stopped regulations or required that they be rewritten to lower costs to the private sector. In Congress, the appropriation process is used to deny the EPA the money needed to implement the CAA. The Congressional oversight process is used to intimidate EPA from aggressively pursuing the CAA goals.

(3) The 1970 CAA demanded a ninety percent reduction in motor vehicle emissions. This anticipated reduction was programmed into the

plans made by the states to reach the NAAQS. The mobile source air pollution program has been relatively successful when compared with other pollution control programs, but still has not achieved a ninety percent reduction in emissions. At the same time, vehicle miles traveled (VMT) and energy consumed by transportation have increased. Thus, more vehicles, driving more miles and emitting more air pollution per mile traveled than projected by programs under the 1970 CAA, have helped create a nonattainment status for much of the United States.

(4) The measures used to control air pollution were not as effective as anticipated: (a) incorrect data was used in many models used in SIP development; (b) linear rollback models did not work well, especially for ozone because its atmospheric formation is complex, and other more sophisticated models also had significant limitations; and (c) unjustified assumptions concerning the effectiveness of various control strategies were used in SIPs.

(5) The CAA regulated new sources much more stringently than existing sources. The expectation was that air quality would improve, over time, as existing sources were replaced. However, the costs of complying with the CAA led industry to maintain existing facilities beyond their expected useful life. Thus, the imposition of new source standards move more slowly than originally expected.

(6) Control measures were not implemented: (a) technology was not available or was too costly to use; and (b) local opposition prevented the quick and effective development of strategies such as I/M and Stage II vapor recovery.

(7) Control measures and other requirements of the CAA were not enforced.

Arnold Reitze, Air Pollution Law 60–61 (1995).

CLASS DISCUSSION PROBLEM: BUILDING THE BOATMANN MANUFACTURING PLANT IN JORDANVILLE

Boatmanns, AG, a large, diversified German manufacturing firm, has determined that it wishes to locate its North American manufacturing and distribution center for its line of computer printers in the State of Wilsonia. The state's position in the central part of the country makes it perfectly suited for such a plant and its skilled workforce provides an available pool of employees for the facility. Boatmanns has entered into discussions with the Southern Wilsonia Economic Development Commission ("Commission") about finding a specific site for the printer plant in the Jordanville metropolitan area. This area, having a population of approximately 375,000, has a great need for economic development since its unemployment rate has remained at least two to three percentage points higher than the national average for the last three years.

Boatmanns proposed Jordanville facility has been modeled after other plants that the company operates both in Europe and in Asia. It employs modern production and pollution control technology yet the plant's specifications indicate that there will be air emissions in the following amounts: (1) Oxidants or ozone pollution—1,000 tons per year (tpy), (2) Nitrogen oxide pollution—500 tpy, and (3) Benzene pollution—2 tpy. The Commission is supportive of Boatmanns proposal but several staff members have expressed concern over the air quality impacts of the facility. The staff has information that the Jordanville metropolitan area has been formally designated nonattainment by the State of Wilsonia for the pollutant ozone. Its design value for ozone is ;5 parts per million while the primary NAAQS is .12 ppm. Other recent data indicates that the area is in attainment for carbon monoxide (CO) but only by a slim margin. There is no NAAQS for benzene.

1. If the Commission finds an otherwise suitable site for the proposed Boatmanns plant within the Jordanville area, will the facility's air emissions preclude or otherwise affect its location? What if Boatmann had a preexisting plant in Jordanville which currently is allowed to emit 2000 tons per year of oxidants. Could the firm voluntarily reduce these emissions by 1000 tpy and then construct the new computer printer plant without undergoing § 173 new source review?

2. What kind of analysis must be done to determine whether the Boatmann plant can be operated in Jordanville? What analytical process does the Clean Air Act § 173 require before a source with these emission characteristics may be allowed to locate in the Jordanville nonattainment area?

3. If Boatmanns must acquire "offset credits" in order to locate in Jordanville,

> a.   How is this offset to be accomplished? Suggest ways for Boatmanns to obtain these reductions. What might be some anticipated complications.

> b.   How are the acquired emission reductions or credits to be measured? What is the "baseline" against which emission offsets are to be credited? Is the baseline to be measured from those emission theoretically allowed under the approved SIP or those actually occurring in practice. Why does this matter?

> c.   Assuming the area is also in nonattainment status for carbon monoxide, could Boatmanns obtain CO offset credits from another source and use them in the offset calculation for the proposed facility? EPA generally bars such interpollutant offsets. Why would the agency take that position? Is it wise? Why not accept a "blend" of offset credits?

> d.   Where can the offset credits be found? Should Boatmanns be allowed to obtain offsets in New York for its new source in Wilsonia (a distance of 850 miles)? What about credits from the adjacent State of Perkins? Should the rule differ depending upon the transport or other characteristics of the pollutant? Should Boatmanns receive full credit for emission reductions at distant sites even if the pollutant is mobile?

e. Should Boatmanns get offset credit for a source that is shut down or curtails its production levels? What if this pre-existing source shut down before Boatmanns sought its permit? EPA generally does not grant offset credit in this situation. Why not? What if Boatmanns was building its new facility as a replacement for an older one which it had closed? Should EPA bar this credit also?

f. Assuming that Boatmanns wishes to introduce 1000 tons per year of oxidants into the non-attainment area, how many tons must it remove by way of offset credits? Would 1000 tons be enough? Does the Act anticipate a greater than one-for-one substitution of pollution? Read § 173(1)(a) [§ 7503(1)(a)]. If so, would 1001 tons be enough? How about 2000 tons? How should this offset ratio be established? EPA's offset guidance documents only requires that the offset show a "positive net air quality benefit in the affected area." What policy should govern this issue? Should the policy explicitly consider other factors such as employment effects, fuel use, land use issues, hazardous waste production, etc. in setting the offset ratio.

4. If Boatmanns can acquire not only the oxidant offsets required by § 173 but have 100 tpy of offsets left over, can these 100 tons per year be retained or "banked" for future use by Boatmanns or sale to another firm? How would such an emissions offset credit "bank" work? Who would oversee its operation? Would these credits, once recognized, be considered "property?" What might be the implications of this?

B. THE NONATTAINMENT AREA AIR QUALITY PLANNING PROGRAM

1. THE 1990 ACT PROVISIONS

Philip D. Reed, Implementation Plans 11–54 to 11–59 in Law of Environmental Protection

S. Novick et al. eds. 1995.

The Clean Air Act Amendments of 1990

Title I of the 1990 Amendments sets out a new program to bring non-attainment areas into compliance with the NAAQS. Congress rewrote section 110(a)(2) and Part D and added special nonattainment SIP requirements for ozone, carbon monoxide, and particulate matter. The centerpiece of the new requirements is the ozone SIP provision, which incorporates several novel concepts. The new Subpart 2 to Part D classifies nonattainment areas on a five-point scale from "Marginal" to "Extreme" and allows progressively more time for each higher class to attain the NAAQS, but also requires increasingly stringent control measures for each higher class. Controls based on federal control guidelines are mandated for more existing sources. Another major innovation is that the reasonable further progress concept is translated into a quantified "milestones" for ozone nonattainment areas. Areas that miss the milestones are to be automatically subject to more stringent "contingency" measures required to be included in the SIP. In addition, they may be moved into a higher class, thereby requiring them to adopt additional controls. The new program will be a dramatic challenge for EPA, the states and the urban areas that are ozone nonattainment areas.

Nonattainment Area Designations and Classifications

The Amendments give EPA more control over the general process for designating nonattainment areas. EPA now may revise the state's proposed designations or trigger the redesignation process. Until nonattainment area SIPs have been approved, it apparently will be virtually impossible for states to have nonattainment areas redesignated to attainment status. Notice and comment rulemaking is not required for designations.

For purposes of implementing the new nonattainment provisions of the Act, designations in place on November 15, 1990 are carried forward. States must submit revised lists of ozone and carbon monoxide nonattainment areas to EPA within 120 days of enactment, but cannot redesignate nonattainment areas to other status in this review. Areas designated nonattainment for particulate matter under the total suspended particulate standard are automatically deemed nonattainment for PM_{10}, but the existing TSP attainment designations for total suspended particulate are preserved for the PSD program.

SIP Review Procedures

The 1990 Amendments revise the basic SIP review process, largely to relieve EPA of extreme administrative burdens created by the original system and to give it greater leverage with the states. When a new NAAQS is promulgated, the states have three years to submit new SIPs. The deadlines for submission of the SIP revisions required by the Amendments are found in the pollutant-specific sections. The Amendments insert a new "completeness" step into the process. From the time a state submission is complete, EPA has twelve months to review and act on it. The Amendments officially authorize the expedient SIP approval options developed by EPA over the years, so that EPA's action on a state plan may be approval, partial approval, conditional approval or disapproval. Partial approval does not relieve the state of any consequences of missing a deadline, however, and conditional approval automatically reverts to disapproval if the conditions are not satisfied within one year. While EPA will have greater flexibility than under the 1977 Amendments, it still may face widespread noncompliance by the state with the new ultimate deadlines and it is not clear that it will be politically any easier to enforce the Act literally to allow the "automatic" penalties to be imposed.

General SIP and Part D Requirements

The Amendments rewrite section 110(a)(2), making several significant changes. The "other" control measures that may be included in a SIP now are defined specially to include economic incentives. In addition, the construction moratorium of old section 110(a)(2)(I) has been deleted. Sanctions for states that fail to live up to their SIP obligations still include cuts in federal highway funding (unless the funding is for safety or air quality projects), but a new sanction, replacing the construction moratorium, is a tougher offset rule; offsets that must be obtained in order to construct major new sources in nonattainment areas must be 2 to 1. EPA retains the authority to issue a notice of deficiency to the states if a SIP is substantially inadequate to meet the requirements of the Act and must promulgate a federal implementation plan within two years of a state's failure to submit a satisfactory plan or to correct deficiencies in a plan on schedule, unless the state corrects the deficiencies before EPA promulgates its plan.

The special Part D SIP requirements for nonattainment areas also are rewritten in the Amendments. The basic attainment deadline for such areas is five years. Non-attainment areas may be classified by the extent to which existing air quality exceeds the NAAQS, with up to an additional five years allowed the more seriously polluted areas for attainment. All nonattainment areas SIPs now must include contingency measures that take effect *automatically* if any applicable reasonable further progress "milestone" or attainment deadline is missed. New source review programs must be tightened. Nonattainment SIPs must remain in force after attainment until EPA has approved a maintenance SIP, which must automatically reactivate the nonattainment SIP and other appropriate contingency provisions in the event that the area regressed into nonattainment. EPA may impose either the funding or offset sanction for noncompliance with SIP deadlines at any time after determining that the state is not in compliance, and must impose one of the two if such noncompliance continues for eighteen months. If the deficiency is not corrected within an additional six months, EPA must also impose the other sanction.

2. THE DESIGNATION OF NONATTAINMENT AREAS

As the material below will indicate, the attainment status of an area is an exceedingly important bit of information having significant implications for the economic growth potential of the region. The 1977 amendments established a procedure for classifying all lands for purposes of the Act. First, it required that the states submit lists of data by early 1978 identifying the attainment status of all AQCRs within their borders. See § 107(d) [§ 7407(d)]. Next, EPA was mandated to promulgate this listing either intact or as modified by the agency. This step was to be accomplished within sixty days of the state's submittal of its list. Finally, states could propose revisions to the attainment listing to EPA for consideration. The 1990 Clean Air Act amendments continue much of present practice.

The attainment status is reported, usually on a county-by-county basis, for each of the pollutants having an NAAQS. EPA has published a state-by-state listing of attainment status in 40 C.F.R. Part 81 (1999), and at http://www.epa.gov/oar/oaqps/greenbk/index.html. This status is reported as either meeting primary or secondary standards, not meeting these standards or unclassifiable. How do the states and EPA know what the actual air quality is on such a particularized basis? Both actual monitoring data and diffusion modeling projections may serve as the basis for nonattainment designation. Some have objected to basing such an important determination such as attainment status upon computer modeling predictions. However, the statute clearly anticipated the use of this data—see § 171(2) [§ 7501(2)]—and the courts have been extremely agreeable in accepting this form of information. See e.g., Republic Steel Corp. v. Costle, 621 F.2d 797 (6th Cir.1980) and Cincinnati Gas & Electric Co. v. Costle, 632 F.2d 14 (6th Cir.1980) (accepting modeling data even when there were some actual monitoring measurements indicating attainment of the NAAQS).

The listing of nonattainment areas does not create a static database. As one might imagine, air quality conditions change over time with alterations in the pattern of pollutant emissions. Under the 1990 Act, both EPA and the states can propose redesignations. Why might these designations be so important? The redesignation of attainment status occurs on a continuing basis, often at the request of the status. EPA is not obligated to accept the state's request. EPA's rejection of the State of Kentucky's petition requesting redesignation of the Kentucky portion of the Cincinnati–Northern Kentucky Moderate Non-attainment Area to attainment status resulted in litigation which ultimately upheld EPA. Commonwealth of Kentucky v. EPA, 1998 U.S. App. LEXIS 21686.

3. NONATTAINMENT PROGRAM STRUCTURE

Sliding Scale Compliance Dates. The 1990 Act requires attainment "as expeditiously as practicable, but no later than 5 years from the date the area was designated nonattainment under section 107(d) * * *" § 172(a)(2). EPA is authorized to extend this period for as much as another 5 years and additionally, a state could request up to two 1 year extensions. The severity of the air pollution problem and feasibility of control measures determines the length of the extension. Secondary NAAQSs must be attained as "expeditiously as practicable," which has been interpreted to be "a reasonable time" in the legislative history. H.R.Rep. No. 101–490 Part I, 101st Cong., 2d Sess. 223 (1990).

The 1990 Act has taken a more customized approach to attainment questions by

• classifying non-attainment conditions according to severity,

• imposing mandatory SIP features depending upon nonattainment category, and

• establishing a sliding scale of extended NAAQS attainment dates which are proportionate to the severity of violation. Of central importance, of course, is the classification into which each individual nonattainment area falls. For instance, ozone nonattainment areas receive the most particularized attention with five levels of nonattainment (marginal, moderate, serious, severe, and extreme) set out. A "design value" is assigned to each area and that rating dictates the particular nonattainment classification. The following chart—derived from § 181(a)—reflects the relationship between each area classification and the new attainment date for *ozone* nonattainment areas.

Area classification	Design value (ppm)	Primary standard attainment date (years after enactment)
Marginal (up to 15% over)	.121 up to .135	3
Moderate (15 to 33% over)	.138 up to .160	6
Serious (33 to 50% over) . .	.160 up to .180	9
Severe (50 to 233% over) . .	.180 up to .280	15
Extreme (more than 233% over)	.280 and above	20

Could a state be required to reach attainment earlier than these dates? The House Report on the Act indicates that these dates were intended as,

> outside limits intended to provide a reasonable target for a large class of nonattainment areas. In the case of each individual nonattainment area, the bill continues the responsibility to attain as expeditiously as practicable. The objective is to achieve the standard as early as possible with effective and enforceable measures and without gaming by the States, industry and others.

H.R.Rpt. No. 101–490 Part 1, 101st Cong., 2d Sess. 229 (1990). Other NAAQS pollutants have less complex classifications with CO and PM–10 having moderate and serious categories with 5 and 10 year attainment dates respectively. See §§ 186(a) [§ 7512(a)] & 188(a) [§ 7513(a)]. Generally, nonattainment areas for sulfur oxides, nitrogen dioxide and lead are placed in single classification and are accorded five years to attain the air quality standards.

Nonattainment Area Air Quality Planning. Under the 1990 law, air quality planning and control requirements are distributed according to the severity of the nonattainment condition; as the area's classification moves to a higher level, the SIP must comply with the requirements of the preceding class plus additional requirements. This graduated control program links a more aggressive array of control elements with the generally longer NAAQS attainment date. Consider the example of ozone nonattainment. For marginal nonattainment areas (the least polluted category), § 182(a) requires states to submit a) a comprehensive emissions inventory within 2 years, b) SIP revisions including EPA-proposed reasonably available control technology, a corrected auto inspection and maintenance program (when one is already required) and a new or modified source review program, c) updated emission inventories at 3 year intervals along with stationary source emission statements and d) general offset requirements of only 1.1 to 1 for new or modified facilities.

When an area has worse air quality in the "moderate" range, these rather minimal requirements for marginal ozone nonattainment areas are augmented to include four additional features. See § 182(b). First, a SIP must be submitted providing for at least a 15% reduction in VOC emissions by 1996. Second, EPA-defined reasonably available control technology (RACT) must be applied on all major stationary sources and included in air pollution permits. Third, all moderate areas must have an auto inspection and maintenance program in place conforming to EPA guidance. Fourth, the state's SIP must require gasoline stations to install and operate Stage II vapor recovery by mid–1993 to 1995. And fifth, the ratio of required emission offsets for new or modified facilities is raised slightly to 1.15 to 1 in moderate areas. As the degree of ozone pollution worsens up the scale to the "extreme" (i.e. Los Angeles), the 1990 statute mandates an extended list of enhanced pollution control requirements including "major sources" defined as small as 10 tons per year, emission offset requirements of 1.5 to 1, clean fuels used in industry, emission reduction milestones, and VOC emission fees of $5,000 per ton. In great degree, Congress has set forth SIP requirements for nonattainment areas in explicit detail reducing EPA and state discretion. Why would Congress have taken such a position requiring SIPs to be formulated in such specific detail? Is this inflexible approach consistent with the changing political landscape in the second half of the 1990s?

4. NONATTAINMENT PROGRAM PERFORMANCE

Nonattainment of the NAAQS remains a serious air quality problem into the new century. In September, 1999 EPA estimated that 105 million people live in areas designated as nonattainment for at least one of the criteria pollutants. By January, 2001 this number had risen to approximately 108 million people. Current information about the number and location of nonattainment areas can be found in EPA's "Greenbook" at www.epa.gov/oar/oaqps/greenbk. The following Table 4–3 taken from EPA data illustrates the relative non-attainment status between criteria air pollutants and the number of persons affected by each one.

Table 4–3.   Nonattainment Status

Pollutant	Original # areas	1999 # areas	1999 Population (In 1000s)
CO	43	20	33,230
Pb	12	8	1,116
NO_2	1	0	0
O_3	101	32	92,505
PM_{10}	85	77	29,880
SO_2	51	31	4,371

EPA National Air Quality and Emission Trends Report, 1999

This chart indicates that ozone pollution affects the greatest number Americans. However, the next chart reveals the severity of the NAAQS violation in relation to the number of exposed persons.

Ozone Nonattainment Area Summary

As of January 29, 2001

Classification	Number of Areas	Number of Counties	Population (1000s)
Extreme	1	4	13,000
Severe (2007)	5	51	31,387
Severe (2005)	4	27	10,666
Serious	14	80	28,962
Moderate	10	36	7,733
Marginal	21	43	7,321
Other	1	9	5,815
SUBTOTAL	56	241	104,884
Section 185A	4	10	2,101
Incomplete Date	15	16	1,236
SUBTOTAL	19	26	3,337
GRAND TOTAL	75	266	108,221

Source: http://www.epa.gov/air/oaqps/greenbk/onsum.html

C.   New Source Review in Nonattainment Areas

From the discussion concerning air quality planning it is certain that nonattainment policy can have a dramatic impact on a community's economic development. Assume that an area has been designated as nonattainment for one or more of the NAAQS, can a new industrial or commercial facility be located which will increase emissions of these pollutants? As a general matter major stationary sources must obtain an air pollution permit prior to commencing construction regardless of whether they are proposed for attainment or nonattainment areas. To allow the construction of the facility would improve local employment and economic development, but it could also worsen air quality conditions. Examine the statutory language of § 173 to identify the policy for new source construction in nonattainment areas. How would it affect your answer to the Boatmann Manufacturing Company class discussion problem?

Excerpts from the Clean Air Act

42 U.S.C. § 7503.

§ 173(a). In General. The permit program required by section 172(b)(6) shall provide that permits to construct and operate may be issued if—

(1) in accordance with regulations issued by the Administrator for the determination of baseline emissions in a manner consistent with

the assumptions underlying the applicable implementation plan approved under section 110 and this part, the permitting agency determines that—

(A) by the time the source is to commence operation, sufficient offsetting emissions reductions have been obtained, such that total allowable emissions from existing sources in the region, from new or modified sources which are not major emitting facilities, and from the proposed source will be sufficiently less than total emissions from existing sources (as determined in accordance with the regulations under this paragraph) prior to the application for such permit to construct or modify so as to represent (when considered together with the plan provisions required under section 172) reasonable further progress (as defined in section 171); or

(B) in the case of a new or modified major stationary source which is located in a zone (within the non-attainment area) identified by the Administrator, in consultation with the Secretary of Housing and Urban Development, as a zone to which economic development should be targeted, that emissions of such pollutant resulting from the proposed new or modified major stationary source will not cause or contribute to emissions levels which exceed the allowance permitted for such pollutant for such area from new or modified major stationary sources under section 172(c);

(2) the proposed source is required to comply with the lowest achievable emission rate;

(3) the owner or operator of the proposed new or modified source has demonstrated that all major stationary sources owned or operated by such person (or by any entity controlling, controlled by, or under common control with such person) in such State are subject to emission limitations and are in compliance, or on a schedule for compliance, with all applicable emission limitations and standards under this Act;

(4) the Administrator has not determined that the applicable implementation plan is not being adequately implemented for the nonattainment area in which the proposed source is to be constructed or modified in accordance with the requirements of this part; and

(5) an analysis of alternative sites, sizes, production processes, and environmental control techniques for such proposed source demonstrates that benefits of the proposed source significantly outweigh the environmental and social costs imposed as a result of its location, construction, or modification.

Any emission reductions required as a precondition of the issuance of a permit under paragraph (1) shall be federally enforceable before such permit may be issued.

Sierra Club v. Larson

United States Court of Appeal, First Circuit, 1993.
2 F.3d 462.

■ BOUDIN, CIRCUIT JUDGE.

In this case, the Sierra Club appeals from the judgment of the district court declining to enjoin construction of the central artery/third harbor tunnel project in Boston. It also petitions to review the action of the Environmental Protection Agency in approving an amendment to Massachusetts state regulations that bears upon the project. We affirm the district court and deny the petition for review.

I.   THE FACTS AND PRIOR PROCEEDINGS

Massachusetts, through its Department of Public Works, has begun construction of a mammoth project that includes rebuilding a major segment of Interstate Route 93 that now runs on a viaduct through downtown Boston and is known as "the central artery." When the central artery tunnel project is completed some years from now, the highway segment in question will be widened, sunk below ground level, and mostly covered. It will connect at the north with a new bridge across the Charles River and at the south with a newly built third harbor tunnel running from South Boston to Logan Airport in East Boston.

The depressed and covered portion of the new highway and the tunnel will be ventilated by ducts and fans in six buildings located on the highway route and near the tunnel portals. Vast amounts of air will be drawn into the covered highway and tunnel, and the mixture of air and motor vehicle emissions will be pumped up through the six buildings and exhausted through stacks ranging from 90 to 225 feet high. Studies indicate that the project will reduce traffic congestion, increase average speeds, and reduce area-wide carbon monoxide and hydrocarbon emissions.

The Sierra Club, a non-profit environmental group, believes that whatever the area-wide effects of the project, it will create new "hot spots" of pollution in certain of the neighborhoods near to the six ventilation buildings. In its view, pollution control equipment, in the nature of after-burners, should be installed in the ventilation buildings. The federal and state governments, which have filed a joint brief in this case, deny that any dangerous hot spots will be created, pointing to studies conducted as part of the project's environmental review. They also assert that after-burner technology is not feasible because of the low concentration of pollutants in the vented air.

In March 1991, the Sierra Club and certain of its members who live in the vicinity of the central artery brought suit in district court against a collection of state and federal officials associated with the project. The gravamen of the suit was the Sierra Club's claim that the ventilation buildings planned for the project comprised a "major stationary source" of air pollution as that term is used in the Clean Air Act, 42 U.S.C. § 7401, *et seq.,* and the counterpart Massachusetts regulations, 310 C.M.R. § 7.00 *et seq.* It is common ground that, if the ventilation buildings were so classified, then the project would require a permit or permits from Massachusetts that have not been secured. To frame this issue entails a brief description of the statute.

The Clean Air Act enacted a complex statutory regime, several times amended, to control and mitigate air pollution in the United States. Broadly speaking, Title I of the statute regulates stationary sources of pollution and Title II regulates mobile sources, most importantly motor vehicles. For specified pollutants, national air quality standards are promulgated by the EPA. 42 U.S.C. § 7409. Whether new construction of polluting facilities is permitted in an area, and what kind of controls are required, depends on whether the area is below or above the standard for each pollutant. Part C, 42 U.S.C. §§ 7470–7492, governs permits where the standard has been attained; Part D applied to so-called nonattainment areas. *Id.* §§ 7501–7515.

In either event, the construction of a "major" new stationary source— normally, one emitting 100 or more tons of pollutant each year, see 42 U.S.C. § 7602(j)—generally requires a permit. 42 U.S.C. §§ 7475(a), 7502(c)(5). In the case of Boston, some of the pollutants that will flow through the proposed ventilation buildings currently exceed national standards so that new major sources are subject to the more stringent class of limitations; other pollutants are below the standards and less stringent limitations apply. By way of example, the Boston area exceeds the national standards for carbon monoxide, and to secure a permit the highway proponents would have to show that a major stationary source can achieve the "lowest achievable emission rate" for that pollutant. 42 U.S.C. § 7503(a)(2).

The Clean Air Act allocates different responsibilities to the EPA on the one hand and to the state on the other. Each state is directed to adopt and submit to the EPA for approval a state implementation plan to achieve and maintain the national standards established by the EPA. 42 U.S.C. § 7410(a). See also id. §§ 7471, 7502. If the state fails to adopt an approvable plan, the EPA must adopt federal regulations for the area. 42 U.S.C. § 7410(c). Massachusetts has an approved state implementation plan. Under the Clean Air Act, "citizen" suits may be brought to enjoin a project that requires a permit under Parts C or D but has not obtained one. 42 U.S.C. § 7604(a)(3).

In this case, in April 1991, the Sierra Club and certain of its members sought a preliminary injunction against construction of the central artery and tunnel project. The request was denied on July 30, 1991. After transfer of the case to another judge, the district court received further briefing and argument. On September 16, 1992, the court granted summary judgment in favor of the government defendants, state and federal, holding that the ventilation buildings did not comprise stationary sources subject to preconstruction permit requirements. The Sierra Club and its named members appealed.

Shortly before the lawsuit, the Massachusetts Department of Environmental Protection submitted to the EPA on January 30, 1991, a new regulation—regulation 7.38, codified as 310 C.M.R. § 7.38 as a proposed amendment to the Massachusetts state implementation plan. This regulations seeks to classify tunnel ventilation systems as "indirect sources" under the Clean Air Act. In the early 1970s, the EPA had begun to require that state implementation plans regulate such facilities as parking lots, highways, and garages that do not emit pollutants themselves but attract numbers of polluting vehicles. Congress responded in 1977 by barring the EPA from regulation of what were called "indirect sources." 42 U.S.C. § 7410(a)(5)(B). However, Congress at the same time gave the states permission, if they so chose, to regulate such indirect sources themselves as part of their state implementation plans. *Id.* § 7410(a)(5)(A), (C).

Massachusetts, exercising this option through regulation 7.38, proposed to regulate roadway/tunnel ventilation systems as indirect sources. The regime involves certification by the building that specified pollution standards will be met, and the Department of Environmental Protection may accept, conditionally approve, or reject the certification after notice and hearing. Monitoring after construction and periodical renewal of the certificate are required. The new regulation also states that the systems are not subject to the preconstruction permitting required for various stationary sources under regulation 7.02, 310 C.M.R. § 7.02.

The Sierra Club opposed the approval of regulation 7.38 when Massachusetts submitted it to the EPA as an amendment to the state implementation plan. The Sierra Club argued that the effect would be indirectly to relieve the project at issue in this case of the more stringent pre-construction approval required of major stationary sources under the Clean Air Act and the Massachusetts regulations that apply to stationary sources. After notice and receipt of public comments, the EPA on October 8, 1992, published notice of its approval, 57 Fed.Reg. 46310 (1992). The Sierra Club then petitioned for review of the EPA's action in this court pursuant to 42 U.S.C. § 7607(b)(1).

Because of the overlapping issues and common subject, this court consolidated the two appeals taken from the district court judgment with the proceeding for direct review of the EPA action. In this opinion, we address [the] statutory issues posed by the appeals from the district court and the additional issues posed by the Massachusetts regulations and by the petition to review the EPA's action approving regulation 7.38.

III. THE STATUTORY ISSUES

The merits of the appeals from the district court judgment turn principally on a narrow point of statutory construction, namely, whether the ventilation buildings that will vent the underground highway and harbor tunnel comprise a "stationary source or sources" within the meaning [of] the Clean Air Act. If so labeled, a permit is required; apparently the amount of pollutant needed to qualify as a "major" source is not at issue. Easily stated, the issue is less resolved: there is little by way of statutory definition, no useful judicial precedent or legislative history offered to us, and a reasonable possibility that Congress never gave any thought to the idiosyncracy posed by these ventilation buildings.

Starting as one normally does with language, parts C and D, which contain the preconstruction permit requirements for major stationary sources, originally contained no definition of stationary source. Instead part D defines a "major stationary source" as "any stationary facility or source" emitting the specified quantity of pollutant. Part C, by cross-reference (see note 1, above), adopts the same language. Part A, concerned with so-called performance standards, other than air quality standards, did use the term "stationary source" in 42 U.S.C. § 7411, defining it as "any building, structure, facility, or installation which emits or may emit any air pollutant." 42 U.S.C. § 7411(a)(3). That definition, however, was adopted "for purposes of this section," *i.e.*, section 7411.

Thus far the breadth of the language appears helpful to the Sierra Club position, since linguistically a ventilation system with a stack could be called a "facility," a "source" or even a "building." The table tilted back the other way in 1977 when Congress amended the Clean Air Act to exclude "indirect sources" from mandatory coverage in state implementation plans. 42 U.S.C. § 7410(a)(5)(A). An indirect source is defined in the statute as

> a facility, building, structure, installation, real property, road, or highway which attracts, or may attract, mobile sources of pollution. Such term includes parking lots, parking garages, and other facilities subject to any measure for management of parking supply * * *.

42 U.S.C. § 7410(a)(5)(C). Asserting that automakers should bear the brunt of reducing tailpipe emissions, Congress imposed the limitations already described on the EPA efforts to regulate the magnets for vehicles rather than the vehicles themselves.

Although indirect sources are not in terms excluded from the definition of stationary sources—the former provision is cast instead as a limitation on EPA authority—the effect of the amendment is to treat indirect sources as a separate category of sources subject to a different legal regime. The states may still "choose[]" to regulate them in state implementation plans, 42 U.S.C. § 7410(a)(5)(A)(i), but the decision whether and how to regulate is left largely to the states. Our best reading of the statute is that, at least after 1977, an indirect source is not to be treated as a stationary source under Parts C and D. Cf. South Terminal Corp. v. EPA, 504 F2d. 646, 669 (1st Cir.1974)("parking structures, which themselves emit no pollutants but instead only attract vehicles which emit pollution, are not stationary sources").

Assuming that a stationary source and an indirect source are exclusive categories, the difficult question remains whether ventilation buildings should be assimilated to the former or to the latter. It is a question that dictionaries cannot answer. The terms are technical rather than common ones, and they were developed against the background of a complex statute with interlocking provisions and specific goals. Nor does legislative history furnish any clue as to Congress' intent for ventilation buildings. Perhaps this small corner among possible applications of the statute was simply overlooked.

Similarly, it is difficult to derive any clear cut answer from analogy or policy. A covered highway or tunnel with a ventilation system is akin to an uncovered highway or open sided garage—clearly, indirect sources—in multiple senses: in each instance the facility or space attracts more cars, pollution in the vicinity may be greatly increased, and the initial source of the pollution is the cars themselves. On the other hand, the possibility exists (no information has been provided to us on the point) that the large scale ventilation systems may be more potent than a highway or garage in concentrating and expelling pollutants in a specific area; and on this ground, if no other, one might distinguish between them and a facility that is ordinarily ventilated without mechanical aid. Thus the analogy hardly dispels all doubt.

Two other arguments pressed by the parties seem to us inconclusive. The Sierra Club points us to a new provision, added to Title I in 1990 without limitation as to its application, which for the first time defines stationary source as meaning "generally any source of an air pollutant except those emission resulting directly from an internal combustion engine for transportation purposes or from a nonroad engine or a nonroad vehicle as defined in section 7550 * * *." 42 U.S.C. § 7602(z). The Sierra Club stresses the word "directly," arguing that the emissions from the ventilation shaft do not fit the "except" clause because the auto emissions are emitted first ("directly," in the Sierra Club's view) into the air of the covered highway or tunnel and only then gathered by fans and spewed out through the ventilators.

The government brief offers its own parsing of this new language, but both sides' arguments about what is "direct" and what is "indirect" emission have the flavor of a Medieval dispute in theology. The reality is that Congress framed this new subsection (z) to deal with an entirely different problem, namely, to include within the stationary source definition mobile sources of pollution, like ships in port and portable asphalt concrete plants, so far as they emit pollutants as part of their stationary activities, e.g., by leaking fuel at dockside (in contrast to engine emissions that occur when the ship or plant travels to a new destination). S.Rep. No. 228, 101st Cong., 1st Sess. 376 (1990). In other words, Congress was not addressing tunnel ventilation when it drew up this new provision.

Conversely, we are doubtful about the government's argument based upon the structure of the statute. Admittedly, Congress did establish two different regimes: that in Title I, with which we are concerned, governed stationary sources; that in Title II created a quite different regime, part of which is familiar to anyone who has a car inspected, to regulate vehicle emissions directly. This symmetry could suggest that tailpipe pollution— the source of the pollutants at issue here—was not meant to fall within Title I at all. The difficulty is that Congress might have not minded two layers of control, and contrivances like the "indirect source" provision in Title I blur the notion that auto pollution is exclusively a Title II problem.

In the end, we think the balance is tipped here by the explicit administrative interpretation of the Clean Air Act adopted by the EPA. In approving the addition of regulation 7.38 to Massachusetts' state implementation plan, the EPA stated:

> Tunnel ventilation systems, which do not generate their own emissions but rather simply funnel emissions from mobile sources, are not stationary sources within the meaning of the Clean Air Act.

57 Fed.Reg. 46310, 46311 (1992). The Supreme Court has told us that in construing a statute the courts should ordinarily show a measure of deference to the agency charged with administering the statute. The case most often cited for that precept is *Chevron*, which involved a different application of the very same "stationary source" provision that is now before us.

The *Chevron* doctrine has been the subject of much debate and, in subsequent decisions, the Supreme Court may have softened its impact somewhat and in some situation. See, e.g., INS v. Cardoza–Fonseca, 480 U.S. 421, 448, 107 S.Ct. 1207, 1221, 94 L.Ed.2d 434 (1987). To be sure, the courts have the last word on statutory interpretation—the question is one of the *weight* to be accorded to agency views—and often the statute's language of history leaves no latitude for the agency. In other cases the issue of interpretation may be so central to the operation of the statute that, whether or not Congress' meaning is clear, it is improbable that Congress meant for the courts to defer to the agency. We do not think these or other qualifications on *Chevron* deflect its impact here.

On the contrary, this statute *is* ambiguous on the issue before us, at least when the words "stationary source" are read together with the "indirect source" proviso and the structural juxtaposition of Titles I and II. The application of the stationary and indirect source language to tunnel ventilation is not the heart of the statute but a fringe issue on which Congress did not clearly express its intent. The Clean Air Act is an immensely complex and technical statute more familiar to the EPA than to anyone else, and the task of making its parts function together harmoniously is entrusted to many actors but above all to the EPA.

In sum this is a case in which *Chevron* and deference to the agency are not makeweights or subsidiary arguments. Rather, in this fairly debatable case, where statutory language is ambiguous, legislative history is silent and policies and analogies can be and have been mustered on both sides, we think that the EPA's unqualified and precise reading is decisive. It is unnecessary to calibrate perfectly the weight to be accorded to the agency view in a case of this species: once "considerable" weight is accorded to EPA's reading of the statute, see Chevron, 467 U.S. at 844, 104 S.Ct. at 2782, it is enough to tip a set of scales otherwise so closely balanced. [See the remaining portion of the opinion the court upheld EPA's approval of regulation 7.38 as part of the Massachusetts SIP, concluded that the regulation was validly adopted by the State of Massachusetts, and determined that regulation 7.38 did not require pre-construction review and approval for ventilation buildings such as the central artery/tunnel project.]

The judgment of the district court is *affirmed*. The petition for review is *denied*.

[When reading the following case, consider its implications for the situation presented in the Boatmann Manufacturing class discussion question. What flexibility does the non-attainment tradeoff policy present? How does it test the creativity of industrial planners and how does it present the potential for future air quality deterioration rather than improvement?]

The CARE case reflects a rather deferential "soft glance" form of judicial review accorded to a non-attainment area tradeoff calculation worked out by a permit applicant and the Virginia air pollution control agency. Notice the four main objections raised against the project. Can you suggest any others? What about the general practice of the state acting in the dual roles of 1) industrial development facilitator (by contributing offset credits) and 2) air quality regulator. Is there an inherent conflict of interest?]

Citizens Against Refinery's Effects, Inc. v. United States Environmental Protection Agency

United States Court of Appeals, Fourth Circuit, 1981.
643 F.2d 183.

■ K.K. HALL, CIRCUIT JUDGE.

Citizens Against the Refinery's Effects (CARE) appeals from a final ruling by the Administrator of the Environmental Protection Agency (EPA) approving the Virginia State Implementation Plan (SIP) for reducing hydrocarbon pollutants. The plan requires the Virginia Highway Department to decrease usage of a certain type of asphalt, thereby reducing hydrocarbon pollution by more than enough to offset expected pollution from the Hampton Roads Energy Company's (HREC) proposed refinery. We affirm the action of the administrator in approving the state plan.

The Act

The Clean Air Act establishes National Ambient Air Quality Standards (NAAQS) for five major air pollutants. 42 U.S.C. § 7409; 40 CFR § 50 (1976). The EPA has divided each state into Air Quality Control Regions (AQCR) and monitors each region to assure that the national standard for each pollutant is met. 42 U.S.C. § 7407. Where the standard has not been attained for a certain pollutant, the state must develop a State Implementation Plan designed to bring the area into attainment within a certain period. 42 U.S.C. § 7410. In addition, no new source of that pollutant may be constructed until the standard is attained. 40 CFR § 51.18 (1973).

The Clean Air Act created a no-growth environment in areas where the clean air requirements had not been attained. EPA recognized the need to develop a program that encouraged attainment of clean air standards without discouraging economic growth. Thus the agency proposed an Interpretive Ruling in 1976 which allowed the states to develop an "offset program" within the State Implementation Plans. The offset program, later codified by Congress in the 1977 Amendments to the Clean Air Act, permits the states to develop plans which allow construction of new pollution sources where accompanied by a corresponding reduction in an existing pollution source. 42 U.S.C. § 7502(b)(6) and § 7503. In effect, a new emitting facility can be built if an existing pollution source decreases its emissions or ceases operations as long as a positive net air quality benefit occurs.

If the proposed factory will emit carbon monoxide, sulfur dioxide, or particulates, the EPA requires that the offsetting pollution source be within the immediate vicinity of the new plant. The other two pollutants, hydrocarbons and nitrogen oxide, are less "site-specific," and thus the ruling permits the offsetting source to locate anywhere within a broad vicinity of the new source.[3]

The offset program has two other important requirements. First, a base time period must be determined in which to calculate how much reduction is needed in existing pollutants to offset the new source. This base period is defined as the first year of the SIP or, where the state has not yet developed a SIP, as the year in which a construction permit application is filed. 41 Fed.Reg. 55529 (1976). Second, the offset program requires that the new source adopt the Lowest Achievable Emissions Rate (LAER) using the most modern technology available in the industry. 41 Fed.Reg. 55528–9 (1976).

The Refinery

HREC proposes to build a petroleum refinery and offloading facility in Portsmouth, Virginia. Portsmouth has been unable to reduce air pollution enough to attain the national standard for one pollutant, photochemical oxidants,[4] which is created when hydrocarbons are released into the atmosphere and react with other substances. Since a refinery is a major source of hydrocarbons, the Clean Air Act prevents construction of the HREC plant until the area attains the national standard.

In 1975, HREC applied to the Virginia State Air Pollution Control Board (VSAPCB) for a refinery construction permit. The permit was issued by the VSAPCB on October 8, 1975, extended and reissued on October 5, 1977 after a full public hearing, modified on August 8, 1978, and extended

---

3. The pertinent section in the Interpretive Ruling reads:

"In the case of emission offsets involving hydrocarbons or NOx, the offsets may be obtained from sources located anywhere in the broad vicinity of the proposed new source (within the area of non-attainment and usually within the source air quality control re-

gion). This is because area-wide oxidant and NO_2 levels are generally not as dependent on specific hydrocarbon or NOx source location as they are on overall area emissions." 41 Fed.Reg. 55529 (1976).

4. Probably the best known photochemical oxidant is ozone.

again on September 27, 1979. The VSAPCB, in an effort to help HREC meet the clean air requirements, proposed to use the offset ruling to comply with the Clean Air Act.

On November 28, 1977, the VSAPCB submitted a State Implementation Plan to EPA which included the HREC permit. The Virginia Board proposed to offset the new HREC hydrocarbon pollution by reducing the amount of cutback asphalt[5] used for road paving operations in three highway districts by the Virginia Department of Highways.[6] By switching from "cutback" to "emulsified" asphalt, the state can reduce hydrocarbon pollutants by the amount necessary to offset the pollutants from the proposed refinery.

EPA requested some changes in the state plan, including certain monitoring changes and verification from the Virginia Attorney General that the offset program was legally enforceable. The plan was transmitted by the EPA Region III director to EPA headquarters on September 9, 1978. Notices of the proposed plan were published on October 10, 1978 and again on May 1, 1979. 43 Fed.Reg. 46554 (1978). 44 Fed.Reg. 25471 (1979). Numerous comments were received, including several from CARE. The EPA administrator carefully considered the comments and approved the Virginia offset plan on January 31, 1980.

CARE raises four issues regarding the state plan. First, they argue that the geographic area used as the base for the offset was arbitrarily determined and that the area as defined violates the regulations. Second, CARE contends that EPA should have used 1975 instead of 1977 as the base year to compare usage of cutback asphalt. Third, CARE insists that the offset plan should have been disapproved since the state is voluntarily reducing usage of cutback asphalt anyway. Fourth, CARE questions the approval of the plan without definite Lowest Achievable Emissions Rates (LAER) as required by the statute. We reject the CARE challenges to the state plan.
* * *

The Geographic Area

CARE contends that the state plan should not have been approved by EPA since the three highway-district area where cutback usage will be reduced to offset refinery emissions was artificially developed by the state. The ruling permits a broad area (usually within one AQCR) to be used as the offset basis.

The ruling does not specify how to determine the area, nor provide a standard procedure for defining the geographic area. Here the Virginia Board originally proposed to use four highway districts comprising one-half the state as the offset area. When this was found to be much more than

---

5. "Cutback" asphalt has a petroleum base which gives off great amounts of hydrocarbons. "Emulsified" asphalt uses a water base which evaporates, giving off no hydrocarbons.

6. The three highway districts so designated comprise almost the entire eastern one-third of the state. This area cuts across four of the seven Virginia Air Quality Control Regions (AQCR).

necessary to offset pollution expected from the refinery, the state changed it to one highway district plus nine additional counties. Later the proposed plan was again revised to include a geographic area of three highway districts.

The agency action in approving the use of three highway districts was neither arbitrary, capricious, nor outside the statute. First, Congress intended that the states and the EPA be given flexibility in designing and implementing SIPs. Such flexibility allows the states to make reasoned choices as to which areas may be used to offset new pollution and how the plan is to be implemented. Second, the offset program was initiated to encourage economic growth in the state. Thus a state plan designed to reduce highway department pollution in order to attract another industry is a reasonable contribution to economic growth without a corresponding increase in pollution. Third, to be sensibly administered the offset plan had to be divided into districts which could be monitored by the highway department. Use of any areas other than highway districts would be unwieldy and difficult to administer. Fourth, the scientific understanding of ozone pollution is not advanced to the point where exact air transport may be predicted. Designation of the broad area in which hydrocarbons may be transported is well within the discretion and expertise of the agency.

The Base Year

Asphalt consumption varies greatly from year to year, depending upon weather and road conditions. Yet EPA must accurately determine the volume of hydrocarbon emissions from cutback asphalt. Only then can the agency determine whether the reduction in cutback usage will result in an offset great enough to account for the new refinery pollution. To calculate consumption of a material where it constantly varies, a base year must be selected. In this case, EPA's Interpretive Ruling establishes the base year as the year in which the permit application is made. EPA decided that 1977 was an acceptable base year. CARE argues that EPA illegally chose 1977 instead of 1975.

Considering all of the circumstances, including the unusually high asphalt consumption in 1977, the selection by EPA of that as the base year was within the discretion of the agency. Since the EPA Interpretive Ruling allowing the offset was not issued until 1976, 1977 was the first year after the offset ruling and the logical base year in which to calculate the offset. Also, the permit issued by the VSAPCB was reissued in 1977 with extensive additions and revisions after a full hearing. Under these circumstances, 1977 appears to be a logical choice of a base year.

The Legally Binding Plan

For several years, Virginia has pursued a policy of shifting from cutback asphalt to the less expensive emulsified asphalt in road-paving operations. The policy was initiated in an effort to save money, and was totally unrelated to a State Implementation Plan.[7] Because of this policy, CARE argues that hydrocarbon emissions were decreasing independent of this SIP and therefore are not a proper offset against the refinery. They argue that there is not, in effect, an actual reduction in pollution.

The Virginia voluntary plan is not enforceable and therefore is not in compliance with the 1976 Interpretive Ruling which requires that the offset program be enforceable. The EPA, in approving the state plan, obtained a letter from the Deputy Attorney General of Virginia in which he stated that the requisites had been satisfied for establishing and enforcing the plan with the Department of Highways. Without such authority, no decrease in asphalt-produced pollution is guaranteed. In contrast to the voluntary plan, the offset plant guarantees a reduction in pollution resulting from road-paving operations.

The Lower Achievable Emissions Rate

Initially, CARE argues that the Offset Plan does not provide adequate Lowest Achievable Emission Rates (LAER) as required by the 1976 Interpretive Ruling because the plan contains only a 90% vapor recovery requirement, places an excessive 176.5 ton limitation on hydrocarbon emissions, and does not require specific removal techniques at the terminal. EPA takes the position that the best technique available for marine terminals provides only a 90% recovery and that the 176.5 ton limit may be reduced by the agency after the final product mix at the terminal is determined.

Since the record shows no evidence of arbitrary or capricious action in approving the HREC emissions equipment, the agency determination of these technical matters must be upheld.

Conclusion

In approving the state plan, EPA thoroughly examined the data, requested changes in the plan, and approved the plan only after the changes were made. There is no indication that the agency acted in an arbitrary or capricious manner or that it stepped beyond the bounds of the Clean Air Act. We affirm the decision of the administrator in approving the state plan.

NOTES AND QUESTIONS

1. *The "Bubble Concept" and Nonattainment Area Policy.* The "bubble concept" has been advanced as a method of tapping facility owner self-interest and knowledge as a spur to pollution control without direct government regulation. Consider the following excerpt by Professor William Rodgers and evaluate his criticisms of the policy.

---

7. "Cutback" asphalt uses an expensive fuel base while "emulsified" asphalt uses wa-   ter.

From a practical and theoretical perspective, the bubble notion is strongly supported by efficiency considerations. It is understood empirically that an industrial plant is a system of constantly changing processes where start-ups and shutdowns affecting the pattern of emissions is a fact of life. It is presumed also that cost-effective adjustments translating process change into emission control are far more likely to be discovered by the operator than a distant regulatory overseer. It is for this reason that retention by the source of discretion in choosing how to achieve a given goal of environmental quality is often accepted as something approaching a first principle. The Clean Air Act endorses in various ways this idea of flexibility in selecting choice of controls.

Additionally, proponents of the bubble invoke the need to reward and give incentives to sources who discover new and different ways to cut down on emissions by process adjustments. This is done by allowing them to use any increments "saved" within the bubble so long as there is no net increase in emissions outside the bubble. Effectively, the bubble grants a regime of private entitlements to the dispersion capacity of the air to any source operating under the comfortable protection of this imaginary dome.

So stated, it is not difficult to anticipate objections to the bubble on fairness grounds. The principal qualm stems from the policy choice to allow the source to use the air beneath the bubble as its own. In one sense, this rewards part polluters for their transgressions. In another, the bubble contradicts the sentiment that the atmosphere is a public commons that should be considered replenished by any air that is "saved" as a result of a curtailment of pollution. Any further allocation under this view would be a matter of public choice not private entitlement. Opponents of the bubble harbor doubts also that the act of "saving" air by reducing pollution, even a subtle exploitation of a complex process, resembles the kind of bold or imaginative effort normally required of successful claimants to natural resources "enhanced" by their efforts. Under this rights view, all "savings" immediately revert to the commons, and every "new source" in a literal sense should be held to high standards of control.

Another possible distinction that could serve as a measure of whether the bubble ought to be applied is a test of whether the affected area is nonattainment or not. In nonattainment areas the added flexibility of the bubble is attended by a suspicion that every increment of "saved" air assigned to polluters is one less increment retired in the service of public health. Where public health standards are not now met, there is little appeal in a treadmill offset policy slowing down the trek to compliance. Where the standards are met, on the other hand, flexibility and cost-effectiveness are increasingly appealing policy considerations. Who cares about adjustments that may be made if compliance is secure? Who needs the transaction costs of a building permit program where there are no great social costs in waiving them? (footnotes omitted)

1 W. Rodgers, *Environmental Law—Air and Water* 338–39, 343 (1986).

2. *Emissions Reduction Using Market Principles.*

L. Hines, The Market, Energy and the Environment

62–65 (1988).

Emissions Trading

The emissions-trading program allows the regulated firm to meet its pollution obligations by trading the abatement of one source of pollution for that of another—reducing sulfur dioxide discharges in coke production, for example, instead of lowering similar discharges in blast furnace operation—as long as the firm's aggregate emissions are not increased. (A large industrial installation may have hundreds of emission sources.) Further, the firm can compensate for over-emissions in one area of production by under-emission performance in another area; a firm can also buy emission credits from an under-polluting firm or bank for sale or future use its own emission credits. In effect, emissions trading engages the firm in a variety of market-like transactions through which it can find the least costly and most expeditious means of meeting its pollution abatement obligation.

How Is Emissions Trading Better?

In what respects is emissions trading considered superior to the command-and-control approach? First, it allows the firm to meet its obligation by reducing cheap pollution sources rather than costly pollution sources within its plant complex or by buying reduced emissions from another firm where the abatement costs are less. Second, by focusing on aggregate emissions, rather than requiring that the EPA regulate each source and that the firm reduce *all* points of excess emissions, the agency's case load is less and the firm's compliance costs are lower. There are other economic-environmental impacts of this approach, but before considering these we need to see how the emissions-trading system works.

How Emissions Trading Works

The emissions bubble. The bubble approach was adopted in response to industry pressures for greater flexibility in satisfying pollution goals, especially by firms with older installations that could not meet Clean Air standards. If the firm employed old-fashioned coking ovens and could reduce its total emissions—its bubble—in non-coking activities, such as blast furnace operation, by as much or more than the difference between the old and new coking process, the EPA would accept this modification as satisfying its abatement obligation. The presumption is that both society and the firm are better off with this adjustment, which is the result of *offsetting* emissions, than when each plant source of pollution has to meet a fixed standard.

The offset. The bubble is the stage upon which the offset act takes place. Although the bubble and the use of offset usually are confined to a single industrial installation, on occasion the bubble may encompass a larger area, covering other firms and different industrial processes. This expands the firms' emission trading market and increases the opportunities for a mutually satisfactory arrangement.

The path of emissions trading has not been entirely smooth since it was instituted by the EPA. The 1975 version of the bubble policy was overturned by the courts and EPA has revised its approach so that it makes compliance with legislative goals easier, rather than affording a way of avoiding them. Emissions trading has grown steadily since this period, resulting in the establishment of an "emissions bank" in Kentucky in 1984 and by late 1985 emissions trades had exceeded 2,500 cases. * * *

Is Emissions Trading All Good?

Viewed purely in terms of the immediate effect upon air quality, emissions trading is likely to improve air quality at a lower cost for the polluter and with less regulatory effort by the federal agency than the traditional command-and-control approach. Not all firms are equally advantaged by the opportunity to offset emissions, however, and the use of this approach can delay the installation of state-of-the-art abatement equipment. Additionally, a firm that meets its abatement obligation by an emissions offset—either from within its own plant or through outside purchase—is likely to face lower production costs than the firm that adds new abatement technology to its plant. Thus the firm that adopts the most advanced abatement equipment is competitively disadvantaged and the improvement in air quality of the region falls short of its full potential. Important though these flaws may be in certain cases, they appear not to be sufficiently widespread to warrant dismantling the emissions trading program. They strongly suggest, however, that the program be reviewed periodically to check its impact upon the polluting industries as well as its contribution to air quality improvement.

In a study of emissions trading, the Government Accounting Office found that there were large transaction and search costs in emissions trading, but that it was generally superior to the command-and-control approach. It summarized its findings as follows:

Creating Pollution Rights

If the recognition of emission reduction credits and the development of exchange institutions such as banks represent the establishment of pollution rights in a legal sense, consider the following questions.

* What formalities must be followed to establish "rights" to ERCs? Who defines these rules? Should there be different rules in each state?

* Are the ERCs property rights which can be freely exchanged between parties?

* What is the duration of an ERC? Using the terminology of conventional land rights, are ERCs estates at will, estates for years, life estates, fee simple absolutes, or some other variety?

* Can the transferor impose restrictive covenants on the ERC that "run with the right" with the intention of binding all successive transferees? What if the covenants bar use of the ERCs by an economic competitor of the transferor?

* Can the ERCs be totally lost if they remain unused and the pollution control agency needs to find emission "reductions" in order to meet future NAAQS attainment dates? Is this an unconstitutional taking of property without just compensation? Can the ERCs be merely reduced to 50% of their emission credit value?

3. *Offset Credits—Offset Ratios.* By definition, nonattainment areas have air quality which violates standards and consequently, adding more emissions from a new or an expanded existing source would seem to make matters worse. Therefore, the CAA policy has required new or modified source owners to obtain "offsets" or offsetting emission reductions as a condition to permit approval. The idea is that the new pollution will be "offset" by equal or greater reductions in actual emissions from other sources in the area. EPA rules specifying which emission reductions qualify as an "offset" are detailed. How much of an offset is required: one unit out for each unit in? The amount of the offset required depends on two factors: 1) the pollutant being added and 2) the severity of the nonattainment condition in the area. The table below reflects the differing offset ratios for ozone nonattainment areas.

Ozone Nonattainment Area Classification	Minimum Emissions Offset Ratio Required
Extreme	1.5 to 1
Severe	1.3 to 1
Serious	1.2 to 1
Moderate	1.15 to 1
Marginal	1.1 to 1

Why did the CAA adopt this graduated policy? If you represented a new source wishing to locate in an ozone nonattainment area, where would you look for offsets?

4. *Offset Credits—Location Issues.* How far from the proposed new source location can Boatmanns look for offset credits usable in the offset calculation? What policy should govern this issue. The 1990 Clean Air Act amendments added that following language to § 173(c) on this issue. It provides,

> (1) The owner or operator of a new or modified major stationary source may comply with any offset requirement in effect under this part for increased emissions of any air pollutant only by obtaining emission reductions of such air pollutant from the same source or other sources in the same nonattainment area, except that the State

may allow the owner or operator of a source to obtain such emission reductions in another nonattainment area if (A) the other area has an equal or higher nonattainment classification than the area in which the source is located and (B) emissions from such other area contribute to a violation of the national ambient air quality standard in the nonattainment area in which the source is located. Such emission reductions shall be, by the time a new or modified source commences operation, in effect and enforceable and shall assure that the total tonnage of increased emissions of the air pollutant from the new or modified source shall be offset by an equal or greater reduction, as applicable, in the actual emissions of such air pollutant from the same or other sources in the area.

(2) Emission reductions otherwise required by this Act shall not be creditable as emissions reductions for purposes of any such offset requirement. Incidental emission reductions which are not otherwise required by this Act shall be creditable as emission reductions for such purposes if such emission reductions meet the requirements of paragraph (1).

Why impose this "proximity" rule to the offset calculation? If this provision were not required what might happen?

5. *Substantive Elements of New Source Review.* Major stationary sources in nonattainment areas are subject to stringent permitting rules and each state must adopt a new source review (NSR) program as part of their SIP pursuant to § 172(c)(5). A new or modified source will be subject to this NSR program. Generally, under definition § 302(j), a "major stationary source" is one emitting or having the potential to emit 100 tons per year; but this threshold is lower in moderate to extreme ozone nonattainment areas. See Sierra Club v. Larson, 2 F.3d 462 (1st Cir.1993) (discussion of major source definition). The definition of "modification" is drawn from the language of § 111(a)(4) dealing with new source performance standards. It includes any physical change in a stationary source 1)which increases the amount of any air pollutant emitted by the source or 2) which results in the emission of any air pollutant not previously emitted. How could an existing source owner escape the burdens of NSR? How could a new source owner design a plant to avoid NSR? Obtaining sufficient offset credits to satisfy the demands of § 173(a)(1) represents only part of the necessary showing for new source approval in a nonattainment area. Consider the other elements of § 173. What policies are advanced by each one?

• *Lowest Achievable Emission Rate.* The Clean Air Act contains numerous labels for various levels of pollution control. Section 173(2) requires that new and modified sources comply with the "lowest achievable emission rate" or LAER as a condition of permitting. What is LAER? The Act— 171(3) [§ 7501(3)]—defines it as the emission rate that reflects the most stringent limitation for the source category that is contained in any SIP or is achieved in practice. LAER may never result in emissions greater than those permissible under an applicable § 111 NSPS. Set on a case-by-case fashion there is generally some consideration of economic, energy or other environmental concerns. Section 178 [§ 7508] gives EPA the authority to issue Guidance Documents defining LAER and the agency has issued a multitude of such documents and EPA maintains a control technology clearinghouse containing data from states on LAER. The Guidance Documents are intended to help the state permit writers to determine LAER in the case-by-case process of NSR.

Consider the following questions. Why does the nonattainment permitting provision require LAER? How might LAER drive § 111 to more stringent levels of control? Does the LAER requirement make new source location in a nonattainment area more of a "privilege" than a "right?" What is an "achievable" emission rate? How should cost of compliance to be considered in this context and should it be different from cost questions in the § 111 NSPS situation?

• *Source Owner Statewide Compliance.* Section 173(3) contains a requirement that the owner or operator of a proposed new or modified source demonstrate that all major stationary sources under its full or partial control, within the state, be either in compliance or on a schedule for compliance with the Clean Air Act. EPA has determined that it is the permit applicant's duty to certify that its sources are in compliance. The idea behind this provision seems clear—the extension of the special privilege of nonattainment area expansion is to be accorded only to those firms with a good record of Clean Air Act compliance. Depending upon how strictly "compliance" is defined, this mandate could motivate sources to come into compliance if they wished to expand in the state. This policy could also have the effect of encouraging multi-facility firms to divest themselves of those facilities unlikely ever to reach compliance. Would that help or hinder the attainment of the NAAQS?

Consider how this "good corporate citizen" requirement could have been made more difficult to meet; e.g., nationwide Clean Air Act compliance, state or nationwide compliance under all environmental laws, or no recent civil or criminal enforcement actions. As attainment of the NAAQS becomes more elusive these and other suggestion might become more attractive.

A final requirement of § 173(a)(4) is that a permit may not be granted if EPA has determined that the entire SIP is not being "adequately implemented" by the state. What could this phrase mean? How much potential power does this provision grant EPA? Might EPA use this as leverage to gain active state participation in SIP development, monitoring and enforcement? This element puts pressure on the states to actively participate in SIP enforcement as a condition of nonattainment area new source permitting.

• *Benefit/Cost Analysis of Proposed Sources.* The 1990 Clean Air Act amendments added the following provision (§ 173(a)(5)) which mandated that the nonattainment new source permit program require,

(5) an analysis of alternative sites, sizes, production processes, and environmental control techniques for such proposed source demonstrates that benefits of the proposed source significantly outweigh the environmental and social costs imposed as a result of its location, construction, or modification.

What kind of analysis does this demand and for what purpose? Why was this cost-benefit analysis inserted into the air law? Who is obligated to perform this analysis and how likely is it that a source proposal will fail? Does this required pre-construction review test directly involve EPA or the state into matters of local land use and economic development decisionmaking?

● *The "Reasonable Further Progress" Requirement.* Notice the language of § 173(a)(1)(A) dealing with required emission offsets. The amount of offsets required for the new source when considered in combination with all other allowable emissions in the region to represent "reasonable further progress" (RFP) towards attainment. What could this mean? Section 171(a) defines RFP as "annual incremental reductions in emissions * * * as are required * * * for the purpose of ensuring attainment [of the NAAQS] * * * by the applicable date." What seems to be the idea here? Is this an anti-procrastination provision rejecting a state's desire to economically expand now and reduce emissions later?

6. *Existing Sources in NonAttainment Areas.* The Boatmann Manufacturing plant problem emphasizes the importance of new or modified source emission offset program to the solution of the nonattainment problem. To what extent, if any, are existing sources regulated in these areas under the Clean Air Act? What can be done to limit emissions from "non-new sources"?

Reasonably Available Control Technology (RACT). The nonattainment problem is ultimately a question of improving ambient air quality and reducing air emissions. A major component of this policy is obtaining emission reductions of existing sources. New source contribution to the nonattainment issue is treated in the problem at the beginning of this section. However, § 172(c)(1) & (2) [§ 7502(c)(1) & (2)] also mandates that states' non-attainment area SIPs make "reasonable further progress" towards the timely attainment of the NAAQS through the adoption, at a minimum, of "reasonably available control technology" (RACT) for existing sources. Why would the Act create a new statutory label for existing source control technology? Read § 171(1) [§ 7501(1)] which defines "reasonable further progress" towards attainment. Does this reveal why a stricter technology standard for existing sources would have been necessary?

What is RACT and who defines it? EPA regulations have provided the following definition for the term as,

devices, systems process modifications, or other apparatus or techniques that are reasonably available taking into account (1) the necessity of imposing such controls in order to attain and maintain a national ambient air quality standard, (2) the social, environmental and economic impact of such controls, and (3) alternative means of providing for attainment and maintenance of such standard.

40 C.F.R. § 100(*o*) (1990). Does this definition help very much? Does "reasonable" in this context refer to cost or to technical practicability? Could EPA require the imposition of NSPS on existing sources in nonattainment areas? EPA has announced a policy of making RACT determinations flexible—a case-by-case standard which the agency defines as "the lowest emission limit that a particular source is capable of meeting by the applicable of control technology that is reasonably available considering technological and economic feasibility." EPA has developed voluminous guidance documents to assist the states in determining RACT in specific situations. The states are given the responsibility for setting RACTs yet they often rely on EPA-issued Control Technique Guidelines on CTGs mentioned below.

In an effort to make air pollution control technology information more widely accessible, the 1990 Clean Air Act amendments require EPA to make data regarding emission control technology available to the States and to the general public through the creation of a central database termed the RACT/BACT/LAER Clearinghouse required by § 108(h). This clearinghouse can be found online at http://www.epa.gov./ttn/catc/ and it contains will contain control technology information derived from the states' SIP submissions and from permits issued to individual sources.

Control Technique Guidelines (CTGs)

Under § 108 EPA is authorized to issue information on air pollution control techniques. Prior to 1990, the agency had issued "control techniques guideline" or CTG documents for 27 categories of existing stationary sources. The 1990 Clean Air Act amendments direct EPA to issue CTGs for an additional 11 categories of VOC emitting stationary sources by 1993. See § 183(a). The 1990's EPA developed CTG documents for the synthetic organic chemical manufacturing industry, wood furniture manufacturing, plastic parts coating, wet offset lithography, cleanup solvents, pesticide application, petroleum and industrial wastewater facilities, consumer/commercial products, architectural/industrial coatings, adhesives, autobody refinishing and marine vessel loading and unloading operations.

CTGs take on added significance since EPA considers them the "presumptive norm" when specifying RACT for existing sources in non-attainment areas. Deviations would have to be justified based upon individualized economic and technical circumstances of a particular source. See H.R.Rep. No. 101–490 Part 1, 101st Cong., 2d Sess. 252 (1990). Increasingly EPA will be the provider of specific technical information for air pollution sources.

7. *Consumer Products and Nonattainment.* How many forms of personal activity give rise to air pollution. Although California and New York had previously acted, section 183(e) for the first time requires EPA to regulate consumer products that contribute to ozone formation. Under this section EPA identified those products accounting for 80% of Volatile Organic Compound (VOCs) emissions form consumer products such as cleaning fluids, paint, varnishes, solvents, hair sprays, windshield wiper fluid, pesticide sprays, and underarm deodorants. Creating four categories of products scheduled for regulation, EPA set "best available control" standards to the first group and made them applicable to manufactures, processors, distributors or importers of the listed products. Treading lightly on public opinion, no obligations are imposed on consumers or other end users. Product regulations for this first group-composed of consumer products, were set in 1998 and they are estimated to result in a reduction of 90,000 tons of VOC pollutants per year. The architectural coatings rule is estimated to prevent 113,500 tons per year of VOCs. The other three groups of commercial and consumer products are slated for regulation by 2003. This CAA effort reflects the fact that the search for emission reductions must focus on smaller and widely dispersed "personal" sources as the major sources become less polluting. The CAA now reaches all the way from coal fired electric power plants to the hair styling gel, nail polish removers, oven cleaners and air fresheners Americans use everyday.

SECTION 6.   KEEPING CLEAN AIR UNPOLLUTED—THE PREVENTION OF SIGNIFICANT DETERIORATION OF AIR QUALITY

A.   INTRODUCTION AND OVERVIEW

Most of the attention to this point has focused upon the problem of air pollution assuming that the developing environmental law is concerned mainly with the improvement of poor air quality that impairs human health. While most of the Clean Air Act's organization is aimed at this problem, the fact remains that air in many areas of the nation is cleaner than that required by the primary and secondary NAAQS. As a general matter the emission of NAAQS pollutants has generally declined in the U.S. over the past 25 years, and by 1993 EPA estimated that 59 million Americans lived in areas experiencing violations of one or more NAAQS. Consequently, many parts of the country have air quality better than NAAQS. Should the Clean Air Act as a matter of policy have any application to those places? Should very unpolluted air be allowed to be "deteriorated" by emissions from plants and autos?

The language of the 1970 Act provided minimal guidance on this question. A general purpose of this statute was "to protect and enhance the quality and the Nation's air resources so as to promote the public health and welfare and the productive capacity of its population." § 101(b) [§ 7401(b)]. This was hardly a clear call to administrative action. While the express textual support for non-deterioration was thin, there were shreds of legislative history vaguely supporting the idea that clean air should not be allowed to get dirty. EPA's initial SIP preparation regulations only required the states to assure that air quality would not violate the secondary standard thereby indirectly allowing deterioration to that level.

In 1972, the Sierra Club brought suit alleging that the Clean Air Act implicitly required SIPs to prevent the "significant deterioration" of air quality in "clean air" areas. The District Court for the District of Columbia agreed with this contention, holding that the Act's state of purpose clause, § 101(b)(1), imposed this obligation. On June 12, 1972 this court issued a 4 page memorandum opinion which directed EPA to prevent the worsening of air quality to the levels of the NAAQS. This decision was affirmed per curium by the D.C. Circuit and upheld on a 4 to 4 vote of the Supreme Court with Justice Powell not participating. Sierra Club v. Ruckelshaus, 344 F.Supp. 253 (D.D.C.1972), affirmed per curium 2 ELR 20656 (1972), affirmed sub nom. Fri v. Sierra Club, 412 U.S. 541 (1973). For an excellent history and critique of this development see Craig Oren, Prevention of Significant Deterioration: Control Compelling Versus Site–Shifting, 74 Iowa L.Rev. 1 (1988).

By 1974, EPA responded to this decision by issuing prevention of significant deterioration (PSD) regulations which established the fundamental structure of the present program. In 1977 Congress required PSD by statute, adding Part C, §§ 161–169 [§§ 7470–79] to the Clean Air Act and modifying the scheme initially established by EPA. Section 161 [§ 7470] now provides an express directive that state plans include measures to prevent the significant deterioration of air quality in areas designated by the states as having ambient air quality better than the national standards or where there is insufficient data to make a determination of the air quality. The 1990 amendments did not make major changes in the PSD program. The PSD program mandated by the Act is composed of three central elements: (1) a specialized permit program for any new or modified "major emitting facility" locating within the clean air region, (2) such a facility must use "the best available control technology" (BACT) for each pollutant regulated by the Act, and (3) the new emissions must not cause violations of prescribed increments over baseline ambient pollutant concentrations.

CLASS DISCUSSION PROBLEM: AIR POLLUTION IN THE UTAH DESERT

The City of Bonaire, Utah is a picturesque Southwestern town of 25,000 people. It is located in southern Utah and connected to the larger cities in the state by interstate highway. The economy of Bonaire is based primarily upon tourism, ranching, farming and, to a lesser degree, light industry. Bonaire is surrounded by great expanses of open land with an occasional mesa or other rock outcropping occurring from place to place. Several large national parks are located within a 15–25 mile radius of Bonaire. Cactus abounds in this nearly desert climate and the air is especially clean. The air quality is so unspoiled that Bonaire has been classified as an attainment area for all of the Clean Air Act NAAQS pollutants. The residents of Bonaire have sought out this isolated and environmentally pristine area for its lifestyle and natural beauty. In the past, several proposals for a number of large industrial developments had been rejected by the city's elected officials and by the voters. However, several recent events have threatened to disturb the status quo in Bonaire, Utah.

Jones Manufacturing Company ("Jones") manufactures various replacement parts for automobiles and it has operated its principal plant in Bonaire for over 20 year. Jones presently employs 200 people at this facility but the company's management believes that several changes to the firm's operations would be beneficial. *First,* in order to become more cost-efficient, Jones would like to replace its existing coal-fired, steam generating boilers with new, more efficient models which could use a wider range of coal as a fuel depending upon whichever grade was least expensive. (Jones Project #1) While this new boiler unit would be less polluting for each unit of steam produced, its higher steam production capacity would actually result in the emission of 15 tons per year of SO_2 more than the older boiler it was replacing. *Second,* Jones wished to expand its operations to include the painting or coating of automobile sheet metal replacement or "crash" parts. (Jones Project #2) To accomplish this the company planned to construct a new paint spraying and drying line at the Bonaire plant. It was estimated that this new line would emit approximately 250 tons per year of volatile organic compounds (VOC) which are causes of oxidant or ozone pollution. Jones proposed to eliminate 150 tons of existing VOC emissions at the Bonaire plant by tightening controls. It also offered to reduce some of its particulate or fugitive dust emissions by better managing its outdoor coal and raw material piles.

In a separate matter, the Utah Electric Illuminating Company ("Utah Electric") began to investigate the Bonaire area as a potential site for a large coal-fired electric generating plant. Abundant local coal supplies, burgeoning regional power demand, and convenient railroad connections had made this location a high priority generating site for Utah Electric. Since this was planned as a major plant, it was expected that at least 1000 tons per year of SO_2 would be discharged into the air even if the most modern pollution control technology were employed. Beyond this, the utility company planned to construct tall smokestacks to disburse the emissions away from Bonaire. Some in the community had predicted that these emissions could travel all the way to Zion and Bryce National Parks and perhaps beyond. The Utah Electric proposals, as well as that of Jones Manufacturing, have alarmed many people in Bonaire and they have come to you for advice. Consider the following questions.

1. What special provisions does the Clean Air Act make for stationary source emissions in areas of the nation having air cleaner than required by the NAAQS? What general policy does this statutory material reflect?

2. a. Does the Clean Air Act's Prevention of Significant Deterioration (PSD) policy govern the Jones Project #1? Why would it? Are there any reasons why the Jones Project #1 would not be required to undergo the rigors of PSD review and be forced to meet the substantive elements of the PSD program?

b. What about the Jones Project #2, would it be subject to the PSD requirements? Should the company be allowed to "offset" or "net out" the new VOC emissions from the painting line with VOC reductions from other points at the Jones Manufacturing facility? What about off-site VOC reductions, should that be allowed? Should Jones be permitted to "net out" the new VOC emissions with reductions in SO_2 or particulates? Why or why not?

3.   What analysis must be undertaken by EPA or the State of Utah prior to permitting Utah Electric to construct and operate its proposed Bonaire plant? Which aspects of PSD review will be especially important in the decision to permit the new coal-fired generating facility? How could the proximity of the proposed plant to Zion and Bryce National Parks complicate matters for Utah Electric?

4.   The permitting of major sources in PSD areas usually involves consideration of the available pollution "increment." How should the increments be allocated? Is the present method of first-come, first-served wise policy in terms of other societal goals such as encouraging full employment, increasing tax base, and building high technology industry. If you were the Director of your state's Air Pollution Control Agency or the Policy Advisor to your Governor, could you devise a policy for distributing these increments? You may wish to consider the following issues. At present, a successful PSD permittee pays nothing for the right to consume all or part of the air quality increment. Should market principles be applied to the allocation of this resource? If so, how? What of the concern for intergenerational equity? Is it valuable and largely-irreplaceable resource? Should there be some "reservation" of a portion of the increment for future distribution?

B.   THE POLICY JUSTIFICATIONS FOR THE PSD PROGRAM

[The following excerpt is extracted from the report of the House Committee on Interstate and Foreign Commerce accompanying H.R. 6161, the 1977 Clean Air Act Amendments. Consider the range of arguments made in support of the PSD policy. Have the committee's views been supported in the time since the report was written? Are there other justifications you can think of for PSD policy?]

Clean Air Act Amendments of 1977

H.R.Rep. No. 95-294, 95th Cong., 1st Sess. 105-137 (1977).
Footnotes omitted.

The need for a national policy of and State policy for preventing significant deteriorations

The committee recognized the strong need for a policy of preventing significant deterioration of air quality. The bases of such a policy include: health and welfare protection, economic and employment considerations, protection of States' rights and avoidance of interstate conflicts relating to air pollution, protection of air quality within unique national lands such as national parks, and avoidance of unnecessary stratospheric and atmospheric modifications due to air pollution.

Health basis for preventing significant deterioration

In its "Forward Plan for Health, 1977–1981," the Department of Health, Education, and Welfare has stressed the fact that preventive methods of dealing with disease represent the best hope of substantially improving the Nation's health in the coming years. * * *

It is with this goal of disease prevention in mind that the committee approached the 1977 Clean Air Act Amendments in general and the issue of prevention of significant deterioration in particular. Some people have attempted to characterize the policy of prevention of significant deterioration as one of protecting trees and wilderness areas at the expense of people. However, in the committee's view, the need to prevent significant deterioration in so-called clean air areas arises in substantial part from the need to protect the public's health.

As ambient pollution levels in our major metropolitan areas have decreased, the seriousness and frequency of pollution-related respiratory diseases have been reduced. Achievement of the ambient standards has resulted in a decrease in the incidence of asthma attacks, emphysema, and upper respiratory ailments.

The beneficial health impact of the ambient standards has been recognized by the American Medical Association and the American Lung Association in testimony before the subcommittee and in resolutions urging no delays or relaxation in meeting these standards. Even more graphically, two recent studies show that a significant decrease in the number of deaths can result from improving air quality to the level of the national primary ambient air quality standards.

Thus, there can be no question that the national ambient air quality standards are necessary and beneficial for protection of the healthy and reduction of risk to the susceptible and chronically ill. However, it is also clear that a combination of ambient standards with a policy for prevention of significant deterioration of air quality is necessary to provide for maximum feasible protection of the public health. Since 1971 when the national ambient air quality standards were set, new and disturbing information has come to light showing that the public's health is being harmed to some extent, perhaps seriously, even at levels below the national standards. The margins of safety, supposedly insured by the standards, seem to have vanished in the face of new data.

The inadequacies of the standards are substantial both with regard to the pollutants which are regulated and with respect to their failure to regulate others. A summary of the shortcomings and limitations of the existing national primary ambient air quality standards demonstrates this.

A. *The margins of safety originally set to prevent the occurrence of known and anticipated health effects have turned out to be very modest or nonexistent.*

B. *The national primary standards are based on the assumption that a no-effects threshold level exists and can be proved; in fact, this assumption of a safe threshold appears to be false.*

C. *The national primary standards are not designed to protect against genetic mutations, birth defects, or cancer which may be associated with air pollution, although these risks may be reduced, to some extent, by reducing pollution to the level of the ambient standards.*

D. *The national primary ambient air quality standards are not designed so as to provide adequate protection against diseases which result from long-term chronic exposures or periodic short-term peak concentrations of pollutants.*

E. *The national primary ambient air quality standards fail to protect against hazards to health resulting from cumulative or synergistic effects of multiple pollutants in the air.*

F. *The national primary ambient air quality standards do not protect against adverse effects which appear to be related to derivative pollutants which result in the atmosphere (such as sulfate-compounds, sulfuric acid aerosols, nitrate compounds, nitric acid aerosols, etc.).*

G. *Health Conclusions*

The foregoing deficiencies in the national primary ambient air quality standards are persuasive and not easily cured. Some have suggested that since the standards are to protect against all known or anticipated effects and since no safe thresholds can be established, the ambient standards should be set at zero or background levels. Obviously, this no-risk philosophy ignores all economic and social consequences and is impractical. This is particularly true in light of the legal requirement for mandatory attainment of the national primary standards within 3 years.

Others have suggested that unless conclusive proof of actual harm can be found based on the past occurrence of adverse effects, then the standards should remain unchanged and no pollution limits should be applicable to areas which are cleaner than the ambient standards.

This second approach ignores the commonsense reality that "an ounce of prevention is worth a pound of cure". Permitting unrestricted deterioration of air quality up to the ambient standards involves trying to cure a condition after it has developed rather than using practical and currently available means to prevent or minimize the condition in the first place. This approach of unlimited air quality deterioration is particularly short-sighted at a time when all indicators point to the likely necessity for tightening the ambient air quality standards to protect public health. This approach is not good preventive medicine. Nor is it good long-term economic policy.

The committee proposal is intended to properly balance these two approaches. Since there is a reasonable basis for anticipation of tightening of the ambient standards, a policy of maximum practicable protection of health has been developed. The committee approach to prevention of significant deterioration (together with the requirement proposed by the committee in section 111 that all new major industrial sources meet an emission standard achievable through the use of best available control technology) will help provide the necessary health protection for all Americans, including those most susceptible to the damaging effects of pollution—the young, the aged, and the infirm. * * *

The welfare basis for prevention of significant deterioration

There is increasing evidence of adverse effect on public welfare from low levels of pollution. Under the Clean Air Act, "public welfare" includes "effects on soils, water, crops, vegetation, man-made materials, animals, wildlife, weather, visibility, and climate, damage to and deterioration of property, and hazards to transportation, as well as effects on economic values and on personal comfort and well-being".

A. Agricultural impacts

* * * Damage directly linked to ongoing fallout of industrial pollution across the U.S. continent, extending hundreds of miles beyond the sources of emission, has already reduced yields in forests and other crops in some areas by as much as 75 percent. Failing new and stringently enforced pollution controls, an energy development program emphasizing increased use of fossil fuels for electrical generation could well spread and accelerate this phenomenon.

The damage is taking place in a number of ways: Sulfur oxides and other pollutants, carried downwind in dry air or precipitated in acid rain, assault plants and trees directly or infiltrate the soil with subsequent impact on the vegetation's genetic structure and resistance to disease. Some pollutants, harmless at low levels of toxicity, interact strongly when combined with others—ozone and sulfur dioxide, for example—"to reach high leaf kill or other damage levels." ("Middle and Long–Term Energy Policies and Alternatives, Part 4," Energy and Power Subcommittee, Mar. 25 and 26, 1976; p. 1)

The evidence is strong that air pollutants have damaging effects on crops at levels below the national standards. For example, studies show that important agricultural crops suffer leaf damage, growth inhibition, or increased mortality resulting from sulfur dioxide levels lower than the national ambient air quality standards. These effects may result in substantial economic impact, such as the reported 15–percent reduction in wheat yield at a sulfur dioxide exposure level of less than half the national standard (Guderian, R. and H. Shatmann, Forschungsber, Landes Nordrhein–Westfaler 1920:3, 1968). Since much of the United States where wheat is grown has SO_2 pollution levels below half the national standard, the importance of not allowing air quality to deteriorate to the standard is clear.

Various studies indicate varying adverse effects of pollutants at levels below the national standards on other grains including barley and oats, as well as on peanuts, soybeans, alfalfa, potatoes, spinach, oranges, tobacco, and pines. * * *

B. Acid rain

Sulfur oxides and nitrogen oxides in the atmosphere also cause a phenomenon known as acid rain. Acid rain can lower the pH of natural waters and soil, damaging both plants, and animals. * * * [T]here is indirect evidence that the pH of precipitation was formerly above 5.7 over wide areas where it is now below 4.5 * * * and at Ithaca, N.Y., in June–July 1971, the average pH of rain was as low as 3.53. (The lower the pH number, the more acidic the solution.)

Economic bases for preventing significant deterioration

A national policy of prevention of significant deterioration, in conjunction with the section 111 requirement that all new major sources install and use best available pollution control technology, is a necessary economic measure designed to encourage wise use of scarce air resources and to preserve the potential for long-term economic growth.

A.   *Prevention of significant deterioration will assure greater opportunities for economic growth and creation of more jobs in all parts of the country while protecting against unhealthy pollution levels.*

B.   *Abandonment of a policy of prevention of significant deterioration will encourage flight of industry—and jobs—from areas where pollution levels are approaching or exceed the minimum Federal standards to cleaner areas requiring less controls on industry.*

C.   *By minimizing the transport of pollutants from one area of the Nation to another, prevention of significant deterioration will guarantee that one region will not suffer economically because it becomes the dumping grounds for another region's air pollution.*

D.   *It is much more economical to prevent pollution before it occurs than it is to require expensive retrofitting of technology on existing plants once dangerous levels of pollution have already been reached.*

E.   *Prevention of significant deterioration will protect the economies of regions of the Nation heavily dependent upon tourism.*

C.   IMPLEMENTING PSD POLICY

Puerto Rican Cement Co. v. U.S. EPA

United States Court of Appeals, First Circuit, 1989.
889 F.2d 292.

■ BREYER, CIRCUIT JUDGE.

The Puerto Rican Cement Co. (the "Company") wishes to build a new cement kiln, replacing older kilns that it now operates at about 60 percent of their capacity. If operated to achieve about the same level of production, the new kiln will pollute far less than the older kilns; but, if the Company operates the new kiln at significantly higher production levels, it will emit more pollutants than did the older kilns. The Environmental Protection Agency, noting that it is *possible* that the new kiln will produce more pollution, has held that the Company cannot build it without obtaining a special kind of EPA approval, required when one wishes to "construct" a "major emitting facility" in a place where the air is particularly clean. (The facility must meet "prevention of significant deterioration" ("PSD") requirements. See 42 U.S.C. § 7475.) The Company appeals. We find that EPA's determination is lawful.

I.

Background

1. *Factual:* The Company's cement plant contains six kilns, which produce a fine powder called "clinker." In 1987 the Company decided to convert Kiln No. 6 from a "wet," to a "dry," cement-making process, and to combine that kiln with Kiln No. 3. At that time, Kilns 3 and 6 were operating at about 60 percent of their combined capacity, producing about 424,000 tons of clinker per year. The converted kiln would have a total capacity of 961,000 tons of clinker per year, or about 35 percent more than the 705,000 ton capacity of Kilns 3 and 6. At any given level of production, the new kiln would emit less air polluting substance than the two older kilns combined, and would use less fuel to boot. However, if the Company decided to operate the new kiln close to its capacity, it might produce both more clinker and more pollution than the old kilns produced when operated at 60 percent of their capacity. In particular, information submitted by the Company suggests the following:

Pounds of Emissions per Ton of Clinker Produced

	NO_x	SO_2	PM
Old (Wet) Process	4.9	6.32	0.234
New (Dry) Process	2.6	4.01	0.133

Fig. 1: Comparative Emissions Rates

Tons of Emissions Per Year

	NO_x	SO_2	PM
Old (Wet) Process			
/Actual (operated at about 60% of capacity)	1100	1340	49.6
/Potential	1745	2230	82.6
New (Dry) Process			
/Actual	578	850	28.2
/Potential (operated at full capacity)	1250	1927	64.0

Fig. 2: Comparative Emissions Amounts

These charts show the rate and amount of emissions of three pollutants: nitrogen oxides, sulfur dioxide, and particulate matter. The "Actual" rate of production is the average rate for Kilns 3 and 6 for the years 1985–86, or 424,000 tons; the "Potential" rate equals 705,000 tons of clinker per year for the old wet process and 911,000 tons of clinker per year for the new dry process. The emboldened numbers are those used by EPA in comparing *actual* emissions of the old kilns with *potential* emissions of the proposed new kiln. The charts make clear that emissions will increase only if the company operates the new kiln at significantly higher production levels.

2. *Legal:* Since the cement plant is located near Ponce, Puerto Rico, where the air quality is better than national ambient air quality standards, new construction is subject to PSD provisions contained in Part C of Title I of the Clean Air Act. See 42 U.S.C. §§ 7470–7479. That part of the Act says that "[n]o major emitting facility ... *may be constructed* in any [such] area" without various specified studies, reviews, demonstrations of compliance with certain substantive standards, and the issuance of a permit. See 42 U.S.C. § 7475 (emphasis added). The Act defines "major emitting facility" as a "stationary source[ ]of air pollutants," including Portland Cement plants that "emit, or have the potential to emit, one hundred tons per year or more of any air pollutant" (such as the facilities at issue here). 42 U.S.C. § 7479(1). It defines "construction" to include "modification," which it says

> means any physical change in, or change in the method of operation of, a stationary source which increases the amount of any air pollutant emitted by such source or which results in the emission of any air pollutant not previously emitted.

42 U.S.C. §§ 7411(a)(4), 7479(2)(C). The Act also provides that EPA itself must review the construction proposal and provide the necessary approvals where, as here, no EPA-approved "state implementation plan" is in effect. See 42 U.S.C. § 7478; 40 C.F.R. 52.21(a).

Because the permitting process is costly and time-consuming, EPA has developed an informal system for determining whether or not a particular construction proposal does, or does not, fall within the scope of the PSD permit law. If EPA decides that PSD review is unnecessary, it issues a "non-applicability determination" (known as a "NAD").

3. *Proceedings:* On July 9, 1987, the Company asked EPA for a NAD. It submitted information to EPA over an eight-month period. On August 30, 1988, EPA denied the Company the NAD. The Company has appealed EPA's determination to this court. Subsequent to the docketing of this appeal the Company and EPA agreed that, if the Company loses this appeal, it will operate its new facility at a sufficiently low capacity to prevent any actual increase in emissions levels. EPA will then issue a NAD, see 40 C.F.R. 52.21(b)(4) (federally enforceable limitations on emissions will be taken into consideration in determining "potential to emit"), but the Company will lose its right to ask for a PSD permit, thereby giving up the possibility of obtaining EPA's approval for an increase of emissions. * * *

III.

The Merits

A.

Interpreting EPA's Regulations

The statute applies its PSD requirements to the Company's proposed modification of its kilns only if the modification will "increase[ ] the amount of any air pollutant emitted." 42 U.S.C. §§ 7411(a)(4), 7479(2)(C). In deciding whether or not the kiln conversion would result in such an increase, EPA calculated the *actual* historical amount of pollutants that Kilns 3 and 6 emitted in the past (which, under the regulations, equals the average emissions over the past two years, see 40 C.F.R. § 52.21(b)(21)(ii)) and compared that with the amount of pollutants that the converted kiln would be *capable* of emitting in the future. Since the Company operated the kilns at only 60 percent of their capacity in 1985–86, the new kiln, though cleaner and more efficient, is obviously *capable* of emitting significantly more pollutants.

The Company argues that the EPA's application of this "actual/potential" method of measurement to its proposed kiln modification represents an improper, arbitrary, and contradictory interpretation of EPA's own regulations. After reading the regulations themselves, we disagree.

First, the language and expressed intent of the regulations both support EPA's interpretation. The regulations provide that a "major modification," subject to PSD review, includes "any physical change in or change in the method of operation of a major stationary source that would result in a significant *net emissions increase* of any pollutant * * *." 40 C.F.R. § 52.21(b)(2)(i) (emphasis added). They go on to define "net emissions increase" as the amount by which the "sum of * * * any increase in *actual emissions*" (plus or minus other "contemporaneous" changes in emissions) "exceeds zero." 40 C.F.R. § 52.21(b)(3) (emphasis added). And, most importantly for present purposes, they define the words *"actual emissions"* in a special way.

They state that

"[a]ctual emissions" means the actual rate of emissions of a pollutant from an emissions unit, *as determined in accordance with paragraphs * * * (ii) through (iv) [below]*.

40 C.F.R. § 52.21(b)(21)(i) (emphasis added). Paragraph (ii) says that

[i]n general, actual emissions as of a particular date shall equal the average rate, in tons per year, at which the unit actually emitted the pollutant during [the preceding] two-year period.

40 C.F.R. § 52.21(b)(21)(ii). But, paragraph (iv) adds that

[f]or any emissions unit which has not begun normal operations on the particular date, actual emissions shall equal the potential to emit of the unit on that date.

40 C.F.R. § 52.21(b)(21)(iv) (emphasis added). The regulations also define "emissions unit" to include *"any part* of a stationary source which ... would have the potential to emit any pollutant." 40 C.F.R. § 52.21(b)(7) (emphasis added).

The Company's proposed modified kiln is "part of a stationary source" and it has the "potential to emit" a pollutant. 40 C.F.R. § 52.21(b)(7). EPA considered it to be an "emissions unit which has not begun normal operations." 40 C.F.R. § 52.21(b)(21)(iv). It therefore counted as its "actual emissions," the modified kiln's "potential to emit" pollution, *id.,* namely, in the case of SO$_2$, 1927 tons per year. It counted the "actual emissions" of the existing kilns as "the average rate * * * at which" they "actually emitted the pollutant during the [preceding] two year period," 40 C.F.R. § 52.21(b)(21)(ii), namely, in the case of SO$_2$, 1340 tons per year. It therefore found an increase in what the regulations call "actual emissions" (1927 minus 1340 equals 587 tons per year). And, after setting off allowable contemporaneous changes, it found that the net increase was significantly greater than zero. See 40 C.F.R. §§ 52.21(b)(2)(i), 52.21(b)(3)(i).

EPA's application of its regulation to the facts of this case complies with the expressed intent of the regulation's writers as well. In a preamble to the regulation, EPA says that, when calculating whether a physical change will bring about a significant net increase in emissions, "the source owner must [first] quantify the amount of the proposed emissions increase. This amount will generally be the *potential to emit* of the new or modified unit." 45 Fed.Reg. 52,677 (emphasis added).

In considering the lawfulness of an agency's interpretation of its own regulations, courts often give that interpretation "controlling weight unless it is plainly erroneous or inconsistent with the regulation." Udall v. Tallman, 380 U.S. 1, 16–17, 85 S.Ct. 792, 801–02, 13 L.Ed.2d 616 (1965) (quoting Bowles v. Seminole Rock & Sand Co., 325 U.S. 410, 414, 65 S.Ct. 1215, 1217, 89 L.Ed. 1700 (1945)); accord Donovan v. A. Amorello & Sons, Inc., 761 F.2d 61, 63 (1st Cir.1985). In this case, EPA needs little help from this principle, for both language and expressed purpose indicate that EPA applied the regulations properly.

Second, the Company argues that EPA's interpretation of the regulation is arbitrary—that the interpretation makes little sense because it would significantly discourage the Company, and others like it, from installing more efficient machinery that, at any production level, emits significantly less pollution. But we cannot agree. EPA has simply taken account of, and given controlling weight to, a different consideration: the fact that a firm's decision to introduce new, more efficient machinery may lead the firm to decide to *increase the level of production,* with the result that, despite the new machinery, overall emissions will increase. Indeed, EPA points out that a firm introducing such machinery can escape PSD review simply by promising that it will ensure its actual emissions do not in fact increase (that is, by promising that it will not run the machinery at such a rate as to create an actual increase in emissions levels.) See 40 C.F.R. 52.21(b)(4) (federally enforceable physical or operational limitations which effect emissions will be taken into consideration in determining "potential to emit").

One can imagine circumstances that might test the reasonableness of EPA's regulation. An electricity company, for example, might wish to replace a peak load generator—one that operates only a few days per year—with a new peak load generator that the firm could, but almost certainly will not, operate every day. And, uncertainties about the precise shape of future electricity peak demand might make the firm hesitate to promise

EPA it will never increase actual emissions (particularly since EPA insists, as a condition of accepting the promise and issuing the NAD, that the firm also promise not to apply for permission for an actual increase under the PSD review process). Whatever the arguments about the "irrationality" of EPA's interpretation in such circumstances, however, those circumstances are not present here. The Company is not interested in peak load capacity; it operated its old kilns at low levels in the past; its new, more efficient kiln might give it the economic ability to increase production; consequently, EPA could plausibly fear an increase in actual emissions were it to provide the NAD. Thus, this seems the very type of case for which the regulations quoted above were written. We can find nothing arbitrary or irrational about EPA applying those regulations to the Company's proposal. * * *

[The cement company unsuccessfully raised two other issues challenging EPA's interpretation of its PSD rules. First, it argued that EPA had inconsistently interpreted its regulations without explanation or justification. Second, it claimed that the PSD rules at issue were unauthorized by the Clean Air Act and therefore unlawful. The court found this latter challenge untimely and in the wrong court.]

IV.

Credit for "Contemporaneous" Decreases in Emissions

The regulations, as we have previously mentioned, measure any increase in emissions by, first, calculating the "actual" increase in emissions, and second, offsetting any "contemporaneous" decrease in emissions, due, say, to other changes the firm has made at the plant * * *. The Company undertook a coal conversion project in 1982–1983, which led to a significant decrease in emissions. The EPA refused to credit the Company with this decrease because, it found, the decrease was not "contemporaneous" with the present proposed project. The Company now argues that the EPA is wrong.

The EPA's regulations, however, make clear that the coal project was not "contemporaneous." They say that a decrease is "contemporaneous" if it occurs between

> the date five years before construction on the particular change commences[,] and * * * the date that the increase from the particular change occurs.

40 C.F.R. § 52.21(b)(3)(iii). Since construction on the kiln modification has not yet "commence[d]", and since more than five years has passed since the coal conversion, the Company cannot bring itself within this "contemporaneous" window. The Company says that it *filed its NAD application* within five years of the time it converted to coal, but that fact is irrelevant; the regulation speaks of "*construction* on the [kiln] * * * change," not of an *application* to make the change. 40 C.F.R. § 52.21(b)(3)(iii). And, the history of the regulation, referring to an alternative, shorter (three year) window measured with respect to "the date an application was complete," makes clear that reference to a construction date (along with the longer

five year window) was intended. See 45 Fed.Reg. 6803 (1980) (soliciting comments on proposed regulations defining "contemporaneous" for purposes of offsetting emissions).

Since the regulation is clear, since it does not count the 1982–83 coal conversion project as "contemporaneous," since the Company made no request of the agency to waive the rule, and since it cannot challenge the lawfulness of this "nationally applicable" regulation in this court, [see] 42 U.S.C. 7607(b)(1), we must reject its claim.

For these reasons, the petition for review is denied and the order of the United States Environmental Protection Agency is affirmed.

NOTES AND QUESTIONS

1. *PSD Area Classification.* As the terminology indicates, PSD does not prevent all deterioration of air quality in clean air areas, only "significant" deterioration. If clean air is that which is better than the NAAQS, how much worsening will be accepted in the name of economic growth and community development? Like all else involved with the Clean Air Act, the answer is not simple.

The Act requires that all clean air areas be placed into one of three classifications (I, II, or III) to reflect the amount of air quality deterioration that is acceptable. Areas have been designated for three of the NAAQS— sulphur dioxide, particulates, and nitrogen dioxide. Class I areas tolerate the least air pollution growth while Class III allow the most. Class I areas have the "narrowest" PSD increment while Class III areas have the "broadest." Obviously the classification of land areas for PSD purposes is of critical importance to economic growth of the region. The air quality increment provides a limited air pollution assimilative capacity and, as such, a control on future growth.

Section 162(a) establishes four categories of federal lands—international parks, national wilderness areas, national memorial parks and national parks—exceeding minimum acreage and in existence in 1977 as "mandatory Class I areas" which must permanently be included in this restrictive category. As of 2001, there were 156 mandatory Class I areas mostly located in the western states and usually as wilderness areas located in National Forests. The CAA § 162(a) prevents these areas from being redesignated to Class II or Class III. Why should these areas have perpetual Class I status? All other PSD areas were initially deemed Class II areas and they could be redesignated to either Class I or Class III status by action of the states. The Act in § 164(a) imposes the following three-part test for redesignation to the least restrictive Class III category. It states that,

> Any area (other than an area referred to in paragraph (1) or (2) or an area established as class I * * *) may be redesignated by the State as class III if—
>
> (A) such redesignation has been specifically approved by the Governor of the State, after consultation with the appropriate Committees

of the legislature if it is in session or with the leadership of the legislature if it is not in session (unless State law provides that such redesignation must be specifically approved by State legislation) and if general purpose units of local government representing a majority of the residents of the area so redesignated enact legislation (including for such units of local government resolutions where appropriate) concurring in the State's redesignation;

(B) such redesignation will not cause, or contribute to, concentrations of any air pollutant which exceed any maximum allowable increase or maximum allowable concentration permitted under the classification of any other area; and

(C) such redesignation otherwise meets the requirements of this part.

EPA's regulations generally set forth a detailed procedure for state redesignation proceedings including broad notice requirements, a multifaceted analytical report, consultation with local elected officials and at least one public hearing. See 40 C.F.R. § 51.24(g)(1999). As CAA § 164(a) indicates that even greater state action is required for redesignation to Class III status. What pragmatic concerns might a state governor have about such a request? What political considerations might be present?

2. *PSD Air Quality Increments.* What are the principal differences in PSD classifications? Why might it matter if an area is categorized Class I or Class II and how could the classification affect economic development?

The designation of clean air areas into the three classes has a direct impact on the amount of air quality deterioration that will be permitted. Section 163(b) sets allowable deterioration increments for increases in ambient concentrations of two pollutants—sulfur dioxide and particulates. The increments represent a statement of available assimilative capacity that can be awarded to new or modified sources wishing to locate within the PSD area. Different increments were established for each land classification with the increments being smallest for Class I and largest for Class III. These increments are as follows:

Pollutant	Maximum allowable increase (micrograms per cubic meter)
CLASS I	
Particulate matter:	
PM$_{10}$, annual geometric mean	4
PM$_{10}$, 24–hr maximum	8
Sulfur dioxide:	
Annual arithmetic mean	2
24–hr maximum	5
3–hr maximum	25

Pollutant	Maximum allowable increase (micrograms per cubic meter)
Nitrogen dioxide:	
Annual arithmetic mean	2.5
CLASS II	
Particulate matter:	
PM_{10}, annual geometric mean	17
PM_{10}, 24–hr maximum............................	30
Sulfur dioxide:	
Annual arithmetic mean	20
24–hr maximum	91
3–hr maximum	512
Nitrogen dioxide:	
Annual arithmetic mean...........................	25
CLASS III	
Particulate matter:	
PM_{10}, annual geometric mean	34
PM_{10}, 24–hr maximum............................	60
Sulfur dioxide:	
Annual arithmetic mean	40
24–hr maximum	182
3–hr maximum	700
Nitrogen dioxide:	
Annual arithmetic mean...........................	50

As part of the PSD new source review, a source impact analysis must be performed to demonstrate compliance with the available air quality increment. The increment becomes the amount of air pollution assimilative capacity left to be "allocated" to users. That is to say that the new or modified source's emissions will not exceed the available increment nor violate the primary or secondary NAAQS. This process has been briefly summarized in the following terms,

The first complete application for construction of a major new source or modification in a PSD area triggers a "baseline date" and a "baseline concentration" for the given pollutant in the "baseline area." The first permittee draws down the available increment. Subsequent applicants for a PSD permit draw upon the amount of increment remaining following the issuance of the first permit and later permits, if any. The "baseline concentration" is defined as the ambient level of the pollutant in question on the baseline date. It is derived from actual emissions, but includes certain adjustments.

The "baseline date" is the earliest date that a major source or modification files a complete application for a PSD permit, and is triggered for each pollutant which the new source would emit in a significant amount. The "baseline area" is also pollutant-specific and includes the designated attainment or unclassifiable area where the new source would locate, as well as any other such area within the state experiencing an impact of one microgram per cubic meter from that proposed source. (footnotes omitted)

P. Wyckoff & G. Foote, New Source Review in *Law of Environmental Protection* 11–150 to 11–151 (S. Novick ed. 1995). As this discussion indicates, the setting of the baseline concentration is of critical importance since the calculation of the available increment rests upon it. An example might make this point clearer. Assume for simplicity that the new source is to be located in a PSD area for particulates (PM–10) and that it will only emit particulate matter. The following chart indicates the available increment for particulates in all three land classes. Remember that there is also an increment for particulates measured by a 24 hour average.

Once the air quality increment is totally consumed, the air may not be further polluted. Also, the NAAQS sets another barrier for air emissions growth which a PSD increment cannot invade. There is evidence that rapid PSD permitting in the 1980s and early 1990s has consumed available increments in many parts of the country. How can a new source locate or a modification occur in that case? What analogy to non-attainment policy would be relevant?

2. *PSD Program New Source Review.* Most states implement the PSD program within their territories under their State Implementation Plans or by delegation of federal authority. EPA exercises supervisory authority to ensure that state PSD permitting practices follow the EPA-approved procedures and that the source is not violating the terms of its permit. If PSD review and substantive standards focus attention on new sources and major modifications, which of them are included in the regulatory "net?" What is pre-construction review in this context? A new source review program lies at the heart of the PSD scheme.

   • *Source Coverage.* The PSD preconstruction review and permitting program is aimed at "major emitting facilities," a subcategory of all new sources. Section 169(1) [§ 7479(1)] defines this term to include a list of twenty-eight kinds of industrial facilities "which emit, or have the potential to emit, one hundred tons a year or more of any air pollutant." These include iron and steel plants, large electric generating plants, refineries, and chemical process facilities. If a source does not fall within these 28 categories, it will be subject to PSD provisions if it has the "potential to emit" two hundred and fifty tons per year or more of any air pollutant. Why would Congress exempt new sources smaller than these from PSD review? Why also would Congress permit the exemption of all new sources which are "non-profit health or education institutions * * *?" See Town of Brookline v. Gorsuch, 667 F.2d 215, 222 (1st Cir.1981) (upholding the exemption of Harvard University-related diesel-operated, cogeneration power plant from PSD analysis).

   Sources emitting either 100 or 250 tons per year are clearly swept in by the § 169(*l*) definition. But what does the term "potential to emit" mean? What are the possible interpretations? Prior to the decision in

Alabama Power v. Costle, 606 F.2d 1068 (D.C.Cir.1979), EPA had suggested a definition of the amount of emissions during source operation at capacity *without* pollution controls. The court disagreed and focused instead upon a concept of "design capacity" which took into account the anticipated functioning of the pollution control equipment. From a practical standpoint, does it matter which definition is used? Which definition captures the largest number of sources? What incentives does this regulatory system give industrial designers? What if a source agreed in its state-issued air permit to restrict emissions to *less than* 100 or 250 tons per year? Such an agreement must be federally-enforceable.

What if a facility has a number of emission points which individually fall *below* the statutory 100/250 tons per year point but when combined exceed that level? When would these multiple emission points be considered a "major emitting facility" and be subject to PSD requirements? EPA has taken the position that all the pollutant-emitting activities undertaken (1) within the same "major group" under the U.S. Government's Standard Industrial Classification Manual and (2) under the same ownership or control must be added together. What are the implications of such a policy?

Remember that the new source review requirements also apply to major modifications of existing sources. A modification can occur, for example, when an existing plant either (1) replaces a part of its equipment or (2) expands with the addition of a new operation. In addition, the modification must significantly increase the plant's overall emissions by more than a *de minimis* amount. EPA has defined *de minimis* ranging from nearly 0 to 100 tons per year depending on the pollutant, with hazardous air pollutants having the lowest threshold. See 40 C.F.R. § 52.21(b)(23).

What if a facility has several emission points and it plans to reduce emissions from one smokestack while at the same time adding emissions from the modification? What about a single replacement that reduces emissions over pre-existing levels? EPA has promulgated regulations that define "source" as "plant" and a PSD permit is required only when there has been a significant net increase in emissions from the plant. There is the "bubble" policy which subjects facility modifications to PSD review only when the net change in emissions is significant. EPA has attempted to encourage the use of such bubbles by reducing the required air quality modeling and by instituting general rules which permit bubbles without the requirement of a SIP revision.

• *Pollutants Covered.* Carefully read § 169(1). What kinds of emissions trigger PSD review? While the Clean Air Act sets the 100 and 250 tons per year levels as "jurisdictional amounts" for the PSD program, *Alabama Power* held that PSD review applied to all pollutants regulated under the Act, not just the criteria pollutants. EPA has declared that, in addition to the NAAQS pollutants, the following emissions are "regulated under the Act": asbestos, beryllium, mercury, vinyl chloride, fluorides, sulfuric acid mist, hydrogen sulfide, total reduced sulfur, and reduced sulfur compounds.

As other air pollutants are regulated under the Act presumably they would be added to this list.

• *Analysis of New or Modified Source Impact on Air Quality.* All new or modified sources wishing to locate in PSD areas must show that they will not "cause or contribute to" a violation of the NAAQS or a PSD increment. EPA regulations require that this showing be made in two steps—1) preapplication air quality monitoring for up to one year and 2) air quality diffusion modeling analysis indicating the impact of the proposed source and other associated emissions. This analysis is intended to determine how much of the available increment would be "consumed" by the proposed new or modified source. EPA has issued its *Guideline on Air Quality Models* to provide for uniform modeling procedures. The applicant must also include an analysis of non-NAAQS air quality and the impairment to visibility, soils and vegetation caused by the new source and associated growth. The costs and time consumed by these application data requirements would certainly encourage an applicant to avoid PSD review if possible.

• *The Best Available Control Technology (BACT) Requirement.* The Clean Air Act conditions the issuance of new or modified source permits in PSD areas upon compliance with a high degree of pollution control technology. See § 165(a)(4) [§ 7475(a)(4)]. The Act, as you know by now, provides a number of verbal formulations for required levels of pollution control. For PSD, this specification is termed Best Available Control Technology (BACT) and is defined in § 169(3) [§ 7479(3)] as the maximum degree of pollution reduction (considering a number of factors) that is achievable. However, BACT must be at least as stringent as the requirements of §§ 111 & 112. Read the BACT definition and compare it to LAER definition in § 171(3) [§ 7501(3)]. Which is more demanding? Is this definition truly "technology forcing" within the conception of § 111?

BACT must be determined for each Clean Air Act "regulated" pollutant emitted by the new source in "significant amounts" and not just for "major" or NAAQS pollutants. What pollutants would be included? The BACT standard for a source is set on a case-by-case basis by the reviewing authority which must take into account "energy, environmental, and economic impacts and other costs." If you were the permit writer, how might this broad array of factors affect your setting of BACT in a particular case? Compare how economic costs are to be considered in the establishment of BACT, LAER, and NSPS. Why would the Act provide for such direct consideration of economic matters in the PSD context?

How does the permit-granting agency (EPA or the state) know what is the best technology that is "available" or "achievable?" What analytical process should be employed to consider alternatives? How could the size of the available air quality increment affect the setting of BACT? In Northern Plains Resource Council v. United States EPA, 645 F.2d 1349 (9th Cir. 1981) the court upheld EPA's choice of a weaker particulate BACT so as to achieve greater SO_2 control. What if there is no NSPS, NESHAPs, or SIP limitation for a particular unregulated pollutant? Can BACT be no control at all? Should a proposed source be able to satisfy BACT by applying control technology to a different facility in the area?

3. *Visibility Protection.* The PSD provisions of the Clean Air Act limit the incremental amount of new pollution brought to clean air areas. What about pollution that impairs visibility regardless of PSD limits? Does the Act deal with such visual issues? In many scenic and pristine areas visibility is an important value yet one which has been impaired by the emissions of single or small groups of sources. Visibility is an especially significant aspect of national parks, forests and wilderness areas. However, the conflict over visibility indicates that these issues are not exclusively the concern of federal lands in the western United States.

In 1977, Congress initiated a special regulatory program to protect visibility in mandatory Class I areas—"areas of great scenic importance"— due to a belief that PSD protection was insufficient. Mandatory Class I areas include national parks exceeding 6,000 acres, wilderness areas and national memorial parks exceeding 5,000 acres and all international parks which were in existence on August 7, 1977. Impairment of visibility has been found to be an issue in 156 of these areas in over 35 states and one territory. Section 169A of the Act [§ 7491] declares a national goal in the prevention of any future, and the remedying of any existing, "manmade" impairment of visibility in such areas. Surprisingly, the additional protections provided by this program were not accorded to other, non-mandatory Class I areas. Why do you think § 169A was designed in this fashion? Why were non-manmade visibility impairments not brought under this program?

● Visibility Protection Post–1977

Following the 1977 CAA amendments, visibility protection was to be accomplished through a state/federal partnership where SIPs were to be amended a) to assess and remedy visibility harm from new and existing pollution sources and b) to develop long term strategies to assure "reasonable further progress" towards the § 169A national visibility goal. Under EPA's 1980 visibility regulations 40 C.F.R. 51.300–51.307 the main focus was the control of "plume blight" that is smoke plumes reasonably attributable by visual observation (or other means) to a specific source or a small group of sources. The focus was on plume blight from speatically, identified air pollution sources. This program required states to take 5 steps;

1. revise SIPs to assure to assure reasonable further progress towards the national visibility goal

2. determine which existing stationary sources should install the "best available retrofit technology" or BART to control emissions impairing visibility,

3. develop, adopt, implement and evaluate long-term strategies for making reasonable progress for meeting the § 169A national visibility goal

4. adopt measures to assess potential visibility effects of new or modified major stationary sources,

5. conduct visibility monitoring in Class I areas.

Most states required to submit visibility SIP revisions missed their deadlines or failed to submit anything. This ultimately resulted in EPA's promulgation a Federal Implement Plan component for them.

● Attacking the Problem of "Regional Haze"

While plume blight from discrete and identifiable sources was the principal focus of EPA's visibility program, it deferred to a later date dealing with the more diffuse problem of regional haze. Regional Haze is visibility impairment produced by many sources and activities which emit fine particles and which are distributed over a larger geographical area. Regional haze had constituted a difficult technical problem in the early 1980's due to inadequate monitoring and air quality modeling techniques needed to correlate causes and effects. In State of Maine v. Thomas, 874 F.2d 883 (1st Cir.1989), the appellate court rejected a citizens suit brought by states to compel EPA to issue regional haze regulations. In 1990, Congress added § 169B which emphasized regulatory reports to Congress and the formation of regional Visibility Transport Regions to deal with multi-jurisdictional problems.

Finally, in 1999, 19 years after the first visibility protection rules EPA issued a final regulation requiring states to eradicated haze conditions in the nation's 156 mandatory Class I national parks and wilderness area. 40 C.F.R. Part 51, subpart P, § § 51.308–309. This regulation—the Haze Rule—will be implemented over a 60 year period—perhaps, the longest regulatory phase—in period ever—and it requires that the states establish long-term strategies for reducing SO_2, NO_X, and fine particulate which contribute to the impairment of visibility. The overall goal of the rule is to attain "natural visibility conditions" by 2064.

Significantly, the regional haze rule may cause states to assign BART or retrofit pollution control requirements to certain existing sources including coal fired utilities, industrial boilers, refineries and iron and steel plants built between 1962–1977. States must identify these "BART-eligible" plants and establish control strategies to provide for progress in achieving natural visibility for each Class I area both within and without the state. The regional haze rule allows the state to impose more stringent BART limits reasonably anticipated to cause or contribute to haze. In May, 2001 EPA proposed guidance to states in deciding which such facilities must install retrofit air pollution controls not later than 2013. During the 1980's, BART limits were rarely imposed by states or by EPA—the Navajo Generating Station in Arizona being a notable exception attributable to its effect on the Grand Canyon. The haze rule also allows the alternative measure of emissions trading to source-by-source BART controls, as long as the trading program achieves greater emission reductions that the individual BART limits. The new regional haze rule SIP revisions must be submitted to EPA from 2004–2008 with revision of haze plans every 10 years thereafter.

SECTION 7. ENFORCING THE CLEAN AIR ACT

A. INTRODUCTION AND OVERVIEW

The discussion to this point has described a complex scheme of air pollution regulation emphasizing specific source controls. SIPs and federal emission limitations under §§ 111 and 112 assign particularized performance responsibilities upon individual sources. Under the logic of the Clean Air Act's design the objectives of achieving the NAAQS, air toxic standards and acid rain requirements depend upon reducing and maintaining source emissions to regulated levels. Automobile and other mobile source performance must similarly be limited. With the enactment of Title V of the 1990 Clean Air Act amendments, Congress has decided to parallel the structure of the Clean Water Act and to obtain compliance with these standards by means of an enforceable permit program. Setting standards does not automatically result in their attainment (especially when there are large economic consequences connected to compliance). "Enforcement" is the term used to describe the means of obtaining compliance with pollution control rules.

How should the government assure compliance with performance obligations imposed under the air pollution statute? In theory, numerous possibilities exist: government subsidy or other incentive for pollution control, voluntary compliance agreements, private emissions trading schemes, etc. However, the Clean Air Act commands compliance with its requirements through a system of sanctions imposed when an emission source fails to perform at the required levels. These include performance commands enforced by way of administrative order and penalty, judicial injunction, monetary civil penalties, criminal punishment, and denial of government contracts. Since voluntary compliance with the Clean Air Act can hardly be assured, enforcement of these regulatory requirements becomes crucial to the success or failure in achieving the goals of the Act. The overall structure of the compliance method is summarized as follows.

> The Act's enforcement scheme has five elements. The first is institutional responsibility for enforcement, which the Clean Air Act splits among EPA, the states, and private citizens. The second element is the enforceable, source-specific emission limit. Third is investigatory authority: The Act provides broad authority to investigate and document possible violations of its provisions. Fourth is the process by which enforcers choose their responses once violations have been detected. The Clean Air Act leaves EPA considerable flexibility in this area of traditionally broad prosecutorial discretion, but imposes some constraints not common in other law enforcement fields. The fifth element of Clean Air Act enforcement is imposition of sanctions on appropriate violators. Each of these pieces of the enforcement puzzle is critical to the overall effectiveness of the system.

P. Reed, State Implementation Plans in *Law of Environmental Protection* 11–66 (S. Novick ed. 1995).

The enforcement of the requirements of federal environmental law has been diffused over a broad range of actions and actors. Governmental enforcement of the Clean Air Act may occur at the federal or state government level while citizen suit enforcement power exists to give local governments and a range of non-governmental interests the ability to assure compliance with the Act. In terms of the federal government, primary responsibility for Clean Air Act enforcement rests with the Environmental Protection Agency's Office of Enforcement and Compliance Assurance acting both from the Washington D.C. headquarters and in each of the agency's ten regional offices. When court action is anticipated, EPA works in conjunction with the Department of Justice Environment and Natural Resources Division in all civil and criminal enforcement cases. Enforcement cases often result in a mixture of efforts of personnel from EPA, DOJ, and the U.S. Attorneys Office working together to resolve a dispute.

Under the Clean Air Act, as with other federal environmental acts, enforcement measures can be taken either within EPA or in court. EPA is increasingly emphasizing compliance assistance; incentives and self auditing policies. In the first instance of agency enforcement, EPA may seek a pollution source's compliance with a Clean Air Act requirement through informal means such as a conversation, site inspection, or written request. Should these efforts result in the desired response from the source owner, no further action is needed. Aside from these informal methods, EPA can issue a formal notice of violation under § 113(a)(1), as a precursor to taking more serious administrative or judicial enforcement steps. Under the Act EPA has a broad range of administrative enforcement powers including the issuance of compliance orders and the assessment of administrative penalties. In more serious, contested cases EPA can initiate an enforcement lawsuit in federal court to receive a judgment imposing civil remedies of either an injunctive or financial nature against a violator of the Act. In addition, the U.S. government may initiate a criminal enforcement action which could result in criminal fines or incarceration.

Enforcement is receiving increased EPA emphasis as part of its general pollution control program. During the 2000 fiscal year, under all of its authorities EPA brought a record 6,027 enforcement actions involving sanctions with the following breakdown:

236 criminal cases referred to DOJ

1,763 administrative complaints

3,660 administrative compliance orders and field citations

368 civil referrals to the DOJ

27 civil referrals for consent decree enforcement.

Penalties for this FY 2000 totaled a record $224 million combined for civil penalties and criminal fines and another $2.6 billion was paid to implement injunctive relief for environmental cleanup, superfund site remediation and improved monitoring.

The Clean Air Act does not centralize its treatment of enforcement issues in one particular part of the statute. In addition, enforcement powers are shared by both governmental and non-governmental entities. Government enforcement authority for stationary source compliance with SIP and national emission limitations is found in § 113 [§ 7413] of the Clean Air Act. Section 113(b) sets forth the list of potential violations subject to government enforcement. Similar enforcement power with respect to mobile sources resides in another part of the statute. See §§ 203–205 [§§ 7522–7524]. Jurisdiction for citizen suit enforcement is found in yet another part of the Act. See § 304 [§ 7604]. Why would the drafters of the Clean Air Act vest these powers in private groups or individuals? Wouldn't they just "get in the way" of ongoing EPA and state enforcement efforts?

Our attention will initially focus upon the governmental enforcement powers contained in § 113. Read this section giving special consideration to §§ 113(a)–(d). What is the structure of the enforcement authority? Why would EPA elect to pursue enforcement by way of administrative order rather than direct resort to judicial intervention? How is state enforcement of Clean Air Act requirements accommodated and does the statute assure coordinated action? See § 116 [§ 7416].

CLASS DISCUSSION PROBLEM: ENFORCING THE CLEAN AIR ACT AT BOWMAR PAPER

Bowmar Paper Corporation ("Bowmar") operates a plant containing its Special Materials Division in Baton Rouge, Louisiana. In this facility Bowmar manufactures a wide range of specialty papers used for such diverse purposes as chemical testing and photographic supply. The Baton Rouge plant functions with an operations permit issued by the Louisiana Department of Environmental Protection ("the Department") which sets specific emission rates and workplace standards for a number of Bowmar's emission points. The permit also states that the plant is subject to all of the provisions of the Louisiana State Implementation Plan (SIP). Although the papermaking facility has been in operation for nearly 10 years, the facility has been visited by inspectors from the Department only twice. Both inspections had merely resulted in weakly-worded Department letters to Bowmar noting a number of operational and emission control failures but only requesting future compliance. At no time did the Department initiate or recommend any formal enforcement action to compel compliance with the Bowmar permit or the related SIP terms.

Recently, EPA's regional office received information from several residents living near the Bowmar plant of (1) unusual and continuing construction activity at the site, (2) new emissions emanating from the site and, (3) reports of increased, serious worker's illness at the plant. A local environmental group has also asserted that it has evidence of a recent upsurge in paralysis, cancer and birth defects in the vicinity of the Bowmar plant. The EPA Regional Counsel has decided to look into the Bowmar case and you have been assigned to conduct the investigation and map out any enforcement strategy that might be warranted. Your initial inquiries to the Louisiana Department of Environmental Protection reveal that the state agency has not inspected the Bowmar plant during the past three years and that it is not aware of any Bowmar request to expand or modify the Baton Rouge facility. Consider the following questions.

1. Assuming that you wanted to examine Bowmar's production and pollution control records and reports, could you get access to them? Could you send an inspection team composed of EPA personnel and private compliance consultants to the Bowmar site to examine the plant and its air pollution control devices to assess SIP and permit compliance? Can Bowmar keep the inspection team out?

2. If through the findings of the inspection team or from other information you determine that Bowmar has violated the terms of its state-issued air permit or other provisions of the Louisiana SIP, what Clean Air Act enforcement steps could you take? What if you learned that Bowmar had constructed a new emission point without notifying the State or EPA and without a new permit? Would you have to initiate a federal lawsuit to order Bowman into compliance and to impose monetary penalties? Could you achieve both of these goals by direct EPA administrative action? Why might you prefer EPA administrative action to litigation?

3. What if you discover that the new, unpermitted expansion of Bowmar's plant emits significant amounts of benzene into the air. Benzene, you discover, is a hazardous air pollutant which has been listed pursuant to § 112 of the Clean Air Act. Could this information, if verified, give rise to criminal prosecutions under the Clean Air Act? Would criminal prosecution be appropriate in this case? Who might be potential defendants and what penalties could be imposed? Would the corporation itself have any potential liability? What additional facts would need to be established by proof in order to obtain a conviction?

4. For purposes of this question, assume that neither the State of Louisiana nor the federal EPA have taken any enforcement action against Bowmar. What if an environmental group obtained credible information that Bowmar had consistently violated terms of its permit or other SIP provisions over the prior three years (215 alleged violations). Could it force EPA to act? Could it initiate an enforcement action in its own right in federal court to seek compliance with the Clean Air Act? What procedures must it follow? Can the environmental group seek monetary penalties against Bowmar? How would they be measured? Could the group recover its litigation expenses incurred in this litigation?

B.   The Structure of Enforcement Under the Clean Air Act

Arnold W. Reitze, Jr., Air Pollution Law
1008–09 (1995).

§ 20.4   Enforcement Provisions Under the 1990 Clean Air Act Amendments

The 1990 CAA Amendments modernize the Act and add provisions similar to those included in amendments to the CWA, TSCA, RCRA, and

CERCLA since the prior CAA Amendments in 1977. The changes also make the CAA easier to enforce. The basic enforcement provision, section 113, expands EPA's enforcement options by providing a range of responses from field citations to criminal prosecution, new sanctions and increased stringency in the existing sanctions, and more clarity in the applicable standards. Through the use of other new CAA provisions, more information on compliance with the standards may be obtained.

Under the old CAA, the use of compliance orders was limited because compliance had to obtained in thirty days. The new law allows compliance schedules of up to one year, which should enhance their utilization. Under the old law, CAA section 120 controlled noncompliance penalties and allowed penalties only prospectively from the issuance of a Notice of Noncompliance. Now, using section 113, penalties can be applied for past violations. EPA's administrative powers are considerably enhanced. There is new authority for EPA to levy administrative penalties of up to $25,000 per day, but generally with a cap of $200,000. These penalties must follow an opportunity for a hearing on the record that meets the requirements of the Administrative Procedure Act. EPA has been given new authority to deal with minor violations. EPA can issue field citations with penalties up to $5000 per violation and needs to provide only an opportunity for an informal hearing. The new field citation program, the CAA equivalent of a traffic ticket, gives EPA an enforcement tool that is easier to use than the civil judicial actions that were the primary enforcement tool under the old CAA.

Sanctions have become more stringent, and fines are now based on title 18 provisions, which allows increases in the maximum size of the fines. The new law authorizes felony sanctions, typically up to five years, rather than the one-year misdemeanor approach used under the old law and authorizes doubling the sanctions for repeat offenders. The new law adds provisions making negligent endangerment for a misdemeanor [§ 113(c)(4)] and knowing endangerment a felony [§ 113(c)(5)]. Knowingly violating a fee requirement under the CAA is now a misdemeanor. The new law in section 113(c) and (h) defines "operator" and "person" to limit criminal prosecution of corporate employees to those who are senior managers or officers except in cases of knowing and willful violations. Section 113(c)(2) has been amended to provide criminal liability for a range of actions relating to keeping documents and supplying information. Prison penalties have been increased from six months to two years.

Under the old CAA, EPA could not act upon SIP violations unless they lasted beyond thirty days. Now, under CAA section 113(a)(1), a one-day violation may be the subject of an EPA response although a thirty-day notice is still required. Penalties can be applied to all violations including those that predate the notice of violations. Section 113(b) now states clearly that the statutory penalties apply per day for *each* violation. EPA can now establish violations with any credible evidence including the use of evidence other than that derived from the applicable test method [§ 113(e)]. This section also adds the requirement that the violator may have to prove when the violation has ended.

The new law also clarified that section 167 administrative orders for new or modified sources may be civilly and criminally enforced using section 113. The new law in CAA section 302 also confirms that moveable stationary sources are subject to stationary source requirements. Only motor vehicles and non-road engines regulated under section 216 are exempt from section 113. Basically everything that needs to be enforced in the CAA, except mobile sources which have their own enforcement provision, is subject to section 113. Section 113 also provides authority to collect fees owed to the United States.

The new law removes two provisions in the old CAA. The old CAA section 113(d)'s delayed compliance order, which could excuse meeting attainment deadlines, has been abolished. The old CAA section 113(e)'s delayed compliance deadline for the steel industry was also abolished.

The 1990 CAA Amendments enhance EPA's enforcement power by increasing its ability to obtain information. CAA section 114 has been amended to clarify EPA's right to require information to be generated and submitted on a regular basis. Under the new section 114(a)(3), owners and operators of sources can be required to identify the standards to which they are subject and to provide certification that they are complying with the standards. CAA section 307(a), dealing with administrative enforcement subpoenas, has been amended to make compliance information subject to the subpoena power.

Excerpt from the Clean Air Act

42 U.S.C. § 7413.

§ 113(b) Civil judicial enforcement

The Administrator shall, as appropriate, in the case of any person that is the owner or operator of an affected source, a major emitting facility, or a major stationary source, and may, in the case of any other person, commence a civil action for a permanent or temporary injunction, or to assess and recover a civil penalty of not more than $25,000 per day for each violation, or both, in any of the following instances:

(1) Whenever such person has violated, or is in violation of, any requirement or prohibition of an applicable implementation plan or permit. Such an action shall be commenced (A) during any period of federally assumed enforcement, or (B) more than 30 days following the date of the Administrator's notification under subsection (a)(1) of this section that such person has violated, or is in violation of, such requirement or prohibition.

(2) Whenever such person has violated, or is in violation of, any other requirement or prohibition of this subchapter, section 7603 of this title, subchapter IV-A, subchapter V, or subchapter VI of this chapter, including, but not limited to, a requirement or prohibition of

any rule, order, waiver or permit promulgated, issued, or approved under this chapter, or for the payment of any fee owed the United States under this chapter (other than subchapter II of this chapter).

(3) Whenever such person attempts to construct or modify a major stationary source in any area with respect to which a finding under subsection (a)(5) of this section has been made.

Any action under this subsection may be brought in the district court of the United States for the district in which the violation is alleged to have occurred, or is occurring, or in which the defendant resides, or where the defendant's principal place of business is located, and such court shall have jurisdiction to restrain such violation, to require compliance, to assess such civil penalty, to collect any fees owed the United States under this chapter (other than subchapter II of this chapter) and any noncompliance assessment and nonpayment penalty owed under section 7420 of this title, and to award any other appropriate relief. Notice of the commencement of such action shall be given to the appropriate State air pollution control agency. In the case of any action brought by the Administrator under this subsection, the court may award costs of litigation (including reasonable attorney and expert witness fees) to the party or parties against whom such action was brought if the court finds that such action was unreasonable.

C. GATHERING INFORMATION

NOTE ON ENFORCEMENT INFORMATION GATHERING

In most enforcement cases EPA notifies the defendant that it is not in compliance with the state's SIP or its permit conditions. How does the agency know? In all probability, EPA has discovered these instances of non-compliance while conducting an inspection of the company's facility. An employee or a neighbor could also tip off the agency.

Collecting information regarding air pollution source performance is an important component of the Clean Air Act regulatory scheme. The critical concept of NAAQS attainment and air toxics standards hinges upon the achievement of SIP requirements and other emission limitations by sources subject to control. The Title V permit program will make stationary source performance requirements clearer by setting them out in an EPA state issued permit. But how does EPA or a state air pollution control agency "know" if facilities under their regulatory control are complying with these air pollution control requirements? Presumably area-wide air quality data could indicate whether the air is becoming cleaner, dirtier, or staying the same. But this information would say little or nothing about whether a specific source was meeting SIP-imposed and permit-required performance obligations. What should a regulatory agency do?

Two approaches come to mind: (1) ask the source to keep track of its performance and to report it to EPA on a regular basis and (2) have EPA go to the location of the source and collect this data on-site by itself. With regard to stationary sources the Clean Air Act allows for both kinds of information gathering through the provisions of § 114 [§ 7414].

● *Monitoring Recordkeeping and Self–Reporting*

In terms of recordkeeping and monitoring, § 114(a)(1) generally permits EPA to require a source to establish and maintain records, to make reports, to install, to use and maintain monitoring equipment, to sample emissions and to provide other information as EPA requests. NSPS often set out specific monitoring recordkeeping and reporting requirements. In addition, the 1990 Act added the requirement that stationary sources submit "compliance certifications" to EPA containing the following information,

(A) identification of the applicable requirement that is the basis for the certification,

(B) the method used for determining the compliance status,

(C) the compliance status,

(D) whether compliance is continuous or intermittent,

(E) such other facts as the Administrator may require.

§ 114(a)(3). If you were an EPA enforcement attorney, how might this information be significant and how might it save EPA time and money in enforcement? This data must be made available to the public under the terms of § 114(c). How might this information also be useful to a community resident or to an environmental organization? Are there analogies in other areas of federal pollution control law? Does this require the source owner or employees to forced self-incrimination?

● *Enforcement Information Gathering—Inspection of Facilities*

Under § 114(a)(2), EPA or "authorized representatives" may enter the premises of source owners and operators and others "subject to any requirement of the Act" not only to collect previously recorded information but also to inspect monitoring methods and equipment and to sample emissions. Inspections can determine compliance not only with SIP or permit requirements but also with monitoring and reporting rules. They can also have access to a facility for the purpose of obtaining data necessary in the development of technology-based standards. EPA and the states conduct facility inspections with a range of thoroughness from the most cursory to a detailed "stack test." EPA may also require a source to sample its own emissions and report the results to the agency. The 1990 amendments gave EPA inspectors new authority to issue "field citations" without formal hearings for minor violations. These citations are backed up with civil penalties of up to $5,000 per day of violation. In the past, the authority to invade corporate property has given rise to numerous questions concerning the extent of agency enforcement power, some with constitutional implications.

● *Search Warrants*

Does EPA have the authority to inspect the premises of a source without first obtaining a search warrant? Read § 114 [§ 7414] and then consider the following statement in Public Service Co. v. United States EPA, 509 F.Supp. 720, 724 (S.D.Ind.1981), a case in which the firm sought a declaratory judgment that two EPA searches were illegal:

> The statute [§ 114] allows the EPA to require extensive monitoring and reporting of emissions data, and would appear to permit warrant-less entry upon regulated premises for purposes of investigating compliance with EPA standards. However, with its decision in Marshall v. Barlow's, Inc., 436 U.S. 307 (1978), the Supreme Court made it clear that a warrant was required, absent consent to entry and inspection, in the fact of similar OSHA legislation purporting to allow warrantless entry. It is clear that under the facts and statutes involved in the present action a warrant was equally required, absent consent, prior to entry upon the PSI premises.

> The level of probable cause required to support an administrative inspection warrant has been the subject of considerable discussion in recent years. It is clear that the probable cause standard for such a warrant is somewhat less stringent than that required in criminal matters. As the court stated in *Barlow's*, supra:

>> Whether the Secretary proceeds to secure a warrant or other process, with or without prior notice, his entitlement to inspect will not depend on his demonstrating probable cause to believe that conditions in violation of OSHA exist on the premises. Probable cause in the criminal law sense is not required. For purposes of an administrative search such as this, probable cause justifying the issuance of a warrant may be based not only on specific evidence of an existing violation but also on a showing that "reasonable legislative or administrative standards for conducting an * * * inspection are satisfied with respect to a particular [establishment]." Camara v. Municipal Court, 387 U.S. at 538.

> 436 U.S. at 320–21 quoted in Burkart Randall Division of Textron, Inc. v. Marshall, 625 F.2d 1313, 1316 (7th Cir.1980). See also See v. City of Seattle, 387 U.S. 541 (1967). Whether an agency inspection is pursuant to a preestablished administrative plan or the result of specific employee complaints is immaterial insofar as the level of probable cause required to support a warrant is concerned.

The search warrant requirement, even in its relaxed form, is unnecessary when the regulated company consents to the inspection by the agency. In practice, most inspections are undertaken with the consent of the source owner. Some firms have attempted to condition their consent upon EPA's acceptance of certain limitations including hold harmless and secrecy clauses, liability waivers, roping off plant areas, and claiming the right to develop any photographs taken. See 1 W. Rodgers, *Environmental Law—Air and Water* 501 & n. 36 (1986). These conditions have not been well received by the courts and they can lead to EPA routinely seeking warrants for sources that insist upon them. Can EPA or a state make warrantless inspections a condition for the issuance of an operating permit? The 1990 Clean Air Act amendments require that each permit issued under the Act "shall set for inspection, entry, monitoring, compliance certification and reporting requirements to assure compliance with permit terms and conditions." See § 504(c).

Must a warrant be procured or consent granted for emissions observations taken outside of or above the facility itself? The Supreme Court has ruled in two air pollution cases on these search and seizure issues that no warrant is required. See Air Pollution Variance Board v. Western Alfalfa Corp., 416 U.S. 861 (1974) (4th Amendment protections do not extend to activities seen from "the open field"). In Dow Chemical Co. v. United States, 476 U.S. 227 (1986), the Court upheld EPA's use of aerial photography of Dow's 2000 acre Midland, Michigan facility as permitted by § 114 and not violative of the 4th Amendment under the "open field" rationale of *Western Alfalfa*. What if EPA inspectors find a non-complying imported automobile offered for sale in an auto dealer's showroom? Is this an illegal search? See Autoworld Specialty Cars, Inc. v. United States, 815 F.2d 385 (6th Cir.1987) (no search involved for the cars were on public display).

What if a source owner fears that certain operational information useful to business competitors might be revealed in disclosures made to EPA? Can it refuse to supply the data or force the agency to keep it "secret," away from public scrutiny? Most of the time, any nonconfidential business information can be released via the Freedom of Information Act. Notice how § 114(c) balances the competing interests.

> *Section 114(c)*. Any records, reports or information obtained under subsection (a) of this section shall be available to the public, except that on a showing satisfactory to the Administrator by any person that records, reports, or information, or particular part thereof (other than emission data), [to which EPA has access] if made public would divulge methods or processes entitled to protection as trade secrets * * *, [EPA shall consider them confidential as under the Trade Secrets Act, 18 U.S.C. § 1905].

Does this give EPA the power to suppress all source-supplied data as a "trade secret?" EPA rules specify how requests for confidentiality are to be treated. See 40 C.F.R. § 2.201. If a trade secret were disclosed by EPA under the provisions of § 114(c) what recourse would the source supplying the data have?

D.   PERMITTING UNDER THE CLEAN AIR ACT

Clean Air Act Amendments of 1989, Senate Committee Report on S. 1630

S.Rep. No. 101–228, 101st Cong., 1st Sess. 346–8 (1989).

TITLE V—PERMITS

INTRODUCTION

Title V of the bill adds a new part B to title III of the Act. The Clean Air Act currently contains no explicit Federal requirement for sources of air pollution to obtain an operating permit. This is a serious gap in the current

Act. Operating permits are needed to (1) better enforce the requirements of the law by applying them more clearly to individual sources and allowing better tracking of compliance, and (2) provide an expedited process for implementing new control requirements.

The failure of the current Act to require operating permits puts it at odds with the other major environmental statutes. The Clean Water Act (CWA) requires permits for discharges into the nation's waters. The Resource Conservation and Recovery Act (RCRA) requires operating permits for treatment, storage, and disposal facilities. Moreover, the RCRA manifest system, which tracks the movement of wastes, functions in many respects as the equivalent of a permit system. The Federal Insecticide, Fungicide, and Rodenticide Act requires the equivalent of permits for pesticides. The Toxic Substances Control Act authorizes permits with respect to chemical substances, and EPA has required them for PCB disposal facilities. The Clean Air Act itself requires construction permits for new or modified major sources of air pollution, and about 35 of the States have their own laws requiring operating permits for most minor and major sources as well.

In order to assure adequate compliance with the Act, there needs to be a Federal operating permit requirement as provided by the title. The operating permit program contained in this Act is based on the essential features of the Clean Water Act's permit program, which has successfully imposed pollution controls on large numbers of sources in a readily enforceable and administratively flexible manner. Although sources of air pollution tend to have more emission points, and thus be more complex, than sources of water pollution, the new air permit program will provide many of the same benefits as the CWA program, without unduly cumbersome requirements.

The first benefit of the title V permit program is that, like the CWA program, it will clarify and make more readily enforceable a source's pollution control requirements. Currently, in many cases, the source's pollution control obligations—ranging from emissions controls and monitoring requirements to recordkeeping and reporting requirements—are scattered throughout numerous, often hard-to-find provisions of the SIP or other Federal regulations. In addition, SIP regulations are often written to cover broad source categories, and may not make clear how a general regulation applies to a specific source. Moreover, in some cases, the source is not required under the SIP or other Clean Air Act provisions to submit periodic compliance reports to EPA or the States. As a result, there is no ready way to identify the extent of a source's compliance and noncompliance.

The air permit program will ensure that all of a source's obligations with respect to each of the air pollutants it is required to control will be contained in one permit document. In many cases, the permit will simply incorporate the requirements of the existing SIP or other Clean Air Act requirements, but in other cases, the permit will tailor and clarify how the general rules apply to the specific source. In addition, the source will file periodic reports, as determined by EPA regulations, identifying the extent to which it has complied with those obligations. Both the permit and the reports must be made publicly available.

This system will enable the State, EPA, and the public to better determine the requirements to which the source is subject, and whether the source is meeting those requirements. Better enforcement will result for all air pollution requirements, including SIP limits, new source performance standards, hazardous air pollution requirements, and acid deposition limits. In addition, this system will benefit stationary sources by providing greater certainty as to what their pollution control obligations are. Permits will also clearly identify baseline requirements for each source, facilitating emissions trading.

Another benefit of the permit program—which will accrue to regulated sources—is the simplification and expediting of procedures for modifying a source's pollution control obligations. In general, under the current Act, for sources subject to a SIP, the vast majority of changes in the source's pollution control obligations, no matter how minor, must be developed by the State and then approved or disapproved by EPA through informal, notice-and-comment rulemaking. This "double-key" system has long been recognized as being laborious and resource-intensive, and has led to unacceptably long delays in EPA action on even relatively minor SIP revisions. See Pedersen, "Why the Clean Air Act Works Badly", 129 U.Pa.L.Rev. 1059 (1981). Typically, EPA has taken 12–14 months to act on a SIP revision, and in some cases, EPA has taken much longer. The new permit program should eliminate this problem for source-specific SIP revisions by placing a strict time limit on EPA review. After the State revises the permit, EPA will have only 90 days to review it; if EPA takes no action, the revised permit will automatically become effective.

The permit program will also greatly augment the State's resources to administer pollution control programs. Throughout the 20–year history of the current Clean Air Act, inadequate State and local agency resources have increasingly hampered pollution control efforts. The permit fees provisions of this title will ameliorate this problem by requiring sources of pollution to pay a share of the costs of state air pollution programs, including, as discussed below, the costs of issuing the permit as well as the costs of modeling, monitoring, and preparation of attainment demonstrations and regulations that form the basis for air pollution control requirements.

Finally, the permit program provides a ready vehicle for the states to assume responsibility for administration of significant parts of the air toxics program and the acid deposition program. States that are delegated responsibility for these programs will use the permit systems to administer them, with the resulting advantages of better enforcement and a means for EPA oversight.

NOTE ON TITLE V PERMITTING

Under Title V of the 1990 Clean Air act amendments, EPA was charged with the responsibility of developing a national, uniform permitting program that could be implemented by state air pollution control agencies. See § 502(b). Title V provides a standardization among the states in permitting requirements. The operating permit rules are found at 40 C.F.R. Part 70 and EPA database with numerous permit policy and guidance documents www.epa.gov/region07/artd/air/title5pg.html. Previously the Act had only required preconstruction permits for new or modified air pollution sources. Now, both major and certain nonmajor sources will be included into the permit program. See § 502(a). Hundreds of source categories that were previously unregulated now must obtain Title V permits. States submitted their programs in 1993 for EPA review and approval within a year. Assuming that the state permitting program is in place by 1994, sources subject to the permitting requirement will receive their permits over the next three years. EPA gave partial approval to permit programs substantially complying with CAA requirements. Should a state default on its obligation to submit, administer and enforce a proper permit program, EPA may establish a federal permitting regime that it would administer.

The Act sets out a number of specific permit features that are worthy of note. *First,* EPA maintains direct and continuing oversight of the state-issued Clean Air Act permits and may formally object within 45 days to a draft state permit if it is "not in compliance with the applicable requirements of [the Clean Air Act]." See § 505(b)(1). This EPA review and veto power tracks the structure of § 402(d)(2) of the Clean Water Act. *Second,* even if EPA does not object, any citizen may petition EPA and restate its objections to the draft permit in an effort to convince EPA to block the permit. Judicial review is available if EPA denies the petition. See § 505(b)(2). *Third,* the state has 90 days from receipt of EPA's objections to revise the draft permit in accordance with EPA's views. If the state fails to act, EPA takes over responsibility for the particular permit. *Fourth,* a source's compliance with its permit terms will shield it from enforcement for alleged violation of the Act. See § 504(f). Much of enforcement will then focus upon permit compliance issues. Permits are now more precise including all limits, conditions and schedules to assure compliance with the requirements of the CAA. However, this permit "shield" has its limits. See 40 C.F.R. § 70.6(f) (defining the permit shield). *Fifth,* a single permit would be needed for a facility with multiple air emission source points (see § 502(c)) and plants will be allowed to make operational changes without the necessity of permit revision if they give at least 7 days notice, do not plan a "modification," and the changes will not result in emissions that exceed those already allowable in the permit (see § 502(b)(10)).

E.   Government Enforcement

United States v. SCM Corporation

United States District Court, District of Maryland, 1987.
667 F.Supp. 1110.

■ Ramsey, District Judge.

The United States brought this action against the SCM Corporation (hereinafter "defendant" or "SCM") at the request of the Administrator of the Environmental Protection Agency (hereinafter "EPA"). The action, brought pursuant to 42 U.S.C. § 7413(b), seeks injunctive relief and the imposition of civil penalties as a result of defendant's alleged violations of the Clean Air Act and the State Implementation Plan approved by the EPA pursuant to the Act. By an Order dated August 14, 1985, the Court permitted Maryland Waste Coalition (hereinafter "MWC"), a local conservation organization, to intervene, pursuant to 42 U.S.C. § 7604(b)(1), in the action brought on behalf of the EPA. MWC's intervening complaint alleges that the interests of its members have been, are being and will be adversely affected by the failure of SCM to comply with State Implementation Plan requirements. MWC seeks declaratory and injunctive relief as well as the costs and fees of bringing its part of this action. * * *

I.   *The Clean Air Act*

[In this section the court summarized the structure of the Clean Air Act and explained EPA's civil enforcement power under § 113] * * *

In 1972, the EPA promulgated primary and secondary NAAQS for particulate matter and other air pollutants. Following the promulgation of those standards, Maryland adopted, and the EPA approved, a Maryland SIP which is published in the Code of Maryland Regulations (COMAR) and in the Code of Federal Regulations. The Maryland SIP, * * * prohibits the discharge of particulate matter in amounts greater than 0.03 grains per standard cubic foot of dry exhaust gas ("gr/SCFD"), * * * (hereinafter the "particulate matter standard"), and further prohibits the emission of sulfuric acid mist in a concentration greater than 70 milligrams per cubic meter of exhaust gas ("mg/m3"). * * * The emission limits for particulate matter and sulfuric acid mist are intended to be "technology forcing". The violation of these provisions of the Maryland SIP is alleged in the case at bar.

II.   *Findings of Fact*

A.   *SCM Corporation*

SCM is a major corporation with operations in chemicals, coatings and resins, paper products, foods and typewriters. SCM Corporation is one of the four leading world producers of titanium dioxide, a white inorganic pigment widely used as a whitener and opacifier in the manufacture of paint, paper, plastic and rubber products. * * * SCM had $2.18 billion in net sales for fiscal 1985. The company paid a cash dividend of $2.00 per share in each of the four years preceding and including 1985. In 1985, total cash dividends equaled $20,000,000.

SCM owns and operates the Adrian Joyce Works in Baltimore, at which titanium dioxide is manufactured both by the sulfate process and by the chloride process. In the sulfate-process manufacturing facility, three calcining kilns are used to process a titanium intermediate, titanium hydrolysate, into crystalline titanium dioxide. Specifically at issue in this case are emissions of particulate matter and sulfuric acid mist from calcining kilns 2 and 3 in light of the Maryland SIP limits for those two pollutants. * * *

[In sections B through I, of the decision the court provided a detailed description of the pollution control efforts at SCM's Adrian Joyce Works in Baltimore, Maryland. From the early 1970's SCM, the State of Maryland, and EPA attempted through a continuing negotiation process to identify a pollution control technology for the plant which would allow it to meet Maryland's particulate and sulfuric acid mist limitations. In 1982 Maryland officials undertook four days of stack testing and found that the results greatly exceeded the SIP requirements (by as much as six times the standard in one test). Consequently, a state enforcement proceeding was initiated against SCM.

After additional stack tests and another year of extended discussions between SCM and state officials, an agreement was reached on a schedule for the installation of "demisters" in the plant's stacks. By the end of 1984 SCM and the state signed a consent order mandating the construction of plant modifications over a schedule and imposing an initial $15,000 civil penalty with additional monetary penalties imposed for failure to meet milestone dates in the order.

During 1984 EPA had been apprized of the on-going negotiations between Maryland and SCM. However, in September EPA referred the matter to the Justice Department for initiation of a civil action and in January of 1985 the action was filed in federal court. During 1985 and 1986 SCM modified the control systems proposed in the consent order in an effort to comply with SIP emission rates. Performance was inconsistent in all three calcining kilns until substantial modernizing changes were made to kiln 3 in June of 1986. EPA's civil action was tried in 1987.]

III. *Questions of Law*

This case presents two important questions of law that must be addressed before the Court can apply the statutory scheme of the Clean Air Act to the facts found.

A. *The Appropriate Penalty Period*

Section 113(b) of the Clean Air Act, 42 U.S.C. § 7413(b), provides in pertinent part:

> The Administrator shall, in the case of any person which is the owner or operator of a major stationary source, and may, in the case of any other person, commence a civil action for a permanent or temporary injunction, or to assess and recover a civil penalty of not more than $25,000 per day of violation, or both, whenever such person—
>
> * * * (2) violates any requirement of an applicable implementation plan * * * (B) more than 30 days after having been notified by the Administrator under subsection (a)(1) of this section of a finding that such person is violating such requirement * * * *

SCM contends that section 7413(b)(2)(B) permits the EPA to obtain penalties only for the period commencing 31 days after the issuance of a Notice of Violation. In this case, the relevant period would begin after May 20, 1984. EPA argues that when the NOV was issued has no bearing on the period for which EPA can collect penalties. The Agency views the issuance of the NOV and the 30–day continuing violation period as a jurisdictional threshold which must be reached in order for EPA to maintain a suit for civil penalties.

EPA supports its interpretation by reference to its "civil penalty policy," a document used by the Agency in computing the minimum penalty the Agency will accept in settlement of enforcement actions under the Clean Air Act. That policy states that "for the purposes of computing both the statutory maximum penalty and the minimum settlement amount, the period of noncompliance begins with the earliest provable day of violation and ends with the projected date of compliance." EPA also believes that the plain language of the statute and the intent of the legislature support the view that issuance of the NOV does not affect the penalty period. Finally, the EPA refers the Court to two recent Clean Air Act cases where federal district courts imposed penalties for each day the government proved that the source operated in violation of the applicable SIP, including days prior to the NOV.

The Court finds that civil penalties are available for days of violation occurring prior to the issuance of the NOV. Section 7413(b)(2)(B) is silent as to the date on which the penalty period begins, but other relevant factors support assessment of penalties for pre-NOV violations. The Court does not find the language of section 7413 to be as "plain" and "unambiguous" as EPA suggests. However, the Court finds that the availability of penalties for pre-NOV violations supports the purposes of the Clean Air Act, enhances the Court's discretion to fashion an appropriate penalty, and is consistent with the decisions of other federal courts.

It is fair to say that the overriding objective of Congress in enacting and amending the Clean Air Act is the abatement and control of air pollution through systematic and timely attainment of air quality standards. * * * One express purpose of the Clean Air Act is "to protect and enhance the quality of the Nation's air resources so as to promote the public health and welfare and the productive capacity of its population." 42 U.S.C. § 7401(b)(1). The availability of penalties for pre-NOV violations furthers that purpose.

The civil penalty provisions of the Act provide incentive to the violator to expeditiously resolve emissions violations. A violating source can avoid civil penalties if it ceases violation within 30 days of the NOV. Failure to comply within 30 days can result in the assessment of substantial penalties for each day of violation. The availability of penalties for pre-NOV violations enhances the incentive to resolve emission problems. More importantly, it provides incentive to avoid violations all together. Assessment of civil penalties for post-NOV violations only allows the source to wait until it is caught before making serious efforts to "clean up its act." Once the NOV is issued, the violating source could perform a cost/benefit analysis, weighing the benefits of operating in violation, without expenditures for further pollution control, against the potential cost of $25,000 per day of violation; a cost that may never be realized or at best will be collected only after an uncertain and time consuming litigation process. Such a practice is certainly not consistent with Congress' Clean Air objectives. Potential penalties for pre-NOV violations add a substantial and less calculable weight to the cost side of the analysis.

Additional support for pre-NOV penalties exists. Congress intended the Courts to exercise substantial discretion in fashioning an appropriate civil penalty. It set a maximum of $25,000 for each day of violation, but counseled the courts to consider the size of the business, the economic impact of the penalty on the business, and the seriousness of the violation. 42 U.S.C. § 7413(b). Broadening the available penalty period to include days prior to issuance of the NOV enhances the court's discretion to fix an appropriate penalty.

Lastly, the Court has considered two recent decisions where civil penalties were assessed for pre-NOV violations. See United States v. Chevron U.S.A., Inc., 639 F.Supp. 770 (W.D.Tex.1985) and United States v. Kaiser Steel Corp., No. 82–2623–IH (C.D.Cal. Jan. 26, 1984). * * * Furthermore, the *Chevron* and *Kaiser Steel* courts apparently assessed penalties for pre-NOV violations without questioning the propriety of such an assessment. However, SCM has not referred the Court, and the Court has not found, any case where the assessment of pre-NOV penalties was considered but refused. The Court recognizes the benefit of consistent construction of the Clean Air Act penalty provisions and where, as here, the construction of the Act by other Courts is in accord with the purposes of the Act, this Court is inclined to adopt a similar construction.

EPA suggests that SCM has been in violation of the Maryland SIP provisions for particulate matter and sulfuric acid mist emissions at kilns 2 and 3 continuously from the effective date of the SIP to the present. Accordingly, and consonant with its interpretation of the civil penalties provision of the Act, EPA contends that this Court may properly assess a penalty in the amount of $50,000 per day (for two violations) for each day between August 7, 1977, (the effective date of the Clean Air Act amendment that provided for civil penalties of $25,000 per day) and the present.

The Court has held that civil penalties may be assessed for days of violation occurring prior to the issuance of a notice of violation. It does not follow, however, that EPA may recover penalties from August 7, 1977, to the present. 28 U.S.C. § 2462 provides:

> Except as otherwise provided by Act of Congress, an action, suit or proceeding for the enforcement of any civil fine, penalty, or forfeiture, pecuniary or otherwise, shall not be entertained unless commenced within five years from the date when the claim first accrued if, within the same period, the offender or the property is found within the United States in order that proper service may be made thereon.

The five-year federal statute of limitations found in section 2462 has been held to apply to citizen suits for civil penalties as well as government actions for civil penalties under the Clean Water Act. See, e.g., Atlantic States Legal Foundation v. Al Tech Specialty Steel Corp., 635 F.Supp. 284, 287 (N.D.N.Y.1986); [other citations omitted]. The Court finds no reason why section 2462 should not apply to an action by the government to obtain civil penalties under the Clean Air Act. Accordingly, civil penalties are available for violations occurring within the five years prior to the filing of this action, or from January 2, 1980, to the present.

B.   *The Burden of Proof*

EPA suggests that under the Clean Air Act, once a source is shown to be out of compliance, it has the burden of demonstrating to the State and the EPA that it has achieved compliance. In the alternative, EPA suggests that the government may have the burden of proving continuing violations but it may satisfy that burden by a combination of intermittent testing results. The Court does not agree with either proposition.

EPA has produced test results showing SIP violations obtained at various intervals of time over a period of years. Most of the test results were obtained many months apart. It argues that there is no evidence that any different situation existed during the days between the dates when the test results were obtained. Therefore, EPA asserts that SCM has been in continuous violation of the Maryland SIP provisions for particulate matter and sulfuric acid mist since the effective date of the SIP.

Support for a similar approach can be found in Chesapeake Bay Foundation, Inc. v. Gwaltney of Smithfield, Ltd., 791 F.2d 304 (4th Cir. 1986), cert. granted, 107 S.Ct. 872, (1987), a Clean Water Act case. In *Gwaltney,* the defendant, Gwaltney of Smithfield ("Gwaltney"), was a holder of a National Pollutant Discharge Elimination System ("NPDES") permit. Such permits are issued pursuant to procedures and regulations under the Clean Water Act, and allow permit holders to discharge various pollutants into navigable waters. Gwaltney's permit fixed both "daily" and "monthly average" discharge limits for certain named pollutants. Id. at 307. Permittees are required to submit discharge monitoring reports ("DMRs"), and Gwaltney's DMRs reported a number of violations of "monthly average" permit limits. The district court held that a violation of a monthly limitation is equivalent to a daily violation for each day of that month. Chesapeake Bay Foundation v. Gwaltney of Smithfield, Ltd., 611 F.Supp. 1542, 1552–53 (E.D.Va.1985). The appellate court agreed.

In addition to monthly averages violations, there were a number of violations of daily standards in months when no violations of monthly averages occurred. Gwaltney's DMRs did not indicate on which day of the month a given violation occurred, and it was possible that some violations occurred on the same day. The district court held that it was permissible to shift the burden of proof to the defendant to demonstrate that there was some "overlap" of violations of daily limitations, in order to reduce the total number of days of violation. Id. at 1556. Again, the appellate court agreed.

This case differs from *Gwaltney* in respects that make the burden of proof approach used in that case inapplicable here. This case does not involve monthly average limits. More importantly, this case does not involve a permit holder which is required by statute or regulations to monitor its emissions and report them through DMRs. The Clean Air Act and Maryland's SIP authorize the administrator of the EPA and the Department of Health and Mental Hygiene to require a source to monitor and report its emissions. See 42 U.S.C. § 7414 *and* COMAR 10.18.01.04B(1). But sources are not otherwise required to test emissions on any periodic basis. It is the monitoring and reporting requirements of the Clean Water Act that justified the shift of the burden of proof and the presumptions employed in *Gwaltney*. "[T]he Act itself places on the permit-holder a burden of showing compliance with the permit's limitations." *Gwaltney*, 791 F.2d at 316. The Clean Air Act does not place such a burden on SCM.

In an enforcement proceeding under the Clean Air Act, the burden of establishing a violation of the applicable regulation is on the government. In *Chevron*, the court placed on plaintiffs, the United States * * * the burden of proving by a preponderance of the evidence each date on which defendant had violated applicable regulations. Likewise, in *Kaiser Steel*, the Court found that the government had proven a total of 33 violations, by date and time of violation. This Court finds no reason to depart from that approach in the case at hand.

EPA maintains that it would not be possible to nail down proof for each day of a claimed continuous violation. The Court agrees. However, EPA had available to it a suitable means to avoid its proof problems. 42 U.S.C. § 7414(a) provides that the administrator may require any person who owns or operates any emission source to sample such emissions (in accordance with such methods, at such locations, at such intervals, and in such manner as the administrator shall prescribe) for the purpose of determining whether any person is in violation of an emission standard or implementation plan, or for the purpose of carrying out any provision of the Clean Air Act * * *. The government could have used the procedure under section 7414 to obtain sufficient evidence of continuous noncompliance. If the Court had before it test results obtained at some logical and uniform interval, as the *Gwaltney* Court had, it would be more inclined to shift to SCM the burden of proving compliance on the dates between test results. But the government did not utilize the section 7414 process and the Court will not shift the burden of proving compliance to SCM on the basis of relatively few test results obtained at intervals of varying length. Civil penalties will be assessed only for each day of violation proved by plaintiffs.

IV. *Conclusions of Law*

   A. *Civil Penalties*

Section 7413(b) provides for a civil penalty of not more than $25,000 per day of violation. EPA has proven the following daily violations of Maryland SIP limits for particulate matter from January, 1980, through the present: [The court listed the date, location and inspector of particulate and sulfuric acid mist violations.]

EPA has proven 14 daily violations of the Maryland SIP limits for particulate matter and 16 daily violations of the Maryland SIP limits for sulfuric acid mist during the relevant penalty period. The maximum available civil penalty for the 30 days of proven violations is $750,000 (30 × $25,000).

Having calculated the maximum civil penalty available, other factors must be considered by the court in determining the appropriate penalty to assess. Section 7413(b) directs that the Court take into consideration (in addition to other factors) the size of the business, the economic impact of the penalty on the business, and the seriousness of the violation. In addition to the factors listed in the statute, other Courts have considered technological or economic infeasibility, good faith, or a lack thereof, on the part of the violating source, the violating source's relationship with the state and governmental delay in bringing the action. * * * The Court will examine each of these factors.

Application of the first two factors, size of the business and economic impact of the penalty, supports the imposition of a substantial penalty. SCM, like Chevron U.S.A., Inc., is a major corporation. "Only a substantial penalty would have any economic impact or serve as any deterrent." Chevron U.S.A., Inc., 639 F.Supp. at 779. Imposition of the entire $750,000 available would result in a penalty equal to less than four percent of the 20 million dollars in cash dividends paid by the company in fiscal 1985.

SCM's violations of the applicable Maryland SIP limits were serious violations. The Court refused to presume, based on the limited test results available, that SCM was in continuous violation of the SIP limits for the purpose of determining days of violation. But, based even on the limited data available, there is little doubt that had stack tests been performed with greater regularity prior to 1986, a substantial number of additional violations might have been identified. The seriousness of SCM's violations is evident, however, even from the relatively few days of violation proved. Test results obtained on the 30 days of proven violations show particulate matter and sulfuric acid mist measurements equal to two, three and four times SIP limits for those pollutants.

The court heard considerable testimony and argument throughout the trial of this matter on the issue of technological infeasibility. It should be noted that technological infeasibility is not a complete defense to Clean Air Act violations * * *. The Clean Air Act, like Maryland's SIP, is intended to be "technology forcing." * * * Technological infeasibility may be considered, however, as a factor mitigating against the imposition of monetary penalties. Ford Motor Co., 814 F.2d at 1104.

In this case, technological infeasibility mitigates, to some extent, against the imposition of a substantial penalty. In its March, 1979, Final Report prepared for EPA, GCA Corporation acknowledged that only one of the four plants in the United States then producing titanium dioxide pigment via the sulfate process employed an emission control system capable of achieving Maryland's 0.03 gr/SCFD standard for particulate matter. The report further notes that "it cannot be unequivocally stated that [SCM] is not using the best available control equipment."

Reference to the GCA report, without more, would suggest that technological infeasibility should be a substantial mitigating factor. But several circumstances, in addition to the many disclaimers and qualifiers in the report itself, counsel against placing great weight on the GCA report. Technological infeasibility cannot be examined without a corresponding inquiry into good faith. "[T]he absence of demonstrable good faith efforts toward compliance should serve to dampen any enthusiasm for technological and economic arguments advanced in defense of a claimed violation." Ford Motor Co., 814 F.2d at 1104 (quoting Indiana & Michigan Elec. Co. v. E.P.A., 509 F.2d 839, 845 (7th Cir.1975)). It is evident that at least prior to 1977, SCM dragged its feet, and did not work expeditiously toward compliance. The July 28, 1976, memo from Leonard Burgess characterizes the various air pollution plans of compliance SCM negotiated with the State as a "means to buy time." The memo further admits that SCM did not "regard the plan dates as commandments * * * and [SCM] worked toward [its] own best interests." SCM made its most impressive efforts to achieve compliance after the State issued its Notice of Violation in January, 1983.

It should also be noted that the GCA report is dated March, 1979. The Court has held that the relevant period for assessment of civil penalties in this case did not begin until January, 1980, five years prior to the filing of this action. Accordingly, it is the period from 1980 to the present that should be examined in connection with any claimed technological infeasibility. In the early 1980's SCM's efforts at its Adrian Joyce Works were directed more toward the development and installation of its waste heat recycle system than toward achieving compliance with emission limits. SCM demonstrated its ability to be a leader in the development of new and effective technology with the development and installation of its waste heat recycle system. That same creative energy could have been employed to develop an effective emission control system. Later, when it was forced to do so, after the issuance of the State's NOV in January, 1983, SCM was able to develop in a relatively brief period of time an emission control system capable of achieving State limits for particulate matter and sulfuric acid mist. The Court recognizes that SCM developed the waste heat recycle system at a time when energy conservation was a, if not "the", national priority. However, that does not excuse the failure to meet SIP limits.

* * *

Finally, some mention of governmental delay should be made. EPA suggests that SCM has been in continuous violation of the Maryland SIP provisions for particulate matter and sulfuric acid mist emissions from the effective date of the SIP, May 31, 1972, to the present. But EPA issued its NOV on April 20, 1984, and it filed this action in January, 1985. The Court does not believe that the government's delay in bringing this action should mitigate against imposition of a substantial penalty; nor should it act to enhance the penalty amount. Suffice it to say that the threat of this action has evidently encouraged SCM to develop an emission control system capable of achieving State limits on particulate matter and acid mist. Earlier action on the part of EPA may have eliminated years of potentially hazardous air pollution.

Having considered the relevant factors the Court imposes the following penalties:

> For the five violations of particulate matter or acid mist limits occurring on days during the period from January, 1980, through January, 1983, the Court imposes $20,000 per violation, for a total of $100,000;

> For the 25 violations of particulate matter or acid mist limits occurring on days during the period from February, 1983, through May, 1986, the Court imposes $10,000 per violation, for a total of $250,000;

> The total civil penalty imposed shall be $350,000.

* * *

[EPA request for injunctive relief was denied. MWC's request for relief and litigation costs were also denied.]

Excerpt from the Clean Air Act

42 U.S.C. § 7604.

§ 304(a) Authority to bring civil action; jurisdiction

Except as provided in subsection (b) of this section, any person may commence a civil action on his own behalf—

> (1) against any person (including (i) the United States, and (ii) any other governmental instrumentality or agency to the extent permitted by the Eleventh Amendment to the Constitution) who is alleged to have violated (if there is evidence that the alleged violation has been repeated) or to be in violation of (A) an emission standard or limitation under this chapter or (B) an order issued by the Administrator or a State with respect to such a standard or limitation,

> (2) against the Administrator where there is alleged a failure of the Administrator to perform any act or duty under this chapter which is not discretionary with the Administrator, or

> (3) against any person who proposes to construct or constructs any new or modified major emitting facility without a permit required under part C of subchapter I of this chapter (relating to significant deterioration of air quality) or part D of subchapter I of this chapter (relating to nonattainment) or who is alleged to have violated (if there is evidence that the alleged violation has been repeated) or to be in violation of any condition of such permit.

(f) "Emission standard or limitation under this chapter" defined

For purposes of this section, the term "emission standard or limitation under this chapter" means—

(1) a schedule or timetable of compliance, emission limitation, standard of performance or emission standard,

(2) a control or prohibition respecting a motor vehicle fuel or fuel additive, or

(3) any condition or requirement of a permit under part C of subchapter I of this chapter (relating to significant deterioration of air quality) or part D of subchapter I of this chapter (relating to non-attainment) 3 section 7419 of this title (relating to primary nonferrous smelter orders), any condition or requirement under an applicable implementation plan relating to transportation control measures, air quality maintenance plans, vehicle inspection and maintenance programs or vapor recovery requirements, section 7545(e) and (f) of this title (relating to fuels and fuel additives), section 7491 of this title (relating to visibility protection), any condition or requirement under subchapter VI of this chapter (relating to ozone protection), or any requirement under section 7411 or 7412 of this title (without regard to whether such requirement is expressed as an emission standard or otherwise);' or

(4) any other standard, limitation, or schedule established under any permit issued pursuant to subchapter V of this chapter or under any applicable State implementation plan approved by the Administrator, any permit term or condition, and any requirement to obtain a permit as a condition of operations.'

which is in effect under this chapter (including a requirement applicable by reason of section 7418 of this title) or under an applicable implementation plan.

NOTES AND QUESTIONS

1. *Enforceable Violations Under the Clean Air Act.* The court in the *SCM* case concludes that civil penalties can be imposed for pollution violations occurring prior to the EPA notice of violation. Is there any plausible reason why a source would not be liable for these violations? Read § 113(b)(2)(B) [§ 7413(b)(2)(B)] carefully. What if a source had violated its emission limitation prior to receiving the EPA notice of violation but had come into compliance either before the notice or during the 30 day notice period. Should this insulate the source from § 113 penalties for established violations? One court has ruled, in the context of a citizen suit enforcement action, that enforcement may not be had for wholly past violations. See Moran v. Vaccaro, 684 F.Supp. 1201, 1203–04 (S.D.N.Y.1988) (applying the result from the Clean Water Act case Gwaltney of Smithfield, Ltd. v. Chesapeake Bay Foundation, Inc., 484 U.S. 49 (1987)). The 1990 amendments have reversed this position with regard to the Clean Air Act. Should this result apply to government enforcement actions? Compare the language of § 113(b) with § 304.

2. *Government Enforcement Options.* The Clean Air Act provides EPA with a range of sanctions with which to seek enforcement of the statute. The primary enforcement techniques—a) administrative orders and penalties, b) injunctions, c) civil and criminal penalties—are prescribed in § 113. There can be significant financial consequences to these enforcement efforts. In FY99 CAA enforcement had the following impact: a) administrative penalties ($5.1 million) b) injunctions ($1.1 billion), c) civil judicial penalties ($104.6 million) and d) criminal penalties ($2.2 million). The enforcement process presents EPA with a series of choices. Once a permit or SIP violation has been identified by EPA, the agency must issue a notice of violation to both the state and to the polluter. If the violation continues for more than 30 days, EPA may (1) issue a compliance order, (2) issue an administrative penalty order or (3) initiate a civil action in an effort to obtain judicially ordered injunctive remedies and civil penalties. See § 113(a)(1)(A)–(C). Criminal fines and penalties are also possible and are included in § 113(c) for a range of violations of the Act, including negligent and knowing violations of a number of provisions. Consistent with other environmental statutes, criminal violations of the Clean Air Act have been upgraded from misdemeanors to felonies.

When a violation is detected in the vast majority of cases, the agency issues an administrative order demanding compliance and imposing civil penalties. EPA may issue such an order assessing penalties (administrative penalty orders) up to $25,000 per day up to a maximum of $200,000. EPA may also impose "field citations" for "minor violations" up to $5000 per day of violation § 113(d)(3). EPA regulations have increased these maximum penalty amounts up to $27,500 and $5,500 per day of violation to take inflation into account 40 C.F.R. § 19.1 Table 1. Review of administratively imposed penalties is in the U.S. District Court. Occasionally, the defendant will challenge the order or will be the subject of a civil enforcement action in federal court. On average between 40–110 of these CAA cases are referred each year. Most cases, however, result in a negotiated settlement usually reflected in a consent decree.

Government enforcement can proceed to federal court with the government seeking two forms of remedy: injunctive relief and civil penalties. Injunctive relief is usually sought to obtain emergency action, to enforce EPA orders and to order a judicial scheduling for compliance with permit or SIP requirements. These injunctions can be enforced themselves by civil penalties in subsequent contempt proceedings. However, judicial enforcement is also used in the first instance to impose civil penalties.

3. *Designing Civil Penalties.* How should EPA or a court decide on the level of financial penalty to be imposed on an air polluter? In § 113(b)(1), the statute provides an upward bound for this determination at $25,000 per day of each violation. At this rate a year long violation would result in potential liability of over $15 million! In many cases this figure sets an impressive maximum potential penalty which is usually not levied. However, in some multi-facility settlements, the amount to be paid can be considerable. See U.S. v. Willamette Industries, Inc. (failure to install pollution controls, report emissions, and obtain air permits for 13 wood product factories resulting in a $90 million settlement in July, 2000). Why would EPA seek a "global" or multi-facility enforcement action? How might that affect the civil penalty calculation?

What rationale should govern the setting of civil penalties? Congress added the following § 113(e) in 1990 to guide EPA and the courts in setting civil penalties. The factors to be considered are,

> the size of the business, the economic impact of the penalty on the business, the violator's full compliance history and good faith efforts to comply, the duration of the violation as established by any credible evidence * * *, payment by the violator of penalties previously assessed for the same violation, the economic benefit of non-compliance, and the seriousness of the violation.

If you were a U.S. District Court judge, how might you employ § 113(e) in fashioning a civil penalty remedy in the class discussion problem? Are there any other factors you might consider when fashioning your remedy?

When EPA obtains a civil penalty from a Clean Air Act violator through court action or administrative imposition, how does the environment benefit? While surprising to some, EPA does not keep the civil or criminal penalty monies as a form of reward for its diligent efforts. All of these penalties revert to the U.S. Treasury and are lost to EPA and do not yield direct environmental improvement. Furthermore, civil penalties are usually considered fines and are not tax deductible for the firm paying them. While paying financial penalties may punish past misconduct and potentially influence future behavior, greater benefit to the environment can result from the use of more flexible and creative remedies.

Since the early 1980s, EPA began to seek alternatives to monetary penalties in enforcement actions which would provide an improvement in environmental quality. The Supplemental Environmental Project or SEP became the alternative to conventional enforcement devices. It is indirectly authorized by Clean Air Act § 113(d)(2)(B). An SEP is a project or other action that a defendant in an enforcement case agrees to conduct as a component of a settlement often in exchange for a reduction or mitigation in a proposed financial penalty. In 1995 EPA issued a SEP policy that reflected the agency's increased emphasis of environmentally beneficial projects as part of case settlements. For FY 1995–1997, EPA has incorporated SEPs into 584 case settlements arising under a wide range of federal environmental statutes including the Clean Air Act. Of those settlements, 27 implemented SEPs with costs of over $1 million. While emphasizing pollution prevention and reduction, SEPs have included a number of disparate projects including funding for local emergency planning councils, an air toxics reduction demonstration study, environmental audits, process changes, energy conservation, enhanced training and reclamation and recycling.

Consider the following questions. As an EPA enforcement attorney, how would you approach the SEP question in settlement negotiations? How might the defendant firm consider the SEP? What are the benefits to the polluter? How should the SEP policy be limited, if at all?

4. *Criminal Enforcement Mechanisms.* Criminal enforcement of the Clean Air Act, as well as other environmental statutes, has been accorded enhanced priority within the federal government during the last decade. Although the Act contained criminal sanctions since 1970, the Department of Justice and EPA only began to allocate resources for this purpose in the early 1980s. The expansion in EPA investigative personnel can be traced to the Pollution Prosecution Act of 1990 which authorized funds for hiring 200 criminal investigators by 1995. In this first decade from 1982 through 1991, under all statutes more than 800 defendants were prosecuted, 605 convicted, 360 years of jail time imposed, 160 years actual served and approximately $75 million in criminal penalties have gone to the Treasury. The following chart illustrates more recent data on criminal enforcement statistics.

Figure 4–2. Office of Criminal Enforcement

Five Year Statistical Comparison

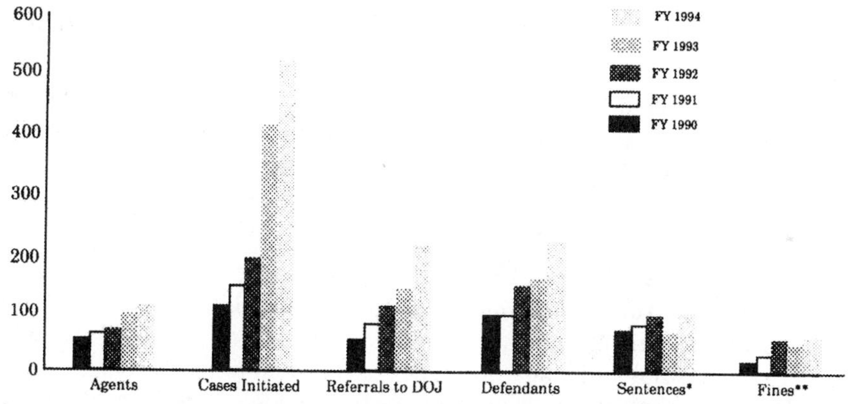

	Agents	Cases Initiated	Referrals	Defendants	Sentences*	Fines**
FY 1990	51	112	56	100	75.3	5.5
FY 1991	62	150	81	104	80.3	14.1
FY 1992	72	203	107	150	94.6	37.9
FY 1993	110	410	140	161	74.3	29.7
FY 1994	123	525	220	250	99	36.8

* Years of Incarceration
** Millions of Dollars

In 2000, EPA's criminal enforcement program initiated 477 cases, referred 236 cases to the Justice Department and charged 360 defendants with criminal offences. Is this increased emphasis on criminal enforcement justified? Who should be threatened with jail time for causing environmental and public health damage? Does the threat of criminal liability constitute a more effective deterrent to air pollution violations than civil enforcement methods? Should the government be cautious in employing criminal sanctions?

The Clean Air Act's criminal penalty provision—§ 113(c)—was substantially upgraded by the 1990 amendments. It now contains five separate criminal offenses under the Act, each a felony (prison term of one year or more) and each with a different maximum penalty. See § 113(c)(1)–(5). Penalties are specified in terms of both incarceration and fine with a doubling of maximum penalties referred for repeat offenders. Of special significance is the increased emphasis placed upon criminal punishment of the release into the ambient air of hazardous air pollutants. Section 113(c)(4) criminalizes the negligent release of such dangerous air pollutant if the release "places another person in imminent danger of death or serious bodily injury * * *"

However, the most severe Clean Air Act punishment—up to 15 years in jail and/or a fine is leveled at any person who (1) "knowingly releases" such hazardous materials into the ambient air and (2) who "knows at the time that he thereby places another person in imminent danger of death or serious bodily injury * * *." See § 113(c)(5). Defendants charged with this crime can also be "organizations" and this broad array of formal and informal entities may be subjected to a fine of up to $1 million for each violation. How hard would it be to convict an individual under § 113(c)(5)? What would a prosecutor have to prove? Consider the following language of § 113(c)(5)(B).

(B) In determining whether a defendant who is an individual knew that the violation placed another person in imminent danger of death or serious bodily injury—

    (i) the defendant is responsible only for actual awareness or actual belief possessed; and

    (ii) knowledge possessed by a person other than the defendant, but not by the defendant, may not be attributed to the defendant; except that in proving a defendant's possession of actual knowledge, circumstantial evidence may be used, including evidence that the defendant took affirmative steps to be shielded from relevant information.

Could this state of knowledge be easily proved? How? In addition, the Clean Air Act contains the following general provision in § 113(c)(5)(D),

    (D) All general defenses, affirmative defenses, and bars to prosecution that may apply with respect to other Federal criminal offenses may apply under subparagraph (A) of this paragraph and shall be determined by the courts of the United States according to the principles of common law as they may be interpreted in the light of reason and experience. Concepts of justification and excuse applicable under this section may be developed in the light of reason and experience.

How effective is this "knowing" release section likely to be?

5. *Economic Punishments—EPA Contractor Listings or Debarment.* If a principal objective of environmental enforcement is the alteration of polluter behavior, why not appeal to the economic self-interest of the offending actor by cutting off lucrative business opportunities with a large purchaser.

Section 306 of the Clean Air Act and § 508 of the Clean Water Act do just that by prohibiting the entire federal government from providing contracts, grants or loans to a firm whose facilities violated clear air or clean water standards. Effective automatically upon conviction, these facilities are listed by EPA until the agency determines they have corrected the conditions which led to the criminal convictions. At its discretion EPA can extend this ban to other facilities owned or operated by the firm. How significant would this contractor listing or debarment be? If you were an EPA enforcement attorney, how would you use this technique?

What about the bulk of firms found out of compliance with Clean Air (or Water) Act requirements that are subject to civil, not criminal, enforcement sanctions. Facilities with records of civil violations may also be listed at the discretion of EPA upon its own recommendation, that of the state or even a member of the public. This is known as a discretionary listing and the process has been infrequently used by EPA. In theory, the possibility of discretionary listing could help achieve settlements in civil enforcement cases.

6. *Citizen Suit Enforcement.* Enforcement of federal law is commonly, but erroneously, thought to be the sole province of the government. However, most federal environmental statutes contain provisions similar to § 304 [§ 7604] allowing "citizens" access to the federal courts to seek enforcement of Clean Air Act pollution requirements. In the environmental area, § 304 has been the model for most other subsequent federal legislation. The following excerpt describes the creation in § 304 in the 1970 Clean Air Act.

> The citizen suit was born in § 304 of the Clean Air Act as amended in 1970, which developed through several versions before being enacted. The enactment of the section was contested; however, the political impossibility of opposing a "pro-environmental" measure at the outset of the environmental decade and the desire to keep environmental legislation bipartisan obscured the debate. Attempts to sidetrack the measure to the Senate Judiciary Committee were clothed with concern for "burdening the [already overcrowded] courts with a large number of lawsuits." Proponents of the idea quickly switched from espousing it as an antidote to an untrustworthy administration, to championing it as the answer to the enforcement agencies' inevitable lack of sufficient resources to address all statutory violations. Although the issues in the debate are obscure, there was a real debate, and tension between proponents and opponents shaped the provision. Thus, citizens were allowed to sue, but could do so only after notifying appropriate regulatory agencies and giving them opportunity to sue first. While citizens were allowed to sue to redress statutory violations, they were not allowed to sue for resulting damages. And private enforcement was encouraged by allowing the award of attorneys fees but frivolous and harassing suits were discouraged by allowing fee awards against any party where appropriate.

J. Miller, *Citizen Suits: Private Enforcement of Federal Pollution Control Laws* 4–5 (1987) (footnotes omitted). In the past, the Clean Air Act's citizen suit provision has not been used as frequently as has the analogous Clean Water Act section. However, changes brought by the 1990 amendments—notably the permitting, monitoring, and self-reporting requirements—may simplify this feature of the air law by clearly specifying pollution source obligations and by making the information reflecting a Clean Air Act violation more accessible to citizen suit plaintiffs.

Read § 304 carefully and consider the following issues.

a. *Definitional Questions.* The Clean Air Act contains a citizen suit provision which mirrors and raises many of the same issues as the corresponding section in the Clean Water Act, § 505. Under § 304 [§ 7604], a civil action may be brought by "any person" against "any person" in three enumerated instances:

(1) to enforce an "emission standard or limitation" or "an order issued by the Administrator or a State with respect to such standard or limitation,"

(2) against the Administrator of EPA to enforce any "non-discretionary duty," and

(3) against any person who ignores the permit requirements of the PSD or non-attainment programs.

§ 304(a)(1)–(3) [§ 7604(a)(1)–(3)]. The 1990 Clean Air Act amendments modified § 304(a) to authorize citizen suits for past violations of the Act "if there is evidence that the alleged violation has been repeated." This language was added to avoid the limits of such suits stemming from the Supreme Court's Clean Water Act decision in Gwaltney of Smithfield, Ltd. v. Chesapeake Bay Foundation, Inc., 484 U.S. 49 (1987).

Section 304 grants jurisdiction to U.S. district courts without regard to the diversity of citizenship or the amount in controversy. Proper venue for the action is exclusively in the district where the source is located. § 304(c)(1) [§ 7604(c)(1)]. The statute of limitations for citizen suits is five years based on 28 U.S.C. § 2492. What will be sufficient to allege standing under § 304? Section 304(a) permits "any person," defined broadly in § 302(e), to bring suit under its provisions. What are the constitutional implications of such a statute arguably creating universal standing to enforce the Act? What would be the practical advantages and disadvantages of such an expansive position on standing? In practice, standing requirements are usually satisfied by allegations that named individuals are adversely affected by the conduct sought to be enjoined or otherwise penalized.

b. *Limitations on Clean Air Act Citizen Suits.* Section 304 establishes two important limitations on the right to bring a citizen suit: (a) the notice requirement and (b) the "diligent prosecution" restriction. Read § 304(b) [§ 7604(b)].

In the first instance, 60 day notice must be given to the state and federal governments and any polluter. What is the purpose of such a provision? What is the effect of failure to comply with the notice requirement? Is the notice requirement a prerequisite to obtaining federal jurisdiction over the matter under § 304? See City of Highland Park v. Train, 519 F.2d 681, 690–91 (7th Cir.1975) (yes). How does one comply with it? See 40 C.F.R. Part 54 (EPA notice regulations specifying written notice rules). The notice requirement has been strictly enforced but plaintiffs fail to give it with a surprising degree of regularity.

The second limit in § 304(b)(1)(B) prohibits citizen suits "if the Administrator or State has commenced and is diligently prosecuting a civil action in a court of the United States or a State to require compliance." What is the purpose of such a provision? Does the language of § 304 mean exactly what it says—the government action must be prosecuted "in a court" in order to bar citizen suits? What if the government is using an administrative rather than a judicial setting to seek compliance? Should this enforcement process completely bar the citizen suit? What are the arguments pro and con? The courts have had difficulty with this issue. In Baughman v. Bradford Coal Co., 592 F.2d 215 (3d Cir.1979), the court found no preclusion by a Pennsylvania enforcement process mainly due to the state agency's lack of remedial powers compared to those available to EPA in federal court. On the other hand, the Second Circuit rejected the remedial equivalency test of *Baughman* and read the "in a court" language of the identical Clean Water Act section as unambiguous. See Friends of the Earth v. Consolidated Rail Corp., 768 F.2d 57, 62–3 (2d Cir.1985). Recent Clean Water Act decisions have barred citizen suits when EPA has issued a compliance order. See Washington PIRG v. Pendleton Woolen Mills, 11 F.3d 883 (9th Cir.1993). Should this citizen suit obstacle be given narrow or a broad reading?

c. *Scope of Enforcement.* What Clean Air Act requirements can be enforced by a § 304 citizen suit? This statute sets forth three potential targets for suit: 1) action against any person alleged to be in violation of "an emission standard for limitation" or a governmental enforcement order, 2) action against the EPA Administrator alleging failure to perform any non-discretionary act or duty, and 3) against any person proposing to construct a facility without a non-attainment or PSD permit or in violation of such a permit.

What is an "emission standard or limitation?" The 1977 and 1990 Clean Air Act amendments expanded the definition of this term in § 304(f). Read the long list of "conditions or requirements" that can be enforced under § 304. Compare the scope of governmental enforcement authority under § 113 with that allotted to citizen suits. Can a citizen suit be brought to directly enforce the NAAQS? If not, then what seems clearly enforceable under § 304(f) [§ 7604(f)]? Is every requirement imposed by a SIP enforceable under § 304? One case, Wilder v. Thomas, 854 F.2d 605 (2d Cir.1988), denied enforcement of New York SIP provisions in a suit claiming that a redevelopment project on 42nd Street would aggravate CO "hotspots" within New York City.

A 1990 amendment to § 304(f) added the following language to the definition for the term "emission standard or limitation,"

> (4) any other standard, limitation, or schedule established under any permit issued pursuant to title V or under any applicable State implementation plan approved by the Administrator, any permit term or condition, and any requirement to obtain a permit as a condition of operations.

How does this amendment affect the potential scope of Clean Air Act citizen suits? Why might this language be important to plaintiffs?

If § 304 allows citizens to sue to force the Administrator to perform any "act or duty" which is not discretionary, what are they? Unfortunately the statute does not provide us with a definition and decisions are made on a case by case basis.

d. *Citizen Suit Remedies*. Imagine the range of remedies that a citizen suit plaintiff might seek in an action under § 304. Injunctive relief undoubtedly comes to mind to force a polluter to come into compliance with its permit or a provision of the state's SIP. An injunction would also be attractive in enforcing EPA's non-discretionary duties. What about civil penalties for Clean Air Act violations? The 1990 amendments made the Act similar to the Clean Water Act in that civil penalties could be awarded as a remedy in a successful citizen suit. The general criteria for judges setting such penalties established in § 113(b) in government enforcement actions also apply to citizen suits.

Prior to 1990, Clean Air Act citizen suit litigants were authorized to obtain only injunctive relief in § 304 actions. With the 1990 amendments to the Clean Air Act, plaintiffs were also permitted to seek civil penalties under the Act. If a citizen suit resulted in the judicial imposition of civil penalties, where would they go? New § 304(g) requires these Clean Air Act citizen suit civil penalties to be deposited into a special penalty fund in the United States Treasury available only to EPA for financing "air compliance and enforcement activities." Would environmentalists have supported such a change? What about EPA?

What about citizen suit settlements with polluter defendants? Does a federal judge have the discretion to order a citizen suit defendant to contribute money to an environmental group or to fund an environmentally-protective project? Congress, in 1990, gave a qualified "yes" to this question. Section 304(g)(2) provides,

> (2) Notwithstanding paragraph (1) [regarding the Treasury penalty fund] the court in any action under this subsection to apply civil penalties shall have discretion to order that such civil penalties, in lieu of being deposited in the fund referred to in paragraph (1), be used in beneficial mitigation projects which are consistent with this Act and enhance the public health or the environment. The court shall obtain the view of the Administrator in exercising such discretion and select-

ing any such projects. The amount of any such payment in any such action shall not exceed $100,000.

Why did Congress limit this alternative to the civil penalty to "benefit mitigation projects" up to $100,000? If you were a federal district court judge, would you welcome this limitation on your equitable discretion?

What if a § 304 citizen suit ends in settlement *prior to* a formal judgment? Can a plaintiff environmental group be allowed to accept a "charitable contribution" or direct a monetary payment from the defendant as part of the price of the settlement? Would such a result advance the purposes of the Act? Could and should Congress ban this practice? In 1990, Congress also required that all proposed consent judgments be sent to the Attorney General for at least 45 days of review and provided that the Government could submit comments or intervene as a matter of right. § 304(c)(3). In what circumstances might the federal government object to a proposed settlement? Would a judge be likely to reject the settlement based on these comments?

e. *Financial Aspects of Citizen Suits: Attorneys Fees to Prevailing Parties.* Section 304 allows the court to award reasonable attorneys fees and expert witness fees whenever "appropriate." These fee-shifting provisions have been the subject of considerable litigation themselves. Of primary importance is the Supreme Court's decision in Ruckelshaus v. Sierra Club, 463 U.S. 680 (1983) which required some degree of success on the merits before the awarding of fees was "appropriate." But sometimes identifying this success is difficult. Should the party be forced to clearly prove success on the merits before recovering fees? What are the arguments, if any, for awarding attorneys fees to unsuccessful parties in Clean Air Act cases.

CHAPTER ELEVEN

WATER POLLUTION CONTROL

SECTION 1. INTRODUCTION AND OVERVIEW

A. WATER QUALITY PROBLEMS

Water is an indispensable natural resource. It is a necessity not only for maintenance of biological and ecological processes, but also for economic well-being. The quotation from Coleridge's "The Rhyme of the Ancient Mariner" of "water, water every where nor any drop to drink" refers to one essential use of water for the preservation of human life. However, water is immensely important for other purposes as well. In the United States, water is used increasingly for domestic and commercial purposes, in manufacturing, for agriculture, and for energy production, mining, and navigation. In addition, many recreational activities require a substantial supply of accessible water. As with air, water is a critical natural resource useful for public and private purposes.

Actually, much of the U.S. economy depends upon clean water. Annually a third of all Americans visit coastal areas spending $44 billion for their 910 million trips. Water is also used for irrigating crops and raising livestock worth nearly $200 billion in annual sales. Commercial fishing and shell fishing require clean water to produce the 10 billion pounds of fish and shell fish from the Great Lakes and the Gulf of Mexico. Finally, manufacturers use 9 trillion gallons of fresh water each year with the soft drink industry alone using more than 12 billion gallons of water a year to produce drinks valued at $58 billion annually. Having clean water provides significant economic as well as environmental benefits to the nation. See Liquid Assets 2000: America's Water Resources at a Turning Point U.S. EPA (2000). This report is available at www.epa.gov/ow/liquidassets.html.

The total amount of water on Earth is essentially constant, and about 97 percent of the world's water is in the ocean. Nevertheless, the hydrologic cycle, involving complex processes of evaporation and precipitation powered by the energy of the sun, making varying amounts of fresh water available to landlocked areas. Water appears to us in apparently separate forms and locations. For instance, surface water occurs in rivers, lakes, streams, wetlands, and estuaries; groundwater is found in zones of saturation below the land surface known as aquifers. Through the hydrologic cycle and other natural processes, there is an interchange of surface, groundwater, and the oceans thereby connecting all three components into an interlocking natural system.

While the quantity of water resources is of great and increasing importance, the maintenance of minimum levels of water quality is essential to the well-being of both human beings and the environment. Water may be used in a wide range of direct and indirect ways often with incompatible effects. We often conclude that water quality is affected by the presence of "pollution," a term more easily used than understood. But then what is water pollution, who is to define it, and how is it to be achieved and preserved? These general questions form the core of our public policy as it concerns water quality and will frame our consideration of water pollution control in this chapter. A report published in 1973 shortly after the enactment of the 1972 Federal Water Pollution Control Act, summarized the then-existing major types and sources of water pollution. It began with the following excerpt,

> Pure water is a manufactured product. Natural water is not pure. Its quality is affected by a variety of geologic, hydrologic, and biologic factors. Natural impurities such as sediments, decaying vegetation, and wastes from wild animal populations impose measurable levels of contamination on many watercourses. Dissolved minerals rendered some of our surface and ground waters unfit for certain uses long before man appeared on the scene. But most of what we call pollution today results from disposal of the waste products of civilization. Controlling man-caused pollution is the central concern of this chapter.

> Pollution sources are of two types: (1) waste discharges from identifiable points (point-sources) and (2) diffused wastes reaching water through land runoff, washout from the atmosphere, or other means (nonpoint-sources). The two differ in that point sources can be controlled directly while nonpoint-sources are extremely difficult to control.

National Water Comm'n, Water Policies for the Future 64 (1973).

In this report, the Commission detailed the point/nonpoint source dichotomy by giving examples of each source of water pollution. Under the heading of point source pollution it identified 1) municipal sewerage systems, 2) storm water runoff, 3) industrial wastes and 4) animal feed lots as major categories. Regarding nonpoint source pollution, the report noted 1) sediment runoff, 2) agricultural chemicals (fertilizers and pesticides), 3) mine drainage, 4) oil and hazardous material spills and 5) miscellaneous sources (animal and vegetable wastes, industrial site runoff, highway salt, vessel discharges and atmospheric deposition).

After nearly thirty years, what is the current status of American water quality? In 2000, EPA's Twelfth National Water Quality Inventory (or § 3056 Report) provided a partial answer to this fundamental question. Relying upon state-supplied information, the bi-annual report contained data on the status on only 23% of the nation's rivers, 42% of the lakes, and 32% of the estuaries. This information was derived from monitored field data or evaluated data. The following chart indicates the percentage of each type of waterway:

	Total Size	Amount Assessed	Good (% of Assessed)	Good but Threatened (% of Assessed)	Polluted or Impaired (% of Assessed)
Rivers (miles)	3.66 million	23%	55%	10%	35%
Lakes (acres)	41.59 million	42%	46%	9%	45%
Estuaries (sq. miles)	.90 million	32%	32%	47%	44%

The designation "good" reflects those waters meeting water quality standards; "good but threatened" means meeting water quality standards but may degrade in the near future; "polluted or impaired" indicates either not meeting water quality standards or occasionally exceeding them. While only reflecting a part of the picture, this information reveals basic information concerning the leading pollutants and the sources of pollution.

The § 305b Report consolidates, on a national level, government information about current water quality problems. It is notable that for each of the three categories of surface waters the leading pollutants and their sources differ. Examine the chart below and determine the diverse nature of American water pollution problems.

	Rivers and Streams	Lakes, Ponds, and Reservoirs	Estuaries
Pollutants	1. Siltation 2. Pathogens (bacteria) 3. Nutrients 4. Oxygen depleting substances	1. Nutrients 2. Metals 3. Siltation 4. Oxygen depleting	1. Pathogens (bacteria) 2. Organic enrichment/ Low dissolved oxygen 3. Metals 4. Nutrients
Sources	1. Agriculture 2. Hydro modification (flow regulation, dredging, dams) 3. Urban Runoff/Storm Sewers 4. Municipal Point Sources	1. Agriculture 2. Hydro modification 3. Urban Runoff/Storm Sewers 4. Municipal Point Sources	1. Municipal Point Sources (POTWs) 2. Urban Runoff/Storm Sewers 3. Atmospheric Deposition 4. Industrial Discharges

What does this chart suggest about the design of American water pollution public policy? In terms of environmental planning and regulation, where should the public and private efforts be made?

B. THE DEVELOPMENT OF AMERICAN WATER POLLUTION LAW

Peter Goplerud III, Water Pollution Law: Milestones From the Past and Anticipation of the Future

10 Natural Resources & Environment 7–12 (1995).

The task of tabulating and assessing the impact of landmarks in any area of the law is daunting. It is particularly so when the task deals with environmental law or any subdivision of the discipline. The period of the last twenty-five years has seen an explosion of legislation, litigation, and activism in environmental law. The period has thus seen many landmarks and choosing the most significant is fraught with danger. Nonetheless an attempt will be made to present, with some description and analysis, the most significant events, cases, legislative creations, and policy break-throughs in water pollution law. As with all areas of environmental law, it is a work in progress with an uncertain future, both near term and long term. There has, however, been a significant foundation laid over the past several decades. To fully understand where we are today, and where we might be headed tomorrow, it is necessary to go back nearly a century.

A Brief Historical Overview

In the historical overview, federal legislation dating back to 1899 was identified as the first law to address water pollution issues. Later, the Federal Water Pollution Control Act of 1948 urged states to establish water quality standards yet the problems of surface waters actually became more pronounced and publicly understood during the 1960s.

The 1970s Environmental Awakening

The beginning of the 1970s marked the true beginnings of environmental awareness on the part of Congress, and perhaps most of the country. Congress enacted numerous laws aimed to mandating environmental planning and pollution control. The 1972 Federal Water Pollution Control Act Amendments, today known as the Clean Water Act, expanded significantly the reach and mandates of the 1948 Act. This statutory scheme has been fine-tuned through amendments enacted in 1977 and 1987. Congress is currently considering significant amendments to the Act, primarily designed to cut costs for both government and polluters. [No statutory changes have occurred.—Eds.]

The 1972 amendments provided three major pollution control mechanisms: (1) control of industrial and municipal discharges (the primary focus of this article); (2) control of oil and hazardous materials spills; and (3) funding for construction of sewage treatment facilities. Congress also established a pair of laudable goals that have proved to be unattainable in many streams and lakes. The goal was for the waters of the United States to be fishable and swimmable by 1983 and to have no discharge of pollutants in the country by 1985. While there are now many lakes and streams that qualify as fishable or swimmable, many bodies of water are still seriously polluted, and there remain thousands of sources that continue to discharge pollutants into the navigable waters.

The amendments also featured a strong measure of cooperative federalism. The responsibilities under the Act were to be divided between the states and the federal government. The federal government, specifically the Environmental Protection Agency (EPA), was to direct and, in some instances, coerce the states to implement and enforce the various programs. A state that chose not to do so faced federal implementation and administration of these programs, a result not desired by most state and local governmental entities.

Unlike previous efforts, the 1972 amendments focused on both water quality standards and effluent limitations. The key to the pollution control mechanism was control at the source and the key to this program was an elaborate permit program for discharges. In addition, water quality standards were to be established and ultimately attained. The Act specifically prohibits the discharge of pollutants from point sources into navigable waters, but provides an exception, codified elsewhere in the Act, for sources that have obtained a permit to discharge. 33 U.S.C. § 1311(a); 33 U.S.C. § 1342. The permit was to include limitations on discharges of pollutants for various industrial and municipal sources throughout the country. When the two sections were read together it became clear that Congress intended to only regulate discharges of pollutants from point sources into navigable waters.

NOTE ON CLEAN WATER ACT COVERAGE

In general, the Clean Water Act requires NPDES permits for point sources that discharge pollutants into bodies of water. This fact is derived from the general "no discharge" policy set forth in § 301(a) that "[E]xcept in compliance with this section and sections 302, 306, 307, 318, 402, and 404 of this Act, the discharge of any pollutant by any person shall be unlawful." Compare this policy with that of the Clean Air Act. Which is sounder public policy? Why did Congress require permits for all dischargers? You might wish to consider the implications of structuring a pollution control system around the permit. To restate the general principle of permitting, an NPDES permit is required for the discharge of pollutants from point sources into waters of the United States. Each component of this statement deserves attention.

● *Discharge of pollutants.* Within the CWA "discharge of a pollutant" is defined as "(A) any addition of any pollutant to navigable waters from any point sources, and (B) any addition of any pollutant to the waters of the contiguous zone or the ocean from any point source other than a vessel or other floating craft." § 502(12) [§ 1362(12)]. This definition emphasizes the making of "additions" of pollutants to water bodies as the element of primary importance. In most cases this form of polluting act is easy to conceptualize. But occasionally there are confusing questions of definition and a court is asked to decide a question of whether CWA permitting rules apply. For instance, is a hydroelectric dam which alters the water's speed and its biological traits a discharger of pollutants? In National Wildlife Federation v. Gorsuch, 693 F.2d 156, 174–5 (D.C.Cir.1982) the court found no addition of pollutants in the operation of a dam. A subsequent case, National Wildlife Federation v. Consumers Power Co., 862 F.2d 580 (6th Cir.1988) agreed even though the dam sent dead fish and fish remains into Lake Michigan. See also No Spray Coalition v. City of New York, 2000 WL 1401458 (city's insecticide spraying is not a pollutant discharge even though incidental drift over water was possible). What principles should guide a court in interpreting these questions?

● *Pollutant.* While the CWA generally defines "pollution" as the "man-made or man-induced alteration of the chemical, physical, biological or radiological integrity of water," § 502(19) [§ 1362(19)], the Act provides a more specific, yet equally broad, meaning of the word "pollutant." A pollutant under the CWA is,

> dredged spoil, solid waste, incinerator residue, sewage, garbage, sewage sludge, munitions, chemical wastes, biological materials, radioactive materials, heat, wrecked or discarded equipment, rock, sand, cellar dirt, and industrial, municipal and agricultural waste discharged into water.

§ 502(6) [§ 1362(6)]. Heat is within the statutory definition. See Piney Run Preservation Ass'n v. Carroll Cty., 50 F.Supp.2d 443 (D.Md.1999).

It is the addition of pollution to water that triggers the NPDES requirement. In addition to the obvious forms of discharge, this requirement also reaches discharges from animal feedlots, aquaculture, silviculture, and separate storm sewers. See 40 C.F.R. § 122.1(b)(2). However, certain discharges are statutorily exempt from the NPDES obligation—vessel sewage and well injection—and others administratively eliminated—radioactive materials regulated by the NRC under the Atomic Energy Act.

● *Point source.* Only discharges of pollutants from point sources are subject to the NPDES requirements. As might be expected, the CWA defines this term as "any discernable, confined and discrete conveyance, including but not limited to any pipe, ditch, channel, tunnel, conduit, well, fissure, container, rolling stock, concentrated animal feeding operation, or vessel or other floating craft from which pollutants may be discharged." § 502(14) [§ 1362(14)]. In Dague v. City of Burlington, 732 F.Supp. 458, 470 (D.Vt.1989), the court found the operation of a municipal landfill violated the CWA since chemical wastes from the landfill were found in an adjacent wetland. The court, following the broad definition of "point source" in United States v. Earth Sciences, Inc., 599 F.2d 368, 373 (10th Cir.1979), held that landfill was a point source since chemical wastes originating from it ultimately reached the wetland via a culvert located on property neighboring the landfill. The city was found to be in violation of the CWA since it lacked a discharge permit. Following the 1987 amendments EPA's NPDES regulations now include "landfill leachate collection systems" as point sources. 40 C.F.R. § 122.2. There are numerous case decisions finding unconventional point sources. See Stone v. Naperville Park District, 38 F.Supp.2d 651 (N.D.Ill.1999) (trap shooting range was a point source discharging lead shot and shattered clay pigeons); Driscoll v. Adams, 181 F.3d 1285 (11th Cir.1999) (timber clearing and development resulted in storm water carrying eroded mud, silt and sand to a creek); and United States v. West Indies Transport, Inc., 127 F.3d 299 (3d Cir.1997) (a floating vessel is a point source when pollutants are discharged when the owner severs the vessel and causes it to sink).

Why would the Clean Water Act concentrate its permitting effort on these point sources and not "non-point" sources as well? Certain discharges are exempted from the NPDES requirements including those sent to a Publicly Owned Treatment Works (POTW) return flows from agricultural irrigation, those sent to privately-owned treatment works, and those regulated under § 404 of the Act.

● *Navigable waters.* NPDES requirements only apply to point source discharges of pollutants into navigable waters. See § 502(12) [§ 1362(12)]. Those not reaching "navigable waters" would ostensibly avoid the permitting obligations. What are navigable waters? The Act defines this term as "the waters of the United States" and its legislative history and subsequent judicial interpretations have given this wording the broadest meaning consistent with the Commerce Clause of the Constitution. See United States v. Riverside Bayview Homes, Inc., 474 U.S. 121 (1985). Even intermittent streams have been found to be navigable waters under the CWA. See Driscoll v. Adams, 181 F.3d 1285 (11th Cir.1999). However, the Supreme Court's ruling in United States v. Lopez, 514 U.S. 549 (1995), has cast some doubts as to the breadth of the Commerce Clause in the environmental context. Although the precise limit of the jurisdictional sweep of the NPDES requirement is not known, it is clear that EPA and the courts have taken an expansive view and will probably continue to do so. It should be noted that some states require permits for discharges not only to surface water but also to groundwater. For instance, under Virginia law all discharges into "state waters" require a certificate from the state water control board. Va. Code § 62.1–44.16. "State waters" are defined in the Virginia statute to include all waters both above and below the ground. Id. at § 62.1–44.3(4). Thus, activities that would not require an NPDES permit would require a state permit if there were a discharge into groundwater. See Allegany Envtl. Action Coalition v. Westinghouse Elec. Corp., 46 Env't Rep. Cas. (BNA) 1126 (W.D.Pa.1998) (CWA does not prohibit unpermitted discharges to groundwater).

● *Federal facilities pollution control.* Are federal facilities subject to NPDES permit requirements? Should there be a difference in the application of pollution control rules between federal and privately-owned point sources? What arguments, if any, would justify exempting a sewage treatment plant serving a Department of Transportation facility from the obligation of obtaining an NPDES permit? What about other kinds of federal facilities? What message would the exemption of federal sources from water pollution control requirements send to non-federal dischargers?

Section 313 [§ 1323] specifically provides that federal facilities are fully subject to federal, state, interstate, and local requirements, including substantive, procedural, and enforcement provisions of the laws. The President may grant exemptions for compliance with any requirements on a year-by-year basis. The President also may issue regulations concerning exemptions for military vessels and equipment. In Romero–Barcelo v. Brown, 643 F.2d 835 (1st Cir.1981), the court held that the Navy Department must obtain either an NPDES permit or a national security exemption before discharging ordnance into coastal waters off Puerto Rico for training purposes despite the fact that there was no showing that the Navy's activities harm the coastal waters. The Supreme Court reversed this judgment on the ground that in granting or denying injunctive relief, the lower courts must "pay particular regard for the public consequences in employing the extraordinary remedy * * *." Weinberger v. Romero–Barcelo, 456 U.S. 305 (1982).

SECTION 2.   INDUSTRIAL POINT SOURCE REGULATION

CLASS DISCUSSION PROBLEM: TROUBLE AT AJAX PAPERBOARD'S CENTRALIA PLANT

Background Information

The city of Centralia and its surrounding suburbs has a population of 450,000. This growing community is located on the East River within 2 miles of the Atlantic Ocean. The city has a diversified economy composed of a mixture of service, manufacturing and governmental activities. While East River has historically supported a wide variety of aquatic and non-aquatic species and water recreational uses, its present condition has been degraded to the point where only limited numbers of resilient "bottom fish" live and where water quality does not permit water contact sports or water supply.

A recent analysis of water quality within the Centralia water basin has revealed the following factors explaining current water quality conditions. 1) The East River reaches Centralia in less than a pristine condition. Upstream cities and factories discharge substantial quantities of pollutants to the river before it reaches Centralia. 2) Centralia's municipal sewer authority operates three treatment works which discharge treated effluent into the East River. Those sewer plants receive both domestic wastes and the waste products of a number of industries which are piped to the sewer plant for treatment. 3) There are 4 major industrial plants which treat their own process wastes (containing a range of pollutants) and discharge them into the East River pursuant to permit issued by the State Water Board. 4) Surface runoff caused by increasing land development, impervious land cover, agricultural practices (pesticides and fertilizer applications) also have affected the water quality.

Citizen groups and the Centralia city government have become increasingly disturbed about the deteriorating condition of the East River. Although other sources of pollution are important, recent attention has been focused upon the local industrial point sources discharging their wastes directly into the river by way of outfall pipes. Of particular concern are the effluents released by the Ajax Paperboard Company (Ajax) plant located one mile upstream from Centralia. Ajax has operated its Centralia facility for the last twenty-five years after acquiring it from the now defunct Diamond Paper Company. At its peak production in 1950 the Diamond Paper mill employed 800 people. Since that time Ajax has closed sections of the plant and employs approximately 250 people in its papermaking facility. In 1972 Ajax installed new papermaking process equipment which it now claims is barely profitable. While the mill worker's union vigorously disputes that assertion, the rumor of Ajax's closing or takeover occasionally surfaces.

The Ajax Centralia plant is an existing facility employing the bleached Kraft process to produce pulp and paper products. This production method generates both conventional (BOD5, Total Suspended Solids, and pH) and toxic (pentachlorophenol and trichlorophenol) effluents which must be discharged into the East River. The Ajax facility has always been known for its characteristic unpleasant odor but it is the plant's impact on the East River which has caused the greatest concern. Citizens and environmental groups have claimed that fish and wildlife taken in the vicinity of the Ajax plant have often been deformed and have had unusual skin ulcers. This alarming report stands in stark contrast with records from the 1920's and 1930's indicating the river supporting a wide variety of sport fish.

You are an attorney representing a newly-formed group—Citizens for a Clean Centralia (CCC)—and you wish to discover what possible discharge controls could be imposed on Ajax's operation. You have learned that two scientific studies have raised concerns about the presence of dioxins, furans, and other chlorinated organic compounds in the discharges from Kraft plants like the Ajax facility. These pollutants are known to be carcinogenic, bioaccumulative and persistent. CCC has asked you to determine generally whether Ajax's effluents are subject to federal regulation under the Clean Water Act. You should address yourself to the following questions:

1. [Regulatory Authority] What authority exists under the Clean Water Act for EPA to establish water pollution control regulations for an existing industrial point source like Ajax Paperboard? What if Ajax were proposing to construct a new papermaking plant at the Centralia site? Does the Act make any distinction between existing and new facilities in terms of pollution control requirements? Why set different regulations for new and existing plants in the same industry?

2. [Regulatory Process] What process does EPA use for setting these water pollution regulations? To what extent is the public involved? What kind(s) of information does EPA need in order to issue the regulations? Where would it obtain this data?

3. [Regulatory Choice] How does the language of the Clean Water Act influence EPA's choice of pollution control requirements in terms of a) the requisite level or kind of technology and b) the considerations of pollution control costs? How important are each of these factors in setting the "best" regulation?

4. [Judicial Review] Can EPA's choice of Clean Water Act pollution control regulations be challenged in court? How and under what terms?

5. [Exceptions] If EPA has issued a uniform discharge regulation or effluent standard for the pulp and paper industry, under what terms, if any, can Ajax receive a waiver or exception from what it considers to be an overly strict standard? Would such a waiver be available?

A.   POINT SOURCE REGULATION

E.I. du Pont de Nemours & Co. v. Train

United States Supreme Court, 1977.
430 U.S. 112, 97 S.Ct. 965, 51 L.Ed.2d 204.

■ MR. JUSTICE STEVENS delivered the opinion of the Court.

These cases present three important questions of statutory construction: (1) whether EPA has the authority under § 301 of the Act to issue industrywide regulations limiting discharges by existing plants; (2) whether the Court of Appeals, which admittedly is authorized to review the standards for new sources, also has jurisdiction under § 509 to review the regulations concerning existing plants; and (3) whether the new-source standards issued under § 306 must allow variances for individual plants.

As a preface to our discussion of these three questions, we summarize relevant portions of the statute and then describe the procedure which EPA followed in promulgating the challenged regulations.

The Statute

The statute, enacted on October 18, 1972, authorized a series of steps to be taken to achieve the goal of eliminating all discharges of pollutants into the Nation's waters by 1985, § 101(a)(1).

The first steps required by the Act are described in § 304, which directs the Administrator to develop and publish various kinds of technical data to provide guidance in carrying out responsibilities imposed by other sections of the Act. Thus, within 60 days, 120 days, and 180 days after the date of enactment, the Administrator was to promulgate a series of guidelines to assist the States in developing and carrying out permit programs pursuant to § 402. §§ 304(h), (f), (g). Within 270 days, he was to develop the information to be used in formulating standards for new plants pursuant to § 306. § 304(c). And within one year he was to publish regulations providing guidance for effluent limitations on existing point sources. Section 304(b)[4] goes into great detail concerning the contents of these regula-

---

4. Section 304(b) provides:

"(b) For the purpose of adopting or revising effluent limitations under this Act the Administrator shall, after consultation with appropriate Federal and State agencies and other interested persons, publish within one year of enactment of this title, regulations, providing guidelines for effluent limitations, and, at least annually thereafter, revise, if appropriate, such regulations. Such regulations shall—

"(1)(A) identify, in terms of amounts of constituents and chemical, physical, and biological characteristics of pollutants, the degree of effluent reduction attainable through the application of the best practicable control technology currently available for classes and categories of point sources (other than publicly owned treatment works); and

"(B) specify factors to be taken into account in determining the control measures and practices to be applicable to point sources

tions. They must identify the degree of effluent reduction attainable through use of the best practicable or best available technology for a class of plants. The guidelines must also "specify factors to be taken into account" in determining the control measures applicable to point sources within these classes. A list of factors to be considered then follows. The Administrator was also directed to develop and publish, within one year, elaborate criteria for water quality accurately reflecting the most current scientific knowledge, and also technical information on factors necessary to restore and maintain water quality. § 304(a). The title of § 304 describes it as the "information and guidelines" portion of the statute.

Section 301 is captioned "effluent limitations." Section 301(a) makes the discharge of any pollutant unlawful unless the discharge is in compliance with certain enumerated sections of the Act. The enumerated sections which are relevant to this case are § 301 itself, § 306, and § 402. A brief word about each of these sections is necessary.

Section 402[7] authorizes the Administrator to issue permits for individual point sources, and also authorizes him to review and approve the plan

(other than publicly owned treatment works) within such categories or classes. Factors relating to the assessment of best practicable control technology currently available to comply with subsection (b)(1) of section 301 of this Act shall include consideration of the total cost of application of technology in relation to the effluent reduction benefits to be achieved from such application, and shall also take into account the age of equipment and facilities involved, the process employed, the engineering aspects of the application of various types of control techniques, process changes, non-water quality environmental impact (including energy requirements), and such other factors as the Administrator deems appropriate;

"(2)(A) identify, in terms of amounts of constituents and chemical, physical, and biological characteristics of pollutants, the degree of effluent reduction attainable through the application of the best control measures and practices achievable including treatment techniques, process and procedure innovations, operating methods, and other alternatives for classes and categories of point sources (other than publicly owned treatment works); and

"(B) specify factors to be taken into account in determining the best measures and practices available to comply with subsection (b)(2) of section 301 of this Act to be applicable to any point source (other than publicly owned treatment works) within such categories or classes. Factors relating to the assess-

ment of best available technology shall take into account the age of equipment and facilities involved, the process employed, the engineering aspects of the application of various types of control techniques, process changes, the cost of achieving such effluent reduction, non-water quality environmental impact (including energy requirements), and such other factors as the Administrator deems appropriate; and

"(3) identify control measures and practices available to eliminate the discharge of pollutants from categories and classes of point sources, taking into account the cost of achieving such elimination of the discharge of pollutants." 33 U.S.C. § 1314(b).

7. Section 402(a)(1) provides:

"Except as provided in sections 318 and 404 of this Act, the Administrator may, after opportunity for public hearing, issue a permit for the discharge of any pollutant, or combination of pollutants, notwithstanding section 301(a), upon condition that such discharge will meet either all applicable requirements under sections 301, 302, 306, 307, 308, and 403 of this Act, or prior to the taking of necessary implementing actions relating to all such requirements, such conditions as the Administrator determines are necessary to carry out the provisions of this Act." 86 Stat. 880, 33 U.S.C. § 1342(a)(1).

Under § 402(b), the Administrator may delegate this authority to the States, but

of any State desiring to administer its own permit program. These permits serve "to transform generally applicable effluent limitations * * * into the obligations (including a timetable for compliance) of the individual discharger[s] * * *." EPA v. California ex rel. State Water Resources Control Board, 426 U.S. 200, 205. Petitioner chemical companies' position in this litigation is that § 402 provides the only statutory authority for the issuance of enforceable limitations on the discharge of pollutants by existing plants. It is noteworthy, however, that although this section authorizes the imposition of limitations in individual permits, the section itself does not mandate either the Administrator or the States to use permits as the method of prescribing effluent limitations.

Section 306 directs the Administrator to publish within 90 days a list of categories of sources discharging pollutants and, within one year thereafter, to publish regulations establishing national standards of performance for new sources within each category. Section 306 contains no provision for exceptions from the standards for individual plants; on the contrary, subsection (e) expressly makes it unlawful to operate a new source in violation of the applicable standard of performance after its effective date. The statute provides that the new-source standards shall reflect the greatest degree of effluent reduction achievable through application of the best available demonstrated control technology.

Section 301(b) defines the effluent limitations that shall be achieved by existing point sources in two stages. By July 1, 1977, the effluent limitations shall require the application of the best *practicable* control technology currently available; by July 1, 1983, the limitations shall require application of the best *available* technology economically achievable. The statute expressly provides that the limitations which are to become effective in 1983 are applicable to "categories and classes of point sources"; this phrase is omitted from the description of the 1977 limitations. While § 301 states that these limitations "shall be achieved," it fails to state who will establish the limitations.

Section 301(c) authorizes the Administrator to grant variances from the 1983 limitations. Section 301(e) states that effluent limitations established pursuant to § 301 shall be applied to all point sources.

To summarize, § 301(b) requires the achievement of effluent limitations requiring use of the "best practicable" or "best available" technology. It refers to § 304 for a definition of these terms. Section 304 requires the publication of "regulations, providing guidelines for effluent limitations." Finally, permits issued under § 402 must require compliance with § 301 effluent limitations. Nowhere are we told who sets the § 301 effluent limitations, or precisely how they relate to § 304 guidelines and § 402 permits.

retains the power to withdraw approval of the state program, § 402(c)(3), and to veto individual state permits, § 402(d). Finally, under § 402(k), compliance with the permit is generally deemed compliance with § 301. Twenty-seven States now administer their own permit programs.

The Regulations

The various deadlines imposed on the Administrator were too ambitious for him to meet. For that reason, the procedure which he followed in adopting the regulations applicable to the inorganic chemical industry and to other classes of point sources is somewhat different from that apparently contemplated by the statute. Specifically, as will appear, he did not adopt guidelines pursuant to § 304 before defining the effluent limitations for existing sources described in § 301(b) or the national standards for new sources described in § 306. This case illustrates the approach the Administrator followed in implementing the Act.

EPA began by engaging a private contractor to prepare a Development Document. This document provided a detailed technical study of pollution control in the industry. The study first divided the industry into categories. For each category, present levels of pollution were measured and plants with exemplary pollution control were investigated. Based on this information, other technical data, and economic studies, a determination was made of the degree of pollution control which could be achieved by the various levels of technology mandated by the statute. The study was made available to the public and circulated to interested persons. It formed the basis of "effluent limitation guideline" regulations issued by EPA after receiving public comment on proposed regulations. These regulations divide the industry into 22 subcategories. Within each subcategory, precise numerical limits are set for various pollutants.[9] The regulations for each subcategory contain a variance clause, applicable only to the 1977 limitations.[10]

Eight chemical companies filed petitions in the United States Court of Appeals for the Fourth Circuit for review of these regulations. The Court of Appeals rejected their challenge to EPA's authority to issue precise, single-number limitations for discharges of pollutants from existing sources. It held, however, that these limitations and the new plant standards were only "presumptively applicable" to individual plants. We granted the chemical companies' petitions for certiorari in order to consider the scope of EPA's authority to issue existing-source regulations. We also granted the Government's cross-petition for review of the ruling that new-source standards are only presumptively applicable. For convenience, we will refer to the chemical companies as the "petitioners."

---

9. Some subcategories are required to eliminate all discharges by 1977. E.g., 40 CFR §§ 415.70–415.76 (1976). Other subcategories are subject to less stringent restrictions. For instance, by 1977 plants producing titanium dioxide by the chloride process must reduce average daily discharges of dissolved iron to 0.72 pounds per thousand pounds of product. This limit is cut in half for existing plants in 1983 and for all new plants. 40 CFR §§ 415.220–415.225 (1976).

10. These limitations may be made "either more or less stringent" to the extent that "factors relating to the equipment or facilities involved, the process applied, or other such factors related to such discharger are fundamentally different from the factors considered" in establishing the limitations. See, e.g., for the two subcategories discussed in n. 9, supra, 40 CFR §§ 415.72 and 415.222 (1976), respectively.

The Issues

The broad outlines of the parties' respective theories may be stated briefly. EPA contends that § 301(b) authorizes it to issue regulations establishing effluent limitations for classes of plants. The permits granted under § 402, in EPA's view, simply incorporate these across-the-board limitations, except for the limited variances allowed by the regulations themselves and by § 301(c). The § 304(b) guidelines, according to EPA, were intended to guide it in later establishing § 301 effluent-limitation regulations. Because the process proved more time consuming than Congress assumed when it established this two-stage process, EPA condensed the two stages into a single regulation.

In contrast, petitioners contend that § 301 is not an independent source of authority for setting effluent limitations by regulation. Instead, § 301 is seen as merely a description of the effluent limitations which are set for each plant on an individual basis during the permit-issuance process. Under the industry view, the § 304 guidelines serve the function of guiding the permit issuer in setting the effluent limitations. * * *

I.

We think § 301 itself is the key to the problem. The statutory language concerning the 1983 limitations, in particular, leaves no doubt that these limitations are to be set by regulation. Subsection (b)(2)(A) of § 301 states that by 1983 "effluent limitations *for categories and classes* of point sources" are to be achieved which will require "application of the best available technology economically achievable *for such category or class.*" (Emphasis added.) These effluent limitations are to require elimination of all discharges if "such elimination is technologically and economically achievable for a *category or class* of point sources." (Emphasis added.) This is "language difficult to reconcile with the view that individual effluent limitations are to be set when each permit is issued." American Meat Institute v. EPA, 526 F.2d 442, 450 (7th Cir.1975). The statute thus focuses expressly on the characteristics of the "category or class" rather than the characteristics of individual point sources. Normally, such classwide determinations would be made by regulation, not in the course of issuing a permit to one member of the class.[17]

Thus, we find that § 301 unambiguously provides for the use of regulations to establish the 1983 effluent limitations. Different language is used in § 301 with respect to the 1977 limitations. Here, the statute speaks

17. Furthermore, § 301(c) provides that the 1983 limitations may be modified if the owner of a plant shows that "such modified requirements (1) will represent the maximum use of technology within the economic capability of the owner or operator; and (2) will result in reasonable further progress toward the elimination of the discharge of pollutants." This provision shows that the § 301(b) limitations for 1983 are to be estab-lished prior to consideration of the characteristics of the individual plant. American Iron & Steel Institute v. EPA, supra, at 1037 n. 15. Moreover, it shows that the term "best technology economically achievable" does not refer to any individual plant. Otherwise, it would be impossible for this "economically achievable" technology to be beyond the individual owner's "economic capability."

of "effluent limitations for point sources," rather than "effluent limitations for categories and classes of point sources." Nothing elsewhere in the Act, however, suggests any radical difference in the mechanism used to impose limitations for the 1977 and 1983 deadlines. See American Iron & Steel Institute v. EPA, 526 F.2d 1027, 1042 n. 32 (3d Cir.1975). For instance, there is no indication in either § 301 or § 304 that the § 304 guidelines play a different role in setting 1977 limitations. Moreover, it would be highly anomalous if the 1983 regulations and the new-source standards[18] were directly reviewable in the Court of Appeals, while the 1977 regulations based on the same administrative record were reviewable only in the District Court. The magnitude and highly technical character of the administrative record involved with these regulations makes it almost inconceivable that Congress would have required duplicate review in the first instance by different courts. We conclude that the statute authorizes the 1977 limitations as well as the 1983 limitations to be set by regulation, so long as some allowance is made for variations in individual plants, as EPA has done by including a variance clause in its 1977 limitations.[19]

The question of the form of § 301 limitations is tied to the question whether the Act requires the Administrator or the permit issuer to establish the limitations. Section 301 does not itself answer this question, for it speaks only in the passive voice of the achievement and establishment of the limitations. But other parts of the statute leave little doubt on this score. Section 304(b) states that "[f]or the purpose of adopting or revising effluent limitations * * * the Administrator shall" issue guideline regulations; while the judicial-review section, § 509(b)(1), speaks of "the Administrator's action * * * in approving or promulgating any effluent limitation or other limitation under section 301 * * *." And § 101(d) requires us to resolve any ambiguity on this score in favor of the Administrator. It provides that "[e]xcept as otherwise *expressly* provided in this Act, the Administrator of the Environmental Protection Agency * * * shall administer this Act." (Emphasis added.) In sum, the language of the statute supports the view that § 301 limitations are to be adopted by the Administrator, that they are to be based primarily on classes and categories, and that they are to take the form of regulations.

* * *

What, then, is the function of the § 304(b) guidelines? As we noted earlier, § 304(b) requires EPA to identify the amount of effluent reduction attainable through use of the best practicable or available technology and to "specify factors to be taken into account" in determining the pollution control methods "to be applicable to point sources * * * within such categories or classes." These guidelines are to be issued "[f]or the purpose of adopting or revising effluent limitations under this Act." As we read it,

18. Section 509(b)(1) makes new-source standards directly review able in the court of appeals.

19. We agree with the Court of Appeals, 541 F.2d at 1028, that consideration of whether EPA's variance provision has the proper scope would be premature.

§ 304 requires that the guidelines survey the practicable or available pollution-control technology for an industry and assess its effectiveness. The guidelines are then to describe the methodology EPA intends to use in the § 301 regulations to determine the effluent limitations for particular plants. If the technical complexity of the task had not prevented EPA from issuing the guidelines within the statutory deadline, they could have provided valuable guidance to permit issuers, industry, and the public, prior to the issuance of the § 301 regulations.

II.

Our holding that § 301 does authorize the Administrator to promulgate effluent limitations for classes and categories of existing point sources necessarily resolves the jurisdictional issue as well. For, as we have already pointed out, § 509(b)(1) provides that "[r]eview of the Administrator's action * * * in approving or promulgating any effluent limitation or other limitation under section 301, 302, or 306, * * * may be had by any interested person in the Circuit Court of Appeals of the United States for the Federal judicial district in which such person resides or transacts such business * * *."

* * *

We regard § 509(b)(1)(E) as unambiguously authorizing court of appeals review of EPA action promulgating an effluent limitation for existing point sources under § 301. Since those limitations are typically promulgated in the same proceeding as the new-source standards under § 306, we have no doubt that Congress intended review of the two sets of regulations to be had in the same forum.

III.

The remaining issue in this case concerns new plants. Under § 306, EPA is to promulgate "regulations establishing Federal standards of performance for new sources * * *." § 306(b)(1)(B). A "standard of performance" is a "standard for the control of the discharge of pollutants which reflects the greatest degree of effluent reduction which the Administrator determines to be achievable through application of the best available demonstrated control technology, * * * including, where practicable, a standard permitting no discharge of pollutants." § 306(a)(1). In setting the standard, "[t]he Administrator may distinguish among classes, types, and sizes within categories of new sources * * * and shall consider the type of process employed (including whether batch or continuous)." § 306(b)(2). As the House Report states, the standard must reflect the best technology for "that category of sources, and for class, types, and sizes within categories." H.R.Rep. No. 92–911, p. 111 (1972), Leg.Hist. 798.

The Court of Appeals held:

"Neither the Act nor the regulations contain any variance provision for new sources. The rule of presumptive applicability applies to new sources as well as existing sources. On remand EPA should come forward with some limited escape mechanism for new sources." *du Pont II*, 541 F.2d, at 1028.

The court's rationale was that "[p]rovisions for variances, modifications, and exceptions are appropriate to the regulatory process." Ibid.

The question, however, is not what a court thinks is generally appropriate to the regulatory process; it is what Congress intended for *these* regulations. It is clear that Congress intended these regulations to be absolute prohibitions. The use of the word "standards" implies as much. So does the description of the preferred standard as one "permitting *no* discharge of pollutants." (Emphasis added.) It is "unlawful for *any* owner or operator of *any* new source to operate such source in violation of any standard of performance applicable to such source." § 306(e) (emphasis added). In striking contrast to § 301(c), there is no statutory provision for variances, and a variance provision would be inappropriate in a standard that was intended to insure national uniformity and "maximum feasible control of new sources." S.Rep. No. 92–414, p. 58 (1971), Leg.Hist. 1476.

That portion of the judgment of the Court of Appeals in 541 F.2d 1018 requiring EPA to provide a variance procedure for new sources is reversed. In all other aspects, the judgments of the Court of Appeals are affirmed.

It is so ordered.

■ MR. JUSTICE POWELL took no part in the consideration or decision of these cases.

B. CWA EFFLUENT STANDARDS FOR INDUSTRIAL POINT SOURCES

Overview of Point Source Controls

One skill needed in the field of environmental law is the mastery of specialized statutory terminology. With its emphasis on increasingly effective pollution control/elimination technology, the CWA uses a number of terms to describe a particular level or kind of technological control to be imposed upon an industrial water pollution source. The terms invariably are converted into acronyms that are frequently used in place of the more convoluted statutory formulations. Unfortunately, as the CWA has evolved the pollution control terms-of-art have also changed.

As the introductory material and the *du Pont* case indicate, the 1972 Act specified two levels of increasingly stringent pollution control—best practicable control technology currently available (BPT) and best available technology economically achievable leading to the elimination of pollution discharge (BAT). Like the Clean Air Act, the CWA tied the achievement of these levels of pollution control to listed dates, originally 1977 and 1983. About 80% of the nation's industrial dischargers met the deadline for BPT. In 1977 Congress amended the CWA by creating a more complex scheme of discharge regulations with extended compliance dates. Following this statutory amendment, the Clean Water Act regulatory scheme took on a four-part organization based upon pollutant categories.

a. *Conventional pollutants*. The Act has defined a special group of pollutants—called "conventional" pollutants—that would no longer be subject to BAT control but rather a new level of control termed the "best conventional pollutant control technology" or BCT. EPA's development of BCT effluent standards pursuant to § 304(b)(4)(B) [§ 1314(b)(4)(B)] was the subject of the *American Paper Institute* case discussed below. Conventional pollutants are comprised of those that are usually associated with POTWs such as biological oxygen demand, suspended solids, fecal coliform, pH, and others formally identified by EPA under § 304(a)(4) [§ 1314(a)(4)]. Oil and grease have been added under this authority. See 40 C.F.R. § 401.16. Attainment of the BCT standards was initially set for 1984 but it was extended by the 1987 amendments to March 31, 1989.

b. *Toxic pollutants*. The 1977 amendments greatly increased the emphasis on the control of toxic water pollutants through the use of technology-based BAT effluent standards. The legislation codified the result of litigation that had resulted in a consent decree ordering EPA to use a BAT approach to the regulation of 65 toxic pollutants discharged by 21 industry groups. See NRDC, Inc. v. Train, 6 Envtl. L.Rep. 20588 (D.D.C.1976) (Flannery decree). EPA has listed toxic water pollutants at 40 C.F.R. § 401.15. Examples of BAT regulated toxic water pollutants discharged by point sources include aldrin/dieldrin, DDT, endrin, toxaphene, benzedrine, and PCBs. The Act and the decree shifted the focus in toxics regulation away from the health-based regulation of § 307. The BAT limitations are to be set according to the general guidance of the criteria in § 304(b)(2). Under the terms of the 1987 CWA amendments, achievement of the BAT effluent standards must be attained by March 31, 1989. In some instances where the receiving water is highly polluted with toxics (a toxic "hot spot"), an Individual Control Strategy or ICS can be imposed which is more stringent than BAT standards.

c. *Nonconventional pollutants*. This category of water pollutants includes all those pollutants which do not fall into the classification of conventional pollutants, toxic pollutants or heat. See § 301(b)(2)(F) [§ 1311(b)(2)(F)]. Examples of nonconventional pollutants are ammonia, chlorides, nitrates, iron, and color. In general, under the 1987 amendments, nonconventional pollutants are subject to BAT limitations with a March 31, 1989 attainment deadline. However, the CWA also provides for a special BAT modification in § 301(g) that is similar to the waiver available to dischargers of heat under § 316.

d. *Heat*. Thermal discharges are considered water pollutants under the CWA and ostensibly are regulated under the general technology-based structure of the Act. In 1974 EPA issued effluent guidelines for heat applicable to the steam electric industry which barred the discharge of heat except from cooling lakes, ponds or towers. This regulation was struck down in Appalachian Power Co. v. Train, 545 F.2d 1351 (4th Cir.1976). Most thermal discharge permits are issued, however, with limits imposed under the authority of the variance provision contained in § 316. Section 316(b) requires that the location, design, construction, and capacity of cooling water intake structures reflect the best technology available for minimizing adverse environmental impact. In August, 2000 EPA proposed regulations that would establish national requirements for these elements at new facilities. See 65 Fed. Reg. 49,060 (2000).

The Clean Water Act directs EPA to set effluent standards on limitations for industrial categories of dischargers. EPA has set such national standards for a large number of polluter categories. These can be found in the Code of Federal Regulations (C.F.R.) arranged by industrial category. The following chart presents the point source effluent standards and the requisite performance standards established by the CWA.

- Industrial Point Sources

  Existing facilities

  —Best Conventional Treatment (BCT)

  —Conventional Pollutants

  —Best Available Treatment (BAT)

  —Toxic and Non–Conventional Pollutants

  New facilities

  —Best Demonstrated Treatment (BDT)

  —All Pollutants

- Publicly Owned Treatment Works (POTWs)

  Primary, Secondary, Tertiary Treatment

Excerpt from the Clean Water Act

33 U.S.C. § 304 (emphasis added).

§ 304(b) For the purpose of adopting or revising effluent limitations under this Act the Administrator shall, after consultation with appropriate Federal and State agencies and other interested persons, publish within one year of enactment of this title, regulations, providing guidelines for effluent limitations, and, at least annually thereafter, revise, if appropriate, such regulations. Such regulations shall—

(1)(A) identify, in terms of amounts of constituents and chemical, physical, and biological characteristics of pollutants, the degree of effluent reduction attainable through the application of the **best practicable control technology currently available** for classes and categories of point sources (other than publicly owned treatment works); and

(B) specify factors to be taken into account in determining the control measures and practices to be applicable to point sources (other than publicly owned treatment works) within such categories or classes. **Factors relating to the assessment of best practicable control technology currently available** to comply with subsection (b)(1) of section 301 of this Act shall include consideration of the total cost of application of technology in relation to the effluent reduction benefits to be achieved from such application, and shall also take into account the age of equipment and facilities involved, the process employed, the engineering aspects of the application of various types of control techniques, process changes, non-water quality environmental impact (including energy requirements), and such other factors as the Administrator deems appropriate;

(2)(A) identify, in terms of amounts of constituents and chemical, physical, and biological characteristics of pollutants, the degree of effluent reduction attainable through the application of the **best control measures and practices achievable** including treatment techniques, process and procedure innovations, operating methods, and other alternatives for classes and categories of point sources (other than publicly owned treatment works); and

(B) specify factors to be taken into account in determining the best measures and practices available to comply with subsection (b)(2) of section 301 of this Act to be applicable to any point source (other than publicly owned treatment works) within such categories of classes. **Factors relating to the assessment of best available technology** shall take into account the age of equipment and facilities involved, the process employed, the engineering aspects of the application of various types of control techniques, process changes, the cost of achieving such effluent reduction, non-water quality environmental impact (including energy requirements), and such other factors as the Administrator deems appropriate. * * *

(4)(A) Identify, in terms of constituents and chemical, physical and biological characteristics of pollutants, the degree of effluent reduction attainable through the application of the **best conventional pollutant control technology** (including measures and practices) for classes and categories of point sources (other than publicly owned treatment works); and

(B) specify factors to be taken into account in determining the best conventional pollutant control technology measures and practices to comply with section 1311(b)(2)(E) of this title to be applicable to any point source (other than publicly owned treatment works) within such categories or classes. **Factors relating to the assessment of best conventional pollutant control technology** (including measures and practices) include consideration of the reasonableness of the relationship between the costs of obtaining a reduction in effluents and the effluent reduction benefits derived, and the comparison of the cost and level of reduction of such pollutants from the discharge from publicly owned treatment works to the cost and level of reduction of such pollutants from a class or category of industrial sources, and shall take into account the age of equipment and facilities involved, the process employed, the engineering aspects of various types of control techniques, process changes, non-water quality environmental impact (including energy requirements), and such other factors as the Administrator deems appropriate.

NOTE ON DESIGNING POINT SOURCE CONTROLS—THE EFFLUENT LIMITATION APPROACH

How should the problem of water pollution be approached? First we must define the nature of the problem. Put as simply as possible, what is water pollution? Is it some level of water quality that is considered to be unacceptable to most people? But what level is that? The supposedly simple questions soon give way to much more difficult social choice decisions. For instance, should all water be clean enough for all persons to be able to safely drink? Clean enough for swimming? for fishing? for transportation? for waste disposal? Should water quality be established at a uniform level throughout the nation? What about groundwater—should it be at a consistent quality level? Who should set this level and what process should be employed? What role, if any, should considerations of economic cost play in the determination of what is unacceptable water pollution?

The CWA defines the term "pollutant" yet the statute does not directly set forth the meaning of water pollution. See Clean Water Act § 502 (33 U.S.C. § 1362). Consider how the Clean Air Act specifies "air pollution" through the NAAQS mechanism and how the regulatory system is organized around the concept of attainment. Why not structure the statutory response to water pollution around a federally-established ambient or environmental standard set on a pollutant-by-pollutant basis? While water quality standards do play a role in the CWA scheme, a major emphasis of the Act is on nationally-uniform, technologically-advanced discharge or effluent standards applicable to categories of point sources.

Can you think of reasons why designing a system solely aimed at attaining uniform water quality standards would be undesirable? Is it because of the multiplicity of point and non-point sources? Is it because of the difficulty in determining the water quality impact of a single point source's discharge on water quality? Is it the impact of such limitations upon economic growth in the area? Is it due to the difficulty of obtaining interjurisdictional cooperation in the designation and enforcement of such standards? Can you imagine other reasons why the Clean Air Act model was not more closely followed in designing the 1972 CWA? Are there non-regulatory alternatives to the CWA effluent standard approach which could reach water quality objectives with a minimum of EPA involvement?

As noted above the CWA adopts a system of increasingly strict pollution control requirements theoretically leading towards the total elimination of point source discharges. As the discussion below will indicate, the degree of source control is defined according to the level of technological achievement within the industry. Usually these discharge or effluent standards are described as "mass" based limits which establish the maximum quantity of pollutants which may be discharged for each unit of production. For instance, BAT limitations in the primary nickel and cobalt subcategory of the Non–Ferrous Metals Point Source Category state that a source may not discharge, on a daily average, more than 16.25 pounds of the pollutant copper for each million pounds of nickel produced. See 40 C.F.R. § 421.233(c). In theory, as control technology improves the amounts of waste copper to be disposed of should approach zero pounds for each million pounds of nickel produced. Alternatively, sometimes effluent standards are expressed in terms of permissible pollutant concentrations in wastewater. These concentration-based effluent standards are stated in terms of milligrams of a pollutant per liter of wastewater regardless of the amount of production. As such, they focus upon the amount of pollutants discharged and not those produced as do mass-based effluent standards. Although such limitations are acceptable to EPA in limited circumstances, they run afoul of the basic anti-pollution policy of the Act. For example, a source could meet such a concentration-based standard by diluting its wastestream with intake water in order to meet the restriction.

EPA's Notice to Review and Promulgate Effluent Guideline Regulations

55 Fed.Reg. 80, 84–86 (1990).

This section of the notice summarizes the various tasks which the Agency [EPA] must complete in a typical effluent guideline rulemaking.

Initially, the Agency must establish the scope of the rulemaking and the dimensions of the rulemaking project by defining the industry category. For some industry categories, such as the Inorganic Chemicals Manufacturing category (40 C.F.R. part 415), the Agency was able to use readily available tools such as the Standard Industrial Classification (SIC) Manual in defining the category to be addressed. For others, such as the Machinery Manufacturing and Rebuilding category ("MM & R"), the process has been more difficult. In defining the MM & R category, the Agency first examined what industrial activities had not been regulated in the "Machinery and Mechanical Products" category as identified in the 1976 consent decree. From that, the Agency identified approximately 89,000 facilities that manufacture or rebuild machinery but that were not covered by previously promulgated guidelines. The Agency then examined whether the Metal Finishing category (40 C.F.R. part 433) would cover these establishments and found that it did cover approximately 13,000 of the 89,000 identified. EPA then examined the products manufactured and processes employed by the remaining 76,000 facilities and by facilities with related processes and facilities. The Agency was unable, from a process or practical basis, to differentiate between manufacturing, maintenance and rebuilding. Accordingly, EPA determined these three classifications should be evaluated together.

Next, the Agency determines the size of the category as it has been defined, using all available sources. Given the diversity of regulatory categories, no one source suffices to establish size. At various times, EPA has used one or more of the following sources: standard published sources, information available through trade associations, data purchased from the Dun and Bradstreet, Inc. data base, other publicly available data bases, census data, other U.S. Government information and any available EPA data base. For MM & R, for example, the Agency found that its original estimate of 89,000 facilities had included only the larger manufacturing facilities. The Agency currently believes this category includes over 278,000 facilities with 10 or more employees, and totals approximately 970,000 facilities. If a category is very large, the Agency will determine whether it can be broken down into appropriate categories or subcategories. If more than one subcategory can be identified, the Agency may need to establish priorities for regulation.

Regulatory information about industry categories is obtained largely through survey questionnaires and on-site wastewater sampling. Survey questionnaires solicit detailed information necessary to assess the statutory rulemaking factors (particularly technological and economic achievability of available controls), water use, production processes, and wastewater treatment and disposal practices. A significant portion of the Agency's questionnaires typically seek information necessary to assess economic achievability.

If the survey questionnaire is expected to go to more than nine entities, clearance from the Office of Management and Budget (OMB) is required under the Paperwork Reduction Act (44 U.S.C. 3501 et seq.). Typically, the Agency will construct a questionnaire and obtain public reaction on it. Often the Agency will pre-test the questionnaire by having one or more facilities complete the draft form. Formal submission to OMB will follow completion of these activities. OMB review can take up to 90 days from official submission of the questionnaire. * * *

Generally, the Agency is able to define its wastewater sampling effort based on information received in response to the questionnaires. While the questionnaire provides information about production processes, water uses and, in general terms, what is found in the industry's wastewater, on-site sampling is required to characterize specifically the pollutants found in discharges. This is because direct dischargers are ordinarily required to do limited, though regular, sampling under the monitoring provisions of their permits, and few indirect dischargers are required to do any frequent testing. Moreover, site visits are necessary to assess pollutant control technology. Scheduling of site visits depends on a number of factors. First, sampling is generally conducted by contractors selected by the strict standards of the government contracting process. The logistics of coordinating the sampling can be extensive. Second, successful site visits require the presence of knowledgeable plant personnel to answer pertinent questions and to assist the sampling team in various ways. Third, site visits are useful only if plants are operating under "normal" conditions; therefore, visits must be scheduled to avoid "down time" periods for maintenance or other interruptions. Finally, scheduling of a site visit may depend on plant production schedules, if a plant produces numerous products or changes its product mix as part of a production cycle.

Sampling and site visits and many other tasks related to the preparation of guidelines, including numerous efforts related to economic, statistical and environmental analyses, are generally accomplished with the assistance of EPA contractors under supervision of Agency program staff. In addition, contract laboratories, rather than EPA laboratories, ordinarily analyze these samples. (EPA laboratories generally are devoted to research and development.) Hiring contractors is a rigorous and somewhat protracted process that is dictated by Federal contracting requirements. * * *

Most of the effluent sampling and analysis that has supported effluent guideline regulations promulgated to date has been conducted and funded by EPA. On occasion, however, these activities have been pursued on a cooperative basis with industry parties. For example, EPA and numerous pulp and paper manufacturers participated in a cooperative effort to sample and analyze effluent, wastewater treatment sludge and pulp from domestic mills that bleach pulp in their production processes. Despite the obvious advantage that such a cooperative situation presents to the Agency in terms of reduced cost, it is not clear that such a process shortens the time required to promulgate a regulation. In fact, the negotiated nature of such a cooperative program may actually lengthen the analytical data collection phase of the regulation development process.

When sampling is completed, wastewater samples are sent to laboratories for analysis.

Responses to questionnaires are generally written on the questionnaire form itself. Together with results from sampling and site visits, the information must be entered into computer files. This is a considerable task that generally precedes the major analytical work and must be performed according to quality assurance procedures. Frequently, this effort is slowed by the need to interpret the information as submitted by the respondent and to reconcile discrepancies. However, only when it is completed, can the Agency conduct the statistical, economic and engineering analyses necessary to develop treatment control options and to select one or more of these options tentatively as the basis for a rulemaking proposal.

Rulemaking proposals, as well as final rules and other rulemaking notices (such as notices of the availability of new data) all undergo thorough internal Agency review before publication in the Federal Register. The process of internal review is designed not only to ensure the quality and completeness of regulatory packages, but to expedite rulemaking by the early identification of issues and resolution of any disagreements among concerned EPA offices.

Within the Agency, an individual "work group" oversees the development of each effluent guideline and the supporting record. The purpose of work groups is to provide for full consultation and coordination on a rulemaking package among all EPA offices (often including regional offices) that participate in the rulemaking. After the work group develops treatment control options for a guideline, the options typically are presented to the Administrator as the basis for the proposed guideline. After "options selection", work groups must reach closure on a rulemaking package that implements the proposal of the selected treatment option before review of the package at higher levels. "Work Group Closure" on a regulatory package that proposes a guideline occurs when the work group concludes that the major issues presented by a rulemaking package are resolved and that the package is generally ready for consideration by the Agency's senior management. A closure meeting usually follows review and revision of several drafts of a rulemaking package. This can take many months.

Following Work Group Closure, several steps must be taken before publication of a proposed guideline. These steps usually begin with revision of the preamble, proposed rule and associated documents in response to the comments raised by concerned offices at Work Group Closure. After the completion of revisions to these documents, which can be quite lengthy, final review begins. This includes a review by senior Agency management known as the "Red Border" process, separate review by OMB under Executive Order 12291, formal recommendation by the Assistant Administrator for Water and signature by the Administrator. This final review is not a mere formality; the Agency usually allows about 4 months to accomplish these steps. Any unresolved issues that remain after Work Group Closure must be settled. Once the Administrator approves the proposal, the rulemaking proposal can be published in the **Federal Register,** opening the public comment period. Comment periods generally are set for 60 to 90 days, but sometimes extend beyond 90 days for particularly complicated proposals.

At the close of the comment period on the proposed rule, the work group reviews the comments to identify significant issues and to initiate the preparation of responses to comments. Responding to comments submitted in guidelines rulemaking is often an enormous task because of the variety of processes and pollutants covered by the proposal, the range of treatment technologies that may be required, the different types of manufacturers in the category to be covered, and the number of parties and citizens affected by the rule. (In the recent rulemaking setting guidelines for the Organic Chemicals, Plastics and Synthetic Fibers category (40 C.F.R. part 414), the Agency received over 15,000 pages of comments.) During this period, the Agency also revises the technical support documents and other analyses in light of comments received.

Ultimately the Agency must decide what modifications to the proposed rule must be made in response to the public comments or in response to new data developed by EPA itself since the proposal. Sometimes it is necessary to re-propose all or parts of a rule or to publish a supplemental notice or notice of data availability. For example, in the Organic Chemicals rulemaking, the Agency issued three notices and requests for comments after the original proposal. If any notices must be issued between the publication of the rulemaking proposal and the promulgation of the final rule, these notices undergo internal review with many of the same requirements before publication and are subject to comment by the public.

Finally, the Agency prepares a final rulemaking package. This package must reflect appropriate resolution of comments received and issues raised since the proposal. Typically, "Options Selection" at the Administrator's level again takes place. In addition, the rulemaking record, which often includes tens of thousands of pages, must be assembled. The final rule is subject to the same review process as rulemaking proposals, including Work Group Closure, review in Red Border, and separate review by OMB before signature by the Administrator.

After publication of a final rule, the Agency must continue to devote significant time and resources to the rulemaking project. For example, the project staff works with staff from EPA regional offices and States on implementation of the guideline. In the event of a challenge in the United States Court of Appeals, the project staff must spend a great deal of additional time assisting in the defense of the rule. Project staff sometimes also become involved in special studies relating to the published rule. Until these post-publication activities end, the resources involved frequently cannot be transferred to the preparation of other guidelines.

NOTES AND QUESTIONS

1. *Selecting Water Pollution Controls.* What authority exists under the Clean Water Act for EPA to establish water pollution control regulations for an existing industrial point source like Ajax Paperboard? When would Ajax have to be in compliance with any newly-established effluent limitation? What if Ajax were proposing to construct a new Kraft papermaking plant at the Centralia site? Does the Act make any distinction between existing and new facilities in terms of pollution control requirements? Why set different regulations for new and existing plants in the same industry.

BCT and BAT. After reading the *du Pont* case, you should know that the principal means of point source control established by the CWA is the effluent standard or effluent limitation. The statutory authority for setting effluent standards is found in sections 301 and 304 of the CWA. Section 301 deals with compliance timing while section 304 concerns EPA standard setting. As for timing, § 301 generally requires compliance "as expeditiously as practicable, but in no case later than three years after the date such limitations are promulgated under [section 304], and in no case later than March 31, 1989." Ignoring the last clause, the general phase-in period allowed is three years subject to waivers and exceptions mentioned later in the chapter. These two provisions must be read in tandem to understand the role Congress has assigned for EPA and the way uniform national effluent limitations are intended to help achieve clean water goals. Notice in the convoluted sentences of § 304 the charge given to EPA to create levels of effluent control—BAT and BCT. Assume for the moment that you are the EPA official in charge of issuing effluent standards. What do you do? What governs your regulatory decisions?

Read sections 304(b)(2) [BAT] and § 304(b)(4) [BCT]. Do these provisions help to guide your administrative judgment? Compare the factors set out for BAT with those for BCT. Considering the statutory language, is there a difference in (1) the range of authorized control techniques and (2) the substantive factors you are to consider in setting the standards? If, as the EPA official, you are to specify the effluent standard, how could you look to this language for support of your regulatory decision? What other information might help support your regulatory decision?

When statutes employ different terms it is expected that different meanings are intended. Examine the language of BPT, BAT, and BCT. What is the difference between "best practicable control technology currently available" in § 304(b)(1)(A) [§ 1314(b)(1)(A)], "best available technology economically achievable" § 304(b)(2)(A) [§ 1314(b)(2)(A)] and "best conventional pollutant control technology" in § 304(b)(4)(A) [§ 1314(b)(4)(A)]? Remember that these cumbersome terms actually direct EPA to select specific levels of pollution control for classes or categories of point sources. Selecting effluent standards for a wide range of facilities in industrial categories is hardly an easy task. Why did Congress direct EPA to set uniform effluent standards on an industry-by-industry basis and then create different levels of control on a pollutant by pollutant basis? What burden does this responsibility impose upon EPA? Does this make sense or is it needless micro management?

(i) Does BPT mean a lowest common denominator approach or can EPA take the average of the "best" in the industrial category? (yes).

(ii) Does BAT allow EPA to require the use of technology that is not currently in use? See Weyerhaeuser Co. v. Costle, 590 F.2d 1011, 1060–1062 (D.C.Cir.1978) (yes).

(iii) Can BAT be derived from a single operating plant or data secured from an experimental or pilot plant? See Association of Pacific Fisheries v. EPA, 615 F.2d 794, 816 (9th Cir.1980) (yes, noting legislative history).

(iv) Is a BAT effluent standard "achievable" if EPA derived it from two plants performances which individually did not meet the new pollution control standard for each pollutant parameter. See Chemical Manufacturers Ass'n v. U.S. EPA, 870 F.2d 177, 238–9 (5th Cir.1989) (yes, viewing single pollutant exceedances by one plant as "irrelevant" as long as the other plant demonstrates the limits are achievable.)

(v) What if there was no EPA-issued BAT effluent standard for the Kraft process pulp and paper industry. Remember that such standards have only been developed for certain listed industrial groups. What effluent standards if any, would apply to Ajax Paperboard?

New Sources: National Standards of Performance. The CWA borrows the concept of new source performance standard (NSPS) from the Clean Air Act. See Clean Air Act § 111 [§ 7411].

(a) "New sources" of water pollution must comply with special national standards of performance which reflect,

> the greatest degree of effluent reduction ... achievable through application of the best available demonstrated control technology, processes, operating methods, or other alternatives, including where practicable, a standard permitting no discharge of pollutants.

§ 306(a)(1) [§ 1316(a)(1)]. This is the verbal formulation for the CWA's stringent level of control. Compare this terminology with that used to define BAT, BCT and BPT. Is it clear from the statutory language that the § 306 new source standards should be the most stringent? What assumptions would support such a policy imposing the strictest standards on new sources? In setting the standards of performance, EPA must take into consideration both the cost of achieving the effluent reduction and non-water quality environmental impacts. § 306(b)(1)(B) [§ 1316(b)(1)(B)]. Should EPA be able to impose a higher degree of pollutant removal under new source standards than with BAT on existing sources? Should there be an explicit cost/benefit analysis required for each NSPS? Why? In practice, new source standards and BAT are often identical. Why would EPA take such an approach? Should it?

(b) What facilities are subject to § 306 standards? Under § 306(a) a "source" is a "building, structure, facility or installation from which there is or may be the discharge of pollutants." A source is "new" when construction began on it *after* the publication of proposed regulations pertaining to it, assuming they are finally adopted. The Act also requires that EPA formally promulgate the new source standards within 120 days after their proposal. § 306(b)(1)(B) [§ 1316(b)(1)(B)].

EPA has been known to miss statutory deadlines on the issuance of regulations. Can you imagine the risk or uncertainty for prospective plant owners who commence construction after the proposal of new source standards yet prior to their final promulgation? Notice EPA's solution to this problem. Its regulations define "new source" as a water pollution source whose construction began after either (a) the promulgation of final § 306 standards or (b) the proposal of standards, but only if they are finally adopted within 120 days of their proposal. How does this solve the problem of agency delay?

(c) New source performance standards have been set at the most stringent level of technical pollution control following the theory that such standards will "force" technology to improve over time. Their theory has been challenged by a number of analysts as being punitive and poor policy. Consider the following quotation from an article by Professors Ackerman and Stewart and evaluate the persuasiveness of their criticisms of new source policy.

BAT controls, and the litigation which they provoke, impose disproportionate penalties on new products and processes. A BAT strategy
typically imposes far more stringent controls on new sources because
there is no risk of shutdown. Also, new plants and products must run
the gauntlet of lengthy regulatory and legal proceedings to win approval; the resulting uncertainty and delay discourage new investment. By
contrast, existing products and processes can use the legal process to
postpone or water down compliance requirements. Also, BAT strategies
impose disproportionate burdens on more productive and profitable
industries because they can "afford" more stringent controls. This
"soak the rich" approach penalizes growth and international competitiveness.

Bruce A. Ackerman & Richard B. Stewart, Reforming Environmental Law:
The Democratic Case for Market Incentives, 13 Colum. J. Envt'l L. 171
(1988).

(d) What are the implications of being categorized a "new source?"
First and foremost, the source must meet the § 306 effluent limitation
reflecting BDT or the best demonstrated control technology. Second, once a
new source has complied with these standards it is insulated from any more
stringent standard for a period of 10 years or its depreciation period
whichever is shorter. § 306(d) [§ 1316(d)]. EPA's regulations make it clear
that this immunity from regulatory change does not apply to more stringent water quality based or toxic effluent standards. See 40 C.F.R.
§ 122.29(d)(2). Third, an EPA-issued NPDES permit containing a § 306
new source standard is subject to the National Environmental Policy Act
and therefore could require the preparation of an environmental impact
statement. See § 511(c)(1) [§ 1371(c)(1)] and 40 C.F.R. § 122.29(c).

Why would Congress require EPA to undertake NEPA review of these
permits and not others? What about NPDES permits issued by the over 40
states having delegated authority? Must EPA or the states themselves
undertake NEPA review prior to permit issuance? EPA NPDES regulations
answer this in the negative with regard to EPA. See 40 C.F.R.
§ 122.29(c)(1)(ii). When enacting § 511(c)(1) Congress believed that the
owners of new sources had flexibility in their facility design not available to
owners of existing plants and that more environmentally optimal projects
would result. See e.g., Municipality of Anchorage v. United States, 980 F.2d
1320 (9th Cir.1992). Does this requirement do much to achieve this goal?

2. *The Administrative Process of Setting Effluent Standards.* What process does EPA use for setting these water pollution regulations? In general,
how is the public involved? If EPA were to establish an effluent standard
for Kraft process paper mills, how could CCC participate in the rulemaking
process? How could CCC be most effective? How is information important
in this regulatory process and who has access to it?

The promulgation of effluent standards is undertaken through an
agency process called informal or "notice and comment" rulemaking mentioned in the chapter on Administrative Law. The following case excerpt
describes EPA's exercise of rulemaking power in the development of

effluent limitations for the non-ferrous metals manufacturing industry. Notice the duration of the rulemaking process and also the role of the regulated industry in the process.

EPA did not approach casually the task of non-ferrous metals rulemaking. In 1977, the agency began gathering data for the proposed rules which was published on February 17, 1983. Data was obtained from plant visits, plant samplings, studies of scientific journals, and consultations with industry. Three hundred and nineteen firms, operating 416 facilities, received questionnaires from EPA asking for information on flow rates, production rates, wastewater treatment, and costs. Each plant visited by EPA also received an opportunity to comment on the trip report prepared by the agency. Various of the petitioners met with EPA both before and after publication of the proposed rules.

The resulting record ran 24,000 pages. EPA solicited public comment on all aspects of the regulations, highlighting points on which the agency wanted additional information. The initial commend period lasted eleven weeks. EPA reopened the comment period twice and accepted late-filed comments from one of the petitioners.

The agency considered the comments and contacted each petitioner with follow-up inquiries. The comments led EPA to re-examine its selections of model technologies and data bases. EPA likewise considered additional data on the treatment of lead and ammonia, as well as continuing to request and evaluate data from plants that had not previously submitted data. The long process of gathering data and the ongoing dialogue with the industry culminated in the final rule promulgated March 8, 1984.

Kennecott v. United States EPA, 780 F.2d 445, 449 (4th Cir.1985).

The setting of CWA effluent limitations gives rise to numerous questions of administrative law often focusing upon the purpose of the notice and comment requirement to the rulemaking structure. For instance, if EPA decides to allow multiple rounds of public notice and comment, must it subject every incremental change in its regulations to further public scrutiny before final action? What would be the likely effect if EPA did extend public comment each time it changed a proposal? Considering the pressing statutory time limits built into environmental statutes, courts have upheld final rules that are found to be a "logical outgrowth" of initial rulemaking proposals and the notice and comment process. See, e.g., Chocolate Manufacturers Ass'n v. Block, 755 F.2d 1098, 1105–07 (4th Cir.1985) (finding a USDA rule to be an "outgrowth" of the proposed rule but not a "logical" one).

What if EPA proposed a BAT effluent limitation for the Kraft pulp and paper industry based upon the use of a particular model control technology (technology A). Thereafter, public comment indicated that the paper industry believed that this effluent standard was unachievable using technology A. EPA then issued final effluent standards requiring the use of technology

A plus technology B, the latter control method only mentioned among numerous alternatives in the EPA Development Document which had accompanied the original proposed rule. Should this satisfy the notice and comment requirements of the Administrative Procedure Act? See Kennecott v. United States EPA, 780 F.2d 445, 453 (4th Cir.1985) (yes).

C. SETTING EFFLUENT LIMITATIONS—OTHER CONSIDERATIONS

How do the policies and the language of the Clean Water Act influence EPA's choice of specific pollution control requirements in terms of a) grouping of similar categories of industrial facilities for uniform treatment under the effluent standards provision of the CWA, b) the requisite level or kind of technology (to be adopted as BAT), and c) the considerations of pollution control costs in the selection of effluent standards? How important are each of these factors in setting the "best" regulation?

(a) *Subcategorization.* The Clean Water Act emphasizes uniformity in the design of water pollution regulations. Why? How far is EPA required to go in classifying industries into subcategories for the purpose of setting uniform effluent standards? EPA's effluent standards subcategorize industries to a remarkable degree. For instance, within the Canned and Preserved Seafood Processing Point Source category are the following subcategories each with its own effluent standard: (1) farm-raised catfish processing plants, (2) five groupings for shrimp processing, (3) seven categories of crab meat processors, and (4) five categories of clam and oyster processors. See 40 C.F.R. Part 408. Why would the question of subcategorization be important to a particular plant such as the Ajax facility? Should the agency be required to take into consideration regional differences, age, climate, and other factors? The courts have generally been quite deferential to EPA's categorization choices finding them not to be an abuse of discretion. Ultimately isn't each discharger a subcategory of one? Is the subcategorization issue of continuing importance with the availability of fundamentally different factor (FDF) and other variances?

(b) *The Selection of Pollution Control Technology and Technology Transfer.* Consider the following discussion in conjunction with the setting of an effluent standard for the Ajax facility. When establishing effluent standards for water pollution sources, EPA must determine that a model pollution control technology exists which, if employed, would allow sources within the industrial category to meet the standard. Where would you look for such "model" pollution control technology? Would you try to find the least polluting facility in the country and use it as the norm?

Must EPA be limited to finding such model technology within the exact industry group for which the effluent standards are being set? Put another way, should the agency be permitted to use pollution control data from industry A to set effluent standards for industry B? Since perfect information does not exist for every industrial category and subcategory, EPA has found it necessary to borrow pollution control technology from one industry and conclude that it is applicable to another. When is it appropriate to transfer pollution control technology from one industry and impose it as

BAT standard for another? Following the holding in CPC Intern., Inc. v. Train, 515 F.2d 1032, 1048 (8th Cir.1975), courts have employed a durable three-part test for making this determination. To decide that technology from one industry can be applied to another EPA must,

a) show that the transfer technology is available outside the industry,

b) determine that the technology is transferable to the industry, and

c) make a reasonable prediction that the technology if used in the industry will be capable of removing the increment required by the effluent standards.

In one case EPA identified a sulfide precipitation technology for the primary metals industry that was in use in Japan and Sweden. The Fourth Circuit upheld the transfer of that technology even though it had been used in Japan to produce arsenic trioxide and not to cleanse industrial wastewater. See Kennecott v. United States EPA, 780 F.2d 445, 453 (4th Cir.1985).

(c) *Cost Considerations in Setting Effluent Standards.* Occasionally changes in industrial processes will both reduce pollutant discharge and unit production costs. When this is the case, industrial managers will happily convert their production processes in order to gain the advantage of lower operating costs and resulting higher profits. However, it is more often the case that the imposition of environmental controls adds to the costs of production without necessarily increasing production efficiency. In this case dischargers are less willing to raise their costs especially if they believe that their competitors are not taking the same steps. Consider the following general questions.

When EPA establishes an effluent standard, how much consideration, if any, should the agency give to the issue of the economic costs of complying with the new regulation? Should pollution control levels be set uniformly at the highest point of technological capability regardless of cost or benefits? While you evaluate these questions consider the following information.

● Cheap vs. Expensive Pounds of Pollution Example

As a general proposition, the cost of removing one pound of pollutant from a wastestream increases as the percentage of pollution removal rises. For example, the cost of removing 80% of pollutant X (80% control) from a factory's discharge might be $0.25 per pound. However, as the level of removal goes up from 80% to 90% (90% control) the incremental cost of control might rise to $0.75 per pound of pollutant X removed. Therefore, the incremental cost of improving pollution control from 80% to 90% effectiveness has tripled. Finally, the incremental costs of removing the last 10% of pollutant X from the plant's wastestream could be much higher— possibly as much as $2.50 per pound. As you can see from this example, the per pound cost of removing pollutant X has increased by a factor of ten as the level of control moved from 80% to 100%. This illustration indicates that there are "cheap" and "expensive" pounds of pollutant X discharged from the same plant.

A continuing public policy problem is determining how far along the pollution control continuum EPA should go. How high should the unit cost of pollution control be and what policy principle should govern EPA's choice. Remember that the uniform BAT effluent standards all are set without regard to the quality of the receiving water. Consequently stringent BAT limits will be imposed without considering the effect of the discharge on water quality.

(i) *Statutory Guidance and Different Definitions of Pollution Control.* The CWA provides limited guidance for the consideration of costs in the setting effluent standards for BPT, BCT, and BAT. Read the following language authorizing the issuance of these pollution control regulations. Do they reflect any clear legislative policy on the procedure for considering costs or the substantive weight to be attached to cost versus benefits in the rulemaking process? If you were redrafting the CWA how would you instruct EPA?

> *BPT*—In assessing technology EPA shall "include consideration of the total cost of application of technology in relation to the effluent reduction benefits to be achieved from such application." § 304(b)(1)(B) [§ 1314(b)(1)(B)].

> *BCT*—EPA must "include consideration of the reasonableness of the relationship between the costs of attaining a reduction in effluents and the effluent reduction benefits derived, and the comparison of the cost and level of reduction of such pollutants from the discharge from [POTWs] to the cost and level of reduction of such pollutants from a class or category of industrial sources." § 304(b)(4)(B) [§ 1314(b)(4)(B)].

> *BAT*—Within a list of seven factors, EPA must take into account, in setting BAT limitations, "the cost of achieving such effluent reduction." § 304(b)(2)(B) [§ 1314(b)(2)(B)].

Cases on the subject have concluded that BPT-setting requires a "limited balancing" of costs against benefits. See e.g. National Ass'n Metal Finishers v. EPA, 719 F.2d 624 (3d Cir.1983). The language creating BCT clearly anticipates an agency cost analysis and a reasonable relationship between costs and benefits. But what about EPA's fixing of BAT standards—should compliance cost factors be of diminished importance in the agency's choice of this control technology? Should EPA try to reach higher levels of pollution control with increasingly stringent BAT standards, irrespective of cost, in an effort to achieve the no-discharge goal of the Act? See § 301(b)(2)(A) [§ 1311(b)(2)(A)].

(ii) *Judicial Review and the Question of Costs.* As indicated above, cases challenging BPT and BCT standards usually carefully analyze EPA's consideration of costs and benefits in proposing effluent standards. See, e.g., Weyerhaeuser Co. v. Costle, 590 F.2d 1011, 1047–48 (D.C.Cir.1978). However, when BAT standards have been judicially reviewed courts have only required that EPA demonstrate that compliance costs have been "considered" along with the range of other statutory factors. Tested under an "arbitrary and capricious" standard of review, most BAT effluent standards and their cost justifications have been upheld. The following excerpt written by Judge (now Justice) Kennedy characterizes these opinions,

> The record discloses that the Agency studied the cost of complying with the 1983 regulations * * *. It set forth the cost of compliance for plants that produced various amounts of effluent per minute, both in terms of capital costs and operation and maintenance costs * * *. The projections include estimates of the costs of construction, labor, power, chemicals and fuel * * *. Although land acquisition costs were not considered, the amount of land necessary for the air flotation unit is minimal. In contrast to our conclusion regarding aerated lagoons, the Agency was not arbitrary in concluding that the DAF unit could be installed on existing plant locations without necessitating additional land acquisitions * * *.

> Finally, it does not appear that the cost of complying with the 1983 regulations is unreasonable. The cost of compliance for the Northwest Canned Salmon subcategory, for example, is estimated to be $157,000 for initial investment and $32,000 of annual expenditures for the average size plants * * *. According to the EPA's economic analysis, the total annual costs of pollution abatement averaged between one and two percent of the total sales figures of each subcategory * * *. Depreciation is available for the capital outlays and tax deductions are available for business expenses. The Agency concluded that the benefits justified the costs, and petitioners have not shown that conclusion to be arbitrary or capricious. See American Iron & Steel Inst., supra, 526 F.2d at 1052–53.

> Although the number of plants estimated to close as a result of the 1983 regulations was not stated clearly to us it appears to be a lesser proportion of affected plants than that which we approved for the 1977 regulations * * *. Since Congress contemplated the closure of some marginal plants, we do not consider the regulations to be arbitrary and capricious.

Association of Pacific Fisheries v. EPA, 615 F.2d 794, 818 (9th Cir.1980). It appears that courts are reluctant to overturn EPA technology determinations even when industry cost estimates vary widely from agency calculations. See Reynolds Metals Co. v. United States EPA, 760 F.2d 549, 565 (4th Cir.1985) (EPA estimate of $50 per pound removal cost versus industry estimate of $17,710 per pound costs).

Does this mean that economic issues are irrelevant? Is EPA free to select high levels of control without being constrained by the enormous unit cost? Apparently some level of excessive cost compared to a minuscule benefit will trigger judicial rejection, but the reported decisions have not identified such a case. In American Petroleum Institute v. EPA, 787 F.2d 965, 973 (5th Cir.1986) the court concluded that, "[T]he point of regulation *ad absurdum* has not been reached in this case, but only because the costs imposed on industry * * * will not be significant." Within the context of the Ajax case, can you hypothesize a situation where a court might invalidate an effluent standard?

(iii) *Critique of the Uniform, Technology–Based Effluent Standard Approach.* The CWA's reliance upon the technology-based effluent standard has placed great emphasis on technological development as the engine for water quality improvement. As the discussion above indicates, the initial selection of the requisite BAT level deemphasizes considerations of cost. Such a view holds that control technology will continue to improve and ultimately lead to the elimination of all discharges. This technologically optimistic scenario also assumes the uniform adoption of these advanced effluent standards across entire industry groups regardless of discharge location or receiving water quality. The following excerpt written by William Pedersen is critical of this approach. Consider the author's viewpoint and suggest possible solutions to the issues raised in the second paragraph.

Pedersen, Turning the Tide on Water Quality, 15 Ecol.L.Q. 69, 82–84 (1988) (footnotes omitted).

A.   *The Inefficiency of Technology–Based Standards*

Economists long have argued that technology-based controls, of which the Clean Water Act provides a nearly perfect example, waste money in two major ways. First, by imposing the same requirements on similar plants everywhere they run the risk of regulating too little to meet water quality goals in some areas and more than necessary in others. As a result, some bodies of water fail to improve in quality or to avoid deterioration. Other requirements are strict beyond any rational link to environmental improvements. The unimpressive overall ratio of benefits to expenditures since 1972 and the remaining cases of unarrested decline in water quality strongly suggest that this model of economically inefficient expenditures fits the Clean Water Act. What case studies there are tend to confirm that impression.

Second, even if one assumes that the effluent load that technology-based standards produce for a body of water is somehow the load that best suits water quality, the industry-by-industry method by which these standards are set assures inefficiency in allocating the costs of reaching that pollution level. Only rarely will the costs of restricting pollutant X in industry A to a specified level—as calculated by rule-making immersed in the details of determining the proper technology-based controls for that industry—equal the costs of restricting pollutant X to the level specified by similarly parochial rulemaking for industry B. Whenever those costs differ, the efficiency of pollution control for a given body of water will suffer to the extent that the overall reduction target could be met by substituting low-cost reductions at a plant in one industry for high-cost reductions at a plant in another. For example, if the cost of controlling a unit of pollution is ten percent less at plant A than at plant B, and the environmental benefits are the same, society will save resources if it shifts the burden from plant B to plant A until marginal control costs at the two plants are equal. Here, too, case studies have shown the economic inefficiency of the Clean Water Act. The courts have declined to intervene on such a basis, ruling that cross-industry cost comparisons cannot support a challenge to an effluent standard for a particular industry.

4. *Flexibility Devices.* If EPA has issued a uniform discharge regulation or effluent standard for the pulp and paper industry, under what terms, if any, can Ajax receive a waiver or exception from what it considers to be an overly strict standard? When should the uniform coverage of CWA effluent standards be waived for the benefit of an individual plant like Ajax?

(a) *Codification of FDF Variances.* In 1987 Congress codified EPA's administrative practice of granting FDF variances by adding § 301(n) to the CWA. The provision applied to effluent limitations and pretreatment standards yet is limited in scope. It places the burden of proving the fundamental difference upon the applicant and requires that four substantive elements be established. Section 301(n) [§ 1311(n)] requires the establishment of the following four factors,

(A) the facility is fundamentally different with respect to the factors (other than cost) specified in section 1314(b) or 1314(g) of this title and considered by the Administrator in establishing such national effluent limitation guidelines or categorical pretreatment standards;

(B) the application—

(i) is based solely on information and supporting data submitted to the Administrator during the rule-making for establishment of the applicable national effluent limitation guidelines or categorical pretreatment standard specifically raising the factors that are fundamentally different for such facility; or

(ii) is based on information and supporting data referred to in clause (i) and information and supporting data the applicant did not have a reasonable opportunity to submit during such rulemaking;

(C) the alternative requirement is no less stringent than justified by the fundamental difference; and

(D) the alternative requirement will not result in a nonwater quality environmental impact which is markedly more adverse than the impact considered by the Administrator in establishing such national effluent limitation guideline or categorical pretreatment standard.

The legislative history of this provision indicates a rather narrow sweep in that the FDF variance should be granted "only rarely and only to create a separate standard for a facility so unique that it would have required a separate subcategory had EPA given it adequate attention in the national rulemaking." See Sen. Comm. on Environment & Public Works, Clean Water Act Amendments of 1985, S.Rep. No. 99–50, 99th Cong., 1st Sess. 19 (1985). In litigation this provision has been interpreted to require "plant specific" FDF variance requests to be considered solely in a FDF variance proceeding and not in a review of national rules. See Chemical Mfrs. Ass'n

v. United States EPA, 870 F.2d 177, 221–222 (5th Cir.1989). The CWA provides for a limited number of other flexibility devices in § 301(c) (BAT variance based for toxic pollutants on cost) and § 301(g) (BAT variance for non-conventional pollutants).

(b) *Setting Effluent Standards*. It has been stated that three questions should be addressed on judicial review: first, whether EPA explained the facts and policy concerns relied on; second, whether the facts have some basis in the administrative record; and third, whether these facts and policy considerations could lead a reasonable person to the same judgment reached by the agency. With these factors in mind read the following case excerpt, including its footnotes, and consider how the court dealt with the petitioners complaints about EPA's choice of BAT technology for offshore oil drilling in Alaskan waters.

American Petroleum Institute v. United States EPA

United States Court of Appeals, Fifth Circuit, 1988.
858 F.2d 261.

■ JERRY E. SMITH, CIRCUIT JUDGE:

I.

The American Petroleum Institute (API) and four individual oil companies petition us to invalidate Environmental Protection Agency (EPA) regulations imposing certain restrictions upon oil companies that drill offshore in Alaskan waters. We have previously upheld the criteria under which such permits are issued. API v. EPA, 787 F.2d 965, 975–77 (5th Cir.1986). In that opinion, we ordered the EPA to substantiate further its pill-substitution[1] regulations. In response, EPA has reissued revised substantiation for BAT—level control[2] of diesel oil, effectively requiring drillers

---

1. Normally, thousands of barrels of "mud" lubricate the drilling pipe and bit and carry the drill cuttings to the surface. The industry is usually allowed to dispose of this mud in the surrounding waters. When the pipe becomes stuck, however, additional lubrication is required. In these cases, a "pill" of oil or other additives is circulated down the drilling hole. Pills are made up of mud buffers on either end of a significant amount of diesel oil or mineral oil. These pills may not be discharged into the surrounding waters, and the industry is usually required to dispose of the pill in approved land hazardous materials management sites. This EPA permit for Alaskan waters effectively condemns the entire mud system to on-land disposal if diesel oil is used in the pill. Our prior opinion more expansively described the functions of drilling muds and pills. 787 F.2d at 971.

2. EPA ordinarily regulates conventional pollutants according to best conventional pollutant technology (BCT); the current list of conventional pollutants, 40 C.F.R. § 401.16, does not include any oils. The agency is empowered to use the more stringent best available technology (BAT) economically achievable for pollutants classified as toxic (pursuant to 33 U.S.C. § 1317(a)(1) and currently listed at 40 C.F.R. § 401.15) or as nonconventional (those not defined as toxic or conventional), although the latter are controlled subject to some modifications to the BAT limitations.

The regulations allow EPA to impose the more stringent BAT limitations to control conventional pollutants and to remove the modifications required for nonconventional pollutants, if that pollutant may be characterized under 40 C.F.R. § 125.3(h)(1) as an

to use mineral oil, rather than diesel oil, as a drilling additive to lubricant mud. Finding that EPA has adequately supported its pill-substitution regulations, we uphold the requirements placed upon permittees. Accordingly, API's petition is denied.

II. The Appropriate Method of BAT—Level Control.

Virtually conceding agency authority, API argues that EPA's permit scheme is flawed because, even if diesel oil may be characterized in such a way as to merit BAT treatment, EPA chose an improper method from among the alternative BAT-level technologies. The continuing controversy in this seven-year litigation is whether mineral oil pill-substitution is the appropriate BAT-level technology.

EPA determined that the best available technology for limiting diesel oil discharges is product substitution, so EPA required the industry to use mineral oil instead of diesel oil in the pills it circulates down wellheads being drilled. If industry prefers, it may continue to use diesel oil pills, but must barge the entire mud system for on-land disposal; while API asserts that the barge alternative is not realistic for Alaskan waters, water discharge is allowed so long as no diesel oil has been used in the pills.

API contends that EPA applied the wrong standard in determining that mineral oil was an appropriate product substitute. In arguing its position, API focuses upon which survey data the EPA relied in determining that mineral oil is an appropriate substitute for diesel oil in pills. EPA followed its regulations in ordering the substitution, and its interpretation of the various surveys and choice between indicated outcomes commands great deference.

Indeed, we review deferentially not only EPA's factual evaluations, but also its statutory and regulatory interpretation and application, and its policy determinations. We have previously instructed API and the agency that the restraint we exercise in such administrative review requires us to uphold agency action when it has appropriately enforced its statutory mandate. *API v. EPA,* 661 F.2d at 349 ("[The agency's] decision need not be ideal or even, perhaps, correct so long as not 'arbitrary' or 'capricious' and so long as the agency gave at least minimal consideration to the relevant facts as contained in the record.") Certainly the data is subject to dispute, but we cannot say that EPA's conclusions are unfounded.

API also argues, without citation to authority, that the product substituted must be "operationally equivalent" to diesel oil before EPA may require the substitution. EPA counters that the substitution must be only

"indicator," that is, a carrier of toxic pollutants. EPA found diesel oil to be an indicator pollutant and determined that the "most appropriate means at this time of regulating the toxic pollutants contained in diesel oil is to prohibit the discharge of muds and cuttings contaminated with diesel oil." 51 Fed. Reg. 29,607.

This issue centers on EPA's characterization of diesel oil as an indicator, a ruling that serves as the predicate for the imposition of BAT-level controls on diesel oil discharges. Scientific research indicates, virtually without dissent, that diesel oil is a toxic carrier, and hence appropriately labeled an indicator pollutant. * * *

"technologically and economically achievable." 33 U.S.C. § 1311(b)(2)(A). Our remand to the agency was confined to the diesel-oil provision, and EPA has now developed evidence to meet our concerns.

Upon remand, EPA considered survey data gathered from wells on which diesel oil and mineral oil pills were used and concluded that the substitution met the "achievability" standard. EPA is correct that API is without legal support for its contention that a technology must be widely used in the industry to be considered as an appropriate product substitute. While acknowledging that mineral oil is used for pills less frequently than is diesel oil, EPA argues that it is presently used in some circumstances and demonstrably can be used effectively in the future. Even if mineral oil is not the industry's choice as an additive for lubricant mud, and even if this plausible substitute is only most rarely seen in practice, studies support feasibility (at an added cost); thus, mineral oil replacement for toxic-carrying diesel oil is "technologically and economically achievable."[4]

However, under existing environmental legislation a process is deemed "available" even if it is not in use at all. Association of Pac. Fisheries v. EPA, 615 F.2d 794, 816 (9th Cir.1980) (upholding imposition of BAT burdens based upon a single study of a specific technology, which was not in actual use in any sector of the industry). Such an outcome is consistent

---

4. API argues that the EPA's substitution of mineral oil for diesel oil is improper because EPA inadequately considered the statutory factors required for BAT-level limitations. Before EPA selects BAT-level limitations, it is required to address both (1) operational considerations, including "the process employed, the engineering aspects of the application of various types of control techniques [and] process changes," and (2) cost, including "the cost of achieving such effluent reduction[,] non-water quality, environmental impact [and] energy requirements." 33 U.S.C. § 1314(b)(2)(B).

In arguing this point, API asserts that mineral oil is not as effective as diesel oil for pill usage, indicating that the substitution does not meet operational standards. API estimates that the use of mineral oil pills could add as much as $30 million to the cost of drilling off the Alaskan coast over the next ten years. In addition, API argues that "one to three wells will be needlessly lost if only the Agency's product substitute (i.e., mineral oil) is used."

It is significant that API attacks the EPA's conclusions and the data upon which it is based in asserting that the EPA's action was arbitrary and capricious. EPA based its ruling on various surveys of pill usage in the Gulf of Mexico, and API disputes the agency's interpretation of that data. Neither the mineral oil evaluation nor EPA's rejection of (allegedly less costly) alternate or additional treatment processes are open for our reconsideration; as long as the policy choices reached are supported in the scientific record, we cannot second-guess the agency's decision. We note, however, that EPA's data and factfinding explicitly addressed the problem that "existing pill recovery techniques have not been shown to be effective in reducing the diesel oil content and toxicity of discharged muds."

* * *

Finally, the parties dispute whether EPA is required to compare the cost of effluent reduction with the degree of pollutant removal. API asserts that EPA is under a duty to make a reasonable determination with regard to cost effectiveness, but, as is further discussed below, EPA is not required to show a direct cost/benefit correlation, but only that a beneficial substitution is "technologically and economically achievable." 33 U.S.C. § 1311(b)(2)(A).

EPA thoroughly documented its factfinding and clearly followed its regulations and the Clean Water Act when redrafting these permits. The evidence amply supports the agency's factual determinations.

with Congress' intent to "push pollution control technology." *Weyerhauser,* 590 F.2d at 1061.

One further concern motivated our inquiry here: API's repeated argument that toxic-carrying diesel pills pose no environmental threat when discharged in the relatively small volumes of mud typical of Alaskan operations.[5] However, the Clean Water Act permits blanket prohibitions and other "stringent pollution restrictions" to be imposed "even where the discharge caused no discernible harm to the environment." *API v. EPA,* 661 F.2d at 344. Accord, Hooker Chem. & Plastics Corp. v. Train, 537 F.2d 620, 622 (2d Cir.1976).

"Analogous to a strict liability standard," *API v. EPA,* 661 F.2d at 344, BAT limitations properly may require industry, regardless of a discharge's effect on water quality, to employ defined levels of technology to meet effluent limitations; a direct cost/benefit correlation is not required, so even minimal environmental impact can be regulated, so long as the prescribed alternative is "technologically and economically achievable." 4 Leg. History of the Clean Water Act of 1977: A Continuation of the Leg. History of the Fed. Water Pollution Control Act, 95th Cong., 2d Sess. 1469–70 (1978). * * *

IV. Conclusion

EPA has amply supported its permit requirements, and we accordingly uphold the pill-substitution regulation. API's petition is DENIED.

NOTES AND QUESTIONS

1. *Judicial Review of Effluent Standards.* If EPA issued an effluent standard applicable to the Ajax facility, how could CCC challenge this regulation in court? Could Ajax challenge it as well? On what basis could a court invalidate EPA's effluent standard?

Effluent limitations promulgated by EPA are subject to pre-enforcement judicial review by any "interested person" in the U.S. Court of Appeals. § 509(b)(1) [§ 1369(b)(1)]. If the application for review is filed within 120 days of the final rulemaking, the CWA makes jurisdiction available where the petitioner resides or does business. Consequently, the

---

5. Citing 40 years in which diesel oil has been discharged "without environmental damage" to the Outer Continental Shelf, API argues that "the discharge of approximately 24 barrels of diesel oil per year [into] the general permit areas encompass[ing] thousands of square miles of open ocean ... will be avoided at an annual cost of nearly $6,000,000.00"; this "infinitesimal" impact at a "monumental" cost is indicative of Region 10's administrators' "perverse" and "obsessive" disregard of correct agency decisionmaking in order to ban effluents with *de minimis* environmental harm and proves that "this limitation is not based upon any adverse impact to the receiving water." Under BCT-level control, EPA is not allowed to impose "treatment for treatment's sake [but must consider] 'the reasonableness of the relationship between the costs of attaining a reduction in effluents and the effluent reduction benefits derived.' " *API v. EPA,* 787 F.2d at 976 (quoting 33 U.S.C. § 1314(b)(4)(B)). However, BAT-level limitations are not subject to such a strict cost/benefit correlation.

case reports of these rulemaking challenges come from many different circuits. Judicial review of the agency's action in issuing the effluent standard is prohibited at the civil or criminal enforcement stage. If two or more plaintiffs challenge the same EPA standard in different circuits, the Act provides for proper venue to be selected through a random selection procedure carried out by the Administrative Office of the United States Courts. § 509(b)(3) [§ 1369(b)(3)].

2.   *The Finality of CWA Rulemaking.* EPA's responsibility for the development of industry-specific water discharge regulations is substantial and consuming a great deal of agency resources. Once an effluent standard for a particular industry group is issued in final form, it has received much analysis and criticism from non-EPA participants in the rulemaking process. As the material in this section also indicates, the final promulgation of the EPA regulation opens the possibility for continued external critique of both the process and substance of the EPA effluent standard in court. Judicial review of agency decisionmaking is a longstanding part of modern administrative law. However, consider the function of the effluent standard within the overall CWA scheme of water quality protection and improvement. These regulations must be used by EPA and state agencies to control point source discharges by statutory deadlines. Should judicial review of these EPA rules be available indefinitely?

Congress in § 509 provided a limited "window" of opportunity for judicial review of CWA regulations. What if no challenge to an EPA effluent standard was brought within the time limits established in § 509? Could they be subsequently attacked in a lawsuit challenging the rulemaking effort? Why would Congress wish to limit judicial review so severely? Do you agree with this policy in general? Consider the implications of such a policy in the following problem.

● Plouf Electroplating Hypothetical

Assume that the process wastewater that Plouf Electroplating Company (Plouf) has discharged into municipal sewers connected to a POTW contained various levels of cyanide, chromium, copper, lead, cadmium, nickel, and zinc in excess of those permitted under EPA's § 307(b) pretreatment standards. EPA learns of this and in a subsequent federal enforcement action filed in U.S. District Court alleging criminal violations of the CWA under § 309(c)(1) & (2), could Plouf and its president Toni Robinson move to dismiss the indictment due to the alleged unlawfulness of the existing electroplating pretreatment regulations? If these regulations had been promulgated several years before the Plouf indictment, could the trial judge consider the defendant's arguments? See United States v. Alley, 755 F.Supp. 771 (N.D.Ill.1990). Read CWA § 509(b)(2) [§ 1369(b)(2)]. Recognizing the need for regulatory finality, could it be argued that § 509(b)(2) is unconstitutional as applied to this case?

3.   *The Impact of Rulemaking Review on the Courts.* While EPA must consider the development of effluent standards for large and complex industry groups an enormously difficult and time-consuming undertaking, courts which review these extensive rules must also commit enormous

judicial resources in their work. In Chemical Manufacturers Ass'n v. U.S. EPA, 870 F.2d 177 (5th Cir.1989), the court considered challenges to EPA's effluent standards for the organic chemical, plastics, and synthetic fibers industries and issued a 90 page opinion. As a preface to upholding most of the regulations, the court noted the following comment about nature of the task before it.

> The case is of such complexity that the parties have submitted briefs totalling more than 3,000 pages and a joint appendix 9,000 pages long distilled from a 600,000–page administrative record. To enable us to render a decision as promptly as possible, the members of the panel have divided responsibility for preparing portions of this opinion, as the District of Columbia Circuit did in *Alabama Power Co. v. Costle.* Judge Garza prepared sections V, VI, and VII of this opinion, as well as all portions discussing issues raised by the NRDC; Judge Rubin prepared sections I and III; and Judge King prepared sections II and IV, except for those portions discussing issues raised by the NRDC.

Is this the best way to develop complex, technological rules? Is judicial review of such regulations a waste of scarce resources? Are judges capable of reviewing these complex technically-based choices? What factors in a rulemaking would you consider most important if you were the judge?

4. *Publicly Owned Treatment Works (POTWs) and Effluent Limitations.* (a) *Treatment Standards.* What pollution control requirements does the Clean Water Act impose upon a source such as a municipal sewage treatment plant? Are governmental sewage treatment facilities even subject to the CWA?

As the introductory material indicates, POTWs or municipal sewage treatment plants continue to be a major water pollution source into the 21st Century. Under § 301(b)(1)(B) of the 1972 Act, publicly owned treatment works (POTWs) were to have attained effluent limits of "secondary treatment" by July 1, 1977. Following the pattern of the two-step regulation of industrial sources, the Act specified a more advanced level of POTW control entitled "best practicable control technology over the life of the works" which was to be attained by 1983. In 1981 Congress repealed this latter technology standard and its associated deadline thereby leaving the imposition of more stringent POTW controls to the states.

Municipal waste water treatment plants are often said to provide either primary or secondary treatment of the sewage effluent. Primary treatment, developed during the late Nineteenth Century, collects sewage in tanks called digesters, applies bacteria to destroy the organic matter, settles solids into a sludge, and releases the chlorine treated liquid into a body of receiving water. Secondary treatment uses more specialized biological or physical/chemical treatment to remove additional organic matter. EPA has defined "secondary treatment" in its regulations as effluent quality meeting minimum standards for biochemical oxygen demand, suspended solids, and Ph. See 40 C.F.R. § 133.102. These control levels can be met by biological and chemical/physical treatment methods with examples of the former being oxidation ponds, lagoons, ditches and trickling filters.

See § 304(d)(4) [1314(d)(4)]. Section 301(i) [§ 1311(i)] allowed municipalities to receive time extensions for the attainment of secondary treatment up until July 31, 1988.

Are there instances in which the across-the-board secondary treatment requirement for municipal dischargers is not enough? Occasionally such higher removal standards are imposed in order to achieve state water quality standards. Tertiary or so-called advanced secondary treatment techniques can be used to remove nutrients like nitrogen and phosphorus. They can also be used to provide further reduction of suspended solids and biochemical oxygen demand. Such techniques are very expensive, however, and special federal funding was provided for up to 85% of the construction costs for innovative or alternative technology. See § 202(a)(2) & (3) [§ 1282(a)(2) & (3)].

(b) *Water Pollution Control Subsidy: Federal Grants for the Construction of Treatment Works.* The CWA is not only a regulatory statute but it has also been a vehicle for providing substantial federal financial subsidies for the planning and construction of local government treatment works. Through the "construction grants" program authorized by Title II of the 1972 Act, §§ 1281–1297, EPA has transferred more than $45 billion dollars in grants to state, regional and local governments for POTW construction and renovation. Structured as a cost sharing program, the federal government initially provided 75% of the cost of planning and constructing new wastewater treatment facilities. During the 1970s and 1980 the CWA construction grants program ranked only second to the highway building program of the Department of Transportation in dollar volume. This program did more than fund the building of sewage treatment plants in that it funded Correction of Infiltration/Inflow, Major Rehabilitation of Sewers, New Collector Sewers, New Interceptor Sewers, Control of Combined Sewer Overflow, Treatment and/or Control of Storm Water. All in all, public funding from all sources for treatment works represented an investment of approximately $128 billion over the last 30 years. Why would the CWA adopt this subsidy policy only for publicly owned sewage treatment works and not for private facilities? Is this a wise policy?

With its 1987 amendments to the CWA, Congress ended the federal construction grants program as of 1990 and substituted for it the federal capitalization of a water pollution control revolving loan fund. Today, these funds have a total asset value of more than $34 billion and it has resulted in over 9,500 low interest loans for water pollution control projects. Funds to establish or capitalize the state revolving funds are to be provided jointly by the federal (83%) and state (17%) governments. See §§ 601–07 [§§ 1881–87.] States would be awarded federal grants to capitalize state water pollution control revolving funds (SRFs) which could make low-cost loans for three purposes: (1) the construction of waste water treatment facilities, (2) the implementation of non-point source management programs, and (3) the development and implementation of estuary conservation and management plans. SRFs would not make direct grants to recipients but rather they would lend money for up to 20 years. As these funds were repaid, the SRF would be replenished and more loans could then be made. The SRF program provides the states with a great deal more flexibility in helping to finance water pollution improvements; much more so than under the prior categorized grants program.

(c) *POTWs and Indirect Dischargers.* The discussion of effluent standards to this point has been primarily concerned with the designing of pollution controls for an industrial facility discharging pollutants into a body of water. However, it must be remembered that the second most significant point source category is that of POTWs. These treatment plants are commonly and mistakenly believed to process and purify only domestic effluents. POTWs serve an additional function of receiving and treating industrial wastes piped to them from factories and other production facilities. EPA has estimated that more than 60,000 industrial plants in 34 primary industrial groups discharge into POTWs. These effluent generators have been termed "indirect dischargers" since their wastes are not literally sent to rivers or streams by them. Why would an industrial source prefer to be an indirect rather than a direct discharger? EPA has adopted nationally applicable pretreatment standards for indirect discharges which track the effluent standards set by the agency for direct dischargers under §§ 310 and 304. These technology-based numerical limits apply in the same uniform fashion as do the BAT, BPT, and new source effluent standards. Accordingly, pretreatment standards are set for both new and existing sources.

SECTION 3. NONPOINT SOURCE POLLUTION

A. BACKGROUND AND OVERVIEW

In 1987, the Clean Water Act was amended to place new emphasis on control of nonpoint source [NPS] pollution as one of the primary goals of the Act. Section 101(a)(7) [33 U.S.C. § 1251(a)(7)] states:

> [I]t is the national policy that programs for the control of nonpoint sources of pollution be developed and implemented in an expeditious manner so as to enable the goals of this Act to be met through the control of both point and nonpoint sources of pollution.

To effectuate this policy, in 1987 Congress enacted CWA § 319 [33 U.S.C. § 1329], requiring each state to assess the impact of NPS pollution on its waters and to develop and submit to EPA a comprehensive management plan to control NPS pollution. Furthermore, the 1987 amendments authorized grant funds for the states and EPA to address NPS pollution and, under section § 304(k)(1), required that EPA enter into agreements with other federal agencies to ensure maximum utilization of federal programs to control NPS pollution.

Legislation enacted prior to the 1987 CWA amendments for the purpose of controlling pollution of the nation's waters reflected the two basic approaches mentioned before: water quality-based control and technology-based control. However, by 1987 it was apparent that technology based point source controls would not be enough to reach the CWA's water quality goals. The § 208 nonpoint source program adopted in 1972 had largely generated studies and reports yet little observable progress on the NPS problem. The generally accepted reasons were: the diffuse nature of NPS pollution, the difficulty in establishing NPS source to water connections and limited data about background or baseline water conditions to measure impacts. NPS pollution was recognized as an important contributor to water quality problem yet its control would affect a number of major economic and governmental interests: agriculture, forestry, mining, land development, and local government. Rather than take a prescriptive or command and control approach, Congress, with § 319, decided to use financial support as the "honey" to trigger effective state and local government responses. Section 319 bore a familiar structure to another 1987 CWA amendment—§ 304(*l*)—which concentrated on the accelerated cleanup of "toxic hot spots." Its architecture focused on the states and it had the following form:

1) § 319(a)(1)(A) identification of waters harmed by NPS pollution

2) § 319(a)(1)(B) identification of NP Sources affecting those waters

3) § 319(a)(1)(C) identification of management practices applicable to NP Sources

4) § 319(a)(1)(D) preparation of a management program to be approved by EPA

The planning process was open by design and it could include a range of methods including permit-based regulation, demonstration projects, education and program funding support. What was lacking? Section 319 did not contain specific performance objectives with specified attainment dates. There was nothing really mandatory about the § 319 program. Also, EPA oversight authority was quite limited; it could not mandate or take over the planning or management program process. Its authority was restricted to steps 1 & 2 only. Not surprisingly, the § 319 program has produced little in the way of concrete results as evidenced by the prominence of NPS pollution on EPA's recent water inventories. See David Zaring, *Agriculture, Nonpoint Source Pollution, and Regulatory Control: The Clean Water Act's Bleak Present and Future*, 20 HARV. ENVTL. L. REV. 515 (1996) (highly critical description of state NPS programs). The future of water quality improvement will depend upon greater NPS pollution prevention. Who should decide? What techniques should be employed? What does recent history tell us? Is this more a technical or political problem?

CLASS DISCUSSION PROBLEM: RESPONDING TO NONPOINT SOURCE POLLUTION

In compliance with the requirements of the Clean Water Act § 319, the state government has designated its Department of Environmental Protection (DEP) as the lead agency for NPS planning and management. In its initial assessment of sources of NPS pollution in the Centralia watershed, DEP has identified the following primary sources:

(1) *Storm water discharges associated with industrial activity and from the separate municipal storm sewer system.* Given the already existing NPS pollution from these sources, DEP water quality administrators are concerned about the potential negative impact on local water quality of the continued development in the northern sector of the city, which is characterized by relatively impermeable soils and steep slopes.

(2) *Both nitrogen and phosphorus, emanating principally from various agricultural activities.* Early spring runoff moves large amounts of phosphorus into the East River, followed a few weeks later by nitrogen carried by high base flows in the River. These high nutrient levels have accelerated eutrophication of the River, by which process high levels of these artificially introduced nutrients increase the growth of vegetation in the river. In addition, nitrate concentrations exceed the drinking water criterion for a significant portion of the year.

(3) *Bacterial contaminants from upstream dairy farming operations.* Small creeks running through the properties of several large dairy farms flow into a small estuary that is the source of crabs and oysters for the surrounding communities. The shellfishing industry has an economic impact from one to two million dollars annually. Shellfishing has recently been threatened with unexpected closure due to excessive fecal coliform bacteria levels in the growing waters, and suspended sediments in the streams and the estuary are increasing. Affected along with the commercial oyster industry are recreational fishing, boating, and numerous other activities traditionally enjoyed by the surrounding communities and attracting substantial numbers of tourists each year.

You are a regional administrator for the state DEP charged with developing that portion of the state NPS management plan which concerns the Centralia watershed. In your initial planning efforts, you should address yourself to the following questions:

1. To what extent could or are the foregoing sources of pollution defined as being point sources of pollution, subject to the requirements of the NPDES program? What interaction between point source regulation and control of nonpoint sources is envisioned by the Clean Water Act?

2. What process does EPA use for review of state NPS plans? What elements must the plan include, and what ongoing requirements exist for plan implementation? What procedures must DEP follow if the state plan is not approved? What regulations has EPA promulgated under the authority of the Clean Water Act that provide guidance to the states on NPS control planning and implementation?

3. What enforcement mechanisms are available under the Clean Water Act or other Federal or state legislation for the control of NPS pollution? How should nonpoint source pollution be controlled?

B. NONPOINT SOURCE WATER POLLUTION—DEFINITIONS AND SOLUTIONS

1. DEFINING NONPOINT SOURCE POLLUTION

In simple terms, nonpoint sources of pollution are any sources not included in the definition of point sources. Point sources are defined by CWA § 502(14) [33 U.S.C. § 1362(14)] as follows:

> The term "point source" means any discernible, confined and discrete conveyance, including but not limited to any pipe, ditch, channel, tunnel, conduit, well, discrete fissure, container, rolling stock, concentrated animal feeding operation, or vessel or other floating craft, from which pollutants are or may be discharged. This term does not include agricultural stormwater discharges and return flows from irrigated agriculture.

In practical terms, NPS pollution does not result from a discharge at a specific, single location (with the exception of agricultural stormwater discharges and irrigation return flows). Rather, it generally results from land runoff, precipitation, snowmelt, atmospheric deposition, drainage, or seepage. When viewed together, point and nonpoint sources of pollution should be considered to encompass all sources of surface water pollution. This is the approach reflected by the TMDL analytical and regulatory process.

The decision whether a given source of pollution is a point source, subject to the requirements of the NPDES permitting program, or a nonpoint source is fact-specific, and has often been decided in a litigation context. Two recent case decisions illustrate the legal significance of the point source/nonpoint source dichotomy.

● Concerned Area Residents for the Environment v. Southview Farm, 34 F.3d 114 (2d Cir.1994).

In this CWA citizen suit, plaintiffs challenged the liquid manure spreading operations of a large dairy farm in western New York as being a point source under the statute. In concluding that Southview Farm was a point source within the meaning of the CWA the appeals court described the pollution emanating from the 1,100 acre and 2,200 animal dairy farm in the following terms.

> Unlike old-fashioned dairy farms, Southview's operations do not involve pasturing the cows. Instead, the cows remain in their barns except during the three times per day milking procedure. Also unlike old-fashioned dairy farms where the accumulated manure was spread by a manure spreader, Southview's rather enormous manure operations are largely performed through the use of storage lagoons and liquid cow manure. The storage lagoons number five on the main farm property ("A Farm"). One four-acre manure storage lagoon has a capacity of approximately six-to-eight million gallons of liquid cow manure.

In connection with this particular manure storage lagoon, South-view has installed a separator which pumps the cow manure over a mechanical device which drains off the liquid and passes the solids out through a compressing process. The solids that remain are dropped into bins for transport while the liquid runs by gravity through a pipe to the four-acre manure storage lagoon. This separated liquid was apparently used for the purpose of washing down the barns where the cows are housed.

Insofar as application of the manure as fertilizer to the land is concerned, there is a center pivot irrigation system for spreading liquid manure over the fields. The diameter of the circle of this irrigation system can be modified to conform to the field on which the application is being made. A series of pipes connects the pivot to the liquid manure storage lagoons. The pivot is self-propelled with the height of the arc from the manure spray being somewhere between 12 and 60 feet.

Southview also spreads its manure with a hard hose traveler which is a long piece of plastic tubing on a large reel. The traveler can be unwound and has a nozzle on the end which can send liquid manure 150 feet in either direction making a 300–foot-wide swath for the purposes of fertilizing farm fields. The height of the arc from the projected spray is "a couple of feet higher" than that of the center pivot irrigator. Since 1988, a piping system consisting of a six-inch aluminum pipe and running under both the state highway and a town road to a lagoon on at least one Southview Farm other than the "A Farm," has transported liquid manure from the storage lagoon to various locations without the use of vehicles.

Southview also uses conventional manure spreading equipment including spreaders pulled by tractors and self-propelled vehicles which, generally speaking, have a 5,000 gallon capacity for liquid manure. These vehicles were used to spread manure from the smaller lagoons on the "A Farm" which do not receive liquid manure processed through the separation system. Southview's manure spreading record reflects the application of millions of gallons of manure to its fields.

34 F.3d at 116. Once determined to be a "point source," permitting and enforcement implications follow.

• Washington Wilderness Coalition v. Hecla Mining Co., 870 F.Supp. 983 (E.D.Wash.1994).

In a similar CWA citizen suit, plaintiff claims that chemicals and heavy metals, which are gold and silver mining waste products, seep through tailings ponds up to 38 acres in size and pollute the ground and surface waters. As such, plaintiff asserted that the tailings ponds were point sources under the CWA and that the Act was enforceable against them. In resolving this issue in the plaintiff's favor, the court struggled with the point source/nonpoint source distinction drawing the following conclusion.

Hecla argues that its tailings ponds are not point sources, but merely "areas of low topography into which mine tailing from mineral processing activities have been deposited and through which water may percolate.'' Noting that a point source is usually a pipe or a ditch, Hecla points out that here we are dealing with a 38 acre man-made pond.

Initially, it is clear that the size of the pond is not relevant to determining whether or not it is a point source. As plaintiff explains, it would be irrational to conclude that the bigger the source of pollution, the less likely it is to be a "source" under the CWA. Cases cited by defendants support the conclusion that man-made ponds, designed to receive tailings, are "conveyances" or "containers" under the definitions in the Clean Water Act. See United States v. Earth Sciences, Inc., 599 F.2d 368, 370 (10th Cir.1979). See also, Committee to Save Mokelumne River v. East Bay Mun. Util. Dist., 13 F.3d 305, 308 (9th Cir.1993) (holding that an NPDES permit is required for "surface runoff that is collected or channeled" into a Mine Run Dam Reservoir).

These cases make clear that the touchstone for finding a point source is the ability to identify a discrete facility from which pollutants have escaped. Particularly persuasive is the reasoning of the Earth Sciences court, adopted by the Ninth Circuit in Trustees for Alaska, 599 F.2d at 370. There, the court noted that "point source" must be interpreted broadly to effectuate the remedial purposes of the CWA. The non-point source designation is limited to uncollected runoff water from, for example, oil and gasoline on a highway, which is difficult to ascribe to a single polluter. Discharges from a pond or refuse pile can easily be traced to their source. Thus, even though runoff may be caused by rainfall or snow melt percolating through a pond or refuse pile, the discharge is from a point source because the pond or pile acts to collect and channel contaminated water.

870 F.Supp. at 989. Significantly, the court also concluded that the mining leachate was a pollutant discharged into "navigable waters" since that term encompassed discharges proved to have migrated through groundwater and ultimately reaching surface waters. *Id.* at 990. Consequently, § 402 NPDES permits would be required and citizen suits could be brought. Cases such as these demonstrate the fuzziness in the distinction between point and nonpoint sources and ultimately the arbitrariness inherent in the CWA system of water pollution control.

2.   THE NATURE OF NPS POLLUTION

Nonpoint sources of pollution result from natural causes, human action, and the interactions between natural events and conditions associated with human use of the land and its resources. The degree to which NPS pollution impacts water quality often depends on a complex interaction of factors. For example, in the case of runoff of agricultural chemicals, the amount of chemicals contributed to local surface waters will depend on intensity and duration of rainfall or snowmelt, length of time between application of chemicals to fields and rainfall occurrence, soil permeability, type and amount of land cover and tillage practices, percent slope of the land, properties of the chemicals, and the methods of chemical application. Control of NPS pollution, therefore, is by necessity a site-specific undertaking.

Some changes in water quality which result from human action may be beneficial. An example would be a moderate temperature increase in a stream cooler than the optimum, which could increase productivity and have a beneficial effect on the aquatic environment. Most changes in water quality due to human practices, however, are not beneficial. Although agriculture is the most pervasive cause of nonpoint source water quality problems, other land uses also contribute to NPS water pollution. Forestry, mining, livestock production, and urban development have all been identified as causing NPS; depending on local land uses, any of these might be the primary source of water quality problems in a given watershed. Consider the comments of the former EPA Administrator William K. Reilly regarding his perception of why it is so difficult to limit nonpoint source water pollution. Then, compare the following excerpt by Professor Oliver A. Houck with Reilly's thesis.

William K. Reilly, The Issues and the Policy: View From EPA

17 EPA Journal 20 (November/December 1991).

These alarming statistics [about nonpoint source pollution] share a common denominator: They are all examples of nonpoint-source pollution—pollution that does not come from distinct, identifiable "point" sources (such as a sewage treatment or industrial plant discharge pipe). Nonpoint-source pollution is runoff from rainwater or snow melt that picks up along the way soil, animal wastes, fertilizers, pesticides, used oil, toxic substances, and street debris. It comes from farms, cities, forests, mining operations, and construction sites. And it carries contaminants into nearby surface or underground waterways—sometimes washing directly into lakes and streams, sometimes entering storm and sanitary sewer systems, where from EPA's regulatory perspective it becomes a point source. However it reaches our waterways, it originates, nonetheless, as nonpoint-source pollution. And almost always, it is subtle, it is diffuse, it is difficult to visualize.

Unlike drama scenes from an earlier era of belching smokestacks spewing black clouds skyward or sewer pipes disgorging viscous, green ooze seaward, nonpoint-source pollution conjures up no vivid images in the mind's eye. Unlike the mere mention of oil spills or beach closings or toxic waste dumps, nonpoint-source pollution fails to inflame or incite to action. Yet this "pointless" pollution is one of the most serious remaining threats to our nation's water quality—and its cumulative effects from many small sources and individual actions are visible and disturbing: algal blooms that choke lakes and aquatic life, fish kills, fishing bans, silt-covered spawning habitat along riverbeds.

A preview of EPA's *1990 National Water Quality Report to Congress* shows that nonpoint-source pollution is the main reason lakes and rivers fail to meet clean water standards for fishing, swimming, and drinking. Agricultural runoff was by far the most extensive source of pollution, responsible for impairing about 60 percent of the degraded rivers and a like percentage of degraded lakes studied. Extraction activities, along with dams, levees, and other hydrologic modifications were also significant contributors, as were storm sewers and urban runoff.

Clearly, the problem is enormous. Yet because this type of pollution is so hard to pinpoint and because almost everybody contributes to the problem, it largely defies traditional command-and-control regulatory approaches that have brought so much success in curbing pollution from specific plants or pipes over the past 20 years.

Incidentally, let me underscore the significant progress we have made in this area—progress that has revealed the previously obscured threat of nonpoint-source pollution. Since 1972, the federal government has spent over $50 billion to upgrade and construct municipal sewage treatment plants. By 1988, EPA reported that almost 90 percent of all municipal sewage treatment plants and a slightly higher percentage of major industrial facilities met federal and state water pollution control requirements.

With the exception of EPA's programs to control pollution from urban and industrial stormwater pipes and from combined sanitary/stormwater overflows through more traditional permitting programs, tackling nonpoint-source pollution poses different challenges and requires new solutions.

I see three hurdles ahead in curbing nonpoint source pollution.

First, a national regulatory program similar to that to control point sources simply won't work. The challenge is, in part, one of promoting changes in longstanding habits and practices—at home, at work, in our communities, on farms, in mining, forestry, and construction operations. Education is key to influencing changes in lifestyles and behaviors to prevent this type of pollution. Nonpoint-source pollution is everyone's problem. It is the responsibility of farms to grow their crops and graze their animals in ways that protect nearby streams and ground water. It is the responsibility of those who harvest timber to do so in ways that prevent soil runoff. It is the responsibility of backyard mechanics to take used motor oil to collection or recycling centers. It's the responsibility of homeowners to apply lawn care chemicals and fertilizers carefully and safely if and when needed. It's the responsibility of car owners to keep their vehicles maintained so they don't leak oil or grease onto the roadway.

Farmers and other landowners, in particular, are understandably wary of intrusive government programs. No effective solutions will work without the whole-hearted involvement of farmers, whose stake in conservation is greater than that of virtually all others, whose very livelihood depends on productive soils and healthy natural systems. Their trust, and their interests, need to be protected.

Second, addressing nonpoint-source pollution effectively may require attention to land use planning. States and localities often find they can't protect water quality without planning for protection of their watersheds—and that means planning for growth. That, of course, is properly a matter for state and local governments, not the federal government. We at the federal level can provide information on how various communities have successfully addressed these challenges—accommodating growth and development in a manner that protects valuable wetlands and habitats and avoids creating nonpoint-source pollution that threatens the health of aquatic ecosystems.

Local enforcement officials need to be alert to prevent runoff from construction sites and ensure that homes and businesses don't unlawfully connect sanitary sewer lines to systems designed to collect only stormwater. State and local governments can require catch basins, buffer strips, and other management practices. The federal government has the responsibility to provide basic scientific information, incentives, technical expertise, and limited funding to state governments to develop effective programs. Research, information, education, technical assistance—all are reasonable federal rules. But it is local building and land use decisions more than anything else that will help cut nonpoint-source pollution.

Third, in some instances—like our incipient efforts to regulate urban stormwater—the costs to control nonpoint-source pollution through traditional approaches are potentially enormous: tens of billions of dollars. I might add that on the stormwater permitting front, the Agency is hearing from states, municipalities, and industries alarmed at the cost and complexity of implementing statutory requirements to regulate stormwater as a point source. With all the concurrent demands on local governments for an entire array of environmental improvements, not to mention other worthy needs, financing nonpoint-source controls is a real challenge.

Oliver A. Houck, The Clean Water Act TMDL Program: Law, Policy, and Implementation 87–94 (1999)

(Footnotes omitted).

From Nonpoint to Point Source Regulation. The great axiom of the CWA is that point sources are strictly regulated while nonpoint sources, in the delicate phrase of one commentator [Professor William H. Rodgers], are "immune from important features of the Act" such as effluent standards, permits, and enforcement (i.e., those features that have made the NPDES program work). The history of nonpoint source pollution control since 1972 is of an attempt, to date largely unsuccessful, to find replacements for these features through voluntary, local programs. The rationales offered for treating nonpoint sources separately under the Act include

(1) the alleged "number and variety of nonpoint sources";

(2) the "site-specific nature" of the pollution; and

(3) the "lack of known control technologies."

One reflection, none of these reasons are terribly convincing, because

(1) we have a great number and variety of point sources as well (several hundred major industrial categories to the setting of technology-based guidelines); and

(2) each industrial discharge, too, has site-specific effects on its receiving water (effects that are irrelevant to the setting of technology-based guidelines); and

(3) the control technologies for nonpoint pollution (e.g., shelter-belts, nutrient caps, retention ponds) are anything but unknown, complex, technologically difficult, or even very costly.

In truth, we do not avoid regulating nonpoint source pollution because are unable to figure out how to do it. Rather, we have deferred to the myth that its impacts are essentially local and of secondary importance, as we have deferred to legislatures dominated by rural constituencies unaccustomed to any regulation and ready to fight. Recently—albeit with glacial slowness—both the myth and the dominance have begun to melt, reopening the question of nonpoint source controls. One answer to the problem is simply to treat a greater number of dischargers as point sources, bringing them into the operational features of the Act.

EPA and Congress have been wrestling with the application of the NPDES program to agriculture, silviculture, and land-based pollution since the adoption of the Act in its modern form. In 1973, the Agency adopted a definition of point sources that included runoff collected or channeled virtually in any way, but then proceeded to exempt discharges from all silviculture, all urban storm sewers, and all but the largest agricultural operations. These exemptions were immediately challenged by a citizen suit and rejected by both the federal district and appellate courts of the District of Columbia. Facing EPA arguments—similar to those noted above—that nonpoint sources were too numerous, diffuse, and difficult to regulate, these courts suggested the use of alternative permit conditions and general permits, and concluded with the inspiration that "[i]magination conjoined with determination will likely give EPA capability for practical administration. If not the remedy lies with Congress."

Congress did not wait to see. Firmly held by the myth that nonpoint source pollution was a local affair, Congress amended the Act in 1977 specifically to exclude irrigated agriculture from point source regulation, and in 1987 went further to exempt all agricultural stormwater discharges. As a result, with the exception of concentrated animal feedlots, agricultural pollution was exempted from the Act even when it came from and through discrete collection systems. The scope of this exemption went largely unchallenged until 1994 when the Second Circuit ruled in *Concerned Area Residents for the Environment v. Southview Farm*, that a large dairy farm, in its entirety, was a point source under the CWA. The court reasoned in the alternative that the machines that spread manure on the farm, and the drainage system conveying these wastes to navigable waters, were point sources as well. This ruling contained the seeds of reclassifying a great deal of mechanized agriculture as point sources, an invitation that EPA has not yet accepted.

Instead, under the impetus of other CWA amendments in 1987 [CWA § 304(m)], EPA has proposed to develop standards for a number of diffuse sources. The most important of these proposals, from the standpoint of abating serious pollution, involve animal feeding operations (AFOs) and municipal storm sewers. Each of these programs could serve to take considerable weight off of remaining nonpoint programs and could give the TMDL approach for polluted waters the additional leverage that comes from the availability of point source—like permits and standards.

[Professor Houck then discussed EPA's efforts during the late 1990's to expand NPDES permitting with effluent guidelines for concentrated animal feeding operations (CAFOs), an industry he found to be previously regulated in an "underinclusive and ineffective" way. This new approach would eventually go into effect because water-quality based controls never were imposed, even though authorized. He concluded that this pattern "says something about the ability of states to control local industry and the ability of states to control local industry and the ability of anyone to control discharges by water quality standards. When things got serious, we turned once again to more extensive BAT." On the second issue of urban storm water runoff he said,

> EPA has approached storm water regulation with the same aware-ness-cum-trepidation that it has agriculture, and for many of the same reasons. The Agency faces cash-strapped municipalities without either the threat of injunction which it holds over industrial sources or the leverage of funding it provides for municipal sewage treatment. Storm water remedies, further, while often obvious and available, smack of the kind of land use control of which no federal agency dares stand accused. On the other hand, urban runoff is major pollution, in coastal areas it is the *dominant* source of water pollution, and it is discharged for the most part through pipes, drains, and other discrete conveyances (i.e. point sources under the CWA).]

NOTES AND QUESTIONS

1. *The Section 319 NPS Planning Process.* What process does EPA use for review of state NPS assessment reports and implementation plans? What elements must the plan include, and what ongoing requirements exist for plan implementation? What procedures must DEP follow if the state plan is not approved? What regulations has EPA promulgated under the authority of the Clean Water Act that provide guidance to the states on NPS planning and implementation?

The required elements of state NPS assessment reports and implementation plans are detailed in CWA § 319(a) and (b). The states must submit both components for EPA approval. Once approval is obtained, the state is then eligible for § 319 grant monies. Section 319(h)(8) requires "satisfactory progress" in implementing the proposed management plan in a given fiscal year before subsequent grants can be made to a state under § 319. Assessment reports are to be submitted before or concurrently with the State Management Program. The criteria developed by EPA for use in evaluating a State's Assessment Report largely track the statutory requirements of § 319.

EPA guidance for the development of State Management Programs indicates that, to the maximum extent practicable, the programs should be developed on a watershed-by-watershed basis. In planning management strategies, the states are not to consider land ownership (Federal/State/local/private). In addition, the states are expected to develop statewide program approaches to address various types of nonpoint sources. The criteria for approval of State Management Programs also parallel the statutory requirements imposed by § 319. After notice and opportunity for public comment and consultation with appropriate Federal and state agencies and other interested persons, an EPA Regional Administrator may disapprove a state's assessment report and/or management program. If a report or program is disapproved, EPA must within 180 days of receiving the proposed report or program notify the state of any revisions or modifications necessary to obtain approval. The state is then allowed three months to revise its submittal. Criteria for disapproval are specified in CWA § 319(d)(2).

Complying with the terms of § 319 does not exhaust a state's planning responsibilities. Other provisions of the CWA also contain planning requirements, and various federal regulations provide guidance pertinent to the NPS planning and implementation process. See CWA § 106, 205, 208, 303(e), 304(f), 305(b) and 40 C.F.R. § 130.6(c)(4)(ii) [mandating regulatory programs for the control of NPS where non-regulatory programs are inadequate or inappropriate] and § 130.6(c)(4)(iii) [requiring that BMPs be identified for nonpoint sources], among others. A Special Coastal NPS Control Program has been required of the 29 coastal states under § 6217 of the Coastal Zone Act. EPA and NOAA jointly administer this program which must contain "enforceable policies and mechanisms" to achieve the statute's policy goals. Apparently, these agencies have met with stiff resistance or at least, weak participation from the states. The major sanction for state failure to submit an approvable program—partial hold back of § 6217 and CWA § 319 program funds—has not been used.

2. *Funding Sources for NPS Programs.* What funding might be available for both the planning and implementation phases of DEP's NPS program? How are funding sources likely to vary in the future?

The traditional funding source for NPS programs has been governmental appropriations for both program administration and for the provision of incentives or cost sharing. A cost-share program, used primarily in the agricultural sector, is a method for sharing installation costs for NPS pollution controls in the form of BMPs between a governmental entity (usually a State) and a farmer or rancher. Many commentators have been highly critical of the use of purely voluntary cost-share programs in the NPS area, especially where used to pay for controls that the farmer could afford without public assistance. Among other problems, enormous government expenditures would be necessary to provide enough cost sharing funds to accomplish pollution reduction goals. For example, it has been estimated that at least $90 million would be needed to address only soil erosion and animal-waste needs in Maryland.

Ultimately, any decision regarding the nature of an NPS control program and funding sources will be a determination of how costs and impacts can be distributed most reasonably. Increasingly, states are implementing programs based on the "polluter pays" principle, i.e., the determination that polluters should be primarily responsible for the direct costs of pollution control. Where the principle is implemented, individual polluters are given an economic incentive to modify their activities. Thus, funding is not only a resource to support pollution controls, but a pollution control mechanism in its own right.

Fees. Potentially, where fees are used to finance environmental programs, there is a direct relationship between the polluter and the costs of mitigation or prevention. A fee may be assessed on an individual, corporation or municipality to cover the costs of 1) regulating the activity (permit fee); 2) cleaning up the activity (discharge fee); or 3) the incremental burden or infrastructure costs associated with new development (impact fee).

Other Funding Options. Possible options for creative funding include the following:

—Investment tax credits for expenditures needed to implement BMPs.

—Cross-compliance measures whereby eligibility for financial and other government benefits are made contingent on implementation of BMPs.

—Performance taxes based on the amount of pollution caused by particular practices.

—Performance standards, specifying minimum runoff or water quality requirements with associated fines for violations of the standards.

—Modification of pricing mechanisms such as irrigation water, fertilizers, or pesticides to discourage overuse.

State–Local Institutional Relationships. State water quality planners should also look to other governmental agencies to determine how their ongoing efforts might fit in with the control of NPS pollution. For example, state programs for subdivision control, pesticide, fertilizer, solid and hazardous waste control and the state soil conservation and extension services are examples of potential candidates for NPS program integration.

In addition to creating alternative sources of revenue and administrative instruments, states can establish innovative state-local institutional relationships to raise funds more effectively. Special districts with fee-setting and taxing authority can serve this purpose. Both special utility districts and water quality districts fall within this categorization.

3. *Enforcement of NPS Controls.* What enforcement mechanisms are available under the Clean Water Act or other Federal or state legislation for the control of NPS pollution?

The Clean Water Act's enforcement section, § 309, does not apply to § 319 NPS programs. Furthermore, § 319 does not actually require states to submit and implement NPS plans: there are no consequences to such a failure other than ineligibility for grant monies made available under the authority of § 319. While the statute states that EPA "shall" prepare an assessment report for any state failing to submit one of its own, there is no similar provision regarding a state's failure to submit a management program. The Act gives EPA no authority either to mandate state NPS control measures or initiate enforcement actions against those found to be causing NPS pollution of another state's waters. Neither does it encourage the states to develop their own enforcement machinery. While 40 C.F.R. § 130.6(c)(4)(ii) requires states to develop regulatory programs for the control of NPS pollution where non-regulatory approaches are found to be inappropriate or ineffective as part of their water quality planning and management process, this section has not been employed in practice.

In Northwest Indian Cemetery Protective Association v. Peterson, 565 F.Supp. 586 (N.D.Cal.1983), affirmed 764 F.2d 581 (9th Cir.1985), affirmed on rehearing 795 F.2d 688 (9th Cir.1986), reversed on other grounds sub nom. Lyng v. Northwest Indian Cemetery Protective Ass'n, 485 U.S. 439 (1988), a federal Court of Appeals affirmed a lower court ruling that California water quality standards could be enforced against nonpoint sources—such as logging activities—on federal lands. Neither court, however, addressed the question of jurisdiction. In Oregon Natural Resources Council v. United States Forest Service, 834 F.2d 842 (9th Cir.1987) the court reaffirmed the right of an environmental organization to challenge violations of state water quality standards, clarifying that jurisdiction could be found under the Administrative Procedure Act (APA), 5 U.S.C. §§ 701–706. The APA provides that "[a] person suffering legal wrong because of agency action or adversely affected or aggrieved by agency action within the meaning of a relevant statute, is entitled to judicial review thereof." Thus, in certain circumstances—i.e. where the activities of a federal agency are causing the violations—state water quality standards can constitute judicially enforceable constraints on land management. Commentators have suggested that antidegradation standards could also be judicially enforceable. It remains unclear, however, whether these decisions will be directly applicable to other federal agency activities or even to forest management outside northern California.

What about using federal funding of state and local government programs as the vehicle for obtaining NPS control? This practice has been termed "cross-compliance" and "grant-conditioning." Cross-compliance measures are one means to achieving control of NPS pollution. An example of an effective cross-compliance measure is presented by Shanty Town

Associates Limited Partnership v. EPA, 843 F.2d 782 (4th Cir.1988). In this case EPA imposed restrictive conditions designed to minimize NPS pollution on CWA Title II funds granted to a municipality for construction of a sewage collection system. The EPA grant conditions made new land development in the grant area considerably less attractive than it earlier had been. The plaintiff, a developer, owned a lot in the area and filed suit to challenge the conditions imposed by EPA on the grounds that they disturbed the delicate balance of federal and state power created by Congress in which the states were responsible for regulation of NPS pollution. The court found that EPA had not exceeded its statutory authority and upheld the practice. This means to forcing the states to adopt adequate NPS pollution control programs may have some utility. What are the drawbacks of such an approach from EPA's perspective? What might be the political ramifications of conditioning federal grants to making regulatory commitments such as these?

SECTION 4. AMBIENT WATER QUALITY CONSIDERATIONS AND WATER POLLUTION CONTROL

To this point, our consideration of the federal strategy of water pollution control has focused nearly exclusively on technology-based point source effluent controls. One would imagine that point source discharges were only regulated by technologically derived effluent standards in a manner totally apart from considerations of water quality. At least one commentator has criticized the CWA for an overemphasis of uniform pollution source control. See Petersen, Turning the Tide on Water Quality, 15 Ecol.L.Q. 69, 82–87 (1988). Although major, this emphasis on technological source controls is but one element of the Clean Water Act structure of pollution control.

Despite the emphasis on effluent standards in water pollution control law, the quality of ambient or receiving water is still an important, if not an ultimate, goal of the Act. In fact, Section 301(b)(1)(C) [§ 1311(b)(1)(C)] states that NPDES permits must assure the achievement of water quality standards. Recent statutory changes have increased the emphasis on water quality concerns. As you study the material in this section, consider how water quality standards could be used to reach the significant environmental quality goals of the Clean Water Act. Recall the aspirational objectives of the statute to eliminate all waste discharges and to achieve "fishable and swimmable" waters throughout the nation and the goal that water not be used for waste disposal. See § 101(a)(1)–(2) [§ 1251(a)(1)–(2)]. There are four provisions in the Act which directly address water quality issues—1) § 302—Water Quality Related Effluent Limitations, 2) § 303—Water Quality Standards and Plans, 3) § 307(a)(2)—Toxic Effluent Standards, and 4) § 403—Ocean Discharge Criteria. The focus of this section of the materials will be on the first two provisions and their impact on individual source permitting and intergovernmental relationships.

CLASS DISCUSSION PROBLEM: THE PROBLEMS OF UNIVERSAL WIDGET COMPANY AND WATER QUALITY STANDARDS

Assume that a major widget manufacturer—Universal Widget Company (UWC)—wished to locate a new widget manufacturing facility in the Centralia area. UWC's consultants have informed the company's management that Centralia was perfectly situated for the location of a new plant due to its proximity to ample supplies of requisite raw materials, ample skilled labor and abundant electrical energy. UWC intends to manufacture metal and wood widgets at its proposed Centralia plant. In order to be self-sufficient, the company plans to mine iron ore and harvest trees in an area near the plant site and to use these materials in its widget manufacturing process. Such an expansion was within the company's strategic plan. It was determined that Centralia was also centrally located in the new marketing region into which UWC wished to expand. Since the UWC widget plant would benefit the local economy, state and local government officials have expressed support for the project.

UWC has been an industry leader in the widget business and its management has prided itself on maintaining a corporate image of being a "good corporate citizen" in terms of environmental matters. This company attitude has preceded the recent interest in producing "environmentally-friendly" products. In all of its recent plant expansions elsewhere UWC has employed the most modern technical processes for the manufacture of widgets and has complied with all applicable environmental regulations. The corporate management intends to continue this practice by adopting, with regard to direct water discharges, the CWA § 306 new source performance standards applicable to the widget industry.

After carefully examining the industrial land market UWC has purchased options on three suitably-sized tracts of land located at different points on the East River. As part of the final stage of its corporate decision to locate in Centralia, the company is now trying to decide which of these three sites should be chosen for construction.

You should assume that the proposed UWC widget plant employing the § 306 technology would discharge pollutant X at the rate of 5 pounds per ton of widgets produced at the plant. The East River water at each of the three different outfall locations has substantially different concentrations of pollutant X—site 1 is pristine water with virtually no pollution at all, site 2 is moderately affected by pollutant X, and site 3 has heavy concentrations of pollutant X. The construction of the UWC facility at any one of these locations will undoubtedly increase the concentration of pollutant X to some degree.

In selecting the preferred industrial location (or choosing to locate elsewhere) consider the following questions:

    1. If UWC complies with EPA's § 306 new source performance standard for the widget industry, can the state pollution control agency require even greater control of the discharge of pollutant X? On what legal basis could this be required? What policies would justify this increased level of pollution control?

2. Would it matter whether UWC selected site 1, 2, or 3 for its new plant? What are the pros and cons of each site? How might state water quality standards affect the choice? What information would UWC need in order to make its locational decision?

a.   What if UWC chose site 1 for its new plant. The water in the river adjacent to that site was generally unpolluted to the degree that the state has classified it as suitable for trout fishing. What if the planned discharge of pollutant X from the UWC facility would violate the state's stringent water quality standard (WQS) for that pristine river segment. Could UWC petition the state to change its WQS to a less restrictive level so as to accommodate the facility?

b.   What if UWC chose site 3 for its new plant? The water in the river adjacent to that site was extremely polluted to the extent that it would only support limited aquatic species. The present uses of the river fell considerably short of those specified by the state's WQS. These poor water quality conditions were the result of discharges from 10 point sources and from varied non-point sources. Can UWC be allowed to locate at site 3 and if so under what conditions?

c.   What might occur if pollutant X was a toxic pollutant and the receiving water was already highly polluted with toxics?

3. What if the surface runoff of acidity and suspended solids from the mining and timber harvesting operations reached the East River or one of its tributaries and raised the pH and turbidity levels above state water quality standards (WQS). Could UWC be forced by litigation, or otherwise, to stop this pollution in order to meet the state WQS?

4. To what extent (if any) could the dispersion of pollutant X be permitted to satisfy any state water quality standard? How would the location of the plant's outfall be important in determining whether the state's water quality standards would be violated? What if UWC were proposing to transport process wastes by way of a lengthy outfall to a site 10 miles offshore and to discharge them into the ocean waters?

A.   WATER QUALITY STANDARDS

The discussion to this point has emphasized the CWA's emphasis on the use of EPA developed, uniform and nationally-applicable, technology-based effluent limitations. But the CWA does not focus exclusively on technology and the administrative process to provide the nation with clean water. It also contains reference to an older theme in American environmental law—ambient water quality-based standards. The Act therefore represents a hybrid of clean water policy; mixing the new (technology based standards) with the old (water quality based standards). It is not that the CWA technology emphasis has failed. Over the past 30 years there have been major gains achieved in terms of discharges subject to permits, the removal of pounds of waste discharged and the number of water bodies with improving quality and improved aquatic life. See Robert W. Adler et. al, The Clean Water Act 20 Years Later 18 (1993). Nearly 30 years after the passage of the modern water pollution control, the statutory goals of "fishable/swimmable" water have not been realized. As one commentator explained,

> Yet, we do not have clean water. To be sure, we have improved water quality since circa 1972—when rivers and harbors were so contaminated they were actually catching fire—but, taken as a whole, we have not had clean water in America in the lifetime of anyone living. Moreover, the more we learn about the actual quality of America's waters today, the worse, in the aggregate, the news. We have been spared knowing how polluted our waters are by the simple fact that we have not made a serious effort to find out. Only 19 percent of the nation's rivers, lakes, and estuaries have been assessed for pollution [as of 1998, eds.], and these for, in most cases, only the most rudimentary contaminants. The data available have led to the rote conclusion that approximately one-third of America's waters do not meet water quality standards. That number may be high, more likely it is low, but if it is even in the ballpark it is bad news for a country that has poured billions of dollars and countless work-years into programs intended to do no less than eliminate pollution and secure clean water nationwide.

Oliver A. Houck, The Clean Water Act TMDL Program: Law, Policy, and Implementation 4 (1999). Professor Houck asserts that the central reason for the CWA policy failure "is that pollution sources not regulated by the Act have bloomed like algae to swallow the gains." *Id*. These pollution sources, though discreet diffuse individually small, are well represented and protected in state government as well as in Congress. Where the large scale, industrial point sources were easier to conceptualize and regulate as "polluters," these hog and chicken farmers, sugar growers, loggers, agricultural irrigators, and suburban land subdivides are more difficult to cast as significant causes of water quality impairment. With the limits of the benefit of technology based standards in view, the CWA's emphasis has begun to concentrate on water quality itself. Is surface water sufficiently clean? During the late 1990's, an EPA Water Program Official, Robert Perciasepe wrote the following in an agency memorandum:

> Almost 25 years after the passage of the [CWA], the national water program is at a defining moment. We—meaning each of you, each of our State, local, and Tribal partners, and all of us in the Office of Water—are making the transition from a clean water program based primarily on technology-based controls to water-quality based controls implemented on a watershed basis.

As the material below indicates, this renewed emphasis on the achievement of water quality standards echoes back to the interstate standards which had originally become a part of federal law with the Water Quality Act of 1965. Codified within CWA § 303 was a process of establishing state water quality standards. This setting of water quality standards has had special meaning since these clean water characteristics become the ultimate objective. If waters remain polluted after employing the technology-based effluent limitations, the state's water quality standards mandate the application of further controls. At least this is what § 303(d) says. Recently, these state adopted water quality standards have assumed much greater importance as policy objectives and as the target for assigning Total Maximum Daily Loads or TMDLs to individual point sources and categories of nonpoint sources.

Excerpt from the Clean Water Act

33 U.S.C. § 1313.

§ 303   Water quality standards and implementation plans

(a) Existing water quality standards

* * *

(3)(A) Any State which prior to October 18, 1972, has not adopted pursuant to its own laws water quality standards applicable to intrastate waters shall, not later than one hundred and eighty days after October 18, 1972, adopt and submit such standards to the Administrator.

(B) If the Administrator determines that any such standards are consistent with the applicable requirements of this Act as in effect immediately prior to October 18, 1972, he shall approve such standards.

(C) If the Administrator determines that any such standards are not consistent with the applicable requirements of this Act as in effect immediately prior to October 18, 1972, he shall, not later than the ninetieth day after the date of submission of such standards, notify the State and specify the changes to meet such requirements. If such changes are not adopted by the State within ninety days after the date of notification, the Administrator shall promulgate such standards pursuant to subsection (b) of this section.

(b) Proposed regulations

(1) The Administrator shall promptly prepare and publish proposed regulations setting forth water quality standards for a State in accordance with the applicable requirements of this Act as in effect immediately prior to October 18, 1972, if—

(A) the State fails to submit water quality standards within the times prescribed in subsection (a) of this section.

(B) a water quality standard submitted by such State under subsection (a) of this section is determined by the Administrator not to be consistent with the applicable requirements of subsection (a) of this section.

(2) The Administrator shall promulgate any water quality standard published in a proposed regulation not later than one hundred and ninety days after the date he publishes any such proposed standard, unless prior

to such promulgation, such State has adopted a water quality standard which the Administrator determines to be in accordance with subsection (a) of this section.

(c) Review; revised standard; publication

(1) The Governor of a State or the State water pollution control agency of such State shall from time to time (but at least once each three year period beginning with October 18, 1972) hold public hearings for the purpose of reviewing applicable water quality standards and, as appropriate, modifying and adopting standards. Results of such review shall be made available to the Administrator.

(2)(A) Whenever the State revises or adopts a new standard, such revised or new standard shall be submitted to the Administrator. Such revised or new water quality standard shall consist of the designated uses of the navigable waters involved and the water quality criteria for such waters based upon such uses. Such standards shall be such as to protect the public health or welfare, enhance the quality of water and serve the purposes of this chapter. Such standards shall be established taking into consideration their use and value for public water supplies, propagation of fish and wildlife, recreational purposes, and agricultural, industrial, and other purposes, and also taking into consideration their use and value for navigation.

(B) Whenever a State reviews water quality standards pursuant to paragraph (1) of this subsection, or revises or adopts new standards pursuant to this paragraph, such State shall adopt criteria for all toxic pollutants listed pursuant to section 1317(a)(1) of this title for which criteria have been published under section 1314(a) of this title, the discharge or presence of which in the affected waters could reasonably be expected to interfere with those designated uses adopted by the State, as necessary to support such designated uses. Such criteria shall be specific numerical criteria for such toxic pollutants. Where such numerical criteria are not available, whenever a State reviews water quality standards pursuant to paragraph (1), or revises or adopts new standards pursuant to this paragraph, such State shall adopt criteria based on biological monitoring or assessment methods consistent with information published pursuant to section 1314(a)(8) of this title. Nothing in this section shall be construed to limit or delay the use of effluent limitations or other permit conditions based on or involving biological monitoring or assessment methods or previously adopted numerical criteria.

(3) If the Administrator, within sixty days after the date of submission of the revised or new standard, determines that such standard meets the requirements of this chapter, such standard shall thereafter be the water quality standard for the applicable waters of that State. If the Administrator determines that any such revised or new standard is not consistent with the applicable requirements of this chapter, he shall not later than the ninetieth day after the date of submission of such standard notify the State and specify the changes to meet such requirements. If such changes are not adopted by the State within ninety days after the date of notification, the

Administrator shall promulgate such standard pursuant to paragraph (4) of this subsection.

(4) The Administrator shall promptly prepare and publish proposed regulations setting forth a revised or new water quality standard for the navigable waters involved—

(A) if a revised or new water quality standard submitted by such State under paragraph (3) of this subsection for such waters is determined by the Administrator not to be consistent with the applicable requirements of this chapter, or

(B) in any case where the Administrator determines that a revised or new standard is necessary to meet the requirements of this chapter.

The Administrator shall promulgate any revised or new standard under this paragraph not later than ninety days after he publishes such proposed standards, unless prior to such promulgation, such State has adopted a revised or new water quality standard which the Administrator determines to be in accordance with this chapter.

(d) Identification of areas with insufficient controls; maximum daily load; certain effluent limitations revision

(1)(A) Each State shall identify those waters within its boundaries for which the effluent limitations required by section 1311(b)(1)(A) and section 1311(b)(1)(B) of this title are not stringent enough to implement any water quality standard applicable to such waters. The State shall establish a priority ranking for such waters, taking into account the severity of the pollution and the uses to be made of such waters.

(B) Each State shall identify those waters or parts thereof within its boundaries for which controls on thermal discharges under section 1311 of this title are not stringent enough to assure protection and propagation of a balanced indigenous population of shellfish, fish, and wildlife.

(C) Each State shall establish for the waters identified in paragraph (1)(A) of this subsection, and in accordance with the priority ranking, the total maximum daily load, for those pollutants which the Administrator identifies under section 1314(a)(2) of this title as suitable for such calculation. Such load shall be established at a level necessary to implement the applicable water quality standards with seasonal variations and a margin of safety which takes into account any lack of knowledge concerning the relationship between effluent limitations and water quality.

(D) Each State shall estimate for the waters identified in paragraph (1)(B) of this subsection the total maximum daily thermal load required to assure protection and propagation of a balanced, indigenous population of shellfish, fish and wildlife. Such estimates shall take into account the normal water temperatures, flow rates, seasonal variations, existing sources of heat input, and the dissipative capacity of the identified waters or parts thereof. Such estimates shall include a calculation of the maximum heat input that can be made into each such part and shall include a margin of safety which takes into account any lack of knowledge concerning the development of thermal water quality criteria for such protection and propagation in the identified waters or parts thereof.

(2) Each State shall submit to the Administrator from time to time, with the first such submission not later than one hundred and eighty days after the date of publication of the first identification of pollutants under section 1314(a)(2)(D) of this title, for his approval the waters identified and the loads established under paragraphs (1)(A), (1)(B), (1)(C), and (1)(D) of this subsection. The Administrator shall either approve or disapprove such identification and load not later than thirty days after the date of submission. If the Administrator approves such identification and load, such State shall incorporate them into its current plan under subsection (e) of this section. If the Administrator disapproves such identification and load, he shall not later than thirty days after the date of such disapproval identify such waters in such State and establish such loads for such waters as he determines necessary to implement the water quality standards applicable to such waters and upon such identification and establishment the State shall incorporate them into its current plan under subsection (e) of this section.

(3) For the specific purpose of developing information, each State shall identify all waters within its boundaries which it has not identified under paragraph (1)(A) and (1)(B) of this subsection and estimate for such waters the total maximum daily load with seasonal variations and margins of safety, for those pollutants which the Administrator identifies under section 1314(a)(2) of this title as suitable for such calculation and for thermal discharges, at a level that would assure protection and propagation of a balanced indigenous population of fish, shellfish and wildlife.

(4) Limitations on revision of certain effluent limitations

(A) Standard not attained. For waters identified under paragraph (1)(A) where the applicable water quality standard has not yet been attained, any effluent limitation based on a total maximum daily load or other waste load allocation established under this section may be revised only if (i) the cumulative effect of all such revised effluent limitations based on such total maximum daily load or waste load allocation will assure the attainment of such water quality standard, or (ii) the designated use which is not being attained is removed in accordance with regulations established under this section.

(B) Standard attained. For waters identified under paragraph (1)(A) where the quality of such waters equals or exceeds levels necessary to protect the designated use for such waters or otherwise required by applicable water quality standards, any effluent limitation based on a total maximum daily load or other waste load allocation established under this section, or any water quality standard established under this section, or any other permitting standard may be revised only if such revision is subject to and consistent with the antidegradation policy established under this section.

(e) Continuing planning process

(1) Each State shall have a continuing planning process approved under paragraph (2) of this subsection which is consistent with this chapter.

* * *

A NOTE ON ESTABLISHING AND REVISING WATER QUALITY STANDARDS

1. *Introduction*

Initially we will consider the provisions of § 303 and the idea of water quality standards. At this point you should read § 303 [§ 1313] with care. Notice that the Clean Water Act does not contain a counterpart to the Clean Air Act's EPA-set NAAQS concept. Consider these general observations and questions. Why didn't Congress structure the Clean Water Act around the attainment of administratively-set environmental quality standards? Why are § 303 water quality standards determined by the states with a degree of federal oversight and control?

The absence of an NAAQS—equivalent does not mean that the Water Act ignores environmental quality objectives for American water resources. Try to understand these components. In this section we will concentrate on the first two concepts: 1) designated water uses, 2) water quality criteria, and 3) an antidegradation clause. The "use" component operates much like a conventional zoning ordinance by specifying particular uses to each water segment. EPA regulations require that all waters, when attainable, be assigned uses consistent with fishable/swimmable standard set forth in § 101(a)(2). See 40 C.F.R. § 131.6(a). The "criteria" portion of the water quality standards are water characteristics, either numerical concentrations or narrative descriptions, sufficient to protect the designated use. The states are granted the authority to establish water uses yet EPA reserves the primary responsibility for defining the criteria.

2. *State Setting of Water Quality Standards*

The Act does not anticipate that water quality standards (WQS) will be ignored by the regulatory agencies. In fact, WQS exist in all 50 states and the U.S. Territories. Every three years the states must review existing water quality standards for all waters within their boundaries and submit them to EPA for approval. See § 303(c)(1)–(2) [§ 1313(c)(1)–(2)]. If EPA determines that a state's adopted WQS does not meet the requirements of the CWA, it can begin a proceeding resulting in the federal promulgation of the standard. EPA approval and disapproval of state WQS can lead to federal court review. See American Wildlands v. Browner, 94 F.Supp.2d 1150 (D.Colo.2000) (upheld approval) and Idaho Mining Ass'n v. Browner, 90 F.Supp.2d 1078 (D.Idaho 2000) (overturns disapproval). EPA has acted to promulgate WQS for Kentucky, Arizona, Nebraska, Mississippi, Alabama, North Carolina and Ohio. In addition, each state must provide EPA with a water quality report every two years that (1) describes existing water quality, (2) inventories all point sources, and (3) identifies the date by which various waters shall reach "fishable and swimmable" status. See § 305(b) [§ 1315(b)]. This bi-annual report is incorporated into EPA's National Inventory every two years. The 1987 amendments also required state analysis and reporting of non-point source pollution causing violation of water quality standards. See § 319(a) [§ 1329(a)].

3. Water Quality in Indian Lands

Who sets WQS for waters located on the lands of Indian Tribes? How are state/tribal WQS conflicts avoided or resolved? Section 518(e) of the CWA contains a provision which allows Indian Tribes to be treated as States for purposes of administering the CWA program in general and the water quality standards program in particular. If certain qualifications are met, Indian Tribes can establish water quality standards for waters under their jurisdiction pursuant to § 303(c) of the CWA.

Section 518 also requires EPA to provide regulations defining a mechanism for the resolution of any "unreasonable consequences" that may arise as a result of differing water quality standards that may be set by States and Indian Tribes located on common bodies of waters. The statute provides for the following guidance in the design of this intergovernment conflict resolution mechanism. It states,

> Such mechanism shall provide for explicit consideration of relevant factors including, but not limited to, the effects of differing water quality permit requirements on upstream and downstream dischargers, economic impacts, and present and historical uses and quality of the waters subject to such standards. Such mechanism should provide for the avoidance of such unreasonable consequences in a manner consistent with the objective of this chapter.

§ 518(e) [§ 1377(e)]. How would you implement this authority if you were drafting EPA's regulations?

Conflicts between tribal governments exercising CWA water quality standard jurisdiction and non-tribal pollution sources located on fee owned land within the Indian reservation has occasionally surfaced. In Montana v. EPA, 137 F.3d 1135 (9th Cir.1998), some land surrounding a large lake on the Flathead Indian Reservation was owned by non-Indian groups including the state and several local governments. Tribal governments applied to EPA for "treated as a state" or TAS status with respect to establishing water quality standards for surface waters on the reservation applicable to all polluting sources even those *not* owned by Indians. The Ninth Circuit upheld EPA's approval of the TAS application stating that tribal water quality regulation was essential due to the serious and substantial threats to tribal health and welfare posed by the activities of non-Indian landowners (including landfills, auto wrecking yards, feedlots, and dumps). By so concluding, the court found EPA's TAS regulations to reflect an appropriate identification of inherent Tribal regulatory authority over non-consenting, non-members. In another decision, City of Albuquerque v. Browner, 97 F.3d 415, 423 (10th Cir.1996), the Tenth Circuit held that a Tribe had inherent authority to set CWA water quality standards at a level more stringent than federal standards.

4.   *Establishing Use Designations*

States are accorded the initial responsibility in setting water quality standards by establishing use classifications for all surface water segments. This water use "zoning" process is undoubtedly important. How are these uses set and how are they significant?

EPA's regulations indicate that in establishing water uses states must take into consideration the use of water for "public water supplies, protection and propagation of fish, shellfish and wildlife, recreation in and on the water, agricultural, industrial, and other purposes including navigation." See 40 C.F.R. § 131.10(a). The use of water for waste assimilation or transport is specifically prohibited. Compare this to the language of § 303(c)(2). Consequently, water uses are usually set *at the level of or better than* the existing use of the water body. In the CWA's not-so-delicate intergovernmental balance, states have the primary responsibility for establishing uses of a waterbody. Each State develops its own use classification system based on the generic uses cited in the CWA. The goals of the CWA setting forth basic uses for support and propagation of aquatic life and recreation in and on the water are used by all States in some form. States may differentiate and subcategorize the types of uses which are to be protected, such as coldwater or warmwater fisheries, or specific species which are to be protected, such as trout or bass. States may also designate special uses to protect sensitive or valuation aquatic life or habitat.

There can be a difference between the existing use and the designated use of a waterbody. An existing use is one which has been attained and it cannot be modified unless they are replaced with uses requiring *more* stringent criteria. On the other hand, designated uses may be changed to a level requiring *less* stringent criteria but only following a Use Attainability Analysis (UAA) discussed below.

5.   *Water Quality Criteria*

Once water *uses* have been established within a state, water quality criteria must be set to protect the designated use. These criteria are intended to link degrees of water pollution to desired levels of water use as a form of performance standard for the chosen water use. EPA intends to fully integrate (1) biological, (2) nutrient, and (3) microbial criteria in the future to better define the meaning of water quality. Criteria are usually expressed either in the form of (1) numerical values of pollutant concentrations or (2) narrative descriptions frequently expressed as water quality free from certain adverse characteristics (e.g., free from toxic pollutants in toxic amounts). An illustrative case can be found in the Iowa Water Quality Standards which provide for both kinds of standards. For example, the Iowa criteria for acidity have been stated as a pH of "not less than 6.5 nor greater than 9.0 * * * [with] the maximum change permitted as a result of a waste discharge * * * [not to] exceed 0.5 pH units." Criteria also include narrative standards expressed without numerical components, for example, "[T]he waters shall contain no substances which will impart any undesirable tastes to fish flesh, or in any other way make fish inedible." See Iowa Administrative Code, Division 567, chapter 61, §§ 61.3(3)(e) & (g). Which form of criteria provides the most consistent results in source permitting? Which requires a great deal of discretion or flexibility?

a. *Where do the states find water criteria?* EPA has published a recommended list of water quality criteria under the authority of § 304(a)(1). EPA has published a completion of criteria for approximately 150 pollutants to provide guidance to the states and Tribes. Some of these pollutants include Atragene, ammonia, bacteria, cadmium, copper, lead, and dissolved oxygen. These criteria present data and scientific judgments on the relationship between pollutant concentrations and environmental and human health effects.

Section 304(a) criteria are published as guidance documents to assist the States in setting water quality standards and they have no independent legal effect. These criteria guidance documents contain two varieties of data: (1) scientific information on the effects of pollutants on human health, aquatic life and recreation and (2) quantitative concentrations or qualitative assessments of pollutants in water which will ensure adequate water quality for a designated use. These criteria are intended to provide the latest scientific information on the effect of a pollutant on human health and aquatic life. States are free to adopt their own general or site specific criteria under EPA's rules. However, in practice EPA's criteria guidance documents have been largely adopted by the states. See 40 C.F.R. § 131.11(b). What if a state wished to impose water quality criteria which were stricter than those in EPA's lists? See Homestake Mining Co. v. U.S. EPA, 477 F.Supp. 1279 (D.S.D.1979) (yes, considering the anti-preemption policy of § 510).

6. *The Results of Establishing State Water Quality Standards*

Over the nearly thirty years of the CWA, the states have slowly adopted the WQS described in the text above. EPA criteria and other technical documents have been helpful guides, but in the end the states were free to select their own WQS—at least, as long as EPA would approve them. As noted, EPA has disapproved some state-initiated WQS and substituted its own for that of the state. The most important point to recognize is that WQS are not identical on a national basis. Uniformity has not been the operative principle with the ambient water standards under the CWA. The existing WQS program has been criticized on a number of grounds "including a high degree of variability in state water quality criteria, equally varying application factors (e.g., flow assumptions), mixing zones, site specific water quality criteria, downgrading uses, degrading waters within uses and the absence of certain critical standards (e.g., sediments and nutrients)." Oliver A. Houck, The Clean Water Act TMDL Program: Law, Policy and Implementation 141 (1999). Compare this to the nationally-uniform and preempted effect of the Clean Air Act's National Ambient Air Quality Standards (NAAQS).

It is also worth noting that a considerable amount of water quality "nonattainment" or impairment exists through the nation. Recall the information in the introductory section of this chapter from EPA's Twelfth Water Quality Inventory indicating a relatively high percentage of polluted or impaired waters in the assessed surface waters included in the report. The actual number of Water Quality Limited Segments (WQLS) or waters not meeting water quality standard was nearly 16,000 in 1996 indicating that the goals of the CWA have not yet been achieved. As you read the materials ahead, try to understand the requirements of CWA § 303(d) and new emphasis on the development of Total Maximum Daily Loads or TMDLs as a means of allocating pollution control obligations to the point and nonpoint sources actually causing the impaired water conditions.

Oregon Natural Resources Council v. United States Forest Service

United States Court of Appeals, Ninth Circuit, 1987.
834 F.2d 842, 844, 848–52.

■ FERGUSON, CIRCUIT JUDGE:

[In 1977 the U.S. Forest Service proposed timber sales in the Willamette National Forest in Oregon and in 1981 the agency sold timber rights in the North Roaring Devil area to a private company. No harvesting of timber took place under this sale and in December of 1985 the Forest Service reoffered the timber under provisions of federal law. In October of 1986 it awarded the timber sale to the Bugaboo Timber Company. Plaintiffs unsuccessfully attempted to appeal the resale to Bugaboo and finally they filed suit in federal court alleging violations of NEPA, the Endangered Species Act, the APA, and the Clean Water Act. The following excerpt from the Ninth Circuit's opinion responds to the district court's grant of summary judgment in favor of the Forest Service (659 F.Supp. 1441 (D.Or. 1987)).] * * *

VI.

Plaintiffs allege that the road building and timber harvesting associated with the timber sale violate Oregon state water quality standards[6] and that the USFS's failure to comply with these standards violates section 1323 of the CWA. The CWA requires each state to develop and implement

---

6. According to plaintiffs, defendants have violated and plan to violate the State of Oregon's Water Quality Standard for nondegradation, which provides that unless the Environmental Quality Commission grants an exemption, "existing high quality waters * * * shall be maintained and protected." Or.Admin.R. 340–41–026(1)(a) (1986). Plain- tiffs further allege violations of a rule proscribing activities in the Willamette Basin which "either alone or in combination with other wastes or activities will cause * * * a 10 percent cumulative increase in natural stream turbidities." Or.Admin.R. 340–41–445(2)(c) (1986).

"water quality" standards to protect and enhance the quality of water within the state. 33 U.S.C. § 1313. The Act also requires all federal agencies to comply with all state requirements. 33 U.S.C. § 1323.

Plaintiffs claim that the district court erred when it concluded that plaintiffs could not bring a CWA action under section 1365 of the Act (the citizen suit provision) because they failed to provide a sixty-day notice. 33 U.S.C. § 1365(b)(1). Plaintiffs argue that their action is not brought pursuant to section 1365 but instead is brought under the judicial review provision of the APA, 5 U.S.C. §§ 701–706, or, in the alternative, that they gave adequate notice under the CWA.

Defendants argue that plaintiffs failed to meet the sixty-day notice under the CWA citizen suit provision or, in the alternative, that plaintiffs are not entitled to bring an action under the CWA because the CWA permits citizen suit enforcement of state water quality standards *only* to the extent that the requirements are conditions of permits issued under the National Pollutant Discharge Elimination System ("NPDES") established under the Act, 33 U.S.C. § 1342. Because plaintiffs do not allege such violations, defendants state that plaintiffs are without a remedy under the Act.[7] Defendants further argue that the CWA provides an exclusive remedy and that plaintiffs cannot seek review under the APA for this type of agency action.

Before we decide whether plaintiffs must comply with the sixty-day notice requirement, we must first resolve the issue concerning whether plaintiffs have a cause of action under the citizen suit provision of the Act, and thus whether the sixty-day notice requirement is applicable. See 33 U.S.C. § 1365(b)(1). Initially, we must consider the language of the citizen suit provision. The provision states that any citizen may commence a civil action "against any person * * * who is alleged to be in violation of (A) an effluent standard or limitation under this chapter." 33 U.S.C. § 1365(a). Section 1365(f) defines "effluent standard or limitation" as "an unlawful act under subsection (a) of section 1311 * * * [or] an effluent limitation or other limitation under section 1311 or 1312 of this title." Plaintiffs concede that section 1311(a) of the Act refers specifically to point source discharges,[8] which are not at issue in this case. Plaintiffs also concede that sections 1311(b)(1)(A) and (B) only apply to point sources.

We are asked, however, to examine section 1311(b)(1)(C), which lists additional enforceable standards, including state water quality standards. The provision states that in order to achieve the objectives of the Act there shall be achieved "any more stringent limitation including those necessary to meet water quality standards, treatment standards * * * or any other

---

7. Indeed, plaintiffs state in their brief that "[t]he reason for using the APA is that the citizen suit provision arguably applies only to permit violations and not to water quality violations, such as those involved here."

8. The term "point source" means "any discernible, confined and discrete con-

veyance, included but not limited to any pipe, ditch, channel, tunnel, conduit, well, discrete fissure, container, rolling stock, concentrated animal feeding operation, or vessel or other floating craft, from which pollutants are or may be discharged." 33 U.S.C. § 1362(14).

Federal law or regulation, or required to implement *any applicable water quality standard established pursuant to this chapter.*" 33 U.S.C. § 1311(b)(1)(C) (emphasis added). It is plaintiffs' contention that because section 1311(b)(1)(C) incorporates state water quality standards established pursuant to section 1313 and does not explicitly refer to point sources, plaintiffs are entitled to sue under the citizen suit provision of the Act to enforce state water quality standards affected by nonpoint sources.[9]

We recognize that nonpoint sources of pollution constitute a major source of pollution in the nation's waters. However, we do not believe that the Act allows for the enforcement of state water quality standards, as affected by nonpoint sources, under the citizen suit provision. When Congress established the National Pollutant Discharge Elimination System (NPDES) in 1972 and concomitantly created a new approach to regulating and abating water pollution, it drew a distinct line between point and nonpoint pollution sources. Point sources are subject to direct federal regulation and enforcement under the Act.[11] See 33 U.S.C. § 1342. Nonpoint sources, because of their very nature, are not regulated under the NPDES. Instead, Congress addressed nonpoint sources of pollution in a separate portion of the Act which encourages states to develop areawide waste treatment management plans.[12] See 33 U.S.C. § 1288. We do not agree with plaintiffs that Congress intended section 1311 to apply to nonpoint sources. Section 1311 of the Act is entitled "Effluent Limitations." 33 U.S.C. § 1311. Effluent limitations are defined as "any restriction established by a state or the Administrator on quantities, rates, and concentrations of chemical, physical, biological, and other constituents which are discharged from *point sources* into navigable waters." 33 U.S.C. § 1362(11) (emphasis added).

Three methods for deriving effluent limitations are identified in section 1311(b)(1). The first method is "application of the best practicable control technology currently available." 33 U.S.C. § 1311(b)(1)(A). The second

9. Nonpoint source pollution is not specifically defined in the Act, but is pollution that does not result from the "discharge" or "addition" of pollutants from a point source. Examples of nonpoint source pollution include runoff from irrigated agriculture and silvicultural activities. See Trustees for Alaska v. Environmental Protection Agency, 749 F.2d 549, 558 (9th Cir.1984).

11. The Act provides that, except under certain specified circumstances, "the discharge of any pollutant by any person shall be unlawful." 33 U.S.C. § 1311(a). A "discharge of a pollutant" is defined in part as "any addition of any pollutant to navigable waters from any *point source.*" 33 U.S.C. § 1362(12) (emphasis added).

12. Congress recently amended the Clean Water Act and added a new provision dealing with nonpoint sources of pollution

which provides grants and assistance to states who develop programs to deal with nonpoint sources. See Water Quality Act of 1987, Pub.L. No. 100–4, § 316, 101 Stat. 52 (Feb. 4, 1987).

In the new amendments Congress also added the following language to section 1251(a) of the Act, which sets forth the goals and policies of Congress. The new language states that:

> (7) it is the national policy that programs for the control of nonpoint sources of pollution be developed and implemented in an expeditious manner so as to enable the goals of the Act to be met through the control of both point and nonpoint sources of pollution.

Pub.L. No. 100–4, § 316(b), 101 Stat. 60 (Feb. 4, 1987).

method is "secondary treatment as defined by the [EPA] Administrator." 33 U.S.C. § 1311(b)(1)(B). The third method includes "any more stringent limitation," including these necessary to meet state water quality standards. 33 U.S.C. § 1311(b)(1)(C). Thus, effluent limitations may be derived from state water quality standards and may be enforced when included in a discharger's permit. We agree with defendants that it is not the water quality standards themselves that are enforceable in section 1311(b)(1)(C), but it is the "limitations necessary to meet" those standards, or "required to implement" the standards.

The title and construction of section 1311(b)(1) lead us to the logical conclusion that the "limitations" set forth in section 1311(b)(1)(C) are "effluent limitations" and, therefore, by definition, applicable only to point sources. See 33 U.S.C. § 1362(11). Having reached this conclusion, we find that plaintiffs do not have a cause of action under the citizen suit provision of the CWA. Therefore, the required sixty-day notice under the Act is not applicable in this case. The district court, therefore, erred in its conclusion that plaintiffs were subject to the notice requirement.

[In the remaining part of the opinion the court determined that the plaintiffs could enforce Oregon's water quality standards against the U.S. Forest Service by way of suit under the Administrative Procedure Act. The court rejected the argument that based upon the Supreme Court's holding in Middlesex County Sewerage Authority v. National Sea Clammers Ass'n, 453 U.S. 1 (1981), the Clean Water Act citizen suit provision was the exclusive means to enforce the Act. Concluding that judicial review was also available under the APA, the Ninth Circuit remanded the case for a decision on the merits.]

[In Northwest Environmental Advocates v. City of Portland, 56 F.3d 979 (9th Cir.1995), the appeals court ruled that CWA citizen suits can enforce state water quality standards included as NPDES permit conditions and not only numeric end-of-the-pipe effluent limitations. The plaintiffs had filed suit against the City of Portland for alleged CWA violations resulting from the city's discharge of raw sewage into the Columbia and Willamette Rivers during periods of heavy rainfall. The court reversed its prior ruling in the case largely based upon the U.S. Supreme Court's holding in PUD No. 1 of Jefferson County v. Washington Dept. of Ecology, 114 St. Ct. 1900 (1994) that a state could condition § 401 certification not only on numerical effluent limits but also on broader state water quality standards such as minimum stream flow requirements. The Ninth Circuit concluded that the CWA's language, its legislative history and case law authorize citizens to enforce permit conditions stated in terms of water quality standards.]

Excerpt from the Clean Water Act
33 U.S.C. § 1313(d).

Water Quality Standards and Implementation Plans
§ 303(d) Identification of areas with insufficient controls; maximum daily load; certain effluent limitation revision

(1)(A) Each State shall identify those waters within its boundaries for which the effluent limitations required by section 1311(b)(1)(A) and section 1311(b)(1)(B) of this title are not stringent enough to implement any water quality standard applicable to such waters. The State shall establish a priority ranking for such waters, taking into account the severity of the pollution and the uses to be made of such waters. * * *

(c) Each State shall establish for the waters identified in paragraph (1)(A) of this subsection, and in accordance with the priority ranking, the total maximum daily load, for those pollutants which the Administrator identifies under section 1314(a)(2) of this title as suitable for such calculation. Such load shall be established at a level necessary to implement the applicable water quality standards with seasonal variations and a margin of safety which takes into account any lack of knowledge concerning the relationship between effluent limitations and water quality. * * *

(2) Each State shall submit to the Administrator from time to time, with the first such submission not later than one hundred and eighty days after the date of publication of the first identification of pollutants under section 1314(a)(2)(1), for his approval of the water identified and the loads established under paragraphs (1)(A), (1)(B), (1)(C), and (1)(D) of this subsection. The Administrator shall either approve or disapprove such identification and load not later than thirty days after the date of submission. If the Administrator approves such identification and load, such state shall incorporate them into its current plan under subsection (E) of this section. If the Administrator disapproves such identification and load, he shall not later than thirty days after such disapproval identify such waters in such state and establish such loads for such waters as he determines necessary the implementation of the water quality standards applicable to such waters and upon such identification and establishment the State shall incorporate them into its current plan under subsection (e) of this section.

Natural Resources Defense Council v. Fox

United States District Court, Southern District of New York, 2000.
93 F.Supp.2d 531.

■ Peter K. Leisure, District Judge:

This case involves the alleged failure for the past twenty years of the State of New York to establish pollution limits, known as total maximum daily loads ("TMDLs"), for waterbodies in the State. Plaintiffs bring this action against the United States Environmental Protection Agency and two of its administrators (collectively, "EPA"), pursuant to the Clean Water Act ("CWA"), 33 U.S.C. §§ 1251, et seq., and the Administrative Procedure Act ("APA"), 5 U.S.C. §§ 501, et seq., alleging that in the face of New York State's failure to act, EPA has unlawfully failed to intervene and establish the TMDLs itself. Plaintiffs raise a number of related claims, including that EPA has acted arbitrarily and capriciously with respect to New York State's 1997 submission of proposed TMDLs for reservoirs that supply drinking water to New York City.

[In a prior decision (NRDC II), the court had granted defendant's motion for summary judgment dismissing all of plaintiff's claims except the one arising under the Administrative Procedure Act. The opinion below disposes of this argument.]

Background

The Court presumes familiarity with the discussion of the Clean Water Act's statutory scheme in its previous decisions in this action. See NRDC II, 30 F.Supp. 2d at 373–74; NRDC, 909 F.Supp. at 156–57. Accordingly, only those elements of the Clean Water Act pertinent to the motions presently before the Court are set forth here.

The instant case involves Section 303(d) of the Clean Water Act, which regulates waterbodies failing to meet water quality standards even upon application of so-called technological pollution controls. See 33 U.S.C. § 1313(d)(1)(A). States are required to create a prioritized list of such waterbodies, and, upon EPA's approval of the priority list, to establish TMDLs for each waterbody concerning pollutants specified by EPA. See 33 U.S.C. §§ 1313(d)(1)(A) & (C).

The Act prescribes the basic elements of a TMDL:

Such load shall be established at a level necessary to implement the applicable water quality standards with seasonal variations and a margin of safety which takes into account any lack of knowledge concerning the relationship between effluent limitations and water quality.

Id. § 1313(d)(1)(C). EPA regulations further provide that a TMDL shall consist of the sum of: (i) the loading allotments for existing and future point sources of pollution (known as "wasteload allocations"), and (ii) the loading allotments for existing and future nonpoint sources of pollution and natural background sources of pollution (known as "load allocations"). See 40 C.F.R. §§ 130.2(e)–(i).

The Act provides that states "shall submit" the prioritized lists of waterbodies and accompanying TMDLs "from time to time, with the first such submission not later than one hundred and eighty days after" EPA identifies relevant pollutants. See 33 U.S.C. § 1313(d)(2). The parties do not dispute that the states' initial TMDLs and lists of waterbodies were due on June 26, 1979.

Upon receipt of lists and/or TMDLs, EPA "shall either approve or disapprove [them] . . . not later than 30 days after the date of submission." Id. § 313(d)(2). Should EPA disapprove either a list of waterbodies or a TMDL,

[it] shall not later than thirty days after the date of such disapproval identify such waters in such State and establish such loads for such waters as [it] determines necessary to implement the water quality standards applicable to such waters. . . .

Id.

Principally at issue in the instant case is New York State's alleged failure to submit TMDLs to EPA for review. The Clean Water Act does not expressly address what duty, if any, EPA bears under such circumstances. See id. § 1313(d). This Court and others have read into the Act a requirement that EPA treat such state inaction as a so-called "constructive submission" of a deficient TMDL, triggering EPA's explicit mandatory duties under the Act to disapprove the "submission," id. § 1313(d)(2), and to establish TMDLs for the state, id. See NRDC, 909 F.Supp. at 157 (explaining doctrine and listing cases).

In NRDC II, the Court identified the issues to be decided in the final stage of this action, and in April 1999 the parties submitted the record upon which the Court will adjudicate plaintiffs' remaining claims. . . . What had its origin as a Clean Water Act case is now primarily a suit under the Administrative Procedure Act. But while these APA claims are legally and analytically distinct from the original CWA claims, the underlying facts and plaintiffs' concerns remain the same. * * *

Plaintiffs seek injunctive relief in the form of a "binding, but reasonable, schedule for bringing Federal Defendants (and New York State) into compliance with the statutory scheme." More specifically, plaintiffs ask the Court for an order directing EPA: i) to establish TMDLs for all waterbodies on New York's 1998 § 303(d) list pursuant to a court-ordered timetable; ii) to promulgate TMDLs for the eight New York City reservoirs for which EPA has approved New York's proposed TMDLs; iii) to approve or disapprove the remaining ten reservoir TMDLs within 30 days of the entry of judgment in this case; iv) to review New York State's Continuing Planning Process; and v) to serve upon the Court and upon plaintiffs semi-annual progress reports regarding EPA's compliance with the proposed order. Plaintiffs also ask the Court to retain jurisdiction over this case "for a period of time necessary to insure compliance with the above-sought relief, to consider any additional motions that may be brought, and to consider an application for an award of fees and costs."

Discussion

* * * In Claims Six and Seven of their complaint, plaintiffs seek review under the Administrative Procedure Act, 5 U.S.C. § 706, of EPA's alleged failure to deem New York State's slow progress in promulgating TMDLs a "constructive submission" of deficient TMDLs, and its failure, in turn, to reject this deficient submission and promulgate its own TMDLs for the State.

Adopting the doctrine introduced by the Seventh Circuit in Scott v. City of Hammond, Ind., 741 F.2d 992, 994 (7th Cir.1984) [hereinafter, "Scott"], the Court in NRDC held that New York State's failure to submit proposed TMDLs to EPA in a timely manner could constitute a "constructive submission" of inadequate TMDLs, which in turn might trigger EPA's duty to intervene under the Clean Water Act.

In NRDC II, the Court dismissed plaintiffs' Clean Water Act claims on this issue, concluding that EPA acted within its discretion under the CWA in not deeming New York State's TMDL activity a "constructive submission" of no TMDLs. See NRDC II, 30 F.Supp. 2d at 377. Although the Court in NRDC made clear that the State's failure to promulgate TMDLs in accordance with the CWA would eventually trigger EPA's duty under the Act to declare a "constructive submission," the Court held in NRDC II that EPA retained discretion to determine at what point the State's intransigence was sufficient to require declaration of a "constructive submission." Because the CWA does not require EPA to take such action by a date certain, or within a particular time frame, the Court found that EPA acted within its discretion under the Act in concluding that it was not yet required to declare a "constructive submission."

The Court must now determine whether EPA's failure to declare a "constructive submission" by New York State, and ultimately to promulgate TMDLs in its stead, requires the Court to compel agency action under the Administrative Procedure Act. In NRDC II, the Court held that Claims Six and Seven properly state a cause of action under the APA, and denied defendants' motion for summary judgment on these claims. The Court observed, however, that recent progress made by New York State and EPA in developing TMDLs for the State was "certainly probative as to whether New York State has taken action sufficient to prevent EPA from being considered in violation of § 706." The Court continued, "Assuming EPA's duty to intervene has been triggered, the nature and extent of that duty must be assessed in light of continuing developments, including progress in state efforts to submit TMDLs. It may be the case, for example, that sufficient state progress after a period of delinquency could reduce the extent of EPA intervention required or even render the need for intervention altogether moot." The Court must now decide whether EPA's omission to deem New York State's delay in promulgating TMDLs a "constructive submission" is arbitrary, capricious, or otherwise not in accordance with law, in contravention of 5 U.S.C. § 706(2)(A). The Court must also decide whether EPA unlawfully withheld or unreasonably delayed agency action, in contravention of 5 U.S.C. § 706(1).

A. Agency Action Arbitrary, Capricious or Otherwise Not in Accordance with Law

"Section 706(2)(A) requires a finding that the actual choice made was not 'arbitrary, capricious, an abuse of discretion, or otherwise not in accordance with law.'" Citizens to Preserve Overton Park, Inc. v. Volpe, 401 U.S. 402, 416, 28 L. Ed. 2d 136, 91 S. Ct. 814 (1971) (quoting 5 U.S.C. § 706(2)(A)). To make this finding, a court "must consider whether the decision was based on a consideration of the relevant factors and whether there has been a clear error of judgment." Id. Moreover, "although this inquiry into the facts is to be searching and careful, the ultimate standard of review is a narrow one. The court is not empowered to substitute its judgment for that of the agency." Id. An agency action can be set aside "if the agency has relied on factors which Congress has not intended it to consider, entirely failed to consider an important aspect of the problem, offered an explanation for its decision that runs counter to the evidence before the agency, or is so implausible that it could not be ascribed to a difference in view or the product of agency expertise." Motor Vehicle Mfrs. Ass'n of U.S., Inc. v. State Farm Mut. Auto. Ins. Co., 463 U.S. 29, 43, 77 L. Ed. 2d 443, 103 S. Ct. 2856 (1983).

" 'The reviewing court must take into account contradictory evidence in the record, but the possibility of drawing two inconsistent conclusions from the evidence does not prevent an administrative agency's finding from being supported by substantial evidence.' When an agency makes a decision in the face of disputed technical facts, '[a] court must be reluctant to reverse results supported by ... a weight of considered and carefully articulated expert opinion.' " Cellular Phone Taskforce, 205 F.3d at 89 (internal citations omitted). Plaintiffs bear the burden of overcoming the presumption of validity of EPA's actions. See, e.g., Environmental Defense Fund, Inc. v. Costle, 211 U.S. App. D.C. 313, 657 F.2d 275, 283 (D.C.Cir. 1981).

The Court made clear in NRDC II that New York State's failure to submit proposed TMDLs to EPA for approval would, after an unspecified period of time, trigger EPA's duty to declare a "constructive submission" of inadequate TMDLs by the State, and trigger EPA's further duty to approve or disapprove this "constructive submission" within 30 days. See NRDC II, 30 F.Supp. 2d at 376–78; see also 33 U.S.C. § 1313(d)(2). * * *

On the merits of Claim Six, plaintiffs argue that, despite recent progress by EPA and the State in establishing TMDLs for New York, the State's failure to promulgate and submit TMDLs for EPA approval over the past two decades has undoubtedly triggered EPA's so-called "deeming duty," i.e., the duty to declare a "constructive submission" of no TMDLs. Defendants maintain that EPA's "deeming duty" has not been triggered, as New York State has made steady progress in developing its TMDL program over the past two decades. Defendants argue that, under the constructive submission doctrine, EPA's "deeming duty" arises only in the face of complete nonfeasance by the State; i.e., in order to declare a constructive submission of inadequate TMDLs, EPA must conclude that the State is ignoring its TMDL obligation entirely. Defendants claim that the administrative record amply supports their conclusion that New York is making progress in formulating TMDLs, and that an agency intervention that amounts to a vote of no confidence is inappropriate and potentially counterproductive. The Court agrees.

Upon review of the administrative record and joint appendix of documents submitted by the parties, the Court is fully satisfied that EPA's decision not to declare a "constructive submission" of no TMDLs by New York State is supported by the record, and is clearly not arbitrary, capricious, or contrary to law.

Although New York did not submit TMDLs to EPA for approval prior to the filing of plaintiffs' suit, it is clear from the record that New York was actively engaged in the preparation of TMDLs as early as the mid–1980s, and maintained close communication with EPA during that time regarding its progress. The record indicates that, in addition to its substantial efforts to comply with other provisions of the Clean Water Act during the 1970s and 1980s, New York began its TMDL planning as early as 1986.

EPA Administrator Carol M. Browner, a named defendant in this suit, has frankly acknowledged what some scholarly observers had previously suggested: that the TMDL program was consciously neglected by EPA until recent years, while resources were dedicated to other components of EPA's water quality control efforts under the CWA. See "Testimony of Carol Browner," Feb. 23, 2000, 2000 WL 11068367 (before the Senate Committee on Agriculture) [hereinafter, "Browner Testimony"].

> The TMDL program was designed to provide a safety net, catching water bodies that were not protected or restored by the implementation of the range of general, broadly applicable, pollution control programs authorized in the Clean Water Act.

> Until the early 1990's, however, EPA and States gave top priority to implementing these general clean water programs and gave lower priority to the more focused restoration authorities of the TMDL program. As a result, relatively few TMDLs were developed and many State lists were limited to a few waters and were not submitted in a timely manner.

Id.

Notwithstanding the fact that EPA was not pushing the states to develop TMDLs during the 1980s, New York was beginning to satisfy its obligation under § 303(d), unlike many states that turned a blind eye to the provision. Nonetheless, it is conceded by defendants that actual efforts to develop, submit, and approve TMDLs that comply with statutory requirements did not begin in earnest until this lawsuit was commenced.

Since that time, the administrative record ... reflect[s] that New York has been entirely cooperative in satisfying its TMDL obligation, and has at no point suggested to EPA that it would or could not shoulder its burden. Indeed, New York has submitted numerous proposed TMDLs during the pendency of this lawsuit, notwithstanding plaintiffs' contention that these submissions are facially inadequate.

In September 1997, EPA and New York State entered into a Memorandum of Agreement ("MOA"), which established an eight-year schedule for promulgation of TMDLs for all 129 water quality limited segments ("WQLSs") included on the State's 1996 § 303(d) list. Under the MOA, the State agreed to establish, with EPA's help, TMDLs for fifty "high priority" WQLSs by December 31, 2001. The State agreed to establish the remaining 79 TMDLs over the four years 2002 to 2005, with 25% to be completed in each of these four years.

On April 14, 1998, New York State submitted its 1998 § 303(d) list to EPA. See id. at 3. The 1998 list identified an additional 400 WQLSs not included in the 1996 list. The 1998 list increased the number of "high priority" WQLSs from 50 to 59, and provided that TMDLs for all but one "high priority" segment would be completed on the timetable established by the 1996 MOA. New York proposed that the TMDL submission deadline for New York/New Jersey Harbor waters be extended from December 31, 2001, to December 31, 2005, in light of the fact that the 1998 list included a use impairment of fish consumption resulting from standard exceedances for priority organics and/or pesticides caused by contaminated sediment and/or urban runoff, whereas the original deadline was based solely on use impairments due to standard exceedances for metals or pollutants associated with combined sewer overflow. The State concluded, and EPA agreed, that the expanded range of use impairments and the corresponding need to promulgate additional TMDLs justified such an extension. See id. New York retained the December 31, 2005, deadline for all non-high priority WQLSs, with the exception of a number of segments denominated "monitored standard exceedances." The State identified those waterbodies where, "because of natural background concentrations of iron, the current standard for [a given] pollutant is exceeded and the scientific basis for the standard is subject to review," and proposed for them a December 2008 deadline, to provide additional time to accommodate this review. On July 2, 1998, EPA approved New York's 1998 § 303(d) list, and on September 30, 1998, EPA accepted the State's proposed deadlines for establishing TMDLs.

Thus, to date, while New York has not promulgated TMDLs for every waterbody on its most recent § 303(d) list, it has unquestionably formulated and submitted some TMDLs, and has dedicated substantial resources to the problem and amply demonstrated its good-faith interest in collaborating with EPA to bring the State's TMDL program to completion. On this basis alone, the Court can conclude that EPA's decision not to declare a "constructive submission" of "no TMDLs" by New York is well-supported by the record. Still, there is more to the story.

Across the nation, EPA's TMDL program is in a state of flux. In her testimony before the Senate Committee on Agriculture, defendant Browner indicated that in 1996, EPA concluded that "there was a need for a comprehensive evaluation of the TMDL program." Browner Testimony, 2000 WL 11068367. This led to the formation of a TMDL committee under the Federal Advisory Committee Act (FACA), 5 U.S.C. app. §§ 1–14. Id. The FACA TMDL committee "was composed of 20 individuals with diverse backgrounds, including agriculture, forestry, environmental advocacy, industry, and State, local, and Tribal governments." Id. The advice of the committee guided EPA's proposed revisions of the TMDL regulations, published for notice and comment in August 1999, and expected to be made final later this year, following EPA's review of public comments. See Proposed Revisions to the Water Quality Planning and Management Regulation, 64 Fed. Reg. 46,012 (1999).

Within the context of these efforts at TMDL reform, and with TMDL litigation pending in numerous courts, EPA still believes that the states reasonably require a total of 8 to 13 years to complete their TMDL development. In fact, the proposed rule suggests extending this timetable to 15 years. States have been asked to take a phased approach to the development of TMDLs, by which they first promulgate TMDLs for the most seriously threatened waterbodies, and address the remainder on a rolling basis, with a fixed deadline for full compliance. Browner observes that these "are mid-course changes to the existing program based on current data and first-hand, on-the-ground knowledge regarding the status of the Nation's waters." Id. The proposal to extend the timetable for TMDL submission to 15 years "recognizes that some States need to develop many TMDLs and that it takes time to develop a useful and effective TMDL." Id.

While EPA's early record on TMDLs is far from admirable, it is clear that EPA is now taking its responsibilities in New York very seriously and taking reasonable strides to bring the TMDL program to fruition. At present, EPA is working closely with New York State to develop TMDLs for each of the State's § 303(d) listed waterbodies, and to honor its obligations under the CWA. Moreover, as noted above, EPA plans to implement extensive changes to the TMDL program later this year.

In addition, EPA and New York State have agreed to negotiate a Performance Partnership Agreement ("PPA") every two years, establishing "the mutual expectations and undertakings of each agency in carrying out the water program in New York State." Each year New York must also submit, and EPA must approve, work plans that "set out the scope of work the State will undertake under various EPA grants of federal assistance to the NYS DEC." Furthermore, the PPA and grant work plans "spell out the specific undertakings each agency will commit to each year" and "identify funding each agency will make available to carry out the activities identified and, where appropriate, the technical assistance that may be required of either agency to perform the work." EPA has made approximately $8.2 million in federal funds available to assist New York directly in developing TMDLs for its waterbodies. The Clinton Administration's Fiscal Year 2001 budget increases TMDL grant funding for the states from $365 million to $410 million.

Finally, EPA will monitor the State's progress in TMDL development by means of a Grant Review and Oversight Group ("GROG"). EPA and New York have entered a Memorandum of Understanding ("MOU") for the establishment of this group. Under the MOU, EPA and the State will meet quarterly to discuss the status of each grant awarded by EPA, and New York's commitments thereunder. According to EPA, this process will provide for early identification of the State's inability to honor any such commitment, and an opportunity for EPA to examine the reasons for the inability, explore possible remedial actions with the State, and seek agreement on a new commitment date where necessary.

While plaintiffs are correct to point out that New York's promises of future action are by themselves insufficient to avoid declaration of a "constructive submission," the Court considers the future plans established by New York and EPA to be an important sign, informed by New York's diligence in the past, that the intrusive injunctive remedies requested by plaintiffs are not warranted here. Not only has New York consistently cooperated in the TMDL effort, but it has pledged itself to a reasonable, even ambitious, timetable for completion of these tasks.

The Court cannot conclude, based on the record before it, that EPA has acted arbitrarily or capriciously, or otherwise contrary to law, in declining to declare a "constructive submission" by New York of no TMDLs. As the Court noted in NRDC II, the "constructive submission" doctrine and the corollary "deeming duty" exist only by judicial gloss on the Clean Water Act. The rationale behind this judicial lawmaking, as first articulated by the Seventh Circuit in Scott, is that "the CWA should be liberally construed to achieve its objectives—in this case to impose a duty on the EPA to establish TMDL's when the states have defaulted by refusal to act over a long period." Scott, 741 F.2d at 998 (emphasis added). The Scott court found that EPA had a duty to intervene because Congress could not have intended that "an important aspect of a federal scheme of water pollution control could be frustrated by the refusal of states to act." Id. at 997. The Seventh Circuit in Scott made clear, however, that the duty to declare a "constructive submission" could be avoided if "EPA promptly comes forward with persuasive evidence indicating that the states are or will soon be, in the process of submitting TMDL proposals."

The intent of the "constructive submission" doctrine is to ensure that EPA will ultimately bear a mandatory duty to act in furtherance of the goals of the CWA if a state refuses to act. Despite New York's understandably slow pace in the face of EPA's early neglect of the TMDL program, the record amply supports EPA's conclusion that New York has not in the past "refused," and is not presently "refusing," to act in furtherance of the TMDL program mandated by the CWA. In fact, the contrary is true. Accordingly, so long as New York continues to participate actively and meaningfully in the effort to promulgate TMDLs for the waterbodies on its § 303(d) priority list, the Court is of the view that the State has not "refused" to act, and EPA therefore is under no duty to declare a "constructive submission" of inadequate TMDLs by New York. The determination as to whether the State's participation is active and meaningful is one for EPA to make, based on the record before it. The Court cannot say, however, based on the administrative record, that EPA has acted arbitrarily or capriciously in concluding that New York's participation has been sufficiently active and meaningful to obviate resort to the "constructive submission" approach. Accordingly, plaintiffs are not entitled to relief at this time on their § 706(2)(A) theory under Claim Six.

[The court also rejected the NRDC's argument that EPA had "unreasonably delayed" agency action in violation of APA § 706(a)(1). While denying plaintiffs their requested relief, the court admonished EPA and the State that if the two substantially departed from the terms of the Memorandum of Agreement the plaintiffs could renew their "constructive submission" case and seek a judicial order for EPA to issue New York's TMDLs. This claim was dismissed without prejudice.]

NOTE ON TMDL LITIGATION

The principal case, *Natural Resources Defense Council v. Fox*, refused to find that the State of New York's delay in filing impaired waters inventories and proposing TMDLs to EPA constituted a "constructive submission" of no TMDL. This result may be explained by the developing rapport between the state and EPA as well as a series of concrete steps taken to make New York TMDLs a reality. However, this outcome stands in contrast to an opposite consistent trend in litigation. In at least thirty other states, environmental organizations have filed citizen suits to require EPA to develop TMDLs alleging that state authorities have failed to do so in a timely fashion. This litigation pattern springs from the Seventh Circuit's 1984 decision in *Scott v. City of Hammond*, 741 F.2d 992 (7th Cir.1984), which had concluded that the "prolonged failure" of a state to submit any TMDL to EPA for approval constituted the "constructive submission" of no TMDL. This result triggered EPA's obligation either 1) to disapprove the defective submission and issue the TMDL itself or 2) persuade the tardy state to act. Hayes v. EPA, 48 Env't Rep. Cas. (BNA) 1078 (N.D.Okla.1998) and Kingman Park Civic Ass'n v. EPA, 29 Envtl. L.Rep. 10716 (D.D.C.1999) are examples of this trend.

More recent cases have gone beyond the threshold question of whether state has submitted any Water Quality Limited Segment (WQLS) inventory and TMDLs to EPA, to more sophisticated questions evaluating the nature and sufficiency of a state submission and the quality of EPA's response. Two cases, Idaho Sportsmen's Coalition v. Browner, 951 F.Supp. 962 (W.D.Wash.1996) and Sierra Club v. Hankinson, 939 F.Supp. 865 (N.D.Ga. 1996), provide good examples. In the Idaho case, the court bristled at the lengthy 25 year TMDL phase in schedule with no fixed deadlines and just "soft" target dates. The Georgia case presented even a more lengthy TMDL adoption rate which reached to over 100 years for the impaired waters on the current listing. The litigation wave may have crested for the moment with the states being forced to take their § 303(d) more seriously and with EPA according to the TMDL program the agency's emphasis it deserves. In July, 2000 EPA issued its TMDL regulations—40 C.F.R. Part 130—with revised definitions of TMDLs, impaired water bodies, specific TMDL elements, changed listing cycle and new public participation requirements. Undoubtedly the provisions of these rules will be tested in the courts. The new TMDL regulations can be found at www.epa.gov/owow/tmdl/finalrule/finalrule.pdf. It is worth noting that the TMDL rules have already found opposition within the halls of Congress. Soon after their promulgation Congress added a TMDL rider to a supplemental appropriations bill containing funds for U.S. military forces in Kosova, Columbia anti-drug efforts and disaster relief. The rider prohibited EPA from implementing the rules until the end of FY01. The next several years will reveal whether the 1972 congressional goals incorporated in § 303(d) will be achieved or deferred.

NOTES AND QUESTIONS

1. *Water Quality Related Effluent Limitations.* In the Class Discussion Problem, if UWC complies with EPA's § 306 new source performance standard for the widget industry, can the state pollution control agency require even greater control of the discharge of pollutant X? On what legal basis could this be required? What policies would justify this increased level of pollution control?

Should the new source performance standards mandated by § 306 ever be considered *inadequate*? Remember the CWA standard for setting the § 306 standards. Can local water quality conditions require the imposition of additional pollution control measures beyond those specified in § 306? Read the following portion of § 302(a) [§ 1312(a)] for part of the answer.

> Whenever, in the judgment of the Administrator or as identified under section 1314(1) of this title, discharges of pollutants from a point source or group of point sources, with the application of effluent limitations required under section 1311(b)(2) of this title, would interfere with the attainment or maintenance of that water quality in a specific portion of the navigable waters which shall assure protection of public health, public water supplies, agricultural and industrial uses, and the protection and propagation of a balanced population of shellfish, fish and wildlife, and allow recreational activities in and on the water, effluent limitations (including alternative effluent control strategies) for such point source or sources shall be established which can reasonably be expected to contribute to the attainment or maintenance of such water quality.

This authorization for water quality related effluent limitations contains several complicating features which have apparently lead to its non-use. Prior to setting these § 302 effluent standards EPA must hold public hearings and it must also perform an assessment of the relative costs and benefits associated with a higher degree of pollution control. Section 302(b) flatly states that for non-toxic pollutants no § 302 standard can be imposed when "there is no reasonable relationship between the economic and social costs and the benefits to be obtained * * * from achieving such limitation." Is this just an admonition against additional pollution control without demonstrable and significant benefits?

How does § 302 relate to the water quality standards set under the authority of § 303? Couldn't compliance with a state's water quality standards require controls more stringent than those required by § 306? In its 1987 amendments to the CWA Congress shed some light on the relationship between these two sections. The Senate report on this legislation stated,

> Ordinarily, State water quality standards established or revised under section 303 designate the uses specified in section 101(a)(2) of the Act, and if implemented through adequate criteria, waste load allocations, and effluent limitations in permits, will protect the level of water quality addressed by section 302(a). The Administrator is to use the authority of section 302(a), however, where compliance with best available technology requirements or the State water quality standards

process are not attaining this level of water quality, due to point sources.

* * *

Section 303 of the Act is the primary mechanism for the development of State water quality standards and effluent limitations based on them. In developing standards under the section, States are authorized to consider the economics of achieving such standards only as allowed under EPA's regulations established pursuant to section 303. Section 302 is not intended to undercut or in any way affect the development of water quality standards under section 303 nor the imposition of section 301(b)(1)(C) of the Act. Rather, it is a supplemental provision which directs the Administrator, with the concurrence of the State, to impose effluent limitations which assure the attainment or maintenance of water quality for the protection of public health, public water supplies, agricultural and industrial uses, and the protection and propagation of a balanced population of shellfish, fish, and wildlife, and recreational activities in and on the water, in situations where the adopted water quality standards do not assure the attainment and maintenance of such uses, including in some instances those waters that are listed under the new section 305(c).

(S.Rep. No. 50, 99th Cong., 1st Sess. 24 (1986).)

Does this make § 302 a special "supplemental" power which EPA can use when state water quality standards are not being achieved? Why not just require EPA to force the states to meet their water quality standards without resorting to § 302?

2. *Total Maximum Daily Loads on TMDLs.* Reading over § 303(d) you should observe that their CWA section makes three main demands of the states. They must,

- identify waters that are and will remain polluted after the application of technology-based effluent standards
- make a prioritized list of these waters based upon the severity of the water pollution
- establish TMDLs for these waters at levels necessary to meet applicable water quality standards accounting for seasoned variations and including a margin of safety to reflect a lack of certainty about discharges and water quality.

The state must then submit their impaired waters inventories and TMDLs to EPA for approval. If disapproved by EPA, then EPA must promulgate both the inventories and the TMDLs by itself, for incorporation into the state's § 303(e) plan. Consider the CWA's language in § 303(d). Is permissive or mandatory? Does anything appear to be missing from the statutory structure of § 303(d)?

Understand the literal scope of application of § 303(d)—it takes up where the water quality benefits of technology-based point source controls end and it views the achievement of the state WQS as the important, ultimate goal. Once a water body is found to or is predicted *not* to achieve WQS even with technologically-based controls, TMDLs are seemingly required. The waterway is referred to as a Water Quality Limited Segment or WQLS. A TMDL is (1) a calculation of the maximum amount of a pollutant that a water body can receive and still meet WQS and (2) an allocation of that pollutant load to the various sources affecting the water's quality. Put another way, a TMDL is the sum of the allowable loads of a single pollutant from all contributing point and nonpoint sources. Notice that the calculation must also include a margin of safety and account for seasonal variations in water quality.

A simplified way to analyze the TMDL concept is through an arithmetic illustration for a pollutant subject to a WQS—pollutant X. The General Formula For Calculating TMDLs is:

WLA	(Waste Load Allocations from Point Sources)
LA	(Load Allocations from Nonpoint Sources)
MOS	(Margin of Safety)
+ MFD	(Margin for Future Development)
TMDL	(Total Maximum Daily Load)

Consider the following waste loading allocation problem.

• TMDL Calculation Hypothetical

Assume that credible technical calculations have determined that this water body can receive up to 250 units of pollutant X and still achieve its WQS. This means that the water can assimilate discharges of pollutant X only up to 250 units and that discharges greater than 250 units will result in a WQS violation making the water body an impaired waterway of a WQLS. First, if the water body currently receives *less than* 250 units of pollutant X, it will not be on the CWA § 303(d) inventory of impaired waters and ostensibly not be subject to TMDLs. Second, if the water body currently receives *more than* 250 units of pollutant X it is not achieving its WQS and should be listed on the state's inventory of WQLSs. Third, assume that the water body currently receives 350 units of pollutant X; 200 units from nonpoint sources and 150 units from point sources. Consider the following questions.

(1) How would you decide to distribute the right to discharge pollutant X into this water body?

(2) What would be the technical issues that would be important to consider in making allocation decisions?

(3) What would be the socio-economic or political considerations that could influence such a decision?

(4) As a state water pollution program official, how would you plan for and account for the Margin of Safety (MOS) and Margin for future Development (MFD) factors?

(5) How would you achieve enforceable reductions in existing loadings of pollutant X from nonpoint and point sources to reach the discharge target of 250 units?

(6) How should this calculation be affected by the existence of natural, background amounts of pollutant X or amounts added to the water from atmospheric deposition?

3. *Water Quality Issues—Anti–Degradation.* In the Class Discussion problem, would it matter whether UWC selected site 1, 2, or 3 for its new plant? What are the pros and cons of each site? How might state water quality standards affect the choice? What information would UWC need in order to make its locational decision?

What if UWC chose site 1 for its new plant? The water in the river adjacent to that site was generally unpolluted to the degree that the state has classified it as suitable for trout fishing. What if the planned discharge of pollutant X from the UWC facility would violate the state's stringent water quality standard (WQS) for that pristine river segment. Could UWC petition the state to change its WQS to a less restrictive level so as to accommodate the facility?

What if existing water quality meets or exceeds the fishable/swimmable standard? Must water quality remain unchanged at this high level indefinitely? If a state wants to encourage economic development and attract industry, can a waterway of pristine quality be given a relatively low classification in order to create a great deal of unused assimilative capacity to be doled out to dischargers? As a general policy matter, should a state be allowed to degrade this high level of environmental quality?

Under EPA rules, states are required to adopt an anti-degradation policy as part of their water quality standards. Federal antidegradation policy was established at least as early as 1968 by the Secretary of Interior and was incorporated into the initial water quality standards regulation issued in 1975. EPA regulations express a three-part policy: (1) existing water quality and uses shall be maintained (Tier 1), (2) water quality better than that which is required for the "fishable/swimmable" standard may only be reduced in certain defined circumstances to allow economic or social development to occur (Tier 2), and 3) high quality waters of exceptional recreational or ecological significance represent an outstanding national resource (ONRs) whose water quality is to be maintained and protected (Tier 3). See 40 C.F.R. § 131.12(a). Section 303(d)(4)(B) was added in 1987 in an attempt to codify EPA's policy. As noted, part 2 of the anti-degradation policy provides for a lowering of high water quality when it "is necessary to accommodate important economic or social development in the area in which the waters are located." 40 C.F.R. § 131.12(a)(2). How should this policy be administered if UWC wished to locate its plant located at site 1? What about site 2? How far should water quality be allowed to degrade? If you were responsible for considering a degradation request, what factors would you consider and how would you reach your decision? Would "any" economic and social rationale be sufficient? What is the Clean Air Act analogy to this problem? Are there any lessons to be learned?

What if UWC chose site 3 for its new plant? The water in the river adjacent to that site was extremely polluted to the extent that it would only support limited aquatic species. The present uses of the river fell considerably short of those specified by the state's WQS. These poor water quality conditions were the result of discharges from 10 point sources and from varied non-point sources. Can UWC be allowed to locate at site 3 and if so under what conditions?

Can a state decide to have lower water quality than is required by the CWA? While the Act sets forth a general fishable/swimmable (§ 101(a)(2)) standard for water quality, EPA's regulations anticipate that the floor for use designation will be at least the existing use of the water body with gradual improvement to meet the fishable/swimmable standard. Should states ever be able to set water quality standards below those required to meet this existing use level? What if the existing water uses fall short of the § 101(a)(2) standard? EPA rules permit a "downgrading" of water quality from higher levels if the state conducts a "use attainability analysis" and it can demonstrate that such attainment is "not feasible."

4. *Toxic Water Pollutants.* What might occur if pollutant X was a toxic pollutant and the receiving water was already highly polluted with toxics?

The 1987 CWA amendments added § 304(l) which established a new procedure for states which would lead to the development of individual control strategies (ICS) applicable to point sources discharging into river segments where water quality standards would not be met in spite of compliance with BAT controls. This was intended to remedy "toxic hot spots." The first step under § 304(l) was to identify those waters in need of ICS. The states were to have submitted these lists to EPA by February of 1989 and receive approval or disapproval by June of 1989. EPA could take over these responsibilities if the state failed to do so. The second step was to identify the specific point sources whose toxic pollutant discharges prevent the attainment of the water quality standards. The third and final component of the § 304(l) program was the establishment of an ICS for each identified point source. The structure of this toxics control program is quite similar to that imposed under § 303(d). Section 304(l)(1)(D) states that

> for each such segment, an individual control strategy which the State determines will produce a reduction in the discharge of toxic pollutants from point sources identified by the State under this paragraph through the establishment of effluent limitations under section 1342 of this title and water quality standards under section 1313(c)(2)(B) of this title, which reduction is sufficient, in combination with existing controls on point and nonpoint sources of pollution, to achieve the applicable water quality standard as soon as possible, but not later than 3 years after the date of the establishment of such strategy.

If the East River near the proposed UWC plant was identified under this § 304(l) process, how long would existing identified sources have to come into compliance with their ICS? Remember the five-year extension provided for in § 302(b)(2)(B) [§ 1312(b)(2)(B)]? If it would discharge toxic pollutants, how should the proposed UWC plant be analyzed and treated under the ICS system?

5. *Nonpoint Source Pollution and Water Quality Standards.* What if the surface runoff of acidity and suspended solids from the mining and timber harvesting operations reached the East River or one of its tributaries and raised the pH and turbidity levels above state water quality standards (WQS)? Could UWC be forced by litigation, or otherwise, to stop this pollution in order to meet the state WQS? What about seeting a TMDL applicable to UWC's mining and timbering nonpoint source runoff?

After reading the excerpt from *Oregon Natural Resources Council v. United States Forest Service,* if your circuit followed that holding, would it be likely that a violation of the state WQS for pH and turbidity caused by UWC's mining and timber operations could be enjoined by suit under CWA § 505? Would the Administrative Procedure Act be helpful?

The question of whether TMDLs could be required to correct WQS violations has been a controversial one. At least one federal court-Pronsolino v. EPA, 91 F.Supp.2d 1337 (N.D.Cal.2000) has ruled that EPA has the authority to establish TMDLs for waters that are impaired solely as a result of nonpoint source pollution. Although some have suggested that it is unclear whether § 303(d) covers nonpoint source pollution, EPA has designed its regulation assuming that it does. See Oliver A. Houck, TMDLs III: A New Framework for the Clean Water Act's Ambient Standards Program, 28 ELR 10421–22 (Aug. 1998). Despite this uncertainty, EPA's July 2000 TMDL regulations require, as one of the required TMDL elements, that load allocations attributable to nonpoint sources of a pollutant be established. See 40 C.F.R. § 130.33(6). What kind of data would be needed to set a TMDL for UWC's nonpoint source loads into the East River? How specific should it be in terms of "causing" an East River WQS violation for pH and turbidity? What if there were other potential nonpoint sources of these two pollutants in the vicinity of UWC? What if they were farms and livestock operations?

6. *Locating Water Pollution Discharges—The Mixing Zone Concept.* In the Class Discussion Problem, to what extent (if any) could the dispersion of pollutant X be permitted to satisfy any state water quality standard? How would the location of the plant's outfall be important in determining whether the state's water quality standards would be violated?

How are water quality standards (WQS) measured and imposed? Consider this example. If you discharged one pound of pollutant X into a river and measured its concentration close to the discharge point, its concentration would likely be so high as to violate WQS. Should compliance with a WQS be determined in the immediate location of the discharge point or at a point some distance away? EPA has created the "mixing zone" concept which allows a pollutant's discharge to be diluted by the ambient receiving water within limits. This excerpt comes from an unsuccessful challenge to permit conditions imposed upon oil company outfalls in Cook Inlet, Alaska. The court discusses the concept of "mixing zone."

> We pause at this point to explain briefly the crucial notion of a "mixing zone." Environmental agencies do—and under present technology, must—permit polluted effluents to be discharged into natural

bodies of water. By definition, the effluent itself does not meet water quality standards; otherwise, it would not be considered polluted. But the receiving water dilutes the effluent, and this dilution increases as the plume of effluent gradually diffuses in the receiving water. The "mixing zone" is simply the area of dispersal in the receiving waters where the pollutants in the effluent are not sufficiently diluted to meet water quality standards. It necessarily follows, then, that the edge or outer circumference of the mixing zone is defined as the boundary at which water quality standards are first met. The size and configuration of the mixing zone is a crucial variable in determining whether or not a given effluent can be discharged. If the permitted mixing zone is tiny— say, one meter in diameter—any effluent whatever will violate water quality standards; if the permitted mixing zone is huge—say, 100 kilometers—a tremendously toxic effluent can be discharged without violating water quality standards. The EPA has never set a general-purpose figure or formula for determining the proper mixing zone; instead, at least in some cases, the Agency appears to use a 100 meter mixing zone as a rule-of-thumb [in its Ocean discharge criteria]. Nor does the ADEC [Alaska Dept. of Envtl. Conservation] have a general-purpose mixing zone formula.

Marathon Oil Co. v. EPA, 830 F.2d 1346, 1349 (5th Cir.1987). See also Puerto Rico Sun Oil Co. v. EPA, 8 F.3d 73 (1st Cir.1993). How could this be significant to UWC? What impact, if any, does this concept have on non-point source pollution caused by UWC mining and timber operations?

SECTION 5. ENFORCING WATER POLLUTION LAW

A. BACKGROUND AND OVERVIEW

During the early period of environmental law (1960's and 1970's), most of the energy expended by agencies such as EPA focused upon basic program development and environmental standard-setting. The field was new and the basic policy directions were being established. Although the initial environmental statutes such as The Clean Water Act contained enforcement authorities, relatively little concentrated effort and resources were devoted to ensuring compliance with the emerging sets of rules and regulations. At the state level, the development of enforcement authority and capabilities lagged even farther behind. Since the mid-to-late 1980s environmental enforcement has become more of a priority at all levels of government and with citizens as well. This section of the chapter deals with enforcing water pollution law. It is especially important to understand the basic theories and techniques because many lawyers who practice environmental law actually work on regulatory compliance and enforcement matters as their primary function.

The word enforcement actually sounds threatening—being forced to do something by someone in authority. Modern enforcement personnel euphemistically describe their work as ensuring regulatory compliance or compliance assurance. By whatever name, environmental enforcement is important to the government, citizens, and the regulated community as well. First and foremost, enforcement reduces polluting activities and helps to actually achieve environmental goals like the CWA's "fishable/swimmable" goal. Secondly, it assures industry groups that all similar facilities are being held to the same standard and that no one obtains a competitive advantage through non-compliance with permit or other regulatory requirements. Creating an equal or level playing field for economic competitors is an important objective.

Traditional enforcement activities focus upon a determination of whether a regulated entity is "in compliance" with its regulatory requirements such as an NPDES permit. Compliance status is usually established by an agency's (EPA) collection of source performance data and this is done by monitoring, inspections, source reporting and the receipt of citizen complaints. From time to time, EPA will set as a priority emphasizing enforcement against certain industries and with regard to certain media. Once the compliance data is collected and verified, problem cases will be identified and a range of different kinds of enforcement actions may be taken. Government agencies operate with limited resources and they concentrate those resources in such a way so as to maximize compliance results. Much enforcement is accomplished by way of EPA/source negotiation and compromise (settlements). Sometimes the agency will use administrative complaints and penalty orders. These administrative actions are far away the most common techniques employed to assure compliance mainly because of cost, efficiency, and flexibility. EPA always reserves the right to use more forceful, non-administrative methods such as judicial enforcement to seek compliance and deterrence objectives. Over the decade of the 1990's EPA would annually refer between approximately 50 to 125 CWA cases to the Department of Justice for civil enforcement. Criminal enforcement referrals are also possible yet less frequent. A final element of the enforcement picture is the citizen suit authorized by CWA § 505 and most other federal environmental statutes. These citizen or environmental group-initiated actions can supplement governmental efforts and can bring significant results improving environmental quality.

In recent years EPA has begun to emphasize compliance incentives and compliance assistance as an adjunct to the traditional enforcement techniques. These new efforts acknowledge that environmental rules can be complex and firms, particularly small businesses, sometimes need assistance to help them comply. EPA's compliance assistance programs focus on the transfer of needed information by way of on-site visits, compliance assistance hotlines, workshops/training presentations, and the distribution of tools such as compliance checklists and guides. Additionally, EPA has encouraged voluntary auditing and self-disclosure of environment violations through its issuance of an Audit Policy. See Incentives for Self-Policing: Discovery, Disclosure, Correction, and Prevention of Violations, 60 Fed. Reg. 66706 (Dec. 22, 1995). The Audit Policy provides incentives for companies to develop environmental audit and compliance management systems to detect, disclose, and correct violations. When firms voluntarily discover and promptly disclose environmental violations to EPA, the agency will waive or substantially reduce (75%) gravity-based civil penalties. Also, for those companies meeting the policies conditions, EPA will not recommend criminal referral to the Department of Justice. While the voluntary audit technique remains controversial, it does reflect the modern trend towards more firm-initiated compliance assurance techniques. With this introduction, the materials below will emphasize the traditional judicial enforcement techniques. These methods continue to be important and to be used by environmental agencies.

B. The Legal Structure of Government Civil Enforcement

CLASS DISCUSSION PROBLEM: GOVERNMENTAL ENFORCEMENT OF THE CLEAN WATER ACT: MULTIPLE ENFORCEMENT ISSUES

One of Centralia's oldest and most established business firms is Wilson Foods (Wilson). Wilson operates a food processing, warehousing and beverage canning facility in Centralia. The wastewater generated by these activities is discharged into the East River. Wilson has obtained a water discharge permit from the State of Euphoria's Department of Environmental Conservation (DEC), the agency which administers the CWA NPDES program. Under the terms of this permit Wilson is authorized to discharge wastewater into the river at specified outfall points but its discharged effluent must also have characteristics that do not exceed numerical limits set by the permit. Under permit terms, Wilson is also obligated to monitor the nature of its waste water, to keep records of its plant operation and to report regularly its pollution control results to DEC in the form of Discharge Monitoring Reports (DMRs). The permit contains no terms or conditions which might be considered unusual for a plant in Wilson's industrial group and of its size.

Recently the DEC and EPA's regional office having responsibility for the State of Euphoria received information in the form of an anonymous letter stating that Wilson was "violating anti-pollution laws." Specifically the letter alleged the company was acting improperly in several ways:

1. the effluent monitoring device on Wilson's main outfall has been intentionally miscalibrated to under-register effluent concentration.

2. that DMRs were sporadically filed with the DEC and usually the reports were 6 months late.

3. that during peak production periods untreated effluent was disposed of by discharges through an unlisted outfall point and by pumping into a sewer line which crossed the Wilson plant site.

4. that Wilson frequently violated the effluent limitations incorporated into its NPDES permit (the plant's DMRs reflected this).

Although the letter was unsigned, it reflected a familiarity with the Wilson plant's design and operation that could only have arisen from first hand experience, possibly coming from a Wilson employee. The DEC believed the letter was credible but due to serious understaffing merely placed the facility on its "careful watch" list. EPA, on the other hand, took the matter so seriously that it assigned the case to a compliance team. Over the past 2 years the EPA enforcement division had noticed a significant variation in the discharge performance described in Wilson's DMRs (sometimes high and other times low). In addition, ambient water quality in the vicinity of the Wilson plant continued to violate Euphoria water quality standards in spite of substantial point source and non-point source control on that East River segment. In the opinion of the EPA regional enforcement director, Wilson needed to be investigated.

Consider the following questions:

A.   As a preliminary step, EPA intends to investigate the Wilson plant in order to inspect the plant's product processes and outfalls and to collect documentary evidence in Wilson's files concerning production and discharge practices. Is EPA authorized to enter the Wilson plant and attempt to recover this data? Could EPA enlist the services of a private engineering consultant to either assist in the inspection or independently conduct it under EPA's direction? Can the information derived from this inspection be made available to the public or can Wilson force EPA not to disclose it?

B.   From the limited facts provided, what enforcement options are available to EPA under the CWA especially under § 309? What can EPA enforce under § 309? If you were EPA's regional attorney, what objectives would you have in contemplating an enforcement strategy with regards to Wilson?

a.   Could EPA administratively order Wilson to comply with its permit conditions? How would such an order be enforced? Could EPA go directly to court to seek injunctive relief without first issuing an order?

b.   Could EPA seek financial penalties against Wilson for any or all of the four "violations" mentioned in the anonymous letter if they were later corroborated with evidence? Could EPA assess such monetary penalties by itself or did it need to seek judicial imposition of these charges?

c.   Could any individual be prosecuted for criminal violation of the CWA for any of the conduct described in the anonymous letter? What range of Wilson corporate officers and employees might be exposed to criminal sanctions?

d.   What if Sam, the Wilson employee who wrote the anonymous letter tipping EPA and DEC to Wilson's violations, were fired when his actions became known? What recourse exists for Sam?

C.   What if the State of Euphoria's DEC has begun to investigate Wilson's compliance status? Does this state action displace EPA's power to enforce? What if the state DEC has commenced an enforcement action against Wilson in state court or through state administrative means? Does this prevent EPA from taking its own action? Does EPA have any recourse against the State of Euphoria if it conducts a weak enforcement program permitting NPDES permit non-compliance to go unchecked?

Andreen, Beyond Words of Exhortation: The Congressional Prescription for Vigorous Federal Enforcement of the Clean Water Act

55 Geo.Wash.L.Rev. 202, 215–222 (1987) (footnotes omitted).

B. A New Beginning: The Federal Water Pollution Control Act Amendments of 1972

Congress completely revised the federal approach to water pollution control when it enacted the Federal Water Pollution Control Act Amendments of 1972. These Amendments established the basic structure of the current Federal Water Pollution Control Act, better known today as the Clean Water Act. The pollution control strategy of the Clean Water Act centers upon a broad prohibition contained in section 301(a), which forbids "the discharge of any pollutant by any person" to waters of the United States, unless the discharge conforms with certain provisions of the Act. Among those provisions are several that call upon the EPA to promulgate effluent limitations that apply to every discharger in a particular category. To implement and monitor compliance with those limitations and other standards, section 301(a) also requires a discharger to obtain a permit and comply with its terms. Such a permit is issued through the National Pollutant Discharge Elimination System (NPDES), established by section 402, which serves as a means for transforming most of the requirements of the Act into specific obligations of the individual discharger.

Enforcement, therefore, is no longer limited to instances where public health is endangered or where the government can show that a particular source of pollution is responsible for violation of a water quality standard. Instead, the Clean Water Act makes it unlawful to discharge a pollutant without a NPDES permit or in violation of such a permit. Furthermore, to enhance the EPA's ability to determine whether a discharger has violated its NPDES permit, Congress authorized the Agency to impose substantial monitoring and reporting requirements on the regulated community. Pursuant to this authority, the EPA requires each permittee to file periodically a discharge monitoring report (DMR) that reveals the levels of pollutants found in the permittee's effluent. The determination of permit violations, consequently, is in many cases a relatively simple affair requiring only a comparison of the permit conditions with the permittee's actual performance as shown by a DMR.

Moreover, the Clean Water Act eliminated the procedural impediments to effective enforcement and created a wide array of sanctions for violations of the Act. In doing so, the Act gives the federal government enormous power to enforce the Act through administrative action and direct access to the courts to seek injunctive relief, civil monetary penalties, and even criminal sanctions. The Act also provides private citizens with a civil right of action to obtain compliance with its requirements.

1. Federal Enforcement

The primary mechanisms provided by the Act for federal enforcement of the NPDES program are found in section 309. Whenever the Administrator of the EPA finds that a discharger has violated the terms of a state-issued NPDES permit, section 309(a)(1) requires the Administrator to react in one of two ways. One option states that the Administrator "shall" notify the discharger and the state government of the alleged violation. If the state fails to take "appropriate enforcement action" within thirty days, the Administrator either "shall issue" an administrative order requiring the discharger to comply with its permit or "shall bring" a civil enforcement suit. This option recognizes that states having a qualified permit program possess primary enforcement responsibility with regard to their permits, while the EPA serves "as a backstop." The second available course of action, however, recognizes that federal enforcement power is concurrent with that of state governments. Under this alternative, the Administrator is to proceed under section 309(a)(3), which provides that he "shall" issue a compliance order or institute civil proceedings without giving notice or awaiting state enforcement. In cases not involving the violation of a state-issued permit, the Administrator is not given the option of deferring to state action. Therefore, where the Administrator finds a violation of a federally issued NPDES permit or a discharger who has failed to obtain a permit, the Administrator is required, pursuant to section 309(a)(3), to issue a compliance order or to bring suit.

Despite the mandatory language used in section 309(a), section 309(b) merely authorizes the Administrator to undertake civil actions "for any violation for which he is authorized to issue a compliance order under [section 309(a)]." In such civil actions, the Administrator may seek injunctive relief as well as civil penalties.

In addition to compliance orders and civil actions, the Clean Water Act provides for a host of other remedial and punitive actions. Section 309(c) authorizes criminal prosecutions for knowing or negligent violations. A conviction under this provision subjects a discharger not only to fines and possible imprisonment, but also to debarment from federal contracting. In addition, the Administrator is authorized, in an emergency, to bring suit immediately to abate any "pollution" that presents a danger to public health or the livelihood of individuals.

2. Private Enforcement

In order to both supplement and induce government enforcement, Congress empowered citizens to gain access to the courts to enforce the pollution requirements of the Clean Water Act. Specifically, section 505— the citizen suit provision—authorizes "any citizen" to commence a civil action against a discharger who is allegedly in violation of an "effluent standard or limitation" or a compliance order issued by either the EPA or a state. Such cases may be brought in federal district courts, which possess jurisdiction to enjoin those violations and impose civil penalties.

At least sixty days prior to the commencement of a private enforcement action, however, the citizen generally must give notice of the violation to the EPA, the state, and the discharger. This notification requirement was intended to give the administrative agencies a chance to enforce the law before allowing a citizen suit to proceed. If at the end of sixty days the EPA or a state agency is not "diligently prosecuting a civil or criminal action," the citizen may file the suit.

To ensure that the EPA complies with its mandatory duties under the Act, section 505 also allows a citizen to bring suit against the Administrator for an alleged failure to perform any nondiscretionary act or duty. District courts have jurisdiction to compel the performance of such duties. However, sixty-days notice must be given to the Administrator before filing suit, apparently to allow the EPA time to act.

Excerpt from the Clean Water Act
33 U.S.C. § 1319.

§ 309(a) State enforcement; compliance orders

(1) Whenever, on the basis of any information available to him, the Administrator finds that any person is in violation of any condition or limitation which implements section 1311, 1312, 1316, 1317, 1318, 1328, or 1345 of this title in a permit issued by a State under an approved permit program under section 1342 or 1344 of this title he shall proceed under his authority in paragraph (3) of this subsection or he shall notify the person in alleged violation and such State of such finding. If beyond the thirtieth day after the Administrator's notification the State has not commenced appropriate enforcement action, the Administrator shall issue an order requiring such person to comply with such condition or limitation or shall bring a civil action in accordance with subsection (b) of this section.

(2) Whenever, on the basis of information available to him, the Administrator finds that violations of permit conditions or limitations as set forth in paragraph (1) of this subsection are so widespread that such violations appear to result from a failure of the State to enforce such permit conditions or limitations effectively, he shall so notify the State. If the Administrator finds such failure extends beyond the thirtieth day after such notice, he shall give public notice of such finding. During the period beginning with such public notice and ending when such State satisfies the Administrator that it will enforce such conditions and limitations (hereafter referred to in this section as the period of "federally assumed enforcement"), except where an extension has been granted under paragraph (5)(B) of this subsection, the Administrator shall enforce any permit condition or limitation with respect to any person—

(A) by issuing an order to comply with such condition or limitation, or

(B) by bringing a civil action under subsection (b) of this section.

(3) Whenever on the basis of any information available to him the Administrator finds that any person is in violation of section 1311, 1312, 1316, 1317, 1318, 1328, or 1345 of this title, or is in violation of any permit condition or limitation implementing any of such sections in a permit issued under section 1342 of this title by him or by a State or in a permit issued under section 1344 of this title by a State, he shall issue an order requiring such person to comply with such section or requirement, or he shall bring a civil action in accordance with subsection (b) of this section.
* * *

(b) Civil actions

The Administrator is authorized to commence a civil action for appropriate relief, including a permanent or temporary injunction, for any violation for which he is authorized to issue a compliance order under subsection (a) of this section. Any action under this subsection may be brought in the district court of the United States for the district in which the defendant is located or resides or is doing business, and such court shall have jurisdiction to restrain such violation and to require compliance. Notice of the commencement of such action shall be given immediately to the appropriate State.

(c) Criminal penalties

(1) Negligent violations

Any person who—

(A) negligently violates section 1311, 1312, 1316, 1317, 1318, 1328, or 1345 of this title, or any permit condition or limitation implementing any of such sections in a permit issued under section 1342 of this title by the Administrator or by a State, or any requirement imposed in a pretreatment program approved under section 1342(a)(3) or 1342(b)(8) of this title or in a permit issued under section 1344 of this title by the Secretary of the Army or by a State; or

(B) negligently introduces into a sewer system or into a publicly owned treatment works any pollutant or hazardous substance which such person knew or reasonably should have known could cause personal injury or property damage or, other than in compliance with all applicable Federal, State, or local requirements or permits, which causes such treatment works to violate any effluent limitation or condition in any permit issued to the treatment works under section 1342 of this title by the Administrator or a State;

shall be punished by a fine of not less than $2,500 nor more than $25,000 per day of violation, or by imprisonment for not more than 1 year, or by both. If a conviction of a person is for a violation committed after a first conviction of such person under this paragraph, punishment shall be by a fine of not more than $50,000 per day of violation, or by imprisonment of not more than 2 years, or by both.

(2) Knowing violations

Any person who—

(A) knowingly violates sections 1311, 1312, 1316, 1317, 1318, 1328, or 1345 of this title, or any permit condition or limitation implementing any of such sections in a permit issued under section 1342 of this title by the Administrator or by a State, or any requirement imposed in a pretreatment program approved under section 1342(a)(3) or 1342(b)(8) of this title or in a permit issued under section 1344 of this title by the Secretary of the Army or by a State; or

(B) knowingly introduces into a sewer system or into a publicly owned treatment works any pollutant or hazardous substance which such person knew or reasonably should have known could cause personal injury or property damage or, other than in compliance with all applicable Federal, State, or local requirements or permits, which causes such treatment works to violate any effluent limitation or condition in a permit issued to the treatment works under section 1342 of this title by the Administrator or a State;

shall be punished by a fine of not less than $5,000 nor more than $50,000 per day of violation, or by imprisonment for not more than 3 years, or by both. If a conviction of a person is for a violation committed after a first conviction of such person under this paragraph, punishment shall be by a fine of not more than $100,000 per day of violation, or by imprisonment of not more than 6 years, or by both. * * *

(4) False statements

Any person who knowingly makes any false material statement, representation, or certification in any application, record, report, plan, or other document filed or required to be maintained under this chapter or who knowingly falsifies, tampers with, or renders inaccurate any monitoring device or method required to be maintained under this chapter, shall upon conviction, be punished by a fine of not more than $10,000, or by imprisonment for not more than 2 years, or by both. If a conviction of a person is for a violation committed after a first conviction of such person under this paragraph, punishment shall be by a fine of not more than $20,000 per day of violation, or by imprisonment of not more than 4 years, or by both. * * *

(d) Civil penalties; factors considered in determining amount

Any person who violates sections 1311, 1312, 1316, 1317, 1318, 1328, or 1345 of this title, or any permit condition or limitation implementing any of such sections in a permit issued under section 1342 of this title by the Administrator, or by a State, or in a permit issued under section 1344 of this title by a State, or any requirement imposed in a pretreatment program approved under section 1342(a)(3) or 1342(b)(8) of this title, and any person who violates any order issued by the Administrator under subsection (a) of this section, shall be subject to a civil penalty not to exceed $25,000 per day for each violation. In determining the amount of a civil penalty the court shall consider the seriousness of the violation or violations, the economic benefit (if any) resulting from the violation, any history of such violations, any good-faith efforts to comply with the applicable requirements, the economic impact of the penalty on the violator, and such other matters as justice may require. For purposes of this subsection, a single operational upset which leads to simultaneous violations of more than one pollutant parameter shall be treated as a single violation.

NOTES AND QUESTIONS

1. *Obtaining CWA Enforcement Information.* As a preliminary step, EPA intends to investigate the Wilson plant in order to inspect the plant's product processes and outfalls and to collect documentary evidence in Wilson's files concerning production and discharge practices. Is EPA authorized to enter the Wilson plant and attempt to recover this data? Could EPA enlist the services of a private engineering consultant to either assist in the inspection or independently conduct it under EPA's direction? Can the information derived from this inspection be made available to the public or can Wilson force EPA not to disclose it?

Information is the basis of enforcement. But how does EPA or the state obtain the necessary information necessary to determine whether a point source is in compliance with its permit or whether the source is a discharger needing a permit? In the CWA context sources are usually required to report their pollution control performance in their regular discharge monitoring reports or DMRs. But is the DMR the only method of obtaining data? Like the other federal environment status, the CWA vests significant authority in EPA to have access to data concerning CWA compliance. Sometimes important compliance information can only be acquired by inspecting facilities themselves and this can give rise to the need for a search warrant.

The basic information gathering powers are found in § 308 [§ 1318]. The CWA mandates a considerable amount of disclosure concerning the operations of a discharging facility. For instance, a permit applicant must submit a list of any toxic pollutant used or manufactured in the plant and not just those discharged from the facility. See NRDC, Inc. v. United States EPA, 822 F.2d 104, 117 (D.C.Cir.1987).

What about legitimate business concerns about disclosure of operations? Could competitors review a company's NPDES permit application, its monitoring data and inspection reports to acquire "useful" information about the business, such as trade secrets? On the other hand, could an individual or an environmental group have access to information gathered by EPA? Section 308(b) deals with the disclosure issue in the following fashion. It states, in part,

> Any records, reports, or information obtained under this section (1) shall, in the case of effluent data, be related to any applicable effluent limitations, toxic, pretreatment, or new source performance standards, and (2) shall be available to the public, except that upon a showing satisfactory to the Administrator by any person that records,

reports, or information, or particular part thereof (other than effluent data), to which the Administrator has access under this section, if made public would divulge methods or processes entitled to protection as trade secrets of such person, the Administrator shall consider such record, report, or information, or particular portion thereof confidential in accordance with the purposes of section 1905 of Title 18.

The section concludes by criminally penalizing the unauthorized disclosure of such trade secrets and by allowing the transfer of trade secret data to other governmental officials.

2. *Enforcement Alternatives Under the Clean Water Act.* From the limited facts provided, what enforcement options are available to EPA under the CWA especially under § 309? What can EPA enforce under § 309? If you were EPA's regional attorney, what objectives would you have in contemplating an enforcement strategy with regards to Wilson?

a. *EPA Options for Enforcement.* Could EPA administratively order Wilson to comply with its permit conditions? How would such an order be enforced? Could EPA go directly to court to seek injunctive relief without first issuing an order?

The Supreme Court's decision in the *Gwaltney* case prevents the CWA § 505 citizen suit to be used punish "wholly past" violations which are not occurring at the time the action is filed. But what about governmental enforcement efforts aimed at such past violations? Are they precluded by the holding in *Gwaltney?* Courts have taken a consistent approach interpreting the limits of *Gwaltney* and finding broad enforcement power in the government.

Should the government have broader enforcement authorities than a plaintiff in a citizen suit? Should there be any enforcement of pure past violations of NPDES permits? What are the pros and cons?

b. *Financial Penalties for Water Pollution.* Could EPA seek financial penalties against Wilson for any or all of the four "violations" mentioned in the anonymous letter if they were later corroborated with evidence? Could EPA assess such monetary penalties by itself or did it need to seek judicial imposition of these charges?

If EPA attorneys believed that Wilson's conduct deserved a financial punishment, what authorities could they use to impose that form of sanction? Read § 309(a)(3) and (b) [§ 1319(a)(3) & (b)]. Would these sections apply to Wilson's alleged violations? Remember that criminal penalties also contain financial punishments. What kind of remedies are available under these provisions authorizing civil actions? Now read § 309(d) [§ 1319(d)]. If you were the federal district court judge considering EPA's request for civil penalties how would you set the penalty? Does § 309(d) define a precise, mandatory financial penalty? Does it provide you with sufficient guidance for exercising your discretion?

What if EPA did not wish to seek enforcement in court? What could it do administratively to penalize *Wilson?* In 1987, Congress amended the enforcement section and added a new § 309(g) which provides for the assessment and collection of administrative penalties. This section is similar to an administrative penalty authority added to RCRA in 1984. Section 309(g)(2) establishes a two-tiered system of civil penalties—Class I and Class II—with different penalty amounts procedures for imposition and judicial review. Does this provision give EPA too much power to punish? Section 309(g)(8) states that a court shall not set aside an administratively developed penalty "unless there is not substantial evidence in the record, taken as a whole, to support the finding of a violation or unless—[EPA's penalty] constitutes an abuse of discretion * * *." Is it likely that administrative orders will be overturned in court?

3. *Pollution Control and the Problem of "Whistleblowers".* Where does information concerning a factory's polluting activities come from? Undoubtedly much of this data is derived from inspection and monitoring efforts undertaken by federal and state governmental authorities and from facility self-reporting. A surprising number of times the initial information comes from citizen complaints. EPA reported that in 1999 it received 5,095 such complaints with the greatest number in the Clean Air program (49%) followed by the CWA (16%) and the FIFRA program (14%).

But what about the situation of an employee "tip" or other information to an environmental agency that leads to some form of enforcement action against the firm? Would an employee be likely to provide damaging, yet accurate information about an employer's conduct? Several factors might discourage this kind of "whistleblowing." Most important would certainly be the fear of employer retribution by way of firing or other punitive action against the employee.

The Clean Water Act addresses this potential problem in § 507 [§ 1367]. It states in § 507(a) that,

> No person shall fire, or in any other way discriminate against, or cause to be fired or discriminated against, any employee or any authorized representative of employees by reason of the fact that such employee or representative has filed, instituted, or caused to be filed or instituted any proceeding under this chapter, or has testified or is about to testify in any proceeding resulting from the administration or enforcement of the provisions of this chapter.

This prohibition on employer retribution is effectuated by a Department of Labor investigation and hearing to determine whether the firing or other discrimination did occur in violation of § 507(a). The Secretary of Labor is authorized under this section to remedy these unlawful employee sanctions with orders requiring reinstatement, compensation and costs. These protections are not available to the employee who deliberately and without direction from the employer violates the CWA.

There is little reported federal litigation involving § 507 due perhaps to the administrative nature of its factfinding and conflict resolution process. However, one case Willy v. Coastal Corp., 855 F.2d 1160 (5th Cir.1988), presents an interesting situation involving the firing of an in-house lawyer for alleged "whistleblowing" conduct. Although the plaintiff filed a state law claim under Texas law for wrongful discharge and several other injuries, his main federal theory arose under the "whistleblower" protection provisions of the CWA and other environmental acts. The following excerpt described Willy's case.

Willy is a lawyer who was employed as in-house counsel from May 1981 until he was fired in October 1984 by defendant-appellee Coastal States Management Co., a wholly-owned subsidary of defendant-appellee The Coastal Corporation. These entities (collectively, Coastal), are involved in the oil and gas industry through other subsidiaries of The Coastal Corporation. Willy claims that he was fired because he insisted that Coastal comply with various state and federal environmental and securities laws and because he would not act in violation of those laws.

Within a month of his dismissal, Willy filed an administrative complaint against Coastal with the United States Department of Labor pursuant to 29 C.F.R. pt. 24 (1984). He argued that by firing him Coastal had violated the "whistleblower" provisions of the [6 federal environmental statutes] * * * The Department of Labor investigated and agreed. The Administrative Law Judge (ALJ) to whom Willy's case was assigned, however, found that Willy had engaged in only intracorporate activity, not communications with a governmental agency, and recommended dismissal of Willy's claim under *Brown & Root, Inc. v. Donovan,* 747 F.2d 1029 (5th Cir.1984) (the "whistleblower" provision of the Energy Reorganization Act, 42 U.S.C. § 5851(a)(3), does not protect an employee from filing an intracorporate quality control report). On June 4, 1987, the Secretary of Labor (Secretary) rejected the ALJ's recommendation and remanded, finding from the record that Willy had been in contact with governmental agencies, presumably federal, before he was fired. The Secretary further "held" that *Brown & Root* was incorrectly decided and that this Court should be given an opportunity to reconsider its decision in light of *Kansas Gas & Electric Co. v. Brock,* 780 F.2d 1505 (10th Cir.1985), * * * The present status of Willy's administrative action is not reflected by the record or briefs.

Id. at 1162–63. Should an employee such as Willy be protected by CWA § 507? Who does a lawyer or other employee owe his/her loyalty to? Is a lawyer in a particularly difficult ethical dilemma?

Would Willy's disclosure breach an ethical duty to his employee/client? In 2001, the American Bar Association's House of Delegates gave preliminary approval to a change in the ABA's Code of Professional Responsibility to permit an attorney to reveal confidential information if it is necessary to prevent "reasonably certain" death or substantial injury. This was viewed as an expansion of those situations (including toxic waste discharge cases) were an attorney could divulge client information without running afoul of ethical rules. How would you advise a friend who had learned of her employer's or client's conduct which violated the CWA? What if the conduct was filing DMRs a month late? What if it was introducing toxic pollutants into a public sewer without permission?

4. *Multi-Governmental Enforcement.* What if the State of Euphoria's DEC has begun to investigate Wilson's compliance status? Does this state action displace EPA's power to enforce? What if the state DEC has commenced an enforcement action against Wilson in state court or through state administrative means? Does or should this prevent EPA from taking its own action? Does EPA have any recourse against the State of Euphoria if it conducts a weak enforcement program permitting NPDES permit noncompliance to go unchecked?

a. State–Federal Enforcement Problems. Section 309 [§ 1319] provides for concurrent state and federal enforcement, even where the NPDES permitting authority has been transferred to the state. What exactly does this mean? What is the relationship between federal and state enforcement efforts? Should a state's exercise of CWA permitting and enforcement power displace EPA and prevent it from acting independently? One case, United States v. City of Colorado Springs, 455 F.Supp. 1364 (D.Colo.1978), has held that even after CWA program "delegation" to the state, EPA retains the authority to seek judicial enforcement under § 309. This result reflects the majority view. But does this principle of overarching EPA enforcement power answer all questions?

One study of shared enforcement authority between EPA and the states has concluded that while state environmental enforcement duties have risen dramatically during the 1980's, the federal/state relationship has not been satisfactory to either party. The states often seek greater flexibility and independence in dealing with enforcement matters and they resent federal supremacy over their efforts which they believe undermines their credibility. One particular problem is the issue of federal "overfiling." Overfiling occurs when EPA determines that a state's enforcement action is inappropriate (a fine is too small, large or non-existent) and EPA then steps in and files its own case. This practice has recently been criticized as creating state/federal conflict and being costly and time consuming. Why might EPA strongly wish to preserve overfiling authority?

The following excerpt presents the view of overfiling from the perspective of regulated industries.

> Overfiling arises due to the federal-state relationship under many federal environmental laws. Several of these laws, including RCRA and federal Clean Air Act, require EPA to promulgate federal regulations and authorize state environmental agencies to operate delegated regulatory programs. When state environmental agencies have received the appropriate "delegation" from EPA, they are responsible for the implementation and day-to-day enforcement of these programs, including issuance of appropriate permits, as well as the prosecution and settlement of regulatory violations.

> Given this framework, it is quite common for corporate environmental manages to work directly with state regulators—and not EPA—to address potential environmental noncompliance matters. For example, an authorized state agency may use letters of warning, notices of violation, administrative orders and other appropriate legal mecha-

nisms to initiate enforcement actions against alleged corporate violations of federal/state environmental laws. These enforcement actions often are resolved through the payment of a fine or civil penalty pursuant to a state administrative consent agreement and final order, or perhaps a consent decree filed with a state court. During the past decade, EPA has begun to more closely monitor these state agency settlements. In some situations, EPA has determined that the settlement was "inappropriate" or did not recover an "inadequate" penalty or fine, and the Agency has filed its own independent overfiling action against the offending corporation.

EPA overfiling confronts companies with substantial legal and practical problems. For example, these cases often involve unanticipated EPA claims for substantially increases penalties for vast violations that already have been settled with state regulators. Such claims can lead not only to potentially greater legal liabilities for corporations, but also can cause a company to be unwilling to quickly settle state-lead enforcement cases if EPA is not involved

Daniel M. Steinway & J. Barton Seitz, EPA Wins Important Ruling on Enforcement Authority, Pollution Engineering Online (January 2001). Overfiling has become a much more visible legal issue following the Eighth Circuit's decision in Harmon Industries, Inc. v. Browner, 191 F.3d 894 (8th Cir.1999), where the court found that because the firm had settled claims brought by the State of Missouri pursuant to a consent decree approved by a state court, EPA was barred from filing its own suit regarding the same violations. The *Harmon* court, interpreting RCRA, found EPA's position to be "not consistent with the plain language of the statute, its legislative history or its declared purpose." *Id*. at 902. *Harmon* has not been followed by later decisions outside of the Eighth Circuit. See United States v. Power Engineering Co., 125 F.Supp.2d 1050 (D.Colo.2000); United States v. LTV Steel Co., 118 F.Supp.2d 827 (N.D.Ohio 2000) (CAA case).

   b.   Res Judicata Problems. Why wouldn't EPA be bound by a prior state court decision concluding a state enforcement action against a polluter? Why wouldn't principles of *res judicata* bar EPA from pursuing a second enforcement action in federal court? Principles of *res judicata* embodied in the Full Faith and Credit Act, 28 U.S.C. § 1738 and U.S. Const. art. 4, § 1, require federal courts to give preclusive effect to state court judgments whenever that state court would give the judgment *res judicata* effect. The requirements for finding *res judicata* effect are set out by state law. In Ohio, for instance, *res judicata* requires that the defendant show, (1) a final judgment rendered on the merits by a court of competent jurisdiction; (2) concerning the same claim or cause of action as that now asserted; (3) between the same parties as are in the current action or their 'privies,' Using this test (or a similar one found in other states), would it be likely that a court would easily find that *res judicata* prevented the second enforcement action brought by EPA? Which of these elements might be difficult to prove? It should be noted that the Eighth Circuit also held in the *Harmon* case that Missouri *res judicata* principles also prevented EPA's federal enforcement action. See 191 F.3d at 904.

The *res judicata* principles mentioned above could also be used to protect a polluter from a second enforcement action brought by the state and not by EPA. In *State Water Control Board v. Smithfield Foods, Inc.*, 261 Va. 209, 542 S.E.2d 766 (2001), the Virginia Supreme Court held that following the res judicata doctrine, the state could not bring an enforcement action against the firm for alleged violations of state water pollution laws *after* EPA had successfully enforced in federal court. Privity was found even though the state did not participate in the federal action and even though EPA's case generally involved violations of different discharge limits than those alleged in the state suit. The *Smithfield Foods* case reveals just how sympathetic some courts are to company complaints of being "whipsawed" by a second enforcement case after the matter had been "settled."

Finally, there has been substantial controversy and confusion over the *mens rea* requirement in the CWA and in environmental law statutes generally. The Fourth Circuit wrote,

> On a first reading of the clause, "any person who knowingly violates section 1311 shall be punished," the order of the words suggest that "knowingly" modifies "violates" so that the clause imposes punishment when one violates the statute with knowledge that he is violating it, i.e., with knowledge of the illegality of his conduct. But the statute's structure, the architecture of which includes a series of sections incorporating other sections, its legislation history, and the body of Supreme Court jurisprudence addressing *mens rea* of federal criminal statutes caution that our first reading may not simply lead us to the proper interpretation. United States v. Wilson, 133 F.3d 251, 261 (4th Cir.1997).

The principal case, *United States v. Sinskey*, takes the mainstream position on the issue. Is it really fair to defendants? Is it necessary to prevent a greater harm?

C. THE LEGAL STRUCTURE OF CRIMINAL ENFORCEMENT OF THE CLEAN WATER ACT

United States v. Sinskey

United States Court of Appeals, Eighth Circuit, 1997.
119 F.3d 712.

■ ARNOLD, CIRCUIT JUDGE.

The defendants appeal their convictions for criminal violations of the Clean Water Act. We affirm the judgments of the trial court.

I.

In the early 1990s, Timothy Sinskey and Wayne Kumm were, respectively, the plant manager and plant engineer at John Morrell & Co. ("Morrell"), a large meat-packing plant in Sioux Falls, South Dakota. The meat-packing process created a large amount of wastewater, some of which Morrell piped to a municipal treatment plant and the rest of which it treated at its own wastewater treatment plant ("WWTP"). After treating wastewater at the WWTP, Morrell would discharge it into the Big Sioux River.

One of the WWTP's functions was to reduce the amount of ammonia nitrogen in the wastewater discharged into the river, and the Environmental Protection Agency ("EPA") required Morrell to limit that amount to levels specified in a permit issued under the Clean Water Act ("CWA"). As well as specifying the acceptable levels of ammonia nitrogen, the permit also required Morrell to perform weekly a series of tests to monitor the amounts of ammonia nitrogen in the discharged water and to file monthly with the EPA a set of reports concerning those results.

In the spring of 1991, Morrell doubled the number of hogs that it slaughtered and processed at the Sioux Falls plant. The resulting increase in wastewater caused the level of ammonia nitrate in the discharged water to be above that allowed by the CWA permit. Ron Greenwood and Barry Milbauer, the manager and assistant manager, respectively, of the WWTP, manipulated the testing process in two ways so that Morrell would appear not to violate its permit. In the first technique, which the parties frequently refer to as "flow manipulation" or the "flow game," Morrell would discharge extremely low levels of water (and thus low levels of ammonia nitrogen) early in the week, when Greenwood and Milbauer would perform the required tests. After the tests had been performed, Morrell would discharge an exceedingly high level of water (and high levels of ammonia nitrogen) later in the week. The tests would therefore not accurately reflect the overall levels of ammonia nitrogen in the discharged water. In addition to manipulating the flow, Greenwood and Milbauer also engaged in what the parties call "selective sampling," that is, they performed more than the number of tests required by the EPA but reported only the tests showing acceptable levels of ammonia nitrogen. When manipulating the flow and selective sampling failed to yield the required number of tests showing acceptable levels of ammonia nitrogen, the two simply falsified the test results and the monthly EPA reports, which Sinskey then signed and sent to the EPA. Morrell submitted false reports for every month but one from August, 1991, to December, 1992.

As a result of their participation in these activities, Sinskey and Kumm were charged with a variety of CWA violations. After a three-week trial, a jury found Sinskey guilty of eleven of the thirty counts with which he was charged, and Kumm guilty of one of the seventeen counts with which he was charged. In particular, the jury found both Sinskey and Kumm guilty of knowingly rendering inaccurate a monitoring method required to be maintained under the CWA, in violation of 33 U.S.C. § 1319(c)(4), and

Sinskey guilty of knowingly discharging a pollutant into waters of the United States in amounts exceeding CWA permit limitations, in violation of 33 U.S.C. § 1319(c)(2)(A); see also 33 U.S.C. § 1311(a). Each appeals his conviction.

II.

Sinskey first challenges the jury instructions that the trial court gave with respect to 33 U.S.C. § 1319(c)(2)(A), which, among other things, punishes anyone who "knowingly violates" § 1311 or a condition or limitation contained in a permit that implements § 1311. That section of the CWA prohibits the discharge of pollutants except in compliance with, among other provisions, § 1342, which establishes the National Pollutant Discharge Elimination System ("NPDES"). The NPDES authorizes the EPA to issue permits that allow the discharge of certain pollutants within specified limitations and with specified reporting and monitoring conditions. As applied in this case, § 1319(c)(2)(A) therefore prohibits the discharge of pollutants in amounts exceeding the limitations specified in an NPDES permit.

The trial court gave an instruction, which it incorporated into several substantive charges, that in order for the jury to find Sinskey guilty of acting "knowingly," the proof had to show that he was "aware of the nature of his acts, performed them intentionally, and [did] not act or fail to act through ignorance, mistake, or accident." The instructions also told the jury that the government was not required to prove that Sinskey knew that his acts violated the CWA or permits issued under that act. Sinskey contests these instructions as applied to 33 U.S.C. § 1319(c)(2)(A), arguing that because the adverb "knowingly" immediately precedes the verb "violates," the government must prove that he knew that his conduct violated either the CWA or the NPDES permit. We disagree.

Although our court has not yet decided whether 33 U.S.C. § 1319(c)(2)(A) requires the government to prove that a defendant knew that he or she was violating either the CWA or the relevant NPDES permit when he or she acted, we are guided in answering this question by the generally accepted construction of the word "knowingly" in criminal statutes, by the CWA's legislative history, and by the decisions of the other courts of appeals that have addressed this issue. In construing other statutes with similar language and structure, that is, statutes in which one provision punishes the "knowing violation" of another provision that defines the illegal conduct, we have repeatedly held that the word "knowingly" modifies the acts constituting the underlying conduct. See United States v. Farrell, 69 F.3d 891, 893 (8th Cir.1995), cert. denied, 134 L. Ed. 2d 228, 116 S. Ct. 1283 (1996), and United States v. Hern, 926 F.2d 764, 766–68 (8th Cir.1991).

In Farrell, 69 F.3d at 892–93, for example, we discussed 18 U.S.C. § 924 (a)(2), which penalizes anyone who "knowingly violates" § 922(o)(1), which in turn prohibits the transfer or possession of a machine gun. In construing the word "knowingly," we held that it applied only to the conduct proscribed in § 922(*o*)(1), that is, the act of transferring or possessing a machine gun, and not to the illegal nature of those actions. A conviction under § 924(a)(2) therefore did not require proof that the defendant knew that his actions violated the law.

We see no reason to depart from that commonly accepted construction in this case, and we therefore believe that in 33 U.S.C. § 1319(c)(2)(A), the word "knowingly" applies to the underlying conduct prohibited by the statute. Untangling the statutory provisions discussed above in order to define precisely the relevant underlying conduct, however, is not a little difficult. At first glance, the conduct in question might appear to be violating a permit limitation, which would imply that § 1319(c)(2)(A) requires proof that the defendant knew of the permit limitation and knew that he or she was violating it. To violate a permit limitation, however, one must engage in the conduct prohibited by that limitation. The permit is, in essence, another layer of regulation in the nature of a law, in this case, a law that applies only to Morrell. We therefore believe that the underlying conduct of which Sinskey must have had knowledge is the conduct that is prohibited by the permit, for example, that Morrell's discharges of ammonia nitrates were higher than one part per million in the summer of 1992. Given this interpretation of the statute, the government was not required to prove that Sinskey knew that his acts violated either the CWA or the NPDES permit, but merely that he was aware of the conduct that resulted in the permit's violation.

This interpretation comports not only with our legal system's general recognition that ignorance of the law is no excuse, see Cheek v. United States, 498 U.S. 192, 199, 112 L. Ed. 2d 617, 111 S. Ct. 604 (1991), but also with Supreme Court interpretations of statutes containing similar language and structure. In United States v. International Minerals & Chemical Corp., 402 U.S. 558, 29 L. Ed. 2d 178, 91 S. Ct. 1697 (1971), for example, the Court analyzed a statute that punished anyone who "knowingly violated" certain regulations pertaining to the interstate shipment of hazardous materials. In holding that a conviction under the statute at issue did not require knowledge of the pertinent law, the Court reasoned that the statute's language was merely a shorthand designation for punishing anyone who knowingly committed the specific acts or omissions contemplated by the regulations at issue, and that the statute therefore required knowledge of the material facts but not the relevant law. Id. at 562–63. The Court also focused on the nature of the regulatory scheme at issue, noting that where "dangerous or ... obnoxious waste materials" are involved, anyone dealing with such materials "must be presumed" to be aware of the existence of the regulations. Id. at 565. Requiring knowledge only of the underlying actions, and not of the law, would therefore raise no substantial due process concerns. Id. at 564–65. Such reasoning applies with equal force, we believe, to the CWA, which regulates the discharge into the public's water of such "obnoxious waste materials" as the byproducts of slaughtered animals.

The act's legislative history, moreover, supports our view of the mens rea required for conviction under 33 U.S.C. § 1319(c)(2)(A). In 1987, Congress amended the act, in part to increase deterrence by strengthening the criminal sanctions for its violation. See, e.g., H.R. Conf. Rep. No. 99–1004 at 138 (1986) and S. Rep. No. 99–50 at 29–30 (1985). To that end, Congress changed the term "willfully" to "knowingly" in that section of the act dealing with intentional violations. See 133 Cong. Rec. H131 (daily ed. Jan. 7, 1987) (statement of Rep. J. Howard), reprinted in 1987 U.S.C.C.A.N. 5, 28, and 33 U.S.C. § 1319, historical and statutory notes, 1987 amendment, at 197 (West supp. 1997). Although Congress did not explicitly discuss this change, it may logically be viewed as an effort to reduce the mens rea necessary for a conviction, as the word "willfully" generally connotes acting with the knowledge that one's conduct violates the law, while the word "knowingly" normally means acting with an awareness of one's actions. Compare Cheek, 498 U.S. at 201, with International Minerals, 402 U.S. at 562–63. See also Babbitt v. Sweet Home Chapter of Communities, 515 U.S. 687, 115 S. Ct. 2407, 2412 n. 9, 132 L. Ed. 2d 597 (1995) (discussing change in Endangered Species Act from "willfully" to "knowingly"), and Hern, 926 F.2d at 767.

Our confidence in this interpretation is increased by decisions of the only other appellate courts to analyze the precise issue presented here. See United States v. Hopkins, 53 F.3d 533, 541 (2d Cir.1995), cert. denied, 133 L. Ed. 2d 725, 116 S. Ct. 773 (1996), and United States v. Weitzenhoff, 35 F.3d 1275, 1283–86 (9th Cir.1993), cert. denied, 115 S. Ct. 939 (1995). Both cases held that 33 U.S.C. § 1319(c)(2)(A) does not require proof that the defendant knew that his or her acts violated the CWA or the NPDES permits at issue.

Contrary to the defendants' assertions, moreover, United States v. Ahmad, 101 F.3d 386 (5th Cir.1996), is inapposite. In Ahmad, 101 F.3d at 388, a convenience store owner pumped out an underground gasoline storage tank into which some water had leaked, discharging gasoline into city sewer systems and nearby creeks in violation of 33 U.S.C. § 1319(c)(2)(A). At trial, the defendant asserted that he thought that he was discharging water, and that the statute's requirement that he act knowingly required that the government prove not only that he knew that he was discharging something, but also that he knew that he was discharging gasoline. Id. at 390. The Fifth Circuit agreed, holding that a defendant does not violate the statute unless he or she acts knowingly with regard to each element of an offense. Id. at 391. Ahmad, however, involved a classic mistake-of-fact defense, and is not applicable to a mistake-of-law defense such as that asserted by Sinskey and Kumm. Indeed, the Fifth Circuit noted as much, distinguishing Hopkins, 53 F.3d at 533, and Weitzenhoff, 35 F.3d at 1275, on the grounds that those decisions involved a mistake-of-law defense. See Ahmad, 101 F.3d at 390–91.

Sinskey, joined by Kumm, also challenges the trial court's instructions with respect to 33 U.S.C. § 1319(c)(4), arguing that the government should have been required to prove that they knew that their acts were illegal.

A 92–count superseding indictment issued on September 27, 1996, charged Van Loben Sels and two other individuals with, inter alia, transportation of hazardous waste without a manifest, in violation of 42 U.S.C. § 6982(d)(5); aiding and abetting, in violation of 18 U.S.C. § 2; negligently discharging, and causing to be discharged, wastewater containing hazardous levels of benzene, and other volatile organic compounds, in violation of 33 U.S.C. §§ 1319(c)(1)(A), 1317(d), and LAMC § 64.30; and conspiracy, in violation of 18 U.S.C. § 371.[4] On December 2, 1997, Van Loben Sels pled guilty to one count of negligently discharging oily wastewater contaminated with hazardous levels of benzene into the Los Angeles sewer system, in violation of 33 U.S.C. §§ 1319(c)(1)(A), and 1317(d), and LAMC § 64.30.

The district court conducted an evidentiary hearing prior to sentencing.[5] The district court originally issued a tentative finding that Sentencing Guideline section 2Q1.1(b)(1)(A) would apply because Gibson admitted to violating WLBT's discharge permit and environmental contamination had occurred. The district court also found that the totality of the circumstances allowed for a downward adjustment of two-levels, from level six to level four. The district court continued the evidentiary and sentencing hearing in order to receive supplemental briefing and evidence concerning two issues: whether the substance that was released was hazardous or toxic; and whether or not there was a discharge into the environment.

The district court found that: (1) it was undisputed that Van Loben Sels had continuously discharged benzene into the environment; (2) the term "environment" includes the POTW, which includes the City of Los Angeles' sanitary sewer system; (3) the Government failed to prove the total contribution of benzene to Terminal Island on any periodic basis, and the percentage of the total contribution that could be attributed to Gibson; and (4) the periodic tests taken by the City of Los Angeles during the entire

---

4. On February 12, 1997, the district court granted the defendants' motion to suppress state search warrants executed on Gibson's facilities in July 1993. Thereafter, all of Van Loben Sels' co-defendants pled guilty and received departures under Sentencing Guideline § 5K1.1 based upon their cooperation with the Government. Van Loben Sels' co-defendant, Lucas T. Dobrzanski, pled guilty to a one-count superseding information charging him with transportation of hazardous waste without a manifest, in violation of 42 U.S.C. § 6982(d)(5), and aiding and abetting, in violation of 18 U.S.C. § 2. Dobrzanski was sentenced on September 22, 1997, to fifteen months imprisonment and twelve months supervised release. Id. Co-defendant Thomas Pruitt pled guilty to conspiracy, in violation of 18 U.S.C. § 371 on March 31, 1998, and was sentenced to six months imprisonment. Co-defendant Dick Dahm pled guilty to negligently discharging, and causing to be discharged, wastewater containing hazardous levels of benzene, and other volatile organic compounds, in violation of 33 U.S.C. §§ 1319(c)(1)(A), 1317(d), and LAMC § 64.30. Dahm was also sentenced on March 31, 1998, to sixty months probation.

5. The Presentence Sentence Report ("PSR") calculated Van Loben Sels' total offense level at 20 which, combined with a criminal history category of I, presented the district court with a sentencing range of 33 to 41 months. Pursuant to Sentencing Guideline section 5G1.1(a), however, Van Loben Sels could not be subjected to a sentence greater than the statutory maximum of twelve months. Accordingly, the PSR recommended that Van Loben Sels be sentenced to twelve months imprisonment and twelve months supervised release with special conditions, and pay restitution in the amount of $35,000, due immediately.

period of the offense showed that no benzene had been discharged as effluent from Terminal Island. Accordingly, the district court rejected the government's position, and refused to apply the six-level upward adjustment under section 2Q1.1(b)(1)(A).

The district court thereupon recalculated Van Loben Sels' base offense level at 8, added a 4–level upward adjustment pursuant to section 2Q1.2(b)(4), because the offense involved the disposal of hazardous waste in violation of a permit, and subtracted 2–levels pursuant to section 3E1.1(a), for acceptance of responsibility. These adjustments resulted in a total offense level of 10. The district court, presented with a range of six to twelve months, sentenced Van Loben Sels to one-month community confinement, five-months home detention, waiver of the $25 fine, and restitution in the amount of $35,000, which became due immediately. The Government timely appeals.

JURISDICTION

The district court exercised original jurisdiction of the case under 18 U.S.C. § 3231. We have jurisdiction of the government's appeal of Van Loben Sels' sentence pursuant to 18 U.S.C. § 3742(b) and 28 U.S.C. § 1291.

DISCUSSION

At issue is whether the district court properly declined to upwardly adjust Van Loben Sels' base offense level pursuant to Sentencing Guideline section 2Q1.1(b)(1)(A). Van Loben Sels did not receive an upward adjustment because the district court assessed the toxicity of the wastewater at the time it left the Terminal Island Treatment Plant, rather than at the point it was initially discharged into the Los Angeles sanitary sewer system at the WLBT.

The district court's interpretation and application of the Sentencing Guidelines is reviewed de novo. See United States v. Merino, 190 F.3d 956, 957 (9th Cir.1999). We review the district court's findings of fact underlying the sentencing decision for clear error. See United States v. Robinson, 94 F.3d 1325, 1326 (9th Cir.1996).

Sentencing Guideline section 2Q1.2(b)(1)(A) provides that "if the offense resulted in an ongoing, continuous, or repetitive discharge, release, or emission of a hazardous or toxic substance or pesticide into the environment, increase by 6 levels." Application note 5 to section 2Q1.2 provides further guidance on this point:

> Subsection (b)(1) assumes a discharge or emission into the environment resulting in actual environmental contamination. A wide range of conduct, involving the handling of different quantities of materials with widely differing propensities, potentially is covered. Depending upon the harm resulting from the emission, release or discharge, the quantity and nature of the substance or pollutant, the duration of the offense and the risk associated with the violation, a departure of up to

two levels in either direction from the offense levels prescribed in these specific offense characteristics may be appropriate.

U.S.S.G. § 2Q1.2 application note 5 (1997).

This Court applies the rules of statutory construction when interpreting the Sentencing Guidelines. See Robinson, 94 F.3d at 1328. If the language of a statute is unambiguous, the plain meaning controls. Id. Correspondingly, commentary in the Sentencing Guidelines that interprets or explains a guideline is binding unless it violates the Constitution or a federal statute, or is inconsistent with that guideline. See id. (citing Stinson v. United States, 508 U.S. 36, 38, 123 L. Ed. 2d 598, 113 S. Ct. 1913 (1993)).

The only previously published case from this circuit interpreting and applying section 2Q1.2(b)(1)(A) is United States v. Ferrin, 994 F.2d 658 (9th Cir.1993). In Ferrin, the defendant was the civilian supervisor of seven hazardous waste handlers at a naval station, and instructed his employees to treat a hazardous substance by mixing the substance with another chemical. When the mixture did not react as the defendant planned, he directed his staff to pour the chemicals into a kitty litter-like absorbent and dump the contents into the municipal dumpster outside the facility. Due to an ongoing investigation of the defendant, however, authorities witnessed the dumping and initiated a cleanup before the waste left the dumpster and contaminated the environment. See id. at 660.

In Ferrin, we explained that because offenses covered by Guideline section 2Q1.2 may or may not result in de facto contamination, the language of Application Note 5 requires a showing that some amount of hazardous substance in fact contaminated the environment to justify an offense level increase under subsection (b)(1). See id. at 663–64. Although we declined to increase Ferrin's offense level based on subsection (b)(1) because there was no actual contamination of the environment due to the fortuitous intervention of the authorities, we nevertheless stated that in most cases reasonable inferences from available evidence will suffice to support a conclusion that the illegal acts resulted in contamination. See id.

In the present case, Van Loben Sels' superseding information expressly states that the City of Los Angeles had adopted local pretreatment standards prohibiting the discharge of benzene and other volatile organic compounds to its POTWs. In essence, these local pretreatment standards applied to Gibson's wastewater discharges from the point source at WLBT on its path to the final treatment stage at Terminal Island.

Moreover, Van Loben Sels' plea agreement states that from August 1991 through March 1993, he was aware of and authorized the transportation of truckloads totaling one million gallons per month of untreated wastewater containing benzene from Gibson's Bakersfield facility to WLBT for discharge into the Los Angeles sanitary sewer system. The district court further found that Gibson had continuously discharged benzene into the environment, which included the City of Los Angeles' sanitary sewer system, by discharging its untreated wastewater at the WLBT POTW collection pipes/connection point. Sentencing Guideline subsection (b)(1)(A) "actually specifies that the discharge, release or emission be 'into the environment.' " Ferrin, 994 F.2d at 658.

The record here supports the district court's finding that hazardous material had been continuously discharged into the environment. This is the appropriate predicate for upward adjustment under subsection (b)(1), see Ferrin 994 F.2d at 664, and thus, it is reasonable to infer from that evidence that Gibson's illegal acts resulted in contamination, necessitating application of section 2Q1.2(b)(1)(A), see id. The district court's refusal to apply subsection (b)(1) on the ground that the Government failed to prove that the effluent from Terminal Island contained hazardous levels of benzene does not control the determination whether the adjustment under section 2Q1.2(b)(1)(A) is applicable. We conclude that the district court's refusal to apply such an adjustment is clearly erroneous in light of its finding that Gibson had continuously discharged benzene into the environment. See Ferrin, 994 F.2d at 663. Accordingly, Van Loben Sels' offense level should have been upwardly adjusted six levels, while empowering the district court with the discretion to depart two levels in either direction "depending upon the harm resulting from the emission, release or discharge, the quantity and nature of the substance or pollutant, the duration of the offense and the risk associated with the violation." U.S.S.G. § 2Q1.2 application note 5.

Other reasons support an upward adjustment for Van Loben Sels. It would be unfair to require the public to absorb any additional cleanup costs attributable to unregulated increases in discharged wastes to either a publicly funded treatment facility or directly into the environment. In addition, without punishment, Gibson's competitors may receive the message that this is acceptable conduct in order to remain economically competitive.

CONCLUSION

The decision of the district court is REVERSED and REMANDED for the limited purpose of RESENTENCING pursuant to Sentencing Guidelines section 2Q1.2(b)(1)(A).

NOTES AND QUESTIONS

1. If self-reporting is the norm, what temptations exist for distortion or outright falsification? Recent criminal enforcement cases, including *United States v. Sinskey*, reflect the fact that the federal government takes an extremely dim view of such efforts to "beat" the system. Falsification of Discharge Monitoring Reports (DMRs) and laboratory analysis for DMRs has triggered criminal prosecutors and resulted in incarceration. In some reported cases, bypass mechanisms have been built to completely avoid monitoring equipment. See e.g., United States v. Hartsell, 127 F.3d 343 (4th Cir.1997) (upholding convictions imposing fines and jail time.) Even senior corporate officers can be convicted of these crimes.

2. *Enforcement of the CWA with Criminal Sanctions.* In the Class Discussion Problem—Part I—could any individual be prosecuted for criminal violation of the CWA for any of the conduct described in the anonymous letter? What about the corporation itself? Why subject corporation to criminal punishment? What range of Wilson corporate officers and employees might be exposed to criminal sanctions?

Should polluters be subject to criminal punishment? This question presents issues of enforcement philosophy—will the threat of criminal penalty deter non-compliant behavior? Congress in enacting § 309(c) apparently has considered the criminal sanctions of incarceration and fine to be necessary components in the array of government enforcement powers. However, until 1987 the wide range of CWA criminal offenses were modestly punished qualifying as misdemeanors. Until the 1980's environmental agencies relied upon civil not criminal penalties to sanction polluters and to achieve compliance with anti-pollution regulations.

During the latter part of the 1980s and throughout the 1990s, the emphasis on criminal enforcement measures increased with the main focus being cases brought under the Clean Water Act, RCRA and CERCLA. Criminal case referral to the Department of Justice has plateaued since the mid–1990s to the present at about 250 cases per year. During this period, jail time imposed at approximately 200 years of sentences per year, and criminal fines varying widely but averaging about $6 million per year. Some states also used criminal enforcement aggressively. See Ed Neatsey and Edward Bonanno, Criminal Environmental Enforcement: The New Jersey Experience, 10 Nat. Envt. Ent. J. 3 (May 1995).

The 1987 CWA amendments substantially increased criminal punishment for water pollution violations. Section 309(c) [§ 1319(c)] contains the criminal enforcement provisions of the Clean Water Act. This section contains 4 categories of criminal conduct: a) negligent violations, b) knowing violations, c) knowing endangerment, and d) making false statements. The legislative trend has been to expand the list of criminal acts, to create new public health crimes and to increase criminal penalties.

a) A conviction of a negligent violation of any one of a list of offenses could result in a fine of up to $25,000 per day and/or imprisonment for up to one year. A second offense under this section may result in a felony conviction, which would double these penalties.

b) If any of the offenses set forth in section 1319(c)(1) are violated "knowingly," the resulting conviction will constitute a felony and will be punishable by a fine of up to $50,000 per day and/or imprisonment for up to three years. Under this provision, penalties are once again doubled for repeat offenders. However, a discharge subject to the provisions of the CWA is required to trigger criminal liability. In an unconventional attempt at applying the criminal CWA sanctions, the Second Circuit ruled that a criminal defendant who had placed hepatitis-contaminated blood vials into the Hudson River was not criminally liable under the CWA for "knowingly" discharging pollutants into navigable waters because a person could not be considered a "point source" under the act. See United States v. Plaza Health Laboratories, Inc., 3 F.3d 643 (2d Cir.1993).

c) The 1987 amendment to the CWA added a knowing endangerment provision—§ 309(c)(3)—modelled after the nearly identical RCRA provision. Upon conviction, any person who knowingly violates CWA provisions and knows at the time that he places another person in imminent danger of death or serious bodily injury may be subject to a fine of up to $250,000 or imprisonment of up to 15 years, or both. Furthermore, a defendant which is an "organization" can receive a fine of up to $1,000,000. This provision is complicated and contains its own definitions, proof requirements and affirmative defenses. See United States v. Borowski, 977 F.2d 27 (1st Cir.1992).

d) The CWA also imposes felony penalties upon "a person who knowingly makes any false material statement, representation, or certification in any application, record, report, plan, or other document filed or required to be maintained [under the Act] or who knowingly falsifies, tampers with, or renders inaccurate any monitoring device or method required to be maintained" under the Act. A conviction under this provision can result in a fine of up to $10,000 and/or imprisonment of up to two years with doubling for repeat offenders.

D.   CLEAN WATER ACT CITIZEN SUIT ENFORCEMENT

CLASS DISCUSSION PROBLEM—CITIZEN SUIT ENFORCEMENT OF THE CLEAN WATER ACT

The Southern Euphoria Regional Sewer District ("Sewer District") operates a large regional waste treatment system in the Centralia metropolitan area. The Sewer District collects domestic and industrial waste, transports it by pipe, treats these wastes at several treatment facilities, and then discharges the treated effluent into the East River. While most of the district's treatment plants have operated in a satisfactory manner, one plant—Piney Run—has been the source of continuing community concern. Built in 1977, the Piney Run wastewater plant was originally designed to treat only domestic waste. It had minimal equipment, no chlorination process, and no means of disposing of the sludge remaining after treatment. A 1986 study recommended a substantial upgrade of Piney Run but because the Sewer District had decided to emphasize the construction of new treatment plants throughout the area, Piney Run was not renovated. Over the years the proportion of high-strength industrial wastewater treated at the plant has substantially increased thereby imposing substantial loads on the plant and adversely affecting wastewater characteristics. Although authorized to require industries sending wastes to Piney Run to pretreat them, the Sewer District has not actively pursued this course.

In 1994 the State of Euphoria Department of Environmental Conservation ("DEC") issued an NPDES permit to the Sewer District for the Piney Run plant authorizing discharge of treated wastewater in accordance with the following limitations.

(a) Dissolved Oxygen: 5 milligrams per liter (mg/1)(minimum);

(b) Total Suspended Solids (concentration): 30 mg/1 (monthly average) and 45 mg/1 (weekly average);

(c) Total Suspended Solids (mass): 171.9 lbs/day (monthly average) and 257.8 lbs/day (weekly average);

(d) Biochemical Oxygen Demand (concentration): 30 mg/1 (monthly average) and 45 mg/1 (weekly average);

(e) Biochemical Oxygen Demand (mass): 171.9 lbs/day (monthly average) and 257.8 lbs/day (weekly average);

(f) pH: 6 to 9; and

(g) Fecal Coliform: 200/100 milliliters (monthly average) and 400/100 milliliters (maximum).

In July of both 1997 and 1998 the Piney Run plant "went septic," experiencing anaerobic conditions resulting in extremely unpleasant odors which caused turmoil in the community. Frequently odors were so noxious that people could not remain in the vicinity and algae clumps and human sewage often floated on the surface on the river. The 1998 breakdown required emergency operations at the plant, including the hauling of excess sludge to other waste treatment plants. Fish kills occurred in the East River in March and May of 1998 and again in May of 1999. The DEC suspected discharges from the Piney Run plant in two of the fish kills and attributed the third to an algal bloom.

You have been hired by two landowners (Yvette and Sylvia) living near the Piney Run facility to see what could be done about the unacceptable conditions. You have discovered that the Discharge Monitoring Reports (DMRs) submitted to the DEC by the Sewer District showed frequent violations of the NPDES permit for the plant and corroborate Yvette and Sylvia's descriptions. On at least two occasions, there was no dissolved oxygen in the discharged water. The average fecal coliform measurement was in violation of the permit every month from January 1996 to June 2000. For twelve of those months, the levels were reported as "too numerous to count." During the same fifty-four month period, the concentration of biochemical oxygen demand reached or exceeded the maximum permitted levels for twenty-nine months, and total suspended solids were excessive for fifty months. Also, discovered in DEC files were nine notices of violation and numerous letters from the DEC to the Sewer District which rated the operation of the Piney Run plant as "unacceptable" and detailed violations noted during the DEC's on-site inspections including recordkeeping and other operational deficiencies.

In 2000 the Sewer District announced an "interim modernization program" (IMP) which would substantially renovate the Piney Run treatment works by 2004. While the Sewer District expressed its commitment to the IMP, some concern exists about its financing.

1. Could Yvette and Sylvia file suit in federal court to compel either EPA or the DEC to initiate an enforcement action to obtain compliance

with the terms of the Sewer District's Piney Run NPDES permit or the issuance of a revised permit with strengthened limitations?

2.   Could Yvette, Sylvia and the group East River Fishery and Recreation Association (the Association) themselves directly obtain enforcement of the NPDES permit in federal court under the CWA? (a) What exactly would they be enforcing? (b) If the CWA provides a cause of action, would Yvette, Sylvia and the Association have standing? (c) Where could the suit be brought? (d) Are there any unusual, and important, procedural obligations the plaintiffs would need to comply with?

3.   What forms of relief could the plaintiffs seek? (a) Could plaintiffs obtain an injunction demanding permit compliance? Could plaintiffs have monetary or civil penalties imposed on the Sewer District? How should the judge set the penalty if one were imposed? (b) What defenses, if any, could the Sewer District raise? Is the CWA § 505 and the concept of citizen enforcement of governmental regulatory programs unconstitutional? (c) Could any of the plaintiffs sue the Sewer District for monetary damages under the CWA? What about such a claim arising under state law? (d) What should your strategy be regarding any potential settlement?

Excerpts from the Clean Water Act
33 U.S.C. § 1365.

§ 505(a) Authorization; jurisdiction

Except as provided in subsection (b) of this section and section 1319(g)(6) of this title, any citizen may commence a civil action on his own behalf—

(1) against any person (including (i) the United States, and

(ii) any other governmental instrumentality or agency to the extent permitted by the eleventh amendment to the Constitution) who is alleged to be in violation of (A) an effluent standard or limitation under this chapter or (B) an order issued by the Administrator or a State with respect to such a standard or limitation, or

(2) against the Administrator where there is alleged a failure of the Administrator to perform any act or duty under this chapter which is not discretionary with the Administrator. The district courts shall have jurisdiction, without regard to the amount in controversy or the citizenship of the parties, to enforce such an effluent standard or limitation, or such an order, or to order the Administrator to perform such act or duty, as the case may be, and to apply any appropriate civil penalties under section 1319(d) of this title.

Sierra Club v. Union Oil Co.
United States Court of Appeals, Ninth Circuit, 1988.
853 F.2d 667.

■ CHIEF JUDGE GOODWIN:

In Union Oil Co. v. Sierra Club, 108 S.Ct. 1102, 99 L.Ed.2d 264 (1988), the Supreme Court vacated our opinion in Sierra Club v. Union Oil Co.,

813 F.2d 1480 (9th Cir.1987), and remanded the matter for further consideration in light of Gwaltney v. Chesapeake Bay Foundation, 108 S.Ct. 376 (1987). On remand, the parties filed three motions: (1) Sierra Club moved to reinstate our judgment; (2) Union Oil moved to remand the entire matter to the district court; and (3) Sierra Club asked this court to take judicial notice of certain public documents. We grant Sierra Club's motion for reinstatement. We deny Union Oil's motion for remand and Sierra Club's request for judicial notice.

This case began when Sierra Club brought a citizen enforcement action under section 505(a) of the Clean Water Act, 33 U.S.C. § 1365(a), against Union Oil for violations of Union Oil's National Pollutant Discharge Elimination System (NPDES) permit. In the complaint, Sierra Club sought injunctive relief and the imposition of civil penalties. Sierra Club alleged seventy-six specific permit violations during the period 1979 to 1983. Later, Sierra Club sought to amend its complaint to allege additional violations before 1979 and after 1983.

The district court denied Sierra Club's request for leave to amend its complaint and denied both parties' motions for summary judgment. After a five-day trial on the issue of liability, the district court found Union Oil not liable for any of the seventy-six past violations, entered a judgment in favor of Union Oil, and dismissed the action with prejudice. Specifically,

> [t]he court excused some of the reported exceedances of permit limitations by application of an upset defense (an excuse for permit violations when circumstances occur that are beyond the reasonable control of the permittee), some on the ground that reports of exceedances were mistakes caused by sampling error, and some by application of a purported de minimus exception to the [Clean Water Act].

Sierra Club, 813 F.2d at 1482. Sierra Club appealed.

On appeal, we reversed the district court's finding of no liability and remanded the case for further proceedings. We determined that Union Oil was liable for seventy-four of the seventy-six past violations, and that the remaining two alleged permit violations required further findings of fact. Id. We found that (1) the upset defense was not available to Union Oil, (2) the district court improperly allowed Union Oil to impeach its own reports of permit violations by showing sampling error, and (3) the district court erred by invoking a "de minimus" exception to the Clean Water Act to excuse violations based on unusual human error. We also reversed the district court's denial of Sierra Club's request for leave to amend its complaint, except as to violations about which Sierra Club knew or should have known when it filed the original complaint.

On December 1, 1987, the Supreme Court decided Gwaltney v. Chesapeake Bay Foundation, 108 S.Ct. 376 (1987). In *Gwaltney,* the Court described what citizen plaintiffs must do to establish federal jurisdiction in suits under section 505(a) of the Clean Water Act; how defendants may challenge jurisdiction in such suits; and what citizen plaintiffs must prove to prevail on the merits.

First, the Court stated that citizens, unlike the EPA, may seek the imposition of civil penalties for violations of the Clean Water Act only in suits brought to enjoin or otherwise abate ongoing violations. *Id.* 108 S.Ct. at 382. Thus, to invoke federal jurisdiction under section 505(a) of the Clean Water Act, a citizen plaintiff must allege "a state of either continuous or intermittent violation—that is, a reasonable likelihood that a past polluter will continue to pollute in the future." Id. 108 S.Ct. at 381.

To protect defendants against frivolous suits, the Court added that the citizen plaintiff's allegations must be made in "good faith." Id. 108 S.Ct. at 385. The citizen plaintiff, however, need not prove the allegations of ongoing noncompliance before jurisdiction attaches. Id. Rather, the allegations need only satisfy the good-faith pleading requirements set forth in Rule 11 of the Federal Rules of Civil Procedure. The citizen plaintiff's allegations must be based on good-faith beliefs, "formed after reasonable inquiry," that are "well grounded in fact." Id. (quoting F.R.C.P. 11).

Next, the Court established that it is the defendant's responsibility to challenge the truthfulness of the allegations of ongoing violations. If the defendant wishes to argue that the allegations are untrue, and that the citizen plaintiff lacks standing to bring the suit, the defendant must move for summary judgment and demonstrate that "the allegations were sham and raised no genuine issue of fact." Id. * * *. If the defendant fails to convince the court that there are no genuine issues of fact after the plaintiff offers evidence to support the allegations of ongoing noncompliance, the case goes to trial on the merits. Id.

Federal courts can also lose jurisdiction over citizen suits when the defendant can show that the case is moot. The burden of proving that the case is moot is on the defendant. The defendant must show that "there is no reasonable expectation that the wrong will be repeated," id. * * * and must make it "absolutely clear that allegedly wrongful behavior could not reasonably be expected to recur," id. * * *

Finally, the Court stated that citizen plaintiffs must eventually prove the existence of ongoing Clean Water Act violations or the reasonable likelihood of continuing future violations to prevail on the merits of a citizen enforcement action. Id. 108 S.Ct. at 386.

In light of *Gwaltney*, Union Oil and Sierra Club make the following arguments on remand. Union Oil urges this court to remand the entire matter to the district court to start over again. Union Oil argues that Sierra Club may not obtain relief until it proves the existence of ongoing NPDES permit violations. Because the district court failed to make findings concerning ongoing violations, Union Oil argues that we should not reinstate our judgment—which imposes liability on Union Oil for seventy-four permit violations—until Sierra Club can prove in district court the existence of ongoing violations.

Sierra Club urges this court to reinstate its judgment. First, Sierra Club argues that, despite the district court's failure to make specific findings, the Sierra Club offered sufficient proof of ongoing violations at trial to impose on Union Oil liability for past violations. Second, Sierra Club asks this court to take judicial notice of ongoing NPDES permit violations documented in public records, if we conclude that the trial record contains insufficient proof.

We chart a middle course between the alternatives suggested by the parties. We think it best to reinstate our judgment, which already remanded the case to the district court for further proceedings, but to amend our opinion to indicate that the district court may not assess penalties against Union Oil for past NPDES permit violations until Sierra Club proves the existence of ongoing permit violations or the reasonable likelihood of continuing future violations. We adopt this approach for the following reasons.

First, *Gwaltney* did not contradict or invalidate anything we said in *Sierra Club.* In fact, *Gwaltney* did not address the issues we discussed. *Gwaltney* explained when courts have jurisdiction over citizen suits under section 505(a) of the Clean Water Act, when such suits become moot, and what citizens must prove to prevail on the merits. *Sierra Club* discussed the upset defense, sampling errors, exceptions to the Clean Water Act's requirements, and when a citizen plaintiff may amend its complaint. Thus, as long as federal jurisdiction was properly assumed, and the case has not become moot, our opinion in *Sierra Club* is necessary to guide further district court proceedings.

Second, Union Oil concedes that Sierra Club satisfied *Gwaltney's* threshold requirements for jurisdiction. Under *Gwaltney,* Sierra Club had to make good faith allegations of continuous or intermittent ongoing NPDES permit violations for jurisdiction to attach. We agree with the district court that Sierra Club's complaint alleged ongoing violations. In rejecting Union Oil's motion for summary judgment, the district court found that:

> [P]laintiff alleges not only past violations by defendants, but continuing violations as well. The complaint alleges an ongoing pattern of frequent and substantial non-compliance with the Act on the part of defendants. In fact, the complaint explicitly states that the "interests of the Sierra Club members have been, *are being,* and unless the relief prayed herein is granted, *will be,* adversely affected by the failure of defendants to comply with their permit." (Emphasis added.) The complaint also alleges "that, without the imposition of appropriate civil penalties and issuance of an injunction, defendants *will continue to violate* their NPDES permit to the further irreparable injury of plaintiff and the public." (Emphasis added.)

Sierra Club v. Union Oil Co., 15 Envtl.L.Rep. (Envtl.L.Inst.) 20,890, 20,891 (N.D.Cal. Jan.11, 1985) (quoting Sierra Club's complaint). Union Oil does not appear to challenge this finding on appeal. Nor does Union Oil argue that Sierra Club's allegations violate Fed.R.Civ.P. 11 or lack any basis in fact. Accordingly, both the district court and this court properly assumed jurisdiction.

The problem Union Oil raises is that our opinion seems to impose liability on Union Oil for past permit violations prior to Sierra Club's proof at trial of the existence of ongoing violations. In *Sierra Club,* we stated that "[t]he district court's finding of no liability for the other seventy-four exceedances alleged in the original complaint is reversed and the case is remanded for determination of penalty." 813 F.2d at 1494. Union Oil asserts that *Gwaltney* precludes a finding of liability when there has been no proof of ongoing violations, and that our opinion therefore conflicts with *Gwaltney.*

Sierra Club seeks to solve this problem by arguing in the alternative that they did prove ongoing violations at trial or that we may now take judicial notice of ongoing violations.

We are not willing to address factual matters not considered by the district court. Union Oil correctly notes that the district court made no factual findings on the issue of ongoing violations or the reasonable likelihood of continuing future violations. Although Sierra Club did present evidence of ongoing violations in its motion for leave to file an amended complaint, and it appears that Sierra Club may be able to prove ongoing violations on remand to the district court, we think it best to leave factual matters in the first instance to the district court.

The fact that the district court has not yet addressed the issue of ongoing violations, however, does not convince us that we should remand this case to the district court without first reinstating our opinion, as Union Oil suggests. Our finding of liability for the seventy-four past violations may be conditioned on Sierra Club's ability to prove ongoing violations before the district court on remand. By reinstating our opinion and amending it to conform to the requirements of *Gwaltney,* we may both preserve the substantive discussions in *Sierra Club* that are not affected by *Gwaltney* and respond to Union Oil's concern that it not be held liable for past violations until Sierra Club can prove the existence of ongoing violations as required by *Gwaltney.*

On the matter of proving ongoing violations, we agree with the Fourth Circuit's recent decision on remand from *Gwaltney* that a citizen plaintiff may prove ongoing violations "either (1) by proving violations that continue on or after the date the complaint is filed, or (2) by adducing evidence from which a reasonable trier of fact could find a continuing likelihood of a recurrence in intermittent or sporadic violations." Chesapeake Bay Foundation v. Gwaltney, 844 F.2d 170, 171–72 (4th Cir.1988), on remand from 108 S.Ct. 376 (1987). We also agree with the Fourth Circuit's definition of what may constitute a continuing likelihood of violations. "Intermittent or sporadic violations do not cease to be ongoing until the date when there is *no real likelihood of repetition.*" Id. at 172 (emphasis added). Thus, the Fourth Circuit linked proof of ongoing violations to the Supreme Court's discussion of mootness in *Gwaltney:*

Consistent with the guidance of the Supreme Court majority and concurring opinions, the district court may wish to consider whether remedial actions were taken to cure violations, the *ex ante* probability that such remedial measures would be effective, and any other evidence presented during the proceedings that bears on *whether the risk of defendant's continued violation had been completely eradicated* when citizen-plaintiffs filed suit.

Id. (emphasis added). We believe this is the correct approach to proving ongoing violations or the reasonable likelihood of continuing violations under *Gwaltney*.

* * *

JUDGMENT REINSTATED AND AMENDED.

[On remand, the district court considered whether the 74 CWA violations were "ongoing" or "reasonably likely to recur" by applying the following test. A violation is determined to be "ongoing" when a court compares self-reported exceedances before the complaint was filed and afterwards. If the same pollution parameter is exceeded, or a violation recurs and the cause has not been completely eradicated then the violation will be deemed "ongoing" and liability attaches. See Sierra Club v. Union Oil Co., 716 F.Supp. 429, 433 (N.D.Cal.1988). After examining the evidence the court concluded that the 74 exceedances were ongoing violations and that Union Oil had not established "no real likelihood of repetition."]

Long Island Soundkeeper Fund, Inc. v. New York City

United States District Court, Eastern District of New York, 1998.
27 F.Supp.2d 380.

■ DEARIE, DISTRICT JUDGE:

Plaintiffs bring this action pursuant to the citizen suit provision of the Clean Water Act ("CWA"), 33 U.S.C. § 1365, alleging defendants New York City Department of Environmental Protection ("DEP" or the "City") and Joel A. Mile, DEP's Commissioner, violated discharge permits issued by the New York State Department of Environmental Conservation ("DEC" or the "State"). Plaintiffs claim that DEP exceeded its permit limitations at eight sewage treatment plants that discharge pollutants into the East River and Jamaica Bay. The State of Connecticut, granted permission to intervene in this action, alleges violations only at those plants that discharge pollutants into the East River. Defendants move to dismiss the complaint or, alternatively, to stay the proceedings pending the resolution of a state court enforcement action brought by the State of New York regarding largely the same permit violations. Additionally, defendants move to dismiss plaintiffs' claims that DEP is violating its settleable solids permit limitations. The motion to dismiss the complaint or to stay the proceedings is denied. The motion to dismiss those claims regarding DEP's settleable solids limitations is granted.

Background

New York State DEC Region 2 is responsible for administering New York City's State Pollutant Discharge Elimination System ("SPDES") permits for the discharge of pollutants into navigable waters. DEC, in accordance with 33 U.S.C. § 1342,[1] implements federal CWA standards through the issuance of these permits. DEC has issued fourteen permits to DEP for fourteen sewage treatment plants. Id. P 3. Each permit limits the amounts of certain pollutants that may be discharged from each facility.

On December 18, 1997, plaintiffs sent a letter to defendant DEP alleging it exceeded the discharge limits in its SPDES permits for the sewage plants in Bowery Bay, Tallman Island, Wards Island, Hunts Point, 26th Ward, Coney Island, Jamaica, and Rockaway. This letter also provided notice to DEP that plaintiffs intended to file a civil action under the citizen suit provision of the Clean Water Act. A copy of this notice letter was sent to DEC and the United States Environmental Protection Agency ("EPA").

Under the CWA, private citizens must provide notice of their intent to sue sixty (60) days before they file their suit. 33 U.S.C. § 1365(b)(1)(B). As plaintiffs' notice letter was sent December 18, 1997, they were legally authorized to file suit on or after February 16, 1998 if no enforcement action had been taken by DEC against DEP for the same violations. See 33 U.S.C. § 1365(b)(1)(B). On February 6, 1998, plaintiffs and DEC agreed that neither party would file any action prior to February 23, 1998. * * *

On February 11, 1998, plaintiffs' attorneys met with DEC officials to discuss defendants' compliance with their permit restrictions. On February 20, 1998, plaintiffs and DEC again agreed to postpone filing any action against defendants so that DEC and attorneys for both plaintiffs and defendants could meet to discuss the alleged violations. Significantly, plaintiffs agreed not to file before March 9, 1998, thereby allowing DEC a clear opportunity to file first and preclude private action.

On March 6, 1998, DEC requested that plaintiffs again postpone filing suit to a date later than March 9, 1998 because DEC was not prepared to file on March 6, 1998 as previously agreed. Plaintiffs would not agree to any further extension. Plaintiffs filed this action at 8:36 a.m. on March 9, 1998, before DEC had taken any enforcement action against defendants. DEC filed its state court action at 9:00 a.m. that same day.

Plaintiffs allege in their complaint that the City discharged fecal coliform, nitrogen, settleable solids, and biological oxygen in amounts greater than the levels authorized in DEP's permits. Plaintiffs seek to enjoin DEP from further violating the permits and request that the Court

---

1. Section § 1342 of Title 33 of the United States Code authorizes state issuance of National Pollutant Discharge Elimination System Permits ("NPDES"). The state issued permits must comply with the standards set forth by the Clean Water Act and federal regulations and may also, as seen here, im- pose more stringent requirements. For the purposes of this opinion "SPDES" is used to refer to the permits issued by the New York State DEC. It is noted that the term "NPDES" has been used in cases, cited to in this opinion, to refer to these state issued permits.

order the City to pay $25,000 in civil fines for each day DEP is in violation. DEC's state court complaint alleges essentially the same violations under New York State Environmental Conservation Law ("ECL") and seeks the same relief.

Discussion

The CWA contains two limitations on a citizen's right to bring a private enforcement action. First, § 1365(b)(1)(A) requires that notice of the alleged violation be provided to the alleged violator, the EPA, and to the state enforcement agency at least sixty days before the citizen suit is filed. 33 U.S.C. § 1365(b)(1)(A). Second, § 1365(b)(1)(B) provides that no private enforcement action may be commenced if the "State has commenced and is diligently prosecuting a civil or criminal action in a court of the United States, or a State" seeking the same relief. 33 U.S.C. § 1365(b)(1)(B).

Defendants concede that plaintiffs satisfied the notice requirement. However, defendants contend that DEC is "diligently prosecuting" its enforcement action in state court pursuant to § 1365(b)(1)(B) and that the citizen suit before this Court must therefore be dismissed. Plaintiffs argue that DEC's state court action does not bar their citizen suit because it was properly filed before DEC filed its state court action.

It is well established that "the starting point for interpreting a statute is the language of the statute itself." Gwaltney of Smithfield, Ltd. v. Chesapeake Bay Found., Inc., 484 U.S. 49, 56, 98 L. Ed. 2d 306, 108 S. Ct. 376 (1987) (quoting Consumer Product Safety Comm'n v. GTE Sylvania, Inc., 447 U.S. 102, 108, 64 L. Ed. 2d 766, 100 S. Ct. 2051 (1980)). Section 1365(b)(1)(B) clearly states that a citizen suit may not be brought against an alleged violator if the "State has commenced and is diligently prosecuting a civil or criminal action" seeking the same relief. 33 U.S.C. § 1365(b)(1)(B) (emphasis added). The language of this statute "clearly contemplates action prior to the filing of a citizen suit." Conn. Fund for the Env't v. Job Plating Co., 623 F.Supp. 207, 215 (D.Conn.1985) (Cabranes, J.).

In Job Plating, a citizen suit was filed on November 17, 1983 against the Job Plating Company alleging it was violating its NPDES permits. Id. at 210. The State of Connecticut then filed a state court action on March 19, 1984. Id. at 211. The defendant moved to dismiss the citizen suit pursuant to § 1365(b)(1)(B), arguing that the State's subsequent state court action amounted to "diligent prosecution" that precluded the citizen suit. Id. at 215. The court, however, found that only where there has been a prior state enforcement action "is it possible to consider whether that action is 'diligent prosecution' that would preclude the filing of the citizen suit." "Actions taken by the state after the filing of a citizen suit may not be considered as constituting 'diligent prosecution' pursuant to [§ 1365(b)(1)(B)]." Id. at 216. No court has held otherwise.

The fact that DEC filed its complaint in state court less than one-half hour after plaintiffs filed their complaint in this Court does not change the fact that plaintiff's suit was filed first. In Connecticut Fund for the Environment v. Upjohn Co., 660 F.Supp. 1397 (D.Conn.1987), the court concluded that a state enforcement action filed three days after a citizen suit was filed in federal court did not preclude the citizen suit from going forward. Id. at 1402–03. The court noted that the "sixty-day waiting period of § 1365(b)(1)(B) gives the government the opportunity to act and to control the course of the litigation if it acts within the time period. If the government delays, then the citizens may go forward...." Id. at 1404. The court concluded that it "must apply an inflexible rule which determines jurisdiction from the time of filing the complaint." Id. at 1404. Here, the State had that same opportunity, but relinquished it by their inaction.

In Chesapeake Bay Foundation v. American Recovery Co., 769 F.2d 207 (4th Cir.1985), the court found that a state enforcement action filed three hours after a citizen suit was filed did not preclude the citizen suit from going forward. Plaintiffs filed their citizen suit on January 23, 1984 at 12:34 p.m.; the state enforcement action was filed at 3:52 p.m. that same day. Id. at 207. The court found that "the verb tenses used in subsection (b)(1)(B) and the scheme of the statute demonstrate that the bar was not intended to apply unless the government files suit first." Id. at 208. The Fourth Circuit concluded that "the government did not act within the sixty-day waiting period and it had not yet filed suit when plaintiffs filed their independent action. Therefore, plaintiffs' suit was not barred." Id. at 208–09.

Defendants rely on two cases in which citizen suits were dismissed even though they were filed before any state enforcement action was taken: Atlantic States Legal Foundation v. Eastman Kodak Co., 933 F.2d 124 (2d Cir.1991) and United States Environmental Protection Agency v. City of Green Forest, 921 F.2d 1394 (8th Cir.1991). However, neither case addresses the same issue presented here. In both cases, a citizen suit filed in federal court was dismissed when a later filed government enforcement action was resolved by consent decree. The dismissal in each case was based on the settlement of the issues and not on the diligent prosecution provision of the CWA. As stated by the Second Circuit in Eastman Kodak, "If the state enforcement proceeding has caused the violations alleged in the citizen suit to cease without any likelihood of recurrence—has eliminated the basis for the citizen suit—[then] ... the citizen suit must be dismissed." 933 F.2d at 127. In Eastman Kodak, the state negotiated an out-of-court settlement that potentially resolved the issues in the case. The court remanded the case to the district court to determine whether there remained "a realistic prospect of continuing violations." Id. If not, the district court was instructed to dismiss the citizen suit as moot. Id. Nothing in Eastman Kodak counsels in favor of dismissing plaintiffs' suit.

In sum, the language of the statute, as confirmed by available case analysis, makes clear that state prosecution of the same claims no matter how diligent, will not preclude a properly filed private action, or require its dismissal. To hold otherwise would undermine the Congress' clear intention to authorize private action under the prescribed circumstances and would remove the incentive benefits built into the legislation for prompt government action.

[The city then made the argument that the federal court should abstain from exercising jurisdiction over the citizen suit because there were parallel enforcement proceedings underway in both state and federal court. The court rejected this *Colorado River* abstention request, construing the doctrine narrowly and finding that CWA citizen suits were a statutory right conferred by Congress.]

Finally, plaintiffs allege that the Jamaica sewage plant violated the limits on settleable solids found in its SPDES permit. Defendants contend that plaintiffs cannot enforce these permit provisions because the settleable solids restrictions were imposed by DEC under state law and are not required under federal law.[3] Defendants argue that the Second Circuit's holding in Atlantic States Legal Found. v. Eastman Kodak Co., 12 F.3d 353 (2d Cir.1993), precludes citizens from suing to enforce permit provisions imposed under state law that are stricter than those required under federal law. The Court agrees.

In Atlantic States, the Second Circuit found that "state regulations, including the provisions of SPDES permits, which mandate 'a greater scope of coverage than that required' by the federal CWA and its implementing regulations are not enforceable through a citizen suit under 33 U.S.C. § 1365." Id. at 359 (quoting 40 C.F.R. § 123.1(i)(2)). The court explained, "States may enact stricter standards for wastewater effluents than mandated by the CWA and federal EPA regulations. These states' standards may be enforced under the CWA by the states or the EPA, but private citizens have no standing to do so." Id. at 358 (citations omitted). The settleable solids limitations at issue in this case are stricter than those required under federal law. Accordingly, plaintiffs have no standing to sue DEP for violating the settleable solids provisions in its SPDES permits. See Upper Chattahoochee Riverkeeper v. City of Atlanta, 953 F.Supp. 1541, 1552 (N.D.Ga.1996) (construing Atlantic States to hold that "private citizens have no standing to enforce broader state regulations contained in NPDES permits"); City of New York v. Anglebrook, 891 F.Supp. 900, 904 (S.D.N.Y. 1995) ("[In Atlantic States,] the Second Circuit held that the district court lacked jurisdiction in a citizen suit where plaintiffs sought to enforce a state permit requirement that was stricter than the Clean Water Act and its implementing regulations.").

---

3. While current federal regulations regarding municipal sewage plants do not include settleable solids restrictions, see 40 C.F.R. § 133.102(a), (b), New York law specifically requires "the removal of substantially all floating and settleable solids." ECL § 17–0509. Plaintiffs do not dispute that New York law expands the scope of current federal limits on settleable solids found in § 133.102(a) and (b). Instead, plaintiffs claim that "a former federal regulation," 40 C.F.R. § 125.58(m) (1979), requires similar limits and therefore "the state-issued permit does not impose a greater scope of coverage than required by the CWA." However, this regulation is no longer in effect. New York law includes restrictions on settleable solids that are not found in current federal law.

For the reasons stated above, defendants' motion to dismiss plaintiffs' citizen suit or to stay the proceedings pending the outcome of the state court action is denied. Defendants' motion to dismiss that part of plaintiffs' suit regarding DEP's settleable solids restrictions is granted.

SO ORDERED.

A NOTE ON POST–GWALTNEY LITIGATION

As the *Union Oil* decision indicates, courts considering CWA citizen suit litigation must confront fundamental jurisdictional questions posed by the U.S. Supreme Court's holding in Gwaltney v. Chesapeake Bay Foundation, Inc., 484 U.S. 49 (1987). Using the language, structure and legislative history of the Act, the Court ruled that § 505(a) does not confer federal jurisdiction over citizen suits for wholly past violations of the CWA. This position has more recently been confirmed by the Court in Steel Co. v. Citizens for a Better Environment, 523 U.S. 83, 106–107 (1998). While clearly rejecting citizen suits for past violations, the Court did not read § 505 to require proof of present or future violations. The majority opinion interpreted the "to be in violation" language of § 505 as requiring only that there be a "reasonable likelihood that a past polluter will continue to pollute into the future." *Id.* at 57. In addition, since the CWA only requires that a § 505 defendant be "alleged" to have violated the Act, the Court held that a "good-faith allegation" of ongoing violation was sufficient for jurisdictional purposes. Since the Court did not provide clear guidance for implementing its decision, soome have feared that the holding would spawn confusion. Others have predicted that the *Gwaltney* decision would severely limit CWA citizen suits in the future. The consistent flow of § 505 cases filed add decided since 1987 has shown that *Gwaltney* has not been the obstacle some had feared. In the lower court cases following *Gwaltney*, courts have had relatively little difficulty applying the "good-faith allegations" and "ongoing violation" requirements mentioned above. These two issues and two more deserve further attention.

(a) Good–Faith Allegations

The Court clearly stated that under the terms of § 505 jurisdiction does not require proof of an ongoing violation but only allegations. The Court noted in *Gwaltney* that summary judgment and the concept of mootness were always available to the defendant in order to challenge jurisdiction and to defend against stale or frivolous claims. Consequently, the "good-faith allegation" requirement of *Gwaltney* has not been a significant deterrent to § 505 litigation. In fact, this requirement has been reduced to a matter of careful pleading since allegations of ongoing violations must appear on the face of the complaint. For example, in Brewer v. Ravan, 680 F.Supp. 1176 (M.D.Tenn.1988), it was held that a plaintiff's allegations stating that defendant violated the CWA on "several occasions more than five years ago" was insufficient to invoke federal jurisdiction since there was no statement that there was a reasonable likelihood that the defendant would violate the Act in the future. Once the ongoing allegation is made, courts appear reluctant to dismiss the action unless it "appears beyond doubt that the plaintiff can prove no set of facts in support of his claim which would entitle him to relief." Atlantic States Legal Foundation v. W.H. Pfarrer Co., 28 ERC (BNA) 1452 (N.D.Ind.1988).

What insures that the allegations will truly be in "good faith?" This standard is governed by Rule 11 of the Federal Rules of Civil Procedure which requires pleadings to be "formed after reasonable inquiry" and "well grounded in fact." Rule 11 provides for sanctions to be imposed against attorneys for filing frivolous suits but it is not an impossible precondition requiring proof that violations will definitely occur in the future.

(b) Ongoing Violations

Gwaltney held that once jurisdiction attached to a § 505 case, the citizen must then prove its allegation that the CWA violation was "continuous or intermittent." 484 U.S. at 57. On remand from the Supreme Court, the Fourth Circuit articulated a standard that a plaintiff may prove an ongoing violation either by 1) proving violations that continue on or after the date the complaint is filed, or 2) adducing evidence from which a reasonable trier of fact could find a continuing likelihood of a recurrence in intermittent or sporadic violations. Chesapeake Bay Foundation, Inc. v. Gwaltney, 844 F.2d 170–71 (4th Cir.1988). This test has been cited with approval and applied by the Second, Third, Fifth, Ninth and Eleventh circuits. See, e.g. Russian River Watershed Protection Committee v. Santa Rosa, 142 F.3d 1136 (9th Cir.1998).

In the *Gwaltney* case, proving the ongoing violation was made easier by the fact that the firm had a long history of frequent permit violations. But a lengthy record of past non-compliance is not a required element of proof as in NRDC v. Outboard Marine Corp., 692 F.Supp. 801 (N.D.Ill.1988), where three permit violations over three years was sufficient proof. To avoid § 505 liability, a defendant must establish that it has taken steps to prevent future recurrences of permit violations. How far must a defendant go? Even if a defendant takes action to prevent future violations, some courts have been reluctant to accept claims that future violations are not reasonably likely. See PIRG v. Powell Duffryn Terminals, Inc., 720 F.Supp. 1158 (D.N.J.1989) (the installation of a new waste water treatment system did not assure continuing future compliance unless the plant "as operated" would meet permit limits). Is the *Powell Duffryn Terminals* court asking far too much?

Is there an ongoing violation when the actual discharge has ended yet residual seepage continues to add pollutants to the water. Several courts have found an ongoing violation in these circumstances. See Umatilla Waterquality Protective Ass'n v. Smith Frozen Foods, 962 F.Supp. 1312, 1322 (D.Or.1997) and Informed Citizens United, Inc. v. USX Corp., 36 F.Supp.2d 375 (S.D.Tex.1999). There do seem to be some limits on a defendant's exposure. In Morris–Smith v. Moulton Niguel Water District, 234 F.3d 1277 (9th Cir.2000), the case was dismissed based on unrebutted evidence that the defendant had modified and upgraded at the offending facility before plaintiffs filed their complaint and therefore future violations were unlikely.

(c) Mootness of a Citizen Suit Claim

CWA citizen suits are often brought to enforce compliance obligations of water pollution sources often contained in the facility's NPDES permit. Assume that citizen suit plaintiffs are successful in establishing standing to bring the action in federal court, what should happen to the case if, after filing the § 505 suit, the polluter voluntarily comes into compliance with its permit conditions? Further, what should happen to the suit if, prior to a final court judgment, the polluting facility is closed, dismantled and put up for sale? Should either of these events make the § 505 case legally moot and allow the court to dismiss the action? These interesting questions serve as the backdrop for an actual case reaching the Supreme Court.

In Friends of the Earth v. Laidlaw Environmental Services, 528 U.S. 167 (2000), the Supreme Court considered a fact situation presenting these mootness issues in combination with question regarding CWA plaintiff's standing. Laidlaw operated a hazardous waste incinerator in Roebuck, South Carolina that included a wastewater treatment plant. The state environmental agency granted Laidlaw an NPDES permit to discharge treated wastewater into the local river. This permit placed limits on Laidlaw's discharge of several pollutants including mercury, an extremely toxic pollutant. The company repeatedly violated the limits set by the state permit. FOE filed a CWA citizens suit alleging noncompliance with the permit and seeking declaratory and injunctive relief as well as an award of civil penalties. After finding that FOE had standing, the district court ruled in favor of FOE concluding that a $505,800 civil penalty was appropriate. However, the court declined to order injunctive relief because Laidlaw, after the suit began, had achieved "substantial compliance" with its permit. The Fourth Circuit reversed the district court by concluding that the case had become moot. It reasoned that all three elements of Article III standing-injury, causation and redress ability—must exist at every stage of the litigation or else the action becomes moot. In the Laidlaw case, the action had become moot because "the only remedy currently available to [FOE]—civil penalties payable to the government—would not redress any injury [FOE has] suffered." This appellate court ruling on the effect of post-filing compliance was inconsistent with decisions of the Second, Third, Seventh, and the Eleventh Circuits.

The Supreme Court, by way of a majority opinion written by Justice Ginsberg, disagreed. First, it clarified the reach of the earlier Supreme Court decision in Steel Company by holding that the prior case had only held that citizen suit plaintiffs lacked standing to seek civil penalties for violations "that have abated by the time of the suit." These "wholly past violations" were outside the scope of CWA citizen suits; but plaintiffs could have standing to obtain civil penalties or "ongoing violations" that could continue into the future if "undeterred." Concluding that FOE had standing to bring the CWA citizen suit, Justice Ginsberg turned to the mootness question and wrote the following,

The only conceivable basis for a finding of mootness in this case is Laidlaw's voluntary conduct—either its achievement by August 1992 of substantial compliance with its NPDES permit or its more recent shutdown of the Roebuck facility. It is well settled that "a defendant's voluntary cessation of a challenged practice does not deprive a federal court of its power to determine the legality of the practice" City of Mesquite, 455 U.S. at 289. "If it did, the courts would be compelled to 'leave the defendant ... free to return to his old ways.'" 455 U.S. at 289, n. 10. In accordance with this principle, the standard we have announced for determining whether a case has been mooted by the defendant's voluntary conduct is stringent: "A case might become moot if subsequent events made it absolutely clear that the allegedly wrongful behavior could not reasonably be expected to recur." United States v. Concentrated Phosphate Export Assn., Inc., 393 U.S. 199, 203, 89 S.Ct. 361, 21 L.Ed.2d 344 (1968). The "heavy burden of persuading" the court that the challenged conduct cannot reasonably be expected to start up again lies with the party asserting mootness. Ibid.

528 U.S. at 188. Consider this language in conjunction with defendant's post-citizen suit filing compliance measures. When would it be "absolutely clear" that wrongful behavior would not reoccur? What steps would or should satisfy this mootness test? Installation of pollution control equipment? Adoption of thorough facility operation and maintenance training? Consent agreements with substantial financial penalties for later noncompliance? Sale of the facility to another company? Plant shutdown and demolition?

The *Laidlaw* decision suggests that once standing has been established by the plaintiff showing that there was a substantial likelihood of a continuing violation, federal judges possessed a range of remedial options to deter future misbehavior by the defendant. Justice Ginsberg noted that unless it was "absolutely clear" that permit violations could not be reasonably expected to recur, the suit was *not* moot and that judges had discretion to frame remedies. She wrote,

In its brief, Laidlaw appears to argue that, regardless of the effect of Laidlaw's compliance, FOE doomed its own civil penalty claim to mootness by failing to appeal the District Court's denial of injunctive relief. This argument misconceives the statutory scheme. Under § 1365(a), the district court has discretion to determine which form of relief is best suited, in the particular case, to abate current violations and deter future ones. "[A] federal judge sitting as chancellor is not mechanically obligated to grant an injunction for every violation of law." Weinberger v. Romero–Barcelo, 456 U.S. 305, 313, 102 S.Ct. 1798, 72 L.Ed.2d 91 (1982). Denial of injunctive relief does not necessarily mean that the district court has concluded there is no prospect of future violations for civil penalties to deter. Indeed, it meant no such thing in this case. The District Court denied injunctive relief, but expressly based its award of civil penalties on the need for deterrence.

As the dissent notes, federal courts should aim to ensure " 'the framing of relief no broader than required by the precise facts.' " Schlesinger v. Reservists Comm. to Stop the War, 418 U.S. 208, 222, 94 S.Ct. 2925, 41 L.Ed.2d 706 (1974). In accordance with this aim, a district court in a Clean Water Act citizen suit properly may conclude that an injunction would be an excessively intrusive remedy, because it could entail continuing superintendence of the permit holder's activities by a federal court—a process burdensome to court and permit holder alike. See City of Mesquite, 455 U.S. at 289 (although the defendant's voluntary cessation of the challenged practice does not moot the case, "such abandonment is an important factor bearing on the question whether a court should exercise its power to enjoin the defendant from renewing the practice").

Laidlaw also asserts, in a supplemental suggestion of mootness, that the closure of its Roebuck facility, which took place after the Court of Appeals issued its decision, mooted the case. The facility closure, like Laidlaw's earlier achievement of substantial compliance with its permit requirements, might moot the case, but—we once more reiterate—only if one or the other of these events made it absolutely clear that Laidlaw's permit violations could not reasonably be expected to recur. The effect of both Laidlaw's compliance and the facility closure on the prospect of future violations is a disputed factual matter. FOE points out, for example—and Laidlaw does not appear to contest—that Laidlaw retains its NPDES permit. These issues have not been aired in the lower courts; they remain open for consideration on remand. (emphasis added)

528 U.S. at 192–95. The key to future mootness claims appears to be court's willingness to find that present noncompliance will not or perhaps, cannot reoccur.

NOTES AND QUESTIONS

1. *CWA Citizen Enforcement Powers.* Could Yvette and Sylvia file suit in federal court to compel either EPA or the DEC to initiate an enforcement action to obtain compliance with the terms of the Sewer District's Piney Run NPDES permit or the issuance of a revised permit with strengthened limitations?

Can the federal government be forced to enforce compliance with the CWA and prevent violations such as those alleged at the Piney Run facility? Read over the language of § 309(a)(1) & (3). Is enforcement discretionary or mandatory under these terms? The mandatory word "shall" appears in § 309(a), however its automatic effect is tempered by the necessity making a "finding" of noncompliance. Why would this be important to Yvette and Sylvia?

Consider the terms of § 505(a)(2) which authorize citizen suits against EPA (not polluters) "where there is alleged a failure of the Administrator to perform any act or duty under this chapter which is not discretionary

* * *." Most cases which have considered this issue of characterizing EPA enforcement judgment have used the "discretionary" label and have dismissed suits against EPA for lack of subject matter jurisdiction. See Dubois v. Thomas, 820 F.2d 943, 946–51 (8th Cir.1987). Also, major attacks on EPA's oversight of the state administration of the NPDES program are not likely to be successful. See Weatherby Lake Improvement Co. v. EPA, 45 Env't Rep. Cas. (BNA) 1191 (W.D.Mo.1997).

Should EPA be under a non-discretionary duty to issue compliance orders when a discharger is violating its permit? Should EPA be under a duty to enforce an existing consent decree? Why might a court be reluctant to intrude into this form of agency judgment? Can you imagine a situation where EPA should be forced by court order to initiate enforcement action? Does the Piney Run hypothetical present such a case? What arguments would you make on this issue?

Could the State of Euphoria be ordered to enforce its NPDES permit against the Sewer District? More specifically, could a CWA citizen suit be brought against a state for failure to enforce the basic provision of § 301(a) that prohibits the discharge of any pollutant except in accordance with an NPDES permit? A number of cases have considered this issue and have given § 505(a) a narrow sweep. The following discussion is typical.

> [T]he court is similarly persuaded that Congress did not intend the citizen suit provision to permit a cause of action against the states for any improper administration of their regulatory duties or for any failure to enforce the provisions of the FWPCA against polluters. Even if the [state] were administering a federally approved permit program here, the proper forum for such a claim would be state court rather than federal court because a state law determination would be involved * * *.

Ringbolt Farms Homeowners Ass'n v. Town of Hull, 714 F.Supp. 1246, 1256 (D.Mass.1989) (action to have state enforce RCRA and CWA against discharge from town's landfill into river). Consequently, state law should not be ignored as a source of authority under mandamus principles.

One possible avenue of approach for plaintiffs in this hypothetical might be under § 402(c) [§ 1342(c)] which allows EPA to withdraw the total NPDES program from the state after futile efforts to have the state to correct the problems. This, too, would be discretionary with EPA and would only result in the restoration of program's control to EPA. Would EPA be anxious to takeover the § 402 program? Why not?

2. *The "Mechanics" of CWA Citizen Suits.* In the Class Discussion Problem, could Yvette, Sylvia and the group East River Fishery and Recreation Association (the Association) themselves directly obtain enforcement of the NPDES permit in federal court under the CWA? (a) What exactly would they be enforcing? (b) If the CWA provides a cause of action, would Yvette, Sylvia and the Association have standing? (c) Where could the suit be brought? (d) Are there any unusual, and important, procedural obligations the plaintiffs would need to comply with?

a. *The Scope of Citizen Suit Enforcement.* Consider the language of § 505(a)(1). It authorizes citizens to enforce either 1) an effluent standard or limitation or 2) a government order issued with respect to such a standard or limitation. What does this mean? Rather than leave this term open to varying interpretation, Congress provided § 505(f) which specifically defines "effluent standard or limitation" and thereby defines the scope of CWA citizen suits. Would the conduct of the Sewer District be encompassed by § 505(f)?

The exact language of § 505(f) is as follows,

> (f) Effluent standard or limitation. For purposes of this section "effluent standard or limitation under this chapter" means (1) effective July 1, 1973, an unlawful act under subsection (a) of section 301 of this title, (2) an effluent limitation or other limitation under section 301 or 302 of this title; (3) standard of performance under section 306 of this title; (4) prohibition, effluent standard or pretreatment standards under section 307 of this title; (5) certification under section 401 of this title; (6) a permit or condition thereof issued under section 402 of this title, which is in effect under this chapter (including a requirement applicable by reason of section 313 of this title); or (7) a regulation under section 405(d) of this title.

Which of the following would be subject to citizen suit enforcement: 1) discharge without an NPDES permit, 2) discharge in violation of permit effluent limits, 3) departures from a permit's schedule of compliance, 4) discharge which causes water quality to violate state water quality standards, 5) failure to keep accurate records and to regularly report effluent monitoring to the government. Some cases have dismissed citizen suits for a lack of federal court jurisdiction to enforce as aspect of the CWA not clearly within § 505(f). See Northwest Environmental Defense Center v. U.S. Army Corps of Engineers, 118 F.Supp.2d 1115 (D.Or.2000) (§ 404 dredge and fill permit nondischarge conditions were *not* "effluent standards or limitations" within the meaning of § 505(f)). Also, as in *Long Island Soundkeeper Fund* permit conditions, in excess of more stringent federal rules, may not be enforced via a § 505 action.

b. *Proper Plaintiffs in CWA Citizen Suits.* Who can bring a federal enforcement action under § 505? Would Yvette, Sylvia and the Association be covered by the statute? Are they all "citizens" under the CWA? The Clean Water Act provides a circuitous answer. Section 505(g) [§ 1365(g)] states that "citizen" means "a person or persons having an interest which is or may be adversely affected." This section presents a number of other questions. If a "citizen" is a "person," then who or what is a "person" under the CWA? Read the definitional section 502(5) for the answer. Could foreign nations such as Canada or Mexico file § 505 citizen suits? See United States v. Hooker Chemicals & Plastics Corp., 101 F.R.D. 451 (W.D.N.Y.1984), affirmed 749 F.2d 968 (2d Cir.1984) (Canadian province is not a "person" under the CWA).

What would be required for the individual and organizational plaintiffs to establish standing to sue under § 505? Suppose that Yvette owned a

house located on the East River downstream from the Piney Run plant and suppose further that Sylvia had occasionally operated her power boat on the river in the vicinity of the facility. Do they have an interest "which is or may be adversely affected?" Is that all that must be established? Sierra Club v. Morton, 405 U.S. 727 (1972), set forth a constitutionally-based "injury in fact" requirement for the establishment of standing. Would either or both of these two plaintiffs be able to satisfy the Sierra Club test?

What about standing for the Association? What arguments could you make for this organization? Hunt v. Washington State Apple Adv. Comm'n, 432 U.S. 333 (1977) set forth a 3–pronged test for organizational standing in § 505 citizen suit cases filed on behalf of the membership:

1) individual group members must have standing to sue in their own rights,

2) the interests sought to be protected are germane to the group's purpose, and

3) neither the claim nor the requested relief requires individual participants.

See e.g., Friends of the Earth v. Chevron Chemical Co., 129 F.3d 826 (5th Cir.1997). In pre–1990's litigation, courts did not demand much in the way of direct proof of member injury. In NRDC v. Outboard Marine Corp., 692 F.Supp. 801, 807 (N.D.Ill.1988), the court stated that,

It is enough for NRDC to show its members use the water into which OMC's allegedly illegal discharges flow * * *. Such standing is not undermined because NRDC's members have not explicitly said they are harmed by OMC's permit violations. It is enough that they identify harm to their aesthetic or environmental interests from the overall pollution of the waterways. If OMC is proved to be violating the terms of its permit, that alone constitutes injury to those using the affected waters.

However, more recent litigation has been considerably more demanding especially on the question of proving particularized injury to an association's members. See e.g., PIRG v. Magnesium Elektron, Inc., 123 F.3d 111 (3d Cir.1997). A considerable number of cases, however, have no problem with the injury in fact requirement. The Ninth Circuit held that injury in fact may be established by daily geographic proximity without recreational use of the area or repeated recreational use with desired future use. See Ecological Rights Fdn. v. Pacific Lumber Co., 230 F.3d 1141 (9th Cir.2000).

c. *Procedural Prerequisites Citizen Suit Litigation.* If any or all of the plaintiffs establish standing, could a § 505 citizen suit be immediately filed? Examine the terms of § 505(b)(1)(A) & (B) [§ 1365(b)(1)(A) & (B)].

i. *Sixty day notice requirement.* Why does § 505(b)(1)(A) require that plaintiffs give notice of their intention to file a citizen suit? EPA, the state, and the alleged CWA violator must all be notified. What purpose does such notification serve? In Ada—Cascade Watch Co. v. Cascade Resource Recovery, Inc., 720 F.2d 897, 908 (6th Cir.1983), Judge Merritt justified the

RCRA 60 days notice provision with a number of reasons: a) it allows time for the government to take action and use the pending citizen suit leverage to obtain compliance, b) it permits technically complex issues to be resolved by expert agencies and not generalist courts, c) it encourages non-judicial dispute resolution and settlement, and d) it alerts the polluter and the government to the perceived seriousness of the violation. Are these convincing justifications?

How important is it for the plaintiffs in the Piney Run case to provide the required 60 days notice? In deciding the analogous notice provision in RCRA the U.S. Supreme Court has held that compliance with the notification rule was necessary to give the federal court jurisdiction and without it the case would have to be dismissed. See Hallstrom v. Tillamook County, 493 U.S. 20 (1989). CWA cases have been consistently dismissed for lack of jurisdiction. See Board of Trustees of Gainesville Township v. City of Gainesville, 1999 U.S. App. LEXIS 33998 (6th Cir.1999) and Washington Trout v. McCain Foods, Inc., 45 F.3d 1351, 1354 (9th Cir.1995) (inadequate notice deprives court of federal jurisdiction). Recent case decisions focus on the adequacy of the notice—that is, they must be sufficiently specific to inform the alleged violation of its error. See e.g. Atlantic States Legal Found., Inc. v. Stroh Die Casting Co., 116 F.3d 814, 819 (7th Cir.1997).

ii. *The Diligent Prosecution Bar.* Read the terms of § 505(b)(1)(B) [§ 1365(b)(1)(B)]. Why would Congress wish to prevent a citizen suit when EPA or the state has "commenced and is diligently prosecuting a civil or criminal action" in a federal or state court to secure compliance with the CWA? Why should the plaintiffs in the Piney Run case be prevented from litigating their own case?

When is the government diligently prosecuting an enforcement action "in a court?" The appellate courts have split on this question. The Second Circuit in Friends of the Earth v. Consolidated Rail Corp., 768 F.2d 57 (2d Cir.1985) and the Ninth Circuit in Sierra Club v. Chevron U.S.A., Inc., 834 F.2d 1517 (9th Cir.1987), have held that enforcement by a state board is not a "court" and does not bar a federal citizen suit. The Third and Sixth Circuits, on the other hand, has ruled that "courts" include administrative tribunals with judicial powers. See Baughman v. Bradford Coal Co., 592 F.2d 215 (3d Cir.1979) and Jones v. City of Lakeland, 175 F.3d 410 (6th Cir.1999). In addition, the filing of a state judicial enforcement action after the initiation of a § 505 action does not bar the citizen suit. However, if a settlement has been reached by prior state action, the citizen suit may be barred. See Williams Pipe Line Co. v. Bayer Corp., 964 F.Supp. 1300 (S.D.Iowa 1997).

3. *Citizen Suit Litigation Issues.* In the Class Discussion problem what forms of relief could the plaintiffs seek? (a) Could plaintiffs obtain an injunction demanding permit compliance? Could plaintiffs have monetary or civil penalties imposed on the Sewer District? How should the judge set the penalty if one were imposed? (b) What defenses, if any, could the Sewer District raise? (c) What should your strategy be regarding any potential settlement? (d) Could any of the plaintiffs sue the Sewer District for

monetary damages under the CWA? What about such a claim arising under state law?

a. *Injunctive Relief Issues.* In NRDC, Inc. v. Texaco Refining and Marketing, Inc., 906 F.2d 934 (3d Cir.1990), the appellate court reviewed the issuance of a permanent injunction issued against Texaco preventing the illegal discharge of industrial waste water from its Delaware City refinery into the Delaware River. The trial court noted that Texaco had filed monitoring data (DMRs) which revealed numerous prima facie permit violations for which no valid defenses existed. Having established Texaco's violations, the district court issued an injunction against future permit violations. The Third Circuit considered whether the district court erred by presuming that the demonstrated violation of the Clean Water Act constituted irreparable harm thereby justifying the issuance of the injunction. Relying on Weinberger v. Romero–Barcelo, 456 U.S. 305 (1982) and Amoco Production Co. v. Village of Gambell, 480 U.S. 531 (1987), the court reversed the trial judge and emphasized that traditional equitable remedial principles were not displaced by the CWA. Amplifying its reasoning, the Third Circuit concluded by noting,

> Thus, it is clear to us that a district court may issue a permanent injunction under the Act only after a showing both of irreparable injury and inadequacy of legal remedies, and a balancing of competing claims of injury and the public interest. *Amoco,* 480 U.S. at 544–47. From our reading of the district court's opinion in this case it is far from certain that such issues were considered and decided upon by the court. Rather, the district court—especially in light of its finding that no violation of the new permit has occurred—appears to have erroneously presumed irreparable harm from the mere fact of statutory violation, thus improperly focusing on the integrity of the permit process rather than the integrity of the Nation's waters. We will remand the case to the district court, therefore, for a proper determination of whether an injunction should issue. However, we do recognize, and so advise the district court on remand, that in applying the traditional equitable standard:
>
> > "Environmental injury, by its nature, can seldom be adequately remedied by money damages and is often permanent or at least of long duration, i.e. irreparable. If such injury is sufficiently likely, therefore, the balance of harms will usually favor the issuance of an injunction to protect the environment." *Amoco,* 480 U.S. at 545.

Did the NRDC make a mistake in arguing for the injunctive remedy without sufficiently establishing the two elements emphasized by the Court of Appeals? Why shouldn't "mere violation" of the CWA ground the issuance of an injunction without the showing required in the *Texaco* case? Would the holding in this case seriously impede government or citizen suit enforcement activities?

b. *Defenses Raised in CWA Citizen Suit Litigation.* As the cases reveal, establishing CWA liability for NPDES permit violations is quite easy. The industrial self-reporting mandated in the DMRs provides the government and citizens with a continuing picture of a firm's compliance status. This DMR information and its comparison to permit conditions often serves as the basis for CWA enforcement actions.

Is there anything a point source with damaging DMR information can do to avoid enforcement liability? The following case raising a wide range of defensive arguments is instructive. In Chesapeake Bay Foundation, Inc. v. Bethlehem Steel Corp., 652 F.Supp. 620 (D.Md.1987), the Chesapeake Bay Foundation, Inc. (CBF) filed a § 505 citizen suit against Bethlehem Steel seeking injunctive relief and civil penalties for the firm's demonstrated non-compliance with its NPDES permit. After presenting evidence of hundreds of permit violations, CBF moved for summary judgment on the question of whether or not Bethlehem Steel violated its permit. In response to this motion, Bethlehem Steel raised numerous defenses to the prima facie case of CWA liability. The following arguments were made.

i. *Res Judicata.* Citing Student Public Interest Research Group v. Georgia–Pacific Corp., 615 F.Supp. 1419, 1432 (D.N.J.1985), Bethlehem Steel argued that CBF was precluded from litigating the alleged violations because they had already been the subject of state enforcement proceedings and its resultant consent decree. The court rejected this defense as argued but asked for additional briefing on the question.

ii. *Diligent Prosecution.* This issue raised the bar of § 505(b)(1)(B) [§ 1365(b)(1)(B)] to the citizen suit action claiming that the State of Maryland had commenced and was diligently prosecuting an administrative proceeding against Bethlehem Steel. The court rejected this defense on the grounds that the Maryland action was commenced *after* CBF filed its citizen suit.

iii. *Upset Defense.* Bethlehem Steel tried to have many of its alleged violations excused as "upsets" which is defined in EPA regulations as an exceptional and temporary state of violation which is beyond the control of the point source. See 40 C.F.R. § 122.41(n)(1). Reviewing the facts of non-compliance before it, the court concluded that the nearly three months of continuous permit violations could not be considered "exceptional" or "temporary" and the upset defense was not available. Although recognized by EPA, in most cases this defense is unsuccessful in court.

iv. *Bypass Defense.* A bypass differs from an upset in that it is the intentional diversion of waste streams from a treatment facility usually for unexpected maintenance purposes or in order to avoid a serious emergency. See 40 C.F.R. § 122.41(m). In this case Bethlehem Steel's permit contained a bypass provision even stricter than the EPA regulation. The court held that these narrow conditions (excessive rainfall) were not met and consequently the bypass defense was unavailable.

v. *Disagreement as to Calculations.* Bethlehem Steel recalculated its discharges over the contested period and alleged that for many reported exceedances the violation had a lesser magnitude or was not a violation at all. In general, the court found these claims unconvincing and refused to overturn the finding of violation.

vi. *Analytical Methods.* Since the discharger is responsible for measuring and reporting its compliance status in its DMRs question are occasionally raised concerning the accuracy of the reported performance. Bethlehem Steel claimed that its autoanalyzer measuring phenols was greatly inaccurate by a factor of 12 to 14 times. While the court followed the general trend denying challenge to the accuracy of DMRs—see Sierra Club v. Simkins Industries, Inc., 847 F.2d 1109 (4th Cir.1988)—it did acknowledge that errors in testing procedure might constitute a defense.

vii. *Statute of Limitations Defense.* What is the relevant statute of limitations on both citizen suit and government enforcement actions? The Clean Water Act does not contain a limitation period and most courts have used the five year statute of limitations period contained in 28 U.S.C. § 2462 which states that

> Except as otherwise provided by Act of Congress, an action, suit or proceeding for the enforcement of any civil fine, penalty, or forfeiture, pecuniary or otherwise, shall not be entertained unless commenced within five years from the date when the claim first accrued....

When would an action be barred by § 2462? A key question with all statute of limitations defenses is "when does a claim first accrue?" Cases have held that the statute does not begin to run when the violations occur but rather when reports are filed with EPA. See Atlantic States Legal Foundation v. Al Tech Specialty Steel Corp., 635 F.Supp. 284, 287 (N.D.N.Y.1986). Also, the federal statute and not a shorter state law statute will apply to the claim. See Georges River Tidewater Ass'n v. Warren Sanitary District, 2000 WL 891969 (D.Me.2000).

viii. *Estoppel Defense.* The court rejected an assertion of a defense based upon the premise that since the State of Maryland was aware of Bethlehem Steel's testing and its difficulties that CBF should be estopped from its § 505 action. Estoppel by state inaction is no defense.

ix. *Impossibility Defense.* Bethlehem Steel asserted that certain permit limitations were later found to be impossible to achieve and that such impossibility should excuse alleged violations. While the court acknowledged that the CWA did not expressly provide for an impossibility defense, it did request additional briefing on the issue.

c. *Citizen Suit Settlement Strategies.* Most litigation never results in formal judicial resolution—it ends in settlement. If you represent the plaintiffs in this § 505 action against the Sewer District, when should you enter into settlement negotiations and, if you settle the case, how should you structure and set the settlement terms? There are a number of possibilities.

i. *Financial Aspects of Settlements.* It must be remembered that in a § 505 action, any judicially-imposed civil penalty is not granted to the citizen plaintiff but rather it is payable to the U.S. Treasury. Where does the defendant's monetary "penalty" go in a citizen suit settled prior to trial? It is possible that the defendant would sign a settlement agreement obligating it to reach CWA compliance at certain specified milestones. In addition, the defendant could agree to make a "donation" to an environmental group, trust or specific improvement project. Why might a corporate § 505 defendant look favorably on such a "charitable" resolution to the citizen suit? In addition, as plaintiff you might wish to consider a conditional settlement that provides for a reduction or elimination of any financial penalty if certain steps are taken within a predetermined time period. Propose a number of settlement proposals and evaluate them from the perspective of the plaintiffs, and defendants, EPA and the state.

The settlement of a CWA citizen suit usually is reflected in a consent order which contains the terms of an agreement reached between the parties. A 1987 CWA amendment adding § 505(c)(3) requires that the United States be given 45 days to review any proposed consent order prior to its entry by the federal court. Why would Congress give the Justice Department this opportunity to review proposed citizen suit settlements? Can't the Justice Department participate in or completely displace any CWA citizen suit under other provisions of § 505? Would the Justice Department ever object to a proposed CWA citizen suit settlement? Why?

In Sierra Club v. Electronic Controls Design Inc., 909 F.2d 1350 (9th Cir.1990), the Ninth Circuit considered the question of whether a Clean Water Act citizen suit settlement could contain an agreement to pay $45,000 to private environmental groups for support of their efforts to maintain and protect water quality in Oregon. Although it did not participate in the litigation, the Justice Department had filed an objection to a proposed consent decree containing this element and it argued that it was illegal since such a payment constituted a civil penalty which the CWA required to be paid to the U.S. Treasury. The district court agreed with the Justice Department and it refused to enter the proposed consent order. The Sierra Club appealed this ruling to the Ninth Circuit. Writing for the appeals court, Judge Goodwin held that the proposed $45,000 payment could not be characterized as a civil penalty since,

> no violation of the Act was found or determined by the proposed settlement judgment. When a defendant agrees before trial to make payments to environmental organizations without admitting liability, the agreement is part of an out-of-court settlement which the parties are free to make.

Id. at 1354. Why might the Justice Department have taken this position? What impact on citizen suit litigation might the district court's opinion have? From a public policy viewpoint, should settlement payments to environmental groups be encouraged or discouraged? Why might a citizen suit defendant prefer such a financial settlement as in *Electronic Controls Design* to a court imposed civil penalty of the same amount?

ii. *Attorneys Fees and Litigation Expenses.* Finally, the plaintiff might be concerned about recovering attorneys fees and other litigation expenses in the settlement. Section 505(c) makes these expenses recoverable, at the court's discretion, by any "prevailing or substantially prevailing party" by court order at the conclusion of litigation. Consequently, if the citizen suit were to be tried and plaintiffs were to prevail, plaintiff would petition the court for the award of litigation expenses supported by well-documented contemporaneous records. In this request, plaintiff would seek to recover a "loadstar" amount representing the number of working hours multiplied times a reasonable hourly rate "prevailing in the community for similar work." Copeland v. Marshall, 641 F.2d 880, 891 (D.C.Cir.1980). This would be established by other attorney affidavits or other recent fee awards. The loadstar amount is occasionally adjusted upward or downward to reflect specific characteristics of the case. See Friends of the Earth v. Eastman Kodak Co., 834 F.2d 295 (2d Cir.1987).

Not infrequently, the successful plaintiff's request for attorneys fees spawns an additional round of litigation when the defendant refuses to pay the amount of fees requested by the plaintiff. In these cases, plaintiff's fee requests are carefully scrutinized for adequate justification with reductions often being ordered. Worse for citizen suit plaintiffs is losing such a suit. In Morris–Smith v. Moulton Niguel Water District, 44 F.Supp.2d 1084 (C.D.Cal.1999), the court held that a defendant "prevailing" in a citizen's suit could recover attorneys fees, but only if the plaintiff's claims were frivolous. How low should the "frivolous" bar be set?

If your citizen suit against the Sewer Authority ended in settlement, how would you negotiate the question of attorneys fees? If you thought your fee request would be resisted, what kinds of recordkeeping practices and documentation would you employ? If you represented the Sewer Authority, how would you examine the plaintiff's fee request?

d. *Damages and State Law Claims.* The question of independent state law remedies occasionally arises in federal CWA citizen suits. The statute contains the following provision.

Section 505 (e) Statutory or common law rights not restricted

Nothing in this section shall restrict any right which any person (or class of persons) may have under any statute or common law to seek enforcement of any effluent standard or limitation or to seek any other relief (including relief against the Administrator or a State agency).

What could be the purpose of § 505(e)? If these state law-derived rights may coexist with the CWA requirements, can they be enforced as part of a federal § 505 action? The answer to this turns on the concept of pendent jurisdiction. Pendant jurisdiction has been defined as the "ability of a federal court to hear and decide a state law claim for which there otherwise would not be jurisdiction that arises from the same facts as a federal question that is properly before the court." E. Chemerinsky, *Federal Jurisdiction* § 5.4.2 (1989). This is a discretionary authority of the federal courts and one requiring a common nucleus of operative fact between the state and federal claims.

While the CWA does not provide plaintiffs with a federal cause of action for water pollution-caused damages, see Evansville v. Kentucky Liquid Recycling, Inc., 604 F.2d 1008 (7th Cir.1979), the scope of pendent jurisdiction enlarges federal judicial power so as to order a wide range of state law remedies. For example, in Jones v. City of St. Clair, 804 F.2d 478 (8th Cir.1986), the Eighth Circuit upheld a pendent state nuisance law award of $15,000 and in City of Norfolk v. Harold, 662 F.Supp. 959 (E.D.Va.1987), the district court considered a pendent claim arising under Virginia's Wetlands Act. Most interestingly, the Fourth Circuit upheld a monetary award springing from finding that a POTWs poorly-treated discharge constituted a "taking" of property under the South Carolina constitution. See Stoddard v. Western Carolina Regional Sewer Authority, 784 F.2d 1200, 1204 (4th Cir.1986). In *Stoddard* the court found that the sewer plant's discharge caused eutrophic lake conditions, odors, and fish kills which constituted both a nuisance and a taking of riparian landowner's property without compensation in violation of Article I, section 13 of the South Carolina constitution. Nearly $300,000 in damages plus litigation expenses were awarded as well. How might these § 505 cases with pendent claims affect your litigation planning if you represented Yvette, Sylvia and the Association?

INDEX

✝

1-56662-937-3

90000